BAILMENT

by

N. E. PALMER

M.A., B.C.L. (Oxon)
of Gray's Inn, Barrister at Law,
Lecturer in Law at the University of Manchester,
Sometime Senior Lecturer in Law at the University of Tasmania

THE LAW BOOK COMPANY LIMITED
SYDNEY MELBOURNE BRISBANE PERTH
1979

Published in Sydney by

The Law Book Company Limited
301-305 Kent Street, Sydney
389-393 Lonsdale Street, Melbourne
27-35 Turbot Street, Brisbane
6 Sherwood Court, Perth

National Library of Australia
Cataloguing-in-Publication entry

Palmer, Norman E.
Bailment.

Index
ISBN 0 455 19610 9

1. Bailments. I. Title

346.025

Typeset by Meredith Trade Lino Pty. Ltd., Burnley, Victoria
Printed by Ramsay Ware Stockland Pty. Ltd.,
North Melbourne, Victoria.

TO JUDITH AND VICTORIA

PREFACE

In writing this book, I have tried to do three things: to provide a guide for practitioners upon the problems of bailment that commonly arise in practice; to provide a source from which students may discover more about a legal relationship normally neglected by other writers; and to place the bailment relation within its proper perspective in the modern sphere of obligations.

I am all too aware that these may prove conflicting objectives. If compelled to choose, I would attach most significance to the third. In accordance with this objective I have cited freely from Commonwealth and American case law and have not hesitated to present decisions which are factually or conceptually interesting alongside those of higher authority. I considered this course to be justified because so much of the modern province of bailment is uncharted and remains in the shape of ideas rather than of settled rules. In the event, I think I have covered every important or interesting Commonwealth decision upon the subject, including many from fairly small jurisdictions such as Ireland, the West Indies and Papua and New Guinea. In addition, the important statutory provisions in England and Australia are discussed. I hope, therefore, that the book will be found useful throughout the English-speaking world.

This does not purport to be a book upon the history of bailment. I have confined historical analysis to a minimum and have concentrated instead upon the character, content and likely development of the relation in the light of modern judicial analysis. If some of the resultant ideas appear precarious, I trust that the book will at least serve to generate debate and will lead to a greater eventual clarity. In this connection, I am happy to rely upon the words of Lord Holt in the great case of *Coggs* v. *Bernard*:

> I have said thus much in this case, because it is of great consequence that the law should be settled on this point; but I don't know whether I may have settled it, or may not rather have unsettled it. But however that may happen, I have stirred these points which wiser heads in time may settle.

For a number of reasons, this proved a very difficult book to write. The somewhat elusive quality of bailment means not only that its principles are frequently neglected in the reaching of decisions, but that those decisions which do base themselves upon its principles are often to be found under some other heading. Important cases have occasionally been indexed under topics as unexpected and diverse as "Administrative Law" and "Post Office", as well as under "Contract", "Tort" and "Personal Property". In this regard, I should like to express my indebtedness to Lloyd's Reports, which have proved an invaluable source of reference for decisions not fully reported elsewhere.

A further difficulty concerned the extent to which I should investigate the relevant principles of contract and tort. So much of bailment rubs shoulders with these other forms of obligation that some discussion of them was inevitable. I have, however, tried to strike a balance and I have assumed that most readers will be familiar with the fundamental rules relating to these other obligations. Despite this, I have included a special chapter on Exclusion Clauses and another on Bailments and Third Parties, both of which discuss broader issues in contract and tort which are relevant but not peculiar to bailment.

The major part of the manuscript of this book was completed and delivered to the publishers between May and November 1976; the remaining Chapters were completed during the early months of 1977. The timing was unfortunate because the second half of 1977 witnessed the passing of the *Unfair Contract Terms Act*, 1977, the *Torts (Interference with Goods) Act*, 1977 and the (Australian) *Trade Practices Amendment Act* 1977. As a result, I had to decide when the book was already in galley form whether to engage in a substantial re-writing. My eventual decision was a compromise. The section in the Chapter on Exclusion Clauses which dealt originally with the *Exemption Clauses (England and Wales) Bill* 1975 has now been thoroughly overhauled to provide an account of the *Unfair Contract Terms Act*. The *Torts (Interference with Goods) Act* has been discussed and analysed at some length in the first Appendix to the book and cross-references to this discussion have been inserted wherever appropriate throughout the text of the book. The *Trade Practices Amendment Act* is of more peripheral importance and I have contented myself with setting out its relevant provisions in a second Appendix.

Case-law also provided some problems during 1977. The Chapter on Exclusion Clauses underwent a further substantial expansion at galley stage to take account of the Court of Appeal's decision in *Levison* v. *Patent Steam Carpet Cleaning Co. Ltd.*[1] and a whole section in the Chapter on Carriage of Goods by Road was rewritten in the aftermath of the House of Lords' decision in *Babco*.[2] As a result of these and other amendments, I think I can claim that, with two exceptions, the book is now up to date till 1st January 1978. The exceptions are, first, the series of statutory instruments made during 1977 under the *Consumer Credit Act* 1974. The disruption involved in inserting these at galley stage would have been unjustifiably great and I hope that the reader will find these readily available elsewhere. Secondly, I have managed to insert a few references to decisions handed down in the early part of 1978. The most notable of these is *Mitchell* v. *Ealing London Borough Council*[3] which affords some valuable reflections upon the liability of the gratuitous bailee. It was, to my regret, impossible to give this decision the full attention it deserved.

I am grateful to many people for the help and advice they have given while I was writing this book. The publishers showed exceptional patience and helpfulness at every stage of the preparation. My occasional research assistants, Steven Churches, Heidi Lehner and Wendy Cull, were an

---

[1] [1977] 3 W.L.R. 90; [1978] Q.B. 69
[2] *James Buchanan & Co. Ltd.* v. *Babco Forwarding & Shipping (U.K.) Ltd.* [1977] 3 W.L.R. 907.
[3] [1978] 2 W.L.R. 999; (1978) *The Times*, February 21st.

invaluable source of ideas as well as of information and gave up many hours (often at short notice) during the early months of writing. Mr. David Yates, Senior Lecturer in Law at the University of Manchester, made some valuable observations on the Chapter on Exclusion Clauses when it was in galley form and was kind enough to allow me to see a proof copy of his monograph on Exemption Clauses in Contracts. Mr. Max Atkinson, Senior Lecturer in Law at the University of Tasmania, sacrificed many hours to read and discuss the typescript with me and saved me from many infelicities. I am particularly grateful to him because, when great demands were being made upon his time as Dean of the Faculty, he was always willing to listen to ideas and to give me the benefit of his exceptional knowledge of the common law.

I am likewise most grateful to my contributors, who kindly undertook exclusive responsibility for certain portions of the book. The Chapter on Carriage of Goods by Sea was the work of Mr. F. D. Rose, Lecturer in Law at University College London, and Mr. H. M. Rigney, student of the Faculty of Law, University of Tasmania. The Chapters on Carriage of Goods by Road, Sea and Rail were contributed by Mr. J. D. Livermore, Lecturer in Law at the Faculty of Commerce in the University of Tasmania. Through no fault of Mr. Livermore's the section in the Chapter on Carriage of Goods by Road relating to recent cases under the *Carriage of Goods by Road Act*, 1965, became out of date at galley stage because of the Court of Appeal's decision in *Ulster-Swift Ltd.* v. *Taunton Meat Haulage Ltd.*[4] and the House of Lords' decision in *James Buchanan & Co. Ltd.* v. *Babco Forwarding & Shipping (U.K.) Ltd.*[5] I therefore re-wrote this section to take account of those decisions. With this one exception the chapters on Carriage are entirely the work of the contributors, and I am indebted to them.

I also received valuable assistance from Mr. P. J. Davies, Lecturer in Law at the University of Manchester, who generously updated and revised at galley stage the section on the *Unfair Contract Terms Act*, 1977, and subsequently compiled the index; and again from Mr. F. D. Rose, who contributed a short section on Tracing. The latter section was unfortunately written before the reporting of the Court of Appeal's decision in *Romalpa*,[6] but I have subsequently managed to incorporate a brief discussion of that case.

Finally, and most of all, I wish to thank my wife, who not only compiled the table of cases but remained patient and generous throughout the three years which it took to write this book.

N. E. PALMER

Manchester,
September 1978.

---

[4] [1977] 1 W.L.R. 625; [1977] 3 All E.R. 641.
[5] [1977] 3 W.L.R. 907.
[6] *Aluminium Industrie Vaassen* v. *Romalpa Aluminium Ltd.* [1976] 1 W.L.R. 676.

TABLE OF CONTENTS

Chapter
XIII. — *continued*

TABLE OF CASES

TABLE OF STATUTES

CHAPTER I

THE NATURE AND ELEMENTS OF BAILMENT

I. INTRODUCTION

Bailment is one of the commonest transactions of everyday life. Its breadth and diversity are enormous. And yet it is unknown to non-lawyers, and frequently neglected by lawyers themselves. The result is that a fertile source of legal development has been largely unexplored.

In part, this neglect can be ascribed to the antiquity of bailment[1] and to its substantial overlap with other fields of obligation. In many respects, bailment stands at the point at which contract, property and tort converge. In its standard form it represents a conveyance of personal property,[2] created by contract and enforceable in tort. Bailment therefore partakes of all three phenomena, and its remedies may correspond with remedies available under other forms of action. But it retains a separate legal personality with much to distinguish it from other concepts. Occasionally in recent years this independent character has provided a refuge for judges who wish to avoid a particular legal consequence dictated by some other form of action with which bailment overlaps.[3] But no judicial attempt has been made to synthesise these differences into a coherent scheme of obligation. Bailment has therefore remained a fragmented subject, and its development has been sporadic and ill co-ordinated.

The essence of bailment is possession. The word derives from the French verb *bailler,* meaning to deliver.[4] The doctrine is confined to personal property and denotes a separation of the actual possession of goods from some ultimate or reversionary possessory right. Thus the owner of goods may make a person his bailee by putting him in posses-

---

[1] On the history of bailment (which will not be separately discussed) see Fifoot, *History and Sources of the Common Law,* pp. 24-34, 157-164; Tay (1966) 5 *Sydney Law Review* 239; Davidge (1925) 41 L.Q.R. 433; Holdsworth, *History of English Law,* passim, especially vol. III, pp. 336-350; Holmes, *The Common Law,* pp. 164-205.

[2] Winfield, *Province of the Law of Tort,* pp. 102-103.

[3] E.g. *Building and Civil Engineering Holidays Scheme Management Ltd.* v. *Post Office* [1966] 1 Q.B. 247, at 261 per Lord Denning M.R. (damages); *Hobbs* v. *Petersham Transport Co. Pty. Ltd.* (1971) 45 A.L.J.R. 356, at 364 per Windeyer J. (burden of proof); *Scruttons Ltd.* v. *Midland Silicones Ltd.* [1962] A.C. 446, at 489-490, and *Morris* v. *C. W. Martin & Sons Ltd.* [1966] 1 Q.B. 716, at 729-730 per Lord Denning M.R. (operation of non-contractual exclusion clauses); *Levison* v. *Patent Steam Carpet Cleaning Co. Ltd.* [1977] 3 W.L.R. 90, per the Court of Appeal (onus of negativing fundamental breach). See also *Davidson* v. *Three Spruces Realty Ltd.* [1977] 6 W.W.R. 460, where the *Levison* case was applied; and *Harold Stephen & Co. Ltd.* v. *Post Office* [1977] 1 W.L.R. 1172, at 1177-1178, 1179-1180

[4] Blackstone, *Commentaries,* 2, p. 451; *Gilchrist, Watt & Sanderson Pty. Ltd.* v. *York Products Pty. Ltd.* [1970] 3 All E.R. 825, at 831. The word "bail" is still used in some areas of France to connote a lease.

1

sion of them for a limited period, and a bailee may create a bailment of goods to their owner by re-granting possession to that owner during the existence of the original bailment. Even a person with no right of possession against the original owner may create an enforceable bailment by conferring a limited right of possession upon a third party, as where a thief bails stolen property to a repairer, or a finder delivers lost property to an expert for valuation.[5] Thus the central theme of every standard bailment is the carving out, by the bailor, of a lesser interest than his own. That interest is possession, and without possession there can be no relationship of bailor and bailee.[6] Conversely, a conveyance which simultaneously confers both possession *and ownership* upon the grantee cannot create a bailment; and an owner of goods cannot constitute himself their bailee at Common Law.[7]

We have remarked upon the linguistic connection between bailment and delivery. This is more a matter of generality than of definition. Under modern theory less importance is attached to the actual mechanics of delivery than to the consequence that the alleged bailee should come into possession of the bailor's chattel. Thus a bailment may arise when the bailee has remained in constant possession of the goods throughout the dispositions which precede his current bailor's ownership. A bailment may also arise when the owner of goods has not consented to their possession by the bailee at all.[8]

Whereas possession is the salient feature of bailment,[9] the mere fact of possession does not necessarily constitute the possessor a bailee. First, such possession may be enjoyed in conjunction with full rights of ownership, in which event the concept of bailment is immaterial and repugnant. Secondly, a bailment cannot rise without a certain mental element on the part of the putative bailee. The precise nature of this mental element is one of the most contentious questions in the law of bailment. The view adopted in this book is that a bailment comes into being whenever one person is knowingly and willingly in possession of goods which belong to another. Authors differ as to whether this is an accurate theory of bailment, but the view we have put forward enjoys the general support of judicial authority. The competing theories will be discussed later in the present chapter.[10]

II. ILLUSTRATION AND EXPANSION

As with any other legal concept, it is easier to give individual examples of bailment than to define its overall perimeter or scope. In *Coggs* v. *Bernard*,[11] which can justly claim to be the seminal modern decision on

---

[5] *Armory* v. *Delamirie* (1722) 1 Stra. 505; and see generally Chapter 22.
[6] Cf. post, p. 78.
[7] Cf. *Harding* v. *Commissioner of Inland Revenue* [1977] 1 N.Z.L.R. 337.
[8] Post, pp. 25-30.
[9] Vaines, *Personal Property* (5th ed.), p. 70; Paton, *Bailment in the Common Law*, p. 5; Winfield, op. cit., p. 101; cf. Stoljar (1955) 7 *Res Judicatae* 160, at 161.
[10] Post, pp. 11 et. seq.
[11] (1703) 3 Ld. Raym. 909, at 912-913; 92 E.R. 107, at 109. The full passage is set out in Chapter 2.

this subject, Lord Holt C.J. set out what he regarded as the six forms of bailment. These were:

the custody of goods without reward;

the loan of goods;

the hire of goods;

the pawn or pledge of goods;

the carrying of goods, or the performance of some other service about them, for reward;

the carrying of goods, or the performance of some other service about them, without reward.

In at least two respects, this analysis is now significantly outmoded. First, all the examples are of consensual bailments; they are confined to two-party transactions and arise upon a direct delivery of goods from one to the other. Indeed, Lord Holt was evidently of the opinion that every bailment resulted from a contract between the parties. Modern authority has repudiated all of these limitations. A bailment may now arise without delivery, without a contract, and apparently without consent on the part of the "bailor". It may arise from the operation of a multi-partite situation, so that it is possible to have an almost infinite chain of head bailors, sub-bailors and sub-bailees. The owner need never have taken possession of the goods before the creation of the bailment. All of these elements represent an advance upon the methods of creating a bailment envisaged by Lord Holt in 1703:

> *McCowan* v. *McCulloch*.[12] D mistakenly takes a suitcase from the luggage rack in a train, thinking that it belongs to a friend. He then makes inadequate attempts to return the case to its owner, and because of his negligence the case is stolen. He is liable as a bailee to its owner.
>
> *Moukataff* v. *B.O.A.C.*[13] P orders his London bank to despatch, by post, £20,000 to his bank in Kuwait. The banknotes are delivered into the custody of the G.P.O., who arrange with an airline to carry them to Kuwait. While they are being loaded on to the plane, one of the airline's loaders steals the banknotes. The airline are liable to D.

The second point of anachronism in Lord Holt's analysis concerns the types of promise which the parties may superimpose upon a bailment without destroying the quality of their relationship as one of bailor and bailee. The transactional aspect which most clearly reflects the modern expansion of the concept is the aspect of re-delivery: i.e., what the bailee may be required to do with the chattel when the bailment comes to an end. Traditionally, a bailment required that the identical goods be returned to the bailor when the purpose for which they were bailed had been fulfilled. At an early stage it was accepted that a transaction would still qualify as a bailment although the identity of the goods was to be altered by the bailee, as where grapes are delivered to be pressed into wine, or corn to be ground into flour.[14] Further, it was recognised

---

[12] [1926] 1 D.L.R. 312.

[13] [1967] 1 Lloyd's Rep. 396.

[14] See, for example, *Oriental Bank Corporation* v. *Hewitt* (1862) 1 S.C.R. (N.S.W.) 220: the defendant, to whom money was given in order that he should purchase gold for the plaintiff, was held upon having purchased the gold to owe in respect

that the bailee need not be obliged to redeliver the goods *to the bailor*, and that a transaction might still give rise to a bailment although the goods were to be delivered to a third party or sold on the bailor's behalf.[15] Finally, the parties to the bailment need not contemplate that the goods should be re-delivered to anyone at all, but should remain permanently with the bailee. The paradigm is the contract of hire-purchase, under which the prospective purchaser acquires goods under a contract of hire with an integral option to purchase. This creates a bailment of the goods until the option is exercised, although the whole object of the transaction is the bailee's acquisition of a full title and the correlative non-return of the goods to the bailor. Indeed, hire-purchase affords a further example of the way in which bailment has adapted to modern circumstances, for the inherent (albeit contingent) element of sale has displaced the conventional rule that the bailee is estopped from denying his bailor's title.[16]

Even more recently it has been recognised that a conditional sale (under which the purchaser agrees to buy goods, and takes possession of them, but does not become their owner until all instalments of the purchase-price have been paid) gives rise to a bailment in the interval between delivery and the passing of title.[17] It therefore follows that the capacities of vendor and purchaser, and bailor and bailee, are not mutually exclusive but can exist concurrently as well as consecutively in relation to a particular subject-matter.[18] The words of a New Zealand judge illustrate the distance travelled (and the territory engulfed) by the concept of bailment in recent years:

> There are few transactions in the terminology of the law whose definition proves so difficult as that of bailment, and few to which so little careful attention has been given in recent years. . . . I think . . . it would be a mistake to conclude that the transaction of bailment is one which has refused, and can still refuse, to undergo the evolution and adaptation which the Common Law imposes upon every legal institution; and although the bailments known to Roman Law were sufficient for Lord Holt C.J., in 1703, I decline to assume that, under the pressures and stresses of modern legal necessity, some new mutation may not have burst into flower, of a quality to startle the author of the Institutes were he privileged to behold it. Such a "sport" may readily be seen in the bailment which is undoubtedly the product of the *Helby* v. *Matthews* type of agreement . . . I think . . . it may be contended that it is possible that development in our own day of the commercial process of the instalment-purchase of goods, with concurrent evolution of the legal concepts of hire-purchase and (in New Zealand) the wider use of the (*conditional sale*), may all

---

thereof the duty of a mere bailee, and could not be sued upon a count for money had and received. See further *R.* v. *Leboeuf* (1864) 9 L.C. Jur. 245 (Quebec); *R.* v. *Craingly* [1931] 3 D.L.R. 640; and post, p. 502.

15 Pollock and Wright, *Possession in the Common Law*, pp. 161-162; *Harding* v. *Commissioner of Inland Revenue* [1977] 1 N.Z.L.R. 337.

16 *Karflex Ltd.* v. *Poole* [1933] 2 K.B. 251, at 263-265 per Goddard J. As to the rule itself, see post, pp. 163 et seq. and App. I.

17 *Motor Mart Ltd.* v. *Webb* [1958] N.Z.L.R. 772.

18 Likewise, when a seller remains in possession after property has passed but prior to delivery: see post, p. 282; *Mgonu* v. *Nzekwe* (1977) C.A. Unrep. July 8.

combine to compel the evolution in the law of bailment of a new type of bailment different in some respects from other types hereto existing.[19]

Thus, modern commercial ingenuity renders it possible to state a definition of bailment which repudiates the need for a re-delivery at the end of the bailment and recognises it as any grant of possession which does not by itself convey the whole of the interest enjoyed (or purportedly enjoyed) by the grantor. Admittedly it may be difficult to establish in particular cases whether the bailor is carving out a lesser interest than his own when he delivers possession or is disposing of the chattel outright. Sometimes the question will be answered by a minor provision in the contract itself, which conflicts with popular expectation and produces a new variety of bailment peculiar to the modern world. For example, every British passport states that it "remains the property of Her Majesty's Government in the United Kingdom and may be withdrawn at any time"; while Clause 10 of the British Rail *Conditions of Carriage of Passengers and their Luggage* similarly declares: "Tickets are the property of the Board and must be produced at any time during the journey or delivered up on demand by any servant of the Board or of any body or person on whose understanding the tickets are available". The consequence in each case is to make the passport or ticket holder a mere bailee; presumably (although the conclusion is rather surprising) the bailment involved is one of hire.[20]

The rule that a delivery of chattels need not contemplate the return of those chattels to the deliveror in order to qualify as a bailment has recently been affirmed in another New Zealand case, which further holds that under ss. 49 and 69A of the New Zealand *Property Act* 1952, it is now possible for an owner to constitute himself the bailee of his own goods.[21] The case provides a further example of the expansion of the concept of bailment in recent years.

But to demonstrate the catholic quality of the modern transaction of bailment is one thing; to reduce its diverse forms to a single denominator is quite another. It is here that one encounters the greatest divergence between traditional theory and modern judicial interpretation. Many of the older writers on bailment founded their definitions upon the most orthodox examples of that concept and rejected (as hybrid or ambiguous cases) the peripheral types of bailment that today provoke the greatest conceptual debate. The point was made by an American commentator in 1931, at a time when the independence of bailment from contract first began to be commonly accepted.

[I]n the field of bailments the common and usual cases have controlled the terminology and classification to such an extent that the less

---

[19] Per Turner J. in *Motor Mart Ltd.* v. *Webb* [1958] N.Z.L.R. 773, at 780, 784-785.
[20] As to the distinctions between bailment and debt and bailment and sale, see post, pp. 96 et seq. As to the legal relationship between the sender and the recipient of a letter, see (1936-1937) 46 *Yale Law Journal* 493. As to the donor's ability to recover an engagement ring, see (inter alia) *Jacobs* v. *Davis* [1917] 2 K.B. 532; *Cohen* v. *Sellar* [1926] 1 K.B. 536; *Fitkevich* v. *Fitkevich* [1976] 2 N.Z.L.R. 414; Goff and Jones, *The Law of Restitution*, pp. 363-364. And see further *Levine* v. *Sebastian* (1911) E.L.R. 311.
[21] *Harding* v. *Commissioner of Inland Revenue* [1977] 1 N.Z.L.R. 337.

usual cases have with difficulty retained their standing as cases of
bailment . . . The endeavour should be to find the element common
to all members of the large group and to disclose the trunk upon
which perhaps several varieties are borne.[22]

An analysis of the nature of bailment should properly proceed upon
two levels: the methods and states of mind essential to its creation, and
the machinery of its enforcement. Winfield once distinguished these as
the "static" and "dynamic" aspects of bailment.[23] By examining them
separately, it should be possible not only to identify the conceptual foundation of bailment but to demonstrate its acknowledged independence
from other forms of obligation. But before we embark upon this inquiry,
it may be proper to digress and to consider in some detail the types of
property upon which the doctrines of bailment react.

III. SUBJECT-MATTER

A. General

The law of bailment is confined to tangible chattels; it has no application
to real property nor (at present) to intangible property such as a chose
in action. Nor can it apply to human beings. In this respect the field of
bailment can actually be seen to have contracted in recent years. Bailments of slaves were a common phenomenon in nineteenth century
American law, and authorities can be found which approach such bailments in much the same way as any other contract of hire for reward.[24]
We do not propose to discuss the law relating to fixtures, nor the problems of ascertaining whether a given article is separate or indivisible from
the land upon which it stands. It is sufficient for our purposes to observe
that a bailment of a chattel is no less a bailment because the bailee
attaches it to land during the period of his use; and that an object which
begins as a fixture upon land may nevertheless form the subject of a
bailment if the parties contemplate its severance and removal. Certain
other types of tangible commodity do, however, demand a closer
examination of their candidacy as the subject-matter of bailment.

B. Negotiable instruments, documents of title, tokens, and "valuable paper"

There can be no bailment of the rights of action represented by such
documents as cheques, mates' receipts or winning lottery tickets, because
those rights are intangible chattels and are therefore not susceptible of
possession. The document itself can be bailed, however, and the courts
have occasionally allowed the bailor by means of an action in tort to
recover not only the value of the document as paper but its surface or
exchange value as well. Thus on a bailment of holiday credit stamps the

---

[22] William King Laidlaw, "Principles of Bailment" (1931) 16 *Cornell Law Quarterly*
286. Cf. Cullen, "The Definition of a Bailment" (1926) 11 *St. Louis Law Review*
257, at 264.
[23] *Province of the Law of Tort*, p. 103.
[24] For a most interesting survey, see Stealey, *Responsibilities and Liabilities of the
Bailee of Slave Labor in Virginia* (1968) III *American Journal of Legal History*,
336.

bailor may be entitled to recover not only the value of the stamps as small pieces of coloured paper but a sum to represent their actual value to him;[25] and on a bailment of a customer list, the bailor may be entitled to restitution for the value of business abstracted by the bailee from his misuse of the list.[26] The problems relative to this kind of bailment are discussed fully in Chapter 3.[27]

C. Animals

Animals may be owned and possessed and may therefore constitute the subject of a bailment. Even dogs, which the Common Law traditionally regarded as vermin,[28] may now be the subject of possessory rights, and many authorities exist in which the bailor of a dog has recovered to the extent of its loss or damage from a defaulting bailee.[29] Wild animals represent a slightly different problem because property must first be acquired by reducing them into possession.[30] Once this has occurred, there is no impediment to the creation of a bailment between the *reductor* and anyone whom he subsequently allows to possess the animal.

D. Corpses and human tissue generally

English law has long set its face against the notion that there may be property in a corpse.[31] Thus it has been held that a doctor cannot be sued in trover for keeping the bodies of two children who had grown together in the womb;[32] that the taking of a corpse is not larceny;[33] that a body may not be disposed of by will;[34] and, in Minnesota, that an undertaker cannot be sued for recovery of the body in an action for replevin.[35] From these and other decisions it might be inferred that there can be no bailment of a corpse, and that no enforceable rights of possession will be recognised over subject-matter of this character. But it has recently been shown that the English decisions are not conclusive,[36] and their antiquity may likewise suggest that they are due for reconsideration. Moreover, there are Commonwealth decisions acknowledging a right of action in negligence and in conversion or detinue by the next-of-kin or

---

[25] *Building and Civil Engineering Holidays Scheme Management Ltd.* v. *Post Office* [1966] 1 Q.B. 247.

[26] *Borden Chemical Co. (Canada) Ltd.* v. *J. G. Beukers Ltd.* (1973) 29 D.L.R. (3d) 337.

[27] *Post,* p. 138.

[28] Pollock and Wright, *Possession in the Common Law,* pp. 235-236.

[29] E.g. *Mackenzie* v. *Cox* (1840) 9 Car. & P. 632; *Phipps* v. *The New Claridge's Hotel Ltd.* (1905) 22 T.L.R. 49 (post, p. 296).

[30] See generally Vaines, *Personal Property* (5th ed.), Chapter 18.

[31] 3 Co. Inst. 110, at 203, 215; *Haynes' Case* 12 Rep. 113; 1 Hawkins P.C. 148; *R.* v. *Sharpe* (1857) Dears & B. 160, at 163; 2 Bl. Com. 429; 4 Bl. Com. 236. Dicta to similar effect appear in *Williams* v. *Williams* (1882) 20 Ch. D. 659, at 663; *R.* v. *Price* (1884) 12 Q.B.D. 247, at 252; *Foster* v. *Dodd* (1867) L.R. 3 Q.B. 67, at 77.

[32] *Handyside's Case* (1750) 2 East P.C. 652.

[33] *R.* v. *Lynn* (1788) 2 Durn. & East 733; *R.* v. *Price* (1884) 12 Q.B.D. 247, at 252; Stephen, *Digest* (5th ed.), p. 252; and see *R.* v. *Sharpe* (1857) 2 Dears & B. 160.

[34] *Williams* v. *Williams* (1882) 20 Ch. D. 659; but see now *Human Tissue Act* 1961 (England).

[35] *Keyes* v. *Konkel* (1899) 78 N.W. 649; cf. *Guthrie* v. *Weaver* (1876) 1 Mo. App. 136 and see also *Edwards* v. *State* (1959) 286 S.W. 2d. 157.

[36] Skegg (1976) 5 *Anglo-American Law Review,* p. 412; and see Meyers, *The Human Body and the Law,* Chapter 5.

other person entitled to the corpse, as against someone who deals with it in a manner contrary to that right.

In *Miner* v. *Canadian Pacific Railway*,[37] where the mother of a deceased youth recovered from the defendant railway for expenses arising out of their negligent delay in delivery of the body, this result was accompanied by a clear recognition that, for certain purposes at least, property may exist in a corpse, and by a clear condemnation of the English authority as unsatisfactory and unreliable.[38] In *Doodeward* v. *Spence*,[39] the High Court of Australia noted the absence of any express decision relative to detinue and doubted the validity of *Handyside's Case* on the ground that it was uncertain as to who was the plaintiff.[40] *Doodeward* v. *Spence* involved the preserved foetus of a two-headed child, still-born some forty years previously, which the appellant had purchased and now sought to recover from the police. The appellant intended to exhibit the body for gain and the respondent had originally taken custody on the ground that such exhibition would offend public decency. The respondent now claimed that no action lay to recover the foetus because no rights of property in human tissue were recognised at Common Law. Counsel for the appellant sought to distinguish earlier authority on the ground that it related to the corpses of humans once living rather than to still-born bodies. However, the Court did not rely upon this distinction in concluding that the action could lie.[41] As Griffith C.J. remarked, the English authority relates primarily to the condition of the human body at death, at which time it may accurately be said to be nullius in rebus:

> But is does not follow from the fact that an object is at one time nullius in rebus that it is incapable of becoming the subject of ownership; for instance, the dead body of an animal *ferae naturae* is not at death the property of anyone, but may be appropriated by the finder. So it does not follow from the mere fact that a human body is not the subject of ownership that it is forever incapable of having an owner.[42]

[37] (1910) 15 W.L.R. 161 (Alberta Supreme Court); varied and damages for mental anguish disallowed, in (1911) 18 W.L.R. 476.

[38] (1910) 15 W.L.R. 167 at 168-9 per Beck J., approving *Pettigrew* v. *Pettigrew* (1904) 207 Pa. 313: " . . . the law recognises property in a corpse, a property, of course, which is subject, on the one hand, to the obligations, e.g. of proper care and prima facie of decent burial appropriate to its condition and the condition of the individual in his lifetime . . . and to the restraints upon its voluntary or involuntary disposal by law (e.g. the existence of the conditions authorising its use for anatomical purposes) or arising out of the fact that the thing in question is a corpse (e.g. no lien can attach: *R.* v. *Fox* (1841) 2 Q.B. 246; a public exhibition contrary to public decency is not permissible: *Russell on Crimes* (7th ed.) . . .); and, on the other hand, the nature and extent of the right or obligation of the person for the time being claiming property (e.g. an executor, a husband-wife, next of kin, medical institute etc.) . . . I cannot see any ground in reason why there should not be appropriate remedies against interference with the right of custody, possession, and control of a corpse awaiting burial, presupposing a right of property therein, subject to the obligations and restrictions which I have indicated". The origins of the traditional theory can be traced to the fact that burial was once the exclusive preserve of the ecclesiastical courts: 3 Co. Inst. 203; and see (1926) 9 *U.Pa. L. Rev.* 404, at 405.

[39] (1908) 6 C.L.R. 406 (Higgins J. dissenting).

[40] Ibid., at 411 (Griffith C.J.); and see per Barton J., at 416.

[41] Ibid., at 415.

[42] Ibid., at 411-412.

In the learned Chief Justice's view, the question was entirely unanswered by earlier authority, and the respondent's contention that the possession of any unburied human person for a purpose other than burial was unlawful (and could therefore be disturbed with impunity) could not be supported. No law prohibited per se the possession of a corpse for such ancillary purposes; if this were so, the possession of mummies, skulls, pathological specimens and other remains by learned societies, students and collectors would be entirely unprotected. Since such possession was not per se unlawful, the law would protect it. The case for a legally inviolable possession was particularly strong if the body possesses attributes of such a nature that its preservation may afford valuable or interesting information or instruction.[43] The reverse may apply, of course, if its retention or exhibition offends public health or decency.

Griffith C.J. was not prepared to commit himself to an exhaustive enumeration of those instances in which a person might enjoy possession, and thus the de facto elements of property, in a corpse. However, in his view such a right indisputably arose . . .

> . . . when a person has by the lawful exercise of work or skill so dealt with a human body or part of a human body in his lawful possession that it has acquired some attributes differentiating it from a mere corpse awaiting burial.[44]

It should, however, be read subject to the superior right of the person entitled to have the body delivered to him for burial, and to the existence of any positive law (such as burial or public health Acts) proscribing the detention of the corpse in the particular circumstances of the case.

From the tenor of this authority, and from various statutes which recognise that there may be possession of human tissue in limited types of case,[45] it seems relatively clear that the law will now acknowledge (at least for certain purposes) the possibility of a bailment of dead body, or of any part thereof. Indeed, it may be hazarded that such acknowledgement should follow whenever human tissue has been delivered by one person to another for a specific and legitimate object. The relative who delivers the body to an undertaker (and who we shall assume, hitherto enjoyed a valid de facto possession) should surely be treated, so far as is practical, in no different a manner from any other person who delivers tangible property to another for a purpose consistent with the notion of bailment. Actions will be unlikely because of the near-impossibility of establishing any economic loss, but this should not inhibit the courts from conferring upon such transactions the normal attributes of a bailment. Indeed, it is possible to foresee cases in which the application of this concept could become very important, in view of the increasing science of organ-transplantation and of the possibility that organs may be bought and sold. The question may also arise from the establishment of organ-banks and other institutions in which bodily components (often,

---

[43] Ibid., at 413-414.
[44] Ibid., at 414.
[45] E.g. *Anatomy Act* 1832: *Human Tissue Act* 1961 (England). See, as to the former Act, *R.* v. *Feist* (1858) Dears & B. 590; and, generally, Meyers, op. cit., p. 107 et. seq.

it may be, those of living persons) are stored until the occasion arises for use.

Similarly, therefore, a person who assumes possession of a dead body should enjoy the same protection as a bailee against any third-party who meddles with it. Thus an undertaker or a hospital authority should be entitled to bring actions in tort against anyone who despoils or misappropriates a body during the period of possession.[46]

Thus, while "it may still be true that a dead body is not property in the common commercial sense of that term",[47] there would seem to be a wide spectrum of events in which a person entitled to a corpse should be legally entitled to vindicate that right. In this respect, it is urged that the approach adopted by the Common Law should be that reflected in a number of American authorities, viz.:

> . . . that the custodian of it has a legal right to its possession for the purposes of preservation and burial [and for any other purpose not contrary to law and permitted by the appropriate individual] and that any interference with that right, by mutilating or otherwise disturbing the body, is an actionable wrong.[48]

E. Fungible property

The doctrines of bailment may apply to money or to any other commodity in which property would normally pass upon delivery, provided it is made clear from the terms of the bailment itself that the goods are to be returned in specie and not merely in an equivalent form. This question is further discussed in Chapter 2.

F. Intangible property

In a recent case from South Australia, Zelling J. purported to discern a bailment of the use of a motor lorry, and held that the bailee was someone other than the person currently in possession of the vehicle itself.[49] The idea is a novel one, and it seems most unlikely that the courts will develop the underlying theory that there may be a bailment of an intangible thing. Thus, information cannot normally be the subject-matter of bailment unless there is some accompanying article (such as a piece of paper) recording that information and providing the necessary tangible foundation for the doctrine of bailment to operate upon. It may be that modern information systems will eventually produce a modification of the conventional rule and will allow, for example, an action by the bailor of information for its recovery from the proprietor of a retrieval system with whom it has been stored. Such a development is not entirely impossible, given the distance travelled by the law of bailment in recent years. But it is probably fruitless to speculate further until at least some authority has arisen. The problems of bailments of intellectual property are discussed again briefly in Chapter 3.

---

[46] Cf. *Edwards* v. *State* (1959) 286 S.W. (2d) 157, a case involving criminal liability, where it was held that the taking of custody of a body by a funeral home in order to prepare it for burial did not constitute a contract to borrow or hire the body for the use and benefit of the funeral home and was not a bailment.
[47] *Larson* v. *Chase* (1891) 50 N.W. 238.
[48] Ibid; and see further (1933-1934) *Indiana Law Journal* 177.
[49] *Roufos* v. *Brewster and Brewster* [1971] 2 S.A.S.R. 218 (dissenting on this point).

IV. CREATION

We shall deal later with the elements of possession. In the present section we are concerned with the extent to which it is synonymous with bailment, and with the additional elements (if any) which must exist alongside the possession of another's chattel in order to justify the conclusion that the possessor is a bailee.

There are six theories as to the essential formative element in bailments. They are as follows:

1. That bailment requires a delivery of possession.
2. That it requires a contract giving rise to possession.
3. That it requires consensus or agreement giving rise to possession.
4. That it requires a voluntary possession.
5. That it requires a knowing (but not necessary voluntary) possession.
6. That it requires possession and no more.

Possession is central to each of these theories; they differ only in the degrees of mental or physical activity which are asserted to be a necessary accompaniment to possession itself. Some of the theories would hold the state of mind of both parties relevant; others would hold only that of the bailee relevant; and the final theory would deny the relevance of either. We shall now examine each in turn.

A. Bailment and delivery

Both semantically and historically it could be argued that bailment involves a delivery of goods from one person (the bailor) to another person (the bailee). Most of the older definitions of bailment seem to require that an overt physical transfer of this kind be present. Bacon, for example, defined bailment as:

> . . . a delivery of personal chattels in trust, on a contract, express or implied, that the trust shall be duly executed, and the chattels redelivered in either their original or an altered form, as soon as the time, or use for, or condition on which they were bailed, shall have elapsed or been performed.[50]

Taken as a component transaction in its own right, delivery would appear to connote both a physical and a mental element: an intention to transfer the possession of goods to a bailee, coupled with an act achieving that result. But these requirements no longer afford a conclusive test as to whether a bailment has arisen because they no longer represent the sole method of creating that relationship. Thus it has been said that one does not deliver goods of the existence of which one is unaware, such as where a desk is sold containing sovereigns in a secret drawer;[51] but once the acquirer of the goods discovers that he is in possession of them, and continues to retain possession when he could dispose of them, it would seem both reasonable and (on modern authority) legitimate to exact from him the duties of a bailee. Likewise in the Victorian case of R.

---

[50] Bacon, *Abridgment,* Tit. *Bailment*; cited with approval (inter alia) by Cohen J. in *Re S. Davis & Co. Ltd.* [1945] Ch. 402, at 405; and see Stoljar (1955) 7 *Res Judicatae* 160.
[51] *Merry* v. *Green* (1841) 7 M. & W. 623, at 631 per Parke B.

v. *Bennie*[52] it was held that a person could not be held guilty of the crime of larceny as a bailee unless some delivery of the chattel had been made to him, but it was stressed that a different conclusion might have been reached had the issue been civil rather than criminal.

> I am dealing with a criminal and not a civil case and in criminal law at any rate words have to be construed with strictness. In my opinion it is essential to constitute a bailment that there should have been a delivery of the chattels made by the bailor to the bailee. That delivery may, in certain cases, be a token delivery and, as at present advised, in the case of a motor car, I think it would be a sufficient delivery for the bailor to deliver the ignition keys or the door keys of the car to the bailee and that would constitute a delivery. It may be that it would be sufficient evidence of a delivery that there was some other action indicating a transfer of delivery taking place, such as placing one's hand on the car coupled with words which in substance indicated that the bailor was delivering the car to the bailee.[53]

Admittedly it may be legitimate to interpret the word bailment more restrictively when it is used in a statute imposing criminal as opposed to civil liability. There is a recent precedent for such discrimination in the case of *Thompson* v. *Nixon*,[54] where it was held (albeit reluctantly) that a finder of goods was not a bailee for the purposes of the *Larceny Act, 1916.*[55] But in *R.* v. *Bennie* the defendant was the holder of goods under a bill of sale, and to add to his undoubted possession of the goods the requirement for some formal antic amounting to actual delivery seems, with respect, unduly technical. Certainly in civil questions he would have been liable as a bailee.[56]

In fact, a person may owe the duties of a bailee irrespective of any conscious transference of the chattel by the putative bailor. For example, finders are answerable for a failure to exercise due care in relation to a chattel which has come, without the owner's intention or instrumentality, into their possession;[57] and this may be so even though the "bailor" has not hitherto known that the chattel existed.[58] Moreover, where goods are given under a mistake or deception to a rogue, there may or may not be a delivery but it seems that the rogue should be considered a bailee for the purposes, at least, of making him responsible for the safety of the goods and of preventing him from disputing the other person's title.[59] Again, there are cases where a vendor who retains possession of goods after sale has been held to be a bailee although the true owner may never

---

[52] [1953] V.L.R. 583. Cf. *R.* v. *Boyd* (1870) 1 A.J.R. 88.
[53] [1953] V.L.R., at 584.
[54] [1966] 1 Q.B. 103; post, p. 26, and see now *Theft Act* 1968, s. 3(1).
[55] But cf. Pollock and Wright, *Possession in the Common Law,* p. 160: "There seems to be no reason to doubt that in general the same thing is a bailment for the purposes of the criminal law, both common and statutory, as in civil matters"; *R.* v. *McDonald* (1885) 15 Q.B.D. 323.
[56] *Fenn* v. *Bittleston* (1851) 7 Ex. 152; *Lethbridge* v. *Echlin* (1893) 5 Q.L.J. 75.
[57] Chapter 22, post.
[58] E.g., where it had lain hitherto undetected upon his land.
[59] *Folkes* v. *King* [1923] 1 K.B. 282; *Pearson* v. *Rose & Young, Ltd.* [1951] 1 K.B. 275; cf. *Lake* v. *Simmons* [1927] A.C. 487; Thornely (1974) 13 J.S.P.T.L. 150-151. Two old New South Wales decisions on criminal liability hold to the contrary: *R.* v. *Parker* (1863) 2 S.C.R. (N.S.W.) 217; *R.* v. *Critchell* (1864) 3 S.C.R. (N.S.W.) 209.

have seen the goods, much less have possessed them and redelivered them to their former owner.[60] Finally, there is the doctrine of attornment.[61] In the words of Pollock and Wright:

> A bailment may arise without any change of physical possession, as for instance where a person is bailee from one person, he may become the bailee of another by attornment, i.e. by agreeing to hold under him, and so it is conceived may a person who holds as a servant or even as a trespasser acquire possession as a bailee by subsequent agreement. Whether any act is necessary to be done to evidence or perfect the agreement in such a case seems not to have been decided.[62]

Even in those cases where a delivery has occurred it has not always taken the form of a physical handing-over from the bailor to the bailee. Quite apart from the notion of constructive delivery (where the means of access or control to goods are transferred without any physical handling of the goods themselves)[63] it is clear that a bailment may arise when possession of A's chattel is given to C by an intermediary, B. B may himself be a bailee of the goods, in which event C will probably assume the character of a sub-bailee.[64] On the other hand, B may be an employee of A's who is not himself a bailee; for instance, a servant sent to take A's coat to the cleaner, or a forwarding agent who is engaged to handle the carriage of A's goods without ever obtaining possession of them. He may alternatively be a dealer who delivers a car to a customer to be held on hire-purchase from a finance-company which never sees or possesses the car before the hirer takes possession; in this event the customer nevertheless becomes the finance-company's bailee.[65] But the principle goes even further than this. The real deliveror may not be an agent or associate of the owner at all; he may, for instance, be a stranger who finds A's watch in the street and hands it to a policeman.[66]

It is clear, then, that one cannot rationalise all cases of bailment in terms of an overt act of delivery from bailor to bailee. A bailment requires that one party should be in possession of goods to which another party enjoys some superior or reversionary right. Delivery, in its literal sense, is only one of the methods whereunder such possession may be acquired.[67]

---

[60] E.g. *Union Transport Finance Ltd* v. *Ballardie* [1937] 1 K.B. 510 at 516; *Worcester Works Finance Ltd.* v. *Cooden Engineering Co. Ltd.* [1972] 1 Q.B. 210; *Demby Hamilton & Co. Ltd.* v. *Barden* [1949] 1 All E.R. 435; cf. *Sharp* v. *Batt* (1930) 25 Tas. L.R. 33.
[61] Chapter 21, post.
[62] *Possession in the Common Law*, p. 134.
[63] Cf. *Kilpin* v. *Ratley* [1892] 1 Q.B. 582; *Rawlinson* v. *Mort* (1905) 93 L.T. 555 (cases of gift); and see *R.* v. *Bennie* (*ante.*, pp. 11-12); Pollock and Wright, op. cit., pp. 57-70; Goodeve, *Personal Property* (9th ed.), p. 42.
[64] Chapter 20, post.
[65] *Belvoir Finance Co. Ltd.* v. *Stapleton* [1971] 1 Q.B. 210, at 218, 221.
[66] Cf. *Helson* v. *McKenzies (Cuba St.) Ltd.* [1950] N.Z.L.R. 878; post, pp. 29, 873.
[67] *Makower, McBeath & Co. Pty. Ltd.* v. *Dalgety & Co. Pty. Ltd.* [1921] V.L.R. 365, at 373 per McArthur J.: "It is not necessary, in order to constitute a bailment, that the goods should in the first instance be delivered by the bailor to the bailee; it is quite sufficient, in my opinion, if the bailee, having in the first instance obtained possession and control of the bailor's goods, without the latter's knowledge or consent, afterwards acknowledges to the bailor that he holds them for him, and

B. Bailment and contract

Most bailments arise from a contract between the bailor and the bailee, and at one time it was assumed that a valid and enforceable contract was essential to the creation of a bailment. Thus, Sir William Jones, writing in 1781, defined bailment as . . .

> . . . a delivery of goods in trust, on a contract express or implied, that the trust shall be duly executed, and the goods redelivered, as soon as the time or use for which they were bailed shall have elapsed or be performed.[68]

This definition, which corresponded largely with that of Bacon,[69] has been adopted and applied in a number of decisions.[70] As recently as the last century writers and judges have adhered to the notion of bailment as a contractual phenomenon. This was accepted by Wyatt Paine in his book on Bailments in 1901;[71] by Holland in 1924;[72] and by Williams in 1926.[73] In *R.* v. *Ashwell*[74] Lord Coleridge added his support to the contractual theory of bailment, despite an earlier decision (*R.* v. *McDonald*)[75] in which a minor was held criminally liable as a bailee. He said:

> I was one of a considerable minority of judges on the second argument of *Reg.* v. *Mcdonald,* and my opinion was, and is, that bailment is not a mere delivery on a contract, but is a contract in itself . . . "The contract of bailment" is not a mere loose and common phrase, but is the accurate expression of a legal idea.[76]

Even today, it is possible to discover judgments which continue to refer to bailment as the (impliedly exclusive) product of contract.[77] But it is clear that this limitation is now outmoded and that a bailment may arise in the absence of any contract obliging or entitling the bailee to take possession.[78] The identification with contract is unsound on historical grounds because bailment is a much older concept than contract; as Professor Carnegie has observed, "there was a relatively fully-fledged law of bailment at a stage when the law of contract had hardly achieved an embryonic existence".[79] The confusion seems mainly to have arisen with

thereafter retains possession and control for him with his consent". See further, Laidlaw (1930-1931) 16 *Cornell Law Quarterly* 286, at 293.

[68] *An Essay on the Law of Bailments,* p. 117; cf. ibid., at p. 1.
[69] Ante, p. 11.
[70] E.g. *R.* v. *McDonald* (1885) 15 Q.B.D. 323, at 327-328 per Cave J.; *Martin* v. *Town 'n' Country Delicatessen Ltd.* (1963) 42 D.L.R. (2d) 449, at 453 per Miller, C.J.M.; *Lesser* v. *Jones* (1920) 47 N.B.R. 318, per Hazen C.J..
[71] At p. 1.
[72] *Jurisprudence* (13th ed.), p. 289.
[73] *Personal Property* (18th ed.), p. 57.
[74] (1885) 16 Q.B.D. 190.
[75] (1885) 15 Q.B.D. 323.
[76] (1885) 16 Q.B.D. at 223.
[77] E.g. *Chapman* v. *Robinson and Ferguson* (1969) 71 W.W.R. 515, at 523; and see the authorities listed on p. 314 n. 81, post.
[78] See the authorities listed on p. 314 n. 82, post, and Ch. 20.
[79] (1966) 3 *Adelaide Law Review* 7; and see Fifoot, *History and Sources of the Common Law,* pp. 24-25: "Bailment, in truth, is sui generis—an elementary and unique transaction, the practical necessity of which is self-evident and self-explanatory, and if in later years it is most often, though not invariably, associated with a contract, this is not and never has been, its essential characteristic. It was a familiar fact, as Detinue and Debt were familiar words, before contract was a generic conception."

the application to bailments of the contractual doctrine of consideration; this is evident in the judgment of Lord Holt C.J. in *Coggs* v. *Bernard*[80] and can be discerned in decisions throughout the preceding century.[81] Combined with the emergent nineteenth century notion (not conclusively exploded until *Donoghue* v. *Stevenson*)[82] that there could be no action for negligence without a pre-existing contract between the parties, it effectively enchained bailment to contract for something like two centuries. Of course, the equation itself involved the supposition that an action on the bailment must be either tortious or contractual, a fallacy which unfortunately persists until the present day.[83] But nineteenth century notions of the primacy of contract completed a process of absorption which it has taken nearly a century to reverse.

Modern authority has affirmed in a wide variety of contexts that a valid bailment may exist without a contract inter partes. We shall concentrate upon cases where the parties are (to some extent at least) in agreement as to the creation of a bailment, but where that agreement is prevented by the absence of some technical requirement from giving rise to a contract.

1. *Incapacity*: The mere presence of a contractual incapacity does not necessarily inhibit the creation of an enforceable bailment. This is especially true when it is the bailor that is alleged to suffer from the incapacity, because modern theories of bailment focus far more upon the obligations, and the necessary states of mind, of the bailee. Thus there may be a relationship of bailor and bailee although the bailor is drunk,[84] or a lunatic,[85] or an infant,[86] at the time the bailment was created.

When the incapacity is alleged to rest in the bailee, the question may be whether it vitiates consent; and for this purpose it may be necessary to draw a distinction between legal and mental capacity. If the parties are agreed upon the creation of a bailment, a purely legal or jural incapacity will not prevent the incapacitated party from becoming a bailee; an infant may be liable as a bailee,[87] and so might a married woman,[88] despite the contractual incapacity that formerly attached to wives under English law.

---

[80] (1703) 2 Ld. Raym. 909, at 919; 92 E.R. 107, at 113. See on this point Tay (1966) 5 *Sydney Law Review* 239, at 242-243.

[81] Though they are not unanimous: see *Riches* v. *Bridges* (1602) Cro. Eliz. 883; *Game* v. *Harvie* (1630) Yelv. 50; *Gelley* v. *Clerk* (1606) Cro. Jac. 188; *Pickas* v. *Guide* (1608) Yelv. 128; *Wheatley* v. *Low* (1623) Cro. Jac. 668; Winfield, op. cit., pp. 93-96; Davidge (1925) 41 L.Q.R. 433. The fallacy apparently stemmed from the misconception that a bailor's action in assumpsit sounds in contract; this is condemned by Davidge, loc. cit., at 439; "But the true reason for all this talk about consideration for gratuitous bailment seems to be forgetfulness of the fact that assumpsit was in origin an action of tort, and will still sometimes lie for one."

[82] [1932] A.C. 562; cf. *Govett* v. *Radnidge* (1802) 3 East 62.

[83] Post, p. 36 et. seq.

[84] *R.* v. *Reeves* (1859) 5 Jur. 716, cited by Pollock and Wright, op. cit., p. 163, where, however, the bailor was tipsy and apparently agreed to the taking of his watch from his pocket by the bailee, mistaking it for an act of kindness; cf. *R.* v. *Rigbey* (1863) 2 S.C.R. (N.S.W.) 176.

[85] *Martin* v. *L.C.C.* [1947] 1 K.B. 628.

[86] *Stevenson* v. *Toronto Board of Education* (1919) 49 D.L.R. 673.

[87] *R.* v. *McDonald* (1885) 15 Q.B.D. 323, not following *Mills* v. *Graham* (1804) 1 Bos. & Pul. (N.R.) 140; *Ballett* v. *Mingay* [1943] K.B. 281; and see post.

[88] *R.* v. *Jane Robson* (1861) 31 L.J. (N.S.) M.C. 22, which "must be taken to have overruled" *R.* v. *Denmour* (1861) 8 Cox 440, per Winfield, *Province of the Law of Tort*, p. 98; likewise, *Smith* v. *Plomer* (1812) 15 East 607.

The relevance of mental incapacity depends upon the breadth of one's definition of bailment. If one accepts the broadest definition of all and characterises bailment as the relationship between an owner and anyone in possession of his chattel,[89] the drunkard and the lunatic would evidently be classified as bailees. If one accepts the narrower definition of bailment as the relationship between an owner and anyone who voluntarily and knowingly accepts possession of his chattel,[90] the relevance of capacity is directed solely to ascertaining the reality of that knowledge and the genuineness of that consent. In either event it is clear that contractual incapacity alone does not preclude recognition of the incapacitated party as a bailee.

The cases relating to infant bailees have created an uneasy distinction between those actions by the bailor which are merely a cloak for the enforcement of some contractual duty undertaken by the infant, and those which disclose an independent liability in tort. The first class of action will not be allowed to succeed unless the contract itself is enforceable; but in cases of the second variety the infant is answerable in the same way as any other tortfeasor. Thus in *Jennings* v. *Rundall*[91] the lessor of a horse to an infant, having stipulated that it should be moderately ridden, was held unable to recover for the infant's misconduct in riding it "wrongfully and injuriously"; but in *Burnard* v. *Haggis*[92] a lessor who had explicitly forbidden the infant to use the horse for jumping was held entitled to recover in tort when the infant lent it to a friend who killed the horse by using it for the proscribed purpose. Likewise in *Victoria U Drive Yourself Auto Livery Ltd.* v. *Wood*[93] the infant hirer of a car was held liable in tort for damage which ensued after he wrongfully lent it to a friend, while in *Dickson Bros. Garage & U Drive Ltd.* v. *Woo Wai Jing*[94] the infant was absolved because his alleged wrong consisted in using the car negligently, contrary to certain stipulated terms in the contract of hire. Various theories have been advanced to explain or reconcile these decisions. The commonest explanation is that the infant is not liable when his misconduct consists solely in his doing, in an unauthorised manner, something authorised by the contract, whereas he *is* liable if he does something entirely outside or forbidden by the contract, which amounts in itself to an independent tort; in other words, the wrong must be something not contemplated by the contract itself.[95] But of course this reasoning is artificial in the extreme. It was applied in *Fawcet* v. *Smethurst*[96] to justify the conclusion that an infant who took a hired car further than was permitted under the contract of hire was not answerable for its subsequent damage, because the cause of action disclosed no independent tort but arose purely

---

89 Post, p. 35.
90 Post, p. 24.
91 (1799) 8 Term. Rep. 335.
92 (1863) 14 C.B.N.S. 45.
93 [1930] 2 D.L.R. 811.
94 (1958) 11 D.L.R. (2d) 477.
95 Treitel, *Law of Contract* (4th ed.), p. 388; Cheshire and Fifoot, *Law of Contract* (3rd Australian ed.), pp. 476-477.
96 (1914) 31 T.L.R. 68.

ex contractu;[97] whereas in *Ballet* v. *Mingay*[98] the infant hirer of a microphone and amplifier, who lent the equipment without authority to a friend and was subsequently unable to return it, was held liable in detinue to the owner because by sub-bailing the goods he stepped beyond the purview of the contract of bailment and therefore committed an independent tort.[99] It may be thought that the deviation involved in the latter case was scarcely more serious or repugnant to the bailment than that achieved in *Fawcett* v. *Smethurst*. The fact is that the agreement will often define what is a tort on the part of the infant by imposing restrictions upon the duration of his use, or by requiring that he should use the goods only for his personal enjoyment; therefore to classify his misconduct as an independent tort may be no more than to recognise and enforce the contract itself. Elsewhere we suggest that an action may lie against the infant for breach of bailment and that such an action (although essentially for breach of a promissory obligation) may escape the taint of contractual personality because bailment is an independent source of action.[1] However, no approach seems hitherto to have been made upon these lines. The infancy cases represent an area in which the exclusive division of actions into tortious and contractual, to the neglect of bailment, is firmly and unfortunately rooted.

2. *Failure of condition precedent*: The possessor of a chattel may be liable as a bailee for its safety although the chattel was delivered in pursuance of a contract which is unenforceable through the failure of some stipulated anterior event. Only in those cases in which the ensuing bailment can be characterised as involuntary may this conclusion be displaced; and such cases will be rare because the very stipulation of the event suggests some contemplation that it may not occur and that the possessor may come into possession without a contract. In any event, it has been argued that even an involuntary bailment falls within the wider orbit of the bailment relation.[2]

In *Bentworth Finance Ltd.* v. *Lubert*[3] a hire-purchase agreement was held unenforceable because the lessors had failed to perform the necessary condition precedent of puttting the hirer in possession of the log-book. The car had been damaged while in the hirer's possession and the lessors failed in their attempt to enforce a term in the contract binding the hirer to compensate them for such damage. But there is nothing in the decision to suggest that the hirer would not have been liable as a bailee if the damage had occurred through her failure to take reasonable care of the vehicle.

---

[97] Cf. *Walley* v. *Holt* (1876) 35 L.T. 631 where, in not dissimilar circumstances, the infant's misconduct was sufficiently aggravated to amount to an independent tort.
[98] [1943] K.B. 281; *Burton* v. *Levey* (1891) 7 T.L.R. 248.
[99] See further *Peters* v. *Tuck* (1915) 11 Tas. L.R. 30, where an infant in whose name money was deposited was held accountable on a count for money had and received, Crisp J. holding that this was in essence a claim *ex delicto* for the infant's conversion of the money. Cf. *Bristow* v. *Eastman* (1794) 1 Esp. 172; *Cowern* v. *Nield* [1912] 2 K.B. 419.
[1] Post, p. 752.
[2] Post, p. 32. cf. *Kolfor Plant* v. *Tilbury Plant* (1977) *The Times*, 17th May.
[3] [1968] 1 Q.B. 680.

3. *Expiry of Contract*: There may originally have been a contract between the parties which has now expired through lapse of the contractual period, or performance, or frustration or breach, leaving one party in possession of the other's goods. That person may still be counted a bailee for the purposes of safeguarding and redelivering the goods, although his obligations may be lighter because of the unprojected nature of his custody.[4]

> There are certain cases of bailment in which the contract, from unexpected reasons, becomes impossible of fulfilment, while the bailee nevertheless remains in possession of the bailor's chattels and becomes subject to duties which arise out of the fact of possession. This occurs when perishable goods are entrusted to a carrier to deliver at a wrong address, or when, by reason of sea peril, the cargo becomes incapable of being carried to its destination. In these cases, it may be quite sound to say that the claim arising from breach of duty is wholly a claim in tort.[5]

Similar observations apply where a purchaser is put in possession of goods substantially different from those which he has contracted to purchase. The contract may be put to an end by his rescission, but he may still be answerable as a bailee for the safety of the goods.[6]

4. *Lack of intention to create legal relations*: The fact that certain terms in the bailment are unenforceable because the parties did not intend to enter a binding contract does not detract from the fundamental character or status of those parties as bailor and bailee. The bailee will still be answerable for the safety of the goods, because this is an obligation which does not depend exclusively upon contract.[7]

5. *Lack of privity*: There may be a subsisting contract in relation to the goods, but one to which the owner or the plaintiff is not a party. In this event, the owner may still be entitled to proceed against the possessor as the bailee of his goods, and the bailee may owe to him all the duties which at Common Law are inherent in the bailment relation.[8] This conclusion should at least follow when the alleged bailee knows that the owner is someone other than the person who has delivered the goods to him and raises no objection, at the time of delivery, to a plural responsibility for them.

6. *Illegality*: Clearly, no court will compel a party to perform an illegal contract, and to this extent a bailment which is for an illegal purpose or is contrary to public policy will be unenforceable in law.[9] Thus a bailment of goods to a carrier, to be carried in a vehicle which both parties know to be illegally loaded, has been held not to give rise to a right of action by the bailor for delay or damage to the goods[10]. Nor, it seems,

---

[4] See generally Chapter 12.
[5] *Steljes* v. *Ingram* (1903) 19 T.L.R. 534, at 535, per Phillimore J.
[6] Cf. *Kolfor Plant Hire Ltd.* v. *Tilbury Plant Hire Ltd.* (1977) *The Times* 17 May.
[7] *Roufos* v. *Brewster and Brewster* [1971] 2 S.A.S.R. 218, at 230 per Mitchell J.
[8] E.g. *Andrews* v. *Home Flats Ltd.* [1945] 2 All E.R. 698; *Morris* v. *C. W. Martin & Sons Ltd.* [1966] 1 Q.B. 716. Cf. *Helson* v. *McKenzies (Cuba St.) Ltd.* [1950] N.Z.L.R. 878 (post, p. 29); *Corbett* v. *Jamieson* [1923] N.Z.L.R. 374.
[9] See generally Treitel, *Law of Contract* (4th ed.), p. 319 et. seq.; *Pearce* v. *Brooks* (1866) L.R. 1 Ex. 213; *Snell* v. *Unity Finance Ltd.* [1964] 2 Q.B. 203.
[10] *Ashmore, Benson, Pease & Co. Ltd.* v. *A. V. Dawson Ltd.* [1973] 1 W.L.R. 828. The prohibition upon enforcement may be relaxed if it is not within the policy of

can the bailor evade this rule by suing the bailee in tort;[11] for although the modern interpretation of the principle ex turpi causa non oritur actio is necessarily narrow,[12] no court will allow the circuitous enforcement of an illegal contract by means of an action for negligence, detinue or conversion.[13] Nevertheless, it would seem that in at least four respects an illegal bailment may be accompanied by enforceable rights or obligations on the part of either party. Thus, the bailor may be entitled to recover the goods for the bailee if he can assert his separate and independent title to them without relying on the illegal transaction.[14] Moreover, the bailee acquires an enforceable possessory interest which he can vindicate against the incursions of the owner or of those of third parties.[15] Thirdly, it may be that the bailee is estopped from disputing his bailor's title, except insofar as he may claim that the assertion of that title necessarily discloses a reliance upon the illegal transaction. Finally, there may be circumstances in which the bailee is answerable in tort, or in an action upon the bailment, for loss or damage to the goods despite the illegality of the contract under which they were delivered. Such an action should be possible when their safekeeping was not the primary contractual objective but arises only from the necessary proximity of the bailee to the goods and his voluntary acceptance of them. Thus whereas the damage

---

the illegalising statute to render the ensuing contract void, or if the bailor is not a participant in the illegality: *St. John Shipping Corporation* v. *Joseph Rank Ltd.* [1957] 1 Q.B. 267; *Archbold's (Freightage) Ltd.* v. *S. Spanglett Ltd.* [1961] 1 Q.B. 374.

11 *Archbold's (Freightage) Ltd.* v. *S. Spanglett Ltd.* [1961] 1 Q.B. 374, at 384 per Pearce L.J.: "His cause of action comes from the contract, and if the contract is such that the court must refuse its aid, the plaintiffs cannot recover their damages." The same conclusion is endorsed by *Ashmore, Benson, Pease & Co. Ltd.* v. *A. V. Dawson Ltd.* [1973] 1 W.L.R. 828, where the plaintiff's principal cause of action was in negligence. See further Dwyer, (1977) 93 L.Q.R. 386, n. 4.
12 *Smith* v. *Jenkins* (1970) 119 C.L.R. 397; cf. *Progress & Properties Ltd.* v. *Craft* (1976) 51 A.L.J.R. (H.C.) 184; *Murphy* v. *Culhane* [1976] 3 All E.R. 533 (C.A.).
13 *Kahler* v. *Midland Bank, Ltd.* [1950] A.C. 24; *Zivnostenska Bank* v. *Frankman* [1950] A.C. 57, especially at 87 per Lord Radcliffe.
14 *Bowmakers Ltd.* v. *Barnet Instruments Ltd.* [1945] K.B. 65: "Prima facie, a man is entitled to his own property, and it is not a general principle of our law that when one man's goods have got into another's possession in consequence of some unlawful dealings between them, the true owner can never be allowed to recover those goods by an action", per du Parcq L.J., at 70. The decision was severely criticised by Hamson (1949) 10 C.L.J. 249, but has been followed regularly: see, e.g., *Belvoir Finance Co. Ltd.* v. *Harold G. Cole & Co. Ltd.* [1969] 1 W.L.R. 1877; *Belvoir Finance Co. Ltd.* v. *Stapleton* [1971] 1 Q.B. 210; *Singh* v. *Ali* [1960] A.C. 167; *Amar Singh* v. *Kulubya* [1964] A.C. 142; *Southern Industrial Trust Ltd.* v. *Brooke House Motors Ltd.* (1968) 112 Sol. Jo. 798; *Pye Ltd.* v. *B.G. Transport Service Ltd.* [1966] 2 Lloyd's Rep. 300; *Joe* v. *Young* [1964] N.Z.L.R. 24; *Evans* v. *Credit Services Investments Ltd.* [1975] 2 N.Z.L.R. 560; *N.Z. Securities & Finance Ltd.* v. *Wrightcars Ltd.* [1976] 1 N.Z.L.R. 77. Cf. *Thomas Brown & Sons Ltd.* v. *Fazal Deen* (1962) 108 C.L.R. 391, where the *Bowmaker* case was distinguished. The plaintiff had bailed gold and gems to the defendant under an arrangement which contravened exchange control regulations. The defendant refused to return them on demand and the plaintiff brought an action in detinue, the limitation period for conversion having expired. The High Court held that the allegation of detinue necessarily disclosed reliance upon the illegal bailment, and debarred the plaintiff from recovering, because proof of the contract itself was necessary to prove an obligation to redeliver. Cf. further *Bigos* v. *Bousted* [1951] 1 All E.R. 92.
15 E.g. *Roberts* v. *Roberts* [1957] Tas. S.R. 84; *Taylor* v. *Chester* (1869) L.R. 4 Q.B. 309; *Harris* v. *Lombard New Zealand Ltd.* [1974] 2 N.Z.L.R. 161.

of goods comprised in an illegal contract of carriage may not be remedi-able, a remedy may lie when the object of the contract was something other than carriage or storage: for instance, where the goods are bailed under an illegal contract of hire, or possibly even an illegal contract of repair. Such a remedy might be a logical extension of the bailor's power to sue upon his separate and independent title.[16]

The fact that a valid bailment may arise out of an illegal contract is illustrated by some American cases, which uphold the fundamental obliga-tions of the bailment notwithstanding that the accompanying contract is void for contravention of Sunday Observance laws.[17]

7. *Lack of consideration*: The most obvious example of a non-contractual bailment is the bailment which is gratuitous: i.e., from which only one party benefits. A gratuitous bailment may take one of two forms. The benefit may rest exclusively with the bailor, as in cases of depositum or mandatum, which involve the unrewarded custody of goods or the unrewarded performance of work upon them. Conversely the benefit may rest entirely with the bailee; a bailment of this kind is known as com-modatum or gratuitous loan. At one time it was thought that gratuitous bailments could be accommodated within the contractual theory of bail-ments by means of some invented or hypothetical consideration. As Pro-fessor Stoljar has remarked, these attempts were amusing and highly artificial.[18] In cases of depositum or mandatum the bailor's consideration was sometimes said to rest in the fact that he had yielded up his possession of the goods,[19] or had trusted the bailee with them,[20] or had conferred upon the bailee a right to exercise the possessory remedies against third parties. But this was hardly a detriment to the bailor, or indeed a benefit to the bailee, when the whole object of the transaction was to provide the bailor with something for nothing.[21] In cases of loan it was easy enough to identify the bailee's benefit, and the Courts were prepared to recognise such a benefit even though it could not be objectively identified; thus in the curious case of *Bainbridge* v. *Firmstone*,[22] where the bailee borrowed two boilers from the owner in order to weigh them, Denman C.J. remark-ed that if the bailee thought he was deriving a benefit from the transaction that would suffice to make him answerable for their damage while in his possession.

---

[16] Cf., however, the observations by Pearce L.J. in the *Archbolds* case, ante, where reliance upon such title was pleaded. Cf. further *Pye Ltd.* v. *B.G. Transport Service Ltd.* [1966] 2 Lloyd's Rep. 300, where bailors were allowed to recover against carriers for negligent loss of a quantity of radio sets notwithstanding that the radios were in the process of being exported in a manner designed to evade the Persian customs, and in contravention of the *Customs and Excise Act* 1952. Browne J. held that no reliance upon the illegal contract of sale was necessary in order to establish an action against the carriers, and allowed recovery on the principle of *Bowmakers* case, (ante).
[17] *Frost* v. *Plumb* (1873) 40 Conn. 111; *Hinkel* v. *Pruitt* (1912) 151 S.W. 43; cf. *Parker* v. *Latner* (1872) 60 Me. 528.
[18] (1955) 7 *Res Judicatae* 160, at 167.
[19] Story, *Bailments*, p. 4.
[20] E.g. *Coggs* v. *Bernard* (1703) 2 Ld. Raym. 909, at 919; *Banbury* v. *Bank of Montreal* [1918] A.C. 626, at 657; and, generally, Pollock (1886) 2 L.Q.R. 37; Tay (1966) 5 *Sydney Law Review* 239, at 242-243.
[21] Tay, ibid.
[22] (1838) 8 Ad. & El. 743.

The defendant had some reason for wishing to weigh the boilers, and he could do so only by obtaining permission from the plaintiff, which he did obtain by promising to return them in good condition.[23]

But it was much harder to perform the reverse analysis and to discern the borrower's consideration under a gratuitous bailment of this kind. In one case, the Court was reduced to saying that the lender's duty in relation to the safety of the chattel was contracted as a result of the purpose of the loan:

By the necessarily implied purpose of the loan a duty is contracted towards the borrower not to conceal from him those defects known to the lender which may make the loan perilous or unprofitable to him.[24]

The result in this case was the imposition upon the lender of a duty lower than a duty of reasonable care and it may be that this narrow, pseudo-contractual duty has survived until the present day.[25] But more recent cases have repudiated the notion of a gratuitous bailment as a contractual relation. In the New South Wales case, *Heaton* v. *Richards*,[26] which involved a bailment by way of mandatum, it was suggested that a contractual rationalisation may still have been possible if the bailment had arisen at the request or instigation of the unrewarded party; for then, as in *Bainbridge* v. *Firmstone,* it might be possible to say that the bailee's own private prospect of advantage was sufficient consideration. Later cases have abandoned such refinements and have suggested that whenever no tangible benefit can be perceived as accruing to one party the bailment will be non-contractual.[27] The resultant conclusion, that gratuitous bailment "has nothing to do with the law of contract at all",[28] has been specifically endorsed by modern tribunals in both New South Wales and New Zealand. In *Thomas* v. *High*[29] a sum of money was gratuitously bailed by the respondent to the appellant, on terms that the appellant should keep it for no reward and return it to the respondent as and when required. The appellant returned certain sums and then refused to surrender the remainder. The respondent sued for money had and received and succeeded at the trial. The appellant appealed, claiming that since the action was essentially one for conversion it disclosed or relied upon an assertion of felony and should be stayed until criminal proceedings had been taken to establish his guilt. This contention had been rejected at the trial because the judge found that the action was founded upon an implied contract, the appellant's promise being to redeliver on demand. The Supreme Court repudiated this conclusion and ordered a new trial. In their view, a gratuitous bailment disclosed no possible action in contract but gave rise to purely tortious remedies against the defaulting bailee. Admittedly in the case of bailment of money the bailor might

---

[23] Ibid., at 744.
[24] *Blakemore* v. *Bristol & Exeter Ry. Co.* (1858) 8 E. & B. 1034, at 1051-1052.
[25] Post, p. 349.
[26] (1881) 2 L.R. (N.S.W.) 73; post, p. 285.
[27] See, in addition to the text, p. (314, n. 82), post.
[28] Paton, *Bailment in the Common Law*, p. 40.
[29] (1960) 60 S.R. (N.S.W.) 401.

waive the tort and sue for money had and received, but his action remained essentially tortious[30] and a gratuitous bailment engendered no
right of action in contract at all. It may be noticed that in this case the
bailment arose at the suggestion of the appellant; however, this did not
inhibit the Court from accepting that he was a gratuitous or unrewarded
bailee.

In *Walker* v. *Watson*[31] the gratuitous bailment took the form of a loan
of the plaintiff's car to the defendant. The car was damaged and the
plaintiff sued in contract for breach of an implied promise to treat the
car with reasonable care and to redeliver it in the condition in which it
was bailed. The defendant claimed that since the plaintiff knew that she
was drunk at the time the bailment was created she should be entitled to
plead contributory negligence or volenti non fit injuria in her defence. At
first instance this defence was rejected on the ground that the plaintiff's
action was an action in contract and that the specified defences were inapplicable to an action for bread of contractual duty[32] This decision was
reversed on appeal, Mahon J. holding that the action was essentially one
for negligence and that no action for breach of contract could be founded
upon a bare gratuitous bailment.

> This, however, is a case of gratuitous bailment. There was no
> element of contract at present. No consideration moved from the
> appellant when she took possession of the car with the consent
> of the respondent. The only duties which arose in consequence of
> the bailment were the ordinary duties which the law imposes as
> incidents of that special relationship. There were no contractual
> terms super-added. The appellant assumed the ordinary duty of a
> bailee to take care of the chattel entrusted to her custody. Any
> action for breach of that duty lay in tort, not in contract.[33]

English decisions have further denied (albeit only by way of dictum)
the identification of gratuitous bailments with contract.[34] Thus in *Morris*
v. *C. W. Martin & Sons Ltd.,*[35] which actually involved a bailment for
reward, Diplock, L.J., declared that neither a gratuitous bailment nor a
bailment by finding gives rise to a contractual relationship between the
parties; and in *Hedley Byrne & Co. Ltd.* v. *Heller & Partners Ltd.*[36] Lord
Devlin suggested that because of this analysis the bailor's remedies under
a gratuitous bailment subsisted solely in tort.

> A promise given without consideration to perform a service cannot
> be enforced as a contract by the promisee; but if the service is in
> fact performed and done negligently the promisee can recover in an
> action in tort. This is the foundation of the liability of a gratuitous
> bailee.

Elsewhere, we hope to show that the denial of any correlation between
gratuitous bailment and contract does not necessarily justify the conclusion

---

[30] Cf. on this point *Chesworth* v. *Farrar* [1967] 1 Q.B. 407; *Peters* v. *Tuck* (1915)
11 Tas. L.R. 30.
[31] [1974] 2 N.Z.L.R. 175; Palmer (1975) 24 I.C.L.Q. 565; post, p. 316.
[32] As to this question, see post, p. 55.
[33] [1974] 2 N.Z.L.R. 175, at 178.
[34] See, in addition to the text, p. 314, nn. 81, 82, post.
[35] [1966] 1 Q.B. 716, at 731-732.
[36] [1964] A.C. 465, at 526.

that the remedies available under a gratuitous bailment are limited to those that are available under the law of tort.[37] To assume this is to deny the independent character of the bailment relation, and to disregard the considerable evidence that bailment is a transaction sui generis with rules that cannot be explained solely or satisfactorily by reference to other forms of action. For the present, it may suffice to point out that other equally recent authorities do support a contractual analysis of gratuitous bailment, and apparently regard the question of consideration as less important than the consensual nature of the relationship. Such an approach is evident in certain dicta of Bray C.J. in the South Australian case of *Roufos* v. *Brewster*,[38] and in the observation of Lord Wilberforce in *New Zealand Shipping Co. Ltd.* v. *A. M. Satterthwaite & Co. Ltd.*[39] that gratuitous bailments are one of a class of everyday contracts which modern law subjects to "a practical approach, often at the cost of forcing the facts to fit uneasily into the marked slots of offer, acceptance and consideration."[40]

With respect, it seems that to classify the gratuitous bailment as a species of contract is to threaten to disfigure the notion of contract itself with no compensating advantage to the concept of bailment. Even if gratuitous bailments were theoretically assimilable within the purview of contract, there would remain other varieties of bailment that are incapable of such analysis. Examples are the sub-bailment and the bailment by finding, neither of which predicates even a consensual relationship between the parties.[41] The result, in conceptual terms, would therefore be the dislocation or fragmentation of bailment and the unjustified expansion of contract. There are further perils in a contractual fiction of bailment. It could lead to the application of a requirement of privity of agreement, whereas under the modern law of bailment there is none; and it could lead to a misleading interpretation of the bailment for reward. At present, the distinction between a contractual and a non-contractual bailment is not synonymous with the distinction between a bailment for reward and a gratuitous bailment. This is so because it is possible to create a bailment for reward which does not disclose a contract between the parties. Such a bailment might arise when the wife of a tenant in a block of flats deposits goods with the landlord for storage,[42] or when a bailee of goods sub-bails them for reward to a third party. In the latter event, the sub-bailee will owe to the original bailor all the obligations that arise at Common Law upon a bailment for reward.[43]

In any event, sufficient has been said to demonstrate the independence of even the consensual bailment from contract: bailment is a legal relationship which, while frequently arising from contract, can exist independently thereof.[44] The true nature of the relationship between bailment

[37] Post, p. 36.
[38] [1971] 2 S.A.S.R. 218, at 223-224, set out at p. 000, post. Cf. Zelling J. at 235, who denied the equation.
[39] [1975] A.C. 154, at 167.
[40] See further p. 314, n. 81, post.
[41] Post, p. 25, and Chapters 20, 22.
[42] *Andrews* v. *Home Flats Ltd.* [1945] 2 All E.R. 698.
[43] *Morris* v. *C. W. Martin & Sons Ltd.* [1966] 1 Q.B. 716; Chapter 20, post.
[44] *Chesworth* v. *Farrar* [1967] 1 Q.B. 407, at 415.

and contract was identified by Winfield,[45] who maintained that bailment was a form of conveyance of personal property, since it gave the bailee a recognised and defensible interest in the subject-matter of the bailment. Contract is no more than the vehicle by which that conveyance is normally effected. To equate bailment with contract is therefore to concentrate unduly upon the static dimension of bailment (i.e. its creation and forms) and to neglect its active dimension (i.e. the machinery of its enforcement). In neither respect is contract a complete or universal solution.

Admittedly, Winfield's approach is conditioned by his analysis of bailment as a form or product of agreement, and he does not finally commit himself as to whether contract could actually be dispensed with.[46] But this is because he was more concerned to show the immateriality of contract to the essential obligations of bailment than to assess its materiality to the original creation of the relationship. Later developments, by reducing still further the relevance of both contract and agreement to bailment, serve only to accentuate the central importance of the possessory interest that results from the bailment relation. Of course, it is more difficult to regard bailments as representing a "conveyance" of personal property when they can arise contrary to the will and consent of the "bailor". But the result of bailment, i.e. the creation of a possessory interest and of a relationship founded upon a form of property, is the same whether the bailment is consensual or unilateral. It is unfortunate that the implications of this view of the central element of bailment have not been more fully explored.[47]

C. Bailment and consensus

When the contractual theory of bailment began to be eroded, there followed a significant interlude during which bailment because identified as the product of some agreement between the parties. Some of the most influential judges and writers lent their support to this analysis. Among the latter were Pollock and Wright, who in their treatise "Possession in the Common Law" (published in 1888) identified a bailee as follows:

> Any person is to be considered as a bailee who otherwise than as a servant either receives possession of a thing from another or consents to receive or hold possession of a thing for another upon an understanding with the other person either to keep and return or deliver to him the specific thing or to (convey and) apply the specific thing according to the directions antecedent or future of the other person.[48]

This definition was accepted without criticism by Paton in his work on bailment in 1952,[49] and was largely echoed in the writings of Winfield in 1931.[50] It enjoys the advantage of accommodating within the perimeter of bailment all those cases wherein the possession of a chattel has been transferred under an agreement which, for some reason, falls short of

---

[45] *Province of the Law of Tort*, pp. 100-103.
[46] Ibid., pp. 98, 100.
[47] See further post, p. 65 et. seq.
[48] At p. 163; adopted by Chitty, *Contract*, vol. II (24th ed.), para 2201, and by Dubinsky J. in *Lawton* v. *Dartmouth Moving & Storage Ltd.* (1976) 64 D.L.R. (3d) 326, at 330.
[49] Op. cit., pp. 4-5.
[50] Op. cit., Chapter 5.

contract. The consensual theory of bailment is accepted by a number of judges[51] and was endorsed by Professor Stoljar as recently as 1955.[52] He maintained that bailments were an essentially contractual phenomenon, not in the conventional sense that they were the product of bargain, but because their central element was the bailee's promise (and corresponding duty) to return the goods to the bailor or some third person. This promise begins to operate only when the bailment is executed and the goods are placed in the bailee's possession; but of course there would be no need for the bailor to enforce a promise as to redelivery before that time. The important factor is that, even under a gratuitous bailment, the promise is enforceable.

> The resulting relation must therefore be regarded as being one of contract, to the same extent that every enforcement of a promise, in an arrangement between two persons, is a matter of contract. The arrangement starts with A's agreeing to lend a chattel, and ends with the legal enforcement of B's promise to return it.[53]

Linguistically, the consensual theory of bailment may be said to carry considerable weight. If bailment be truly dependent upon delivery it would be remarkable to have a delivery (and thus a bailment) without an agreement between the parties. But we have already seen that neither the physical nor the mental elements of delivery are essential to the modern transaction of bailment;[54] and it may be added that there are many possessors, who are under a duty to return the chattel to the owner, whom Professors Stoljar would not identify as bailees.[55] The misfortune of the consensual theory of bailment is, quite simply, that it has been overtaken by events. These events are more strongly judicial than academic in character, and have largely (although not entirely) occurred within the past ten or fifteen years. When Professor Stoljar propounded his wider contractual theory in 1955, the only prominent obstacles to a complete identification of bailment with contract were the "incapacity" cases (involving infants and married women) and the cases of gratuitous bailment. The former could be reconciled with a wider contractual theory of bailment on the ground that the contract-negating element was largely technical in character and that both here and in the case of a gratuitous bailee the law nevertheless enforced the bailee's promise to return the chattel. Professor Stoljar in fact saw the gratuitous bailment cases as "the really difficult prototypes of bailment."[56] But even these were at least consensual in character, and infinitely more difficult examples of modern bailment have since arisen. There are now a number of cases in which it is recognised that the parties may enter into a relationship of bailment without agreement, or indeed without communication of any kind at all. Some of these cases also demonstrate that the bailor's consent to the bailee's possession of his chattel is no longer an essential feature of bail-

---

[51] E.g. A. L. Smith and Collins L.JJ., in *Turner* v. *Stallibrass* [1898] 1 Q.B. 56, at 58, 59; Schultz J.A. in *Martin* v. *Town 'n' Country Delicatessen Ltd.* (1963) 42 D.L.R. (2d) 449, at 461-462.
[52] (1955) 7 *Res Judicatae* 160.
[53] Ibid., at 165.
[54] Ante, p. 11.
[55] E.g. finders, as to which see Stoljar loc. cit., at p. 169.
[56] Loc. cit., pp. 163-164.

ment; and some of them are considerably older than the consensual theory of bailment itself.

1. *Finding*:[57] It is now clearly established that cases of finding give rise to a bailment, at least to the extent that the finder owes substantially the same Common Law duties in relation to the chattel as an ordinary consensual bailee. Since the definition of bailment is of primary value in assessing the liabilities attendant upon that relation, and since the great majority of cases are concerned with the duties of the bailee, it seems acceptable now to characterise finding as a case of bailment. In cases of criminal liability, the general trend has admittedly been opposed to this conclusion; and despite a dictum by Lord Goddard in 1951[58] that a finder who subsequently decided to appropriate goods might be guilty of larceny as a bailee, as recently as 1965 it was held that the finder was not a bailee for this purpose.[59] However, the decision in that case was reached with marked reluctance and on the authority of a decision which dated from the time when bailment was still largely regarded as a contractual relation;[60] indeed, Sachs J. observed that had it not been for such prior authority he would readily have accepted the classification, even for criminal purposes, of the finder as a bailee.[61] More recent civil cases have clearly stated that finding gives rise to a form of bailment despite the absence of a common delivery. This was the opinion of Diplock L.J. in *Morris* v. *C. W. Martin & Sons Ltd.*[62] and of Lord Pearson in *Gilchrist Watt & Sanderson Pty. Ltd.* v. *York Products Pty. Ltd.*[63] Admittedly, the equation is not complete, for at least one of the primary rules of bailment (viz., the rule that the bailee is estopped from denying his bailor's title)[64] is unworkable in cases of finding; this is partly because the rule stems from the time when bailments occurred only by way of delivery and the estoppel could be rationalised as part of the consideration for the delivery itself. But there is a sufficient community of responsibility, and a sufficient difference between this responsibility and that owed under the general law of tort, to justify describing cases of finding as, for most practical purposes, cases of bailment.

> In 2 *Halsbury's Laws* [3rd ed.], p. 99, para. 198, which refers to these cases of finding, is headed "When finder of chattel is bailee". This expression is not etymologically accurate, because the word "bailee" is derived from the French 'bailler' meaning to deliver or hand over, and there is no delivering or handing over to a finder. But there is a common element, because both in an ordinary bailment and in a "bailment by finding" the obligation arises because the taking of possession for the safe keeping of the goods.[65]

[57] Chapter 22, post.
[58] *Walters* v. *Lunt* [1951] 2 All E.R. 645, at 647.
[59] *Thompson* v. *Nixon* [1966] 1 Q.B. 103; Hadden [1965] C.L.J. 173.
[60] *R.* v. *Matthews* (1873) 12 Cox C.C. 489.
[61] [1966] 1 Q.B. at 110.
[62] [1966] 1 Q.B. 716, at 731-732.
[63] [1970] 3 All E.R. 825, at 831-832.
[64] Post, p. 163 and see now App. I post.
[65] *Gilchrist Watt & Sanderson Pty. Ltd.* v. *York Products Pty. Ltd.* [1970] 3 All E.R. 825, at 831 per Lord Pearson. Cf. older authorities which, while admitting that the bailee's duties are substantially the same as those arising under an ordinary bailment, feel constrained by the requirements of delivery or consensuality to state

The principal difficulty confronting this equation arises from the identification of the bailor. Is it the owner of the goods, or the person who has
lost them? When the finder hands the goods to a third party for safekeeping, is that third party the bailee of the finder, or of the owner, or of anyone else who has an interest in the goods? All three may be different and
all three are possible contestants in an action to enforce the duties of the
finder-bailee. It may well be that the problems of ascertaining the bailor
in a case of bailment by finding explain the original reluctance of the
courts to equate finding and bailment at all. But this difficulty is not a
serious one and affords no decisive deterrent to the equation in question.
In the great majority of cases the finder bailee's duties will be enforceable
solely by the owner because he alone will have an interest in their enforcement; in the rare cases in which some other party is interested, a
solution can generally be reached by looking to the circumstances, and
perhaps to the state of knowledge, in which the finder assumed possession.

Finders are not involuntary bailees,[66] unless they already have possession of the goods before they find them and then retain them no longer
than they have to.

2. *Sub-bailments and quasi-bailments*:[67] Occasionally the facts of a given
case may rise to a form of tripartite bailment, in which the ultimate possessor of goods takes delivery of them from (or on the instructions of)
someone other than the owner. Normally this intermediary will be acting,
or purporting to act, on the owner's behalf. If the intermediary himself
is a bailee we would normally characterise the subsidiary delivery as a
sub-bailment and the eventual possessor as a sub-bailee;[68] if, on the
other hand, the intermediary acquires no intervening possession of his
own, we would normally characterise the ultimate delivery as a quasi-
bailment, and the eventual possessor as a quasi-bailee.[69] It is now established that a delivery of this kind may give rise to a bailment at Common Law between the owner and the ultimate possessor, although there
is neither contract, agreement or communication between them It seems,
moreover, that their relationship is one of bailment for the purpose of
estopping the possessor from denying the owner's title,[70] as well as for the
purpose of rendering him answerable for the safety of the goods.

3. *Other bailments without the consent of the owner*:[71] All three of the
foregoing varieties of bailment could, at a pinch, be rationalised as a form
of consensual arrangement if it were accepted that the finder and the
sub- or quasi-bailee take possession by the implied consent of the owner.

---

or to imply that the finder is not a bailee: *Newman* v. *Bourne & Hollingsworth
Ltd.* (1915) 31 T.L.R. 209; *Helson* v. *McKenzies (Cuba St.) Ltd.* [1950] N.Z.L.R.
878; *Makower, McBeath & Co. Pty. Ltd.* v. *Dalgety & Co. Ltd.* [1921] V.L.R.
365, at 373-374; and see Paton, op. cit., p. 118; Stoljar (1955) 7 *Res Judicatae*
160, at 169; Hadden [1965] C.L.J. 173.

---

[66] Cf. *Helson* v. *McKenzies (Cuba St.) Ltd.* [1950] N.Z.L.R. 878.
[67] Chapter 20, post.
[68] E.g. *Morris* v. *C. W. Martin & Sons Ltd.* [1966] 1 Q.B. 716.
[69] E.g. *Arcweld Constructions Pty. Ltd.* v. *Smith* (1968) Unrep. Vic. Sup. Ct.; post,
     p. 837.
[70] Post, p. 175.
[71] Post, p. 878.

This fiction is at least sustained to the extent that the honest finder is not guilty of trespass in taking possession of the goods.[72] But in other respects the theory is misleading and otiose; and it seems clear, for instance (despite Australian and Canadian dicta to the contrary)[73] that an enforceable sub-bailment may be created although the principal bailor has not consented to the sub-bailee's possession of the goods.[74] Moreover, there are a number of other authorities which have discerned the creation of a bailment although the taking into possession of the owner's goods was entirely without his authority or consent. Thus there may be a bailment where a person takes a suitcase from a train mistaking it for a friend's;[75] where goods are taken from a mental patient upon her admission to hospital;[76] where an apparently well-intentioned passer-by takes a watch from a tipsy man;[77] where a person seizes goods in order to protect them from a fire;[78] when a wharfinger takes possession of goods unloaded at the quay-side;[79] when a landlord distrains upon his tenant's goods;[80] or when an owner of land distrains upon an animal damage feasant.[81] Admittedly, some of these cases bear a closer affinity to the consensual bailment than others, and in one Australian case it was held that no bailment arose for the purposes of the criminal law when a wallet was taken from a drunkard.[82] But the case dealt with criminal rather than civil liability and is of some antiquity; against it may be placed the more recent Western Australian authority in which a policeman who seized camels and detained them wrongfully was assumed to owe to their owner the duties of a bailee.[83]

It is true that some of these cases refer to the resultant bailment as a merely analogous or constructive example of the species;[84] in this respect, they may be regarded as sanctioning the recognition of a form of "limited-purpose" bailment, whereunder some but not necessarily all of the conventional obligations arising under an orthodox bailment are present. The significant feature is that, for most practical purposes, the relationship of the parties is directly equivalent to that of the bailor and bailee; and that, but for this analogy, the bailee would not have owed the distinctive duties to which he electively became subject.

The advantages of liberating bailment from agreement are essentially the same as those of emancipating bailment from contract. To subject

---

[72] Post, p. 857.
[73] *Chapman* v. *Robinson and Ferguson* (1969) 71 W.W.R. 515; *Wood Motors Ltd.* v. *McTavish* (1972) 21 D.L.R. (3d) 480, at 482-483; *Roufos* v. *Brewster and Brewster* [1971] 2 S.A.S.R. 218, at 234.
[74] Post, p. 786.
[75] *McCowan* v. *McCulloch* [1926] 1 D.L.R. 312.
[76] *Martin* v. *L.C.C.* [1947] 1 K.B. 628.
[77] *R.* v. *Reeves* (1859) 5 Jur. 716.
[78] *R.* v. *Leigh* (1800) 2 East P.C. 694.
[79] *Makower, McBeath & Co. Pty. Ltd.* v. *Dalgety & Co. Ltd.* [1921] V.L.R. 365; *Gilchrist Watt & Sanderson Pty. Ltd.* v. *York Products Pty. Ltd.* [1970] 3 All E.R. 825.
[80] *Chesworth* v. *Farrar* [1967] 1 Q.B. 407; cf. Blackstone, 2 Comm. 451; Vaines, *Personal Property* (5th ed.), p. 77; *Hopkins* v. *Kong Lee* (1892) 14 A.L.T. 41.
[81] Vaines, loc. cit.; cf. *Sorrell* v. *Paget* [1950] 1 K.B. 252.
[82] *R.* v. *Rigbey* (1863) 2 S.C.R. (N.S.W.) 176.
[83] *Mazullah Khan* v. *McNamara* (1911) 13 W.A.L.R. 151.
[84] See in particular *Makower, McBeath & Co. Pty. Ltd.* v. *Dalgety & Co. Ltd.* (ante).

bailment to the limitations of agreement would have the unfortunate consequence of importing a notion of privity into an area in which it is misleading and unnecessary. As Professor Tay and the modern authorities have shown,[85] bailment now primarily connotes the relationship between a person (the bailee) and a thing (the subject-matter of the bailment). From this initial relationship there arises a collection of interpersonal duties which are owed by the bailee to whomsoever can be identified as his bailor, and vice-versa. It is not necessary that the original steps which give rise to this reciprocity of duties should be based upon agreement, and modern authority confirms that even when an agreement exists the bailor need not be a party to it in order to enforce the duties of the bailee.[86]

But if bailment be independent of agreement, the question must arise as to who occupies the rôle of bailor, and who can enforce the duties of the bailee. In most cases of non-consensual bailment this question will cause no difficulty. The "bailor" will be the owner, or the person from whose possession the goods are taken; and in cases in which these two parties are different it would seem reasonable to exact from the bailee the same duties in respect of each. Likewise, when goods are delivered by an intermediary, the recipient should be regarded as the bailee not only (if this is the apparent intention of the parties) of the deliveror himself but of the party who owns the goods, at least when the recipient knows that this is someone other than the deliveror. In other cases, it should (as we have already suggested) be relatively simple to derive from the circumstances of the bailee's possession the identity of the party or parties to whom he owes his duties as bailee.

One case in which the consensual theory of bailment was invoked to produce an unjust result was the New Zealand decision in *Helson* v. *McKenzies (Cuba St.) Ltd.*[87] Here, a customer lost money in a shop and another customer handed it to an assistant for safekeeping. Through the negligence of the management the money was handed to an imposter and was permanently lost. It was held that the store were not liable as bailees to the owner[88] because the only bailment (i.e. delivery) that took place was between them and the honest customer who originally found the money. This customer was not the owner's agent for the purposes of creating a bailment to the store and no such bailment between the store and the owner could therefore arise. This case was decided at a time when bailment could still be asserted to rest (broadly) upon contract, and when the notion of a sub-bailee's double liability had not become established. It appears, with respect, that the case should be decided differently today. When a person accepts goods from a non-owner and knows that they belong to someone other than the immediate deliveror, he should owe the duties of a bailee to the owner himself as well (if this intention is clear from the circumstances of the delivery) to the deliveror. A plural

---

[85] Tay (1966) 5 *Sydney Law Review* 239; *Roufos* v. *Brewster & Brewster* [1971] 2 S.A.S.R. 218, at 235 per Zelling J.; post, p. 30.
[86] E.g. *Morris* v. *C. W. Martin & Sons.* [1966] 1 Q.B. 716.
[87] [1950] N.Z.L.R. 878. Cf. *Corbett* v. *Jamieson* [1923] N.Z.L.R. 374.
[88] She recovered in conversion, but her damages were substantially reduced for contributory negligence: post, p. 135.

responsibility of this kind may be said to be one of the terms upon which the bailee's undertaking of custody is impliedly based, and upon which his possession is assumed. In exceptional cases, the bailee may refuse to undertake any responsibility to the ulterior owner and may, by making such refusal one of the essential conditions upon which he takes delivery, effectively debar any action against him by the owner, irrespective of contract.[89] But without some clear and effective declaration of the terms of his own possession, no agreement between the relevant parties would seem necessary to make him liable to the owner as a bailee.

4. *Bailment and the voluntary assumption of possession*: The judicial analysis of bailments seems therefore to have reached the stage at which any person who voluntarily assumes possession of goods belonging to another will be held to owe at least the principal duties of the bailee at Common Law. This analysis is broadly supported by Halsbury[90] and Chitty,[91] although both authors point out that non-consensual bailments represent a novel and perhaps anomalous addition to the species. But other commentators have gone further and have variously denied the need for consent or knowledge on the bailee's part in order to discern a bailment.

The middle theory of bailment as a voluntary and intelligent acceptance of chattels, in which attention focuses exclusively upon the mental state of the alleged bailee, is an attractive one because it helps to demarcate areas of distinctive duty while emancipating those duties from the restrictive requirements of privity, agreement or consideration. Most voluntary bailees, whether they possess the relevant chattel under a contract or not, owe a duty towards that chattel which either would not have arisen at all, or would be in some significant respect different, were it not for the fact of their possession.[92] Indeed, it is the traditional absence of any such duty on the part of the involuntary bailee, as much as the theory that no man can become a bailee against his will, that has probably arrested the further judicial development of bailment into areas of involuntary possession and has led both judges and commentators to stress the need for a willing possession of chattels.[93]

So far, we have discussed this theory of bailment as the product of modern judicial innovation. One author has taken the view that the theory is not, in fact, a novel one but represents "an interesting and fruitful return to the original foundations from which the law of bailment took its departure". This analysis is pursued by Professor Tay in an article in the Sydney Law Review.[94] Arguing primarily from an historical perspective, she contends that bailment and detinue were originally co-extensive, and that any person could historically be considered a bailee who had such possession of goods as could render him liable in an action for detinue.

[89] *Johnson Matthey & Co. Ltd.* v. *Constantine Terminals Ltd.* [1976] 2 Lloyd's Rep. 215; post, p. 810. As to the relevance of the sub-bailee's knowledge of the owner's existence under an extended bailment, see post, p. 819.
[90] *Laws* (4th ed.), vol. ii, para.
[91] *Contract* (24th ed.), vol. II, paras, 2201, 2217.
[92] Post, pp. 39, 852.
[93] As to the conceptual position of involuntary bailment, see post, p. 32. et. seq.
[94] (1966) 5 *Sydney Law Review* 239.

It was only the later evolution of assumpsit, and the procedural division of detinue into detinue sur bailment and devenerunt ad manus, that allowed bailment to be mistakenly drawn off into the realm of consensual obligations. But bailment was independent of agreement because its essence lay in the notion of an "undertaking". By this is meant, not an undertaking in the more modern sense of a promise or assurance given to a particular person, but an undertaking in the sense of an assumption of a duty or the commencement of a task. Thus, in bailment, the bailee's duty depends upon his having undertaken possession of the bailor's goods, rather than upon his having given, in the form of an agreement, any undertaking to the bailor himself. This interpretation is supported by Beale in the wider area of undertaking generally:

> An undertaking is the entrance of two parties into such relationship as that one party, on account of the bare relationship unaided by agreement, has a new duty to perform toward the other; he *undertakes* a new duty.[95]

According, therefore, to Professor Tay the relationship of bailor and bailee depends purely upon the bailee's having entered into a relationship with the bailor's chattel. That relationship consists in possession, and a knowing possession of another man's goods is the root and essence of bailment. Bailment therefore requires "neither an agreement with, nor any knowledge of the person of, a particular bailor". Citing *Thornhill's* case,[96] she observes:

> Here, then, we have the non-contractual and non-consensual view of a person's liabilities in detinue. He may admittedly have legal possession of the chattel, but the chattel belongs to another or another has the better right to possess it. He has been made aware of the continuing right of another by a demand for delivery. He now has a duty towards the demandant, not because of any express or implied undertaking toward the demandant, not because of any agreement between them, but simply because he accepted possession of a thing in which another had a continuing interest. Only if the defendant claims that he has a continuing right to detain do agreements and undertakings become relevant, not to the plaintiff's charge but to the defendant's reply. It is by entering into a relationship with a thing, and not by entering into a relationship with a person, that the defendant becomes subject to duties. It is thus that the finder has the same primary duty as the consensual bailee.[97]

There are two principal difficulties confronting an acceptance of Professor Tay's theory as the proper historical analysis of bailment. The first is that the word bailment originated as a particular sub-division of detinue, to accommodate cases based upon the very element which Professor Tay contends to be unnecessary: viz., a delivery from person (the bailor) to another (the bailee). This explains the expression bailment itself which, as we have seen, originates from the French verb "to deliver". Thus Professor Tay's theory, while claiming to be based upon historical deriva-

---

[95] *Gratuitous Undertakings* (1891-1892) 5 *Harvard Law Review* 222, cited by Tay loc. cit., at 242.
[96] (1344) Y.B. 17 & Edw. 3 (R.S.) 150.
[97] Tay, loc. cit., at 244.

tions, relies upon an interpretation of bailment which seems wider than that originally accorded to it.

Professor Tay answers this objection by pointing out that there was no fundamental difference between an allegation of detinue sur bailment and an allegation of detinue on the plea of devenerunt ad manus. Detinue sur bailment was merely a stronger case of detinue, or a stronger way of framing the action. The agreement or delivery which was inherent in such a plea was not essential to the liability of the party in possession, and in all fundamental respects both forms of action were congruent: "the primary duty arises from the acceptance of possession".

> We have seen that in the early law the term "bailment" was used to make a distinction within detinue. But this distinction, we have argued, has no fundamental importance in the law: consent and agreement between the parties help only to define the extent of the duty, they do not create it . . . It is for this reason that the term "bailment" is most conveniently used not to cover delivery upon agreement, but to refer to that general situation in which a man has duties arising from his temporary possession of another's chattel.[98]

Even on purely historical grounds there is some dispute as to the early correlation of detinue and bailment. Fifoot, for example, remarks that the evidence for any intimate association between the two types of obligation is scarce, and concludes: "The content of the fourteenth century cases confirms the suspicion that bailment was not the single root of detinue."[99]

But ultimately one's view of this early relationship depends upon the circular issue of what one means by bailment. It is on the extreme limb of this latter question that the second objection to Professor Tay's theory is founded; for her equation between detinue and bailment leads her at one point to extend the orthodox relationship of bailor and bailee to cases of "involuntary bailment". If, by this, she means a possession of goods that is involuntary ab initio, then apart from some rather colourable American authority, there is no case-law supporting this extension of bailment under modern law at all.

5. *Bailment and the knowing possession of chattels*: The one significant difference, therefore, between Professor Tay's notion of bailment and that currently acknowledged by the courts is that Professor Tay seems to consider the possessor's consent to possession irrelevant to his status as a bailee. In other words, she would apparently deny the ambiguity of the expression "involuntary bailment" and would class the involuntary but knowing possessor of chattels as a true bailee.

In fact, the expression "involuntary bailment" can mean one of two different things; the relationship between an owner of goods and a person who has given no *original* consent to their possession (such as the recipient of unsolicited goods) and the relationship between an owner and a person whose originally voluntary possession has become involuntary through lapse of time (such as a carrier who is unable through no

---

[98] Tay, loc. cit., at 245.
[99] *History and Sources of the Common Law*, p. 29.

fault of his own to deliver goods at their destination).[1] It is acceptable to regard the latter class of possessor as a bailee because there is at least some vestige of consent to the position he now occupies; indeed the risk of uncollected goods is probably an occupational hazard of carriers and artificers alike. But the same is scarcely true of the originally involuntary bailee.

Two interrelated arguments have been advanced in favour of aggregating such instances of possession with the wider orbit of the bailment relation. Professor Tay founds her argument upon the formulation of a duty which is based upon possession, is common to voluntary and involuntary bailees alike, and is in her view the essence of bailment.

> The primary duty of a man who takes into his possession the chattel of another without challenging the other's title is the same whether he be a hirer, a borrower, a finder or an "involuntary bailee": he has a duty to safeguard and redeliver.[2]

However, the inclusion within this formula of bailments which are involuntary ab initio is open to at least three objections. The first is that an involuntary bailee does not (unless he is defrauded or duressed into doing so) "take into his possession the chattel of another": the chattel is thrust upon him, and into his possession, independently of any conduct or desire on his part. Secondly, the involuntary bailee is under a duty to redeliver the goods only when the "bailor" can sue for detinue; and for detinue to issue the defendant must have refused to comply with a demand for their surrender.[3] A possessor who fails to heed such a demand and continues in possession of the goods when he could readily relieve himself of them is scarcely, from that moment, an involuntary bailee. Thirdly, the traditional view of an involuntary bailee's obligations denies that he is under any duty of care towards them unless he chooses to effect a redelivery.[4] His only liability is for intentional and, possibly, reckless damage. Thus it could scarcely be contended that he owes any responsibility to "safeguard" them at all.

In fact, Professor Tay's approach to involuntary bailments is notably ambivalent, and elsewhere in her analysis she contends that to become a bailee "I must in some way consent to having possession, though in some situations the law may give me little leave to reject it".[5] Possibly, therefore, her earlier reference to involuntary bailment was meant to signify only those cases in which an originally voluntary possession becomes involuntary by lapse of time. A less equivocal advocate of the bailment quality of involuntary bailments was Professor Laidlaw, from whom Professor Tay derived much contemporary support. In Laidlaw's view, it was incorrect to regard the involuntary bailee as owing no duty towards the goods; he would probably be liable at least if he showed "extreme active negligence" in their custody, and he would ultimately come under an

---

[1] See generally Chapter 12.
[2] Tay, loc. cit., at 245.
[3] Post, p. 149.
[4] Post, p. 381.
[5] Tay, loc. cit., at 252.

obligation to redeliver them.[6] The latter point can be dismissed on the ground that the obligation in question can crystallise only when the bailee has declined to surrender the goods in response to the owner's demand. The former point has greater validity, because there is at least some authority and considerable common-sense in favour of basing the involuntary bailee's liability for safekeeping upon a broad definition of reasonable care.[7] Since this is the standard exacted from most conventional bailees, there may therefore be said to exist sufficient affinity between the two classes of bailment to justify their inclusion within one general group. Indeed, a not dissimilar argument may be advanced upon the more conventional view of the involuntary bailee's liability, as excluding mere acts of negligence and encompassing only intentional damage. Since, on this approach, both voluntary and involuntary bailments have peculiar (albeit different) rules of liability, and since both sets of rules depend upon possession, it might be urged that there is sufficient similarity between both classes to justify the latter's inclusion within the conceptual realm of bailment.[8] But the functional value of bailment as a distinctive source of obligation is that it (a) imposes duties that would not otherwise exist; and (b) imposes duties which, despite minor internal variations, are fundamentally similar. According to present authority, the "bailment" which is involuntary ab initio would appear, on these criteria, to fail to qualify as a member of the general group. Either the rules as to liability are markedly different from those which govern the voluntary bailment, or they may be explicable as a single function of the ordinary law of tort.[9]

In fact, for most practical purposes, the argument whether this relationship counts as a bailment proper is a fairly pointless one. The inclusion of the originally involuntary bailment within the general group would be valuable only if it meant that rules peculiar to orthodox bailments could be applied by analogy to the new member or if the rules of involuntary bailment could be employed to cast some light upon bailments as a whole. The latter prospect is scarcely likely to materialise because of the uncertain and exigual nature of the rules themselves. Moreover, if the occasion ever arose to consider whether some other facet of bailment apart from the duty of care (such as the bailee's estoppel, or his peculiar burden of proof) should be applied to cases of involuntary bailment, it seems likely that a conclusion would be reached upon considerations of expediency and justice rather than by relying upon the general features of a class of obligation to which involuntary bailments may or may not belong.[10] The question is therefore of little practical or contemporary value and it would seem that the considerable body of authority which denies the bailment quality of an originally voluntary bailment[11] is (despite the fact that it dates from the time when the predominant conception of bailment was as a con-

---

[6] W. K. Laidlaw, "Principles of Bailment" (1930-1931) 16 *Cornell Law Quarterly* 286, at 306.
[7] Post, p. 381 et seq.
[8] Post, pp. 380-381.
[9] Ibid.
[10] At pp. 381 and 390, we suggest that the estoppel rule should not apply but that the burden of proof should be similar to that arising under an ordinary bailment.
[11] E.g. *Lethbridge* v. *Phillips* (1819) 2 Stark. 478; *Neuwith* v. *Over Darwen Co. Operative Society* (1894) 63 L.J.Q.B. 290; post, p. 381.

tractual or at least a consensual relation) doctrinally acceptable today. Involuntary bailments may, because of their inherent eccentricity, perhaps be classed as pseudo-bailments, and for this reason we afford them a place within our overall classification; but their inclusion has no real value other than that of tidiness. In most cases the identification of an involuntary bailment will justify the conclusion that there is no bailment at all.

6. *Bailment and possession simpliciter*: It is no part of Professor Tay's thesis that a person who is in possession of another's goods without his knowledge (such as an occupier upon whose land they are lost) should be considered a bailee. Indeed, she examines in depth those cases in which the courts have been compelled to decide whether a possessor should reasonably have been aware of the fact of his possession, and can therefore be subjected to the liabilities of a bailee.[12] But several other commentators have proposed a formulation of bailment which would encompass every situation in which one person is in possession of a chattel to which another person has a superior possessory right. Such is the functional approach taken by an anonymous annotator to the *Stanford Law Review* in 1959.[13] According to this author:

> Since the term [bailment] is applied to a variety of transactions a realistic definition would view the term as referring collectively to the rules of law that govern the relationship between a possessor and one who has a prior or superior possessory interest, usually the owner.

This approach, which is shared to some degree by Laidlaw[14] and Williston,[15] would perceive a relationship of bailment not only between an owner and an "involuntary bailee" but between an owner and any person who is unwittingly in possession of the owner's goods. Judicially it has only rarely been sought to argue that an unconscious possession of goods gives rise to a bailment, partly because an unconscious possessor would owe no duty in relation to the goods, and partly because the enforcement of any possessory right in relation to them (e.g. by an occupier against a finder) is not dependent upon the presence of an orthodox bailment.[16] There is indeed some argument for aggregating all instances of non-proprietary possession under a single division for the purpose of clarifying the incidents of possession itself. However, this exercise would seem to be best conducted by an examination of the concept of possession per se rather than via some fictional equation

---

[12] Tay (1966) 5 *Sydney Law Review* 239, at 252-253.

[13] (1959) 12 *Stanford Law Review* 264, at 266.

[14] (1930-1931) 16 *Cornell Law Quarterly* 286, at 306-307; cf. at 290.

[15] *Contracts*, para 1032, who claimed that a bailment arose whenever someone had lawful possession of a chattel of which he was not the owner; disapproved by Tay, loc. cit., at 252-253.

[16] The American authority most commonly cited for the equation between possession and bailment is *Foulke* v. *New York Consolidated R.R.* (1920) 228 N.Y. 269, 127 N.E. 137: "It is the element of lawful possession, however created, and duty to account for the thing as the property of another that creates a bailment, regardless of whether such possession is based upon contract in the ordinary sense or not." But it does not seem that the discovery of a bailment was essential to this decision. A similar confusion (but with the opposite result) can be glimpsed in *Bridges* v. *Hawksworth* (1851) 21 L.J.Q.B. 75. For a more modern and restrictive American view of bailment, see *Berglund* v. *Roosevelt University* (1974) 310 N.E. (2d) 773; post, p. 232.

between that concept and bailment. Neither historical derivation nor modern judicial usage sanctions this equation, and it has yet to be demonstrated that such an approach would be of value to an understanding of bailment itself. It is therefore submitted that unwitting possessors or "bailees by concealment",[17] such as occupiers upon whose land goods are lost, or bona fide purchasers of goods who take delivery without realising that they have not obtained a good title, are not bailees, and that there would be neither authority nor purpose for stating that they were. In short, possession and bailment are not synonymous.

V. ENFORCEMENT: BAILMENT AND TORT

We have already demonstrated that a bailment may exist independently of contract, and may therefore give rise to remedies that cannot be characterised as contractual. This realisation has often induced the courts to state that a non-contractual bailment gives rise solely to remedies in tort. If this conclusion were true it would effectively reduce the importance of bailment in the modern field of obligations, for most torts to chattels (for example, negligence and conversion) do not depend upon the tortfeasor's possession of the chattel and are therefore not peculiar to bailment. The role of bailment would be limited to that of a mere duty-structure within which the ordinary principles of tortious liability apply.

This conclusion appears to have been confirmed in *Morris* v. *C. W. Martin & Sons Ltd.*,[18] where Salmon L.J. stated that the primary duties of the bailee at Common Law were to take proper care of the chattel bailed and to refrain from converting it. In *B.W.I.A.* v. *Bart*,[19] this and similar dicta of Diplock L.J. in the same decision were taken as authority for the rule that a non-contractual bailee could not be liable for a negligent delay in the delivery of goods, because this was not a wrong redressed by the ordinary law of tort.[20] Further assumptions that a gratuitous bailee's duties are merely one function of the general law of tort have been made in a wide variety of cases.[21] Coupled with the non-essentiality of contract to bailment, these pronouncements lend much force to the assertion that bailment is predominantly a tortious relation.

In fact, the Common Law liabilities of a bailee (and, to a lesser extent, those of a bailor) may be significantly different from those which would be imposed under the general law of tort. The distinctions between bailment and tort relate both to the creation of particular duties and to the

---

[17] See Chapter 6.
[18] [1966] 1 Q.B. 716, at 738; see also Diplock L.J. at 731-732.
[19] (1966) 11 W.I.R. 378 (Guyana C.A.); post, p. 822.
[20] But cf. *Miner* v. *Canadian Pacific Railroad* (1910) 15 W.L.R. 161; (1911) 18 W.L.R. 476; *Caltex Oil (Aust.) Pty. Ltd.* v. *The "Willemstad"* (1976) 11 A.L.R. 227.
[21] E.g. *Steljes* v. *Ingram* (1903) 19 T.L.R. 534 at 535, per Phillimore J. (ante, p. 18); *Hedley Byrne & Co. Ltd.* v. *Heller & Partners Ltd.* [1964] A.C. 465, at 526 per Lord Devlin; *Thomas* v. *High* (1960) 60 S.R. (N.S.W.) 401; *Walker* v. *Watson* [1974] 2 N.Z.L.R. 175; *Philip Morris (Australia) Ltd.* v. *The Transport Commission* [1975] Tas. S.R. 128.

machinery of their enforcement. These differences may be summarised by comparing the action on a bare bailment with the two forms of tortious liability to which it bears the closest resemblance: i.e., negligence and detinue.

A. Liability for negligence and the bailee's duty of care

The majority of reported cases on bailment concern actions by the bailor against the bailee for breach of the latter's duty to take proper care of the goods. Actions of this kind differ from ordinary actions in negligence in several respects.

1. *Origins of duty*: Winfield perceived two criteria of differentiation in that tortious duties are owed to persons generally whereas the duties of a bailee are owed to his bailor; and in that tortious liability is primarily established by law, irrespective of the consent of the parties, whereas liability under a bailment is primarily fixed by the parties themselves.

> When once they have entered into the relation, a good many legal consequences follow and some of them were probably never contemplated by either bailor or bailee. But just the same sort of thing occurs with many of the obligations that arise from contract, yet no one doubts that it is by the parties to it, and not by the law, that the obligations arising from contract are primarily imposed. What happens in the way of secondary duties which are annexed to bailments by the law does not concern us here. A bailee, like a contractor, may protest against some of them as harsh and not contemplated by him when he became a bailee, but that does not alter the fact that primarily it was he, and not the law, that brought into being the legal relation to which these consequences are attached. Bailment originates in an agreement, express or implied, and tortious liability does not.[22]

It will be noted that Winfield's second distinction between bailment and tort is coloured by his conception of bailment as a consensual relation. Indeed, he dismisses the possibility that an action for breach of bailment may originally have been tortious in character on the ground that "we are concerned with the law here and now". To modern eyes, Winfield's here and now has become a there and then. Even if one rejects the theory that involuntary bailments are proper examples of the bailment relation, the modern view of bailment as a voluntary possession of chattels lends some support to Professor Tay's argument that bailment and tort are fundamentally and originally similar.

> The customary distinction between the "grand divisions" of contract and of tort is made in these terms: a contractual duty is one which is owed to a specific person in consequence of an agreement entered into with that person; a tortious duty is one owed impartially to the whole world in consequence of entering into a specific situation, though it can be claimed upon only by those who have become linked with the duty-bearer through that situation. On this view, the primary duty of the bailee as set forth in these pages [i.e. to safeguard and redeliver] is a tortious duty: the duty of the bailee

---

[22] *Province of the Law of Tort*, pp. 99-100.

requires neither his agreement with, nor his knowledge of, the bailor.[23]

In fact, it was not necessary for Winfield to conclude that agreement is fundamental to bailment. His only authorities were the involuntary bailment cases, which related only the *bailee's* consent to possession.[24] It was not an inevitable conesquence of the principle that "a man cannot without his knowledge and consent be considered as a bailee of property"[25] to hold that a person who voluntarily *assumes* possession of goods can be excluded from the category of bailees merely because the owner had not consented to such possession.[26] Even in 1931, authority to the contrary could be cited.[27]

Thus far, there would seem to be a clear preference for Professor Tay's analysis over that of Professor Winfield. This preference (prompted largely by recent accelerations in the scope and diversity of bailment) inevitably weakens Winfield's first distinction between tort and bailment, as well as his second. But certain aspects of the creation of a bailment detract from a definition of the relationship as purely or fundamentally tortious, and suggest that a bailee may define or declare his status and responsibilities in a manner which, while removing his liability from the realm of tort, does not bring him within the narrower zone of a bailee by contract or agreement. One example is the sub-bailee who, by means of the contract of sub-bailment, excludes all responsibility for loss of the goods towards the head bailor, with whom he has neither contract, agreement or communication of any kind. Even if the head bailor has forbidden the sub-bailor to enter into a subsidiary agreement of this kind, it seems that he will be bound thereby.[28] Likewise, there may be cases in which a sub-bailee has no reason to suspect the existence of a principal bailor and in which it would be unfair to exact from him a double responsibility towards both principal and secondary bailor.[29] In such a case there may be no relationship at all between sub-bailee and principal bailor. Although some of these examples can be explained (like the influence of reward, or knowledge of the character of the bailee) as matters which "do not go to the essence of the bailment or the primary duty of the bailee" but are merely "ancillary, surrounding circumstances determining the appropriate degree of care", others would seem to go further and negate ab initio the very existence of a bailment between the particular parties even though the bailee is knowingly in possession of the alleged bailor's goods, and even though there is no agreement to

---

[23] (1966) 5 *Sydney Law Review* 239, at 245.
[24] Most notably, *Lethbridge* v. *Phillips* (1819) 2 Stark. 544; post, p. 381.
[25] Winfield, op. cit., 100.
[26] Laidlaw (1930-1931) 16 *Cornell Law Quarterly* 286, at 290: "But the principle that "one cannot be made the bailee of another's property without his consent" does not require that there be a contract, or even that there be a mutual agreement. It means nothing more than that a person should not have obligations thrust upon him without reason and ought not to be required to use care towards property when he did not know that he was possessed of it."
[27] Ante, p. 28.
[28] *Johnson Matthey & Co. Ltd.* v. *Constantine Terminals Ltd.* [1976] 2 Lloyd's Rep. 215; and see generally Chapters 20, 26, post.
[29] Cf. *Lee & Sons Pty. Ltd.* v. *Abood* (1968) 89 W.N. (N.S.W.) (Pt. 1) 430; and see generally p. 810 et. seq., post.

contrary effect between them. At best such a person may be an involuntary bailee and there is as yet no judicial authority for saying that such cases are bailments.

2. *Special or peculiar duties*: Certain liabilities would not arise if there were not a bailment between the parties, even though the defendant's conduct could reasonably have been expected to cause the plaintiff's loss. Perhaps the best example is the duty to protect goods from theft. As a general rule of tort there is no such duty;[30] certainly none arises under the principles of occupiers' liability[31] and (leaving aside the special case of the boarding-house proprietor)[32] it is most unusual to find decisions which impose such liability other than by way of contract or through the fact that the defendant is a bailee. But the liability of a bailee for the theft of goods which he has accepted into his custody does not depend upon contract. The bailment may be gratuitous[33] or the plaintiff and the defendant may be respectively principal bailor and sub-bailor.[34]

Another illustration, although less unique than the foregoing, concerns liability for independent contractors. In tort, there is no general vicarious liability for the acts of independent contractors unless certain narrow conditions are fulfilled.[35] Under the law of bailment, where the bailee deputes his task of safekeeping to an independent contractor, such liability may be imposed regardless of whether these conditions apply or not.[36] Admittedly, the principal decision rationalises this liability as arising under an implied term of the contract of bailment,[37] but it seems beyond question that an identical liability would be imposed, for instance, between a sub-bailee for reward and a principal bailor. Again, this is a liability that arises independently of the general law of tort.[38]

A third example is the rule that a bailee is estopped from denying his bailor's title.[39] The foundation of this rule may well be contractual[40]

---

[30] Post, p. 223; *Johnson Matthey & Co. Ltd.* v. *Constantine Terminals Ltd.* [1976] 2 Lloyd's Rep. 215.
[31] Post, p. 214.
[32] Chapter 24, post.
[33] Post, p. 309 (the position is not yet settled, but authority seems balanced in favour of this view, and it seems logically preferable).
[34] Post, p. 785 et. seq. For a comparatively early illustration, see *Lee Cooper Ltd.* v. *C. H. Jeakins & Sons Ltd.* [1967] 2 Q.B. 1, which imposed such liability as a simple extension of the rule in *Donoghue* v. *Stevenson* [1932] A.C. 562, and was criticised by Weir [1965] C.L.J. 186. However, it seems preferable to regard such liability as a special obligation arising from the peculiar character of bailment, because of the anomaly of rationalising such cases as aspects of the ordinary law of tort. It has been suggested that cases of loss by theft under non-contractual bailments represent examples of the recovery of purely economic loss other than in contract: Clerk and Lindsell, *Torts* (14th ed.), para. 1044.
[35] See generally Clerk and Lindsell, op. cit., para. 256 et. seq.
[36] E.g. *Philip Morris (Australia) Ltd.* v. *The Transport Commission* [1975] Tas. S.R. 128 (obiter); *British Road Services Ltd.* v. *Arthur V. Crutchley & Co. Ltd.* [1968] 1 All E.R. 811; post, p. 829 et. seq.
[37] *The British Road Services* case, ante, especially per Lord Pearson at 820.
[38] It seems that liability of this kind may be distinguished from ordinary vicarious liability on three grounds: first, as stated, it can extend to independent contractors; secondly, the "employee" need not be personally guilty of a tort against the bailor; thirdly, it may be that the act which leads to the injury or loss need not be committed within the employee's course of employment: post, p. 475 et. seq.
[39] Post, p. 163 et. seq.
[40] Cf. Blackburn J. in *Biddle* v. *Bond* (1865) 6 B. & S. 225, at 232.

but it clearly applies to gratuitous bailments and probably to sub-bailments as well.[41] Again, this is a form of duty that arises quite independently of the law of tort and does not depend upon the existence of a contract between the parties.[42]

3. *Enforcement of particular duties*: Even when bailment and tort give rise to concurrent liabilities, there may be considerable functional disparity between an action based upon the bailment and an action in tort. In cases which allege a failure by the bailee to take sufficient care of the goods the principal differences are as follows.

(a) Burden of proof: In an action for negligence the general rule is that the plaintiff must prove breach of the duty of care. When goods are injured or lost while in the possession of a bailee, this rule is displaced and the bailee must prove *either* that he took the appropriate care of them *or* that his failure to do so did not contribute to the loss.[43] Various reasons have been given for the location of this burden. According to Atkin, L.J., its justification lies in the fact that, since the bailee is in possession, he is best able to provide an explanation of the misadventure and he is most likely to have been at fault if such an explanation is not forthcoming.[44] A more elaborate explanation was given by Sachs L.J. in *B.R.S. Ltd.* v. *Arthur V. Crutchley Ltd.*[45]

> The Common Law has always been vigilant in the interests of bailors whose goods are not returned to them by the bailee for a number of reasons; insofar as that vigilance relates to the onus of proof, one of the reasons stems from the fact that normally it is only the bailee who knows what care was being taken of the goods, and another from the number of temptations to which a bailee may succumb. Those temptations may vary in each generation according to the nature of the transaction and in these days of rising costs include that of the bailee wishing to pay as little for security as he can "get away with", and the complacency that can arise from the feeling "after all, we are insured". The present case provides a good example of the need to scrutinise closely the claim of a bailee that he has discharged the onus of proof to which reference has been made.

The bailee's burden of proof is well established and, while not imposing a duty to provide an exact explanation of the injury,[46] is clearly distinguishable from the burden of proof in an ordinary action for negligence or breach of contract. We later attempt to demonstrate that it applies to sub-bailees[47] and gratuitous bailees[48] as well as to ordinary consensual bailees for reward. But, perhaps because Atkin L.J.'s explana-

---

[41] Post, p. 175.
[42] Cf. now the *Torts* (*Interference with Goods*) *Act* 1977 (England), ss. 7 and 8.
[43] *Travers & Sons Ltd.* v. *Cooper* [1915] 1 K.B. 73; *Fankhauser* v. *Mark Dykes Pty. Ltd.* [1960] V.R. 376; and see further the authorities discussed at p. 440 et. seq., post. At one time the burden appears to have been placed upon the bailor; see, for instance, *Finucane* v. *Small* (1795) 1 Esp. 315 and *Cooper* v. *Barton* (1810) 3 Camp. 5n., N.P. But these cases are clearly no longer reliable.
[44] *The Ruapehu* (1925) 21 Lloyd's Rep. 310, at 315.
[45] [1968] 1 All E.R. 811, at 822.
[46] Post, p. 442; cf. *Copland* v. *Brogan* 1916 S.C. 277.
[47] Post, p. 809 et. seq.
[48] Post, p. 311 et. seq.; cf. *Thomas* v. *High* (1960) 60 S.R. (N.S.W.) 401, at 404, 407.

tion for the burden is similar to that commonly used to explain the doctrine of res ipsa loquitur, there has been a tendency to equate the two doctrines and thereby to erode one of the peculiar responsibilities of a bailee.[49]

The relationship between res ipsa loquitur and the bailee's burden of proof is somewhat uncertain, partly because, even assuming that the two doctrines are separate, they will often have an identical effect. An illustration of their substantial overlap may be found in the case of *Ludgate* v. *Lovett*,[50] where the hirer of a van was held liable to the owner for damage to that van resulting from an accident on a motorway. Both parties were wholly unable to explain the accident: the vehicle had been regularly serviced by its owner and a tyre, which had burst, was proved to have done so only towards the end of the series of events which led to the damage. The defendant, being unable to adduce evidence rebutting fault on his part, was held liable on the principle of res ipsa loquitur, Edmund Davies L.J. remarking that this was as clear a case of res ipsa loquitur as he had ever seen.[51] Moreover, the defendant failed on his counterclaim for injuries resulting from the accident because he was unable to prove that these injuries resulted from a want of care on the part of the owner. The case may be open to criticism on the ground that the lessor's warranty of safety may be a strict one,[52] and on the ground that res ipsa loquitur is a distinct doctrine from that which dictates the bailee's burden of proof. But these are really criticisms of the way in which the case was argued. The significant feature of *Ludgate* v. *Lovett* is that both parties accepted throughout that it was appropriate to argue it solely on the basis of res ipsa loquitur, and the Court of Appeal decided it exclusively on that ground. Indeed, they seem to have equated the two doctrines, and it may well have made no difference on the facts as to which of them was pleaded.

Now it is evident that the weaker the doctrine of res ipsa loquitur in a given jurisdiction, the greater the differences that are likely to exist between this and the bailee's burden of proof. Thus in Australia, where a defendant may rebut the presumption of res ipsa loquitur by (inter alia) pointing to possible alternative cause of injury which is consistent with the facts and does not involve negligence on his part, it has been repeatedly recognised that different effects flow from this doctrine and from the bailee's burden of proof.[53] In the words of Scholl J., the bailee's burden is legal and not merely evidential.[54] It is harder to displace than the inference raised by res ipsa loquitur, and unless it be displaced

---

[49] E.g. *The Coast Prince* [1967] 2 Lloyd's Rep. 290; *Easson* v. *L.N.E. Ry. Co.* [1944] 1 K.B. 421, at 422-423.
[50] [1969] 1 W.L.R. 1016.
[51] Ibid., at 1021.
[52] Post, p. 724 et. seq.
[53] *Paterson* v. *Miller* [1923] V.L.R. 36, at 41; *Fankhauser* v. *Mark Dykes Pty. Ltd.* (ante), at 377-378; *A.A. Radio Taxi Trucks Pty. Ltd.* v. *Curyer* [1965] S.A.S.R. 110, at 111; *Hobbs* v. *Petersham Transport Co. Pty. Ltd.* (1971) 45 A.L.J.R. 356, at 364.
[54] *Fankhauser* v. *Mark Dykes Pty. Ltd.*, at 377; the full quotation is set out post, p. 441.

the bailee will be answerable.[55] The same burden applies whether a bailor sues in detinue, case or assumpsit.[56]

Equally, in Canada, the Supreme Court has recently acknowledged the differing operation of the two doctrines in borderline situations. In *National Trust Corporation Ltd.* v. *Wong Aviation Ltd.*[57] a qualified but inexperienced pilot disappeared alone with a hired plane while on a flight around Toronto. The owner of the plane (Wong) and Wong Aviation (the company to which he had leased it and who had re-leased it to the aviator) both sued his executors for the value of the plane. Wong based his case solely upon the doctrine of res ipsa loquitur; apparently because, not being in direct contract with the aviator, he considered himself disabled from suing on the bailment and reduced to suing in tort. This view (which was apparently shared by the Supreme Court)[58] is criticised elsewhere.[59] Wong Aviation relied upon two causes of action: first, breach of bailment, relying on the bailee's conventional burden of proof, and secondly negligence, relying on res ipsa loquitur. Both plaintiffs failed.

So far as concerned the two claims in tort, the Court considered that the defendant executors had effectively displaced any inference of negligence by adducing evidence of other possible causes of the loss. The loss of the aircraft could have been caused by many other factors as equally consistent with no negligence as with negligence on the part of the deceased.[60]

This disposed of the allegation of res ipsa loquitur, and incidentally showed that the Canadian view of that doctrine is closely similar to that adopted by Australian courts.[61] In dismissing the claim based upon breach of bailment, the Court held that the bailee's ordinary burden may be displaced in cases where both he and the chattel are lost and where no first-hand explanation of the loss is accordingly forthcoming.[62] The appropriate burden in such an event was that appropriate to cases of allegedly self-induced frustration, as laid down by Lord Wright in *Joseph Constantine S.S. Co. Ltd.* v. *Imperial Smelting Corporation Ltd.*:[63] viz. that the person alleging fault must prove it unless the circumstances raise a prima facie case. Thus, on the instant facts, the case came back to one of res ipsa loquitur and on that basis the bailment claim, like the claim based on simple negligence, failed.

In laying down this principle the Supreme Court was dealing with an exceptional situation; and there is clear evidence that the judges regarded res ipsa loquitur as distinct from the bailee's burden of proof. This distinction is implicit in their acknowledgement that res ipsa loquitur may operate as a sort of long-stop for bailors when the bailee's general

---

[55] Except in those unusual cases where the bailee can prove that his negligence did not contribute to the loss.
[56] *Paterson* v. *Miller* [1923] V.L.R., 36 at 41.
[57] (1969) 3 D.L.R. (3d) 55.
[58] Ibid., at 56-57.
[59] Post, p. 801 cf. *The Suleyman Stalskiy* [1976] 2 Lloyd's Rep. 609.
[60] (1969) 3 D.L.R. (3d) at 61.
[61] See post, p. 839.
[62] (1969) 3 D.L.R. (3d), at 62-63.
[63] [1942] A.C. 154.

burden of proof has, in exceptional cases, been displaced; an acknow-ledgement that may be compared with the perhaps preferable observation of Laskin J. in the Ontario Court of Appeal, that res ipsa loquitur has no place in the law of bailment.[64] At all events, both in Canada and Australia the two types of burden are clearly distinguishable. At least one judge has attributed this distinction to the fact that bailment is a cause of action sui generis, independent both of contract and of tort.[65]

In England, the precise effect of res ipsa loquitur is uncertain, and it may be that this principle imposes a heavier obligation on the defendant in an action for negligence than is the case in other Commonwealth jurisdictions.[66] But even in England, the plaintiff in such an action must have shown at the end of the day that the defendant was negligent. The bailor need show nothing of the kind and yet (provided the bailee has failed to prove reasonable care) will almost invariably succeed. Of course in the majority of cases there will be a substantial degree of evidence either way; but it is clearly arguable that under English law the ordinary action for negligence, assisted by the doctrine res ipsa loquitur, is different from the action against a defaulting bailee.

(b) Degrees of care: Conventionally, the measure of diligence to be exacted from a bailee is governed primarily by the existence and location of any benefit or reward. Thus it is said that a mandatary or depositary is liable only for gross negligence,[67] whereas a borrower must exercise the utmost diligence and is liable even for slight neglect.[68] In one instance at least, the location of benefit may also be said to govern the responsi-bility of the bailor; for on traditional theory the lender of a chattel, since he derives no benefit from the bailment, is not liable for mere negligence in failing to know and to apprise the borrower of its defects but is answerable only for a failure to disclose to the borrower those defects of which he is actually aware.[69]

If the traditional degrees of negligence retain their validity under the modern law of bailment, they clearly distinguish the action against a gratuitous bailee from an ordinary action in tort. Even the providers of gratuitous services have been held, under the general law of negligence, to owe a duty of reasonable care.[70] Of course, the direction of such decisions strongly suggests that the same all-purpose standard will be applied to cases of gratuitous bailment, and that the question of reward is now merely a single element in the overall quantification of reasonable

[64] (1966) 56 D.L.R. (2d) 228, at 232.
[65] *Hobbs* v. *Petersham Transport Co. Pty. Ltd.* (1971) 45 A.L.J.R. 356, at 364 per Windeyer J.
[66] Post, p. 839; Cross, *Evidence* (4th ed.), pp. 131-134.
[67] E.g. *Coggs* v. *Bernard* (1703) 3 Ld. Raym. 909, at 913; and see further post, pp. 288, 330.
[68] *Coggs* v. *Bernard* (1703) 2 Ld. Raym. 909, at 913; post, p. 368.
[69] *Coughlin* v. *Gillison* [1899] 1 Q.B. 145; post, p. 349.
[70] E.g. *Hedley Byrne & Co. Ltd.* v. *Heller & Partners Ltd.* [1964] A.C. 465 (gratuitous advice); *Birch* v. *Thomas* [1972] 1 All E.R. 905 (gratuitous carriage of passenger); and see post, Chapter 10.

care. A number of recent cases support this approach and repudiate such Romanesque notions as "gross" or "slight" neglect.[71] But Commonwealth jurisdictions are not unanimous on the point and it is still possible to discover authorities in which the degrees of negligence are preserved.[72] Insofar as gross and slight negligence are still acceptable and coherent calibrations of liability, it is clear that the defendant in a non-possessory negligence action is subject to neither of these gradations. It may therefore be doubted whether the general assimilation of gratuitous bailments into the simple rules of tortious liability does full justice to the varied allotment of benefit and duty which these bailments are traditionally assumed to impose.[73]

(c) Exclusion clauses: It is now recognised (at least in England) that an exclusion clause may take effect between a principal bailor and a sub-bailee although there is no contract or agreement between the parties to that effect. This consequence may follow upon two distinct principles. First, the principal bailor may have consented to the sub-bailment on such terms;[74] secondly, the sub-bailee may have inserted the exclusion into the subsidiary bailment as one of the essential terms, or as part of the consideration, under which he assumed possession.[75] In the latter case (at least insofar as the relevant duty is one which would not have arisen but for the sub-bailment) it is immaterial that the principal bailor has not consented to, or may even have prohibited, the sub-bailment on those terms.

The foregoing authorities represent exceptions to the general rule that a person who is not a party to a contract may not take advantage of an exclusion clause contained therein, or may not be subjected to the burden of such a provision. These exceptions would appear to be peculiar to the law of bailment. Certainly they cannot be rationalised in terms of contract or agreement, and it is submitted that they are equally distinct from the tortious defence of volenti non fit injuria. This observation can be made with confidence in regard to the second exception, because the operation of the defence is independent of the plaintiff's consent. It seems, however, that even the first exception is independent of the tortious defence in question.[76]

Elsewhere we suggest that the first of these principles may be analogous to the transmission of covenants with land, and may be rooted in the

---

[71] Perhaps most notably *Houghland* v. *R. R. Low (Luxury Coaches) Ltd.* [1962] 1 Q.B. 694; *James Buchanan & Sons Ltd.* v. *Hay's Transport Service Ltd.* [1972] 2 Lloyd's Rep. 535; and see post, pp. 288, 230, 368.

[72] Ibid.

[73] The idea of degrees of negligence stems from the importation into the English Law of bailment of the doctrines of Roman Law. This occurred most notably, via Bracton, in *Coggs* v. *Bernard* (1793) 2 Ld. Raym. 909, per Lord Holt C.J. But more recently it has been affirmed that these doctrines correspond to those under English Law and have become incorporated therein: *Nugent* v. *Smith* (1875) 45 L.J. Q.B. 19, at 22 per Brett J.; *Taylor* v. *Caldwell* (1863) 3 B. & S. 826, at 839 per Blackburn J.

[74] *Morris* v. *C. W. Martin & Sons, Ltd.* [1966] 1 Q.B. 716; *Gillespie Bros. Ltd.* v. *Roy Bowles Transport Ltd.* [1973] Q.B. 400 at 412; post, p. 1000 et seq.

[75] *Johnson Matthey & Co. Ltd.* v. *Constantine Terminals Ltd.* [1976] 2 Lloyd's Rep. 215; post, p. 1004.

[76] Post, p. 1000.

defendant's possessory interest;[77] an interest which is not shared by defendants in ordinary actions for negligence. At least one judge has ascribed the defence to the independent character of bailment.[78]

(d) Extra-compensatory damages: The rule that a bailee is estopped from disputing his bailor's title enables a bailor to sue for the full value of goods which have been lost or destroyed by the bailee's negligence even though the bailor does not own the goods personally and is not answerable to the owner for the relevant loss.[79] Bailment therefore represents an exception to the general principles of tort (and contract) that a plaintiff may recover only to the extent of his immediate personal loss.[80]

On one interpretation of bailment, a further peculiarity may be said to exist in that a bailee may recover against a third-party tortfeasor for damage or destruction of the chattel bailed, again irrespective of whether the bailee has suffered any personal loss or is liable to the bailor as a result of the injury.[81] This rule is not confined to conventional bailees such as carriers and warehousemen but may be invoked by finders, salvors and even thieves. In fact the generality of the principle suggests that it is not peculiar to bailment but is one facet to the rule that, as against a wrongdoer, possession is title. It therefore seems to belong to the field of possession rather than to the field of bailments proper, and it is only be equating the two concepts and by disregarding the necessity for any mental state on the part of the bailee that one can rationalise the principle as peculiar to bailments. Admittedly finders, salvors and thieves can be considered bailees in that they are voluntarily in possession of chattels which they know to belong (in the broad sense) to another,[82] but knowledge of another's ownership and the consent to possession do not appear to be pre-requisites to the operation of the remedy in question.

It should, however, be noted that the bailee has an insurable interest in the property bailed and can recover under a policy of insurance to the full extent of an injury to the goods, irrespective of whether he is liable to the owner or other bailor for such injury.[83] Admittedly, he holds the proceeds of such recovery on trust for the bailor, but the initial right of recovery again represents a right to extra-compensatory damages which is (in general) peculiar to bailments.

(e) Promissory obligations of non-contractual bailees: Although it is now generally acknowledged that gratuitous bailments are not a contractual phenomenon, there is considerable authority for the view that an unrewarded bailee (such as a depositary or a mandatary) may be liable for the breach of any super-added promise which he has made with regard

---

[77] Post, p. 65 et seq.
[78] Lord Denning, M.R., in *Scruttons Ltd.* v. *Midland Silicones Ltd.* [1962] A.C. 446, at 489-490, and in *Morris* v. *C. W. Martin & Sons Ltd.* [1966] 1 Q.B. 716, at 729-730.
[79] Post, p. 177.
[80] *The Albazero* [1976] 3 All E.R. 129, at 136.
[81] As to this question, see Chapters 4 and 22, post.
[82] Ante, p. 26.
[83] Post, p. 193; aliter a mere licensee: *Bank of Ireland* v. *Northern Assurance Co. Ltd.* (1925) 21 Lloyd's L.R. 203 and 333.

to the subject-matter of the bailment, even though that promise is not enforceable by means of an action in tort.[84] Such promises cannot be enforced while the agreement is still executory but would appear to crystallise, and to become enforceable, once the bailee takes possession. They cannot be rationalised as contractual because the bailor supplies no consideration to support them, and they seem, if anything, to be relics of the old action in assumpsit, whereunder the party giving an undertaking could be made liable for breach thereof, without consideration, once he had embarked upon performance. They represent a form of liability for non-feasance which is therefore apparently independent of contract and unenforceable under any modern action in tort. Examples drawn from the authorities are the promise by a mandatary to perform the work for which the chattel was bailed;[85] the promise by a gratuitous custodian to exercise a greater degree of care for the goods (or assume a greater liability for their loss or injury) than would be exacted from him in tort;[86] and the promise by a gratuitous bailee of a document not to disclose its contents to any third party.[87]

Admittedly, modern authority is not unanimously in favour of the enforcement of promissory obligations against gratuitous bailees, and it may transpire that this is one aspect of bailment that has been crushed out of existence by the competing actions in contract and in tort. Moreover, the third example was given as a form of contractual obligation and may in fact be enforceable by an action (for conversion) in tort. But the relative abundance (and modernity) of some of the authorities which support the enforceability of such promises suggest that the principle does in fact survive and is entitled to a place within the modern sphere of obligations quite separate from contract or tort.

If express promises, transcending the bailee's liability in tort, are enforceable under a gratuitous bailment, it would seem to follow that in appropriate cases equivalent promises could be implied. Moreover, we suggest elsewhere that it may even be legitimate to imply promissory obligations into a non-consensual bailment, such as the relationship between a principal bailor and a sub-bailee.[88] Although the parties in such a case are parties to no agreement, the privity of bailment that exists between them may provide an acceptable foundation for the implication of certain extra-tortious responsibilities, whenever these may be deemed essential to the efficacy of the extended bailment relation. Thus a sub-bailee for work and labour may be deemed to have warranted to the owner of the goods that his labour and materials will be of good quality and reasonably fit for their purpose. Even a non-consensual bailment provides a relationship of some kind between the parties, and the courts should perhaps feel entitled to amplify that relationship by

---

[84] *Mitchell* v. *Ealing L.B.C.* (1978) *The Times*, 21st February; post, p. 322.
[85] *Oriental Bank Corporation* v. *The Queen* (1867) 8 S.C.R. (N.S.W.) 122, at 125 per Faucett J.
[86] *Kettle* v. *Bromsall* (1738) Willes 118, at 121; *Trefftz & Sons Ltd.* v. *Canelli* (1872) L.R. 4 P.C. 277; Carnegie, 3 *Adelaide Law Review* 7, at 10-11.
[87] *Roufos* v. *Brewster and Brewster* [1971] 2 S.A.S.R. 218, at 223-224.
[88] Post, p. 821 et. seq.

means of implied terms, notwithstanding that the enforcement of those terms is incapable of analysis as an action in contract or in tort.

Hitherto we have confined our attention to the augmented or extra-tortious liability of the non-contractual *bailee*. It may be, however, that similar principles are applicable to exact promissory or extra-tortious obligations from the bailor under a non-contractual bailment. To some extent, as we have seen, this is already true: thus, on conventional theory, the lender's obligation is not tortious but contractual and may even extend to liability for economic loss;[89] and we later suggest that a lender may be bound upon delivery by a promise to allow the borrower the use of his chattel for a particular specified term.[90] The tenor of the authorities suggests that, within consensual bailments at least, the transfer of possession makes up for the absence of consideration, and renders actionable those promises (express or implied) that are not ordinary facets of liability in tort and would not be enforceable under an ordinary action in contract. From this fact, and from the further fact that there can be a bailment without privity of contract or of agreement between the parties, it may be possible to argue that a non-contractual *bailor* should be subject in appropriate cases to a heavier standard of liability than would be imposed under the ordinary law of tort.

In *Morris* v. *C. W. Martin & Sons Ltd.*[91] the Court of Appeal held that a sub-bailee for work and labour owed to the principal bailor the duties of a bailee for reward, notwithstanding that the sub-bailee's payment for the service in question emanated not from the principal bailor himself but from the intermediate bailee. The result was not the imposition upon the sub-bailee of duties substantially beyond those normally owed in tort, because the sole question was as to the sub-bailee's liability for acts of conversion by his servants,[92] and the only duties recognised as applying to sub-bailees were the duty to safeguard the goods with reasonable care and the duty to refrain from converting them. However, if the source of reward is irrelevant to establishing whether a bailee owes the duties of a bailee for reward, the same reasoning might apply to an identification of the responsibilities of the bailor; and in cases where the liability of the bailor is in issue, the fact that he is a bailor for reward may significantly increase his duties towards the bailee beyond those that would be exacted in tort. A bailor for reward will often, in fact, be a lessor: i.e. a person who leases his chattel in return for a monetary reward. A lessor, on the preferable view of the authorities, is under a strict liability for the safety and fitness of the chattel leased; he cannot evade this responsiblity merely by proving that he took reasonable care.[93] Normally this obligation will be enforceable in contract and will represent an implied condition or warranty within the contract of hire.

---

[89] *Blakemore* v. *Bristol & Exeter Ry. Co.* (1858) 8 E. & B. 1034, at 1051-1052; post, p. 360.
[90] Post, p. 364.
[91] [1966] 1 Q.B. 716.
[92] Quaere, however, whether this is not closer to a contractual form of liability: post, p. 486 et. seq.; *Adams (Durham) Ltd.* v. *Trust House Ltd.* [1961] 1 Lloyd's Rep. 380, at 386.
[93] Chapter 19, post.

But if, on the analogy of *Morris* v. *C. W. Martin & Sons Ltd.,* it is possible to be a lessor for reward vis-à-vis a particular hirer, without any supporting contract, then it should be possible for such a hirer to enforce the lessor's strict obligation of safety and fitness without recourse to contract and in a manner not allowable under the conventional rules of tort. Thus a sub-hirer may, at least when the sub-hire is authorised, be entitled to sue the principal lessor and to exact from him a strict liability for the condition of the chattel as a "bailor for reward", even though the principal lessor's reward emanates not from the sub-hirer himself but from the intermediate hirer.

A conclusion not dissimilar from this was recently reached by the Supreme Court of Montana. In *Lovely* v. *Burroughs Corporation*[94] the plaintiff, an accountant, ordered a new computer from the defendant corporation. The proposal was that the defendants should sell the machine to a third party and that the plaintiff should then take it on lease from the purchaser. The computer was delivered to the plaintiff but proved to be unsatisfactory; no formal lease was ever executed and the defendants remained owners of the computer, although the plaintiff did despatch one rental cheque to the leasing company before the computer was eventually removed by the defendant. The plaintiff claimed against the defendants for damage suffered through the defectiveness of the computer, alleging breach of a strict warranty of reasonable fitness for purpose under the bailment or hiring for reward. The defendant's reply that there could be no hiring for reward because their remuneration was to come from the leasing company and not from the plaintiff was rejected by the Court, who refused to discern a merely gratuitous bailment between the parties:

> At the very least, a bailment for mutual benefit arose as both parties received the benefits of the transaction . . . Plaintiffs had the use of the computer while the defendant had the expectation of profit from a lease directly with the plaintiff or a sale to the third-party leasing company . . . To argue that defendant gratuitously placed a $38000 computer at the disposal of the plaintiffs without expectation of profits does not square with the facts.[95]

Admittedly, the foregoing case is not precisely congruent to the situation we have envisaged, in which the parties at either end of a chain of hiring and sub-hiring may owe stricter obligations or enjoy greater remedies than are possible in tort. The case was decided under a statute which imposed such a warranty upon one who lets chattels for reward, and there may well have been a direct or collateral contract between the parties.[96] But in principle there seems no reason why an importation of the theory in this case, that one may be a bailor for reward without a contract with the relevant bailee, could not be effected in jurisdictions where the lessor's duties are governed by the Common Law and in cases where the bailor and the bailee have no prior communication. In short, the theory may demonstrate the status quality of the relationship between bailor and bailee.

94 (1974) 527 P. (2d) 557.
95 Ibid., at 560.
96 Cf. *Andrews* v. *Hopkinson* [1957] 1 Q.B. 229.

(f) Deviation: A bailee deviates from the terms of the bailment when he substantially departs from the prescribed course of performance. Thus, a deviation is committed when a bailee sub-bails goods without authority, or stores or carries them in a place or by a route other than that permitted, or detains them after the agreed period of custody has elapsed.[97] The doctrine of deviation is peculiar to bailments,[98] and renders the bailee liable for all ensuing loss or damage to the chattel irrespective of negligence on his part; but it has been invoked by way of analogy in non-bailment cases, mainly for the purpose of holding that the party in breach thereby forfeits the protection of any exclusion clause contained in the contract.[99]

The concept of deviation is essentially a contractual phenomenon, and it primarily denotes a difference between contractual bailments and other contracts rather than between bailment and tort. Under traditional theory, the bailor whose bailee has committed a deviation need not rescind the bailment in order to bring it to an end. Deviation generates an automatic discharge of the bailment, whereas the apparent rule in non-bailment contracts is that there is no discharge until rescission, even after a fundamental breach.[1] Of course, the bailor may affirm the bailment if he so chooses.

In fact, however, there is some authority for the view that a deviation may be committed by a gratuitous (i.e. non-contractual) bailee;[2] and Professor Carnegie has suggested that a similar liability may be imposed under an extended bailment, as between a principal bailor and a sub-bailee.[3] The resultant liability would appear to be neither tortious nor contractual; a deviation is not necessarily a conversion[4] and will give rise (if at all) to an action in detinue only if the goods are destroyed or lost, as opposed to merely damaged. Moreover, it operates quite independently of any negligence on the part of the bailee.

B. Bailment and detinue

Although it is impossible to rationalise every aspect of a bailee's common law liability as a simple application of the tort of negligence, some of the aspects which cannot be thus rationalised are capable of explanation as functions of a separate tort, the action in detinue. Detinue imposes the same burden of proof upon a defendant who is alleged to have lost goods, or to have negligently caused their destruction, as is imposed under an ordinary action for breach of bailment:[5] a fact which lends considerable

---

[97] Post, pp. 517-518.
[98] Coote, *Exception Clauses*, p. 83.
[99] See generally Chapter 25.
[1] See the authorities discussed by Legh-Jones and Pickering (1971) 87 L.Q.R. 515, at 520 et. seq.; and by Coote [1970] C.L.J. 221; and see further *Hain S.S. Co. Ltd.* v. *Tate & Lyle, Ltd.* [1936] 2 All E.R. 597, at 601, per Lord Atkin; *Milk Bottles Recovery* v. *Camillo* [1948] V.L.R. 344.
[2] Post, p. 322; *Knight* v. *Wilson* 1946 S.L.T. (Sh. Ct.) 26.
[3] (1966) 3 *Adelaide Law Review* 7, at 11; and see generally Chapter 20.
[4] *Lilley* v. *Doubleday* (1881) 7 Q.B.D. 510, at 511-512, where the question was left open; and see Chapter 19.
[5] *Goodman* v. *Boycott* (1862) 2 B. & S. 1; *Reeve* v. *Palmer* (1858) 5 C.B.N.S. 84; *Houghland* v. *R. R. Low (Luxury Coaches) Ltd.* [1962] 1 Q.B. 694; *Makower, McBeath & Co. Pty. Ltd.* v. *Dalgety & Co. Ltd.* [1921] V.L.R. 365; *Paterson* v. *Miller* [1923] V.L.R. 36, at 41.

support to the view that detinue was once the functional dimension of bailment.[6] Moreover, a defendant may be liable in detinue if his lack of reasonable care has resulted in the loss of the goods by theft,[7] whereas (as we have seen) there is no general liability in negligence to that effect. Finally, the action may issue only against those defendants who were in actual or constructive possession of the goods at the material time. Although this requirement is construed more loosely than the requirement of possession in a bailee,[8] it nevertheless lends further credence to a modern equation of bailment with detinue.

In other respects, however, detinue is an incomplete explanation of the obligations that arise under a bailment at common law. First, of course, it has no bearing upon the normal liabilities of the bailor, such as his responsibility for the defective condition of the goods. Secondly, detinue cannot issue when goods have been merely damaged, as opposed to destroyed or lost.[9] Thirdly, liability in detinue necessitates a prior demand by the plaintiff for the return of the goods;[10] an action for breach of bailment can arise without one. Fourthly, the plaintiff who relies upon a possessory right in detinue must prove an immediate right of possession arising out of some proprietary right in the goods:[11] but the latter qualification may be inessential to an action for breach of bailment. Fifthly, the liability of a bailee for failure to take reasonable precautions to rescue goods which have been initially lost without his negligence is not, apparently, a liability in detinue.[12] Sixthly, it may be that a sub-bailee is not liable in detinue to the principal bailor if the goods are not lost through his neglect, because this aspect of liability in detinue is confined to cases in which the goods were delivered by the plaintiff to the defendant.[13] This difference perhaps underlines the semi-contractual nature of this aspect of the action in detinue[14] and (since bailment is now independent of contract or agreement) may further indicate the distance between detinue and the wider sphere of bailment itself.

In any event, it is clear that there are considerable differences between liability in detinue and liability under a bailment, and that these differences cannot entirely be explained by characterising the bailee's liability as issuing under some other tort. The same observations are true of liability in conversion, which is neither dependent upon a bailment inter partes nor a comprehensive foundation for the liabilities that arise therefrom.

---

[6] Ante, p. 30.

[7] E.g., *Houghland* v. *R. R. Low (Luxury Coaches) Ltd.* [1962] 1 Q.B. 694.

[8] *Alicia Hosiery Ltd.* v. *Brown, Shipley & Co.* [1970] 1 Q.B. 195.

[9] Post, p. 148.

[10] Post, p. 149.

[11] Post, p. 150.

[12] *Coldman* v. *Hill* [1919] 1 K.B. 443, at 449 per Bankes L.J.

[13] Clerk and Lindsell, *Torts* (14th ed.), paras. 1177-1178. In *Lee Cooper Ltd.* v. *C. H. Jeakins & Sons Ltd.* [1967] 2 Q.B. 1, it was assumed that the only tortious action available would be one in negligence but the plaintiff did not appear to have prefaced his action by a demand for the return of the goods. Weir [1965] C.L.J. 186, at 190, assumes that the need for an original delivery can be dispensed with by a subsequent demand; see also *Goodman* v. *Boycott* (1862) 2 B. & S. 1.

[14] Clerk and Lindsell, *Torts* (14th ed.), para. 1177.

VI. ENFORCEMENT: PSEUDO-CONTRACTUAL ASPECTS OF NON-CONTRACTUAL BAILMENTS

The possibility that a non-contractual bailee may be guilty of deviation inevitably raises questions as to whether the non-contractual bailment is not more closely akin to a contractual relationship than to a scheme of obligation in tort. Certainly this observation may be sustained to a large degree in the case of the ordinary gratuitous bailment, because despite the lack of consideration there is an obvious consensus or agreement between the parties; and in fact the courts have been willing on occasions to adopt basic contractual principles in order to establish the obligations of the parties to such a bailment. Thus there are suggestions that the rules of agency[15] and illegality[16] may apply, mutatis mutandis, to gratuitous bailments as they do to bailments arising by way of contract; and it seems likely that similar rules as to duress, misrepresentation and capacity would be applied if and when the occasion arose. Moreover, there is considerable authority for the view that superadded promises in the part of a gratuitous bailee (for example, to assume a greater liability for the goods than would be imposed at common law) are enforceable in much the same way as contractual promises, despite the absence of consideration.[17]

The equation is harder to make in the case of an extended bailment relation, because, although both parties may have consented to such a relation, there will generally be no agreement or communication between them. But in at least one respect sub-bailments are closer to contract than gratuitous bailments, because the law allows the head bailor to "borrow" any consideration paid by the intermediate bailee to the sub-bailee in order to extract from that sub-bailee the duties of a bailee for reward.[18] We argue in the ensuing pages that certain obligations akin to obligations in contract may legitimately be imposed between such parties notwithstanding the lack of any contractual relation;[19] in fact, to some extent, this seems already to have occurred. The liability of a non-contractual bailee for his servants' conversions, the prohibition upon his denial of the bailor's title, the operation in his favour of non-contractual exclusion clauses and even his peculiar burden of proof, may all represent originally contractual obligations which have been applied by analogy to bailments that are independent of contract. It may therefore be possible to argue (as did Cullen in 1926) that the source of the duties and obligations in bailment is "contractual, express, implied or constructive".[20] Certainly many aspects of the liability of a gratuitous or non-consensual bailee are more closely akin to liability in contract than to anything else.

But rather than draw upon an expanded conception of contract for the conceptual basis of bailment, it seems preferable to regard bailment as

[15] *Chapman* v. *Robinson and Ferguson* (1969) 71 W.W.R. 515; *Helson* v. *McKenzies (Cuba St.) Ltd.* [1950] N.Z.L.R. 878.
[16] *Walker* v. *Watson* [1974] 2 N.Z.L.R. 175, at 180.
[17] Post, pp. 313, 339.
[18] *Morris* v. *C. W. Martin & Sons Ltd.* [1966] 1 Q.B. 716.
[19] See especially Chapter 20, post.
[20] *Definition of a Bailment* (1926) 11 *St. Louis Law Review* 257, at 265.

something complete and sui generis: and the differences we have elicited appear to substantiate this conclusion. Bailment, in its entirety, is neither a synonym, nor a derivative, nor a diminutive of any other juristic image, but a personality unto itself. It may be formed or enforced without recourse to contract, and in a manner that is not wholly explicable by reference to the law of tort. It cannot for all purposes be equated with its central element, possession, for there are many cases in which a man may be in possession of another's chattel and yet not be a bailee. It has elements akin to the law of real property,[21] but these again are not a complete theorisation of the modern relation of bailment. The relationship is independent and unique.

VII. The Nature of Actions in Bailment

It emerges from the foregoing analysis that duties arise under a bailment in two principal ways: by implication of law, as a result of the possessory relationship, or by virtue of an agreement between the parties. When the agreement is simultaneously a contract, there will be a contractual right of action to enforce any obligations which the parties have superadded to those owed at common law. Thus, if a bailee by contract undertakes to assume a strict liability for the goods, or to store them by a particular method, an action will lie in contract for breach of that promise. But if such a promise is enforceable against even a non-contractual bailee (for example, a mandatary or unpaid custodian)[22] it would seem to follow that promissory obligations undertaken pursuant to any form of bailment are not exclusively contractual in character. Contract, under an executed bailment, becomes an accessorial remedy, because the promise could have been enforced without it. The central or primary remedy becomes an action for breach of bailment.

The independence of bailment as a source of obligation can be alternatively argued by reference to the bailee's duties at common law. The most obvious example is the duty of care. When the bailment is contractual, the bailor who complains of a breach of this duty may sue in contract (for breach of the promise to redeliver the chattel in the condition in which it was bailed) or in tort (for negligence or detinue).[23] Generally, there is no rule dictating which form of action he shall adopt and he may elect between them; to deny him the power of choice would, as Winfield once observed, be to allow the plaintiff to suffer and the defendant to benefit from the fact that the defendant has committed two wrongs instead of one.[24] Admittedly, there is some question as to whether the plaintiff in a non-bailment case, who is in a

---

[21] Post, p. 65.
[22] E.g. *Trefftz & Sons Ltd.* v. *Canelli* (1872) L.R. 4 P.C. 277.
[23] *Paterson* v. *Miller* [1923] V.L.R. 36; *Tozer Kemsley & Millbourn (Australasia) Pty. Ltd.* v. *Collier's Interstate Transport Service Pty. Ltd.* (1956) 94 C.L.R. 385; *John F. Goulding* v. *Victorian Railways Commissioners* (1932) 48 C.L.R. 157; *The Coast Prince* [1967] 2 Lloyd's Rep. 290. As to the separate quality of the promise to redeliver, see further, p. 464 et. seq., post. Cf. *Steljes* v. *Ingram* (1903) 19 T.L.R. 534, at 535; *Thomas* v. *High* (1960) 60 S.R. (N.S.W.) 401, at 406.
[24] *Province of the Law of Tort*, p. 79 et. seq.

contractual relationship with the defendant, can frame his action alternatively as an action in tort.[25] The most recent appellate authority suggests clearly that he may;[26] but in any event the main authority to the contrary recognises an exception for cases of bailment.[27] The main reason for this exception is that the bailee's liability is not founded solely upon contract but arises from his voluntary possession of the chattel.[28] This also helps to explain why a bailee may be sued even after his deviation has automatically discharged the contract pursuant to which the goods were bailed.[29] The bailment survives the contract and he may be sued thereupon.

For some purposes, admittedly, it is essential to divide actions exclusively into those in contract and those in tort, and to allocate an action for breach of bailment to either of these exhaustive categories. This necessity arises when the legislature lays down imperative and distinctive rules for contract and tort and overlooks the possibility that an action in bailment may be independent of either[29a]. In such a case the

[25] See, for example, *Steljes* v. *Ingram* (1903) 19 T.L.R. 534 (action against architect held to be an action in contract for the purposes of the County Courts Act, 1888); *Bagot* v. *Stevens Scanlan & Co. Ltd.* [1966] 1 Q.B. 197 (action against architect held to be an action in contract for the purposes of the Limitation Act, 1939); cf. *McConnell* v. *Lynch-Robinson* [1957] N.I. 70 (action against architect assumed to be an action in tort for the purposes of the law as to contribution); *Jarvis* v. *Moy, Davies & Co.* [1936] 1 K.B. 399 (action against stockbroker held to be an action in contract for the purposes of the County Courts Act, 1919); and see further *Groom* v. *Crocker* [1939] 1 K.B. 194; *Clark* v. *Kirby-Smith* [1964] Ch. 506; *Belous* v. *Willets* [1970] V.R. 45 (actions against solicitors held to be actions in contract); cf. *Heywood* v. *Weller & Partners* [1976] Q.B. 446, and see now per contra *Midland Bank Trust Co. Ltd.* v. *Hett, Stubbs and Kemp* (1977) *The Times* December 2nd.

[26] *Esso Petroleum Co. Ltd.* v. *Mardon* [1976] Q.B. 801, relying (inter alia) upon *Boorman* v. *Brown* (1842) 3 Q.B. 511; *H. Parsons (Livestock) Ltd.* v. *Uttley Ingham & Co. Ltd.* (1977) *The Times* 18 May, per Lord Denning M.R. See further *Midland Bank Trust Co. Ltd.* v. *Hett, Stubbs and Kemp* ante; *Vacwell Engineering Co. Ltd.* v. *B.D.H. Chemicals Ltd.* [1971] 1 Q.B. 88 at 108; *Govett* v. *Radnidge* (1802) 3 East 62; *Fish* v. *Kapur* [1948] 2 All E.R. 176; *White* v. *John Warwick & Co. Ltd.* [1953] 1 W.L.R. 1285; *Jackson* v. *Mayfair Window Cleaning Co.* [1952] 1 All E.R. 215; *Anderson* v. *Rhodes* [1967] 2 All E.R. 850; *Matthews* v. *Kuwait Bechtel Corporation* [1959] 2 Q.B. 57; *McInerney* v. *Lloyd's Bank Ltd.* [1974] 1 Lloyd's Rep. 246; Poulton (1966) 82 L.Q.R. 346; Fridman (1977) 93 L.Q.R. 422; Winfield, *Province of the Law of Tort*, Chapter 4. The statement by Scrutton L.J. in *Hall* v. *Brooklands Auto Racing Club* [1933] 1 K.B. 205, at 213, that "when the defendant has protection under a contract, it is not permissible to disregard the contract and allege a wider liability in tort" (recently applied by the New South Wales Court of Appeal in *Allan J. Panozza & Co. Pty. Ltd.* v. *Allied Interstate (Qld) Pty. Ltd.* [1976] 2 N.S.W.R. 192) must be taken to be confined, as Denning L.J. observed in the *John Warwick* case (ante) at 1294, to cases where the plaintiff has plainly contracted to exempt the defendant from liability in tort. See generally Chapter 25, post.

[27] *Bagot* v. *Stevens Scanlan & Co. Ltd.* [1966] 1 Q.B. 197, at 204-206; and see Poulton (1966) 82 L.Q.R. 346, at 353-360, 365-366; Winfield, op. cit., p. 63: "Lawyers were thoroughly familiar with negligence as one mode of bungling a contract or a bailment long before it became an independent tort. Nor has it ever ceased to retain this earlier signification, though it has acquired the later one. Here then was one fruitful source of coincidence of contract with liability in tort, and it shows no sign of exhaustion at the present day." The carriers' cases are the most obvious example of a bailor's ability to proceed against a contractual bailee in tort: see post, p. 555.

[28] *Turner* v. *Stallibrass* [1898] 1 Q.B. 56.

[29] Ante, p. 49.

[29a] Cf. *Harold Stephen & Co.* v. *Post Office* [1977] 1 W.L.R. 1172 at 1177-1178 and 1179-1180 (C.A.).

courts will ascertain whether the plaintiff could have maintained the action without relying on the contract, or whether the contract alone produced the duty which is now alleged to be broken. If the former is the case, the action will be characterised as one in tort. The process is an artificial one which has little relevance to the legal quality of bailment in more general contexts. Thus it has been held that an action for breach of the duty of care owed by a bailee for mutual advantage is an action in tort for the purposes of the *Limitation Act* 1939[30] and the *County Courts Act* 1888.[31] No doubt the same characterisation would be applied a fortiori to an action against a gratuitous bailee.

> I think some confusion may possibly arise from the expression of the rule on this subject as being that the test is whether the plaintiff is obliged, in order to maintain his action, to rely on a contract. The relation of bailor and bailee must arise out of some agreement of the minds of the parties to it; but that agreement of minds is not the contract contemplated by that mode of expressing the rule to which I refer. Such an agreement of minds is presupposed in the case of any relation which brings about the common law liability of a bailee to his bailor. Where such a relation is established, the result of the cases appears to be that, if the plaintiff can maintain his action by shewing the breach of a duty arising at common law out of that relation, he is not obliged to rely on a contract within the meaning of the rule; but, if his cause of action is that the defendant ought to have done something, or taken some precaution, which would not be embraced by the common law liability arising out of the relation of bailor and bailee, then he is obliged to rely on a contract within the meaning of the rule. A distinction has been drawn between acts of misfeasance and non-feasance which has given rise to some difficulty; but it seems to me that, whether the matter complained of is one of misfeasance or non-feasance, the question really is whether it is embraced within the ambit of the common law liability arising out of the relation between bailor and bailee. If it is, then the plaintiff is not driven to rely on a contract within the meaning of the rule on the subject of costs. But, if it is not, then the plaintiff must rely on a contract in order to shew a cause of action, and the action is therefore one founded on contract.[32]

Conversely, it has been held that on action by the bailor of a car against a car-park operator for the latter's failure to safeguard the

---

[30] *Chesworth* v. *Farrar* [1967] 1 Q.B. 407; cf. *John F. Goulding Pty. Ltd.* v. *Victorian Railways Commissioners* (1932) 48 C.L.R. 157.

[31] *Turner* v. *Stallibrass* [1898] 1 Q.B. 56; see also *Bryant* v. *Herbert* (1878) 3 C.P.D. 389; *Tattan* v. *G.W. Ry. Co.* (1860) 2 El. & El. 844; *Pontifex* v. *Midland Ry. Co.* (1877) 3 Q.B.D. 23.

[32] *Turner* v. *Stallibrass* [1898] 1 Q.B. 56, at 59-60 per Collins L.J. The explanation of the distinction which has probably received the greatest acceptance among modern authority is that of Greer L.J. in *Jarvis* v. *Moy, Davies & Co.* [1936] 1 K.B. 399, at 405: "where the breach of duty alleged arises out of a liability independently of the personal obligation undertaken by contract, it is tort, and it may be tort even though there may happen to be a contract between the parties, if the duty in fact arises independently of that contract. Breach of contract occurs where that which is complained of is a breach of duty arising out of the obligations undertaken by the contract." This was approved in *Chesworth* v. *Farrar* [1967] 1 Q.B. 407, at 414, and in *Bagot* v. *Stevens Scanlan & Co. Ltd.* [1966] 1 Q.B. 197, at 204.

vehicle with reasonable care is an action founded upon a contract for the supply of services within the meaning of the Victorian *Small Claims Tribunal Act* 1973;[33] and that an action against a bailee for money had and received, although based upon the bailee's conversion of the chattel, is quasi-contractual and not an action in tort for the purposes of the *Limitation Act*.[34] Clearly the classification of an action for breach of bailment as contractual or tortious depends largely upon the purpose of the statute dictating the classification and upon the context in which the classification is to be made. The action may be an action in tort for the purposes of one statutory rule and not for the purposes of another.

The fact that such a classification must occasionally be made because the legislature has divided actions exclusively into those in contract or tort is not, however, conclusive evidence against the independent character of an action for breach of bailment. As Winfield observed, "in trying to arrange the legal system we need not be terrified by legislative insistence upon "contract or tort and nothing else" in a limited class of cases".[35] We have already seen that actions for breach of bailment may be entirely distinguishable from actions in contract or tort. It is submitted that these distinctions are not the fragmentary relics of a moribund form of action but are evidence of a coherent and unitary source of modern obligation. Thus, even when an action in bailment runs parallel to an action in contract or tort, its independent character should be recognised, and its content should be worked out without undue regard to any similarity with other forms of action. It would follow that a breach of the contractual bailee's duty of care could give rise to actions in contract, tort or bailment,[36] and that a breach of the non-contractual bailee's duty could give rise to an action in bailment as well as a simple action in tort. We have already seen that the two are not identical for all purposes. Even when their operation is substantially similar, it does not follow that they can be universally equated.

If, even in this concurrent sphere, the action for breach of bailment retains its separate identity, it becomes necessary to explore the identity for the purpose of rules which normally operate upon a distinction between contract and tort. To some extent, this inquiry necessitates an assessment as to whether, in a given context, the action against a bailee is more akin to a contractual action than to a tortious action, or vice versa. It also involves an examination of some of the differences between contract and tort. A few examples of the problem are appended.

A. Contributory negligence and volenti non fit injuria

Although the question cannot be regarded as settled, the balance of authority suggests that contributory negligence and volenti non fit injuria

---

[33] *Walsh* v. *Palladium Car Park Pty. Ltd.* [1975] V.R. 949.
[34] *Chesworth* v. *Farrar* [1967] 1 Q.B. 407, at 416-418. Cf. *Mears* v. *Sayers* (1974) 41 D.L.R. (3d) 424, as to the assignment of the bailor's rights of action.
[35] *Province of the Law of Tort*, p. 101.
[36] Recent (albeit tacit) recognition of this possibility is afforded by the New South Wales Court of Appeal in *Allan J. Panozza & Co. Pty. Ltd.* v. *Allied Interstate (Qld) Pty. Ltd.* [1976] 2 N.S.W.R. 192. Cf. *Harold Stephen & Co. Ltd.* v. *Post Office ante*, where the C.A. left open the question whether s. 29(1) of the *Post*

are not defences to an action for breach of contract.[37] In cases where a bailor sues for breach of the bailee's duty of reasonable care, some courts have drawn a distinction between gratuitous and contractual bailments. Thus it has been held in New Zealand that an action against a gratuitous borrower is an action for negligence and that the specified defences can accordingly apply;[38] whereas it has been held in Victoria that an action against a hirer for failure to take reasonable care of the chattel hired is an action in contract and that contributory negligence is no defence.[39] On the other hand, dicta elsewhere suggest that both defences can apply to bailments for reward.[40]

At first sight, it would seem strange that an action which is essentially for negligence could, by alteration of its form, avoid the application of defences that are normally open to negligent defendants. But in considering whether these defences should be available under the separate action for breach of bailment, the principal impression is that they would generally be irrelevant. The known capacity of a bailee can often be taken to qualify his duty of care, so that a case like *Walker* v. *Watson*,[41] for example, could equally have been decided on the ground that the bailor was entitled to exact from the drunken bailee only such a degree of care as he knew to be within her diminished capability.[42] An approach of this kind effectively negates the significance of volenti to actions in bailment, and it could be further argued that contributory negligence is likewise immaterial in this context: the bailor's negligence operates as a qualification of the bailee's duty of care, and the question becomes a simple one as to whether that qualified duty has been

---

Office Act 1969 could be circumvented by bringing an action in bailment as opposed to one in "tort".

[37] *Becker* v. *Medd* (1897) 13 T.L.R. 313; *Vaile Brothers* v. *Hobson Ltd.* (1933) L.T. 283, at 284; *Quinn* v. *Burch Bros. (Builders) Ltd.* [1966] 2 Q.B. 370; *Belous* v. *Willetts* [1970] V.R. 45; *A. S. James Pty. Ltd.* v. *C. B. Duncan* [1970] V.R. 705; *Harper* v. *Ashton's Circus Pty. Ltd.* [1972] 2 N.S.W.L.R. 395; *Southland Harbour Board* v. *Vella* [1974] 1 N.Z.L.R. 526; *Walker* v. *Watson* [1974] 2 N.Z.L.R. 175; but cf. *Sayers* v. *Harlow U.D.C.* [1958] 1 W.L.R. 623; *Grein* v. *Imperial Airways* [1937] 1 K.B. 50; *De Meza* v. *Apple* [1974] 1 Lloyd's Rep. 508; *Artingstoll* v. *Hewens Garages Ltd.* [1973] R.T.R. 197 at 201; Tasmanian authority has held that contributory negligence is a defence to an action for negligent breach of contract: see *Queen's Bridge Motors Pty. Ltd.* v. *Edwards* [1964] Tas. S.R. 93; *Smith* v. *Buckley* [1965] Tas. S.R. 210 per Crisp J.; *W. & G. Genders Pty. Ltd.* v. *Noel Searle (Tasmania) Pty. Ltd.* (1977) Unrep., 22 February per Crawford J. which contains a useful survey of the authorities. Quaere, however, whether the same approach should not be made to this question as was adopted by Samuel J. in considering whether contributory negligence applies to an action for conversion: viz., to enquire whether this was ever a total defence before the relevant apportionment legislation was passed: *Wilton* v. *Commonwealth Trading Bank of Australia* [1973] 2 N.S.W.R. 644; post, p. 136.
[38] *Walker* v. *Watson* [1974] 2 N.Z.L.R. 175; Palmer (1975) 24 I.C.L.Q. 565; see also *Thomas* v. *High* (1960) 60 S.R. (N.S.W.) 401.
[39] *A. S. James Pty. Ltd.* v. *C. B. Duncan* [1970] V.R. 705, at 719 et. seq. Likewise *Aseltine* v. *McAnally* [1950] O.W.N. 229, and see also *Coupe Co. Ltd.* v. *Maddick* [1891] 2 Q.B. 413, at 415-416; *Thomas* v. *High*, ante, at 406.
[40] E.g. *Saunders (Mayfair) Furs Ltd.* v. *Chas. Wm. Davies Ltd.* [1966] 2 Lloyd's Rep. 78, at 83; *Minichiello* v. *Devonshire Hotel (1967) Ltd.* (1976) 66 D.L.R. (3d) 619, at 625-626; but cf. *Brabant & Co.* v. *King* [1895] A.C. 632, at 641; *Talley* v. *G.W. Ry. Co.* (1870) L.R. 6 C.P. 44, at 52; *Vosper* v. *G.W. Ry. Co.* [1928] 1 K.B. 340.
[41] [1974] 2 N.Z.L.R. 175.
[42] Ibid., at 180; and see Chapter 13.

satisfied.[43] But in peripheral cases a power of apportionment may be useful and it may be equitable to reduce the quantum of the bailor's damages according to the part he has played in the bailee's acknowledged breach of duty. A tentative example may be drawn from a Canadian case,[44] where the operators of a car-wash wrongfully left the bailor's car in the street when they had performed their work upon it. They took care not to leave the ignition key in the car but were unaware that the bailor had left a spare key in the glove compartment. The car was stolen and the bailees were held liable in full for its loss; but it could at least be argued that the bailor had to some degree contributed to that loss. In any event, it seems that the independent action for breach of bailment may provide one method of averting the often unfair principle that volenti and contributory negligence are not defences to actions in contract, at least when the plaintiff founds his case upon a central duty of care. This, like the ensuing examples, represents an area in which the character of bailment has been insufficiently explored. Such an exploration can only be made when cases arise in which its character is fully argued.

B. Conflict of laws

Widely different choice of law rules govern a cause of action according to whether it is contractual or tortious. In cases of contract, the relevant system is normally the proper law; in cases of tort, the plaintiff must fulfil the "double-barrelled" rule in *Phillips* v. *Eyre*,[45] a rule which has been variously and confusingly interpreted.[46] Many actions against bailees (for example those relating to the carriage of goods by sea) will proceed upon an assertion of contract and will fall subject to the contractual choice of law rules. If the bailee has committed a specific tort, however, there would seem to be no conclusive objection to allowing the bailor to proceed alternatively in tort.[47] When, as may one day occur, the plaintiff sues upon a simple allegation of breach of bailment, it may be surmised that the courts will lean more to a contractual choice of law rule than to one based upon the law of tort.[48] Certainly this approach would be justified in the cases of consensual but non-contractual bailment such as depositum or commodatum because the transaction is arguably more akin to a contract than to an ordinary situation in tort, and because an application of the proper law of the bailment would seem to provide a clearer and more convenient selection than the competing rule in *Phillips* v. *Eyre*. The same reasoning might also be urged in respect of the sub-bailment for reward, which although independent of agreement inter partes has at least some qualities of a contractual relationship and may give rise to implied or promissory obligations that are not comple-

---

[43] Or, whether the plaintiff has fulfilled his duty to mitigate.
[44] *Edelson* v. *Musty's Service Station and Garage* [1956] O.W.N. 848.
[45] (1870) L.R. 6 Q.B. 1.
[46] *Boys* v. *Chaplin* [1971] A.C. 356; Dicey and Morris, *Conflict of Laws* (9th ed.), Chapter 18.
[47] Cf. *Matthews* v. *Kuwait Bechtel Corporation* [1959] 2 Q.B. 57; *Allan J. Panozza & Co. Pty. Ltd.* v. *Allied Interstate (Qld.) Pty. Ltd.* [1976] 2 N.S.W.R. 192.
[48] Cf. *Sayers* v. *International Drilling Co.* [1971] 1 W.L.R. 1176; *The Sindh* [1975] 1 Lloyd's Rep. 372; *The Makefjell* [1976] 2 Lloyd's Rep. 29; Knight (1977) 26 I.C.L.Q. 664.

mented by the law of tort. It may be that the courts would confine this contractual fiction to bailments that are consensual, or semi-consensual in character, or to those obligations based upon bailment which are more essentially "promissory" than "tortious". Whatever the approach eventually taken, it can at least be argued that in this sphere (as in others already recognised) bailment suggests a method of enabling courts to avoid one rule in favour of another which is more convenient or equitable. The proper law of the bailment may in fact be one such rule.

In *Kahler* v. *Midland Bank Ltd.*[49] the appellant was the owner of securities in a Canadian company. He never acquired possession of them prior to the action because they were purchased in London in 1927 and remained on deposit with Messrs. Samuel Montagu; the appellant himself was resident in Czechoslovakia and remained there for some twelve years after the purchase of the shares. In 1938 the appellant's Czechoslovakian bank (the Zivnostenska Bank) credited the shares to the appellant's newly-opened deposit account with them, and wrote to the respondent (Midland) Bank instructing them to receive the shares from Samuel Montagu on Zivnostenka's account. The respondents acceded to this request in a letter which referred to Zivnostenska as their customer and noted that the shares had now been credited to them. In 1939, as a condition of being allowed to leave Czechoslovakia, the appellant transferred his account from the Zivnostenska to the Bohemian Bank. Zivnostenska advised the respondents of this transfer and the respondents then notified the Bohemian Bank that the securities were now held on their account. The assumption of the House of Lords seems to have been that the relevant sequence of bailment therefore ran as follows:

(a) K (Bailor)	⟶			S.M. (Bailee)
(b) K (Bailor)	⟶	Z (Bailee)	⟶	S.M. (Sub-bailee)
(c) K (Bailor)	⟶	Z (Bailee)	⟶	M. (Sub-bailee)
(d) K (Bailor)	⟶	B (Bailee)	⟶	M. (Sub-bailee)

When the war was over, the appellant (now resident in the U.S.A.) asked the respondents to surrender the securities to him. They refused on the ground that the B. Bank (with whom the appellant had contracted for the keeping of the shares) were prevented from the proper law of that contract from ordering delivery to the appellant and that they (the respondents), as bailees of the B. Bank, could stand in no better position than their bailor. The appellant sued them in detinue (an earlier action for breach of contract having been discontinued) and his claim was rejected by the House of Lords. Their Lordships held that the proper law of the contract of bailment between B and the appellant was Czechoslovakian and that the appellant was prevented by this

[49] [1950] A.C. 24.

contract from showing the immediate right to possession upon which his action for detinue depended. Lords Reid and MacDermott, who dissented from this conclusion, did so only on the ground that the proper law of the contract between B. and the appellant was English and not Czechoslovakian. None of their Lordships saw fit to consider whether the proper law of the sub- or extended bailment between the appellant and the respondents was something other than the proper law of the contract between the appellant and B. This was probably because the sub-bailee's liability to a principal bailor, and the notion that a distinct relationship of bailment could exist between two such parties, were not authoritatively confirmed until 1965. The majority of their Lordships merely saw the appellant's demand for redelivery as an invitation to them to enforce a contract which was illegal under its proper law, and this they refused to do. Indeed, Lord MacDermott expressly denied that there was a bailment between the parties to the present action and accordingly felt that the respondents were entitled to plead jus tertii because the appellant was a stranger to the bailment.[50] But later authority confirms that a bailment may arise, without contract or even agreement, between a principal bailor and a sub-bailee, and it seems that the sub-bailee may well be estopped from disputing his bailor's title.[51] Moreover, it is difficult to see how a relationship of bailment could have existed between, on the one hand, the respondents and either B or Z, and on the other hand, the appellant and either B or Z, when neither B nor Z ever owned or possessed the securities. In fact, there may only have been one bailment throughout, and that was between the parties to the action. The decision in *Kahler's* case is an unfortunate example of the way in which a court may become mesmerised by the presence of some contractual relationship into disregarding the special quality of a concurrent or contangent bailment within the same parameter of facts, thereby losing sight of the different obligations which that bailment may generate.[52] It may well be that if the performance of a contract of bailment is illegal under its proper law the bailor cannot ignore that contract by bringing an action in rem.[53] But perhaps even a contractual bailment may, in exceptional cases, give rise to two different systems of governing law according to whether it is the contract or the bailment that is sued upon; and this disunity of systems is much more likely to occur when the three transactions are a principal contract of bailment, an extended non-contractual bailment, and a contract of sub-bailment to which the original bailor is not even a party.

C. Actions against the Crown

At Common Law the Crown could not be sued in tort and could be sued in contract only by petition of right. Statute has now removed both of these disabilities[54] and the distinction between contract and tort has

[50] Ibid., at 38.
[51] See p. 175 and Chapter 20, post.
[52] The decision is doubted by Dicey and Morris, op. cit., p. 815; and see further at pp. 928-929.
[53] *Zivnostenska Bank* v. *Frankman* [1950] A.C. 57, at 87 per Lord Radcliffe.
[54] In England, the *Crown Proceedings Act* 1947, sections 1 and 2.

declined in significance in this context. It seems that an action against the Crown for breach of its duty of care as a bailee was normally regarded as an action in tort for this purpose.[55] In *Brabant & Co.* v. *King*[56] this liability was extended to acts of non-feasance when "the parties charged with non-feasance are under obligation to an individual member of the public to perform the duty which they have neglected to his prejudice, in consideration of their being remunerated by him for its performance". It seems, however, that a similar liability for negligence by omission might be exacted from the Crown in those areas (admittedly rare) in which it is a gratuitous bailee, or a sub-bailee for reward.

For many reasons, it may still be preferable for a bailor to frame his action in contract rather than in tort, even under the extended liability of the *Crown Proceedings Act* 1947. The classes of employee for whom the Crown may be vicariously liable,[57] and the requirement that the servant himself must be liable in tort to the plaintiff,[58] severely limit the utility of the Act to plaintiffs in tort. Thus it seems that the Crown might not be liable in tort for the negligence of a borrowed servant, leading to the loss of the bailor's goods by theft. In this and in other potential situations it may be advisable to proceed in contract; and if the bailment is contractual in character such an action should be allowed as a means of enforcing even the fundamental duties of the bailee at Common Law. Where, however, the bailment is non-contractual, the bailor who sues for breach of the bailee's common law duties would seem at first sight to be limited to an action in tort, and the bailor who sues for breach of some super-added or pseudo-contractual obligation would appear to have no action at all. A possible solution to this dilemma may exist in Section 2(1) (c) of the Act, which allows the plaintiff to proceed against the Crown.

> . . . in respect of any breach of the duties attaching at common law to the ownership, occupation, *possession* or control of property.

This subsection seems primarily to have been designed to impose upon the Crown the principles of occupiers' liability, and there is some difficulty in construing it as covering all of the Crown's duties as a potential non-contractual bailee. The fundamental duties of the bailment (i.e. to take reasonable care of the chattel, and to abstain from converting it) would seem to be readily enough encompassed by 2(1) (c), which has the advantage of not being subject to the proviso as to the independent liability of any servant or agent. But extra obligations may need to satisfy two apparent conditions in order to qualify for enforcement under s. 2(1) (c): first, that liability under them is liability "attaching at Common Law" within the meaning of s. 2(1)(c) itself, and, secondly, that such liability qualifies as liability "in tort", as contem-

---

[55] But it seems that in mixed cases of contract and tort a fiat would generally be granted enabling the plaintiff to bring a petition of right: Halsbury, *Statutes,* vol. 8, p. 846. Cf. the Canadian decisions in *Long* v. *R.* (1922) 63 D.L.R. 134; *Kaufman Metal Co.* v. *R.* [1951] 1 D.L.R. 801; *Massein* v. *R.* [1935] 1 D.L.R. 701; *Corse* v. *R.* (1892) 3 Ex. C.R. 13.
[56] [1895] A.C. 632.
[57] Sections 2(3) to 2(6).
[58] Section 2(1).

plated by the prefatory words to s. 2(1). Although the satisfaction of these requirements may be difficult, it is submitted that a court could legitimately hold that they were satisfied for the purpose, for instance, of enforcing a pseudo-contractual undertaking by the Crown as an extended bailee to be liable for the conversions of its independent contractors.

In *Levy Bros.* v. *The Queen,*[59] the Crown was held liable under s. 3(1)(a) of the *Crown Liability Act* 1952-1953 (Can.) for the conversion of goods by one of its servants while acting in the course of his employment. The servant was an employee in the Customs Postal Branch and the goods were a parcel of diamonds delivered to that office pending entry and payment of customs duty. Section 3(1)(a) was equivalent to s. 2(1)(a) of the English Statute, which provides that the Crown is liable in respect of torts committed by its servants or agents provided (as was clearly the case in the present proceedings) the servant or agent himself would be liable. The Supreme Court of Canada left open the question whether the Crown would additionally have been liable, as a bailee, under the Canadian equivalent of s. 2(1)(b).[60] It is submitted that such a conclusion would have been justified, and may provide a method of enforcing against the Crown, as a non-contractual bailee, those obligations which do not qualify as giving rise to claims in tort within the meaning of s. 2(1)(a).

The liability of the Post Office for loss or damage to goods handed to them for delivery is governed by special rules, beyond the ambit of the present work.[61]

D. Rights of contribution

In tort, a person liable for damage may recover contribution from any other tortfeasor who would, if sued, have been liable for the same damage; and this right applies whether the party from whom contribution is claimed is a joint tortfeasor or not. This result is achieved by s. 6(1)(c) of the English *Law Reform (Married Women and Tortfeasors) Act* 1935, which abrogates the rule in *Merryweather* v. *Nixan.*[62] The section does not, however, apply to contracting parties, so that a defendant sued for breach of contract cannot claim contribution from another contracting party unless their obligation arises under a joint contract.[63] This limitation can produce inequitable results and tentative proposals are afoot in England for its statutory modification.[64]

Clearly it could prove desirable to classify the optimum number of actions against bailees as actions in tort, in order to avoid the contractual rule. Certainly, in the peripheral area of bailees' liability for

---

[59] (1961) 26 D.L.R. (2d) 760.
[60] Ibid., at 764.
[61] See generally *Triefus & Co.* v. *Post Office* [1957] 2 Q.B. 352; *Wadsworth* v. *P.M.G.* (1939) 56 T.L.R. 1; *Building and Civil Engineering Holidays Scheme Management Ltd.* v. *Post Office* [1966] 1 Q.B. 247; *Moukataff* v. *B.O.A.C.* [1967] 1 Lloyd's Rep. 396; *Post Office Act* 1969 (U.K.), ss. 29-30; *Harold Stephen & Co. Ltd.* v. *Post Office* [1977] 1 W.L.R. 1172, esp. at 1177-1178, 1179-1180.
[62] (1799) 8 Term. Rep. 186.
[63] *McConnell* v. *Lynch-Robinson* [1957] N.I. 70; and see further *Dominion Chain Co.* v. *Eastern Construction Co. Ltd.* (1976) 1 C.P.C. 13.
[64] Law Commission Working Paper No. 59, *Contribution* (1975); Law Commission Report No. 79, *Contribution,* (1977).

the acts of servants, independent contractors and secondary bailees generally, the courts have apparently been untroubled by the fact that the contributor's liability may not in fact be tortious and therefore incapable of engendering a duty to contribute.[65] This seems reasonable when the second tortfeasor's liability is akin, for example, to ordinary principles of vicarious liability, but it may prove harder to achieve when the only liability he could have owed the victim was under some promissory, non-contractual obligation based upon the implied terms of the extended bailment. Moreover, an original bailee may be liable either in contract or in tort, and if sued in the former might again appear precluded from enforcing a right of contribution under the 1935 Act. It is submitted that an action against a primary bailee should be classified so far as possible as an action in tort for this purpose when it relates to the fundamental duty to safeguard the goods; but again the difficulty may be that his liability is contractual and does not correspond with any established tort at all. The only solution would then be to argue that the duty in question is not essentially contractual because it may be enforced without consideration; but this alone may not convince the court that the damage is suffered "as a result of a tort". Of course, many of the foregoing problems are academic because the first bailee may have a contractual (or even non-contractual) right of indemnity against the second bailee;[66] but this conclusion may not always follow, and it is to be hoped that some consideration of the special problems of bailment will be reflected in any reform of the law in this area.

E. Damages

There is some evidence of a special principle for the assessment of damages which flow from a breach of bailment. In *Building and Civil Engineering Holidays Scheme Management Ltd.* v. *Post Office*[67] Lord Denning M.R. expressed the rule as follows:

> At common law in a case of bailment, the general principle is restitutio in integrum, which means that the party damnified is entitled to such a sum of money as will put him as good a position as if the goods had not been lost or damaged. This is subject, however, to the qualification that the damages must not be too remote, that is, they must be such damages as flow directly and in the usual course of things from the loss or damage, see *The Argentino* [(1888) 13 P.D. 191, 196, 200]. If the party damnified suffers damage of a special kind, he is entitled to recover it, subject to the qualification that the damages must not exceed such damages as would be produced in the ordinary course of things by the act complained of, see *Cory* v. *Thames Ironworks* [(1868) L.R. 3 Q.B. 181]. When goods are lost or damaged in transit, the damage ordinarily produced is, in the case of loss, the cost of replacement; or in the case of damage, the cost of repair. That is the amount which, in the absence of contract, the bailor can recover. He cannot

---

[65] See, e.g., *Eastman Chemical International A.G.* v. *N.M.T. Trading Ltd.* [1972] 2 Lloyd's Rep. 25, at 35; *Arcweld Constructions Pty. Ltd.* v. *Smith* (1968) Unrep., Vic. Sup. Ct.; post, p. 837.

[66] Cf. *Everett's Blinds Ltd.* v. *Thomas Ballinger Ltd.* [1965] N.Z.L.R. 266.

[67] [1966] 1 Q.B. 247, at 261-262; cf. per Pearson L.J. at 265.

recover indirect or consequential damages (such as loss of profits on a business)[68] because those can only be recovered in cases on contracts proper, where notice of special circumstances is brought home, see *British Columbia Saw-Mill* v. *Nettleship* [(1866) L.R. 3 C.P. 499, at 506].

In fact, it is uncertain how far the rule expressed by Lord Denning differs from the ordinary rule as to remoteness of damage in actions for breach of contract. Generally, questions of damage in bailment cases have fallen to be decided simply according to whether the action is in contract or in tort. When the bailor complains of a breach of duty additional to the duties imposed upon the bailee at Common Law (such as a promise to carry goods by a particular route or to deliver them within a specific time) the action is normally characterised as an action in contract and the contractual assessment of damages will apply.[69] When the bailor complains of negligence in the custody or carrying of goods, he would seem to enjoy alternative remedies in tort or contract and the level of damages will be that appropriate to the form of action he has chosen.[70] When he sues for some other tort (such as conversion or detinue) damages will be assessed on the principles peculiar to that tort.[71] None of these situations provides a solution to those cases in which a bailee's right of action is neither contractual or tortious, and it may be argued that even the foregoing situations themselves could justifiably be classed as actions in bailment for the purpose of some special principle peculiar to transactions of that character. Generally, how-

[68] See on this point *Anderson* v. *N.E. Ry. Co.* (1861) 4 L.T. 216; *Henderson* v. *N.E. Ry. Co.* (1861) 9 W.R. 519; cf. *Re Trent & Humber Co., ex parte Cambrian Steam Packet Co.* (1868) 4 Ch. App. 112.

[69] E.g. *The Heron II* [1969] 1 A.C. 350; cf. *Lilley* v. *Doubleday* (1881) 7 Q.B.D. 510, at 511-512; *Parsons* v. *Uttley Ingham* [1978] 1 All E.R. 825.

[70] For example, it should be possible for the bailor to recover damages in contract from a carrier or artificer for mental anguish or loss of enjoyment caused by the bailee's negligent destruction or delay of the goods, notwithstanding that such damages may be irrecoverable in tort: cf. *Miner* v. *Canadian Pacific Railroad* (1910) 15 W.L.R. 161; (1911) 18 W.L.R. 476 (ante, p. 8), where the action against the carrier was framed as an action in negligence and damages for mental suffering were disallowed; *Jennings* v. *Wolfe* [1950] 3 D.L.R. 442, where a keen sportsman who had shot a grizzly bear and delivered its skin to a taxidermist to be stuffed was held, upon its loss by the bailee, to be entitled to recover only its market value and not damages for its sentimental trophy value. It is likely that in an action for breach of contract these cases would be decided differently today: see generally Rose (1977) 55 *Canadian Bar Review* 333; cf. *Ichard* v. *Frangoulis* [1977] 2 All E.R. 461; *Harris* v. *Lombard New Zealand Ltd.* [1974] 2 N.Z.L.R. 161 (where damages for loss of enjoyment were awarded against a repossessing finance company for a wrongful sale of the chattel).

[71] As to the measure of damages in conversion and detinue (which will not be separately examined) see Fleming, *Torts* (5th ed.), pp. 67-71; Clerk and Lindsell, *Torts* (14th ed.), paras. 1150 et. seq. The statement by Bramwell B. in *Chinery* v. *Viall* (1860) 5 H. & N. 288, at 295, "that a man cannot by merely changing the form of action entitle himself to recover damages greater than the amount to which he is in law entitled according to the true facts of the case and the real nature of the transaction", must be limited to those cases in which the plaintiff is seeking by means of a revised form of action to recover more than his actual loss. Such cases will be rare because it now seems established that the measure of changes both in conversion (the tort involved in *Chinery* v. *Viall*) and in detinue is not based universally upon the value of the chattel but is limited to the plaintiff's actual loss: see *Greenwood* v. *Bennett* [1973] Q.B. 195; *Butler* v. *Egg Board* (1966) 114 C.L.R. 185; *Bryanston Leasings* v. *Principality Finance Ltd.* [1977] R.T.R. 45.

ever, this special principle has passed unheeded: the courts have adhered
to the more conventional divisions of contract and tort and there are few
cases of bailment which cast any significant light upon the principles of
damage peculiar to bailees.[72] It may be hazarded that certain non-
contractual forms of liability, such as the action for breach of a
gratuitous bailee's promise to store goods in a particular place, will more
readily be equated with contract for the purpose of assessing damages
than with tort; but again this is an area of bailment that remains almost
entirely uncharted.

F. Judgments in foreign currency

For a short time, it may have been justifiable to conclude that contract
differed from tort insofar as damages in a currency other than sterling
could be awarded in the former action but not in the latter.[73] However,
a recent decision of the Court of Appeal allows recovery in a foreign
currency upon an action for negligence.[74] Until the validity of this conclusion is tested at the highest level, it must be assumed that there
is now no material bar to the award of damages in a foreign currency
upon any action for breach of bailment. If, on a later occasion, differences
between tort and contract do emerge in this context, it may again become
necessary to ascertain to which of these forms of action an action on
the bailment is closer. No doubt different conclusions might be reached
according to the nature of the obligation sought to be enforced. The
present uncertainty does at least allow sufficient latitude for a court to
do substantial justice between the parties whenever a case of the kind
in question arises.

G. Miscellaneous cases

We have already noted that an action for breach of the bailee's duty of
care has been characterised as an action in tort for the purposes of the
Limitation Act 1939, and of the *County Courts Act* 1888.[75] In *Thomas*
v. *High*[76] it was held that an action against a gratuitous bailee for the
non-return of money could not (because of the absence of consideration)
be classed as contractual and was essentially an action in conversion.
Moreover, this characterisation would apply on the facts of the case
even though the bailor sued alternatively on a count for money had and
received. On this point the decision may be contrasted with *Chesworth*
v. *Farrar*,[77] where the Court of Appeal held that an action for money
had and received was not an action in tort (but in quasi-contract) for
the purposes of the *Limitation Act*. The question of characterisation arose
in *Thomas* v. *High* because the defendant bailee claimed a stay of action.

---

[72] For illustrations of problems of damages in bailment cases, see *Martin* v. *L.C.C.*
[1947] 1 K.B. 628; *Macrae* v. *Swindell's* [1954] 2 All E.R. 260; *Booth* v. *Wellby*
(1928) 165 L.T. Jo. 213; *Dash* v. *Faulkner* (1886) 2 T.L.R. 255; *Arcweld
Constructions Pty. Ltd.* v. *Smith* (1968) Unrep. Vic. Sup. Ct.; *Grenn* v. *Brampton
Poultry Co.* (1958) 13 D.L.R. (2d) 279; *Chinery* v. *Viall* (1860) 5 H. & N. 416.
[73] *The Volturno* [1921] 2 A.C. 544; *Miliangos* v. *George Frank (Textiles) Ltd.*
[1975] A.C. 943.
[74] *The Despina R.* (1977) *The Times,* 21 June.
[75] Ante., p. 54.
[76] (1960) 60 S.R. (N.S.W.) 401.
[77] [1967] 1 Q.B. 407.

He contended that the claim was based on fraud, and should therefore be stayed until he was prosecuted for felony. The magistrate had regarded the action as a suit for breach of contract and had regarded the relationship between a bailor and gratuitous bailee as contractual. The Supreme Court in banco rejected this classification and remarked that the bailor's rights under such a bailment were purely rights of action in tort. A new trial was therefore ordered and the magistrate's verdict set aside, because the refusal of the defendant to return the money on demand was evidence of a conversion.

With respect, it is submitted that the court was in error in observing that a bailor's remedies under a gratuitous bailment lie exclusively in tort. An action may lie for breach of bailment in cases where the bailee's liability is incapable of being rationalised as tortious or contractual. To state that tort is the sole foundation of action upon a gratuitous bailment, or (as Ferguson J. did) that the duties of a bailee for reward "arise out of contract"[78] is to neglect the special character of bailment and to contribute to its extinction in favour of more modern forms of action.

VIII. BAILMENT AND PROPERTY[79]

We have hitherto excluded from our consideration of the nature of bailment any examination of its role within the broader field of property. This is largely because our analysis has concentrated upon modern judicial interpretations of the scope and content of bailment, and within such interpretations there is a marked absence of reasoning based upon conclusions drawn from the law of property itself. It is, however, impossible to understand and to predict the development of bailment without some investigation of its function and standing as a source of property rights.

A bailment gives rise to a form of property because it creates a division of interests in rem within the compass of a single chattel. The division is chronological rather than geographical; as in the case of leaseholds, a bailment divides the ownership of the res "on a plane of time".[80] The bailee obtains a legal interest in the form of possession, which is in many respects equivalent to an estate in land and in the case of some bailments at least (such as pawns, liens and probably contracts of hire) this interest is preserved although the bailor disposes of his interest during the bailment to a third party.[81] The bailor retains a reversionary interest in the form of his residual or eventual right to possession, which normally (but not necessarily) exists concurrently with his ownership of

---

[78] (1960) 60 S.R. (N.S.W.) 401, at 406.
[79] Paton (1950) 23 A.L.J. 591; *Bailment in the Common Law*, p. 29 et. seq.
[80] Lawson, *Introduction to the Law of Property*, p. 118; and see *Rich* v. *Aldred* (1705) 6 Mod. Rep. 216, where Lord Holt observed: "If A bails goods to C, and after gives his whole right in them to B, B cannot maintain detinue for them against C, because the special property that C acquires by the bailment was not thereby transferred to B." This statement was cited with approval in *Franklin* v. *Neate* (1844) 13 M. & W. 481 at 486 by Rolfe B., who went on to remark that "there does not seem to be any solid ground of distinction, in this respect, between a bailment by way of pawn and any other bailment."
[81] Lawson op. cit. pp. 72-73; and see post, Chapter 26.

the goods; and here, again, this interest is generally preserved although the bailee disposes of the goods to a third party.[82] In the terminology of the older authorities, the bailor has the "general" and the bailee the "special" property in the subject chattel.[83] It is for this reason that Winfield favoured the categorisation of bailment as part of the law of property, and repudiated the contract-analysis as affording an incomplete theory of bailment.[84] Stoljar objects to this classification as lacking in practical value.[85] We hope to show that it may be extremely valuable as a vehicle for clarifying the rights and identities of bailor and bailee.

> However we define a bailment, the central feature is the delivery of possession to the bailee. Possession is essentially an interest in the law of property—indeed from a purely analytical point of view, bailment is more analogous to a lease than a contract, in the sense that a property interest, less than ownership, is transferred. Many of the rights of the bailee flow from his grant of possession.[86]

One such right, of course, is the power of the bailee to recover for injury to the chattel during the term of bailment.[87] This right, the conceptual origins of which are obscure, is founded upon the doctrine that, as against third-parties, possession amounts to title. It entitles the bailee to damages for the full extent of the impairment, regardless of personal loss. It subsists although the bailment-contract is illegal,[88] and can prevail in appropriate cases against the owner or other bailor as well as against a third party, although, in the latter case, the bailee is apparently restricted to recovering for his actual loss.[89]

Bailments and leases compared

For present purposes we shall make the parallel as close as possible and shall assume that the bailment in question is the hire of a chattel.

---

[82] To pass a good title, the disposition by a bailee without authority to sell must fall within one of the exceptions to the principle *nemo dat quod non habet*: see generally Atiyah, *Sale of Goods* (5th ed.), Chapter 19; Vaines, *Personal Property* (5th ed.), Chapter 9. Note further that under contracts of hire-purchase the hirer enjoys an equity to the extent of the instalments already paid, and that this equity may be deducted from any damages awarded against him or a third party for conversion of the chattel during the currency of the agreement: *Belsize Motor Supply Co. Ltd.* v. *Cox* [1914] 1 K.B. 244; *Whiteley* v. *Hilt* [1918] 2 K.B. 808; *Wickham Holdings Ltd.* v. *Brooke House Motors Ltd.* [1967] 1 All E.R. 117; *Belvoir Finance Co. Ltd.* v. *Stapleton* [1971] 1 Q.B. 210; *N.Z. Securities & Finance Ltd.* v. *Wrightcars Ltd.* [1976] 1 N.Z.L.R. 77 (where the bailment in question was a simple lease); *Western Credits* v. *Dragon Motors Ltd.* [1973] W.A.R. 184. Cf. *Astley Industrial Trust Ltd.* v. *Miller* [1968] 2 All E.R. 36, at 44, and see generally (1976) 126 New Law Jo. 70.

[83] E.g., *Taylor* v. *Chester* (1869) L.R. 4 Q.B. 309; *A. L. Hamblin Equipment Pty. Ltd.* v. *Federal Commissioner of Taxation* [1974] *Australian Tax Cases* 4310, at 4318 per Mason J.; Bordwell, "Property in Chattels" (1915-1916) 29 *Harvard Law Review* 374, 501, 731. Cf. *The Odessa* [1916] I A.C. 145, at 158-159 per Lord Mersey.

[84] *Province of the Law of Tort*, pp. 100-103; Williams (1915) 31 L.Q.R. 80.

[85] (1955) 7 *Res Judicatae* 160, at 161.

[86] Paton, op. cit., pp. 30-31.

[87] *The Winkfield* [1902] P. 42; Chapter 4, post.

[88] Ante, p. 18.

[89] *Brierley* v. *Kendall* (1852) 17 Q.B. 937; *City Motors (1933) Pty. Ltd.* v. *Southern Aerial Super Service Pty. Ltd.* (1961) 35 A.L.J.R. 206; *Standard Electronic Apparatus Laboratories Pty. Ltd.* v. *Stenner* [1960] N.S.W.R. 447. Cf. *Roberts* v. *Roberts* [1957] Tas. S.R. 84; *Harris* v. *Lombard New Zealand Ltd.* [1974] 2 N.Z.L.R. 161.

The functional and commercial similarities between the lease of land and the hire of a chattel are self-evident.[90] In both cases the present occupier of the property pays for its use and enjoyment under a contract which grants him possession but not full rights of ownership: he is in posesssion of something that "belongs" to another, with that other's full permission and consent. The property is employed as a source of income by the "owner" and is to this end partitioned, both legally and chronologically, between him and the user or occupant. The grantor has a reversionary interest, the grantee has a present right of occupation. Indeed, the contract of hire may be said, like the lease, to grant both tenure and estate to the hirer. The appropriateness of these and other elements in the real-property vocabulary, as applied to the context of chattels, is defended by Lawson. As one of the very few modern authors to pursue the comparison in question, Lawson's opinions demand to be cited in extenso. On the subject of tenure, he argued as follows:

> Tenure has no place in the law of personalty. Nevertheless, a very close analogy to the relation of landlord and tenant is to be found in that between bailor and bailee. Whenever a physical movable is delivered by one person to another for a purpose upon the understanding that it is to be returned upon the accomplishment of the purpose, there is a bailment. Now between the bailor, who hands over the thing, and the bailee, who receives it, there is a personal relation, for the bailee is under a duty to the bailor to take reasonable care of the thing and to return it in due course. But a bailment for a term also confers possession on the bailee, to the exclusion of the bailor. Thus the bailee, and not the bailor, can alone recover possession from a dispossessor. If the bailment is at will, the bailee's position is precisely the same, though it is said on rather doubtful authority that the bailor also has possession, with the rights it confers. So far there is nothing to differentiate in principle a bailment for a term from a lease of land. Moreover, such interest as the bailee has in the chattel is derived from that of the bailor, as is shown by the rule that, just as a lessee cannot be heard to deny his lessor's title, so a bailee cannot be heard to deny that of his bailor. Thus a bailment presents the same sort of mingling of real and personal relations as a lease, and to say that there is tenure between bailor and bailee would be no great offence against terminological propriety.[91]

Likewise, Lawson has claimed that the relationship of bailment can be seen, without undue distortion, as a dimension of the doctrine of estates.

> Bailments do indeed raise very interesting theoretical questions which do not seem to have called for a solution. They have usually been discussed in terms of ownership and possession, but as conferring possession they differ in no way from leases of land. Do they then, like leases, confer real rights to their objects and are they in fact, though not ostensibly, subject to a doctrine of estates in the same rather imperfect way?
>
> Some bailments, for example by way of pledge, undoubtedly confer real rights good against purchasers from the owner of the chattel.

---

[90] Lawson, *Introduction to the Law of Property,* pp. 109-110, 118-119; and see *Stoljar,* loc. cit.
[91] Ibid., at 63.

Bailments at will, under which the bailor can resume possession at any moment, cause no difficulty. Of course the purchaser can oust the bailee. There is authority for saying that if a person charters a ship for a term, any other person, such as a purchaser, who has notice of the charter-party must take the ship subject to it. Apart from ships, which in many ways strongly resemble land, there seems to be no authority on the question whether a purchaser could oust a bailee for a term such as a hirer for a fixed period. In fact a would-be purchaser would almost always have notice of the bailment and, unwilling to risk the trouble and doubtful success of an attempt to oust the bailee, would probably either refuse to buy or pay only for the right to have the thing after the bailment came to an end.

In that case he would really be buying a reversion. That term is commonly used in such a connexion. But is it rightly so used? There are one or two cases which allow the owner of a chattel out of possession, and therefore not entitled to bring an action of trespass, to bring an action for damage to the reversion, that is to say, permanent physical damage to the thing itself. Thus there is warrant for the use of the word reversion. The only doubt—it goes mainly to classification and does not effect the substance of the law —is whether by calling the owner's interest in the chattel the reversion the law subjects it to a doctrine of estates. Perhaps the best answer that can be given to that question is that the doctrine of estates was not invented to deal with terms of years, to which it has always been applied with some difficulty and with more than the usual amount of artificiality, and that bailments of chattels present no greater difficulty. Certainly the interconnected elements of time and quantum which went to make the doctrine of estates are present in both.[92]

Lawson, admittedly, was postulating a general parallel between lease and hire. But the essential similarities between bailments and leases are such that it is substantially irrelevant whether the bailment used as a comparative model is one of hire or serves some other purpose such as storage or pledge. The notion of warehousing or even of pledging land[93] is so remote as to render such a comparison superficially laughable. But in essence a bailment and a lease are similar, whatever the purpose for which the goods are bailed and whether or not that purpose is capable of reflection in the use of land.

Thus, a doctrine of attornment exists under both transactions,[94] and there is a similar rule that the possessor (bailee or tenant), is estopped from denying his bailor's or landlord's title.[95] The elements of possession

---

[92] Ibid., at 72-73.
[93] But cf. the old concept of the mortuum vadium.
[94] As to this rule in bailments, see Chapter 21, post.
[95] As to this rule in bailments, see post, p. 163 et. seq. As to leases, note the recent decision of the Court of Appeal in *Industrial Properties (Barton Hill) Ltd.* v. *A.E.I. Ltd.* [1977] 2 W.L.R. 726. A further, somewhat tentative parallel is suggested by recent dicta of the House of Lords in *Mardorf Peach Co., Ltd.* v. *Attica Sea Carriers Corporation of Liberia* [1977] 1 All E.R. 545. In this case the respondents had sought (at too late a stage for the point to be decided) to argue that a withdrawal clause in a time charterparty, empowering the ship-owners to withdraw the vessel for non-payment of hire "semi-monthly in advance", was comparable to a forfeiture clause in a lease and might therefore be subject to equitable relief. Lord Salmon (at p. 557) was inclined to agree with Lord Denning

in each case are similar; for example, the rule that a servant does not normally acquire possession of his master's goods[96] is reflected in the case of land by this rule:

> A servant or bailiff, or any person occupying land or buildings in a merely ministerial character, does not acquire possession. And it makes no difference that he may carry on a business of his own at the same place.[97]

The principle that a lessee for a term of years acquires possession without entry[98] is probably complemented in the case of a bailment without actual delivery, provided the bailor has vacated possession and no third-party has intervened to oust the bailee.[99] Again, at common law it is impossible for an owner of land or of chattels to create a lease or bailment thereof to himself.[1] Both lessees and bailees have the right to sue for trespass,[2] even where necessary as against the owner. In either case, the owner may have an action for damage to his reversionary interest.[3] The lessee has a proprietary interest in the land, and it has been suggested that an equivalent interest is enjoyed by the hirer.[4] Both

---

M.R. in the Court of Appeal ([1976] 2 All E.R. 249, at 245, 246) that the clause could be characterised as a forfeiture clause but that a commercial case of this nature was not an appropriate medium for equitable relief. However, he preferred to leave the question open. Lord Simon of Glaisdale (at pp. 553-554) was more sympathetic and, while declining to express a concluded opinion, pointed to a number of cases in which withdrawal clauses had been identified as forfeiture clauses. In his view: "Obviously there are differences between the lease of land or buildings and the hire of a ship under a time charter — although service tenancies should not be forgotten. The question would be whether they are material differences in relation to the power of equity to relieve against the effect of a 'forfeiture clause' in the respective contracts. In some respects the law of contract already treats a ship as if she were a piece of realty". However, at pp. 550-551 and 553 Lord Wilberforce expressly repudiated the equation between withdrawal and forfeiture clauses, declaring that the use of the word 'forfeiture' in earlier shipping authorities — most notably *The Petrofina* [1949] A.C. 76 at 90 — did not involve an attribution of legal consequences"; and pointing out the substantial differences between a lease of land and a time charterpart — most notably, that the latter is really little more than a contract for the provision of services. This leaves open the possibility of invoking the parallel in cases of charterparties by demise and in contracts of hire generally, where there is a true bailment and the charterer (like the tenant) gets exclusive occupation of the property in question.

---

[96] Chapter 7, post.

[97] Pollock and Wright, *Possession in the Common Law*, p. 56, citing *White* v. *Bailey* (1861) 10 C.B.N.S. 227.

[98] Pollock and Wright, ibid.

[99] Cf. *Quiggin* v. *Duff* (1836) 1 M. & W. 174.

[1] *Rye* v. *Rye* [1962] A.C. 496 (as to leases); cf. *Harding* v. *Commissioner of Inland Revenue* [1977] 1 N.Z.L.R. 337.

[2] See, as to tenants, Evans, *Law of Landlord and Tenant*, pp. 177-178, where it is observed that the tenant can recover only to the extent of any impairment of his own enjoyment or amenities. In this respect, the tenant's position differs from that of the bailee, as to which see Chapter 4.

[3] As to bailors, see post, pp. 153 et. seq. The landlord's action is an action in trespass and not, as in the case of the bailor, an action on the case. It may issue against the tenant, provided damage to the reversionary interest is proved: Evans, op. cit., p. 173. For the explanation as to why the lessor is said to retain possession of the demised property (and is therefore able to sue in trespass) see Lawson, *Introduction to the Law of Property*, pp. 118-119.

[4] *A.L. Hamblin Equipment Pty. Ltd.* v. *Federal Commissioner of Taxation* [1974] *Australian Tax Cases* 4310, at 4318 per Mason J. who described such a conclusion as "persuasive"; Paton, op. cit., pp. 30-31. But cf. Barwick C.J. in the

leases and hirings contain implied covenants as to quiet possession.[5] The landlord under an illegal lease, like the bailor under an illegal bailment, may sue to recover the land if he can demonstrate an independent title thereto.[6] It has even been suggested that the finder (i.e. a non-consensual bailee) should obtain a species of property which enables him to recover the chattel although he has temporarily lost possession.[7] Such property may be of wider comparative relevance in that it suggests a parallel with the adverse possession of land. On a more modern level, there is an obvious similarity between the extensive landlord and tenant legislation and the protection accorded to certain categories of hirer under the *Consumer Credit Act* 1974. Finally, the lessor's interest in both leases and bailments may be disposed of to a third party; and in some cases at least the acquirer inherits as against the possessor the rights and duties which were formerly owed or enjoyed by the lessor.[8] A useful example in the case of chattels is the power of someone who buys goods from a pawnor to demand redemption, on tender of the amount of the debt, from the pawnee.[9] It is probable that the same result would obtain in a purchase of goods subject to a lien. Rights may therefore run with chattels as well as with land.

In many of the foregoing examples the points of similarity are precise and stem from the close conceptual and functional affinity between bailments and leases in general. It is doubtful, however, whether they alone suggest any fundamental framework for a coherent modern theory of bailment. A more significant analogy concerns the power of a purchaser from the bailor or landlord to sue for antecedent breaches of obligation by the tenant or bailee. In the case of leases, it is now established that the landlord's assignee acquires along with the reversion to the land the right to sue for breaches of covenant committed by the tenant before the assignment took place.[10] This power, which is now contained in s. 141 of the *L.P.A.* 1925 but which apparently existed at Common Law,[11] extends even to covenants to pay rent.[12] There is some evidence of a similar doctrine in relation to chattels which are the subject-matter of a bailment.

Hamblin case, at 4314, and *Australian Provincial Assurance Co. Ltd.* v. *Coroneo* (1938) 38 S.R. (N.S.W.) 700, at 714-715, where it is said that the hirer's interest is merely possessory, and Jordan C.J. specifically repudiates the parallel with leasehold interests.

---

[5] As to the convenant in cases of hire, see post, p. 721 et. seq. A possible difference may exist in that the covenant survives in cases of hire notwithstanding that the hirer has been evicted by title paramount: this is evidently the position in relation to sales after *Microbeads A.C.* v. *Vinhurst Road Markings Ltd.* [1975] 1 All E.R. 529. A covenant of title exists in cases of pledge: see *Cheesman* v. *Exall* (1851) 6 Ex. 341.

[6] *Amar Singh* v. *Kulubya* [1964] A.C. 142; and see *Edler* v. *Auerbach* [1950] 1 K.B. 359; Treitel, *Law of Contract* (4th ed.), pp. 332-333.

[7] Holmes, *The Common Law*, p. 238; post., p. 854. Cf. *Barker* v. *Furlong* [1891] 2 Ch. 173.

[8] Post.

[9] *Franklin* v. *Neate* (1844) 13 M. & W. 481.

[10] *Re King* [1963] Ch. 459; *London and County (A. & D.) Ltd.* v. *Wilfred Sportsman Ltd.* [1971] Ch. 764; *Arlesford Trading Co. Ltd.* v. *Servan Singh* [1971] 1 W.L.R. 1080.

[11] *Re King* (ante).

[12] See the *London and County* and *Arlesford Trading Co.* cases, ante. Cf. as to contracts of hire, *Bowyer* v. *Robinson* (1843) 2 L.T.O.S. 123; post., p. 75.

Thus it has been held that when title-deeds are lost by a bailee before the plaintiff becomes entitled to them, the bailee is liable in detinue to the plaintiff for failing to return them;[13] and that when documents of title are misdelivered by a bailee, the subsequent proprietor of these documents may likewise sue in trover or detinue although the act which disables the bailee from returning them occurred before his entitlement to them arose.[14] Likewise, we have already seen that the purchaser of a pawnor's "reversion" may sue to enforce his right to redeem the goods.[15] All three decisions may be taken as authority against Blackburn J.'s assertion in the first of them that "as a general rule, causes of action already accrued do not run with the property in goods or deeds"[16] and as authority for the view that at least some obligations undertaken by a bailee may be enforced by later disponees of the reversion in a manner akin to that allowable under leases of land.[17]

Admittedly, the authority of these and similar cases is somewhat weakened by a recent decision of the English High Court. In *Margarine Union G.m.b.H.* v. *Cambay Prince S.S. Co. Ltd.*[18] the plaintiffs were the purchasers of 2000 tons of copra. Their portion was part of a larger cargo which, at the time of sale, was afloat on the defendant's ship. Through the negligence of the shipowners the cargo became contaminated, but this occurred before the purchasers had acquired, by separation from the bulk, property in any part thereof. Subsequently they sued for the damage and relied in part upon the decisions discussed above. Roskill J., having held that their lack of ownership at the material time precluded their succeeding upon an ordinary action for negligence,[19] further held that the older cases could all be rationalised as cases in which the relevant tort had been committed subsequently to the plaintiff's acquisition of title. They did not, therefore, support the contention that a later acquisition of property in goods that are the subject of a bailment

---

[13] *Goodman* v. *Boycott* (1862) 2 B. & S. 1, where counsel for the plaintiff had argued (at p. 3) that "The property in the deeds accompanies the title to the land, and passes with the land to the devisee and their loss is in the nature of damage done to the land. By analogy to the cases of covenants which run with the land—such as covenants to repair—which pass with the reversion to the heir or devisee, this action is maintainable." The defendant based his case upon the fact (inter alia) that there was no privity of bailment between the parties. Wightman J. (at 7-8) remarked that the case would have been different if it were alleged that the deeds had been destroyed before the plaintiff became entitled to them; for then "the plaintiff would never have had any property in the deeds at all and, consequently, could not be entitled to maintain an action to recover the possession, or damages for withholding it."

[14] *Bristol & West of England Bank* v. *Midland Ry. Co.* [1891] 2 Q.B. 653 (where the plaintiffs were pledgees of the documents of title); see also *Pirie* v. *Warden* (1871) Ct. of Sess., 3rd series, IX Macpherson, 610; *Short* v. *Simpson* (1866) L.R. 1 C.R. 248.

[15] *Franklin* v. *Neate* (1844) 13 M. & W. 481.

[16] (1862) 2 B. & S. 1, at 9.

[17] Cf. Chapter 26 post, and see further, *Glenwood Lumber Co. Ltd.* v. *Phillips* [1904] A.C. 404; *Land Mortgage Bank of Victoria* v. *Jane Reid* [1909] V.L.R. 284, at 290-291.

[18] [1969] 2 Q.B. 219.

[19] Approved on this point by Lord Denning M.R. in *Spartan Steel & Alloys Ltd.* v. *Martin & Co. (Contractors) Ltd.* [1973] Q.B. 27, at 36; cf. *Caltex Oil (Aust.) Pty. Ltd.* v. *The "Willemstad"* (1976) 11 A.L.R. 227.

confers a right to sue for torts committed before such property was acquired.[20]

It may be doubted whether Roskill J.'s interpretation of the earlier authorities does justice to the principle they were intended to state, and it is uncertain whether his analysis satisfies the observation of Crompton J. in *Goodman* v. *Boycott*[21] that if the plaintiff were unable to sue nobody else could. It might be argued that the original bailor could still sue under the contract of bailment between himself and the miscreant bailee. Certainly this result should follow when the injury is known to all parties at the time of the sale, for then the bailor loses by having to sell the goods more cheaply while the purchaser (presumably) loses nothing at all. Even when the loss is not reflected in the sale, the original bailor may well be entitled to recover extra-compensatory damages under the bailment, relying upon the bailee's incapacity to plead jus tertii. But this procedure could be unsatisfactory if it excludes the purchaser from any right of action and forces him to rely upon the honesty of the seller (bailor) in accounting to him for the proceeds of the suit. The difficulty could be removed if, at the time of the action, the bailee can be said to have become the bailee of the purchaser, for then he would be estopped from pleading jus tertii, even perhaps in relation to a title antecedent to the present relationship of bailment. Normally a bailment does not arise between bailee and purchaser until the former has attorned.[22] But it may be possible to discern a substitutional relationship of this kind without attornment and by analogy with the assignment of a lessor's reversion. This solution would not have assisted the plaintiffs in the *Margarine Union* case because by the time they were in a position to become bailors (i.e. when they acquired property in the copra) the goods were no longer in the defendants' possession. However, in the case of specific goods which remain throughout in the bailee's possession during a series of sales of the reversion, it could be argued that the creation of a bailment relationship between the bailee and a subsequent purchaser implies an undertaking on the former's part to answer without qualification for an injury committed to the goods by his default, whether arising after that relationship or before it. Certainly this would be the position when there has been an attornment, and it may be that the same should apply when a second bailment arises by any other method. If a plural

---

[20] [1969] 2 Q.B. at 246-250. Other authorities subsequent to those discussed in the text, namely *London Joint Stock Bank Ltd.* v. *British Amsterdam Maritime Agency Ltd.* (1910) 16 Com. Cas. 102 and *Hannan* v. *Arp* (1928) 30 Ll. L.R. 306, were cited in support of this analysis. The interpretation has some force when applied to the *Bristol & West of England Bank* case (ante) because counsel for the plaintiffs seems to have conceded in argument that it was the conversion by non-return upon demand, and not the original conversion by misdelivery, upon which the plaintiff's claim was founded; quaere, however, whether successive conversions can be recognised as founding fresh causes of action: cf. *Spackman* v. *Foster* (1883) 11 Q.B.D. 99.

[21] (1862) 2 B. & S. 1, at 8; cf. Blackburn J. who thought that the executors could sue on the original bailment: ibid., at 10. Blackburn J. clearly thought that the wrong complained of in this case was not one occurring subsequently to the plaintiff's ownership of the deeds: ibid. Cf. Wightman J. at 8, who stressed that the action "is not to recover damages for losing the deeds, but for the detention of them."

[22] Chapter 21, post.

responsibility may be imposed upon a sub-bailee who knows that his immediate deliveror is not the owner of the goods,[23] it might be argued that a similar responsibility might also apply in limited cases to an original bailee who knows that his original bailor is no longer the owner. Such a concluson would not contravene the decision in *Margarine Union* because the defendants' possession never coincided with the plaintiffs' ownership and the defendants were therefore never the plaintiff's bailees.

At this point the parallel between bailments and leases begins to take on some material value, because it is possible to maintain that similar rules should govern the transmission of convenants as between assignees of the original parties. In the case of a lease, the Common Law acknowledged that both the benefit and the burden of covenants contained in the lease could pass to later alienees of the original leasehold interests in at least three out of four potential situations.

1.   Landlord
          ↓
          Tenant   ———————→   Assignee

In this case the original tenant has assigned his term to A. According to the rule in *Spencer's Case*,[24] A takes the benefit of all those covenants which touch and concern the land, and is likewise subjected to the burden of such covenants, at least insofar as the latter relate to things in esse as opposed to things in posse.[25] If this be true of leases, it may also be arguable in the case of bailments.

2.   Bailor
          ↓
          Bailee   ———————→   Assignee

When a hirer under a finite term assigns his remainder in that term to a third party (and we shall assume for present purposes that this occurs with the consent of the lessor), it could therefore be argued that the hirer's assignee can enforce all the relevant covenants contained in the original bailment, and is subject to at least some of the burdens likewise covenanted by the hirer under the original hiring. An example of the former type of covenant might be the lessor's strict implied undertaking that the chattel is reasonably safe and fit for use. We have suggested earlier in the present chapter that the conferment of the benefit of this undertaking upon a secondary hirer may be attained by a flexible employment of the concept of bailment for reward, or by means of some pseudo-contractual implication within the secondary relationship between the lessor and the new bailee.[26] The analogy with leases suggests a further method. In the diagram above there is clear privity of estate between the lessor and the hirer's assignee, and there is also (which may not be the same thing) privity of bailment. In both leases and bailments there are qualities which straddle the dividing-line between property and contract. In the case of a lease, these qualities permit the enforcement of undertakings which, although contractual in origin, may be invoked

---

[23] Chapter 20, post.
[24] (1583) 5 Co. Rep. 16.
[25] The latter qualification is abolished by s. 79(1), L.P.A., 1925.
[26] Ante, pp. 46, 48; and see Chapter 20, post.

by or against persons other than the original contracting parties. Logically there seems no reason why similar rules as to the transmission of covenants with the term itself might not apply in cases of bailment. Of course, the parallel need not be total, not least because different covenants might arise according to whether the lease relates to chattels or to land. This is illustrated by our example, for at common law there is no implied warranty that leased premises are reasonably fit for their purpose;[27] and even in the case of chattels, the hirer's assignee may have difficulty in showing (if that be necessary) that he relied upon the lessor's skill and judgment. But other covenants, whether implied (such as a covenant of quiet possession) or express (such as a covenant to repair) would transpose themselves quite readily into a bailment between a lessor and the hirer's assignee.

The same applies to covenants which impose a burden on the hirer. If the hirer promises, for example, not to use the chattel for certain purposes, or to keep it in repair, it would seem reasonable to enforce a similar covenant against an assignee with knowledge of the covenant. Contract would be irrelevant in this context because the assignee of the original interest, by acquiring that interest, stands in the shoes of the assignor.[28] Again, we suggest other methods for attaining the same result, but the parallel with leases is so obvious that it is regrettable to find that it has not been more deeply explored.

3.   Assignee   ←————   Landlord
                                         ↓
                                      Tenant

In this example the landlord has assigned his reversion. The assignee may enforce at common law any implied covenant (i.e. any covenant which results automatically from the relationship of landlord and tenant) contained in the original lease.[29] A parallel may be perceived with bailments in the case of *Franklin* v. *Neate*,[30] where the pawnee's duty to restore the chattel upon tender of the debt was held to be enforceable by the purchaser of the pawnor's "reversion". In that case Rolfe B. stated that no right would have accrued to the plaintiff to enforce the pawnee's duty to take reasonable care of the chattel;[31] for that duty arose under the contract of bailment, to which the plaintiff was not a party. Although contract and bailment are no longer correlative, it was almost certainly true that the pawnee was not the plaintiff's bailee for this purpose,

---

[27] *Sutton* v. *Temple* (1843) 12 M. & W. 52; [1975] Juridical Review 133; cf. *Gabolinscy* v. *Hamilton City Corporation* [1975] 1 N.Z.L.R. 150.
[28] Cf. Weir [1977] C.L.J. 24, at 27, discussing *The Albazero* [1976] 3 All E.R. 129.
[29] *Wedd* v. *Porter* [1916] 3 K.B. 91, at 100-101.
[30] (1844) 13 M. & W. 481.
[31] Ibid., at 485-486: "Again, it is said, suppose the chattel is injured by default of the pawnee, while in his custody, who is to sue the pawnee, the original pawnor or the purchaser? The answer is obvious. The person with whom the contract is made, that is, the original depositor, is the proper plaintiff, if the action be for a breach of contract express or implied, unless a new one be made with the purchaser: the owner for the time being is the proper plaintiff, if the injury be by the destruction or conversion of the chattel: just as, in the case of a carrier, the original employer is the person to sue for the loss for negligent carriage, or other breach of contract—the other subsequent purchaser for the conversion after the purchase." As to the latter observations, cf. *The Albazero* [1976] 3 All E.R. 129, discussed in Chapter 4, post.

because generally a bailee does not become the bailee of a purchaser from his original bailor until he has attorned to the latter; and in *Franklin* v. *Neate* no such attornment had evidently taken place. The case may show, therefore, that obligations may be enforced against bailees which transcend the perimeter of the bailment relation. Alternatively, it may be arguable that a relaxation of the requirement of attornment may occur in certain cases, and that a bailee may by acquiescence or implied agreement owe certain duties qua bailee, either substitutionally or concurrently, to an assignee of the original bailor.[32]

4.   Assignee   ←———   Bailor
                                                           ↓
                                                        Bailee

At common law, the burden of covenants contained in a lease did not run with the reversion. The rule was inconvenient and was gradually abolished by statute.[33] In the case of bailments, the position of the bailee is somewhat more advantageous, and there are at least two respects in which he may loosely be said to be entitled to enforce covenants against the purchaser of the bailor's reversion. Firstly, an attornment by a bailee to a purchaser from the original bailor is said to create a bailment upon the same terms between attornor and attornee, so that exclusion clauses in the original contract of bailment may be raised as a defence by the bailee against an action (e.g. for negligence) by the subsequent purchaser.[34] Secondly, the purchaser of a chattel which is subject to a pre-existing contract of hire may be bound to honour that contract of hire even though he is not a party to it.[35] In the first case, the conclusion is evidently based on the assumption that the purchaser becomes the bailor and that the original bailor withdraws from the bailment relation. In the second case, the relationship of the bailee and the purchaser may or may not, according to circumstances, be that of bailor and bailee. In neither case, perhaps, is the parallel exact, but each discloses at least some suggestion that the burden of covenants contained in a bailment may be transmitted to an assignee of the bailor's interest in a manner akin to that which follows, under statute, in the case of an assignment of the landlord's reversion. It may be that other types of covenant (e.g. quiet possession, or reasonable fitness for use) could also be transmitted in this way.

5.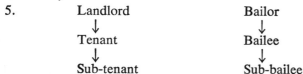

[32] In *Bowyer* v. *Robinson* (1843) 2 L.T.O.S. 123, the lessor of a church organ assigned his reversion and the hirer paid rent to the assignee for two years. It was held that the assignee, not being party to the original contract, could not enforce the obligation to pay rent; quaere, however, whether the hirer had not, by paying rent, attorned to him and thereby become his bailee.
[33] See now s. 142(1), L.P.A., 1925.
[34] *H.M.F. Humphrey Ltd.* v. *Baxter Hoare & Co. Ltd.* (1933) 149 L.T. 603; *Britain & Overseas Trading (Bristles) Ltd.* v. *Brook's Wharf & Bull Wharf, Ltd.* [1967] 2 Lloyd's Rep. 51, at 60.
[35] Post, p. 973 et seq. cf. *Swiss Bank* v. *Lloyd's Bank* (1978) *The Times* May 16.

Even without privity of contract or estate, there is one situation in which a leasehold covenant may be enforced by the landlord against a person deriving title from the lessee. When the tenant creates a sub-tenancy, and thereby alienates the right of occupation for less than the period of his own original term, the sub-tenant may be bound by restric-tive covenants in the original lease in accordance with the doctrine in *Tulk* v. *Moxhay*.[36] The requirement that a covenantee who desires to enforce this doctrine should retain adjoining land capable of benefiting from the covenant is apparently overcome, in the case of leases, by characterising the landlord's reversion as a sufficient interest for the purpose of the rule.[37]

Again it could be argued that an equivalent rule should prevail in cases of sub-bailment, and that the sub-bailee should be bound at the suit of the bailor by any negative stipulation contained in the original bailment, at least where he takes the chattel with notice thereof. This problem arose in the Canadian case of *Chapman* v. *Robinson and Ferguson*,[38] where the court had to decide whether the lender of a car could enforce a prohibition on re-lending against a bailee from the original borrower. A solution was eventually found in the fiction of a contract between bailor and sub-bailee. Elsewhere we suggest that the same conclusion could have been reached more simply by treating the prohibition as one of the essential terms of the sub-bailment.[39] A further method lies in the analogy of a landlord's action against an under-lessee. Most secondary bailments (for example, where a bailee for repair sub-bails to a second repairer) do not amount to an outright "assignment" of the original bailee's interest because he will retain a certain reversion, even though this may amount to no more than a requirement that the goods are to be returned to the bailor through him. It would be desirable if negative covenants were enforceable against sub-bailees in this way. Indeed, it is unfortunate that the analogy of *Tulk* v. *Moxhay* does not likewise permit the enforcement of positive covenants against the sub-bailee, such as an undertaking that his skill and materials should be reasonably fit for their purpose, or (in the case of a deputed contract of carriage) that he will actually carry the goods. Again, we suggest else-where that positive obligations of this kind may be enforced and recog-nised by implication within the sub-bailment relation.[40] The parallel with leases suggests a narrower form of redress, but one which ought not to be wholly disregarded.

The foregoing analysis is necessarily superficial, and it must be conceded that the transplantation within bailments of doctrines peculiar to leasehold interests cannot be made without certain difficulties and adaptations. One problem concerns the necessity to decide whether an assignment of either party's interest under the bailment can cause original

---

[36] (1848) 2 Ph. 774; see *Clements* v. *Welles* (1863) L.R. 1 Eq. 200; *Hall* v. *Ewin* (1887) 37 Ch. D. 74; *John* v. *Holmes* [1900] 1 Ch. 188.
[37] *Regent Oil Co. Ltd.* v. *J. A. Gregory (Hatch End) Ltd.* [1966] Ch. 402, per Harman L.J.
[38] (1969) 71 W.W.R. 515.
[39] Post, p. 373.
[40] Post, p. 821.

covenants to run only when it creates between the assignee and the assignor's original counterpart the relationship of bailor and bailee; or whether the transmission of undertakings in this context can operate outside the perimeter of any subsisting bailment relation. Another difficulty lies in deciding whether the original bailment itself is cancelled and replaced by an assignment of the kind in question. In many cases the answer to the latter question may be in the negative—the original bailment will survive (and with it, inter alia, the bailee's liability for the misconduct of his assignee) because it is the intention of the parties that it should. In fact, these problems are arguably no more serious than those which the common law originally faced when devising the rules about transmission of covenants in leases and it would seem no more difficult in the case of bailments to synthesise principles which, while relying for analogy upon leases, are in some ways distinguishable by virtue of the different character of the transaction.

Two objections may be made to the analogy in question. The first is that leasehold principles have never been applied to chattels and that if doctrines of this kind were inherent in the law of personal property they would have surfaced long ago. In a crude form, they possibly have; but a better answer to this objection is that formerly it was scarcely worthwhile to apply leasehold principles to bailments of chattels because of the transitory nature of most chattels.[41] Nowadays it may be otherwise; certain chattels of a functional character, such as computers, aircraft, industrial plant and ships, have a substantial life-span. They are frequently let on hire for the whole of their working lives and the identity of both lessor and hirer may alter many times during this period. The finance lease epitomises the phenomenon. It can hardly be said that, because problems akin to those in leases have never before arisen with regard to chattels, a court is now conceptually precluded from looking to leasehold solutions in cases where these problems are substantially the same.

> The law cannot provide in advance a detailed solution for every conceivable specific problem. It must develop principles and techniques which can be applied uniformly over fields of varying extent. Hence the need to generalize.
> Now the full extent to which a general principle or technique can properly be made to apply is hardly ever apparent from the start. Accordingly, generalization tends to be progressive; partial generalizations are seen to yield to wider generalizations. The process is often easy enough, though awkward exceptions may have to be admitted. Sometimes it is difficult because, whereas the common elements in two bodies of doctrine or technique may now seem to outweigh in importance the differences between them, at an earlier period the differences seemed so serious that generalization was expressly rejected.
> This has been the case with realty and chattels. Above all, extremely fruitful generalizations such as the notion of tenure and the doctrine of estates have been excluded on principle from the law of chattels, for the very good reason that what at the time would have been the

[41] Lawson, op. cit. pp. 59-60.

most important inferences to be drawn from those generalizations were clearly not applicable to chattels. But those inferences, as will be seen later, can no longer be drawn for realty either, and so the question must now be raised whether the elements common to the law of realty and the law of chattels are not important enough to justify new attempts to generalize more thoroughly the whole law of property, and in particular to apply to the somewhat rudimentary law of chattels the highly developed doctrines and techniques hitherto commonly recognized to apply only to realty. A conviction that such attempts are justified must explain what may at first sight appear to be an excessive preoccupation with obscure problems raised by bailments, and especially with the questions whether the notion of tenure and the doctrine of estates can be applied to them.[42]

The second objection is that land is immovable, that chattels are movable, and that different considerations accordingly apply to each. The validity of this objection can be tested only upon the facts of individual cases. Certainly it is easier to identify land and to ascertain whether anyone other than the owner is legitimately in possession. But even with land the problems of identifying individual interests have led to a system of registration, and it cannot be said that all the objections to a statutory registration of chattel interests are especially compelling.[43] In general, there would not seem to be anything endemic in bailments which raises any insuperable difficulty to an assimilation (at least in part) of the rules evolved for real property and for leases.[44] It is hoped that the "extremely fruitful generalizations" to which Lawson referred may one day be authoritatively made.

IX. THE MEANING OF POSSESSION

A. Is possession essential to bailment?

It is almost universally agreed that no-one can become a bailee without possession of a tangible chattel. Apart from the opinion of Zelling J. that there may be a bailment of the use of a thing,[45] practically the only modern dissentient is Byles J. Speaking obiter in *Fowler* v. *Lock*,[46] he observed that "it may not be necessary to the existence of a bailment [by way of hire] that possession of the chattel should vest in the bailee; it is enough if he have only the use and enjoyment of it". The factor which Byles J. apparently saw as preventing the hirer from acquiring possession in a case of this type was the supply of a servant by the lessor to operate and maintain the chattel. In fact, recent authority has viewed transactions of this kind as governed by the same criteria as apply to all other cases of bailment, and has refused to discern a bailment unless possession has vested in the putative hirer.[47] It may be that for some

---

[42] Ibid., at p. 60.
[43] See Goode, *The Consumer Credit Act, 1974*, p. 7.
[44] Lawson, op. cit., 177-178.
[45] *Roufos* v. *Brewster and Brewster* [1971] 2 S.A.S.R. 218, at 234. Cf. Bray C.J. at 227; *Sexton* v. *King* [1957] St. R. Qd. 355 at 365-366.
[46] (1872) L.R. 7 C.P. 272, at 282.
[47] Post, p. 246 et. seq.

purposes (for example, the implication of a term that the chattel be reasonably fit for use)[48] the transfer of possession makes no material difference to the obligations of the parties. But in other contexts more peculiar to the existence of bailment (such as the bailee's right to sue for trespass, or the incidence of his special burden of proof) it is clear that the fundamental requirement of possession will not be relaxed.[49]

In *Kahler v. Midland Bank Ltd.*[50] the House of Lords regarded two Czechoslovakian banks (the Z. Bank and the B. Bank) as successive bailees of certain securities belonging to the plaintiff but deposited throughout in London. For most of the time the securities were held by the respondent bank in the depot of the Czechoslovakian banks, but it is extremely doubtful whether this sufficed to place either of the latter in possession. The more logical analysis is that the respondent Bank were the bailees of the securities and that they (as independent contractors) took and retained possession upon the instruction of the Z and B Banks as purely contractual intermediaries. It would be difficult to assert that possession was in the Z and B Banks during the material time, if this involved the converse proposition that the respondents were never the possessors. Although, even within the restricted area of bailment, it may sometimes be possible to show that different persons are in possession for different purposes, it would probably have been more simple and accurate to have decided *Kahler's case* independently of any assumption that Z. and B. were bailees.

Nevertheless, the fact that a person *no longer* has possession of another's chattel will not necessarily debar him from owing the obligations of a bailee. This is certainly true, of course, if the one-time possessor has ceased to be in possession as a result of his own default.[51] But it may also be true if the one-time possessor, having discharged part of the work for which he was granted possession, exercises an authority to sub-bail the goods to a third person. In many cases he will remain answerable for the manner in which the chattel is treated by the sub-bailee.[52]

Some cases have gone further and have implied that the duties of a bailee may be owed although the alleged bailee has *never* taken possession. Again, this conclusion seems more readily sustained when the failure to acquire possession is due entirely to the fault of the alleged bailee himself. Thus the liability of a bailee may be owed by one who,

[48] *Southland Harbour Board* v. *Vella* [1974] 1 N.Z.L.R. 526; *Silverman* v. *Imperial London Hotels Ltd.* (1927) 137 L.T. 57; 43 T.L.R. 260.
[49] It should be noted that in cases of pawn or pledge the courts have sometimes acknowledged the pledging of a mere chose in action, and have therefore extended the perimeter of this variety of bailment to include intangible things; see Paton, op. cit., p. 354; cf. *Bristol & West of England Bank* v. *Midland Ry. Co.* [1871] 2 Q.B. 653. But the general rule is that no pledge can arise without delivery of the security—*Ayers* v. *South Australian Banking Co.* (1871) L.R. 3 P.C. 548—and even the pledge of a chose in action apparently requires delivery of an instrument representing or symbolising the goods: see *Carter* v. *Wake* (1877) 4 Ch. D. 605; *Harrold* v. *Plenty* [1901] 2 Ch. 314 at 316.
[50] [1950] A.C. 24.
[51] E.g. *Goodman* v. *Boycott* (186) 2 B. & S. 1; *Houghland* v. *R. R. Low (Luxury Coaches) Ltd.* [1962] 1 Q.B. 694.
[52] Post., p. 829 et. seq.

having been ordered to take possession of goods, negligently omits to
do so with the result that they are taken up and possessed by a thief;[53]
or by one who, although under a personal duty to assume possession,
wrongfully deputes this task to another, with the result that he acquires
no intervening possession between that of the bailor and that of the
third party.[54] In such cases it seems legitimate and reasonable to depart
from the strict rule of possession and to make the defendant answerable
as a bailee. If, on the other hand, the defendant never acquires possession
because he exercises a legitimate authority from the bailor in instructing
that possession be assumed by a third party, the defendant's subsequent
liability to the bailor would rest exclusively in contract or tort and
would seem to have nothing to do with bailment at all.[55]

B. When are chattels possessed?

It is significant that, throughout their treatise on possession in the
common law, Pollock and Wright nowhere attempt to provide a comprehensive definition of that concept. Possession denotes a relationship
between a person and a thing, to which relationship the law attaches
different consequences and which may therefore vary considerably according to the context in which the issue is raised.[56] We do not intend to
analyse the concept deeply, but merely to indicate some of the circumstances in which it has caused problems in the law of bailment. Of course
it is possible to be in possession of chattels without any actual or
imputable knowledge of their existence, but in such cases (as we have
remarked) it is contrary to principle to characterise the possessor as
a bailee.[57]

Possession need not imply immediate physical custody, provided the
bailee enjoys both the means and the mentality of some immediate
control. An obvious modern illustration may be found in a criminal
case. In *R. v. Purdy*[58] the Court of Appeal held that a police-officer who
left an arrest warrant in a police car some fifty or sixty yards away while
making an arrest had the warrant in his possession for the purposes of
s. 102(4) of the *Magistrates' Courts Act* 1952. "It did not cease to be
in his possession merely because, though he still of course had control
of it, he did not actually, physically have it in his pocket or on his
person".[59] Although it must always be borne in mind that possession
under the criminal law (and as employed in a statute) may differ significantly from possession in the civil law,[60] there can be no doubt that the
policeman in this case would have been held to be in possession of the
article for the purposes of suing an intruder for trespass or conversion,

---

[53] *Quiggin v. Duff* (1836) 1 M. & W. 174; cf. *O'Neill v. McCormack & Co.* (1913)
15 W.A.L.R. 33.
[54] *Edwards v. Newland & Co.* [1950] 2 K.B. 534.
[55] See the unreported Victorian decision in *Arcweld Constructions Pty. Ltd. v.
Smith* (17 Sept., 1968), discussed post., at p. 837 et. seq.
[56] See generally Harris, *Oxford Essays in Jurisprudence*, Chapter IV.
[57] As to the concept of bailment by concealment, see Chapter 6, post.
[58] [1975] Q.B. 288.
[59] Ibid., at 297 per Roskill L.J.
[60] For recent indications to this effect, see *R. v. Van Swol* (1974) 4 A.L.R. 386;
D.P.P. v. Brooks [1974] A.C. 862; *Sullivan v. Earl of Caithness* [1976] 2
W.L.R. 361.

or of being liable for its negligent loss or damage, had the occasion arisen. Indeed, the principle may be taken much further than was necessary in *R. v. Purdy*; a man may remain in possession of his goods although he has left them locked in his house while he travels for many years on the other side of the world; likewise if he leaves the house unlocked, or even leaves them standing in his garden: "There is no magic in four walls".[61]

Conversely, certain types of retention or detention, although accompanied by immediate physical custody, are considered almost as a matter of law not to give rise to a bailment. Examples are the use of cutlery by guests at a dinner, the handing of a photograph to a friend for him to admire, the examination of goods in shops and the picking up and inspection of lost goods by a potential finder.[62] Other cases are more doubtful: they include the leaving, by workmen, of tools overnight in a house in which they are working;[63] the assumption of control over the transit of goods by a forwarding-agent;[64] the provision of storage lockers by hospitals, hostels or employers;[65] and the handling of goods in transit by baggage-porters, stevedores and similar personnel.[66] Each case can be decided only by reference to its particular facts, and it is perilous to generalise.

Possession, therefore, is a ductile and intuitive concept; so much so, in fact, that Stoljar has rejected it as a foundation for any meaningful theory of bailment.[67] We hope to have shown that it enjoys considerable value in enabling conclusions to be drawn about the character of bailment as a source of proprietary interests. Moreover, at least in those cases in which a bailment is said to arise by some direct and active delivery from the bailor to the bailee, there exists a substantial body of illustrative authority which allows one to state with relative certainty whether, in a given case, a transfer of possession has taken place.

Possession differs in birth from in life, in procreation from continuation. More particularly, the degree of physical control which is necessary to constitute a transfer or assumption of possession is generally greater than that which is necessary to sustain a possession already acquired. In order to come into possession of a chattel it may therefore be necessary to prove not only a delivery, or some permitted access thereto, but that this has resulted in "a high degree of physical control" over the chattel in question, to the exclusion (at least) of the bailor.[68] So stringent a quality need not attach to one who seeks to establish the *continued*

---

[61] Pollock and Wright, op. cit., p. 38.
[62] Pollock and Wright, op. cit., p. 58; Lawson, op. cit., p. 34; Vaines, op. cit., p. 49; Stoljar, loc. cit., p. 170.
[63] Cf. *MacDonald* v. *Whittaker Textiles (Marysville) Ltd.* (1976) 64 D.L.R. (3d) 317; *Berglund* v. *Roosevelt University* (1974) 310 N.E. (2d) 773.
[64] As to whether the forwarding-agent is a bailee, see post, p. 835.
[65] Cf. *Deyong* v. *Shenburn* [1946] 1 K.B. 227; *Edwards* v. *West Herts Group Hospital Management Committee* [1975] 1 W.L.R. 415; *Hubbard* v. *Sisters of St. Joseph* [1952] 3 D.L.R. 852; and see generally Chapter 5, post.
[66] E.g. *Scruttons Ltd.* v. *Midland Silicones Ltd.* [1962] A.C. 446; stevedores held not to be bailees "sub, bald or simple". And see *Duncan Furness & Co. Pty. Ltd.* v. *R. S. Couch & Co.* [1922] V.L.R. 660.
[67] (1955) 7 *Res Judicatae* 160, at 161.
[68] Harris, op. cit., pp. 74-75.

possession of a chattel to which his original possession is undisputed.[69] Two cases, one ancient and one modern, exemplify the original requirement.

Young v. *Hichens.*[70] The plaintiff was fishing for pilchards. He had drawn his net partially around the fish in question, leaving open a space of about seven fathoms, and was about to close this space with a stop net. In addition, two of his boats were "splashing the water" with the object of deterring the fish from venturing out of the hole. The defendant rowed up and helped himself to certain of the pilchards. *Held,* the plaintiff could not maintain trespass because the fish were not in his possession at the time of the appropriation. "It does appear almost certain that the plaintiff would have had possession of the fish but for the act of the defendant; but it is quite certain that he had not possession . . . until (*he*) had actual power over the fish".[71]

Balmoral Supermarket Ltd. v. *Bank of New Zealand, Ltd.*[72] The plaintiffs' employee took a sum of $4000 to the defendant bank to deposit it. Of this, all but $660 was in cash. She emptied the cash on to the counter in front of the defendant's teller and the teller began to count a small bundle of notes. Two robbers then entered and stole all the cash except a small wad of about $100. The plaintiffs claimed that the loss should fall on the bank because [inter alia] the money had passed into its possession at the time of the robbery. They failed. "In the present case there was never full legal possession of the money in the bank to the exclusion of the plaintiff. At any time before the money had been counted, and it may be before the banking slip had been receipted, the plaintiff's employee could have called for a return of the money placed on the counter for the purposes of counting".[73] In cases where a delivery is attempted, that delivery must be perfected in order for a bailment to take effect.[74]

The nature of the chattel, and its situation, may likewise be relevant in considering whether it has become the subject of a bailment.

J. Lowenstein & Co. Ltd. v. *Durable Wharfage Co. Ltd.*[75] Copper ingots were stored on a barge moored alongside the defendants' wharf. The barge did not belong to the defendants but to a lighterage-company, the third parties in the action. It was battened down, sheeted and locked and the defendants' nightwatchman was on duty, but the ingots were stolen. The defendants were exonerated from liability for this loss because they were not, at the material time, bailees. "The only facility provided by the defendants in this case was for the copper to be passed over their wharf directly on to

[69] *Bird* v. *Fort Frances* [1949] 2 D.L.R. 791 at 800; *McFayden* v. *Wineti* (1908) 11 G.L.R. 245; Chapter 22, post.
[70] (1844) 6 Q.B. 606; Pollock and Wright, op. cit., pp. 37-38.
[71] Ibid., at p. 610; cf *Aberdeen Arctic Co.* v. *Sutter* (1862) 4 Macq. 355 (H.L.)
[72] [1974] 2 N.Z.L.R. 155; cf. *Chambers* v. *Miller* (1862) 18 C.B.N. S. 125.
[73] [1974] 2 N.Z.L.R. at 158.
[74] Cf. pp. 105 et. seq., post, as to whether property in currency passes upon delivery, and see the observations on this point by McMullin CJ. at [1974] 2 N.Z.L.R. 158. "Nor do I think that, even if possession had passed, ownership had passed. Although property in currency generally passes with its possession, this is not necessarily so and the principle must remain that property passes when it is intended by the parties that it shall pass."
[75] [1973] 1 Lloyd's Rep. 221.

the . . . barge moored alongside, and the contract was in my view purely one of handling".[76]

The facts of this case were not dissimilar from those involved in the numerous "licence" cases, where an owner who leaves his chattel with permission upon the land of another is held not to be a bailor to the landowner but a mere licensor over the land upon which it is left.[77] Sometimes, however, it will be the chattel-owner who is the licensor and the user, or alleged bailee, who is the licensee.

> *Southland Harbour Board* v. *Vella.*[78] The appellants hired loading machinery to a shipping company. The machine was attached to the floor of a shed belonging to the appellants. The shed was, throughout the period of the machine's use, under the appellants' "general control" and their servants had regular access to it. *Held* the transaction did not create a bailment of the machine but a relationship of licensor and licensee. However, the same implied warranty of reasonable fitness applied as would have been implied in a case of true hiring.

In this case, admittedly, the machinery seems to have been a fixture rather than a chattel in its own right. But the obstacle to any discovery of a bailment was not so much the problem of delivering so bulky and stationary a chattel, for clearly this could be accomplished by conferring upon the shipping company the means of immediate and exclusive control. Rather, the impediment lay in the shared or non-exclusive nature of the shipping company's access to and dominion over the machinery. This problem can arise in the case of small chattels, usually when it is uncertain whether the owner (bailor) has relinquished his own control of the goods. Thus there is no bailment to a taxi-driver when the passenger travels with his luggage beside him on the back seat, but there may be when the luggage is stowed in the roof-rack, the front-compartment or the boot.[79] Again, there is generally no bailment when the owner of a car allows another to drive him in it,[80] but there may be a bailment when the owner delivers his car to a factory for repair and then allows an employee of the factory to drive him to the station in it.[81] It is all a question of fact and degree, but the question of control, and the distance between the owner and his chattel, are clearly relevant factors.

The problems of exclusivity of control quite often arise with regard to large, faveolate chattels such as ships, in relation to which it is perhaps more logical to talk of occupation in the manner of land rather than possession in the manner of chattels. A number of cases confirm that it is possible for different persons to be in possession of different parts of a ship at the same time.[82]

---

[76] Ibid., at 226. Cf. *Thomas* v. *Day* (1803) 4 Esp. 262; *Wetmore* v. *McKenzie* (1877) 1 P. & B. 557 (Can.); *Seaspan International Ltd.* v. *The "Kostis Prois"* (1973) 33 D.L.R. (3d) 1.
[77] These cases are discussed in Chapter 5, post.
[78] [1974] 1 N.Z.L.R. 526; cf. *Williams* v. *Jones* (1864) 3 H. & C. 256 and 602.
[79] *Hancock* v. *Cunnain* (1886) 12 V.L.R. 9; cf. *Munro* v. *Auckland Transport Board* 5 M.C.D. 43 (New Zealand).
[80] *Wood Motors Ltd.* v. *McTavish* (1971) 21 D.L.R. (3d) 480.
[81] *Chowdhary* v. *Gillot* [1947] 2 All E.R. 541.
[82] E.g. *R.* v. *Halifax Shipyards Ltd.* (1956) 4 D.L.R. (2d) 566; *Ellis* v. *Scruttons Maltby Ltd.* [1975] 1 Lloyd's Rep. 564.

Theoretically, therefore, it is possible to create a bailment in which possession is divided not chronologically but geographically upon the subject-chattel. With a chattel like a ship this is easily envisaged. The smaller the article, and the less closely it resembles a piece of land in its divisibility, the harder it is to conceive a possessory condominium of the kind suggested. One possible application of this theory arises in the case of chattels leased, or chartered, in the company of an operator. Here it may perhaps logically be said that the operator, on behalf of his master, retains possession of those parts of the machine which he alone is empowered to touch or to operate, while the "hirer" (who will generally be responsible for the safekeeping of the machine and entitled to direct its deployment) possesses the remainder. However, this approach creates considerable difficulty and has not hitherto been adopted by the courts.[83]

On the other hand, it is equally possible to have an alternating possession; that is, one which moves like a pendulum between one party and another as circumstances change and each custodian successively reasserts his presence and control. In the case of ships that are occupied by repairers, this seems to be in many cases the likelier conclusion.

> *The Ruapehu.*[84] Shipowners claimed against repairers for fire-damage occurring while the ship was in the repairers' dry-dock. The repairers argued that they were not bound, as bailees, to prove that the fire occurred without negligence on their part, because the material parts of the ship were in their possession only during working hours. The fire broke out at 3.30 am and they alleged that the ship was in the possession of the plaintiffs, through their servants, from evening until morning. The Court of Appeal found that the facts were in any event sufficient proof of negligence on the part of the repairers, and they upheld the conclusion of the trial judge that they were liable for the damage. However, Atkin L.J. observed that in cases of this kind the traditional burden of proof might require some modification. Such modification was not necessary in the present case because the fire itself, upon his view of the facts, actually started during working hours.
>
> "How far is the position altered by the presence of the owners' servants? I do not think that the rights reserved to the owners to retain the use of the vessel for certain purposes prevents the transaction from being one of bailment; but I think that the principle of onus of proof must in such a case be modified though not destroyed. The original principle seems to be grounded on a common sense view of the facts. The bailee knows all about it: he must explain. He and his servants are the persons in charge; the bailor has no opportunity of knowing what happened. These considerations, coupled with the duty to take care, result in the obligation on the bailee to show that that duty has been discharged. Applying this to a case like the present, where for the period of the working hours the ordinary conditions of a complete bailment in fact prevail, and the bailee's servants are in charge and know all about it, but during the rest of the 24 hours the bailor's servants are in

[83] Post, p. 260 et. seq.
[84] (1925) 21 Ll. L.R. 119 and 310; and see *R.* v. *Halifax Shipyards Ltd.* (1956) 4 D.L.R. (2d) 566.

charge and know all about it, it would seem to follow that the onus of proof cast upon the bailee only applies to damage originating during the period of working hours. It seems to me impossible to throw upon the bailee the onus of accounting for injury happening while he and his servants are away and the bailor is there; and at the same time unreasonable to alter the rule if the injury happens while the bailee or his servants are there and in charge, even though some of the bailor's servants may be there as a term of the bailment.

Approaching the case therefore from this point of view a very material question in this case would appear to be, when did the fire originate? If during working hours the onus would be upon the defendants to show that it was not occasioned by their negligence; if during non-working hours then the plaintiffs must discharge the onus of showing that the injury was caused by the defendants' negligence. In working hours I include overtime."[85]

When the location of possession is in doubt, it will be presumed to reside in the party who has title to the goods.[86] But this rule (which is rarely invoked in cases of ordinary bailment) takes effect only when the presence and apparent custody of both parties are equally consistent with a vesting of possession in either. Of course, it is possible to have a joint bailment, where possession resides (at least originally) in two or more joint bailees. The remedies of the parties in this situation are discussed in Chapter 3.

As a general rule, a servant does not obtain possession of his master's chattels.[87] This rule is subject to wide exceptions and it may be questioned whether it retains any practical value.

There are authoritative statements that a gratuitous bailee, or a bailee at will, does not acquire possession of the subject-chattel because possession remains in his bailor.[88] It is submitted, however, that these statements are misconceived.[89] The law permits a fiction of possession in the bailor for the purpose of allowing him to sue in trespass any third-party who violates the bailee's own possession.[90] But the fact that the bailee's own interest is essentially possessory is shown by his ability to recover for injury to the goods (without proof of personal loss) against a stranger,[91] and is consistent with the principles of bailment generally. A right to immediate possession is better characterised as generating a constructive rather than an actual possession.

---

[85] (1925) 21 Ll. L.R. at 315-316.
[86] *Ramsey* v. *Margrett* [1894] 2 Q.B. 18, at 24 per Esher M.R.; *Re Magnus* [1910] 2 K.B. 1049; *French* v. *Gething* [1922] 1 K.B. 236; *Canvey Island Commissioners* v. *Preedy* [1922] 1 Ch.; *Hislop* v. *Hislop* [1950] W.N. 124; *Koppel* v. *Koppel* [1966] 2 All ER. 187; *In re Brick* (1899) 18 N.Z.L.R. 496; cf. *Youngs* v. *Youngs* [1940] 1 K.B. 760; *Re Cole* [1964] Ch. 175.
[87] Chapter 7, post.
[88] E.g. *Ancona* v. *Rogers* (1876) 1 Ex. 285, at 292 per Mellish L.J.; *United States of America and Republic of France* v. *Dollfuss Mieg & Cie, and Bank of England* [1952] A.C. 582, at 611 per Lord Porter (cf. Earl Jowitt at 605); *Wilson* v. *Lombank Ltd.* [1963] 1 W.L.R. 1294; *Woodage* v. *Moss* [1974] 1 W.L.R. 411 at 415; *Sullivan* v. *Earl of Caithness* [1976] 2 W.L.R. 361, at 363, citing Lord Parker C.J. in *Towers & Co. Ltd.* v. *Gray* [1961] 2 Q.B. 351, at 361.
[89] Paton, op. cit., Preface and pp. 6-9; Lawson, op. cit., p. 118.
[90] Post, p. 118 et. seq.
[91] Chapter 4, post.

X. The Termination of Bailment

A distinction must be drawn between, on the one hand, the termination of a contract underpinning a bailment and the revival of a bailor's right of immediate possession, and on the other hand the cessation of the bailee's responsibility for the goods *as a bailee*. When the bailee performs an act fundamentally at variance with the terms of the bailment (for example, by deviating from an agreed route) no formal conduct is required on the part of the bailor in order to determine the accompanying contract or to crystallise his immediate right to possess.[92] But the bailee's liability outlives the contract, and this is so whether the contract is discharged by the bailee's own breach, or by the operation of some external event amounting to frustration, or by mere expiration of time. Admittedly, his responsibility may vary according to the circumstances in which the contract is terminated, and in cases where neither the termination itself nor the fact that he is still in possession of the goods is due to the fault of the bailee, that responsibility may be significantly lighter. The fact remains that his obligations are essentially those of a bailee and arise essentially out of the continuing bailment relation.[93]

In the ordinary case, the bailee's duties do not entirely cease until he has redelivered the goods to the bailor or to any other person to whom he has agreed to redeliver them. This means that his own possession must be vacated in favour of the authorised deliveree, and in particular cases this requirement will give rise to difficult questions of fact. Generally such questions will be solved in the same way as questions relating to the perfection of an original delivery from bailor to bailee.

Thus, a bailee may be relieved of responsibility if the bailor repossesses the goods by some unilateral act, as where a railway passenger takes his suitcase from the luggage-van during the course of a journey and thereafter keeps it beside him in the carriage,[94] or where a servant of the bailor takes redelivery of goods from a warehouse-clerk and leaves them in some public part of the warehouse while he goes in search of others.[95] But if the bailee adopts some specific method of re-delivery (such as transportation to the bailor's residence) his obligation to take care of the goods extends until the bailor is put in possession or until his explicit instructions are wholly fulfilled.[96] It is not enough merely to leave the goods exposed and vulnerable to theft in a place from which the bailor

---

[92] *Cooper v. Willomatt* (1845) 1 C.B. 672; *Fenn v. Bittleston* (1851) 7 Ex. 152; *Bryant v. Wardell* (1848) 2 Ex. 479; *R. v. Poyser* (1851) 2 Den. 233; *Plasycoed Collieries Co. Ltd. v. Partridge, Jones & Co. Ltd.* [1912] 2 K.B. 345, at 351; *Whitely v. Hilt* [1918] 2 K.B. 808; *Scotton v. Bridge & Co. Ltd.* (1919) 19 N.S.W.L.R. 70; *North Central Wagon & Finance Co. Ltd. v. Graham* [1950] 2 K.B. 7; *Reliance Car Facilities Ltd. v. Roding Motors Ltd.* [1952] 2 Q.B. 844; *Union Transport Finance v. B.C.A.* [1978] 2 All E.R. 385.

[93] See, for example, *Steljes v. Ingram* (1903) 19 T.L.R. 534, at 535; *Heugh v. L. & N.W. Ry. Co.* (1870) L.R. 5 Ex. 51; *Mitchell v. Davis* (1920) 37 T.L.R. 68; *Darling Ladies' Wear Ltd. v. Hickey* [1949] 2 D.L.R. 420 (reversed on other grounds [1950] 1 D.L.R. 720); *E. G. Chown & Son v. Moreland* (1975) N.Z. Unrep. 17 Nov.; *Lilley v. Doubleday* (1881) 7 Q.B.D. 510. Cf. *Fong v. Tinkess* [1941] 4 D.L.R. 295.

[94] Cf. *Talley v. G.W. Ry. Co.* (1870) L.R. 6 C.P. 44.

[95] *Barton Ginger & Co. Ltd. v. Wellington Harbour Board* [1951] N.Z.L.R. 673.

[96] *Becker v. Lavender & Co. Ltd.* (1946) 62 T.L.R. 504.

may collect them,[97] unless the agreement of the parties specifically countenances such a course of action.

There may, however, be intervals during the overall period of the bailment, during which the bailee is not responsbile for the goods because he
has in turn bailed them to some third-party on the terms that this shall
create a substitutional bailment between that third-party and the original
bailor and shall determine temporarily the original relationship of bailor
and bailee.[98] Whether a secondary bailment has this effect is a question of
fact, derived from the intention of the parties. It seems likelier that the
effect in question will follow if the secondary bailment occurs at the
request of the bailor, rather than for the convenience of the bailee.[99]

In exceptional cases a bailment may be determined by the operation of
external events which do not destroy the goods but merely render them
less mobile. This was the result in the New Zealand case of *Percy Bros.* v.
Fly and Young,[1] where a horse was killed by a carriage when the bailee
was walking it along a public road to return it to its owner. The accident
occurred through no fault of the bailee and his responsibility was held
to cease from that moment. It should be noted, however, that in such
circumstances the bailee would normally be under a duty to inform the
bailor of what had occurred and to take reasonable steps for the protection of the chattel.[2] Both of these conditions were fulfilled in the
case in question.

---

[97] *Forbes* v. *Aberdeen Motors Ltd.* 1965 S.C. 193; cf. *Furbank* v. *Anderson* (1966)
57 W.W.R. 647.

[98] E.g. *Roufos* v. *Brewster and Brewster* [1971] 2 S.A.S.R. 218; *E. A. Marr & Sons
(Contracting) Pty. Ltd.* v. *Broken Hill Pty. Co. Ltd.* [1970] 3 N.S.W.R. 206;
Joseph Abrams Ltd. v. *Coady and Vint* (1963) 40 D.L.R. (2d) 257; *Valley Auto
Wrecking & Demolition Ltd.* v. *Colonial Motors Ltd.* [1977] 1 W.W.R. 759.

[99] As recognised in the *Valley Auto* case, ante; see generally Chapter 20, post.

[1] [1917] N.Z.L.R. 451, affirming [1916] N.Z.L.R. 837; cf. *British Crane Hire
Corporation Ltd.* v. *Ipswich Plant Hire, Ltd.* [1975] Q.B. 303, where the bailment
was held not to have been determined and the expenses of recovering the machine
were awarded against the hirer.

[2] Post., p. 447.

CHAPTER 2

CLASSIFICATIONS AND DISTINCTIONS

I. THE SUBDIVISIONS OF BAILMENT

Many attempts have been made to classify bailments and to allocate individual examples to a rational and coherent plan. To some extent, this task is influenced by the accepted definition of bailment. There are many peripheral varieties which are either ignored by the older classifications or fit uneasily into them. To accommodate such varieties within an overall scheme requires at least the creation of additional categories and perhaps a recasting of the entire pattern. In fact no general pattern is entirely satisfactory, just as no comprehensive definition of bailment can be certain of encompassing every variation upon the fundamental theme.

The earliest significant attempt to impose a logical order on the field of bailments was made by Holt C.J. in *Coggs* v. *Bernard*.[1] He propounded a six-fold classification, governed primarily by the purpose for which the goods were bailed and the question whether the benefit was mutual or unilateral:

> And there are six sorts of bailments. The first sort of bailment is a bare naked bailment of goods delivered by one man to another to keep for the use of the bailor; and this I call *depositum,* and it is that sort of bailment which is mentioned in *Southcote's Case.*[2] The second sort is, when goods or chattels that are useful, are lent to a friend gratis, to be used by him, and this is called *commodatum*, because the thing is to be restored in specie. The third sort is, when goods are left with the bailee to be used by him for hire; this is called *locatio et conductio*, and the lender is called *locator* and the borrower *conductor*. The fourth sort is when goods or chattels are delivered to another as a pawn, to be a security to him for money borrowed of him by the bailor; and this is called in Latin *vadium*, and in English a pawn or a pledge. The fifth sort is when goods or chattels are delivered to be carried, or something is to be done about them for a reward to be paid by the person who delivers them to the bailee, who is to do the thing about them. The sixth sort is when there is a delivery of goods or chattels to somebody, who is to carry them, or do something about them gratis, without any reward for such his work or carriage, which is this present case. I mention these things, not so much that they are all of them so necessary in order to maintain the proposition which is to be proved, as to clear the reason of the obligation which is upon persons in cases of trust.[3]

[1] (1703) 2 Ld. Raym, 909; 92 E.R. 107.
[2] *Southcote* v. *Bennet* (1601) Cro. Eliz. 815.
[3] (1703) 2 Ld. Raym. 909, at 912-913; 92 E.R. 107, at 110.

Although there seems to have been no particular reason for the order in which these six varieties of bailment were enumerated, it cannot be denied that Holt C.J's. descriptive classification corresponded with the major contemporary manifestations of the bailor-bailee relationship and proved markedly influential upon subsequent discussions of the subject. Even today, it is not easy to think of types of bailment that are not accommodated by his categorisation, and the broad sweep of his analysis is one which has been adopted, with certain refinements, in the present treatment of the subject. Nevertheless, Holt C.J's. division is governed by a fundamentally consensual concept of bailment and by the most obvious social or commercial examples of that concept. It therefore pays no regard to the more hybrid or peripheral kinds of bailment and, by leaving them out altogether, suggests that they do not belong to the realm of bailment at all. Admittedly, this observation is based in part upon developments which have occurred since *Coggs* v. *Bernard,* and is therefore a statement of Holt C.J's. failure to foresee these developments rather than a criticism of his failure to observe them as a contemporary force. The fact remains that a large number of bailments, of a more or less orthodox character, are excluded from his classification. These include bailments by finding, bailments which arise upon a wrongful or mistaken seizure of property, "mutual loans",[4] bailments which arise when a landlord levies distress upon his tenant's goods or when a finance company calls in its security, bailments existing between an owner of goods and a sub-bailee, and bailments which, although redounding to the mutual benefit of the parties, are not the product of a direct bargain or do not involve a "reward to be paid" from bailor to bailee or vice-versa. Nor is it clear that certain bailments of a more modern but conventional kind (such as the contract of hire-purchase, the issue of a ticket to a railway passenger on condition that he surrender it at the end of his journey, or the delivery of a tool to a workman in order that he can perform certain work with it) can find a place within the foregoing classification. Although it would be unfair to criticise Holt C.J's. analysis merely for failing to be water-tight or comprehensive, it seems that if the value of classification rests in the ear-marking of variant obligations within a basic unitary concept, the analysis is not complete. By concentrating exclusively upon the kinds of bailment that arise from some privity of bargain inter partes, the learned Chief Justice's approach neglects the extended or constructive bailment; by concentrating upon the more conventional types of consensual bailment he neglects certain others which fall within the consensual definition; and by stressing only the elements of purpose and reward he discounts certain other criteria which may affect the obligations of the parties.

The question of reward does indeed supply one of the most fundamental and obvious differentiations between different categories of bailment. The differentiation may be dual or triple. One the first level it divides bail--ments into those that are gratuitous and those that are for the mutual benefit of the parties. A gratuitous bailment is, on this analysis, a bailment from which only one party benefits: the other party supplies his services

---

[4] See *Bryce* v. *Hornby* (1938) 82 Sol. Jo. 216; post, p. 286.

(or his chattels) free. Thus, the loan of a chattel or the unrewarded performance of work upon it (mandatum) would qualify as gratuitous bailments whereas the hire of a chattel or the carriage, storage or performance of labour upon goods in return for a remuneration would qualify as a bailment for reward. The alternative analysis proceeds by identifying the party or parties who benefit from the bailment: it therefore groups bailments according to whether they are for the sole benefit of the bailee, for the sole benefit of the bailor, or for the benefit of both. The loan of a chattel falls into the first category, the unrewarded custody or performance of labour upon a chattel falls into the second and hire or storage or labour for reward falls into the third.

Classifying bailments according to the criterion of benefit or reward affords a valuable first guide to understanding the subject; and because it aids clarity of exposition, this system has been adopted in the present work. Possibly, however, this method of distinction is not as clear-cut or as useful as would initially appear. Partly this is due to the difficulty of finding or denying some element of reward in marginal cases. Is it, for instance, possible to say that the benefit arising from the loan of a chattel is entirely one-sided, when the bailor is at least relieved of the task of storing and safeguarding it during the period of the loan? Probably the answer depends upon the nature and usefulness of the chattel; if it is cumbersome and of no immediate use to the bailor the courts should be readier to treat the bailment as one for mutual benefit. Greater problems arise with bailments by finding and bailments which occur through the wrongful seizure of property. With finding, the traditional approach has been to treat the finder as a gratuitous bailee, but his expected benefit from the act of taking custody of the goods may well justify a contrary assumption. With wrongful seizures, the element of benefit may be affected by the degree of innocence with which the seizure was made.[5] None of these problems should afford a decisive deterrent to employing the tests of gratuitousness or reward if it were certain that these tests denoted different areas of responsibility and different fields of obligation. But despite the large amount of older authority which does regulate the duties of both bailor and bailee according to whether they benefit from the bailment, modern decisions seem generally to discard these gradations of liability in favour of a general responsibility for negligence. While this simplification is open to question, it cannot but detract from the value of a classification which proceeds exclusively according to reward. The detraction is not fatal because specific aspects of responsibility do survive in which the gratuitous quality of the bailment may prove to be a determining feature,[6] but the value of the distinction would no longer appear to be as fundamental as it once was. This is particularly so if (as we argue in the ensuing pages) a promissory enlargement of the bailee's common law responsibility is possible not only upon a contractual bailment but upon a gratuitous bailment and a non-contractual bailment for

---

[5] See Chapter 8.
[6] See the examples listed in Chapter 8; and *Tappenden* v. *Artus* [1964]. 2 Q.B. 185, at 201. (gratuitous borrower, unlike hirer, may have no implied right to create a lien).

reward.[7] In this respect the gratuitousness of the transaction would be immaterial.

The presence of consideration has nevertheless been recognised by the learned editor of *Williston on Contracts*[8] as the cardinal distinguishing feature between modern varieties of bailment. The learned editor propounds a four-fold classification into:

1. Gratuitous bailments for the bailor's sole benefit.
2. Gratuitous bailments for the bailee's sole benefit.
3. Bailments for mutual benefit.
4. Bailments to which the law, for reasons of policy, attaches exceptional obligations.[9]

It is conceded to be uncertain whether certain kinds of non-consensual or involuntary bailments are to be included within these categories or whether such transactions do, in fact, disclose a bailment at all. On balance, the editor appears to accept that the resultant bailment is of a constructive character and gratuitous; presumably the gratuitousness is vis-à-vis the bailee, although this would seem unfair where he and not the bailor was the author of the bailment.[10]

More recently, American authorities have shown a tendency to classify bailments according to the manner in which they arise rather than according to their content. One such method of classification divides bailments into three categories: express, implied and constructive. An express bailment is one whereunder the parties have explicitly agreed to adopt the relation of bailor and bailee with regard to a particular subject matter: the bailment may be for any purpose (provided the purpose is consistent with the notion of bailment) and may last for any length of time. Examples of an express bailment would be a contract for warehousing of goods or the delivery of an article to an artificer for cleaning or repair. It would not appear necessary that the bailment should arise ex contractu in order to be express:[11] the necessary qualifications are fulfilled as much by a transaction of depositum or mandatum as by the hire of a chattel or the hire of custody for reward. Thus this classification runs transversely to the old classification of bailments as gratuitous or for reward.

An implied bailment, on the other hand, may be said to occur when the parties have not expressly agreed to occupy the relation of bailor and bailee but have by their conduct created a mutual agreement that that relationship should exist between them. In such a case there may often be a physical delivery without any specific statement of its purpose or intended duration; or there may be no actual delivery at all, as where the implied bailee merely takes possession of the bailor's property in his

[7] E.g. of the kind recognised in *Andrews* v. *Home Flats Ltd.* [1945] 2 All E.R. 698; post, p. 276.

[8] (2nd ed.) vol. 9, para. 1032. See also *Corpus Juris Secundum* Vol. 8 Title *Bailments*, which adopts the first three of Williston's categories.

[9] The principal occupants of this category would be carriers and innkeepers, both of whom owe a strict liability at Common Law: but the latter at least do not have to be bailees and their liability is not founded technically upon bailment. See Chapter 23, post.

[10] E.g., where he mistakenly took possession of the plaintiffs' goods on the assumption that he was entitled to them; cf. *McCowen* v. *McCulloch* [1926] 1 D.L.R. 312.

[11] Cf. *Hope* v. *Costello* (1927) 297 S.W. 100, at 103.

absence on the justified assumption that the bailor wishes him to do so. Thus, an implied bailment may arise when a waiter removes a diner's coat from the back of his chair and places it on a rack or in the cloak-room, or when a visitor to a restaurant leaves his car in the restaurant car-park.[12] An implied bailment may also arise when there is an express bailment of a particular object or receptacle but a merely tacit acceptance of its contents: for example, when a car is bailed to a parking-lot operator containing a valuable quantity of jewels,[13] and the operator can be deemed to have agreed to accept the contents although there is no articulated pact to that effect. Again, it would not seem necessary that the implied bailment should be the product of a contract inter partes. The central feature is that is arises out of an agreement and is inferred whenever it is necessary to make commercial sense of the relationship between the parties. Very often, of course, an implied bailment will occur between two parties who are already contractually related and to whose contractual relationship the bailment is a necessary or reasonable in-cident. The test of an implied bailment must therefore be whether each of the parties was reasonably entitled to infer, from the conduct of the other and from the elements necessary to the efficacy of their relation-ship, that the relationship of bailment had arisen between them. An implied bailment may, of course, be either gratuitous or for the mutual benefit of the parties.

The two foregoing categories envelop all the orthodox species of bail-ment, from vadium (or pledge) to locatio conductio rei (or hire) and depositum (or gratuitous safekeeping). The third category is a hybrid or residual one, designed to accommodate a number of diverse relation-ships which enjoy one or more of the properties of a conventional bail-ment but do not fit into the central pattern of consensual relations. They are called constructive bailments and have been defined as arising:

> Where the person having possession of a chattel holds it under such circumstances that the law imposes upon him the obligation of de-livering it to another.[14]

The constructive bailment lacks one or more of those elements in a conventional bailment which make it possible to base the rights of the parties upon an express or implied agreement. Indeed, there may be overt disagreement between the parties as to the creation of that relationship, or (more commonly) a total absence of communication prior to the transfer of possession.[15] Generally there will be an absence of consent on the part of either bailor or bailee to the taking or vacation of possession. Such non-consent may be exclusive to the bailor (as where A borrows B's bicycle without B's permission) or exclusive to the bailee (as where C sends unsolicited goods on sale or return to D),[16] or may be shared in equal degree by both parties. Thus, a constructive bailment may be im-

---

[12] As to whether possession is taken in such circumstances, see generally Chapter 5.
[13] E.g. *Minichiello* v. *Devonshire Hotel* (1967) *Ltd.* (1976) 66 D.L.R. (3d) 619; post, p. 449.
[14] *Hope* v. *Costello* ante, at 103.
[15] Cf. *Hope* v. *Costello,* where constructive bailments are distinguished on the ground that there need be no actual or constructive delivery.
[16] See generally p. 379 et seq., post.

posed when E loses goods which are found by F and mistakenly delivered by him to G, or when a flood removes H's goods from his land and sweeps them downstream to the land of J. But even parties who are perfectly willing to stand in the relationship of bailor and bailee (or at least who acquiesce in the transfer of possession which produces that relationship) may be parties to a constructive bailment if there is no agreement or communication to that effect between them. The commonest example is the relationship between a principal bailor and a sub-bailee:[17] another might exist in the case of an honest finder to whose possession of goods the loser would raise no objection at all.

Clearly in all these cases there is some relation between the parties and some duties are owed; equally clearly, it is artificial to base either their relationship or the resultant duties upon an implied agreement. The value of having a category of constructive bailments lies not so much in the automatic assessment of the reciprocal obligations of the parties which can occur once a bailment is assigned to that category, because constructive bailments can differ greatly in this respect inter se. Rather its value lies in its acknowledgement of those cases in which the fact of being in possession of another person's goods can generate duties which would not arise but for such possession, and in which the courts are thus enabled to treat the possessor in some respects, or for some limited purpose, as occupying the position of a bailee. In effecting this treatment the courts will pay further regard to the manner in which possession came to be assumed; but one central element in the manner of its assumption (i.e. the absence of an agreement or of any meeting of the minds to that effect) is of prior relevance in allotting the bailment to the category of constructive bailments in the first place.

It is, of course, a matter of controversy whether certain constructive bailments (such as the ordinary involuntary bailment) are properly characterised as bailments at all. Quantifying the value of this classification is, however, less important than quantifying the resultant liabilities of the parties. In practice it makes no difference whether the defendant in a case like *Hope* v. *Costello* is exonerated because she was not a bailee of the plaintiff's furs or because she had performed the exigual duties which attached to her as an involuntary bailee thereof.[18] But the recognition of a category of constructive bailments, having in common only the fact of possession and the absence of agreement, is worthwhile for two reasons. It leads to a greater understanding of the outer boundaries of bailment and of the peculiar effect upon liability of bare possession; and, by grouping together a miscellany of examples which may have little more in common that the original qualification for assignment to that category, it encourages a more fruitful comparison or alikening of individual cases and a more consistent system of results.

---

[17] See further at Chapter 20, post.
[18] In fact the plaintiff lost her case because she alleged a conventional bailment by way of *depositum* in the form of an implied *contract*.

The division of bailments into express, implied and constructive, is made in a number of recent American cases[19] but would appear to have had little impact upon Commonwealth authority. It is, moreover, discarded by the editors of *Corpus Juris Secundum* in favour of a division according to reward. This preference is naturally engendered by the accepted notion of bailment as a consensual relation,[20] although the authors do acknowledge a category of constructive bailments which are distinguishable from those which arise by way of contract. On the whole this category is narrower than the category we have proposed, but of course constructive bailment is a variable zone which expands or contracts according to the latitude of one's definition of bailment:

> Although bailments are generally founded on a contractual relation
> . . . the agreement of the parties may be quasi and constructive and
> an actual contract or one implied in fact is not always necessary to
> create a bailment. There is also a class of bailments which arise by
> operation of law.[21] Such a constructive or involuntary bailment arises
> where the person having possession of a chattel holds it under such
> circumstances that the law imposes on him the obligation of delivering
> it to another, where a person has lawfully acquired possession of
> personal property of another otherwise than by a mutual contract of
> bailment, or where a person has lawfully acquired the possession of
> personal property of another and holds it under circumstances where-
> by he should, on principles of justice, keep it safely and restore it
> or deliver it to the owner. In the case of a constructive bailment it is
> not necessary that there be either an actual or a constructive delivery.
> The lawful possession of the chattel and the duty to account for it
> as the property of another is sufficient.[22]

One criticism of such a category is that it is too wide or amorphous to be valuable; another that it may fail to indicate exhaustively when a bailment should be imposed by law. But these are expressions of discontent with the vagueness of bailment itself rather than a condemnation of any individual classification. Clearly, even the term constructive bailment might not include cases in which the alleged bailee does not know that the property belongs to another; and no doubt other exceptions could be made. The fact remains that this classification leads to a wider understanding of the subject, or at least of its problems, than any other.

Further minor categorisations can be made for the purpose of establishing particular obligations within particular kinds of bailment. Thus a distinction may be drawn between bailments in which the bailor is providing a service for the bailee, and those in which the bailee is providing a service for the bailor. In practice this distinction will substantially correspond with the question as to who receives monetary compensation or benefit and who receives something else; but the correspondence is not total because one party may receive no benefit at all, and even when both parties benefit no money may change hands. Into the first category would

---

[19] E.g. *Berglund* v. *Roosevelt University* (1974) 310 N.E. (2d) 773 (where the third category was described as "implied-in-law"); and see (1959) 12 *Stanford Law Review* 264, at 268 et seq.
[20] C.J.S. Vol. 8. 314.
[21] This is acknowledged to include finders: ibid., at 362.
[22] Ibid.; annotations omitted.

fall contracts of hire and bailments by way of commodatum (or loan); into the second, the storage of goods and the performance of labour upon them. This categorisation could be useful as a first means of establishing the party who owes strict obligations to ensure that the goods or his services are suitable for their purpose, and perhaps of accentuating the fact that these obligations may exist within a bailment alongside which there exists no concurrent contract. But in this regard at least it must be read subject to the prior distinction between gratuitousness and reward rather than as a fundamental division in its own right.

A further distinction exists between contractual and non-contractual bailments. In some ways this is preferable to the categorisation of express, implied and constructive bailments, because it recognises that not all consensual bailments (for example, the gratuitous deposit of goods) are the product of an express or implied contract. But to group such non-contractual bailments alongside the hybrid bailment arising between a finder and a loser, or an owner and a sub-bailee, is scarcely more satisfactory than a system which requires their identification as contracts. The owner-sub-bailee relationship will probably take the form of a bailment for reward, whereas the essential absence of consideration makes the bailment by way of depositum gratuitous; depositor and depositee will at least have negotiated and reached agreement, whereas owner and sub-bailee may not even be aware of one another's identity. In this respect, the difference between the various species of non-contractual bailment may be more fundamental than the difference between each species and the bailment that arises by way of contract. Nevertheless, a three-fold division which first isolates contractual bailments from the remaining varieties and then segregates consensual, non-contractual bailments from the residue possesses the advantage of dissociating bailment from both contract and agreement,[23] while simultaneously acknowledging that either of these phenomena may be influential, or indeed decisive, upon the obligations of the parties. It is therefore suggested that the most satisfactory modern classification may be as follows:

1. Bailments which arise from the agreement of the parties:
   (a) bailments based upon express or implied contract
   (b) bailments based upon consensus falling short of contract.
2. Non-consensual or constructive bailments.
   (a) bailments which arise without the consent of the bailor
   (b) bailments which arise without the consent of the bailee
   (c) bailments to which both parties consent but in the creation of which there has been no prior communication or agreement.

To some extent, we have adhered to this classification in the present treatment; but a classification which is designed to present a coherent overall conspectus of the subject-matter is not necessarily one which provides the most logical sequence for a discussion of internal differences between members of that subject. Partly for this reason and partly because of its traditional significance, we have attempted to combine the above division with the more orthodox one between gratuitousness and reward.

[23] As advocated by Tay (1966) 5 *Sydney Law Review* 239.

II. Bailment Distinguished from other Transactions

A. Bailment and sale

A bailment passes no general property in the subject chattel[24] and cannot by itself make the bailee owner of the goods. If the bailment contains an option for him to purchase the goods, the exercise of that option terminates his status as a bailee.[25] With contracts of sale, on the other hand, the passing of property is the primary object of the transaction and the failure to pass title has been held to produce a total failure of consideration.[26] Thus there is a clear conceptual distinction between bailment and sale, which, for the most part, renders the two relations mutually exclusive.

Nevertheless it may be possible for the two transactions to operate successively upon a single chattel and between the same parties. Thus, in a contract of hire-purchase the bailee will enjoy the power of becoming owner upon exercise of his option to purchase, while remaining until such exercise a mere bailee by way of hire. But even during the pre-option period the law regards him more as a potential purchaser than as a mere bailee: an identification that is shown, for example, in the judicial attitude to penalty clauses or the commission of a fundamental breach of contract by the owner.[27] Hire-purchase is a hybrid and peculiar form of bailment, bearing perhaps a greater affinity to methods of outright disposition than to the strict division of interests that arises upon a traditional bailment.

Further, a contract may take the form of a bailment while amounting for all practical purposes to an outright sale, even where there is no question of the bailee's exercising any option to purchase. This is exemplified by the finance lease,[28] whereunder a chattel may be hired for its entire expected life-span for a cost which is scaled to the value of the chattel itself. Certain contracts of hire are now treated in a manner equivalent to consumer credit agreements under English law,[29] but in general a long-term hiring arrangement continues to be regarded as a bailment rather than a sale. This may be contrasted with the approach in some American states, where such transactions have been equated with sales for the purposes of applying the rules of the Uniform Commercial Code. In England, the ambiguity of distinguishing between sales and hirings for a variety of purposes in which identical rules would seem appropriate has long been commented upon.[30] The fact remains that the lease of a chattel creates a bailment and not a sale if it is explicitly stated that the supplier remains at all times the owner and that the lessee is entitled merely to enjoyment and possession. The character of the transaction as a bailment is not altered by the fact that the hirer may, by paying the hiring charges regularly, continue in indefinite possesion of the chattel, or by the

---

[24] *Atkin* v. *Barwick* (1719) 1 Stra. 165.
[25] This is, of course, most commonly illustrated by the hire-purchase agreement.
[26] *Rowland* v. *Divall* [1923] 2 K.B. 500.
[27] See generally Vaines, op. cit., p. 374 et seq.; Cmnd. 4596 (1971) paras. 5.2.2. et seq.
[28] Post, p. 717.
[29] Post, p. 760 et seq.
[30] See generally, Chapter 19, and Law Commission Working Paper No. 71. (1977).

fact that the charges for hiring are evidently a computation of its value.

Decisions in this area fall into two principal categories: those in which it is unclear whether the delivery of goods contemplates the return in specie of those goods themselves or merely of equivalent goods; and those in which it is unclear whether the supplier or deliveror has reserved the right to demand the return of the goods at all. Into the first category fall the 'wheat' cases, and into the second fall the 'bottle' cases. Of course the principles involved in these decisions extend beyond their immediate subject-matter. We shall examine each in turn.

1. *The wheat cases*: The essence of bailment is that the bailed property should be returned to the bailor or applied in accordance with his instructions when the bailment terminates. The goods need not be in their precise original form when this event occurs in order for the transaction to qualify as a bailment; if this rule were imposed, it would remove many bailments (such as those for repair or alteration) from the sphere of that relation altogether.[31] What is necessary is that the goods themselves, whether in altered or original form, should be returnable and not merely some other goods of equivalent character or value.[32] There must be a clear physical heredity between what has been delivered to the bailee and what must be returned.

This rule has given rise to difficulty in the area of milling or storage contracts where consumable goods are delivered by their owners for a process of treatment which necessarily involves the intermingling of those goods with similar merchandise belonging to other parties. The facts of *South Australian Insurance Co. Ltd. v. Randell*[33] epitomise the problem. A firm of millers were attempting to enforce a claim against their insurers in respect of a quantity of wheat and flour which had been destroyed by fire on their premises. The insurers' defence was that the millers held the wheat as mere bailees for the farmers who delivered it to them to be ground, and that the terms of the relevant policy did not cover goods that were subject to a bailment because the millers had not insured them specifically as "Goods held in trust or on commission".[34] The millers denied that they were bailees. They showed that their established trade practice, known to all farmers with whom they dealt, was to intermingle individual deliveries of wheat within a central pool and to use this pool as their current stock. The intermixture took place immediately upon receipt of the wheat and in the presence of the farmer who delivered it. Once it had occurred, the millers might sell any part of the wheat, or grind any part into flour at their sole discretion; the farmer's part of the bargain was that he could at any time demand payment for an equal quantity of wheat to that originally delivered at the price which was current at the time of demand. Sometimes the millers made advances to farmers upon individual

---

[31] Post, p. 502.
[32] *Chapman Bros. v. Verco Bros. Ltd.* (1933) 49 C.L.R. 306, at 314, 316 per Rich and Starke JJ.
[33] (1869) L.R. 3 P.C. 101.
[34] As to the conditions upon which a bailee may recover insurance moneys for goods held subject to a bailment see post, p. 193.

deliveries. It was not directly shown that any farmer could demand an equal quantity of wheat.[35]

The Privy Council held that the above course of dealing clearly failed to create a bailment of each consignment of wheat, and gave rise instead to a sale of such consignments, subject (if one took the construction most favourable to the insurers) to the seller's right to repurchase an equivalent quantity at a future time. Even if individual farmers could, under the terms of trade, demand the return of an equivalent quantity of wheat, they could not demand the identical consignment and thus had not cast the millers in the position of bailees. The case was no different from the deposit of money with a banker, and the fact that the millers made a small charge "for storage" did not affect the complexion of the agreement.[36]

> The delivery was not for the peculiar or primary purpose of storage *simpliciter*, as in the case of a bailment of property to be returned to one Bailor, or of any part to one or more of several joint Bailors; but the wheat was delivered by each farmer independently, to be stored and used as part of the current stock or capital of the miller's trade. There seems to be no ground upon which a Banker is held not to be a Trustee, or a Banker's current capital not to be trust property, that is not applicable in principle to the case of the miller and his current stock of wheat, which is his trading capital.[37]

The same conclusion was later reached by the High Court of Australia in *Chapman Bros v. Verco Bros. & Co. Ltd.*[38] The facts were similar to those in *Randell's* case and the wheat was again described in the receipts as "received for storage"—but the millers' conditions of trade stated inter alia that they would, at any time desired by the farmer, purchase and pay for the wheat, or would redeliver an equivalent quantity to the farmer on demand. Again, as in *Randell's* case, there was a small charge for storage; but the wheat was kept stored in the bags in which it was delivered and not commingled in a single pool. Despite the fact that the overall transaction perhaps bore a closer resemblance to the ordinary bailment by way of custody than was true of *Randell's* case (at least up to the point when a farmer desired the millers to purchase his wheat) the High Court held that the original delivery operated to pass property in the wheat and did not merely serve to make it the subject of a bailment. A principal reason for this conclusion was the fact that the wheat was delivered in unmarked bags and was all of the same quality: a single farmer had no right to demand redelivery of the specific bags he had delivered and would know that compliance with such a demand was impossible. Evatt J. delivered a dissenting judgment, pointing out that the millers in the *Randell* case had enjoyed a much greater liberty in dealing with the wheat than did the present respondents, and that under the present respondents' terms of trade the risk of destruction was to remain with the individual farmer until the respondents purchased his wheat. Since property and

---

[35] (1869) L.R. 3 P.C. at 108.
[36] Ibid., at 111.
[37] Ibid., at 113-114.
[38] (1933) 49 C.L.R. 306. Cf. *New Zealand Loan & Mercantile Agency Co. Ltd.* v. *Wright* [1930] N.Z.L.R. 630.

risk are normally located in the same person, this provision afforded some ground for arguing that the wheat did not upon delivery become the property of the respondents: indeed, if it did, it is difficult to see what the subsequent sale gave them.[39] The fact remains that the farmers, upon delivery of their bags of wheat, appear quite unequivocally to have abandoned their property in them in favour of a right to demand a monetary payment or an equivalent consignment from stock. Canadian decisions confirm the trend of Australian case-law in this area,[40] and stress the need for redelivery in specie as a central feature of bailment.

The distinction between bailment and sale is important in cases of this kind because the deliveree's liability for damage or destruction varies according to the nature of the transaction. If he is a bailee, he is liable only if the destruction or damage occurs as a result of his failure to take reasonable care; if, however, the goods have become his own property on condition that he will re-sell an equivalent quantity to the deliveror on demand, his liability upon the latter undertaking is absolute.[41] An alternative way of describing the distinction is to say that the bailee's promise as to redelivery is contingent upon his failure to employ reasonable care[42] whereas the banker's or the re-seller's applies in any event.

2. *The bottle cases*: There is no clear authority as to the nature of the transaction which arises when goods are purchased in a container and a small "deposit", refundable on return, is paid by the customer in respect of the container itself. Normally this situation occurs in relation to liquid comestibles which are supplied in a bottle. In *Geddling* v. *Marsh*[43] three possible characterisations of the transaction were advanced: (a) that there was a gratuitous bailment of the bottle, in the nature of a loan; (b) that the bottle was sold to the customer subject to a promise that it would be re-purchased on return; and (c) that the bottle was hired to the consumer. No conclusion was reached on this question because it was sufficient for the court's purpose merely to hold that the bottle had been supplied *under* the contract for sale of its contents. This rendered the suppliers liable for a defect in the bottle by virtue of s. 14(1) of the *Sale of Goods Act* 1893[44] which required that goods supplied under a contract of sale should be reasonably fit for their purpose. Thus it may be that in the context of the supplier's liability for defective containers the exact analysis of the transaction is of little significance. But in other respects (such as the customer's right to exercise unfettered dominion over the container, and to deal with it as he pleases) it could be highly material to discover whether he has become the owner of it or a mere bailee.

Clearly a straightforward and unambiguous reservation of ownership

---

[39] Ibid., at 323 et seq.
[40] E.g. *O'Flynn* v. *Carson* (1908) 7 W.L.R. 463 (liquor); *Lawlor* v. *Nichol* (1898) 12 Man. R. 224; *Cargo* v. *Jovner* (1899) 4 Terr. L.R. 64; *Re Williams* (1871) 3 U.C.Q.B. 143; *Stephenson* v. *Ranney* (1852) 2 U.C.C.P. 196; *Clark* v. *McClellan* (1892) 23 O.R. 465 (wheat); and see *Crawford* v. *Kingston and Johnston* [1952] 4 D.L.R. 37.
[41] *South Australian Insurance Co.* v. *Randall* (1869) L.R. 3 P.C. 101, at 111-112.
[42] But cf. post, p. 464 et seq.
[43] [1920] 1 K.B. 668.
[44] Now s. 14(3).

at the time of delivery will negate the passing of title to the deliveree and constitute him a mere bailee of the container. This result was achieved in the old case of *Manders* v. *Williams*[45] where casks containing porter had been delivered by the plaintiff brewers to a publican, on the express condition that when empty the casks should be returned to the plaintiffs at the publican's expense or paid for by the publican. It was held that after the casks were emptied (and before the publican purchased and paid for them) he became a mere bailee at will and the plaintiffs enjoyed an immediate right of possession. This enabled them to bring an action of trover against the Sheriff of Camarthen who had seized the casks under a fi. fa.

The same principle applied in *Penfolds Wines Pty. Ltd.* v. *Elliott*,[46] where the reservation of title was achieved (inter alia) by the appellants' embossing on their wine-bottles the words "This bottle always remains the property of Penfolds Wines". The High Court held that this announcement not only rendered the original acquirer of each bottle a mere bailee but imposed the same limitation of relationship upon any subsequent possessor. Thus, if a person obtained a bottle and dealt with it in a manner contrary to the title reserved by the appellants, he could be liable for conversion.[47]

Other decisions in Australia,[48] New Zealand[49] and Ireland,[50] and an unreported decision of the English King's Bench,[51] likewise confirm the power of the manufacturer of beverages to proclaim that title in his containers should not pass alongside title in the beverages themselves. In some of these cases the necessary announcement was reinforced or replaced by a printed condition within the customers' own invoices; in some the owners of the bottles extracted a deposit, whereas in others they did not. In the Irish case, Andrews L.J. specifically held that the fact of a deposit, even one which exceeded the cost of the bottle to the owners, did not entitle the retailer-bailee to resell the bottle at any price he cared to name. Just as with the deposit paid upon a hired car, the deposit in this case was no more than a "guarantee for safe return". On the other hand, the fact that the deposit is considerably less than the value of the bottle may be strong evidence against a contract of sale, while the total absence of a deposit may suggest that the bottle is non-returnable and therefore that it becomes the customer's own property. But there is nothing inconsistent, in theory, in a bailment whereunder the bailee need never return the chattel but must abstain from dealing with it in a particular way.[52]

Most of the foregoing cases involved a systematic and large-scale misuse or detention of one beverage-manufacturer's bottles by a rival

---

[45] (1849) 4 Ex. 339.
[46] (1946) 74 C.L.R. 204. (High Court of Australia.)
[47] See generally on this point pp. 130, 147 post.
[48] *Curtis* v. *Perth & Freemantle Bottle Exchange Co. Ltd.* (1914) 18 C.L.R. 17; *Milk Bottles Recovery Ltd.* v. *Camillo* [1948] V.L.R. 344; and see *Model Dairy Pty. Ltd.* v. *White* (1935) 41 A.L.R. 432.
[49] *New Zealand Breweries Ltd.* v. *Grogan* [1931] G.L.R. 412; *New Zealand Breweries Ltd.* v. *McKendrick Bros. Ltd.* [1937] N.Z.L.R. 112.
[50] *Cantrell & Cochrane Ltd.* v. *Neeson* [1926] N.I. 107.
[51] *Barlow & Co.* v. *Hanslip*, [1926] N.I. 113 n. (Avory and Rowlatt JJ.).
[52] E.g. the bailment by way of hire-purchase?

manufacturer or supplier. They provide little assistance in solving the more ordinary case of a private consumer who acquires the bottle from a retailer and wishes to deal with it in a certain way, or who wishes for some other reason to know the precise nature of the transaction concerning the bottle. Two general points can be briefly made. If the bottle itself contains a declaration that it remains the property of the manufacturer or of some other person, or if the consumer is advised by some other method that property in the bottle is not intended to pass to him, he becomes a mere bailee. Even in the absence of such notification, the principle nemo dat quod non habet may operate to prevent him from becoming the owner. Thus if the manufacturer supplies bottles to the retailer on the terms that the retailer is a mere bailee, and the retailer purports to sell the bottle to the consumer, the retailer is attempting to dispose of a greater interest than he enjoys and the contract of sale may be nugatory; indeed the innocent purchaser may even be liable to the bailor in conversion.

Most containers do not nowadays display a declaration as to their ownership and in the ordinary course of events there can be no doubt that property in them passes to the consumer along with their contents. The point was made obiter by Lord Clyde in the Scottish case of *Leitch & Co. Ltd.* v. *Leydon*:[53]

> I do not think that it can be doubted that—apart from special conditions attached to the contract of sale of the goods—the containers in which goods are bought and sold (paper bags and wrappings, sheets, cartons, tins, jars, bottles, sacks and cases) pass in property to the purchaser of the goods. In practice they are either covered by the price charged for the goods, or they form the subject of an additional charge or price; but it is not unusual for the seller to attach a special condition to the contract by which he engages to make a refund if the purchaser chooses to return them. In either case the buyer acquires on completion of the contract a title to the property in the container.

In view of this, it is perhaps surprising to find a decision by Vaisey J. holding that a customer who purchased a bottle of Lucozade and paid a refundable deposit of threepence on the bottle did not thereby become the owner of the bottle but merely held it under a contract of hire.[54] The decision was given in relation to an action under the *Restrictive Trade Practices Act* 1956, and it may well be that in an ordinary civil action between retailer and consumer a different conclusion would be reached. Certainly it is a remarkable contract of hire under which the hirer pays a fixed charge for the use of a thing and may keep the thing for as long as he, at his sole discretion, chooses: for there is no clear statement that the bailor of the bottle could compel its return to him.[55]

---

[53] 1930 S.C. 41, at 52-53; affirmed 1931 S.C. (H.L.) 1. See also 1930 S.C. 41, at 58-59 per Lord Sands.
[54] *Beecham Foods Ltd.* v. *North Supplies (Edmonton) Ltd.* [1959] 1 W.L.R. 643; cf. *Doble* v. *David Greig Ltd.* [1972] 1 W.L.R. 703, where the refundable deposit on a bottle of Ribena was evidently regarded as part of the price for the purposes of a prosecution under s. 11(2) of the *Trade Descriptions Act* 1968.
[55] At [1959] 1 W.L.R. 646, Vaisey J. expressed doubts on this question but seemed to think that they were immaterial to the present dispute.

Of course, the bailor may desire to restrict in some other way the bailee's right to deal with the chattel, but this might be accomplished no less effectively in the context of a contract of sale.

The ordinary principle that a sale of goods includes a sale of their container may of course be displaced in a variety of ways. Apart from an express declaration to that effect the supplier may rely upon the practice of his particular trade and the common understanding of those who engage therein.[56] To take an obvious example, nobody could seriously claim that the sale of a pint of beer in a public house entitles the drinker to keep the glass. Presumably, although no separate consideration is charged, the publican bails the glass under a transaction akin to a contract of hire, assuming that the glass passes into his customer's possession in the first place. The value of the container and the cost of its replacement are of course important considerations in this regard.[57]

The sensitivity of manufacturers about the use to which their containers are put has encouraged them on occasions to advance arguments which suggest (in a manner akin to the price-fixing cases) that covenants should run with chattels. Normally a sub-purchaser is not affected by conditions in the principal contract of purchase because there is no privity between him and the person for whose benefit the original conditions were imposed.[58] The same rule would apply to a non-party to the original contract who merely handled the goods without acquiring possession; and this would be so whether the original contract was one of bailment or sale. But a sub-bailee may be bound by some such condition, as one of the terms of his bailment with the principal bailor, if bailment is accepted as a relationship which generates obligations for the enforcement of which privity of contract is unnecessary. This issue, which we discuss in depth elsewhere,[59] could operate in the context of a manufacturer and a private consumer so as to compel the consumer to treat the bottle in which he had purchased a product in a manner consistent with his bailment. For this to occur, however, it would generally be necessary for the manufacturer to prove that the consumer knew at the time of purchase from the retailer that the bottle was held by the retailer, and was to be held by him, subject to a bailment. The absence of such knowledge might make the consumer an involuntary bailee and this would exonerate him from the duty to redeliver it to the owner; but it would not normally entitle him to retain it as against an owner who called to collect it.[60] The more important question is whether his ignorance of the original bailment can operate to free him of that bailment altogether and confer upon him a full title in the goods.

The general answer is that such a conclusion is prohibited by the doctrine nemo dat quod non habet. If the retailer has no title in the

---

[56] Per Lord Clyde in *Leitch & Co. Ltd.* v. *Leydon* 1930 S.C. 41, at 53.
[57] It seems that merely to emboss the manufacturer's name on the bottle is, without more, insufficient notification that title is reserved and that the bona fide acquirer holds as a mere bailee.
[58] Post, p. 821; and cf. now *Swiss Bank* v. *Lloyd's Bank* (1978) The *Times*, May 16.
[59] Chapters 20 and 26.
[60] *Leitch & Co. Ltd.* v. *Leydon* 1931 S.C. (H.L.). 1, at 11 per Lord Blanesburgh.

bottle he cannot confer title on the consumer, regardless of whether the customer is unaware of the limitations on the retailer's interest. There are, however, clear suggestions in two Australian cases that the owner may be estopped from asserting his title if his conduct has induced the ultimate acquirer to believe that such title has been transmitted to an intermediate party from whom the ultimate acquirer purports to receive it.[61] Similar observations were made by Lord Sands in *Leitch & Co. Ltd.* v. *Leydon*:[62]

> A person who is told that, if he is not going to return the battle, he must pay the penny, regards the bottle as his own subject to no obligation. Nobody imagines that he is guilty of any misappropriation if he throws such a bottle into the sea, or uses it as a target, or breaks it up to place upon the top of his garden wall as a discouragement to trespassers, or below the base of the wall as an annoyance to invading rats. Doubtless as regards the ownership of an article the person in temporary possession of it on handing it over to another can convey no higher right of property than that which he himself possesses. But the complainers who launch their bottles upon the wide sea must be taken to be familiar with the normal incidents of the trade, and if this involves that those who purchase from them part with the bottles to many customers with no obligation to return and merely the promise of a penny if the bottle is brought back, I do not think that the complainers are entitled, as against a person who so acquires them, to claim every bottle as being their property.

These observations were regarded with some favour in the subsequent appeal to the House of Lords. Lord Buckmaster expressed himself in some doubt as to whether the manufacturers in that case had not "parted with the possession of those bottles on terms which they must be assumed to know would not be made binding on the ultimate purchaser, and clothed their customer with the full apparent power of making a good title to the bottle".[63] Similar reservations were expressed by Viscount Hailsham and Lord Warrington of Clyffe.[64] In specific cases, it may even be possible to argue that the manufacturer has abandoned his property in the container.[65]

The decision in *Leitch & Co. Ltd.* v. *Leydon* shows that a third party who acts contrary to the original limitations upon which the container was bailed (and who is not himself a bailee upon similar terms) cannot be bound by those limitations if they are contained in a contract to which he is a stranger, and cannot otherwise be made answerable for their violation unless, in so doing, he commits a specific tort. The respondent in this case was a grocer who filled bottles handed to him by customers from a soda-fountain in his shop. The bottles had been delivered from the manufacturers to various retailers on the condition

---

[61] *Curtis* v. *Perth & Freemantle Bottle Exchange Co. Ltd.* (1914) 18 C.L.R. 17, at 23, 28-29; *Penfolds Wines Pty. Ltd.* v. *Elliott* (1946) 74 C.L.R. 204, at 211-212. In the *Curtis* case (ante), at p. 23 of the Report, Griffith C.J. observed that once the estoppel came into effect it could enure in favour of all the world, even a later purchaser who had notice of the original limitation.
[62] 1930 S.C. 41, at 58-59.
[63] 1931 S.C. (H.L.) 1, at 7-8.
[64] Ibid., at 6, 14.
[65] Cf. *Barlow & Co.* v. *Hanslip* [1926] N.I. 113 n.

(inter alia) that they remained at all times the property of the manufacturers and must be returned to them. The grocer's customers probably
acquired them from individual retailers and probably did not have notice
of this condition; all they knew was that there was a deposit on the bottle,
refundable on return. The Scottish House of Lords held that the grocer
had committed no identifiable wrong by filling the bottles and that an
injunction could not be granted against him. This may be contrasted
with the decision of the Australian High Court in *Penfolds Wines Pty.
Ltd.* v. *Elliott*,[66] where in similar circumstances the defendant was held
liable in conversion, but an injunction was refused.

In those cases where the customer can be established to be a mere
bailee of the container in which goods are supplied, it seems clear that
he should be considered a bailee for reward. *Cantrell & Cochrane Ltd.*
v. *Neeson*[67] apparently takes the contrary view but this seems misconceived; the supplier benefits from the consumer's use of the receptacle
because it is unlikely that the product could be marketed without it, and
because the container itself is an obvious source of attraction. It is
therefore submitted that the preferable view, as stated by Vaisey J. in
Beecham Foods Ltd. v. *North Supplies* (*Edmonton*) *Ltd.*,[68] is that the
transaction is one of hire.

To some extent, modern marketing methods have reduced the likelihood that problems of this character will recur. The use of the returnable
glass bottle, for example, is expensive and capable of causing a serious
risk to health unless thoroughly washed and inspected on its return to
the factory. Partly as a result, there has been an increase in disposable
containers over the past decade and an increase in the number of bottles
which are sold on "no deposit, no return." Thus it is likelier today that
the purchaser of a beverage will become the owner of its container rather
than a mere bailee. The fact that problems remain may be inferred, for
instance, from the South Australian *Beverage Container Act* 1975, which
evidently seeks, for reasons of policy, to encourage a return to the
returnable container.

3. *Other Cases*: Work and labour contracts may occasionally raise problems as to whether the party who is to perform work upon a chattel
supplied by another is a bailee of that chattel or acquires it under some
outright disposition in order to resell it to the original supplier when the
work is completed. In the great majority of cases the artificer will be a
bailee and property in the supplied subject-matter will remain throughout
in his "employer".[69] The contrary assumption appears to have been
made in *Dixon* v. *London Small Arms Co. Ltd.*,[70] where the respondents
had agreed to supply a quantity of rifles to the War Office at a price
which excluded the cost of the steel barrels and stocks, these being

---

[66] (1946) 74 C.L.R. 204; post, p. 130.
[67] [1926] N.I. 107.
[68] [1959] 1 W.L.R. 643; see also *Milk Bottles Recovery Ltd.* v. *Camillo* [1948]
V.L.R. 344, where Lowe J. refers variously to a hiring and a loan; and
Geddling v. *Marsh* [1920] 1 K.B. 668, at 672, where Bray J. evidently favoured
regarding the contract as one of hire. The question of gratuitousness and reward
is discussed generally in Chapter 8, post.
[69] See generally, Chapter 14.
[70] (1876) 1 App. Cas. 632 (H.L.).

supplied by the War Office itself. The finished article infringed the appellant's patent and he sought compensation from the respondents. In allowing his claim it was explicitly assumed by Lord Cairns L.C.[71] that property in the finished rifles passed to the Government upon acceptance of the work and that the price paid in respect of the whole article was paid under a contract of sale. Thus it seems that property in the stocks and barrels passed to the respondents prior to that time. A similar inference can be drawn from the speeches of Lords Hatherley and Selborne,[72] although Lord Penzance and Lord Hagan[73] were more reluctant to commit themselves, and the point itself was not apparently essential to the decision. Whether or not a transaction of this kind is to be construed as a bailment locatio operis faciendi or as a sale and re-sale clearly depends upon the intention of the parties; the relative value of the materials supplied and the method of computing the cost of the work are clearly material factors.

Occasionally there may be agreement that property in a particular chattel is to pass but uncertainty as to the exact time of its passing; thus at any given time the deliveror may claim that the chattel was the deliveree's property and at the deliveree's risk while the deliveree may claim that he held it as a mere bailee. This problem arose in the Queensland case of *Knoblauch* v. *McInnes*,[74] where the plaintiff company supplied stoves and gas coppers to a firm of builders for installation in their new homes. Agreement was reached that the stoves should be paid for when the houses in which they were installed were sold, and in a letter the builders stated that they would "of course, be fully responsible for any depreciation or damage to the stoves while they are in the houses prior to sale". It was held that property in the stoves passed to the builders upon delivery and that they did not, in the interval between delivery and the sale of their houses, hold them as mere bailees.

B. Bailment and debt

Property in money passes generally upon delivery; thus the relationship between a bank and its client is, with regard to money deposited, one of debtor and creditor rather than of bailor and bailee.[75] The reason why most recipients of money are not bailees (whether they take the money under a loan or under instructions to deal with it in a particular way) is that they are not obliged to return the identical notes or coins to the bailor; their duty may be discharged by the tender of an equivalent sum. The point was succinctly made by Cockburn C.J. in a criminal case, where the treasurer of a Money Club was prosecuted for the offence of larceny as a bailee. The defendant had collected members' subscriptions for almost a year and then attempted to stage a burglary of his house on

---

[71] Ibid., at 644.
[72] Ibid., at 648, 650, 660.
[73] Ibid., at 654, 657.
[74] [1935] St. R. Qd. 28 (Full Supreme Court).
[75] *South Australian Insurance Co.* v. *Randell* (1869) L.R. 3 P.C. 101, at 111. Aliter where the money has not yet been checked and accepted by the bank but is still undergoing this process as the material time: see *Balmoral Supermarket Ltd.* v. *Bank of New Zealand* [1974] 1 N.Z.L.R. 155.

on the evening of the pay-out. In dismissing the prosecution's case, Cockburn C.J. observed:

> Here the prisoner was not bound to return the specific coins he received. Does not the word, bailee, imply that the thing received is to be specifically returned? A bailee must either return the article received or something into which it has been converted in accordance with the terms of the bailment.[76]

The same principle can be discerned in a number of old criminal cases, in which a curate acting as unofficial treasurer for a Missionary Society,[77] a debt-collector employed without reward to collect money owing to his employer,[78] and the agent of an administrator of an estate, who received on the instructions of his principal a cheque from an insurance company without any accompanying mandate as to how he should apply it,[79] have been held not be bailees of the relevant money for the purposes of the criminal law. It appears that the word bailee was used in the relevant criminal statutes in its ordinary sense,[80] and that the foregoing decisions are likewise material to questions of civil liability between the bailor and bailee.

There are, on the other hand, a number of cases in which persons in a similar position to the defendants in *R. v. Hassall* and *R. v. Garrett* have been treated for the purposes of civil liability as mere bailees of money and not as debtors of the party who delivered it to them. Thus, the Honorary Treasurer of the North Camberwell Radical Club[81] and the Treasurer of the Polish Fraternal Aid Society of St. John Cantius[82] have both been exonerated from liability for the theft of society funds in their possession on proof that they were not guilty of gross or ordinary neglect. If the relationship between the treasurer and the society had been one of debtor and creditor, one would have expected the treasurer's liability to be absolute No doubt it is possible to spell out a transaction of debt in which the debtor is discharged in certain eventualities from the duty of repayment, but it is unlikely that this could be accomplished otherwise than by clear express terms.

The difference between the cases may suggest that the identification of a bailment varies according to the context in which it is sought to be identified and according to the policy of the rule under which the question is raised. Alternatively, the difference may be taken merely to emphasise that whether a given case which involves the delivery of money for a specific purpose creates a bailment is entirely a question of fact, and that it is upon their individual facts that each of the cases depends. In the ordinary course of events, it would be remarkable if the Treasurer of a Society were permitted to commingle club funds with his own and to apply them to his own purposes provided only that he

---

[76] *R. v. Hassall* (1861) Le. & Ca. 58, at 62; 169 E.R. 1302, at 1304.

[77] *R. v. Garrett* (1860) 2 F. & F. 14; 175 E.R. 938.

[78] *R. v. Hoare* (1859) 1 F. & F. 647; 175 E.R. 890.

[79] *R. v. Andrews* (1896) 2 A.L.R. 226. Cf. *R. v. Horne* (1881) 2 L.R. (N.S.W.) 187; *Ex p. Green* (1910) 27 W.N. (N.S.W.) 33.

[80] *R. v. Hassall* (1861) Le. & Ca. 58, at 63-64 per Cockburn C.J.; Pollock & Wright. *Possession in the Common Law*, p. 160; cf. *Thompson v. Nixon* [1965] 2 All E.R. 741.

[81] *Troke v. Felton* (1897) 13 T.L.R. 252 (post, p. 295).

[82] *Polish Fraternal Aid Society v. Kapusta* [1938] 4 D.L.R. 724.

restored an equivalent sum at the appropriate time. The members of the Society would no doubt take the view that, however honest the Treasurer may be, such a practice would lead to temptation and could produce a confusion of accounts from which the society would be bound to suffer. The consequential definition of the Treasurer's status as a mere bailee may limit his power of disposal of the funds but it also limits his liability for their loss. This is illustrated by *Walker* v. *British Guarantee Association,*[83] where the trustees of a building society sued the Treasurer for breach of his covenant to pay punctually into the society's account all moneys received for the society. Before the Treasurer could pay in one particular amount of money he was robbed of it by "irresistible violence", in circumstances which clearly negatived any personal default. The trustees' action failed because the Treasurer was held to be a mere bailee of their funds and not their debtor. Lord Campbell C.J. observed that if the conclusion for which the trustees had contended were sustained, the Treasurer's liability would be greater than that of a common carrier and he would be liable for such manifestations of vis major as an earthquake swallowing up his bag of gold.[84]

In certain cases, the nature of the society may provide an indication of the status of a custodian of their money. The loan club treasurer in *Hassall*[85] was empowered to lay out the money in small loans for the benefit of the society; in most of the other cases the treasurer's duty was clearly not one of investment but merely one of safekeeping. A solicitor no doubt deals generally with his client's money as a debtor rather than as a bailee, but where money is handed to him for a specific purpose such as the purchase of an identified piece of land there may be evidence that he held that money (at least where it is in the form of a cheque) as his client's bailee.[86]

A bailment of money therefore arises only when a specific, tangible sum is accepted by a person on an express or implied mandate to return the identical money at some given future time or to apply it, without alteration or substitution, in its exact original form for some purpose directed by the bailor.[87] The purposes for which the money is received may be as varied as the forms of bailment generally: thus a banknote may be given by way of pledge,[88] or for safekeeping (particularly if it is rare or valuable) or for payment in specie to an identified third-party[89] or to be held by a stakeholder.[90] In any one of these eventualities property may not pass to the transferee and he will hold the currency under a bailment. An obvious modern example is the carriage of bullion by a firm of security contractors. The same rules apply to negotiable property which has monetary value.[91]

---

[83] (1852) 18 Q.B. 277; 118 E.R. 104. See also *Thomas* v. *High* [1960] S.R. (N.S.W.) 401, at p. 403, 406
[84] Ibid., at p. 287, 107.
[85] (1861) Le. & Ca. 58; ante.
[86] *R.* v. *Geake* (1896) 2 A.L.R. 162. (Victorian Full Supreme Court.)
[87] *R.* v. *Mason* (1890) 16 V.L.R. 327, explaining earlier cases.
[88] *Taylor* v. *Chester* (1869) L.R. 4 Q.B. 309.
[89] *R.* v. *Mason* ante.
[90] Cf. *R.* v. *Buckmaster* (1887) 20 Q.B.D. 182.
[91] *R.* v. *Mason* ante; cf. *R.* v. *Tidemann* (1871) 5 S.A.L.R. 15.

Occasionally, the terms upon which a sum of money is delivered may leave it uncertain whether the deliveror's instructions relate necessarily to the specific coins or notes or to some equivalent sum supplied in substitution therefore at the deliveree's discretion. This problem arose in a South Australian case,[92] where the appellant was handed a sum of money in notes by an acquaintance and was requested by the acquaintance to buy her a wireless set. Instead of applying the specific notes for this purpose, the appellant entered into a hire-purchase agreement in her own name for the purchase of a wireless and spent the original sum of money on herself. Richards J. held that in order for a bailment of money to be constituted:

> . . . the *instructions given* must be such that the proposed bailee would, as a reasonable person, understand that the identical coins, or notes, or cheque delivered is to be used for the bailor's purpose: though the instructions might, at least in part, be implied from the circumstances.[93]

No such instructions could be discerned in the present case and the defendant was therefore (with some reluctance) acquitted of larceny as a bailee.[94] As Richards J. remarked, an instruction of this kind may well have been intended by the deliveror of the notes, but it was insufficiently expressed for the court to state definitely that there had arisen a bailment. Richards J. declined to commit himself as to the significance of what the alleged bailee understood the bailor to mean when the notes were originally delivered. It may be that a bailment in the criminal sense requires a fuller acceptance and realisation of the existence of the relationship than is necessary under civil law.

The net result is that a delivery of money for use in accordance with the deliveror's instructions will only rarely give rise to a bailment.[95] This conclusion is all the more true, of course, when money is transferred by way of loan, for the object of the loan would be confounded if the recipient were obliged to restore the identical notes or coins. In *R.* v. *Ashwell*[96] the Court for Crown Cases Reserved held that no bailment arose when the defendant, having asked for the loan of a shilling, was handed a sovereign by mistake; a fact he did not discover until later. Smith J. reached this conclusion on the ground that when the sovereign was delivered no condition at all was attached to its delivery other than that a coin of like value should be returned to the lender at a future date;[97] Coleridge C.J. on the narrower ground that there was no contract between the parties.[98] Under modern theory a bailment may exist without any kind of consensual relation between the parties whatever, but to perceive a bailment in a case such as *R.* v. *Ashwell* would presumably require a clear understanding by the recipient that if the deliveror had know that he had delivered a sovereign, he would have required its

---

[92] *Reece* v. *Harris* [1943] S.A.S.R. 127; 18 A.L.J. 81.
[93] Ibid., at 130.
[94] Cf., on the facts, *R.* v. *Mason* ante; *R.* v. *Ward* (1938) 38 S.R. (N.S.W.) 308.
[95] *Slattery* v. *The King* (1905) 2 C.L.R. 546, at 561 per Griffith C.J.
[96] (1885) 16 Q.B.D. 190.
[97] Ibid., at 198-199.
[98] Ibid., at 223-224; but cf. ante, p. 14.

return in specie. This would, of course, be very difficult to prove unless the sovereign possessed a unique or special value.[99]

C. Bailment and contracts of service or agency

According to traditional theory, a servant has mere custody of his master's property and does not become a bailee. In Chapter 7 we challenge this assumption and argue that a person may become the bailee of a chattel while occupying simultaneously the position of servant or agent towards the bailor. The reason for this apparent ambiguity is that the two relationships are imposed for different purposes and identified by different tests. Thus they may coexist without conflict within a single situation.

While, however, the foregoing analysis may produce acceptable results in the context of a master's action against his servant for loss or damage to the master's goods, the fact remains that, for most other purposes, bailees cannot be regarded as the servants of their bailors. This may be inferred by examining the purposes for which the courts may wish to discover a relationship of master and servant and the criteria by which that relationship may be established. The existence of the relationship may fall in question for a number of reasons: to establish the servant's rights under the alleged contract of service, to answer questions of tax liability or insurance benefit, or to impose vicarious liability upon the alleged employer. The identification of the relationship occurs by the use of certain compound criteria: the degree of control asserted by the "employer" over his employee's performance of the task for which he is engaged, the extent to which the employee is assimilated into the employer's general organisation and workforce, the method of payment, the regularity and proposed duration of the employment and the powers of termination or dismissal. Clearly, the use of these criteria will dictate in the great majority of cases that an ordinary bailee of goods—such as a hirer, a repairer, a warehouseman or a carrier—is not to be simultaneously identified as the servant or agent of the bailor. This is borne out by decided cases, which hold that a bailee cannot render his bailor vicariously liable for any tortious misconduct which occurs during the performance of the bailment and cannot, by such contributory misconduct, reduce the damages payable to the bailor by an independent, third-party tortfeasor.[1] In the normal course of events the bailee is an independent contractor and the court will refuse to identify him with the bailor for the purpose of allocating responsibility for the bailee's misdeeds. For this reason the relationships of bailor and bailee and master and servant can be regarded, for most practical purposes, as mutually exclusive: many servants are so closely supervised that they cannot acquire possession of their masters' chattels, while most bailees are so loosely controlled that they cannot be deemed to be servants. Nevertheless, the two questions should be answered separately; when inquiring whether the user of a chattel is

---

[99] Cf. *Thompson* v. *Nixon* [1965] 2 All E.R. 741 (finder of non-monetary chattels, who decided to steal them *after* taking possession, not guilty of larceny as a bailee). Of course, it must be remembered that the criminal cases discussed in this section are no longer representative of the English criminal law since the passing of the *Theft Act* 1968.
[1] The cases are listed post, p. 961.

a servant or agent of the owner, it is not enough to show that for the purpose of liability for damage to the chattel the law regards him as a bailee. This is particularly so in cases of casual delegation, where one person drives another's car in order to perform some task or duty imposed upon the owner. In such a case the owner may well be liable to a third party for the mandatary's misperformance of his mandate, but it seems beyond doubt that the mandatary will be regarded as his bailee.[2]

Generally it is impossible to regard the hirer of a chattel as in any sense the servant or agent of the owner: if anything, the relevant service is provided by the owner to the hirer. The position becomes less clear-cut, however, when the hirer employs the chattel for purposes of commercial reward and pays part of that reward, in substitution for a hiring-charge, to the owner. In such a case the hirer may be thought to be working for the benefit of the owner, and there may be sufficient common interest in the enterprise to justify regarding the hirer as a servant or agent of the owner. The problem is exemplified by a long sequence of English decisions involving the bailment of taxi-cabs between owners and drivers.[3] Instead of paying the driver fixed wages, the owner may keep a proportion of the takings or may allow the driver to keep all the takings in return for a guaranteed daily sum. The owner will normally tax, maintain and insure the cab but will not have any immediate control over the way the driver conducts his business. Undoubtedly the driver may be regarded as a bailee for the purpose of rendering him liable for any damage inflicted on the cab, but the owner may not necessarily escape being vicariously liable for torts committed while the driver is going about his business. Such liability depends upon whether the driver is his servant or agent under the various judicial and statutory tests which have been laid down as determining that relationship. These tests are not precisely synonymous with those that seek to establish whether the driver is a bailee.

In fact, the English decisions on this point have managed to evade the issue by holding that the *London Hackney Carriages Act* 1843 creates a statutory presumption that the driver of a hackney-carriage or taxi-cab drives as the servant of the owner so as to make the latter liable for torts committed in the course of driving. Thus, the proprietor is liable for personal injuries negligently inflicted by the taxi-driver upon members of the public,[4] and for the loss of a passenger's luggage through the negligence of the driver.[5] Doubts were expressed in some of these

---

[2] See generally p. 242 et seq., post, and Bowstead, *Agency* (13th ed.), p. 6, where it is acknowledged that certain kinds of agent (e.g. auctioneers) will also be bailees of their principals' property.
[3] No contract of service exists between taxi-driver and passenger: post, p. 249.
[4] *Venables* v. *Smith* (1877) 2 Q.B.D. 279; *King* v. *London Improved Cab Co.* (1889) 23 Q.B.D. 281; *Keen* v. *Henry* [1894] 1 Q.B. 292; *Gates* v. *R. Bill & Son* [1902] 2 K.B. 38 (where the relevant liability was held not to be confined to *registered* proprietors); *Bygraves* v. *Dicker* [1923] 2 K.B. 585 (where the same liability was held to apply under the *Town Police Clauses Act* 1847); *Smith* v. *General Motor Cab Co. Ltd.* [1911] A.C. 188, at 191-192 (obiter); *Steel* v. *Lester* (1877) 3 C.P.D. 121, at 125-126 (obiter). Cf. *Kemp* v. *Elisha* [1918] 1 K.B. 228.
[5] *Powles* v. *Hider* (1856) 6 E. & B. 206; 119 E.R. 841, where it was held that the driver must be deemed to have authority to undertake the safe carriage of

decisions as to whether the same relationship would have been held to exist at Common Law,[6] and it seems likely that without the statute no vicarious liability would be held to exist on modern principles.[7] However, each case would have to be judged upon its own facts, and these may in fact differ considerably inter se.

Australian courts have refused to construe their own statutes in equivalent terms and have preferred to regard the relationship of master and servant not as a matter of legislative fiction but as a question of fact.[8] In answering this question, they have looked primarily to the control which the owner has asserted over the driver and the degree of independence with which the latter is entitled to act. The normal conclusion is that the driver is a bailee of the cab and that the owner is not vicariously liable for his negligence; but a contrary result was reached in *Fenn* v. *Sagar*[9] where Wolff J. discovered a relationship of master and servant on the grounds, inter alia, that the cab-owner had extensive powers of dismissal over his drivers, operated his business by way of a telephone service which required the driver in question to attend his premises and answer calls as they came, expected the driver's regular attendance and (upon first hearing of the relevant act of negligence) took it upon himself to offer the victim compensation. With the modern phenomenon of the radio-controlled taxi, which operates largely on instructions from a central headquarters, the driver's discretion may be sufficiently reduced to qualify him as a servant of the proprietor. Alternatively, this inference may be counterbalanced by the method of payment and it may even be possible to regard such instructions as a service provided for the benefit of the driver.

In answering questions of vicarious liability, Australian judges have occasionally relied upon English cases in which some other issue required analysis of the relationship between owner and driver.[10] In such cases, the driver has almost unanimously been held to be a bailee. The earliest significant decision is *Fowler* v. *Lock*,[11] where the cab-driver sued for breach of the owner's warranty that the horse supplied with his cab should be reasonably safe.[12] The terms of the transaction were that the plaintiff paid eighteen shillings per day for the use of the cab and was entitled to keep the surplus takings: he was under no obligation to ply for hire and could (within reason) deal with the cab as he pleased. The owner argued that the relationship was one of master and servant and that no warranty of safety should therefore be implied. This argument was accepted by Willes J. who dissented from the majority view and

---

passengers' goods on behalf of the owner, and that a contract arose between owner and passenger to that effect.

[6] E.g. *Venables* v. *Smith* (1877) 2 Q.B.D. 279, at 282-283, where Cockburn C.J. states that the "statute alters what would otherwise be the parties true relationship".
[7] Cf. *Morgans* v. *Launchbury* [1973] A.C. 127.
[8] *Clutterbuck* v. *Curry* (1885) 11 V.L.R. 810; *McKinnon* v. *Gange* [1910] V.L.R. 32; *Dillon* v. *Gange* (1941) 64 C.L.R. 253; *Fenn* v. *Sagar* (1955) 57 W.A.L.R. 12.
[9] (1955) 57 W.A.L.R. 12.
[10] E.g. per Starke J. in *Dillon* v. *Gange* ante, at 263.
[11] (1872) L.R. 7 C.P. 272.
[12] See generally, Chapter 19.

relied upon *Powles* v. *Hider*;[13] in his view the relationship should be analysed in the same way for all purposes, and the analysis adopted in the vicarious liability cases should be adopted in dealing with the rights of the owner and the driver inter se. Byles J. disagreed and regarded the identity of the parties as of cardinal importance. He pointed out that the vicarious liability case of *Powles* v. *Hider* was influenced by the wording of the statute, and concluded that the plaintiff in the present case was clearly a bailee for hire because he had complete and exclusive control and disposition of the horse. Similar observations were made by Grove J., who further agreed with Byles J. that the defendant would still have been liable if the appropriate relationship had been one of master and servant.

On appeal (briefly reported as a note)[14] the Court of Exchequer Chamber seems to have been divided. This division was not material to the outcome of the case because those members of the court who thought that there was a bailment thought also that the plaintiff had taken upon himself the risk of the horse's unfitness, so that no warranty should be implied. The case was however remitted for trial on the ground that the facts were insufficiently adduced to enable the courts to make a final decision, and no judgment was delivered as to the relation of the parties. At the trial, the jury found that the horse and cab were entrusted to the driver as a bailee and that the owner had not taken reasonable care to ensure that the horse was fit for its purpose. The defendant appealed but the Court of Common Pleas refused to disturb the verdict and upheld judgment for the plaintiff.[15] No further opinion was expressed as to the status of the driver as servant or bailee.

In fact, there can be little doubt that the driver in *Fowler* v. *Lock* was a bailee rather than a servant. This is largely confirmed by a later decision of the House of Lords. In *Smith* v. *General Motor Cab Co. Ltd.*[16] the driver of a cab was injured in an accident while driving. He was not one of the company's regular drivers but an "odd man", who drove for them when their regular drivers were indisposed and paid them seventy-five per cent of his takings. Although he was required to wear livery, he was allowed full discretion as to the manner and place of work and was not obliged to work for the owners at all if he did not want to. The House of Lords, rejecting his claim for workman's compensation, held that he did not qualify as a servant of the company but was a mere bailee of their vehicle. Lord Shaw remarked that while inter se the owners and the driver were bailor and bailee, "Quoad the public, the relation of the cab-driver to the cab-owner was . . . one of agency; so that, for negligence in the conduct of his business, both principal and agent might naturally be responsible to the public";[17] a conclusion which was presumably founded on the statutory agency imposed by the Act of 1843. Lord Atkinson observed:[18]

[13] (1856) 6 E. & B. 206; 119 E.R. 841; ante, p. 110.
[14] (1874) L.R. 9 C.P. 751 n.
[15] (1874) L.R. 10 C.P. 90.
[16] [1911] A.C. 188; see also *Doggett* v. *Waterloo Taxi Cab Co. Ltd.* [1910] 2 K.B. 336; cf. *R.* v. *Solomons* [1909] 2 K.B. 980.
[17] [1911] A.C. 192.
[18] Ibid., at 191-192.

It may be necessary to point out that the decision of your Lordships' house on this appeal does not in any way touch the question of the liability of the cab-proprietor to third parties, passengers, way-farers, or others, for the acts of the driver. It may well be that though the relation between the taxi-cab owner and his driver inter se be that of bailor and bailee, the driver may still quoad third parties be treated as the agent of the proprietor authorized to ply for hire in the streets for reward to the latter; and the proprietor be thereby rendered liable for those acts of the driver which were within the scope of the latter's authority. The general result of the cases of *Fowler* v. *Lock*,[19] *Venables* v. *Smith*,[20] *King* v. *London Improved Cab Co.*,[21] *Smith* v. *Bailey*[22] and *Gates* v. *R. Bill and Son*,[23] cited in *Doggett's Case*,[24] is that in the case of horse-drawn cabs, where drivers were given them in charge under terms resembling those admitted to exist in the present case, the relation between the pro-prietor and driver was that of bailor and bailee, but that *quoad* third parties the drivers were, under the provisions of the *Metropolitan Hackney Carriage Act* 1843 (admittedly applicable to taxi-cabs) deemed to be servants of the proprietors.

A similar conclusion was reached by Vaisey J. in *London General Cab Co. Ltd.* v. *Inland Revenue Commissioners*,[25] where the proprietors of a fleet of taxi-cabs sought exemption from profits tax under the *Finance Act* 1937, on the ground that they were statutory undertakers rendering a service for the carriage of the public. In dismissing their appeal, Vaisey J. held that the relationship between the company and each individual driver was for this purpose, and possibly for the majority of purposes, that of lessor and hirer. He conceded that a different interpretation might apply according to the context in which the relationship was analysed:

> I think that a good deal of ground may still remain to be explored, this being one of those cases in which a quite simple, ordinary, every-day relationship, contractual or quasi-contractual, is found on examination to be, from the legal point of view, of an extremely complicated, and in some respects ambiguous, character. I have formed the conclusion that the authorities are not altogether easy to reconcile and every case, no doubt, will have to be considered in the light of its own particular circumstances. It may well be that in one case the driver is the agent of the owner, in another case he may be the servant of the owner, and a third case may be one of a simple bailment. I also think that it may be two or more of those classes of association when viewed from different angles, that it to say, the driver may be, for the purpose of the National Insurance Act, 1946, a servant of the owner, and for the purpose of the returns of income tax he may be regarded as an independent contractor . . . It may be very difficult to predicate that the relationship is for all purposes (whatever it may be for some purposes) within any one of the categories which I have suggested.[26]

[19] (1872) L.R. 7 C.P. 272.
[20] (1877) 2 Q.B.D. 279.
[21] (1889) 23 Q.B.D. 281.
[22] [1893] 2 Q.B. 403, at 405.
[23] [1902] 2 K.B. 38.
[24] [1910] 2 K.B. 336.
[25] [1950] 2 All E.R. 566.
[26] Ibid., at 570. See also *Checker Taxi-cab Co., Ltd.* v. *Stone* [1930] N.Z.L.R. 169, where the cab-owners under the sort of arrangement discussed in the text were

The same observations are theoretically applicable to any situation in which one person engages another to use, or to deal with, his chattel. The contract of service primarily denotes control over the servant, whereas the contract of bailment primarily denotes control over the subject chattel. It is therefore possible, although admittedly rare, for a person to be both a servant and a bailee.

In the area of restitution, there are strong reasons for treating even an independent contractor as equivalent to a servant or agent when he holds the plaintiff's chattel under a bailment. Thus, it has been held that a bailee for sale owes a fiduciary duty to account for the profits of the bailment, and that such proceeds may be traced into the hands of a third party.[27] It may be legitimate to extend this principle to all bailments; certainly a bailee should be accountable when the profit results from his own misuse of the goods.[28]

The bailee's servant will rarely, if ever, become a bailee in his own right of the bailor's goods. In *Fairline Shipping Corporation Ltd.* v. *Adamson*,[29] Kerr J. would have been prepared to discover a bailment between the original bailor of perishable goods and the managing-director of the latterly defunct company which had undertaken their storage, but the learned judge found on the facts that the managing-director never acquired exclusive possession of the goods. This conclusion did not, however, debar Kerr J. from holding the director liable for their deterioration through failure to maintain the temperature of the store, on the separate ground that, by writing to the bailors in a manner which suggested that he was now undertaking the task of storage, the director made himself responsible for ensuring that they were safeguarded with reasonable care.

D. Bailment and licences

Sometimes the owner of a chattel may leave it upon another person's land with the permission of the landowner, or may even attach it to another person's chattel,[30] in circumstances which do not confer possession of his chattel upon that other person. In such a case the owner of the chattel is said to be a mere licensee (or sometimes, a lessee) of the space in which the chattel resides and his purported or apparent delivery will not give rise to a bailment. The distinction between bailments and licences depends upon a multiplicity of factors, all of which are discussed in Chapter 5.

held entitled to recover in full from a third party whose negligence contributed to the damage of the cab, notwithstanding that the collision was caused in part by the negligence of their own driver. This conclusion was reached on the ground that he was not a partner but a bailee; cf. *Aldridge* v. *Paterson* (1914) 33 N.Z.L.R. 997.

[27] *Aluminium Industrie Vaasen* v. *Romalpa Aluminium Ltd.* [1976] 1 W.L.R. 676; post, p. 155.
[28] Post, p. 142 et seq. Cf. *Everett's Blinds Ltd.* v. *Thomas Ballinger Ltd.* [1965] N.Z.L.R. 266, at 271-272, where Tompkins J. refused to equate a contract of bailment with a contract of employment for the purposes of the rules of indemnity.
[29] [1975] Q.B. 180; Diamond (1975) 38 M.L.R. 198.
[30] As in *Seaspan International Ltd.* v. *The Kostis Prois* (1973) 33 D.L.R. (3d) 1.

E. Bailment and trusts

Although many definitions of bailment, particularly the older ones, define it as a delivery of goods on trust,[31] there are in fact, substantial differences between bailments and trusts. Thus, a trust may relate to land as well as to personal property; it may relate to money which is not to be returned in specie: and it will make the trustee the legal owner of the trust estate, whereas of course the bailee has mere possession.[32] Nor are these differences reduced by the fact that a bailee may occasionally become a constructive trustee of the proceeds of the bailment.[33]

Whether the parties have created a bailment or a trust depends upon their intention, as evidenced by such factors as the contemplated destination of the property, the evidence as to legal ownership and the deliveror's power (if any) to revoke or vary the transaction. If A delivers money to B to be delivered specifically to C, it may be that B is simultaneously a bailee of the money from A and a trustee for the benefit of C: indeed, it may even happen that B becomes C's bailee, at least if there is anything resembling an attornment by B.[34] In most cases, however, the radical differences between bailment and trust will render them easily distinguishable.

Sometimes the beneficiary under a trust may be characterised as a bailee of the trust property. This may occur when the beneficiary is given a limited interest in indisposable personalty such as family heirlooms, in which event he may be characterised as a bailee for the remainder-man; alternatively, the beneficiary may be regarded as a trustee in his own right for the ulterior legatees, subject to his own anterior beneficial interest.[35] On balance, it seems preferable to avoid recourse to the law of bailment in cases of this kind.

F. Bailment and chartering

Occasionally a contract for the supply or enjoyment of a chattel will bind the supplier to provide a servant entrusted with its management or operation: an example is the charter of a bus by a society for its annual outing. In such a case, the presence of the servant will generally mean that possession of the chattel remains in his employer and that the

---

[31] E.g. Bacon's *Abridgement*, Bailments; approved in Halsbury's *Laws* (4th ed.), vol. ii, para. 1501, and by Cohen J. in *Re S. Davis & Co. Ltd.* [1945] Ch. 402, at 405.

[32] See further Paton, *Bailment in the Common Law*, p. 5-6; Snell, *Equity* (27th ed.), 89.

[33] For a decision in which a trust company were held to be bailees and not trustees of certain share certificates deposited with them for safekeeping, see *Elgin Loan & Savings Co.* v. *National Trust Co. Ltd.* (1905) 10 O.L.R. 41 (Ontario C.A.)

[34] It is on grounds similar to this that Underhill on *Trusts* (11th ed.), p. 6 distinguishes bailments and trusts, viz. that under a bailment the bailee's duty can be enforced only by the party at whose request the service was undertaken: sed quaere. See further *Flewellin* v. *Rave* (1610) 1 Bulst. 68; *Harris* v. *de Bervoir* (1624) Cro. Jac. 687.

[35] *In re Swan, Witham* v. *Swan* [1915] 1 Ch. 829; cf. the position of the life tenant in *Eddis* v. *Chichester Constable* [1969] 2 Ch. 345, and see *Foster* v. *Crabb* (1852) 12 C.B. 136; *Wright* v. *Robotham* (1886) 33 Ch. D. 106.

charterer is not technically a bailee.[36] This distinction is discussed at greater length elsewhere in the present work.[37]

In the case of ships and aircraft, the existence of a bailment depends upon the type of charterparty involved. The main distinction is very clearly drawn in a recent Law Commission Working Paper:[38]

> . . . there are two main categories of charterparty, the charterparty by demise and the charterparty not by demise. The former operates as a lease of the ship (*or aircraft*) itself, to which the services of the master and crew may or may not be superadded. The master and crew, if provided, become for all intents the servants of the charterer and through them the possession of the ship is in him. Under a charter not by demise, on the other hand, the ship-owner agrees with the charterer to render services by his master and crew to carry goods which are put on board his ship by or on behalf of the charterer; the possession of the ship remains in the original owner. A charter by demise is in effect a contract for the hire of a chattel, and is governed by the general principles of the Common Law relating to contracts of hire . . . Charterparties not by demise, that is to say time charters and voyage charters, are contracts for the rendering of services by the owner, not for the hiring out of his ship.

[36] Cf. the observations of Byles J. in *Fowler* v. *Lock* (1872) 26 L.T. 476, at 479.
[37] Post, p. 246 et seq.
[38] Working Paper No. 71, *Implied Terms in Contracts for the Supply of Goods* (1977), p. 24.

CHAPTER 3

THE REMEDIES OF THE BAILOR*

Several causes of action may be open to the bailor whose chattel is lost, damaged, misused or destroyed while it is in the hands of a bailee. It is not the object of this chapter to discuss these remedies in detail, but to illustrate their operation and inter-reaction in the context of the bailment relation. At the outset it must be observed that most (if not all) of these potential remedies are borrowed from the general law and are not peculiar to bailments; and that in many situations they may exist concurrently, so that the availability of one remedy will not necessarily exclude another. Which of them the bailor chooses will depend upon the nature of the wrongdoing, the identity of the wrongdoer, the quality of the bailment itself, and the type of loss—if any—that has been sustained.

I. TRESPASS

Any unauthorised interference with another person's chattel may amount to trespass, provided the act causing the harm or deprivation is immediate and direct[1] and the wrongdoer has acted either intentionally or negligently.[2] A mere asportation without damage or permanent deprivation

*Since the ensuing chapter was written, an Act has been passed in England which is based upon the Law Reform Committee's proposals for reform to the law of interference with chattels: Cmnd. 4774 (1971). References to this Act (the Torts (Interference with Goods) Act 1977) have been inserted wherever possible within the present chapter. The Act itself is set out in Appendix 1 of this book.

[1] Salmond on Torts (16th edn.), p. 92, explains that the act must be such "as amounts to a direct forcible injury within the meaning of the distinction drawn in the old practice between the writ of trespass and that of trespass on the case." Actual physical contact may, however, be unnecessary, as in the case of chasing cattle: Farmer v. Hunt (1610) 1 Brownl. 220; Durant v. Childe (1611) 1 Brownl. 221; cf. New v. McMaster (1863) 2 S.C.R. (N.S.W.) 323; or propelling an object against the chattel: Fleming, The Law of Torts (4th ed.), p. 49. It seems that whereas the throwing of poisoned bait to a dog will be trespass, the laying of bait will not: Hutchins v. Maughan [1947] V.L.R. 131.

[2] In England, it is uncertain whether the modern action for trespass to chattels includes negligent as well as intentional interference. Fleming, op cit., p. 50, considers that inadvertent damage now falls exclusively within the province of negligence, a view which draws support by analogy from certain statements of Lord Denning M.R. in Letang v Cooper [1965] 1 Q.B. 232, at 239-240, 244-245, concerning injury to the person. Cf. Salmond, op. cit., pp. 92-93; Winfield and Jolowicz, Torts (10th ed.), p. 403; Clerk & Lindsell, Torts (13th ed.), para. 1183; Leame v. Bray (1803) 3 East 593; 102 E.R. 724; Covell v. Laming (1808) 1 Camp. 497. In Everitt v. Martin [1953] N.Z.L.R. 298, Adams J. seemed prepared to accept both states of mind as appropriate to trespass but implied that actual physical damage would be necessary in the case of inadvertent contact. However, in Venning v. Chin [1975] 10 S.A.S.R. 299 the South Australian Full Supreme Court held that either state of mind would suffice for an action of trespass of the person. In their view Letang v. Cooper was inconsistent with the Australian High Court's decision in Williams v. Milotin (1957) 97 C.L.R. 465, and the latter

will suffice,[3] whether or not the defendant honestly and mistakenly believes that he has the right to remove the chattel[4] and regardless of whether he does so solely for the benefit of the owner.[5] Physical impairment of the chattel[6] or its total destruction are likewise sufficient grounds of action, although damage caused by omission or neglect is not, predominantly because of the necessity for some direct or proximate contact.[7]

Whether the wrongdoer is a third-party or the bailee himself, an action in trespass will rarely provide the bailor with an efficacious and satisfactory remedy. The reasons for this are threefold and will be discussed in ascending order of importance.

First, it is still uncertain whether the action will lie for an unauthorised meddling with the chattel which does not cause actual physical damage. In the absence of a positive asportation, the owner's failure to establish such damage may prove fatal to his case. In *Penfolds Wines Pty. Ltd.* v. *Elliott*[8] (where the remedy sought was an injunction) Latham C.J., explicitly acknowledged that a non-damaging invasion of a chattel would sound in trespass. This view is supported by other authorities[9] and is emphatically to be preferred, for otherwise an owner might be without redress in the event of an imperceptible process of erosion or deterioration by a series of wrongful dealings. But authority exists to the contrary and Fleming has doubted whether the rule which renders trespasses to land actionable per se can legitimately be transported into the realm of

case should prevail. This probably represents the modern Australian rule for trespass to goods. Cf. Bailey, (1976) 5 *Adelaide Law Review* 402; *West* v. *Peters* [1976] *Australian Current Law Digest* 174.

[3] *G.W.K.* v. *Dunlop Rubber Co. Ltd.* (1926) 42 T.L.R. 376; *O'Connor* v. *Sheriff of Queensland* (1892) 4 Q.L.J. 213 (5 days' deprivation: £150 damages for "gross outrage"): cf. *Harvey* v. *Birrell* (1878) 12 S.A.L.R. 58.

[4] *Wilson* v. *Lombank Ltd.* [1963] 1 W.L.R. 1924; *Moore* v. *Lambeth County Court Registrar (No. 2)* [1970] 1 Q.B. 560; *Colwill* v. *Reeves* (1811) 2 Camp. 575.

[5] *Kirk* v. *Gregory* (1876) 1 Ex. D. 55. Here the defendant, fearing for the safety of certain property, removed it from one room of a house to another. It was held that he had comitted a trespass, and nominal damages of 1s. were awarded. See, however, the judgments of Bramwell and Amphlett BB., where it is conceded that a reasonable belief in the necessity of the precautions taken would have afforded a defence. This defence was actually sustained in *Proudman* v. *Allen* [1954] S.A.S.R. 336.

[6] The classic instance is that given by Alderson B. in *Fouldes* v. *Willoughby* (1841) 8 M. & W. 540, at 549, viz., scratching the panel of a carriage.

[7] *Hillier* v. *Leitch* [1936] S.A.S.R. 490; and see Milsom, "Not doing is no trespass" [1954] C.L.J. 105. In *Hillier* v. *Leitch* it is said that, for this reason, a master cannot be liable for the trespasses of his servants; cf. Street C.J. in *Elliott* v. *Barnes* (1951) 51 S.R. (N.S.W.) 179, at 181-182.

[8] (1946) 74 C.L.R. 204, at 214-215: "The handling of a chattel without authority is a trespass . . . Unauthorized user of goods is a trespass . . . even though the (chattel) be returned unharmed." Starke J. did not discuss the matter but associated himself with the decision of Dixon J. who seemed prepared to assume that the act of filling the bottles was potentially trespassory; cf. Williams J. at 241-242, who spoke only of trespass by asportation, and McTiernan J. who did not express an opinion on the question at all.

[9] *Leitch & Co. Ltd.* v. *Leydon* [1931] A.C. 90, at 106; Salmond, *op. cit.*, p. 93; Pollock, *Torts* (15th ed.), pp. 265 et seq; Street, *Torts* (6th ed.), p. 31; Law Reform Committee, Eighteenth Report (Conversion and Detinue) (Cmnd. 4774), paras. 17, 21.

chattels.[10] If a ladder propped against a wall,[11] or a bullet discharged across the surface,[12] may constitute trespass to land, it is difficult to see why a similar rule should not protect the owner of personal property; especially as such intermeddling may eventually make the chattel dangerous. One may hazard that the school of thought which favours action without proof of actual damage will (when such a case arises) prevail.[13]

United States jurisdictions have, incidentally, adopted the contrary view and have held that while asportation without ensuing damage amounts to trespass,[14] non-asportative interference can ground trespass only on proof of actual impairment.[15] This is supported by the Second Restatement[16] and justified by reference to the owner's ability to use reasonable force to protect his property, even against harmless interference.[17]

Secondly, it seems that in England the erosion of trespass to chattels as a tort of strict liability[18] has carried with it the procedural disadvantage of requiring a plaintiff to prove affirmatively that the wrongful dealing was intentional or negligent.[19] A bailor, on the other hand, need only

---

[10] Fleming, *op. cit.*, p. 50, citing *Slater* v. *Swann* (1730) 2 Stra. 872; *Everitt* v. *Martin* [1953] N.Z.L.R. 298.

[11] *Westripp* v. *Baldock* [1938] 2 All E.R. 779; [1939] 1 All E.R. 279; cf. *Walsh* v. *Elson* [1955] V.L.R. 276; [1955] A.L.R. 857.

[12] *Davies* v. *Bennison* (1927) 22 Tas. L.R. 52.

[13] Certain authorities favour a distinction for this purpose between intentional trespass (which should be actionable per se) and negligent or inadvertent trespass, for which proof of actual damage should be required: *Everitt* v. *Martin* (supra), at 302-303; *Clerk & Lindsell*, op. cit., para. 1181; Winfield & Jolowicz, op. cit., pp. 403-404. See also *Letang* v. *Cooper* [1965] 1 Q.B. 232, at 244-245, where Diplock L.J. said that in actions for unintentional trespass to the person actual injury was necessary. The rule as stated in the text may be justified by reference to the case of pets (or other articles of sentimental value) which the owner will for legitimate reasons desire not to be handled by strangers. Note also that an action for non-damaging trespass will clearly lie in the case of chattels (such as ships) which are capable of being trespassed upon in manner akin to land: cf. *Dean* v. *Hogg* (1834) 10 Bing. 345; post, p. 249.

[14] *Wintringham* v. *Lafoy* (1827) 7 Cow. (N.Y.) 735.

[15] *Marentille* v. *Oliver* (1808) 2 N.J.L. 358; *Paul* v. *Slason* (1850) 22 Vt. 231; 54 Am. Dec. 75; *Graves* v. *Severens* (1868) 40 Vt. 636; *Gliddon* v. *Szybiak* (1949) 95 N.H. 318; 62 A. (2d) 233.

[16] Para. 218, comment (f).

[17] See, for instance, Prosser, *Cases on Torts*, p. 89. This argument is hardly likely to appeal to the bailor, who will usually lack the control necessary to adopt such an expedient.

[18] *N.C.B.* v. *Evans* [1951] 2 K.B. 861; and see the authorities listed by Vaines, *Personal Property* (5th ed.), p. 22.

[19] Although, as Winfield and Jolowicz point out (op. cit., p. 404 n. 15), this does not specifically emerge from the decision in *N.C.B.* v. *Evans* (supra), it is supportable by reference to decisions concerning trespass to the person, especially *Fowler* v. *Lanning* [1954] 1 Q.B. 426 and *Long* v. *Hepworth* [1968] 1 W.L.R. 1299; see also *Holmes* v. *Mather* (1875) L.R. 10 Ex. 261, at 267; *River Wear Commissioners* v. *Adamson* (1877) 2 App. Cas. 743, at 767; *Gayler and Pope* v. *B. Davies & Son* [1924] 2 K.B. 75; cf. *Cook* v. *Lewis* [1952] 1 D.L.R. 1; *Hollebone* v. *Barnard* [1954] 2 D.L.R. 278. Salmond, op. cit., pp. 93, 138. In Cmnd. 4774 para. 18, the matter is reported as still not free from doubt but probably as stated in the text. However, in *Venning* v. *Chin* [1975] 10 S.A.S.R. 299, both Bray C.J. and Jacobs J. held that in an action for trespass to the person the onus is on the defendant to disprove negligence, except in cases of accidents occurring on the highway. This rule as to the general burden of proof in trespass had already been upheld in Australia in *MacHale* v. *Watson* (1964) 111 C.L.R. 384 and has also been applied in Canada: *Bell Canada Ltd.* v. *Bannermount Ltd.* (1974) 35 D.L.R. (3d) 367. It was, however, conceded in *Venning* v.

establish the facts of delivery intact and subsequent damage or loss to place the onus of negativing negligence on the bailee.[20]

Thirdly, both the nature of trespass, and the interests it was designed to protect, substantially disqualify most bailors from invoking it against either their bailees or intermeddling strangers. Trespass is, historically and conceptually, a wrong to possession.[21] Thus, it is said that an owner out of possession may not maintain trespass in respect of damage or abuse to his chattel. While as a generalisation this statement is true, it needs to be qualified and explained in relation to the revocable bailment, or what is sometimes called the bailment-at-will.

A. Sufficiency of the immediate right to possess

Where a chattel is transferred for a set term (for example, the hire of a car for a week) the authorities are agreed that neither trespass nor trover will issue against the wrongdoer during the currency of the term.[22] The proper plaintiff in such cases is the bailee; for it is he who enjoys possession and it is he who must prima facie account to the bailor at the end of the bailment. The position may differ, however, where there is a simple, revocable bailment: for instance, the loan of a bicycle to a friend or the gratuitous deposit of goods with one who undertakes to deliver them on demand. Now at one time it was thought that the immediate right to possession of a chattel was enough in all cases to ground trespass. Thus, Bowen L.J. in *Johnson* v. *Diprose*:

> A person who brings an action for trespass to goods must either be in possession of them at the time of the alleged trespass or entitled to the immediate possession.[23]

This is assuredly the case in actions for conversion or detinue. But the equation between these remedies and trespass has been vigorously resisted, most notably by Pollock and Wright:[24]

> In some cases the owner of a thing who has never yet acquired the possession of it, or an owner who has parted with the possession, is nevertheless, in virtue of his right to possession, entitled to sue or prosecute a stranger who takes the thing, and it is of much practical and theoretical importance to discover in what cases a mere right to possession suffices for this purpose, and on what ground.

Chin that in cases of highway "accidents" the burden is always on the plaintiff to establish negligence and presumably the same rule must apply to property damage occurring on the highway.

---

[20] Ante, p. 40.

[21] *Ward* v. *Macauley* (1791) 4 T.R. 489, at 490; 100 E.R. 1135, per Lord Kenyon C.J.

[22] See the numerous authorities set out in Pollock and Wright, *op. cit.*, p. 166, n. 2, and (as to trespass alone) *Henry Berry & Co. Pty. Ltd.* v. *Rushton* (1935) 29 Q.J.P.R. 169; *Penfolds Wines Pty. Ltd.* v. *Elliott* (1946) 74 C.L.R. 204; *Wilson* v. *Lombank Ltd.* [1963] 1 W.L.R. 1294. In both of the last two decisions the rule was implicitly accepted but found not to apply. In *Henry Berry & Co. Pty. Ltd.* v. *Rushton* (supra), at 175-176, there is the suggestion that the lack of an immediate right to possess will not debar an action where there is damage to the bailor's reversionary interest; sed quaere. Cf. *Wertheim* v. *Cheel* (1885) 11 V.L.R. 107.

[23] [1893] 1 Q.B. 512, at 516; a similar statement occurs in the judgment of Henchman J. in *Henry Berry & Co. Pty. Ltd.* v. *Rushton* (supra), at 175, citing *Salmond on Torts* (8th ed.), p. 354; cf. 16th ed., p. 94.

[24] Op. cit. at 145.

There are expressions in some cases and in text-books to the effect that a person with a right to possession of a thing, though without possession, can always maintain trespass, as (except where the right is suspended, e.g. in a bailment for a term—*Gordon* v. *Harper* 1796, 7 T.R.9) he certainly can trover or detinue, against a stranger who takes the thing: and if this is correct the gist of the action of trespass must be the wrong to the right of possession. But it is difficult to see how there can be a forcible and immediate injury vi et armis to a mere legal right; and there are some parts of the law of trespass and theft which are inexplicable on such a view.

The true position, as Wright goes on to remark,[25] is that a right to possession will justify an action in trespass only when the person whose possession is violated is in some way a delegate or representative of the plaintiff. In other words, the possessor must be an agent, servant or bailee under a revocable bailment before trespass can be sustained against the interloper. Where these conditions are satisfied, a bailor may retain, concurrently with his bailee, the right to sue for trespass any stranger who has wrongfully violated the bailee's own possession.

B. Revocable bailment

The bailment must be one which is "revocable by the bailor at his pleasure either unconditionally or upon a condition which he may satisfy at will."[26] The basic instance is obvious. A lends his car to B, stipulating that he may call for its return at any time. C steals or damages the car while B is in possession. A (as well as B) can sue C in trespass.

A bailment need not be gratuitous in order to qualify under this rule. The right to possess may be immediate where a bailee for reward is granted possession until a certain event has occurred, such as the emptying of a cask;[27] or where he forfeits his right to possess by virtue of an act repugnant to the bailment;[28] or where the work he is to perform upon the chattel has been completed and he has no lien over it;[29] or where the bailment is ostensibly for a fixed term but the bailor reserves the right to requisition the chattel at any time during that period.[30] In each of these cases, the bailor might sue for trespass once the 'revesting' event has occurred.

C. Violation of the bailee's possession

Trespass, then, may be invoked by a bailor only when the bailee's possession rests, so to speak, vicariously in him.[31] In such a case the

---

[25] Ibid., at 144-145.
[26] Ibid., at 166.
[27] *Manders* v. *Williams* (1849) 4 Exch. 343.
[28] See, for instance, *Donald* v. *Suckling* (1866) L.R. 1 Q.B. 585; *Whiteley Ltd.* v. *Hilt* [1918] 2 K.B. 808; *Moorgate Mercantile Co. Ltd.* v. *Finch* [1962] 1 Q.B. 701; *Union Transport Finance* v. *British Car Auctions* [1978] 2 All E.R. 385.
[29] Cf. *Wilson* v. *Lombank Ltd.* [1963] 1 W.L.R. 1294, where the facts were of the kind described but Hinchcliffe J. preferred to hold (perhaps wrongly) that the owner of the chattel retained possession throughout.
[30] Cf. *Nominal Defendant* v. *Morgan Cars Pty. Ltd.* (1974) 48 A.L.J.R. 174.
[31] Some authorities (for instance, Winfield and Jolowicz, p. 405; Salmond, p. 95) go so far as to say that in these cases the "bailor" never loses possession at all; sed quaere. Cf. Fleming, pp. 50-51, who is clearly of the opinion that the bailee-at-will has actual possession; Clerk and Lindsell, para. 1182, where the

injury to the delegate counts as an injury to his superior and both will have a remedy. The converse is that where there has been no actual violation of the bailee's possession (for instance, where he has himself invited or permitted the misuse of the chattel) there can be no action in trespass by the bailor. Neither his immediate right to possession nor his ownership of the chattel will avail him because the protection of these interests is not the object of the remedy; they are merely the link that make the bailee's possession (for the purposes of the remedy) that of his bailor. Thus: A lends his car to B, retrievable on demand; B dishonestly hands the car to C and allows him to use it for motor-racing; A cannot sue C in trespass.

A similar problem came before the High Court of Australia in *Penfolds Wines Pty. Ltd.* v. *Elliott.*[32] The plaintiffs were wine-merchants, selling their wine in bottles upon which were embossed the words: "This bottle always remains[33] the property of Penfolds Wines Ltd." In addition, they gave their customers invoices stating that only the contents of the bottles were sold and not the bottles themselves, and sold the wine on the condition that the container should not be used for any purpose other than the retailing of the plaintiffs' wine. The defendant had for some time been selling other brands of wine in bottles belonging to the plaintiffs, which his customers brought to him to be filled. On the occasion in question, however, the bottles had been delivered to him not by the customer (who was an inspector employed inter alia by the plaintiffs) but by the defendant's brother. It was accepted that the defendant did not purport to sell the bottles themselves, but only the wine with which he had filled them. The plaintiffs sought an injunction, alleging (inter alia) that each separate act of filling one of their wine-bottles for an unauthorised purpose constituted a trespass to that bottle. Latham C.J., citing *Johnson* v. *Diprose*[34] and other authorities, favoured granting the injunction on the grounds that an immediate right to possess (accruing to the plaintiffs through their customer-bailee's misuse of the bottles) can found an action in trespass.[35] Dixon J. disagreed, pointing out that it is not the immediate right to possess but possession itself that is protected by trespass; and that without an infringement of the bailee's possession no right in trespass arises to be transmitted to the bailor. The appropriate remedy in such a case is conversion. Were trespass so liberal a cause of action as the plaintiffs had contended, there would have been no need for the remedy of conversion to have developed as it did.[36]

view is taken that the bailor retains "sufficient possession" to entitle him to sue third parties; Cmnd. 4774, para. 18, which refers to "the fiction" that the bailor at will is still in possession of the chattel.

[32] (1946) 74 C.L.R. 204.
[33] Or, occasionally, "is".
[34] [1893] 1 Q.B. 512.
[35] (1946) 74 C.L.R. 204, at 214-217.
[36] Ibid., at 224-228; supported by Starke and Williams JJ. Dixon J. acknowledged that there is "slender but ancient" authority for the rule that where a third party does not take delivery from the bailee but merely takes the goods out of the bailee's possession by the bailee's licence, this will qualify as a trespassory taking and may entitle the bailor to sue the third party. Dixon J. concluded that

It follows that a bailor who, without right, removes goods from his bailee's possession, or damages them during the currency of the bailment, will be answerable in trespass as the suit of the bailee.[37] This is so whether the bailor owns the chattels in question, or has merely delivered them for a limited purpose, with or without the authority of the true owner.[38]

Conversely, it is no trespass for a bailee to misuse or misappropriate the chattel of his bailor, for such an act implies no offence to the bailee's own possession.[39] To this, however, there are two exceptions, based on very old authority. The first occurs when the bailee has "broken bulk"— that is, has opened the parcel or other container in which the goods were delivered to him, so as to alter in law the nature of the thing which he received. The second occurs when the bailee has completely destroyed the chattel.[40] Although these exceptions enjoy some recognition in recent authority,[41] there are no decisions within the last century in which they have been directly applied.

In any event, the mere performance of an act repugnant to the bailment (albeit an act which entitles the bailor to determine the relationship forthwith) will not ground trespass against the miscreant bailee.[42] Thus when Dixon J. remarked in *Penfolds Wines Pty. Ltd.* v. *Elliott* that: "A delivery of possession by the bailee, however wrongful as against the bailor, could not work an invasion of the bailee's own possession, so as to found trespass"[43] his observations were true not only in the context of a bailor's action against a stranger but also in the context of his proceeding in trespass against his own bailee.

D. Trespass and the jus tertii

The crucial quality of trespass as an offence to possession again becomes evident when one examines the circumstances in which the trespasser may successfully plead title in a third person as an answer to an action in trespass. Here the law draws a distinction between those trespassory acts which involve interfering with the goods while they are in the

---

"whether this refinement would now be maintained as valid need not be considered": ibid., at 228.

---

[37] As in *Standard Electronic Apparatus Laboratories Ltd.* v. *Stenner* [1960] N.S.W.R. 447, where the bailee had a lien over the goods in respect of work performed upon them; *Roberts* v. *Roberts* [1957] Tas. S.R. 84, where the bailor purported to repossess under a hire-purchase agreement which contravened the rules as to minimum deposit and was therefore void as against the hirer: the statement in question was made obiter and upon the assumption that the agreement was still on foot at the time; *Keenan Bros. Ltd.* v. *C.I.E.* (1962) 97 I.L.T.R. 54; *Singh* v. *Ali* [1960] A.C. 167 Cf. *Roberts* v. *Wyatt* (1810) 2 Taunt. 268, which was actually an action in trover by the bailee but which illustrates the same principle.

[38] For an example of the bailor who is not an owner, see the *Standard Electronic* case, supra. Since even a wrongdoer with possession may sue in trespass (*Woadson* v. *Nawton* (1727) 2 Stra. 777) it may be assumed that any bailee from that wrongdoer may sue him in trespass for wrongful dispossession.

[39] Pollock and Wright, *op. cit.*, pp. 131-132, 135-137, 157.

[40] Ibid., pp. 132-133.

[41] See the judgment of Dixon J. in *Penfolds Wines Pty. Ltd.* v. *Elliott* (1946) 74 C.L.R. 204, at 227-228, and *Fenn* v. *Bittleston* (1851) 7 Ex. at 159-160.

[42] Pollock and Wright, op. cit., pp. 132-133.

[43] (1946) 74 C.L.R. 204, at 228.

plaintiff's possession, and those to which the plaintiff pleads a mere immediate right of possession in grounding his claim. In the former case, that is, where the plaintiff was in actual possession of the goods, the defendant cannot plead jus tertii.[44] In the latter, he may do so because, in the words of Salmond, the plaintiff: ". . . must recover on the strength of his title, and proof of the jus tertii will destroy the only thing upon which he relies."[45]

The rule is capricious,[46] and represents a further severe disadvantage to the bailor, who will invariably be, ex hypothesi, out of possession. It is ironic that the one class of person who may not raise this defence to a plaintiff out of possession is the bailee,[47] against whom a bailor will only very rarely (if at all) enjoy an opportunity of proceeding in trespass anyway.

II. CONVERSION[48]

Unlike trespass, conversion is essentially an offence to property: "it is, and always has been, primarily an action for the protection of owner-ship."[49] Accordingly, it may be maintained by anyone who enjoys either the possession of goods or the immediate right to possess;[50] in the latter case, irrespective of whether the intermediate possessor permits or connives at the act of conversion[51] or whether the plaintiff is the owner.[52] But a postponed right of possession (such as that of an owner of goods during the currency of a lease) is insufficient, so that a bailor cannot, during the continuance of the term, maintain conversion against a third party who intermeddles with the chattel and treats it as his own.[53] If,

---

[44] *Wilson* v. *Lombank* [1963] 1 W.L.R. 1294; *Standard Electronic Apparatus Laboratories Ltd.* v. *Stenner* [1960] N.S.W.R. 447.

[45] Op. cit., p. 95. The rule is supported by *Butler* v. *Hobson* (1838) 4 Bing. N.C. 290; *Leake* v. *Loveday* (1842) 4. M. & G. 972; *Gadsden* v. *Barrow* (1854) 9 Exch. 514; *Buckley* v. *Green* (1863) 3 B. & S. 566; *Richards* v. *Jenkins* (1886) 17 Q.B.D. 544; *Henry Berry & Co. Pty. Ltd.* v. *Rushton* (1935) 29 Q.J.P.R. 169.

[46] Cmnd. 4774, para. 53.

[47] *Biddle* v. *Bond* (1865) 6 B. & S. 225; see further, p. 163 et. seq., post, and cf. now ss. 7-8, *Torts (Interference with Goods) Act* 1977.

[48] Law Reform Committee, *Eighteenth Report (Conversion and Detinue)* Cmnd. 4774 (1971); Fleming, *The Law of Torts* (4th ed.), pp. 51-73; Salmond, *Torts* (16th ed.), pp. 95-113.

[49] Cmnd. 4774, para. 13. Cf. Morison, Sharwood and Phegan, *Cases on Torts* (4th ed.), p. 127, and see now s. 2(2) *Torts (Interference with Goods) Act* 1977.

[50] *Bute (Marquess of)* v. *Barclay's Bank Ltd.* [1955] 1 Q.B. 202; *Wilton* v. *Commonwealth Trading Bank of Australia Ltd.* [1973] 2 N.S.W.L.R. 644, at 651; *Federal Savings Credit Union Ltd.* v. *Centennial Trailer Sales Ltd.* (1973) 37 D.L.R. (3d) 146; for further authority, see Fleming, pp. 61-63.

[51] Cf. the position in trespass; p. 122, ante.

[52] See the *Marquess of Bute* case (supra); *Armory* v. *Delamirie* (1721) 1 Stra. 505; 93 E.R. 664.

[53] See the authorities listed in Pollock and Wright, *Possession in the Common Law,* p. 166, and especially *Gordon* v. *Harper* (1796) 7 T.R. 9; *Donald* v. *Suckling* (1866) L.R. 1 Q.B. 585; *Lord* v. *Price* (1874) L.R. 9 Ex. 54. Australian cases to the same effect are *Wertheim* v. *Cheel* (1885) 11 V.L.R. 107; *Glen* v. *Abbott* (1880) 6 V.L.R. (L.) 483; *Short* v. *City Bank Ltd.* (1912) 15 C.L.R. 148. It follows that the hirer under a hire purchase agreement cannot maintain conversion if the goods, having been lawfully repossessed for his default in meeting the instal-ments, are wrongfully sold by the owner before the statutory procedures have been observed. Until he makes payment, the hirer lacks the necessary immediate

however, the bailee has wrongfully brought the relationship to an end by an act wholly repugnant to the bailment[54] (and conversion of the subject matter is clearly such an act) the remedy may lie not only against him but against anyone else who deals with the goods. Circumstances which can cause this right to accrue include the unauthorised loan of the chattel to a third party;[55] the selling of the subject matter of the bailment;[56] its use in a forbidden manner by the bailee;[57] the occurrence of an event specified in the contract, such as the seizure of the goods by way of execution,[58] or the emptying of casks[59] by a bailee; or the mere immediate right of recall enjoyed by a bailor under a bailment at will.[60] Very often, of course, the conduct which revives the bailor's right of possession will in itself constitute a conversion. This is particularly so where the unauthorised act results in the loss or destruction of the chattel.[61] But misuse and conversion are not synonymous. It may be that a further, more serious interference with the bailor's property will be required before his immediate right to possess can be sublimated into an action for conversion.[62] Moreover, the terms of the agreement may themselves be subject to provisions of the general law which render a purported right of possession unenforceable. Thus conversion may not lie where the relevant system of law renders recovery of the goods illegal[63] or (to

right to possess: *Carr* v. *James Broderick & Co. Ltd.* [1942] 2 K.B. 275; *Harris* v. *Lombard New Zealand Ltd.* [1974] 2 N.Z.L.R. 161; cf. *Consumer Credit Act 1974* (U.K.), ss. 91, 170(1); Goode, *Consumer Credit Act 1974*, paras. 21.35-21.38. The rule prohibiting a bailor with only a suspended right to possession from suing is criticised by Warren (1936) 49 *Harvard Law Review* 1084, at 1100 et. seq. and by the Law Reform Committee, who recommend its abolition: Cmnd. 4774, para. 34.

[54] He will not, of course, cease to owe the duties of a bailee but will lose his finite tenure of the goods. See ante, p. 000.
[55] *Chapman* v. *Robinson* (1969) 71 W.W.R. 515; *Bringloe* v. *Morice* (1676) 1 Mod. Rep. 210; 86 E.R. 834.
[56] *Shelley* v. *Ford* (1832) 5 C. & P. 313; *North Central Wagon and Finance Co. Ltd.* v. *Graham* [1950] 2 K.B. 7. As to the different effects of sales by lien-holders and pledgees, see Fleming, op. cit., pp. 62-63.
[57] *Penfolds Wines Ltd.* v. *Elliott* (1946) 74 C.L.R. 204, at 214, 217-218, 227, 241-242; *Andrews* v. *Nominal Defendant* (1968) 89 W.N. (Pt. 2) (N.S.W.) 113; *United Transport Finance* v. *B.C.A.* [1978] 2 All E.R. 385.
[58] *Jelks* v. *Hayward* [1905] 2 K.B. 460.
[59] *Manders* v. *Williams* (1849) 4 Ex. 339.
[60] In *Chapman* v. *Robinson* (1969) 71 W.W.R. 515 it was stated that the unauthorised sub-loan of a vehicle merely gave the bailor a right to revoke the bailment which had not, at the time of the subsequent damage, been exercised. The conclusion was that the bailee continued to enjoy the authority to deal with the chattel and could thus create a valid sub-bailment between the bailor and the sub-bailee; accordingly the former could proceed against the latter for damage to the vehicle. The decision must be regarded in the light of the particular result which it was desired to achieve; and it is submitted that the plaintiff's immediate right of possession, in the context of an action in conversion, would have been deemed to arise from the moment the misuse occurred without any formal revocation on her part. In any event, it seems that despite this decision and a statement by Zelling J. in *Roufos* v. *Brewster and Brewster* [1971] 2 S.A.S.R. 218, at 234, no authority on the part of the intermediate bailor is required before an enforceable sub-bailment can be created: post, p. 786.
[61] *Moorgate Mercantile Co. Ltd.* v. *Finch* [1962] 1 Q.B. 701 (hire car, being used to carry smuggled goods, seized by the customs); see further, p. 753 et. seq., post.
[62] See p. 126 post.
[63] *Kahler* v. *Midland Bank Ltd.* [1950] A.C. 24, criticised at p. 58, ante. The case actually involved an action in detinue.

employ a more specific example) where a hire-purchase agreement purports to give the owner an immediate right to possess upon default by
the hirer.[64] Whereas detinue apparently requires that the immediate right
to possess should be founded upon a proprietary right,[65] it seems that
conversion is not thus limited.[66]

It follows that conversion is a much wider and more flexible remedy
than trespass, particularly in the context of actions brought by a bailor
against a bailee;[67] indeed, it has almost wholly supplanted the earlier
form of action. Its utility is augmented by the measure of damages,
which, although primarily based upon the value of the chattel converted,
has recently enjoyed an appreciable degree of expansion and adaptation
by the Courts.[68] The real difficulty lies in isolating those types of conduct
which amount to conversion from those lesser interferences which do not.

A. What is conversion?

Conversion has been defined by Atkin J. as:

> . . . dealing with goods in a manner inconsistent with the rights
> of the true owner . . . provided that it is also established that there
> is an intention on the part of the defendant in so doing to deny the
> owner's right or to assert a right which is inconsistent with the
> owner's right.[69]

Provided the necessary degree of deprivation or adverse interference
is satisfied, liability may therefore be incurred innocently; conversion
does not depend upon any deliberate or malicious abjuration of the
plaintiff's title, nor is it excluded by any permission given to the converter
by a third party (whether an intermediate possessor or an owner with
no right of immediate possession), to deal with the goods in the manner
complained of.[70] The key to this strict liability may be found in the

---

[64] See *Consumer Credit Act* 1974 (U.K.), s. 87 and, for equivalent Australian
legislation, Else-Mitchell and Parsons, *Hire Purchase Law* (4th ed.), p. 109 et.
seq.; *Consumer Transactions Act* 1972-1973 (S.A.), ss. 21, 24, 27.

[65] *Jarvis* v. *Williams* [1955] 1 W.L.R. 71; *Singh* v. *Ali* [1960] A.C. 167, at 176.

[66] *Harris* v. *Lombard New Zealand Ltd.* [1974] 2 N.Z.L.R. 161; Cmnd. 4774, para.
9; Fleming, op. cit., p. 61, n. 7, asserts the contrary, but with reservation.

[67] See p. 121, ante.

[68] Ante, p. 63.

[69] *Lancashire and Yorkshire Ry. Co.* v. *MacNicoll* (1919) 88 L.J.K.B. 601: approved
by Scrutton L.J. in *Oakley* v. *Lyster* [1931] 1 K.B. 148, at 153; by Lord Porter in
Caxton Publishing Co. Ltd. v. *Sutherland Publishing Co. Ltd.* [1939] A.C. 178, at
201-202, and by Bray C.J. in *The Queen* v. *Hansford* [1974] 8 S.A.S.R. 164, at
169; but note the remarks of Davidson J. in *Glass* v. *Hollander* (1935) 35 S.R.
(N.S.W.) 304. Other well-known definitions are those of Lord Porter in *Caxton
Publishing Co. Ltd.* v. *Sutherland Publishing Co. Ltd.* (supra), at 202: "an act
intentionally done inconsistent with the owner's right, though the doer may not
know of or intend to challenge the property or possession of the true owner" and
of Bramwell B. in *Hiort* v. *Bott* (1874) L.R. 9 Ex. 86, at 89: "it is where a man
does an unauthorised act which deprives another of his property permanently
or for an indefinite time". And see Salmond, op. cit., pp. 96-97, adopted by
Cmnd. 4774, para. 38.

[70] Illustrations of this principle are abundant; for some typical situations, see
Hiort v. *Bott* (1874) L.R. 9 Ex. 86 (defendant indorsing delivery order to third
party with object of returning goods to owner); *Consolidated Co. Ltd.* v. *Curtis
& Son* [1892] 1 Q.B. 495 (auctioneers selling goods by order of grantors of bill
of sale); *Jerome* v. *Bentley & Co. Ltd.* [1952] 2 All E.R. 114 (innocent purchaser
receiving goods under sale from fraudulent intermediary); *Blenheim Borough and
Wairau Rice Board* v. *British Pavements (Canterbury) Ltd.* [1940] N.Z.L.R. 564

function of conversion as an instrument for the protection of ownership. Because of this, "questions as to the fault of the defendant are irrelevant, the principle adopted being that 'persons deal with the property in chattels or exercise acts of ownership over them at their peril'."[71] The rule is a harsh one and cruel cases abound.[72]

It now seems clearly established that the defendant need not have acquired possession of the goods at the material time to be guilty of their conversion.[73] Certainly, liability in conversion is not peculiar to bailees, however widely one frames one's definition of bailment.

There are thousands of reported cases on conversion, most of which turn upon their particular facts. In an adjectival discussion of this nature, only the broadest analysis can be given. A preliminary observation which may help to explain some of the cases is that the characterisation of conduct as a conversion will often depend upon two distinct facts: the nature of the defendant's conduct and the consequences thereof. If a carrier wrongfully delegates the task of transporting a particular consignment and the goods are stolen by the sub-contractor, the carrier will probably be held liable in conversion: *at least,* where his selection of the deputy has been negligent.[74] If, on the other hand, the sub-bailment is provoked by an unforeseen emergency, the main contractor takes every care to ensure that the sub-bailees are honest, and the goods are duly delivered, it would seem unlikely that an action for conversion against the principal carrier would succeed. The crux of the question has been admirably stated by Fleming:[75] since the measure of damages in conversion is (prima facie) the full value of the chattel, the act complained of must be a sufficiently serious infringement of the plaintiff's right of control to justify "the drastic sanction of compelling the wrongdoer to buy the plaintiff out."

> The controlling factor therefore seems to be, not necessarily the defendant's act viewed in isolation, but whether it has *resulted in a major interference* with the owner's rights so serious as to warrant a forced sale. Hence, a particular type of intermeddling is probably not, under any and all circumstances, necessarily a conversion. What

(bona fide removal of shingle under mistaken belief that the necessary authority had been granted); *Hollins* v. *Fowler* (1875) L.R. 7 H.L. 757 (defendant selling cotton on behalf of rogue believing him to be the true owner).

---

[71] Cmnd. 4774, para. 13, citing Cleasby B. in *Hollins* v. *Fowler* (1872) L.R. 7 Q.B. 616, at 639. Because of this function, the Law Reform Committee has recommended the retention of strict liability in conversion, albeit with mitigaton in special cases; ibid., para. 14, and conclusions thereto.

[72] An oft-cited example being *Stephens* v. *Elwall* (1815) 4 M. & S. 259; but see Cmnd. 4774, para. 41.

[73] Ibid., para. 8; *Hiort* v. *Bott* (1874) L.R. 9 Ex. 86; *Oakley* v. *Lyster* [1931] 1 K.B. 148; *Douglas Valley Finance Co. Ltd.* v. *S. Hughes (Hirers) Ltd.* [1969] 1 Q.B. 738; *Kitano* v. *Commonwealth of Australia* (1974) 2 A.L.R. 83.

[74] *Garnham, Harris and Elton Ltd.* v. *Alfred W. Ellis (Transport) Ltd.* [1967] 2 All E.R. 940; Vaines, *Personal Property* (5th ed.), p. 109. It is not necessary to show that the defendant intended the dispossession to be permanent, if it is in fact wrongful and the chattel is lost as a result: *City of Wellington* v. *Singh* [1971] N.Z.L.R. 1025. Indeed, there need be no permanent deprivation at all, although its absence may be material to the matter of damages: *Penfolds Wines Pty. Ltd.* v. *Elliott* (1946) 74 C.L.R. 204, at 243.

[75] Op. cit., at p. 51.

may be decisive are such additional factors as the extent and duration of the interference, the harm done to the chattel, and, not least, the defendant's intent.[76]

Certain species of conduct are, of course, clearly identifiable as conversions: an unauthorised sale[77] or pledge[78] or execution of a bill of sale over the chattel,[79] stealing[80] and destruction,[81] are obvious examples. Equally clearly, it is not conversion merely to damage or lose a chattel negligently[82] or even to inflict deliberate damage in a manner which does not alter its identity. Between these two extremes (which may, of course, be morally indistinguishable) there lies a wide margin of disputed territory in which conversion stands revealed as the most intuitive and perhaps the most discretionary of all torts.

Thus, the mere taking of the chattel, or a mere refusal to allow the owner to recover it, may be conversion, according to whether the asportation is accompanied by an intention of exercising "a temporary or permanent dominion",[83] and whether the refusal is an unqualified contradiction of the owner's right to the chattel.[84] Receipt under an unlawful disposition is generally conversion, although there is authority to the contrary in the case of a pledgee who has made no assertion of title contrary to that of the plaintiff.[85] The Law Reform Committee have

---

[76] Ibid., p. 54, citing Prosser (1957) *Cornell Law Quarterly* 168.
[77] *Consolidated Co. Ltd.* v. *Curtis & Son* [1892] 1 Q.B. 495; *Glass* v. *Hollander* (1935) 35 S.R. (N.S.W.) 304; *Hollins* v. *Fowler* (1875) L.R. 7 H.L. 757; *Willis* v. *British Car Auctions Ltd.* (1978) *The Times* January 14th. According to the Law Reform Committee (Cmnd. 4774, para. 41) no delivery under the sale is necessary to complete the cause of action; cf. Fleming, op. cit., p. 56, who speaks of "sale and delivery" as constituting conversion, and observes that ordinarily a failure to deliver will affect neither possession nor title (citing *Lancs Wagon Co.* v. *Fitzhugh* (1861) 6 H. & N. 502). It is probable that either title or possession must be transferred: in the latter case, an imperfect or attempted sale will suffice, and the tort may be committed where the documents of title, as opposed to the subject-matter itself, have been transferred: Cmnd. 4774, ibid. Cf. *Australian Assurance Co. Ltd.* v. *Coroneo* (1938) 38 S.R. (N.S.W.) 700.
[78] *Parker* v. *Godin* (1728) 2 Stra. 813; *Singer Manufacturing Co. Ltd.* v. *Clark* (1879) 5 Ex. D. 37.
[79] Or even a mere hiring, if the chattel be handed over pursuant to it cf. *Australian Assurance Co. Ltd.* v. *Coroneo* (1938) 38 S.R. (N.S.W.) 700 (where there was no delivery) and *Federal Savings Credit Union Ltd.* v. *Centennial Trailer Sales Ltd.* (1973) 37 D.L.R. 146, where the mere execution of a conditional sales agreement between a chattel mortgagor and the defendant was held sufficient to give the mortgagees an immediate right to possess and to entitle them to sue in conversion.
[80] *Armory* v. *Delamirie* (1721) 1 Stra. 505; 93 E.R. 664.
[81] Cmnd. 4774, para. 44; *Richards* v. *Atkinson* (1723) 1 Stra. 576; *M'leod* v. *M'Ghie* (1841) 2 Man. & G. 771.
[82] But cf. *Torts (Interference with Goods) Act* 1977, s. 2(2).
[83] Cmnd. 4774, para 39; *Penfolds Wines Pty. Ltd.* v. *Elliott* (1946) 74 C.L.R. 204, 218; *Wellington City* v. *Singh* [1971] N.Z.L.R. 1025; *Fouldes* v. *Willoughby* (1841) 8 M. & W. 584 (no liability where ferryman removed plaintiff's horses from ferry and put them ashore).
[84] Cmnd. 4774, para. 40; see *McCurdy* v. *P.M.G.* [1959] N.Z.L.R. 533; *England* v. *Cowley* (1873) L.R 8 Ex 126; *Ramki* v. *Maragh* (1966) 10 W.I.R. 113; cf. *Chicago I. & L. Ry. Co.* v. *Pope* (1934) 188 N.E. 594 (criticised in (1933-1934) 9 *Notre Dame Law Review* 3337) which seems to hold that an unequivocal refusal to allow the owner access to his goods is not conversion.
[85] *Spackman* v. *Foster* (1883) 11 Q.B.D. 99; *Miller* v. *Dell* [1891] 1 Q.B. 468. It is pointed out in Cmnd. 4774 para. 42 that this distinction between pledges and sales is hard to justify, and is not adopted in the American Restatement (s. 223). To

recommended retaining the general rule and extending it to all cases in which goods have been received or collected under an unauthorised disposal; subject, however, to the principle that "a bailee who has accounted for the goods to his bailor should be exempt from liability to any other person."[86] The misuse of a chattel in a manner calculated to produce an appreciable interference with the owner's interest or dominion will also generally qualify as conversion, as where a vehicle used for smuggling is forfeited to the Crown[87] or where a defendant uses the bottles of another person in which to deliver his milk.[88] But here the dichotomy between the misconduct itself and the consequences thereof becomes especially important and confusing. It now seems clear, despite early assertions to the contrary,[89] that the mere, inconsequential misuse of another's chattel does not by itself amount to conversion, at least where there is no threatened or effective intention on the part of the misuser to treat it for all material purposes as his own. Thus, merely to use another man's pen, or to deviate from the agreed route while carrying his goods or using a vehicle hired from him,[90] should not without ensuing loss entitle the owner to demand the full value of the goods mishandled. Even where they are damaged as a result, the appropriate remedy would seem not to be conversion but an action for breach of bailment, based upon the strict liability resulting from the bailee's deviation from the agreed terms of the relationship.[91] On the other hand, the total loss of the goods as the result of an act of misuse may persuade the Courts to regard the abuse as a conversion, at least where there has been no orthodox bailment upon which to found an implied agreement to compensate for such loss. Of course, the motives of the defendant may be no less relevant than the nature or consequences of his conduct. If he intends to arrogate to himself the full use and apparent ownership of a chattel, or to impair substantially the full enjoyment of that ownership, then even a trivial act directed to that end may be enough. Without malicious intention, more positive conduct or interference may be required. But it must always be remembered that conversion is not traditionally a tort of intention. Conversely, it seems to be accepted that a mere assertion of ownership, without any accompanying conduct which

sustain it would invite difficulties in relation to other dispositions, for instance, liens or rights of sale improperly exercised under the various *Disposal of Uncollected Goods Acts.* Of course, if the recipient acquires a good title under the disposition, no remedy will lie against him. See now *Torts (Interference with Goods) Act* 1977, s 11(2).

---

[86] Cmnd. 4774, para. 43.

[87] *Moorgate Mercantile Credit Co. Ltd.* v. *Finch* [1962] 1 Q.B. 701.

[88] *Model Dairy Co. Ltd.* v. *White* (1935) 41 Arg. L.R. 432; *Milk Bottles Recovery Ltd.* v. *Camillo* [1948] V.L.R. 344. The mere risk of loss may, if serious, be enough.

[89] Fleming, op. cit., p. 59.

[90] See the authorities discussed by Paton, *Bailment in the Common Law,* pp. 303-304, and Blaugrund (1935-1936) 21 *Cornell Law Quarterly* 112, who remarks: "At some point the deviation is so marked, so serious, that the only reasonable inference is that (the bailee) intends to assume dominion. But to hold the mere slight deviation a conversion seems utterly contrary to sound legal theory and commonsense."

[91] Cf. *Scott-Mayer Commission Co.* v. *Merchants Grocer Co.* (1921) 226 S.W. 1060: 12 A.L.R. 1316, cited in Blaugrund, loc. cit., n. 23; see post, p. 753.

threatens or amounts to an impairment of the rights of the true owner, does not justify the imposition of liability in conversion.[92]

A decision which illustrates the problematical quality of the marginal and less total varieties of conversion is *Penfolds Wines Pty. Ltd.* v. *Elliott,*[93] the facts of which have already been stated.[94] In addition to suing in trespass for the defendant's misuse of their bottles, the plaintiffs sought an injunction for conversion. By a majority of three to two, the High Court dismissed their action, but in such a manner as to render it difficult to extract any uniform ratio. According to Latham C.J. (with whom Williams J. concurred) the actual use of the bottles for the use of the defendant and his brother was a conversion;[95] it amounted, in the words of Pollock on *Torts,*[96] to an "unauthorised assumption of the powers of the true owner"; and "(a)ctually dealing with another's goods as owner, for however short a time and however limited a purpose, is therefore conversion." Moreover, there was a further act of conversion when the defendant handed the bottles over to the plaintiff's inspector, Moon, even though the latter transaction did not amount to a purported sale.[97] Since damages were not an adequate remedy, he thought an injunction should be granted.

Starke J., although expressing general concurrence with the opinion of Dixon J., was content to assume that the actions of the defendant were a conversion, and delivered judgment on the basis that the remedy sought by the plaintiffs was not justifiable in the circumstances.[98] McTiernan J. adopted a similar approach, although in his view conversion had been affirmatively proved. It is not entirely clear whether the learned judge considered that each of the disputed actions (i.e. filling the bottles and disposing of them) constituted the tort in isolation, or whether it was their combined effect which justified that result; but it seems that in his opinion the first of these was by itself sufficient.[99]

It was left to Dixon J. to put the case against conversion. He did so in a passage which is worth setting out in detail:

> The essence of conversion is a dealing with a chattel in a manner repugnant to the immediate right of possession of the person who has the property or special property in the chattel . . . But damage to

[92] Fleming, op. cit., pp. 60-61; Cmnd. 4774, para. 45; cf. *Oakley* v. *Lyster* [1931] 1 K.B. 148, where (at 150) Scrutton L.J. appears to favour the contrary rule. Fleming contends that this statement must be confined to the circumstances of that case, where the defendant had some degree of control over the subject matter of the conversion and had "backed up his assertion by using some of it himself and by stopping the owner and his purchaser from removing it." This analysis was cited with approval by Wells J. in *The Queen* v. *Hansford* (1973-1974) 8 S.A.S.R. 164, at 193. Cf. *Federal Savings Credit Union Ltd.* v. *Centennial Trailer Sales Ltd.* (1973) 37 D.L.R. (3d) 146. The rule as stated in the text is confirmed by the *Torts (Interference with Goods) Act*, 1977, s. 11(3).
[93] (1946) 74 C.L.R. 204.
[94] Ante, p. 122.
[95] (1946) 74 C.L.R. 204, at 219.
[96] (14th ed.) 286.
[97] (1946) 74 C.L.R. 204, at 219. Latham C.J. appeared to doubt whether there was not, in fact a sale of the bottles to Moon, but on the definition of conversion he was applying the precise nature of the disposition was immaterial. Cf. Dixon J. at 223; McTiernan J. at 233.
[98] Ibid., at 221-222.
[99] Ibid., at 234-235.

the chattel is not conversion, nor is use, nor is a transfer of possession otherwise than for the purpose of affecting the immediate right to possession, nor is it always conversion to lose the goods beyond hope of recovery. An intent to do that which would deprive "the true owner" of his immediate right to possession or impair it may be said to form the essential ground of the tort. There is nothing in the course followed by the respondent in supplying wine to his customers who brought bottles to receive it involving any deprival or impairment of property in the bottles, that is of the immediate right to possession.[1]

More specifically, the redelivery of the bottles to the persons from whom the defendant had received them was not conversion because it did not purport to transfer any right of property, and the filling of the bottles was not conversion because it did not involve "the exercise of any dominion over them, however transitory." Even the two cases of delivery to the inspector, Moon, did not amount to a sale; there was accordingly no attempted transfer of property and no impairment of the plaintiff's right to immediate possession.[2]

It is important to understand what is meant by an impairment of the owner's immediate right to possession. Legally, that right is never extinguished or reduced unless the circumstances in which the defendant has transferred the chattel amount to an exception to the rule nemo dat quod non habet. And yet there will be many cases of conversion in which the disputed disposition does not have this effect. The important question seems to be whether, in transferring the chattel, the defendant has taken it upon himself to act in a manner which is inconsistent with, and is, in a practical sense, calculated to deny or to defeat the immediate right to possess. Such a right is clearly useless if the transferee of the chattel is untraceable; conversely, the transferor should not escape liability merely because the owner enjoys an effective remedy against a third person. Thus, an act may amount to conversion although its effect is to strengthen the owner's chances of recovering the chattel rather than to reduce them, if the object of the act was to deal with the chattel in a manner which contradicted or weakened his title or claim to the goods. Moreover, the content of an act of conversion may itself be inseparable from the terms and context of the bailment under which the chattel was originally delivered. The bailment may, in other words, specifically forbid certain conduct which, if performed by a stranger to the agreement, would not necessarily be unlawful. In such a case, what is a conversion on the part of one defendant may be wholly legitimate on the part of another[3]

---

[1] Ibid., at 229.
[2] Ibid., at 230. On the question whether mere misuse is conversion, contrast further *Craig v. Marsh* (1935) 35 S.R. (N.S.W.) 323 and *McKenna & Armistead Ltd. v. Excavators Pty. Ltd.* [1957] S.R. (N.S.W.) 515 (post, p. 143).
[3] The First American Restatement, *Torts* (1934), para. 228, stated that the unauthorised use of a chattel by a bailee did not amount to conversion unless it was a material breach of the contract of bailment; if there were no material breach the bailee should be liable only for damages, para. 256. One decision applying this rule was *Donovan v. Barkhauser Co.* (1929) 227 N.W. 940; 200 Wis. 194, where a bailee who, contrary to orders, repaired a car, was held not liable for conversion. The approach was criticised by Blaugrund (1935-1936) 21 *Cornell Law Quarterly* 112, for failing to define conversion and for offering a misleading metaphor: ". . . it is not a question of whether or not the law of contracts has

B. The innocent handler

Undoubtedly, the greatest problems under the present law of conversion concern the "innocent handler". The difficulties seems to revolve around three principal ideas:

(a) that a person will often handle, or deal with goods, without asserting title on his own behalf and without altering or impairing the property of the owner;

(b) that such conduct will often be performed pursuant to a relationship which imposes upon the defendant a duty of obedience to perform the act complained of;

(c) that occasionally an act which does impair the owner's claim will have been performed with the very object of restoring the goods to him; an object which is frustrated by the conduct of a third party whom the defendant innocently enabled to perpetrate the deprivation.

The first two situations are distinguishable from the third, and have been the subject of certain ambiguous essays in mitigation. Thus, it is said that a merely "ministerial" handling of goods (i.e., one which changes only the position of the goods and not the property in them) is not a conversion, if performed at the request of an apparent owner who has the actual control of the goods.[4] According to Blackburn J. the handler will be relieved if (i) he deals with the goods at the request of the actual custodian in the bona fide belief that the person is the true owner, or has the true owner's authority, and (ii) the act of the defendant is of a kind which would be excused if done by the authority of the person in possession, if he were the finder of the goods or entrusted with their custody.[5] This test is not easy to apply and there is at least one case in which a defendant escaped liability although the imputed conduct involved transferring the goods to a third person in pursuance of a sale by the defendant's employer.[6] Despite criticism from other quarters,[7] the Law Reform Committee have recommended against a statutory reversal of this decision.[8] But the defendant's conduct must still (it seems) satisfy the general requirements of changing no more

---

called such a breach material but whether the breach is such as interferes, not with some rights of the owner, but with a substantial portion of his rights and interests in chattel". See further, p. 753, post. Cf. 2nd Restatement, *Torts* (1965), para. 228.

---

[4] Cmnd. 4774, para. 46.

[5] *Hollins* v. *Fowler* (1875) L.R. 7 H.L. 757, at 766-767.

[6] *National Mercantile Bank Ltd.* v. *Rymill* (1881) 44 L.T. 767 (auctioneer delivered goods to third person knowing that his client, who had originally deposited them with him for sale, had privately sold them to that third person, and having been instructed to make the delivery: aliter, if the defendant had actually effected the sale or, of course, if he had known of the adverse claim: Fleming, op. cit., p. 57; and see *Willis* v. *British Car Auctions Ltd.* (1978) *The Times* January 14th.

[7] Salmond, op. cit., p. 105, considers the decision inconsistent with both *Hollins* v. *Fowler* (supra) and *Stephens* v. *Elwall* (1815) 4 M. & S. 259, though it is conceded that there may be a distinction between the last of these cases and the decision in *Rymill* in that in the latter case "the goods were sent out of the jurisdiction to America which even today would be considered to have made it substantially more difficult for the true owner to recover them": Cmnd. 4774, para. 41. See also *James* v. *Oxley* (1939) 61 C.L.R. 433, and the *Willis* case, ante.

[8] Cmnd. 4774, para. 47. No change to the general rule is effected by the *Torts (Interference with Goods) Act* 1977.

than the location of the goods where the act in question results from a measure of discretion on its part, or represents a departure from the ordinary role played by institutions of the same character. In *Ernest Scragg & Sons Ltd.* v. *Perseverance Banking & Trust Co Ltd.*[9] the respondent bank, acting on behalf of an Israeli company, ordered machines from the appellants. The goods were duly shipped to Israel and the documents of title were forwarded to the respondents. They, instead of behaving in the usual manner of bankers and paying for the goods, sent the documents to the Israeli company. Lord Denning said:[10]

> That is the plainest possible conversion. It is not a mere ministerial act. It is assuming dominion over the goods themselves by means of the documents of title.

The line between ministerial and assertive acts is hard to draw; Fleming has suggested that the result should depend upon whether the innocent handling involves so serious an assumption of control that it deserves to be treated as an involuntary purchase.[11] Certainly there will continue to be cases in which this test is satisfied without any degree of moral blame on the part of the defendant. The Law Reform Committee have declined to recommend any radical change in the law on this subject, for a variety of reasons: the relative injustice of discriminating between the innocent handler and the innocent acquirer; the existence of the defence in *Rymill's* case to mitigate some of the rigours of the strict doctrine of conversion; the fact that many of the handlers subject to such liability will be carrying on business where this is an occupational hazard which may frequently be insured against; and the impracticability of operating any system of apportionment where the plaintiff's negligence has contributed to his loss.[12] But recognising that the proposed fusion of trespass and conversion into a single tort might impair the immunity of the innocent ministerial handler, they suggest that:

> . . . an act by a defendant which would not, on the ground that it was an innocent handling, have given rise under the existing law to liability in conversion, would not be deemed to be wrongful for the purposes of the proposed new tort, and the provision we recommend is that for the purposes of the proposed new tort an act of interference with property is not wrongful if it is shown that:
> (1) it was done on the instructions of the person in possession of the property; and
> (2) there was nothing in the circumstances to indicate to the defendant that the person in possession was not entitled to give such instructions; and
> (3) the instructions were such as a hirer of the property or, as the case may be, a person undertaking its custody for reward, might reasonably be expected to be entitled to give without specific authority from his bailor.[13]

Well-intentioned misdeliveries involve a different set of problems, because they generally produce a change in possession and an impairment

---

9 [1973] 2 Lloyd's Rep. 101.
10 Ibid., at 103.
11 Op. cit., p. 57.
12 Cmnd. 4774, para. 48.
13 Ibid., para. 50. Cf. ante, p. 132, n. 6.

of the owner's right to possess. It is clear that, in general circumstances, an innocent but active misdelivery of goods to a person not entitled to them will render the deliveror liable in conversion.[14] This result can follow where the defendant mistakenly assumes the transferee to be the owner[15] or where the defendant relies upon a promise by the transferee to return the goods to the person entitled.[16] It has been suggested[17] that liability should not be imposed where the act is done with the honest intention of giving effect to the owner's right over the chattel and is of a kind which any reasonable man would have done in the defendant's place; for in such cases there is no conduct necessarily constituting a denial of the plaintiff's right, and no act inconsistent therewith.[18] But this approach has yet to find favour with the courts and it is unlikely that any positive, unnecessary interference which facilitates the misappropriation of goods and amounts to a temporary assumption of the owner's rights by the defendant would (however well-intentioned) escape characterisation as a conversion.

Even where there is an unauthorised transfer, it must be one which disturbs the plaintiff's right of possession and is causally connected with the ensuing loss. In *Kitano* v. *Commonwealth of Australia*[19] the plaintiff was a Japanese national who was part owner of a yacht, the remaining shares being vested in M (the sailing master) and N and F (the other members of the crew). Upon arrival of the yacht in Darwin, all of them except for the plaintiff expressed their desire to return to Japan. He, having other intentions, obtained an export licence from the Commonwealth Authorities, thinking that this would prevent the other three from acting without his permission. He was also given an assurance that no customs clearance would be issued for the next twenty-four hours. However, the sailing master (M) obtained a clearance to leave the port, and the yacht sailed away without the plaintiff. His claim in conversion against the Commonwealth was rejected by the High Court on two grounds relevant to the present discussion. First, it was held that the issue by the Customs of a clearance to M, although wrongful, did not disturb the existing rights of possession of the plaintiff and M to the yacht. Secondly, even if the clearance were to be regarded as a transfer

---

[14] *Ashby* v. *Tolhurst* [1937] 2 K.B. 242; Fleming, op. cit., p. 57; *Joule Ltd.* v. *Poole* (1924) 24 S.R. (N.S.W.) 387. The strict liability does not, however, apply where the bailee delivers to the addressee or other person to whom he is instructed to deliver the goods, although that person may not, in fact, be entitled to them; *M'Kean* v. *M'Ivor* (1870) L.R. 6 Ex. 36. Where the bailee is unable to deliver goods and is obliged to keep them for longer than the contemplated period, it seems that he will be liable for any subsequent mis-delivery only if he did so dishonestly or negligently: *Duff* v. *Budd* (1822) 3 Brod. & Bing. 177; *Stephenson* v. *Hart* (1828) 4 Bing 476; *Heugh* v. *L.N.W.R.* (1870) L.R. 5 Ex. 51; (1921-1922) 6 *Minnesota Law Review*.

[15] *Helson* v. *McKenzies (Cuba St.) Ltd.* [1950] N.Z.L.R. 878 (shop employee handing lost handbag to person claiming to be owner); *Hollins* v. *J. Davy Ltd.* [1963] 1 Q.B. 844; *Sydney City Council* v. *West* (1965) 114 C.L.R. 481.

[16] *Hiort* v. *Bott* (1874) L.R. 9 Ex. 86; p. 126, ante.

[17] Burnett (1960) 76 L.Q.R. 364, at 371-372.

[18] Burnett seeks in this way to establish parity between the position of parties like the defendant in *Hiort* v. *Bott* (supra) and the duties of an involuntary bailee: as to the latter, see p. 387 et. seq., post.

[19] (1973) 2 A.L.R. 83. Cf. *Hiort* v. *Bott* (ante); *Bryanston Leasings* v. *Principality Finance Ltd.* [1977] R.T.R. 45.

by the customs to M of a right or title to possession, it was a transfer to a person who as co-owner was entitled to possession, and thus no tort had been committed against the plaintiff:

> In my view, by issuing the certificate the customs did not deal with the *Akitsushima* in a manner inconsistent with the rights of the plaintiff as a co-owner; nor can it be said that what it did was done with the intention of denying those rights. The issue of the certificate enabled M to sail the yacht away without breaching s. 118[20] but it did not give him possession of the yacht . . . The issue of the clearance did not operate as a delivery of possession of the yacht from customs to M. He and his companions already had possession . . . The deprivation sustained by the plaintiff was his exclusion from possession which was effected, not by issue of the certificate, but by the action of his companions in sailing the boat away.[21]

C. Contributory negligence as a defence to conversion

Many cases of conversion involve two entirely innocent parties: the owner, whose chattel has been misappropriated by a fraudulent intermediary, and the defendant, who has acquired it in good faith either directly or indirectly from the intermediary himself.[22] In such a case, it is invariably the defendant who (unless he can establish one of the exceptions to the nemo dat principle) will suffer: "The Courts have always favoured the original owner at the expense of the innocent purchaser."[23]

Because of the harshness of this principle, and because the owner will often have parted with the chattel in circumstances which suggest a lack of circumspection on his part, the idea has been advanced of allowing the defendant in cases of innocent conversion to plead the plaintiff's negligence as a ground for reducing his liability, under the various contributory negligence statutes in force in England and Australia.[24] Apportionment of the ensuing loss has been advocated both judicially[25] and academically[26] as the fairest and most appropriate solution to this problem, where the plaintiff's own carelessness has contributed to his loss and the defendant had neither knowledge of, nor the intention to deny, the title of the plaintiff. Indeed, such a defence has actually been sustained in two decisions, from New Zealand[27] and England[28] respectively. In the first of these cases, the plaintiff lost her handbag (containing some £422) in the defendants' store. Another customer handed it in to an employee of the defendants. Without inspecting its contents, and relying only on a description, he delivered it to a third person who claimed to be the owner. The Court of Appeal upheld the plaintiff's claim for conversion

---

20 Customs Act 1901-1971 (Com.).
21 (1973) 2 A.L.R. 83, at 98. Cf. s. 10, *Torts (Interference with Goods) Act,* 1977.
22 For a characteristic case, see *Lewis* v. *Averay* [1971] 3 W.L.R. 603.
23 *Wilton* v. *Commonwealth Trading Bank Ltd.* [1973] 2 N.S.W.L.R. 644, at 666 per Samuel J.
24 In England, the *Law Reform (Contributory Negligence) Act* 1945.
25 By Devlin L.J. in *Ingram* v. *Little* [1961] 1 Q.B. 31, at 73-74.
26 Burnett (1960) 76 L.Q.R. 364; Roebuck (1969) *University of Tasmania Law Review* 191; Glanville Williams, *Joint Torts,* pp. 210-212 (the same author did, in fact, draft such a provision into the Irish *Civil Liability Act* 1961, s. 34).
27 *Helson* v. *McKenzies (Cuba St.) Ltd.* [1950] N.Z.L.R. 878 (N.Z.C.A.).
28 *Lumsden* v. *London Trustee Savings Bank Ltd.* [1970] 1 Lloyd's Rep. 114 (High Court, Donaldson J.).

but reduced her damages by three-fourths. Their decision is unsatisfactory for two reasons. First, it is difficult to see the causal connexion
between the plaintiff's negligence (said to consist in her leaving a
handbag containing so large a sum of money upon the counter) and the
ultimate misdelivery by the defendants.[29] They knew that they were in
possession of property which was not their own and that they were
under no obligation to deal with it in the particular way they chose; the
case is far removed from that of an innocent purchaser who, merely by
purchasing and taking delivery, may commit a conversion.[30] It was the
lack of such connection, and the causal exhaustion of the plaintiff's
original inadvertence, that formed the foundation of the dissenting
judgment of Finlay J. in the Court of Appeal,[31] although the learned
judge did not appear to doubt that as a general principle the New Zealand
Contributory Negligence Act 1947 could apply between the parties.
Secondly, no authority has cited in support of this contention and none
of the judges gave reasons for so holding;[32] partly, perhaps, because
counsel for the defendants denied throughout that there had been a
conversion in the first place.

Lumsden v. *London Trustee Savings Bank Ltd.*[33] involved an action
for the conversion of cheques; a field which, it has been suggested, "is
a corner of its own"[34] and from which it may be unsafe to predicate
conclusions applying to the conversion of chattels generally.[35] The
decision is not unambiguous[36] and the only authority cited which was
directly in point was that of *Helson's* case. It would be a bold court
which sought to rely upon these authorities alone.

Against these decisions must be placed the exhaustive and careful
analysis of Samuel J. in *Wilton* v. *Commonwealth Trading Bank Ltd.*,[37]
where a directly opposite conclusion was reached. Samuel J's judgment
(which dealt with an action for the conversion of cheques, but is not
specifically limited to such cases) was the first to properly consider
whether contributory negligence had ever been a total defenec to an
action for conversion before the passing of the provisions for apportionment in the *Law Reform (Miscellaneous Provisions) Act* 1965.[38]

Samuel J. admitted[39] that his conclusion was based "more upon
silence or dicta than upon any case which precisely decides the point",
but found himself persuaded by the frequent expressions of opinion to the

---

[29] Cf. (1921-1922) 35 *Harvard Law Review* 873, where it is said that the defendant
sued for misdelivery under an involuntary bailment will not generally be able to
plead contributory negligence because of the last opportunity doctrine. This
doctrine has, as a substantive principle, now been discredited in England: see
Winfield and Jolowicz, *Tort* (10th ed.), p. 113. But there must still, of course, be
a connection between the two events.
[30] See p. 128 et seq., ante.
[31] Relying principally upon *Davies* v. *Mann* (1842) 10 M. & W. 546; 152 E.R. 588.
[32] See the masterly analysis of this decision by Samuel J. in *Wilton* v. *Commonwealth Trading Bank Ltd.* [1973] 2 N.S.W.L.R. 644, at 653-654.
[33] [1971] 1 Lloyd's Rep. 114.
[34] Salmond, op. cit., p. 106, n. 48.
[35] Note the protection afforded to a collecting bank by s. 4 of the *Cheques Act* 1957.
[36] Cmnd. 4774, para. 101, n. 3.
[37] [1973] 2 N.S.W.L.R. 644, at 653-667.
[38] This being the relevant N.S.W. statute.
[39] [1973] 2 N.S.W.L.R. 644, at 666.

effect that mere carelessness on the part of an owner of property cannot, without more, divest him of his title to the goods.[40] Accordingly, the defence of contributory negligence could not now be invoked to reduce the damages recoverable by a plaintiff whose neglect had allegedly contributed to the defendant's innocent (albeit negligent) receipt and appropriation of the plaintiff's cheques.[41] Samuel J. went on to hold that, even if this conclusion were wrong, the defendants had failed to discharge their onus of proving that the plaintiff's negligence had in fact been causally connected with the ultimate conversion.[42] His approach to the general issue is, to some extent, reinforced by the decision of the House of Lords in a more recent case concerning estoppel in pais.[43]

There can be little doubt that, in Australia at least, the decision in *Wilton's* case will be regarded as determining the question. The result coincides with the policy urged in England by successive Law Reform Committees.[44] In their Report on Conversion on Detinue, the Committee endorsed their criticisms of this defence as stated in the earlier report and remarked that, if it were admitted:

> . . . much judicial time would be occupied, to little advantage, in considering what particular precautions are required from householders against burglars, or from an ordinary citizen against pickpockets, or from a store proprietor against shoplifters.[45]

Accordingly, it seems improbable that legislation will be implemented in England to authorise the apportionment of responsibility for losses in actions for conversion, or that any judicial reform will take place to the same effect.[46]

However, it should be pointed out that the negligence of the plaintiff may be material in raising an estoppel against his assertion of title[47]

---

[40] Among the authorities relied upon were: *Bank of Ireland* v. *The Trustees of Evans' Charities in Ireland* (1855) 5 H.L. Cas. 389, at 413 (Lord Cranworth L.C.); *Scholfield* v. *The Earl of Landesburgh* [1896] A.C. 514, at 521, 522 (Lord Halsbury L.C.); *Farquarson Bros. & Co. Ltd.* v. *King & Co. Ltd.* [1902] A.C. 325, at 329-331, 335, 337 (Lord Halsbury L.C. and Lord MacNaghten); *Lloyd's Bank* v. *The Chartered Bank of India etc* .[1929] 1 K.B. 40, at 60. (Scrutton L.J.): *Lloyd's Bank Ltd.* v. *E. B. Savory & Co.* [1933] A.C. 201, at 236 (Lord Wright): *Jerome* v. *Bentley & Co.* [1952] 2 All E.R. 114, at 118 (Donovan J.); *Central Newbury Car Auctions Ltd.* v. *Unity Finance Ltd.* [1957] 1 Q.B. 371, at 379 (Denning L.J.). See also the *Twitchings* case, infra.

[41] The N.S.W. Act, like the English and the New Zealand, extended the defence to all cases where a person suffered damage as a result partly of his own fault and partly of the fault of any other person(s), "fault" being defined as "negligence, or other act or omission which gives rise to liability in tort or would, apart from this Part, give rise to the defence of contributory negligence": s. 9, ibid.

[42] [1973] 2 N.S.W.L.R., at 667-671.

[43] *Moorgate Mercantile Co. Ltd.* v. *Twitchings* [1976] 2 All E.R. 641; and see *Willis* v. *British Car Auctions Ltd.* (1978) *The Times*, January 14th, per Lord Denning M.R.

[44] 12th Report, *The Transfer of Title to Chattels* (1966) Cmnd. 2958; 18th Report, *Conversion and Detinue* (1971) Cmnd. 4774. And see now *Torts (Interference with Goods) Act*, 1977, s. 11(1), which confirms these views.

[45] Cmnd. 4774, para. 81: see also para. 48; ante, p. 133. But cf. para. 101, where it is conceded that there may be strong arguments for extending the defence to collecting banks: it is felt, however, that such a reform would best be considered in the context of a review of banking law and not upon the more general level with which the Committee was presently concerned.

[46] This has since been endorsed by s. 11(1) of the *Torts (Interference with Goods) Act*, 1977.

[47] Vaines, *Personal Property* (5th ed.), Chapter 9.

or in disentitling him, where he has lent his signature to a document, from raising the defence of non est factum.[48] Both of these defences are beyond the scope of this book.

D. Conversion of documents and tokens

Special problems are caused by the conversion of articles which possess a low intrinsic worth but a high potential or exchange value. Although there can only be conversion of a chattel, and not of an intangible thing,[49] it is clearly unsatisfactory to disregard the consequential value of such tokens when assessing damages for their conversion. The defendant who destroys a season ticket, or a cheque, or even a winning football coupon[50] is clearly damnifying the owner to a far greater extent than the value of the paper itself. Accordingly, the courts have begun to allow plaintiffs in actions for conversion to recover, in effect, the value of the rights or benefits which the document or other token represents, and which have, as the result of the defendant's conduct, been impaired.

To a large extent, this involves a question of damages[51] rather than an examination of what constitutes a conversion. But the latter question may become material in a number of ways: first, because so many documents are dependent upon questions of time for their validity and, secondly, because they may be made valueless without any degree of physical destruction. It may accordingly be necessary to decide whether such misconduct as delay in the delivery of an ephemeral token, or the arrogation of the rights or opportunities it represents without any tangible impairment of the token itself, should constitute conversion.

Nevertheless, the principal issue is undoubtedly the quantification of loss. In the case of cheques, the courts have long permitted the expedient of suing for conversion of the piece of paper upon which the cheque is written, but allowing as damages the amount of the cheque.[52] In a recent decision,[53] Roskill J. held that this principle should be confined to documents which were, or were in the nature of, negotiable instruments, or what are sometimes called quasi-negotiable instruments, such as bills of lading.[54] Accordingly, he declined to assess damages against the Post

---

[48] See *Saunders v. Anglia Building Society Ltd.* [1971] A.C. 1004; *Petelin v. Cullen* (1975) 6 A.L.R. 129; *United Dominions Trust Ltd. v. Western* [1976] 2 W.L.R. 64.
[49] *The Queen v. Hansford* [1974] 8 S.A.S.R. 164, at 169 per Bray C.J.; cf. *Roufos v. Brewster* [1971] 2 S.A.S.R. 218, at 234 per Zelling J.
[50] Cf. *B.W.I.A. Ltd. v. Bart* (1966) 11 W.I.R. 378; p. 822, post.
[51] Ante, p. 63.
[52] *Lloyd's Bank Ltd. v. The Chartered Bank of India etc.* [1929] 1 K.B. 40, at 56 per Scrutton L.J.; *Morrison v. London County and Westminster Bank Ltd.* [1914] 3 K.B. 356, at 365-366 per Lord Reading C.J.; *The Queen v. Hansford* [1974] 8 S.A.S.R. 164, at 169 per Bray C.J.
[53] *Building & Civil Engineering Holidays Scheme Management Ltd. v. Post Office* [1964] 2 Q.B. 430.
[54] Ibid., at 445: "It is not necessary here to consider whether the same rule will apply to such documents as docks or warehouses warrants". Cf. *Bavins Jnr. & Sims v. London and South Western Bank Ltd.* [1900] 1 Q.B. 270, distinguished by Roskill J. at 446. In *Ernest Scragg and Sons Ltd. v. Perseverance Banking and Trust Co. Ltd.* [1973] 2 Lloyd's Rep. 101, Lord Denning M.R. applied the rule relating to cheques to a conversion of documents of title to goods, which had been sold by the plaintiffs but not yet paid for. He awarded an amount equivalent to the price of the goods; adding that since their price was the same in this case as damages for conversion, there was no need for the plaintiffs to elect between the two.

Office for the conversion of a quantity of holiday credit stamps on any ground other than "their value as small pieces of printed paper and no more."[55] This decision was reversed on appeal[56] on the ground that the appropriate cause of action was not conversion but a special statutory cause of action arising under s. 9(2) of the *Crown Proceedings Act* 1947.[57] In the course of his judgment, Lord Denning M.R. observed:

> One thing is quite clear. The Post Office is a bailee of the registered packet and when you examine this new statutory cause of action you will find that it is very much like the action which the common law gives on a bailment . . . An action against a bailee can often be put, not as an action in contract, nor in tort, but as an action on its own, sui generis, arising out of the possession had by the bailee of the goods . . . The incidents of this cause of action are not to be found by look- ing at the old books on detinue and trover . . . At common law in a case of bailment, the general principle is restitutio in integrum, which means that the party damnified is entitled to such a sum of money as will put him in as good a position as if the goods had not been lost or damaged . . . subject, however, to the qualification that they must be such damages as flow directly and in the usual course of things from the loss or damage . . .[58]

In fact, it seems that Roskill J.'s opinion as to the level of recovery in conversion may have been misconceived[59] and that this remedy would in any event allow for damages to be assessed above and beyond the mere intrinsic value of the token or document itself.[60] In the words of the Law Reform Committee, "the true measure of damages in respect of a token may vary according to the circumstances from a face value to a trivial cost of replacing the token itself."[61]

The fact remains, however, that before this measure can be applied, it must be shown that the defendant's conduct amounted to a conversion. In the case of paper or tokens with a value limited by time this could be exceedingly difficult. Suppose, for instance, that the defendant 'borrows' a season ticket for a particular journey and then returns it to the owner. This would presumably be conversion because he has exercised the rights of the owner and because it is not necessary that he should have per- manently deprived the other of his ticket;[62] although if mere damage to a chattel falling short of destruction is not conversion it is a little difficult to understand why the mere partial consumption of the value of the ticket should constitute the tort. But suppose, on the other hand, that the defendants in *Building & Civil Holidays Scheme Management Ltd.* v. *Post Office*[63] had negligently delayed delivery of the stamps so that, by

[55] [1964] 2 Q.B., at 447. Order of payment out to plaintiffs of 1s. in court.
[56] [1966] 1 Q.B. 247.
[57] See *Post Office Act* 1969, s. 30.
[58] [1966] 1 Q.B. 247, at 260-261.
[59] Cmnd. 4774, para. 90.
[60] Salmond, op. cit., p. 102; Cmnd. 4774, at para. 91, where the following examples are given: ship, rail and air tickets, theatre and luggage tickets, travellers' cheques, bank and other credit cards, club membership cards, car log books, book tokens, trading coupons and stamps, and gaming chips. To which one might add, football coupons and lottery tickets.
[61] Ibid.
[62] Ante, p. 129.
[63] Supra.

the time they arrived, they were worthless. Of course, such conduct could be actionable as a breach of contract, but this would be of little value to a non-contracting party who had suffered heavily from the negligent delay, even where he was the owner of the tokens. This was, in fact, the position in *British West Indian Airways Ltd.* v. *Bart*,[64] where the plaintiff handed his winning football coupon to a local distributor for transmission to England. The distributor in turn handed it to the defendant airline but, due to the latter's inefficiency, the coupon was rendered valueless by delay. The Guyanan Court of Appeal dismissed the claim, holding that the only right of action against a sub-bailee lay in tort and that in the present case no tort had been committed.

It is not suggested that the best solution for cases of this kind necessarily lies in some modification of the tort of conversion. The mere negligent loss of goods is not conversion[65] and it would seem logical to apply this rule a fortiori to cases of negligent delay. But whereas a plaintiff whose goods have been negligently lost by a bailee may have an action for detinue,[66] the plaintiff whose goods have been negligently delayed will not.[67] Without a contract, the traditional Common Law remedies would appear to be valueless. There may well be other examples of conduct which will render a document valueless without providing a discernible remedy in tort.

For this reason, Lord Denning's advocacy of a separate principle for bailments is attractive. If pushed beyond the immediate frontier of damages, it could remove the necessity of proving that the defendant's conduct under a non-contractual bailment falls within the established categories of tort. Instead, recovery would depend upon proof of a failure to comply with the terms of the bailment, and these terms could be established by reference to all the circumstances of the transaction; including (where appropriate) the terms of any contract between the bailee and an intermediate bailor. To cast the bailee's Common Law duties exclusively within the mould of established torts could severely hamper the satisfactory enforcement of remedies for the economic destruction of tokens or documents that are held subject to a gratuitous bailment, a sub-bailment or even an unvaried bailment for reward.

A recent decision from the Supreme Court of British Columbia shows how easily the tort of conversion can sometimes be adapted to meet new and unusual demands. In *Borden Chemical Co. (Canada) Ltd.* v. *J. G. Beukers Ltd.*[68] the defendants were indebted to the plaintiffs to the tune of $30,000 for supplies of a chemical called Cling, in respect of which they had been appointed the plaintiff's distributors. As security for their delinquent account (and, it was held, for no other purpose)[69] they assigned to the plaintiffs their accounts receivable, which involved handing the

---

[64] (1966) 11 W.I.R. 378; post, p. 822.
[65] *Attersol* v. *Briant* (1808) 1 Camp. 409; *Lee Cooper Ltd.* v. *C.H. Jeakins & Sons Ltd.* [1967] 2 Q.B. 1.
[66] Post, p. 149.
[67] Unless, perhaps, the delay is a substantial one and he makes his demand for the goods a substantial time before it is over.
[68] (1973) 29 D.L.R. (3d) 337.
[69] Ibid., at 341.

plaintiffs a copy of their customer list. The plaintiffs, having acquired possession of this list, used it to deal directly with the customers on their own account, and the defendants issued a counter-claim for conversion of their "entire distribution system". McKay J. held that there had been a conversion, but only of the customer list, and approving Salmond's statement that the appropriate level of damages is the value of the converted property together with damages for its detention,[70] he awarded the defendants $20,000. In arriving at this figure, he took into account the value of the list to both companies, the fact that the plaintiffs would have paid a reasonable sum to acquire it, and the fact that supplies of Cling to the defendant company had already been cut off before the latter's bankruptcy.

There can be little doubt that this result was a desirable one, and that the approach adopted in *Borden's* case could alleviate many of the problems of a mishandling of documents in a non-contractual situation.[71] But there are limits to its efficacy and it seems unlikely that a court would readily characterise every misuse of intellectual or economic property as a conversion of the document which symbolises or contains it.[72] To do so would involve the artificiality not only of equating the intangible benefits of a document with the material personality of that document itself, but of asserting that conduct which may involve no physical touching or impairment of that document (for instance, allowing a third party to look at it) can of itself constitute conversion.[73] In the absence of any specific principle of restitution, it may be preferable to construct the plaintiff's remedy around the terms, both express and implied, of the bailment under which the document was originally delivered and to hold that any loss sustained by the bailor, as the result of a breach of that bailment is recoverable from the bailee. In this way, the existence of a bailment would provide fluid principles for the identification of conduct as remediable without the need to allot that conduct to one of the present spectrum of torts. Both the existence of the wrong and (as Lord Denning has suggested) the quantification of the loss would depend upon the peculiar rules of that relation. In such a way, it may

---

[70] 15th ed., p. 146; cf. 16th ed., p. 579.

[71] Cf. the problem posed by Bray C.J. in *Roufos* v. *Brewster and Brewster* [1971] 2 S.A.S.R. 218, at 223-224, set out at p. 319, post.

[72] A fortiori where there is no document. The decision in *Borden* may be contrasted with the Californian case of *Olschewski* v. *Hudson* (1927) 87 Cal. App. 282; 262 Pac. 43. Here the plaintiff (trustee in bankruptcy to a laundry company) sued the executor of a former driver employed by the company for conversion of a laundry route. The driver had knowledge of the list of customers but it was not proved that he actually possessed any such list. The conversion allegedly consisted in the driver's refusal to turn over a list of customers to the bankrupt's vendee, and his sale of this route to a third party. The court held that trover could not be maintained for interference with an intangible property right. See also *Mackay* v. *Benjamin Franklin Co.* (1927) 288 Pa. 207; 135 Atl. 613: trover does not lie for the appropriation of ideas unaccompanied by wrongful dealing with the documents containing them. This decision is discussed in (1926-1927) 40 *Harvard Law Review* 1017. Both cases seem to accept, in principle, that an action for conversion of ideas or information may proceed upon a misuse of an actual document embodying them.

[73] Cf. *Thurston* v. *Charles* (1905) 21 T.L.R. 659, where damages of £400 were awarded in trespass against a defendant who showed a private letter without authority to a third person.

be possible to secure restitution of benefits by a wrongdoer where the owner has himself suffered no loss. Certainly, it could be undesirable for the plaintiff's action in a case like *Borden's* to be dependent upon specific loss, and unfortunate perhaps if he were unable to recover the amount of profit made by the wrongdoer, whether or not that profit would otherwise have accrued to him In those cases of bailment, at least, which involve the provision of services to the bailor by the bailee (and this is arguably every bailment that produces a duty of care) there are powerful arguments for aggregating the duties owed by the bailee with those owed by an ordinary servant or agent[74] and for casting the bailee's duties in a fiduciary rather than a purely compensatory mould.

E. Restitution of benefits where there is no accompanying loss to the plaintiff

In *Strand Electric and Engineering Co. Ltd.* v. *Brisford Entertainments Ltd.*[75] the defendants detained and used a number of portable switchboards belonging to the plaintiffs. The plaintiffs, who leased out such equipment as part of their normal business operations, claimed that their damages should include a sum equivalent to the market hiring rate for the equipment. The trial judge upheld this claim, but made deductions for the period during which the defendants could reasonably have examined the plaintiffs' right to call for the goods, and for the fact that the plaintiffs would have been unlikely to have leased all the items of equipment during the period of the detention. This assessment was varied on appeal. The Court of Appeal held that where the goods detained are of a kind which the defendant normally leases for reward, and the defendant has enjoyed the beneficial use of them during the relevant period, the plaintiff's loss is to be assessed by reference to what it would have cost the defendant, on the normal market, to hire goods of that description for an equivalent period. Somervell L.J. pointed out that to award a lesser sum would be to allow the defendants to profit from their own wrong.[76]

Both Somervell and Romer L.JJ. regarded such an amount as no more than the loss suffered by the plaintiff[77] and considered the value of the benefit received by the defendant from his unlawful user as irrelevant to this assessment. Both declined to commit themselves as to whether a similar principle should apply in cases where the goods are of a nonprofit earning character or, being of such character, are not normally employed by the plaintiff for that purpose. Denning L.J., while concurring on the specific point at issue, went further and formulated a general principle for the restitution of benefits obtained by the unpermitted user of a chattel. In his view, any wrongdoer who makes use of a chattel which is not his own must pay a reasonable hire for it, irrespective

---

[74] Cf. *Aluminium Industrie Vaassen* v. *Romalpa Industries Ltd.* [1976] 2 All E.R. 552 (bailee for sale held to occupy fiduciary position for the purposes of the rules as to tracing).

[75] [1952] 2 Q.B. 246.

[76] Ibid., at 250. Presumably the same principle would apply in relation to a period over which the defendant converts goods by using them for his own benefit.

[77] Ibid., at 252, 256; cf. Denning L.J. at 253.

of whether the hirer has suffered loss as a result, or whether such loss amounts to less than the notional hiring charge. This liability (which Denning L.J. did not express to be limited to cases where the plaintiff normally employed the goods in a profit-earning capacity) was founded upon the benefit received by the defendant. It therefore did not extend to cases in which the goods were merely detained and not used.[78]

Although Denning L.J. formulated his rule in terms of "a wrongdoer", it is submitted that the principle of restitution should not be restricted to situations in which the benefitting party has committed a specific tort against the plaintiff. The deliberate misuse of goods will not always be accompanied by their unlawful detention and in many cases will not constitute conversion.[79] Nor will it necessarily amount to a trespass as against the owner; for instance, where a defendant who has become a subsidiary bailee has misused the goods with the permission of an original bailee.[80] To enchain the plaintiff's right of restitution to his ability to prove an established wrong could expose many situations in which the defendant would be free to profit from his moral, if not legal, transgression.

One decision in which this was allowed to occur was *McKenna & Armistead Pty. Ltd.* v. *Excavations Pty. Ltd.*[81] Here, a seller in possession of goods used them for his own business purposes prior to the date fixed for delivery. The Court doubted whether this constituted conversion but was prepared to award damages, under the terms of the bailment, for deterioration resulting from the unauthorised use. Having decided, however, that there was no evidence upon which an assessment of such deterioration could be based,[82] the Court went on to refuse to award a reasonable hiring fee as advocated by Denning L.J. in the *Strand Electric* case. The ground for so holding was that the defendants were not, at the material time, under a duty to deliver the goods to the plaintiff and were accordingly neither depriving them of possession nor causing them any loss.[83]

It is submitted that this decision, by confining itself to the narrow facts of the *Strand Electric* case and by disregarding the wider principle enunciated by Denning L.J. (a principle at no point explicitly discountenanced by his fellow members of the Court of Appeal) produced an unnecessarily rigid and unfortunate result. The regrettable nature of the decision is accentuated by the fact that the defendants were direct bailees for reward from the plaintiffs and enjoyed their user of the goods in direct breach of that bailment. The notion that a bailee who misuses goods without causing loss to his bailor is entitled to keep the resultant saving or profit unless, perhaps, his conduct amounts to a conversion, is one which seems repugnant to justice and which indicates the need

---

[78] Ibid., at 254-255. See also *Capital Finance Ltd.* v. *Bray* [1964] 1 W.L.R. 23, at 329; cf. *Hutseal* v. *I.A.C. Ltd.* (1973) 48 D.L.R. (3d) 638.
[79] Ante, p. 130.
[80] Ante, p. 121.
[81] [1957] S.R. (N.S.W.) 515.
[82] They were secondhand goods.
[83] It was conceded (at 519) that the plaintiffs might have been able to demand the goods upon hearing of the misuse, but this was dismissed as a relevant consideration because no such demand had been made.

for a more catholic, or trans-conceptual, approach to the liability of defaulting bailees. It contrasts unfavourably with the decision in *Borden Chemical Co. (Canada) Ltd.* v. *J. G. Beukers Ltd.*,[84] where the damages awarded bore little relation to the loss sustained by the plaintiff[85] and concentrated primarily upon the benefit to the defendant; in this case, corresponding with the value *to them* of the document that had been converted. Although the court in that case held the defendants liable in conversion, it seems that it would be both unnecessary and undesirable to limit the principle of restitution to such cases. The defendants in *Borden* were bailees who, by breaching the bailment and misusing the bailed property, had made a profit which was not reflected in any loss to the bailor. Since bailees have peculiar opportunities for the misuse of property entrusted to them and are (in a loose sense) in the service of their bailors, it is submitted that they should be regarded for this purpose as occupying a fiduciary position.[86] A fiduciary must disgorge profits received in the course of his duties irrespective of whether he has intercepted them from the person to whom his fiduciary duty is owed,[87] and there is no reason why the same strict accountability should not apply to a bailee. Such accountability should include, where appropriate, not only a reasonable hiring fee for the goods but any further profit or advantage accruing as a result of the unauthorised user.[88] A recent decision lends some colour to this view. In *MacAlpine & Son Ltd.* v. *Minimax Ltd.*[89] the plaintiffs bailed the damaged remains of two fire extinguishers (which were alleged to have exploded on their premises) to the defendants, who had originally supplied them and had requested their temporary return for the purpose of compiling a report in respect

---

[84] (1973) 29 D.L.R. (3d) 337; ante, p. 140.

[85] In fact, they went bankrupt and could not have used the customer list anyway.

[86] As they may be for others: see *Aluminium Industrie Vaassen* v. *Romalpa Aluminium Ltd.* [1976] 2 All E.R. 552; post, p. 155.

[87] *Keech* v. *Sandford* (1726) Sel. Cas. Ch. 61; *A.G.* v. *Goddard* (1929) 98 L.J.K.B. 743; *Reading* v. *A.G.* [1951] A.C. 507; *Regal (Hastings) Ltd.* v. *Gulliver* [1942] 1 All E.R. 378; *Boardman* v. *Phipps* [1967] 2 A.C. 46; *Industrial Development Consultants Ltd.* v. *Cooley* [1972] 2 All E.R. 162; *Peso Silver Mines Ltd.* v. *Cropper* (1966) 58 D.L.R. (2d) 1; *Canadian Aero Service Ltd.* v. *O'Malley* (1974) 40 D.L.R. (3d) 371.

[88] In the *Strand Electric* case [1952] 2 Q.B. 246, at 255 Denning L.J., after remarking that it was unnecessary to allocate the owner's remedy for recovery of hiring-charges to any formal category, continued: "I can imagine cases where an owner might be entitled to the profits made by a wrongdoer by the use of a chattel, but I do not think this is such a case." In the absence of any reason for this opinion, it may be suggested that the *Strand Electric* case is distinguishable from the situation posed in the text in that the plaintiff and defendant were not parties to an orthodox consensual bailment arising by direct delivery inter partes: the plaintiffs had originally loaned the switchboards to B. Ltd., who had agreed to purchase the defendants' theatre and were let into possession thereof prior to completion. The switchboards were delivered to the premises and the defendants came into possession of them when they subsequently resumed possession of the theatre. Thus, they had not originally bargained for possession (though they fought hard to retain it) and may have been considered exempt from a rule of accountability of profits which (it is submitted) should affect ordinary bailees. But while it might be harsh to impose a duty to restore profits upon every category of 'quasi-bailee' (e.g. a finder who cannot find the owner and uses the goods for many years before they are rediscovered) it does not seem that the present case was an especially meritorious one for exemption from this form of restitution.

[89] [1970] 1 Lloyd's Rep. 397, esp. at 421-422.

of threatened litigation by the plaintiffs. The extinguishers were never returned and the plaintiffs sued in detinue. Thesiger J. refused to confine the resultant damages to the value of the damaged extinguishers themselves and ordered delivery up of the completed report. He said:

> Any report received afterwards was one obtained by the use of the plaintiff's property, and both in justice and equity the defendants were under an obligation to show it to the plaintiffs. I see no reason why, in the circumstances, it was not equivalent to money had and received for the use of the plaintiffs. I think support for the plaintiffs' submission to me is to be found in the observations of Denning L.J. [as he then was] in *Strand Electric and Engineering Co. Ltd.* v. *Brisford Entertainment Ltd.* [supra]. If, as suggested in *Mayne & McGregor on Damages* [12th ed., p. 619, para. 715] "the plaintiff could always recover, beyond his proved loss, to the extent of the benefit conferred on the defendant by his use of the goods", I can see no reason why I should not give judgment as I am asked [for delivering up the report].

Again, this was a case of detinue, but there seems no reason why the same result should not have applied where the defendants' "use of the plaintiffs' property" did not fall within any of the established categories of tort but merely amounted to a breach of the terms upon which the profit-producing chattel was originally bailed. Indeed, there are strong reasons for regarding the restitutionary aspect of such liability as a separate cause of action in itself, even in those cases where the receipt of the unjust benefit stems from the commission of a tort. As a general rule, plaintiffs in conversion (and presumably detinue) can recover no more than their actual loss.[90] It is submitted that, rather than to expand and obscure the already vexed issue of damages that can be awarded for conversion and detinue, the courts should approach the question of a bailee's duty to account (and indeed the duty to account owed by any third party) through the entirely separate medium of unjust enrichment, thereby also liberating that duty from the necessity for the commission of any tort.

F. Bailments and conversion[91]

The principles which characterise an act as conversion, and identify the plaintiff's title to sue, are of general application; they do not depend upon either party's being party to a bailment. For the most part, their assimilation into the bailment context is straightforward and unexceptional. Thus, a bailor who enjoys the immediate right to possess may sue both his bailee and any third party who commits an act of conversion; and a bailee who rebails the chattel to his bailor for a limited purpose or period may maintain conversion for conduct occurring after the agreed events have expired.

However, a number of special observations should be made about the operation of this remedy against a bailee:

(1) It is said that a bailee does not commit conversion by putting the

---

[90] Ante, p. 63.
[91] See *Torts (Interference with Goods) Act* 1977, s. 2(2).

goods in the care or custody of his servant,[92] even, it seems, where this delegation is not explicitly countenanced by the bailor. The traditional reason is that the servant does not acquire possession and there is accordingly no interference with the bailor's right to possess; the bailee does not alter his own position in relation to the goods.[93] But it is suggested that this rule must be read subject to the nature of the transfer and to the possibility that a servant may, in certain circumstances, be constituted a bailee.[94] In most cases, a bailor can be taken to have consented to the delegation of the bailee's duty to a competent and honest servant. Where the servant is not of this description, or where such delegation is in any event prohibited by the terms of the bailment, the risk to the goods or the deliberate misdealing with them may well constitute a conversion, whether the servant actually gets possession or not. This is an area in which it is impossible to be dogmatic, for each case must clearly depend on its own facts.

(2) A bailee who holds over on the expiration of the bailment does not per se become a converter.[95] Whether he is guilty of conversion depends upon the intention with which he retains the goods and the sort of conduct by which he effects that retention. He continues, in any event, to owe the duties of a bailee, and if the delay in redelivery is due to his own fault he will become an insurer of the goods.

(3) On the other hand, it seems clears that a bailee who, wrongfully and without authority, sub-bails the goods to an independent third party, does commit a conversion. In this case he has parted with possession and has, at least potentially, impaired the bailor's ability to recover the goods. In *Garnham, Harris and Elton Ltd.* v. *Alfred W. Ellis (Transport) Ltd.*,[96] there was held to be a conversion where the sub-contractors were chosen negligently and the goods were subsequently stolen. It is submitted that, even without these additional factors, the unauthorised nature of the sub-bailment may have sufficed to raise a case in conversion against the principal bailees. However, much may depend upon the degree of risk to the goods and the circumstances under which the sub-bailment was made. A conscionable breach of orders in an unforeseen emergency is clearly entitled to a more favourable interpretation than a breach brought about by laziness or inefficiency. In such a case, the court may be willing to deny that there has been a conversion and to hold the bailee liable only for actual losses consequent upon his deviation (if any) from the terms of the bailment. Again, however, it will be largely a question of fact.

So far as concerns the sub-bailee himself, it is submitted that liability depends upon whether he knew that the sub-bailment was unauthorised. If he did not, he should be regarded as occupying a similar position to the finder, who does not convert merely by taking the chattel into his

---

92 *Canot* v. *Hughes* (1836) 2 Bing. N.C. 448, where the "servant" in question was an attorney; cf. *Alexander* v. *Southey* (1821) 106 E.R. 1183.
93 Fleming, op. cit., p. 57.
94 Chapter 7, post.
95 Cmnd. 4774, para. 40.
96 [1967] 2 All E.R. 940.

custody. It may be otherwise, however, where the sub-bailee asserts a lien in respect of work he has performed on the goods.

(4) Involuntary bailees[97] appear to be exempt from the traditionally strict liability in conversion and, provided they deal with the chattel in good faith, to be liable only if negligent. Such at least has been held to be the rule where the bailee is attempting to restore the goods to their owner,[98] and it seems that this principle is of general application.

(5) The identification of conduct as conversion can cause difficulties where the defendant is a sub-bailee who knows of a particular prohibition within the original bailment. Suppose, for instance, that A bails bottles to B forbidding him to fill them with wine not manufactured by A; and that B sub-bails the bottles to C, who knows of the original prohibition. Taken in the abstract, a filling of the bottles by C may or may not amount to conversion. The question is whether its identity as such is strengthened or established by C's knowledge (as a sub-bailee) that this is something A has forbidden B to do. This problem arose in *Penfolds Wines Pty. Ltd. v. Elliott*,[99] where Latham C.J. clearly considered the terms of the earlier bailment relevant to the liability of the secondary bailee:

> I assume (and I think rightly) in favour of the defendant that his brother, who obtained the bottles from a retailer of the plaintiff's wines, was a sub-bailee of the bottles with the same rights as against the plaintiff as the original bailee (the retailer) including a right to use the bottles for the purpose of once using etc. the wine made by plaintiff contained in the bottles, but not including any right to use the bottles for other wine or to deliver them to any person other than the plaintiff. If the defendant's brother is regarded as being a sub-bailee holding the bottles *upon the same terms as the original bailee,* his delivery of the bottles to the defendant to be filled with wine other than the plaintiff's wine and to be returned to him was . . . therefore "a determination of the lawful [sub] bailment and caused the possessory title to revert to the bailor and entitled him to maintain an action of trover" . . . the contract between the bailor and the bailee was never meant to authorise the bailee "to do more than use the chattels and not to give the use to a third person" . . . In the present case *the terms of the bailment* expressly prohibited the use of the bottles for purposes other than those expressed, and the transfer of the possession of the bottles for such a purpose was a prohibited act: it was unquestionably wrong and determined the bailment, and therefore would have entitled the plaintiff to sue the defendant's brother in trover.[1]

In many cases, of course, the sub-bailee's misconduct will be of a kind that constitutes conversion in any event, irrespective of any known prohibition which the bailor has imposed upon an intervening bailee. In others, his knowledge of a particular way in which the bailor desires his chattel not to be handled may suffice to make him guilty of conversion, irrespective of whether he personally holds the goods under a sub-bail-

---

[97] Discussed in Ch. 12, post; arguably not bailees at all.
[98] *Elvin Powell & Co. Ltd.* v. *Plummer Roddis Ltd.* (1933) 50 T.L.R. 158; post, p. 388.
[99] (1946) 74 C.L.R. 204; ante, pp. 122, 130.
[1] Ibid., at 217-218. Cf. Dixon J. at 224, 229-230.

ment. But in residual cases, his possession of the chattel may suffice to create in him positive obligations, the breach of which may constitute a sufficiently wrongful act between him and the original bailor to make his conduct actionable. If it is thus actionable, the further question arises as to whether the appropriate remedy is one for a breach of the terms of the bailment or an action for conversion. Opinion is divided as to whether the commission of this tort should depend upon the terms of any contract between the parties.[2] If affirmative duties can be undertaken under a sub-bailment, irrespective of contract, it may follow that these obligations likewise possess a value in characterising the sub-bailee's conduct as a conversion; alternatively, it may follow that the latter remedy is otiose in these circumstances and that the demands of individual cases can be justly met by the independent action upon the bailment: an action which (like the brother's obligations in the *Penfold* case) does not depend upon contract and may be entirely separate from tort. As to the imposition of such affirmative duties, there is no direct authority in favour[3] and one decision against.[4] The sub-bailee is said, of course, to be under a duty not to convert but there is no authority suggesting that the terms upon which he accepted the goods may, as between himself and the principal bailor, define what is or is not a conversion. It will be submitted later[5] that such obligations should (in certain circumstances) be recognised. When they do, a breach of them may render the sub-bailee liable for conversion in circumstances where, if no sub-bailment existed, no such liability could itself exist.

(6) In the opinion of the Law Reform Committee,[6] a bailee who returns the goods to the person from whom he received them, or delivers them to a third party in accordance with the bailor's instructions, is not liable for conversion. This view has the support of Blackburn J. in *Hollins* v. *Fowler*,[7] and seems acceptable, at least where the bailee has no knowledge of any adverse title and does not himself effect the sale or other disposition under which delivery to a third party is made.[8]

(7) At Common Law a bailee is estopped, except in limited circumstances, from denying the bailor's title to the goods and pleading jus tertii. This principle will be considered in more detail elsewhere.[9]

III. DETINUE[10]

The action of detinue is of great antiquity and is the characteristic remedy of bailors against defaulting bailees.[11] It will lie whenever a person in

---

[2] Ante, p. 127.
[3] Apart from the dictum of Latham C.J. supra.
[4] *B.W.I.A.* v. *Bart* (1966) 11 W.I.R. 378; see post.
[5] Post, p. 821.
[6] Cmnd. 4774, para. 46.
[7] (1875) L.R. 7 H.L. 757, at 766-767; ante, p. 127. See also *Penfolds Wines Pty. Ltd.* v. *Elliott* (1946) 74 C.L.R. 204, at 229.
[8] See further p. 163, post.
[9] Post, p. 163. cf. *Torts (Interference with Goods) Act* 1977, ss. 7-8.
[10] Detinue is abolished by s. 2(1) of the *Torts (Interference with Goods) Act* 1977: facets of the same relationship; cf. Fifoot, *History and Sources of Common* see also s. 2(2), discussed in Appendix I, post.
[11] Quaere whether detinue and bailment were originally the static and dynamic

actual or constructive possession of goods detains or fails to deliver them without lawful excuse, in defiance of someone who enjoys an immediate right to possess. It is a much narrower remedy than conversion, which may be committed in many ways which do not involve an adverse detention of goods. There are several further important distinctions between detinue and conversion.

In order to succeed in an action for detinue, the plaintiff must show that he first demanded the goods from the defendant, and that this demand was unequivocally refused.[12] No such prefatory requirement exists in an action for conversion.[13] Its relevance in detinue is primarily to questions of limitation, for time does not run until demand and refusal have established an unlawful keeping.[14] But it possesses a supplemental value in that it provides an opportunity for the defendant to avoid litigation and to hand the chattel over without being compelled to defend an action in court. To this extent, it is suggested that a recent decision of the Appellate Division of the Alberta Supreme Court,[15] which holds that a demand and refusal are unnecessary if in the ensuing action the defendant pleads an adverse title to the plaintiff's and shows that any demand would have been refused, should be applied sparingly in future decisions.[16] The case in question rested upon slender authority[17] and, insofar as it is acceptable at all, should perhaps be confined to those situations where the defendant has received (either from the plaintiff or from a third party) "full information" about the defect in his title or the strength of the competing claim.[18] The fact that the defendant, when forced into a corner by the sudden issue of a writ, chooses to defend the action by alleging an adverse title does not necessarily mean that he would have declined to observe an earlier demand (or at least to discuss a compromise) had he been given the chance. In any event, the demand requirement is a just and reasonable one[19] which provides innocent detainers with a fair warning of adverse interests and may often discourage litigation. It should be preserved so far as is consonant with the

---

Law, p. 26 et. seq., who denies the equation and Tay (1966) 5 *Sydney Law Review* 239, who supports it. The necessity for a demand and refusal before the writ can issue lends some support to the view that every modern defendant to an action for detinue is in some respects at least, a bailee. See ante p. 33.

[12] *Gledstane* v. *Hewitt* (1831) 1 Cr. & J. 565, at 570; *Cullen* v. *Barclay* (1881) 10 L.R. Ir. 224; *King* v. *Walsh* [1932] I.R. 178; *Lloyd* v. *Osborne* (1899) 20 L.R. (N.S.W.) 190; 15 W.N. (N.S.W.) 267; *Canterbury College* v. *Mountfort* (1909) 11 G.L.R. 513; *Ball* v. *Sawyer-Massey Co. Ltd.* [1929] 4 D.L.R. 323; *Shentag* v. *Gauthier* (1972) 27 D.L.R. (3d) 710.

[13] *Bruen* v. *Roe* (1665) 1 Sid. 264; *Mires* v. *Solebay* (1678) 2 Mod. 242, at 244-245; 86 E.R. 1050, at 1051; Fleming, op. cit., p. 54.

[14] See e.g., *Re Tidd, Tidd* v. *Overall* [1893] 3 Ch. 154; but note *Limitation Act* 1939, s. 3(1); Cmnd. 4774, para. 84.

[15] *Baud Corp. N.V.* v. *Brook* (1974) 40 D.L.R. (3d) 418.

[16] (1975) 53 *Canadian Bar Review* 121.

[17] Apart from one unsupported dictum of Swift J. in *London Jewellers Ltd.* v. *Sutton* (1934) 50 T.L.R. 193, at 194 (reversed sub-nom. *London Jewellers Ltd.* v. *Attenborough* [1934] 2 K.B. 206) the only authorities cited were American decisions on replevin. Cf. *Macleod* v. *Scramlen* (1910) 14 W.L.R. 262.

[18] This was the ground upon which O'Brien J. was prepared to waive the demand and refusal requirement in *Employer's Fire Assurance Co.* v. *Cotten* (1927) 245 N.Y. 102; 156 N.E. 629; 51 A.L.R. 1462 (New York Court of Appeals).

[19] *Gillett* v. *Roberts* (1874) 57 N.Y. 28.

interests of justice and the policy of the rule itself, and relaxed only in exceptional cases.

The refusal must be unqualified, or, if qualified, must disclose an intention to detain the goods irrespective of the claims of the plaintiff. Clearly, a refusal to hand over goods until reasonable inquiries have been made will be considered a reasonable qualification and will not, by itself, render the defendant liable in detinue.[20] In *Lloyd* v. *Osborne*[21] the Supreme Court of New South Wales held, by a majority of three to two, that the defendant's failure to reply to a letter from the plaintiff's solicitor requiring him to deliver the goods at once to the plaintiff or her agent did not, on the facts, constitute a refusal within the meaning of the rule:

> Under certain circumstances, that is to say if the demand was sufficient, taking no notice of it might be equivalent to a refusal. But the demand [in this case] is not sufficient. The letter . . . does not say where [the goods] are to be delivered, nor does it say who the agent is.[22]

Another difference between detinue and conversion lies in the fact that in detinue the plaintiff's immediate right to possession must arise out of a proprietary interest in the goods.[23] Clearly a bailor who is the owner of goods, and whose right of possession is immediate, will enjoy the right to sue in detinue, whether the detainer be his original bailee or any third party who has come into possession. But the ability to sue is not confined to those who enjoy a general property in the goods: an immediate right of possession arising out of some special property[24] (such as the revived reversion of a principal bailee under a sub-lease of chattels) will suffice, so that the hirer could sue in detinue any person to whom he had lawfully sub-leased the goods and who insisted on detaining them in defiance of their agreement.[25] Even when the principal bailee has lost his right to possess as against the original bailment (e.g. by performing an act repugnant to the original bailment) it does not follow that his right to sue in detinue is simultaneously lost: the subsidiary bailee, having received possession from him, is estopped from denying his bailor's title.[26] Indeed, it seems that even a thief may bring detinue (or trespass, or conversion) against someone who is not the true owner;[27] certainly a finder can.[28] The right to possess is a relative and not an abstract thing.

Although mere negligence cannot amount to a conversion, a defendant in detinue will not escape liability merely by proving that the goods have

---

[20] *Clayton* v. *Le Roy* [1911] 2 K.B. 1031; *Garrett* v. *Arthur Churchill Ltd.* [1970] 1 Q.B. 92.

[21] (1899) 20 L.R. (N.S.W.) 190.

[22] Ibid.

[23] *Rosenthal* v. *Alderton* [1946] 1 All E.R. 583, at 584; *Jarvis* v. *Williams* [1955] 1 W.L.R. 71; *Singh* v. *Ali* [1960] A.C. 167, at 176; *Harris* v. *Lombard New Zealand Ltd.* [1974] 2 N.Z.L.R. 161, at 166; Cmnd. 4774, para. 9.

[24] *Singh* v. *Ali* (supra).

[25] Clear acknowledgment that bailees can sue in detinue was given by Evershed M.R. in *Jarvis* v. *Williams* (supra). For example of a bailee proceeding in detinue against his bailor, see *City Motors (1933) Ltd.* v. *Southern Aerial Super Service Pty. Ltd.* (1961) 106 C.L.R. 477; [1962] A.L.R. 184.

[26] See p. 186, post.

[27] *Richard* v. *Nowlan* (1959) 19 D.L.R. (2d) 229; cf. *Buckley* v. *Gross* (1863) 3 B. & S. 566.

[28] *Armory* v. *Delamirie* (1721) 1 Stra. 505 (an action in trover); see Chapter 22, post.

been lost, or by denying that they are now in his possession. Once delivery has been proved, he must show that any loss of possession occurred without fault on his part, and that he exercised the appropriate measure of care required of him as bailee.[29] It is uncertain whether the same rule applies to defendants who are not bailees stricto sensu, but on balance it may well. In any event, the plaintiff's demand will arguably place upon the detainer a duty to safeguard the goods until judgment, and the failure to exercise this duty will be akin in many respects (including, perhaps, the burden of proof) to that of an ordinary bailee. Even where the loss precedes the demand, it is thought that those possessors who occupy a similar position to an orthodox bailee (e.g. the finder) are liable for failing to take care of the goods, and can be sued for detinue.[30] It should be otherwise, however, when the defendant never had cause to suspect that the chattel was not his own before the loss occurred.[31]

It has been said that detinue (unlike conversion) will issue only against a defendant who, at the time of the alleged detention, is in possession of the goods.[32] However, this observation must be qualified for two reasons. First, of course, the defendant may already have lost the goods, or caused them to be destroyed, at the time when the demand is made. Secondly, it does not appear that actual possession is essential, for the defendant may have sub-bailed the goods to an independent third-party who, in a contest between him and the defendant, would clearly be considered to be the party in possession. The essential feature is that the defendant, in cases where the goods still exist and he has not negligently lost them, should continue to be in *control* of them at the time when the demand is made. This test is satisfied if they are in the hands of a bank or warehouseman who holds to his order, or if they are stored in premises to which the defendant (although not the occupier) has ready access. The rule is therefore more accurately stated in the terms that the detainer must have actual or constructive possession of the goods.[33] Where actual possession vests in a third party, the defendant must either be entitled to immediate possession against him or capable of acquiring such a right by his own conduct alone.

Further differences between the two forms of action consist in the date at which damages are to be assessed,[34] although this distinction is now of diminishing importance,[35] and the fact that detinue can issue for specific restitution of goods; conversion, on the other hand, signifies a claim for a sum of money only. It may, at this point, be convenient to set out the various forms of relief that can be granted in an action for detinue or conversion.

---

[29] *Reeve* v. *Palmer* (1858) 5 C.B. (N.S.) 84; 141 E.R. 33; cf. *Jones* v. *Dowle* (1841) 9 M. & W. 19.
[30] Chapter 22, post.
[31] See Chapter 6, post.
[32] Cmnd. 4774, para. 8; cf. p. 127, ante; *Fitzgerald* v. *Kellion*, [1978] A.C.L.D. 137.
[33] *Alicia Hosiery Ltd.* v. *Brown, Shipley & Co.* [1970] 1 Q.B. 195.
[34] As to this, see p. 63 ante.
[35] Cmnd. 4774, para. 9.

A. Forms of relief in conversion and detinue[36]

These were conflated and summarised by Diplock L.J. in *General and Finance Facilities Ltd.* v. *Cooks Cars (Romford) Ltd.*[37] His analysis accentuates the fundamentally different nature of the two causes of action, and the impact of this difference upon the orders that can be obtained:

(i) Conversion is a purely personal cause of action and can only result in a judgment for pecuniary damages, which will generally embrace the value of the chattel at the date of the conversion and any consequential damage which is not too remote. Often, but invariably, this will be the same measure as in detinue. Until satisfied, such a judgment does not divest the plaintiff of his property, but he may not call on the assistance of the court to recover the chattel. A judgment in conversion, as we have remarked earlier,[38] is essentially a compulsory sale to the defendant, although its effects are suspended until the judgment is satisfied.

(ii) Detinue on the other hand, "partakes of the nature of an action in rem", and its characteristic quality is a demand for specific restitution. Under modern law judgment in detinue may take one of three forms:

(a) Where the chattel is an ordinary commercial article, or the defendant no longer has the chattel, the adopted form will generally be an order that the defendant pay the value of the chattel (assessed according to the relevant criteria) plus damages for its detention.[39] In such a case, he has no option of returning the goods to the plaintiff. The plaintiff may elect for a judgment in this form as of right if the defendant has failed to do so at the time of judgment. This form of order is closely akin to that in conversion, although the level of damages may differ. Once it is made, neither party can insist on a return of the chattel.

(b) Alternatively, the court may order the return of the chattel, *or* recovery of its value, plus damages for its detention. Here the defendant does enjoy the option of returning the chattel. In addition, the order entitles the plaintiff to apply to the court to enforce specific restitution by writ of delivery, or attachment or sequestration, as well as to recover damages for its detention by a writ of fi fa. The judgment should specify separately the assessed value of the chattel and the damages for its detention. This seems to be the commonest form.[40]

(c) In unusual circumstances, the court may order return of the chattel and damages for its detention. This will normally occur only where the chattel is of especial rarity or value to the plaintiff.[41]

The Law Reform Committee have recognised the value of the availability of specific restitution in actions for detinue and have recommended that the proposed new tort of wrongful interference of chattels be formulated so as to preserve this facet of that remedy.[42]

---

[36] But cf. *Torts (Interference with Goods) Act* 1977, ss. 3-4.
[37] [1963] 1 W.L.R. 644, at 648-651; cited with approval in *Schentag* v. *Gauthier* (1972) 27 D.L.R. (3d) 710, at 716-717.
[38] Ante, p. 133.
[39] It seems that the county court judge's order for specific restitution was not justified in *Greenwood* v. *Bennett* [1972] 3 All E.R. 586.
[40] Cmnd. 4774, para. 92.
[41] For an example, see *Hymas* v. *Ogden* [1905] 1 K.B. 246.
[42] Cmnd. 4774, paras. 93-97.

IV. THE PROTECTION OF REVERSIONARY INTERESTS[43]

The principles which prevent the bailor who has merely a postponed right to possession from suing a third-party in trespass, detinue or conversion need not inhibit him entirely from recovering damages for injury to the chattel. It is now established that an action on the case may lie for damage to his reversionary interest. The seminal decision is that of the Court of Common Pleas in *Mears* v. *L. & S.W. Railway Co.*[44] The owner of a barge leased it on hire to one Russell. During the currency of the lease, the defendants were employed to unload a boiler from the barge. Their negligence in performing this operation caused the boiler to fall, with the result that the barge was damaged and out of commission for a considerable time. Erle C.J. held that an action could lie for any "permanent injury done to a chattel while the owner's right to the possession is suspended": in such an event, the temporary interest of the hirer created no bar to the action. Williams J. concurred, endorsing the need for permanent injury and implying that the action would lie against anyone who caused such injury by means of a "wrongful act".[45]

The remedy is a valuable one, particularly perhaps for rental and finance companies which seek to recover from negligent third parties for damage to chattels leased on hire or hire-purchase.[46] It can extend to conduct which causes permanent loss as distinct from permanent injury or destruction; for example, where the third-party's negligence enables a thief to steal the goods.[47] It has also been applied as against a sub-bailee whose servant stole the subject-matter of the bailment.[48] The general rule is well entrenched, being accepted by all the leading text-book writers and having been applied in more than a dozen Commonwealth decisions since 1862.

The principle encompasses directly inflicted as well as indirect damage,[49]

---

[43] The appropriateness of the word 'reversion' in the context of a bailment of chattels is discussed by Lawson, *Introduction to Law of Property*, at pp. 72-73.

[44] (1862) 11 C.B.N.S. 850; 142 E.R. 1029; see also *Lancashire Waggon Co.* v. *Fitzhugh* (1861) 6 H. & N. 502. In *Drive-Yourself Lessey's Pty. Ltd.* v. *Burnside* [1959] S.R. (N.S.W.) 390, at p. 395, counsel appears to have regarded *Meux* v. *G.E. Ry. Co.* [1895] 2 Q.B. 387 as an application of this principle, but it is clear that even if there were a bailment to the servant in that case it was a bailment at will. Bailors at will are entitled to recover for all damage: *Nicolls* v. *Bastard* (1835) 2 C.M. & R. 659; 150 E.R. 279; *Manders* v. *Williams* (1849) 4 Ex. 339; 154 E.R. 1242; *Fletcher* v. *Thomas* [1931] 3 D.L.R. 142.

[45] (1862) 11 C.B.N.S. 850, at pp. 854, 855; 142 E.R. 1029 at p. 1031. The Court drew some support from a statement of Pollock C.B. in *Tancred* v. *Allgood* (1859) 4 H. & N. 438, at p. 444; 157 E.R. 910, at p. 913, that "Probably any temporary damage done while the plaintiff's possession was suspended . . . is not the foundation of an action."

[46] *Dee Trading Co. Pty. Ltd.* v. *Baldwin* [1938] V.L.R. 173; *Industrial Acceptance Corporation Ltd.* v. *Quinn* [1973] Qld. lawyer 325; cf. *Drive-Yourself Lessey's Pty. Ltd.* v. *Burnside* [1959] S.R. (N.S.W.) 390 (p. 214 et. seq., post) and see Fleming (1958) 32 A.L.J. 267.

[47] But the remedy may not necessarily apply to a case of mere wrongful taking (*Mukibi* v. *Bhasavar* [1967] E.A. 473; Cmnd. 4774, para. 34) for this will not necessarily impair the bailor's reversionary interest; see further *infra*.

[48] *Moukataff* v. *B.O.A.C.* [1967] 1 Lloyd's Rep. 396, at 415.

[49] *Lancashire Waggon Co.* v. *Fitzhugh* (1861) 6 H. & N. 502; see also *Drive-Yourself Lessey's Pty. Ltd.* [1959] S.R. (N.S.W.) 390, at p. 413, where Herron J. implies that negligently-inflicted damage is only one of the several types of misconduct

and therefore caters for those injuries which, but for the bailor's lack of possession, would be trespassory against him.[50]

In theory, no injury need be permanent provided the chattel is capable of repair. However, it is clear that the availability of the action on the case is not confined to situations in which the chattel has been, for all practical purposes, destroyed. One possible definition of "permanent injury" in this context is an injury which the bailee is not bound to rectify and which will therefore, presumably, remain unrectified until the bailor regains possession. Although this definition has some usefulness in determining whether the bailor has actually lost anything, it would seem on balance to be unsatisfactory, because it allows the terms of the bailment to govern the liability of a wrongdoer who is not a party thereto.

In fact, it appears that the requirement of permanent injury merely demands that the injury be one which would not be righted (or would not right itself) in the ordinary course of events before the bailor's right to possession revives. Trivial damage, which the bailee is either bound to repair or can normally be relied upon to repair (such as a puncture to a hired car) might therefore fail to qualify, whereas other items of damage ostensibly no less trivial (like a dent to the fender) would. In *Penfolds Wines Pty. Ltd.* v. *Elliott*[51] Dixon J. acknowledged that a bailor with an immediate right of possession could recover for "less lasting" damage than a bailor whose right to possession was postponed; but he went on to say that even the latter could recover for "some injury enuring to (his) detriment." Provided such injury has enured in fact, the remedy should therefore lie. It was not available in *Penfolds* case because the defendant had not damaged the plaintiff's bottles but had merely filled them with wine.[52]

The English Law Reform Committee have recommended that their proposed new remedy of wrongful interference with chattels should apply in favour of owners of reversionary interests whose right of possession

that may be actionable: "The respondent, as bailor of the motor-car to Taylor, was entitled to sue the appellants as a wrongdoer during the period of the bailment, and the right included a right to sue for all damages caused by the appellant's negligence. The bailor's right to sue is in case and not in trespass . . ." In *Henry Berry & Co. Pty. Ltd.* v *Rushton* [1937] St.R. Qd. 109, at p. 117, Henchman J. after stating that a person with a suspended right to possession could not sue for trespass, went on to observe that such a person could sue if ". . . by reason of the conversion or trespass he has actually been deprived, permanently or temporarily, of the benefit of his reversionary interest. Thus he can sue if the chattel has been destroyed, or if it has been so disposed of that a valid title has become vested in a third person, as by sale in market overt, or if after his reversionary interest has fallen into possession, he is prevented from obtaining possession by reason of the previous act of conversion."

---

50 Ante, p. 120.
51 (1946) 74 C.L.R. at pp. 230, 231. None of the other members of the High Court considered this aspect of the plaintiff's claim.
52 Cf. Herron J. in *Drive-Yourself Lessey's Pty. Ltd.* v. *Burnside* [1959] S.R. (N.S.W.) 390, at p. 413: "all damage"; Henchman J. in *Henry Berry & Co. Pty. Ltd.* v. *Rushton* [1937] St.R. Qd. 109, at 117: if a bailor has been "actually deprived, permanently or temporarily, of the benefit of his reversionary interest." In *Moukataff* v. *B.O.A.C.* [1967] 1 Lloyd's Rep. 396, at p. 416, Browne J. allowed the remedy to issue in a case of loss by theft where the goods "had by then been permanently lost, in the sense that there was then no reasonable prospect of any further recovery."

is suspended, and accordingly that the separate action on the case should
be merged within this larger remedy.[53]

The measure of damages under this action is the damage to the
plaintiff's reversionary interest and not, for instance, the value of the
chattel.[54]

V. FOLLOWING PROPERTY—TRACING[55]

For several reasons, a bailor may prefer a proprietary to a personal
action. For example, a personal claim may be statute-barred where a
proprietary one is not;[56] judgment will carry interest from the date when
the property comes into a defendant's hands rather than from the date
of judgment;[57] he may obtain an order for the preservation of his property
pending trial;[58] he may wish to recover property which has increased
in value; and, in particular, he will have priority over general creditors
of a defendant who becomes bankrupt with the property in his hands.[59]

---

[53] Cmnd. 4774 (1971) para. 34. Cf. now s. 1, *Torts (Interference with Goods)
Act*, 1977.

[54] *Tancred* v. *Allgood* (1859) 4 H. & N. 438; *Henry Berry & Co. Pty. Ltd.* v.
Rushton [1937] St.R. Qd. 109 at p. 117. Cf. *Dee Trading Co. Pty. Ltd.* v. *Baldwin*
[1938] V.L.R. 173, where repair-costs were awarded against the negligent third-
party although these were "probably" recoverable from the hirer.

[55] We shall not deal separately with the subjects of accession and interfusion and
with questions as to the ownership of altered or commixed goods. For discussion
of these and related issues, the reader is referred to Paton, *Bailment in the
Common Law*, Chapter 10; Vaines, *Personal Property* (5th ed.), Chapter 19;
Guest (1964) 27 M.L.R. 505; Slater (1959) 37 Can.BarRev. 597; Lee (1945) 19
Temple Univ. L.Q. 89; the New Zealand decision in *Thomas* v. *Robinson* [1977]
1 N.Z.L.R. 385, discussed in [1977] *New Zealand Law Journal* 168 et. seq.,
Express Coach Finishers v. *Caulfield* 1968 S.L.T. (Sh.Ct.) 11; *Munro* v. *Willmott*
[1949] 1 K.B. 295; and *Torts (Interference with Goods) Act* 1977, ss. 6, 9(2).

[56] See *Sinclair* v. *Broughman* [1914] A.C. 398.

[57] See *Re Diplock's Estate* [1948] Ch. 465 (affirmed sub. nom. *Ministry of Health* v.
Simpson [1951] A.C. 251).

[58] In England, under R.S.C. Ord. 50 r. 3.

[59] The last consideration has assumed particular importance since the decision of the
Court of Appeal in *Aluminium Industrie Vaasen B.V.* v. *Romalpa Aluminium
Ltd.* [1976] 2 All E.R. 552; see Goode (1976) 92 L.Q.R. 360 and 528; [1977]
J.B.L. 139. In the light of this decision (which bids fair to create profound reper-
cussions in the field of commercial law) it now seems likely that, within the
commodity market, sellers of goods will adopt the practice of entering an
express reservation of title to themselves within the contract of sale, such
reservation to apply until the full purchase price has been discharged. A reservation of this kind need not, if appropriately framed, prevent the purchasers from
reselling the goods *as principals* to any sub-purchasers but it will (again, if
appropriately framed) render the relationship between the original seller and the
original purchaser that of bailor and bailee until the original purchase debt is
discharged. This relationship may in turn qualify as a fiduciary relationship for
the purposes of the equitable rules as to tracing, and will accordingly entitle the
seller-bailor to trace the proceeds of the goods into the hands of the purchaser-
bailee or (as in the present case) into those of his receiver in bankruptcy when
the goods are resold. In this way, the original seller achieves priority over the
general creditors of the original purchaser and has a proprietary right to recover
the sum representing the proceeds of re-sale. "I see no difficulty in the contractual
concept that, as between the defendants (*the original buyers*) and their sub-
purchasers, the defendants sold as principals, but that, as between themselves and
the plaintiffs (*the original sellers*), those goods which they were selling as
principals within their implied authorities from the plaintiffs were the plaintiff's
goods which they were selling as agents for the plaintiffs to whom they

In order to obtain a proprietary remedy the plaintiff must be able to follow or (in equity) to trace the property to which he asserts his right. This becomes important in cases where the nature of property is altered, e.g., where goods are exchanged for other goods.

In *Scott* v. *Surman*,[60] the plaintiffs consigned tar to a factor who resold it, receiving payment in the form of promissory notes. On the factor's bankruptcy, his commissioners-in-bankruptcy assigned the promissory notes to the defendants who confirmed the sale and received payment. It was held that the plaintiffs were not limited to the role of general creditors of the bankrupt but could maintain an action for money had and received to their use against the defendants, thus permitting use of the action to secure a prior claim on the factor's insolvency.[61] Clearly such a claim is preferable to a mere personal action of a proprietary nature, such as an action for damages for conversion.[62] However, the common law right to follow property, the basis of which is unknown,[63] is limited to cases in which the bailor's property is "physically" identifiable. This does not mean that the original property must be identifiable as such but that the means must exist for ascertaining that property whether in its original or altered form. This requirement is satisfied where one article is exchanged for another, or an article is sold and the proceeds are used for specific investments or retained in a separate fund. However, the deficiency of the legal right becomes apparent where property is converted into money for by its very nature this is currency and is not easily distinguishable from other money unless kept in a separate account or unless it exists in a particular form (e.g. specific coins).

Thus there would seem to be no provision at common law for the common case where money is mixed in a bank account. In this situation, the bank generally becomes the owner of the money at law although where B pays A's money into C's account, A may claim from C as money had and received to his use. When A's money has passed through B's account into C's hands the position is more difficult. In *Banque Belge* v.

---

remained fully accountable. If an agent lawfully sells his principal's goods, he stands in a fiduciary relationship to his principal and remains accountable to his principal for those goods and their proceeds. A bailee is in like position in relation to his bailor's goods. What, then, is there here to relieve the defendants from their obligation to account to the plaintiffs for those goods of the plaintiffs which they lawfully sell to sub-purchasers? The fact that they so sold them as principals does not, as I think affect their relationship with the plaintiffs; nor, as at present advised, do I think . . . that the sub-purchasers could on this analysis have sued the plaintiffs on the sub-contracts as undisclosed principals for, say, breach of warranty of quality": per Roskill L.J. [1976] 2 All E.R. 552, at 563-564.

---

60 (1742) Willes 400.

61 Cf. Scott (1966) 7 U.W.A.L.R. 463; Cuthbertson (1967) 8 U.W.A.L.R. 402; Babafemi (1971) 34 M.L.R. 12.

62 Where that may be brought: cf. *Taylor* v. *Plumer* (1815) 3 M. & S. 562. A plaintiff with a mere personal claim will take only a dividend on the defendant's bankruptcy. With respect to personal claims in equity, see *Ministry of Health* v. *Simpson*, supra; Jones (1957) 73 L.Q.R. 48; Goff & Jones, *The Law of Restitution*, pp. 408-410.

63 The traditional explanation, naturally popular when the "implied contract" theory of restitution was popular, was that it depended on the plaintiff's ratification: see *Sinclair* v. *Brougham* (supra), p. 441. But cf. *Taylor* v. *Plumer*, supra.

Hambrouck,[64] the Court of Appeal permitted such money to be followed. Bankes L.J. said this was permissible at common law because only A's money was involved. Scrutton L.J., who allowed tracing in equity,[65] said that no tracing was possible at law if money is mixed with other money. Atkin L.J. disagreed, stressing that the whole question depends on whether the means of ascertainment fail. On his reasoning, the common law would be extended to permit a plaintiff to recover the product of his original property.

To meet the difficulty of the mixed fund, equity developed the right to trace.[66] This has the advantage of assisting equitable owners, whose rights were, of course, not recognised at common law. It has the general disadvantage of being confined to cases in which there is a fiduciary relationship with a person through whose hands the property has passed to the defendant so that some equitable proprietary interest attaches to it.[67] In the former situation, the plaintiff obtains priority over general creditors; where he traces against an innocent volunteer he ranks pari passu. The relationship, the necessity for which has been criticised,[68] exists between bailor and bailee.[69]

There are several limitations on the right to trace in equity. First, as at common law, the property must be identifiable. In equity, this includes identification as part of a mixed fund or as latent in property acquired by means of such a fund. But it is of no avail if money has been dissipated on a specific object, such as a dinner, or if an innocent volunteer into whose hands the fund has come has used it to improve other property he owns—the money has disappeared.[70] Secondly, the equitable right is exercisable only by one who has only an equitable interest and not by one who is owner both at law and in equity; this follows from the requirement of a fiduciary relationship. Thirdly, where tracing takes place against an innocent volunteer or into other property, the plaintiff must have a proprietary interest. These two requirements are, arguably, unnecessary limitations on the principle of unjust enrichment.[71] Finally, the right must not have been lost: because the property disappears, or has come into the hands of a bona fide purchaser without notice of the right, or in any other case in which it might be held that it is inequitable to permit tracing.[72]

---

[64] [1921] 1 K.B. 321.
[65] See infra.
[66] The case for fusion of the legal and equitable rights is discussed by Babafemi (1971) 34 M.L.R. 12; cf. Pearce (1976) 40 Conv. (*N.S.*) 277. See also Goff & Jones, op. cit., p. 56, where it is argued that both a legal and an equitable owner should be able to follow property into a mixed fund subject to the defences of bona fide purchase and change of position.
[67] *Re Diplock*, supra. See Maudsley (1959) 75 L.Q.R. 234; Higgins (1966) 6 U.W.A.L.R. 428; Oakley (1975) 28 C.L.P. 64.
[68] For criticism of the requirement, see Goff & Jones, op. cit., pp. 41-43.
[69] *Re Hallett's Estate* (1880) 13 Ch. D. 696, at 709 per Jessell M.R. See also Sealy [1962] C.L.J. 69; [1963] C.L.J. 119; *Aluminium Industrie Vaasen B.V.* v. *Romalpa Aluminium Ltd.* [1976] 2 All E.R. 552 (ante, p. 155).
[70] *Re Diplock* supra, at 521, 547.
[71] See e.g., *Hanbury's Modern Equity* (9th ed.), pp. 423-424.
[72] Other examples include cases where an innocent volunteer uses money to pay off debts or to improve his land. In the first case, the debt is extinguished, any security for it ceases to exist and so the bailor cannot claim to be subrogated

Subject to the defence of bona fide purchase, a plaintiff can either, quite simply, trace the identifiable produce of the sale of his original property into an unmixed fund or, if other property is bought with the proceeds, he may elect either to take the property purchased or to have a charge over it for the amount of his money which has been expended on it.[73] In principle, if the plaintiff's property or money is mixed with that of his fiduciary agent, the former should have a declaration of charge over the whole of the mixed property for the value of his contribution. This would mean that he will receive his money plus interest in priority to general creditors of the defendant but that the latter would keep any and all profits accruing to the fund. To meet this problem, the High Court of Australia in *Scott* v. *Scott*[74] allowed the plaintiff an alternative remedy in this situation—a claim to a share of the fund in the proportion which "his" original funds bore to the mixed fund as a whole at the time of mixing. Where the fund decreases in value, the bailor will wish to retain his right to a charge; where it increases, he will reap the benefit to which he is entitled by claiming a proportionate share.

Problems most commonly arise where money is mixed in banking accounts and the balance in the account falls or fluctuates.[75] The plaintiff will have a charge over the whole or any part of the fund in the account which is identifiable as having been part of the fund with which his money was confused. Thus, where money is drawn out of the fund, and spent, the charge subsists over the remainder as it is assumed that the defendant's own money is drawn out first.[76] However, where early withdrawals are dissipated, the charge will remain over investments purchased with the remainder.[77] These rules yield where an intention is manifested to deal with different parts of the fund separately. Similarly, since the plaintiff's right decreases to the lowest intermediate balance in the account derived from the mixed fund, any payments into the account will only feed the mixed fund to the extent intended.[78] These rules will serve to protect the bailor's money (or property converted into money) in his bailee's hands, albeit at the expense of the latter's general creditors who will presumably have granted him credit on an estimation of his financial stability which may have depended to some extent on his funds being inflated with the bailor's money.

Finally, we must consider the bailor's position where the bailee (or an innocent volunteer) has mixed the former's money with money belonging to one or more third parties. Where the mixing takes place in an active, unbroken bank account from which withdrawals are made, the arbitrary

to rights of the creditor: *Re Diplock* (supra), at 59. Just as there may be room for the operation of the subrogation doctrine in this case, there is arguably room in the second case for giving the plaintiff a declaration of charge: cf. Pettit, *Equity and The Law of Trusts* (3rd ed.), pp. 468-469.

---

[73] *Re Hallett* supra, at 709 per Jessel M.R.
[74] (1963) 37 A.L.J.R. 345. See also *Re Tilley's Will Trusts* [1967] Ch. 1179, at 1189.
[75] As a general rule, where property is mixed, a beneficiary is entitled to all that property which a trustee is unable to prove is his own: *Lupton* v. *White* (1808) 15 Ves. 432.
[76] *Re Hallett's Estate*, supra.
[77] *Re Oatway* [1903] 2 Ch. 356.
[78] *Rosco* v. *Winder* [1915] 1 Ch. 62.

rule in *Clayton's* case[79] applies. Under this rule, which evolved to ascertain the liabilities of partners in banking firms,[80] it is presumed that withdrawals from the account are made in the same order as payments into it (i.e. first in, first out). Thus, subject to a clear intention to the contrary where a withdrawal is seen to be for a specific purpose,[81] a bailor whose money is paid into the defendant's account at an early stage is more likely to find that his money has been withdrawn and spent (and has, therefore, disappeared) than one whose money is mixed in the account at a later stage, albeit this may mean the balance remaining in the account is deemed to belong to the defendant alone.

In situations outside the ambit of *Clayton's* case the general rule is that reductions are borne pari passu and that contributors are entitled to a charge pari passu over property bought or investments made out of the fund.[82] The same rule applies where the money is mixed with that of an innocent volunteer thus placing him in a favourable position in relation to the whole fund and protecting, arguably to an unnecessary extent,[83] his interest therein.

VI. JOINT BAILORS AND BAILEES[84]

Occasionally there may be a joint bailment, as where two parties who are jointly interested in a chattel deposit it with a third.[85] In such a case the general rule is that a demand by one joint bailor, made without the authority of the other, is insufficient to compel the return of the chattel to him and will not expose the bailee to an action for detinue for refusing to accede to the demand. In *Atwood* v. *Ernest*[86] Maule J. explained the rule as follows:

> Now, where several joint owners of a chattel deliver it to a third person, he may detain it until all the joint-owners require him to return it. If some of them ask him to return it, and others desire him to keep it, the bailee is not liable to an action at the suit of those who ask for a return. If that were not so, each might have an action, and so the bailee might be harassed with as many actions as there were joint-owners.[87]

[79] *Devaynes* v. *Noble, Clayton's Case* (1816) 1 Mer. 529. See McConville (1963) 79 L.Q.R. 388.
[80] Maitland, *Equity*, p. 219.
[81] *Re Diplock* (supra), at 551-552.
[82] *Sinclair* v. *Brougham* [1914] A.C. 398 (depositors and shareholders); *Re Diplock* (supra), at 533-534, 539.
[83] See Goff & Jones, op. cit., pp. 52-53.
[84] *Halsbury, Laws* vol. ii, paras. 1504 and 1505; Paton. op. cit., pp. 402-403.
[85] For a decision in which a joint bailment of livestock to the bailor and another person was upheld under the New Zealand *Law of Property Act* 1952, see *Harding* v. *Commissioner of Inland Revenue* [1977] 1 N.Z.L.R. 337.
[86] (1853) 13 C.B. 881; but cf. *Broadbent* v. *Ledward* (1839) 11 Ad. & E. 209, where a dictum by Lord Denman C.J. suggests a contrary rule. As Halsbury (loc. cit.), points out, the dictum is insupportable on such an interpretation.
[87] (1853) 13 C.B. 881, at 889. Of course, the bailment may contain an express stipulation displacing the conventional rule: Halsbury, loc. cit. The rule may also be displaced if the party making the demand has a special property in the entire chattel, giving him the sole right to its possession: see *Nyberg* v. *Handelaar* [1892] 2 Q.B. 202.

The rule was upheld by the Court of Appeal in *Wright* v. *Robotham*,[88] where title-deeds had been deposited with the defendant solicitors by the owner in fee simple of an estate. The owner later settled the estate and it became vested in the plaintiffs and the settlor's heir-at-law. The plaintiffs wished to sell part of the property and demanded that the solicitors deliver up the deeds, but they (knowing that the heir-at-law could not be found to collaborate in the demand) refused. The Court, apparently treating the case as one of joint bailment, upheld their refusal as correct, but ordered that the deeds be deposited in court for the benefit of all parties entitled. Likewise, in *Harper* v. *Godsell*[89] a pawnee to whom goods had been pledged by four partners was held not liable in conversion for failing to deliver them to the assignee of three of the partners without the authority of the fourth, even though the assignee had discharged the debt for which the goods were security. The Court held that, irrespective of whether the plaintiff was a joint tenant or a tenant in common, when he sought to put an end to the pledge "he could at most only do so as to his interest in it".

> Now it is a principle as old as Littleton (Co. Litt. 200a) that one joint tenant cannot maintain trover against his co-tenant for the goods while they are in the co-tenant's possession. When the property is wrongfully destroyed, the action may be maintained. Here, the wine was sold under the power of sale, as it had not been redeemed. It was not destroyed. If Porro [the fourth partner] himself had sold the wine the plaintiff could not have sued him in trover for so doing and as the defendant sold the wine under an authority from Porro, I think the plaintiff cannot sue the defendant in trover for so selling the wine.[90]

May v. *Harvey*[91] affirms the general rule, but on the facts of that case it was held not to apply. The assignee of a lease agreed with the assignor that, to save the expense of a counterpart, the lease should be deposited with the defendant's son, who appears to have acted throughout as his father's agent. A commission of bankrupt subsequently issued against the assignee and the lease was demanded from the defendant. His defence that there had been a joint bailment, and that no valid demand could issue without the concurrent authority of the assignor, was rejected. The Court held that the bailment was not joint because it did not appear that at the time of the deposit the bailee had any notice of the agreement between assignor and assignee; moreover, both the original bailee and the defendant (his father) had dealt with the lease as though it were the property of the assignee alone.

Where the bailee under a joint bailment breaches the bailment by delivering the goods on the authority of one bailor alone, the bailor who thus requested the delivery cannot join in an action for breach of the bailment.[92] Since it is necessary for all joint bailors to join in an action

---

[88] (1886) 33 Ch. D. 106; cf. *Foster* v. *Crabb* (1852) 12 C.B. 136.
[89] (1870) L.R. 5 Q.B. 422.
[90] Ibid., at 428 per Blackburn J. Note, however, that the learned judge went on to remark that so far as concerned the surplus proceeds of the sale the defendant must account to the estate of the firm.
[91] (1811) 13 East. 197; cf. *Nathan* v. *Buckland* (1818) 2 Moore C.P. 153.
[92] *Brandon* v. *Scott* (1857) 7 E1. & B1. 234.

for misdelivery of the chattel, the result would be that no action for detinue would lie against the bailee in the situation we have outlined. But as Lord Campbell C.J. observed in *Brandon* v. *Scott*[93] "there would be a clear remedy in equity for the breach of trust in delivering the joint property to one only of the cestui que trusts".

Occasionally a joint bailment of chattels may be said to arise although some of the chattels in question (such as the contents of a box) belong separately and not jointly to the individual bailors. This inference was drawn in *Metcalfe* v. *London, Brighton & South Coast Railway*.[94] Goods belonging to two brothers were delivered by a third person in a padlocked box to the defendant railway. The box was addressed to one of the brothers and it was he who paid for the carriage. The Court held that there was evidence of a joint bailment, in respect of which an action might be brought by both brothers jointly for the loss of the goods. Willes J. said arguendo[95] that it was a very unworthy argument to claim that because items in the box belonged to different brothers separately there could be no joint bailment; and he pointed out that the only effect of holding to the contrary would be to harass the defendants (who had raised the point) with two actions instead of one.[96] In his view there was a joint bailment because the goods had been delivered by a person who might reasonably be considered to be the servant or agent of both bailors, and because the box itself was in the joint use of both for the purpose of the journey. Cockburn C.J. agreed and stated that there was "abundant evidence" of such a bailment.[97] Williams J. further pointed out that there was also joint consideration. If the action had been brought in contract it would properly have been brought jointly, and "although this is not an action on the contract but for a breach of duty still it is founded on contract and must follow the general rules as to joinder which govern actions ex contractu".[98]

Once joint bailors have made a joint demand for delivery of the goods, and that demand has been refused, they may bring separate actions for detinue (or conversion, if appropriate) against the bailee.[99]

The converse situation to that discussed above arises when a single bailor bails his chattel to two or more bailees, to be held by them jointly. In *Davey* v. *Chamberlain*[1] a chaise was hired jointly to two bailees and was driven negligently by one of them while the other was sitting next to him, smoking. The chaise collided with the plaintiff's horse and killed it. Lord Ellenborough C.J. held that both hirers were jointly liable:

> . . . if two persons were jointly concerned in the carriage, as if both had hired it together, . . . the care of the King's subjects required that both should be answerable for any accident arising from the

93 Ibid., at 237.
94 (1858) 4 C.B.N.S. 307.
95 Ibid., at 318.
96 Ibid., at 321.
97 Ibid., at 318-319.
98 Ibid., at 320-321.
99 *Bleaden* v. *Hancock* (1829) 4 C. & P. 152; cf. *Kitano* v. *Commonwealth of Australia* (1973) 2 A.L.R. 83 (ante, p. 134).
1 (1803) 4 Esp. 229.

misconduct of either in the driving of the carriage, while it was so in their joint care.[2]

It can be assumed that the same principle applies to any action brought by the bailor for negligent misuse of the chattel,[3] at least when the misconduct of one bailee occurs in the performance of the bailment.[4] In fact, the details as to liability in this context can probably be best worked out as implications within the bailment agreement itself, and there can be little doubt that business efficacy would generally favour a joint rather than a several liability.[5]

Actions by co-owners: At Common Law there is some doubt as to whether, and in what circumstances, one co-owner can bring trespass or trover against another.[6] Section 10 of the *Torts (Interference with Goods) Act* 1977 now seeks to dispel this confusion by providing as follows:

> (1) Co-ownership is no defence to an action founded on conversion or trespass to goods where the defendant without the authority of the other co-owner—
> (a) destroys the goods, or disposes of the goods in a way giving a good title to the entire property in the goods, or otherwise does anything equivalent to the destruction of the other's interest in the goods, or
> (b) purports to dispose of the goods in a way which would give a good title to the entire property in the goods if he was acting with the authority of all co-owners of the goods.
> (2) Subsection (1) shall not affect the law concerning execution or enforcement of judgments, or concerning any form of distress.
> (3) Subsection (1)(a) is by way of restatement of existing law so far as it relates to conversion.

VII. Other Remedies

The foregoing concludes our account of those major remedies that exist for the vindication of interests in chattels; but of course the bailor may enjoy other remedies drawn from the general law of tort. Foremost among these remedies is the action for negligence; a large proportion of actions against bailees are framed in negligence because, in most cases, the bailee's primary duty is to safeguard the goods with reasonable care. But even when based upon a lack of such care, the bailor's action may

---

[2] Ibid., at 230; aliter if one defendant had been a mere passenger: cf. *Wood Motors Ltd.* v. *McTavish* (1974) 21 D.L.R. (3d) 480, where the driver himself was held not to be a bailee.

[3] *Victoria U-Drive Yourself Auto Livery Ltd.* v. *Wood* [1930] 2 D.L.R. 811, at 813, 817. Cf. *Morris* v. *Armit* (1887) 4 Man. L.R. 152, which may be a simple illustration of the bailee's vicarious liability for third parties whom he allows to deal with the chatel rather than a true case of joint bailment. The Court cited with approval *Schouler on Bailments,* p. 142: "The hirer must answer not only for loss and injury inflicted upon the thing by himself in person, but also for the injurious acts of those whom he voluntarily admits, so to speak, into the use of the thing."

[4] Halsbury, loc. cit., citing *Morris* v. *C. W. Martin & Sons Ltd.* [1966] 1 Q.B. 716.

[5] Cf. *Coupe Co. Ltd.* v. *Maddick* [1891] 2 Q.B. 413, at 415 per Cave J.

[6] See *Holliday* v. *Camsell and White* (1787) 1 T.R. 658, and the discussion by Paton, op. cit., p. 403.

differ in several important respects from that enjoyed by a plaintiff non-bailor against an ordinary negligent tortfeasor.[7] Moreover, an action for breach of bailment may be possible irrespective of negligence on the part of the bailee.

The bailor may also, where appropriate, have a remedy against the bailee or a third party for breach of the defendant's duty as an occupier;[8] for nuisance or for breach of the rule in *Rylands* v. *Fletcher*;[9] for slander of title or passing off; or even, perhaps, under the special action on the case propounded by the High Court of Australia in *Beaudesert Shire Council* v. *Smith*.[10] Discussion of these remedies is superfluous, but it would seem that where the bailor's right of possession is suspended at the time of the alleged tort the above-mentioned remedies should issue only when his reversionary interest has been permanently injured.[11]

The bailor may also enjoy an action in contract; normally this will be against his bailee, and the possible concurrence between this and other remedies is discussed in Chapter 1. Occasionally, however, there will be a contractual remedy against a third party.

Finally, of course, there is the separate action for breach of bailment. Enough has already been said to demonstrate that the normal remedies in tort and contract do not encompass every situation in which a bailee may be liable. The residual remedies may be said to comprise the law of bailment, together with those wider aspects of liability (for example, in negligence) which overlap with other specific torts.

VIII. BAILEES AND THE JUS TERTII[12]

> There are numerous cases in connexion with wharfs and docks, in which, if the party entrusted with the possession of property were not estopped from denying the titles of the person from whom he received it, it would be difficult to transact commercial business.

Thus spoke Martin B. in *Cheesman* v. *Exall*.[13] The rule that precludes a bailee from pleading jus tertii, and thus from evading liability for damage or non-delivery on the grounds that the goods belong to someone other than the bailor, is a long-established one, which has been accepted for over a century in Canada[14] and New Zealand[15] as well as in England.[16]

---

[7] E.g. burden of proof: ante, p. 40.

[8] Post, p. 214 et seq.

[9] (1866) L.R. 1 Ex. 265; (1868) L.R. 3 H.L. 330.

[10] (1966) 120 C.L.R. 145; this doctrine was recognised obiter as applicable to injuries to interests in chattels in *Kitano* v. *Commonwealth of Australia* (1973) 2 A.L.R. 83, at 98-99.

[11] Cf. ante, p. 153.

[12] Cf. *Torts (Interference with Goods) Act* 1977, ss. 7-8.

[13] (1851) 6 Ex. 341, at 346.

[14] *Holton* v. *Sanson* (1861) 11 U.C.C.P. 606; *Le Bel* v. *Fredericton Boom Co.* 9 N.B.R. 198; *Stewart* v. *Gates* (1881) 2 P.E.I. 432; *Schentag* v. *Gauthier* (1972) 27 D.L.R. (3d) 710; *Canadian National Railway Co.* v. *Hammill* (1974) 43 D.L.R. (3d) 731; cf. *Leighton* v. *Bohan* (1866) 11 N.B.R. 440, where the question did not fall to be decided.

[15] *Peacock* v. *Anderson* (1878) 4 N.Z. Jur. (N.S.) S.C. 67.

[16] Early decisions to this effect are cited in *Biddle* v. *Bond* (1865) 6 B. & S. 225; 122 E.R. 1179.

The rule is based on obvious and necessary considerations, which can readily be tested by considering any alternative principle:

> [T]o allow a depositary of goods or money, who has acknowledged the title of one person, to set up the title of another who makes no claim or has abandoned all claim, would enable the depositary to keep for himself that to which he does not pretend to have any title in himself whatsoever.[17]

Of course, the implementation of the rule can place the bailee in serious difficulties, as where he is faced by two competing claims for the goods and is afraid of delivering them to the wrong person. In such a case it would be tempting to retain the goods and to refuse to hand them to either party until a valid title had been proved. But such an expedient would be both dangerous and unnecessary for the majority of bailees. It would be dangerous because a refusal to redeliver to the bailor may well amount to a conversion. It would be unnecessary partly because a redelivery to the bailor may not constitute a conversion vis-à-vis the third party,[18] but (far more important) because the bailee may institute interpleader proceedings,[19] whereunder the true owner would be identified and the goods formally allocated to him.

The bailee's inability to plead jus tertii applies irrespective of the particular remedy the bailor is seeking against him, whether it be conversion, detinue, negligence or even trespass. It is immaterial that the bailor may have obtained the goods illegally or may have been acting throughout in wilful derogation of the rights of the third party.[20] Even a thief, it seems, can create a enforceable bailment of goods he has stolen,[21] and the policy of the bailee's estoppel would seem consistent with its application to such a bailment.

In some situations, the bailee's difficulties may be exacerbated by the fact that he is uncertain as to who, at the relevant time, is his bailor. Such a problem arose in *Rogers, Sons & Co.* v. *Lambert & Co.*[22] The plaintiffs had purchased copper from the defendants, who continued to hold it as warehousemen subject to usual warehousing charges. Some time later the plaintiffs sold the copper to a third party and endorsed their delivery orders to the buyers, but these were never presented to the defendants and no attornment to the third parties ever took place. The

---

[17] *Betteley* v. *Reed* (1843) 4 Q.B. 511, at 517 per Lord Denman C.J.
[18] Ante, p. 148; but cf. *European & Australian Royal Mail Co. Ltd.* v. *Royal Steam Packet Co.* (1861) 30 L.J.C.P. 247; post, p. 170. Much may depend upon the degree of information he possesses as to the third party's rival claim. If he has credible notice of such a claim, his most sensible course is to interplead. If he does not interplead it seems that he redelivers at his peril: *Winter* v. *Bancks* (1901) 84 L.T. 504; Salmond, *Torts* (16th ed.), p. 104.
[19] See *Common Law Procedure Act* 1860 (U.K.); cf. *Dollfus Mieg* v. *Bank of England* [1949] 1 Ch. 369 (appeals decided on different grounds [1950] 1 Ch. 383; [1952] A.C.) where no interpleader could issue because the bailors were foreign sovereigns.
[20] *Biddle* v. *Bond* (supra), at 1182 (E.R.). It seems that the rule extends not only to the property originally bailed but to its produce or progeny, provided no property in the latter has vested in the bailee: *Horne* v. *Richardson* (1970) 64 Q.J.P. 47.
[21] *Chapman* v. *Robinson and Ferguson* (1969) 71 W.W.R. 515, at 522.
[22] [1891] 1 Q.B. 318; see also *Gibbs, Bright & Co.* v. *Ralph* (1892) 14 A.L.T. 80; *Ogle* v. *Atkinson* (1814) 5 Taunt. 759; 15 R.R. 647; *In re Savoy Estate Ltd., Remnant* v. *Savoy Estate Ltd.* [1949] 1 Ch. 622.

plaintiffs subsequently notified the defendants that they had cancelled the endorsement on the delivery orders and demanded delivery to themselves, but the defendants refused, claiming that the plaintiffs no longer had an interest in the copper, and admitting that they were retaining it for their own benefit and protection. The plaintiffs sued for damages and their claim succeeded. Their status as bailors had not been determined by their giving a delivery order to the third-party for this could be withdrawn, as between the plaintiffs and the defendants, at any time: "and they did withdraw it by demanding the goods."[23] It would have been otherwise if the defendants had already attorned to the third parties,[24] for then the plaintiffs would have ceased to be bailors and the defendants' estoppel would have applied between them and the third parties alone.[25] Any unqualified failure to deliver to the third parties would therefore have amounted to a conversion, and it would have been no defence for the warehousemen to plead that the third parties had no proper title.[26]

Exceptions to the rule are four-fold. Three of the exceptions are of general validity; the fourth applies only in the context of hire-purchase agreements.

A. Eviction by title paramount

If the true owner appears, and demands the goods from the bailee, the bailee is bound to deliver them and may be liable for conversion or detinue if he does not,[27] for he has no better title than his bailor.[28] In such an event the bailee possesses a complete and final answer to any subsequent action against him by the bailor; he may, in fact, invoke the title of the third party, and the consequences that have enured from it, as a defence.[29] The classic case of this defence is *Biddle* v. *Bond*,[30] where the plaintiff wrongfully seized goods belonging to one Robbins by way of distress for rent, and delivered them to the defendant (an auctioneer) for sale. When the sale was about to begin, the defendant received a notice from Robbins stating that the distress was void, showing that no relationship of landlord or tenant existed between him and the plaintiff and demanding the goods or their proceeds. The sale proceeded as planned because the defendant had no time to investigate these alle-

---

23 Ibid., at 324 per Lord Esher M.R.; cf. *European & Australian Royal Mail Co. Ltd.* v. *Royal Steam Packet Co.* (1861) 30 L.J.C.P. 247; post, p. 170.
24 See Chapter 21, post.
25 See [1891] 1 Q.B. 318, at 320 (arguendo); *Henderson & Co.* v. *Williams* [1895] 1 Q.B. 521; *Ross* v. *Edwards & Co.* (1895) 73 T.L.R. 100.
26 *Henderson & Co.* v. *Williams* (supra); *Ross* v. *Edwards & Co.* (supra), at 101.
27 *Wilson* v. *Anderson* (1830) 1 B. & Ad. 450; aliter where the bailee merely declines on a reasonable doubt and requests a reasonable time for inquiry: *Pillott* v. *Wilkinson* (1864) 3 H. & C. 345; *Lee* v. *Robinson and Bayes* (1856) 25 L.J.C.P. (N.S.) 249; Paton, op. cit., pp. 392-393.
28 *Biddle* v. *Bond* supra, at 1181 (E.R.).
29 *Shelbury* v. *Scotsford* (1603) Yelv. 22; *Rogers & Co.* v. *Lambert & Co.* [1891] 1 Q.B. 318. But this will be of no avail where the third party lacks a sufficient title, even where the bailee has redelivered under an order of the court; Paton, op. cit., pp. 390, 396. In such a case he will probably be in breach of his duty as a bailee for failing to inform the bailor of a rival claim: *Ranson* v. *Platt* [1911] 2 K.B. 291.
30 (1865) 6 B. & S. 225; 122 E.R. 1179.

gations, but he subsequently refused to pay the proceeds to the plaintiff, and the plaintiffs sued him for their return. In dismissing the action, Blackburn J. remarked that the defendant would have no defence to an action for conversion or money had and received brought by Robbins; he was therefore compelled to yield to Robins' claim,[31] and it would be unjust and contrary to principle to make him liable to the plaintiff for doing so. The estoppel against setting up a jus tertii ceases when the bailment on which it is founded is determined by what is equivalent to an eviction by title paramount.[32]

In the old case of *Shelbury* v. *Scotsford*[33] the court held that proof of eviction vi et armis et contra voluntatem "does in law discharge the promise" the bailee originally makes to redeliver the chattel, and entitles him to plead the true property in a third party. But it is clear from modern authority that there need be no violent, physical expulsion from the chattel in order for the bailee's estoppel to be determined by eviction. This much emerges from *Biddle* v. *Bond*[34] and from the New South Wales decision in *Edwards* v. *Amos*,[35] where Herron J. remarked:

> It is not necessary in my view that there should be actual force used. The rule is the same where a lawful demand is made by the true owner against which the bailee has no defence.

In fact, it seems that an eviction may be deemed to have occurred whenever the bailee returns the goods to the true owner upon the latter's demand, whether under threat of action or not.[36] But, of course, to do so without clear proof of the third party's interest would place the bailee in considerable jeopardy, for a mistaken but honest belief in the identity of the owner would afford him no defence in any later action brought against him by the bailor. In most cases, the safest course is to interplead.[37]

Where, on the other hand, the bailee decides to continue in possession, he will not be able to demonstrate an eviction simply by virtue of his knowledge of a rival claim to the goods,[38] or because somebody has made an adverse claim against him.[39] In this situation, there must be clear evidence of authority from the rival claimant, empowering him to resist the bailor's claim on his behalf. It is here that the first exception to the bailee's estoppel begins to shade into the second.

---

[31] Note that he had not actually paid over the money, but "from the evidence of Robbins . . . the Court drew the inference of fact that the defendant withheld the proceeds from the plaintiff and defended this action, relying on the right and by the authority of Robbins, and not hostilely to him": (1865) 122 E.R. 1179, at 1180.

[32] Ibid., at 1182; *Ross* v. *Edwards & Co.* (1895) 73 T.L.R. 100, at 101 (where it is remarked that the parties may make a special contract to the contrary effect).

[33] (1603) Yelv. 22; 80 E.R. 17.

[34] (1865) 6 B. & S. 225; 122 E.R. 1179; also *Ross* v. *Edwards & Co.* (supra), where the eviction resulted from a judgment on interpleader proceedings brought by the bailees.

[35] (1945) 62 W.N. (N.S.W.) 204, at 205.

[36] Salmond, op. cit., p. 105; *Edwards* v. *Amos* (supra); cf. *Eastern Construction Co. Ltd.* v. *National Trust Co. Ltd.* [1914] A.C. 197. And see infra, p. 171.

[37] *Edwards* v. *Amos* (1945) 62 W.N. (N.S.W.) 204, at 206.

[38] *Betteley* v. *Reed* (1843) 4 Q.B. 511.

[39] *Thorne* v. *Tilbury* (1858) 3 H. & N. 534.

B. Defence by authority of the proper owner

The bailee who, in refusing to redeliver goods to the bailor, acts under
the authority of the true owner, is not bound by the ordinary principles
of estoppel and may in effect raise the jus tertii. In such a case, he must
demonstrate that he is defending "upon the right and title, and by the
authority" of the true owner.[40] Once again, it is not enough that he has
become aware of the title of a third person or that an adverse claim has
actually been made upon him.[41] The distinction was lucidly drawn by
Lord Esher M.R. in *Rogers, Sons & Co.* v. *Lambert & Co.*:[42]

> The defendants refused to give up the copper to the plaintiffs. They
> did not say "you have sold the copper to a third person, and you have
> given him delivery orders, and he has claimed the copper from us,
> and, therefore, we are not safe in delivering it to you, and we must
> either deliver it to him, or we must ask you for an interpleader order."
> Indeed, they could not obtain an interpleader order, because no-one
> had presented the delivery orders to them. They did not say "we know
> that you have indorsed the delivery orders, and handed them over
> to such a firm, and upon their behalf we decline to give up the cop-
> per to you, and we shall defend any action which you may bring
> against us, not in our own interest, because we have none, but for
> them." On the contrary, the defendants . . . said expressly: "We
> are holding the copper for ourselves" . . . The defendants would have
> succeeded if they had defended the action on behalf of these persons.
> But they have not done so; and if, therefore, they are held liable, it
> is because they have not chosen to defend themselves in the way in
> which the law recognises.

Of course, the person on whose behalf the bailee defends the action
must be the rightful owner, so that this course of action still involves
some measure of risk to the defendant. Moreover, the exception is
displaced, and the ordinary estoppel continues to operate, when the bailee
has originally accepted delivery of the goods with full knowledge of the
adverse claim.[43] As Lush L.J. remarked,[44] a bailee who knows of two
adverse claims to the goods and who elects to take the part of one of
the claimants (e.g. by selling the goods as that person's) is estopped
from afterwards denying that claimant's title. No such election had been
made in *Biddle* v. *Bond*,[45] where the auctioneer merely sold the goods

---

[40] *Thorne* v. *Tilbury* (1858) 3 H. & N.S. 534, at 537 per Pollock C.B.; cited with
approval by Blackburn J. in *Biddle* v. *Bond* (1865) 122 E.R., at 1182; *Ex parte
Davies; In re Sadler* (1881) 19 Ch. D. 86, at 90-91. See further *Edwards* v.
Amos (1945) 45 W.N. (N.S.W.) 204, at 206 per Herron J.: "Some difficulty has
been created by the use of the words 'If he defends upon the right and title and
by the authority of the true owner'. In my view, this means that the defendant
in an action for conversion must show a bona fide claim by a named person
and a reliance upon the title of that specified person. It is not enough for
instance, that the bailee has become aware of the title of a third person, unless
he claims not to act for himself, but on the authority of such third person. For
example, where the third person had no claim or had abandoned all claim: see
Betteley v. *Reed* (1843) 4 Q.B. 511; *Rogers, Sons & Co.* v. *Lambert & Co.*
[1891] 1 Q.B. 318, at 328". And see also *Sheridan* v. *New Quay Co.* (1858) 4
C.B. (N.S.) 618.
[41] *Biddle* v. *Bond* (supra).
[42] [1891] 1 Q.B. 318, at 323.
[43] *Ex parte Davies, In Re Sadler* (1881) 19 Ch. D. 86.
[44] Ibid., at 93.
[45] (1865) 6 B. & S. 225; 122 E.R. 1179.

under a pre-existing authority between him and the bailor, shortly after notice was given of the third party claim. But in the present case, an auctioneer had deliberately elected to sell the goods for one of the two known claimants, and was accordingly bound by that election.

The idea of election may conceivably have been applied to alleviate the "almost Gilbertian" situation that arose in *Remnant* v. *Savoy Estate Ltd.*[46] The action concerned a quantity of furniture which had originally belonged to Mr & Mrs Remnant but which they had sold in 1907 to Sir Charles Friswell. The Remnants were allowed to continue in possession of the goods and some time later Mrs Remnant lent them to a company (Savoy Estates) which her husband had been instrumental in forming, and which used the furniture in connection with one of its hotels. In 1940 a receiver was appointed at the instigation of certain debenture holders and he applied for leave to sell the furniture. Mrs Remnant resisted this on the ground that the furniture in question had been given to her by Sir Charles Friswell. Her action failed before the Court of Appeal because she could not prove the gift. Undeterred, Mrs Remnant issued a further summons, claiming not only the furniture comprised in the Court of Appeal action but also certain other items not covered in the earlier litigation. Evershed J. held that as regards the bulk of the furniture the question was res judicata and could not be re-opened; however, he allowed her to amend her summons so that it now referred only to those items which had not been the subject of the Court of Appeal's decision. This summons then came before Vaisey J., who dismissed it on the ground that Mrs Remnant had failed to establish that any furniture existed over and above the subject matter of the earlier judgment.

Now between the judgments of Evershed and Vaisey JJ. there had appeared upon the scene a further set of claimants, in the form of the personal representatives of Sir Charles Friswell. They claimed *all* the furniture in the possession of the receiver, and not merely those items (if any) that were excluded from the decision in the Court of Appeal. Vaisey J. heard their summons together with Mrs Remnant's, and awarded the furniture to them. He did so because title had already been conclusively established to rest in Friswell and no other course was open to him than to restore it to his estate. From this decision the company (in the form of its receiver and one of its debenture-holders) appealed.

One of the problems facing the Court of Appeal, when the case came before them for the second time, was that when the company, through the appellants, had resisted the claims of Mrs Remnant in the earlier Court of Appeal litigation, it had done so on the ground that title to the furniture rested in Friswell or his estate. (In fact, it seems to have raised the jus tertii and there is no apparent indication as to why, as bailees from Mrs Remnant, it was allowed to do so).[47] Could the company now turn round to the representatives and say, "although we championed your cause for the purpose of resisting Mrs Remnant, we now contend

46 [1949] 1 Ch. 622, at 630; Paton, op. cit., pp. 393-394.
47 Cf. Evershed M.R. at 634.

that the gift to her was valid and that is she, rather than you, who is the true owner?" To allow them to do so, of course, would have meant not merely permitting the receiver to allege something entirely inconsistent with his earlier allegations as to title,[48] but also permitting him to defeat one claim through the instrumentality of another claim which he had already, in the earlier Court of Appeal action, effectively detonated. He was, in other words, attempting to have his cake and eat it. His conduct fell almost exactly within the description outlined over a hundred years earlier by Lord Denman C.J. as the reason for denying the bailee a right to plead jus tertii.[49]

In fact, the question of the bailee's estoppel did not require a final answer from the court, who decided the case on the grounds that the earlier Court of Appeal decision was res judicata not only between the receiver and Mrs Remnant, but between him and Friswell's estate, and that the receiver, as an officer of the Court, was in any event bound to deliver up the furniture to the person entitled, so that whether that person was Mrs Remnant or the personal representatives it was clear that the company itself had no right to retain the goods.[50] Nor indeed had the company alleged any such right,[51] for it had merely sought to exploit the relative weakness of each of the competing claims.

The Court of Appeal did, however, comment upon a suggestion made by counsel for the representatives that the receiver, by defending the earlier action on the title of Sir Charles Friswell, had in effect attorned to him as a bailee and was therefore, in this capacity, estopped from denying the title of his constructive or adoptive bailor, since he did not do so on the authority of Mrs Remnant. Evershed M.R. thought that there might be great difficulty in this approach,[52] and both he and Somervell L.J. declined to express a concluded opinion upon it.[53] The Master of the Rolls agreed that the effective emasculation of any subsequent claim by Mrs Remnant had produced a situation analogous to that outlined in *Betteley* v. *Reed*;[54] and he seemed to accept that it would be undesirable if a person who possessed no title to goods might effectively acquire one merely by setting up the title of a third party who had abandoned all claim to the goods *or who could make no claim to them* (e.g. by being estopped from doing so). He conceded, however, that there could be difficulties in characterising the appellants as bailees of Friswell for the purposes of the rule.[55] Somervell J. agreed (albeit tentatively) that the principle in *Biddle* v. *Bond*[56] might by a comparatively minor extension be regarded as covering the issue".[57]

---

[48] Which was, in the circumstances, a perfectly proper approach; [1949] 1 Ch. 622, at 635-636 per Evershed M.R.
[49] *Betteley* v. *Reed* (1843) 4 Q.B. 511, at 517; ante p. 164. See [1949] 1 Ch. 622, at 635.
[50] Note that the representatives had in fact expressed the intention giving the goods to Mrs Remnant.
[51] [1949] 1 Ch., at 633.
[52] Ibid., at 634.
[53] Ibid., at 638.
[54] (1843) 4 Q.B. 511, at 517; ante, p. 164.
[55] [1949] 1 Ch., at 635-636.
[56] (1861) 6 B. & S. 225; 122 E.R. 1179; ante, p. 165.
[57] [1949] 1 Ch. at 638.

Jenkins L.J. accepted that the company (after the elimination of Mrs Remnant) held the goods as bailee for Friswell's representatives but made no comment on the question of jus tertii as between these parties. It is submitted that the bailee's estoppel could have legitimately been applied in this case, if necessary upon an analogy with the statements of Lush L.J. in *Ex parte Davies; In re Sadler*[58] and that the company, having elected to take the part of Friswell in the original litigation, could have been prevented from later resiling from this commitment on the authority of that case.

Some older authorities appear to suggest that a bailee may refuse to deliver up goods whenever property lies in someone other than the person from whom he has received them.[59] In the light of modern authority, this is clearly an oversimplification, but there is one decision which holds that the grant of an immediate right to possession by the bailor to a third party can afford the bailee a legitimate defence for refusing to redeliver to the bailor.[60] At first sight this would appear to conflict with *Rogers, Sons & Co.* v. *Lambert & Co.*,[61] where the fact of the sale to third parties did not entitle the warehouseman (who had not attorned to them) to deny his bailor's title. But the cases are distinguishable and the *European Mail* case can be reconciled with modern authority on several grounds. In many cases where there is a transfer of an interest in goods by a bailor (or his total elimination from the bailment relation) the most appropriate conclusion will be to regard the transfer as effecting a change in the parties to the bailment. The purchaser or other grantee of an immediate interest from the bailor may then become, in turn, the bailor proper, and it will be his title that the continuing bailee is estopped from denying. Admittedly, a warehouseman will not inherit a substitutional bailor until he attorns, but in other cases the safest definition of the bailor may be the person who in fact and to the knowledge of the bailee is entitled to the goods. Certainly, the bailee will normally owe to him the duties of a bailee,[62] and the rule relieving him of a double estoppel is justifiable at least in these cases (like the *European Mail* case) where the restoration to an original bailor would constitute a conversion between the bailee and the third party.

In such a case it is the conduct of the original bailor himself which incapacitates him from taking advantage of the general principle, and he can have not just complaint if the bailee chooses to acknowledge the change he has brought about.[63] Generally this result will be attainable

---

[58] (1881) 19 Ch. D. 86, at 93; ante, p. 167.

[59] E.g. *Ogle* v. *Atkinson* (1815) 5 Taunt. 759; 15 R.R. 647, at 650. The statement is obiter because the bailor did in fact enjoy a complete title; see Paton, op. cit., pp. 394-395. It is difficult to understand why the bailees in *Remnant* v. *Savoy Estate Ltd.* [1949] 1 Ch. 622 were permitted to plead the jus tertii of Friswell in the earlier actions before Uthwatt, J. and the Court of Appeal.

[60] *European & Australian Royal Mail Co. Ltd.* v. *Royal Steam Packet Co.* (1861) 30 L.J.C.P. 247 (mortgage of ship by bailors).

[61] [1891] 1 Q.B. 318; ante, p. 164.

[62] Cf. Ch. 22, post.

[63] Ibid., at 253: "The principle against the plaintiffs on this point is, that if the defendants gave back the ship they would be liable to an action of trover by the mortgagees, and the plaintiffs, to whom the promise was made, have so changed their situation as to make it an actionable wrong done by the

within the context of the particular agreement, express or implied, between the original bailor and the bailee: thus, as Willes J. observed in the *European Mail Co.* case:[64]

> At the time the defendants entered into this contract the plaintiffs were owners of the vessels, and the contract to give up was made with reference to that relation, and on the faith that the plaintiffs would be the persons entitled, subject to this, that they might appoint other persons to receive, or might interfere so as to prevent the defendants from giving up the ship, or, at least, without peril to themselves. On this ground, I think that the defendants are excused; they could not give up the vessels without subjecting themselves to an action, and that is not what they contracted to do; therefore, on this point my judgment is for the defendants.

C. Redelivery of the goods to the proper owner

It is clear from the foregoing that the first two exceptions are not always clearly distinguished and that in many cases a bailee may claim protection under either or both of these rules.[65] Greater uncertainty surrounds the ability of the bailee to confer upon himself the right to impugn his bailor's title by identifying the true owner or person entitled to immediate possession and, without eviction or even demand, delivering the goods to him. Superficially, this course would seem unobjectionable insofar as it does not involve the bailee's exploiting the relative claims of two competing owners in order to keep the goods for himself.[66] Of course, he would not be protected in any event if he mistakenly identified the owner;[67] the question is rather whether he should be entitled to act in contravention of his implied promise of redelivery at all.

The rule that he should be so entitled is supported by the dictum of Herron J. in *Edwards* v. *Amos*[68] and by certain American authority.[69] On the other hand, it was held in *Elkin & Co. Pty. Ltd.* v. *Specialised Television Installations Pty. Ltd.*[70] that where the true owner has bailed goods, it is no defence to an action brought by him that the bailee has

---

defendants if they keep their promise. That is an excuse by reason of which the plaintiff have done"; per Erle C.J. See also *Sheridan* v. *New Quay Co.* (1858)

4 C.B. (N.S.) 618.
[64] (1861) 30 L.J.C.P. 247, at 253.
[65] One decision which seems to have decided on both principles is *Biddle* v. *Bond* (1865) 6 B. & S. 225; 122 E.R. 1179.
[66] This was given as the reason for the bailee's estoppel in *Betteley* v. *Reed* (1843) 4 Q.B. 511, at 517; supra, p. 164.
[67] *Tozer Kemsley & Millbourn (Australasia) Pty. Ltd.* v. *Collier's Interstate Transport Service Ltd.* (1956) 94 C.L.R. 384, where it is held that the defendant also carries the burden of showing that he delivered to the bailor or some person authorised by him to receive the goods.
[68] (1945) 62 W.N. (N.S.W.) 204; ante, p. 167.
[69] See *Yokohama Specie Bank* v. *Geo. S. Bush & Co.* (1922) 209 Pac. 676; (1922-1923) 21 *Michigan Law Review* 344, where, however, the trial court's decision that the defendant bailee should be relieved was reversed on the ground that it did not conclusively appear from the pleadings that the bailee yielded the goods on a sustainable claim of paramount title.
[70] [1961] S.R. (N.S.W.) 165; 77 W.N. 844.

handed them to a third party who, as between himself and the owner, has the contractual right to possession.[71]

Accordingly, it would seem that this exception should be limited to cases where full ownership is vested in the deliveree; and (perhaps) that the bailee's defence should arise only where three has been a claim against him falling short of eviction. Although there are stronger grounds for relieving the bailee who delivers in reliance upon a third-party ownership than there are in the case of a bailee who relies upon such ownership as a ground for retraining the property against his bailor, the safest course continues to be to interplead.

D. Hire-purchase cases

Since hire-purchase is in essence a contract of deferred purchase, and since the hirer clearly expects and bargains for the ultimate transmission of title, the law permits this variety of bailee to invoke the lack of property in the lessor as a defence against actions for payment and as a cause of action in its own right.[72]

1. *Jus tertii and the constructive or quasi-bailee*: The cases in which the bailee's estoppel was formulated were all examples of orthodox, consensual bailments in which the bailee had either accepted delivery from the plaintiff or had attorned to him. A more questionable relationship arose in *Remnant* v. *Savoy Estate Ltd.*[73] and here, as we have seen, there was considerable doubt as to whether the appellants were bailees of Friswell's estate for the purpose of the rule. Further difficulties arise when one considers the application of the bailee's estoppel to those varieties of quasi- or constructive bailment which have only in recent years been regarded as importing that relationship at all. There seem to be four principal areas in which the operation of the rule is subject to special considerations.

(a) *Bailments by finding*: These do not arise by direct delivery inter partes and cannot, except upon the most artificial analysis, be said to occur with the consent of the owner. The principal, and probably the only, manner in which they equate with orthodox, consensual bailments lies in the bailee's duty of care and his correlative onus of proof.[74] In fact, cases of finding involve bailments without bailors and it is established that the finder-bailee is entitled to require any claimant to prove that he has a better right to the goods than the finder himself. Of course such a right will not necessarily depend upon the claimant's being the owner. But the elaborate protection which the law gives to a finder's possession is inconsistent with, and must prevail over, the rule prohibiting a bailee

---

[71] Cf. *Gibbs, Bright & Co.* v. *Ralph* (1892) 14 A.L.T. 80; that if a warehouseman delivers to someone other than the person to whom he has given his bond certificate, he is liable to the certificate-holder for all the goods represented in it, even where the present holder is an assignee without notice to the warehouseman.

[72] See *Supply of Goods (Implied Terms) Act* 1973 (U.K.), s. 8(1)(a), as amended by Schedule 4, para. 35; *Consumer Credit Act* 1974; *H.P. Act* 1960-1965 (N.S.W.), s. 5; *H.P. Act* 1959 (Vic.), s. 5; *H.P. Act* (Qld) 1960, s. 5; *H.P. Act* 1959 (W.A.), s. 5; *H.P. Act* 1959 (Tas.), s. 9; *H.P. Ord.* 1961-1966 (A.C.T.), s. 10; *H.P. Agreements Act* 1960-1966 (S.A.), s. 5; *Consumer Transactions Act* 1972-1973 (S.A.), ss. 8(1), 24. Cf. p. 4, ante.

[73] [1949] 1 Ch. 622; ante, p. 168.

[74] See generally Chapter 22, post.

from raising jus tertii in an action to dispossess him of the goods. Were the law otherwise, it might become impossible to determine who was entitled to the goods, and there would be the greatest difficulty in deciding who were bailors for the purposes of the rule. Accordingly, the bailee's estoppel has no place in the context of bailments by finding, except perhaps in those rare instances where a finder subsequently acknowledges a right to the goods on the part of a claimant, in which case he might be said to have attorned to him. Even here it is unlikely that such a claimant would be allowed to take advantage of the estoppel if the result were to be the compulsory delivery of the goods to a person with no actual right. If he has such a right, it will stand or fall by its own merits and there is no need for the estoppel to be invoked. If he does not, there is no reason why he should recover the goods, whether the finder has subsequently acknowledged his putative ownership or not. Only where the bailee could be said to have derived some additional advantage from the bailment relation (e.g., where the claimant pays him warehousing charges until he collects the goods) is there any possibility of the proposed rule working unjustly. Greater injustice may, however, arise even in this situation if the finder is compelled, by delivering the goods to the claimant, to commit an act of conversion. The law in this area cannot be said to be certain, but it is submitted that the application of the jus tertii principle as between finders and persons who in fact have no right to the goods should occur only in very exceptional circumstances, if it is to be allowed to occur at all.

(b) *Involuntary bailments*: These represent an even more questionable group than bailments by finding, for there is considerable doubt as to whether they are bailments for any purpose or in any sense of the word.[75] They arise whenever a person is knowingly but unwillingly put in possession of goods belonging to another. In such a case, the traditional reasons for applying the bailee's estoppel would appear to be lacking. These reasons were stated by Blackburn J. in *Biddle* v. *Bond*[76] to be as follows:

> (i) In cases of attornment the bailee represents to a purchaser of the goods that property in them has, in effect, passed to him; this may induce the purchaser to change his position[77] and it is therefore clearly undesirable to allow the bailee to go back on his word.[78]
>
> (ii) In cases of bailment by direct delivery, the bailor represents that the goods are his and the bailee, by taking them, impliedly promises that this representation will not be questioned; the bailor, in other words, yields the goods on the faith that the bailee will not deny his title later. " . . . the bailor represents to the bailee that he may safely accept the bailment. On that representation the bailee promises to redeliver."[79]

Neither of these justifications seem appropriate to the case of involuntary bailments ab initio, where the recipient has made no express

---

[75] Chapter 12, post.
[76] (1861) 6 B. & S. 225; 122 E.R. 1179, at 1182.
[77] As in *Hawes* v. *Watson* (1824) 2 B. & C. 540.
[78] The representation is "analogous to a warranty of title for good consideration to the purchaser", per Blackburn J. in *Biddle* v. *Bond* (supra).
[79] *Ross* v. *Edwards & Co.* (1895) 73 L.T. 100, at 101 per Lord McNaghten.

or tacit representation that the bailor's title will remain unquestioned. The policy of the law has been to pitch the duties of an involuntary bailee at the lowest conscionable level, and it appears reasonable that a sender of unsolicited goods, for example, should be put to proof of his title in any action for their recovery. Admittedly, it seems anomalous that such a bailor should be unable to plead estoppel whereas a thief who has entered into a voluntary bailment is entitled to do so. But the involuntary bailee is probably more akin in this respect to a finder than to a voluntary bailee, and in cases where there is no shadow of an inducement to the bailor to part with possession it seems more appropriate to apply the rule relating to finders than to that which governs the more conventional species of bailment.

The only guidance on this point seems to come from a somewhat unsatisfactory decision of the Nova Scotian Supreme Court in 1921.[80] The facts of this case are set out elsewhere.[81] Three members of the Court agreed that there was no duty of care on the part of the defendant and in so holding seemed to accept that he was merely an involuntary bailee. The two remaining judges dismissed the appeal on the grounds that ". . . it has not been shewn that the plaintiff has suffered any damage inasmuch as I do not think under the evidence the car can be said to be his property."[82]

Unfortunately, this seems to be presented in the report as a separate rather than an additional ground of decision and the learned judges do not specify the kind of bailment under which a bailor must prove himself to be the owner in order to succeed. Insofar, however, as the case can be construed as authority for a denial of the traditional estoppel in cases of involuntary bailment, it is submitted that it represents a sound and acceptable rule.[83]

Different considerations apply, of course, where an originally voluntary bailment becomes involuntary by lapse of time or other events.[84] In this instance, the initial acquiesence of the bailee should be sufficient to bring him within the operation of the orthodox rule and his ability to plead jus tertii should be limited to those situations in which (a) there has been an eviction by title paramount; (b) the bailee defends by authority of the true owner; (c) the bailee has redelivered to the true owner; or (d) the normal estoppel is displaced by the express or implied terms of the agreement between the parties.

Midway between these two extremes lies the concealed bailment;[85] that is, the situation where goods are transferred which contain other property concealed or unknown to the bailee and to which his consent

---

[80] *Fournier* v. *McKenna* (1921) 57 D.L.R. 725.
[81] Post, p. 208.
[82] (1921) 57 D.L.R. 725, at 726 per Mellish, J., Longley J. concurring.
[83] Admittedly, such a rule could operate harshly against those parties who are not responsible for the creation of the involuntary bailment, but it seems likely that cases of this kind in which the bailor is not the owner will be rare. This is an area in which policy would seem to demand a uniform rule and it would seem consonant with the primacy of possession that (for instance) the thief's title should lapse once the goods go out of his control.
[84] Discussed at p. 393 et. seq., post.
[85] See Chapter 6, post.

does not extend. Although, superficially, these cases would seem to be indistinguishable from orthodox involuntary bailments, it is submitted that the fairer rule might be to impose the conventional estoppel upon such a bailee. He has, at least, consented to possession of the containing chattel and has induced the bailor to surrender possession on the strength of that consent. His duty of care may be low or even non-existent but he must at least be taken to have promised that (unless he is incapacitated from doing so) he will restore the property intact.

(c) *Bailments by non-consent of owner*: Sometimes there will be a direct expropriation of goods without the consent of the person who, until that time, enjoyed possession. The "bailee" in such a case may be acting in the owner's interests (as where A seizes B's goods to save them from a fire)[86] or he may be acting for more selfish reasons: to enforce a security,[87] to steal the goods, or even because he thinks they are his own.[88] In several cases a person acquiring possession in this way has been held to owe the former possessor a duty to take reasonable care of the goods and to abstain from converting them, and to discharge, where necessary, the customary burden of proof.[89] Although in all these examples there is no element of inducement or bargain between the notional bailor and his bailee, it is clear that the policy of the bailee's estoppel is best served by denying the expropriator in such cases a right to plead jus tertii. In fact, this result is attained by virtue of a wider and more universal principle whereunder any person in possession of goods can sue for their damage or detention and need not first establish his right to them. This principle, which is clearly of greater importance to bailees than to bailors, is discussed in the following chapter.[90]

(d) *Sub-bailees*: There is now substantial authority for the view that a sub-bailee owes to his original bailor all the duties which at common law are imposed upon a direct bailee.[91] However, the decisions in point touch only upon the sub-bailee's duty of care and upon such allied questions as liability for delay in transit or the perennial burden of proof. So far as concerns the operation of the sub-bailee's estoppel, the only commentator to consider this question has assumed that this will apply both between sub-bailees and principal bailors, and between sub-bailees and their immediate bailors.[92] This result seems consonant with the overall assimilation of sub-bailments into the law which governs bailments generally, although it could have unfortunate consequences for a sub-bailee who, having returned the goods to one of a chain of preceding bailors, is then sued by another and is unable to deny his right to the goods. This seems, in fact, to be the only situation in which a bailee is compelled to serve two masters and to carry the burden of a double

---

[86] *R.* v. *Leigh* (1800) 2 East. P.C. 694.
[87] *Chesworth* v. *Farrar* [1967] 1 Q.B. 407.
[88] Cf. *McCowan* v. *McCulloch* [1926] 1 D.L.R. 312.
[89] Supra, nn. 86-88.
[90] But cf. *Torts (Interference with Goods) Act* 1977, ss. 7-8.
[91] *Morris* v. *C. W. Martin & Sons Ltd.* [1966] 1 Q.B. 716; see further Chapter 20, post.
[92] *Chitty on Contracts* (23rd ed.), Vol. II, para. 169.

estoppel. He will not always be entitled to interplead[93] and the rule which exonerates a bailee from conversion if he redelivers to his bailor may prove difficult to apply where the relevant bailors number more than one. It is submitted that redelivery to the immediate bailor should normally be regarded as a sufficient discharge of the sub-bailee's obligations, at least where the sub-bailee has no reasonable cause to doubt the sub-bailor's title or is not purporting to affect the title to the goods by redelivering them to him. Likewise, where the goods are demanded by the principal bailor, it should normally be sufficient for the sub-bailee to prove that the claimant was in fact the principal bailor and that he redelivered to him; unless perhaps the sub-bailee knew or had cause to know that in so doing, he was impairing any rights the intermediate bailor had over the goods, such as an actual or potential lien. It must be admitted, however, that it would be much simpler if the relationship between principal bailor and sub-bailee were *not* regarded as a bailment for the purposes of the rule in *Biddle* v. *Bond,*[94] and if the bailee's estoppel in such cases were to be confined to the relationship between intermediate and ultimate bailees on the one hand, and principal and intermediate bailors on the other. Once again, this is an area of bailment that awaits authoritative clarification.

(e) *Quasi-bailors*:[95] Where a bailment of goods is arranged by an intermediate party, such as a forwarding-agent, who does not take personal possession of the goods, it appears that he stands neither in the relationship of bailee to the original bailor nor in the relationship of bailor to the eventual bailee. Accordingly the intermediary's title may be denied by the bailee and the intermediary himself can deny the bailor's title. But the approach of the courts has not always been consistent in this context and it may be possible in any event to found an estoppel upon the implied agreement of the parties.[96]

---

[93] E.g. where at any given time there is only one claimant upon goods in his possession.
[94] (1861) 6 B. & S. 225; 122 E.R. 1179. But cf. *Torts (Interference with Goods) Act* 1977, ss. 7-8.
[95] The meaning of this expression is explained post, at p. 791.
[96] See further p. 831 et. seq., post, and cf. *Kahler* v. *Midland Bank Ltd.,* [1950] A.C. 24, especially per Lord MacDermott at 37-38.

CHAPTER 4

THE REMEDIES OF THE BAILEE

I. POSSESSION AS TITLE

Until I heard Mr. Macassey's able and ingenious argument, it never occurred to me to doubt that the law is that either bailee or bailor may sue a wrongdoer for the entire damage done to the chattel bailed. And after careful consideration of the argument and examination of the authorities, I adhere to my previous opinion.[1]

A bailee's possession entitles him to exercise any of the remedies to which possession is a prerequisite,[2] or to which it is one of several grounds of potential qualification.[3] His lack of full ownership does not preclude him, moreover, from recovering the full value of the chattel or the full cost of its impairment; the rule in such circumstances is that "as against a wrongdoer, possession is title".[4] Thus, if the goods are wrongfully taken from him or are damaged while in his possession, he may sue the wrongdoer in trespass, conversion or detinue just as if he were the bailor under a revocable bailment or an owner whose goods had never, before the wrongdoing, left his possession.

The exercise of these remedies will be governed, mutatis mutandis, by the same rules as apply in the case of the bailor; the components of each remedy will not be separately examined.[5] But the special nature of the bailee's position and the limited fiction of ownership that possession confers upon him necessitate some closer analysis of the foundations and consequences of his remedial equipment.

II. THE DEVELOPMENT OF THE RULE

It was only in the present century that the bailee's rights of action against a wrongdoer were finally established. Although decisions granting him an action in trover for the full value of the goods can be traced from the beginning of the nineteenth century,[6] it was at first unclear whether his use of this or any remedy was conditional upon his liability

---

[1] *Mangan* v. *Leary* (1877) 3 N.Z. Jur. (N.S.) C.A. 10, at 16 per Gillies J.
[2] As with trespass: ante., p. 117.
[3] E.g. detinue and conversion: ante, pp. 124, 148.
[4] *The Winkfield* [1902] P. 42, at 60 per Collins M.R.
[5] See Chapter 3.
[6] E.g. *Burton* v. *Hughes* (1824) 2 Bing. 173; *Jeffries* v. *G.W. Ry. Co.* (1856) 5 E. & B. 802; *Pritchard* v. *Blick* (1858) 1 F. & F. 404 N.P.; *Swire* v. *Leach* (1865) 18 C.B. (N.S.) 479; *Bennett* v. *Flood* (1864) 3 N.S.W.S.C.R. 158 (where the plaintiff was a drover of sheep); and see further Pollock & Wright, *Possession in the Common Law*, p. 166n; post, note 20; contra, *Chinery* v. *Viall* (1860) 5 H. & N. 288, at 295 per Bramwell, B., explained in *Attack* v. *Bramwell* (1863) 3 B. & S. 502.

to the bailor; if it were not, he would stand to recover more than he had lost, while the wrongdoer would be forfeiting more than the extent of his immediate damage.

The fact that the bailee's right of action could extend to an action on the case and could subsist irrespective of any liability on his part to the bailor was acknowledged by the New Zealand Court of Appeal in *Mangan* v. *Leary*.[7] A hired horse and carriage were damaged, while in the possession of the bailee, by the negligence of the defendant. The court allowed the bailee to recover the full cost of the damage, refusing to limit his recovery to the extent to which his own rights of enjoyment under the bailment had been impaired. One practical reason for the rule was given by Williams J.:

> [I]f one man entrusts another with the possession of movable chattels, he arms him with the powers necessary to protect them against wrongdoers, and these powers cannot be efficiently exercised if the wrongdoer could set up the right of a third person, and escape wholly or in part from the consequences of his wrong. If it were otherwise, as moveable property can be readily destroyed or made away with, the bailor would have to follow the bailee, and be always at hand to protect his interests against possible wrongdoers. The application of the rule may give rise to difficulty and inconvenience in certain cases, but I think on the whole that the balance of convenience is in its favour.[8]

The decision therefore confirmed that in an action brought by the plaintiff in possession of a chattel it was not open to the defendant wrongdoer to plead jus tertii; he could not set up the title of the bailor either as a total defence to the action or in diminution of the damages he was liable to pay the bailee. In so deciding, *Mangan* v. *Leary* was not especially novel even in the limited context of the action on the case.[9] But it is interesting as a transitional decision which illustrates the uncertainty felt by some judges on this question in the last quarter of the nineteenth century. Certainly, other members of the New Zealand Court of Appeal were less enthusiastic about the principle than Williams J. and more sensitive to its defects. Johnston J. remarked that he would not have concurred in its application if the matter had not been covered by authority,[10] and Richmond J. predicted that it might ideally be limited to cases in which the terms of the bailment manifestly entitle the bailee to act as the bailor's representative in an action against the wrongdoer.[11] In his view, it would often be preferable to allow the bailee to recover only to the extent of his limited interest.

Fourteen years later, similar reservations were translated into

---

[7] (1877) 3 N.Z. Jur. (N.S.) C.A. 10.

[8] Ibid., at 17.

[9] Earlier decisions allowing case were *Rooth* v. *Wilson* (1817) 1 B. & Ald. 59, a case of gratuitous bailment in which each of the four judges (with the possible exception of Lord Ellenborough C.J.) appeared to regard the accountability of the bailee to his bailor as irrelevant to the liability of the wrongdoer to the bailee, and where even Lord Ellenborough's judgement is reconcilable with the majority view; *Mangan* v. *Leary* (ante, n.1.), at 12-13 per Prendergast C.J.; *Croft* v. *Alison* (1821) 4 B. & Ald. 590; *Freeman* v. *Birch* 3 Q.B. 492n.

[10] (1877) 3 N.Z. Jur. (N.S.) C.A. 10, at 15-16.

[11] Ibid. at 14-15.

decision by the English Queen's Bench Division. In *Claridge* v. *South Staffordshire Tramway Co.*[12] the facts were almost identical to *Mangan* v. *Leary*; a horse, bailed to the plaintiff auctioneer with permission to him to use it, was injured through the negligent driving of a tram, and the court held that the plaintiff could recover nothing from the tortfeasor because he had lost nothing as a result of the damage. Liability should, in the Court's view, be conditional upon one of three events: impairment of the plaintiff's immediate interest under the bailment; some ground (presumably either tortious or contractual) rendering him liable to the bailor for the damage sustained by the chattel; or the absence of anyone apart from the bailee who is in a position to sue. In the present case none of these elements existed and the bailee's action was accordingly dismissed:

> I cannot understand why a bailee should be allowed to recover damages beyond the extent of his own loss simply because he happened to be in possession.
> It has been contended that because the plaintiff was bailee of a horse to which an injury was done, while in his possession, by a third person, he is entitled to recover from the wrongdoer the amount of the depreciation of the horse, notwithstanding that the injury was inflicted under circumstances which imposed no liability upon the plaintiff as towards his bailor. The mere statement of that proposition is enough to show that it cannot be true.[13]

Only one authority was cited in *Claridge*[14] and the weight of precedent was undoubtedly opposed to the robust principle it purported to lay down. It was therefore hardly surprising that the decision lasted less than a decade before it was overruled. This came in *The Winkfield*,[15] although the validity of *Claridge* had already been doubted as early as 1895 by A.L. Smith L.J. in *Meux* v. *G.E. Ry. Co.*[16]

> *The Winkfield*: Two ships collided in fog off Table Bay. One of them sank, taking down with it a quantity of mail and parcels which had been posted in South Africa and were en route to Southampton. The owners of the other ship admitted liability for a moiety of the damage and paid the appropriate sum into court. The Postmaster-General (acting on his own behalf and on behalf of the Postmaster-General of Natal and Cape Colony) sued the owners of the delinquent vessel for the value of the lost mail. It was assumed for the purposes of decision that the Postmaster-General was the bailee of the mail, rather than that any separate possession resided in the owners of the ship on which it had been carried.[17]

The Court of Appeal held that the owners of the negligent ship were liable in full for the value of the mail. It made no difference that the Postmaster-General could not have been sued by the bailors, or

---

[12] [1892] 1 Q.B. 422.
[13] Ibid., at 424, per Hawkins and Wills JJ. respectively.
[14] *Rooth* v. *Wilson* ante: see post, p. 294.
[15] [1902] P. 42.
[16] [1895] 2 Q.B. 387; but note that *Claridge's* case was actually followed in *Brown* v. *Hand-in-Hand Fire Insurance Society Ltd.* (1895) 11 T.L.R. 538.
[17] [1902] P. 42, at 53-54. An attempt to plead that the Postmaster-General was not in possession was made by counsel for the defendants, at 49: but it was held that the matter had been raised too late for proper consideration.

senders, because this immunity arose under a transaction to which the tortfeasor was a total stranger and was quite irrelevant to his own identification as a wrongdoer. Possession, the court held, constitutes title against a wrongdoer and "the latter cannot set up the jus tertii unless he claims under it."[18] This had long been the law in relation to goods dispossessed from a finder[19] and there was clearly no reason to distinguish for this purpose between the finder and the bailee. Collins M.R. cited with approval a statement of Lord Campbell in *Jeffries* v. *G.W. Ry. Co.*[20] that "a person possessed of goods as his property has a good title against every stranger, and . . . one who takes them from him, having no title in himself, is a wrongdoer, and cannot defend himself by shewing that there was title in some third person, for against a wrongdoer possession is title". While declining to deliver an opinion upon the true historical derivation of the bailee's rights of action, Collins M.R. held that it was a patent misreading of the ancestry of that principle to confine the bailee's action to those cases in which he was liable personally to the bailor for the loss or damage sustained.[21]

> [T]he root principle of the whole discussion is that, as against a wrongdoer, possession is title. The chattel that has been converted or damaged is deemed to be the chattel of the possessor and of no other, and therefore its deterioration or loss is his loss, and to him, if he demands it, it must be recouped. His obligation to account to the bailor is not really ad rem in the discussion. It only comes in after he has carried his legal position to its logical consequence against a wrongdoer and serves to soothe a mind disconcerted by the notion that a person who is not himself the complete owner should be entitled to receive back the full value of the chattel converted or destroyed. There is no inconsistency between the two positions: the one is the complement of the other. As between bailee and stranger possession gives title — that is, not a limited interest, but absolute and complete ownership and he is entitled to receive back a complete equivalent for the whole loss or deterioration of the thing itself. As between bailor and bailee the real interests of each must be inquired into, and, as the bailee has to account for the thing bailed, so he must account for that which has become its equivalent and now represents it. What he has recovered above his own interest he has received to the use of his bailor. The wrongdoer, having once paid full damages to the bailee, has an answer to any action by the bailor.[22]

The rule propounded by Collins M.R. has stood without judicial question since *The Winkfield* was decided, and has been acknowledged

[18] [1902] P. 42, at 54.

[19] *Armory* v. *Delamirie* (1721) 1 Stra. 504; see post, p. 852 et seq.

[20] (1856) 5 E. & B. 802, at 805; but see on this point Warren, *Trover and Conversion* (1936), p. 11, who points out that Lord Campbell spoke of the plaintiff as being in possession of the goods *as his property* and Wightman J. *as his own*. Other authority cited in support included *Burton* v. *Hughes* (1824) 2 Bing. 173; *Swire* v. *Leach* (1865) 18 C.B. (N.S.) 479; *Turner* v. *Hardcastle* (1862) 11 C.B. 683. See also *Rooth* v. *Wilson* and *Croft* v. *Alison* (both cited ante, n. 9); *Johnson* v. *Stear* (1863) 33 L.J.C.P. 130; *Brierley* v. *Kendall* (1852) 17 Q.B. 161.

[21] [1902] P. 42, at 58-59; see generally Holmes, *The Common Law*, pp. 167-170; Warren, *Trover and Conversion*, p. 4 et seq.

[22] [1902] P. 42, at 60-61.

on at least two occasions by both the House of Lords and the Privy Council.[23] A bailee in possession of a chattel may sue for any injury inflicted upon that chattel and may recover in full the cost of replacement or repair irrespective of whether the chattel has been destroyed or merely damaged;[24] irrespective of whether he has suffered any personal loss as a result of the wrongdoer's misconduct; irrespective of whether the injury sustained by the chattel exceeds the value of the bailee's own limited interest; irrespective of whether he is answerable to the bailor for the damage or loss in question; and irrespective of whether he is a gratuitous bailee with "bare" possession, or a bailee for reward with a finite tenure of the chattel, still subsisting when the wrong occurred.[25] The remedy brought by the bailee in possession can extend not only to trespass, case or conversion, but to negligence,[26] detinue[27] and even, it appears, breach of contract. Thus if the defendant contracts with the bailee of a quantity of steel to build a road in order to enable the steel to be moved under cover, and through his failure to perform this contract the steel becomes corroded, the bailee may recover the value of the steel or damages for its depreciation notwithstanding his own immunity in any action, based upon the deterioration, which may be brought by the bailor.[28] A similar rule might apply when plumbing contractors perform work incompetently in a warehouse, with the result that water pipes burst and goods belonging to many different bailors are destroyed.[29]

There appear to be three situations in which the bailee's possession will be inadequate to protect him against a contrary assertion of title by the wrongdoer. These are as follows:

---

[23] *Hepburn* v. *A. Tomlinson (Hauliers) Ltd.* [1966] A.C. 451, at 468 per Lord Reid; *The Albazero* [1976] 3 All E.R. 129, at 136 per Lord Diplock; *Glenwood Lumber Co. Ltd.* v. *Phillips* [1904] A.C. 405, at 410-411 per Lord Davey; *Eastern Construction Co. Ltd.* v. *National Trust Co. Ltd.* [1914] A.C. 197, at 210 per Lord Atkin. See also *Spartan Steel & Alloys Ltd.* v. *Martin & Co. (Contractors) Ltd.* [1973] Q.B. 27, at p. 36, per Lord Denning, M.R.; *Hamblin Equipment Pty. Ltd.* v. *Federal Commissioner of Taxation* [1974] *Australian Tax Cases* 4310 at p. 4318, per Mason, J.

[24] *Mangan* v. *Leary* ante, n. 1; *McCauley* v. *Karooz* (1944) 61 W.N. (N.S.W.) 165; *Tanenbaum* v. *W. J. Bell Paper Co. Ltd.* (1956) 4 D.L.R. (2d) 177, at 214-215; *Thorne* v. *MacGregor* (1973) 35 D.L.R. (3d) 687, at 691-692.

[25] The gratuitous bailee's right of action was upheld in *Rooth* v. *Wilson* ante; *Mangan* v. *Leary* (ante), at 11-12, 13, 17; *McCauley* v. *Karooz* ante; *Fletcher* v. *Thomas* [1931] 3 D.L.R. 142, at 143-144 (obiter): the last two decisions involved a borrower, but the same principle applies to the mandatary or depositary.

[26] *Shaw, Savill & Albion Co. Ltd.* v. *Timaru Harbour Board* (1888) 6 N.Z.L.R. 456 (reversed on other grounds (1889) N.Z.P.C.C. 180); *Courtenay* v. *Knutson* (1966) 26 D.L.R. (2d) 768; *B.R.S. Ltd.* v. *Arthur V. Crutchley & Co. Ltd.* [1968] 1 All E.R. 811; *Cotton Co. Ltd.* v. *Coast Quarries Ltd.* (1913) 11 D.L.R. 219; *Compton* v. *Allward* (1912) 1 D.L.R. 107 (affirmed 1 W.W.R. 1012); and see *Fletcher* v. *Thomas* ante; *McCauley* v. *Karooz*; *Thorne* v. *MacGregor* ante, n. 24; cf. *Green* v. *The Jockey Club* (1975) 119 Sol. Jo. 258.

[27] Detinue is assumed to lie as against the wrongdoer in *The Albazero* [1976] 3 All E.R. 129, 136; *Glenwood Lumber Co. Ltd.* v. *Phillips* [1904] A.C. 405 and *Eastern Construction Co. Ltd.* v. *National Trust Co. Ltd.* [1914] A.C. 197; see also Cmnd. 4774, para. 51, where this remedy is said to be "probably" available.

[28] *Tanenbaum* v. *W. J. Bell Paper Co. Ltd.* (1956) 4 D.L.R. (2d) 177.

[29] *Terminal Warehouses Ltd.* v. *J. H. Lock & Sons Ltd.* (1958) 12 D.L.R. (2d) 12. As to whether the bailee may claim interest on the loss, see *The Rosalind* (1920) 37 T.L.R. 116.

III. Exceptions to the Rule

(a) when the wrongdoer defends the action on behalf of, and with the authority of, the true owner;

(b) when the conduct of which the bailee complains was originally committed with the authority of the true owner; and

(c) when the wrongdoer has, since the time of wrongdoing, become the owner of the goods.

The first two exceptions seem to be universally admitted[30] and correspond broadly to the equivalent power of a bailee to plead jus tertii.[31] The third exception is little more than a dimension of the second, except that the title therein pleaded is not that of a tertius but that of the defendant himself. It is illustrated by the decision of the Privy Council in *Eastern Construction Co. Ltd.* v. *National Trust Co. Ltd.*[32] where the plaintiffs held land under a lease which reserved all title in timber to their lessors, the Crown. The defendants entered the land and cut a large quantity of timber, removing some and leaving some behind. The Crown then authorised the removal of the timber remaining and charged the defendants for what they had taken. It was held that this constituted a full assignment to the defendants of all the Crown rights in the timber and, as against the title produced by this assign- ment, the plaintiff-occupiers could not assert their mere possession a⸀ grounds for conversion or detinue:

> [I]t is obvious that if, before action brought by [the bailee] against the wrongdoer, the bailor has clothed that wrongdoer with the owner- ship of the goods, the bailee cannot recover from the wrongdoer, thus converted into the true owner, the value of the goods, no more than he could recover their full value from the bailor himself. In such an action the defendant would not be setting up a jus tertii, but, as donee or assignee of the tertius, a jus sui.[33]

It has been said that another exception exists to the rule, in that the defendant may escape by showing that he has already returned the goods to the true owner.[34] But this seems confined to cases in which the bailee was not in possession of the goods at the material time.[35] The power to plead jus tertii is, in fact, somewhat modified when the defendant has not violated an existing possession but has merely impaired what the plaintiff alleges to be an immediate right to possess.[36]

IV. When the Bailee is out of Possession

The protection of a subsisting possession against the plea of jus tertii is not peculiar to the conventional bailee; equivalent powers of action

---

[30] See Cmnd. 4774, para. 51; *The Winkfield* [1902] P. 42, at 54.

[31] Ante, p. 163 et seq.

[32] [1914] A.C. 197.

[33] Ibid., at 210; cf. at 211, where it is pointed out that had the plaintiffs pursued their original plea of trespass the defendants' full ownership of the timber "would have been no answer whatever".

[34] Salmond, *Torts* (16th ed.) 111.

[35] *Wilson* v. *Lombank Ltd.* [1963] 1 W.L.R. 1294; sed quaere as to whether the plaintiff was properly held to have been in possession in this case.

[36] See post.

are enjoyed, for example, by the finder, the involuntary possessor, and the thief.[37] The normal justification for the rule, as Lord Campbell once remarked, is that it tends to a more tranquil society by safeguarding peaceable possession against the incursions of strangers.[38] But when possession has been lost or delegated at the material time, or has never been received, different considerations apply. The protection of a person whose possession is lost or suspended is less essential to the peace of the community because there is no possibility of a direct or violent incursion against him and because there will always be an alternative possessor whose possession will be protected in the ordinary way. In such a case, the plaintiff who is out of possession must rely upon his immediate right to possess; by so doing, he apparently puts the strength of his title in issue and enables the jus tertii to be pleaded.[39]

The defendant who is entitled to raise this plea enjoys an advantage on two levels; the jurisdictional and the quantitative. With finders, thieves and certain other peripheral categories of bailee, it may often suffice for the wrongdoer to rely upon the first of these advantages and to merely challenge the plaintiff to substantiate his immediate right to possess. If such a right cannot be established and the plaintiff cannot prove violation of an existing possession, semble his action for conversion of lost or stolen property may fail.[40] Such preliminary problems are less likely to trouble the conventional bailee, who can generally invoke some transaction conferring upon him an authority to possess; his source of authority will be the original bailment and he will draw his "title" from the owner.[41] Thus, so far as his qualification to sue is concerned, it will not normally avail the defendant to plead jus tertii because the tertius will have consented to the bailee's possession and this will form the very basis of his immediate right to possess. But if the jus tertii is raised, not as a means of impugning the bailee's entitlement to sue but as a means of limiting damages to the value of the bailee's immediate interest, there is some prospect that the defendant will succeed. Technically, of course, this was the situation in *The Winkfield*,[42] where the plaintiff Postmasters-General appear to have sub-bailed the mail to the owners of the sunken ship. The judgment of the Court of Appeal did not explore this problem because it was raised too late in the day,[43] and it is a somewhat ambitious inference to say that the principle laid down in that case may apply whether or not the bailee was in possession at the time of the delinquency.[44] The preferable view may be that the

---

[37] Post, p. 852 et seq.
[38] *Jeffries* v. *G.W. Ry. Co.* (1856) 5 E. & B. 802, at 805.
[39] Cmnd. 4774, para. 53: post, p. 184.
[40] See further, p. 853 et seq., post.
[41] This assumes of course that (a) the bailee has done nothing to forfeit his own right of possession and to cause that of the bailor to revive; (b) that any subsidiary disposition by the bailee, such as a sub-bailment, does not suspend his right to possess. If the latter event has occurred, the original bailee must bring an action on the case: ante p. 153.
[42] [1902] P. 42.
[43] Ibid., at 54.
[44] This theory is put by the learned editor of Winfield on *Tort* (9th ed.) p. 446n., following Mayne and MacGregor, *Damages* (12th ed.), pp. 607-608; see also Cmnd. 4774, para. 55.

dispossessed bailee can recover only the value of his limited interest,[45] unless the circumstances of the bailment have granted him a power to act as the owner's representative.[46]

Authority on this point is scarce, but it does suggest that the mere right to possess for a limited period will be insufficient to justify full recovery under the principle of *The Winkfield*. Unfortunately, the only modern decision to insist upon possession as a correlative to this principle was one in which the bailee was suing only for the value of his limited interest; and the requirement of possession seems to have been extended even to claims of this limited character.

> *Courtney* v. *Knutson*:[47] In this case the wrongdoer had already satisfied the claim of the bailor for damage to his reversionary interest and the bailee was claiming not for the full cost of damage but merely for his loss of the use of the chattel during the period of the bailment. His claim was upheld, but it was stressed that this was only because he had possession of the chattel at the time of the wrongdoing; a mere contractual right to its use, or mere custody and control of it, would have been insufficient.

Another Canadian decision suggests, however, that the requirement of possession may be liberally construed:

> *Terminal Warehouses Ltd.* v. *J. H. Lock & Sons Ltd.*:[48] Because of defectively installed refrigeration pipes, a quantity of goods stored in a warehouse were permeated with water and damaged. The warehouseman was held entitled to recover from the installation company for damage occasioned to goods belonging to a *tenant* of the warehouse. Laidlaw J. A. observed: ". . . it is my opinion that it is not proper to consider the question of the rights or liabilities as between the plaintiff and the owner of the goods. That view is supported by *The Winkfield* . . . It may be that the plaintiff did not have possession in law of the damaged goods, but, there was possession in fact in the sense that the goods were lawfully on the premises of the plaintiff at the time damage was done to them by a wrongdoer. The plaintiff had sufficient interest in them to maintain an action to recover from a wrongdoer the amount of any damage done to them by a wrongdoer and, if a settlement has been made by the plaintiff in respect thereto, it is entitled to recover the amount paid by it in settlement for the damage."[49]

---

[45] Salmond, *Torts* (16th ed.) 576.
[46] This rider is suggested by the judgment of Richmond J. in *Mangan* v. *Leary*, 1877 3 N.Z. Jur. (N.S.) C.A. 10, at 14-15. Cf. *Barker* v. *Furlong* [1891] 2 ch. 172.
[47] (1960) 26 D.L.R. (2d.) 768 (British Columbia Supreme Court); cf. *Bloxam* v. *Hubbard* (1804) 5 East 407, discussed post, n. 54; *West* v. *Palmer* [1943] 3 D.L.R. 400.
[48] (1958) 12 D.L.R. (2d.) 12 (Ontario Court of Appeal).
[49] Ibid., at 18. When a servant of the bailee, who has been entrusted with the chattel, misappropriates it and is involved in an accident through the negligence of a third party, the bailee should be entitled to recover the full damage from that third party on two grounds: first, that despite the servant's unauthorised conduct, possession of the chattel remains in the bailee for this purpose, via his servant, at the time of the accident; secondly, that since the "modern and sensible" rule is to make the bailee answerable to the bailor for such damage, to allow him to recover the full quantum of that damage from the third party is to allow him to recover no more than his actual loss: see Truman J.A., (dissenting, but not on this point) in *Webb* v. *Moore's Taxi Co.* [1942] 4 D.L.R. 154, at 164-166.

This approach was not adopted by the other members of the Court, who based their opinion upon the landlord's liability to the tenant and not upon the landlord's remedy as a bailee; to them, the question was simply one of remoteness of damage. This may have been a safer ground on the present facts for it was clear that if the plaintiff did not have possession he did not have an immediate right to possess. The elastic quality of Laidlaw J.A.'s concept of the word "possession" in this context suggests that anything falling short of this remedial qualification would, in his view, be insufficient. Certainly if there be neither possession in this extended sense nor an immediate right to possess at the time of the injury the plaintiff should be unable to recover.

> *Glenwood Lumber Co. Ltd.* v. *Phillips*:[50] The respondent, who became the lessee of certain land from the Crown on 20 January 1899, claimed damages from the appellants for the cutting and removal of timber from the land. Most of the timber had been cut before the lease was granted, at a time when the appellants had suspected that they and not the respondent would be granted the lease; but cutting had continued until 23 January 1899 and the logs were not removed until after the respondent became the lessee. The Privy Council rejected the appellants' contention that they should be liable in damages only for that part of the timber which was cut after 20 January, because "the action was in substance for trespassing on the respondent's lands and for detinue of the logs removed from his lands after January 20th, 1889."[51] To such a claim it was no reply for the appellants to allege that under the lease title in the timber was reserved to the Crown, for *The Winkfield* made it clear that in an action by the possessor such arrangements were irrelevant. The decision does, however, suggest that if the appellants had cut *and removed* the bulk of the timber before the respondent went into possession as lessee on 20 January, no action could have lain at his behest in respect of that part of the timber.

Other decisions, upon a wide plane of relevance, appear no more conclusive. In *Margarine Union G.m.b.H.* v. *Cambay Prince S.S. Co. Ltd.*[52] it was held that nothing short of some proprietary interest in the goods, or an immediate right to possess, would entitle a buyer to whom property had not yet passed to maintain an action for their damage; mere contractual arrangements between seller and buyer (such as, in this case, a provision that prior to the passing of property the goods should be at the buyer's risk) were held insufficient to grant him a recognisable interest on which to sue. The case therefore acknowledged that an immediate right to possess would suffice but nowhere contemplated that this could confer a right to recover beyond the plaintiff's immediate personal loss. *The Albazero*,[53] which *was* concerned with the exercise of such a right, discussed its possible application only through the medium of an action for breach of contract. This may be relevant where the bailee out of possession is complaining of the

---

[50] [1904] A.C. 405.
[51] Ibid., at 410.
[52] [1969] 1 Q.B. 219: the problems involved in this decision are discussed in more depth, ante, p. 71 et seq.
[53] [1976] 3 All E.R. 219 (H.L.): see post.

defendant's failure to perform some contractual undertaking in respect of the goods, but it will be unusual for this situation to arise without the defendant's becoming, in turn, a bailee from the plaintiff; and in this event (as we point out below) there are stronger grounds for prohibiting a plea of jus tertii on the defendant's part. When the plaintiff complains only of the commission of a tort against the chattel, it seems that the mere right to possess the goods should entitle him to recover only for the value of his limited interest.[54]

Two further points should be made. The first is that the bailee may have created a sub-bailment under which his right of possession is temporarily suspended: in this event, there can be no action for detinue or conversion against an independent wrongdoer but he may still enjoy an action on the case for damage to his reversionary interest.[55] Again it seems that this is limited to the value of his personal reversion and does not extend to the entire residual interest in the chattel unless (as is normally the case) he is answerable to the owner for the misconduct of the sub-bailee. Secondly, the wrongdoer himself may be a bailee, as where X has bailed to the plaintiff and the plaintiff has sub-bailed to the defendant. In such a case, the sub-bailee owes to the original bailee all the duties that traditionally arise upon bailment, and is therefore estopped from denying his bailor's title.[56] This prohibition would presumably encompass not only an attempt to impugn the principal bailee's locus standi as a plaintiff in conversion but also any attempt to diminish his damages on the ground that he was not the true owner. Under the bailment, full reparation for damage or loss may apparently be recovered: at least where the wrong is tortious and the injury is physical in character,[57] and possibly where the wrong is purely contractual and the depreciation of the goods is exclusively economic.

V. Can the Non-owner of Goods Recover More Than Compensatory Damages in Contract?

The law on this point is not entirely clear, and in our discussion of extended bailments[58] we suggest that under a purely contractual action

---

[54] This view is supported by *Bloxham* v. *Hubbard* (ante, n. 47) where the assignees in bankruptcy of the part-owner of a ship brought trover against the defendant and recovered only to the extent of the bankrupt's interest; neither he nor the assignees were in possession at the material time. The decision is doubted by Mayne and McGregor, *Damages* (12th ed.), pp. 607-608, but seems more consistent with authority than the alternative view. Cf. *Armory* v. *Delamirie* (1721) 1 Stra. 504 (where the possessor may be assumed to have retained possession at the time of the misappropriation); *Green* v. *The Jockey Club* (1975) 119 Sol. Jo. 258 (which is very briefly reported and suggests a right of full recovery under a sub-bailment which preceded the defendant's default).

[55] See ante, p. 153. Detinue may in any event be out of the question because it may require a right of possession which emanates from some proprietary right: ante, p. 150.

[56] Ante, p. 163. The same estoppel appears to operate as between principal bailor and sub-bailee; but see now App. I, post.

[57] See *Morris* v. *C. W. Martin & Sons Ltd.* [1966] 1 Q.B. 716, at 728; *Minichiello* v. *Devonshire Hotel (1967) Ltd. (No. 2)* (1978) 79 D.L.R. (3rd) 656; *Freeman* v. *Birch* (1833) 3 Q.B. 492.

[58] Chapter 20.

for economic depreciation the intermediate bailee may be prohibited from recovering more than his actual loss which, if he is not the owner and is not answerable to the owner, will generally be nominal. The general rule, recently re-stated by Lord Diplock in *The Albazero*,[59] is that damages in contract (as in tort) are purely compensatory; their object is to repair the plaintiff's personal loss and not to provide indirect compensation for other victims of the wrongdoing who were not parties to the contract. To this rule, certain exceptions exist: one is the bailee's right to sue a wrongdoer on the strength of his possessory title;[60] another is the right of subrogation in insurance;[61] a third is the bailee's power to recover the full value of the bailed property under a policy of insurance;[62] and a fourth, not separately mentioned by Lord Diplock, is that acknowledged by the Court of Appeal in the recent but contentious decision in *Jackson* v. *Horizon Holidays Ltd.*[63]

It is perhaps no coincidence that two of the four exceptions involve contracts of bailment; and it is the bailment relationship which affords an explanation of the fifth exception to the general rule of damages, discussed at some length by Lord Diplock.[64] There are, among the authorities, a number of cases which suggest that a consignor of goods may recover substantial damages for their damage or depreciation in transit, despite the fact that property has already passed to the consignee at the time of the alleged breach of contract. This will not represent the characteristic inference to be made from the consignment of goods by a seller, because the general presumption appears always to have been that the bailor in this situation was the consignee and that the consignor was merely acting as the consignor's agent in effecting the contract of carriage. However, this general presumption seems to have been rebuttable, provided it could be shown that a special contract had been made between the consignor and the carrier, whereby the carrier undertook liability for the carriage of the goods irrespective of any later disposition of the consignor's interest.[65] One such case was *Duncan* v. *Lambert*,[66] where a consignor of whisky was allowed to recover its value from a sea-carrier although property in the whisky had already passed to the consignee by the time it was lost.[67] The reasoning behind this decision was obscure, and in *The Albazero*[68] Lord Diplock (with whom the other members of the House agreed) held that *Duncan* v. *Lambert* is not authority for the view that the mere existence of a contract between consignor and carrier entitles the consignor to recover

---

[59] [1976] 3 All E.R. 129, at 132 (H.L.).
[60] See *The Winkfield*; unfortunately, Lord Diplock, when referring to this principle at [1976] 3 All E.R. 129, 136, does not clarify whether it extends to a bailee with merely an immediate right to possess at the material time.
[61] [1976] 3 All E.R. 129, at 136.
[62] Post, p. 193 et seq.
[63] [1975] 3 All E.R. 92.
[64] [1976] 3 All E.R. 129, at 134-138.
[65] See the authorities discussed in *The Albazero* at first instance: [1974] 2 All E.R. 906, at 910, and in the Court of Appeal: [1975] 1 W.L.R. 491, at 518.
[66] (1839) 6 Cl. & Fin. 600 (H.L.).
[67] The consignor had, in fact, already compensated the consignee before bringing his own action against the carrier.
[68] [1976] 3 All E.R. 129, at 134-138.

substantial damages in excess of the loss he has personally sustained. In order to justify such recovery, the consignor must go further and bring himself within the following limited principle:

> . . . that in a commercial contract concerning goods where it is in the contemplation of the parties that the proprietary interests in the goods may be transferred from one owner to another after the contract has been entered into and before the breach which causes loss or damage to the goods, an original party to the contract, if such be the intention of them both, is to be treated in law as having entered into the contract for the benefit of all persons who have or may acquire an interest in the goods before they are lost or damaged, and is entitled to recover by way of damages for breach of contract the actual loss sustained by those for whose benefit the contract is entered into.[69]

Lord Diplock further remarked that such an intention could not be elicited when the original contract of carriage contemplates that the carrier shall enter into a separate contract of carriage with the subsequent owner of the goods.[70] A fortiori, the same rule should apply where the contractual rights of the character under a charter party are not identical with those of the bill of lading holder whose goods are lost or damaged. In this case the consignee has an independent and different personal remedy against the carrier and there is no justification for the auxiliary device of enabling the consignor to recover, and to hold on trust for the consignee, the measure of damage to the consignee's interest. This was in fact the position in the present case, where the carriage did not involve a bailment of the goods to a carrier but the charter of a ship to the plaintiffs, who were the original owners of the goods. Moreover, in this case the succeeding owners were debarred from bringing a claim in contract because they had failed to do so within the yearly limitation period. But on the foregoing principle, the charterers were held unable to recover damages on their behalf.

When we attempt to apply this reasoning to the situation where a bailee of goods is seeking to enforce a contractual obligation against a sub-bailee, and to recover by means of this action a greater measure of damages than he has personally suffered, two observations spring to mind The first is that Lord Diplock's formulation is irrelevant to this problem, because he was speaking only of cases in which property has passed to the ulterior party *after* the initial contract has been made whereas, in our problem, the owner remains the owner throughout and the interests of all the relevant parties remain constant. The second observation is to inquire why the ordinary consignor-carrier situation cannot be answered upon the principles of bailment; for, as Lord Diplock himself remarks,[71] in cases of bailment there is the additional legal factor that a defaulting bailee cannot plead jus tertii and cannot deny his bailor's title. Why, then can it not simply be said that the carrier, as the bailee of the consignor, is liable in full for any injury to the

---

[69] Ibid., at 137.
[70] Ibid., at 138.
[71] Ibid., at 132.

goods irrespective of whether that injury is suffered by the consignor himself or a third party, because the carrier is estopped in law from pleading that third party's title by way of defence?

The answer is given by Lord Diplock, and it is an answer to both of the preceding questions. To say that the carrier is precluded from impugning the consignor's title assumes that both parties stand in the relationship of bailor and bailee. But the mere fact that the consignor has delivered (or baillé) the goods to the carrier does not necessarily suffice to create a bailment between them. In most cases, the bailment will be between carrier and consignee (at least, from the time the consignee becomes the owner); and Lord Diplock's rule, although not confined in its formulation to cases of bailment, is really a method of determining whether, in cases where this relationship *is* in question, the carrier is the consignor's bailee. To ask whether the parties intend that the consignor should recover third-party damage in an action for breach of contract is, on one view, synonymous with inquiring whether the parties intend to stand in a relationship of bailment, with the corresponding restrictions that this imposes upon the defences which can be raised by the bailee. But it follows that when the relationship of bailment can be established by reference to circumstances other than those laid down by Lord Diplock, or when the situation in which a bailment is alleged does not involve a post-contractual change of title, the limitations imposed by Lord Diplock are irrelevant and the bailor should be able to rely upon the bailee's inability to plead jus tertii to recover the full cost of damage or depreciation whether or not this redounds to him personally and whether or not the contract fulfils all the qualifications posited by Lord Diplock. If a bailee *in possession* can recover above his personal interest for mere breaches of contract by a third party,[72] it would seem logical to extend this power to the primary bailee when the misconduct of a secondary bailee in possession has led to loss or impairment. At all events, the contract may fall within the description recognised by the Court of Appeal in *Jackson* v. *Horizon Holidays Ltd.*[73] and the principal bailee may accordingly be entitled to recover damages on behalf of all those persons for whose benefit the contract was avowedly made. But it seems preferable not to absorb this situation too closely into the rules of contract because the secondary bailment may be gratuitous and because the inability to plead jus tertii (which, despite its similarity in effect, is quite distinct from the *Horizon* principle) is exclusive to the relationshp of bailor and bailee.

In conclusion, it may be noted that the only cases in which a bailor-non-owner has successfully recovered the full value of the chattel from a subsidiary bailee appear to be those in which the plaintiff was answerable in full to the owner and therefore in fact recovered no more than the extent of his personal loss.[74]

[72] Ante, p. 181.
[73] [1975] All E.R. 92.
[74] See generally Chapter 20, post; but cf. the dictum by Lord Denning M.R., as to the rights of Beder in *Morris* v. *C. W. Martin & Sons Ltd.* [1966] 1 Q.B. 716, at 728; the inadequately reported decision in *Green* v. *The Jockey Club* ante, n. 54; and the *Minichiello* case, ante, n. 57.

VI. The Consequences of Recovery

If the bailee or other possessor recovers in full from a wrongdoer for damage or loss to the chattel, he holds the surplus of the amount recovered, over and above the extent to which his own interest is impaired, on trust for the bailor.[75] Full recovery by the bailee precludes any further action by the bailor against the wrongdoer.[76] If, however, the *bailor* first recovers from the wrongdoer the quantum of injury to his reversionary interest, this will not prevent the bailee from subsequently suing for damage to his own limited interest under the bailment.[77] It should follow that when the first action is brought by the bailee, who recovers no more than the extent of his personal loss, this would constitute no bar to a later action by the reversioner for damage to his own permanent interest.[78]

VII. Proposals for Reform

The bailee's power of full recovery for wrongs inflicted on the chattel has many advantages; it discourages the proliferation of actions and answers the problem that the bailor may be absent from the scene of the wrongdoing, or even ignorant of its occurrence until it is too late for him to assert an effective personal remedy. In this event, he will have armed the bailee with the power to protect his interests and need not bother to vindicate those interests in person.[79]

The converse, of course, is that the bailor may be incapacitated from bringing an action on his own behalf, even if he wants to. Once the bailee has recovered in full from the wrongdoer, further action against him is barred. This rule, while undoubtedly equitable from the wrongdoer's point of view,[80] is less satisfactory from that of the bailor. It forces him to rely upon the honesty or solvency of the bailee in making over the surplus proceeds of the preceding litigation, and it inhibits the bailor from conducting, or settling, the case in his own way. No doubt in many cases these perils will be averted by an agreement between bailor and bailee as to who is to litigate and in what manner. But such collusion will not always be possible, especially when the bailor is

---

[75] *The Winkfield,* at 55; *Eastern Construction Co. Ltd.* v. *National Trust Co. Ltd.* [1914] A.C. 197, 210; *Turner* v. *Hardcastle* (1862) 11 C.B. (N.S.) 683; *Mangan* v. *Leary,* at 13-15; *The Albazero* [1976] 3 All E.R. 129.

[76] *The Winkfield,* at 61; *Mangan* v. *Leary,* at 14, 17; *Nicholls* v. *Bastard* (1835) 2 C.M. & R. 659, at 660 per Parke B.; *Eastern Construction Co. Ltd.* v. *National Trust Co. Ltd.* ante, at 210.

[77] *Courtney* v. *Knutson* (1960) 26 D.L.R. (2d.) 768; cf. Cmnd. 4774, para 57.

[78] Cf. *Brinsmead* v. *Harrison* (1871) L.R. 6 C.P. 584; *Mangan* v. *Leary,* at 17 per Williams J.

[79] Per Williams J. in *Mangan* v. *Leary,* at 17.

[80] It is not, apparently, extended to every wrongdoer, but only to those who infringe the possession of a bailee, and the problems of double liability as against, for example, the defendant who converts goods in the possession of a thief or purchaser under an invalid title, and who may still be sued by the true owner after he has made restitution or paid damages to the immediate possessor, were a strong influence in the Law Reform Committee's recommendations that jus tertii should, in limited circumstances, be pleaded: Cmnd. 4744, para. 58 et seq. See now *Torts (Interference with Goods) Act* 1977.

absent at the time of the wrong and for a long time afterwards or when (as may be the case with the sender of a letter) he is one of a vast number of bailors, all unknown to the bailee. The very rule that allows the bailee to draw all the separate threads of interest together and conjoin them in a single consolidated action may well be the rule that allows those threads to be drawn, in the bailor's opinion, too tightly.

One of the most enthusiastic critics of an unadulterated application of the rule in *The Winkfield* was an American, Edward Warren.[81] In a memorable passage, he summarised the accepted effect of the rule as follows:

> B (*the bailee*), who has a 1% interest, may take control of the litigation, without the express or implied consent of A (*the bailor*), who has a 99% interest, thereby barring A from any remedy against the wrongdoer, and requiring A to look to B for the 99%. *The Winkfield.* This is bad enough.[82]

In Warren's view, the rule in *The Winkfield* pays insufficient regard to the interests of the owner, whose share in the chattel will generally be appreciably greater than that of the bailee and who ought at least to be given some choice as to whether the bailee should sue to recover the extent of that larger share. It is not sufficient, he argued, to show that the owner enjoys a right to recover the surplus proceeds of litigation from the bailee: the possession of those proceeds may place an irresistible temptation before the bailee and one to which the owner had never dreamed of exposing him: "A bailee with whom the bailor is willing to trust the possession of a $2000 automobile is not necessarily a person with whom the bailor would be willing to trust $2000 in ready cash". Even when the bailee is honest, the problem of apportionment is likely to cause contention and here, again, the bailee has the whip hand because the money is in his possession.[83] Of the three parties involved in the conventional *Winkfield* action, the owner or bailor was the least effectively protected of all; and he, said Warren, was the person who should be given the greatest consideration. The solution lay in limiting the bailee's right of full recovery to those cases in which he does so with the express or implied consent of the bailor.[84] This solution is favoured by a few early American cases[85] and received the support of Richmond J. in *Mangan* v. *Leary*;[86] but as Warren remarks, it is probably too late in most jurisdictions to hope for the importation of this refinement into the Common Law.[87]

More recently, the English Law Reform Committee have decided in

---

[81] *Trover and Conversion* (1936), pp. 12-21.
[82] Ibid., p. 21. See also the equivalent statement by Johnston J. in *Mangan* v. *Leary*, at 15-16: ". . . it would be both inconvenient and unjust to allow a bailee, whose claim might be most trifling, to intervene as dominus litis to the exclusion, if he were first in time, of the bailor whose injury might be far more serious."
[83] *Trover and Conversion*, pp. 13-14.
[84] Ibid.: see p. 14, where *The Winkfield* itself is described as a case in which such consent could fairly be implied, and p. 16.
[85] *Johnson* v. *Inhabitants of Holyoke* (1870) 105 Mass. 80, 81; *Finn* v. *Western R.R. Co.* (1873) 112 Mass. 524.
[86] (1877) 3 N.Z. Jur. (N.S.) C.A. 10, at 14-15.
[87] Op. cit., p. 16.

favour of reducing the primacy of possession and of restricting considerably the remedies that can be exercised by a party relying upon a
mere possessory title. Rejecting the suggested parallel with land, they
preferred to modernise the rule as follows:

> that a plaintiff relying on a possessory title in an action for wrongful
> interference should be required in his statement or particulars of claim
> to state the circumstances in which he came into possession, or ac-
> quired an immediate right to possession, of the chattel which is the
> subject-matter of the action. He should also be required to identify
> an other person who to his knowledge has or claims any proprietary
> or possessory interest in the chattel, and we think that the above rule
> should be applied to any *tertius* who becomes joined under our above
> proposals in an action for wrongful interference and claims any in-
> terest in the subject-matter of the action.[88]

In the Committee's view, the law should seek to attain three objectives:
the avoidance of a multiplicity of actions, the limitation of a plaintiff's
damage to his actual loss, and the protection of defendants from double
liability. They therefore proposed a series of amendments to the Common Law rules which govern the right to raise jus tertii.[89] Some of these
proposals are of little more than peripheral interest to the remedies of
the orthodox bailee, but for the sake of completeness they are summarised in toto:

(a) Any third party with an interest in an action for wrongful interference with chattels (such as the bailor in an action by the bailee)
should be entitled to apply to be joined in the action; joinder would
normally be as a co-defendant, and would enable all issues between
the parties to be resolved.

(b) A defendant sued twice in respect of the same wrong should
not derive a total defence from the fact that he has already paid out
the full cost of the interference in an earlier action but should be
enabled to join the first plaintiff as a co-defendant, or to proceed
against him independently for restitution. However, this principle should
not extend to cases where the full recovery was by a bailor or bailee
of the chattel.[90]

(c) A general right should be introduced to plead jus tertii, both as
a defence and in diminution of damages, provided the defendant serves
notice on both the plaintiff and the tertius and makes the latter a party
to a summons for directions. In this way the tertius can be joined in
the action and his rights identified: if he fails to attend to the summons
or comply with the directions he should thereupon be debarred from
making any further claim on the defendant.

(d) Plaintiffs relying on a possessory title must identify the source
and authority of their possession and any residual or competing interests.[91]

---

[88] Eighteenth Report. *Convention and Detinue* (1971) para. 70. In *Berger* v. *34th
Street Garage* (1948) 84 N.Y.S. 2d, 348, discussed in (1949) 34 *Cornell Law
Quarterly* 615, the Court refused to accept Warren's proposed modification of
the rule in *The Winkfield* and held that the bailee may sue irrespective of whether
his bailor has expressly or impliedly consented to the action.
[89] Ibid., paras. 62-77 and 128 (9).
[90] Ibid., paras. 76, 128 (9) (f).
[91] See ante.

(e) A plaintiff with limited title should not generally be entitled to recover damages above his actual loss, but this general principle may be reversed when he sues with the authority of those whose interests make up the full ownership of the chattel. For this purpose a plaintiff in possession or with an immediate right to possession of the chattel at the time of the wrongful interference shall be presumed to have authority to sue from the other part-owners unless it be shown that they have objected to his recovering damages on their behalf.

At the time of writing, no Bill has been presented on the strength of the Committee's proposals, but legislation may well be passed in England before the present work is published.[91a]

VIII. INSURANCE[92]

The bailee has an insurable interest in the subject-matter of the bailment and, under an appropriately worded policy, can recover from the insurer the full value of the goods rather than the lower measure of his limited interest or his own liability to the bailor.[93] This rule, which forms an exception to the general principle of insurance as an instrument of indemnity, was acknowledged as early as 1856. In *Waters and Steel v. The Monarch Life Assurance Co.*[94] a wharfinger and warehouseman who had insured goods in his warehouse against fire was held entitled to recover their value from the defendant insurers notwithstanding that his own interest in them was limited to a lien for cartage and storage. The defendants claimed to limit their liability to (i) those goods in the warehouse which belonged to the plaintiff and (ii) the value of his lien over the remainder; but this was dismissed on the wording of the policy, which had referred to "goods in trust or on commission therein." It was held that it was not illegal for a bailee to insure more than his own interest in the bailed property,[95] nor was it fatal to the enforcement of the policy that he had done so without the knowledge of the bailors. "What the surplus after satisfying [his] own claim might be, could only be ascertained after the loss, when the amount of [his] lien at that time was determined; but [he was] interested in every particle of the goods."[96]

The principle has been frequently upheld in England and Australia,[97] and is similar in purpose to the rule in *The Winkfield*;[98] it is commerci-

---

[91a] See now ss. 7, 8, *Torts (Interference with Goods) Act* 1977.
[92] Roberts (1973) 123 N.L.J. 849.
[93] *Hepburn v. A. Tomlinson (Hauliers) Ltd.* [1966] A.C. 451 (H.L.).
[94] (1856) 5 E. & B. 870; approved by the House of Lords in *Hepburn* v. *A. Tomlinson (Hauliers) Ltd.* ante., at 472.
[95] Aliter, where he intends from the beginning to keep the whole of the policy-moneys for his own benefit, per Lord Hodson in *Hepburn* v. *A. Tomlinson (Hauliers) Ltd.* ante.
[96] (1856) 5 E. & B. 870, at 882 per Crompton J.
[97] In addition to the decisions already cited, see *L. & N.W. Ry. Co.* v. *Glyn* (1859) 1 E. & E. 652; *Castellain* v. *Preston* (1883) 11 Q.B.D. 380; *Calder* v. *Batavia Sea & Fire Insurance Co. Ltd.* [1932] S.A.S.R. 46; *Maurice* v. *Goldsbrough Mort & Co. Ltd.* [1939] A.C. 462 (P.C.); *The Albazero* [1976] 3 All E.R. 129, at 136-137 (obiter, H.L.).
[98] See ante, p. 179.

ally convenient and averts the need for multiple insurance in respect of the same goods.[99] It is established that the bailee holds the surplus of the policy-moneys, after deduction of the proportion of his own interest, on trust for the bailor.[1]

Whether the policy actually covers the full proprietary interest in the goods, or merely extends to the limited interest of the bailee, depends not upon the bailee's unilateral intention in effecting it but upon the construction of the policy itself.[2] The intention of the bailee, beyond its expression within the terms of the policy, is relevant only insofar as the insurer might prove that the bailee intended to keep the full proceeds for his personal benefit and not to distribute them to the owner. In this event, the bailee's interest in the surplus proceeds "is gaming and he cannot recover"; but the burden of proving the necessary intention rests upon the insurer.[3] It is not necessary for the contract of insurance to show an intention by the bailee to contract as trustee or agent for the owner.[4]

---

[99] *Hepburn* v. *A. Tomlinson (Hauliers) Ltd.* (ante, n. 93), at 468, 480; and see the decision of the Court of Appeal, *sub. nom. A. Tomlinson (Hauliers) Ltd.* v. Hepburn [1965] 2 W.L.R. 634, at 644, 650, 656.

[1] Ibid., and see the decisions cited ante, n. 97. As to the division of the proceeds between bailee and owner, see *Maurice* v. *Goldsbrough Mort & Co. Ltd.* [1939] A.C. 462. In this case, woolbrokers who had insured wool which had been consigned to them for sale on a commission basis were held not to be entitled to deduct from the policy-moneys the commission and charges they would have been entitled to make had the wool not been destroyed. Their deductions were limited to costs for services actually rendered and expenses actually incurred before the destruction. See further *Re Pastoral Finance Association Ltd.* (1922) 23 S.R. (N.S.W.) 43, where the proper level of deduction was held not to extend to warehousing charges; *Sidaways* v. *Todd* (1818) 2 Stark. 400.

[2] *Hepburn* v. *A. Tomlinson (Hauliers) Ltd.* [1966] A.C. 451, at 468-470 per Lord Reid, disapproving *Irving* v. *Richardson* (1831) 2 B. & Ad. 193 and dicta of Bowen L.J. in *Castellain* v. *Preston* (1883) 11 Q.B.D. 380, at 397-399; see also per Lord Hodson at 473-474 and per Lord Pearce at 474, 476, 482. As to the meaning of the words "while temporarily housed during the course of transit" within a bailee's policy, see *Crows Transport Ltd.* v. *Phoenix Insurance Co. Ltd.* [1965] 1 All E.R. 596 (C.A.).

[3] *Hepburn* v. *A. Tomlinson (Hauliers) Ltd.,* at 481-482. Cf. the judgments in the Court of Appeal [1965] 2 W.L.R. 634, where the following elements seem to have been regarded as influential in discovering an intention to insure the full value of the goods: the fact that the bailee has contractually undertaken with his bailor to effect insurance; the fact that he and the bailor possess concurrent interests in the goods so that a single blanket policy would be both economical and convenient; the fact that the policy appears to be on goods rather than on the bailee's liability; the fact that the cover claims to be "full" and "comprehensive"; and the previous course of dealing between bailee and insurer. Cf. further *Reilly Bros.* v. *Mercantile Mutual Insurance Co. Ltd.* (1928) 31 W.A.L.R. 57, where the bailee's right of recovery was lost because he had, within the meaning of the policy, parted with an interest in the goods.

[4] *Hepburn* v. *Tomlinson (Hauliers) Ltd.,* and see the judgments in the Court of Appeal [1965] 2 W.L.R. 634. The insured will not, apparently, have an insurable interest where goods are merely left on his land with his permission in circumstances in which he is not responsible for their safety: *Bank of Ireland* v. *Northern Assurance Co. Ltd.* (1925) 21 Lloyd's L. R. 203 and 333, especially per Lord Sumner at 335.

CHAPTER 5

POSSESSION AND PERMISSION

I. Bailments and Licences Distinguished

Most bailments are created or discharged upon premises occupied by the bailee and this fact, whilst not an essential feature of bailment, is clearly a strong pointer to a change in the bailor's possession. However, the mere leaving or depositing of chattels upon land occupied by another, even with his knowledge or at his invitation, does not necessarily make the occupier a bailee. The law has repeatedly drawn a distinction between bailments and licences; the former requiring a transfer of possession and a voluntary acceptance of the Common Law duty of safe-keeping;[1] the latter amounting to no more than a grant of permission to the user of a chattel to leave it upon the licensor's land on the understanding that neither possession shall be transferred nor responsibility for guarding the chattel accepted.[2] The distinction is easy to state but difficult to draw, or, rather, it is difficult to place specific cases on one side or the other. By far the most common manifestation of the problem occurs with car-parking situations, where one party (usually but not necessarily the owner)[3] will take advantage of the occupier's invitation to supply temporary accommodation for his car whilst he is elsewhere. Only rarely will this service be gratuitous; the occupier may charge a fee, or may offer parking space as an inducement to members of the public to frequent his restaurant or public-house or other establishment,[4] and much may depend upon such minutiae as whether, and at whose instigation, the car-owner left the vehicle unlocked; the geography of the car-park; the presence of

---

[1] This may, of course, be qualified by exempting conditions; see Chapter 25, post.

[2] The word licence in this context is misleading, for the true relationship of the parties may be that of invitor and invitee. However, this fact will be of relevance only (if at all) in the context of damage to chattels arising by virtue of a breach of an occupancy duty by the landowner, as to which, see p. 214, post. In the ensuing analysis, the term "licence" is therefore used to connote any relationship between an occupier and the personal property of his lawful entrants which does not amount to a bailment.

[3] See *Walton Stores Ltd.* v. *Sydney City Council* [1968] 2 N.S.W.R. 109, where the plaintiffs' car was parked on the defendants' premises by a manager of the plaintiff company; and cf. *Drive Yourself Lessey's Pty. Ltd.* v. *Burnside* (1959) 59 S.R. (N.S.W.) 390, discussed at pp. 214, 813, post. Where the immediate deliveror is himself a bailee, the occupier who receives possession from him will usually become a sub-bailee. The sub-bailment relationship is discussed at length in Chapter 20, post.

[4] The better view is that a bailment arising in these circumstances is one for reward although there is no direct payment for the facility; see the conflicting opinions of Miller C.J.M. and Schultz J.A. in *Martin* v. *Town 'n' Country Delicatessen Ltd.* (1963) 42 D.L.R. (2d) 449, at 453, 464-465 and the approach taken by Harris C.J. in *Murphy* v. *Hart* (1919) 46 D.L.R. 36, which supports the view stated above; Chapter 8, post.

attendants, and the time at which the charge for parking was payable. Another illustration concerns the deposit of coats in restaurants and here, too, much may revolve around questions such as the proximity of the customer to his garment and whether he or an employee of the defendant deposited it in the place from which it was stolen.

One of the most succinct (and sonorous) statements of the overall distinction is that given by Sherburne J., in the Vermont case of *Zweeres* v. *Thibault*[5] in 1942:

> Where personal property is left upon another's premises under circumstances from which either relation might possibly be predicated, the test is whether or not the person leaving the property has made such a delivery as to amount to relinquishment, for the duration of the relation, of his exclusive possession, control and dominion over the property, so that the person upon whose premises it is left can exclude, within the limits of the agreement, the possession of all others. If he has, the general rule is that the transaction is a bailment. On the other hand, if there is not such delivery and relinquishment of exclusive possession, and his control and dominion over the goods is dependent in no degree upon the co-operation of the owner of the premises, and his access thereto is in nowise subject to the latter's control, it is generally held that he is a tenant or lessee of the space upon where the goods were kept. . . . In a doubtful case consideration should be given to the manifested intention of the parties whether the care of personal property or only the rental of a place to put it was contemplated.

Once possession has been established as residing in the occupier of the land, the law imposes upon him the duties of safe-keeping that are common to all bailees, provided of course that the arrangement took place with his consent, and subject to any exclusions of liability that he may have superimposed. Identifying this change of possession has, however, caused considerable difficulty, for although the parties' intention should always be a material element,[6] this will rarely be decisive and the courts have had to fall back on the physical facts and circumstances of each individual case. The result is a multiplicity of factors which may, either singly or in permutation, provide a pointer to future decisions. With increased urban congestion and restrictions upon parking in public places the car-parking cases represent a recurrent legal difficulty which is likely to escalate before it abates altogether.

The two leading English decisions on this question are forty and twenty-six years old respectively. Although their authority cannot be questioned, changing circumstances have begun to give them a slightly

---

[5] (1942) 112 Vt. 264; 23 A. 2d. 529; 138 A.L.R. 1131. United States decisions on this subject are, as may be expected, numerous. For an interesting pre-war survey, see Jones, "The Parking Lot Cases" (1938) 27 *Georgia Law Journal* 162. Some useful illustrative decisions are to be found in *Sandler* v. *Commonwealth Station Co.* (1940) 307 Mass. 470; 30 N.E. 2d. 389; 131 A.L.R. 1170 (where an attempt is made to classify the various situations arising); *Lewis* v. *Ebersole* (1943) 244 Ala. 200; 12 So. 2d. 543; *Thompson* v. *Mobile Light & R. Co.* (1921) 211 Ala. 525; 101 So. 177; 34 A.L.R. 921; *Doherty* v. *Ernst* (1933) 284 Mass. 341; 187 N.E. 620; *T.T. Consumer Services Corporation* v. *Travellers' Indemnity Co.* (1972) 256 So. 2d. 75; *Simons* v. *First National Bank of Denver* (1971) 491 P. 2d. 602.

[6] Except insofar as possession may change hands irrespective of any intention to that effect; this point is elaborated at p. 210, post.

antiquated look, and in recent years they have been as often distinguished as directly applied. Nevertheless, they continue to be of value and any understanding of this subject is enhanced by a consideration of their facts.

Ashby v. *Tolhurst.*[7] The plaintiff parked his car (worth £37) on a triangular space, open on two sides, occupied and operated as a carpark by the defendant. He paid a shilling to the attendant and was given a ticket which contained exclusory provisions and was prefaced by the words "Sea Way Car Park, Car Park Ticket". During his absence the attendant allowed a stranger to take away the car and it was never recovered. The Court of Appeal held that the defendants were not liable for the loss. There had been no bailment, no delivery of possession and no implied agreement on the defendants' part to redeliver only on production of the ticket. "All the defendant did was to leave his car on the car park, paying the sum of 1s. for the privilege of doing so."[8]

Tinsley v. *Dudley.*[9] The plaintiff called in for a drink at the defendant's public house, leaving his motor-cycle in the adjacent yard. The area was approached through double gates which were standing open at the time but could be closed and locked. Across them were painted the words, "Wheatsheaf: Covered Yard and Garage". There was no fee to be paid and no attendant on duty. The plaintiff was separated from his motor-cycle for nearly two hours, and for some of that time was not drinking at the inn. *Held*, the defendant was not liable for the theft of the machine. The Court of Appeal found that it had never been delivered into his possession and pointed out that the mere fact that the plaintiff was an invitee and not a licensee did not necessarily mean that such delivery had taken place. ". . . the liability of the defendant here depends upon possession or custody; and I cannot see that the distinction between licensee on the one hand and invitee on the other can of itself . . . be relevant to the question, whether there existed some sort of bailment."[10] Moreover, an occupier of premises was under no duty at Common Law to protect the personal property of his invitees from theft in the absence of special agreement to that effect.

In both of these cases it was stressed that everything depends upon the immediate facts. Accordingly, it would appear that the most useful method of analysing the decisions in this area is to segregate the sort of facts, or groups of facts, that have been recognised as having some bearing on the question. The following seem to enjoy a primary significance in identifying the existence of a bailment between the parties.[11]

---

[7] [1937] 2 K.B. 242; cf. the very similar South African decision in *Empire Car Park* v. *Michael* [1952] 3 S.A. 374.

[8] Per Romer L.J. at 255; the Court also found that, in permitting the thief to drive away in the car, the attendant had not been guilty of conversion. See further on this point p. 220, post.

[9] [1951] 2 K.B. 18; cf. *O'Dea* v. *O'Hara* (1895) *South Australian Advertiser*, May 17th.

[10] Per Evershed M.R. at 25; and see Jenkins L.J. at 30-32; Danckwerts L.J. at 33.

[11] Cf. the factors enumerated by Estey J.A. in *Heffron* v. *Imperial Parking Co. Ltd.* (1974) 46 D.L.R. (3d) 642, at 648-649.

A. Transfer of the means of access or control over the chattel

The likeliest example is the car ignition key. Where a man parks his car on a parking-lot and, at the request of the attendant, hands over the keys, there is a strong probability that the courts will discover a bailment, particularly where he has used the place before under similar circumstances. In *Shorter's Parking Station Ltd.* v. *Johnson*[12] this fact seems to have been decisive. The plaintiff had, over a period of five years, regularly parked his car at the defendants' premises for a consideration which, at the revelant time, was £5 per month. The premises were covered and it was the plaintiff's regular practice to leave the keys in the ignition-switch so as to enable the defendants to move the car about at their convenience. This procedure appears to have originated at their request, and was followed on the morning in question. The plaintiff left the car just inside the building and it was stolen. The defendants denied that they had been in possession and cited *Ashby* v. *Tolhurst*[13] to show that a mere car-parking arrangement will not normally give rise to a bailment. In rejecting this contention, Hardie Boys J. relied upon two Canadian cases where, in similar circumstances, the operators had been made liable as bailees,[14] and stressed that the common purposes of plaintiff and defendant, established by years of dealing, clearly necessitated that the latter should enjoy possession of the car while on their premises.[15] Such was the inferred intention of the parties "both for the convenience of the owner of the car and for the carrying out of the business of the garage-firm",[16] and the transfer of keys was obviously vital to the fulfilment of that intention.

Even where there is no regular course of dealing between the parties, the owner who accedes to a request to leave his keys in the car or with an attendant will generally be taken to have entrusted possession to the occupier of the land. Thus, where the attendant wishes to re-park a car and obtains keys for that purpose (or, presumably, for any other purpose relative to the transaction) his employers will be deemed to be in possession and will be liable if the car is stolen through their servants' default. In such a case, it would seem to be immaterial that the keys were never used. In *Brown* v. *Toronto Auto Parks Ltd.*[17] Barlow J. drew a distinction between customers who parked their cars on the open part

---

[12] [1963] N.Z.L.R. 135.

[13] [1937] 2 K.B. 242.

[14] *Way Sagless Springs Co. Ltd.* v. *Bevradio Theatres Ltd.* [1942] 3 D.L.R. 448; *Appleton* v. *Ritchie Taxie Co. Ltd.* [1942] 3 D.L.R. 546. There have been many other Canadian decisions in which the transfer of keys has been accorded a material significance; see, for instance, *Brown* v. *Toronto Auto Parks Ltd.* [1955] 1 D.L.R. 525; *Samuel Smith & Sons Ltd.* v. *Silverman* (1961) 29 D.L.R. (2d) 98 (where the point was conceded); *Dewart* v. *400 Parking Systems Ltd.* [1954] O.W.N. 154; *Schnelle* v. *City Parking Canada Ltd.* [1972] W.W.R. 550; *Gray* v. *Canwest Parking Ltd.* (1956) 52 W.W.R. 56; *Williams & Wilson Ltd.* v. *O.K. Parking Stations Ltd.* (1971) 17 D.L.R. (3d) 243; *Heffron* v. *Imperial Parking Co. Ltd.* (1974) 46 D.L.R. (3d) 642; *Minichiello* v. *Devonshire Hotel (1967) Ltd.* (1976) 66 D.L.R. (3d) 619.

[15] [1963] N.Z.L.R., at p. 138.

[16] Ibid., at 136.

[17] [1955] 1 D.L.R. 461, 463, the actual decision was reversed on appeal ([1955] 1 D.L.R. 525) but only upon the question whether property left in the car was the subject of a bailment; see on this point Chapter 6, post.

of the defendant's ground and those who paid to use the "lock-up" positions; in the latter case, there would have been no right of access and no corresponding duty of safe-keeping. Once possession has been assumed by means of this control, it should continue until the car is redelivered to its owner. Thus, merely secreting the keys under the front seat or in the glove compartment would not determine the bailment, for the defendants' responsibility for the situation they have chosen to create subsists until that situation is ended.[18]

Difficulty may arise when the plaintiff is a regular user of the car-park and there is no general requirement that he should deposit his keys with the attendant. If, on one isolated occasion, such a request is complied with, the conflict between his ordinary experience and the particular circumstances of the occasion may prove difficult to resolve. In two Canadian cases, the normal practice was held to prevail and the court found that the defendants were not bailees. In *Palmer* v. *Toronto Medical Arts Building Ltd.*[19] the Ontario Court of Appeal relied on the fact that the attendant was employed only to help disabled visitors and to keep the traffic moving; his offer to take the keys and park the appellant's car for him was a mere act of courtesy and not behaviour from which an undertaking to safeguard the car against theft could be inferred. Moreover, the car could be retrieved without reference to him and there was no system in force whereby customers were obliged to present tickets or go through any other checking procedure when leaving the car-park. This was considered to negate any presumption (which the appellant, relying on American authorities, sought to raise), to the effect that the delivery of keys was prima facie evidence of a bailment.

Martin v. *Town 'n' Country Delicatessen*[20] was a similar case. The plaintiff drove up to a restaurant on Sadie Hawkins Night and, finding the car-park crowded, accepted the attendant's offer to take the keys and park the car when an occasion arose. He was a regular customer and knew that cars were normally parked and locked by visitors at their own discretion. The Manitoba Court of Appeal examined the functions for which the attendant had been appointed and concluded that these were inconsistent with the plaintiff's suggestion that the defendants were purporting to undertake safe-keeping of the car:

> It is not unusual for attendants at courtesy parking lots to offer assistance in the orderly parking of cars, as was obviously done in the instant case. Surely this service to patrons would not place liability on the owners of the lot which they have not otherwise assumed.[21]

The court doubted whether the attendant had, in any event, the authority to bind the defendant by his promise to park the car.[22] It seems, with

---

[18] Unless, perhaps, the plaintiff has agreed that they should be thus returned once the purpose for which they are transferred has been fulfilled. See *Martin* v. *Town 'n' Country Delicatessen Ltd.* (1963) 42 D.L.R. (2d) 449; *Mobile Parking Stations v. Lawson* (1974) 298 So. 2d. 266.

[19] (1960) 21 D.L.R. (2d) 181; criticised in (1975) 33 *University of Toronto Faculty of Law Review* 100, at 101.

[20] (1963) 42 D.L.R. (2d) 449.

[21] Ibid., at 454 per Miller C.J.M., delivering the majority opinion.

[22] Ibid., at 453.

respect, that the relevant question is not whether the attendant enjoyed the necessary authority but whether the plaintiff was reasonably entitled to assume that he possessed such authority and that the defendants were adopting the role of a bailee. As Lord Denning M.R., said in *Mendelssohn* v. *Normand Ltd.*,[23] dealing with the situation where the attendant had promised to lock the plaintiff's car:

> In other words he promised to see that the contents were safe . . . What is the effect of such a promise? It was not within the *actual* authority of the attendant to give it but it was within his ostensible authority. He was there to receive cars on behalf of the garage company. He had apparent authority to make a statement relating to its custody. Such a statement is binding on the company.[24]

The majority also thought it likely, from the facts of the *Town 'n' Country* case, that the attendant had agreed only to replace the keys in the car when it was parked and not to hold them till the plaintiff returned.[25] Thus, the bailment may already have ended by the time the car was stolen. But by failing to prove that the attendant was not implicated in its disappearance, it is hard to see how the defendants could, even on this construction, have discharged their onus as bailees. In any event this view of the facts does not seem justified. In the dissenting judgment of Schultz J.A. the point is made that the delivery of the keys was subject to specific conditions: first, that the attendant would keep possession of them and secondly, that he would redeliver them on demand.[26] Such an arrangement was consistent only with an assumption of possession by the defendants, with the consequent responsibility for safe custody and the avoidance of theft. It is hard to escape the conclusion that this case was wrongly decided, and that the majority were unduly influenced by the fact that, since parking was without charge, any other result would have been, in their opinion, inequitable.[27]

Mendelssohn v. *Normand Ltd.*[28] is a stronger case, since the plaintiff explicitly warned the attendant of the presence of a suitcase on the back seat of the car and extracted a promise that the car would be locked when parked. The defendants were held liable as bailees, notwithstanding that the plaintiff had used the garage many times before without being required to surrender his keys and that a ticket given to him on entering prohibited any oral variation of its terms by employees of the company. It should be noted that the parking fee was payable on leaving the garage and not on entering; which is itself suggestive of an assumption of control over the vehicle whilst on the defendant's premises.[29]

It would appear, then, that where the surrender of keys is at the defendant's request and where those keys must be retrieved from an attendant before the customer can leave, the usual inference will be in favour of a

---

[23] [1970] 1 Q.B. 177.
[24] Ibid., at 183.
[25] (1963) 42 D.L.R. (2d), at 453-454.
[26] Ibid., at 462.
[27] Ibid., at 458; cf. Jenkins L.J. in *Tinsley* v. *Dudley* [1951] 2 K.B. 18, at 32.
[28] [1970] 1 Q.B. 177: see also *Minichiello* v. *Devonshire Hotel (1967) Ltd.* (1976) 66 D.L.R. (3d) 619.
[29] See further pp. 201, 203, post.

bailment unless the plaintiff should have known that the request was unauthorised and that the defendant's intention was opposed to an assumption
of care and control.

The same result should follow where the deposit is solely for the plaintiff's convenience, provided that the attendant has ostensible authority to
take possession of the goods. In many cases, the question will resolve itself
into whether or not the defendant has undertaken a duty relating to the
vehicle for the discharge of which possession is necessary. In *B. G. Transport Service Ltd.* v. *Marston Motor Co. Ltd.*[30] drivers of lorries were
permitted to leave their keys with an attendant but were not required to do
so.[31] The plaintiffs' driver took advantage of this facility and they were
subsequently collected by a thief. The defendants were exonerated because
they had no intention of moving or otherwise interfering with the vehicles
(unless "an emergency arose") and had imposed no system of checking or
ticketing by which to restrain drivers from taking their vehicles away.[32]

B. Procedures for recovery

Closely allied to the transfer of control is the method of restoring that
control to the owner. In several cases the existence of a system whereby
persons retrieving vehicles are scrutinised before being allowed to leave
has been considered to be conclusive evidence that the operator was a
bailee of the property. The leading Australian case is *Council of the City
of Sydney* v. *West*,[33] where a ticket was given containing the warning:

> This ticket must be presented for time stamping and payment before
> taking delivery of the vehicle.

Although no keys were delivered and the defendants appear to have
reserved no power to move or otherwise deal with the car, it was unanimously held that they were bailees of the vehicle. Coupled to this was an
implied promise not to redeliver the car except on production of the
appropriate ticket; an implication which may be contrasted with the
approach taken in *Ashby* v. *Tolhurst*,[34] where the ticket was more in the

---

[30] [1970] 1 Lloyd's Rep. 371.

[31] The defendants apparently preferred drivers to do so, but did not insist; cf.
Alberta U Drive Ltd. v. *Jack Carter Ltd.* (1972) 28 D.L.R. (3d) 114.

[32] A problem which does not appear to have been raised in any Commonwealth
authority occurs when the plaintiff, knowing that he has occasionally been requested
to leave the keys in his car at a particular car-park, does so without being asked
on a particular occasion. In *Doherty* v. *Ernst* (1933) 284 Mass. 341; 187 N.E.
620, facts similar to this were held to create a bailment. This would appear to be
the preferable view, for it gives priority to the reasonable apprehensions of the
plaintiff as induced by the defendant's conduct; it also accords with the tenor of
the decision in *Shorter's Parking Station Ltd.* v. *Johnson* [1963] N.Z.L.R. 135;
see further *Halls* v. *Piestik* [1955] O.W.N. 641. Where the customer retains his
keys, the general tenor of the authorities is to regard this factor as militating
strongly but not conclusively against a bailment, since other facts may exist which
indicate control. Recent American decisions favouring a mere licence in these circumstances include *Parking Management Inc.* v. *Gilder* (1974) 327 A. 2d. 323
(D.C. Court of Appeals); *Simons* v. *First National Bank of Denver* (1971) 491
P. 2d. 589; *Mobile Parking Stations* v. *Lawson* (1974) 298 So. 2d. 266; cf. *Coe
Oil Service Inc.* v. *Hair* (1973) 283 So. 2d. 734.

[33] (1964) 82 W.N. (Pt 1) (N.S.W.) 139 (N.S.W. Sup. Ct. F.C.); affirmed on appeal,
(1965) 114 C.L.R. 481. See also *Davis* v. *Pearce Parking Station Pty. Ltd.* (1954)
91 C.L.R. 642.

[34] [1937] 2 K.B. 242.

nature of a receipt, payment was in advance and the Court of Appeal rejected the idea that the defendants were undertaking to deliver only to the ticket-holder. *West's* case was followed in *Walton Stores Ltd.* v. *Sydney City Council.*[35] The car-park here was of the multi-storey type and payment was extracted, as in *West's* case, on a time basis, when the plaintiff came to recover his car; a slightly different clause appeared on the ticket, which avoided the use of the word "delivery" but still demanded that it be presented before the car could be recovered. Asprey J.A., said:

> The steps to be taken to enable the plaintiff to regain physical possession of its motor car from the defendant's building involved more than its removal by simply driving it away. Its removal required a bilateral transaction in the terms of the document. It may be that the defendant did not have a lien at common law upon the vehicle for its parking charges (cf. *Hatton* v. *Car Maintenance Co.*[36] and see now the *Warehousemen's Liens Act* 1935) but the contract which regulated the legal relationship of the parties plainly evinced their intention that the holder of the card or ticket had either to pay or tender payment of the amount of the charges for the storage of the vehicle before he was entitled to demand possession of it.[37]

Thus, a defendant who imposes stringent security precautions to prevent the evasion of charges is more likely to find himself responsible for the vehicles on his premises than the operator who lacks such a system and works on a more haphazard basis. But it is not the effectiveness of the procedures that count so much as the intention behind them, and if it can be shown that a defendant contemplated retaining exclusive control until any fees were discharged, the inference that he is a bailee should not readily be displaced simply by proving that his methods of enforcement were deficient.

Considerable emphasis is placed upon this element in recent decisions and there are several cases where the lack of such a procedure has been held to be fatal to the existence of a bailment.[38] It is obviously a powerful factor and, in those cases in which it exists, will nearly always be decisive, but its absence will not automatically negate a bailment as the circum-

---

[35] [1968] 2 N.S.W.R. 109.
[36] [1915] 1 Ch. 621.
[37] [1968] 2 N.S.W. R. 109, at 113; see also *Walsh* v. *Palladium Car Park Pty. Ltd.* [1975] V.R. 949, at 957-959, where it was held that an action for breach of the bailment of a car to a parking lot operator was an action arising under a contract for the provision of services within the meaning of the Victorian *Small Claims Tribunal Act* 1973. In this case there was a direct fee for parking, but it is submitted that the same result should follow whenever the defendant's benefit consists in the owner's use of a shop, theatre, restaurant, etc. operated by the defendant. Bailments by way of custody alone do not appear to constitute contracts for the provision of services within the meaning of s. 74 of the *Trade Practices Act* 1974 (Commonwealth): (1977) 26 I.C.L.Q. 169 (N. E. Palmer, F. D. Rose); cf. Law Commission No. 69, paras. 119-124.
[38] E.g. *Palmer* v. *Toronto Medical Arts Building Ltd.* (1960) 21 D.L.R. (2d) 181; *B.G. Transport Service Ltd.* v. *Marston Motor Co. Ltd.* [1970] 1 Lloyd's Rep. 371; and see *Preston* v. *Ascot Central Car Park, The Times,* January 28th, 1954; *B.R.S. (Contracts) Ltd.* v *.Colney Motor Engineering Co. Ltd., The Times,* November 27th, 1958. American decisions to similar effect are *Hartford Fire Insurance Co.* v. *Doll* (1926) 5 La. App. 226; *Galowitz* v. *Magner* (1924) 208 App. Div. 6; 203 N.Y.S. 421; *Leonard Bros.* v. *Standifer* (1933) 65 S.W. (2d) 1112, where the car park was attached to a store and the bailment was held to be gratuitous; sed quaere.

stances attending the creation of the relationship may be just as relevant as those dictating the manner in which it shall end.

C. Fees and charges

The fact that the plaintiff is charged for leaving his chattel on the defendant's premises will not, of itself, be of particular relevance. In many of the decisions in which there was a mere licence, including the leading case of *Ashby* v. *Tolhurst*,[39] a charge had been exacted and it is clear that no assumption of duty can automatically be inferred from the presence of a consideration which may relate to a facility other than an undertaking of custody. Conversely, there have been cases where a bailment was established although no separate charge was made for safe-keeping, as in *Ultzen* v. *Nicols*,[40] where the act of a waiter in taking a diner's overcoat and placing it on a hook behind him was held to be sufficient evidence of taking possession for the duties of a bailee to be imposed on his employers.[41] But the *quantum* may be significant in assessing the extent of the occupier's undertaking, according to Bean J. in *B. G. Transport Service Ltd.* v. *Marston Motor Co. Ltd.*,[42] who considered that "the cheap rate for twenty-four-hour parking in London" was a material reason for refusing to discern a bailment; and in *James Buchanan Ltd.* v. *Hay's Transport Services Ltd.*,[43] Hinchcliffe J. listed this as one of the factors to be examined in arriving at an overall conclusion, although on the facts before him he concluded that the present bailment was gratuitous.[44]

The greatest significance of this element lies not so much in its existence as in its timing, for all the cases of licences for good consideration have involved charges made at the time of depositing rather than that of withdrawal.[45] If, as is most commonly the case nowadays, the charge is to be computed and paid at the end of the relationship, this will be strong evidence that the occupier intends to retain the chattel and owes the duties correlative to possession.[46]

---

[39] [1937] 2 K.B. 242; see also *B.G. Transport Service Ltd.* v. *Marston Motor Co. Ltd.; Preston* v. *Ascot Central Car Park Ltd.; B.R.S. (Contracts) Ltd.* v. *Colney Motor Engineering Co. Ltd.* (n. 38, ante); *Helton* v. *Sullivan* [1968] Qd. R. 562; *Halbauer* v. *Brighton Corporation* [1954] 1 W.L.R. 1161; 2 All E.R. 707; *Bata* v. *City Parking Canada Ltd.* (1974) 43 D.L.R. (3d) 190; *Wilmers & Gladwin Pty. Ltd.* v. *W.A.L. Building Supplies Pty. Ltd.* (1955) 55 S.R. (N.S.W.) 442; *Greenwood* v. *Council of the Municipality of Waverley* (1928) 28 S.R. (N.S.W.) 219.

[40] [1894] 1 Q.B. 92. For further examples of garments deposited in stores, restaurants and similar establishments, see pp. 205-207, post.

[41] Per Charles J.; the decision of Wright J. proceeded on the assumption that there was a bailment, the point not apparently having been taken at the trial. In *Tinsley* v. *Dudley* [1951] 2 K.B. 18, at 28, it is pointed out that *Ultzen* v. *Nicols* is not wholly free from doubt, although Evershed M.R. regarded it as justifiable on its facts.

[42] [1970] 1 Lloyd's Rep. 371, at p. 378.

[43] [1972] 2 Lloyd's Rep. 535, at p. 542.

[44] Ibid., at 543. Sed quaere; cf. Chapter 8, post.

[45] This observation is primarily intended to apply to the car-parking cases, but would appear to fit most if not all of the analogous situations, e.g. *Greenwood* v. *Council of the Municipality of Waverley* (1928) 28 S.R. (N.S.W.) 219; cf. the *Wilmers & Gladwin* case (1955) 55 S.R. (N.S.W.) 442, where payment was made in arrears but was for a flat rate.

[46] But not necessarily conclusive; occasionally the nature of the land and other circumstances will produce a contrary inference, e.g. as in *Helton* v. *Sullivan*

D. Physical geography

The layout and security of a car-park or other premises may be a material factor, but it is unlikely to be decisive where retrieval is not subject to additional procedures, even though the construction is substantially designed to deter intruders. Thus in *B.R.S.* v. *Colney Engineering Co. Ltd.*,[47] where the premises took the form of a large, floodlit yard surrounded by a six-foot high fence topped with barbed wire, but there was a flat parking rate of 1/6d and no surrender of keys, it was held that there was no bailment. In *Ashby* v. *Tolhurst*,[48] Lord Greene M.R. clearly attached some importance to the fact that the site was open and accessible on two sides although this was not his primary ground for deciding that the relationship there was one of licensor and licensee. In *Walton Stores Ltd.* v. *Sydney City Council*,[49] Asprey J.A. observed that any supposed distinction between a car-park and a garage[50] was no longer of consequence in determining the operator's obligations and considered that the nature of the present building (a multi-storey car-park) "would point towards the conclusion that there was a delivery of possession". It would probably be harder to establish a bailment in the case of open land, but other criteria—such as a time charge or a specific promise—might still displace the first impression that this was a simple grant of permission. On the other hand, if the site is open to a large number of people for a variety of purposes, such as a caravan-site, it would be unreasonable to expect the occupier to exercise vigilance for the safe custody of vehicles or other property left thereon, even when payment has been made by the owner for the privilege of using the land.[51] A different result might obtain, however, where a caravan-site is closed down for the winter, the gates are locked and individual caravans are removed to a separate area in return for a storage charge.[52]

[1968] Qd. R. 563, discussed in n. 52, post. This cuts both ways, for it may mean that the occupier has no lien over the chattels in question.

---

[47] *The Times,* November 27th, 1958; a similar situation existed in *B.G. Transport Service Ltd.* v. *Marston Motor Co. Ltd.* [1970] 1 Lloyd's Rep. 371; cf. *James Buchanan Ltd.* v. *Hay's Transport Services (London) Ltd.* [1972] 2 Lloyd's Rep. 535.

[48] [1937] 2 K.B. 242; *Empire Car Park* v. *Michael* [1952] 3 S.A. 374.

[49] [1968] 2 N.S.W.R. 109, at 112-113.

[50] Such as Evershed M.R. appeared to be making in *Tinsley* v. *Dudley* [1951] 2 K.B. 18, at 26-28; cf. *Davis* v. *Pearce Parking Station Pty. Ltd.* (1954) 91 C.L.R. 642, at 647.

[51] See *Halbauer* v. *Brighton Corporation* [1954] 1 W.L.R. 1161; 2 All E.R. 707. In this case, the caravan in question was actually situated in a storage area during the time in question, but the period of "winter storage" had already come to an end and visitors had recommenced using the site.

[52] This had been the position in *Halbauer* v. *Brighton Corporation* before the camp had re-opened for the summer season. Two of the judges in the Court of Appeal (Singleton and Denning, L.JJ.) were of the opinion that had the theft occurred during that time, and assuming that certain exclusory clauses in the camp regulations were not applicable, the defendants would have been liable as bailees; Morris L.J. inclined to the opposite view (at 712-713) chiefly on the grounds that the relevant regulation clearly pointed to a non-assumption of possession and safe-keeping on the part of the defendants. As to this criterion, see p. 209 et seq., post. Sometimes the size of the land and the locomotive character of the chattels may point to a mere licence. In *Helton* v. *Sullivan* [1968] Qd. R. 562 it was held that there was no bailment where the plaintiff

E. Proximity of the owner

If the car-owner remains in his car while it is parked, it will obviously be all the more difficult for him to maintain that possession has passed to the parking-operator. One of the reasons why it would have been incorrect to infer a bailment in *Halbauer* v. *Brighton Corporation*[53] was the fact that during the summer months most caravans were occupied and accessible to their owners and their visitors, who could come and go without reference to the site-owners. But it seems that merely to allow the plaintiff access to, or even entry into, his vehicle will not preclude a bailment where there is a clear intention to prevent removal of the chattel unless certain conditions are observed. Thus in a multi-storey car-park, it may be that the bailment does not cease until the car is checked out and the charge paid, even in these cases where the car-owner drives it to the exit and thus has immediate control before the defendants have relinquished their overall custody of the car.[54]

The question of proximity may be important with regard to a restaurant's liability for the loss of customers' property. In *Ultzen* v. *Nicols*[55] a coat was removed to a hook behind the customer's table and this was deemed sufficient evidence of a change in possession. During argument, Wright J. asked counsel for the plaintiff whether the same result should follow where a waiter places a coat on a chair by the customer's side. The reply was that this would be a weaker instance, but one nevertheless for the jury to decide.[56] Counsel cited *Richards* v. *London, Brighton & South Coast Ry. Co.*[57] to establish an analogy between the waiter who sees to the disposition of a diner's coat and the porter who takes a railway passenger's luggage out of the station to a waiting cab. Emphasis was placed on the fact that the coat was hung up at the waiter's own initiative and that such courtesies were all part of the service from which an establishment hopes to derive its reputation and, ultimately, its profit. According to Charles J.

depastured a herd of 359 mixed cattle on two large tracts of land owned by the defendants, for a fee of $50 per month. Matthews J. decided on the evidence that "contracts for agistment of large numbers of cattle on grazing areas in this State do not bear the character or implication of bailments unless one finds agreed terms in that behalf". Contracts for agistment have generally been assumed to give rise to bailments; see, for instance, *Smith* v. *Cook* (1875) 1 Q.B.D. 79; *Broadwater* v. *Blot* (1817) Holt N.P. 547; *Grazing & Export Meat Co. Ltd.* v. *Anderson* [1976] 1 N.Z.L.R. 187; cf. *Mears* v. *Sayers* (1974) 41 D.L.R. (3d) 424, where the cattle were at the relevant time in winter quarters; *Robinson* v. *Waters* (1920) 22 W.A.R. 66, at 67-68.

---

[53] [1954] 1 W.L.R. 1161; 2 All E.R. 707.

[54] Cf. *Thornton* v. *Shoe Lane Parking Ltd.* [1971] 2 Q.B. 163; *Leva* v. *Lam* (1972) 25 D.L.R. (3d) 513; *Mercer* v. *Christiana Ferry Co.* (1930) 34 Del. 490; 155 Atl. 596. In *James Buchanan & Co. Ltd.* v. *Hay's Wharf (London) Ltd.* [1972] 2 Lloyd's Rep. 535, the finding of a sub-bailment does not appear to have been inhibited by the fact that the sub-bailor's servant had regular access to the uncoupled tractor parked in the same yard as the stolen trailer, and slept in it for two nights prior to the theft.

[55] [1894] 1 Q.B. 92; see the discussion of this case by Evershed M.R. in *Tinsley* v. *Dudley* [1951] 2 K.B. 18, at 28, where it is pointed out that both Charles and Wright JJ. "felt grave doubt" about the propriety of the finding by the County Court judge that there was a bailment here.

[56] [1894] 1 Q.B. 92, at 93.

[57] (1849) 7 C.B. 839; 18 L.J. (C.P.) 251; cf. *Cavenagh* v. *Such* (1815) 1 Price 328; 145 E.R. 1419.

this case was different only in degree from one where a waiter stood at the door of the dining-room taking the coats of guests before they entered.[58]

The same decision was reached in the Nova Scotian case of *Murphy* v. *Hart*,[59] where the diner left his overcoat and hat in a recess between the shop and the refreshment parts of the defendant's establishment. Harris C.J. cited American authority[60] to show that where a customer in a shop, restaurant, swimming pool, or any other establishment where it is reasonably likely that he would have to remove garments,[61] takes advantage of the facilities provided for depositing them (however poor these facilities may be) a duty arises in the proprietor to exercise care to protect the garment from theft.

English and Australian cases are sparse on this point, and it may well be that the courts would be less willing to impose a bailment in the absence of a conscious active assumption of control by the proprietor or his staff. Some of the North American cases seem to go so far as to impose a duty on all restaurant owners to provide safe-keeping for customers' effects,[62] but it is arguable that this should follow only where the management has shown positively that it is exerting control over the property in question. In *Samuel* v. *Westminster Wine Co.*[63] it was held that the mere depositing of a coat, by its owner, on the hook or rack provided would not operate to create a bailment, although it has been suggested that the opposite may apply where a separate room is set aside for that purpose.[64] Such a situation existed in the New York case of *Webster* v. *Lane*,[65] where a dentist was held liable as a bailee for the loss of a customer's fur wrap left in the reception room while she was undergoing treatment:

> . . . we think we may take judicial notice of the fact that the patients of a dentist are not placed in a dental chair for treatment while they have their overcoats or wraps on. It seems clear, therefore, that the defendant undertook voluntary custody of the coat as an accommo-

---

[58] [1894] 1 Q.B. 92, at 94. But cf. *Apfel* v. *Whyte's Inc.* (1920) 110 N.Y. Misc. 670; 180 N.Y. Supp. 712, where in very similar circumstances there was held to be no bailment; the proximity of the plaintiff being considered a more important factor than the action of the servant.

[59] (1919) 46 D.L.R. 36.

[60] Notably, *Bunnell* v. *Stern* (1890) 122 N.Y. 539.

[61] Assuming, of course, that the arrangement is not illegal or contrary to public policy.

[62] See *Bunnell* v. *Stern*; *Dilberto* v. *Harris* (1894) 95 Ga. 571; 23 S.E. 112 (customer placing hat on hook in barbers' shop; proprietors held liable as bailees); *Hunter* v. *Reed Bros.* (1899) 12 Pa. Super 112 (bailment where clothes left in changing-booth at defendants' emporium). It has been said that the invitation to remove clothing carries a warranty as to its security; (1936-1937) 3 *University of Pittsburgh Law Review* 51; but cf. infra.

[63] *The Times*, May 16th, 1959; American cases to similar effect are *Simpson* v. *Rourke* (1895) 13 N.Y. Misc. 230; 34 N.Y. Supp. 11; *Wiley* v. *Childs Co.* (1918) 211 Ill. App.; *Gilson* v. *Pa RR.* (1914) 92 Atl. 59. *Pattison* v. *Hammerstein* (1896) 17 Misc. Rep. 375, 39 N.Y.S. 1039 (patrons removing wraps in box at theatre and hanging them on hooks provided; *held,* no bailment).

[64] Vaines, *Personal Property* (5th ed.), p. 80; *Davis* v. *Educated Fish Parlours* [1966] C.L.Y. 539; *The Guardian*, July 26th, 1966.

[65] (1925) 125 Misc. 868; 212 N.Y.S. 298; affirmed without opinion (1927) 222 N.Y. Supp. 919.

dation to his patient and as part of the service for which he was
being paid.[66]

Likewise, in *Davis* v. *Educated Fish Parlours Ltd.*[67] there was held to
have been a bailment when the plaintiff's husband handed the plaintiff's
coat to the waitress and asked her to put it in the cloakroom. This cloakroom took the form of a space or recess at the end of the restaurant, not
separate from the main body of the dining-area; but the necessary assumption of a duty of safe-keeping was deemed to exist in that the cloakroom
was locked at the rear (to prevent outsiders from entering surreptitiously)
and the other members of the party had already, on entering the restaurant,
been taken there and invited to deposit their coats.

On the other hand, in *Maher* v. *Chapin's Lunch Co.*[68] it was held that
there was no transfer of possession where a customer was directed by the
restaurant-manager to hang his hat and coat on a hook provided for that
purpose behind the lunch counter. Most modern American authorities have
recognised the need for "exclusive possession" before liability under a
bailment can be predicated.[69] One impediment to discovering this in a
restaurant or shop situation, apart from the physical proximity of the
owner, is the lack of any method of checking out property when it is
reclaimed; the customer can walk out with his (or someone else's) property whenever he pleases. Thus, for instance, it would be unlikely that a
customer in a department store who left her own dress in the changing-
room while showing a potential purchase to a friend in the main body of
the shop could recover against the emporium as bailees.[70] At the other
extreme, however, establishments like theatres or dance halls which have
separate cloakrooms with attendants and ticketing systems are clearly
bailees.[71] It is all a question of degree and the readiness with which the
owner can survey or regain his property is closely relevant to this inquiry.[72]

---

[66] But cf. *Theobald* v. *Satterthwaite* (1948) 190 P.2d. 714 where, in very similar
circumstances, the proprietors of a beauty-salon were held not to be bailees of
a customer's coat.
[67] Supra.
[68] (1935) 119 Pa. Super 213; 180 Atl. 739.
[69] Thus, in *Nolde* v. *W.D.A.S. Broadcasting Station* (1933) 108 Pa. Super 242; 164
Atl. 805, there was held to be no bailment where a guest artiste left her coat
on a stand in the studio reception room, to which the public had access.
[70] Especially if (as is often the case nowadays) the changing-room is of the com-
munal variety. American cases to contrary effect include *Hunter* v. *Reed Bros.*
(1899) 12 Pa. Super. 112; *Woodruff* v. *Painter* (1892) 150 Pa. 91; 24 Atl. 621;
cf. *Wamser* v. *Browning, King & Co.* (1907) 187 N.Y. 87; 79 N.E. 861; *Warner*
v. *Elizabeth Arden Ltd.* (1939) 83 Sol. Jo. 258, where jewellery was left in a
handbag in a changing room at a beauty salon and the proprietors' lack of
knowledge or consent to its being left was held to refute the existence of a
bailment.
[71] *Wellington Racing Club* v. *Symons* [1923] N.Z.L.R. 1; [1922] G.L.R. 478; cf.
Corbett v. *Jamieson* [1923] N.Z.L.R. 374. In *Stevenson* v. *Toronto Board of
Education* [1919] 49 D.L.R. 673, a school authority were deemed to be bailees
of a child's coat left in the girls' cloakroom, but were held not liable as it was
proved that they had taken reasonable care. The decision may be contrasted with
Scriven v. *Middlesex County Council* (1950) 100 L. Jo. 360 (Westminster
County Court) where the defendants were held not liable for the theft of a
coat which had been left in a school cloakroom by a student attending an adult
education class. See also *Poulton* v. *Notre Dame College* (1976) 60 D.L.R.
(3d) 501.
[72] For much the same reason, hospital authorities have been held not to be bailees
of jewellery and other property carried about the person of patients, even when

F. Staffing

The presence of attendants may suggest a bailment for several reasons: because they exercise a real or ostensible authority to assume custody of the chattel on general or particular occasions;[73] because an overt act on their part may amount to an acceptance of possession;[74] and because they may be employed to operate a checking procedure indicative of a retention by the employers until formalities are observed.[75] But here again their presence may not be decisive, for they may be employed only to take money or to supervise parking. If they confine themselves to these activities, or deviate from them in such a way as to demonstrate that no consequent care or safe-keeping is undertaken by their employers, no duty will be owed. It may be noted that certain public conveniences in London and other parts of England display prominent signs warning that attendants are prohibited from taking custody of clients' goods. Any attendant breaking this rule presumably takes as a bailee in his own right.[76]

G. Purposes to which possession a necessary incident

One of the reasons given by Romer L.J. for declining to find a bailment in *Ashby* v. *Tolhurst*[77] was that there was no reason why the defendants needed to gain possession in order to discharge their duty towards the car. The reverse may apply where some task is to be performed in relation to the property, and possession is a necessary or at least a usual accoutrement of that function:

> If, for instance, the car had been left at the car-park for the purpose of being sold or by way of pledge or for the purposes of being driven to some other place or indeed for the purposes of safer custody, delivery of the car, although not actually made, would readily be inferred.[78]

To some extent this begs the question, because whether a duty is owed may itself depend upon whether there has been a transfer of control to the defendant. Nevertheless, if some ancillary function is to be performed, this will often provide a strong pointer to assumption of possession. Occasionally, it may be negated, as in the Nova Scotian case of *Fournier* v. *McKenna*.[79] Here, the plaintiff left a car in the defendant's garage for

the latter are unconscious; *Gumina* v. *Toronto General Hospital Trustees* (1920) 19 O.W.N. 547; *King* v. *Sisters of St. Joseph* [1952] 3 D.L.R. 852. Cf. *Helton* v. *Sullivan* [1968] Qd. R. 562, at 565-566, where the fact that under a letting of land for agistment the occupier would normally expect the chattel-owner to employ a man to keep an eye on the stock was accorded some significance in refusing to discern a bailment.

---

[73] See pp. 199-201, ante.
[74] See the restaurant and other cases discussed under the previous sub-heading.
[75] See pp. 201-203, ante.
[76] Cf. *Palmer* v. *Toronto Medical Arts Building Ltd.* (1960) 21 D.L.R. (2d) 181 where, at 187, it is remarked: "Possession of the vehicle remained in the plaintiff throughout. While performing the gratuitous service of parking the plaintiff's car the attendant did so as the agent of the plaintiff and his temporary de facto possession is to be regarded as the plaintiff's possession."
[77] [1937] 2 K.B. 242.
[78] Ibid., at 255; cf. *Appleton* v. *Ritchie Taxi Co. Ltd.* [1942] Q.R. 446, at 449 per Gillanders J.; *The Narada* [1977] 1 Lloyd's Rep. 256.
[79] (1921) 57 D.L.R. 725.

repairs. The defendant warned him that if he left it in a certain part of the building (used for storing derelict vehicles and junk) he would not be responsible for it. The plaintiff ignored this and a later instruction to take away the car. The defendant subsequently moved it outside in order to lay a concrete floor and the car was damaged by exposure. *Held,* he was not liable for the loss.[80]

In *Shorters Parking Station Ltd.* v. *Johnson,*[81] it was observed that transfer of possession was a necessary incident to the proper performance of the defendants' business as garage-operators, as well as for the plaintiff's convenience. The result should be the same when the relevant purpose is exclusively within the contemplation of the occupier, be it the exaction of fees, the maximising of his available space or the increased attractiveness of his establishment.[82]

H. Tickets and other documentation

The terms and self-description of this sort of literature may or may not help to decide whether there has been a bailment. In *Ashby* v. *Tolhurst*[83] counsel for the plaintiff argued strenuously that the careful and extensive exclusions of liability on the ticket were a clear indication that the defendants were under some initial liability; in other words, that an exemption clause should be presumed to have something to bite on. Scott L.J. sympathised with this argument,[84] but he and the other members of the Court of Appeal found it unacceptable. In their view, it was refuted by the description on the face of the ticket itself—"Car-park ticket"—and the fact that the defendants had taken such pains to demonstrate their refusal to accept responsibility at all.

> You cannot infer a contract by A to perform a certain act out of circumstances in which A has made it perfectly plain that he declines to be under any contractual liability to perform that act.
> In the result on the proper interpretation of these conditions I entirely agree that the dominating words are "All cars are left in all respects entirely at their owner's risk". These words, I think, are unambiguous and in themselves exclude the idea of any contract of bailment.[85]

Such reasoning is unlikely to be persuasive in a more modern context where other factors exist to indicate control. In *Samuel Smith & Sons* v. *Silverman,*[86] there was a similar head-clause, printed prominently on the ticket, but because the plaintiff had obeyed a request to leave his keys in the car the defendants rightly conceded a bailment. In *Davis* v. *Pearce*

---

[80] The case is a peculiar one and may well be an illustration of the "involuntary bailment". Cf. *Helton* v. *Sullivan* (p. 204, n. 52) where a delivery of possession in the cattle was clearly not necessary to give business efficacy to the contract of agistment.

[81] [1963] N.Z.L.R. 135, at 136.

[82] Cf. *Martin* v. *Town 'n' Country Delicatessen Ltd.* (1963) 42 D.L.R. (2d) 449, at 462, 464; the question may be relevant to whether the bailment is gratuitous.

[83] [1937] 2 K.B. 242, at 246.

[84] Ibid., at 257.

[85] Ibid., at 255, 258 (Romer and Scott L.JJ.). See also Morris L.J. in *Halbauer* v. *Brighton Corporation* [1954] 1 W.L.R. 1161; 2 All E.R. 707, at 713.

[86] (1961) 29 D.L.R. (2d) 98.

Parking Station Pty. Ltd.[87] the use of the words "delivery" and "redelivery" on the ticket were held to connote a change in possession despite the presence of carefully-drawn clauses purporting to relieve the defendants of all responsibility for loss or damage.[88] Most large car-parks now adopt such exculpatory provisions but it is no longer seriously argued that they are, by themselves, determinative of a continued possession in the customer.[89] The decision in *Ashby* v. *Tolhurst* must on this point be confined to cases where the ancillary circumstances are equally inconsistent with the character of bailment.

From a negative aspect, it could be inferred that an occupier who excludes some, but not all, of his potential responsibilities, or whose notices are more in the form of a warning as to the Common Law position than a definition of his individual liability, has initially assumed the duties of a bailee.[90] But here again other factors are likely to be decisive and it would be a foolhardy motorist who relied on this argument alone. Clauses that define the quality of the relationship, such as that in *Davis* v. *Pearce Parking Station Pty. Ltd.*,[91] must be distinguished from those that seek to mitigate the consequences of failing to discharge an obligation otherwise established. Even the former must be consistent with the facts of the case. Nevertheless, there will still be cases in which the terms of the contract are important as supporting evidence—for instance, *B. G. Transport Service Ltd.* v. *Marston Motor Co. Ltd.*,[92] where a "no responsibility" clause was one of the judge's four reasons for holding that there was in this case a mere licence.

A decision which appears to contradict much of the foregoing is that of the Ontario Court of Appeal in *Bata* v. *City Parking Canada Ltd.*,[93] which has been described as possibly representing "the inevitable triumph of parking lot owners in absolving themselves completely from liability to users".[94] The plaintiff, at an attendant's request, left the keys in his car; the car was later stolen and, when recovered, was found to be damaged. There was nothing to suggest that the attendant's request was unusual and the general concatenation of circumstances clearly pointed to a bailment. How-

---

[87] (1954) 91 C.L.R. 642.
[88] Cf. *Council of the City of Sydney* v. *West* (1965) 114 C.L.R. 481, where the clause had been modified and the word "redelivery" deleted; *Walton Stores Ltd.* v. *Sydney City Council* [1968] 2 N.S.W.R. 109, where the clause spoke of the vehicle being "removed" and not "delivered" on presentation of the ticket and *Walsh* v. *Palladium Car Park Pty. Ltd.* [1975] V.R. 949, where the clause said that the defendants "may deliver" the vehicle "to any person producing this card" or to anyone else whom the defendants in their sole discretion considered entitled or authorised to collect it. In all three cases there was held to be a bailment. A delivery to someone other than the owner may amount to a fundamental breach of the parking-contract, thus rendering any exclusion clauses ineffective; see the preceding cases and *Heffron* v. *Imperial Parking Co. Ltd.* (1974) 46 D.L.R. (3d) 642; *Penny* v. *Grand Central Car Park Pty. Ltd.* [1965] V.R. 323.
[89] But see post.
[90] Cf. *Hollier* v. *Rambler Motors (A.M.C.) Ltd.* [1972] 2 Q.B. 71, where the clause was of this kind but other factors also indicated a bailment.
[91] Ante; here, of course, it was defined *against* the car-park operator.
[92] [1970] 1 Lloyd's Rep. 371, at 378.
[93] (1974) 43 D.L.R. (3d) 190; cf. *Schnelle* v. *City Parking Canada Ltd.* [1972] 2 W.W.R. 550.
[94] (1975) 33 *University of Toronto Faculty of Law Review* 100.

ever, the Court found otherwise, relying on the following words which were prominently displayed on a sign in the car-park:

> Charges are for use of parking space only. This company assumes no responsibility whatever for loss or damage due to fire, theft or otherwise, to the vehicle or its contents, however caused.

Whilst it may not necessarily be true that the terms of the contract can be relevant only to the effect of a bailment and not to its creation,[95] it is submitted that the *Bata* case, insofar as it allows exculpatory words to produce a definition of the parties' relationship flagrantly at odds with the established facts, is misconceived. The fundamental criterion must always be whether possession in the chattel has been transferred to the defendant, and a refusal to accept the consequences of such a transfer can scarcely be said to gainsay its occurrence. Intention, when thus expressed, must be consistent with the physical facts and circumstances of the case.

I. Commercial standing

In *James Buchanan Ltd.* v. *Hay's Transport Service (London) Ltd.*[96] it was held that the parties' previous relationship and the defendant's reputation were significant factors in establishing a bailment. In this case, the owner and the occupier were not in a direct contractual relationship. The plaintiffs had bailed their whisky to a carrier for transportation to Tilbury Docks. On the journey from Glasgow to Essex the lorry developed mechanical trouble and was uncoupled in the first defendants' yard at Barking. The first defendants were a sister company of the carriers and there was a long-standing arrangement for the use of the yard by the carriers whenever necessary. The tractor portion was driven away on various errands and the trailer left standing until, a few days later, it was stolen. Hinchcliffe J. held that in all the circumstances a bailment had arisen and the yard-owners were liable for the loss of the whisky.

> When all is said and done, Hay's Wharf are specialists in ware-housing, wharfingers and transportation: Duncan Barbour & Son Ltd. is an associated company: and when the plaintiffs, a top-class firm of whisky distillers, employ one of the companies in the Hay's Wharf Group, they do expect to receive Rolls-Royce treatment, and that arrangements will be made to the advantage of both defendants.[97]

The case is different from the ordinary car-park situation in that there was no parking fee, no ticket to be obtained and presented on departure, no signs or printed notices of exemption and only a very qualified version of the traditional attendant. It shows how the plaintiffs' reasonable expectation of the sort of service they might expect from a firm of the first defendants' character was relevant to the question of whether a bailment had come into being at all ,and not merely (as is usually the position) to whether those duties had been adequately discharged.

On a broader level, we have already seen how a course of dealing between the parties before the loss occurred may be either indicative of, or inconsistent with, a bailment according to the circumstances.[98]

---

[95] Ibid., as suggested at 102; cf. p. 209, ante.
[96] [1972] 2 Lloyd's Rep. 535.
[97] Ibid., at p. 542.
[98] Ante, p. 198, et seq.

J. Space-renting agreements

Where an occupier grants the owner of a chattel the exclusive right to use a particular identified portion of his premises for storage or safe-keeping, this agreement will frequently provide conclusive evidence against the creation of a bailment. The reason is that the exclusion of the occupier is inconsonant with the high degree of physical control necessary to constitute a delivery of possession. Thus, it would seem that there is no bailment where a lodger in a boarding-house leaves articles in his room whilst absent from the premises;[99] that a householder does not become the bailee of furniture stored in a locked room;[1] that a hospital authority is not a bailee of personal effects left in the room of a resident house-physician;[2] and that a bank is not a bailee of items stored in a rented safe-deposit to which the customer has the only key.[3]

Even where the occupier has not specifically divested himself of the right to enter the area, but a specific part of his premises has been set aside for the plaintiff's personal use, there will generally be no bailment. In *Deyong* v. *Shenburn*[4] it was conceded that a theatrical producer and licensee did not become the bailee of clothes left in an actor's dressing-room. In *Wilmers & Gladwin Pty. Ltd.* v. *W.A.L. Building Supplies Pty. Ltd.*[5] the defendants were sub-lessees of part of a large building, the floor space of which had been marked off into bays. They agreed to let two of the bays in their section of the building to the plaintiffs, the agreement being described in the invoices as "Rental storage space". They retained their key to the building and, when the plaintiffs wished to deposit goods, would send over an employee to open the door and assist in carrying them inside. It was held that they were not bailees of the goods thus deposited. They had not contracted for their custody and safe-keeping but had merely:

> . . . made available to the plaintiff's company and given it the right to enter, use and occupy two bays on this open floor for the purpose

---

[99] Although the circumstances may point to an implied agreement to safeguard the goods without acquiring possession; see Chapter 24, post.

[1] *Peers* v. *Sampson* (1824) 4 Dow. & Ry. K.B. 636.

[2] *Edwards* v. *West Herts Group Hospital Management Committee* [1957] 1 W.L.R. 415; 1 All E.R. 541.

[3] This appears to be the permissible inference from *People* v. *Merchantile Safe Deposit Co.* (1914) 143 N.Y. Supp. 849, which involved a statute imposing certain duties on banks having customers' securities "in possession or under control". But American authority is divided on the question of whether there is a bailment when both bank and customer retain a key and neither can gain access without the other; see (1913-1914) 27 *Harvard Law Review* 597; (1924-1925) 34 *Yale Law Journal* 795; (1924-1925) 10 *Cornell Law Quarterly* 255. The position cannot be regarded as settled in England or Australia, but the bank's overall control is likely to be held to be determinative of a bailment: see Tay (1964) 6 *Malaya Law Review* 229; *Giblin* v. *McMullen* (1868) L.R. 2 P.C. 317.

[4] [1946] K.B. 227. Both here and in the *Edwards* case, ante, it was held that there is normally no implied term in a contract of service obliging the employer to exercise reasonable care to safeguard his employee's property. But special circumstances may occasionally impose such a duty, and justify a finding that the employer is a bailee; see *Hubbard* v. *Sisters of St. Joseph's* [1944] 1 D.L.R. 190; *Johnson & Towers, Baltimore, Inc.* v. *Babbington* (1972) 288 A. 2d. 131 (Maryland Court of Appeals); *Grana* v. *Security Insurance Group* (1972) 72 Misc. 2d. 265; 339 N.Y.S. 2d. 34.

[5] (1955) 55 S.R. (N.S.W.) 442.

of sheltering goods belonging to the plaintiff and keeping the same there at the plaintiff's disposition and under its control.[6]

In such a case, even though the relationship was not strictly one of lessor and lessee, there was manifestly no delivery of possession. The Court relied on *Ashby* v. *Tolhurst*,[7] *Tinsley* v. *Dudley*[8] and the earlier New South Wales case of **Greenwood** v. *Council of the Municipality of Waverley*,[9] where the deposit of clothes in a hired locker in one of the defendants' bathing sheds was held to raise insufficient evidence of a bailment, despite the fact that the attendant retained the key while the owner was away.

The continued or intermittent presence of the owner of goods will clearly militate strongly against any transfer of possession, at least where those goods are left on an area specifically assigned to his use. A different result may obtain where he is away for a long period and the goods are effectively under the occupier's continuous control. Such a case was *Blount* v. *War Office*,[10] where the defendants, who had requisitioned a house, allowed the plaintiff to store property in one of the rooms, which was locked for the purpose. They were held to be bailees of the goods and liable when some of them were stolen.

K. Summary

As the foregoing analysis has shown, one can rarely answer this question with complete certainty. Certain features appear regularly in the decisions but, taken overall, enjoy only a limited and variable significance. Often they are effective in establishing a bailment only when combined with other factors not, in themselves, conclusive. Consequently, the side of the line upon which a given case may fall is largely intuitive—"a matter of impression". Some cases give no reasons at all but seem essentially correct;[11] others are more explicit but more questionable[12] and seem barely reconcilable with authority pointing the other way. What seems plain is that, in the ordinary run of events, the unattended hotel or restaurant car-park will clearly not produce a bailment, while the modern multi-storey car-park with its careful checks on incoming and outgoing cars and cumulative fee in return for parking space and tickets to be presented before being allowed to depart, will almost invariably do so. Other cases will fall between the two.

---

[6] Ibid., at p. 448. See also *Lesser* v. *Jones* (1920) 47 N.B.R. 318, where a car-owner was allowed to leave it in a private garage, no particular space was assigned, and he was given a key to the building to retrieve the car whenever he chose: *held*, there was no bailment; *Alberta U Drive Ltd.* v. *Jack Carter Ltd.* (1972) 28 D.L.R. (3d) 114; *St. Paul Fire & Marine Insurance Co.* v. *Zurich Insurance Co.* (1971) 250 So. 2d. 451; *Protean Enterprises (Newmarket) Pty. Ltd.* v. *Randall* [1975] V.R. 327.

[7] [1937] 2 K.B. 242.

[8] [1951] 2 K.B. 18.

[9] (1928) 28 S.R. (N.S.W.) 219; cf. *Timaru Borough Council* v. *Boulton* [1924] N.Z.L.R. 365.

[10] [1953] 1 W.L.R. 736; 1 All E.R. 1071.

[11] For instance, *Jenkyns* v. *Southampton Mail Packet Co.* (1919) 35 T.L.R. 264, 435 (passenger engaged free-lance porter to carry his luggage aboard defendants' steam-ship; porter deposited it in part of deck used for storing luggage, with apparent consent of ship's staff; *held*, defendants were bailees).

[12] E.g., *Martin* v. *Town 'n' Country Delicatessen Ltd.* (p. 199, ante); *Bata* v. *City Parking Stations Canada Ltd.* (p. 210, ante).

II. Alternative Remedies

Even where there has been no delivery of possession, the chattel-owner may have other remedies against an occupier of land for loss or damage to his chattel. The availability of these remedies in a given case will depend upon a range of factors, of which the most notable are the nature of the injury, the active conduct (if any) of the occupier or his servants and the terms of any special agreement between the parties.

A. Occupier's liability for theft or damage in relation to visitors' chattels

Apart from certain, narrow exceptions,[13] it is clearly established that an occupier is not liable for the loss of his visitor's property by theft, unless he has become a bailee. In *Tinsley* v. *Dudley*[14] Jenkins L.J. remarked on the complete absence of any authority supporting such liability and observed that such a rule, had it existed, would have undoubtedly have applied to the facts of *Deyong* v. *Shenburn*,[15] where liability was negatived by the Court of Appeal. Such a principle would, in his view, produce "a liability of a most comprehensive and sweeping character, and would have entered into a very great number of cases if it existed".[16] It is significant that since *Tinsley* v. *Dudley* depositors of chattels on land belonging to another have tended to confine their allegations to those of bailment and have not attempted to resurrect the issue of occupiers' liability for theft.[17]

All the cases in which the chattel-owner has been held to be a mere licensee, and therefore without a remedy, have involved loss by theft or, occasionally, physical damage consequent upon theft.[18] Where the negligence of the occupier has caused actual physical damage to the chattel, however, and this damage is sustained while on the premises, both English and Australian authority would appear to concur in giving the chattel-owner a remedy, whether he is a licensee or invitee of the occupier, or indeed has bailed the goods to him.. This is undoubtedly the rule in Australia. In *Drive Yourself Lessey's Pty. Ltd.* v. *Burnside*[19] the hirer of a car paid a

---

[13] Post, ch. 24 and p. 223.

[14] [1951] 2 K.B. 18, at 31.

[15] [1946] K.B. 227; see p. 212, ante.

[16] Cf. *Fong* v. *Tinkess* [1941] 4 D.L.R. 295.

[17] In *Edwards* v. *West Herts Group Hospital Management Committee* [1957] 1 W.L.R. 415; 1 All E.R. 541, the existence of an occupancy duty to guard against theft was again raised but the Court of Appeal, following the earlier statement of Jenkins L.J., rejected it; cf. Bowett (1956) 19 M.L.R. 172, at 183; North, *Occupiers' Liability*, pp. 106-107, where the imposition of such a duty at Common Law is canvassed in cases where "the occupier ha(s) reason to be aware of the presence of thieves". Since s. 1(3)(b) of the *Occupier's Liability Act*, 1957, refers only to damage to property, it seems improbable that even under the statutory liability an occupier is answerable for loss by theft (*A.M.F. International Ltd.* v. *Magnet Bowling Ltd.* [1968] 1 W.L.R. 1028, at 1050) or indeed for total loss arising from other causes: as to which, see North, op. cit., pp. 111-112. See generally Salmond, *Law of Torts* (16th ed.), pp. 266-267; Clerk and Lindsell, *Torts* (14th ed.), para. 1044, where the view is taken that the Act creates no duty (such as a duty to guard against theft) which was not owed at Common Law.

[18] *Martin* v. *Town 'n' Country Delicatessen Ltd.* supra, *Adams (Durham) Ltd.* v. *Trust Houses, Ltd.* [1966] 1 Lloyd's Rep. 380; *Bata* v. *City Parking Stations Canada Ltd.* (1974) 43 D.L.R. (3d) 190; cf. *Samuel Smith & Sons Ltd.* v. *Silverman* (1961) 29 D.L.R. (2d) 98; *Fournier* v. *McKenna* (1921) 57 D.L.R. 725.

[19] [1959] S.R. (N.S.W.) 390; discussed by North, op. cit., pp. 98-105.

fee to leave it in a car-park operated by the defendants. The area was overhung by cliffs, and the defendants knew that rocks occasionally fell from these cliffs, damaging vehicles below. They had taken no reasonable steps to prevent this from happening, or to warn visitors of the danger. A large boulder descended on the car, causing considerable damage, and the plaintiffs (the owners of the vehicle) were held entitled to recover. Street C.J. and Owen J. based their decision upon the defendants' breach of their duty of care as occupiers of the property; Herron J. upon the ground of simple negligence, under the rule in *Donoghue* v. *Stevenson*.[20] In the words of Street C.J.:

> . . . the invitation clearly extended to cover the car, and therefore imposed an obligation upon the appellants to take reasonable care to see that their premises were safe for use as a parking area, or to warn prospective entrants of any unusual danger hidden from the entrant but of which the appellants were aware or ought reasonably to have been aware.[21]

In England, the question is governed by s. 1(3)(b) of the *Occupiers' Liability Act* 1957, understanding of which necessitates recourse to the pre-existing Common Law. Here confusion has arisen from certain dicta by two Masters of the Rolls, Lord Greene and Sir Raymond Evershed. A statement by the latter in *Tinsley* v. *Dudley*[22] appears to suggest that liability for damage to property occurs only when such damage is "incidental or ancillary to personal injury". Lord Greene would seem to take the matter still further, for in *Ashby* v. *Tolhurst*[23] he remarked that the relationship of licensor and licensee:[24]

> . . . would carry no obligations on the part of the licensor towards the licensee in relation to the chattel left there, no obligation to provide anybody to look after it, no liability for any negligent act of any person in the employment of the licensor who happened to be there.

Against this may be placed the dictum of Jenkins L.J. in *Tinsley* v. *Dudley*, which implies no restriction on the occupier's liability for damage to property to cases where the damage is related to personal injury;[25] the fact that Lord Greene M.R. would also have been prepared to exonerate the defendants in *Ashby* v. *Tolhurst* from liability for misdelivery,[26] which is questionable in the light of modern authority;[27] and the existence of a substantial range of authority supporting the wider view of an occupier's

---

20 [1932] A.C. 562.
21 [1959] S.R. (N.S.W.) 390, at 399.
22 [1951] 2 K.B. 18, at 25; the statement is not unambiguous, and may not in fact refer to property damage at all.
23 [1937] 2 K.B. 242, at 249.
24 Note, however, that the relationship in *Ashby* v. *Tolhurst* was almost certainly one of invitation rather than one of licence in the literal acceptation of that term; see *Tinsley* v. *Dudley* supra, at 26 per Evershed M.R.; cf. Danckwerts J. at 33, who appeared to think that in the present case the plaintiff was no more than a licensee as regards the presence of the motor-cycle on the defendant's premises; sed quaere.
25 [1951] 2 K.B. 18, at 31.
26 [1937] 2 K.B. 242, at 252.
27 Post, p. 220.

liability for damage to visitor's goods.[28] Admittedly, the cases directly in point appear to be dealing (as was the Court of Appeal in *Tinsley* v. *Dudley*) with invitees rather than licensees. Thus, a distinction may be said to exist in England between the two classes of entrant even after 1957, for s. 1(3) of the Act imposes on an occupier a duty in respect of property:

> . . . in like manner and to the like extent as the principles applicable at Common Law 'between' an occupier of premises and his invitees or licensees.

No such distinction was accepted by the court in *Lessey's* case, who thought that the Common Law duty should be the same throughout and should follow that outlined by Jenkins L.J. rather than the narrower rule of Evershed M.R. The preferable view, as Dr. North has proposed,[29] would be to acknowledge that the English Common Law position is identical to that in Australia, thus enabling the courts to hold that s. 1(3)(b) of the 1957 Act preserves an already-established Common Law liability for damage to property caused by the unsafe condition of premises, whether occurring in conjunction with or independently of personal injuries, and applicable to all classes of lawful entrant. It would be absurd if the collapse of a ceiling in a ladies dress-shop would entitle those victims who were wearing their own apparel at the time to recover for damage while those who were semi-clad and had left their garb in the changing rooms were bereft of redress.[30]

In any event, it should be reiterated that a relationship characterised as one of licensor and licensee for the purposes of distinguishing it from a bailment will not necessarily be characterised in the same way when it comes to distinguishing it from that of invitor and invitee. If the test of invitation be "whether the occupier derives an economic advantage from the visit",[31] it seems that all fee-paying car-parks (as well as those attached to stores and restaurants) betoken a higher status of entrant than the humble licensee. If a motorist getting free air for his tyres at a service station be an invitee,[32] so a fortiori should the motorist who pays a shilling to use the Seaway Car-Park.

Two further points arising under this class of liability must be briefly mentioned. First, it seems that an occupier's liability for damage to chattels is not confined to those items of property that belong to the entrant, but may extend to chattels of which the entrant is a mere bailee; in the latter case, the occupier will be answerable to the true owner provided the chattel is of such a kind that he can reasonably be taken to have consented to its

---

[28] *Lancaster Canal Co.* v. *Parnaby* (1839) 11 A. & E. 223; *Norman* v. *G.W. Ry. Co.* [1915] 1 K.B. 584; *The Cawood III* [1951] P. 270; *Workington Harbour and Dock Board* v. *Towerfield (Owners)* [1951] A.C. 112; *Grossman* v. *The King* [1952] 1 S.C.R. 571; *Redwell Servicing Co.* v. *Lane Wells Canadian Co.* (1955) 16 W.W.R. 615. See further North, op. cit., pp. 95-101; *Edwards* v. *West Herts Group Hospital Management Committee* [1957] 1 W.L.R. 415, at 417, 422.
[29] *Occupiers' Liability*, at 99.
[30] Or if a prospective purchaser could recover whereas someone who had entered solely in order to use the lavatory could not; cf. *Fleming* v. *British American Oil Co.* [1953] 1 D.L.R. 70; *Pearson* v. *Coleman Bros.* [1949] 2 K.B. 359.
[31] Fleming, *Torts* (4th ed.), p. 383.
[32] Fleming, op. cit., p. 384.

presence on his land.[33] Dr. North has suggested that, while this is un-doubtedly the position in Australia, it is doubtful whether the *Occupiers' Liability Act* of 1957 should properly be applied to such damage.[34] Admittedly, s. 1(3)(b) of the Act includes within its provisions "the property of persons who are not themselves (the occupier's) visitors". But to construe s. 1(3)(b) as extending the common duty of care to goods owned by third-parties would appear to involve one of two assumptions: *either* that an owner of chattels can be a "lawful visitor" upon premises which, physically, he never enters at all, merely by owning goods which themselves come on to those premises; *or*, that a duty can be owed under the Act to a non-entrant. The latter approach arguably runs counter to the main objective of the Act, which is "to determine the duties owed by an occupier to his *lawful visitors*";[35] it also requires one to assume that such liability exists at Common Law, an assumption which is, under English law, doubtful.[36] In Dr. North's view:

> Any action (*for damage to the property of third-parties*) under the *Occupiers' Liability Act* 1957 should be available only to the actual entrant and, therefore, s. 1(3)(b) ought to be read as to apply only to such an action.[37]

On the other hand, the learned editors of Salmond,[38] and Winfield[39] both subscribe to the view that the non-entrant owner can sue under the Act in respect of damage of this kind. Their opinion is shared, moreover, by the authors of a recent Law Commission Working Paper on Liability to Trespassers, who incline to the view that the express language of the Act:

> . . . either assumes, or is intended to create, a relationship between the occupier and the owner of the property brought on the land by a lawful entrant.[40]

Even if s. 1(3)(b) were held not to apply here, it seems that the occupier should, in appropriate circumstances, be liable to the chattel-owner under the ordinary principles of negligence laid down in *Donoghue v. Stevenson*.[41] It is upon this foundation that Dr. North would prefer to

---

[33] *Drive Yourself Lessey's Pty. Ltd.* v. *Burnside* [1959] S.R. (N.S.W.) 390; a fortiori, where the immediate depositor is merely a servant who does not have legal possession: cf. *Meux* v. *G.E. Ry. Co.* [1895] 2 Q.B. 387, which appears to illustrate the principle stated, with *Becher* v. *G.E. Ry. Co.* (1870) L.R. 5 Q.B. 241, where the defendants were not deemed to have consented to the presence of the plaintiff's goods on their railway; and see further *Jenkyns* v. *Southhampton Mail Packet Co.* (1919) 35 T.L.R. 264, at 435; *Walton Stores Ltd.* v. *Sydney City Council* [1968] 2 N.S.W.R. 109.

[34] North, op. cit., p. 101 et seq.

[35] Ibid., at 102.

[36] But see the *Meux* case supra, which can be construed as permitting the non-entrant owner to recover.

[37] Op. cit., p. 105.

[38] *Torts* (16th ed.), p. 267.

[39] *Torts* (10th ed.) p. 186 (though the support is tentative); cf. Clerk and Lindsell, *Torts* (14th ed.), para. 1044, where the point is not discussed but the citation of s. 1(3)(b) suggests that the non-entrant's right of recovery is taken for granted.

[40] W.P. No. 52, para. 44, note 94.

[41] [1932] A.C. 562; *Drive-Yourself Lessey's Pty. Ltd.* v. *Burnside* [1959] S.R. (N.S.W.) 390, per Herron J.; see further, p. 219 et seq., post.

base an occupier's liability to non-entrants whose chattels have been damaged on the former's land.[42]

Secondly, many of the so-called licence cases involve not merely a licensor-licensee relationship nor even one of invitation, but frequently, (where money is paid or some other consideration is present) a contract relating to the use of the land. At Common Law, such contracts were generally deemed to impose a higher duty on the occupier than the duty to exercise reasonable care; the precise degree of duty depending upon a rather confusing parcel of distinctions which, fortunately, are not germane to the present discussion.[43] The difference between this and an invitor-invitee relationship is irrelevant in the area of damage to goods, because even at Common Law the onerous duties owed by an occupier to his contractual visitors applied only to their personal safety and freedom from injury.[44] In relation to any chattels those visitors might have brought with them on to the land, the test seems to have been a universal one of reasonable care.[45] Section 5(1) of the English *Occupiers' Liability Act 1957* effectively confirms this position by extending the common duty of care to all persons who:

> . . . bring or send goods to any premises in exercise of a right conferred by contract with a person occupying or having control of the premises . . .

The insertion of the word "send" in s. 5(1) may again be assumed to cover the situation where A's goods are bought on C's land by B in pursuance of a contract between A and C.[46] It should be also observed that s. 5(1) does not apply (inter alia) to any obligation arising by or by virtue of (a) any contract of bailment; or (b) any contract for the hire of any vehicle, vessel, aircraft or other means of transport; or (c) any contract for the carriage of goods for reward by any such means.[47] Thus in each of these three cases the ordinary rules of the particular bailment in question (modified, where appropriate, by statute) will continue to apply. Dr. North's contention[48] that, by referring only to *contracts* of bailment, s. 5(3) condemns the gratuitous bailment to the operation of s. 5(1) and thereby reverses the traditional burden of proof, seems to overlook the fact that s. 5(1) will, in any event, apply only where there is a contract entitling the bailor to bring or send goods on to the premises in the first place.

B. Negligent damage to chattels

There seems no reason why the occupier should not be liable for damage occasioned by his negligence, whether this amounts to a breach of his duty as an occupier or not. Not all situations in which such damage has occurred will have resulted from a breach of "the duty which an occupier of premises owes to his visitors in respect of dangers due to the state of the

---

[42] Op. cit., p. 105. Of course, if the entrant is a bailee of the chattel, he will enjoy an action under the Act.
[43] See Fleming, op. cit., pp. 379-383.
[44] North, p. 153 n.
[45] *Searle* v. *Laverick* (1874) L.R. 9 Q.B. 122; post, p. 455.
[46] Quaere whether the contractual right must be in the plaintiff; presumably it must.
[47] Section 5(3).
[48] Op. cit., at pp. 157-158.

premises or to things done or omitted to be done of them"[49] or of "the duty imposed by law in consequence of a person's occupation or control of premises and of any invitation or permission . . . to another to enter or use the premises".[50] The distinction between an occupancy duty and one arising independently of occupation is difficult to draw,[51] but Clerk and Lindsell have suggested that "superadded negligence, such as dropping a sack of sugar on the visitor from a crane, running into him in a car or locomotive, shooting him, or pouring tea over him" should fall beyond the conventional purview of occupiers' liability.[52] Presumably the same rule of recovery should apply when negligent acts of this kind cause damage rather than injury.

It has been observed how in *Drive Yourself Lessey's Pty. Ltd.* v. *Burnside*,[53] Herron J. applied the ordinary principles of negligence in holding the defendants liable. English authority is scarce, but support may be found in a dictum of Denning L.J. in *Halbauer* v. *Brighton Corporation*.[54] Remarking that during the summer period the defendants were not bailees of the caravan but merely licensors of the space on which it stood, he continued:

> The corporation . . . were, no doubt, under a duty to use reasonable care in their own sphere of operations. If their servants negligently ran into the caravan, they would be liable for the resulting damage.[55]

It is therefore suggested that an occupier upon whose land goods are left in circumstances not creating a bailment should be liable for negligently occasioned damage to those goods not only where he has broken his duty as an occupier but whenever a general duty of care has been breached through his default. Whilst it may be reasonable to infer from the existence of a license that the occupier is declining responsibility for

---

[49] O.L.A. 1957, s. 1(1).
[50] O.L.A. 1957, s. 1(2).
[51] For an interesting modern example, see *N.Z. Insurance Co. Ltd.* v. *Prudential Assurance Co. Ltd.* [1976] 1 N.Z.L.R. 84, where a visitor to premises of which the occupant had recently committed suicide was killed by drinking the remains of the fatal dose of poison, which was standing in a tumbler in the kitchen.
[52] *Torts* (14th ed.), para. 1013.
[53] [1959] S.R. (N.S.W.) 390.
[54] [1954] 1 W.L.R. 1161; 2 All E.R. 707, at 711; see also *Leva* v. *Lam* (1972) 25 D.L.R. (3d) 513.
[55] Two decisions go so far as to suggest that the occupier must exercise affirmative precautions to prevent the goods from loss or damage through natural causes as well as refraining from active conduct which is likely to damage the goods. In *Seaspan International Ltd.* v. *The Kostis Prois* (1973) 33 D.L.R. (3d) 1, at 7-9, Hall and Laskin JJ. held (dissenting on this point) that the owners of a ship who allowed a barge to be moored alongside were under "an obligation of reasonable care and supervision to see that the barge remained fast" although they were not bailees. In *Fairline Shipping Corporation Ltd.* v. *Adamson* [1975] Q.B. 180, Kerr J. held that the freeholder of a cold store, who was also the managing director and sole effective employee of a company to which he had agreed to lease the store, was liable for the loss of the plaintiff's goods resulting from a failure to keep the temperature constant, although he lacked possession and was not therefore a bailee: "I do not think that the refinements of the concept of legal possession and bailment are or should be determinative of liability in the tort of negligence." Cf. Diamond (1975) 38 M.L.R. 198, who suggests that the decision may be authority for a principle of *respondeat inferior,* and *Protean Enterprises (Newmarket) Pty. Ltd.* v. *Randall* [1975] V.R. 327. On the facts the defendant could probably be regarded as owing a duty of care, but the result may not be one of general application.

loss by theft, a similar inference can scarcely be permissible where the act complained of is the destruction or impairment of the chattel through causes occasioned by the occupier and within his power of reasonable prevention. For such liability to be negated, clear warning should be necessary.

C. Conversion and misdelivery

A person may be guilty of conversion without having acquired possession of the chattel converted.[56] All that is required is an intentional act incompatible with, and repugnant to, the owner's title. Thus it would seem that if a licensor commits, through his servants, a positive act of misdelivery, he should be liable to the owner for the value of the chattel. In *Ashby* v. *Tolhurst*[57] the Court of Appeal held that there was no conversion where the attendant merely acquiesced in the removal of the vehicle and did not actively participate in its misappropriation. Had there been an act of misdelivery, the result may have been that not only the attendant but also his employers would have been liable for the conversion. This was clearly the opinion of Romer L.J., who said:

> Although the car was not delivered to the defendants, I apprehend that the servant acting within his authority might have bound the defendants by an act of conversion if he had purported to deal with the car as the owner.[58]

Unfortunately, the position is obscured by the divergent bases of judgment in *Morris* v. *C. W. Martin & Sons Ltd.*[59] According to Lord Denning M.R., an employer is liable for the conversions of his servants whenever he has entrusted or delegated to them a duty of care over the chattel. Such a duty may arise by virtue of a bailment for reward or from other circumstances producing an analogous responsibility.[60] But the essence of a licence in this context is that the employer is accepting no duty of the kind in question (i.e. to guard against theft) at all. It has been regularly acknowledged that a master is not liable merely because the servant's employment affords him the opportunity of stealing or otherwise converting the property of another.[61] The law requires some closer relationship between the task or duty to be performed and the chattel which has been converted. Bailment for reward is the primary instance of such a relationship. The bailee may delegate his duty of care lawfully, but he does so at his peril, in that responsibility for its fulfilment remains squarely on his shoulders. A licence, on the other hand, imports no duty to safeguard the chattels in question against loss by theft. Thus, it would seem to follow, adopting Lord Denning's analysis, that the denial of a remedy is cases like *Ashby* v. *Tolhurst* extends not only to those situations where the conversion is

---

[56] Ante, p. 127.

[57] [1937] 2 K.B. 242.

[58] At 256; cf. Greene M.R. at 249, who would appear to discount liability even for conversion. The passage is set out p. 215, ante.

[59] [1966] 1 Q.B. 716.

[60] At p. 728.

[61] See *de Parrell* v. *Walker* (1932) 49 T.L.R. 37; *Ruben and Ladenberg* v. *Great Fingall Consolidated* [1906] A.C. 439; *Leesh River Tea Co. Ltd.* v. *British India Steam Navigation Co. Ltd.* [1967] 2 Q.B. 250; *Morris* v. *C. W. Martin & Sons Ltd.* supra, at 727-728, 735, 737, 740-741.

committed by a stranger but to those where the converter is a servant of the licensor himself, whether acting "in the course of his employment" or not.

The judgments of Diplock and Salmon L.JJ. present a somewhat different picture. According to them, liability depends upon the conversion having occurred whilst the servant is performing one of that class of acts which he has been instructed to perform for the purpose of discharging (or helping to discharge) the task originally entrusted to his employers.

> . . . he [the master] has put the agent in his place to do that class of acts and he must be answerable for the manner in which that agent has conducted himself in doing the business which it was the act of his master to place him in.[62]

Although in the present case the relevant duty arose under a bailment, it does not follow that a bailment is essential for this principle to apply. Any delegated function which involves dealing with the chattel in question should suffice. The difficulty lies in segregating these acts of conversion which arise out of the performance of an actual or ostensible duty relating to the stolen chattel, and those which are independent of such a duty. Sometimes the identity of the misfeasant employee will supply an answer. Thus, if the mink stole in *Morris* v. *C. W. Martin & Sons Ltd.* had been stolen by one of the defendant's employees who was not employed to clean the garment or to have the care and custody of it, the defendants may well have escaped liability.[63] If, on the other hand, the defendants had not become bailees at all but had merely been called in to clean the stole upon premises occupied by a third person, it would seem reasonable that they should answer for any conversion committed by the servant through whom they sought to discharge this responsibility, regardless of whether they were under a general duty to protect the property from theft by third-parties. To say that an employer who owes no responsibility to prevent such loss is, ex hypothesi, protected from the depredations of his own servants is to narrow the doctrine of vicarious liability unjustifiably. All that is necessary is that (i) he should be under an actual or apparent duty to deal with the chattel in some way; (ii) that he should delegate this duty to his servant; and (iii) that the servant should, by a sequence of conduct arising from, or in purported discharge of, this duty, commit an act of conversion. Thus, if a television repairman steals a television he is called in to repair, his employers should be liable, for the loss occurred whilst he was performing one of the class of acts in respect of which their duty lay. Likewise where a car-park attendant misdelivers a vehicle in the course of his actual or apparent duty and his employers are not bailees. But, if, on the other hand, a window-cleaner enters a house and steals a painting,[64] or if stevedores take advantage of their task to steal part of the fabric of a ship,[65] the employer should escape, for he has delegated no duty in respect of the stolen property to the servant in the first place.

Practically the only authority in point comes from the Supreme Court of Alberta. In *Alberta U Drive Ltd.* v. *Jack Carter Ltd.*[66] the plaintiffs (a

---

[62] [1966] 1 Q.B. 716, at 735 (Diplock L.J.); see also Salmon L.J. at 738.
[63] Ibid., at 737, 741.
[64] Cf. *de Parrell* v. *Walker* supra.
[65] As in the *Leesh River Tea Co.* case, ante.
[66] (1972) 28 D.L.R. (3d) 114.

car-rental company) left one of their vehicles upon the fore-court of the defendants' garage, in circumstances which were held not to create a bailment. The car was stolen by a former employee of the defendants who, it appeared, had ceased to work for them approximately one hour before the car was deposited upon the fore-court, and who returned surreptitiously for this purpose on the following day. The vehicle was later recovered in a totally wrecked condition. The servant had occasionally acted for the defendants in the capacity of "car-jockey", collecting the plaintiffs' cars from various points and delivering them to the defendants' parking lot. It was on one such occasion that he was believed to have procured a duplicate key to the vehicle which was subsequently stolen.

Riley J. exonerated the defendants on the following grounds: first, although they had been clearly negligent in failing to check the servant's antecedents, the size of their staff and the extent of their operations excused this omission: "one can hardly apply that principle to modern day business with an employer employing many thousands of employees, many of whom are performing menial tasks";[67] secondly, since the relationship was solely one of licensor and licensee, the defendants were under no duty to employ a trustworthy servant anyway;[68] indeed, following Greene M.R., in *Ashby* v. *Tolhurst*,[69] they owed no obligation towards the plaintiffs at all; and thirdly, the conversation did not occur during the term of the servant's employment; even the act of duplicating the key (which was not the immediate cause of the loss) was "quite outside the powers impliedly vested in him by the service".[70] Accordingly, it would be improper to impose on the defendants vicarious liability for a theft substantially committed at a time when they no longer employed the perpetrator.

The case can probably be justified on the last of these grounds, although even here it is disfigured by an apparent conviction that the master is never liable for wrongful acts which a servant commits for his private benefit alone.[71] The rule relating to negligent selection of employees is doubtful and appears to conflict with English authority;[72] again, there is no reason for confining this type of liability to bailees, for many of the cases in point have imposed it irrespective of bailment. Insofar as the Alberta decision denies a remedy where the servant of a licensor commits a conversion in the course of his employment, it is clearly obiter and an English or Australian court may well decline to follow it.[73]

---

[67] At 124-125.
[68] At 126.
[69] [1937] 2 K.B. 242, at 249.
[70] (1972) 28 D.L.R. (3d) 114, at 127, citing Batt, *Master and Servant* (5th ed.), p. 339.
[71] At 127-128; cf. *Lloyd* v. *Grace, Smith & Co.* [1921] A.C. 716; *Uxbridge Permanent Building Society* v. *Pickard* [1939] 2 K.B. 248; *British Ry. etc. Co.* v. *Roper* (1940) 162 L.T. 217; *United Africa Co.* v. *Saka Owoade* [1955] A.C. 130; *Van Geel* v. *Warrington* [1929] 1 D.L.R. 94; *Morris* v. *C.W. Martin & Sons Ltd.* [1966] 1 Q.B. 716.
[72] *Williams* v. *Curzon Syndicate Ltd.* (1919) 35 T.L.R. 475; *Mintz* v. *Silverton* (1920) 36 T.L.R. 399; *de Parrell* v. *Walker* (1932) 49 T.L.R. 37; *Adams (Durham) Ltd.* v. *Trust Houses Ltd.* [1960] 1 Lloyd's Rep. 380; *Hillcrest General Leasing Ltd.* v. *Guelph Investments Ltd.* (1970) 13 D.L.R. (3d) 517.
[73] Cf. Lord Atkin in *Weaver* v. *Tredegar Iron & Coal Co. Ltd.*, [1940] A.C. 955, who speaks of liability being imposed whenever "a person has *in his charge* the goods or belongings of another in such circumstances that he is under a duty

D. Special circumstances creating a duty to guard against theft

There are a number of miscellaneous cases in which parties other than bailees have, on special facts, been held liable for the loss of a plaintiff's chattels by theft. A decorator who negligently leaves the front door of a house unlocked whilst he is away or in a different part of the house will be liable for property stolen in consequence of this default, not only to the other contracting party[74] but, it seems, to any other members of the household in question.[75] Likewise, a firm of security contractors who are engaged to patrol a warehouse without ever acquiring possession of the property stored within will be liable if their failure to exercise proper surveillance results in the property being burgled;[76] and an employer who negligently fails to check a servant's record or credentials will be liable for such ensuing loss of property as may have been foreseeable had he exercised reasonable circumspection and care.[77]

In *Scarborough* v. *Cosgrove*,[78] a female lodger at a boarding-house told the proprietor that she had brought her jewels with her and enquired about security precautions. He explained that no separate key could be given but assured her that the jewels would be quite safe left in her bedroom. The Court held that there was an implied contract whereby the defendant undertook to take reasonable care in looking after the jewels.[79] A similar principle has been adopted in other cases of boarding-house proprietors whose premises do not attract the strict liability of an innkeeper at Common Law.[80]

Applying these authorities to the situation where goods are left by way of licence on another person's land, it follows that an occupier's lack of possession in the goods will not necessarily exonerate him from liability for their loss by theft. The cases in which such liability is likely to be imposed will, however, be exceptional, and almost invariably the result of a contract expressly or impliedly creating a duty of safe-keeping. If, for instance, in the *Wilmers & Gladwin* case the plaintiffs had accepted an invitation to contribute towards the cost of a security-guard employed by the defendants, it should have been possible to argue that a duty arose whereunder the defendants were liable for the consequences of any short-

---

to take all reasonable precautions to protect them from theft of depredation" and he "entrusts that duty to a servant". This would seem to justify imposing such liability upon a broader class of defendant than the bailee alone.

[74] *Stansbie* v. *Troman* [1948] 2 K.B. 48.
[75] *Petrovitch* v. *Callingham's Ltd.* [1969] 2 Lloyd's Rep. 386.
[76] *B.R.S. Ltd.* v. *Arthur V. Crutchley Ltd.* [1968] 1 All E.R. 811
[77] See footnote 72, supra, and *Makower, McBeath & Co. Pty. Ltd.* v. *Dalgety & Co. Ltd.* [1921] V.R. 365.
[78] [1905] 2 K.B. 805.
[79] In *Morris* v. *C. W. Martin & Sons Ltd.* [1966] 1 Q.B. 716, at 727 (Lord Denning M.R.) and *Tinsley* v. *Dudley* [1951] 2 K.B. 18 (Jenkins L.J.); this decision is explained on the grounds of implied contract. North (p. 109) accepts this analysis, and points out that the distinction is relevant to the application of *Occupiers' Liability Act* 1957 s. 5; aliter, where the boarding-house keeper becomes a bailee: s. 5(3). The existence of a contract may also be important to the recovery of purely economic loss (see North, pp. 112-114) although for the purposes of an action in tort total loss by theft will probably be regarded as more akin to destruction: Clerk & Lindsell, *Torts* (14th ed.), para. 1177.
[80] See Chapter 24, post.

coming in the vigilance of their employee. If, on the other hand, the defendants had merely failed to lock the door of the warehouse overnight or had carelessly admitted strangers, their immunity would presumably be preserved. The difference between this situation and *Stansbie* v. *Troman*[81] is hard to detect, but seems to exist in the different duties impliedly undertaken by the respective defendants. A licence, ex hypothesis predicates no duty to protect the licensee's goods from theft, even where the danger has itself been created by the defendant after the goods were deposited.

Therefore, as Dr. North has remarked, there is at common law "only a very restricted liability placed on an occupier as regards the loss of a visitor's property through the act of a third party, and such obligations as exist are not placed on him qua occupier".[82]

III. BAILEES AND LICENSEES

Occasionally, the grant of a right to use or occupy structures belonging to the grantor will produce not a bailment of the structure in question but a license in favour of the user. Generally the determining feature will be the mobility of the structure; if, in particular, it remains attached to the owner's land, it will not normally constitute personalty and cannot therefore be the subject of a bailment.[83] Other factors may also be relevant, such as the presence of the owner's servants while the chattel is in use.[84] On the other hand, the mere fact that the structure was originally attached to the owner's land prior to delivery, or was subsequently attached by the user to his own land, will not necessarily militate against a bailment. The existence and quality of the licence will, of course, affect the owner's (or occupier's) duty of care with regard to injuries suffered by the user or his servants, in those jurisdictions in which there is no legislation equivalent to the *Occupiers' Liability Act* 1957.[85]

---

[81] [1948] 2 K.B. 48.
[82] *Occupier's Liability*, at p. 111.
[83] See *Williams* v. *Jones* (1865) 3 H. & C. 602; 195 E.R. 668; the decisions in *McCarthy* v. *Young* (1861) 6 H. & N. 329; 158 E.R. 136 and *Blakemore* v. *Bristol and Exeter Ry. Co.* (1858) 8 E. & B. 1034; 120 E.R. 385 (discussed in Chapter 11) are probably best regarded in this light.
[84] *Southland Harbour Board* v. *Vella* [1974] 1 N.Z.L.R. 526.
[85] See further *Southland Harbour Board* v. *Vella* ante, and North, op. cit., passim.

CHAPTER 6

POSSESSION AND KNOWLEDGE

The concept of possession is a variable one in which considerations of policy and relative justice play a significant part. In no sphere is this diversity more evident than in assessing the legal relationship between knowledge and possession. For many purposes, particularly those of the criminal law, courts have consistently held that a person's possession of goods is postponed beyond his receiving physical custody until he is aware of what he has received. Thus, in *Merry* v. *Green*[1] it was held that the possession of valuables, concealed within the secret drawer of a desk purchased at an auction, did not pass to the purchaser with the desk itself, so as to acquit him of a charge of larceny when he later discovered and appropriated them, unless he had reason to believe at the time of the sale that he was buying the desk together with its contents. In *R.* v. *Hudson*[2] it was held that the recipient of a letter misaddressed to him by the Ministry of Food did not acquire possession of a cheque contained in the envelope until he opened the envelope itself; he was accordingly guilty of larceny because "As soon as he saw what he had got, he made up his mind to steal it". In *R.* v. *Wright*[3] the Court of Appeal reversed a conviction for being in possession of drugs under s. 5(2) of the *Misuse of Drugs Act* 1971, where the defendant, having been handed a container in which, at the time of delivery, he did not know or have cause to suspect that there were drugs, threw it away immediately as he had been instructed to do. Much will depend, of course, upon the context in which possession is sought to be established and upon the consequences of finding that it exists.

But although the proposition does not apply for all purposes, it is clear that a person may in certain circumstances be in possession of goods although he is unaware of their nature, their location or even their very existence.[4] Many authorities, civil and criminal, can be cited in support, most of them, it is true, giving the unwitting possessor a remedy against

---

[1] (1841) 7 M. & W. 623; 151 E.R. 916; cf. *Cartwright* v. *Green* (1803) 8 Ves. 405; 32 E.R. 412, where possession in the desk was transferred merely for purposes of repair: *held*, the taking of its contents, concealed in a secret drawer, amounted to larceny.

[2] [1943] 1 K.B. 458; see further *R.* v. *Ashwell* (1885) 16 Q.B.D. 190; *R.* v. *Riley* (1853) Dear. 149; *R.* v. *Middleton* (1873) L.R. 2 C.C.R. 38; Paton, pp. 11-14 437-442; cf. *Theft Act* 1968. The decisions are no longer effective under English law and are cited only for their illustrative value.

[3] (1975) *The Times*, November 11th.

[4] Cf. Lord Goddard C.J. in *Russell* v. *Smith* [1958] 1 Q.B. 27, at 34-35, who denied "that a man can take into his possession, or come into possession of a thing of which he has no knowledge". Harris points out (*Oxford Essays in Jurisprudence*, pp. 105-106) that whereas this may be true in relation to the rule that a thief must "take" the chattel to be guilty of larceny the observation does not hold good with regard to other possessory rules.

an interloper[5] or holding that such interloper is guilty of theft if he appropriates the goods to his own use.[6] But being in possession is not synonymous with being a bailee. Even the strongest proponent of the non-consensual view of bailment has not denied that there must be, if not an unqualified assent to the possession of the chattel, at least some degree of actual or imputable knowledge as to its existence on the part of the bailee.[7] A farmer upon whose land a valuable bracelet is dropped by a picnicker may well be entitled to recover this chattel from a wayfarer who finds it before he does,[8] but this does not mean that the farmer is under any duty to take care of the bracelet or to keep an eye open for it when he ventures out upon his tractor. This could hardly be the law when he has no reason to suspect that it might be there.[9]

Occasionally, of course, the facts which prevent the alleged bailee from acquiring knowledge of the chattel will also prevent him from acquiring possession. Thus, where a landlord allows goods to be left in a locked room rented by his tenant, the intention to exclude the landlord will probably mean that possession remains in the tenant.[10] But the mere denial of access to goods will not necessarily preclude their immediate custodian from being a possessor. This is particularly so where their outer covering is in some way portable or transferable by direct delivery. Where goods are delivered in a container to which the owner keeps the key, or where a bank rents out a safe deposit to which only the hirer is allowed admission, the overall or external dominion of the deliveree may arguably suffice to place him in possession.[11]

At one time it was thought that a delivery of this kind could not possibly create a bailment because the owner had not trusted the deliveree with the goods. The fallacy of this was exposed by Holt C.J. in *Coggs* v. *Bernard*:

> As for 8 Edw. 2. Fitz. Detinue 59, where goods were locked in a chest, and left with the bailee, and the owner took away the key, and the goods were stolen, and it was held that the bailee should not answer for the goods. That case they say differs because the bailor did not trust the bailee with them. But I cannot see the reason of that difference, nor why the bailee should not be charged with goods in a chest, as well as goods out of a chest. For the bailee has as little power over them, when they are out of a chest, as to any benefit he might have by them, as when they are in a chest; and he has as great power to defend them in one case as in the other.[12]

[5] These authorities are discussed at p. 865 et seq., post.
[6] *R.* v. *Rowe* (1859) 8 Cox C.C. 139; *Hibbert* v. *Mackiernan* [1948] 2 K.B. 142; *R.* v. *Woodman* [1974] Q.B. 754; cf. *Minigall* v. *McCammon* [1970] S.A.S.R. 82.
[7] Tay (1966) 5 *Sydney Law Review* 239, at 252-253; cf. Laidlaw (1931-1932) 16 *Cornell L.Q.* 236.
[8] At least when the wayfarer is a trespasser and arguably when he is not; but there may be a distinction between goods attached to or buried beneath the realty, and goods mere lying on its surface. See p. 865 et seq., post.
[9] *Bridges* v. *Hawkesworth* (1815) 15 Jur. 1079; 21 L.J.Q.B. 75; *Consentino* v. *Dominion Express Co.* (1906) 4 W.L.R. 498; *Grafstein* v. *Holme and Freeman* (1958) 12 D.L.R. (2d) 727.
[10] *Peers* v. *Sampson* (1824) 4 Dow. & Ry. K.B. 636; 2 L.J. (O.S.) K.B. 212.
[11] Ante, p. 212, see also *Grafstein* v. *Holme and Freeman* (1958) 12 D.L.R. (2d) 727; *Minigall* v. *McCammon* [1970] S.A.S.R. 82, at 89, 91-92.
[12] (1703) 2 Ld. Raym. 909, at 914; 92 E.R. 107, at 110.

Later cases have confirmed that a mere inability or absence of right on the part of the deliveree to observe or obtain access to every part of the bailed property does not relieve him of his duties of a bailee. Thus in *Hartop* v. *Hoare*[13] there was a bailment where jewels were handed over for custody in a sealed bag with orders not to break the seal; in *The Winkfield*,[14] where sealed letters were placed in the possession of the Post Office for delivery; in *Houghland* v. *R. R. Low (Luxury Coaches) Ltd.*,[15] where a locked suitcase was carried by the defendant coach-company; and in *Allison Concrete Ltd.* v. *Canadian Pacific Ltd.*,[16] where a pay-loader was hired, with a driver, on the condition that only the driver should be allowed to operate and service the machine. Scores of other cases endorse this proposition and emphasise the commercial impossibility of adopting the contrary view. Were the rules as to possession so strict as to require unrestricted surveillance of the subject-matter before the custodian could become a bailee, the concept of bailment could only rarely apply to such common phenomena as container-transport, baggage-transit, left-luggage offices, warehousing of packaged goods and the chartering of equipment and manpower. Such a view might also exacerbate the problem of divided bailments, whereunder the bailee would become a bailee only of those parts of the property which he could see, touch or move around.[17]

Equally clear, however, is the necessity for some knowledge on the part of the bailee as to the sort of obligation he is undertaking. A denial of such knowledge may not prevent him from acquiring possession,[18] but it might relieve him of many, if not all, of his responsibilities as a bailee. To take an extreme example, it could hardly be said that the economy tour operator who carries his passengers' luggage in the boot of a coach should be liable for the loss of a suitcase which, unbeknown to him, contained priceless works of art. The predominant philosophy of bailment as a voluntary, if not a consensual, undertaking demands not only that actual possession of the goods, such as would be sufficient to sustain an action in conversion or detinue, but also some reasonable notification of their general quality and value, be brought home to the bailee.

The problems of undisclosed goods, or surreptitious bailments, can probably be approached without injustice in a variety of ways.[19] It is submitted, however, that the most appropriate and effective analysis is to test deliveries of this kind by reference to the cardinal attributes of bailment itself; if, therefore, these standards are not fulfilled there can be no bailment and the defendant is not liable *as a bailee*. He may, on very rare occasions be liable under general tortious principles, but generally the absence of a bailment will mean that he owes no further or supplementary duties in relation to the goods.

---

[13] (1743) 2 Stra. 1187; 26 E.R. 828.
[14] [1902] P. 42.
[15] [1962] 1 Q.B. 694.
[16] (1974) 40 D.L.R. (3d) 237.
[17] See p. 246, post.
[18] See the finders' cases, at p. 865 et seq., post.
[19] For instance, by arguing that the bailor has, through his concealment, impliedly consented to a lower degree of care than would otherwise be necessary; or that it would not be reasonable in any event to expect a bailee to exercise care in respect of goods when he has no knowledge of their existence.

Here two principles, never widely separated, appear to coalesce. The first is that there can be no true bailment without a voluntary assumption of possession:[20] the second, and less distinctly articulated, is that a bailee must know what he is possessing—both that it is not his and, roughly, what it is.[21] The involuntary bailee, such as the recipient of an unsolicited manuscript, normally knows what he has got; indeed this knowledge may place a significant part in his reluctance to keep it. The deceived bailee, or bailee by concealment, has no such knowledge and will usually lack either the ability or the stimulus to acquire it; for him, the relevant information comes only when it is too late and the property has been damaged or lost. Both principles unite in denying the customary remedies of bailment where there has been no effective consent to the full implications of the relation. The problem lies in locating those situations where that consent can be implied.

It is probably not remarkable that the commonest instances of this difficulty arise in the context of car-parking agreements. Where such an agreement produces a bailment of the car, and the vehicle or its contents are later stolen, very fine distinctions may have to be drawn between the sort of things that a bailee might reasonably have contemplated would be in the car, and those that he would not.

On occasions, it has been argued that specific knowledge of the nature of the contents is necessary and that without this there can be no bailment. In *Moukataff* v. *B.O.A.C.*[22] a bank despatched banknotes to the plaintiff by airmail, for which purpose they were placed in special orange bags. The bank delivered them to the Post Office who in turn handed them over to B.O.A.C. upon whose plane the notes were to go to Kuwait. While they were being loaded on the plane, the notes were stolen by one Ilbury, a loader employed by B.O.A.C. He did this by slitting the bags open and concealing their contents upon his person. B.O.A.C. claimed, inter alia, that they were bailees only of the mailbags themselves and not (because they did not know what was in them) of their contents; alternatively, that they were only involuntary or gratuitous bailees. This contention was shortly dismissed by Browne J. who said:

> These submissions seem to be unrealistic. B.O.A.C. knew that the mailbags contained mail and in particular they knew that the red-labelled registered mailbags contained articles of value belonging to the senders, and it seems to me almost absurd to describe B.O.A.C. as involuntary bailees.[23]

Again, it has been held that where the driver of a car leaves it at a garage with a warning to the attendant to lock the car because there is a suitcase of valuables on the back seat, the attendant's employers will be liable not only (in appropriate circumstances) as bailees of the car but also of such of its contents as have been drawn to the bailee's attention and to which his assent has been given.[24] In such case, there is no need for the

---

[20] See generally Chapter 12, post.
[21] *Consentino* v. *Dominion Express Co.* (1906) 4 W.L.R. 498; p. 233, post.
[22] [1967] 1 Lloyd's Rep. 396.
[23] At p. 415.
[24] *Mendelssohn* v. *Normand Ltd.* [1970] 1 Q.B. 77; *Minichiello* v. *Devonshire Hotel (1967) Ltd.* (1976) 66 D.L.R. (3d) 619 (post., p. 449).

bailee to have been given a specific inventory of the items stolen, provided they fall broadly within the description or other indication made by the bailor at the time of delivery.

Even where no explicit notification has been given, it seems that the bailee of a car will be liable for the theft of such contents or accessories as it might reasonably have been expected to contain. Certainly, the general drift of Canadian authorities is to this effect. Thus, in *Bowes* v. *Super-Service Stations Ltd.* [25] a garage-proprietor was held liable for the theft of a camera from a car which had been delivered into his custody and which he had wrongfully left in the street instead of being taken into the defendant's premises. Although there was no evidence that any members of the defendant's staff had seen the camera in the car on this particular occasion, and the plaintiff had not drawn it to their attention, the defendants' manager knew that on previous occasions the camera had been left in the car. According to Ilsley C.J.:

> . . . all cars left at garages or service stations have contents and I do not think that the defendant can validly contend that it has no responsibility for the contents of cars left on its premises by agreement.[26]

The plaintiff therefore received damages of $400, the value of the camera. It may be queried whether the same expectation would have been present, and the same result should have followed, if the defendants had had no previous knowledge of the possible presence of such an expensive piece of equipment in the car. Clearly, a knowledge of the plaintiff's occupation, his purpose in leaving the car, his financial standing and previous conduct may all be relevant factors in arriving at the appropriate conclusion.

Heffron v. *Imperial Parking Ltd.*[27] is a rather more everyday case. Here, the plaintiff recovered for the loss of clothing, an electric razor, a tape player, tools and a radio (total value $308) which were stolen from his car after the defendants had negligently released it to a third party. Estey J.A. held that these articles were constructively within the bailment because they:

> . . . were generally of a type which one might reasonably be expected to carry in an automobile . . . it, therefore, is not unreasonable for a parking lot operator to assume that a great many of the cars left in his custody will contain this kind of personal property in reasonable quantity.[28]

On the other hand, in *Brown* v. *Toronto Auto Parks Ltd.*,[29] Laidlaw J.A. refused to include $44 worth of books, left by the plaintiff in his car, within the general bailment of that vehicle to the defendants. He gave as his reason the fact that there was no evidence showing the defendants knew of

[25] [1955] 3 D.L.R. 193.
[26] At p. 197.
[27] (1974) 46 D.L.R. (3d) 642.
[28] At p. 653; see also *Appleton* v. *Ritchie Taxi Co.* [1942] 3 D.L.R. 546, where the plaintiff recovered for the loss of a spare wheel, a car radio, tools, personal luggage, golf-clubs and a tennis racket, all stolen from his car. The value of the goods totalled $268, but damages of $120 were awarded for the purely procedural purpose of bringing the case with the jurisdiction of the district court.
[29] [1955] 2 D.L.R. 525.

the existence of the books or of their presence in the car. "There was no actual knowledge, and there was no constructive knowledge, of the bailee that it was to become a custodian of these goods."[30] But this explanation is difficult to accept and it may be thought that the articles in question should have been deemed to be within the defendants' reasonable contemplation at the time when the car was handed over to them for safe-keeping. Indeed one might go further and suggest that whenever it is likely that goods of a certain value will be left in vehicles, the bailee should be liable for any goods of that approximate value, whether they were of the precise kind that might have been surmised to be there or not.[31]

A number of American decisions indicate a tendency to restrict the circumstances in which a plaintiff might argue that the defendant's acceptance of their container implies acceptance of its contents. Thus spoke Fox P., of the Supreme Court of Appeals of West Virginia, in 1942:[32]

> . . . the delivery of the automobile at the parking lot and its acceptance by the attendant in charge created the relationship of bailor and bailee as to the automobile, and the tools and fixtures connected therewith . . . We think it also included any other property in plain view, or of which the bailee had notice, express or implied.
> . . . Reason and authority suggest that in every case the bailee should be liable for such property as he undertakes to store and return to the owner. He should not be made liable for property of which he has no knowledge. This does not mean that actual knowledge must be brought home to him in every case. There is ample room for what may be termed implied or constructive notice. For example, he would be charged with constructive knowledge that a piece of baggage probably contained property of some value, although he might not know the particular type of property or the value thereof contained therein. He probably would not, in the absence of actual notice, be liable for extremely valuable property such as jewellery, or a type of property not ordinarily carried as baggage and left in a vehicle. . . . If drivers of automobiles desire to hold keepers of parking lots and garages liable for property left in automobiles committed to their charge, the party to whom the car is so committed should be notified of any concealed baggage. If such baggage is in plain view, no notice is required because, when in plain view, it is treated as part of the property accepted for safekeeping.

There is a considerable divergence between this approach, requiring a fairly high degree of disclosure, and the approach taken by Ilsley C.J. in *Bowes* v. *Super-Service Stations Ltd.*[33] American courts, adhering to the

---

[30] At p. 528.
[31] A parallel question concerns the strict liability of inn-keepers for property *infra hospitium*. In *George* v. *Williams* (1956) 5 D.L.R. (2d) 21 the defendant inn-keeper was exonerated from liability for the theft of an overnight travelling bag, certain personal belongings contained therein, and some clothing from the plaintiff's car. The theft took place at night when the car was parked in the hotel carpark. The Ontario C.A. held that the car itself was *infra hospitium* but that the goods inside it were not: the distinction being that the chattels stolen "unlike accoutrements such as knee-robes or cushions" were not "articles associated with the car for its more comfortable use". This decision is criticised by Murray (1956) 34 *Can. Bar Rev.* 1203.
[32] *Barnette* v. *Casey* (1942) 124 W. Va. 143; 19 S.E. 2d. 621.
[33] [1955] 3 D.L.R. 193.

stricter view, have accordingly held that parking-station proprietors are not liable for the loss of such articles as suitcases containing personal apparel,[34] robes,[35] valuable merchandise contained in a truck,[36] commercial travellers' samples,[37] baby-clothes, structural belts and tools[38] and mink stoles[39] unless the defendant's attention has been drawn to them, and his consent obtained, at the time of delivery. On the other hand, liability has been imposed where attention was drawn by the plaintiff to the presence of a bag on the back seat of his car and a promise to safeguard it was given;[40] and recovery has occasionally been allowed for items like suitcases left in the car even though their existence was not identified to the proprietor or his attendants.[41]

It seems likely that an English or Australian court will adopt the more liberal approach evident in cases like *Heffron* v. *Imperial Parking Co. Ltd.*[42] and will take judicial notice of the fact that certain commonplace articles are customarily left in parked cars; accordingly, the acceptance for safe-keeping of the vehicle itself may carry a collateral obligation to safeguard such of its contents as might reasonably be expected to be therein. However, the goods must clearly be of a character, value and quantity likely to be found in a normal situation of the kind in question. The nature of the area in which the parking lot is situated may be relevant here: for instance, if it is near a university, one might reasonably expect books to be left in cars; if it is in a commercial area, articles like travellers' samples, bulk-loads in transit and work equipment would constitute a more probable type of contents. Another factor might, of course, be the risk involved; the more valuable the item, the less likely it is that an owner will leave it inside his car in his absence, without specifically warning the putative bailee of its existence.[43] Even the value of the vehicle itself may prove significant in assessing its likely contents.

Not all cases involve automobiles. In one American decision[44] the plaintiff's fur piece was handed over by one of her friends to the attendant at a cloakroom of a dancing school. The fur was concealed inside the friend's coat and was delivered in a bundle of which only the outer coat and a hat were visible. The fur was later lost and the plaintiff sued for its value. It was

---

[34] *Barnette* v. *Casey*, supra.
[35] *Rogers* v. *Murch* (1925) 253 Mass. 467; 149 N.E. 202.
[36] *Schulte, Inc.* v. *North Terminal Garage Co.* (1953) 291 Mass. 251; 197 N.E. 16.
[37] *Willis* v. *Jensen* (1933) 82 Utah 148; 22 P. 2d. 220.
[38] *Palotto* v. *Hanna Parking Garage Co.* (1946) 68 N.E. 2d. 170.
[39] *U.S. Fidelity & Guaranty Co.* v. *Dixie Parking Service Inc.* (1971) So. 2d. 248 (where the fact that the fur was specifically drawn to the attendant's notice was neutralised by a prominent notice to the effect that employees were not authorised to accept personal effects for deposit. The court held that, as a general rule, a public garage is liable only for the vehicle itself unless by special agreement the depositary accepts responsibility for articles contained therein).
[40] *Mulhern* v. *Public Auto Parks Inc.* (1938) 296 Ill. App. 238; 16 N.E. 2d. 157; likewise, *Mendelssohn* v. *Normand Ltd.* [1970] 1 Q.B. 177.
[41] *Mee* v. *Sley System Garages* 124 Pa. Super. 230; 188 A 626; *Stevens* v. *St. Botolph Holding Co.* (1942) 316 Mass. 238; 55 N.E. 2d. 450; *Kole-Tober Shoes Inc.* v. *Hoery* (1971) 491 P. 2d. 589.
[42] (1974) 46 D.L.R. (3d) 642.
[43] Even when there is a bailment, the bailor's damages may be reduced by his contributory negligence or by the doctrine *volenti non fit injuria; Walker* v. *Watson* [1974] 2 N.Z.L.R. 175; cf. ante p. 55.
[44] *Samples* v. *Geary* (1927) 292 S.W. 1066; (1928) 28 *Columbia Law Review* 497.

held that since the defendant had no knowledge of its existence there could be no bailment in respect of the fur. Although this decision was reached by applying the contractual theory of bailments, it is probable that the same result would have been reached by regarding bailment as the voluntary entry into a relation with the chattel itself, irrespective of consensuality.

> Since the relation of bailee and bailor is founded on contract, there must be a meeting of the minds to make the contract valid. In this case, the fur piece being concealed, the bailee did not know it was there, the minds of the parties did not meet, and there was no acceptance by the defendant of the article in question.

Similar American cases have denied a remedy where a trunk containing expensive jewellery was left with a hotel by a departing guest;[45] where a box which the owner claimed to contain "papers and other valuables" in fact contained $700 in cash;[46] and where a customer laid aside in the changing room of a shop a garment in the pocket of which there was an expensive diamond ring.[47] On the other hand, plaintiffs have been permitted to recover for such likely articles as fob-watches[48] and cash to the value of $41[49] contained in garments left with defendants in circumstances creating a bailment of the garment itself. It is all a question of what the bailee can reasonably expect, both in the light of his own common-sense and experience and from the nature of his invitation to the plaintiff to deposit his goods.[50]

An interesting recent decision comes from the Appellate Court of Illinois. In *Berglund* v. *Roosevelt University*[51] the plaintiff was the editor and photographer of a student newspaper; he was salaried by the defendant university and allowed the use of an office and a darkroom on its premises. Without disclosing the fact to the defendants, the plaintiff left his camera and ancillary equipment in an unlocked filing cabinet in the darkroom and locked the door. The defendants operated a security force which, late every evening, saw everybody off the premises and locked the main doors, thereupon handing over the security operation to the university cleaning staff. The equipment was stolen and the plaintiff sued for breach of an implied bailment, but the Court rejected his claim. In the words of McNamara J.:

---

[45] *Waters* v. *Beau Site Co.* (1920) 114 Misc. 65; 186 N.Y. Supp. 731.
[46] *Riggs* v. *Bank of Cameo Prairie* (1921) 200 Pac. 118.
[47] *Hunter* v. *Reeds Sons* (1899) 12 Pa. Super. 112; likewise, *Warner* v. *Elizabeth Arden Ltd.* (1939) 83 Sol. Jo. 268.
[48] *Woodruff* v. *Painter* 24 A. 621.
[49] *Hunter* v. *Reeds Sons*, supra.
[50] See further *Roche* v. *Cork, Blackrock & Passage Ry. Co.* (1889) 24 L.R. Ir. 250, where it was held that a passenger could recover for the loss of the sum of £10 contained in a bag deposited in the defendant railway's cloakroom for the charge of 1d. In this case there were no conditions on the ticket, but a common method of encouraging disclosure of valuable chattels is, of course, to exclude liability by notice unless they and their value are declared at the time of their deposit: See *Handon* v. *Caledonian Ry. Co.* (1880) 7 R. (Ct. of Session) 966; *Lyons & Co.* v. *Caledonian Ry. Co.*, 1909 S.C. 1185; *U.S. Fidelity & Guaranty Co.* v. *Dixie Parking Service Inc.* (1971) So. 2d. 248. Exclusion of liability does not, however, per se prevent the recipient from becoming a bailee; *Parker* v. *S.E. Ry. Co.* (1877) 2 C.P.D. 416, at 420; a fortiori, where the clauses are merely clauses of limitation rather than exclusion. A consignor who fails to reveal the nature of goods to a common carrier may be unable to recover on the grounds of fraud; see p. 557 et seq., post; *Batson* v. *Donovan* (1820) 4 B. & A. 21.
[51] (1974) 310 N.E. 2d. 773.

> The characteristics common to every bailment are the intent to create a bailment, delivery of possession of the bailed items, and acceptance of the items by the bailee . . . Knowledge on the part of the bailee is essential to prove proper delivery and acceptance. Physical control over the property allegedly bailed and an intention to exercise that control are needed to show that one is in possession of the bailed item . . . And before acceptance can be inferred . . . there must be evidence to show notice or knowledge on the part of the bailee that the goods are in fact in his possession.[52]

Although, as we have seen, specific notification may not be necessary where knowledge can be implied, the case for requiring it may be appreciably stronger where (as in the present case) it is customary for persons depositing articles to disclose the fact and to obtain permission to do so from the party alleged to be a bailee.

The foregoing principles should apply not only where an alleged bailee is unaware of the existence of a chattel or of its presence in his possession, but also where he enjoys acknowledged possession of a chattel which he does not know, and does not have reasonable cause to know, is the property of another. Thus there should generally be no duty of care where an alien package becomes embroiled in the internal postal system of a company[53] or where the bona fide purchaser of a chattel, having no reason to suspect a defect in his title, negligently damages it. Of course, in the latter instance the owner would normally enjoy a remedy in conversion arising from the defendant's receipt of the chattel under the purported sale.[54]

The relationship between involuntary bailments and bailments by concealment

Although the two cases are not exactly parallel, it is submitted that the rules relating to involuntary bailments may become relevant in assessing the duties of a bailee by concealment in two principal respects.

(a) Where the bailee by concealment finds out what he has been given, and his state of mind continues to be one of "non-consent" to an assumption of the full responsibilities of a bailee, the relationship between him and the owner should be deemed to be one of involuntary bailment. Thus, he may not be liable for theft or damage resulting from a failure to take reasonable care of the chattel,[55] and should be liable for conversion only in the same circumstances as a possessor whose refusal to accept the property existed from the original transfer of possession.[56]

(b) Whether the circumstances are as in (a) or not, it would appear that the bailee by concealment should not be liable for the conversion of a concealed chattel unless he acted unreasonably in committing the act complained of. It may be questioned, of course, whether conversion can be committed in any event by a defendant who is unaware of the very existence of what he is supposed to be converting. In many cases this objection might provide a conclusive answer to a claim for conversion,

---

[52] At pp. 775-776; and see *Collins* v. *Boeing Co.* (1971) 483 P. 2d. 1282.
[53] *Consentino* v. *Dominion Express Co.* (1906) 4 W.L.R. 498; cf. *McCowan* v. *McCulloch* [1926] 1 D.L.R. 312.
[54] Ante, p. 128.
[55] Post, p. 384.
[56] Post, p. 387.

and would render unnecessary an inquiry as to whether the defendant took reasonable care. But in other cases, there might be a lack of reasonable care in failing to ascertain the presence of the chattel before committing the alleged conversion. A bailee might, in other words, have no reason to know of the existence of a concealed chattel at the time when it is delivered into his possession, but might reasonably be expected to have acquired such knowledge before handing the goods over to a third party. Thus, if a customer's handbag is left in the changing-room of a beauty-parlour in circumstances which create a bailment of the handbag itself but not of a valuable diamond ring inside it,[57] and the proprietor, without examining the contents, hands the bag to another customer who claims it as her own, there may well be conversion of the ring and the proprietor will be answerable for his failure to take reasonable care.[58]

It is clear that the plaintiff under a concealed bailment cannot evade the issue by pleading negligence, for such liability depends upon a duty to take care and in the present case there is none.[59] The same principle would presumably apply to actions for negligent trespass. Trespass by intent represents a harder case and it may be thought that the defendant who, for instance, deliberately destroys a container and its contents should take those contents as he finds them and should not be entitled to escape merely because they were more valuable than he though. So far as concerns detinue, the intentional nature of this tort, and the necessary (albeit limited) degree of notice constituted by the plaintiff's prior demand, probably justify making the concealed bailee liable for unlawful detention of the goods, even though he did not suspect their true nature or even, in some cases, their very existence. Defendants should not be encouraged to compute in advance the cost of committing intentional torts or to plead in retrospect that such cost was greater than they had reason to believe. But different considerations may apply where the defendant had reason to believe that the goods were his own or were not the plaintiff's to demand.

---

[57] As seems to have been the position in *Warner* v. *Elizabeth Arden Ltd.* supra., n. 47.
[58] Cf. *Helson* v. *McKenzies (Cuba St.) Ltd.* [1950] N.Z.L.R. 878.
[59] Inter alia because there will no foreseeability as to the relevant loss. Cf. *Re Polemis and Furness, Withy & Co.* [1921] 3 K.B. 560 and the eggshell skull cases: Clerk and Lindsell, *Torts* (14th ed.), paras. 343 et seq.

CHAPTER 7

SERVICE, AGENCY AND POSSESSION

I. THE GENERAL RULE

It has been stated on innumerable occasions that a servant who, as a concommitant of his employment, acquires custody of his master's goods does not in ordinary circumstances become a bailee.[1] Possession is deemed to remain in the master in such circumstances and the servant, having a mere custody or temporary control, neither enjoys the possessory remedies nor (it would seem) owes the strict duties of a bailee. Thus, in *Hopkinson* v. *Gibson*[2] it was held that a colonel who had purchased horses for the Army could not bring trover in respect of them because possession was in his master and he was a mere servant or agent, rather than a bailee.[3] The rule has been criticised, among others by Holmes,[4] who has traced it to the incapacity of slaves to own or possess property independently of their masters.[5] Undoubtedly, it can produce very capricious results.[6]

Despite these criticisms, and the fact that on occasions the rule has been disregarded[7] or even superseded,[8] as a general principle it appears

---

[1] *Mires* v. *Solebay* (1678) 2 Mod. 242; 86 E.R. 1050, *Cavenagh* v. *Such* (1815) 1 Price 328; 145 E.R. 1419; *Alexander* v. *Southey* (1821) 5 B. & Ald. 247, at 248-249; 106 E.R. 1183; *Randelson* v. *Murray* (1838) 8 A. & E. 109; 112 E.R. 777; *Davis* v. *Vernon* (1844) 6 Q.B. 443; *Associated Portland Cement Manufacturers* (1910) *Ltd.* v. *Ashton* [1915] 2 K.B. 1; *Makower, McBeath & Sons Pty. Ltd.* v. *Dalgety & Co. Pty. Ltd.* [1921] V.R. 365, at 371-373; *The Jupiter III* [1927] P. 122, at 131, 250; *Richard* v. *Nowlan* (1959) 19 D.L.R. (2d) 229; *Joseph Abrams Ltd.* v. *Coady and Vint* (1963) 37 D.L.R. (2d) 587, at 590-591; *Wilton* v. *Commonwealth Trading Bank of Australia Ltd.* [1973] 2 N.S.W.L.R. 644, at 651; *Peter Jackson Pty. Ltd.* v. *Consolidated Insurance of Australia Ltd.* [1975] V.R. 480, at 484. The same rule is supported by most leading writers, e.g. Clerk & Lindsell, *Torts* (14th ed.), para. 1124; Pollock & Wright, *Possession in the Common Law*, pp. 56-60, 138-140, 162 et seq., 191 et seq.; Paton, *Bailment*, p. 4. For further authority, see infra.; for the possession of goods found by servants in the course of their employment, see p. 862, post. The foregoing list does not purport to be exhaustive.
[2] (1805) 2 Smith 202; Pollock & Wright, p. 139.
[3] The burden of proving that the plaintiff in a possessory action is a mere servant rests upon the defendant: *Richard* v. *Nowlan* (1959) 19 D.L.R. (2d) 229.
[4] *The Common Law*, p. 226.
[5] This is disputed by Pollock & Wright, pp. 58-59; see further Stoljar, (1955) 7 *Res Judicatae* 160, at 170, who argues that the rule is based on practical considerations.
[6] As an example of the sort of fact situation which could render absurd a master's inability to treat his servant as a bailee (although the case actually concerned employees' compensation) see *Chan* v. *S.Y.C. Ltd.* [1974] 1 N.Z.L.R. 329.
[7] *Beauchamp* v. *Powley* (1831) 1 M. & Rob. 38; 174 E.R. 14; cf. *Lamprell* v. *Markham* (1844) 2 L.T.O.S. 377.
[8] As in *R.* v. *Harding* (1929) 46 T.L.R. 105; 21 Cr. App. 166. In (1930) 46 L.Q.R. 135 this decision is regarded as sweeping away the 600 year old distinction between a servant's custody and possession: sed quaere. The question in the case was whether the appellants, who had broken into a house and forced a servant

to have survived unimpaired.[9] Thus, in *Wiebe* v. *Lepp*[10] it was held that a servant who was engaged to drive his master's truck could not be liable *as a bailee* when, having warned his master that the truck was emitting a peculiar noise, he was instructed to continue driving, with the result that the engine overheated. Matas J.A. acknowledged that a servant was still under a duty to take reasonable care of his master's chattels, but held that in the present case that duty had been discharged.[11] In *Marshall* v. *Dibble*,[12] the same rule was applied to exonerate a clerk who, in the course of his duties, signed for a registered packet and placed it in a pigeon-hole behind the counter in the office where he was employed, in accordance with his master's general instructions. The New Zealand Supreme Court held that he ceased to be a bailee from the moment he put the packet in the pigeon-hole, at which time it passed into the possession of his employers.[13] He was therefore not liable for whatever happened to the packet after that event, whether he were guilty of non-feasance or not; nor, on the facts, was he liable for conversion. In *Associated Portland Cement Manufacturers* (1910) *Ltd.* v. *Ashton*[14] the Court of Appeal held that a ship-master who worked a barge on a system of thirds (whereby he received two-thirds of the gross freight and paid the crew and expenses while the owners received one-third and paid towage, harbourage, brokerage and insurance) was a servant rather than a bailee, so that the owners were liable on the charterparty he had signed. The continued existence of the rule is further endorsed by the numerous modern decisions which treat the relationships of master and servant and bailor and bailee as mutually exclusive,[15] and (impliedly) by those which hold that a bailor's damages against a third party are not liable to be reduced by the contributory negligence of his bailee.[16]

---

to hand them her master's coat, had deprived her of any special property in the coat. It was held that they had. But possession, as we have seen, may carry different connotations in the criminal, as against the civil, law and there is little in *R.* v. *Harding* to support an abolition of the civil rule.

---

[9] Although its operation in peripheral cases has not always been consistent; thus, whereas the honorary treasurer of a political club (*Troke* v. *Felton* (1897) 13 T.L.R. 252) and an incumbent (*Wilkinson* v. *Verity* (1871) L.R. 6 C.P. 206) have both been treated as bailees, there is some authority for the view that a bailiff (*Giles* v. *Grover* (1832) 9 Bing. 128, at 153) and an attorney (*Canot* v. *Hughes* (1836) 2 Bing. N.C. 448) are not to be thus regarded. It is submitted that the result in the latter case must be confined to the context in which it arose, viz. whether the client had committed conversion by letting the goods out of her possession. In this situation, there are strong reasons for holding that possession has not been surrendered to the attorney, at least provided that he enjoys no lien. A different result is clearly justified when the client wishes to proceed against the attorney as a bailee.

[10] (1974) 46 D.L.R. (3d) 441.

[11] Ibid., at 446; cf. *Joseph Abrams Ltd.* v. *Coady and Vint* (1963) 37 D.L.R. (2d) 587, and see *Superlux* v. *Plaisted* [1958] C.L.Y. 195, where the Court of Appeal held that the supervisor of a team of vacuum-cleaner salesmen, who left 14 vacuum cleaners overnight in a car parked outside his house, was in breach of his duty of reasonable care and so liable for their loss.

[12] [1920] 39 N.Z.L.R. 497; cf. *Grey Cabs* v. *Neil* [1947] N.Z.L.R. 62; *Perkins* v. *Stead* (1907) 23 T.L.R. 433.

[13] See further, p. 238 et seq., post.

[14] [1915] 2 K.B. 1.

[15] Ante, p. 109 et seq.; *Gibson* v. *O'Keeney* [1927] I.R. 66; see p. 243 post.

[16] Post, p. 961.

II. EXCEPTIONS TO THE RULE

However, the mere fact that the custodian is a servant of the owner will not necessarily prevent him from becoming a bailee. Admittedly, the circumstances in which this might happen will be rare, for as Pollock and Wright observed in 1888:

> We do not know of any case in which a delivery by the master and the servant with intent to deliver possession as well as custody has been proved as a matter of fact. The holder of goods may make his servant a bailee if he think fit, and the holder of land may make his bailiff a tenant at will; but the law does not regard this as a normal state of things, and probably rather strict proof would be required. There is no reason however to doubt that such an intent, if sufficiently proved in a particular case, would be effectual in law.[17]

The exceptional cases seem, in fact, to fall into three main categories. First, the master may have loaned the chattel to his servant for purposes entirely unconnected with the servant's employment and solely for the benefit of the employee. In such a case the normal inference may be displaced and the master, quite apart from escaping liability on vicarious grounds for the servant's negligence in using the chattel,[18] may be held to have made his servant a bailee. In *Wood Motors Ltd.* v. *McTavish*[19] an automobile salesman had permission from his employer to drive any of his employer's cars for his personal use or to allow his wife or prospective purchasers to drive them. The salesman borrowed a car to make a private journey and, on the return trip, asked an acquaintance to drive. The car was wrecked and the plaintiff-owner sued both salesman and driver for the damage. The action against the salesman was subsequently discontinued, but Bridges C.J. remarked: ". . . although McTavish was employed by the plaintiff, the circumstances under which he had the use of the automobile created a bailment between him and the plaintiff."[20]

Secondly, and whether the delivery is exclusively for the servant's benefit or not, the distance between the master and his chattel, combined with the nature of the servant's instructions, may inferentially render the servant a bailee. Thus, according to Pollock and Wright, the servant's custody: ". . . may . . . sometimes as against strangers be treated as a possession in cases where the servant's charge is to be executed at a distance from the master and where the manner of the execution is necessarily left in a great degree to the discretion of the servant."[21]

It is difficult to assess how far this exception will be taken, particularly since Hill J. has remarked that it is impossible in modern conditions to regard the master of a ship as a bailee[22] and contemporary communications

---

[17] Op. cit., at p. 60.
[18] *Britt* v. *Galmoye and Nevill* (1928) 44 T.L.R. 294; *Higbid* v. *R. C. Hammett Ltd.* (1932) 49 T.L.R. 104; cf. *Carberry* v. *Davis* [1968] 1 W.L.R. 1103; 2 All E.R. 817.
[19] (1971) 21 D.L.R. (3d) 480. (New Brunswick Supreme Court).
[20] Ibid., at 482.
[21] Op. cit., pp. 139-140; cf. *R.* v. *Deakin* (1800) 2 Leach 862; 168 E.R. 530.
[22] *The Jupiter III* [1927] P. 122, 131; affirmed [1927] P. 250; see to like effect *Boson* v. *Sandford* (1690) 1 Shower 101, at 102; 89 E.R. 477, at 478; cf. *Moore* v. *Robinson* (1831) 2 B. & Ad. 817; 109 E.R. 1346.

have rendered the possibility of control over the servant significantly greater. In two cases in which an owner of property sued a railway company for damage occasioned while his servant was travelling on the dedendant's line with the property in his custody, no clear statement was given as to whether the servant was a bailee.[23] It may be, for instance, that a master who hands the candlesticks to his butler before departing on a world cruise, and tells him to sleep with them under his bed every night, or a company which requires its representatives to keep their company cars on their own premises when not in use,[24] would be held to have transferred legal possession and to have constituted the servant a bailee. Much seems to depend upon the intentions of the parties and the particular context in which the question of possession is raised. But it should be recalled that the location of possession is not exclusively a matter of intention and that any such intent must conform with the facts and circumstances of the delivery.

Thirdly, it is said that the servant will possess his master's goods when they are delivered to him by a third party to hold or apply on behalf of his master; such possession, say Pollock and Wright, continues: ". . . until he has done some act by which the thing is appropriated to the master's use."[25]

An example of this situation arose in *Marshall* v *Dibble*[26] where the clerk was held to have been bailee of the packet in the short space of time between receiving it and placing it in the pigeon-hole behind the counter. Most of the relevant cases, however, concern criminal liability and revolve around whether the servant has taken the goods out of the possession of his master. Wright lists nearly 20 examples of such cases,[27] two of which will suffice as an illustration of the difficulty in identifying the change from servant's to master's possession:

> A bank clerk received bonds from a customer and without placing them in the usual receptacle in the cellar appropriated them. *Held*, not a taking from the master's possession at common law. . . .[28]
> A servant sent with his master's cart for goods receives the goods for his master into his master's cart and again takes them from these. *Ruled*, a taking from the master's possession.[29]

It is difficult to extract a coherent principle from these decisions and uncertain whether such a principle (if it exists) would be authoritative on questions of civil liability.[30] There are few civil decisions directly in

---

[23] *Becher* v. *G.E. Ry.* (1870) L.R. 5 Q.B. 241; *Meux* v. *G.E. Ry.* [1895] 2 Q.B. 387 (although A. L Smith L.J.'s reference in the latter case to *Claridge* v. *South Staffordshire Tramway Co.* [1892] 1 Q.B. 412 clearly lends colour to the view that the servant was a bailee; a result which, in the context of the servant's liability to the master, should have been discernible in both cases).

[24] Cf. *Comino* v. *Lynch* [1959] Q.W.N. 49; *Morse* v. *Hicks* [1955] 3 D.L.R. 265,

[25] Op. cit., p. 60.

[26] [1920] N.Z.L.R. 497; cf. *Wilton* v. *Commonwealth Trading Bank of Australia Ltd.* [1973] 2 N.S.W.L.R. 644, at p. 651, where Samuel J. appears to doubt the proposition, at least in the context of the master's action against a third party.

[27] Op. cit., pp. 191-195.

[28] *R.* v. *Waite* (1743) 1 Leach. 28; 2 East P.C. 570; cf. *R.* v. *Bazely* (1799) 2 Leach. 835; 2 East P.C. 571.

[29] *R.* v. *Norval* (1844) 1 Cox 95; see also *R.* v. *Harding* (1807) R. & R. 125.

[30] Indeed, Pollock & Wright point out (at p. 60) that the criminal rule regarding goods in transit *via* a servant from a third party belongs exclusively to that

point and those that exist seem to consider the issue of possession only as a subsidiary to some other question; usually, that of vicarious liability. Thus in *Perkins* v. *Stead*[31] the High Court appeared to uphold a finding by the County Court judge that the purchaser of a new car who, being uncertain how to drive it, agreed to have it delivered by a servant of the dealer, acquired possession of the vehicle from the moment the servant set off on the journey and was vicariously liable for his negligent driving en route. Unfortunately, the decision is unsafe on the question of vicarious liability and it is hard to tell what connection the court saw between this and the issue of possession. Nevertheless, it is at least arguable that the decision was, on this point, correct.

In *Peter Jackson Pty. Ltd.* v. *Consolidated Insurance of Australia Ltd.*[32] the question was whether a servant who had decided to steal a sum of money from his employers, but who deviated from his normal route in carrying the money from his employer's place of business to the bank only when a substantial part of the journey had been completed, had stolen the money on his employer's premises (when he first received it with intention to steal) or away from those premises (when he first deviated from the customary route). Crockett J. held that the theft occurred on the latter occasion and delivered the following dictum:

> A servant entrusted with his master's property (unless it has not already been in the master's possession) never has "legal" possession of the property. Hence, he is not considered a bailee in the usual sense of that term.[33]

The problem with the servant cases lies in the diversity of issues in which the matter of possession can fall to be considered. In some of these cases it would be desirable to hold that the servant is a bailee whereas in others it plainly would not. The older decisions (disregarding those in criminal cases) are mainly concerned with the right to exercise the possessory remedies, and here it is probably better that these should belong exclusively to the master.[34] Likewise, there are sound reasons of policy for holding that a bailee who grants custody to his servant does not dispossess himself of the chattel and is not, therefore, guilty of conversion. On the other hand, it seems anomalous that a master whose servant takes a vehicle out on to the open road and brings it back in pieces should not be able to rely upon the ordinary bailor's advantages of proof but must (subject to the doctrine of res ipsa loquitur) adduce affirmative evidence

branch of the law: this rule they epitomise (at p. 196) as follows: "So long as the thing is with the servant merely in transitu towards the master, the master has not yet the possession as against the servant, but the servant has the possession as against the master." In the civil law this proposition must be read subject to the servant's having performed an act which appropriates the chattel to his master' use: supra.

[31] (1907) 23 T.L.R. 433.
[32] [1975] V.R. 480.
[33] Ibid., at p. 484.
[34] Cf. *Moore* v. *Robinson* (1831) 2 B. & Ad. 817; 109 E.R. 1346; *Richard* v. *Nowlan* (1959) 19 D.L.R. (2d) 229. *Aliter*, when the master is absent and is unable to defend the property in person?

of the servant's fault.[35] To this extent, one might argue that the question of a servant's possession should be determined in no different manner from that of any other person and that the anachronistic rule denying him possession of his master's goods should be confined in future to cases where the facts are in any event inconsistent with such possession.[36]

But such an approach takes account only of disputes arising in the master-servant relationship. In disputes arising between the master and a third party very different considerations might apply.[37] Suppose, for instance that X delivers his television to S to be taken to the shop of S's master, M, for repairs. S (who finishes his rounds too late to take the television to the shop) takes it home where it is destroyed by a fire which occurs mysteriously during the night.[38] It would probably be preferable to treat the master as a bailee of the television and to cast upon him the onus of showing that neither his own default nor that of the servant to whom he delegated the task contributed to the damage.[39] Possession of

[35] It may be objected that the accident could equally probably result from a failure on the employer's part to maintain the vehicle adequately, or from some other self-induced cause (see *Wiebe* v. *Lepp* (1974) 46 D.L.R. (3d) 441, supra, p. 236). But this objection might apply equally in the case of a hired or lent chattel and there is no doubt that in these circumstances the onus of proof is on the bailee. If the servant is injured and wishes to sue for damages, there may well be a presumption of negligence entitling him to rely on the doctrine of res ipsa loquitur: cf. *Ludgate* v. *Lovett* [1969] 1 W.L.R. 1016 where the operation of the two doctrines arose under a contract of hire. The burden would, of course, vary according to the circumstances and, in cases where the servant has possession, it is not unduly harsh to expect him to establish that he took reasonable care. See *Superlux* v. *Plaisted* [1958] C.L.Y. 195, where none of the preceeding objections was relevant since the loss occurred through theft. The servant was held liable for breach of his duty of reasonable care, but it is unclear from the brevity of the report whether the burden was upon him or the plaintiff employers.

[36] In *Sammy Dail* v. *Bergeron* (1974) 293 So. 2d. 894 (Louisiana Court of Appeal) the proprietor of a service-station sought to recover the value of a cash register and contents from a seventeen-year-old employee who had been left in sole charge of the service-station overnight. The register had disappeared and was clearly stolen. The Court, relying on the (1870) Louisiana Civil Code, held that the infant could not be compelled to discharge the burden of proof arising under a bailment because, being both an infant and a servant, he was incapable of being a bailee. It was agreed, however, that affirmative proof of the attendant's negligence would entitle his employer to recover. It is submitted that neither of the reasons advanced in this case should be conclusive at Common Law, but that the same result would probably be reached (a) because the standard of care required of an infant is correspondingly lower and the circumstances very probably revealed a lack of care on the part of the alleged bailor; (b) because the employee may not in any event have enjoyed possession of the chattel. It would be undesirable, for instance, if personnel like security guards and night-watchman, whose powers of access and dealing with their employers' property are necessarily limited, should be cast in the role of bailees. In any event an abolition of the rule that a servant may never possess his master's property would not lead, in most cases, to a different result from that obtained under the old Common Law rule: for instance, servants would rarely if ever be held to possess tools and implements supplied to assist their work on their employer's premises: cf. *Griffiths* v. *Arch Engineering Ltd.* [1968] 3 All E.R. 217.

[37] *Wilton* v. *Commonwealth Trading Bank of Australia Ltd.* [1973] 2 N.S.W.L.R. 644, at 651.

[38] Cf. *Thomas National Transport (Melbourne) Pty. Ltd.* v. *May & Baker (Australia) Pty. Ltd.* (1966) 115 C.L.R. 353, where the collector was an independent contractor and the main contractors were held liable for a fundamental breach of contract in failing to remove the goods to their own depot at night.

[39] Default would, of course, include not only negligence but a radical departure from the agreed terms of the bailment.

the set by the servant, however logical in the context of an indemnity action, would appear to preclude this result.[40]

There can be little doubt that, in a case like this, the courts would hold the employer to be in possession of the goods, and disregard the intervening custody of the servant. Authority exists in the judgment of Atkin J. in *Newman* v. *Bourne & Hollingsworth Ltd.*[41] where a shop-walker found the plaintiff's brooch lying on a counter and, instead of taking it to the lost property office, put it in his desk. In holding his employers liable for the ensuing loss, Atkin J. rejected the County Court judge's finding that the brooch never came into their possession but remained in that of their servant. In his view, "in the circumstances of modern business the possession of the employee could hardly fail to be the possession of the employer."

If, on the other hand, goods are delivered to a servant in circumstances which make it clear that the latter has neither actual nor ostensible authority to accept them, or is otherwise undertaking an exclusively personal responsibility, the possession will be the servant's own. Unless, therefore, the employer is guilty of direct negligence, or the servant's misconduct can be classified as falling within the course of his employment, the bailer's remedy will lie only against the servant. This appears to have been the position in the old case of *Butler* v. *Basing*[42] where a carrier was exonerated from liability for the loss of goods delivered to one of his carters for a reward to be given to the employee alone.[43]

Thus it may be seen that whether a servant is a bailee may vary according to the nature of the dispute and the identity of the parties thereto.[44] There need be nothing inconsistent in this diversity for bailment, like possession, is a versatile concept which can be readily adapted to suit

---

[40] The master may be vicariously liable for the servant's negligence but this differs in at least one respect (viz. burden of proof) from his liability as a bailee.

[41] (1915) 31 T.L.R. 309, at 310. See also *Boys* v. *Pink* (1838) 8 C. & P. 361; *Wilton* v. *Commonwealth Trading Bank of Australia Ltd.* supra; *Helson* v. *McKenzies (Cuba St.) Ltd.* [1950] N.Z.L.R. 878; *White* v. *Alton-Lewis Ltd.* (1975) 49 D.L.R. (3d) 189; p. 874, post.

[42] (1827) 2 C. & P. 613; cf. *Beauchamp* v. *Powley* (1831) 1 M. & Rob. 38; 174 E.R. 14; *Palmer* v. *Toronto Medical Arts Faculty Building Ltd.* (1960) 21 D.L.R. (2d) 181, at 188. In *Union Steamship Co.* v. *Ewart* (1894) 13 N.Z.L.R. 9, a lamp-trimmer employed on one of the appellants' ships was allowed by his employees to undertake the carriage and custody of clients' dogs and to keep any fee they paid him. The appellants, in response to a telephone call, advised the respondent that the charge for this service would be five shillings and told him to deliver his dog to the lamp-trimmer. They did not tell the respondent that the operation was in the nature of a perquisite to their servant, or that they did not consider themselves personally responsible for the goods. It was held that the appellants were bailees of the dog and liable if they could not show that its loss occurred without their own or their servant's neglect. See further *Otago Aero Club (Inc.)* v. *John H. Stevenson Ltd.* [1957] N.Z.L.R. 471.

[43] In many cases the employer will be exonerated on the ground that he has not consented to possession of the goods and cannot therefore be liable as a bailee: see Chapter 6, ante; p. 379 et seq., post; Paton, pp. 242-242. Of course, the fact that possession of goods is in his employer will not protect the negligent servant from liability in tort to their owner; cf. *Fairline Shipping Corporation Ltd.* v. *Adamson* [1975] Q.B. 180, criticised by Diamond (1975) 38 M.L.R. 198.

[44] Quaere, whether the grounds for making the servant a bailee are stronger where he enjoys no viable principal; cf. *Corbett* v. *Jamieson* [1923] N.Z.L.R. 374; *Fairline Shipping Corporation Ltd.* v. *Adamson*, supra.

the needs of particular cases without prejudice to its conceptual integrity to the effectiveness of the remedies it provides.

Temporary agents and casual delegation

The arguments against denying the employee possession of his master's goods in circumstances which conform with such possession are all the stronger where the employee is not in the general service of the master, or part of his regular workforce, but is performing a single act of service on an isolated occasion. Here it is submitted that the question of vicarious liability is entirely separate from and immaterial to the question of whether the agent is liable as a bailee. Most of the cases dealing with this sort of situation involve the former question and have little to say with regard to the rights and duties of the agent under a bailment.[45] Thus, in *Ormrod* v. *Crosville Motor Services Ltd.*[46] the Court of Appeal held that the owner of a car, which was being driven from Birkenhead to Monto Carlo for the joint benefit of the owner and the parties travelling in it, was liable for the negligence of the driver. No reference was made to the question of possession and there can be little doubt that in an action between owner and driver for damage to the car the driver would (and should) have been liable as a bailee. In *Hewitt* v. *Bonvin*[47] the purpose for which the vehicle was being driven was entirely for the benefit of the driver and the owner had no interest in the journey; he had not, in the words of the House of Lords in a later decision, delegated any task or duty to the driver in respect of which the journey was being undertaken.[48] In exonerating him from liability, du Parcq L.J. uttered the following statement, which, it is submitted, supports the view that the relationship of agency and the transfer of possession are consistent phenomena which need not be mutually exclusive:

> It must be added that, in the present case, agency is not negatived merely by the fact that the appellant had parted with the possession of the car to his son. It is, I think, plain on both principle and authority, that the owner, or other person having control of a vehicle may be responsible for the acts of the person driving it, on the ground of agency, even though he was not present in or near the vehicle so as to be able to exercise control over the driver.[49]

In cases where the vehicle or other chattel has passed out of the owner's physical control and is exclusively within that of the driver, it would be absurd not to exact from that driver the duties of a bailee. The company director driving a company car,[50] the casual acquaintance performing a

---

45 See, in addition to the cases discussed in the text, *Scobie* v. *Steele & Wilson Ltd.* 1963 S.L.T. 45; *Carberry* v. *Davis* [1968] 1 W.L.R. 1103; 2 All E.R. 817; *Morgans* v. *Launchbury* [1973] A.C. 127; *Vandyke* v. *Fender* [1970] 2 Q.B. 292; *Nottingham* v. *Aldridge* [1971] 2 Q.B. 739; *Klein* v. *Caluori* [1971] 1 W.L.R. 619; 2 All E.R. 701; *Rambarran* v. *Gurrucharan* [1970] 1 W.L.R. 556; 1 All E.R. 749; *Samson* v. *Aitchison* [1912] A.C. 844; *Pratt* v. *Patrick* [1924] 1 K.B. 488; *Parker* v. *Miller* (1926) 42 T.L.R. 408.
46 [1953] 1 W.L.R. 1120; 2 All E.R. 753; (1954) 70 L.Q.R. 253.
47 [1940] 1 K.B. 188.
48 *Morgans* v. *Launchbury* [1973] A.C. 127.
49 [1940] 1 K.B. 188, at p. 195, citing *Thompson* v. *Reynolds* [1926] N.I. 131; cf. Mackinnon L.J. at 193, and see *Parker* v *Miller* supra.
50 Held to render his employers vicariously liable, although not technically a servant or agent, in *Scobie* v. *Steele & Wilson Ltd.* 1963 S.L.T. 45.

gratuitous mandate for the owner and the truck driver delivering goods from Sydney to Melbourne are all persons acting in the interests of the owner and for whose acts that owner may justifiably be held vicariously liable. To relieve such persons from the consequences of bailment merely because they are, for vicarious purposes, servants or agents, would be not only mischievous but could obscure the jurisprudential quality of many of the more casual and temporary varieties of bailment. *Lenkeit* v. *Ebert*[51] provides a convenient example. The defendant was asked by the plaintiff (at whose party he was) to take the plaintiff's truck and drive another of the plaintiff's guests to the station. Whilst doing so, at speed, he contrived to capsize and wreck the vehicle and the plaintiff sued him for breach of duty as a bailee. The Queensland Full Supreme Court held that there was a gratuitous bailment and exonerated the defendant only because the evidence did not support a finding of gross neglect. But there can be no doubt that the defendant was, simultaneously, the agent of the plaintiff and that the plaintiff would have been vicariously liable for third-party damage or injury committed by his bailee en route. To have held that these two relationships were mutually exclusive would have produced a different and less satisfactory result. The question of agency was rightly not pleaded in *Lenkeit* v. *Ebert* and was clearly immaterial to the decision. The considerations which justify the imposition of vicarious liability upon a principal are quite different from those which should govern whether the agent can sue for trespass to the chattel or is vested with the bailee's burden of proof.[52]

No decision illustrates better than *Roufos* v. *Brewster and Brewster*[53] the confusion that can arise when the courts attempt to apply the orthodox

---

[51] [1947] St. R. Qd. 126; p. 333, post. See also *Walker* v. *Watson* [1974] 2 N.Z.L.R. 175, where the borrowers of a car were treated as gratuitous bailees although there is at least a possibility that the bailor would have been vicariously liable for his negligence.

[52] In *Gibson* v. *O'Keeney* [1927] I.R. 66, the Northern Ireland Court of Appeal clearly suggested that the two relationships of principal and agent and bailor and bailee were exclusive alternatives and that they could not be combined in one situation; but the distinction was drawn solely for the purpose of determining whether the owner of a car was liable for the torts of the borrower (her son) and, as in *Ormrod* v. *Crosville Motor Services Ltd.* [1933] 1 W.L.R. 1120; 2 All E.R. 753, no question arose as to the liability of the borrower as bailee. There is, of course, substantial authority for the view that a bailor is not vicariously liable for the torts of his bailee and for the converse proposition that a bailor's damages against a third party cannot be reduced by the negligence of his bailee, but the decisions in question all involve bailments to hirers, independent contractors or persons for whose exclusive benefit the bailment is made: see, for instance, *Wellwood* v. *King* [1921] 2 I.R. 274 (vehicle bailed to repairer); *Krahn* v. *Bell* [1930] 4 D.L.R. 480 (borrower); *Fletcher* v. *Thomas* [1931] 3 D.L.R. 142 (borrower); *Checker Taxi-Cab* v. *Stone* [1930] G.L.R. 137 (hirer); *Pierard* v. *Wright* [1933] N.Z.L.R.S. 120 (hirer or borrower); *France* v. *Parkinson* [1954] 1 W.L.R. 581; 1 All E.R. 739 (hirer); *Drive-Yourself Lessey's Pty. Ltd.* v. *Burnside* [1959] S.R. (N.S.W.) 391, at 413 (hirer); cf. Fleming (4th ed.), p. 236. In none of these cases, therefore, was there such fulfilment of the bailor's purposes or control over the bailee to justify an identification of interests. It does not follow that there can never be a bailment between an owner and a person for whose conduct he would be vicariously liable, nor that a person who occupies for certain purposes the role of bailor cannot be vicariously liable for the torts of the person who, for those purposes, is characterised as his bailee. See *Roufos* v. *Brewster and Brewster* infra.

[53] [1971] 2 S.A.S.R. 218.

rule to a servant who is not in the regular employment of the owner. The appellant had agreed to arrange for the return of the respondents' lorry from Adelaide to Coober Pedy. He chose for this task one Joanni, who was about to enter the appellant's own employment and was prepared to make the journey for no further reward than the chance of free transportation. By arrangement with the respondents, the appellant also loaded some of his own goods on the truck. The vehicle capsized en route and the question at issue was which of the two principals—appellant or respondents—should bear the cost of the damage. The South Australian Supreme Court held that the loss fell on the respondents because the bailment to the appellant ended when the lorry left his possession in the custody of Joanni. Bray C.J. favoured the view that Joanni drove the vehicle "as the servant of the respondents", a view which led him to state obiter that Joanni would not therefore have become a bailee of the truck. But he did altogether exclude the possibility that Joanni himself might have become a bailee of the respondents, while clearly regarding the first solution as the correct one.[54] Mitchell J. acknowledged that prior to the departure from Adelaide (when Joanni and another person had driven the lorry from a repairer to the appellant's premises) the lorry was in the appellant's "constructive possession". Thereafter "Joanni was in my view the agent of the respondents . . . and the bailment of the lorry was to Joanni."[55]

According to Zelling J., who dissented on the primary issue, the pre-departure bailment to the appellant subsisted throughout the periods in which the lorry was in the custody of Joanni. The learned judge doubted whether the journey to Coober Pedy involved a sub-bailment by the appellant to Joanni because the appellant appeared to lack any authority to sub-bail.[56] He held that there was a concurrent bailment: ". . . a bailment of the use of the truck to Roufos to transport his goods to Coober Pedy and a concurrent bailment of the truck to Joanni to drive it to Coober Pedy."[57]

In his view, Joanni had not become the servant of the respondents; and if he were a sub-bailee from the appellant (which he would surely have had to have been if he were to be any kind of bailee and the appellant were to remain liable) it was under that type of extended bailment whereunder the original bailee remained liable for failing to restore the goods.[58]

Thus, within the space of one decision it is possible to collect three different views: (1) that Joanni was a servant non-bailee; (2) that he was an agent as well as a bailee; (3) that he was partly a non-bailee and partly a bailee of an unspecified kind, but probably not a sub-bailee, for whose acts the prior bailee remained liable. The decision cannot truly be

[54] Ibid., at 225-227. The learned judge also thought that the respondents would have been liable for third-party damage occasioned by Joanni en route.
[55] Ibid., at 231.
[56] Sed quaere. Although similar statements appear in the decision of Bridges C.J. in *Wood Motors Ltd.* v. *McTavish* (1971) 21 D.L.R. (3d) 480, at 482-483, the modern view of bailment as a non-consensual arrangement (a view supported by Zelling J. at 235) would appear to discount the requirement of authority in the creation of an enforceable sub-bailment.
[57] [1971] 2 S.A.S.R. 218, at 234.
[58] Ibid., at 235.

said to clarify the question or to introduce coherence into this difficult area of the law.

The confusion can be removed by recognising that the "servant" rule in bailments has never been directly applied to situations of agency or casual delegation, and by allowing the possession of such functionaries to be assessed under general principles. In many cases in which the owner is physically separated from his chattel the result would be that his agent (for whom the owner remains vicariously liable) is a bailee. To hold otherwise could involve the peculiar consequence that the agent, while not generally a bailee, might become one as soon as he departs from the route laid down by his master, or otherwise uses the chattel for an unauthorised purpose.[59] For a court to have to draw such fine distinctions as these would, in the circumstances, be undesirable.

Conversely, of course, there would normally be no bailment where the owner remains physically in the presence of the chattel, or near enough to dictate some measure of control; thus, to take an obvious example, a master who remains in the driving seat while his agent drives his car would generally be held to have continued in possession.[60] But the opposite result may follow where the driver is in the employment of a third person—for instance, where an owner, having taken his car to a garage for repairs, requests a lift to the station and is given one in his own car with an employee of the garage driving.[61]

Of course, there are substantial difficulties in distinguishing an agent from an independent contractor, which is the category into which almost every bailee must fall. The criteria here are controversial and diverse and beyond the immediate scope of this book.[62] It should, however, be noted that certain authorities have compounded the confusion by implying that a sub-bailor is vested with the possession of his sub-bailee.[63] Insofar as they extend the servant rule to independent contractors, and suggest that even this category of employee does not acquire possession of chattels delivered to it by an employer, these authorities seem clearly misconceived. A sub-bailor may (in terms of his liability to the principal bailor) be in the same position as if he had retained possession,[64] but this is not the same thing as saying that such possession is actually vested in him. Bailment is generally a non-delegable duty; possession is an eminently transferable thing.

---

[59] This may be a permissible inference from *Peter Jackson Pty. Ltd.* v. *Consolidated Insurance of Australia Ltd.* [1975] V.R. 480, at 484, although Crockett J. seemed to consider that a servant could never acquire possession of goods which have already been possessed by his master. Cf. p. 184 ante.

[60] *Wood Motors Ltd.* v. *McTavish* (1971) 21 D.L.R. (3d) 480; cf. *Smallich* v. *Westfall* (1970) 269 A. 2d. 476, where it was held that the mere fact that a bailor shares the use of the chattel with his bailee does not necessarily terminate the bailment.

[61] *Chowdhary* v. *Gillot* [1947] 2 All E.R. 541. Cf. *Price* v. *Le Blanc* (1957) 7 D.L.R. (2d) 716.

[62] See Clerk & Lindsell, *Torts* (14th ed.), paras. 222 et seq.; Winfield and Jolowicz, *Tort* (10th ed.), p. 518 et seq.

[63] *Thomas National Transport (Melbourne) Pty. Ltd.* v. *May & Baker (Australia) Pty. Ltd.* (1966) 115 C.L.R. 353, at 382-383; *Hobbs* v. *Petersham Transport Co. Pty. Ltd.* (1971) 45 A.L.J.R. 356, at 361; cf. at 359, 363, and *Edwards* v. *Newland & Co.* [1950] 2 K.B. 534.

[64] Chapter 20, post.

III. Special Cases

There are two particular areas in which the relationship between the owner of a chattel and a servant who is employed to use or handle the chattel seems likely to cause controversy. These will now be considered in some depth.

A. Men and machines: The provision of equipment and manpower

Under a contract of simple hire, the owner transfers possession in his chattel to a bailee who retains it for his personal (and usually exclusive) use. Often, however, in both consumer and inter-corporate transactions, the owner will concurrently provide a driver or other operative entrusted with the task of working the borrowed machine. This type of contract is normally designated a leasing or hiring of machinery. The supply of ancillary personnel solves two main difficulties; the hirer may be unable or unwilling to operate the machine himself, and the owner may be equally reluctant to entrust an expensive chattel to a possibly untutored stranger. A simple example of this kind of transaction is the hire of a car, or a fleet of cars, together with drivers for a wedding or a funeral; or the chartering of a bus by a society for an outing. A more sophisticated instance, and one in which conceptual problems are likelier to arise, concerns the lease of heavy-duty plant, like a crane or an excavator, with a driver whose functions will frequently include the exclusive right to service and operate the machine. This sort of arrangement is more productive of litigation for several reasons. The plant will often be cumbersome and its operation dependent upon the co-ordinated efforts of a group of men: this increases the risk of damage to the machinery and its surroundings. It will often be required to operate in areas of crowded activity, where the risks of industrial injury are already high; and it will frequently be put to work at times of exigency, when contract dates are to be met and schedules completed, so that a whole jigsaw of liabilities may depend upon the performance of one machine and its driver.

Many of the cases arising in this area take the form of actions in negligence against the driver and his employer, and the courts are regularly called upon to decide who, at the material time, was a particular operative's master. It is now settled that the primary test to be applied to this question:

> . . . is to ask who is entitled to tell the employee the way in which he is to do the work upon which he is engaged. If someone other than his general employer is authorised to do this he will, as a rule, be the person liable for the employee's negligence. But it is not enough that the task to be performed should be under his control, he must also control the method of performing it.[65]

---

[65] *Mersey Docks & Harbour Board* v. *Coggins & Griffith (Liverpool) Ltd.* [1947] 1 A.C. 1, at 17, per Lord Porter; but "Many factors have a bearing on the result. Who is paymaster, who can dismiss, how long the alternative service costs, what machinery is employed, have all to be kept in mind": ibid. cf. Lord Simon, at 12, and Lord Uthwatt, at 21. This test has been widely accepted and applied; see, for instance, the decisions in *Garrard* v. *A. E. Southey & Co.* [1952] 2 Q.B. 174, at 177; *L. R. Harris (Harella) Ltd.* v. *Continental Express Ltd.* [1955] 1 Lloyd's Rep. 251, at 258; *Ready Mixed Concrete (East Midlands) Ltd.* v. *Yorkshire Traffic Area Licensing Authority* [1970] 2 Q.B. 397, at 405; *Savory* v. *Holland & Hannen & Cubitts (Southern) Ltd.* [1964] 1

Applying this test, the general rule is that the servant remains the servant of the general employer throughout.[66]

The question of whether a bailment comes into being through the combined delivery of manpower and machinery from the owner to a "hirer" is a complex and difficult one, which is often decided by default and even more often taken for granted. The question is important for two main reasons. First, the machinery may have became damaged in circumstances which render it impossible to identify either the cause of the damage or the negligent party. In such a case, the owner will be relieved of the need to prove negligence against the hirer or his servant if that hirer was, in fact, a bailee.[67] Secondly, disputes may arise as to who is bound to pay for returning the machine, or for retrieving it from the scene of an accident. In this event, the duty of the customer will (prima facie at least) depend upon whether he has become a bailee of the machine.[68] Admittedly, most commercial organisations nowadays make express provision for such an occurrence, and place this responsibility firmly upon the hirer. In one recent case,[69] where a crane had sunk into marshy ground, the contract contained the following clauses, which were held to be determinative of the hirer's obligation to bear the cost of recovery:

> SITE CONDITIONS: . . . (6) The Hirer shall take all reasonable precautions to ensure that the Crane can safely be taken into and kept upon or at the site and in particular to ensure that the ground is in a satisfactory condition to take the weight of the Crane and/or its load. The Hirer shall where necessary supply and lay timber or other suitable material for the Crane to travel over and work upon and shall be responsible for the recovery of the Crane from soft ground.............
> (8) . . . The Hirer shall be responsible for and indemnify the owner against . . . All . . . expenses in connection with or arising out of the use of the plant. . . .

W.L.R. 1158; 3 All E.R. 18; *Bhoomidas* v. *Port of Singapore Authority* [1978] 1 All E.R. 956 (P.C.); cf. *Herdman* v. *Walker (Tooting) Ltd.* [1956] 1 W.L.R. 209; 1 All E.R. 429; *McArdle* v. *Andmac Roofing Co.* [1967] 1 W.L.R. 356, at 361; 1 All E.R. 583. Decisions adumbrating a similar principle before 1947 include *McDonald* v. *The Commonwealth* (1946) 46 S.R. (N.S.W.) 129; *M'Cartan* v. *Belfast Harbour Commissioners* [1911] 2 Ir. Rep. 143; *Waldock* v. *Winfield* [1901] 2 K.B. 596; *Poulson* v. *John Jarvis & Sons Ltd.* (1920) 89 L.J. (K.B.) 305; *Donovan* v. *Laing, Wharton and Down Construction Syndicate Ltd.* [1893] 1 Q.B. 629; *Crafter* v. *Burns* [1939] S.A.S.R. 152; *Dayman* v. *Gleader* [1939] S.A.S.R. 277; *A. H. Bull & Co.* v. *West African Shipping Agency & Lighterage Co. Ltd.* [1927] A.C. 686; cf. *G. W. Leggott & Son* v. *C. H. Normanton & Son* (1928) 140 L.T. 224; *Moore* v. *Palmer* (1886) 2 T.L.R. 781; *Century Insurance Co. Ltd.* v. *Northern Ireland Road Transport Board* [1942] A.C. 509.

[66] *Savory* v. *Holland & Hannen & Cubitts (Southern) Ltd.* [1964] 1 W.L.R. 1158, at 1163; 3 All E.R. 18, per Lord Denning M.R. This case did not involve the transfer of a machine with the borrowed servant. In such a case, the presumption is all the more difficult to rebut: see infra.

[67] *The Ruapehu* [1925] 21 Lloyd's Rep. 120, at 310, 315 (Atkin L.J.); *Dollar* v. *Greenfield, The Times,* May 19th, 1905, p. 3; *Travers* v. *Cooper* [1915] 1 K.B. 73; *Coldman* v. *Hill* [1919] 1 K.B. 443. See, generally, Chapters 1 and 19, and cf. *National Trust Co. Ltd.* v. *Wong Aviation Ltd.* (1969) 3 D.L.R. (3d) 55.

[68] *British Crane Hire Corporation Ltd.* v. *Ipswich Plant Hire Ltd.* [1975] 1 Q.B. 303.

[69] The *British Crane* case, supra.

Nevertheless, such provision will not always be conclusive. It may fall foul of the rules of incorporation,[70] or adverse construction,[71] or fundamental breach; and in England at least, it may also fall victim to a Common Law test of reasonableness which Lord Denning M.R. has regularly applied to the validity of exemption and indemnity clauses.[72] In such a case, one is thrown back upon the Common Law rules of bailment and must therefore ascertain whether, on a true analysis, the transaction creates such a relationship at all.

Much of the confusion in this area stems from the elastic, colloquial use of the word "hire". Technically, one hires a chattel only if one becomes a bailee and this involves, inevitably, acquiring possession. However, it is not unusual to speak of hiring taxicabs, hiring men and hiring a great many other things of which one does not in fact obtain possession. That this has obscured the quality of the relationship between bailor and bailee may be readily demonstrated.

Hyman v. *Nye*[73] involved what would nowadays be called a consumer transaction. The plaintiff paid a sum of money for the use of a carriage, horses and driver from a job-master. The contract was for a journey from Brighton to Shoreham and back, but the plaintiff, apparently, had the power to order the driver to travel by any route within reason. He was injured when a part of the carriage disintegrated and he sued, originally, in negligence. The Court of Queen's Bench, reversing Hawkins J., allowed his claim despite the plaintiff's failure to prove that the job-master had been negligent in allowing the carriage out on the road. Mathew J. did so on the ground that the bailor for reward is under the same duty as a seller in respect of the fitness of the goods he supplies,[74] Lindley J. upon a rather precarious analogy with cases deciding that suppliers of transportation services (such as railway and stage-coach operators) were under

---

[70] Contrast the *British Crane* case with *D. J. Hill Pty. Ltd.* v. *Walter H. Wright Pty. Ltd.* [1971] V.R. 749; *Grayston Plant Ltd.* v. *Plean Precast Ltd.* (O.H.) 1975 S.L.T. Notes (O.H.) 83.

[71] Including the especially strict onus placed upon a party who seeks to exclude liability for negligence; see *Phillips* v. *Clark* (1857) 2 C.B.N.S. 156; *Rutter* v. *Palmer* [1922] 2 K.B. 87; *Alderslade* v. *Hendon Laundry Ltd.* [1945] 1 K.B. 189; *Canada Steamship Lines* v. *R.* [1952] A.C. 192; *Walters* v. *Whessoe Ltd.* (unreported, Nov. 18th, 1960); *White* v. *John Warwick & Co. Ltd.* [1953] 1 W.L.R. 1285; 2 All E.R. 1021; *Council of the City of Sydney* v. *West* (1965) 114 C.L.R. 481; *T.N.T. (Melbourne) Pty. Ltd.* v. *May and Baker (Australia) Pty Ltd.* (1966) 115 C.L.R. 353; *Spalding* v. *Tarmac Civil Engineering Ltd.* [1966] 1 W.L.R. 156; 1 All E.R. 209; *Wright* v. *Tyne Improvement Commissioners* [1968] 1 W.L.R. 336; 1 All E.R. 807; *Hollier* v. *Rambler Motors (AMC) Ltd.* [1972] 2 Q.B. 71; *Gillespie Brothers Ltd.* v. *Roy Bowles Transport Ltd.* [1973] 1 Q.B. 400; *The Eurymedon* [1974] 1 All E.R. 1015; *Smith* v. *South Wales Switchgear* [1978] 1 All E.R. 18; *British Crane Hire Corporation Ltd.* v. *Ipswich Plant Hire Ltd.* [1975] 1 Q.B. 303; post, p. 926.

[72] *Thornton* v. *Shoe Lane Parking Ltd.* [1971] 2 Q.B. 163; *Gillespie Brothers Ltd.* v. *Roy Bowles Transport Ltd.*, supra; *British Crane Hire Corporation Ltd.* v. *Ipswich Plant Hire Ltd.*, supra; *Levison* v. *Patent Steam Carpet Cleaning Co. Ltd.*, [1978] Q.B. 69. Cf. *Blake* v. *Richards & Wallington Industries Ltd.* [1974] K.I.R. 151, at p. 155; *Kenyon, Son & Craven Ltd.* v. *Baxter, Hoare & Co. Ltd.* [1971] 1 W.L.R. 519; 2 All E.R. 708, and Buckley L.J. in *Gillespie's* case, at 205. In all but the *Gillespie* and *Levison* cases, Lord Denning's test might be construed as extending only to the question of incorporation and not to the issue of substantive validity; see [1974] N.I.L.Q. 338.

[73] (1881) 6 Q.B.D. 685.

[74] At p. 690; though with a possible caveat as to latent defects, at p. 691.

a duty to take care and skill to render their vehicles safe for use.[75] Neither judge examined the true nature of the transaction to see whether it actually imported a bailment. Mathew J. seemed to take the fact for granted. Even Lindley J., whose judgment rested upon decisions where no such relationship had arisen, referred throughout to the parties as letter and hirer. Because of their divergent analyses the point did not really arise for consideration, but it could easily have been crucial: for example, if the vehicle had become embedded in a ditch through no fault of the driver, and the question arose as to who was bound to pay for its retrieval; or if a stranger had made off with the vehicle and the owner was trying to make the hirer answerable for the loss.

On the facts of *Hyman* v. *Nye*, Lindley J. may well have been justified in his apparent refusal to treat the case as one of bailment.[76] The hirer's control was limited to the somewhat abstract power of instructing the driver where to travel; his right to use the chattel was confined to the passive condition of being driven in it.[77] Although not quite so clear-cut, the transaction closely resembled the hire of a taxicab, in which the passenger neither acquires possession nor becomes the master of the driver.[78] One might inquire, echoing the words of Lord Greene M.R. in *Ashby* v. *Tolhurst*,[79] whether the passenger could maintain an action for trespass or conversion if a third party misappropriated the chattel. Although this is, as he said, to beg the question, the improbability of the consequence casts doubt upon the logic of the premise.

It was precisely this question that arose in the old case of *Dean* v. *Hogg and Lewis*.[80] The second defendant hired the steamboat "Adelaide" for a pleasure trip along the Thames to Richmond. The boat was supplied with a captain (furnished and employed by the owner) whose task was to navigate the vessel. As the boat was about to depart from the quay in London, the plaintiff (who was not a member of the defendant's party) came aboard. By the time he discovered his mistake the boat had already cast off and a member of the party advised him to remain. However, rumours spread about his presence and the ladies in the party grew alarmed. The first defendant ordered him to leave and upon the plaintiffs refusing,[81] violently bundled him into a boat alongside. The plaintiff sued for assault and the defendants relied upon their Common Law right to

---

[75] At pp. 687-688, citing *Christie* v. *Griggs* (1840) 2 Camp. 80; *Readhead* v. *Midland Ry. Co.* (1867) L.R. 2 Q.B. 412.

[76] Apparent in spite of his use of the words letter and hirer. He did not cite any of the existing cases on hire of chattels, the most notable being *Jones* v. *Page* (1867) 15 L.T. 619. The plaintiff's statement of claim specifically averred that the plaintiff had been using "a carriage of the defendant in the custody and care of the defendant's servant".

[77] An allegation that he interfered with the reins was negated by the jury; (1881) 6 Q.B.D. at 686.

[78] *Stevenson, Jordan and Harrison* v. *Macdonald* [1953] 1 T.L.R. 101, at 111 (Denning L.J.); *Laugher* v. *Pointer* (1826) 5 B. & C. 547; 29 R.R. 319; 108 E.R. 204 (Abbot C.J.); cf. *Wood Motors Ltd.* v. *McTavish* (1971) 21 D.L.R. (3d) 480.

[79] [1937] 2 K.B. 242, at 250.

[80] (1834) 10 Bing. 345; 38 R.R. 443; see also *Robertson* v. *Amazon Tug and Lighterage Co.* (1881) 7 Q.B.D. 685; *Thompson* v. *Fowler* (1893) 23 O.R. 644; cf. *Moore* v. *Robinson* (1831) 2 B. & Ald. 817.

[81] Apparently, because he objected to the fellow's brusqueness.

expel trespassers, using reasonable force. This defence failed because, in the view of Tindal C.J., the defendants never had possession of the boat. This conclusion was reached on an accumulation of facts: the contract of hire, although granting the second defendant the sole right to enjoyment of the vessel, nowhere contemplated giving him exclusive possession —indeed such a transfer was unnecessary to the fulfilment of the contract; the captain and crew continued in the service of the owners; there were parts of the boat to which the defendants were actually forbidden entry; and nothing could have prevented the captain from carrying goods belonging to third parties, insofar as they did not inconvenience the defendant and his friends. The case contains two interesting statements of the law by counsel, which show a degree of sophistication occasionally lacking in later decisions in this area:

> . . . whether or not the possession of a vessel passes out of the owner to a charterer, depends upon no single fact or expression, but upon the whole of the language of the contract as applicable to its attendant circumstances.[82]
>
> The liability of the owner for the consequences of accidents is no test of his having a possession incompatible with a right in the hirer to maintain trespass for an intrusion on his qualified property.[83]

When applied to the commercial leasing of plant and machinery, the problem becomes less readily soluble. Few modern cases deal specifically with this point, although there are many in which the borrower for reward of a machine and its driver is described in passing as "the hirer". These cases are, for the most part, indecisive, since the dispute does not centre upon the creation of a bailment. For instance, in *Spalding* v. *Tarmac Civil Engineering Ltd.*[84] and *Wright* v. *Tyne Improvement Commissioners*,[85] actions were brought by servants of the borrower[86] against the owners of cranes; in the first case, on grounds of the defective state of the chattel and the negligence of the driver; in the second, on grounds of the driver's negligence alone. In *Spalding*, the plaintiff joined the borrowers as defendants, claiming that they were the temporary masters of the operator, and liability was apportioned between them at sixty to forty per cent; in *Wright*, the owners recovered from the borrowers by way of indemnity clause. In neither case was the existence of bailment a necessary issue. Their significance lies in their habitual description of the borrower as the hirer, a designation undoubtedly accorded to him under the contract but not based upon any serious examination of the question of possession. It is improbable that the vocabulary of the contract would provide an authoritative answer to this question,[87] any more than it would be con-

---

[82] 38 R.R. at 444, citing *Christie* v. *Lewis* (1821) 2 Brod. & B. 410; 23 R.R. 483, *Tate* v. *Meek* (1818) 8 Taunt. 280: 19 R.R. 518, and *Saville* v. *Campion* (1819) 2 B. & Ald. 503; 21 R.R. 376. "As applicable to" must be taken to mean "consistent with".
[83] 38 R.R. at 445.
[84] [1966] 1 W.L.R. 156; 1 All E.R. 209.
[85] [1968] 1 W.L.R. 336; 1 All E.R. 807.
[87] But cf. *Crafter* v. *Burns* [1939] S.A.S.R. 152, at 156; *Bata* v. *City Parking Canada Ltd.* (1974) 43 D.L.R. (3d) 190.
[86] Or, as in *Spalding's* case, of the local authority employing the borrower.

clusive in a dispute as to who is the operator's master.[88] In fact, in *Spalding v. Tarmac Civil Engineering Ltd.* there were strong grounds for supposing that, in working hours at least, possession resided vicariously in the owners. Although the driver was to be treated as the borrower's servant,[89] the contract forbade the borrowers to repair, adjust or drive the crane, so that in normal events they would be prohibited from even touching it. Moreover, the borrowers did not even occupy the land upon which, when not in use, the machine stood. The work-site was an airfield, belonging to the local authority. While the borrowers (who were the main contractors) might conveniently be said to have been in occupation for some purposes,[90] it is clear that no possessory inference could be drawn purely from the presence of the machine on their site. Indeed, there was little to distinguish the case from those where one pays for a service which necessarily includes the use of a tool or a machine, for instance, the householder who engages a man with a rotary hoe to dig his back garden. Only in unusual circumstances will the householder become a bailee of this equipment.

The case against the transfer of possession in the *Spalding* case was all the stronger since the driver remained, in accordance with the traditional presumption, the servant of the owner. But even if this had not been so, a servant might still exercise, on behalf of his general master, the function of excluding all others from the machine, while being in the temporary employment of the very person he is engaged to exclude.

In *British Crane Hire Corporation Ltd.* v. *Ipswich Plant Hire Ltd.*,[91] the Court of Appeal came closer to an analysis of the problem, but even there the issue was irrelevant because of the terms of the contract. A dispute arose as to who should pay for the cost of recovering a crane from marshy ground and the Court encountered no difficulty in holding that, by terms incorporated into the agreement, this fell upon the hirers. They went on to observe that, even without these provisions, the hirers would probably have been liable for the expense of recovery. In so doing, they assumed (and probably correctly) that the defendants were bailees of the crane. But they did not explain why this was so, and it would be unsafe to presume that this result necessarily follows whenever one party pays for the use of another party's plant and manpower. It may be noted, in passing, that the driver in this case remained throughout the servant of the owners.[92]

One important and neglected factor in these cases is the length of the period of hire. Usually it will stretch over days or even months and, of course, the machine will not be perpetually in use throughout that time. Overnight it will normally be left upon the hirer's premises and the fact that it may be locked in and guarded, along with his other equipment, is

---

[88] *Mersey Docks and Harbour Board* v. *Coggins & Griffith (Liverpool) Ltd.* [1947] A.C.1. Cf. *Ferguson* v. *John Dawson & Partners (Contractors) Ltd.* [1976] 3 All E.R. 817.

[89] But only for the purposes of indemnity; see Clause 8 of the Contract of Hire, which made him "for all purposes in connection with [his] employment in the working of plant . . . the servant . . . or agent . . . of the hirer", and cf. Sellers L.J. [1966] 1 W.L.R. at 160, on the relationship apart from the contract.

[90] Cf. *H. N. Emanuel Ltd.* v. *G.L.C.*, [1971] 2 All E.R. 835.

[91] [1975] Q.B. 303; [1974] 1 All E.R. 1059.

[92] At 308, 311 and 1060, 1063.

strongly suggestive of an assumption of care and control on his part. However, even this may not be decisive. The leaving of the vehicle may amount to no more than a licence, and the hirer's obligation may be no greater than that of any other person who grants permission for the use of his premises for a certain purpose. So long as the vehicle is ready for work the next day, he has little interest in where it is kept and may harbour it only as a favour to the owner. Moreover, in many cases the equipment is not left on the hirer's land at all, but merely at the scene of the excavation, for example, by the roadside. It would be misconceived to infer possession in the hirer from its presence upon a piece of land over which he personally may enjoy no more than a licence.

Even in those cases where the machine is stored with the hirer overnight, there may be merely an alternating bailment; in other words, the hirer may be responsible for its safety when it is unoccupied and at rest, but the owner when it is being exclusively operated by his servant. As Atkin L.J. has pointed out,[93] the rationale of a bailee's burden of proof consists in the fact that when a chattel is in his exclusive possession, he is the person most likely to be able to explain its loss or damage and it is he, in the absence of such explanation, who is most likely to have been at fault. Thus, in the case before him, it was held that the repairers of a ship were in the position of bailees on those occasions when they alone were in possession of the vessel, but that this condition terminated (and their onus of proof became suspended) when the crew came aboard at night.[94] Likewise with the lease of machinery, it may be argued that damage during working hours is no more likely to be the fault of the hirer's ordinary servants than that of the owner's skilled operator, and therefore that the burden of proof should remain with the owner.

An interesting line of authority comes from South Australia. The *Road and Railway Transport Act* 1930-1935, made it an offence for a driver to "carry goods for hire" without the appropriate licence.[95] The effect of this section could be avoided if it were shown that, instead of carrying the customer's goods for hire, the vehicle and driver were lent to the customer under circumstances creating a bailment of the lorry. This would mean that the bailee was then carrying his own goods in what was (temporarily) his own lorry, and no offence would be committed. As Richards J. expressed it in *Dayman* v. *Gleader*:

> The real issue in the case is whether the goods were being carried by Messrs. Gibb (*the owner of the lorry*), or were being carried by Sleigh (*the customer*) in a truck which had been bailed too and was in Sleigh's possession. If the former, Gleader (*the driver of the lorry*) was driving a vehicle for the purpose of carrying goods for hire; if the latter, he was quoad hoc working for a person who has a special property in the vehicle, and there was no infringement of the section.[96]

[93] *The Ruapehu* [1925] 21 Lloyd's Rep. 119, at pp. 310, 315-316.
[94] For a similar Canadian authority applying this principle see *Queen* v. *Halifax Shipyards Ltd.* (1956) 4 D.L.R. (2d) 566.
[95] The requirement applied only to travel on a "controlled route".
[96] [1939] S.A.S.R. 277, at 282.

Having thus identified the issue, the court proceeded to decide it solely on the basis of whether Gleader had become the servant of Sleigh. Richards J. went on to remark:

> The case turns on the answer that should be given to the question— Was he carrying them out as Sleigh's servant or as Messrs. Gibb's servant? Or in other words, Was he driving for Sleigh or for Gibb?[97]

The same approach was adopted by Angas Parsons J., who considered it "not inmaterial" to examine who would have been vicariously liable for torts committed by Gleader while driving the lorry and inferred that such liability must have fallen on the owners of the lorry.[98] Therefore, Gleader was the servant of Gibb, and Sleigh could not have become bailees of the lorry. The technique was not without its precedent, for the same court had applied a similar test in *Crafter* v. *Burns*,[99] decided only a few months earlier, and had arrived at a similar conclusion.

At first sight, this reasoning seems excessively simplistic. It is perfectly possible for a bailment to exist without a corresponding change in the servant's allegiance. If servanthood were the solitary test, a hirer of plant and man-power would hardly ever become a bailee, for it has often been remarked that a servant supplied with a complex machine will remain almost invariably in the service of the owner.[1] However, when regarded in the light of their peculiar facts, these decisions can be seen to be justified in their equation of service and possession. The Act was aimed at those who carried goods for hire. Technically, therefore, it could be evaded in several ways, any one of which would take the character of the contract beyond the province of the Act. It might be done by proving that possession in the lorry passed to the hirer, so that it was he and not the owner who was carrying the goods; or it might be done by showing that the driver was his servant, so that any fee paid for the loan of a functionary rather than the performance of a service. But the safest and most convincing way consisted in proving both of these facts, for it would have been very unlikely, in the circumstances of each case, that one would exist without the other. Perhaps this explains why Cleland J., in his judgment in *Crafter* v. *Burns,* spoke of the two questions as indissociable and as well as, in the circumstances, synonymous:

> In order to appreciate the scope and meaning of sec. 14 of the *Road and Railway Transport Act* 1930-1935, it may be well to point out that notwithstanding the terms of that section, a man may lawfully carry his own goods in his own vehicle driven by his own servant, and he may also hire a vehicle for that purpose and hire the services of a driver to drive it, provided that the driver of the vehicle becomes his own *servant, agent* or *employee*.[2]

All the italicised words really mean is that the hirer should be able to direct the course of the work, for without such control he may lack any true possession of the vehicle. It is not necessary that all the elaborate distinctions between the task to be done and the mode of its performance

---

[97] Ibid.
[98] Ibid., at 280-282.
[99] [1939] S.A.S.R. 152.
[1] E.g. in *Garrard* v. *A. E. Southey & Co.* [1952] Q.B. 174, at 179.
[2] [1939] S.A.S.R. 152, at 158.

should be applied to such a case, for once the chattel is delivered into his possession these can only be material to the hirer's vicarious liability and not to his control over the machine. However, it was on the basis of such a distinction that the Court reached its result. Every case cited concerned the loan of a servant and the question of who was his master pro hac vice. There was no reference to any decision which dealt with the requirements of possession.

There is another reason, however, why the Courts treated the two questions as co-terminous. This was not the ordinary case of hire where a machine and its driver come to work on the hirer's land, or in an environ over which he exercises some control. The driver was engaged to travel for long distances, unaccompanied by the hirer or his regular servants. In such a case, there are fewer facts upon which to found a decision as to who was the bailee of the truck. Admittedly, the contract in *Crafter* v. *Burns* made the hirers responsible for keeping it in repair and retaining custody of it, and forbade them from allowing anyone else to drive it. On the other hand, this was a "voyage" rather than a "time" chartering in that the hirers paid a flat rate for the lorry to carry a load from one point to another. They never had the truck on their premises or even saw it; all they knew that that it would load, at a certain brickfield, deliver the materials at their work-site fifty miles away, and from that time cease to be their responsibility. In such a situation practically the only fact which could be of relevance was the identity of the driver's master. Delivery of the lorry to the hirer's servant might then amount to delivery to him. On whomsoever's behalf the driver retained the chattel that person was the bailee.[3]

The facts were substantially similar in *Dayman* v. *Gleader*,[4] except that there was no written contract and the truck actually called at the hirers' premises to be loaded, which might more readily suggest a delivery into the hirers' possession. However, the Court, perhaps over-stressing the service factor and disregarding the more traditional elements of possession, again held that no bailment was created.

The argument in both cases, therefore, was that as soon as the contract period began the driver became transformed into a servant of the hirers, and that any subsequent delivery to the driver, or his continued control of the vehicle after that time, was received and applied on behalf of his transitory master. In this connection, it may be recalled that according to Sir Frederick Pollock:

> . . . a servant does not possess by virtue of his custody, except in one case, namely when he receives a thing from the possession of a third person to hold for the master: and then he is held to possess as a bailee until he has done some act by which the thing is appropriated to the master's use.[5]

---

[3] This approach emerges most clearly in the judgment of Murray C.J. at first instance, [1939] S.A.S.R. 7, at 11-12.
[4] [1939] S.A.S.R. 277.
[5] Pollock and Wright, *Possession in the Common Law*, p. 60. See, on this point, *Marshall* v. *Dibble* [1920] N.Z.L.R. 497; cf. *Grey Cabs Ltd.* v. *Neil* [1947] N.Z.L.R. 62; *Roufos* v. *Brewster and Brewster* [1971] 2 S.A.S.R. 218; ante, p. 238.

Presumably, sufficient evidence of such appropriation would be deemed to exist once the driver called to collect the hirers' goods for carrying, if not from the moment he set off towards the pick-up point.

Because of their peculiar facts, the decisions in *Crafter* v. *Burns* and *Dayman* v. *Gleader* throw little light upon the relevance of a change of service to possessory matters in the conventional hire of plant and manpower. They may serve to establish that a hirer becomes the bailee of a crane from the moment it leaves the owners premises if (and only if) the driver becomes his servant from that time; but this is unlikely to be of great value because most heavy plant is carried, not driven, to its place of employment and the contract will, in any event, usually specify the time from which the hirer's obligation is to commence.[6] Moreover, it is not necessarily a reliable guide; there need be nothing inconsistent in the proposition that, whereas the driver becomes the hirers' servant for the purposes of vicarious liability, he remains an agent of the owner for the purpose of excluding all others from exercising any control over the machine. The latter fact may be the more relevant to a question of possession.

A more generalised statement of the effect of service may be found in the judgment of Cleland J. in *Dayman* v. *Gleader*. The learned judge (who dissented in both cases because, in his view, the driver had become the hirers' servant) said:

> The word "hire" as used by the parties should be given its popular and ordinary meaning, but at the same time it must be conceded that the word "hire" may take its colour from the surrounding circumstances. If in any given case the owner of a vehicle (although expressed to be "hired") retains its possession through its own servant such a vehicle is not "hired" because the owner and not the hirer has the possession.[7]

A servant, then, may assume the role of a fence or a lock or some other inanimate instrument, whereby the hirer is excluded from the vehicle and effectively prevented from exercising any direct, physical dominion over it. But this need not mean that such a result can only be attained by keeping the driver in the particular service of the owner. Who is the master, and who the bailee, are separate questions to which different answers may consistently be given. One need look no further than the *British Crane* case[8] for evidence of this. Although the findings that the hirer became a bailee and that the operator remained in the service of the owner were both delivered obiter, and without any analysis of the factors previously discussed, there is no doubt that as a matter of principle the issues may be divided.

The South Australian authorities may be contrasted with several cases from Canada. In *Coast Crane Co. Ltd.* v. *Dominion Bridge Co. Ltd.*[9] the Supreme Court of British Columbia found that a hirer had not become the bailee of a crane and that the servant with whom it was supplied

---

[6] For an example of such a clause, see *Blake* v. *Richards & Wallington Industries Ltd.* [1974] K.I.R. 151, at 153-154.
[7] [1939] S.A.S.R. 277, at 290-291.
[8] [1975] 1 Q.B. 303.
[9] (1961) 28 D.L.R. (2d) 295.

remained in the general employment of the owner. The question of bailment was directly relevant here because the plaintiffs were suing for damage to their machine and the burden of proof depended upon who, at the material time, was in possession. The defendants denied that they were bailees and the plaintiffs relied in the alternative upon an implied term of reasonable care on the defendants' part in any contract of hire falling short of a bailment. The problem was compounded by the fact that the driver did not work exclusively for the defendants but (subject to their permission) for other contractors at work on the site; moreover, the whole project was under the control of the British Columbia Power Commission and it was to them, the defendants claimed, that delivery (if any) was made. As Verchere J. remarked:

> These issues make necessary consideration of the evidence relating to the possession, control and handling of the crane by the defendant and others before and after as well as during the period of this hiring.[10]

In his view, the evidence established the following facts:

(1) That the driver had the right (implicitly understood by the plaintiff who supplied him) to do or refuse to do all things necessary for the maintenance and safety of the crane; for example, refusing to carry excessively heavy loads or refusing to work on an angle. The plaintiffs "thus exercised control over the crane to this extent",[11] if they thought him right in his refusal, they would have backed him up by withdrawing the crane.

(2) The plaintiffs exercised a measure of control over the driver by virtue of their general instructions to him and his ultimate responsibility to them. This was inconsistent with a hiring, "for which entire responsibility for safety and use was transferred to and vested in the hirer". The driver was "the plaintiffs' agent for the purpose of operating its crane when it was on hire and thus ensuring for it that it was safeguarded at all times".[12]

(3) That the plaintiffs knew that on occasions the crane was deployed on the instructions of other contractors on the site. The plaintiffs were, in fact, "quite willing to send their crane to the defendant and to permit its use by others as the defendant might arrange, but the defendant was to be responsible for the hiring cost as far as the plaintiffs were concerned".[13]

In the light of these facts, the Court accepted the defendant's contention that the two essentials of bailment—delivery and possession—were lacking. Admittedly, the judge was impressed by two unusual circumstances: the crane was in the defendant's actual use for only two hours of the first week, and the defendants seemed to be acting regularly in the character of go-betweens for the other firms on the site. Nevertheless, the significant thing about his decision is his use of the servant-factor merely as a means to establishing the ends of possession. It was only one element in the inquiry. It was one of the criteria by which possession

---

[10] At p. 299.
[11] At p. 300.
[12] At p. 301.
[13] At p. 304; cf. *E. A. Marr (Contracting) Pty. Ltd.* v. *Broken Hill Pty. Co. Ltd.* [1970] 3 N.S.W.L.R. 206.

might be identified. And nowhere in this part of his judgment does he advert to the traditional distinction between a power to order what is to be done, and a power to order how it shall be done, which is laid down as the prime test of servitude in *Mersey Docks and Harbour Board* v. *Coggins and Griffith Ltd.* It is not until Verchere J. reaches the second question (i.e., whether the driver was acting negligently at the time and whether the defendant, as his employer pro hac vice, should be vicariously liable) that this test, which was given so predominant an emphasis in the South Australian cases, is mentioned and applied.

The decision therefore illustrates (as *Dayman* v. *Gleader* and *Crafter* v. *Burns* do not) that the question of whether a servant is in the particular, temporary employment of the hirer is separate from the question of whether that hirer has become a bailee of the chattel. The issues may overlap but neither they, nor the liability they purport to impose, are congruent. The weight to be given to a change in the servant's allegiance will vary according to the other facts and circumstances of the case: where the machine was operating, whether it was shared among the hirer and other contractors, where it was kept overnight, the control exercised by the hirer's regular servants, the time at which the bailment was due to begin and, perhaps, the particular issue to be decided. Indeed, there is some authority for saying that the two questions are entirely unrelated. In *Savory* v. *Holland & Hannen & Cubitts Ltd.* Diplock L.J. observed:

> The doctrine of master and servant pro hac vice today seems to me to be relevant only to a question of vicarious liability: it is a mere adjunct of the doctrine of respondent superior for determining whether A is the superior of B.[14]

Admittedly, it was not the creation of a bailment that the learned judge was seeking to alienate from the sphere of master and servant, but the imposition of occupiers' liability upon the borrowers of a servant. The servant in this case was not accompanied by any machinery and the statement has, as a generalisation, been doubted.[15] Nevertheless, in at least one subsequent case of bailment the Court seems to have attached little weight to the identity of the operator's master. In *Great Lakes Steel Products Ltd.* v. *M. E. Doyle Ltd.*[16] the defendants hired from the plaintiffs a crane and an operator for a period of not less than one month. While it was being used (under the supervision of the defendants' foreman) to move a rotor it toppled over and was damaged. The operator had been taken on to the defendants' payroll and was reported as one of their employees to the Workmen's Compensation Board for physical injuries compensation. The trial judge (Hartt J.)[17] was unable to find that either the driver or the foreman directing him had been negligent, but held that this did not relieve the defendants of their onus of proving, as bailees of the crane, that the accident occurred without any fault on their part. This conclusion was upheld by the Ontario Court of Appeal, who stressed that there was nothing inconsistent in these findings; they merely illustrated the

---

[14] [1964] 1 W.L.R. 1158, at 1165.
[15] Winfield and Jolowicz, *Tort* (9th ed.), p. 532n; cf. 10th ed., pp. 522-523.
[16] (1969) 1 D.L.R. (3d) 349. Cf. *Gemco Equipment Ltd.* v. *Western* (1965) 54 W.W.R. 513.
[17] (1967) 65 D.L.R. (2d) 39.

advantage enjoyed by the owner over the bailee. Nobody contested the existence of a bailment or argued the relevance of the driver's change of allegiance (if any); but in the course of his judgment, Schroeder J.A. observed:

> The fact that Kroker, a skilled crane operator, was required by the respondent plaintiff to operate the crane while it was in use by the appellant is of no special significance and does not modify the transaction so as to derogate from its quality as a contract of bailment. It is clear from the evidence that Kroker's sole duty was to manipulate the controls of the crane's mechanism in co-operation with the employees of the Doyle Company, and more particularly under the orders and directions of its foreman and superintendent, Hardy, who gave Kroker the necessary signals in directing the movement of the load. It was Hardy who chose the site on which the crane would rest during the hoisting operation. The six riggers employed by the appellant company were the persons who placed the requisite slings and rigging on the rotor and attached it to the cable at the end of the boom. These same workmen put the stabilizers of the crane in place and determined their angle with relation to the body of the hoisting machine. All this was done under the supervision of Hardy. . . . It is clear that Kroker did not concern himself with the performance of these and related duties. As he stated, they did not fall within the ambit of his responsibility which was confined to manipulating the controls of the crane in obedience to signals or oral directions given to him by the Doyle Company's superintendent.[18]

Whether or not these facts made Kroker the servant of Doyle is not important. Quite possibly they did.[19] What is important is the idea that the purely internal dominion which a skilled operative exercises over his machine does not necessarily prevent the borrower from becoming a bailee. This principle must not be carried too far—for instance, a chauffeur must do as he is told in many respects, such as route, speed, etc. but it is unlikely that the man who hires him becomes a bailee of the car with which he is supplied. Nevertheless, it is clear that a distinction between the global, general control of the hirer and the internal, mechanical control of the operator may, in an appropriate case, yield the most pragmatic result.

Other Canadian decisions tend to confirm that the exclusive power of an operator to drive a machine will not generally prevent the hirer from becoming a bailee. In so doing, they suggest that the decision in *Coast Crane Co. Ltd.* v. *Dominion Bridge Co. Ltd.*,[20] although supportable on its special facts, represents the exception rather than the rule. In *Catalytic Construction of Canada Ltd.* v. *Austin Co. Ltd.*[21] there was no discussion of this question but the Ontario Court of Appeal accepted the trial judge's conclusion that the chartering of a crane and driver, under circumstances which gave the defendants exclusive control of the work-operation, cast upon them the ordinary onus of a bailee for reward. The Court also stated *obiter* that the operative became the servant of the hirer,[22] but, as in

---

[18] (1969) 1 D.L.R. (3d) 349, at 352-353.
[19] Although, in view of the general presumption, this would be an almost unique event.
[20] (1961) 28 D.L.R. (2d) 295.
[21] (1956) 6 D.L.R. (2d) 193.
[22] At 196.

the *Coast Crane* case, this fact was used solely to determine who would have been liable for the servant's negligence and not as a material element in ascertaining whether there had been a transfer of possession. In *Allison Concrete Ltd.* v. *Canadian Pacific Ltd.*[23] the British Columbia Supreme Court distinguished the *Coast Crane* case on the grounds that there the working day had ended and the crane had been parked by its operator, without the direction of the defendant, upon the dam from which it fell and suffered damage. In the present case, however, the machine was still in use and under the directions of the defendants when the damage occurred. According to Aikins J. there was clearly a bailment: the contract was one of hiring and one does not hire without gaining possession (a somewhat inverted line of argument); delivery had been made; the accident had occurred during the period for which the vehicle had been hired, and was in use at the time; and during that time, nobody else could assert a right of possession of the crane or lawfully take it from the control of the defendant. The learned judge went on:

> I have not overlooked the consideration that by the contract the payloader was to be operated exclusively by the plaintiff's operators. This does not, in my view, touch the issue of possession: the contract was one of hiring with a condition that the machine be run exclusively by operators sent with the machine and in the general employment of the plaintiff. The defendant had the right to dictate the tasks to be performed by the machine and when and where it would do assigned tasks. The plaintiff's operators were to run the machine. It was within their discretion, not the defendant's, to decide how the machine should be manipulated to perform assigned tasks. I do not think this right to control the machines in performing assigned tasks derogates from the defendant's right of possession.[24]

Of course, if the defendants had been able to prove that the mishap occurred solely because of the negligence of the operator, *and* that the operator remained throughout the servant of the bailors, they would have escaped liability even under the bailment. However, the Court concluded that no such negligence had been established and therefore declined to give an opinion upon the identity of the operative's master at the crucial time. There was no indication that Aikins J. considered this issue relevant or helpful to the question of whether there was a bailment.

It seems, then, that a contract for the supply of equipment and manpower of this variety will generally produce a bailment, regardless of the exclusive powers of operation and maintenance conferred on the supplier's operative, so long as the general course of work is to be directed by the person chartering the machine and the accident occurs during that time.

Such an approach should not, however, be permitted to erode the need for a critical assessment of the various factors in every individual case. In most cases the divided dominion between what happens inside the driver's cab and what takes place outside will be obscured by additional criteria, not least of which will be the discretion reserved to the servant in obeying these external directives. It is clear that a transaction may dictate a *chronological* reservation of access to the owner and yet remain (during the time

[23] (1974) 40 D.L.R. (3d) 237.
[24] At pp. 244-245.

such reservation does not apply) a bailment of that chattel. As Atkin L.J. said in *The Ruapehu*:

> I do not think that the rights reserved to the owners to retain the use of the vessel for certain purposes prevents the transaction from being one of bailment . . .[25]

The chattel involved in this case was a ship, which is more capable of being occupied and sub-divided than a smaller and more mobile machine. When one attempts to apply this reasoning in support of a *geographical* condominium over a chattel such as a crane, and to argue that the hirers become bailees of those parts which they can control but that possession of the other sections remains with the owner, conceptual problems immediately arise. Is it juristically accurate to say (even assuming such a dichotomy could logically be made) that one only becomes a bailee of those parts of a composite chattel that one may touch, operate or lawfully move about? The answer would appear to be no. The custodian of a locked suitcase is no less a bailee of its contents because he cannot touch them or does not have access to them.[26] The car-park proprietor who becomes a bailee of a car does not escape liability for the loss of the contents of that car merely because he personally had no right to handle them.[27] Moreover, this type of segmentation has, apparently, been discountenanced by Atkin L.J. in the case already cited. In his view it was:

> . . . unreasonable to alter the rule [imposing the bailee's burden of proof] if the injury happens while the bailee or his servants are there and in charge, even though some of the bailor's servants may be there as a term of the bailment.[28]

Thus, however logical it may be to say that the hirers shall be deemed to be bailees of those parts of the crane which they are most likely to have damaged, but that possession shall remain with the owner in those parts where the damage is most likely to be the work of the driver, there can be no doubt that this approach raises conceptual as well as evaluative difficulties. And yet such a distinction would appear to be the logical converse of the statement of Schroeder J.A. cited above. It is unlikely, for instance, that if the crane in that case had been apparently damaged by purely incompetent operating (such as a failure to replenish the oil level, or seizing the engine, or some other matter exclusively within the driver's knowledge) that the Court would not have relieved the hirers of their burden of proof and decided the case upon the dual issues of whether there was negligence by the servant, and whose servant he was at the time.[29]

---

[25] [1925] 21 Lloyd's Rep. at 315.

[26] See, for instance, *Houghland* v. *R. R. Low (Luxury Coaches) Ltd.* [1962] 1 Q.B. 694.

[27] Cf. *Mendelssohn* v. *Normand Ltd.* [1970] 1 Q.B. 177, where the bailee was warned of the existence of the contents; *Moukataff* v. *B.O.A.C.* [1967] 1 Lloyd's Rep. 396; Chapter 6, ante.

[28] [1925] 21 Lloyd's Rep., at 316; applied in *The Queen* v. *Halifax Shipyards Ltd.* (1956) 4 D.L.R. (2d) 566, where it was, however, emphasised that the bailee must enjoy *exclusive* possession. For a recent application of the latter rule in a different context, reference should be made to *Fairline Shipping Corporation Ltd.* v. *Adamson* [1975] Q.B. 180, at 189 (Kerr J.).

[29] Bearing in mind that the contract would normally prohibit the hirer from making any investigation of this kind. Aliter, of course, if it expressly imposed such liability on the hirer and was construable as extending to negligence by the

The problem is that bailment is too unwieldy and agglomerative a concept to be of much practical value in a situation of this kind. However applied, it is likely to cause injustice. The choice lies between modifying the concept out of recognition, or circumventing it and relying upon the traditional burden of proof, or accepting that it cannot be wholly rationalised and that a man may, in fact, be a bailee for some purposes and not for others. It may well be, as Kerr J. has recently remarked, that one should refuse to accept that "the refinements of the concepts of legal possession and bailment are or should be determinative of liability in the tort of negligence."[30] But this should not induce a court to discount the very considerable advantage that the bailor possess in terms of the bailee's burden of proof.

Conclusions

(1) Under a contract for the supply of machinery and manpower, it may be important to ascertain whether the "hirer" occupies the position of a true bailee for a number of reasons:

(a) to establish upon whom the onus lies of explaining the cause of an accident; if the relationship comprehends a bailment, the burden will rest upon the hirer of proving that the ensuing damage was not due to any default on the part of him or his servants.

(b) to determine whether the hirer is bound to pay the cost of returning the machine or recovering it from the scene of an accident; if he is a bailee, this responsibility will generally fall upon him.

(c) to ensure that the terms normally implied into contracts of simple hire will likewise obtain for the benefit of the hirer; it may be that certain of these terms will exist irrespective of a transfer in possession,[31] but the customer who can bring his contract within the conventional purview of simple hire will almost certainly be in a stronger position and relieved of the need to prove negligence.

(d) to clarify whether the duty of servicing and maintaining the machine falls upon owner or hirer; it would appear to be the general rule (although one readily displaced by the circumstances of the case) that the owner under a contract of hire does not undertake to keep the chattel in repair during the contract period.[32] This presumption would probably not apply where the owner retains possession throughout.

(e) possibly, to establish whether the hirer is a person "entrusted" with the machine for the purposes of the rule in *Morris* v. *C. W. Martin & Son Ltd.*[33]

---

owner's servant. No doubt an owner whose crane had been tampered with by the hirer would expect in such circumstances to enjoy a right of action in trespass against him.

[30] *Fairline Shipping Corporation Ltd.* v. *Adamson* [1975] Q.B. 180, at 189.
[31] See, for instance, *Mowbray* v. *Merriweather* [1895] 2 Q.B. 640 where, although the contract was perhaps not strictly one of hire, a warranty of reasonable fitness was implied akin to that in a contract of hire. See further, Chapter 19 and ss. 68-73 *Trade Practices Act* 1974 (Commonwealth), which apply in general to any contract for the supply of goods, this expression being defined to include leases as well as hirings.
[32] *Hadley* v. *Droitwich Construction Co. Ltd.* [1968] 1 W.L.R. 37; [1967] 3 All E.R. 911.
[33] [1966] 1 Q.B. 716; see Chapter 13, post.

(f) possibly, to ascertain whether the hirer can pass on the benefit of any exemption clauses to sub-bailee.[34]

(g) to establish the hirer's entitlement to sue in trespass or conversion for loss or damage to the machine.

Each of these duties may be answered by the express terms of the contract, but these terms cannot, it is submitted, affect the existence of a bailment. This can only be determined objectively by the court.

(2) The fact that the operator has become a servant pro hac vice of the hirer may be a highly relevant fact in this inquiry but should not, except perhaps in extreme cases, be regarded as solely determinative. Nor should the sole test be whether the hirer is empowered to direct the external movements of the machine. These facts must be considered in conjunction with other criteria, of which the most important are:

(a) the discretion reserved to the driver relating to the movements of the machine, and the extent to which his general master would endorse the exercise of this discretion;

(b) whether the plant was allowed to be used for the benefit and on the instructions of other users;

(c) whether the hirer owns or occupies the land on which the work is performed;

(d) the extent of the driver's private or personal dominion over the machine;

(e) the arrangements relating to the plant while not in use;

(f) whether it was collected by the hirer or delivered by the owner; or whether it was driven to work by the servant, and in what capacity he was acting at the time;

(g) the nature of the damage or other cause of action, its likely source and whether it would be equitable in all the circumstances to invest the hirer with the burden of proving non-default.

Throughout this analysis it should be borne in mind that a true bailment imputes an exclusive possession. The result may be that many contracts traditionally described as hirings may not produce this relationship at all.

(3) The owner who fails to establish a bailment may nevertheless pursue various other possible approaches in order to render the hirer liable for damage to his machine. These will include:

(a) if the operator was in the particular service of the hirer at the time, and the damage appears to be due to his deficient handling, making the hirer vicariously liable for the torts of his temporary servant;

(b) if the damage appears due to the negligence of the hirer's regular servants (e.g. by careless directions to the driver, or a collision caused on the work-site), by likewise making the hirer vicariously liable;

(c) in appropriate circumstances, by pleading a breach of the hirer's duty as occupier of land;

(d) suing in other torts (e.g. trespass, *Rylands* v. *Fletcher*) as appropriate.

[34] See Chapter 20, post.

B. Contracts of carriage and contracts of hire[35]

The foregoing discussion has concentrated upon a hirer's liability for damage to vehicles or other moveable structures while they are under contract to him. Occasionally, however, the chartering of a vehicle and driver will raise questions, not as to whether there has been a bailment of the vehicle itself, but whether possession in its cargo (for the transportation of which the vehicle was hired) rests in the charterer or in the supplier of the van. To take a common example, the owner of goods (possibly a shopkeeper whose own vehicle has broken down) may want them delivered at various points within a certain area and may ask a hire-company to supply a vehicle and driver to perform the deliveries in accordance with the hirer's instructions. A number of questions may thereupon arise as to his relationship with the company:

(i)   Who is vicariously liable for the driver's negligent driving?
(ii) Does the hirer become a bailee of the van?
(iii) Who is in possession of the contents of that van while it is going about the hirer's business?
(iv) How relevant are questions (i) and (ii) to question (iii)?

No firm, general answer can be given to these questions. It may, however, be observed that although the identity of the servant's master is merely one of the facts to be considered when attempting to identify the person in possession, the case for equating employment and possession may be appreciably stronger where the servant is operating at a distance from his master and fewer alternative facts exist to indicate the necessary assumption of control. Thus, if it is found that the hire-company remains the employer of the driver while he is on his rounds, it will generally be safe to assume that the vehicle itself remains in their possession, simply because the hirer's degree of control is appreciably lower than if, for instance, the vehicle had been operating on his own land. Morevoer, if the hire-company remains in possession of the vehicle, it is likely that it will also be the bailee of the contents and liable to show that any loss thereof occurred without its default.[36]

However, this will not always be the case. It is theoretically possible that possession in a container may be segregated from possession in its contents, and that the owner of the former may nevertheless not be held to be a bailee of the latter. Examples are rare, but an illustration may be found in *Makower, McBeath & Co. Pty. Ltd. v. Dalgety & Co. Ltd.*,[37] where McArthur J. held that the transfer by a bailee of goods to a customs-cage in the possession of the harbour authorities did not operate to determine the bailment. A further example might arise where a servant is carrying goods for a third party without his master's authority; in such a case the master's possession in the vehicle may be distinguished

---

[35] See the useful discussion by Hill, *Freight Forwarders,* paras. 265-280.
[37] [1921] V.L.R. 365; cf. *D.P.P.* v. *Brookes* [1974] A.C. 862.
[36] *Gillespie Bros. Ltd.* v. *Roy Bowles Transport Ltd.* [1973] 1 Q.B. 400; *Gallaher Ltd.* v. *B.R.S. Ltd.* [1974] 2 Lloyd's Rep. 440; *Philip Morris (Australia) Ltd.* v. *Transport Commission* [1975] Tas. S.R. 128, are characteristic modern examples.

from the possession in the goods enjoyed either by the third party or (preferably) by the servant as his bailee.[38]

Nevertheless, the primary distinction to be made is between a contract of carriage, whereunder the carrier retains possession in his vehicle and receives the hirer's chattels under a bailment for reward, and a contract for the hire of services, whereunder the driver may be transferred into the employment of the hirer and the only bailment is of the vehicle from its owner to its temporary lessee. Such an analysis will in most cases suffice to determine conclusively where possession in the cargo is located. Unfortunately, the decisions are not entirely consistent in their approach to the primary issue.

A very common example of the problem occurs in the tripartite situation of consignors, forwarders and carriers. The consignor will have engaged the forwarders to effect delivery of goods and the latter (in most cases quite legitimately) will have delegated this task to a carrier by way of sub-contract. Sometimes the carrier will hire his van to the forwarder with a driver who becomes temporarily the forwarder's servant; on other occasions (and far more commonly) the carrier will be acting as an independent enterprise and both servant and vehicle will remain in his employment and possession. There is some authority for the view that, irrespective of whether the driver has become the servant of the forwarder, the carriers will remain liable for any loss occurring while the goods are being carried. Thus, in *Learoyd Bros. Ltd.* v. *Pope & Sons Ltd.*[39] Sachs J. after holding that the carriers were liable as sub-bailees for the loss of the plaintiff's goods, went on to remark that it would have made no difference if the relationship between them and the forwarders had disclosed a contract of hire rather than a contract of carriage. This remark requires some amplification. If the effect of the contract had been to transfer both vehicle *and driver* into the service of the head contractors, it is hard to see how the defendants could have been liable as *bailees* of the contents of the lorry, for possession would presumably have vested in the head-contractors through their temporary servant. Admittedly, it is not inconsistent with the transfer of a servant pro hac vice to hold that possession in the machine with which he is supplied remains with the general employer; there are many cases in which a chattel has been held to have been bailed although the servant remains in the service of his general employer[40] and, in theory, the reverse should be possible. Even if this were so, however, it may still have been the case that possession in the *contents* of the vehicle, as opposed to the vehicle itself, resided throughout in the head-contractors. If the sub-contractors were not bailees, it is hard to see how they could have been liable in negligence to the owners of the goods, unless their liability consisted in supplying a lorry, which was known to be inadequate for the purpose for which it was lent, for the purposes of enabling the head contractors to carry the plaintiff's goods.[41] It is not

---

[38] *Butler* v. *Basing* (1827) 2 C. & P. 613; *Roufos* v. *Brewster and Brewster* [1971] 2 S.A.S.R. 218 post, p. 271.

[39] [1966] 2 Lloyd's Rep. 142, at 148-149.

[40] E.g. *British Crane Hire Corporation Ltd.* v. *Ipswich Plant Hire Ltd.* [1975] 1 Q.B. 303; p. 251, ante.

[41] [1966] 2 Lloyd's Rep. 142, at 149-150.

wholly improbable that a duty might be implied in such a case—perhaps on an analogy with *White* v. *Steadman*[42]—although the instances in which a non-bailee has been liable in negligence for the theft of a person's goods are extremely rare,[43] and this is not a conclusion at which one could arrive without exhaustive analysis.

There is, admittedly, one decision which appears at first sight to render the supplier of a servant liable for his negligence irrespective of whether his service is temporarily transferred to the hirer and even though his general master has not become the bailee of the goods. In *Abraham* v. *Bullock*[44] the defendants were held liable for the negligence of their servant in leaving a carriage unattended while it contained jewellery belonging to the plaintiff. The plaintiff had hired the vehicle, with driver, to carry one of his representatives on his rounds. Shortly before the theft the representative left the carriage to visit a shop, leaving the driver in attendance and the jewels locked inside. The driver went away and the carriage and contents were stolen. The Court of Appeal found for the plaintiffs without discussing whether there had been a bailment to the defendants: they had contracted to supply a competent driver and were answerable for his neglect.[45]

Now if the driver in *Abraham* v. *Bullock* had become the temporary servant of the plaintiff, there would have been no ground for rendering the defendant vicariously liable for the act of negligence and liability would have had to depend upon purely contractual obligations. In such an event, of course, the decision is of little value to a consignor wishing to proceed against a carrier, because there will almost invariably be no contract between the parties; the consignor's only hope of success in such a case would be an action in tort against the carrier for negligently providing an incompetent or dishonest servant. In fact, two of the three members of the Court of Appeal appear to have proceeded on the basis that the driver continued in the service of his general master, without making it clear whether they considered this factor central to their decision. But the third member, Mathews L.J., specifically held that the servant's allegiance had not been transferred.[46] In so doing, he put the decision upon what is, with respect, thought to be the stronger ground of vicarious liability rather than on the basis of an absolute warranty by the defendants of their servant's competence at all times.[47]

---

[42] [1913] 3 K.B. 340; cf. *Eastman Chemical International A.G.* v. *N.M.T. Trading Ltd.* [1972] 2 Lloyd's Rep. 25, where there are suggestions that a principal contractor impliedly warrants the fitness and security of his sub-contractor's vehicles.

[43] P. 223 et seq., ante.

[44] (1902) 86 L.T. 796.

[45] Counsel for the defendant denied the existence of a bailment: sed quaere. The case could probably have been safely decided on this ground, since the servant was left in exclusive control of the carriage and its contents during the absence of the traveller, provided the servant remained in the service of his general master.

[46] At p. 798.

[47] Counsel for the defendants cited *Donovan* v. *Laing, Wharton and Down Construction Syndicate Ltd.* [1893] 1 Q.B. 629 in support of the contention that the plaintiffs were the masters *pro hae vice* of the driver. On the surface this does not seem an unattractive argument, but the later decision in *Cheshire* v. *Bailey* [1905] 1 K.B. 237 clearly held in very similar circumstances that the driver remained in the service of his general employer. Paton, at pp. 183-184, considers

Alternatively, the driver in *Learoyd Bros. Ltd.* v. *Pope & Sons Ltd.*[48] might have remained the servant of the defendants while their van was bailed to the head-contractors. This seems unlikely, but it is a result implicitly endorsed by many of the cases on the hire of plant and machinery.[49] In such a case, the defendants might again have been prevented from becoming bailees of the cargo but they could be made liable either vicariously for the negligence of their servants or directly on the ground of having supplied a defective vehicle.

To some extent, therefore, the question of bailment may be immaterial to the carrier's liability in that he remains responsible for the negligence of his servant in the course of his employment irrespective of whether possession of the goods remains in the owner or not. But of course it will be advantageous to plead bailment whenever possible because it entails a reversal of the ordinary burden of proof. Moreover, the question may become relevant in deciding whether the contents of the vehicle are in the custody of the forwarding agent for the purpose of applying an exclusion clause framed in such terms.[50]

There can be little doubt that the characteristic solution in any consignor-forwarder-carrier situation will be one that favours a contract of carriage between the forwarder and the carrier rather than a hiring of the services of the carrier's equipment and manpower in a manner which places both under the forwarder's control. Accordingly, the forwarder will either have effected a sub-bailment of the goods or will never have gained possession of them at all.[51] This was the situation in *W.L.R. Traders Ltd.* v. *British & Northern Shipping Agency Ltd.*[52] The forwarders here were sued neither as bailees, nor as the employers of the carriers' driver, but purely for breach of an alleged obligation to insure the goods. Pilcher J. rejected this argument and went on to hold that the carriers themselves were liable as bailees for reward for failing to prove that the loss of the consignment occurred without their negligence.[53] In so doing, he accepted that the driver remained the servant of his general employer and had not temporarily entered the service of the forwarding agents. The learned judge also held that the driver was negligent despite having obeyed his employers' instructions when leaving the lorry. Since these instructions appeared inadequate, it may further be concluded that his employers were guilty of direct or personal negligence, as well as being liable on vicarious principles.

In *A. F. Colverd & Co. Ltd.* v. *Anglo-Overseas Transport Co. Ltd.*[54] there was a similar situation but the conclusions reached by Barry J. were

that there was, however, no bailment of the plaintiffs' goods to the employer. Contrast the position when no accompanying personnel of the hirer's is present when the vehicle makes its rounds; in such an event both the service of the driver and possession of the contents would continue to reside in the general employer: *Bontex Knitting Works Ltd.* v. *St. John's Garage* [1943] 2 All E.R. 690.

---

[48] [1966] 2 Lloyd's Rep. 142.
[49] *Ante*, p. 246 et seq.
[50] See *infra*.
[51] I.e., there will be a quasi-bailment. This term is explained at p. 791, post.
[52] [1955] 1 Lloyd's Rep. 554.
[53] At pp. 560-561.
[54] [1961] 2 Lloyd's Rep. 352.

rather more ambivalent. Forwarding-agents (the first defendants) had engaged the second defendants' van and driver to collect the plaintiff's watches from Heathrow and deliver them to the plaintiff's premises in London. It would appear that the entire operation was handled by the second defendants and that the first defendants never acquired physical custody of the goods. While making his deliveries, the second defendants' driver temporarily left the vehicle to go for lunch, having locked the trailer but not the cab, and taking the ignition-key with him. The van was stolen and the first defendants relied on a clause in their contract with the plaintiffs which exempted them from liability for loss or damage:

> . . . unless such loss or damage occurs whilst the goods are in the actual custody of the Company and under its actual control and unless such loss or damage is due to the wilful neglect or default of the Company or its own servants.[55]

They pleaded (i) that the goods were not in their custody but in that of the carriers, (ii) that there had been no wilful neglect on the part of the driver, and (iii) that he was not, at the material time, their servant. Most of the judgment of Barry J. is concerned with the question of whether there had been a fundamental breach on the part of the forwarders; a question which the learned judge answered in the negative.[56] In so doing, he held that the first defendants were bailees of the watches for reward; that the driver remained throughout in the service of the carriers; and that the first defendants were nevertheless vicariously liable for his negligence in leaving the vehicle unattended.[57] He therefore endorsed the plaintiffs' contention that:

> . . . as the first defendants had contracted to transport and deliver the watches . . . they were under a duty to fulfil this obligation and they are not excused from this duty by carrying it out through a sub-contractor.

However, since in the present case the exclusion clause had not been displaced, the first defendants were exonerated and the plaintiffs' claim failed. Taken literally, these findings would appear to involve the proposition that whenever a forwarding-agent (or any other enterprise) arranges for the entire process of carriage and delivery to be handled by an independent contractor whose servants remain in their general master's employment, the forwarding agent becomes a bailee of the goods without ever having seen them or reduced them into his control. There can, however, be no doubt that the van in which they were being transported remained in the possession of the carriers and it is almost impossible to resist the conclusion that the goods were likewise in their possession. The balance of modern authority is against the forwarder's becoming, in ordinary circumstances, a bailee.[58] It would have been interesting to have seen

[55] Clause 11, Standard Trading Conditions, Institute of Shipping and Forwarding Agents.

[56] [1961] 2 Lloyd's Rep. 352, at 363.

[57] At pp. 360, 363.

[58] *Jones* v. *European & General Express Co. Ltd.* (1920) 4 LL.L. Rep. 127; *Evans (J) & Sons (Portsmouth) Ltd.* v. *Andrea Merzario Ltd.* [1975] 1 Lloyd's Rep. 162: rev'd. on other grounds, [1976] 2 All E.R. 930; cf. Hill, *Freight Forwarders,* 42; Hudson (1975) 91 L.Q.R. 447, at 449.

what Barry J. would have made of the position of the carriers in this case; unfortunately, the plaintiffs had abandoned their action against them before the case came up for trial. It is possible that Barry J. would have felt obliged to deny a bailment between these two parties on the ground that they were not in any contractual relation; but although the point was not authoritatively decided until *Morris* v. *C. W. Martin & Sons Ltd.,*[59] both *W.L.R. Traders Ltd.* v. *British & Northern Shipping Agency Ltd.*[60] and *L. Harris (Harella) Ltd.* v. *Continental Express Ltd.*[61] clearly sanctioned an action in these circumstances for breach of bailment between consignor and carrier. The proper approach in *Colverd's* case would surely have been to hold that although as a general rule neither a bailee nor (as is the case of a forwarding-agent) a quasi-bailee escapes liability by delegating the task for which he was employed, in the present case the goods were not in the "custody" of the forwarders at the relevant time and the exemption clause applied.

Of course, there may be occasions on which the relationship between forwarders and carriers amounts to a bailment of the vehicle and a drafting of its driver into the service of the forwarders, rather than a straightforward contract of carriage. Such an inference may be easier to draw when the arrangement between the parties is long-standing and the periods of hiring substantially longer than would be the case with purely spasmodic engagements; where the vans are sign-written with the forwarder's name and both operate from and return to his premises; where the forwarder is given a high degree of control over the servant and assumes most of the ordinary duties of the master-servant relationship, such as payment, insurance, provision of uniforms etc.; and where he likewise assumes responsibility for the maintenance and insurance of the vehicles in his service. Where the overall conclusion is in favour both of a hiring of the vehicle and the creation of a temporary master-servant relationship between forwarder and driver, it will almost invariably follow that the forwarder continues throughout to be the bailee of any cargo transported in the vehicle, and very special facts will be required to displace this presumption. But it must be remembered that employment and bailment are separable issues. It may be the case that the forwarder becomes the bailee of the carrier's van without becoming the master of the carrier's servant. This is unlikely where the vehicle is not operating under his permanent surveillance, as for instance would be a crane or other item of heavy-duty equipment, or on his land. But factors such as a two-way radio system and a detailed itinerary or list of instructions to the driver might conceivably be considered to reduce the vehicle into the charterer's possession while leaving the operator in the employment of the driver, for the degree of control necessary to constitute the former is probably less than would be required to effect a change of employment, although of course the two may be closely related. In such an unlikely event, possession of the cargo would, it is submitted, more probably rest in the bailees of the van than in the employers of the driver; but it is impossible to postulate any definite

[59] [1966] 1 Q.B. 716.
[60] [1955] 1 Lloyd's Rep. 554.
[61] [1961] 1 Lloyd's Rep. 251.

general rules and all the circumstances must be weighed before coming to a conclusion. These could vary considerably from case to case.

An even more unlikely alternative would involve a change of employment without a bailment of the vehicle to the "hirers". In this case, again, possession of the contents of the vehicle would probably follow possession of that vehicle itself. But it must be emphasised that the employer of the driver, whether he be additionally a bailee of the cargo or not, will remain vicariously liable for negligence or conversion committed while discharging the task in hand. In this case, as in the situation outlined in the preceding paragraph, the consignor of the goods will therefore enjoy a choice of defendants; his most favourable course of action will of course be against the bailee, although it is possible that a quasi-bailee whose task is to transport goods without ever gaining possession of them will be counted as a bailee (much in the same way as a sub-bailor) for the purposes of identifying the appropriate burden of proof.[62]

In any event, it is clear that in most cases a bailment of the vehicle will, if it exists, be accompanied by a change in the employment of the driver; and that the latter is very difficult to prove. One case where this result might have been thought to follow was *L. Harris (Harella) Ltd.* v. *Continental Express Ltd.*[63] The first defendants, forwarding-agents, ran what was described as a postal service, whereunder they arranged for the despatch of customers' goods to various countries in return for a fee which covered everything but the actual cost of postage. Clause 1 of their consignment notes announced that they would: ". . . act solely as forwarding Agent and will only accept and arrange for the transport of the goods . . . subject to all the conditions . . . of . . . any . . . Carrier . . . by or through whom they may be conveyed . . ."

The plaintiffs who wished to engage the first defendants' services, filled out some of these forms and sent them to the first defendants. The following day, a van arrived which collected and took away the plaintiff's goods. The circumstances relating to the vehicle were succinctly described by Paull J. as follows:

> The van was coloured the same colour as are all the vans which collect for the first defendants and on the side of the van was the first defendants' name. There was no indication on the van that it was not a van owned by them. In fact, the van was owned by the second defendants and the driver was a man (I hasten to say a perfectly honest man) engaged by and paid by the second defendants. The first defendants owned one van which was marked and used in a manner similar to this van. The first defendants hired from the second defendants, under a long term hire contract, three vans, of which the van in question was one. It was a term of the hire that the second defendants should provide a driver for each van. These vans (including the first defendants' own van) had what may be called regular collecting rounds. All goods after collection were brought to the first defendants' head office in the Old Bailey and from there the goods were dispatched to their destination, the same vans being normally used to take the goods to the docks or the

airport or the station or the post office. At the time of the theft the
driver had not finished his collection round and the goods in question,
therefore, had not reached the first defendants' head office for dispatch.[64]

The plaintiffs, seeking to evade the first defendants' exclusion clauses,
claimed that these did not apply when the first defendants were acting, or
purporting to act, as carriers, and that on the present occasion the arrangement between first and second defendants amounted both to a hiring of
the vehicle and to a transfer of the driver into the service of the first
defendants. The evidence for this was strong, because the relevant contract
(as counsel for the plaintiffs pointed out) entitled the forwarders to give
to the driver all reasonable instructions for the fulfilment of his duties,
including instructions as to itinerary, the packing of goods, and relative
speeds to be followed; bound them to pay his wages and to insure the
goods; and (as we have seen) required the vehicles to be depicted and
represented as the first defendants' own. In the event, Paull J. declined
to adopt the interpretation of the relevant clause in the consignor-
forwarder contract advanced by the plaintiffs; he therefore did not consider it necessary to decide in their action against the first defendants
whether the first defendants had become the employer of the driver. But
in considering the action against the second defendants, he rejected the
latter's contention that:

> . . . at the time when the goods were stolen, the driver, although the
> general servant of the second defendants, was in the employment
> of the first defendants and, in consequence, the goods never came
> into the possession of the second defendants and, therefore, there
> can be no claim against them.[65]

His conclusion was reached mainly through reliance upon the traditional presumption and through construction of the terms of the contract
between first and second defendants. The apparent consequence was that
the second defendant were bailees and liable for negligence on the part of
their employee. It may be queried whether a party who, in the contemplation of the other contracting party, is to collect and deliver the goods
personally, and who gives every impression that this is in fact the case,
should be enabled to escape the consequences of bailment merely by
undisclosedly delegating the task to another. Such delegation may not be
a fundamental breach, but one wonders whether some concept of bailment
by estoppel might not legitimately be employed in such a case.

In fact, it now seems unlikely that the failure of a forwarding agent (or
other person employed to provide transportation) to acquire possession
will by itself relieve him of the necessity of proving that the loss occurred
without the fault of the person to whom he delegated performance. Much
will, of course, depend upon the capacity in which the forwarder is
engaged, for if it is clearly contemplated that his duty is merely to arrange
transport, his liabilities will be discharged (negligence excepted) as soon
as he has done so. But where the forwarder or other intermediary is
employed to carry, albeit with an option to delegate the task in whole or

---

[64] At p. 255.
[65] At p. 257.

in part if he so determines, he remains liable for the manner in which the obligation is discharged whether he ever obtains possession of the goods or not.[66] Accordingly, the foregoing discussion is primarily relevant to the carrier's liability, for if the carrier does not acquire possession of the goods he cannot be liable as a bailee, and if his servant becomes temporarily the servant of the forwarder, the ground for imposing vicarious liability likewise disappears. Having said this, it must however be reiterated that in the great majority of cases the driver will remain in the service of the carrier and the carrier will become a bailee. The recent decision in *Gillespie Bros. Ltd.* v. *Roy Bowles Transport Ltd.*[67] is a characteristic example.

One case which accentuated the problems of divided dominion, albeit upon facts that are unlikely to recur, was *Roufos* v. *Brewster and Brewster*.[68] It will be remembered that the appellant, when arranging for the delivery of the respondents' truck from Adelaide to Coober Pedy, was allowed to put some of his own goods on the vehicle. Who, if anybody, was the bailee of those goods? The question was not material to the decision but two members of the Supreme Court put forward a solution consistent with his or her approach to the central issue. The answer given by Bray C.J. shows the weakness of the general conclusion, for he was obliged to rebut the inference that the respondents would have been liable to the appellant for the damage to his goods:

> If Joanni was, as the claim alleges, though, as I have said, there was no attempt to prove it, incompetent to drive the truck, it may be that any action by the appellant could be met by the plea of *volenti*. It may be that the goods were entrusted by the appellant to Joanni, his potential employee, apart from his appointment of Joanni as the respondents' agent to drive the truck, and that Joanni thereupon became the bailee of the goods from the appellant and that for any damage to the goods the appellant must look to Joanni alone. It may be an implied term of the arrangement on the telephone that the driver selected by the appellant to drive the truck should carry the appellant's goods at the appellant's risk. If improper loading played any part in the accident, that would also cause the failure in whole or in part of any claim by the appellant as the truck was loaded by his servants or agents under his instruction. But I prefer to express no final opinion on any of these matters.[69]

According to Mitchell J.:

> There may have been . . . a separate bailment by Roufos to Joanni of the former's goods, but we are not concerned with questions arising between Roufos and Joanni except in so far as they may throw light upon the question which arises between Roufos and Mr. and Mrs. Brewster.[70]

66 Post, p. 000.
67 [1973] 1 Q.B. 400. See also *Thomas National Transport (Melbourne) Pty. Ltd.* v. *May & Baker (Australia) Pty. Ltd.* (1966) 115 C.L.R. 353, where it is submitted that the sub-contractor clearly became a bailee, despite the statement by Windeyer J. at 382-383, that the main contractors "by its agents who were sub-contractors, obtained possession of the goods"; cf. at 387.
68 [1971] 2 S.A.S.R. 218: p. 243, ante.
69 At p. 226.
70 At pp. 231-232.

Zelling J. advanced no solution to this peripheral issue but it may be assumed that his discovery of a continuing bailment of the use of the truck to Roufos involved the continued possession by Roufos of his goods while they were in the custody of Joanni. The decision therefore illustrates, albeit rather cloudily, that a common purpose in the employment of an agent by two separate owners of chattels may involve the notion that both principals retain possession of their respective chattels even though the one is contained in the other and the agent has effective custody of both.

CHAPTER 8

GRATUITOUS BAILMENTS AND BAILMENTS FOR REWARD

In this short chapter we shall examine the standards by which a bailment is to be classified as gratuitous or for reward. It is difficult to extract any overall principles because of the tremendous variety of situations in which this classification has been applied. Moreover, many of the cases reflect a desire to categorise a particular bailment in such a way as to achieve what, in the court's view, is the most equitable result.

Before commencing this inquiry, it is proper to indicate why it should be necessary at all. It must be conceded that the significance of reward has declined considerably in recent years. To what extent it is now a redundant issue remains, however, undecided.[1] As the ensuing chapters will endeavour to show, modern courts are increasingly reluctant to regulate the degree of care expected of a bailee according to whether he benefits from the bailment. Nevertheless, the trend is not uniform and the existence of mutual benefits is still accepted in some quarters as a material element in the obligations of the parties.

The following appear to be the primary differences between a gratuitous bailment and a bailment for reward:

A. Standards of care

According to orthodox theory, the measure of a bailee's responsibility for a chattel is governed (in the absence of special contract) by the existence and location of any benefit received. Thus, it is said that the non-paying borrower must guard against even slight negligence, whereas the depositary or unpaid custodian is liable only where his negligence is gross.[2] Likewise, the lender of a chattel has been held liable only for those defects of which he knew or which he recklessly concealed at the time of delivery.[3] Although later cases have tended to erode these gradations, they continue to command support, particularly, perhaps, in assessing a borrower's duty towards the borrowed chattel.[4]

B. Vicarious liability

Again, the question is undecided, but there is some authority for the view that a gratuitous custodian of goods is liable for the conversions of

---

[1] Contrast, for instance, the statements of the Court of Appeal in *Houghland* v. *R. R. Low (Luxury Coaches) Ltd.* [1962] 1 Q.B. 694 and in *Morris* v. *C. W. Martin & Sons Ltd.* [1966] 1 Q.B. 716, discussed at pp. 306-310, post.

[2] *Coggs* v. *Bernard* (1703) 2 Ld. Raym. 909; 92 E.R. 107; see further pp. 288-306, 368-372, post.

[3] *Coughlin* v. *Gillison* [1899] 1 Q.B. 145; see further pp. 349-363, post.

[4] At least in Canadian jurisdictions; see *Wilmot Hatheway Motors Ltd.* v. *Degrace* (1969) 1 N.B.R. (2d) 858; *Desjardins* v. *Theriault* (1970) 3 N.B.R. (2d) 260. Cf. *Port Swettenham* v. *Wu* (1978) *The Times*, June 22.

his servants, or for their negligence resulting in a conversion by a third party, only where he was personally negligent in employing or failing to supervise them. Indeed, Lord Denning M.R. has gone further and implied that the depositary is under no liability to protect the goods from theft at all, provided he has kept them "as his own".[5] It will be submitted later that such an approach is outmoded and without proper foundation.[6] Nevertheless, it is supported by what appears to be the only Australian decision to consider the question at all.[7]

C. Supplementary duties of bailor or bailee

Obviously, it will be easier to enforce promises over and above those imposed by the Common Law if the promisee can show that the arrangement is contractual. However, bailment is an older notion than contract and it seems likely that such promises become binding upon delivery although the promisee has furnished no consideration to support them.[8] The reason for this apparent anomaly is to be found in bailment's early association with the action of assumpsit. To the extent that affirmative, consensual duties are clearly enforceable by contract and only possibly enforceable under a gratuitous bailment, the presence of mutual benefits nevertheless remains a significant question. It may also be relevant to the implication of terms not expressly contained in the agreement, e.g. the warranty of fitness for purpose in the case of a contract of hire.[9]

D. Disposition by bailee

If a bailee sub-bails without authority, the absence of reward on the part of the sub-bailee may have significant effects on the sub-bailor's position. An old decision from Queensland suggests that he does not lose his lien over the goods by virtue of such an act.[10] It is also possible, since the gratuitous bailee himself has no lien, that such a disposition would not amount to conversion, whereas if it gave the sub-bailee rights over the chattel it would.[11] Indeed, this analysis would apply whether the alleged converter was an original bailee or not. Coincidentally, the question of reward will often mark the distinction between an immediate right of possession in the bailor and a right which is merely deferred. But the two questions are not congruent and it is possible even under a gratuitous bailment for the bailee to enjoy a secure right of possession over an agreed period.[12]

---

[5] *Morris* v. *C. W. Martin & Sons Ltd.* [1966] 1 Q.B. 716, at 725.
[6] See pp. 306-310, post.
[7] *Makower, McBeath & Co. Pty. Ltd.* v. *Dalgety & Co. Ltd.* [1921] V.L.R. 365, at 374.
[8] See pp. 313, 339 et seq., post.
[9] See pp. 280, 718, post.
[10] *Whitehead* v. *Sunley* (1878) 5 Q.S.C.R. 143; cf. *Hunter* v. *Sunley* (1878) 5 Q.S.C.R. 159.
[11] See generally p. 126 et seq., ante.
[12] Pp. 364-368, post. For a further potential difference between gratuitous bailments and bailments for reward, see *Tappenden* v. *Artus* [1964] 2 Q.B. 185, at p. 201 (post, p. 1009).

E. Burden of proof

Quite a number of Australian cases ordain that under a gratuitous safe-keeping the proof of negligence rests upon the bailor. English authority takes the contrary view and seems preferable. Nevertheless, the question may still be regarded in Australia as technically undecided.[13]

I. BAILMENTS FOR REWARD AND THE DOCTRINE OF CONSIDERATION

Strictly, the word reward is misleading in this context, for it suggests that the advantage in question must be pecuniary. Any benefit, financial or otherwise,[14] will suffice to identify a bailor or bailee as one for reward, although such benefit may not bring him within a particular sub-group; thus, it has been suggested that there is no true contract of hire unless the "payment" given for the use of a chattel is monetary.[15] The benefit may be direct, the result of a specific bargain between the parties, or indirect, as in the case of a loan of equipment between individual members of a work-force, where the "mutual prosecution of the common work" is benefit enough to make the transfer non-gratuitous.[16] Provided, therefore, the bailor or bailee has an interest in or derives an advantage from the performance or creation of the bailment, the sufficiency of his advantage will be immaterial; any benefit, however small or incidental, will be enough.[17] Nor, it seems, will be courts sub-divide the overall bailment into particular aspects or phases and hold, for instance, that where a charge is imposed only for storing goods, any handling of them is a gratuitous act and commands a lower degree of care.[18] It may be inferred that the same considerations apply to bailors as well as bailees. Thus, if A, ostensibly for the sole advantage of the borrower, lends his car to B, A may be considered a bailor for reward whenever he has some motive or expectation that the arrangements will redound to his benefit, e.g. where he wants the car to be used during his absence.[19]

---

13 But see now *Port Swettenham* v. *Wu* (1978) *The Times,* June 22 (P.C.).
14 See n. 25, post.
15 Per Zelling J. in *Roufos* v. *Brewster & Brewster* [1971] 2 S.A.S.R. 218, at 233-234; but see contra, *Leggo* v. *Welland Vale Manufacturing Co. Ltd.* (1901) 2 C.L.R. 45; Story, s. 377; *Derbyshire Building Co. Pty. Ltd.* v. *Becker* (1962) 107 C.L.R. 633; p. 718, post.
16 Per Chapman J. in *Griffiths* v. *Arch Engineering Ltd.* [1968] 3 All E.R. 217, at 220; the statement was obiter because his Lordship did not consider that possession in the equipment had actually been transferred. A similar position existed, and similar observations were made, in *Oliver* v. *Sadler & Co. Ltd.* [1929] A.C. 584, discussed at p. 354, post. Cf. *Fraser* v. *Jenkins* [1968] N.Z.L.R. 816 and see further p. 357, post.
17 *Roufos* v. *Brewster & Brewster,* supra, at 223, 225 appears to support this view: see also *Mansfield Importers and Distributors Ltd.* v. *Casco Terminals Ltd.* [1971] 2 Lloyd's Rep. 73, at 77 (British Columbia Supreme Court).
18 *Mansfield Importers and Distributors Ltd.* v. *Casco Terminals Ltd.,* supra, at p. 76. But cf. *Price* v. *Leblanc* (1957) 7 D.L.R. (2d) 716, which may be wrong on this point.
19 Quaere, however, whether he should be strictly liable for its defects as may be the case with a professional lessor of vehicles. See p. 724, post. See further *Bainbridge* v. *Firmstone* (1838) 8 A. & E. 743; 112 E.R. 1019, where the defendant asked to be allowed to weigh the plaintiff's boilers and damaged them while doing so. Denman C.J. remarked at p. 1020: "The defendant had some reason for wishing to weigh the boilers, and he could do so only by obtaining

There are several ways in which the nature of the reward may be distinguished from the contractual requirement of consideration. First, its source of origin is immaterial. A person who is hired to take custody of goods will owe to their owner the duties of a bailee for reward irrespective of whether the person who has hired and paid him is the owner or some third person.[20] In such a case there will exist privity of bailment, even though the notional bailor has no contractual relation with the ultimate bailee. Secondly, the benefit itself, even where the parties are in direct communication, may be so fortuitous or remote that it does not amount to consideration in the proper sense of that term.[21] It could hardly be said, for instance, that the increased attractiveness of his establishment that a shopkeeper enjoys through taking care of customers' lost goods constitutes consideration on the part of a visitor to the store, especially one who does not in fact intend to make a purchase.[22] Here again, the benefit may derive from quite another source than the bailor. But it would seem that the benefit must be at least within the contemplation of the benefited party for him to qualify as a bailor or bailee for reward. A purely fortuitous or objective advantage to a depositary, not within his intention at the time

permission from the plaintiff, which he did by promising to return them in good condition."

---

[20] In *Andrews* v. *Home Flats Ltd.* [1945] 2 All E.R. 698, the wife of a tenant in a block of flats was held able to recover against the landlords for the loss of her trunk, which had been deposited by agreement in the room set aside for that purpose (cf. *Coons* v. *First National Bank of Philmont* (1926) 218 App. Div. 283; 218 N.Y. Supp. 189 (3rd Dept.); in *Morris* v. *C. W. Martin & Sons Ltd.* [1966] 1 Q.B. 716, a sub-bailee who accepted a fur stole for cleaning from an intermediate bailee has held to owe to the owner of the stole a duty to safeguard it with reasonable care and not to convert it; on sub-bailments generally, see Chapter 20, post. These cases should be contrasted with *Brown* v. *National Bank of Australasia Ltd.* (1890) 16 V.L.R. 475, where the deposit of debentures with a bank for safe-keeping by three trustees at the same time as one of the trustees (who was also an executrix) opened a private account was held not to render the bailment of the debentures one for reward. The decision may be justified on the grounds that there was no connection between the deposit and the alleged benefit because it seems that even under modern theory the latter must be the incentive for the former before there can be a bailment for reward: "The opening of the private account was in pursuance with a contract made with the defendants by Mrs. Brown in her private capacity and not as executrix", per Higinbotham C.J. at p. 480. However, it is difficult not to believe that the two were causally as well as chronologically related and that the bank regarded the opening of the account as a benefit accruing from the overall transaction. The decision is also marred by the view that permission given by the same trustee to the bank to collect the interest on the debentures could not constitute a reward because the other trustees were not party to the agreement, and "consideration must move from the promisee" (at pp. 480-481). The underlying thesis here is an equation between bailments and contract, which is now no longer accepted. There are strong grounds for holding that the bank in this case were not gratuitous bailees but bailees for reward. As to banks generally, see p. 282, post.

[21] Street, *Foundations of Legal Liability*, Vol. II, p. 81, describes the necessity for a causal relation between a promise and its consideration as follows: "The consideration must draw the promise from the promisor and the promise must be the inducement which causes the promisee to incur the detriment which constitutes the consideration. The two factors must be so far mutual that each way be looked upon in a way as being both the cause and effect of the other."

[22] A source of benefit suggested by counsel in *Helson* v. *McKenzies (Cuba St.) Ltd.* [1950] N.Z.L.R. 878, at 897. It was apparently accepted by Gresson J. but not by Finlay J.; see further, pp. 281-282, post, and cf. *De La Bere* v. *Pearson Ltd.* [1908] 1 K.B. 280.

of taking charge of the goods, would not alter the quality of the bailment even though other persons would have considered the arrangement beneficial, e.g. a non-art-lover who is persuaded to keep a valuable Cubist painting on his wall while the owner has the decorators in, or a warehouseman whose warehouse is saved from burglary by the presence of goods stacked up against the windows. Somewhere at the back of the benefiting party's mind there must exist, albeit subconsciously, some prospect of advantage; or at least the circumstances must be such that it can reasonably be expected to be there.

On the other hand, if the bailee stipulates for what appears to the bailor to be a reward (or vice-versa) it should make no difference that this was inadequate or that the other party undertook the service as an act of limited charity.[23] Again, the advantage may be contingent and may never in fact come to fruition, as where a factor agrees to sell goods and is allowed to keep the proceeds over a certain level, but can only sell them for less.[24] It is even possible that a bailment may be for reward although the advantage is incapable of being reckoned in monetary terms.[25]

Most of the cases outlined here will admittedly represent contracts as well as bailments for reward. But it may be that there is a contract but no reward. If A asks B to store his goods without payment, but promises to reimburse B for any damage caused by the goods, howsoever arising, A's promise may be sufficient detriment to constitute consideration but it is hard to see wherein lies the advantage or benefit to B.[26]

II. THE NATURE OF REWARD

Most modern bailments involve a direct monetary payment either from bailor to bailee (as with the hire of custody) or vice-versa (as with the hire of a chattel). In both cases the party receiving the reward is acting for his own advantage and his responsibilities may be correspondingly higher. As we have seen, neither the inadequacy of the reward nor its source will inhibit a court from discovering a bailment for reward, provided it is clear that the payment in question was in fact made as incentive or compensation for the bailment. If a custodian accepts goods from a party who is not their owner, and is paid for storing them or performing work upon them, the duties he owes as a bailee for reward may extend not

---

[23] See n. 17, supra.
[24] A bailment on these terms (where the goods were stolen before sale) was conceded to be a bailment for reward in *Gutter* v. *Tait* (1947) 177 L.T. 1.
[25] There is no decision directly in point, but it is not improbable that the Courts would take such a view. However, in two cases involving bailments of cars, the first to a mandatary who used it to transport lady-friends and the second to girls who promised to return and spend the night, the bailments were classified as solely for the benefit of bailor and bailee respectively: *Campbell* v. *Pickard* (1961) 30 D.L.R. (2d) 152; *Walker* v. *Watson* [1974] 2 N.Z.L.R. 175.
[26] Treitel (4th ed.), p. 94 argues that such an agreement cannot be enforced if merely executory. cf. the situation in *McCarthy* v. *British Oak Insurance Co. Ltd.* [1938] 3 All E.R. 1, where it was held that the loan of a car to a borrower who agrees to pay for the petrol he uses is not a contract of hire. In this case, there would appear to be a contract without any corresponding benefit to the *bailor*. It is probable that such a transaction would be characterised as a gratuitous loan.

only so far as the immediate bailor is concerned but also towards the owner.[27] Indeed, the ultimate custodian in a chain of sub-bailments may have entered into as many separate relationships of bailments for reward as there are intervening bailees.

Generally, it is common to talk about reward in the context of the bailee's responsibilities and it is here, of course, that the question possesses its primary importance. However, it is quite as likely that it will affect the liability of a bailor. Thus, the unpaid lender of a chattel will be liable (at most) for negligence while the remunerated lender may be held to have warranted its safety and fitness for use.[28] In any event, every bailment for monetary reward will involve a corresponding non-pecuniary advantage on the part of the other party. Thus the use of the car, or the cleaning of a coat, or the carriage of vegetables all exemplify the sort of non-financial benefit that will make the recipient a party to a bailment for reward. Such benefits may also represent the sole advantage enjoyed by either party under a gratuitous bailment; the borrower, the non-paying depositor and the mandator all enjoy some species of reward (or benefit) entitling them to be classified as bailors or bailees for reward, even though the benefits are not reciprocal and their counterparts derive no profit from the transaction. Advantage or reward is thus most material as a description of one particular party to a bailment rather than as a description of that relationship itself.

Nevertheless, the expression "bailment for reward" possesses a principal value in indicating those bailments that are for the mutual advantage of the parties. In such cases, it is usually possible to point to some concrete advantage accruing to the bailee independently of his general business operations. Often, however, it will be the very nature of those operations that determines or identifies the existence of his advantage. To this extent, it can be artificial and misleading to separate the question of benefit from the character of the bailee and the capacity in which he is acting.

A. Bailments in the course of professional or commercial operations

A person conducting a commercial enterprise (such as a shipping agency, a transport service, a restaurant or a hotel) will often perform, as adjuncts to the primary service, ancillary services for which no direct charge is exacted. If these services involve the taking possession of goods, it seems clear that the ensuing bailment will not be classified as gratuitous but as one for the mutual advantage of the parties. The bailee will derive (or will hope to derive) a benefit in the form of the increased attractiveness of his establishment, and the prospects of advancing his reputation which such services entail. Thus, there would be a bailment for reward where a bus or railway company agrees to transport passengers' luggage for no additional charge;[29] where the proprietors of a hotel operate a free bus

---

[27] Subject to a possible caveat where he does not know that the goods belong to someone other than the immediate bailor; see pp. 810-813, post.
[28] See pp. 349-363, 724-743, post.
[29] *Cohen* v. *S.E. Ry. Co.* (1877) 2 Ex. D. 253, at 258 (Mellish L.J.). In *Houghland* v. *R.R. Low (Luxury Coaches) Ltd.* [1962] 1 Q.B. 694, the County Court judge had found that there was a gratuitous bailment where the defendants carried the plaintiff's suitcase in the boot of one of their coaches; this finding was

to carry guests and their belongings to and from the hotel;[30] where a hospital authority takes charge of a patient's possessions;[31] where the organisers of a dog show accept custody of an animal for exhibition;[32] where the secretary of a club or the manager of a hotel accepts for safe-keeping the property of a member or guest;[33] where a dentist assumes possession of a patient's coat while she is undergoing treatment;[34] where an accountant has possession of a client's ledgers and papers in the course of his professional work;[35] and where the attendant at a swimming-bath agrees to look after a patron's valuables while he is in the water.[36]

regarded with considerable doubt by Omerod L.J. at p. 697, and seems misconceived. cf. *Carlisle* v. *G.T.R.* [1912] 1 D.L.R. 130. Of course, there must be a delivery of possession in the first place; see *Burnett* v. *Ritter* (1925) 276 S.W. 347, where it was held that the handing of a hand-bag to the conductor of an autocar for him to put on the baggage rack or the running board created a bailment, with the result that the operators were liable for negligence when the bus caught fire and the hand-bag burned.

30 This inference may be drawn from the disapproval of *Hamilton* v. *Consolidated Hotels Ltd.* (1969) 12 M.C.D. 427 (where the facts were as stated in the text) in *Transport Ministry* v. *Keith Hay Ltd.* [1974] 1 N.Z.L.R. 103. Both of these cases dealt not with questions of bailment but with the problem of whether there was a "carriage for reward" within the Transport Act 1962, and in the latter case it was remarked that carriage may be for reward "although no one is legally bound to pay for it . . . it is ultimately a question of fact". Clearly the two requirements are not identical but it would seem that the logic of these decisions should apply *a fortiori* to the question of whether there is a bailment for reward. See further: *Albert* v. *Motor Insurers' Bureau* [1972] A.C. 301.

31 *Martin* v. *L.C.C.* [1947] K.B. 628; cf. pp. 207-208, ante. The position would appear to be no different where the hospital authority is subject to the *National Health Act* 1946; see Vaines, *Personal Property* (5th ed.), pp. 95-96, nor indeed when any bailee is under a legal duty to take custody of goods, unless of course the imposition of the duty is accompanied by qualifying provisions. Cf. *Compagnie de l'Union des Abattoirs de Montreal* v. *Leduc* (1900) Q.R. 10 Q.B. 289.

32 *Andrew* v. *Griffin* [1918] 1 W.W.R. 274, 532; cf. *Coltart* v. *Winnipeg Industrial Exhibition Association* [1912] 4 D.L.R. 108; *Webb* v. *Agricultural Society of New South Wales* (1893) 14 L.R. (N.S.W.) 333, where the point was not discussed but the Society's liability was assumed to lie in negligence (despite a headnote which implies that gross negligence would be required).

33 The point is not specifically decided in *Phipps* v. *New Claridge's Hotel Ltd.* (1905) 22 T.L.R. 49 or in *Williams* v. *Curzon Syndicate Ltd.* (1919) 35 T.L.R. 475, but clearly follows on principle from the foregoing; see also *Daniel* v. *Hotel Pacific Pty. Ltd.* [1953] V.L.R. 447. It seems also that there would be a bailment for reward where the goods are delivered to the hotel reception desk not by the owner but by a third party for the owner to collect; see *Peat* v. *Roth Hotel Co.* (1934) 253 N.W. 546: ". . . the bailment was 'reciprocally beneficial to both parties' . . . The ring was accepted in the ordinary course of business by defendant in rendering a usual service for a guest."

34 *Webster* v. *Lane* (1925) 125 Misc. 868; 212 N.Y.S. 298, discussed at p. 206, ante.

35 *Woodworth* v. *Conroy* [1976] 1 All E.R. 107 (accountant has lien).

36 *Timaru Borough Council* v. *Boulton* [1924] N.Z.L.R. 365. Other examples might include the landlord of a block of flats who operates an no-charge service for storing tenants' trunks: *Andrews* v. *Home Flats Ltd.* [1945] 2 All E.R. 698; an employer who becomes the bailee of his servants' work-tools: *MacDonald* v. *Whittaker Textiles* (1976) 64 D.L.R. (3d) 317; a carrier who is left for a year in possession of goods he has carried for reward and whose notices warn customers that the goods may be sold after three months to defray expenses, including warehouse rental: *Cairns* v. *Robins* (1841) 8 M. & W. 258; 151 E.R. 1934; a carrier who stores goods prior to transporting them: *White* v. *Humphery* (1847) 11 Q.B. 43; a railway company which, having carried goods for reward, returns the empty containers for no extra charge: *Aldridge* v. *G.W. Ry. Co.* (1864) 15 C.B.N.S. 582 (cf. *Heugh* v. *L.N.W.R.* (1870) L.R. 5 Ex. 51, at 55-56); and the organisers of a dance who arrange for a cloakroom with attendant to be available for the benefit of dancers: *Wellington Racing Club* v. *Symons* [1923] 1 N.Z.L.R. 1.

Surprisingly, there are authorities which contradict this principle and appear to insist upon an immediate, tangible advantage on the part of the bailee. Thus, it has been held in Canada that a restaurant is merely a gratuitous bailee of customers' cars left for no extra fee on a "courtesy" parking-lot.[37] It is submitted that such an approach is manifestly wrong. If the proprietor performs an act, or offers some facility, as part of his customary operations and as a means of attracting prospective customers or accommodating existing ones, it can only be assumed that that service is performed, wholly or in part, for the furtherance of his business interests. In the same decision, Schultz J.A. registered a strong dissent[38] and cited with approval the American case of *Warren* v. *Geater*,[39] wherein it was remarked:

> A transaction is a "bailment for hire", although nothing is paid directly by bailor, where it is a necessary incident of business in which bailee makes a profit.

In the earlier Canadian decision in *Murphy* v. *Hart*,[40] Harris C.J. entertained no doubt that the deposit of a customer's coat in an alcove in a restaurant created a bailment for the mutual advantage of the parties, for:

> . . . while no price was paid directly or specifically to the defendant for the care of the plaintiff's overcoat, it was part of the accommodation for which the defendant received his recompense for his customers. It is obvious that the defendant derived some advantage in the way of increased trade by making his premises attractive and the providing of a place in which customers could leave their coats and hats while eating was a necessary incident to the business just as it is in the case of a barber shop or a bathing house.[41]

A further benefit may have existed in that the restaurant itself was left free of impedimenta, cluttering the aisles and tables and taking up necessary space; all factors which would tend against the efficiency and attractiveness of the establishment in question.

There can be no doubt that an English or Australian court would subscribe to the same approach.

A converse situation involves repairers and other operators of service industries who lend a chattel to a customer while his own is receiving attention. In *Sanderson* v. *Collins*,[42] Collins M.R. and Romer L.J. considered that such an arrangement was for the mutual advantage of the parties. Several Canadian cases take the opposite view and classify the client as a gratuitous borrower, with a correspondingly higher duty of

---

[37] *Martin* v. *Town 'n' Country Delicatessen Ltd.* (1963) 42 D.L.R. (2d) 449. See also *Grey Cabs Ltd.* v. *Neil* [1947] N.Z.L.R. (where Johnson J. thought that the bailment was for the mutual advantage of the parties but nevertheless treated the defendants as a gratuitous bailees); *Bullen* v. *Swan Electric Engraving Ltd.* (1906) 22 T.L.R. 275, at 277, where a similar approach was made by Walton J. to the storage of engraving plates by engravers with whose interests the custody coincided; *James Buchanan & Co. Ltd.* v. *Hay's Transport Services Ltd.* [1972] 2 Lloyd's Rep. 535, discussed at p. 211, ante; *Palmer* v. *Toronto Medical Arts Building Ltd.* (1960) 21 D.L.R. (2d) 181, at 189.
[38] (1963) 42 D.L.R. (2d) 449, at 458.
[39] (1943) 176 S.W. (2d) 242.
[40] (1919) 46 D.L.R. 36.
[41] Ibid., at 38.
[42] [1904] 1 K.B. 628, at 630, 633.

care,[43] but the better view is that the lender is a bailor for reward.[44] As a general rule, it is safe to assume that commercial concerns do not perform favours for nothing.

A bailee may even, on the foregoing principles, be deemed to be rewarded although there is no wider contract between him and the bailor. In *Makower, McBeath & Co. Pty. Ltd.* v. *Dalgety & Co. Ltd.*[45] the defendants were licensed wharfingers and ships' agents, who took possession of goods belonging to the plaintiff after delivery from the ship's side. The goods were put in a customs' cage, in circumstances which were found to keep them in the possession of the defendants, and were subsequently lost. The defendants were not directly remunerated for these services but were nevertheless held to owe the duties of a bailee for reward. As McArthur J. pointed out, the company became a licensed wharfinger in its own interest and for its own benefit as the agent of the shipowners. Although the absence of direct payment made the advantage hard to estimate in monetary terms, there could be no doubt that the company thought it was in its interests to act thus and for present purposes they could be considered to be the best judges of those interests.

This case may be contrasted with the Guyanan decision in *Karnani* v. *Booker's Shipping (Demerara) Ltd.*,[46] where Bollers C.J. was prepared to hold that shipowners became gratuitous bailees of cargo when it had been released from the ship's tackle and transported by them to the transit shed on the wharf. However, he conceded that the position might be affected by the provisions of s. 1 of the *Bills of Lading Act* 1855 (U.K.) whereby the consignee inherits the rights and obligations of the shipper under the bill of lading. In any event, it is submitted that where a ship-owner or other carrier offers a composite service of this kind the relevant reward should not be confined to particular stages in the performance of that service but should apply to the whole transaction.[47]

In *Helson* v. *McKenzies (Cuba St.) Ltd.*,[48] Hutchinson J. held that the proprietors of a shop, to whom a customer's handbag was handed by another customer who found it lying on a counter, were gratuitous bailees. On appeal, counsel for the plaintiff argued that the bailment was properly classifiable as one for reward, because:

---

[43] *McDonald* v. *Stirskey* (1879) 12 N.S.R. 520; *Riverdale Garage Ltd.* v. *Barrett Bros.* [1930] 4 D.L.R. 429; cf. *Bijou Motor Parlours Ltd.* v. *Keel* (1918) 39 D.L.R. 410.

[44] *Queens' Sales & Service Ltd.* v. *Smith* (1963) 48 M.P.R. 364; and see *Whitfield* v. *Cooper* (1972) 298 A. 2d 50, where a passenger in the borrowed car recovered against the repairer under strict liability; *Miller* v. *Hand Ford Sales Inc.* (1959) 340 P. 2d 181, where the repairer was characterised as a mere lender.

[45] [1921] V.L.R. 365. Cf. *Port Swettenham* v. *Wu* (1978) *The Times*, June 22.

[46] (1972) 18 W.I.R. 231, at 239-240.

[47] Quaere whether there will be a bailment for reward where the bailee's contract with the bailor has already been performed when the bailment occurs. A number of Canadian cases dealing with hotels storing departing guests' baggage approach the question on the assumption that the bailment is gratuitous; see, for instance *Palin* v. *Reid* (1884) 10 D.A.R. 63; *Sutherland* v. *Bell and Schiesel* (1911) 18 W.L.R. 521; *Brewer* v. *Calori* (1921) 29 B.C.R. 457. But it seems that the prospective advantage of the guests being encouraged to return to the hotel or other institution should constitute sufficient reward.

[48] [1950] N.Z.L.R. 878.

The service given by the respondent is directed towards maintaining the goodwill of the public and the respondent had an interest in acquiring and building up a reputation with the public for its care in looking after customers' lost articles.[49]

Finlay J. disagreed, holding not only that this was a gratuitous bailment but that the parties to it were the respondents and the customer who first found the bag.[50] The remarks on this point, which were obiter dicta, are marred by an anachronistic equation between bailment and contract and are, with respect, open to question. It may be thought that a finder who voluntarily takes goods into his possession will normally enjoy at least a prospective benefit in the chance that the true owner will fail to claim the goods. Bailments by finding could therefore be classed as bailments for reward, except perhaps in unusual cases where the chattel is unattractive and the finder acts from generous motives alone.

A peculiar area of difficulty has arisen from the practice of bankers to accept custody of clients' valuables without making a specific charge for so doing. Logically, this should attract no different principle from those situations in which other commercial undertakings, such as hotels and restaurants, perform a similar service. There is, however, a considerable body of authority (most of it 19th century) which assumes that the bank is a gratuitous bailee.[51] It seems unjustified to create an exception to the general principle in this instance and the modern propensity is to regard the bank as a bailee for reward.[52] Such an approach can scarcely be impeached, at least where the bailor already has an account or other business dealings with the bank. Even where the deposit is an isolated transaction, there may be grounds for concluding that the "publicity" value of such a transaction is benefit enough to constitute the bank a bailee for reward.

B. Bailments pursuant to contracts of sale

These may arise either before or after the sale itself. If a seller retains goods for the buyer after property has passed, he does not become a gratuitous bailee simply because no specific charge is exacted for storage. However, if the buyer fails to collect on the agreed delivery date or (where no such date is agreed) within a reasonable time, the bailment may then become gratuitous.[53] Section 20 of the *Sale of Goods Act* 1893,

---

[49] Ibid., at 897.

[50] Ibid., at 905-906; cf. Gresson J. at 914-918, who agreed that the sole bailment was between the finder and the respondents but seemed attracted by the view that this was a bailment for reward.

[51] *Mayor of the City of Fitzroy* v. *National Bank of Australasia Ltd.* (1890) 16 V.L.R. 342; *Brown* v. *National Bank of Australasia Ltd.* (1890) 16 V.L.R. 475; *Giblin* v. *McMullen* (1869) L.R. 2 P.C. 317; *Leese* v. *Martin* (1873) L.R. 17 Eq. 224, at 235. Cf. *Re United Service Co., Johnston's Claim* (1870) 6 Ch. App. 212.

[52] *Kahler* v. *Midland Bank Ltd.* [1948] 1 All E.R. 811, at 819-820 (Scott L.J.); Vaines, *Personal Property* (5th ed.), p. 94; Paton, p. 95; Paget, *Law of Banking* (8th ed.), p. 190 where, however, it is doubted whether there is a contractual obligation on the part of the banker to receive his clients' goods for custody. Cf. Perry, *Law and Practice Relating to Banking* (2nd ed.), pp. 26-27.

[53] Benjamin, *Sale* (8th ed.), pp. 197-198; see also *Ross* v. *Hannan* (1891) 19 S.C.R. 227; *Ferguson* v. *Eyer* (1919) 43 O.L.R. 190; cf. *Sharp* v. *Batt* (1930) 25 Tas. L.R. 33; *Demby Hamilton & Co. Ltd.* v. *Barden Ltd.* [1949] 1 All E.R. 435. In *Greaves* v. *Ashlin* (1813) 3 Camp. 426 it was held that where a buyer does not collect within a reasonable time the seller may charge him warehouse rental.

provides that (unless otherwise agreed) the risk in the goods passes to the buyer at the same time as the property therein. This rule may be displaced where delivery has been delayed through the fault of one party, whereupon the goods are at his risk as regards any loss which might not have occurred but for the fault: s. 20(1). However, nothing in the foregoing affects the duties of either buyer or seller as a bailee of the goods: s. 20(2). The net result seems to be that a seller of uncollected goods, where the actual or putative delivery date has passed, will be liable only for a failure to observe the standard of care of a gratuitous bailee.[54]

Different considerations arise in the case of a delivery on approval or a delivery on sale or return. Here, the bailment is for the mutual benefit of the parties. The potential buyer gets the benefit of inspecting the goods while the potential seller enjoys the opportunity of making a sale. A good example of this kind of bailment arose in the Canadian case of *Fairley & Stevens* (1966) *Ltd.* v. *Goldsworthy.*[55] The defendant visited the plaintiff's car lot and expressed interest in a 1967 Ford Fairlane 500. Having agreed on a price, he was allowed to take the car to show to his wife before finalising the sale; and it was clear that the contract was conditional on her approval. The defendant used the car for three days and drove it at high speeds in very bad conditions, with the result that it was severely damaged. Dubinsky J. thought that there may well have been evidence of a completed sale, since the defendant's wife had already seen and approved the car. However, on the pleadings he entertained no doubt that the bailment was one for the mutual advantage of the parties and that the bailee was liable for having failed to take reasonable care. He went on to remark[56] that even if contrary to this ruling, the bailment were gratuitous, it would have amounted to an unrewarded loan to the defendant and not to a gratuitous safe-keeping, and that even if the arrangement were one of depositum the defendant was clearly guilty of gross negligence. The case nevertheless illustrates that a prospective purchaser who takes goods on trial is not in the position of one who gratuitously and without personal advantage takes care of goods belonging to another.

C. Wrongful possession

In the West Australian case of *Mazullah Khan* v. *McNamara,*[57] a police constable arrested the plaintiff on a charge of assault and took into custody four camels that were in the plaintiff's possession. The charge was later altered to one of robbery of the camels and the plaintiff was acquitted, but the constable still refused to deliver them up pending instructions. Eventually three were returned, the fourth having died during detention. McMillan J. held on the facts that the constable never held the camels as

---

[54] Aliter where, contrary to the general presumption, property has passed in goods which have yet to be put in a deliverable state by the seller: *Wallace* v. *Safeway Caravan Pty. Ltd.* [1975] 3 Qd. Lawyer 224.

[55] (1973) 34 D.L.R. (3d) 554 (Supreme Court of Nova Scotia, Appellate Division); see also the very similar case of *Kitchen* v. *Goodspeed & Davison Ltd.* (1965) 53 D.L.R. (2d) 140, and Greig, *Sale of Goods*, pp. 218-219. There is also of course a bailment for reward where goods are deposited with a dealer for sale on commission; *Rutter* v. *Palmer* [1922] 2 K.B. 87.

[56] (1973) 34 D.L.R. (3d) 554, at 568.

[57] (1911) 13 W.A.L.R. 151.

gratuitous bailee of the plaintiff but took and retained custody of his own initiative in the belief that they might belong to a third person. He therefore awarded the plaintiff the value of the camel at the date of the seizure. The grounds of judgment appear to have been that a "bailee" who acquires possession by a wrongful act is liable for any damage or depreciation suffered by the chattel while it continues in his possession.[58] The court acknowledged that the position would have been different if the defendant, having originally taken possession by a wrongful act, had continued to hold the camels at the request of the plaintiff; in such a case he would have been a gratuitous bailee.[59]

This case may be contrasted with the Nova Scotian decision in *McCowan* v. *McCulloch*,[60] where one of the defendants boarded a train in order to assist a friend in unloading her luggage. Unfortunately he took the plaintiff's suitcase by mistake, a fact which he did not discover until he had driven several miles from the station. He then delivered it to the fireman on a boat which was going in the same direction as the train, with instructions to redeliver to the plaintiff. The suitcase disappeared and the defendant was held liable as a gratuitous bailee for failing to show reasonable care. From the facts as disclosed in the report, he may also have been guilty of conversion, although this point was apparently not pleaded.

It may be thought that the Australian case is preferable, for the wrongful possessor is arguably in an analogous position to the bailee who deviates from the terms of the bailment and should thus be liable for all ensuing loss, irrespective of negligence on his part. On the other hand, such an approach makes no distinction between the bailee whose original possession is innocent and the bailee who has deprived the original possessor by a deliberate and wrongful act. It would be harsh to impose the duties of a bailee upon someone who at the material time, did not know and had no reason to know that the goods in his possession belonged to someone else. The fairest solution seems to be as follows: that a person who knows his possession is wrongful should be responsible for all losses resulting from that possession, irrespective of subsequent fault; that a person who intends to take possession of another's goods but does not know the possession is wrongful should owe the duties of a bailee for reward, in that he must generally be assumed to have seized the goods for a purpose beneficial to himself;[61] that a person who intends to take possession, but under an innocent and reasonable mistake that the goods are his own or those of somebody who has authorised him to take possession, should not be liable as a bailee at all;[62] and that a person in the third category who later discovers the true ownership should be liable as a gratuitous bailee. Liability for conversion would, of course, exist independently of these considerations, for it does not depend upon an intention

---

[58] See ibid., at 155. There is no mention in the report of the plaintiff having proceeded in conversion or detinue and counsel's argument seem to approach the question solely by analogy with the rules of bailment: ibid., at 152.
[59] Ibid., at 154-155.
[60] [1926] 1 D.L.R. 312.
[61] Cf. *Canadian Imperial Bank of Commerce* v. *Doucette* (1968) 70 D.L.R. (2d) 657, mentioned at p. 285, post.
[62] Quaere what the position would be where the mistake was unreasonable; presumably, the defendant should be liable as a bailee for reward?

to convert; moreover, it can scarcely be said that someone who by his own act takes possession of goods should be considered an involuntary bailee.[63] In most cases of wrongful dispossession this remedy would be sufficient to protect the rights of the party dispossessed without recourse to the principles of bailment at all.

D. Miscellaneous cases

The reports contain many other examples of bailments which are beneficial to both parties without any monetary consideration changing hands. Thus there is a bailment for mutual advantage where one party, wishing to travel to a certain place, agrees that he will drive another's lorry there in return for free transportation;[64] where one tradesman lends another a tool for the furtherance of work in which the parties are jointly interested;[65] where a bank seizes by way of security the personal property of a defaulting debtor;[66] where a workman performs unpaid work upon a chattel in return for being allowed to use it as a demonstration model; where an employer requires his employees to leave their own tools on his premises overnight;[67] where the owner of a painting lends it to an art gallery for exhibition although he does not intend to sell it;[68] where the owners of a computer deliver it to an accountant in the expectation that a third party will buy it from them and lease it to him;[69] and where one party under an agreement for work and labour makes certain tools and, in consideration for being allowed to use them, agrees to make certain other articles for the benefit of the employer.[70] In *Heaton* v. *Richards*[71] however, the Supreme Court of New South Wales refused to discover any consideration or reward where the plaintiff promised to defray the defendant's expenses and to allow him to print his name on the title-page in return for the defendant's printing and binding a book compiled by the plaintiff. The court vigorously rejected the argument that the plaintiff's giving up of his possession in the manuscript was good consideration and held that the arrangement involved neither a

---

[63] But cf. p. 393 et seq., post.

[64] *Roufos* v. *Brewster and Brewster* [1971] 2 S.A.S.R. 219 impliedly supports this, although only Zelling J. was prepared to hold that the bailment to the defendant had not, at the material time, determined (see especially at 233-234). The defendant did not in this case drive the lorry personally but instructed a third party to do so and the opinion of the majority was that this party became the servant or agent of the owners for the duration of the journey.

[65] *Griffiths* v. *Arch Engineering Ltd.* [1968] 3 All E.R. 217, at 220; *Oliver* v. *Sadler & Co. Ltd.* [1929] A.C. 584 (in neither of which, however, does there appear to have been the transfer of possession necessary to a bailment); *Smith* v. *Stockdill* [1960] N.Z.L.R. 53; *Derbyshire Building Co. Pty. Ltd.* v. *Becker* (1962) 107 C.L.R. 633; *Southland Harbour Board* v. *Vella* [1974] 1 N.Z.L.R. 526.

[66] *Canadian Imperial Bank of Commerce Ltd.* v. *Doucette* (1968) 70 D.L.R. (2d) 657. See also *Chesworth* v. *Farrar* [1966] 2 All E.R. 107 (distraining landlord held to be a bailee for reward) and cf. *Mitchell* v. *Ealing L.B.C.* (1978) *The Times*, February 21st (landlord left in possession of squatter's goods after evicting squatter held liable as gratuitous bailee).

[67] *Johnson & Towers, Baltimore Inc.* v. *Babbington* (1972) 288 A. 2d 131. Cf. *MacDonald* v. *Whittaker Textiles (Marysville) Ltd.* (1976) 64 D.L.R. (3d) 317.

[68] *Vigo Agricultural Society* v. *Brumfield* 52 Am.R. 657, discussed by Beven, *Negligence* (2nd ed.), p. 920; sed quaere.

[69] *Lovely* v. *Burroughs Corporation* (1974) 527 P. 2d. 557.

[70] *Leggo* v. *Welland Vale Manufacturing Co. Ltd.* (1901) 2 O.L.R. 45.

[71] (1881) 2 L.R. (N.S.W.) 73.

detriment to him nor a benefit to the defendant. Older cases[72] were distinguished on the ground that they involved a request by the bailee and did not arise at the instigation of the bailor. Although this distinction is questionable (and the defendants may in any event have been in breach of their duty as gratuitous bailees), the decision seems to represent another example of a promise [73] which, while enforceable against the promisee, does not convert the ensuing bailment into one for the mutual advantage of the parties.

A peculiar situation arose in *Jenkins* v. *Smith*.[74] An employee of the plaintiff permitted the defendant to drive the plaintiff's tractor-trailer, while at the same time taking possession of the defendant's own vehicle and driving it himself. The plaintiff's vehicle was damaged and the defendant was held liable for the loss. Hart J. found that "the defendant wanted the plaintiff's driver to try out his new diesel-rig, just as much as the driver wanted to test it".[75] In his view both bailments were gratuitous and in the nature of commodatum, with the result that the defendant was liable for failing to show reasonable care. Although the decision may be justified on the grounds that the plaintiff himself derived no advantage from this arrangement, it may be thought that where, in ordinary circumstances, there is a "double bailment" of this kind, each aspect of the transaction should be judged in the light of the overall relationship and should be classified as for the mutual advantage of the parties.[76]

E. Conclusion

Any benefit or advantage, however prospective or conjectural, will suffice to make the intended recipient a bailor or bailee for reward, provided that it was with such advantage in mind that he entered into the bailment, or continued that relationship where it could otherwise have been determined. The courts are increasingly ready to read reward into the relationship and the circumstances in which a commercial undertaking will be considered a gratuitous bailee or bailor must now be supposed to be very rare.

---

[72] E.g. *Whitehead* v. *Greetham* (1825) 2 Bing. 464; *Bainbridge* v. *Firmstone* (1838) 8 A. & E. 743.
[73] I.e., the promise to reimburse.
[74] (1969) 6 D.L.R. (3d) 309.
[75] Ibid., at 318.
[76] *Bryce* v. *Hornby* (1938) 82 Sol. Jo. 216 impliedly supports this approach. The parties exchanged pieces of jewellery by way of loan and the defendant lost the plaintiff's piece while she was wearing it in her hat. Goddard J. observed that the case did not appear to fall within any of Holt C.J.'s categories in *Coggs* v. *Bernard* (1703) 2 Ld. Raym. 909; 98 E.R. 108, and found against the defendant for failing to prove that the loss did not result from her want of reasonable care.

CHAPTER 9

DEPOSITUM, OR GRATUITOUS SAFEKEEPING

I. INTRODUCTION

Modern authorities on the duties of an unrewarded custodian of goods are comparatively rare. In part this may be ascribed to the increasing readiness of the courts to characterise a bailment as one for the mutual benefit of the parties, even in the absence of direct payment or of any express stipulation for the bailee's benefit within the bargain itself. Again, the increased modern facilities for professional storage and safekeeping render it less likely that claims for loss or damage to chattels will have cause to be litigated against a purely gratuitous bailee. Even those recent cases which have chosen to regard the bailment in question as gratuitous may be questioned on this ground, although in the event this seems to have made no difference to the ultimate result.[1]

Nevertheless, the contract—if such it be—of depositum still represents a very common phenomenon. It may range from an agreement between neighbours, whereby one party promises to look after the other's canary while its owner is on holiday, to the long-term storage (by a seller or a warehouseman) of goods which the owner has failed to collect. Admittedly, the more commercial the transaction, the less likely it is to be classified as gratuitous. But the wide circle of relationships that may still fall within the definition of depositum make it especially unfortunate that so many of its qualities remain at the present time uncertain.

Definition

The three distinguishing characteristics of the modern relationship of depositum are: first, a voluntary assumption of the possession of goods; secondly, a duty imposed by law or by agreement upon the possessor to safeguard those goods and to redeliver them to the person entitled to them on demand; and thirdly a complete absence of remuneration or other benefit, direct or indirect, accruing to the depositee in return for the service he has undertaken.

As is usually the case, it is the peripheral or uncommon situation which renders this species of bailment so amorphous and elastic. The great preponderance of modern examples of depositum fall within a much narrower orbit than that outlined above. Usually the depositor will be the owner, the possession will be transferred by immediate and direct delivery, and the transaction will have arisen out of an agreement between these parties.

[1] *Houghland* v. *R. R. Low (Luxury Coaches) Ltd.* [1962] 1 Q.B. 694; *James Buchanan & Co. Ltd.* v. *Hay's Transport Services Ltd.* [1972] 2 Lloyd's Rep. 535; cf. *Seaspan International Ltd.* v. *The Kostis Prois* (1973) 33 D.L.R. (3d) 1, at 5.

But this may not necessarily be the case. The "bailor" may himself be a prior bailee and may have delivered the goods to the depositee under a gratuitous sub-bailment.[2] The depositary himself may be the owner, as where the lessor of a chattel gratuitously undertakes to store it, and to return it to the lessee, during the continuance of the contract of hire. There may be neither delivery or agreement, for possession of the goods may have been seized by a person who mistakenly thinks that he is their owner[3] or by a friend of the owner to protect them from some sudden emergency[4] or by a finder.[5] All these examples fall within the broad conception of the contract of deposit.

This chapter will deal only with the normal, consensual kinds of depositum. Unrequested assumptions of possession will be considered separately[6] since they appear to represent constructive rather than orthodox varities of bailment. For present purposes we are concerned with consensual undertakings of custody, such as the free storage of chattels among acquaintances or organisations or (a peculiarly important modern example) the duties of a seller of goods when the buyer has failed to collect them on the appointed date or (when no such date has been fixed) within a reasonable time.

Just as it is the exclusive presence of benefit or reward in the bailor that distinguishes depositum from the hire of custody, so it is the location of that benefit that distinguishes it from commodatum. The latter involves a loan of a chattel solely and exclusively for the benefit of the borrower; he is allowed (at least, personally) to use it and the lender gains nothing material in return. With depositum the advantage is entirely on the side of the depositor. If the depositary is allowed to use or enjoy the chattel, the gratuitous nature of his undertaking is lost.

Again, depositum covers only the gratuitous duty of safe-keeping. If other obligations are superadded, such as the unrewarded performance of work on the chattel while it is in the bailee's possession, the relationship ceases to be that of depositum and becomes instead one of *mandatum*.[7]

II. The Depositary's Standard of Care

According to Holt C.J., a depositary whose misconduct is neither fraudulent nor wilful is liable only for gross neglect of the chattel.[8] The same

---

[2] As in *James Buchanan & Co. Ltd.* v. *Hay's Transport Services Ltd.*, supra; cf. *E. A. Lee & Sons Pty. Ltd.* v. *Abood* (1968) 89 W.N. (N.S.W.) 430; *Thomas National Transport (Melbourne) Pty. Ltd.* v. *May & Baker (Australia) Pty. Ltd.* (1966) 115 C.L.R. 353, at 374-375; post, p. 793 (sub-bailments for reward).

[3] *McCowen v. McCulloch* [1926] 1 D.L.R. 312.

[4] Cf. *R.* v. *Leigh* (1800) 1 Leach. 411, n.9.

[5] Quaere, in fact, whether the finder should be regarded as a gratuitous bailee: see p. 873, post; *Kowal v. Ellis* (1977) 76 D.L.R. (3d) 546.

[6] Chapter 22, post.

[7] See further p. 329 et seq., post.

[8] *Coggs* v. *Bernard* (1703) 2 Ld. Raym. 909, at 913; 92 E.R. 107, at 110; see also Gould J. at 909, 107, *Moore* v. *Mourgue* (1776) 2 Cowp. 479; 98 E.R. 1197.

general rule is stated by Sir William Jones[9] and by Paine,[10] and clearly represents the prevalent opinion until at least the middle of the last century. Unfortunately, this approach raises difficulties on a number of levels.

First, there is the abstract problem of deciding what constitutes gross negligence on the part of a bailee. Obviously, one can imagine situations in which the lack of care is extraordinary or extreme: a writer on banking has recently provided the example of a banker who leaves securities overnight in the street,[11] and more than one judge has warned that:

> It is a mistake to suppose that things are not different because a line of strict demarcation cannot be drawn between them.[12]

But whether the majority of cases will indeed fall clearly into one of the separate categories of gross and ordinary negligence or not, it is evident that on many occasions a gratuitous custodian will be uncertain as to the degree of care expected of him. The difficulties of applying and, more especially, of defining the test of gross neglect argue strongly for its abandonment in favour of a more universal and coherent standard of liability, even though this may place a heavier burden on the bailee in question.

Secondly, the formulation of this test in any event produced a number of qualifying elements, which serve to reduce the distinction between gross and ordinary neglect still further. Thus, it is said that much will depend upon the character of the bailee as well as the nature of the bailment; so that what constitutes gross negligence on the part of a proficient and trustworthy person of good reputation will not necessarily serve to visit liability upon a person of lesser abilities.[13] Again, there is the occasional, rather elliptical, suggestion that a failure to observe the general duties normally attendant upon a bailee of the defendant's standing and character (for instance, a banker) will in itself be evidence of gross neglect.[14] Although the element of subjectivity in these statements is beneficial, it probably erodes still further the dichotomy professed by Holt C.J. and other older authorities.

Thirdly, there are clear signs over the past century that the courts are resiling from this ambivalent requirement and would now prefer to found the bailee's liability upon a simple failure to exercise reasonable care, having regard to all the circumstances of the case. Although progress has been made in this direction in both England and Canada, there is at

---

[9] *Bailments* (4th ed.), p. 31 et seq.

[10] *Bailments* (1901), pp. 11, et seq., cf. Story, ss. 61, et seq. (reasonable care).

[11] Perry, *Law and Practice Relating to Banking* (2nd ed.), p. 27.

[12] *Beal* v. *South Devon Ry. Co.* (1864) 3 H. & C. 337, at 341; 159 E.R. 560, at 562, per Crompton J.; *Giblin* v. *McMullen* (1868) L.R. 2 P.C. 317, at 337, per Lord Chelmsford; *Kirk* v. *Commissioner for Railways* (1876) 4 Q.S.C.R. 160, at 162-164 per Cockle C.J. and Lilley J.

[13] *Coggs* v. *Bernard* (1703) 2 Ld. Raym. 909, at 914-915; 92 E.R. 107, at 110-111 per Holt C.J.; *Shiells* v. *Blackburne* (1789) 1 Hy. Bl. 158; 126 E.R. 94; *Wilson* v. *Brett* (1843) 11 M. & W. 113; 152 E.R. 737; cf. *Walker* v. *Watson* [1974] 2 N.Z.L.R. 175, where the bailment was by way of loan to two drunken girls and the defences of contributory negligence and volenti non fit injuria were invoked.

[14] *Giblin* v. *McMullen* (1868) L.R. 2 P.C. 317, at 339 per Lord Chelmsford; *Brown* v. *National Bank of Australasia Ltd.* (1890) 16 V.L.R. 475.

present no Australian authority directly in point.[15] To the extent that an Australian court would be likely to participate in this move towards conformity, any discussion of the meaning of gross negligence must assume a rather archaic flavour. But to the extent that the matter is still technically undecided, such a discussion is justifiable on the grounds of regrettable necessity.

A. The meaning of gross negligence

This may be analysed in two ways: first, by looking at such generalised statements as the courts have made upon the subject, and secondly, by examining particular instances in which the standard of gross neglect has been applied. The latter probably provides a more articulate picture but its usefulness is necessarily limited by the individuality of the situations in question, and by the realisation that each case must rest ultimately on its own peculiar facts.

Modern analyses of the concept of gross negligence are rare. One of the few judges to venture into this area (and he did so with marked reluctance) was Henn Collins J., who observed obiter in *Martin* v. *London County Council*[16] that gross negligence may loosely be described as "some sort of carelessness which appears to the plain man of common sense as being gross."[17]

This *dictum* seems, however, to adhere more to the popular meaning of gross negligence than to its contemporary judicial interpretation. There has, in fact, been a noticeable softening in the judicial translation of this concept since the time of *Coggs* v. *Bernard*. In *Mayor of the City of Fitzroy* v. *National Bank of Australasia Ltd.*[18] counsel for the defendant bank still thought it worthwhile to argue that gross negligence requires "something equivalent, or almost equivalent, to fraud", and was able to cite authority (mostly American)[19] for this proposition. But in almost the preceding breath he had formulated the test as being whether the bank had taken "the ordinary degree of care they would take of their own goods"; and there can be little doubt that the eventual finding against his client was founded upon the latter, less clement ground of liability.

> The learned judge told the jury that the defendants . . . were gratuitous bailees and, as such 'bailees, were only liable for gross neglect. He directed them that it was the duty of the bank to employ reasonable competent officers, and provide a proper' place reasonably safe for keeping these documents, and that the bank were also bound to

---

[15] Post, p. 302 et seq.

[16] [1947] K.B. 628, at 631.

[17] Cf. *Beauchamp* v. *Powley* (1831) 1 M. & Rob. 38, at 40; 174 E.R. 14 per Lord Tenterden C.J.: "great, and somewhat extraordinary, negligence"; *Doorman* v. *Jenkins* (1834) 2 A. & E. 256, at 261-262; 111 E.R. 99, at 102, per Taunton J.: "nothing more than a great and aggravated degree of negligence, as distinguished from negligence of a lower degree"; *Cashill* v. *Wright* (1856) 6 E. & B. 891, at 899; 119 E.R. 1096, at 1099 per Erle J.: "It is such a degree of negligence as excludes the loosest degree of care, and is said to amount to dolus."

[18] (1890) 16 V.L.R. 342, at 360-361.

[19] *Foster* v. *Essex Bank* (1821) 17 Mass. Rep. 479; *Scott* v. *National Bank of Chester Valley* (1874) 72 Penn. 472; *First National Bank of Lyons* v. *Ocean National Bank* (1875) 60 N.Y. Rep. 786; *Smith* v. *First Nationl Bank of Westfield* 99 Mass. 605.

exercise proper supervision over the officers and to make reasonable rules for their guidance in keeping the documents; and he left it to the jury to say whether the defendants had discharged their duty in this respect. We think that this direction was substantially correct . . . The jury found that the defendants were guilty of negligence . . . This finding . . . was, in our opinion, a proper finding . . .[20]

In *Giblin* v. *McMullen*,[21] Lord Chelmsford considered that, despite what had been said in *Wilson* v. *Brett*[22] and other cases dealing with this subject, there was a difference between the varying degrees of negligence, and that the term gross negligence might usefully be retained as descriptive of that difference.[23] Nevertheless, he concided that for all practical purposes the failure to exercise reasonable care, skill and diligence will amount to gross neglect, and he suggested that in the present case a "want of that ordinary diligence which men of common prudence generally exercise about their own affairs"[24] would, if it had existed, have justified a finding of gross negligence against the defendants.

In *Kirk* v. *Commissioner for Railways*[25] the question of gross negligence arose not upon a gratuitous bailment but in the course of construing an exclusion clause which exonerated the defendants for all except "gross and wilful default". Lutwyche J. observed that no case had been cited to show that there was no difference between the various degrees of negligence, and said in conclusion that "the distinction has been drawn and acted upon for a long series of years, and it is well, unless there be some overruling authority not to depart from ancient landmarks."[26] Lilley J. (the trial judge) said on appeal:

> I put the case fully to the Jury—first, was there negligence? and I told them that their answer to that would depend upon the degree of duty which the law and the contract . . . imposed upon the Defendant; and that duty, I told them, was that the Defendant under this contract, having engaged for the exercise of the ordinary care of a competent person, . . . should exercise that ordinary care; and that, if he failed to exercise that, I told the Jury, that I thought it would not be a violent presumption if they found that there was gross negligence.[27]

A similar equation was vouchsafed by Cockle C.J. who considers that "when words importing degrees of negligence are used, they must be taken to be used with an implied reference to the degree of care which ought to be shown."[28] From these and other authorities it may be inferred that, even where there has been judicial acceptance of the terminology of gross negligence, this has generally been accompanied in recent years by an equation of that concept with ordinary and reasonable notions of care. To some extent, this impression is reinforced by an analysis of those

---

20 (1890) 16 V.L.R. 342, at 367 (Higinbotham C.J.).
21 (1868) L.R. 2 P.C. 317.
22 (1843) 11 M. & W. 113; 152 E.R. 737.
23 (1868) L.R. 2 P.C. 317, at 336-337; "The epithet 'gross' is certainly not without its significance."
24 Ibid., at 337-338.
25 (1876) 4 Qd. S.C.R. 160.
26 Ibid., at 163.
27 Ibid., at 164.
28 Ibid., at 162.

situations in which an explicit standard of gross negligence has been held to have been entablished. Thus in *Doorman* v. *Jenkins*,[29] it was held that **the question was properly left to the jury** where a coffeehouse keeper left a sum of money deposited with him by the plaintiff, together with a larger sum of his own, in a cash-box in his tap-room, which room was open to the public on the day in question. Taunton J., after remarking that the question in the present case was purely one for the jury, and that the presence of some of the defendant's own money in the cash-box was "perfectly immaterial", continued:

> If there was no negligence, if the box was locked up and put in a safe place, and proper care taken of it, there were circumstances which the defendant had the best means of knowing and, knowing them, he might have exonerated himself. In the absence, therefore, of evidence to that effect, I think that there was a prima facie case of gross negligence, which required an answer on the defendant's part. The phrase "gross negligence" means nothing more than a great and aggravated degree of negligence, as distinguished from negligence of a lower degree.[30]

Similarly, in *Mytton* v. *Cock*,[31] it was held that there was sufficient evidence upon which a jury might properly reach a verdict of gross negligence where the defendant kept the plaintiff's cartoon in a room next to a stable, one wall of which was damp and caused the painting to peel; and in *Mayor of the City of Fitzroy* v. *National Bank of Australasia Ltd.*[32] it was again held that the question was properly left to the jury, because:

> The defendants kept the debentures in question for a long time without inspection, in a less secure place than that which they, with the special facilities they possessed, thought a reasonable and proper and secure place for keeping property of their own and of their customers of like description.[33]

Although each of these cases involved a serious lapse on the part of the bailee, it may be doubted whether the carelessness shown was really extravagant or gross in the popular acceptation of that term. Even in *Mayor of the City of Fitzroy* v. *National Bank of Australasia Ltd.*,[34] where the bank clearly fell far below their own standards of safe-keeping, there were mitigating features: the stolen property seems to have been kept in some kind of safe and was removed from its resting-place by a theftuous employee who had worked for the bank for several years and whose honesty they had no reasonable cause to suspect. Careless though the bank undoubtedly were, it is questionable whether their neglect was flagrant or glaring:[35] a fortiori whether it was equivalent to recklessness or fraud.

---

[29] (1834) 2 A. & E. 256; 111 E.R. 99; for a similar Canadian case, see *Parent* v. *Plante* (1912) 12 R.L. 349.

[30] (1834) 2 A. & E. 256, at 261-262; 111 E.R. 99, at 102.

[31] (1738) 2 Stra. 1099; 93 E.R. 1057.

[32] (1890) 16 V.L.R. 342.

[33] Ibid., at 367.

[34] Supra.

[35] These words are given by the *Concise Oxford Dictionary* (5th ed.), p. 543, as synonyms for gross.

Thus it may be thought that in many of those cases where a court has specifically applied the test of gross negligence and found it satisfied, a less vituperatively-phrased standard of liability would have yielded the same result. While nominally requiring a greater degree of default, decisions like *Doorman* v. *Jenkins*[36] seem in the final analysis to have depended upon a simple failure to show ordinary and proper care; at least, they can be read consistently with such a criterion.

On the other hand, there are several cases in which a coherent distinction appears to have been drawn between the two varieties of neglect and it has been found that the defendant's conduct, while negligent, was not grossly so. One such decision was *Shiells* v. *Blackburne*[37] (technically an example of mandatum rather than depositum) where it was held that the erroneous entry by the defendant of the plaintiff's case of leather at a custom-house, in circumstances which resulted in the plaintiff's parcel being seized, was not necessarily an act of gross negligence; and despite a finding to that effect by the jury, a new trial was ordered. The court remarked that if the defendant had been a person whose occupation customarily involved dealing with goods through the customs, such an error would have constituted gross neglect. There is, accordingly, early recognition of the fact that such neglect must be assessed in the light of the defendant's special skills and aptitude, and that a failure to exercise the degree of competence or circumspection normally expected of a person of the defendant's character may be regarded as gross negligence in him.

Other cases drawing a factual distinction between gross and ordinary negligence are *Sharp* v. *Batt*,[38] where it was held that a failure by the seller of uncollected apples to wrap them as protection against "black spot" was negligent but did not amount to gross neglect; *Kirk* v. *Commissioner for Railways*,[39] where the jury found that the discharge of sparks from the funnel of a steam-engine, which caused the straw in a wagon to catch fire and the plaintiff's cattle to be burnt, was likewise the product of negligence but not of "gross or wilful neglect"; and *O'Dea* v. *O'Hara*[40] where it was remarked obiter that an innkeeper in whose yard bicycles had been left might have been liable on this basis as a gratuitous bailee. Likewise, in *Doorman* v. *Jenkins*,[41] Patterson J. was careful to point out that whether the defendant had taken reasonable care, although a useful preliminary question in establishing gross negligence, is by no means decisive because the two issues are separate and distinguishable.

Nevertheless, the fact remains that in many of the cases where the courts have upheld the varying gradations of negligence, there has been a tendency to assimilate the depositary's degree of responsibility into an ordinary and reasonable standard of care, particularly in the case of

---

[36] (1834) 2 A. & E. 256; 111 E.R. 99.
[37] (1789) 1 Hy. Bl. 158; 126 E.R. 94; and see *Lenkeit* v. *Ebert* [1947] St. R. Qd. 126; post, p. 333.
[38] (1930) 25 Tas. L.R. 33. See also *The Oriental Bank Corporation* v. *The Queen* (1876) 6 S.C.R. (N.S.W.) 122, at 125.
[39] (1876) 4 Qd. S.C.R. 160.
[40] (1895) *South Australian Advertiser* 17th May.
[41] (1834) 2 A. & E. 256, at 264; 111 E.R. 99, at 102.

"professional" bailees who on a single occasion, are found to be acting gratuitously. Often the equation will be explicit, as in *Brown* v. *National Bank of Australasia Ltd.*,[42] where Higinbotham C.J. held that the defendants should escape because they had demonstrated "the exercise by them of such a moderate amount of care as a reasonable prudent owner would give to his own property."[43] Moreover, this equation coincides, and has for many years run concurrently, with the increasing propensity to abandon the concept of gross negligence altogether and to found the depositee's liability solely upon a failure to take reasonable care.

B. The standard of the reasonable and prudent man

For over a century, gross negligence has been under attack as a notion which is variously meaningless, tautologous and misleading. One of the most pertinent assaults on its identity occurred in *Grill* v. *General Iron Screw Collier Co.*,[44] where Willes J. said as follows:

> Confusion has arisen from regarding negligence as a positive instead of a negative word. It is really the absence of such care as it was the duty of the defendant to use. A bailee is only found to use the ordinary care of a man, and so the absence of it is called gross negligence. A person who undertakes to do some work for reward to an article must exercise the care of a skilled workman, and the absence of such care in him is negligence. Gross, therefore, is a word of description and not of definition. . . .[45]

Elsewhere, it has been remarked that gross negligence is nothing more than negligence with the addition of a vituperative epithet;[46] a concept that should be excluded as far as possible from the Civil Law of obligations[47] and "actually surplusage".[48]

Even before these conscious abjurations of the idea of degrees of fault, English courts were beginning to frame the depositee's liability in simple terms of reasonable care. As early as 1817 Lord Ellenborough remarked that a failure to show a "proper degree of care" or the commission of "such negligence as would make him liable" would entitle the depositary to recover from a third party who had carelessly damaged the bailed property;[49] and in the previous year he had clearly and squarely based

---

[42] (1890) 16 V.L.R. 475.
[43] Ibid., at 482-483; note, however that the learned judge equated a failure to attain this standard with gross negligence and insisted that proof of such negligence would be necessary.
[44] (1866) L.R. 1 C.P. 600.
[45] Ibid., at p. 612.
[46] *Wilson* v. *Brett* (1843) 11 M. & W. 113, at 115-116; 152 E.R. 737, at 739, per Rolfe, B.; *Schermer* v. *Neurath* (1880) 54 Md. 491; *Jenkins* v. *Motlow* (1853) 1 Sneed (Tenn) 248; see also *Austin* v. *Manchester, Sheffield and Lincolnshire Ry. Co.* (1850) 10 C.B. 454; *Cashill* v. *Wright* (1856) 6 E. & B. 891; 119 E.R. 1096, at 899, 1099. *Beal* v. *South Devon Ry. Co.* (1864) 3 H. & C. 337; 159 E.R. 560; *Powell* v. *Graves & Co.* (1886) 2 T.L.R. 663; *Bryce* v. *Hornby* (1938) 82 Sol. Jo. 216; *Houghland* v. *R.R. Low (Luxury Coaches) Ltd.* [1962] 1 Q.B. 694; post, p. 298.
[47] *Pentecost* v. *London District Auditor* [1951] 2 K.B. 759, at 763-767, cited with approval by Dubinsky J., in *Fairley & Stevens (1966) Ltd.* v. *Goldsworthy* (1973) 34 D.L.R. (3d) 554, at 565, and in *Lawton* v. *Dartmouth Moving & Storage Ltd.* (1976) 64 D.L.R. (3d) 326, at 332-333.
[48] (1935-1936) 24 Kentucky Law Journal 334 (J. A. Evans).
[49] *Rooth* v. *Wilson* (1817) 1 B. & Ald. 59; 106 E.R. 22; cf. *Sullivan* v. *Kelleher* (1896) 30 I.L.T. Jo. 205.

the liability of a gratuitous carrier on the lack of reasonable and ordinary care.[50] In 1846 (12 years after *Doorman* v. *Jenkins*),[51] Tindal C.J. and both Erle and Cresswell JJ. gave specific recognition to the fact that the gratuitous custodian's responsibilities are lighter than those of a bailee for reward,[52] but only Erle J. sought to elucidate the difference and he did so in terms which apparently subordinate the importance of reward to the character and capacity of the bailee:

> The degree of attention to the safety of the thing with which the bailee is entrusted, is regulated by 'a reference to the character he fills.[53]

In 1864, however, there was unequivocal endorsement of the standard of reasonable care. In *Ronnenburg* v. *Falkland Islands Co.*,[54] the defendants' agent offered to allow the plaintiffs to use a ship belonging to the defendants as a place in which they might store their gunpowder. After the powder had been taken on board, the defendants decided that they needed the ship for another purpose and so transferred the powder to a half-decked boat called the Lily. The Lily was unsuitable for the purpose and was sunk at anchor by a storm. Williams J. held for the plaintiffs on alternative grounds: either that the transfer to the Lily was a breach of the bailment and thus constituted a trespass to the plaintiff's goods; or that the defendants continued to owe a duy of reasonable care as bailees after the trans-shipment to the Lily, which obligation they had clearly, in the present case, failed to discharge.[55] Byles J., although he had reservations as to whether the original storage created a bailment to the defendants or a loan of the ship to the plaintiffs, concurred in holding that a bailment of the powder arose, at the latest, when the powder was transferred to the boat; that this engendered a duty to take reasonable care of the goods; and that in the circumstances such care had not been taken.[56]

The turning-point seems to have occurred in the decades immediately before and after the turn of the century. It was during these years that the standard of the reasonably prudent man in relation to his own property first received widespread approval.

Troke v. *Felton*[57] is a good example of the genre. The defendant was Honorary Treasurer of the North Camberwell Radical Club. He received a sum of £68 by way of subscriptions and takings and, in accordance with his custom over the preceding four years, kept it in a cupboard in his bedroom before taking it to the bank. The money was stolen and the defendant argued that since he was not guilty of gross negligence he should not be answerable for the loss. Mathew J. seems, however, to have exonerated him on the ground that his conduct was that of the reasonable and prudent man. He remarked that the defendant was honest and of

---

[50] *Nelson* v. *Macintosh* (1816) 1 Stark. 237; 171 E.R. 458.
[51] (1834) 2 A. & E. 256; 111 E.R. 99; ante, p. 292.
[52] *Ross* v. *Hill* (1846) 2 C.B. 877; 135 E.R. 1190.
[53] Ibid., at 893, 1197.
[54] (1864) 17 C.B.N.S. 1; 144 E.R. 1; but cf. *Job* v. *Job* (1877) 6 Ch. D., 562; *Jobson* v. *Palmer* [1893] 1 Ch. 71 (trustees); *Moffatt* v. *Bateman* (1869) L.R. 3 P.C. 115 (gratuitous carriage of persons).
[55] (1864) 17 C.B.N.S. 1, at 6; 144 E.R. 1, at 3.
[56] Ibid., at 3, 7.
[57] (1897) 13 T.L.R. 252.

integrity and that the plaintiffs must have anticipated that he would keep the money in his house for twenty-four hours.

In *Turner* v. *Merrylees*[58] the same test was applied, this time to the defendant's disadvantage. The plaintiff's phaeton had been left (apparently by agreement) in the stables of a castle which he had rented to the defendant. The defendant moved it to an outhouse where it suffered badly from damp. Collins and Wright JJ. upheld the finding of the County Court in favour of the plaintiff because there was "abundant evidence" that the damage was due to a want of reasonable care; Wright J. expressing the view that the result might have been otherwise if the defendant had not moved the carriage but had merely neglected to inspect it.

Phipps v. *New Claridge's Hotel Ltd.*[59] was probably not a case of gratuitous bailment at all. The plaintiff had bought three dogs and was allowed by the assistant-manager of the hotel where he was staying to leave them in a locked room in the basement, the keys being kept by the defendants. Later that evening, the plaintiff returned to find that one of the dogs (called Tibby) had disappeared. The defendants were held liable because they failed to show that they had taken reasonable care. No mention was made, in Bray J.'s short judgment, of this being a gratuitous bailment and the defendants do not appear to have argued (as did the defendants in *Troke* v. *Felton* and *Turner* v. *Merrylees*) that they were liable only for gross neglect.

A similar anomaly surrounds *Bullen* v. *Swan Electric Engraving Co. Ltd.*[60] Here again there were grounds for concluding that the storage of certain engraving-plates by the defendants was an arrangement for the mutual benefit of the parties because, as Walton J. pointed out, if the plaintiffs had wanted any further engravings to be printed, the fact that the plates were in the defendant's possession would have made it more likely that they would be given the work.[61] Nevertheless, the case was approached on the basis that it was one of gratuitous safe-keeping and the defendants argued that they should be liable only for gross negligence, which they defined as "something analogous to wilful default".[62] However, they succeeded on the broader ground that they had proved that they had taken "as much care as a prudent man would use in keeping his own property"[63] and were therefore relieved of the need to establish how exactly the loss occurred. This decision was upheld in the Court of Appeal,[64] Sir Gorell Barnes agreeing that a gratuitous bailee must show that the loss has occurred through no want of reasonable care on his part: "that is to say as much care as a prudent man would use in keeping his own property."[65] Exactly the same classification was applied by Scrutton J. in *Wiehe* v. *Dennis Bros. Ltd.*,[66] despite his earlier reflection that the bailment of a Shetland Pony to the defendants was just as much in their interests as in

[58] (1892) 8 T.L.R. 695.
[59] (1905) 22 T.L.R. 49.
[60] (1906) 22 T.L.R. 275.
[61] Ibid., at 277.
[62] Ibid., at 276.
[63] Ibid., at 277.
[64] (1907) 23 T.L.R. 258.
[65] Ibid., at 259.
[66] (1913) 29 T.L.R. 250.

those of the plaintiff. The defendants had contracted to supply the pony, together with harness and cart, to the plaintiff for delivery to Princess Juliana of the Netherlands. Until the cart was completed, they were permitted to retain possession of the pony and to use it for raising funds for the Dumb Friends League. At a ball in aid of this charity the pony was injured in mysterious circumstances and the defendants contended that as gratuitous bailees they had taken "all reasonable care". In the view of Scrutton J. they had failed to establish such degree of care and were accordingly liable for the loss.

In theory, it might still have been possible at this time to argue that a difference existed between gross and ordinary negligence, and that most of the cases denying this difference could either be explained on other grounds or had involved defendants who had conceded the point without argument.[67] But in recent years the pendulum has swung convincingly in favour of a universal test of reasonable care. As an American judge remarked in 1949:

> **While it is 'generally held** that a gratuitous bailee is liable only for gross negligence, so far as the failure to exercise reasonable care is concerned, very few courts have attempted a definition of that term— Primarily, 'gross negligence connotes the failure to exercise a slight degree of care. But in the well considered case of *McLaughlin* v. *Sears, Roebuck & Co.,*[68] which involved a gratuitous bailment of certain automobile tires on the part of a garage operator, the expression 'gross negligence' was held to denote the failure to exercise reasonable care, which conclusion we think is supported by the current authority 'and weight of reason.[69]

Later English authority is almost unanimously behind this equation. Thus, in *Blount* v. *War Office,*[70] the War Office were held liable for failing to show towards the plaintiff's goods the care of a reasonable man quam suis rebus; and in *James Buchanan & Co. Ltd.* v. *Hay's Transport Services Ltd.*[71] precisely the same test was applied to the relationship between a gratuitous sub-bailee and an owner:

> I am quite satisfied that this sub-bailment was a gratuitous one, but I take the view that the standard of care is the 'same. It is that which a

---

[67] Thus, in *Mitchell* v. *Davis* (1920) 37 T.L.R. 68, Swift J. stated that a gratuitous depositary was bound only to show the absence of gross neglect. cf. *Newman* v. *Bourne & Hollingsworth Ltd.* (1915) 31 T.L.R. 209 where Atkin and Ridley JJ. held that gross negligence was no more than a failure to exercise such care as a reasonable and prudent man would show in all the circumstances of the case. Note, however, that this was a case of finding, in relation to which there are powerful grounds for characterising the finder as a bailee for reward: p. 873 post.

[68] 188 S.C. 358; 199 S.E. 413.

[69] *Wilson* v. *Etheredge* (1949) 214 S.C. 396; 52 S.E. 2d. 812; see also *Kubli* v. *First National Bank of Pleasantville* (1925) 199 Iowa 1944; 200 N.W. 434; *Maddocks* v. *Riggs* (1920) 106 Kan. 808; 190 Pac. 12; p. 330, post.

[70] [1953] 1 W.L.R. 736; 1 All E.R. 1071; the same standard is endorsed by *Bryce* v. *Hornby* (1938) 82 Sol. Jo. 216, but this case probably involved a bailment for the mutual advantage of the parties (see ante, p. 286). See further *Demby Hamilton & Co. Ltd.* v. *Barden* [1949] 1 All E.R. 435, at 438.

[71] [1972] 2 Lloyd's Rep. 535. The same rule was stated in *Mitchell* v. *Ealing L.B.C.* (1978) *The Times* February 21st.

reasonable man would take of his own goods in similar circumstances.[72]

But perhaps the most commonly-cited authority for this view is the decision of the Court of Appeal in *Houghland* v. *R. R. Low* (*Luxury Coaches*) *Ltd.*[73] where the plaintiff was suing for the loss of her suitcase from one of the defendants' motor-coaches. Counsel for the defendants, in a somewhat nostalgic argument, claimed that because the plaintiff had not affirmatively proved gross negligence she should fail. Apart from its adherence to the theory of degrees of negligence, this argument involved the assumption that on an action for breach of *depositum* the burden of proving fault rests with the bailor; a contention which, in England at least, certainly does not represent the law. Dealing with the question of gross negligence, Ormerod L.J. observed:

> I am bound to·say that I am not sure what is meant by the term "gross negligence" which has been in use for a long time in cases of this kind—because it appears to me that the·standard of care required in a case of bailment, or any other type of case, is the standard demanded by the·circumstances of that particular case. It seems to me that to try and put a bailment, for instance, into a watertight compartment—such as gratuitous bailment on the one hand,·and bailment for reward on the other—is to overlook the fact that there might well be an infinite variety of cases, which might come into one or the other category. The question that we have to·consider in a case of this kind, if it is necessary to consider negligence,·is whether in the circumstances of this particular case a sufficient standard of care·has been observed by the defendants or their servants.[74]

At first sight, this would appear to dispose of the matter for all time. But *Houghland* v. *R. R. Low* (*Luxury Coaches*) *Ltd.* is not so strong an authority as it would initially appear. The Court of Appeal were themselves uncertain whether the bailment of the suitcase was properly classified as gratuitous and it seems remarkable that the County Court judge should have so held. More important, however, is the fact that the defendants were unable to adduce any explanation whatever for the loss of the suitcase, so that on either standard of responsibility they would have failed.[75] It follows that the above statement is in any event only obiter dictum.

Nor has it been universally accepted, even in England, that a gratuitous bailee enjoys no relaxation of the care expected of an ordinary bailee simply by virtue of his lack of reward. Certain dicta in *Morris* v. *C. W. Martin & Sons Ltd.*[76] imply that regardless of other relevant circumstances, such as the character of the bailee and the nature and value of the chattel, the absence of remuneration can produce substantive differences between

---

[72] Ibid., at 543; and see *Hedley Byrne & Co. Ltd.* v. *Heller & Partners Ltd.* [1964] A.C. 465, at 526, per Lord Devlin: "A promise given without consideration to perform a service cannot be enforced as a contract by the promisee; but if the service is in fact performed and done negligently, the promisee can recover in an action in tort. This is the foundation of the liability of a gratuitous bailee."

[73] [1962] 1 Q.B. 694.

[74] Ibid., at 697-698.

[75] (1963) 79 L.Q.R. 19; Vaines, *Personal Property* (5th ed.), 94.

[76] [1966] 1 Q.B. 716, at pp. 725, 737.

the duties of a depositee and those of a custodian for reward. Thus, it is suggested that the depositee is under no duty to protect the goods from theft or to answer for the conversions of his servants, unless he has been careless in employing those servants in the first place. Whether these statements are accurate is open to debate, but they do at least illustrate the anxiety of some judges to place limits on the responsibility of a gratuitous custodian which are not present in the case of a bailee for reward. Indeed, Lord Denning M.R. has gone so far as to state that the depositary is obliged only to keep the goods as his own;[77] a standard which, as will be seen, enjoyed a short vogue in earlier law but is rarely mentioned in modern authority. To some extent, the unspecific dicta of the Court of Appeal in *Morris* v. *C. W. Martin & Sons Ltd.* detract from the more vehement utterances delivered in the same court three years earlier.

Contemporary English writers exhibit a similar reluctance to apply exactly the same test of liability to the gratuitous as to the rewarded bailee. Both Chitty[78] and (to a lesser extent) Halsbury[79] adopt the criterion of reasonable care while stressing that the depositary's obligations may be lighter than those of his professional counterpart. However, neither of them suggests any concrete, general distinction. The only difference actually advanced at all seems to be that a depositary is bound only to use such abilities and facilities as he has, whereas the bailee for reward is answerable whenever the nature of his undertaking suggest a higher quality of service than he is really equipped to provide.[80] A neighbour who agrees to look after another's tiara, and does her best to keep it safe, cannot be expected to instal burglar-alarms or night-watchmen, however valuable the goods may be; but a bank may well be liable for such a failure, and generally it will make no difference whether they were being paid for the service or not.[81]

The requirement that a depositary should take such care of the bailed chattel as a reasonable man would exercise in similar circumstances must probably now be regarded as established in English law, although almost every recent decision favouring this standard touches upon the question only by way of dictum and at least one decision appears to point the other way. Assuming however, that this unsatisfactory array of authority is predominant, a number of secondary observations ought to be made.

First, there is no significant difference between the care a reasonable and prudent man normally bestows on his own goods and that which he normally bestows on goods belonging to another. The decision in *Houghland* v. *R. R. Low (Luxury Coaches) Ltd.*[82] tends to support the latter criterion, thus apparently removing the last vestigial difference between the depositary's duty and that of a bailee for reward. But statements such as "the care the circumstances demand" must not be construed too severely. The absence of reward may not be especially significant in itself, but it will often mark the difference between a bailee who accepts goods

---

[77] Ibid., at 725.
[78] *Contracts* (23rd ed.), Vol. II, p. 86.
[79] (4th ed.), Vol. II, para. 1515.
[80] Paton, p. 109.
[81] Cf. *Lewis* v. *McMullen* (1866) 4 W.W. & a'B. 1, at 8.
[82] [1962] 1 Q.B. 694. Cf. *Port Swettenham* v. *Wu* (1978) *The Times*, June 22.

for custody in the ordinary cause of business (and whose experience and expertise should therefore be materially greater) and one who does not normally (or at least professionally) conduct operations of this kind. Even where the depositary is a professional custodian, there may be strong reasons for exacting a lesser standard of vigilance when he is acting without reward. His normal facilities may be fully engaged and he could hardly be expected to put aside paying customers' goods for the benefit of a person to whom he is doing a favour. Again, it would seem unfair that he should be coerced into performing gratuitously what he would normally do only for reward. If, for instance, a buyer of goods fails to collect them on the delivery-date, or (where no such date is fixed) after a reasonable time, the seller may become a gratuitous bailee.[83] To hold that there is no effective difference between the responsibilities he owed prior to that time and those he owes afterwards seems to entitle buyers to extract indefinite periods of free warehousing without any reduction in the standard of care they can demand of the reluctant bailee. Perhaps the courts should be readier to infer, in cases like this, that the bailment is not merely gratuitous but has also become involuntary.[84]

Leaving aside the problem of the gratuitous professional bailee, who may perhaps be letting himself in for more than he bargained for, it seems that the universal formula of "such care as is demanded by the circumstances of the case" can generally be manipulated to produce the just result. As to what these circumstances are, a useful statement comes from the American decision in *McLaughlin* v. *Sears, Roebuck & Co.*:[85]

> . . . what is reasonable care must materially depend upon the nature, value and quality of the thing bailed, its liability to loss and injury, the circumstances under which it is deposited, and sometimes upon the character and confidence and particular dealings of the parties.

Generally, then, it will not be sufficient for a defendant to show that he took the same amount of care of the plaintiff's goods as he did of his own, if that amount is less than a normal person of prudent habits would exercise in regard to the property. In other words, the test is primarily objective rather than subjective. An example of the distinction may be found in *Doorman* v. *Jenkins*[86] where, even under the old criterion, the defendant could not escape by showing that some of his own money had been stolen along with the plaintiff's; or in *Turner* v. *Merrylees*,[87] where it did not help the defendant that he had put his own dog-cart in the same outhouse as the plaintiff's phaeton. Conversely, in the Kentucky case of *Hargis* v. *Spencer*,[88] where the defendant agreed to look after the plaintiff's bag of gold while the latter was in gaol, it was held that it was not an act of gross negligence for her to leave it in a locked trunk where she kept her own money. Although the court specifically

---

[83] Chapter 7, ante.
[84] Chapter 12, post: the warehouseman may have a remedy under the relevant *Disposal of Uncollected Goods Act*, although the English (1952) Act would not apply to a person in his position. Cf. now App. I, post.
[85] 188 S.C. 358; 199 S.E. 413, see also Wyatt Paine, p. 13.
[86] (1834) 2 A. & E. 256; 111 E.R. 99.
[87] (1892) 8 T.L.R. 695.
[88] (1934) 254 Ky. 297; 71 S.W. (2d) 666.

denied that a depositary owes a duty to take such care as a person of reasonable prudence would take of his own goods, the judgment illustrates that what may amount to a conscientious application of the defendant's own standards will not *necessarily* be enough for the court.[89]

It may, in passing, be noted that certain English[90] and American[91] authorities reflect a transitional phase in this evolution by allowing a depositee to escape where he has shown the same degree of care as he *personally* uses towards his own property of a similar nature and in like circumstances. In at least one of these decisions, the application of this standard involved a reversal of the trial-judge's requirement of "such care as a reasonably prudent man would have exercised under the circumstances".[92] While this doctrine almost certainly does not represent the general rule in modern English law, it is evident that the standard outlined in cases like *Bullen* v. *Swan Electric Engraving Co. Ltd.*[93] must be read subject to the known capacities and character of the depositee at the time of delivery. Thus a bailee may be relieved for falling below the level of reasonable and natural prudence if his bailor knows him to be "an idle, drunken fellow"[94] or notoriously inattentive of his own property or perhaps even of known criminal associations. Indeed, the same result may follow even where a depositary is notoriously jealous of his own goods if the bailor knows him to be more than ordinarily inefficient in his care of those which belong to others. Although it seems strange to allow a man to take advantage of his own bad reputation in order to escape liability for failure to behave with reasonable care, this is an escape which theoretically may exist in other spheres than bailment; for instance, where a seller is seeking to show that no buyer would ever rely on his skill and judgment. The circumstances in which such a defence will succeed must necessarily be rare, and few bailees would consciously encourage such an adverse renown for the purposes of avoiding liability on a single occasion. Moreover, it may be imagined that the courts will not venture too deeply into the bailee's character and his depositor's knowledge thereof, where all the external manifestations of his conduct or sphere of operations are such as to justify an expectation of reasonable care.[95]

---

[89] Of course the converse may equally be true; see *Home Insurance Co.* v. *Southern Specialty Sales Co.* (1969) 225 So. 2d. 776, where it was pointed out that merely because the depositary is careless of his own property this does not necessarily mean that he is careless of the subject-matter of the deposit.

[90] *Jones* v. *Lewis* (1751) 2 Ves. Sen. 240; *Coggs* v. *Bernard* (1703) 2 Ld. Raym. 909; 92 E.R. 107, per Holt C.J.: *Lewis* v. *McMullen* (1866) 4 W.W. & a'B. 1, at 8; *Morris* v. *C. W. Martin & Sons Ltd.* [1966] 1 Q.B. 716, at 725, per Lord Denning M.R.; cf. *The William* (1806) 6 Ch. Rob. 316; Paton, pp. 107-110.

[91] *Rubin* v. *Huhn* (1918) 229 Mass. 126; 118 N.E. 290; *Boyden* v. *Bank of Cape Fear* (1871) 65 N.C. 13; cf. *Kubli* v. *First National Bank of Pleasantville* (1925) 199 Iowa 1944; 200 N.W. 434.

[92] *Rubin* v. *Huhn*, supra.

[93] (1906) 22 T.L.R. 275; (1907) 23 T.L.R. 258; ante, p. 296.

[94] *Coggs* v. *Bernard* (1703) 2 Ld. Raym. 909, at 914-915; 92 E.R. 107, at 110-111 per Holt C.J. See also *Neuwith* v. *Over Darwen Cooperative Society Ltd.* (1894) 63 L.J.Q.B. 290, at 292; *Insurance Commissioner* v. *Joyce* (1948) 77 C.L.R. 39, at 46; post, p. 460.

[95] Jones, *Bailments*, p. 46; and see *James Buchanan & Co. Ltd.* v. *Hay's Transport Services Ltd.* [1972] 2 Lloyd's Rep. 535.

C. The Australian position

In England, it seems clear that Paton's prophesy has been fulfilled and that the test of reasonable care has won the day.[96] Broadly the same pattern can be discerned in Canadian jurisdictions, where courts have successively held that gross negligence must be established;[97] that gross negligence means a failure to exercise the care that a reasonable man would show towards his own property;[98] and that reasonable care is the true and only test.[99]

In Australia, there is a marked dearth of decisive authority and it may still be argued with some confidence that the depositary is liable only for gross neglect. Indeed, one old decision seems almost to deny that he owes any duty at all, at least where the bailment occurs at the request of the depositor; but the case (which was one of mandatum rather than depositum) can be explained on the ground that there was no satisfactory evidence of neglect.[1] The remaining decisions seem to fall into three main categories:

(a) those where the standard applied is that of gross neglect, but the court has equated this with the degree of care that a reasonable and prudent person of similar character would have taken in similar circumstances;

(b) those where the standard is that of gross neglect and there is no such qualifying metaphor;

(c) those where the standard is that of reasonable care.

---

[96] *Bailment in Common Law*, p. 110.
[97] *Holmes* v. *Moore* (1867) 17 L.C.R. 143; *Palin* v. *Reid* (1884) 10 O.A.R. 63 (gross negligence being "actual clear negligence"); *Green Fuel Economizer Co.* v. *Toronto* (1915) 8 O.W.N. 541; *Grinsberg* v. *Vanstone Motors Ltd.* [1949] O.W.N. 345; [1950] O.W.N. 200; *Grafstein* v. *Holme and Freeman* (1958) 12 D.L.R. (2d) 727, at 739; *Palmer* v. *Toronto Medical Arts Building Ltd.* (1961) 20 D.L.R. (2d) 181; *Martin* v. *Town 'n' Country Delicatessen* (1963) 42 D.L.R. (2d) 449, at 453.
[98] *Consentino* v. *Dominion Express Co.* (1906) 4 W.L.R. 498, at 505-508; *Brewer* v. *Calori* (1921) 29 B.C.R. 457; *Munn* v. *Wakelin* (1944) 17 M.P.R. 447.
[99] *Sutherland* v. *Bell & Schiesel* (1911) 18 W.L.R. 521; *Wright* v. *Standard Trust Co.* (1916) 29 D.L.R. 391; *Ferguson* v. *Eyer* (1918) 43 O.L.R. 190; *McCowan* v. *McCulloch* [1926] 1 D.L.R. 312; *Mumford* v. *Northern Trusts Co.* [1924] 2 W.W.R. 745; *Stevenson* v. *Toronto Board of Education* (1919) 49 D.L.R. 673; *Martin* v. *Town 'n' Country Delicatessen* (1963) 42 D.L.R. (2d) 449, at 467, *Fairley & Stevens (1966) Ltd.* v. *Goldsworthy* (1973) 48 D.L.R. (3d) 554, at 568; *Seaspan International Ltd.* v. *The Kostis Prois* (1973) 33 D.L.R. (3d) 1, at 5 (obiter). The same standard is now accepted in most American states: see, for instance, *Home Insurance Co.* v. *Southern Specialty Sales Co.* (1969) 225 So. 2d 776.
[1] *Heaton* v. *Richards* (1881) 2 L.R. (N.S.W.) 73. The plaintiff sued the Government printer for failing to carry out certain printing which the defendant had gratuitously promised to perform, and for the loss of portions of the plaintiff's manuscript while in the defendant's possession. The first count failed for lack of consideration (see p. 340, post): as regards the second, Manning J. found for the defendant because there was no consideration for his alleged promise to return the manuscript, while Martin C.J. and Hargrave J. reached the same conclusion on the ground that the plaintiff had adduced no evidence of neglect. The latter approach, whilst appearing to place the onus on the bailor, is nevertheless preferable.

Into the first category fall the banking cases,[2] where the attributes and facilities of the defendant were such that one could have expected a fairly elevated degree of precaution, even in regard to gratuitously-kept property; whether such an equation would have been applied to an occasional, private bailee is not immediately clear from those decisions, and it may well be that they must be confined to defaults by professional bailees. Into the second category fall such cases as *Sharp* v. *Batt*[3] (not, technically, a case of bailment at all);[4] *Lenkeit* v. *Ebert*[5] and a dictum of Way C.J. in *O'Dea* v. *O'Hara*.[6] Taken alone, these decisions seem to indicate that Australian courts still favour some species of gross negligence test, albeit liberalised in particular areas. Against them may be placed their relative antiquity; a collection of dicta from more recent judgments;[7] and the general run of modern English and New Zealand[8] authority. Numerically, if not qualitatively, the older criterion would still appear to be in the lead.

What is significant, however, about all these authorities is that none of them was decided after 1962.[9] Accordingly, there has been little

---

[2] *Giblin* v. *McMullen* (1868) L.R. 2 P.C. 317; *Mayor of the City of Fitzroy* v. *National Bank of Australasia Ltd.* (1890) 16 V.L.R. 342; *Brown* v. *National Bank of Australasia Ltd.* (1890) 16 V.L.R. 475; cf. *Lewis* v. *McMullen* (1866) 4 W.W. & a'B. 1; *Port Swettenham* v. *Wu* (1978) *The Times*, June 22.

[3] (1930) 25 Tas. L.R. 33.

[4] The seller was not a bailee because the buyer's default had prevented property in the apples from passing.

[5] [1947] St. R. Qd. 126; p. 333, post.

[6] (1895) *South Australian Advertiser* (May 17th); cf. *Webb* v. *Agricultural Society of New South Wales* (1893) 14 L.R. (N.S.W.) 333, where the head-note seems to go further than the judgment warrants, in requiring gross negligence; *Mazullah Khan* v. *McNamara* (1911) 13 W.A.R. 151, which arguably provides some tacit support for a lesser degree of care on the gratuitous bailee. Both in *The Oriental Bank Corporation* v. *The Queen* (1867) 6 S.C.R. (N.S.W.) 122, at 125, and in *Daniel* v. *Hotel Pacific Pty. Ltd.* [1953] V.L.R. 447, at 456, 458, there is acknowledgement that different standards of care are to be imposed upon bailees for reward and gratuitous bailees.

[7] *Makower, McBeath & Co. Pty. Ltd.* v. *Dalgety & Co. Ltd.* [1921] V.R. 365, at 372-376, per McArthur J. (where it is suggested that at least in the selection and supervision of his servants the depositary must exercise reasonable care); *Dalgety & Co. Ltd.* v. *Warden* [1954] St. R. Qd. 251, at 253 per O'Hagan J. (whose fellow judges are inconclusive on this point); *Thomas* v. *High* [1960] S.R. (N.S.W.) 407, per Ferguson J.; *Thomas National Transport (Melbourne) Pty. Ltd.* v. *May & Baker (Australia) Pty. Ltd.* (1966) 115 C.L.R. 353, at 374-375, 387-388 per Windeyer J. (who remarks that according to the pleadings the sub-bailee owed the duties of a depositary or mandatary and should therefore be absolved upon proof that he took "proper care"; in fact, the sub-bailee in this case was indisputably a bailee for reward: see Chapter 8, ante and p. 793 et seq., post. Cf. *Port Swettenham* v. *Wu* (1978) *The Times*, June 22.

[8] The test of reasonable care was endorsed obiter by Gresson J. in the New Zealand Court of Appeal in *Helson* v. *McKenzies (Cuba St.) Ltd.* [1950] N.Z.L.R. 878, at 923-924; cf. Hutchinson J. in the Supreme Court, at 887-893, who favoured the standard of gross negligence but characterised the defendants as a gratuitous *involuntary* bailee. Most of the remaining New Zealand authorities seem to involve bailments for the mutual advantage of the parties: *Marshall* v. *Dibble* [1920] N.Z.L.R. 497; *Wellington Racing Club* v. *Symons* [1923] N.Z.L.R. 1; *Timaru Borough Council* v. *Boulton* [1924] N.Z.L.R. 365; *Grey Cabs* v. *Neil* [1947] N.Z.L.R. 62; cf. *Munro* v. *Auckland Transport Board* (1969) 5 M.C.D. 43 (gross negligence) and see further *Pilcher* v. *Leyland Motors Ltd.* [1932] N.Z.L.R. 449, at 465; *Karnani* v. *Bookers' Shipping (Demerara) Ltd.* (1972) 18 W.I.R. 231, at 240.

[9] Except the least conclusive: *Thomas National Transport (Melbourne) Pty. Ltd.* v. *May & Baker (Australia) Pty. Ltd.* (1966) 115 C.L.R. 353, supra.

opportunity so far to assess the impact of *Houghland* v. *R. R. Low (Luxury Coaches) Ltd.*[10] upon modern Australian doctrine. There is, however, one post-1962 authority which attempts to quantify the effect of Ormerod L.J.'s dictum. *Lee & Son Pty. Ltd.* v. *Abood*[11] is not a case of depositum but of sub-bailment for reward, and Goran D.C.J. came only to touch upon the duties of a depositary in the course of considering an argument that a sub-bailee whose reward comes not from the head bailor but from an intermediate bailor can owe towards the former only the duties of a gratuitous bailee. Remarking that the degree of care required of such a bailee is still uncertain but that in England it seems generally to be that of the commonly prudent man, he continued:

> In *Houghland* v. *R. R. Low (Luxury Coaches) Ltd.*, Ormerod L.J. says that the test is whether in all the circumstances of the particular case the defendant has observed a sufficient standard of care. If the phrase "all the circumstances" includes the circumstance that the bailment is gratuitous, with the greatest respect to the learned Lord Justice, this test to some extent at least must beg the question. I, therefore, take the phrase to connote the facts of the case excluding the fact that the bailment is gratuitous . . . Wherever the onus of proof falls in the case of a gratuitous bailment, I am unable to find in the present matter to find anything like "gross" negligence on the evidence before me. Apart from this standard, however, there is the significant fact that the defendants damaged their own truck at the same time as the (*plaintiff's*) compressors were damaged. This is not necessarily enough to absolve them from blame, but it is of some significance, in my mind, when applying the tests laid down in such cases . . . I find on a review of the whole of the circumstances that the defendants did exercise the degree of diligence required of them under this count and as a result the plaintiff must fail . . .[12]

Unfortunately, this does little to clarify matters, since it appears to oscillate between the three overlapping formulae of gross negligence, reasonable care, and the care that the depositee in question takes of his own property. Since in this case the defendants were professional carriers, it would appear reasonable that they should have been expected to show a reasonable degree of care; that is, the degree of care that could normally be expected of an organisation of their occupation and character. But it cannot be said that *Lee and Sons Pty. Ltd.* v. *Abood* is clear authority either way, and it is unlikely to provide any material assistance to a future Australian Court called upon to decide the same issue.[13]

Despite the weight of authority to the contrary, it seems likely that an Australian court will in future suscribe to the standard of reasonable care. In many ways this would be a desirable solution. Not only would it bring Australian law into probable conformity with other Commonwealth

---

[10] [1962] 1 Q.B. 694.
[11] (1968) 89 W.N. (N.S.W.) 430 (District Court).
[12] Ibid., at 433-434.
[13] It seems, if anything, to favour a lower degree of care on the part of a gratuitous bailee, because the plaintiffs eventually recovered from the defendants, on the same facts, as bailees for reward. Cf. *Wallace* v. *Safeway Caravan Pty. Ltd.* [1975] 3 Qd. Lawyer 224, at 232, where Gibney D.C.J. remarked obiter that "the standard of care required of a bailee is the standard determined by the circumstances of the particular case".

jurisdictions and remove for all time the problem of assessing whether a particular act of negligence was ordinary, slight or gross. It would also render redundant for most practical purposes an inquiry as to whether a bailment was gratuitous or for reward.[14]

On the other hand, it may be questioned whether the notion of gross negligence is really so anomalous and meaningless as its critics would suggest. Certainly, no judge since Lord Chelmsford has really bothered to advance the arguments in its favour.[15] Although in abstract terms it may be unwieldly and elusive, there is no real evidence to show that juries have encountered much difficulty in applying it in practice; indeed, much of the original unpopularity of the concept might be attributed to its tendency, in the judges' view, to produce the wrong result. A layman should have no more difficulty in distinguishing between gross and ordinary negligence than he should have in differentiating between these qualities in any other context. That he would do so by allocating gross neglect to a category nearer to recklessness than to ordinary inadvertence probably explains why gross negligence has become so unfashionable in recent years. Admittedly the abandonment of this concept is in keeping with the modern juristic approach to those who perform gratuitous services generally. But as Montague Smith J. once pointed out, gross negligence and its counterparts really connote standards of care rather than gradations of default.[16] To speak, in the context of bailment, in terms of greater or lesser care is neither illogical nor incoherent; to do so might produce fairer results than the application of a single, all-purpose standard.[17]

Gross negligence, as a juristic notion, has existed for many years outside the field of bailments. It has enjoyed a tolerably intelligible record in certain aspects of Common Law manslaughter[18] and has been employed, without embarrassment or alarm, in recent judicial discussions of the degree of care which must be shown by a mortgagee exercising his powers of sale[19] and the duties of an occupier towards trespassers.[20] Even under modern law, there seems to be some endorsement of the idea that negligence can come in greater or lesser degrees of severity; thus it may be necessary to decide whether a particular act of negligence is sufficiently grave to constitute a fundamental breach of contract, and the pattern of this inquiry may not be wholly unlike that adopted formerly in identifying gross neglect.[21] If a modern court can make this differentiation for one

---

[14] Chapter 8, ante.
[15] *Giblin* v. *McMullen*, (1868) L.R. 2 P.C. 317.
[16] *Grill* v. *General Iron Screw Collier Co.* (1866) L.R. 1 C.P. 600, at 614; see also *Kirk* v. *Commissioner for Railways* (1876) Qd. S.C.R. 35, at 38, per Cockle C.J.
[17] The argument that the duty of care defines the persons to whom it is owed is clearly immaterial where, as on a bailment, the object of the duty is pre-defined.
[18] *R.* v. *Cato* [1976] 1 All E.R. 260 is a recent application.
[19] *Cuckmere Brick Co. Ltd.* v. *Mutual Finance Ltd.* [1971] Ch. 949, at 965, 971.
[20] *Herrington* v. *British Railways Board* [1972] A.C. 877, at 921, 928; cf. at 938, 943.
[21] *Kenyon, Son & Craven Ltd.* v. *Baxter Hoare & Co. Ltd.* [1971] 1 W.L.R. 519; 2 All E.R. 708; *Mendelssohn* v. *Normand Ltd.* [1970] 1 Q.B. 177; Vaines, *Personal Property* (5th ed.), pp. 105-107; cf. *Thomas National Transport (Melbourne) Pty. Ltd.* v. *May & Baker (Australia) Ltd.* (1966) 115 C.L.R. 353. An older illustration of the forfeiture of protection for acts of gross negligence may be seen in *Stephenson* v. *Hart* (1828) 4 Bing. 476.

purpose it seems strange that it cannot do it for another. The following are some examples of conduct by depositaries which is probably negligent but arguably not gross neglect. It may be doubted whether in either of them the depositary should be held liable for the loss:

(1) Mr A asks Mrs B, a neighbour, to look after a fur coat which he has bought his wife as a surprise for her birthday. Mrs B puts the coat in her wardrobe, but, on leaving the house to go shopping, forgets to lock the front door. The coat is stolen, along with property of her own.

(2) Mr E finds Mrs F's handbag outside his front gate and takes it indoors. Shortly afterwards, a woman calls and asks him whether he has found her handbag. She describes it in detail and Mr E hands it over. He does not ask for identification, nor does he look in the bag to ascertain the true owner's identity. The caller turns out to be a thief.[22]

D. Vicarious liability

It is still uncertain to what degree a depositary is liable for the conversions or negligent misdeeds of his employees. Most of the older authorities suggest that while the master must answer for the negligence of his servants where that negligence causes damage or destruction of the bailed property, no liability is incurred where:

(a) the servant himself converts the chattel, or

(b) the servant's lack of vigilance enables a third party to do so *unless* the master has been personally negligent in selecting, employing or failing to supervise that servant in the first place.

Thus, in *Brown* v. *National Bank of Australasia Ltd.*,[23] Higinbotham C.J. clearly considered that one of the defendant's employees had been negligent in allowing the felonious clerk Onyons to perpetrate his defalcations. However, having satisfied themselves that the defendants had taken all the supervisory precautions they possibly could, neither Higinbotham C.J., nor the other members of the court, found it necessary to examine whether the bank should bear responsibility for their employee's omission, or whether it amounted to the kind of neglect that could properly be characterised as gross.

In *Makower, McBeath & Co. Ltd.* v. *Dalgety & Co. Ltd.*,[24] McArthur J. took this to be one of the distinctions between a gratuitous safekeeping and one for reward. In his view, where a gratuitous bailee entrusts the bailed property to his servant for safekeeping and it is lost through the servant's negligence, the gratuitous bailee is not liable if he can prove that a reasonable and prudent man would have entrusted such an article to such a servant. Since in the present case (as in *Brown* v. *National Bank of Australasia Ltd.*) the bailee's whole system appeared to have been reasonably safe and proper, it would have followed, had he been considered a gratuitous bailee, that he would have escaped liability for a theft which seemed to have been caused, on a balance of probabilities, by a temporary want of vigilance on the part of his employees.

[22] Cf. *Helson* v. *McKenzies (Cuba St.) Ltd.* [1950] N.Z.L.R. 878.
[23] (1890) 16 V.L.R. 475.
[24] [1921] V.R. 365, at 375-376.

An analogous rule can be elicited from various *dicta* of members of the Court of Appeal in *Morris* v. *C. W. Martin & Sons Ltd.*[25] According to Lord Denning M.R. a householder would not be answerable if his servant converted a coat belonging to a visitor "because he was not under any duty to prevent it being stolen, but only to keep it as his own".[26]

Diplock L.J. said:

> I should add that we are not here concerned with gratuitous bailment. That is a relationship in which the bailee's duties of care in his custody of the goods are different from those of a bailee for reward. It may be that his duties being passive rather than 'active, the concept of vicarious performance of them is less apposite. However this may be, I express no views 'as to the circumstances in which he would be liable for conversion of the goods by his servant.[27]

It cannot be said that these statements are especially helpful in assessing the modern extent of a depositary's responsibility for loss of his bailor's goods. There have been cases in which, contrary to Lord Denning's impression, the depositary has been held responsible for the theft of those goods by third parties[28] and it seems strange that a standard of responsibility requiring him to keep the bailed goods as his own should be thought to absolve him in the even of any "external" depredation. Again, it is hard to see why a gratuitous bailment should necessarily connote passive rather than active duties, and how this can affect the bailee's liability for conversion. Although the depositary will not, by definition, generally be under any duty to treat the goods or to perform work upon them, he must still observe some degree of care in safe-guarding them, and this will in many cases involve a certain amount of active precaution. Insofar as he delegates this duty to his servant, it may be concluded that he should be answerable whenever that servant abuses his trust and converts the chattel.

Nor is there any compelling authority for the proposition that a depositary is liable for the negligence of his servants in the course of their employment only when he has been personally negligent in engaging or in failing to supervise them. Both *Brown* v. *National Bank of Australasia Ltd.*[29] (where the question was not discussed) and *Makower, McBeath & Co. Pty. Ltd.* v. *Dalgety & Co. Ltd.*[30] appear to have taken the matter for granted and it may be questioned whether the same result would have been reached if the claim had arisen in respect of damage (rather than theft) resulting from the servant's omission; for instance, if an employee, while moving the goods, had carelessly dropped them. The distinction proposed by McArthur J. raises the problem of deciding whether a particular servant in the depositary's employment is of suf-

---

[25] [1966] 1 Q.B. 716.
[26] Ibid., at 725. Cf. *Port Swettenham* v. *Wu* (1978) *The Times*, June 22.
[27] Ibid., at 737.
[28] *Bullen* v. *Swan Electric Engraving Co. Ltd.* (1906) 22 T.L.R. 275; (1907) 23 T.L.R. 258 and *Phipps* v. *New Claridge's Hotel Ltd.* (1905) 22 T.L.R. 49 are possible examples; *Troke* v. *Felton* (1897) 13 T.L.R. 252 and *James Buchanan & Co. Ltd.* v. *Hay's Transport Services, Ltd.* [1972] 2 Lloyd's Rep. 535 are clear applications of the rule.
[29] (1890) 16 V.L.R. 475.
[30] [1921] V.L.R. 365.

ficiently high standing to impress his master with the consequences of his own negligence; it would therefore mean that many actions against corporate depositaries would stand a very slender chance of succeeding. In any event, there is a considerable amount of tacit authority favouring the imposition of liability on vicarious as well as personal grounds for the negligence of an officer employed by the depositee. In *Houghland* v. *R. R. Low* (*Luxury Coaches*) *Ltd.*[31] the plaintiff's suitcase was lost from one of the defendants' coaches in circumstances which were held to create an inference of negligence against them. A coach was broken down and had stood unattended for three hours before the arrival of a relief vehicle, to which passengers transferred their own luggage. Before the loss was discovered, several passengers had already alighted from the relief vehicle and the driver had given them such suitcases as they had told him were their own. The defendants were wholly unable to explain the loss and the Court of Appeal upheld the County Court Judge's finding against them, Ormerod L.J. remarking that an action in detinue requires affirmative proof that the loss of the chattel has not occurred through any default on the part of the defendant before it can be successfully resisted. Likewise, if sued in negligence, a gratuitous bailee must adduce sufficient evidence of his own observance of the necessary standard of care to succeed. Now it is clear from the facts of this case that if there was any negligence at all it was on the part of the coach-driver, who was (presumably) a fairly low-ranking member of the defendant's hierarchy. Admittedly, the relief coach had been delivered by no less a person than their managing-director and there was some suggestion that he should have assisted in supervising the transfer of luggage rather than leaving it to the other driver and going off for his tea. But there was no suggestion that anything revolved around so fortuitous a circumstance and the case is clear authority for the view that a depositee is vicariously liable for losses caused by a lack of proper vigilance on the part of his ordinary employees, regardless of whether the general system of the defendant has been shown to be adequate or not.[32]

Most of the relevant decisions in this area do, admittedly, concern actions for damage to chattels rather than actions for loss by theft. Of the latter, a high proportion involve allegations of direct rather than vicarious negligence on the part of the depositary, for instance, *Troke* v. *Felton*[33] and *Dalgety & Co. Ltd.* v. *Warden.*[34] In none of these has it ever been argued that the depositary's liability is confined to damage or destruction of the chattel and does not extend to theft. Such a contention is clearly inconsistent with many decided cases and cannot, despite the support of Lord Denning M.R., seriously be sustained. Where the theft has been occasioned by the negligence of the depositary's servants, but there has been no deficiency of selection or supervision on his part, there would again appear to be much authority in favour of making the master liable

---

[31] [1962] 1 Q.B. 694.
[32] Indeed, Ormerod L.J. explicitly referred to the need to establish a "sufficient standard of care" on the part of "the defendants *or their servants*"; ibid., at 698.
[33] (1897) 13 T.L.R. 252.
[34] [1954] St. R. Qd. 251.

(provided the negligence occurred in the course of his servant's employment). Although the very essence of such cases will often be that the
cause of the loss is impossible to identify with certainty, vicarious liability
would appear to have been imposed in *Phipps* v. *New Claridge's Hotel
Co. Ltd.*,[35] *Newman* v. *Bourne & Hollingsworth Ltd.*,[36] *Blount* v. *War
Office*[37] and *Ultzen* v. *Nichols*,[38] and to have been acknowledged as a
potential ground of liability in *Bullen* v. *Swan Electric Engraving Co.
Ltd.*[39] Taken in conjunction with the decision of the Court of Appeal in
Houghland v. *R. R. Low* (*Luxury Coaches*) *Ltd.*,[40] they amount to
clear authority for the rule in England that a depositee's liability for theft
is not confined to situations in which he personally has fallen below the
required standard of care.

Once again, the position in Australia is technically undecided, and the
solitary statement of McArthur J. in *Makower, McBeath & Co. Pty.
Ltd.* v. *Dalgety & Co. Ltd.*[41] would seem to indicate a divergence from
English law. But the unqualified acceptance in Australia of many English
decisions suggesting the contrary view, coupled with the difficulty of
ascertaining whether the negligent servant in any given case is a menial
factotum or a manifestation of his master's will, encourages the speculation that an Australian court will in future hold the depositary vicariously
liable for the defaults of all his employees, however lowly, whenever such
defaults are committed within the course of their employment.

As regards conversions and misappropriations by servants of the
depositary, the authorities are much scantier and no less indecisive.
Many of the cases already cited were potentially of this character, but
the lack of evidence makes it impossible to categorise them definitely as
examples of the rule that no bailee, rewarded or otherwise, can delegate
with impunity his duty of safe-guarding the chattel. In *Williams* v.
Curzon Syndicate Ltd.,[42] the manager of the club was asked by a
member to keep certain jewellery in the safe in his office. The night-
porter, an old and dangerous thief who had been employed by the club
without any proper inquiry into his antecedents, stole the jewellery. The
defendants (owners of the club) were held liable on the grounds that their
failure to use due care in engaging the thief was the immediate cause of
the loss. Although the express finding of negligence would appear to
gainsay any general principle rendering a depositary liable for the thefts
of his servants, it must be remembered that the thief in this case was
not entrusted with the goods and was not charged with their safe-keeping;
so that even under the enlarged orbit of liability imposed by cases like
Lloyd v. *Grace, Smith & Co.*[43] and *Morris* v. *C. W. Martin & Sons
Ltd.*[44] the defendants would, but for their own negligence, probably have

35 (1905) 22 T.L.R. 49.
36 (1915) 31 T.L.R. 209.
37 [1953] 1 W.L.R. 736; 1 All E.R. 1071.
38 [1894] 1 Q.B. 92 (probably a bailment for reward).
39 (1906) 22 T.L.R. 275; (1907) 23 T.L.R. 258.
40 [1962] 1 Q.B. 694.
41 [1921] V.L.R. 365, at 375-376.
42 (1919) 35 T.L.R. 475; see also *Mintz* v. *Silverton* (1920) 36 T.L.R. 399.
43 [1911] 2 K.B. 489; [1912] A.C. 716.
44 [1966] 1 Q.B. 716.

escaped.[45] It may also be surmised that *Williams* v. *Curzon Syndicate Ltd.* was not, on modern principles, really a case of gratuitous bailment at all.

Ironically, the one decision which appears to supply the necessary logic for rendering the depositee liable in such cases seems in the same breath to deny that very conclusion.[46] If, with Lord Denning, we approach the matter by examining the duty laid on the depositary, it must follow that any attempt on his part to delegate that duty that cannot absolve him from responsibility for the defaults of the deputed performer. In other words:

> . . . when a principal has in his charge the goods or belongings of another ·in such circumstances that he is under a duty to take all reasonable precautions to protect them from theft or depredation, then if he entrusts that duty to a servant or agent, he is answerable for the manner in which that servant or agent carries out his duty. If the servant or agent is careless so that they are stolen by a stranger, the master is liable. So also if the servant or agent himself steals them or makes away with them.[47]

Precisely the same result must ensue from the alternative analyses of Diplock and Salmon L.JJ. If the depositary puts an employee in his place to discharge his duties in respect of the chattel, and the manner in which that servant conducts himself in performing those duties is to convert the chattel, then what the servant does, albeit dishonestly, is done in the course of his employment.[48] It should make no difference that the bailment is gratuitous or that the master's duties are confined to safe-keeping and do not extend to other acts like cleaning or repairing.

And yet both Lord Denning M.R. and Diplock L.J. were clearly reluctant to apply the same rule to the gratuitous bailee. Their unwillingness to carry the decision in *Morris* v. *C. W. Martin & Sons Ltd.* to its logical conclusion in such an area seems to be based, in the final analysis, upon a sentiment of policy which considers it undesirable to visit the depositary with all the normal varieties of liability attendant upon a bailment for reward. Such a sentiment is certainly understandable but it is difficult to support. If the courts had really wished to distinguish between the two classes of bailee, they would have endorsed and perpetuated the standard of gross neglect. Now that such a standard seems discredited, there is no reason to suppose that the gratuitous custodian's liabilities are not an exact facsimile of those that are owed by the bailee for reward, and that the depositary is not liable for the conversions of his servants (be they committed honestly or otherwise) whenever he has nominated or deputed those servants to the discharge of his own original duty of safe-keeping.[49]

---

[45] *Leesh River Tea Co. Ltd.* v. *British India Steam Navigation Co. Ltd.* [1967] 2 Q.B. 250.
[46] *Morris* v. *C. W. Martin & Sons Ltd.* [1966] 1 Q.B. 716.
[47] Ibid., at 728.
[48] Ibid., at 737 (Diplock L.J.).
[49] *Armory* v. *Delamirie* (1722) 1 Stra. 505; 92 E.R. 664, arguably supports the rule, although there are grounds for contending that the bailment (if any) in this case was not gratuitous.

E. The burden of proof

Here one encounters yet another aspect of despositum in which the Australian law is uncertain and may possibly diverge from the prevalent
English rule. The uncertainty can possibly be ascribed to the confusion
existing in England at the time when the principal Australian authorities
were decided. It has already been observed that, around the turn of the
19th century, there were a number of English decisions which placed the
onus of proving negligence upon the bailor.[50] In *Doorman* v. *Jenkins*,[51]
Patteson J. applied the requirement to cases of depositum, and none of
the other members of the court expressly dissented from this view;[52]
Roux v. *Wiseman*[53] appears to similar effect. But it was the decision in
Powell v. *Graves*[54] which really gave this doctrine its modern authority.
The facts of that case probably provide the strongest clue to the principle
it enshrined. The defendants had paid £5 for a picture and had presented
it as a gift to the plaintiff's father. Many years later the plaintiff, who had
inherited the picture, left it with the defendants for safekeeping while he
went abroad. On his return, the picture could not be found; the defendants thought it might have been lost during a fire in their premises, but
were wholly unable to give any concrete evidence as to the circumstances
of its disappearance. They also hotly disputed the value and authenticity
of the picture. Coleridge and Manisty JJ., reversing the County Court
judge's award of £50 damages, clearly indicated that the burden of
proving negligence (although not, apparently, *gross* negligence) lay with
the bailor in cases of depositum and that this burden had not been discharged:

> There must be affirmative evidence of negligence to make them, as
> gratuitous bailees, liable for its loss.
> The evidence of negligence in the defendants was of the most meagre
> character possible to be set up against them as gratuitous bailees.[55]

This precarious view of the law did not survive for long in England.[56]
Although no clear ruling can be found in either *Troke* v. *Felton*[57] or
Turner v. *Merrylees*,[58] the decisions of both Walton J. and the Court of
Appeal in *Bullen* v. *Swan Electric Engraving Co. Ltd.*[59] are clear authority
against it, and Farwell L.J. explicitly said that the decision in *Powell* v.

---

[50] Ante, p. 40.
[51] (1834) 4 A. & E. 256; 111 E.R. 99.
[52] The decision seems to have been misconstrued on this point by the authors of
the Law Commission's *Second Report on Exemption Clauses* (No. 69); 1975,
para. 145.
[53] (1857) 1 F. & F. 45.
[54] (1886) 2 T.L.R. 663.
[55] Ibid.
[56] It was, however, approved by Perdue J.A. (dissenting) in the Manitoba Court
of Appeal in *Consentino* v. *Dominion Express Co.* (1906) 4 W.L.R. 498, at
505; cf. at p. 507, where he appears to favour placing the onus of disproof
upon the gratuitous bailee. Modern Canadian decisions cast the burden upon
the depositary: see, for instance, *Mansfield Importers & Distributors Ltd.* v.
Caseo Terminals Ltd. (1971) 14 D.L.R. (3d) 358; [1971] 2 Lloyd's Rep. 73,
at 77.
[57] (1897) 13 T.L.R. 252, cf. *Polish Fraternal Aid Society* v. *Kapusta* [1938] 4
D.L.R. 724.
[58] (1892) 8 T.L.R. 695.
[59] (1906) 22 T.L.R. 275; (1907) 23 T.L.R. 258.

Graves, as reported, could now hardly be sustained.[60] Later cases, most notably *Houghland v. R. R. Low (Luxury Coaches) Ltd.*[61] and *James Buchanan Ltd.* v. *Hay's Transport Services Ltd.,*[62] concur in placing squarely upon the defendant the burden of proving that he took the care of a reasonable and prudent man. Thus, it will no longer avail him simply to show that the goods have been stolen or otherwise mislaid. But if he can show that, in all the circumstances, he behaved with reasonable vigilance and care, he will be relieved of liability even though he is unable to establish or identify the precise cause of the injury or loss.[63]

An Australian court would probably conform to this rule, support for which may be found in dicta of McArthur J. in *Makower, McBeath & Co. Pty. Ltd.* v. *Dalgety & Co. Ltd.,*[64] and in the decision of the Queensland Supreme Court in *Dalgety & Co. Ltd.* v. *Warden.*[65] But no clear guidance emerges from the authorities and many of the older cases appear to favour, if anything, the opposite view,[66] a view which was explicitly adopted in a case of mandatum.[67] In two later cases, one before the High Court[68] and the other before the District Court of New South Wales,[69] doubts were expressed as to whether an unrewarded bailee carries the burden of disproving negligence, but no concluded opinion was expressed. A recent decision of Mahon J. in the New Zealand Supreme Court seems likewise to proceed on the assumption that the bailor under a gratuitous loan must prove that the borrower was negligent before being entitled to recover for damage to his chattel.[70]

Although the reversal of the orthodox burden of proof might palliate some of the harsher results of basing the depositary's liability on the lack of reasonable care, it is suggested that to distinguish between rewarded and unrewarded bailments in this way would be anomalous and confusing. It would, for instance, mean that if the bailor were suing for negligently-caused damage to his chattel, he would have to advance evidence of default; whereas if he were suing in detinue for its total loss, the burden (as in all cases of detinue) would fall upon the bailee.[71] In any event, the non-existence of reward is immaterial to the traditional

---

[60] (1907) 23 T.L.R. 258, at 259.
[61] [1962] 1 Q.B. 694.
[62] [1972] 2 Lloyd's Rep. 535; *Mitchell* v. *Ealing L.B.C.* (1978) *The Times* February 21st; *Port Swettenham* v. *Wu* (1978) *The Times,* June 22 (p.c.).
[63] *Bullen* v. *Swan Electric Engraving Co. Ltd.,* supra.
[64] [1921] V.R. 365, at pp. 374-375.
[65] [1954] St. R. Qd. 251, at 254 per O'Hagan J.; the judgment of Hangar A.J. is less conclusive.
[66] *Heaton* v. *Richards* (1881) 2 L.R. (N.S.W.) 73; *O'Dea* v. *O'Hara* (1895) *South Australian Advertiser,* May 17th; *Mayor of the City of Fitzroy* v. *National Bank of Australasia Ltd.* (1890) 16 V.L.R. 342; *Giblin* v. *McMullen* (1868) L.R. 2 P.C. 317; cf. *Brown* v. *National Bank of Australasia Ltd.* (1890) 16 V.L.R. 475; *Paterson* v. *Miller* [1923] V.L.R. 36.
[67] *Lenkeit* v. *Ebert* [1947] St. R. Qd. 126: but see p. 343, post.
[68] *Thomas National Transport (Melbourne) Pty. Ltd.* v. *May & Baker (Australia) Ltd.* (1966) 115 C.L.R. 353, at 374-375, 387-388 per Windeyer J.
[69] *Lee & Sons Pty. Ltd.* v. *Abood* (1968) 89 W.N. (N.S.W.) 430, at 433-434, per Goran D.C.J. See also *Thomas* v. *High* (1960) 60 S.R. (N.S.W) 401, at 404, 407; *Linton* v. *Haynes and Facey* (1974) 21 W.I.R. 255.
[70] *Walker* v. *Watson* [1974] 2 N.Z.L.R. 175.
[71] *Reeve* v. *Palmer* (1858) 5 C.B. (N.S.) 84.

justification for making the bailee negative fault, which is that he, the person in possession, is most likely to know what has gone wrong.

III. Ancillary and Additional Obligations of the Depositary

In addition to safe-guarding the property with the requisite standard of care, a depositary must observe certain other duties incidental to that responsibility. Thus he must redeliver the goods on demand, either to the depositor or to a third party in accordance with the depositor's instructions.[72] If a place for redelivery has been agreed, it seems that the depositary must make the goods available at that place. If there is no express agreement to this effect, the court may infer one from the attendant circumstances of the deposit, but generally it will be reluctant to impose additional duties and a readiness to redeliver at the depositary's place of custody will be held sufficient.

Other duties may be imposed according to the nature of the goods and the duration of the deposit, without necessarily transforming the arrangement from depositum to mandatum. Thus, the depositary would normally be expected to feed a horse, or milk a cow, or water a plant, or exercise a dog, or to summon the necessary assistance in the event of an animal becoming ill or (possibly) giving birth. Likewise a failure to remove the goods from a place of sudden danger, to utilise the normal facilities for coping with an emergency, or to inform the owner or the police of the disappearance of the goods, would probably be held to be a dereliction of the depositary's duty.[73] On the other hand, it would not ordinarily be feasible to expect the depositary to take out insurance, unless perhaps his general occupation were such that goods on his premises would be likely to be covered in any event.[74] Nor should the fact that the goods were covered by a policy of his own necessarily oblige him to pursue a claim in respect of them, unless he knew (or ought to have known) that they were not otherwise insured, or unless he had no opportunity to confirm that the depositor would be prosecuting a claim of his own. Much will depend, of course, upon the professional character of the depositary and the facilities at his disposal.

All these examples are really no more than correlatives of the primary duty to safeguard and redeliver. But further obligations may be imposed by the agreement which are not necessarily incidental to the central undertaking. These superadded duties fall into two principal categories:

(1) Those where the depositary promises to exercise a greater degree of care than would normally be implied by law;

[72] *Anon*, (1642) March, 202: Pl. 242; 82 E.R. 475; *Wilkinson* v. *Verity* (1871) L.R. 6 C.P. 206. The rule applies even though the depositary knows that the bailor is not the owner: *Saville* v. *Tankred* (1748) 1 Ves. Sen. 101; 27 E.R. 918; ante, p. 163 (bailee's estoppel).
[73] Cf. *Philpott* v. *Kelley* (1835) 3 A. & E. 106; 111 E.R. 353, where it was held that a bailee was not in breach of his duty in bottling wine which was becoming impaired by remaining in the wood.
[74] Cf. *Wright* v. *Standard Trust Co. Ltd.* (1916) 29 D.L.R. 391, where it was held that the defendant's failure to examine his policy put him in breach of the standard of the reasonable and prudent man; and see (1978) 81 D.L.R. (3d) 587.

(2) Those where the depositary promises to do, or desist from doing, something in relation to the chattel.

Most of the situations falling in the second category will involve mandatum rather than depositum, but this is not necessarily so; for instance, the promise may be negative in character, such as an agreement not to disclose the contents of a document to any third party. The extent to which such promises are enforceable, and the grounds upon which such enforcement will be allowed, raise problems as to the true juristic nature of gratuitous bailments and, ultimately, of bailments as a whole.

A. Depositum as a species of contract

Traditionally, two assumptions about gratuitous bailments have been made. The first is that (so far as concerns enforcement) they must necessarily fall into one of the two categories of contract or tort. The second is that ancillary obligations can be enforced only if the proper classification is that of contract.[75] Inevitably, the individual character of bailment has been eclipsed by these assumptions, and its growth correspondingly retarded.

Whatever the position under early law, it is clear that after *Coggs* v. *Bernard*[76] the gratuitous bailment became emphatically identified with contract. This identification continued throughout the 19th century, being applied to commodatum[77] and mandatum[78] as well as to gratuitous safe-keepings.[79] For many years it ran concurrently with the notion that all bailments were necessarily contractual, and that without a contract, no relationship of bailment could exist.[80] As late as the 1940s and 1950s, some judges were still defining bailment in contractual terms,[81] despite an increasing weight of authority denying this equation.[82]

---

[75] Paton, *Bailment in the Common Law,* pp. 40, 100-101, 132, 150-151; *Heaton* v. *Richards* (1881) 2 L.R. (N.S.W.) 73; *Walker* v. *Watson* [1974] 2 N.Z.L.R. 175.

[76] (1703) 2 Ld. Raym. 909; 92 E.R. 107.

[77] *Bainbridge* v. *Firmstone* (1838) 8 A. & E. 743; 112 E.R. 1019; *Blakemore* v. *Bristol & Exeter Ry. Co.* (1858) 8 E. & B. 1035; 120 E.R. 385.

[78] *Streeter* v. *Horlock* (1822) 2 Bing. 34; 130 E.R. 15; *Whitehead* v. *Greetham* (1825) 2 Bing. 464; 130 E.R. 585.

[79] *Brown* v *National Bank of Australasia Ltd.* (1890) 16 V.L.R. 475, at 482, 483.

[80] *R.* v. *Ashwell* (1885) 16 Q.B.D. 190, per Lord Coleridge C.J. But by this time the equation had begun to be discredited: see *R.* v. *Robson* (1861) Le. & Ca. 93; 8 Jur. N.S. 64; *R.* v. *McDonald* (1885) 15 Q.B.D. 323; ante, p. 14.

[81] *In re S. Davis & Co. Ltd.* [1945] Ch. 402; *Rosenthal* v. *Alderton* [1946] 1 All E.R. 583, at 584; *Ballett* v. *Mingay* [1943] K.B. 281, at 283; *Kahler* v. *Midland Bank Ltd.* [1948] 1 All E.R. 811, at 820; (aff'd [1950] A.C. 24); *Edwards* v. *Newland & Co. Ltd.* [1950] 1 All E.R. 1072, at 1074-1075; *Helson* v. *McKenzies (Cuba St.) Ltd.* [1950] N.Z.L.R. 878, at 905-906, 916, 918, 921-924; *Tinsley* v. *Dudley* [1951] 2 K.B. 18, at 26, 28, 30; *Martin* v. *Town 'n' Country Delicatessen Ltd.* (1963) 42 D.L.R. (2d) 449, at 453; *Chapman* v. *Robinson and Ferguson* (1969) 71 W.W.R. 515, at 523; *Roufos* v. *Brewster and Brewster* [1971] 2 S.A.S.R. 218, at 223-224; *New Zealand Shipping Co. Ltd.* v. *A. N. Satterthwaite & Co. Ltd.* [1974] 1 All E.R. 1015, at 1020; and see Stoljar (1955) 7 Res Judicatae 160; *Warner* v. *Elizabeth Arden Ltd.* (1939) 83 Sol. Jo. 268.

[82] *Meux* v. *G.E. Ry. Co.* [1895] 2 Q.B. 387; *Makower, McBeath & Co. Pty. Ltd.* v. *Dalgety & Co. Ltd.* [1921] V.R. 365; *Elder, Dempster & Co. Ltd.* v. *Paterson, Zochonis & Co. Ltd.* [1924] A.C. 522; *Andrews* v. *Home Flats Ltd.* [1945] 2 All E.R. 698; *Scruttons, Ltd.* v. *Midland Silicones Ltd.* [1962] A.C. 446; *Martin Town 'n' Country Delicatessen Ltd.* (1963) 42 D.L.R. (2d) 449, at 461-462;

In the case of depositum, this approach necessarily raised the question as to what consideration the bailor had supplied to support the bailee's undertaking. Various answers were given to this question over the years, most of them versions of or variations upon the theory first advanced by Holt C.J. in *Coggs* v. *Bernard*:[83]

> And so a bare being trusted with another man's goods must be taken to be a sufficient consideration: if the bailee once enter upon the trust, and take the goods into his possession.[84]

Eventually, the process became inverted. Victorian judges, knowing that gratuitous bailments gave rise to enforceable obligations and believing that such obligations could arise only by virtue of contract, began to read consideration into the agreement as a matter of course, thus rationalising the apparent existence of a class of obligations which were not supported by an exchange of benefits; agents' warranties of authority provide a similar, contemporary example.[85]

The fact that the consideration perceived as a result of this process was, on most occasions, illusory, did not prevent Scott L.J. in 1948,[86] or Lord Wilberforce in 1974,[87] from acknowledging that the gratuitous bailment created a species of implied contract between the parties. Statements in the New Zealand Court of Appeal in 1950 seem to extend this analysis to finders as well as to bailees by agreement, at least for the purpose of identifying the parties to the bailment.[88]

Inevitably, however, the artificiality of this approach produced a reaction. Some reformulation of the basis of the gratuitous bailee's liability became particularly apposite after the decision in *Morris* v. *C. W. Martin & Sons Ltd.*[89] recognised that a sub-bailee may owe an original bailor all the traditional duties of a bailee for reward, even though his consideration emanates solely from the intermediate bailee and he has no communication, much less any contract, with the original

---

Morris v. *C. W. Martin & Sons Ltd.* [1966] 1 Q.B. 716 (and subsequent authority: see Chapter 20, post); *Chesworth* v. *Farrar* [1967] 1 Q.B. 407; *B.R.S.* v. *Arthur V. Crutchley Ltd.* [1968] 1 All E.R. 811, at p. 820; *Gilchrist, Watt & Sanderson Pty. Ltd.* v. *York Products Pty. Ltd.* [1970] 1 W.L.R. 1262; 3 All E.R. 825; *Roufos* v. *Brewster and Brewster* [1971] 2 S.A.S.R. 218, at 235; *Seaspan International Ltd.* v. *The Kostis Prois* (1973) 33 D.L.R. (3d) 1, at 4-5; *Fairline Shipping Corporation Ltd.* v. *Adamson* [1975] Q.B. 180, at p. 189. See further p. 14 et seq., ante.

83 (1703) 2 Ld. Raym. 909, at 920; 92 E.R. 107, at 114; see also *Blakemore* v. *Bristol & Exeter Ry. Co.* (1858) 120 E.R. 385, at 391; *Hart* v. *Miles* (1858) 4 C.B.N.S. 371; *Banbury* v. *The Bank of Montreal* [1918] A.C. 626, at 657.

84 It should be stressed that Holt C.J. was not using the word consideration in its modern sense but simply as a means of justifying the obligation to take care of the goods, enforceable by assumpsit. Tay, (1966) 7 *Sydney Law Review* 239, p. 243; Fifoot, *History and Sources of the Common Law*, pp. 156-157. But the statement in question became translated into support for modern doctrine during the ensuing century and a half.

85 Bowstead on *Agency* (14th edn.) 379.

86 *Kahler* v. *Midland Bank Ltd.* [1948] 1 All E.R. 811, at 819-820.

87 *New Zealand Shipping Co. Ltd.* v. *A. N. Satterthwaite & Co. Ltd.* [1975] A.C. 154, at 167.

88 [1950] N.Z.L.R. 878, at 905-906, 921-924.

89 [1966] 1 Q.B. 716.

bailor. Indeed, in that case Diplock L.J. observed that neither gratuitous bailments nor bailments by finding import a contract between the parties.[90]

From this discredited parentage with contract, the conclusion has been drawn that the bailor's rights under a gratuitous bailment must exist solely in tort; in conversion if the bailee has misappropriated the chattel; in negligence if he has returned it in a damaged or impaired state; in detinue or negligence if, through his carelessness, he is unable to return it at all. Thus, in *Thomas* v. *High*,[91] the New South Wales Full Supreme Court held that an action for the return of a gratuitously-held sum of money was essentially an action for conversion, and may have to be stayed until the defendant had been prosecuted for felony; and in *Walker* v. *Watson*[92] the Supreme Court of New Zealand held that an action against the drunken borrower of a car for damage to the vehicle was no more than an ordinary action in negligence, with the result that the bailee could legitimately plead contributory negligence or volenti non fit injuria in defence to the bailor's claim. In both cases there was explicit endorsement of Paton's statement[93] that gratuitous bailment "has nothing to do with the law of contract at all". Even in cases of bailment for reward, the courts have classified an action for breach of the bailee's Common Law duties as an action in tort for the purposes of the County Courts Acts[94] and for the purposes of limitations of action.[95] The identification between actions on the bailment and actions in tort would appear to be advanced, if not complete.[96]

Such an analysis, although convenient for most purposes, nevertheless raises problems on both a conceptual and a practical level. Conceptually, as we have already seen,[97] there are substantial differences between the bailment relationship and that of plaintiff and defendant in an ordinary action of tort. Pragmatically, the exclusive analysis of gratuitous bailments in terms of tort would seem to threaten the enforceability not only of those instances of depositum which involve a promise of greater care on the part of the depositary, but also of all cases of mandatum, where

---

[90] Ibid., at 731-732.
[91] [1960] S.R. (N.S.W.) 401; 76 W.N. 641.
[92] [1974] 2 N.Z.L.R. 175; (1975) 24 I.C.L.Q. 565.
[93] *Bailment in the Common Law*, p. 40.
[94] *Turner* v. *Stallibrass* [1898] 1 Q.B. 56.
[95] *Chesworth* v. *Farrar* [1967] 1 Q.B. 407.
[96] See further *Tattan* v. *G.W. Ry. Co.* (1860) 29 L.J. (N.S.) Q.B. 184; *Pontifex* v. *Midland Ry. Co.* (1877) 3 Q.B.D. 23; *Bryant* v. *Herbert* (1878) 3 C.P.D. 389; *Fawcett* v. *Smethurst* (1914) 31 T.L.R. 85; *Williams* v. *Fox, Johnson & Co. Ltd.* [1942] 4 D.L.R. 143; *Jackson* v. *Mayfair Window Cleaning Ltd.* [1952] 1 All E.R. 215; *B.W.I.A. Ltd.* v. *Bart* (1966) 11 W.I.R. 378; but cf. *Minichiello* v. *Devonshire Hotel (1967) Ltd. (No. 2)*, (1978) 79 D.L.R. (3d) 656; *Lovely* v. *Burroughs Corporation* (1974) 527 P. 2d 557 (strict liability upon non-contractual bailor "for reward"); *Walsh* v. *Palladium Car Park Pty. Ltd.* [1975] V.R. 949 (action for breach of bailment for reward is a claim arising out of a contract for the provision of services for the purposes of the *Small Claims Tribunal Act* (Vic.) (1973); *Mears* v. *Sayers* (1974) 41 D.L.R. (3d.) 424 (action for damage to bailed property may be validly assigned; for the purposes of deciding whether the action qualified as a chose in action and the assignment was champertous, the character of the action as one in contract or in tort was considered immaterial); *Chesworth* v. *Farrar*, supra, at 416-418 (bailor's claim for money had and received against bailee who sold goods held under a distress lay in contract rather than in tort).
[97] Ante, p. 36 et seq.

the bailee has promised to perform work on a chattel for the sole advantage of the bailor. In fact, there is substantial authority favouring the validity of these additional obligations; not, admittedly, in all cases, but at least where the bailee has embarked upon the undertaking and has already taken possession of the goods.

The question of mandatum will be specifically examined in the following chapter, although most of the considerations relevant to an enlarged agreement of depositum will be equally germane to one of mandatum, For the present, we shall confine our discussion to promises of greater safe-keeping than the law would normally impose under a gratuitous custody, and to ancillary promises which, because of their passive or incidental quality, do not serve to transport the relationship into the realms of mandatum.

There are many older decisions which imply that a depositary's liability is determined primarily by the scope of his promise or undertaking.[98] Those which date before *Coggs* v. *Bernard*[99] cannot, however, be synthesised into a general proposition for various reasons; there was until that time a recurrent belief that the bailee's liability was absolute and many of the examples of "special contracts" were designed to reduce rather than to augment the bailee's original obligation.[1] Again, much seemed to depend upon the form of action employed in a particular case, although it should be noted that if the action chosen was assumpsit, recoverability would ex hypothesi depend upon the extent of the defendant's promise. While it has been shown that later authorities erred in regarding the action in assumpsit as a contractual cause of action,[2] this classification undoubtedly enabled 19th century courts to enforce, in their eyes legitimately, any superimposed duty assumed by the bailee.

Thus, in *Coggs* v. *Bernard*,[3] it was expressly recognised that a man may, by promising to return goods in as good a condition as that in which he received them, bind himself even on a gratuitous bailment to a higher degree of care than the law would otherwise exact; and that where he promises to keep the goods safely at all events "that is a warranty, and will oblige the bailee to keep them safely against perils, where he has his remedy over, but act against such where he has no remedy over."[4]

Likewise, in *Kettle* v. *Bromsall*,[5] where the plaintiff claimed to have entrusted the defendant with the custody of certain valuable antiques, it was agreed that whether the defendant should be liable for the theft of

---

[98] For a useful analysis of these decisions (which are too numerous for discussion in the present work) see Holmes, *The Common Law*, pp. 175-199; Paton, *Bailment in the Common Law*, pp. 68-81; Fifoot, *History and Sources of the Common Law*, pp. 154-183.
[99] (1703) 2 Ld. Raym. 909; 92 E.R. 107.
[1] See in particular *Southcote* v. *Bennet* (1601) 4 Co. Rep. 83b; Co. Lit. 89; 76 E.R. 1061, and Coke's note thereto.
[2] Davidge, (1925) 41 L.Q.R. 433; Holdsworth, *H.E.L.*, Vol. III, pp. 449-450; Fifoot, *History and Sources of the Common Law*, pp. 331-334, Milsom, *Historical Foundations of the Common Law*, pp. 278 et seq.
[3] (1703) 2 Ld. Raym. 909; 92 E.R. 107.
[4] Ibid., at 912, 109 per Powell J. See the comments by Tay, (1966) 5 *Sydney Law Review* 239, at 242 et seq.
[5] (1783) Willes 118; 125 E.R. 1087.

those goods from his pocket without his privity or default depended upon the terms upon which the delivery had been made. According to Willes L.C.J., a promise to keep safely would render the depositary liable even in the event of the goods being taken from him by force, whereas a promise to keep only as his own proper goods would absolve him in such an event.[6] Although these observations are questionable in their interpretation of the liability imposed by a promise to keep safely and securely,[7] they provided further authority for the view that a depositary's traditional duty may be augmented or decreased by the terms of his private bargain.

A more recent case, *Trefttz & Sons Ltd.* v. *Canelli*[8] did not deal with an increased standard of care but with an alleged promise on the part of the depositary to redeliver only to certain persons and on certain conditions. A merchant owed money to the appellants and an arrangement was reached whereby he deposited certain bills with the respondent, who thus constituted himself a voluntary depositary of the bills and undertook to be responsible for them to the appellants "until the effective encashment of them, which remains entrusted to (the merchant)". The appellants claimed that the bills had been wrongly released, enabling the merchant to encash them, and that the respondent should have taken care to get possession of any resulting moneys accruing from the encashment. The Judicial Committee of the Privy Council reached their conclusion solely upon the construction of the agreement. They did not examine the question of consideration and appeared to entertain no doubt that the obligation claimed by the appellants would, if truly implicit in the agreement, have been enforceable. However, in their view the respondent's duty had been discharged and no further undertaking to hold and secure the proceeds of the encashment could be implied. They pointed out that the onus of establishing both the agreement and the breach thereof fell upon the appellants. As to the respondent's claim that he would have been liable only for gross negligence anyway no opinion was given.[9]

None of these authorities is particularly strong in the context of modern forms of action. Nevertheless, there is contemporary authority for the enforcement of a depositary's ancillary promises in the dictum of Bray C.J. in the South Australian case of *Roufos* v. *Brewster and Brewster*:[10]

> . . . where all the indicia from the point of view of abstract jurisprudence of an agreement in fact between competent parties are present, should the common law refrain from calling the transaction a contract simply because of difficulties caused by the doctrine of

---

[6] Ibid., at 1088 (E.R.).
[7] Cf. *Coggs* v. *Bernard*, supra.
[8] (1872) L.R. 4 P.C. 277: see Carnegie, (1966) 3 *Adelaide Law Review* 7.
[9] Other decisions which may be taken as suggesting that additional promises by the depositary are enforceable are: *Moore* v. *Mourgue* (1776) 2 Cowp. 479; 98 E.R. 1197 (where Lord Mansfield remarked that the gratuitous bailee is liable for *breach of orders*, gross negligence or fraud); *Whitney* v. *Lee* 8 Metcalf 91; *Miller* v. *Bank of Holly Springs* (1922) 95 So. 129 (U.S.A.); *Delagorgendiere* v. *Acaster* (1908) 7 W.L.R. 467 (Can.); *Marais* v. *Anderson* (1909) E.D.C. 76 (S. Africa); *Mitchell* v. *Ealing L.B.C.* (1978) *The Times*, Feb. 21.
[10] [1971] 2 S.A.S.R. 218, at pp. 223-224; cf. *Heaton* v. *Richards* (1881) 2 L.R. (N.S.W.) 73.

consideration? Absence of consideration may mean that a purely executory agreement for a gratuitous bailment is not an enforceable contract in the eyes of the law; but where the *res* is handed over to the bailee I should have thought that that was sufficient consideration, even in the case of a gratuitous deposit or gratuitous work on the *res* or gratuitous carriage. It is not, as I see it, necessary that the detriment involved in parting with possession should entail any economic disadvantage to the bailor, and irrelevant that in fact he may derive some advantage from handing over the *res* and the bailee none . . . If a gratuitous bailment carried out in consequence of an agreement in fact is not a contract, there will be difficulty in giving effect to the conditions actually attached by the parties to the bailment. It will not always be possible to find an action in tort appropriate to the breach of such a contract, especially where there is no physical damage to the *res*. Let us suppose A deposits documents with B for safekeeping and B agrees to accept them gratuitously and promises not to disclose them to anyone else. In breach of that promise he allows C to inspect them and C uses his knowledge so gained to the financial disadvantage of A. Is it conceivable that A would have no action against B? And what action could he have but one for damages for breach of contract?[11]

There are various ways of rationalising the imposition of liabilities upon a depositary over and above those which he would owe in tort. One is to subscribe to the elderly fairy-tale that the bailor's trust in his bailee amounts to sufficient consideration to support a promise on the part of the bailee. Another is to say that the bailee's possession grants him certain remedial advantages, e.g., the right to sue in trespass, which are benefit enough to make the agreement a genuine contract; on this interpretation, few bailments would ever be gratuitous. A third is to accept, along with Professor Sutton, that despite the lack of consideration gratuitous bailments impose "a contract by virtue of law" upon the bailee as soon as he assumes possession.[12] A fourth is to rely on the debatable equitable principle that no man will be allowed to renege from his promise where the promisee has altered his position in reliance thereon and where it would be manifestly inequitable to allow the promisor to resile.[13]

Each of these explanations has its advantages and disadvantages. It is submitted that an alternative, and preferable, method of assimilating decisions like *Kettle* v. *Bromsall* into modern theory is to regard them as turning upon the special nature of bailment, and as peculiar to that concept. The action of assumpsit, upon which these earlier authorities depended, did not require consideration. It evolved from the early forms of tort (possibly deceit, possibly trespass on the case)[14] to cater for the situation where, although no active misfeasance had occurred, the

---

[11] Cf. *Borden Chemical Co. (Canada) Ltd.* v. *J. G. Beukers Ltd.* (1973) 29 D.L.R. (3d.) 337 where, in not dissimilar circumstances, a remedy was given in conversion.

[12] Consideration Reconsidered, p. 160.

[13] According to Professor Atiyah, this reliance might constitute consideration: (1975) 38 M.L.R. 65. According to Lord Denning M.R., it could be sufficient to raise a promissory estoppel: *Evenden* v. *Guildford City Association Football Club Ltd.* [1975] I.C.R. 367, at 374.

[14] Fifoot, op. cit., pp. 333-334.

plaintiff had suffered through reliance on the defendant's promise or inducement. The process was well summarised by Holmes:

> If the chattel could be returned *in specie*, detinue afforded no satisfaction for damage which it might have suffered through the bailee's neglect. The natural remedy for such damage was the action on the case. But before this could be made entirely satisfactory there were certain difficulties to be overcome. The neglect which occasioned the damage might be a mere omission, and what was there akin to trespass in a nonfeasance to sustain the analogy upon which trespass on the case was founded? Moreover, to charge a man for not acting, you must show that it was his duty to act. As pleadings were formerly construed it would not have been enough to allege that the plaintiff's goods were damaged by the defendant's negligence. These troubles had been got over by the well-known words, *super se assumpsit*. . . . Assumpsit did not for a long time become an independent action of contract, and the allegation was simply the inducement to an action of tort. The ground of liability was the defendant had started upon the undertaking, so that his negligent omission, which let in the damage, could be connected with his acts as a part of his dealing with the thing. . . . Of course it was not confined to cases of bailment.[15]

But although the original foundations of assumpsit were tortious rather than contractual, and it was only by error that later authorities equated it with contract and superimposed the need for consideration, there is some justification for the view that assumpsit bears a closer similarity to contract than to tort.[16] Both are consensual, both depend upon privity of communication, and both proceed upon the notion of a promise or undertaking. The modern action for detinue or negligence is not thus circumscribed.[17] There can be little doubt, as we shall see from the discussions of mandatum, that gratuitous promises relative to chattels are enforceable once the promisor acquires possession. The same impression is received from modern authority like *Trefttz & Sons Ltd.* v. *Canelli*[18] and *Roufos* v. *Brewster and Brewster*.[19] Nor can it seriously be doubted that they are desirably so enforced. The doctrine of consideration fits uneasily into this enforcement and would be considerably weakened thereby. Since consideration is immaterial to a valid bailment, it might legitimately be discarded even in those situations where the relationship is overlaid with promises for the benefit of one party alone. Such situations might then stand revealed as vestigial relics of the old assumpsit, enforceable irrespective of contract or tort and consonant with the independent character of the modern relation of bailment.[20]

---

[15] *The Common Law*, p. 183.

[16] Cf. Stoljar, (1955) 7 *Res Judicatae* 160.

[17] Except insofar as detinue cannot lie without a prior demand: ante, p. 149.

[18] (1872) L.R. 4 P.C. 277.

[19] [1971] 2 S.A.S.R. 218.

[20] Cf. Davidge, (1925) 41 L.Q.R. 433, at 439: "But the true reason for all this talk about consideration for gratuitous bailment seems to be forgetfulness of the fact that assumpsit was in origin an action of tort and will still sometimes lie for one." In *Carte* v. *Flury Buick Jeep Inc.* (1973) 506 P. 2d. 701 it was held that the bailor has a choice of remedies for injury to his property: in assumpsit for breach of contract or an action based on tort.

B. Exclusion of liability by bailee

The absence of contract need not, of course, inhibit a depositary from limiting or excluding his liability towards the bailor. Despite the statements of Denning and Morris L.JJ. in *Adler* v. *Dickson*[21] that an injured party can be effectively deprived of his rights at common law only by contract, the contrary principle has been consistently acknowledged in a wide range of gratuitous undertakings.[22] Examples of its operation within the context of depositum are rare, probably because it does not occur to the ordinary depositee that he may reduce his liability at all. However *Brown* v. *National Bank of Australasia Ltd.*[23] furnishes such an illustration. Here, the bank accepted custody of debentures in a letter which concluded: "It must be distinctly understood that the bank accepts no responsibility whatsoever in taking charge of these debentures." According to Higinbotham C.J. this clause would not have protected the defendants had they been guilty of gross negligence but might have protected them from losses caused by the negligence of their staff.[24] Since, however, the learned judge also thought that the negligence of the bank's officers in this case did not furnish evidence upon which the jury could properly be invited to found a conclusion of gross neglect,[25] it is hard to discover any head of liability to which the present clause could have applied. In recent years, the words "whatsoever" or "howsoever caused" seem to have assumed a wider effect than that which they were given in the instant case.[26]

Leaving questions of interpretation aside, it is clear that the depositary may, by appropriate wording, impose stringent conditions upon his acceptance of the goods;[27] and may even exclude liability for them altogether. Presumably, the construction of such special agreements will, as in the case of contractual exclusions, take effect contra proferentem, and the onus will be upon the depositary to show that the clause in question covered the particular loss sustained. On the other hand, a court might

---

[21] [1955] 1 Q.B. 158, at 184, 198; see also *White* v. *Blackmore* [1972] 3 All E.R. 158, at 166.

[22] *Ashdown* v. *Samuel Williams Ltd.* [1957] 1 Q.B. 409; *Hedley Byrne & Co. Ltd.* v. *Heller & Partners Ltd.* [1964] A.C. 465; *Buckpitt* v. *Oates* [1968] 1 All E.R. 1145; *Genys* v. *Mathews* [1966] 1 W.L.R. 758; [1965] 3 All E.R. 24; *Gore* v. *Van der Lann* [1967] 2 Q.B. 31; *New Zealand Shipping Co. Ltd.* v. *A. N. Satterthwaite Ltd.* [1975] A.C. 154, at 182, per Lord Simon of Glaisdale.

[23] (1890) 16 V.L.R. 475.

[24] Ibid., at 481-482; see also per Williams J., at 483.

[25] Ibid., at 483.

[26] Until the trend was reversed by *Smith* v. *South Wales Switchgear* [1978] 1 All E.R. 18. The need for banks to impose some safeguarding provision in cases of gratuitous deposit was accentuated by the case of *Langtry* v. *London & Westminster Bank Ltd.* (unreported, 1896) where the defendants were sued for the misdelivery of a box of jewels to a person posing as a depositor; the case was eventually settled out of court. In (1896) 17 *Journal of the Institute of Bankers* 455-456, there is a discussion of the bank's liability in such a case and a common form of receipt devised by a Sub-Committee of the Central Association of Bankers; the drafting committee considered (a) that it would be impracticable for banks to enter into a special contract with every depositor, (b) that the bank would be relieved if it took reasonable care. But the preferable modern view is that liability in conversion on a misdelivery is strict: ante, p. 132.

[27] *Webb* v. *Agricultural Society of New South Wales* (1893) 14 L.R. (N.S.W.) 333; cf. *Andrew* v. *Griffin* [1918] 1 W.W.R. 274, 532.

relax these ordinary principles of construction where the depositary is a private person or does not enjoy a perceptible superiority of bargaining power over the depositor.[28]

C. Modification of bailee's responsibility by conduct of bailor or bailee

Despite the absence of consideration, most gratuitous bailments continue to bear a very close resemblance to a contract between the parties. They will, in most cases, be consensual arrangements, and the parties may vary their agreement in a number of ways: by providing for a greater or lesser standard of care on the part of the depositary or by assigning additional or incidental duties to the basic relationship. In those cases where the bailment is consensual, it may therefore be appropriate to consider whether certain contractual concepts, designed to amplify or effectuate the agreement between the parties, can legitimately be used in clarifying the responsibilities of a bailee.

An obvious example is deviation or "fundamental breach". A bailee for reward who radically departs from the itinerary or place of safe-keeping, or who otherwise breaches his contract in a particularly serious way, may become an insurer of the goods once that event has occurred; thus, if he wrongfully sub-bails them, and they are destroyed while in the possession of the sub-bailee, the original bailee is answerable, regardless of whether there was any carelessness on the part of his sub-bailee.[29] He has, in other words, stepped outside his contract, and anything that ensues from this act will be his responsibility, irrespective of fault.

There is little modern authority favouring the application of this principle to gratuitous bailments, although its adoption would certainly seem to make sense. At first sight, *Ronnenburg* v. *Falkland Islands Co.*[30] appears to be such a case, for the bailees removed the plaintiffs' gunpowder from the agreed place of storage and placed it in a far less suitable vessel. However, it is clear that the court did not hold them liable purely on the basis of deviation, but because their conduct in thus removing the gunpowder was demonstrably negligent or, alternatively, an act of trespass against the plaintiffs. Whether the same result would have followed if the powder had been removed without its owner's consent to an equally safe vessel, and thence been lost through no fault of the defendants, cannot be answered from the decision itself.

The same difficulty attends *Turner* v. *Merrylees*,[31] where the defendant removed the plaintiff's phaeton from its agreed resting-place to an outhouse. Here again, there was abundant evidence that the defendant was negligent in effecting the removal. Wright J.'s observation that he might have escaped liability if he had merely left the phaeton where it was cannot mean that, once he moved it, he became an insurer, any more than it can mean that a depositary's duties arise only from misfeasance and not from passive neglect. If it means anything at all, this remark must signify that whereas to move the vehicle was negligent, to leave it where it stood was not.

---

28 Chapter 25, post.
29 *Edwards* v. *Newland* [1950] 2 K.B. 534; post, p. 473.
30 (1864) 17 C.B.N.S. 1; 144 E.R. 1; ante, p. 295.
31 (1892) 8 T.L.R. 695.

There have, however, been occasional cases of gratuitous loans in which the borrower who has wrongfully allowed a third party to use the chattel, has been held to become an insurer. In *Bringloe* v. *Morice*[32] the only question decided was whether the conduct of the defendant was trespassory, and the court concluded that it was; in *Chapman* v. *Robinson*,[33] although the court was required to deal only with the liability of the sub-bailee, it remarked obiter that the original borrower would have been liable for lending him the chattel in the first place.

Likewise, there is a certain amount of authority favouring the view that a depositary who wrongfully uses the bailed property, or applies it for a purpose not within the terms of the bailment, "thereby determines the bailment and becomes responsible for all consequences".[34] According to Wyatt Paine,[35] the determination of a naked bailment by an inconsistent act on the part of the gratuitous bailee:

> . . . is based on the doctrine that the performance of the unwarranted act operates like a disclaimer of tenancy at common law, and consequently not only determines the bailment, but also renders the tortfeasing bailee liable in an action of trover for the conversion of the goods.

If an agreement between the parties to a gratuitous bailment is to be enforceable at all, it would seem logical that a total departure from the terms of that bailment should render the bailee liable for losses consequent thereon. The wrongful act may not, in the light of modern authority, be trespassory, and unless accompanied by some denial of title will not constitute a conversion.[36] A depositary who promises to keep the goods in a particular place, or to carry them by a particular route, or to give them only his personal attention and not to delegate the task, should not be allowed with impunity to subject those goods to a danger they would not otherwise have suffered, by virtue of his wrongful act. Since that wrongful act may not be tortious (and even perhaps where it is) it is submitted that the analogy of contract should be applicable to provide the bailor with a remedy in all cases of deviation by his bailee, and to render the bailee answerable for a fundamental disregard of his undertaking, whether that disregard was accompanied by negligence or not.

Such liability may be justified as a necessary implication in the agreement or because a conscious disregard of the terms of his undertaking

---

32 (1676) 1 Mod. Rep. 210; 86 E.R. 834.
33 (1969) 71 W.W.R. 515, at 519; see also *Isaack* v. *Clarke* (1615) 2 Bulst. 306; 80 E.R. 1143, at 309, 1145.
34 *Miles* v. *Cattle* (1830) 6 Bing. 743; *Von Minden* v. *Pyke* (1865) 4 F. & F. 176 E.R. 678; *Wills* v. *Browne* [1912] 1 D.L.R. 388 (all cases of *mandatum*); *Munn* v. *Wakelin* (1944) 17 M.P.R. 446; *Knight* v. *Wilson* 1949 Scots L.T. 26 (though the seller of uncollected goods in this case may not have yet become a gratuitous bailee); *McKenna & Armistead Pty. Ltd.* v. *Excavations Pty. Ltd.* [1957] S.R. (N.S.W.) 515 (where the same observation applies, particularly as the delay in delivery was due to the fault of the seller). See also *Mitchell* v. *Ealing L.B.C.* (1978) *The Times* February 21st, where the rule in *Shaw & Co.* v. *Symmons & Sons* [1917] 1 K.B. 199 was held to apply to a gratuitous bailee.
35 Op. cit., at **34**.
36 *McKenna & Armistead Pty. Ltd.* v. *Excavations Pty. Ltd.*, supra; *Penfold's Wines Pty. Ltd.* v. *Elliott* (1946) 74 C.L.R. 204.

makes a bailee guilty of fraud. It seems preferable, however, to accept it as a peculiar feature of gratuitous bailments, which may produce obligations not strictly classifiable as either tortious or contractual, but which, because of bailment's early associations with the action of assumpsit, bear a close analogy to contractual principles and are enforceable in much the same way.

Certainly the depositary who is induced to accept the goods by fraud or duress on the part of the depositor should be under no responsibility for them, except perhaps as an involuntary bailee. If the misrepresentation was merely negligent or innocent, the position is more doubtful, but it is again submitted that the bailee should be entitled to repudiate or sue for damages in analogous manner to one who becomes a bailee by contract. Possibly it would be easier to find mutual consideration in a situation of this kind. Of course, the bailee may in such circumstances enjoy a remedy in tort, but the consensual nature of his obligation suggests that these remedies should not be exhaustive.

D. Detention, delegation and misuse

The classes of conduct which are permitted or forbidden to a depositary will depend on the circumstances of the case. However, in the absence of special facts, it seems that the depositary is not entitled to delegate his responsibility to a third person. Whether such conduct renders him liable for all losses occurring to the goods while in the hands of the delegate has already been discussed.

The depositary is bound to return the goods on demand, or to deliver them over to a third party at the bailor's instruction, at least where such delivery over has been agreed beforehand or does not involve the depositary in any extra labour or expense.[37] Failure to comply with a demand for return may render him liable in detinue to the bailor and may also render him liable for any subsequent loss.

The circumstances of the delivery and the nature of the chattel will also determine whether the bailee is entitled to use it during the period of the bailment. Although certain kinds of physical enjoyment or employment of the chattel may be justified by reference to these facts— and may even be incumbent on the bailee as part of his basic obligation —it again seems clear that there is no prima facie right on the part of the depositary to use the chattel for his own advantage. Such a right must be implied from the agreement and may often, of course, render the bailment non-gratuitous. Where no such right exists, the bailee may be guilty of conversion and should, as suggested above, be strictly liable for losses resulting from his misuse, whether he has committed any tort or not.

E. Profits or progeny

There is no Commonwealth authority in point, but both Story[38] and Paton[39] are agreed that produce or increments accruing to property during the deposit must be restored to the bailor. Generally, this is likely only

[37] Ante, p. 313.
[38] Section 97.
[39] At p. 100.

to occur in the case of living things, such as the offspring of animals or the fruits of a plant or shrub.[40] In this regard, there is a recent decision of the Court of Appeal[41] (dealing with cows held under a hire-purchase agreement) which states as a general rule that at least so far as concerns leased animals produce follows possession. Thus, in that case, the hirer was allowed to keep calves born to the cattle during the period of the bailment. However, the Court pointed out that such a result was subject to a contrary intention, and it seems likely that in cases of gratuitous custody such intention will almost invariably be held to be present.

Where the depositary profits from misusing the chattel (e.g., where he hires out a car for reward) it is submitted that he holds the proceeds as constructive trustee for the bailor, whether or not he has committed a conversion. In this respect, there is a clear analogy between the bailor-bailee relationship and that of master and servant. The depositary may, of course, exercise the possessory remedies against a third party[42] irrespective of whether he is liable over to his bailor,[43] but he will be liable to account for the proceeds, after deducting the value (if any) of his immediate interest. It is unlikely that this interest, being in the vast majority of cases both revocable and burdensome, will give rise to any entitlement to damages per se.

IV. DUTIES OF THE DEPOSITOR

Express promises on the part of the depositor, whether they count as a reward to the depositary or not, would generally constitute consideration; the bailee could in such an event have a contractual right to enforce them. Thus, if A asks B to store his chemicals for no reward, and promises to reimburse B for all damage caused by the goods, whether the result of A's negligence or not, B should be able to enforce this promise by an action for breach of contract. Likewise, if A promises not to call for them before a certain time, there would then arise the unusual phenomenon of a gratuitous bailment which did not give the bailor an immediate right to possess.[44]

However, such promises will be unusual. The greater problem is to decide whether non-tortious obligations on the part of the depositor are to be implied into the agreement. On this point there seems to be no authority and it may follow that the depositor's liabilities sound exclusively in tort. Logically, the theory of gradations of fault would suggest that a depositor should be liable for even slight neglect, as was the gratuitous borrower of a chattel. In both cases the benefit is solely that of the defendant and the division of bailments in *Coggs* v. *Bernard*[45] seems to accept this as determinative of a higher level of care. But with the

---

[40] *Grant's Farming Co. Ltd.* v. *Attwell* (1901) 9 H.C. 91 (S. Africa).
[41] *Tucker* v. *Farm and General Investment Trust Ltd.* [1966] 2 Q.B. 421.
[42] *Rooth* v. *Wilson* (1817) 1 B. & Ald. 59; 106 E.R. 22.
[43] *The Winkfield* [1902] P. 42.
[44] Cf. Paton, p. 101, who doubts whether such a promise is enforceable. There seems to be no reason why a court should not discern reciprocal consideration in a case like this.
[45] (1703) 2 Ld. Raym. 909; 92 E.R. 107.

absence of authority and the modern rejection of standards of negligence, it seems that the bailor will be liable for negligence alone. Ancillary obligations, such as reimbursing the depositary for expenditure on the chattel, are equally difficult to fit into the modern pattern of obligations. Unless the bailee is acting as an agent of necessity or the bailor can be brought within the doctrines of implied assumpsit or unjust enrichment such expenditure would appear to be irrecoverable.[46] It is submitted that implied assumpsit should be invoked whenever possible to encompass such an event. The depositary does not (pace Story)[47] enjoy a lien over the goods[48] and the rules of quasi-contract may only rarely afford him a remedy.[49]

---

[46] If the bailor sues for detinue or conversion, and the bailee's labour has improved the chattel, the measure of damages will normally represent the value of the chattel before any improvements have been effected by the defendant: *Munro* v. *Willmott* [1949] 1 K.B. 295; *Greenwood* v. *Bennett* [1973] Q.B. 195. Likewise, on an award of specific restitution, an allowance will be made. But it seems unlikely that the same principles will apply where there has been no tangible improvement to the goods, e.g. where the defendant's labour and expense merely prevent it from being destroyed or seized by a third party.

[47] Section 121.

[48] *Leese* v. *Martin* (1873) L.R. 17 Eq. 224; aliter, perhaps, if he improves the chattel?

[49] Cf. *R.* v. *Howson* (1966) 55 D.L.R. (2d) 582, at 593-594.

CHAPTER 10

MANDATUM, OR GRATUITOUS WORK AND LABOUR

I. DEFINITION

In many respects, mandatum is the most unusual variety of bailment and the variety which most persuasively demonstrates the singular character of bailments as a whole. It results whenever one person bails goods to another on the understanding that the recipient will perform a gratuitous service in relation to them and redeliver them to the bailor (or at his direction) when the service is completed. Generally, the task will be performed upon the chattel itself, which will accordingly be benefited, altered or preserved as a result. But the concept of mandatum is not limited to transactions of this kind. There have been cases in which a bailment of money to be applied for a certain purpose has been classified as *mandatum*,[1] and it appears that even the delivery of a chattel to be used in the performance of a gratuitous service for the bailor will be characterised in the same way. Examples might arise when A lends B his car in response to B's offer to drive A's friends home,[2] or where C hands to D documents which will enable D to compile gratuitously C's income-tax return.[3]

There are obvious similarities between bailments by way of mandatum and those other, gratuitous undertakings which do not create a bailment between the parties. The older cases draw no material distinction, in question of misfeasance, between the duties of a person who is handed a specific sum of money in order to effect an insurance[4] and a person who promises to do so in return for a promise of future reimbursement.[5] Modern authority endorses the view that these duties are substantially the same. In both cases the promisor will be liable if he performs the covenanted task with less than the required degree of competence or care and

---

[1] E.g. *Wills* v. *Brown* [1912] 1 D.L.R. 388. Gratuitous carriage is, of course, an undisputed example of mandatum. Cases involving the gratuitous transportation of money include *Parry* v. *Roberts* (1835) 3 Ad. & El. 118; 111 E.R. 358; *Copland* v. *Brogan* 1916 S.C. 277.

[2] *Lenkeit* v. *Ebert* [1947] St. R. Qd. 126.

[3] Quaere whether a transaction can amount to mandatum if the undertaking is purely negative; for example, a promise by the gratuitous bailee of a document not to disclose its contents. Probably it is preferable to regard this as mandatum, with the result that this aspect of the undertaking may fall subject to a different burden of proof: see p. 343, post. There is authority for the view that breach of such a promise may entitle the promisee to recover in contract (*Roufos* v. *Brewster and Brewster* [1971] 2 S.A.S.R. 218, at 224) or in conversion (*Borden Chemical Co. (Canada) Ltd.* v. *J. G. Beukers Ltd.* (1973) 29 D.L.R. (3d) 337) from the gratuitous bailee.

[4] *Whitehead* v. *Greetham* (1825) 2 Bing. 464; 130 E.R. 385 (where the bailee promised to purchase an annuity).

[5] *Wilkinson* v. *Coverdale* (1793) 1 Esp. 75; 170 E.R. 284; *Moore* v. *Mourgue* (1776) 2 Cowp. 479; 98 E.R. 1197 (possibly not a case of gratuitous service).

in the case (at least) of non-bailees the standard exacted is that of the reasonable man.[6] More difficult questions arise when the promisor neglects or refuses to perform at all. Where there is no bailment, the absence of consideration will generally disable the promisee from enforcing the promise for as long as the agreement remains executory.[7] In exceptional cases, he may possess a remedy in tort for fraud or negligent mis-statement,[8] but in spite of recent liberalisation[9] the latter remedy remains quite closely circumscribed.[10] He may also contend that his reliance upon the promise constitutes valid consideration, but here again the authorities are generally opposed to enforcement on such grounds.[11] If, on the other hand, the promisee has already begun to perform the work, it seems likely that the courts will discern a contract "imposed by law" to complete it.[12] Certainly there may be powerful reasons for permitting recovery when the plaintiff is put to expense through the gratuitous promisor's failure to carry the work through to its conclusion, and a number of older decisions suggest that such promises are enforceable once the promisor embarks upon performance.[13]

In the context of gratuitous bailments, it is submitted that the arguments for disregarding the absence of consideration are strengthened by the independent quality of the bailment relation, and that the promisor is entitled to enforce from the moment that the bailee takes possession. Modern authority is admittedly rare and the decisions delivered during

---

[6] *Kostiuk* v. *Union Acceptance Corporation Ltd.* (1968) 66 D.L.R. (2d) 430; *Pilcher* v. *Leyland Motors Ltd.* [1932] N.Z.L.R. 449, per Smith and Ostler JJ.; the remaining members of the New Zealand C.A. based their decision solely on the fact that the defendant's promise had been given for good consideration. See further: *W. A. Bennett Ltd.* v. *Puna* [1956] N.Z.L.R. 629; *Hedley Byrne & Co. Ltd.* v. *Heller & Partners Ltd.* [1964] A.C. 465; *Rondel* v. *Worsley* [1969] 1 A.C. 191; cf. *Argy Trading Ltd.* v. *Lapid Developments Ltd.* [1977] 1 W.L.R. 444.

[7] *Thorne* v. *Deas* (1809) 4 Johns (N.Y.) 84; *Pilcher* v. *Leyland Motors Ltd.* [1932] N.Z.L.R. 449, at 466 (Ostler J.); *Skelton* v. *L. & N.W. Ry. Co.* (1867) L.R. 2 C.P. 631, at 636 (Willes J.); *Hedley Byrne & Co. Ltd.* v. *Heller & Partners Ltd.* [1964] A.C. 465, at 526 (Lord Devlin); and see ante, n. 5. If the defendant negligently leads the plaintiff to assume that the work has been done and the plaintiff suffers injury, damage to property or even purely economic loss through his reliance on this belief, there may be an action in negligence: *Sharp* v. *Avery and Kerwood* [1938] 4 All E.R. 85; *Clayton* v. *Woodman & Son (Builders) Ltd.* [1962] 2 Q.B. 533; *Smith* v. *Auckland Hospital Board* [1965] N.Z.L.R. 191; *Dutton* v. *Bognor Regis U.D.C.* [1972] 1 Q.B. 373; *Anns* v. *Merton London Borough Council* [1977] 2 W.L.R. 1024; *Caltex Oil (Aust.) Pty. Ltd.* v. *The "Willemstad"* (1976) 11 A.L.R. 227; *Bowen* v. *Paramount Builders (Hamilton) Ltd.* [1977] 1 N.Z.L.R. 394; cf. *Argy Trading Ltd.* v. *Lapid Developments Ltd.* [1977] 1 W.L.R. 444.

[8] *Hedley Byrne & Co. Ltd.* v. *Heller & Partners Ltd.*, ante.

[9] *Esso Petroleum Co. Ltd.* v. *Mardon* [1975] 1 Q.B. 819; aff'd [1976] Q.B. 801; [1975] C.L.J. 194; *Arenson* v. *Beckman, Casson Rutley & Co.* [1975] 3 All E.R. 901.

[10] *Mutual Life and Citizens' Assurance Co. Ltd.* v. *Evatt* [1971] A.C. 793; Clerk & Lindsell, *Torts* (14th ed.), paras. 866a et seq.

[11] Cf. Atiyah (1975) 38 M.L.R. 65.

[12] *Pilcher* v. *Leyland Motors Ltd.* [1932] N.Z.L.R. 499, at 466-467 (Osler J.).

[13] *Elsee* v. *Gatward* (1793) 1 Term Rep. 143; 101 E.R. 82; *Balfe* v. *West* (1853) 13 C.B. 466; cf. *Fish* v. *Kelly* (1864) 17 C.B.N.S. 194. A modern illustration might be that of a barrister who failed to appear to conduct a case for a client: cf. *Rondel* v. *Worsley* [1969] 1 A.C. 191. Clerk & Lindsell, op. cit., para. 963 seem to conclude that since there is no contract between barrister and client, the client is reduced to an action in tort, which in this case would presumably be non-existent.

the past century seem divided on this issue.[14] But if the foregoing submission is correct, there is a difference between bailments by way of mandatum and other gratuitous undertakings, where the promisor's duty to perform becomes binding (if at all) only when he has begun the task in question.

It is not, at first sight, easy to demarcate bailments by way of mandatum from gratuitous deposits. The latter will often generate positive obligations incidental to the primary duty of safe-keeping; thus, the unrewarded custodian of perishables may be obliged to check and adjust the temperature in which they are kept, and all depositaries must exert some measure of effort to guard against destruction or theft. Conversely, the mandatary will be bound to take care of the chattel in addition to executing the commission for which it was entrusted to him. Sir William Jones distinguished the two relations by saying that mandate lies in feasance whereas depositum lies simply in custody.[15] But this is of little immediate assistance where the deposit involves affirmative conduct of the kind we have described. A better description of the difference was given by Story, in whose opinion:

> The true distinction between them is, that, in the case of a deposit, the principal object of the parties is the custody of the thing, and the service and labour are merely accessorial: in the case of a mandate, the labour and services are the principal objects of the parties, and the custody of the thing is merely accessorial. The distribution of the subject into different heads may, on this account be not unjustifiable, and it is certainly convenient.[16]

The mandatary does, of course, acquire possession of the goods and can therefore exercise the appropriate remedies for any violation of that possession;[17] even, it seems, where his own misconduct has placed him in the position of an insurer.[18] As with every other class of bailee, the mandatary's exercise of these remedies is no longer dependent upon his being liable to the bailor for the loss or damage in question; he will, however, be liable to account to him for the proceeds of such action over and above the quantum of his immediate interest.[19]

There are probably fewer modern cases on mandate than of any other variety of bailment; indeed, its chief claim to renown rests on the fact that it was the species involved in the great case of *Coggs* v. *Bernard*.[20] But modern illustrations do exist, particularly in the area of gratuitous carriage of goods. It is probably not without significance that this area provides the most positive evidence of a progression from the old standards of care towards a general test of negligence in determining the mandatary's liability. There is reason to assume that this criterion will eventually be

---

[14] Post, p. 339 et seq.
[15] *Bailments*, p. 53.
[16] Section 140; *Wills* v. *Brown* [1912] 1 D.L.R. 388; Beven, *Negligence* (2nd ed.), p. 923; *Helson* v. *McKenzies* (*Cuba St.*) *Ltd.* [1950] N.Z.L.R. 878, at 916.
[17] Story, *Bailments*, s. 150 et seq.
[18] Cf. *Miles* v. *Cattle* (1830) 6 Bing. 740; 8 L.J. (O.S.) (C.P.) 271, criticised by Story, s.152.
[19] Ante, p. 177 et seq.
[20] (1703) 2 Ld. Raym. 909; 92 E.R. 107.

extended to encompass all varieties of mandate. However, on the present authorities it is difficult to be sure.

II. The Duties of the Mandatary

A. Duties of competence and care

Logically, it should be possible to differentiate between the two aspects of mandate and to argue that different standards of performance apply in respect of each. This is undoubtedly the case with the hire of work and labour.[21] The bailee is absolutely bound to provide workmanship of the agreed standard,[22] and is strictly liable for defects in any materials he has supplied in conjunction with the work.[23] On the other hand, he is liable only for a want of reasonable care in keeping the chattel during the period of employment.[24]

No such differentiation seems to have been consciously applied under transactions of mandate. It is true that Sir William Jones, relying on principles of the civil law, considered the mandatary to be under a strict obligation to bring to the task such diligence and proficiency as were necessary for its adequate completion.[25] But this approach was vigorously contested by Story[26] and by Beven.[27] It now seems clear that whatever abstract standard of care governs the mandatary's safe-keeping of the chattel applies to his execution of the labour he has undertaken. This does not mean, however, that the same types of conduct will necessarily satisfy both duties. A mandatary may be deemed to have warranted special skill in respect of one branch of his undertaking (e.g. the repair of a watch) but not in respect of the more general duty of custody common to all bailees.[28]

As to the degree of care and competence which the mandatary must show in his dealings with the chattel, there is an obvious parallel between the developments in this field and those relating to gratuitous deposits.[29] But these developments are far from conclusive and the dearth of modern decisions may justify a continued endorsement of the hallowed ratios between responsibility and reward.

In *Coggs* v. *Bernard*[30] there is little direct authority on the Common Law duties of a mandatary, because the court was primarily concerned with the effect of the defendant's special promise "salvo et secure elevare".

---

[21] Chapter 14, post.
[22] E.g. *Kimber* v. *William Willett Ltd.* [1947] 1 K.B. 570; cf. s. 74, *Trade Practices Act* 1974 (Cth); post, p. 518.
[23] E.g. *Stewart* v. *Reavell's Garage Ltd.* [1952] 2 Q.B. 545; *Gloucester County Council* v. *Richardson* [1969] 1 A.C. 480; *Young & Marten Ltd.* v. *McManus Childs Ltd.* [1969] 1 A.C. 454; cf. *Helicopter Sales Pty. Ltd.* v. *Rotorwork Pty. Ltd.* (1974) 3 A.L.R. 85 (High Court of Australia).
[24] E.g. *Hollier* v. *Rambler Motors (A.M.C.) Ltd.* [1972] 2 Q.B. 71.
[25] *Bailments*, at p. 53, et seq.; he was prepared to exempt gratuitous carriers from the general rule; see p. 335, post.
[26] Sections 173 et seq.
[27] *Negligence* (2nd ed.), pp. 924-927.
[28] See p. 334 et seq., post.
[29] Chapter 9, ante.
[30] (1703) 2 Ld. Raym. 909; 92 E.R. 107.

Lord Holt appeared to cast the mandatary's liability in terms of ordinary neglect, but his words were not wholly unequivocal and there is reason to believe that he saw no effective difference in this respect between depositum and mandatum:

> And if a man acts by commission for another gratis, and in the executing of his commission behaves himself negligently, he is answerable. . . . This undertaking obliges the undertaker to a diligent management. . . . And if a man will do that, and miscarries in the performance of his trust, an action will lie against him for that, though nobody could have compelled him to do the thing.[31]

Gould J. seemed to favour the standard of gross neglect, although it is sometimes difficult to dissociate those parts of his judgment which deal with mandates generally from those which deal with the immediate defendant's undertaking.[32] His judgment favours liability for ordinary neglect only where the mandatary has promised to carry the goods "safely and securely" or has made some other promise of equivalent weight. Where, on the other hand, the mandate is merely general or unqualified, the bailee is liable only for gross neglect.

Powell J. took, if anything a less clement view: "And the bailee in this case shall answer accidents if the goods are stolen: but not such accidents and casualties as happen by the act of God, as fire, tempest etc."[33] He based this opinion upon the extent of bailee's warranty: "And a man may warrant a thing without any consideration. And, therefore when I have reposed a trust in you, upon your undertaking, if I suffer, when I have so relied upon you, I shall have my action."[34]

However, the example he gave (of a tenant offering to occupy a house in return for a promise to yield it up in the same state of repair) is certainly one in which a modern court would feel able to find consideration.[35] Powell J. was clearly of the opinion that a general bailment (that is, one in which the bailee had not specially undertaken additional liabilities) does not bind the bailee to keep safely at all events.[36] But he did not explicitly consider the duty to be exacted from a simple mandatary and it is difficult to extract from *Coggs* v. *Bernard* any universal, or even preponderant, support for a general standard of gross neglect.

Nevertheless, this was the criterion of liability adopted in many decisions over the succeeding years.[37] In applying it, the judges appear to have drawn no fundamental distinction between the execution of the task and the incidental custody which this necessitated. The standard of gross negligence

---

[31] Ibid., at 113 (E.R.).
[32] Ibid., at 107-108.
[33] Ibid., at 108.
[34] Ibid.
[35] Cf. *A.R. Williams Machinery Ltd.* v. *Muttart Builders Supplies Winnipeg Ltd.* (1961) 30 D.L.R. (2d) 339; (1961) D.L.R. (2d) 187; post, p. 371.
[36] (1703) 92 E.R., at 109.
[37] *Moore* v. *Mourgue* (1776) 2 Cowp. 479; 93 E.R. 1197; *Shiells* v. *Blackburne* (1789) 1 H. Bl. 158; 126 E.R. 94, *The Rendsberg* (1805) 6 Rob. Adm. R. 142, 155; *Dartnall* v. *Howard* (1825) 4 B. & C. 345; 107 E.R. 1888; *Whitehead* v. *Greetham* (1825) 2 Bing. 464; 130 E.R. 385; *Beauchamp* v. *Powley* (1831) 1 M. & R. 38; 174 E.R. 14. *Shillibeer* v. *Glynn* (1836) 2 M. & W. 143; 150 E.R. 704; cf. *Bourne* v. *Diggles* (1814) 2 Chit. 311; *O'Hanlan* v. *Murray* (1860) 12 Ir. C.L.R. 161.

found acceptance in England as late as 1915[38] and in Australia as recently as 1946.[39] It is supported, at least nominally, by Story,[40] Beven[41] and Wyatt Paine.[42] The following are examples of its operation in particular cases. It will be noted that not all of them are unambiguous, and that on occasions the judges use the terms negligence and gross negligence interchangeably.

Beauchamp v. *Powley*:[43] The defendant was a coachman who took delivery of a parcel to be delivered without reward. It never arrived and the defendant was unable to explain its loss, since he claimed to have forgotten all about it. Lord Tenderden C.J. doubted whether there was sufficient evidence to support a count in trover, but held that the defendant should be liable for gross negligence, if the jury found that his conduct fitted that description. "Nothing was to be paid for its conveyance: but still, if the coachman received it, it was his duty to take care of it, and deliver it at the office in Holborn to which it was addressed . . . (but) . . . if there was not great, and somewhat extraordinary negligence, on his part, the verdict ought to be for him."[44]

Dartnall v. *Howard*:[45] The plaintiff engaged the defendant attorneys to invest a large sum of money in the purchase of an annuity. The money was lost through the defendants' failure to take a sufficient security and the plaintiff sued in assumpsit for the loss. Abbot C.J. held that the action should fail because the pleadings had omitted to allege that the defendants were retained *as attorneys*, or that they were to have any reward for their pains. Accordingly, the defendants could not be charged with any additional responsibility which might otherwise have been attributed to them in their professional character. "Can we say that it is the absolute duty of any person so employed, without pay, and without remuneration . . . not to take a security of an insufficient nature? . . . The only duty that is imposed under such a retainer and employment as is here mentioned is a duty to act faithfully and honestly, and not to be guilty of any gross or corrupt neglect in the discharge of that which he undertakes to do. But a man may, when acting most faithfully and most honestly, happen to take an insufficient security, without gross or culpable negligence on his part; he may have been misled, he may have been deceived, he may have taken such care as an ordinary man would take with regard to the subject-

---

[38] Smith, *Leading Cases* (12th ed.), pp. 207 et seq.
[39] *Lenkeit* v. *Ebert* [1947] St. R. Qd. 126; cf. *Heaton* v. *Richards* (1881) 2 L.R. (N.S.W.) 73.
[40] Sections 173 et seq.
[41] *Negligence* (2nd ed. 1895), pp. 924-929.
[42] *Bailments* (1901), p. 58 et seq.
[43] (1831) 1 M. & R. 38; 174 E.R. 14.
[44] Quaere whether the coachman was a servant, and thus precluded from becoming a bailee. The report says that the parcel was delivered to him by the servant of Fagg, who was one of the proprietors of the coach: cf. Chapter 7, ante. A further peculiarity of this case consists in the fact that the plaintiff was the person to whom the parcel was to be delivered, and not the person who had delivered it to the coachman. Counsel's objection that there was no privity between plaintiff and defendant, and that the defendant did not know of the plaintiff's existence, was disregarded in Lord Tenterden's judgment. The case may represent an early example of the principal bailor's right of action against a sub-bailee, discussed in Chapter 20, post.
[45] (1825) 5 B. & C. 345; 107 E.R. 1088.

matter intrusted to him, and yet doing all that, his endeavours may have failed . . .".[46]

Parry v. *Roberts*:[47] The defendant, having agreed to carry a sum of money for the plaintiff without reward, afterwards claimed that he had "lost the money among the whores" and offered to repay it. Upon his failing to do so, the plaintiff sued on a count for money had and received. The defendant objected that the proper count was gross negligence and that this question could not be raised on a count for money had and received. The court accepted that an action for gross negligence would lie against a mandatary, but held that it was not open to the defendant to evade the present count merely by alleging his own gross neglect. The facts of the case were equally consistent with a misapplication of the money on his part and he had failed to establish the facts upon which he relied. Had he done so, there could be no action for money had and received, but in the present circumstances the onus was upon him and he had failed to discharge it. "If he is to avail himself of his own wrong to defeat an action which otherwise would lie, he must give clear proof of it."[48]

Lenkeit v. *Ebert*:[49] The defendant agreed to drive one of the plaintiff's guests to the station in a vehicle belonging to the plaintiff; all three were guests at a party in the plaintiff's home. The defendant drove off at a high rate of speed and overturned the vehicle while negotiating a curve in the road. The plaintiff's action failed because there was, in the eyes of the Court, no evidence from which a finding of gross negligence could be inferred. The vehicle was old and was fitted with unmatching tyres on the front wheels. The onus of establishing gross negligence was on the plaintiff[50] and in these circumstances it could not definitely be said that the damage resulted from the defendant's excessive speed or any other act of gross negligence on his part. Nor was this a case in which the mandatary was under an increased responsibility by virtue of the mandator's reliance upon his special skill; the task was simple and the responsibility slight.[51]

Piper v. *Geldart*:[52] The plaintiff sued for the destruction by fire of a quantity of furniture and household goods which the defendant was transporting for him free of charge. There was no direct evidence as to the immediate cause of the fire, but the vehicle was shown to have been travelling at an excessive speed and it seems likely that this resulted in friction which ignited the contents. The majority of the New Brunswick Supreme Court (Appeal Division) held that gross negligence was established and appeared to accept that the onus of proof rested with the defendant. Harrison J. held that the bailee in all cases is bound to show reasonable care and skill, but agreed that there was ample evidence of negligence on the present facts.[53]

---

[46] Ibid., at 1089 (E.R.) cf. *Bourne* v. *Diggles* (1814) 2 Chit. 311; *Whitehead* v. *Greetham* (1825) 2 Bing. 464; 130 E.R. 385; *O'Hanlan* v. *Murray* (1860) 12 Irish C.L.R. 161.
[47] (1835) 3 Ad. & El. 118; 111 E.R. 358.
[48] Ibid., at pp. 121, 359 per Lord Denman C.J.
[49] [1947] St. R. Qd. 126.
[50] Per Philp J. at 131; sed quaere; cf. p. 311, ante; p. 343, post.
[51] Cf. *Shiells* v. *Blackburne* (1789) 1 H. Bl. 158; 126 E.R. 94, post, p. 336.
[52] [1954] 2 D.L.R. 97.
[53] Ibid., at 105.

Campbell v. *Pickard*:[54] The owner of a car asked a friend to collect it from a garage and deliver it to him at the Winnipeg Yacht Club. While carrying out the task, the friend drove at speed across a blind intersection when the lights were at red. The vehicle was badly damaged in a collision and the plaintiff (on behalf of his insurance company) claimed against the friend for the resulting loss. The Manitoba Court of Appeal held that the bailment was one of mandatum, and that its character as such was not altered by the fact that the defendant, on his way to the Club, had picked up two young ladies.[55] Accordingly, he was liable only for gross negligence[56] or something "not arising merely from some want of foresight or mistake of judgement, but from some culpable default."[57] In the majority view, such fault had been established and the plaintiff was entitled to succeed, the defendant's conduct amounting to "a very marked departure from the standard by which responsible and competent people in charge of motor cars habitually govern themselves."[58]

However, as in the case of depositum,[59] there are a number of factors which quality or detract from the traditional conception of the mandatary's liability as something comparable to recklessness or fraud. The first of these is the flexible, subjective moderation of the mandatary's liability according to his known capacities and to any special skill he has professed. Sometimes this variation will operate in the mandatary's favour, as where the mandator entrusts a complicated task or an expensive chattel to a person of known incompetence. As Mathew J. remarked in a different context, "A man who lights gas is hardly the person to entrust with the care of a double-bass violin."[60]

But it seems that the rule relieving a mandatary who uses only such ability and skill as he possesses may be displaced where his conduct, or the nature of the task he has undertaken, suggests a greater degree of proficiency than he actually enjoys. In such a case, there is authority for the view that he must bring to the task such care and skill as his profession suggests, and be liable if he falls below that standard.[61] This, in fact, appears to have been the reasoning upon which Jones based his assertion that most mandataries (other than carriers) were liable for any want of competence in the performance of their undertaking, whether or not this involved what would popularly be considered gross neglect. To pretend a greater ability that one possesses, in reliance upon which the mandator

---

[54] (1961) 30 D.L.R. (2d) 152.
[55] Quaere, whether this did not amount to a deviation.
[56] *Coggs* v. *Bernard* (1703) 2 Ld. Raym. 909; 92 E.R. 107.
[57] Citing *Giblin* v. *McMullen* (1868) L.R. 2 P.C. 317.
[58] Citing *McCulloch* v. *Murray* [1942] 2 D.L.R. 189, at (1961) 30 D.L.R. (2d) 170 per Freedman J.A.
[59] Ante, p. 301.
[60] *Neuwith* v. *Over Darwen Co-Operative Society Ltd.* (1894) 63 L.J.Q.B. 290, at 292. Cf. Latham C.J. in *Insurance Commissioner* v. *Joyce* (1948) 77 C.L.R. 39, at 46: "If a person deliberately agrees to allow a blacksmith to mend his watch, it may well be said that he agrees to accept a low standard of skill. But even in such a case, the blacksmith is bound to act sensibly, though he is not subject to the responsibilities of a skilled watchmaker."
[61] *Wilson* v. *Brett* (1843) 11 M. & W. 113; 152 E.R. 756. This doctrine is not peculiar to bailments; see, for instance, *Low* v *Foss* [1845] Res. & Eq. J. 40 (N.S.W. Supreme Court); *Mutual Life and Citizens' Assurance Co. Ltd.* v. *Evatt* [1971] A.C. 793.

yields up and suffers damage to his chattel, is a breach of faith for which the mandatary should suffer. In such a case, he should be liable for any lapse, however slight, from the standard he has held himself out as capable of attaining.

> Nor will a want of ability to perform the contract be any defence for the contracting party: for though the law exacts no impossible things, yet it may justly require that every man should know his own strength before he undertakes to do an act; and that, if he deludes another by false pretensions to skill, he shall be responsible for any injury that may be occasioned by such delusion.[62]

However, Jones favoured exempting the gratuitous carrier from this strict principle on the ground that gratuitous carriage "is a very different thing from a mandate to perform work." In his view, the gratuitous carrier should be liable only for gross negligence, and should be relieved from the stricter warranty of competence which he would impose upon the jeweller, the farrier and the watch-repairer.

Story condemns this distinction as meaningless,[63] and criticises Jones' wider principle of liability as a misconceived importation of the civil law.[64] In his view:

> The true rule of the common law would seem . . . to be that a mandatary who acts gratuitously in a case where his situation or employment does not naturally or necessarily imply any particular knowledge or professional skill, is responsible only for bad faith or gross negligence.[65]

However, the qualification implicit in these words, and the subsequent tenor of Story's analysis, show that there is less effective difference between his opinions and those of Jones than might originally be supposed. Story concedes that the conduct or character of the individual mandatary may amount to an implied promise to use a greater degree of skill or care than the Common Law would exact from a man of lesser abilities; just as, for instance, the defendant's express promise in *Coggs* v. *Bernard*[66] was held to increase his liability for damage to the casks. It seems, in most cases, that a mandatary who undertakes a task for which he is known to possess professional skills or extraordinary competence should be held to have undertaken to exercise the degree of proficiency he is known to (and does) possess.

Thus it would follow that there is in most cases a direct proportion between the nature of the task and the skill that a mandatary promises to use in its performance. The more esoteric the task, the likelier the mandator is to conclude that the mandatary is impliedly professing the necessary degree of special skill;[67] conversely, a task for which no training or skills are necessary and which many untutored persons might perform (as with Jones's example of gratuitous carriage), would be less likely to produce an

---

[62] *Bailments*, p. 53.
[63] Section 177: "To carry jewels safely may be a far more valuable service, and require far more vigilance than to clean the gold which enchases them."
[64] Sections 178-181.
[65] Section 182a.
[66] (1703) 2 Ld. Raym. 909; 92 E.R. 107.
[67] *Harmer* v. *Cornelius* (1858) 5 C.B.N.S. 236; Wyatt Paine, at 60-61.

assumption that the mandatary is asserting a particular aptitude. Moreover, the definition of gross negligence will vary in any event according to the character of the mandatary and his actual competence at the task in question, whether these qualities are known to the mandator or not. As Smith points out,[68] "in the case of a skilled person, that may well be considered gross negligence which, in an ordinary unskilled person, would be only a slight want of care."

The point is neatly illustrated by *Shiells* v. *Blackburne*[69] where the defendant (a general merchant) consigned to Madeira two cases which he mistakenly entered in the customs register as containing wrought leather. In fact, one case did not contain wrought but dressed leather, and belonged to a bankrupt named Godwin who had asked the defendant to despatch it to Madeira on his behalf. The court, treating the service as gratuitous, held that the defendant was not liable for the subsequent seizure of the cases by the customs as a result of the erroneous entry. The act which led to the seizure was not, when viewed in the light of the defendant's experience and expertise, an act of gross negligence or fraud: "he acted bona fide"[70] and "it is not consistent either with the spirit or policy of the law to make him liable.[71] Wilson J. pointed out that even the clerks themselves sometimes made erroneous entries, and Lord Loughborough observed that a higher standard might have been expected from a person whose occupation involved him in regular dealings with the customs, and who might therefore be expected to be familiar with the rules concerning entries:

> If in this case a ship-broker, or a clerk in the Custom-House, had undertaken to enter the goods, a wrong entry would in them be gross negligence, because their situation and employment necessarily imply a competent degree of knowledge in making such entries; but when an application, under the circumstances of this case, is made to a general merchant to make an entry at the Custom-House, such a mistake as this is not to be imputed to him as gross negligence.[72]

Accordingly, the issue of gross negligence is inseparable from the character of the mandatary: it will also, of course, vary in relation to the value and location of the goods and the facilities which the mandatary is known, or can reasonably be expected, to have at his disposal.[73]

In all this, the definition of gross neglect shows a tendency to move towards a simple lack of proper and reasonable care. Admittedly, there are some differences. In *Shiells* v. *Blackburne* Heath J. took the view that a non-professional, called in to perform a task such as surgery, may be exonerated whether he employs improper remedies to the best of his ability or even fails to exert such little skill as he has.[74] Story suggests that even a professional may escape liability for "errors of conduct or action, into

---

[68] *Leading Cases* (12th ed.), p. 262.
[69] (1789) 1 H. Bl. 158; 126 E.R. 94.
[70] Ibid., at 96 (E.R.) per Heath J.
[71] Ibid. (E.R.) per Wilson J.
[72] Ibid.; see also *Beal* v. *South Devon Ry. Co.* (1864) 3 H. & C. 337; 159 E.R. 560; *Kostiuk* v. *Union Acceptance Corporation* (1968) 66 D.L.R. (2d) 430, at 434.
[73] Cf. p. 460, post.
[74] Ibid., at 96 (E.R.).

which a man of ordinary prudence might have fallen,"[75] and there are cases in which the defendant seems to fall clearly between the two degrees of negligence, and to be guilty of ordinary but not of gross neglect.[76] But to the general tenor of the older authorities, that a mandatary who does his best in all the circumstances will be exonerated, unless he has acted in such a way as to make it clear that his best is not enough, more modern decisions have tended to add the corollary that little short of that upper standard will suffice, and that the mandatary must throughout the performance of his obligations act with reasonable care.

Numerically, the decisions in favour of a criterion of reasonable care continue to represent the minority; Paton (writing in 1952) was clearly of the view that the principle of gross negligence still had the advantage over its rival.[77] But even among older authorities one can find the mandatary's liability being framed in terms or ordinary negligence, as witness two early 19th century cases dealing with the gratuitous unloading[78] and gratuitous transportation[79] of goods. It was not until some years later, however, that the scale of liability laid down by *Shiells* v. *Blackburne*[80] was directly and critically questioned. In a Scottish decision in 1916[81] the Lord Justice-Clerk considered that the English rule of gross negligence (which in his view still applied) was at variance with the law of Scotland;[82] and that under Scottish law a gratuitous carrier was bound to show, if not how the loss occurred, at least that it was not due to a lack of "the necessary reasonable care."[83] In this case, the court upheld a claim by the plaintiff schoolmaster (one Primrose Copland) for the loss by a gratuitous carrier of a sum of money which he had collected for the plaintiff from a bank. The defendant was wholly unable to explain the loss and the court inferred that he had failed to exercise the care which a prudent man would have taken with regard to a valuable packet of this kind.

The primary counter-balance in cases of mandate came with the decision of the Court of Appeal in *Houghland* v. *R.R. Low* (*Luxury Coaches*) *Ltd.*,[84] which has been fully discussed in Chapter 9. As we have pointed out, this decision is less conclusive than would initially appear. The service in question (the carriage of a passenger's suitcase by a coach operator) was clearly non-gratuitous and the defendants failed upon their inability to adduce any evidence to demonstrate the cause of the loss. But the approach taken in this case is in keeping with wider developments in the law of tort and with the general tendency at least in English jurisdictions to discard the degrees of care. Thus, whereas older decisions restrict the liability of

---

[75] Section 182a.
[76] The most obvious is probably *Lenkeit* v. *Ebert* [1947] St. R. Qd. 126.
[77] At 137.
[78] *Gibson* v. *Inglis* (1814) 4 Cowp. 72; 171 E.R. 23 (but note that Lord Ellenborough considered this a case in which the defendants had impliedly asserted, as in *Coggs* v. *Bernard*, that the goods would be carried safely).
[79] *Nelson* v. *MacIntosh* (1816) 1 Stark 237; see also *Wilkinson* v. *Coverdale* (1793) 1 Esp. 75; 170 E.R. 284; *Chapmann* v. *Morley* (1891) 7 T.L.R. 257; *Commonwealth Portland Cement Co.* v. *Weber, Lohmann & Co.* [1905] A.C. 66.
[80] (1789) 1 H. Bl. 158; 126 E.R. 94, at 107.
[81] *Copland* v. *Brogan* 1916 S.C. 277.
[82] Ibid., at 282.
[83] The English rule would consider the latter sufficient; see p. 442, post.
[84] [1962] 1 Q.B. 694; ante, p. 298.

a gratuitous carrier of passengers to gross neglect,[85] modern cases place the carrier's liability squarely on the basis of a lack of reasonable care.[86] Other providers of gratuitous services have likewise been brought within the principle of *Donoghue* v. *Stevenson*,[87] even (in appropriate circumstances) where the loss is purely economic.[88] A number of Canadian cases make the mandatary liable for failing to exercise such care as could have been expected from a reasonable and prudent man.[89] In New Zealand it has been held that where a customer finds a lost article in a department store and hands it to an assistant to be returned to the owner, the relationship between the finder and the store is one of mandate and the store operator is liable for want of reasonable care.[90] This is, perhaps, a logical development from the notion that a bailor's remedies (in the absence of any special contract) subsist solely in tort.[91]

The inconclusive authority of *Houghland* v. *R. R. Low (Luxury Coaches) Ltd.*[92] and the somewhat qualified recognition accorded to that case in *Lee & Sons Pty. Ltd.* v. *Abood*[93] render any speculation about the future trend of Australian decisions rather precarious. The latest direct Australian authority casts the mandatary's liability in gross negligence;[94] there seems to be little practical difficulty in distinguishing, on particular facts, between this and a lack of reasonable care. On the other hand, the modern distaste for concepts of comparative negligence appears to be firmly rooted.[95] It is probably only a matter of time before all bailees are finally subjected to a universal rule of reasonable care.

Of course, whichever standard is applied, it will not necessarily avail the mandatary to show that he took the same amount of care of the mandator's property as he did of his own. This is clear from *Doorman* v. *Jenkins*.[96] Against this proposition must be placed the opinion of Lord Den-

---

[85] *Skelton* v. *L. & N.W. Ry. Co.* (1867) L.R. 2 C.P. 631; *Moffatt* v. *Bateman* (1869) L.R. 3 P.C. 115, approved in *Lenkeit* v. *Ebert* [1947] St. R. Qd. 126.

[86] For a recent example among many, see *Birch* v. *Thomas* [1972] 1 All E.R. 905. In some North American jurisdictions there are "guest" statutes which explicitly preserve the rule of gross negligence: for a recent decision in point, see *Thompson* v. *Fraser* [1955] 3 D.L.R. 145 (Canadian Supreme Court); *Plachta* v. *Richardson* (1975) 49 D.L.R. (3d) 23.

[87] [1932] A.C. 562; cf. p. 349, post, on the lender's liability for defective chattels.

[88] *Hedley Byrne & Co. Ltd.* v. *Heller & Partners* [1964] A.C. 465; *Banbury* v. *Bank of Montreal* [1918] A.C. 626, at 657.

[89] *Harris* v. *Sheffield* (1875) 10 N.S.R. 1. (Nova Scotia Court of Appeal); *Wills* v. *Brown* [1912] 1 D.L.R. 388 (Ontario C.A.) *Piper* v. *Geldart* [1954] 2 D.L.R. 97, per Harrison J.; cf. *Tindall* v. *Hayward* (1861) 7 U.C.L.J. 242; *Northern Elevator Co. Ltd.* v. *Western Jobber's Clearing House* (1914) 20 D.L.R. 889, where the standard applied was the subjective one of the care the defendant took of his own property. The criterion of reasonable care was adopted in the Kansas decision of *Maddock* v. *Riggs* (1920) 106 Ka. 808; 190 Pac. 12; see also *Gottlieb* v. *Wallace Wall Paper Co.* 156 N.Y. App. Div. 150; 140 N.Y. Supp. 1032; (1920-1921) 34 *Harvard Law Review* 82.

[90] *Helson* v. *McKenzies (Cuba St.) Ltd.* [1950] N.Z.L.R. 878, at 905, 916 (obiter).

[91] *Walker* v. *Watson* [1974] 2 N.Z.L.R. 175.

[92] [1962] 1 Q.B. 694; cf. *Morris* v. *C. W. Martin & Sons Ltd.* [1966] 1 Q.B. 716; ante, p. 298.

[93] (1968) 89 W.N. (N.S.W.) (Pt 1) 430; ante, p. 304.

[94] *Lenkeit* v. *Ebert* [1947] St. R. Qd. 126; ante, p. 333.

[95] Ante, p. 294.

[96] (1834) 2 Ad. & El. 256; 111 E.R. 99; ante, p. 300. Cf. *Harris* v. *Sheffield* (1875) 10 N.S.R. 1, where such evidence seems to have been used to assist the finding that the defendant took reasonable care; *Tracy* v. *Wood* 3 Mason R.132; Story, ss. 178-181.

ning M.R., that the gratuitous bailee need only keep the bailed goods "as his own".[97] But this view was expressed obiter and enjoys little support among modern authority.[98]

B. The duty to perform

The mandatary's liability will, of course, extend not only to positive acts of negligence but to any failure to take such precautions as are reasonably necessary for the discharge of his duty of safe-keeping.[99] Older authorities hold that he will also be liable for failing to perform the promised work, provided that he has already taken possession.[1] These authorities can be supported in terms of contractual liability by accepting that the bailor's parting with possession,[2] or his trust in the mandatary,[3] or his reliance upon the latter's promise,[4] are good consideration. But despite recent tendencies to mitigate this doctrine, some modern writers continue to assume that the promise given by a mandatary will be unenforceable against him.[5] To do so is to disregard the distinctive quality of bailments, which may give rise to promissory obligations that are incapable of being rationalised in contractual terms and are unsupported by conventional consideration. The mandatary's liability to perform once delivery has been made is supported by dicta in at least two modern decisions[6] and, impliedly, by a decision of the English High Court in 1891. In *Chapmann* v. *Morley*[7] the plaintiff was indebted to the defendant and was ordered to make repayment, through the court, of £1 a week. After the order had been made, the defendant wrote to the plaintiff suggesting that he pay the money direct to him and promising to ensure personally that the money would be passed through the court. The plaintiff made the payments as requested but the defendant neglected to pay them through the court and the plaintiff was imprisoned for debt. He was awarded £50 damages, ostensibly in an action for negligence, and despite the defendant's apparently unrebutted assertion

---

97 *Morris* v. *C. W. Martin & Sons Ltd.* [1966] 1 Q.B. 716, at 725.

98 Cf. *Port Swettenham* v. *Wu* (1978) *The Times*, June 22. (p.c.).

99 *Baxter & Galloway Ltd.* v. *Jones* (1903) 23 C.L.T. 258; 6 O.L.R. 360; 20 W.R. 573 (Can.).

1 *Wheatley* v. *Low* (1623) Cro. Jac. 668; 79 E.R. 578; *Harris* v. *de Bervoir* (1624) 687; 79 E.R. 596; *Boson* v. *Sandford* (1690) 1 Shower 101, at 104; 89 E.R. 477, at 479; *Coggs* v. *Bernard* (1703) 2 Ld. Raym. 909; 92 E.R. 107 (semble: but the statements of Holt C.J. on this point, at 919, 113, are not unambiguous; cf. Gould and Powell JJ. at 910, 108, who seem to provide clearer support); *Wilkinson* v. *Coverdale* (1793) 1 Esp. 75; 170 E.R. 284; *Streeter* v. *Horlock* (1822) 1 Bing. 34; 130 E.R. 15; *Oriental Bank Corporation* v. *The Queen* (1867) 6 S.C.R. (N.S.W.) 122, at 125. Cf. *Boorman* v. *Brown* (1842) 3 Q.B. 511 which, while supporting an action in tort for non-feasance, seems to assume a prior contractual duty to perform.

2 *Coggs* v. *Bernard*, ante.

3 Cf. *Banbury* v. *Bank of Montreal* [1918] A.C. 626, at 657.

4 Ante, p. 315.

5 E.g. Treitel, *Law of Contract* (4th ed.), pp. 93-94.

6 *Pilcher* v. *Leyland Motors Ltd.* [1932] N.Z.L.R. 449, at 464-467 (Ostler J., cf. Smith J. at 467-468); *Roufos* v. *Brewster and Brewster* [1971] 2 S.A.S.R. 218, at 223-224. See also *W. A. Bennett Ltd.* v. *Puna* [1956] N.Z.L.R. 629; *Argy* v. *Lapid* [1977] 1 W.L.R. 444; Seavey, (1951) 64 *Harvard Law Review* 913; *New Zealand Shipping Co. Ltd.* v. *A. M. Satterthwaite & Co. Ltd.* [1974] 1 All E.R. 1015, at 1020; ante, p. 313 et seq.

7 (1891) 7 T.L.R. 257.

that he was a mere volunteer.[8] If anything, the decision seems to grant a remedy for a total failure to perform the terms of the mandate, which presumably became binding upon the defendant from the moment he received the money. It must be conceded, however, that the fact that the delivery arose at the defendant's request suggests the existence of some mutual benefit.

Against these authorities must be placed the decision of the Supreme Court of New South Wales in *Heaton* v. *Richards*[9] where, as we have seen,[10] the plaintiff was held unable to recover for breach of the defendant's gratuitous promise (supported by delivery of the subject matter) to print the plaintiff's manuscript. The decision proceeded solely on the issue of consideration and there were suggestions that liability for non-performance may have resulted if the delivery occurred at the request of the defendant, insofar as he may then have acquired some notional benefit from the transaction.[11] On the present facts, however, the action was branded as an "experiment in litigation" and the plaintiff's arguments were almost contemptuously dismissed. It is submitted that this decision was wrongly decided and that an unrewarded bailee's acceptance of the chattel should bind him not only to an enlarged degree of liability for its safe-keeping,[12] but to any positive obligation which he has voluntarily undertaken in relation to it. Possession, in other words, is the trigger which transforms a nudum pactum into a binding obligation. Such an approach is in keeping with the hybrid character of bailments[13] and their capacity to procreate rights and duties that cannot be explained entirely in terms of contract or of tort.

If the foregoing represents the true doctrine under modern law, it may be necessary to qualify it in two respects. First, there should be a substantial connection between the chattel and the task to be performed, for it would be undesirable if gratuitous promises were suddenly to become enforceable upon delivery of a chattel of no more than token significance to the service in question. Secondly, a lack of intention to create legal relations should possibly militate against the binding quality of the mandatary's obligation between the time of his acceptance of the goods and his commencing to perform. If such intention exists at the time of delivery, the promise should be binding forthwith; if not, the commencement of the

---

[8] Cf. the discussion between counsel and the members of the Court of Appeal as to liability for "negligent" false imprisonment in *Rondel* v. *Worsley* [1967] 1 Q.B. 443, at 492.

[9] (1881) 2 L.R. (N.S.W.) 73.

[10] Ante, p. 285.

[11] (1881) 2 L.R. (N.S.W.) 73, at 77 (Martin C.J.), and at 78 (Manning J.).

[12] Ante, p. 317.

[13] Cheshire & Fifoot, *Law of Contract* (3rd Australian ed.), pp. 79-81. A dictum contrary to the ratio of *Heaton* v. *Richards*, and which was not cited in the latter decision, is to be found in the judgment of Faucett J., in *The Oriental Bank Corporation* v. *The Queen* (1867) 6 S.C.R. (N.S.W.) 122, at 125: "The contract alleged is that if the suppliants will deliver certain goods, the Crown will carry them. If that contract is executory, it is *nudum pactum*, and could not be enforced by the one against the other. But the Crown having accepted the goods incurs a new liability; the liability of a gratuitous bailee. The Crown is therefore bound to carry; and the count alleging a breach of that implied contract is good."

undertaking seems to represent a fairer point of crystallisation.[14] Thus, if A offers to paint B's house and B immediately lends him the brushes, A's mere acceptance of them should not automatically bind him to complete the undertaking. But this does not mean that A, having begun the work, should be entitled to abandon it unfinished, or to perform it incompetently; nor does it mean that A should be entitled to treat the brushes, while they are in his possession, with less than the requisite standard of care.

Even with these qualifications in mind, it seems curious that the mere acceptance of a chattel upon (or with) which a task is to be performed should generate a binding obligation. A fairer rule might be to synchronise this obligation with the performance by the mandator of an act of reliance upon the promise, or with the commencement of the work by the mandatary, so that the mandatary would be precluded from withdrawing only in those cases where to do so would prejudice the mandator. In some cases, such an approach would cause the obligation to arise before the mandatary takes possession of the goods, as where A, relying upon B's promise to repair his car, incurs expense by procuring spare parts which he would not otherwise have bothered to procure. But it seems clear that there can be no binding, executory relationship of mandate.[15] Story regarded the rule as well established[16] and criticised Jones' assertion[17] that it might be displaced where exceptional damage accrues to the mandator as the result of a refusal to perform. The modern doctrine of consideration seems to endorse Story's view as the correct one. The disappointed mandatary might enjoy an action for fraud or negligent mis-statement against the potential mandatary, but he cannot enforce the mandate itself.

So far as concerns the mandator, the authorities suggest that he can withdraw from the engagement at any time before the task has been executed. Thus in *Lyte* v. *Peny*[18] the bailor of money to be paid in specie to a third person was held entitled to revoke before the payment had been made.[19] Generally, this rule will operate without hardship to the mandatary, who will be willing enough to be prematurely relieved of his undertaking. However, it is submitted that the mandator's right to revoke should in turn be subject to two qualifications. First, it may be necessary to imply into the agreement an undertaking on his part not to withdraw without giving reasonable notice; it would, for instance, be unreasonable if the bailor of an expensive and complicated machine, having bailed it to a friend to be gratuitously serviced, should be entitled to demand its return in the condition in which it was delivered before the work is completed. Secondly, the mandator should bear any expense incurred by a

---

[14] Cf. Paton, p. 132, who assumes that he can withdraw at any time.
[15] *Coggs* v. *Bernard* (1703) 2 Ld. Raym. 909; 92 E.R. 107, at 108, 113; *Roufos* v. *Brewster and Brewster* [1971] 2 S.A.S.R. 218, at 223-224; Story, s. 171(b) n. 2.
[16] Section 166.
[17] At p. 53 et seq.
[18] (1541) 1 Dyer, 49a; 73 E.R. 108; *Taylor* v. *Lendey* (1807) 9 East 49; 103 E.R. 492; *Williams* v. *Everett* (1811) 14 East 582; 104 E.R. 725.
[19] Cf. *Atkin* v. *Barwick* (1719) 1 Stra. 165; 93 E.R. 450, where the delivery was held to be supported by consideration and therefore irrevocable, but it was agreed that without this element the commission could have been withdrawn. This case was discussed critically in *Harman* v. *Fisher* (1774) Cowp. 117; 93 E.R. 998.

mandatary in complying with a reversal of his original instructions. Clearly, a mandatary is entitled to resist the imposition of duties and inconveniences over and above those which he has originally undertaken. Where the mandator refuses to reimburse his mandatary for such expenditure, the mandatary should be entitled to pursue the course of action for which he was originally engaged or to cease work and await the recaption of the goods, whichever is the more convenient to him.

C. Delegation, deviation and delay

The rules here are precisely analogous to those which govern the depositary.[20] Thus, whether a mandatary is entitled to delegate the work or to sub-bail the chattel will depend upon the express terms of the agreement or, where none are present, upon whether such permission can be inferred. Generally, the specialised nature of the work and the mandator's knowledge of his mandatary will lead to the conclusion that the duty is a personal one and cannot be sub-contracted. Thus, as in cases of locatio operis faciendi, the mandatary who wrongfully delegates will become an insurer of the goods while they are in the third party's possession and will be prevented from relying on any exemption clause unless it specifically covers that kind of conduct.[21] The same rules will apply whenever the mandatary does an act which is fundamentally at variance with the terms of the bailment, whether it consists in keeping the goods in a different place from that agreed, deviating from an agreed itinerary or retaining the goods without lawful excuse after the bailment has expired.[22]

In certain circumstances, of course, it may be possible to infer a permission granted to the mandatary to delegate the whole or any part of his undertaking. Possibly such an inference is more likely to occur in relation to the custodial aspects of his obligations than with regard to the performance of the task in question. In each case it is a question of fact to be decided by reference to all the circumstances of the case. Even where such delegation is permitted, the substituted performant must be selected with the same degree of care as must be shown by a mandatary when performing the duty in person. When delegation takes place, it would appear that the mandatary (as with a bailee for reward)[23] remains liable for the defaults of his sub-contractor,[24] whether these are directly attributable to the misconduct of the mandatary or not.

---

[20] Ante, p. 322 et seq.

[21] E.g. *Davies* v. *Collins* [1945] 1 All E.R. 247; *Martin* v. *H. Negin Ltd.* (1945) 172 L.T. 275; *Causer* v. *Browne* [1952] V.L.R. 1; [1952] A.L.R. 12; p. 515, post.

[22] *Miles* v. *Cattle* (1830) 6 Bing. 740; 8 L.J. (O.S.) (C.P.) 271; *Von Minden* v. *Pyke* (1865) 4 F. & F. 533; 176 E.R. 678; *Wills* v. *Brown* [1912] 1 D.L.R. 388; cf. *Nelson* v. *MacIntosh* (1816) 1 Stark. (N.P.) 227; Beven, pp. 914-915; *Harris* v. *Sheffield* (1875) 10 N.S.R. 1.

[23] E.g. *B.R.S. Ltd.* v. *Arthur V. Crutchley Ltd.* [1968] 1 All E.R. 811; *Hobbs* v. *Petersham Transport Pty. Ltd.* (1971) 45 A.L.J.R. 356.

[24] Cf. *Von Minden* v. *Pyke*, ante at 535, 679, where it is suggested that a lawful delegation terminates the mandatary's responsibility for the period of the delegation. But this was almost certainly a case of non-gratuitous bailment and it is submitted that the dictum is misconceived.

D. Liability for defaults of servants

The question whether a gratuitous bailee is liable (vicariously or otherwise) for the negligence or conversions of his servant has been fully discussed in Chapter 9. It is submitted that the conclusions reached in that chapter apply with equal force to instances of mandate. Any loss or damage resulting from misconduct committed by a servant of a mandatary, while acting within the scope of his employment or in the discharge of any delegated duty towards the chattel, should be borne by the master on analogous principles to those which govern a bailee for reward.[25]

E. The burden of proof

In *Lenkeit* v. *Ebert*[26] the Queensland Full Supreme Court held that the mandator must adduce affirmative proof of the mandatary's gross negligence in order to succeed. In addition he must demonstrate the connection between this and the injury complained of.[27] This decision is at variance with the general policy of English,[28] Scottish[29] and (possibly) Canadian[30] decisions, although it seems to be in general accord with the Australian approach in cases of depositum.[31] It is submitted that to isolate cases of mandatum, or even gratuitous bailments generally, from the operation of the normal burden of proof would be contrary to the policy which gave rise to that burden originally. The mandatary should carry the onus of proving either that in his custody of the goods he exercised the requisite degree of care, or that any departure from this standard was not causally connected with the bailor's loss. He need not, however (as was suggested tentatively in one Scottish decision[32]) go further and explain the precise cause of the loss, provided the court is satisfied that it did not result from a want of the necessary care or was unconnected with any lapse from that standard.[33]

The foregoing observations can be made with confidence in respect of the custodial aspects of the mandatary's undertaking; that is, his incidental responsibility for the safe-keeping and redelivery of the goods.

---

[25] *Wills* v. *Brown* [1912] 1 D.L.R. 388; *Houghland* v. *R. R. Low (Luxury Coaches) Ltd.* [1962] 1 Q.B. 694; cf. *McLeod* v. *Eberts* (1850) 7 U.C. Q.B. 244. Quaere whether *Armory* v. *Delamirie* (1722) 1 Stra. 505 is an example of the rule stated in the text. There was probably a bailment to the jeweller and at least a possibility that the bailment was gratuitous, but he seems to have been personally implicated in the conversion.

[26] [1947] St. R. Qd. 126.

[27] Ibid., at 131 (per Philp J.).

[28] *Houghland* v. *R. R. Low (Luxury Coaches) Ltd.* [1962] 1 Q.B. 694; the older decisions are either inconclusive on this point or favour placing the onus on the bailor, but they were decided at a time when the modern doctrine had not been properly established even in cases of bailment for reward; see, e.g. *Doorman* v. *Jenkins* (1834) 2 Ad. & El. 256; 111 E.R. 99; ante, p. 311.

[29] *Copland* v. *Brogan* 1916 S.C. 277.

[30] *Piper* v. *Geldart* [1954] 2 D.L.R. 97; technically the question may still be regarded as open in Canada because so many of the cases date from the last century.

[31] Ante, p. 312.

[32] *Copland* v. *Brogan* 1916 S.C. 277, at 282.

[33] To a lesser extent, the same result may be reached by the doctrine of res ipsa loquitur: cf. *Piper* v. *Geldart* [1954] 2 D.L.R. 97. But the two doctrines are different and it is possible to fail on res ipsa loquitur while succeeding on the bailee's burden of proof. See generally, p. 40 et seq., ante.

So far as concerns his performance of the work for which he was engaged, the position would seem to be different. The bailee's onus of proof has been held only to apply to those aspects of a bailment which are central to that relationship, and not to any super-added responsibilities which the parties may have chosen to engraft upon it. Thus, whereas a claim for damage caused by the negligent storage of perishables would impose upon the bailee the onus of proving that he took the necessary precautions for the preservation of the goods, a claim for inadequate repairs or cleaning might not relieve the bailor of proving that the work was performed without the degree of care or skill that was contemplated by the bailment. The point is well made by Scholl J. in a Victorian decision:[34]

> Where the plaintiff . . . founds his claim on breach of the separate obligation to do work on the chattel with reasonable care and skill no question will ordinarily arise of the defendant having to exculpate himself by showing that defective work, or other damage to the chattel occurred without fault on his part . . . In the end, the test upon which the difference of onus depends seems to me to be whether what the plaintiff complains of is a breach of the defendant's promise to redeliver the goods at the end of the bailment, or is a breach of what was really a super-added and collateral promise by the defendant to do work on or in relation to the goods.

These observations were made in the context of bailments for reward, but it is submitted that an analogous rule should apply in cases of mandate. Where the mandator's complaint centres purely upon the standard of workmanship (as where he claims that a book is unsatisfactorily bound, or that a tailor has made alterations to his suit in an unauthorised manner) there is no reason for displacing the orthodox contractual rule that the plaintiff must prove the breach; he must show that the workmanship is inferior to the standard he had been entitled to expect, and in so doing he may have to prove that the defendant exercised less than the necessary amount of care and skill. Where, on the other hand, the goods are lost, or are returned in a condition which suggests that the default arises not from the work performed but from a lapse in the necessary standard of safe-keeping, the proof of their condition will be sufficient to cast upon the bailee the onus of negativing neglect. In cases where the facts suggest a breach of both aspects of the bailee's undertaking, the mandatary will not be relieved of responsibility simply because the bailor has failed to prove that the labour aspect was performed without the necessary care or skill. The custodial aspect being a continuing one, there will be many situations in which an inadequate performance of the labour undertaken will also amount to a breach of the mandatary's duties as a custodian of the goods.[35] If, in such a case, the bailee fails to prove that he discharged these duties with the necessary amount of care, or that his omissions in this regard did not contribute to the loss, the bailor should succeed. The result may be that in many cases only misconduct which does not, in an objective

---

[34] *Fankhauser* v. *Mark Dykes Pty. Ltd.* [1960] V.R. 376, at 379.
[35] An obvious example is *Campbell* v. *Pickard* (1961) 30 D.L.R. (2d) 152; ante, p. 334.

sense, damage the goods (as opposed to altering them in a manner the mandator does not like) will cast the burden of proof upon the mandator.

F. Profits and progeny

The rules here seem to be the same as those which govern bailments by way of depositum.[36] Story[37] states that the mandatary does not, without special agreement become entitled to the produce of any chattel which was bailed for the purpose of the mandate. Under modern theory, the same conclusion will generally be reached in the context of the agreement between the parties.[38]

G. Assumption and exclusion of liability

It is beyond question that the mandatary is entitled to impose exculpatory provisions relating to each or every aspect of his undertaking. It is arguable that acceptance of these terms represent the mandator's consideration under what accordingly becomes a binding contract between the parties. But such exclusions can in any event be imposed irrespective of contract.[39] The normal rules of construction and incorporation will presumably apply, except insofar as the courts may feel inclined to regard more benevolently the exclusions imposed by one who is performing a gratuitous service.

The substantial authority in favour of enforcing promises of augmented responsibility in cases of depositum[40] would seem to apply a fortiori to cases of mandatum, where the binding quality of the service undertaken seems incapable of subsumption under the principles of contract or of tort. *Coggs* v. *Bernard*[41] was such a case, where the bailor was able to enforce a promise by his mandatary to assume a heavier obligation for the safety of the casks than would have been imposed at Common Law. Modern authority is slight, but it would seem to follow that a promise which is relied upon by the mandator, and on the strength of which he yields possession, should be enforceable from the time that the mandatary's larger obligation becomes binding upon him; that is, when he enters into possession.

Although there are obvious difficulties in classifying mandatum as contractual, it seems that in some circumstances that the relationship should be subject to analogous rules with regard to questions as frustration, repudiation, misrepresentation and fundamental breach. Thus, where, for instance, either party dies before the execution of the commission, the arrangements should be deemed to be dissolved;[42] and (as we have suggested already) any fundamental departure from the terms of his obligation should have effects upon the mandatary's position comparable to those which would attend a contractual bailee.

---

[36] See p. 324, ante.
[37] Section 194; Paton, p. 138.
[38] *Grant's Farming Co. Ltd.* v. *Attwell* (1901) 9 H.C. 91 (S. Africa) states as a general rule that the gratuitous bailee must account for profits derived from the use of the chattel on depositum.
[39] Ante, p. 321.
[40] Ante, p. 317.
[41] (1703) 2 Ld. Raym. 909; 92 E.R. 107.
[42] For a full account of the circumstances which might release the mandatary from his undertaking, see Story, s. 202 et seq; summarised by Paton, p. 132.

H. Redelivery

The mandatary must redeliver the goods when the work is completed or at the time agreed. Redelivery will be to the mandator or to any third person to whom the mandatary has agreed to convey or deliver the goods. The finer details of this aspect of the mandatary's duties will depend upon the agreement between the parties. Generally, it may be hazarded that the mandatary is under no duty to transport the goods to the mandator's residence but must make them available for collection by the mandator at all reasonable times, or after a 42a reasonable demand. The goods must, of course, be restored in the condition in which the mandatary received them, subject to any lawful excuse.[43] When goods have been given to the mandatary for delivery over to a third party, and he refuses to deliver them, either the original bailor or the third party may be entitled to proceed against him for their detention.[44]

III. The Duties of the Mandator

Story conceded[45] that there were no Common Law authorities on this point, and this observation seems true today. There are two principal areas in which a mandatary is likely to wish to proceed against his mandator. The first concerns liability for defective or dangerous goods supplied in connection with the mandate. As we observed in Chapter 9, it would be consistent with older theory to make the mandatary or depositor liable for even slight neglect in failing to warn the bailee of any defect in the goods; such an approach would be in keeping with the gradations of care imposed upon bailees by Lord Holt in *Coggs* v. *Bernard*.[46] But in the absence of authority, it is likely that the mandator is liable for negligence alone. In this respect, there may be no difference between the bailor who derives sole benefit from the bailment and the bailor who derives no benefit at all.[47] Of course, the mandator may increase his liability by special contract, although there appears to be no reported decision in which this has been done. More questionable is the mandator's power to reduce or exclude liability by means of a promise exacted from the mandatary when the goods are handed over. Presumably, the exemption would be held to be one of the conditions upon which the mandator assumed possession, and binding upon him in much the same way as the larger agreement itself.[48] Of course, if mandatum can be characterised as contractual there is no difficulty in enforcing such provisions.[49]

The second area concerns the recovery by a mandatary of money spent in the course of his engagement. Story considers that the mandator must

---

[42a] *Mitchell* v. *Ealing L.B.C.* (1978) *The Times*, Feb 21.
[43] He will not normally be liable for ordinary wear and tear.
[44] *Harris* v. *de Bervoir* (1624) Cro. Jac. 687; Paton, p. 132.
[45] Section 196.
[46] (1703) 2 Ld. Raym. 909, at 913; 92 E.R. 107, at 110 et seq.; it would include liability for failing to know of the defect, where such knowledge could have been acquired by the exercise of extraordinary care.
[47] See p. 349, post.
[48] Cf. p. 364, post (commodatum).
[49] Cf. p. 314, ante; p. 364, post.

pay all expenses arising from the mandatary's performance of the mandate.[50] Of course, such expenses must be reasonably necessary and reasonable in size, but they need not represent the minimum that could have been expended, in order for the mandatary to qualify for an indemnity:

> If a party requests a friend to carry goods for him a stage-coach to another town, for which goods carriage-hire is usually paid, a like duty to pay the bill is presumed. And even if the expenses should exceed what the owner himself would have paid, still, if they are such as were reasonably incurred, he is liable therefore: and under particular circumstances he may also be compellable to pay interest thereon . . . It follows of course . . . that, if the expenses are necessary or extravagant, or arise from the gross negligence or fraud of the mandatary, or from his exceeding his authority, they are not reimbursible.[51]

Such reimbursement can probably be justified on the grounds of an implied contract between the parties; alternatively, it should be possible under ordinary principles of restitution. When the mandatary's expenditure is extraordinary in the sense that it is not contemplated by the terms of his agreement, the right to recover will presumably be limited to these situations in which he can establish agency of necessity between himself and the mandator.

[50] Section 197.
[51] Ibid.

CHAPTER 11

COMMODATUM, OR GRATUITOUS LOAN

Commodatum denotes the loan of a chattel for the exclusive benefit of the borrower, on the condition that he will return the chattel to the lender, or redeliver it at his instructions, in accordance with the agreement between the parties. The bailee acquires possession and can therefore exercise the possessory and proprietary remedies against third parties during the currency of the bailment.[1] Generally, however, his tenure of the chattel will be at the will of the bailor and subject to the latter's peremptory revocation. It is uncertain whether an agreement to lend for a particular term, coupled with delivery of the chattel, can be enforced against the bailor. Although there is difficulty in discerning the bailee's consideration for such a promise, it will be submitted later that his assumption of possession should be subject to the terms upon which it was made and that the bailor should not be permitted to resile from the undertaking.[2]

Generally, the benefit will consist in the bailee's right to use the chattel for its conventional purpose, but this will not necessarily be the case. The mere presence of the chattel may prove advantageous to him, or he may have in mind some other function for it, to which he attaches a peculiar or personal importance.[3] The important element is that the lender should derive no benefit from the transaction, for in such a case (except where the benefit is purely fortuitous and unintended) the gratuitous quality of his undertaking is lost. Thus, where A agrees for no reward to exercise B's horse, the relationship will normally be one of mandatum rather than commodatum,[4] unless A derives sufficient benefit from the arrangement for it to amount to a bailment for the mutual advantage of the parties.[5] It follows that a bailment is not classifiable as commodatum merely because it entails an obligation or promise on the bailee's part to use the chattel; the use must be for his benefit, and he must be the only party to the bailment to derive an advantage therefrom.[6]

---

[1] See p. 177, ante; Story, s. 280; *Fletcher* v. *Thomas* [1931] 3 D.L.R. 142; *Richard* v. *Nowlan* (1959) 19 D.L.R (2d) 229, at 232, 235.

[2] See p. 364, post.

[3] *Bainbridge* v. *Firmstone* (1838) 8 Ad. & EL. 743; 112 E.R. 1019 (defendant borrowed boilers in order to weigh them; the Court of Queen's Bench did not specifically characterise the bailment as commodatum but held that the use to which the defendant wished to put the boilers was sufficient consideration for his assumpsit to return them in good condition). See further: Story, ss. 224-225.

[4] *Wilson* v. *Brett* (1843) 11 M. & W. 113.

[5] In the case of an exchange by way of mutual loan, it is suggested that the over-all transaction should be treated as one for the mutual advantage of the parties: see *Bryce* v. *Hornby* (1938) 82 Sol. Jo. 216; p. 286, ante.

[6] See the example given by Story (7th ed.), s. 226: if a horse be agisted and the bailee agrees to exercise it to keep it fit, the bailment is still in the nature of depositum (assuming no other reward is given) rather than of commodatum.

The chattel must of course be returnable at the end of the borrowing, for otherwise there is no bailment.[7] Where goods are lent partly for use and partly for consumption, there will be a bailment of those parts which, on the expiry of the purpose for which they were lent, must be returned to the bailor or applied as he directs.[8]

I. THE DUTIES OF THE BAILOR

A. Safety and fitness of the chattel

The lender's liability for loss or damage resulting from the unsafe character of his chattel remains a remarkably undocumented subject. In *Coggs* v. *Bernard*,[9] as may be expected, Lord Holt defined the duties of the borrower by reference to the benefits received[10] and ventured no opinion as to the standard of care expected of the bailor. It was not until a century and a half later that this question was seriously considered by any English court. Since that time, there has been an increasing judicial acknowledgement that the bailor's duty forms part of the general duty of reasonable care owed by one man to his neighbour.[11] But this view has hitherto appeared only in dicta, and older authorities, more specifically in point, impose a lighter obligation.

In *Coughlin* v. *Gillison*[12] the plaintiff was one of a number of men engaged to ballast a ship owned by the defendants. The gang to which he belonged asked the captain whether they could borrow a donkey-engine standing on the foredeck. The captain agreed on condition that the workmen found a competent engineman to operate it; and this they did. The machine exploded, injuring the plaintiff, who sued the defendants on the ground of gross negligence and failure to warn of the relevant defect. His action was dismissed by Hawkins J. and by the Court of Appeal, on the ground that a gratuitous lender is liable only for failing to warn the borrower of those defects in the chattel of which he has actual knowledge, and not for negligence in failing to apprise himself of the condition of the chattel.[13]

This decision, although on its surface straightforward, is not without its ambiguities. First, there may have been no bailment at all: the facts suggest rather an interchange of tools amongst workmates which, it has been held, does not necessarily give rise to a change of possession.[14]

Of course, when commodatum is described as for the "exclusive" use of the bailee, this does not mean that persons who are not parties to the bailment may not profit by the transaction: for instance, the borrower may himself be entitled to lend the chattel to a friend, or to carry him in a borrowed car. See p. 372, post.

---

[7] For American cases, see Story, s. 282.
[8] This may be the appropriate analysis where beverages are sold in bottles which are expressed to be returnable to the retailer: see *Geddling* v. *Marsh* [1920] 1 K.B. 668, where the point was not finally decided, and p. 99 et seq., ante.
[9] (1703) 2 Ld. Raym. 909; 92 E.R. 107.
[10] 92 E.R., at 111.
[11] *Donoghue* v. *Stevenson* [1932] A.C. 562.
[12] [1899] 1 Q.B. 145.
[13] Ibid., at p.147 (A. L. Smith L.J.), 148 (Rigby L.J.) and 149 (Collins L.J.).
[14] *Griffiths* v. *Arch Engineering Ltd.* [1968] 3 All E.R. 217, at 220; (p. 963, ante); but cf. *Fraser* v. *Jenkins* [1968] N.Z.L.R. 816.

Even if the possession in the engine left the defendants it may well have passed, not to the gang, but to the operator, who was presumably not a servant but an independent contractor, and who probably had the greatest measure of control at any given time.[15] Secondly, there is much to be said for counsel's assertion[16] that the bailment was not gratuitous, since the defendants clearly had an interest in expediting the ballasting: here again, it has been held that the transfer of tools in pursuance of the mutual prosecution of the common work would not constitute the borrower a gratuitous bailee.[17]

More significant, however, is the manner in which the avowed standard of liability was interpreted and applied. All three judges expressed the orthodox view that only a failure to warn of *known* defects would render the defendant liable; indeed, A. L. Smith L.J. described such knowledge as "essential". The same judge stressed that even gross negligence in failing to find out the defect would not suffice, but added:

> I will go this far — that if gross negligence is shown on the part of the bailor in not communicating to the bailee *that which he knew* of the insufficiency of the article bailed, an action is maintainable; but the law does not go further than that.[18]

The judgment of Rigby L.J. appears, however, to detract from this standard. In Rigby L.J.'s view, actual concealment of known material defects was necessary, or at least such negligence in failing to disclose "the facts relating to the article lent" as would amount to the same thing. Thus:

> If the article lent had been put on one side and not used for years, and then lent without any intimation to the bailee of this fact, the case might approximate to one of actual concealment.[19]

At this point, the learned judge appears to move towards a closer equation between negligence in failing to be aware of the defect and negligence in failing to communicate such knowledge. Admittedly, in both cases the neglect must be extreme but it no longer represents a neglect based upon communication of known facts, towards the knowledge of which neglect is irrelevant.

Collins L.J. drew a clearer separation between the two varieties of neglect: in his view, gross negligence was relevant only when it involved a failure to communicate defects of which the bailor was aware.[20] The only difference in substance between his opinion and that of A.L. Smith L.J. is that the latter then proceeded to observe that in his view the defendants had not been guilty of gross negligence, or indeed of any

---

[15] But cf. A. L. Smith L.J. at 147, who refers to the machine being "handed over" to the gang. If there were a bailment to them, presumably they were all joint bailees; but the bailment may well have been to their employers and they, as servants, may have been precluded from acquiring possession; see Chapter 7, ante.
[16] [1899] 1 Q.B., at 146.
[17] See the *Arch Engineering* case [1968] 3 All E.R., at 220; cf. Collins L.J. [1899] 1 Q.B., at 149.
[18] [1899] 1 Q.B. 145, at 147 (italics inserted).
[19] Ibid., at 148.
[20] Ibid., at 149.

negligence at all.[21] Clearly, neither judge considered that a careless ignorance of the condition of the chattel would be enough to render the bailor liable. The nearest the decision approaches to this view is in the judgment of Rigby J., and even here the remarks are consonant with a requirement of recklessness in failing to ascertain the defect.[22]

The principal authority upon which the Court of Appeal relied was *Blakemore* v. *Bristol and Exeter Ry. Co.*[23] That decision ought to establish symmetry between the parties to a gratuitous loan by laying upon the lender responsibility for:

> . . . defects in the chattel with reference to the use for which he knows the loan is accepted, of which he is aware, and owing to which directly the borrower is injured . . . By the necessarily implied purpose of the loan a duty is contracted towards the borrower not to conceal from him those defects known to the lender which may make the loan perilous or unprofitable to him.[24]

It will be seen from this quotation that the court regarded the gratuitous loan as a contract: the borrower's consideration being the fact that he would be liable for gross negligence or want of skill.[25] It was this, rather than the low standard of care, that defeated the plaintiff's claim in the present case, for the defendants managed to show that the chattel in question (a crane) had not been lent to him but to one of their customers, and that the plaintiff had merely assisted in operating the machine at the request of the customer himself. Thus, even though the defendants knew of the defect, they owed no duty to the plaintiff to warn him of its existence:

> . . . that duty, under the circumstances, could only arise from the contract in law between the lender and the borrower; and to that contract James Blakemore was no ways privy.[26]

A similar approach was evinced in *McCarthy* v. *Young*,[27] where the defendant engaged one Portlock to demolish a wall and allowed him to use a scaffold previously erected by the defendant. The plaintiff, a labourer employed by Portlock, was injured while on the scaffold, owing to the collapse of a rotten putlog.[28] His action failed because the

---

[21] Ibid., at 148. Mr N. S. Marsh, writing in (1950) 66 L.Q.R. 39, at 43-44, contends that the decision postulates an unreal distinction between lessors and lenders, because two of the three judges were prepared to hold that knowledge of the conditions from which the defect could be inferred was equivalent to knowledge of the defect itself. But in the case of A. L. Smith L.J., this observation seems to have no foundation: the only judgment lending colour to the equation was that of Rigby L.J. The ratio of *Coughlin* v. *Gillison* is a perfectly clear one and the duty it imposes is readily distinguishable from the standard of reasonable care.

[22] Cf. Clerk and Lindsell, *Torts* (14th ed.), para 938.

[23] (1858) 8 E. & B. 1034; 120 E.R. 385.

[24] 120 E.R., at 391 per Coleridge J. To similar effect are the older *dicta* on gifts: *Gautret* v. *Egerton* (1867) L.R. 2 C.P. 371; *Longmeid* v. *Holliday* (1851) 6 Ex. 761, at 768 (Parke B.).

[25] It seems that Coleridge J. misquoted Holt C.J. in *Coggs* v. *Bernard* on this point, for it is clear that in the Chief Justice's view the borrower would be answerable for even slight neglect: see (1703) 92 E.R. 107, at 111, and p. 368, post.

[26] 120 E.R., at 392.

[27] (1861) 6 H. & N. 329; 158 E.R. 136.

[28] Or cross-support.

defendant was not proved to have known of the defect; he would not, therefore, have been liable to Portlock himself, and the plaintiff, as an outsider, could stand in no better position than the person to whom the article was actually lent.[29]

Blakemore's case was, however, distinguished in the Victorian decision of *Sheridan* v. *The Board of Land and Works*.[30] The plaintiff was injured while using a crane at the defendants' railway station. At the time, he was loading logs for his employers upon the defendants' trucks. Higinbotham J. cited three decisions subsequent to *Blakemore's* case[31] to show that this was no mere license or gratuitous bailment but the supply of an article for the performance of work in which the owner was interested; accordingly, the plaintiff should be deemed to have used the crane at the invitation of the defendant, and the latter was under a duty to use reasonable care to prevent damage from defects in the article of which he knew or ought to have known.[32] In so concluding, he appeared to accept entirely that the rule as stated in *Blakemore's* case was correct and that a gratuitous lender would be liable only for those defects of which he was aware. On the other hand, Williams J. (who dissented on the principal issue) interpreted *McCarthy* v. *Young*[33] as imposing liability for "gross negligence, or a defect in the crane of which they were at the time aware."[34] which seems at variance both with the decision in that case and with its interpretation in *Coughlin* v. *Gillison*.[35]

Taken together, these three decisions did not amount to very strong authority. Neither of them involved a true bailment; one of them deals with the question purely by way of dictum and the other two are confounded by the imagined rule that no action in negligence could be brought in the absence of a contract between the parties.[36] In this respect, the rule in *Blakemore's* case, by treating the gratuitous loan as a contract, was an extension or concession to plaintiffs, but one so limited by its requirements of privity that it was bound to be discarded. It might be argued that if *Blakemore* and its satellite decisions are no longer reliable upon the question of the parties to whom the lender's duty is owed, they are less dependable in their attempt to answer the extent of that duty itself.[37] Indeed, it has been contended that neither in *Blakemore* nor in *McCarthy* v. *Young* was it necessary for the court to propound the principle as to knowledge of defects and that each of them could have been dismissed

---

[29] The court did not have to decide whether, in fact, the plaintiff enjoyed the same right as Portlock or counted as a stranger to the lending. Possibly the latter was the case under the contemporary state of the law: but cf. *King* v. *G.W. Ry. Co.* (1871) 24 L.T. 583, and the *Sheridan* case, post.

[30] (1883) 9 V.L.R. (Law) 421.

[31] *Indermaur* v. *Dames* (1866) L.R. 1 C.P. 274; *Smith* v. *London and St. Katherines Dock Co.* (1868) L.R. 3 C.P. 326; *Heaven* v. *Pender* (1883) 11 Q.B.D. 503.

[32] (1883) 9 V.L.R. (Law), at 431-432; see also Stawell C.J. at 433-434.

[33] (1861) 6 H. & N. 329; 158 E.R. 136.

[34] (1883) 9 V.L.R. (Law), at 427.

[35] [1899] 1 Q.B. 145.

[36] This is a simplification of the rule, which was itself a misconception; see *Donoghue* v. *Stevenson* [1932] A.C. 562.

[37] No attempt was made in *Coughlin* v. *Gillison* [1899] 1 Q.B. 145 to argue that the plaintiff was a stranger to the original loan, although it is by no means evident that the loan was specifically to him.

on the question of privity alone; this, coupled with the fact that in *Coughlin* v. *Gillison*[38] there was no evidence of any neglect at all, is put forward as supporting this conclusion:

> The privileged position of the gratuitous bailor or donor had not been a deliberately conceived exception to the general principle of liability, but merely an illustration of the undeveloped state of the law in the nineteenth century.[39]

Accordingly, it is suggested[40] that the general duty of care enunciated by the decision in *Donoghue* v. *Stevenson*[41] should be taken as having superseded these earlier authorities and should now be regarded as governing the liability of the lender.

In fact, there are a number of authorities prior to 1932 which, although generally affirming the validity of *Coughlin* v. *Gillison*,[42] show a perceptible tendency to limit its effect. In the Ontario case of *MacTague* v. *Inland Lines Ltd.*[43] the plaintiff was the wife of a workman killed while in the employment of the first defendants. It appears from the report that these defendants were engaged in moving a vessel for the second defendants, the Canadian Pacific Railway, who loaned to them for that purpose a quantity of tackle; the equipment included a bolt which had been weakened by being left outside overnight in sub-zero conditions. A cable parted, causing the death of the plaintiff's husband, and the jury found both defendants negligent. Clute J. rejected Canadian Pacific's argument that they were merely gratuitous bailors on the interesting ground that there was no bailment: furthermore, those of their servants who assisted in the operation did not become the employees of the first defendants for the duration of the work.[44] Even assuming that there was a gratuitous bailment of the plant to the first defendants, however, he held that the previous decisions were distinguishable. Unfortunately, the report does not state the reasons for this opinion. Probably the second defendants' knowledge of the fact that the bolt had been subjected to injurious treatment was regarded as sufficiently akin to Rigby L.J.'s illustration in *Coughlin* v. *Gillison*[45] to justify imposing responsibility for a failure to warn of those conditions. Possibly, they knew of the defect in any event. The decision is clearly unsatisfactory but exemplifies the judicial dislike of the orthodox rule.

In *Shrimpton* v. *Hertfordshire County Council*[46] a school authority engaged a jobmaster to provide a vehicle to transport children to school. An accident was caused by the failure to provide a conductor which, it was found, meant that the vehicle was not reasonably fit for use. The judgment of Lord Loreburn L.C. states flatly that a person who provides anything for the use of another is bound to provide a thing reasonably

---

[38] Ante.
[39] (1950) 66 L.Q.R. 39, at 47.
[40] Ibid.
[41] [1932] A.C. 562.
[42] [1899] 1 Q.B. 145.
[43] (1915) 80 O.W.N. 183.
[44] Ibid., at 185; this was presumably designed to show that CPR remained in possession, through their servants, of the equipment.
[45] [1899] 1 Q.B., at 148; see p. 350, ante.
[46] (1911) 104 L.T. 145; 27 T.L.R. 251.

safe for the purpose for which it was intended. Accordingly, the defence, which had sought to rely on *Gautret* v. *Egerton*,[47] failed. The judgments appear to draw no distinction between the hiring and the lending of chattels and it is uncertain whether or not their Lordships considered that the duty of the supplier would be discharged by the taking of reasonable care.[48]

In *Chapman* (*or Oliver*) v. *Saddler & Co.*[49] the victim was a porter whose work consisted in unloading bags from rope slings as they were despatched from a ship by stevedores. The separate groups of porters and stevedores were employed by different companies but there was a regular arrangement that they should participate in unloading and to this end the stevedores permitted the porters to use their ropes and slings. It was one of these that broke and killed the plaintiff's husband. The House of Lords, in a somewhat opaque series of judgments, held that the widow should succeed because, although no contract existed between the victim and the tortfeasor, in the special circumstances of the case a duty was created to take reasonable care to ensure that the tackle was fit for use. However, Lord Atkin specifically said that this was not a case of gratuitous bailment, and that if it had been, "the bailor would only have been liable for a defect actually known to him."[50]

Evidently, this special rule had survived *Heaven* v. *Pender*.[51] The difficulty after *Chapman* (*or Oliver*) v. *Saddler & Co.* lay in identifying the circumstances in which it applied. Did Lord Atkin's dictum mean, as *MacTague* v. *Inland Lines Ltd.*[52] had suggested, that the "known defects" rule applied only in cases of bailment, where there had been a transfer of possession from lender to borrower? If so, the limitation would appear to run contrary to both *Blakemore's* case and *McCarthy* v. *Young,* in neither of which did there appear to be a true bailment and in neither of which was the word bailment mentioned.[53] If, on the other hand, as seems more likely, Lord Atkin was indicating that the present arrangement was for the mutual benefit of the parties, he must either have meant that the facts disclosed a bailment for mutual advantage or that the question of bailment was immaterial—in which case it would have been unnecessary to distinguish these facts from situations where a gratuitous bailment existed. If bailment were irrelevant to the operation of the known defects rule, he need only have said that the present case

[47] (1867) L.R. 2 C.P. 371.
[48] Lord Loreburn L.C., seems to speak in terms of an absolute duty, but Lord Halsbury's speech suggests more a test of reasonable care (though the report is garbled). Even today, it is unclear whether under English law the lessor of a chattel for reward is under a strict duty or merely a duty to take reasonable care: see Chapter 19, post.
[49] [1929] A.C. 584.
[50] Ibid, at 596, distinguishing *Langridge* v. *Levy* (1837) 4 M. & W. 337 on the ground, inter alia, that it contained proof of fraud.
[51] (1883) 11 Q.B.D. 503.
[52] (1915) 80 O.W.N. 183.
[53] Even if the borrower obtained exclusive possession of the structures in those cases (which seems improbable: cf. *Southland Harbour Board* v. *Vella* [1974] 1 N.Z.L.R. 526), they may have been fixtures and bailment applies only to moveable chattels.

did not involve a gratuitous loan. In fact, it is highly unlikely that there was a bailment in the *Chapman* case at all.[54]

But these were only minor erosions or evasions of a principle which, during the first quarter of the present century, seems to have been universally regarded as correct:[55] indeed, Wyatt Paine, writing in 1901, went so far as to conclude that:

> . . . a general license to use an article, without an immediate permission from the proprietor on each occasion, cannot be understood to raise an obligation on his part to mention any fault or defect in the chattel which may arise between the successive users . . .[56]

which was surely rather generous if the owner became aware of the defect before the fatal user occurred.

Undoubtedly the most radical potential upheaval to *Blakemore's* case came with the decision in *Donoghue* v. *Stevenson*.[57] The formulation of the neighbour principle, and the discarding of the precept that a contractual obligation was prerequisite to an action for negligent performance, opened the way for an expansion of the lender's obligation to one of reasonable care. So far, however, the courts have leaned but tentatively towards this conclusion. Admittedly, no specific reference was made in *Donoghue* v. *Stevenson* to the problem of gratuitous loans, and most of the statements in that case were limited to the context of manufacturers and consumers. On the other hand, the definitions of those to whom a duty of care was owed were wide enough to encompass a borrower, and Lord Thankerton remarked upon the difficulty of cataloguing in advance every human relationship which might engender a duty of care.[58]

The case of lending is, of course, technically distinguishable on two grounds. First, it does not involve an initial contract of supply to which the ultimate consumer is a non-party. A gratuitous loan implies a shorter chain of supply and, according to modern theory,[59] a total absence of contractual relations: as well, it may be suggested, as a general lack of intention to create them. Secondly, there is a dearth of profit-motive; whereas in *Donoghue* v. *Stevenson* the defendant was doing the act complained of in the course of earning his living, the lender generally possesses no such commercial experience. It is not just a question of con-

---

[54] See the comments on this decision in (1930) 46 *Canadian Bar Review* 2; (1950) 66 L.Q.R. 42-43. In fact, Lord Atkin uttered the dictum in the course of disputing a statement in the court below that the defendants *"were in the same legal position as* gratuitous bailors". This again suggests that the existence of a bailment was not considered essential to the rule in *Coughlin* v. *Gillison* [1899] 1 Q.B. 145; which is almost certainly correct.

[55] It was invoked, for instance, in the orthodox form by counsel for the defendants in *Geddling* v. *Marsh* [1920] 1 K.B. 668, at 670-671, although the court did not mention the principle and decided the case on other grounds.

[56] *Bailments*, p. 85.

[57] [1932] A.C. 562.

[58] Ibid., at 603; cf. Lord Atkin, at 580. Mr. N. S. Marsh (1950) 66 L.Q.R. at 43 points out that (i) Lord Atkin made no reservation in favour of the gratuitous bailor as he had done three years earlier, and (ii) that both he and Lord MacMillan in *Donoghue* v. *Stevenson* (at 598, 609) specifically preserved the exception to the general rule enounced in cases like *Cavalier* v. *Pope* [1906] A.C. 428 and *Bottomley* v. *Bannister* [1932] 1 K.B. 458; cf. *Dutton* v. *Bognor Regis U.D.C.* [1972] 1 Q.B. 373; *Defective Premises Act* 1972; *Anns* v. *Merton London Borough Council* [1977] 2 W.L.R. 1024; see p. 359, post.

[59] See p. 364, post.

sideration but one of practice and expertise. Many people are habitual manufacturers but few are habitual lenders. Of those who are, many may not be truly gratuitous lenders at all.[60]

Whether these distinctions are material or not is another matter. In such attentuated situations as the question has arisen since 1932, the courts have shown themselves willing to impose a duty of reasonable care upon the lender. One such case was *Griffiths* v. *Arch Engineering Ltd.*[61] Chapman J. found that the specific situation (shared equipment by workmates employed by different masters) there was no gratuitous bailment of a grinding machine to the plaintiff. In so doing he appeared to accept that the rule as to known defects was confined in any event to gratuitous *bailments*.[62] He went on to remark, speaking of the defendant's argument that they need only have given warning of defects known to them:

> I venture to feel some doubt about these propositions,[63] even assuming that I were capable of carrying my mind back to the legal atmosphere prevailing in 1931 . . . I think that many of the old cases which still find places in our textbooks are no longer of direct relevance. They are part of the history of the law of negligence and may serve as useful illustrations, but a lot of water has flowed under the bridge since 1931 . . . Things dangerous in themselves have gone into limbo as a category since *Read* v. *J. Lyons & Co. Ltd.*[64] . . . Nor does it assist the law of negligence to attempt to pigeon-hole injured people according to precisely-drawn categories such as purchasers, children, friends or neighbours or purchasers, tenants, hirers,[65] invitees, licensees, ordinary bailees, bailees for reward, bare users etc.[66]

In Chapman J.'s view, there are two questions uniform to each of these cases: was there a reasonably foreseeable risk and was the defendant one of whom reasonable precautions might have been expected to have been taken? In other words, mere negligence, and not knowledge of the miscreant defect, is the issue now in cases of lending as it is in cases of manufacture and repair.

This view is echoed by another recent case. In *Campbell* v. *O'Donnell*[67] the Supreme Court of Ireland held that a householder who had lent a ladder to two interior decorators engaged by him was not liable when the ladder (which was being used as a trestle to stand upon) collapsed and caused injury.[68] The decision is not conclusively in favour of the test of reasonable care because there was no evidence to show that the defendant had knowledge of the defect; moreover, the ladder was being used for a

---

[60] See the discussion in Chapter 8, ante, especially at p. 280.

[61] [1968] 3 All E.R. 217.

[62] Which the present case was not, since the defendants retained possession of the machine throughout: ibid., at 220.

[63] Munkman, *Employer's Liability* (6th ed.), pp. 147-149; 2 *Halsbury's Laws* (3rd ed.), para. 218.

[64] [1947] A.C. 156.

[65] Sed quaere: the lessor's duty may be higher than reasonable care: see p. 724 et seq., post.

[66] [1968] 3 All E.R., at 220.

[67] [1967] I.R. 226.

[68] It was explicitly conceded that the case was one of gratuitous bailment; had it not been, the matter may have been open to argument.

purpose not contemplated by the lender, so that whatever duty was originally upon him had already been rendered immaterial. Walsh J.[69] cited with tentative approval the statement in Fleming on *Torts*[70] that "the modern attitude has become distinctly unsympathetic to continuing discrimination against gratuitous relations" and instanced *Hedley Byrne & Co. Ltd.* v. *Heller & Partners Ltd.*[71] He also cited, with apparent approval, a statement of Denning L.J., that the pre-1932 cases on the liability of donors were out of date[72] and distinguished *Coughlin* v. *Gillison*[73] on the ground that there was no evidence of any negligence in that case. The other decisions, he considered, could also be interpreted "in the light of their particular grounds."[74] But he concluded that it was unnecessary to decide whether the lender is generally subject to the duty of reasonable care, because of the facts already mentioned and because no reasonable examination would have revealed the defect. The judgment of Fitzgerald J. is similarly inconclusive. In his view, the duty of the lender:

> . . . must depend upon the nature of the article, the circumstances under which it is lent, the purpose for which it is lent, and the character, capacity and experience of the person to whom it is lent.[75]

Probably this is reduceable to a universal test of reasonable care.

The decision of the New Zealand Court of Appeal in *Fraser* v. *Jenkins*[76] seems to disclose a similar approach, although with certain qualifications. A bricklayer was injured by the condition of a circular saw, which he was using to cut wedges. The saw had been loaned to him by a builder upon whose site he was working, although his actual employer was not the builder but the second respondent. It was established that both bailor and bailee were aware of the relevant defect (which consisted in the lack of a guard) and the question was whether the borrower's knowledge will necessarily exonerate the lender. The court adopted the view that there must be a necessary appreciation of the defect by the bailee, which in this case was clearly established. They went on to observe that although cases may arise "in which there is room for a more extensive neighbourly duty of care than arises from the more conventional view of the law,"[77] the present decision did not fall within that category. To some extent, therefore, the case may be taken as manifesting a similar approach to that of Fitzgerald J. in *Campbell* v. *O'Donnell* and as exacting from the bailor such care and warning as is reasonably necessary in the circumstances of the case. It is however debatable whether the present bailment was not properly classifiable as one for reward.

---

[69] At 229-230.
[70] (3rd ed.), p. 487; see now (4th ed.), p. 452.
[71] [1964] A.C. 465, at 525 et seq. per Lord Devlin.
[72] *Hawkins* v. *Coulsdon and Purley U.D.C.* [1954] 1 Q.B. 319, at 333. See further *Levi* v. *Colgate Palmolive Ltd.* (1941) 41 S.R. (N.S.W.) 48; *Pease* v. *Sinclair Refining Co.* (1939) 104 F. (2d) 183; *Ball* v. *L.C.C.* [1948] 2 All E.R. 917, reversed on other grounds [1949] 2 K.B. 159.
[73] [1899] 1 Q.B. 145.
[74] [1967] I.R., at 230.
[75] [1967] I.R., at 231.
[76] [1968] N.Z.L.R. 816.
[77] Ibid., at 824.

Alongside the dicta in these recent decisions may be placed the opinion of Denning L.J., upon the parallel case of gifts[78] and the modern propensity to discard the question of reward as a material factor in imposing a duty of reasonable care.[79] Moreover, there are several decisions in the reports which, although at least potentially identifiable as cases of gratuitous lending, have been decided completely without reference to *Coughlin* v. *Gillison*[80] and its accomplices. Thus in *Jones* v. *Barclay's Bank Ltd.*,[81] where a plumber who had been called in to repair the defendants' pipes was lent a ladder in order to inspect the loft, the case was decided upon a simple application of the rule in *Indermaur* v. *Dames*;[82] in *Lettich* v. *Ocvirk*[83] the plaintiff was injured while helping his landlady to erect a storm window, using a ladder loaned by her for that purpose: he recovered on the basis of a duty of care imposed under *Chapman (or Oliver)* v. *Saddler & Co.*;[84] in *Rossiter* v. *Canada Safeway Ltd.*[85] the plaintiff sued the defendant supermarket for negligence in supplying a defective shopping-trolley: the action failed on the facts but there was no suggestion that the defendants did not owe a duty of reasonable care; and in an American case[86] it was likewise held that a householder's liability to a stonemason, to whom the householder had lent a ladder for the purpose of repairing a chimney, arose only if the defendant "knew of or by the exercise of due care should have known" of the defect in the ladder.[87]

---

[78] See ante, n. 72.

[79] See, for instance, the modern decisions on the duties of the unrewarded depositary, discussed at p. 294 et seq., ante.

[80] [1899] 1 Q.B. 145.

[81] [1949] W.N. 266; cf. *Woodman* v. *Richardson & Concrete Ltd.* [1937] 3 All E.R. 866; *McGrath* v. *Leckie* (1932) 45 B.C.R. 534.

[82] (1866) L.R. 1 C.P. 274: ". . . with respect to such a visitor . . . (i.e. an invitor) . . . he, using reasonable care for his own safety, is entitled to expect that the occupier shall on his part use reasonable care to prevent damage from unusual danger, which he knows or ought to know". cf. *Pemberton National Park Board* v. *Johnson* [1966] W.A.R. 61.

[83] (1968) 65 D.L.R. (2d) 690.

[84] [1929] A.C. 584; p. 354, ante.

[85] (1967) 59 W.W.R. 304.

[86] *Williams* v. *Herrera* (1972) 496 Pa. (2d) 740 (New Mexico Court of Appeals).

[87] Ibid., at 744. The decision is interesting because the court held that para. 392 of the Restatement (Second), *Torts,* did not apply to the facts of the present case. That section applies only when the defendant supplies a chattel "to be used for the supplier's business purposes". In such a case, he is liable for physical harm arising from the proper use of the chattel if he has failed *either* to take reasonable care to make the chattel safe for such use *or* to take reasonable care to discover its dangerous condition and character and to inform those whom he should expect to use it. But in the present case the loan was purely for the plaintiff's personal use. It seems then that the relevant section was para. 405, which imposed liability when the supplier knows or has reason to know "that it is or is likely to be dangerous for the use for which it was given or lent". Sutin J. stressed that the defendant was under no positive obligation to inspect the ladder for defects but implied that a reasonable suspicion of defects would be enough to incur liability. The general drift of earlier American decisions is, however, in favour of the rule in *Blakemore's* case (see Marsh, (1950) 66 L.Q.R. 39, at 40, n.12); and thus limiting liability to defects of which the lender actually knows. cf. *Metz* v. *Haskell* (1966) 417 Pa. (2d) 898, where the loan of the ladder was for the defendant's benefit and liability was held to rest upon negligence; *Miller* v. *Hand Ford Sales Inc.* (1959) 340 Pa. (2d) 181 (where in similar circumstances the old rule as to known defects was held to apply).

Of course, none of these decisions is conclusive against the principle in *Coughlin* v. *Gillison*; in each of them, it could be argued that the loan was for the mutual benefit of the parties, if not (as in *Lettich* v. *Ocvirk*) for the benefit of the lender alone. But quite apart from the fact that similar considerations as to benefit could have applied to *Blakemore* v. *Bristol and Exeter Ry. Co.*[88] and *McCarthy* v. *Young*,[89] it is clear that many of these later decisions suggest not only a disregard for the "known defects" principle but also a variety of methods for its circumvention. One such method, of course, is the use of the rules relating to occupiers' liability.[90] This would undoubtedly have provided a more appropriate ground for dealing with cases like *McCarthy* and *Blakemore* (which clearly involved the condition of structures or premises rather than that of chattels in the literal sense) had such principles been clearly formulated at the time. But the very evolution of these principles, and the manner in which they developed, may argue against the supercession of the known defects rule by the general duty of care. When such rules began to crystallise,[91] and the duties of an occupier towards his lawful visitors became dependent upon the class of visitor in question, the responsibility of a lender of chattels stood revealed as a close parallel to the duty owed by an occupier towards his licensees. Admittedly, the latter duty was often ambiguously phrased, but its general burden was a responsibility to warn against all known but concealed structural dangers, regardless of when and how they originated.[92] This was not a duty of reasonable care; the licensor was not liable for defects of which he ought to have known but merely for those of which he knew or, at most, had reason to know.[93] In England, of course, the rule has now been abolished and supplanted by the common duty of care;[94] it certainly did not disappear with the decision in *Donoghue* v. *Stevenson*.[95] Now, of course, the common duty of care will often provide a means of evading whatever remains of *Coughlin* v. *Gillison* and of making the "lender" of a piece of equipment or a structure liable for want of reasonable care.[96] But many cases of gratuitous

---

[88] (1858) E. & B. 1034; 120 E.R. 385.

[89] (1861) 6 H. & N. 329; 158 E.R. 136.

[90] Particularly, of course, in England after the passing of the *Occupiers' Liability Act* 1957. *Jones* v. *Barclay's Bank Ltd.* ante. is a clear example of this approach in a pre-1957 situation.

[91] *Indermaur* v. *Dames* (1866) L.R. 1 C.P. 274 is generally regarded as the seminal decision.

[92] Fleming, *Torts*, p. 395, citing *Lipman* v. *Clendinnen* (1932) 46 C.L.R. 550, at 564-565. Certain cases support the imposition of liability for inferred or imputable knowledge, but arguably only in these extreme situations which might be said to correspond to the dictum of Rigby L.J. in *Coughlin* v. *Gillison* [1899] 1 Q.B. 145, at 148, cited at p. 350, ante. See on this point *Pearson* v. *Lambeth B.C.* [1938] 1 K.B. 212; *Vale* v. *Whiddon* (1950) 50 S.R. (N.S.W.) 90; cf. *Fairman* v. *Perpetual Building Society Ltd.* [1923] A.C. 74; *Hawkins* v. *Coulsdon and Purley U.D.C.* [1954] 1 Q.B. 319.

[93] Fleming, p. 397.

[94] Section 2(1), *Occupiers' Liability Act* 1957; see generally North, *Occupiers' Liability*.

[95] [1932] A.C. 562.

[96] At least, where it is to be used on his own land. As to the position where there is a *contractual* licence, and injury occurs to an independent contractor engaged by the licensee (or to the servant of an independent contractor), it seems that in jurisdictions where the doctrine in *Francis* v. *Cockerell* (1870) L.R. 5 Q.B. 501 is not replaced by a common duty of care, the warranty of reasonable

loans will not involve an occupancy duty at all. Of these it may be said that their original foundation, relying as it did upon a strong affinity with the license cases, is, like those cases, exempted from assimilation into the general duty of care. Such an analogy may answer Mr Marsh's suggestion[97] that there was no clearly conceived principle relating to lenders which could survive the decision in *Donoghue* v. *Stevenson*.[98] Moreover, it will be observed that in Australia there is no legislation comparable to the English Act of 1957. The result could be the continued validity of the rule that, in non-occupancy as well as in occupancy situations, the lender is liable only for those defects of which he is actually aware.[99]

One final observation should be made. It has already been remarked that the earlier decisions tended to regard gratuitous loans, like gratuitous bailments generally, as contracts.[1] This had its limiting features but in one sense it could possibly have led to a wider liability than that which would accrue by virtue of an action in tort. There are suggestions in *Blakemore's* case that the duty of the lender extended not only to safety but to the general suitability of the article for the purpose for which it was borrowed:[2] the contract obliged him to disclose these known defects which would make the loan "perilous *or unprofitable*" to the borrower. From this it might be concluded that if the borrower suffered economic loss, such as penalties for delay, loss of profits, etc., through the known unsuitability of a tool or piece of machinery, such loss might be recoverable on ordinary contractual principles from the lender. To abolish the contractual standard of liability and replace it simply by an action in negligence would be to limit the recovery of economic loss considerably: for it seems clear that such loss will generally be recoverable in tort only if dependent upon physical injury or damage.[3] Admittedly, the decision in *Hedley Byrne & Co. Ltd.* v. *Heller & Partners Ltd.*[4] permits recovery for economic loss as the result of negligent mis-statements, but may be limited to cases where there is a special relationship between the parties;[5]

---

fitness imposed by that decision may apply consecutively against the licensee and the licensor: *Southland Harbour Board* v. *Vella* [1974] 1 N.Z.L.R. 526.

[97] (1950) 66 L.Q.R., at 47.
[98] [1932] A.C. 562.
[99] Subject, presumably, to the "dangerous chattels" doctrine evolved before 1932. When the chattel belongs to the category of things that are dangerous *per se*, there is, it seems, a special duty to take care to safeguard against injury or damage. In general situations it appears that this doctrine has become defunct: see, e.g., the dictum of Chapman J., cited at p. 356, ante. As applied to the gratuitous lender it seems to add little to the doctrine in *Coughlin* v. *Gillison* ante, n. 91. As Winfield and Jolowicz point out (p. 205, n. 24), although the liability in respect of dangerous chattels has been said not to rest upon knowledge (*Burfitt* v. *Kille* [1939] 2 K.B. 743, at 747) the classification of a chattel as dangerous means, if anything, that everyone is presumed to know that it is dangerous.
[1] Ante, p. 351.
[2] (1858) 120 E.R. 385, at 391. cf. *Jewell* v. *Connolly* (1897) Q.R. 11 S.C. 265.
[3] *Spartan Steel and Alloys Ltd.* v. *Martin & Co. (Contractors) Ltd.* [1973] 1 Q.B. 27; see generally Salmond, pp. 206-207. But cf. *Caltex Oil (Aust.) Pty. Ltd.* v. *The "Willemstad"* (1976) 11 A.L.R. 227.
[4] [1964] A.C. 465; itself perhaps more of a contractual right of action than one in tort — see Atiyah, *Accidents, Compensation and the Law*, pp. 75-76.
[5] *Mutual Life and Citizens' Assurance Co. Ltd.* v. *Evatt* [1971] A.C. 793; see further *Anderson & Sons Ltd.* v. *Rhodes* [1967] 2 All E.R. 850; *Dutton* v.

and despite the fact that actions have recently been allowed for losses due to statements in pre-contractual negotiations,[6] it is by no means certain that the same rule would apply in a simple borrower-lender context.[7] If expansion of the lender's liability for injury is considered desirable, it might be questioned whether the same feeling applies to a contraction of his liability for economic loss.

In fact, there is a clear recent authority from New Zealand[8] to the effect that gratuitous loans (and gratuitous bailments generally) have nothing to do with the law of contract at all and that the remedies of the parties exist solely in tort. In this case, the bailor was suing the bailee and the immediate question was whether the bailee could set up the defences of contributory negligence and volenti non fit injuria. The judgment of Mahon J. did not expressly consider the reverse situation and it may be doubted whether a purely tortious analysis of gratuitous bailments is in any event correct.[9] There are strong arguments in the case of consensual bailments for applying certain contractual principles (e.g., deviation) by way of analogy, even where the bailment is gratuitous and there is an absence of conventional consideration.[10] There are also recent dicta which re-affirm support for the contractual view of such bailments.[11] Accordingly, it is by no means certain that the earlier characterisation of loans of chattels as a contractual phenomenon is discredited. The result may be that the lender's duty remains his narrow, contractual one of revealing only those defects which are known to him.[12] In many cases this would cease to cause hardship because of the courts' increasing willingness to classify a bailment as one for reward.[13] The bailor's duty would then be one of reasonable care (or higher)[14] and it would seem appropriate in such an event that the so-called borrower should be entitled to recover on contractual principles for economic loss.[15]

It must, however, be conceded that modern opinion seems to favour

---

Bognor Regis U.D.C. [1972] 1 Q.B. 373; *Sutcliffe* v. *Thackrah* [1974] A.C. 727; *Arenson* v. *Casson, Beckman, Rutley & Co.* [1975] 3 All E.R. 901.

[6] *Dillingham Constructions Pty. Ltd.* v. *Downs* [1972] 2 N.S.W.L.R. 49; *Esso Petroleum Co. Ltd.* v. *Mardon* [1975] 1 Q.B. 819; [1976] Q.B. 801; *Howard Marine & Dredging Ltd.* v. *A. Ogden & Sons Ltd.* [1978] 2 W.L.R. 515.

[7] Cf. Borrie, *Commercial Law* (4th ed.), pp. 151-152, where it is suggested that the decision might provide a remedy in the context of a hire-purchaser suing a dealer for misrepresentations, but it is admitted that there is no authority for such a proposition. Cf., however, *Capital Motors Ltd.* v. *Beacham* [1975] 1 N.Z.L.R. 576.

[8] *Walker* v. *Watson* [1974] 2 N.Z.L.R. 175; (1975) 24 I.C.L.Q. 565.

[9] See p. 20 et seq., ante, where this question is considered in greater depth.

[10] See pp. 322, 342, ante.

[11] E.g. *Roufos* v. *Brewster and Brewster* [1971] 2 S.A.S.R. 218, at 223-224 (per Bray C.J.); *New Zeadand Shipping Co. Ltd.* v. *A. N. Satterthwaite & Co. Ltd.* [1974] 1 All E.R. 1015, at 1020 per Lord Wilberforce.

[12] Of course, there is nothing anomalous in a contractual duty to take reasonable care.

[13] See Chapter 8, ante.

[14] See Chapter 19, post.

[15] Suppose, for instance that Factory A, which has a long record of mutual assistance with Factory B, borrows from Factory B a generator which is defective and which causes loss of profits etc. It would surely be fair in such a case to make Factory B liable, at least where they were negligent in failing to know or to warn of the defect.

the imposition upon a lender of the general duty of care.[16] In some respects this is desirable, for it could be paradoxical if the lender were liable in negligence to a bystander and not thus liable to the borrower himself; nor would it be easy to extend the "known defects" doctrine to all parties (including sub-borrowers) injured by the chattel, whether they came within the original contract or not. It is to be hoped, however, that the test of reasonable care would be leniently applied and that the character and aptitudes of the lender will be given appropriate weight.[17] Moreover, there is nothing to suggest that the lender, although deprived of the benefit of his implied contract to be liable only for known defects, cannot make an express contract to that effect. There is substantial authority in favour of such an approach in the field of gratuitous services[18] and such a course seems clearly open to the unpaid depositary.[19] Lenders may therefore be advised to attach such a clause to every chattel they may have cause to lend.

1. *The borrower's knowledge*: Whether commodatum be characterised as a contractual relationship or as one within which the ordinary rules of tort apply, it seems that a borrower who takes the chattel with knowledge of its defects (or in such circumstances as would lead a reasonable man to conclude that those defects exist) will be precluded from recovering against the bailor. In tort, this result will be achieved through the medium of the defences of contributory negligence and volenti non fit injuria. These defences may not apply in answer to an action for breach of contract[20] but the bailor would presumably be relieved on the ground that his contractual liability extended only to those defects which were not fully apparent to the borrower at the time the contract was made. In cases of hire, it is probable that a failure to rely on the owner's skill and judgment will deprive the hirer of his remedy.[21] It seems proper to impose a similar rule with regard to borrowers and to deny a remedy where the defectiveness of the chattel was so obvious that no reasonable borrower would have overlooked it and no reasonable lender would have assumed that he had done so. This approach equates with the degree of care which may be expected of a bailee who is known to be careless or unqualified. Insofar as there may be difficulty in exonerating the bailor

[16] Although many textbook writers prefer to leave the question open: see, for instance, Salmond, pp. 305-306, who remarks that the old rule had long been settled by good authority; see also Clerk and Lindsell, paras. 939, 1624, 536, 900; cf. Winfield and Jolowicz, p. 204 (who argue strongly for the new rule) and Paton, p. 153, who contends that House of Lords authority is necessary to overturn the old.

[17] Winfield and Jolowicz, loc. cit., point out that gratuitousness is an important factor in assessing the appropriate standard of care.

[18] See, for instance, *Hedley Byrne & Co. Ltd.* v. *Heller & Partners Ltd.* [1964] A.C. 465; *Ashdown* v. *Samuel Williams Ltd.* [1957] 1 Q.B. 409; *New Zealand Shipping Co. Ltd.* v. *A. N. Satterthwaite & Co. Ltd.* [1974] 1 All E.R. 1015, at 1030 per Lord Simon of Glaisdale.

[19] Cf. *Unfair Contract Terms Act 1977*, ss. 1 (i) (b), 2.

[20] *Southland Harbour Board* v. *Vella* [1974] 1 N.Z.L.R. 526; *Walker* v. *Watson* [1974] 2 N.Z.L.R. 175; *A. S. James Pty. Ltd.* v. *C. B. Duncan* [1970] V.R. 705; cf. ante., p. 55.

[21] Chapter 19, post; cf. Turner (1972) 46 A.L.J. 560, 619. The authorities appear to favour the view that the onus of disproving this should rest upon the bailor and the same rule seems appropriate in cases of gratuitous loans.

under contractual principles, it is suggested that this may best be achieved by analogy with the normal rules of bailees' liability, whereunder a bailee may be liable for such a degree of care and circumspection as the other party can reasonably expect, unless a clear undertaking to the contrary is shown.

The only recent decision to examine this question specifically is *Fraser* v. *Jenkins*.[22] Here the appellant was suing (by way of alternative) in negligence, but was shown to have had knowledge of the defect. In dismissing his appeal, Richmond J. acknowledged that it may sometimes be necessary for the lender to show more than a mere awareness of the defect on the borrower's part; the circumstances may, for instance, require that he issue a warning or take other additional steps in the interests of the safety of the bailee.[23] But where, as in the present case, the borrower clearly appreciates the risk attendant upon the defect, his assumption of that risk should preclude any later redress. It is almost beyond question that this view will be favoured in future decisions, even those (which seem likely to be rare) which adopt the contractual analysis of commodatum.[24]

2. *The Trade Practices Act* 1974: Sections 69 to 72 of the Federal *Trade Practices Act* imply into every contract for the supply of goods from a corporation to a consumer certain widely-drawn undertakings on the part of the supplier.[25] Liability under these undertakings is strict and cannot be excluded.[26] The expression "contract for the supply of goods" is defined by s. 4 to include sale, exchange, hire-purchase, lease and hire. Although this definition does not purport to be exhaustive, it is submitted that for the purposes of the Act bailments by way of commodatum should not be regarded as contracts for the supply of goods. Apart from other considerations, the use of the expression "contract *for*" the supply of goods clearly contemplates binding executory arrangements within which characterisation commodatum seems incapable of falling. It is possible in any event that most corporation-consumer lendings will count as bailments for mutual advantage and therefore as hirings, although the two are not synonymous.[27]

---

[22] [1968] N.Z.L.R. 816.

[23] Ibid., at 824. The learned judge here relied upon an analogy with the law relating to licensees, which had already developed in a similar direction, before the passing of the *Occupiers' Liability Act,* in cases of children or persons of defective intelligence.

[24] A similar principle would, of course, protect the lender when the borrower uses the chattel for a purpose not contemplated by the loan: *Campbell* v. *O'Donnell* [1967] I.R. 226.

[25] Section 69(1)(b) (implied warranty as to quiet possession): s. 69(1)(c) (implied warranty as to freedom from encumbrance); s. 71(2) (implied condition that goods reasonably fit for use). s. 71(1) (implied condition that goods of merchantable quality): s. 72 (implied warranty that goods correspond with sample). Cf. s. 69(1)(a) (title) which applies only where title "is to or may pass" and s. 70 (description) which applies only where the goods are exposed for sale or hire. See generally subsection (2); Palmer and Rose (1977) 26 I.C.L.Q. 169.

[26] Section 68.

[27] Chapter 8, ante; but cf. *Queens Sales & Service Ltd.* v. *Smith* (1963) 48 M.P.R. 364, at 368, 372-373 where Ilsley C.J. and Coffin J. suggested that the duties of a garage company which lent a car to a customer while his own was being repaired were those of a lessor.

B. Other obligations

Story[28] described the duties of a lender as "few, and merely accessorial". Leaving aside his responsibility for the fitness and safety of the chattel, it is immediately clear that the extent to which any ancillary or super-imposed obligations are enforceable will depend in large part upon whether commodatum is a contract. If it is, the borrower's consideration will be sufficient to support any promise made by the lender. It it is not, the question is much more doubtful.

The principal situation which will give rise to this problem occurs when the lender promises to allow the borrower to use the chattel for a fixed and definite term. Can the lender withdraw this permission and repossess the chattel at will, or must he wait until the promised term expires? There is remarkably little authority on this point. The following seem to be the competing solutions:

(a) The remedies which obtain a gratuitous loan are purely tortious and have nothing to do with the law of contract at all. This, as we have seen, enjoys the support of recent authority which was concerned with the bailor's rights of action against the bailee[29] and did not specifically consider the potential enforcement of ancillary promises against the bailor. It is subject to the obvious exception that an additional promise by the borrower (e.g. to compensate for all loss to the chattel, however arising) will be enforceable in contract against him. In such a case, although the bailee's promise may not constitute a benefit to the lender, it is clearly a detriment to the bailee and therefore good consideration.

Under the "purely tortious" theory, the borrower's lack of considera-tion spells the death of contract and the reduction of the bailee to suing in tort for unwarranted dispossession. To sue in trespass or conversion, he would have to show that it was he and not the bailor who enjoyed the immediate right to possession. Any right purportedly given to him by the terms of the commodatum would be unforceable in contract and therefore incapable of vindication in tort. The bailor can go back on his word.

The tortious analysis of gratuitous loans is supported by the similar analysis accorded to gratuitous bailments generally. This support seems, if anything, to be increasing.[30] There would be little purpose in rehearsing here the arguments for and against this theory. Suffice it to say that in many respects gratuitous bailments resemble contracts and partake of contractual remedies in their enforcement. The tortious analysis is an oversimplification and one which arguably fails to do justice to the true substance of the relation.

(b) Gratuitous loans are contracts and therefore enforceable as such, both as to their essential obligations (e.g. to reveal defects, or to return the chattel) and as to any further duties the parties may care to super-impose. This theory is supported by the older decisions[31] and, impliedly,

[28] Section 270.
[29] *Walker* v. *Watson* [1974] 2 N.Z.L.R. 175.
[30] See, generally, p. 000, et seq., ante.
[31] E.g. *Blakemore* v. *Bristol and Exeter Ry. Co.* (1858) 8 E. & B. 1034; 120 E.R. 385; ante, p. 351.

by some new ones.[32] Its efficacy depends, of course, upon the degree of support which the tortious analysis will command in future decisions. Despite the attractions of the contractual theory, its present implications are in something of a state of disarray. Story[33] accepts the theory but denies the conclusion; in his view, the lender (save perhaps in very exceptional circumstances) can revoke at any time. Paton[34] denies the theory and, with it, the result; in substance, therefore, his conclusion is the same as Story's. Older decisions[35] declare that the borrower's consideration lies in his duty to take care of the goods and his liability for failure to do so. More recent authorities seem to suggest that conventional consideration is not necessary anyway[36] and that gratuitous bailment is a special kind of contract exempt from certain of the general contractual rules.

In fact, there may be grounds for arguing that commodatum approaches closer to an orthodox contract than other gratuitous bailments such as depositum and mandatum. Although the lender is deprived of the use of goods, he is at least getting unpaid storage during the period of the borrowing: no such practical advantage attends the depositary, whose primary benefit is probably the unlikely one of being able to exercise the possessory remedies. With the modern tendency to mitigate the doctrine of consideration,[37] the recognition of commodatum as a mutually beneficial arrangement (at least in some circumstances) may not be wholly out of the question. Acknowledgement of the fact that bailments need not be contracts need not involve denying the contractual relation between the parties to a gratuitous loan.

Of course, if this argument were accepted it could lead to the disappearance of commodatum altogether. A more serious objection is that the revival of the contract theory could bring in its wake the application of certain other contractual principles inimical to the nature of bailment. One of these is the doctrine of privity, and we have already seen the injustice that this caused in *Blakemore* v. *Bristol and Exeter Ry. Co.*[38] Moreover, it is generally accepted that commodatum cannot be executory, which rule would be flouted if the borrower's promise to take the goods on loan were to be translated as a valuable promise of custody. There are probably much stronger reasons for allowing a prospective lender to resile from his agreement when the bailee has not yet entered into possession.

In view of the receding likelihood that the contractual theory of commodatum will continue to find acceptance, it seems necessary to seek other principles upon which the bailor's promise of a finite term may be enforced. These may be found within the general rules of Equity, or they may form part of the special system of law relating to bailments.

---

[32] E.g. *New Zealand Shipping Co. Ltd.* v. *A. N. Satterthwaite & Co. Ltd.* [1974] 1 All E.R. 1015, at 1020; *Roufos* v. *Brewster and Brewster* [1971] 2 S.A.S.R. 218, at 223-224; see generally p. 14, et seq., ante.
[33] Section 270 (7th ed. 1863).
[34] At 150-151.
[35] Most notably, the *Blakemore* case, ante, n. 31.
[36] See the *Satterthwaite* and *Roufos* cases, ante, n. 32.
[37] (1975) 24 I.C.L.Q. 565, at 571-572; (1975) 38 M.L.R. 65.
[38] (1858) 8 E. & B. 1034; 120 E.R. 385; ante, p. 351.

In both cases, the principles are obscure and success is far from assured.

(c) There is a prospect that Equity would permit the borrower to resist a claim for early repossession whenever the lender's promise of a finite term was calculated to induce the borrower to make a material change in his position, and did have that effect. Older authority would seem more favourable to this view than the weight of decisions in the twentieth century. For instance, in *Hammersley* v. *de Biel*,[39] Lord Cottenham L.C. laid down a general principle which was wide enough to cover a lender's ancillary promises:

> A representation made by one party for the purpose of influencing the conduct of the other party and acted on by him, will in general be sufficient to entitle him to the assistance of this Court for the purpose of realising such representation.[40]

Later authority, however, detracted from this wide principle and tended to confine *Hammersley* v. *de Biel* to those situations where there was a contract between the parties.[41] The same authority has confined the doctrine of estoppel by representation[42] to statements as to an existing state of fact, and has excluded from its operation mere statements as to intention. The conventional doctrine of consideration would seem to preclude an advance upon these lines.[43]

So far as concerns equitable or promisory estoppel, the stumbling-block would appear to be that there are (ex hypothesi) no existing legal relations between promisor and promisee at the time when the agreement is made.[44] The reverse could be true if the promise is made after the borrower is placed in possession, for then the parties will be in the relationship of bailor and bailee and there is authority for the view that the pre-existing relationship postulated by Denning J. (as he then was) need not be contractual.[45] To make the validity of such promises depend upon whether they are made before or after delivery seems capricious, but it is in keeping with the general principle that an enforceable gratuitous bailment can never be executory, and with the distinctive role of possession in bailments generally.

---

[39] (1845) 12 Cl. & F. 45; 8 E.R. 1312; the decision did not involve bailment but a promise by a prospective father-in-law to leave his daughter a sum of money.

[40] Ibid., at 61n., 1320n. respectively.

[41] See *Citizens' Bank of Louisiana* v. *First National Bank of New Orleans* (1873) L.R. 6 H.L. 352, and the excellent discussion by Professor Sutton, *Consideration Reconsidered*, pp. 72-75.

[42] *Jorden* v. *Money* (1854) 4 H.L.C. 185.

[43] Paton, p. 151; but see contra, Atiyah (1975) 38 M.L.R. 65, who argues that recent developments support the view that a promisee's reliance, to his detriment, upon a promise may constitute good consideration.

[44] *Central London Property Trust Ltd.* v. *High Trees House Ltd.* [1947] 1 K.B. 130; but cf. *Evenden* v. *Guildford City Association Football Club Ltd.* [1975] I.C.R. 367, at 374. It is uncertain in any event whether the doctrine of promissory estoppel represents a principle of Australian Law: Sutton, *Consideration Reconsidered*, Chapter 5.

[45] E.g. *Roberson* v. *Minister of Pensions* [1949] 1 K.B. 227; *Durham Fancy Goods Ltd.* v. *Michael Jackson (Fancy Goods) Ltd.* [1968] 2 Q.B. 839; *Evenden* v. *Guildford City Association Football Club Ltd.* [1975] I.C.R. 367, at 374; cf. *Ajayi* v. *R. T. Briscoe (Nigeria) Ltd.* [1964] 1 W.L.R. 1326, at 1330; *Cook Islands Shipping Co. Ltd.* v. *Colson Builders Ltd.* [1975] 1 N.Z.L.R. 442, at 437-438; *Argy* v. *Lapid* [1977] 1 W.L.R. 444.

There remains a somewhat remote analogy with what has been called the doctrine of acquiescence in relation to land.[46] The general drift of the decisions in this area is to the effect that if I, as an owner of land, knowingly permit another to build upon it, or to make improvements thereto, under the impression that it is his own, "a court of equity will not allow me afterwards to assert my title to the land on which he had expended money on the supposition".[47] Insofar as this doctrine depends upon the principle of unjust enrichment,[48] it is far removed from the plight of the borrower whose expectations as to the period of the loan have been frustrated. However, in at least one decision it was expressed to apply where the promisee expends money *or does some other act* on the faith of the mistaken impression.[49] Insofar as the doctrine is merely one aspect of estoppel by representation, the borrower may again fall victim to the objection that the representation that he would be allowed to remain in possession was not one of fact but one of intention.[50] For the present, two observations should be made.

First, some of the cases contain statements which, if applied to the analogous field of personal property, could be advanced to support the grant of an irrevocable license to the borrower for the period in question, provided he entered into possession in reliance on that promise or, because of it, subsequently altered his position to a material degree.[51] Secondly, a recent decision of the Court of Appeal[52] shows that a person who expends money and labour in improving a chattel which he does not know belongs to another, and as regards which the owner has made no representation to him at all, may nevertheless obtain restitution for the benefits he has expended, by virtue of the principles of unjust enrichment. If the philosophy of the acquiescence cases can be adapted so liberally to the law of personal property in cases of unjust enrichment, it may be thought that a similar adaptation could be made in the area of non-contractual licenses. The law in this field, and its relevance to the notion of irrevocable licenses in chattels, remains however in an obscure condition.

---

[46] Goff and Jones, *The Law of Restitution*, pp. 95-99.

[47] *Ramsden* v. *Dyson* (1866) L.R. 1 H.L., at 140-141 per Lord Cranworth L.C. See also *Huning* v. *Ferrers* (1711) Gib. 85; *Dillwyn* v. *Llewellyn* (1862) 4 De G.F. & J. 517; *Plimmer* v. *Wellington Corporation* (1884) 9 App. Cas. 699; *Inwards* v. *Baker* [1965] 2 Q.B. 29; *Chalmers* v. *Pardoe* [1963] 1 W.L.R. 677; 3 All E.R. 552. The doctrine can apply when the representee builds upon his own land: *I. R. Ives (Investment) Ltd.* v. *High* [1967] 2 Q.B. 379.

[48] Sutton, op. cit., pp. 69-70.

[49] *Willmot* v. *Barber* (1880) 15 Ch. D. 96, at 105-106 per Fry J. See also *Adaras Developments Ltd.* v. *Marcona Corporation* [1975] 1 N.Z.L.R. 324, at 338.

[50] But cf. *Greater Sydney Development Association Ltd.* v. *Rivett* (1929) 29 S.R. (N.S.W.) 356; Sutton, op. cit., pp. 70-72. Of course, the promisor may be held to have misrepresented his intention: *Automobile and General Finance Co. Ltd.* v. *Hoskins Investment Ltd.* (1934) 34 S.R. (N.S.W.) 375, at 392-393. Some authorities see the doctrine as a species of implied contract: see Goff and Jones, op cit., p. 98, n. 13 and *Raffaele* v. *Raffaele* [1962] W.A.R. 29; (1963) 79 L.Q.R. 238 (D. E. Allan).

[51] E.g. *Plimmer* v. *Mayor of Wellington* (1884) 9 App. Cas. 699, at 714; *Crabb* v. *Arun D.C.* [1975] 3 All E.R. 865, at 871, 877; *Evenden* v. *Guildford City Association Football Club Ltd.* [1975] I.C.R. 367, at 374.

[52] *Greenwood* v. *Bennett* [1973] Q.B. 195; cf. *Express Coach Finishers Ltd.* v. *Caulfield* 1968 S.L.T. (Sh. Ct.) 11.

(d) If, as seems to be the case, an unpaid depositary may be liable for the breach of any agreement between the bailor and himself,[53] it would be logical to extend this treatment to unrewarded lenders. The depositary who, for instance, deviates from the terms of his undertaking, becomes an insurer of the goods he has received from the bailor. Such liability cannot be explained purely in terms of tort and is not, according to modern theory, the consequence of any contractual relationship between the parties. It must therefore depend upon the peculiar principles of bailment. It is suggested that, by analogy with the bailee's assumpsit in such cases, an unrewarded bailor should be bound by any undertaking he has made with regard to the chattel, and in reliance upon which the bailee has entered into possession. Although bailment primarily connotes an entry into a relationship with a chattel, the true bailment relation is a bilateral one in which the salient element of possession marks the dividing-line between executory promises and affirmative obligations. From the bailor's angle, these obligations depend upon the nature of the bailment and the terms upon which it is assumed. These terms may be contractual, but they may emanate from the status of the parties and may even exist irrespective of agreement.[54] If the gratuitous bailee's responsibilities are to be determined by reference to the promises upon which he induced the bailor to relinquish possession, it should follow that the bailor's duties will depend upon the promises whereby he ensured that such possession was assumed.[55]

Under this analysis, proof of the bailee's entry into possession in reliance upon an assurance by the bailor might translate that assurance into a binding commitment, whether it related to the period of the loan or to some other promise ancillary to the chattel, e.g. to service it regularly or to stand as an insurer for its safety and fitness for use.

II. THE DUTIES OF THE BORROWER

According to Story,[56] these are fourfold: to take proper care of the chattel, to use it for the purpose for which it was lent, to return it at the appointed time and to restore it in a proper condition. Of these, the first is the most important.

A. The standard of care

Traditionally, the measure of care demanded of a borrower is the converse of that required of the depositary: he must show utmost diligence and is liable for even slight neglect. Thus spoke Lord Holt in *Coggs* v. *Bernard*:[57]

> . . . the borrower is bound to the strictest care and diligence . . . because the bailee has a benefit by the use of them, so as if the bailee

---

[53] These principles are discussed at p. 313 et seq., ante.
[54] Cf. *Lovely* v. *Burroughs Corporation Inc.* (1974) 527 P. (2d) 557.
[55] Note that the question may be of importance to the bailor in his action against a third party. Unless he has an immediate right of possession, he will have to prove damage to his reversionary interest; p. 153, ante.
[56] Section 236.
[57] (1703) 92 E.R. 107, at 111.

be guilty of the least neglect, he will be answerable . . . Bracton says, the bailee must use the utmost care, but yet he shall not be chargeable, where there is such a force as he cannot resist.

However, as with the depositary's duty of care, this standard has undergone a familiar process of erosion over the years. A number of the older authorities adhere to the scale of liability laid down by Lord Holt,[58] although in practice it was not always consistently applied; thus in *Blakemore* v. *Bristol and Exeter Ry. Co.*[59] one finds the borrower's duty phrased in terms of gross negligence, an error which has permeated certain Canadian reports in more recent years.[60] The most recent authority seems to be that of Mahon J. in the New Zealand case of *Walker* v. *Watson*.[61] The respondent lent his M.G. sports car to two girls whom he knew to be drunk, and stipulated that only the less inebriated of them should drive. The car was damaged and he sued the appellant (who was the appointed driver) in contract for breach of bailment. His object in doing so was to avert a possible defence of contributory negligence or volenti non fit injuria. It was held that an action for damage to a gratuitously-bailed chattel sounds in negligence and the stated defence could apply:

> There was no element of contract present. No consideration moved from the appellant when she took possession of the car with the consent of the respondent . . . The appellant assumed the ordinary duty of a bailee to take care of the chattel entrusted to her custody.

Any action for breach of that duty lay in tort, not in contract.[62]

In fact, it is likely that the same result should have been reached upon a contractual theory of commodatum, since it has been stated that a borrower is liable to use only such care and skill as the lender knows to be within his capacity.[63] No discussion occurred as to the theory of degrees of care and the only decisions cited on this point were cases of bailment for reward.[64] On the wider issue of the identity of gratuitous bailments the decision is open to question.[65] On the narrower issue, it is possible that this was a bailment for mutual advantage, since it seems that the object of the loan was to enable the appellant to visit her parents and get their permission to her spending the night with the respondent.[66]

Practically the only other decisions in point are Canadian. Some of

---

[58] E.g. Jones, at 65-66; Story, s. 237 et. seq.; Wyatt Paine, p. 83; Street. *Foundations of Legal Liability*, Vol. II, p. 281; *Vaughan* v. *Menlove* (1837) 3 Bing. (N.C.) 468.

[59] (1858) 8 E. & B. 1035, at 1050-1051; 120 E.R. 385, at 391.

[60] See, for instance, the argument of counsel in *A. R. Williams Machinery Co. Ltd.* v. *Muttart Builders' Supply (Winnipeg) Ltd.* (1961) 30 D.L.R. (2d) 339, at 343, and the decision of the County Court judge in *Wood Motors Ltd.* v. *McTavish* (1972) 21 D.L.R. (3d) 480; cf. *Fairley & Stevens (1966) Ltd.* v. *Goldsworthy* (1973) 34 D.L.R. (3d) 554, at p. 568 (Dubinsky J.).

[61] [1974] 2 N.Z.L.R. 175.

[62] Ibid., at 178.

[63] Jones, op. cit., p. 567.

[64] *Morris* v. *C. W. Martin & Sons Ltd.* [1966] 1 Q.B. 716 (where the passage cited referred to varying degrees of care); *Gilchrist, Watt & Sanderson Pty. Ltd.* v. *York Products Pty. Ltd.* [1970] 1 W.L.R. 1262; 3 All E.R. 825.

[65] See p. 313, ante.

[66] [1974] 2 N.Z.L.R., at 176.

these acknowledge the borrower's liability for slight neglect;[67] thus, according to Latchford C.J. in the Ontario Court of Appeal:

> The borrower must exercise the utmost diligence in his use of the chattel borrowed and is liable for the least degree of negligence. This does not mean that the exactissima diligentia of the Roman Law is called for, such as that in case of accidental fire the commodatarius must save the borrowed chattel though he lost his own: but he must show that there was no negligence on his part occasioning the loss.[68]

But even here one may perceive a tendency to equate this duty with the standard of the reasonable and prudent man. Other cases have accentuated this equation[69] and have largely transformed the borrower's responsibility into one of reasonable care. In *A. R. Williams Machinery Co. Ltd.* v. *Muttart Builders' Supply (Winnipeg) Ltd.*[70] Ferguson J. acknowledged the authority of Latchford C.J.'s observation and specifically exonerated the defendants of slight negligence, but he did so in terms which suggest no distinction between this criterion and the standard of reasonable care.[71] In *Fairley & Stevens (1966) Ltd.* v. *Goldsworthy*[72] Dubinsky J. remarked upon the trend towards clarification or standardisation of the bailee's duty of care and held that the duty in the present case would be the same whether the relationship were one of commodatum, depositum, or bailment for mutual advantage.[73] In *Jenkins* v. *Smith*[74] Hart J. held that in a case of mutual loan between the defendant and a servant of the plaintiff (the plaintiff himself not benefiting from the arrangement):

> By the application of the doctrine of *re ipsa loquitur* and under the rule that a bailee must disprove negligence, . . . there is a burden on the defendant to establish that the loss suffered by the plaintiff was not due to any negligence on his part.[75]

Clearly there is in Canada an advanced propensity towards a single, all-purpose duty of care.

On the other hand, there are recent Canadian decisions which continue to use the language of Lord Holt and to suggest that a distinction still exists between slight and ordinary neglect.[76] There has been no situation yet in which the bailee's misconduct could be properly characterised as

---

[67] *Riverdale Garage Ltd.* v. *Barrett Bros.* [1930] 4 D.L.R. 429; cf. *Bijou Motor Parlours Ltd.* v. *Keel* (1918) 39 D.L.R. 410.

[68] *Riverdale Garage Ltd.* v. *Barrett Bros.* ante, at 430; cf. Story, ss. 245-250.

[69] *Smith* v. *Moats* (1921) 56 D.L.R. 415; *Gibson* v. *Wilson* (1922) 67 D.L.R. 410; *Anderson* v. *Royer* [1928] 3 D.L.R. 248.

[70] (1961) 30 D.L.R. (2d) 339; on appeal, (1961) 31 D.L.R. (2d) 187.

[71] Ibid., at 345: "I can find no negligent act or omission on the part of the defendant or its servants in respect of which it could be reasonably argued that the defendant could or should, as a reasonable person, have foreseen the damage which happened."

[72] (1973) 34 D.L.R. (3d) 554, at 562, 568; ante, p. 000.

[73] Of course, if gross negligence be established (as it was in this case) it will necessarily include the lesser degrees of neglect.

[74] (1969) 6 D.L.R. (3d) 309.

[75] Ibid., at 321.

[76] *Chapman* v. *Robinson and Ferguson* (1969) 71 W.W.R. 515, at 518; *Wilmot Hatheway Motors Ltd.* v. *Degrace* (1969) 1 N.B.R. (2d) 858; *Desjardins* v. *Theriault* (1970) 3 N.B.R. (2d) 260.

a want of extraordinary, but not of ordinary, care. Until such a case occurs, the question may theoretically be regarded as open.

There are no recent Australian or English authorities and the present stature of Lord Holt's criterion can only be inferred from general principles. In the case of depositum, the clear tendency in England is to gravitate away from the different standards of care, although not without some opposition.[77] In Australia, the tendency is less compelling and considerable support survives in favour of the traditional degrees of negligence.[78] Much will, of course, depend upon the respect which these gradations will command in future decisions upon bailment generally; much may also depend upon whether the lender's duty is eventually assimilated into the ordinary duty of reasonable care. It is probable that the borrower's duty will eventually become standardised, to conform with the responsibility owed by bailees under every class of bailment. Until this happens, it cannot really be said that there is any compelling authority more recent than *Coggs* v. *Bernard*.[79] There may continue to be cases in which the courts will wish to apply a stricter standard to the borrower than to the hirer, and there can be little doubt that the authority still exists to enable them to do so. As to what slight negligence encompasses, it would probably be fruitless to speculate until such cases arise.

Of course, the borrower may enlarge his liability by special contract and bind himself either to an increased standard of care or to an absolute responsibility for any accidents which befall the chattel. An illustration of this principle may be found in *A. R. Williams Machinery Co. Ltd.* v. *Muttart Builders Supply (Winnipeg) Ltd.*,[80] where the defendants agreed to be responsible for any "repairs and damages" occurring or rendered necessary to a fork-lift truck they borrowed from the plaintiffs. The vehicle was destroyed by fire without negligence on the defendants' part but they were held liable in contract for the loss:

> . . . in consideration of the plaintiff loaning the machine to the defendant . . . the machine was to be returned to the plaintiff after it had served its purpose, in the same condition as received less ordinary wear and tear.[81]

The borrower is not liable at Common Law for ordinary wear and tear, but he may enter a binding agreement to the contrary.[82] Thus if he promises to return the chattel "in equivalent condition" it seems that he undertakes responsibility for all deteriorations, even those which result from his normal and authorised user of the chattel.[83]

---

[77] See p. 294 et seq., ante.
[78] See p. 302 et seq., ante.
[79] (1703) 2 Ld. Raym. 909; 92 E.R. 107. cf. *Bryce* v. *Hornby* (1938) 82 Sol. Jo. 216 where the loan was part of a mutual arrangement and the defendant failed because she could not establish reasonable care.
[80] (1961) 30 D.L.R. (2d) 339; aff'd, (1961) 31 D.L.R. (2d) 187.
[81] Ibid., at 348; *Edwards on Bailments* (3rd ed), s. 380; Story (9th ed), s. 252; *Grant* v. *Armour* (1894) 25 O.R. 7; *Harvey* v. *Murray* (1884) 136 Mass. 377.
[82] Story, s. 268; *Blakemore* v. *Bristol and Exeter Ry. Co.* (1858) 8 E. & B. 1035; 120 E.R. 385.
[83] *Vendair (London) Ltd.* v. *Giro Aviation Co. Ltd.* [1961] 1 Lloyd's Rep. 283 (a case of hire). See further p. 750, post.

The borrower must, however, pay all expenses arising out of the day-to-day maintenance of the chattel. Thus, he must feed a horse[84] and, presumably, bear the cost of such minor events as punctures to a borrowed car, or the necessary servicing of a borrowed machine, during the currency of the bailment. He is not, however, liable for what Story[85] called "extraordinary" expenses, as where a horse falls sick and requires extensive medical attention or an expensive part of a vehicle needs replacement without the fault of the borrower. The dividing line seems to depend upon whether the maintenance effects a permanent and substantial improvement to the chattel or is merely part of the everyday range of activity necessary to keep it in working order.

If the borrower does incur expense in effecting an improvement or repair for which he is not liable, there is some doubt as to whether this is recoverable from the lender. Generally there will be no recovery where the work is done without the request or permission of the lender, because it would be inequitable to impose liability for improvements undertaken behind his back, and for which he may well have made other arrangements. There may be an implied assumpsit, or a remedy in quasi-contract, where the lender cannot be contacted and the repair is essential for the preservation of the chattel, as has been suggested in a recent Canadian decision dealing with involuntary bailment.[86] But Paton[87] takes the contrary view, and cites the position of the finder[88] as an analogy. In any event, it is clear that there is no Common Law duty on the lender to service or maintain the chattel during the period of the loan.[89]

Liability for acts of servants: The borrower will be liable not only for any direct or personal failure to comply with the requisite standard of care, but for any loss or damage caused by the tortious acts of his servants, while acting in the course of their employment or while discharging any of the duties owed by the borrower and delegated to them. This result is impliedly endorsed by some of the Canadian authorities[90] and is consistent with the suggested rule in cases of depositum,[91] although it must be conceded that modern authority is slight.

B. Unauthorised use

The borrower must not use the chattel for any purpose which is expressly or impliedly forbidden by the terms of the bailment. Whether a particular use is prohibited will depend upon the circumstances and the apparent intention of the parties. In *Bringloe* v. *Morice*[92] a distinction was drawn between hirers and borrowers for the purposes of deciding whether the

---

[84] *Handford* v. *Palmer* (1820) 2 B. & B. 359; 129 E.R. 1005.
[85] Section 256.
[86] *R.* v. *Howson* (1966) 55 D.L.R. (2d) 582, at 593 (Laskin, J.A.).
[87] See p. 154.
[88] Post, p. 877.
[89] *Pomfret* v. *Ricroft* (1671) 1 Saund. 321; 85 E.R. 454; Paton, loc. cit.
[90] E.g., *Wilmot Hatheway Motors Ltd.* v. *Degrace* (1969) 1 N.B.R. (2d) 858. Cf. *South Island Motors, Ltd.* v. *Thacker* [1931] N.Z.L.R. 1104 (post, p. 485) which it is submitted, is unreliable on this question.
[91] Ante, p. 306.
[92] (1676) 1 Mod. Rep. 210; 86 E.R. 834.

bailee is entitled to allow a stranger to the bailment to use the chattel. In the court's opinion, a hirer may lend the chattel to a competent third person but a borrower may not.[93] But as Wyatt Paine points out,[94] this observation is too general. In many cases, the loan will be valueless unless the borrower is enabled to delegate the operation or superintendence of the chattel to a servant or other third party.[95] The nature of the chattel and the purpose for which it was lent must be taken into account in determining whether its use was intended to be personal to the borrower or delegated with reasonable care. Even the past and present relationships of the parties may be relevant, as in *Chapman* v. *Robinson and Ferguson*[96] where it was held that a 19-year-old girl who was permitted to drive her mother's car while the mother was on holiday did not thereby inherit the right to lend the car to any other person. Although such a restriction had not been expressly imposed when the keys were handed over, the girl had never been allowed to lend the car to her friends before and no consent would have been given (if asked for) on the present occasion. This case may be contrasted with *Queens Sales & Service Ltd.* v. *Smith*[97] where the defendant was allowed to use a vehicle belonging to the plaintiff dealers in the interval between his old car being traded in and the new one arriving. It was held that his permitting a friend to drive the car did not amount to an unauthorised user for two reasons: the dealers' agent knew that the defendant had a friend whom he often allowed to drive his own car and, more important, such permission was clearly within the contemplated purposes for which the vehicle was lent. This case was not, in fact, one of commodatum since the majority found that the arrangement was for the mutual advantage of the parties,[98] but it seems that similar principles will apply where the bailment is solely for the benefit of the bailee. In each case, the question is the importance attached by the bailor to the personality of the bailee and the extent to which he must be taken to have contemplated the use of the chattel by a stranger to the bailment.

If the borrower sub-bails the chattel without authority or uses it in any other unauthorised manner (including, where appropriate, allowing a third person to operate the chattel in circumstances which do not create a subsidiary bailment) he becomes an insurer and is liable for any loss or damage occurring during the period of misuse. An early expression of this principle was given by Lord Holt in *Coggs* v. *Bernard*:[99]

> . . . as if a man should lend another a horse, to go westward, or for a month; if the bailee go northward, or keep the horse above a month,

---

[93] Unless the loan was for fixed term: ibid. Cf. *Dennison* v. *Gavaza* (1885) 18 N.S.R. 490.

[94] At p. 83.

[95] Cf. *Camoys* v. *Scurr* (1840) 9 C. & P. 383. (Prospective purchaser of a horse entitled to allow competent third party to ride it for the purposes of getting his opinion.)

[96] (1969) 71 W.W.R. 515, at 519. (Alberta District Court).

[97] (1963) 48 M.P.R. 364 (Nova Scotia Supreme Court).

[98] See especially Ilsley C.J. and Coffin J. at 368, 372-373, who went so far as to characterise the agreement as a hiring.

[99] (1703) 2 Ld. Raym. 909, at 913; 92 E.R. 107, at 111. See also *Bringloe* v. *Morice* (1676) 1 Mod. Rep. 210; 83 E.R. 834; *Isaack* v. *Clarke* (1615) 2 Bulst. 306, at 309; 80 E.R. 1143, at 1145.

if any accident happen to the horse in the northern journey, or after
the expiration of one month, the bailee will be chargeable; because he
has made use of the horse contrary to the trust he was lent to him
under, and it may be if the horse had been used no otherwise than
he was lent, that accident would not have befallen him.

The context of this illustration suggests that Lord Holt regarded unauthorised user as a species of that slight neglect for which, in his opinion,
the borrower was liable. Neglect, in these terms, would signify not so
much carelessness as disobedience to, or disregard of, the terms of the
bailment.[1] But later decisions appear to approach the question by way
of an analogy with the doctrine of deviation in contract. Thus, in
Chapman v. *Robinson and Ferguson*[2] Belzil D.C.J. refers to bailment as
being part of the law of contract[3] and observes that when the sub-
borrower:

> . . . breached the terms of the bailment by permitting the defendant
> Robinson to drive, he then became an insurer and liable to (the
> original borrower) for the damage caused to it by the negligence of
> the defendant Robinson, irrespective of his own negligence.[4]

Certainly an unauthorised dealing entitles the lender to visit the borrower
for all loss or damage occurring to the chattel during the period of misuse,
regardless of whether there is actual negligence on the bailee's part in
creating or permitting the continuance of the misuse. In this respect
there is a close similarity between commodatum and the ordinary bailment for reward.[5] It is questionable whether commodatum really denotes
a contract as opposed to some analogous relation, but even assuming
this analysis to be wrong there are clear reasons for applying by way of
analogy the contractual principle that a party who deviates from the
terms of his performance becomes from that moment an insurer. This

---

[1] Cf. Bacon's Abridgement, *Bailments,* C., where it is remarked that the bailor's
remedy is an action on the case; *Bringloe* v. *Morice,* ante, where the elected remedy
was trespass.
[2] (1969) 71 W.W.R. 515; cf. *Pratt* v. *Waddington* (1911) 20 O.L.R. 178.
[3] Ibid., at 523. See also *Queens Sales & Service Ltd.* v. *Smith* (1963) 48 M.P.R. 364.
[4] Ibid., at 522.
[5] See, for instance, *Edwards* v. *Newland & Co.* [1950] 2 K.B. 534. Note, however,
that the principle of termination of a bailment by a repugnant act has occasionally been invoked to allow bailors to recover in trespass for an infant's
misuse of their chattel, where there was no enforceable contract between the
parties: *Burnard* v. *Haggis* (1863) 14 C.B.N.S. 45; 31 L.J.C.P. 189; *Walley*
v. *Holt* (1876) 35 L.T. 631; cf. *Jennings* v. *Rundall* (1799) 8 T.R. 335; 4 R.R.
680. But in *Fawcett* v. *Smethurst* (1914) 31 T.L.R. 68, where there was a clear
and literal deviation by the infant hirer from the terms of the bailment, recovery was denied because the only offence committed by the bailee arose ex
contractu and the contract was unenforceable: he had not by his conduct
become an "independent tortfeasor". It may be suggested that this is one field
in which the coincidence of bailment and contract should not be taken to too
literal a conclusion and that a remedy might legitimately have been given on
the principles of bailment even though the agreement, when regarded as a
contract, was unenforceable. All the cases in point deal with infants' contracts
of hire. If an infant *borrows* a chattel and exceeds the terms of the bailment
there is no reason why he should not become an insurer, because the wrong
does not, strictly speaking, arise ex contractu: cf. *Ballett* v. *Mingay* [1943]
K.B. 281. If this be the position in cases of borrowing, it seems odd that the
same rule should not apply to bailments for reward. On modern principles, it
may be that no action for trespass will lie in these circumstances because there
is no offence to the bailor's possession; see p. 121 et seq., ante.

reasoning should apply not only in a bi-partite situation, but where the original borrower sub-bails on identical terms to those under which he initially received the chattel. The third party would then become a gratuitous sub-bailee and should owe to the owner the same duties as if he took directly from him rather than through an intermediary.

It is at this point, however, that the contractual analysis of commodatum creates difficulty. If there be no privity of contract between the original lender and the ultimate borrower, how can the former invoke any restrictions placed upon the ultimate borrower by the terms of the sub-bailment in order to make him an insurer? In *Chapman* v. *Robinson and Ferguson* this difficulty was surmounted by invoking the principles of agency. The plaintiff lent her car to her daughter, with a prohibition on re-lending. The daughter lent it to Ferguson, instructing him not to allow Robinson to drive. This instruction was disobeyed, and while Robinson was driving the vehicle it was damaged beyond repair. The plaintiff's action against Ferguson, based on the assertion that his misuse of the chattel made him an insurer, succeeded on the following grounds. Although the plaintiff's daughter had no authority to sub-bail the car, her breach of this prohibition did not terminate the bailment between her and her mother but merely gave the latter a right to revoke it. The sub-bailment was not, however, revoked but ratified by the plaintiff's pleadings, with the result that it became retroactively authorised and served to create a direct bailment between the plaintiff and Ferguson, through the agency of the daughter. Accordingly, any breach of the terms of that bailment made Ferguson absolutely liable to the plaintiff for the ensuing loss.

Belzil D.C.J. remarked[6] that one of the alternatives open to the plaintiff would have been the assertion of a common law (as opposed, presumably, to a contractual) relationship of bailment with Ferguson by virtue of the decision in *Morris* v. *C. W. Martin & Sons Ltd.*[7] The apparent difficulty with this approach is that, in the only decision to consider the question, the duties of the extended bailee under this principle have been held to be confined to the avoidance of negligent damage and abstention from conversion.[8] This may have obliged Ferguson to disprove negligence in his handing-over of the car, but would not operate to make him an insurer.[9]

Such an approach seems unfortunately restrictive, for it relies upon too rigid a separation of the bailee's remedies into the contractual and the tortious. In many areas the principles of bailment transcend these limitations and permit a remedy which cannot accurately be characterised according to the conventional forms of action. Indeed, one example is the liability of a deviating borrower which, (if commodatum is not contractual) seems to be incapable of subsumption under the principles of either contract or tort. If a principal bailor can be prevented, by the authorised terms of a sub-bailment, from proceeding in tort against the

---

[6] (1969) 71 W.W.R. 515, at 519.
[7] [1966] 1 Q.B. 716; post p. 793 et seq.
[8] *B.W.I.A. Ltd.* v. *Bart* (1966) 11 W.I.R. 378.
[9] Quaere, whether he was not guilty of conversion.

ultimate bailee,[10] it might legitimately follow that any affirmative obligations undertaken by the sub-bailee, which were, to his knowledge, imposed by the sub-bailor on the authority or at the insistence of the principal bailor, are likewise enforceable against him. This principle will, admittedly, be of little value in the context of unauthorised sub-bailments. The principal bailor will generally prefer to rely on the intermediate bailee's role as an insurer or the ultimate bailee's liability in conversion.[11] Moreover, it would be unfair to permit the principal bailor to take advantage of restrictions he has not originally authorised. Where the entire sub-bailment falls into that category, there are clearly problems in asserting that any limitations on the sub-borrower's use were imposed by the authority of original lender. It may be possible for the principal bailor to adopt or ratify the restriction, although this could be unfair if it were to result in the sub-bailee's suddenly becoming an insurer *vis-a-vis* two bailors instead of the original one. In any event, it seems that where the sub-bailee knows of a greater restriction on the first bailee's power to deal with the chattel than the first bailee imposes upon him, the sub-bailee cannot reasonably complain if, by breaking the latter, he is treated as having knowingly breached the former, and is made liable to the original bailor for all ensuing loss.

Whether this principle is acceptable in the context of unauthorised sub-bailments or not, it should be available to the bailor who authorises the subsidiary transaction and who insists that the restriction be imposed. If A bails to B and authorises a sub-bailment to C on terms which restrict A's right to recover for damage to the chattel, it seems in England at least that, regardless of contract, A is bound by these terms in any later action against C.[12] If this is so, it should follow that A can enforce against C any duty which A has authorised B to impose and was known by C to have been authorised by A when C became a sub-bailee of the chattel.[13] Such a restriction becomes one of the essential conditions upon which C occupies the position of sub-bailee and enforceable against him irrespective of any contractual relation.[14]

Even where the borrower is entitled to allow another person to use or acquire possession of the chattel, he must of course select the person with the same amount of care as he must use in dealing with the chattel personally.[15] This part of the general duty of care imposed by the relationship of commodatum, which applies to delegations of the borrower's responsibility as well as to any attempt on his part to discharge that responsibility in person.

---

[10] Post, p. 1000.
[11] (1969) 71 W.W.R. 515, at 519. In *Chapman's* case the plaintiff did not want to sue her own daughter.
[12] See p. 1000 et seq., post.
[13] This question is discussed at greater length in Chapters 1 ante and 20 post.
[14] Some support for this view may perhaps be found in the judgment of Latham C.J. in *Penfolds Wines Pty. Ltd.* v. *Elliott* (1946) 74 C.L.R. 204, at 217-218, where the question centred upon a sub-bailee's liability for conversion and the class of acts that would cause the principal bailor's immediate right of possession to revive.
[15] See *Queens Sales & Service Ltd.* v. *Smith* (1963) 48 M.P.R. 364, at 368-369 per Ilsley C.J. which dealt, however, with a bailment for mutual advantage.

C. Redelivery to the lender

The borrower must return the chattel to the lender at the appointed time and place. Failure to redeliver will place the borrower *in mora* and will mean that he becomes an insurer in respect of any loss or damage occurring to the chattel after the appointed time, whether this be the result of the borrower's neglect or not; such failure will not, however, determine the bailment by itself. Story[16] considered that any accessions to, or produce from, the borrowed chattel must also be returned to the lender. A recent English decision dealing with the hire-purchase of animals states that, as a general rule, property in the progeny of leased animals passes to the party in possession.[17] The circumstances of the lending will almost invariably be sufficient to displace this rule in cases of commodatum.

The borrower who has expressly promised to redeliver the chattel to a particular place will be bound by his promise, for there is clearly consideration in the lender's original delivery. Where no venue is specifically agreed, the borrower must do what is reasonable. Generally, this will mean returning the chattel to the lender's abode or place of business; there is certainly no duty, under normal circumstances, upon the lender to come and collect it. If the lender has moved a great distance away from his former residence, or is untraceable, Story[18] considers that there is no obligation on the borrower to take the chattel to him there. In such a case he may redeliver to an authorised agent of the lender[19] or may be given specific guide-lines under one of the State *Disposal of Uncollected Goods Acts*.[20] Failing this, he seems entitled, as a bailee whose bailment has become involuntary by lapse of time, to take whatever steps are reasonable to return or dispose of the chattel; conversely, he is bound to continue to treat the chattel with reasonable care.[21] This standard may, of course, relax or become extenuated as time passes and the goods become progressively more of an inconvenience. The borrower is probably entitled, provided there is no express agreement to the contrary, to continue using the chattel for as long as he is unable to redeliver it, although in this case he will continue to be bound by the borrower's high standards of care.

D. Return in a proper condition

There is little encompassed by this duty that has not been covered under the previous headings. When the borrower's lack of the necessary care results in the chattel's being damaged, he will of course be liable for that loss. In cases which do not strictly involve damage, the question as to what is a proper condition will depend upon the circumstances of the case and any agreement between the parties. This, it will generally be

---

[16] Section 260.
[17] *Tucker* v. *Farm and General Investments Trust Ltd.* [1966] 2 Q.B. 421 (C.A.).
[18] Section 261; the same writer also points out that on occasions it will be more consistent with the borrower's duty of care for him not to return the chatttel at the appointed time or place: ibid., s. 263.
[19] Story, s. 262; a promise by the borrower to redeliver to a third party is clearly binding on him and should be enforceable by the third party.
[20] See the W.A., Tas. and N.S.W. Acts, at pp. 400, 407, 424, post.
[21] See p. 394 et seq., post.

incumbent on the bailee to re-assemble the chattel, even where the bailment includes a permission to dismantle it, and to restore it in as readily useable a condition as that in which he received it, so far as is consistent with the terms of the bailment and the measure of diligence that he must exercise in its safe-keeping. A man who borrows a power-drill is not entitled to return it in pieces, even though the dismantling has caused no damage and has not resulted from any negligence or wilful misuse on his part.

Burden of Proof: Although the recent decision in *Walker* v. *Watson*,[22] by characterising the lender's remedy for damage as a simple action in negligence, suggests that the burden of proof is upon him, it is clear both from the several Canadian decisions[23] and from the general principles of bailment that the borrower must show that the loss or damage occurred without default on his part. He need not demonstrate the precise cause of the loss, but he must show affirmatively that he exercised the appropriate standard of care.

---

[22] [1974] 2 N.Z.L.R. 175. See also *Thomas* v. *High* (1960) 60 S.R. (N.S.W.) 401, at 404, 407; and cf. now *Port Swettenham* v. *Wu* (1978) *The Times,* June 22nd.
[23] Ante, pp. 311-313; a good example is *Wilmot Hatheway Motors Ltd.* v. *Degrace* (1969) 1 N.B.R. (2d) 858.

CHAPTER 12

INVOLUNTARY BAILMENT

I. DEFINITION

An involuntary bailee may be defined as a person whose possession of a chattel, although known to him and the result of circumstances of which be is aware,[1] occurs through events over which he has no proper control and to which he has given no effective prior consent. The circumstances in question may be set in motion by the owner or other person enjoying prior possession—as where unsolicited goods are sent by post to a potential customer—or by factors beyond the control of either party, as where A's timber is carried downstream to B's land and deposited there against B's will.[2] In recent years, the abuses of inertia selling, by which unsolicited goods are sent to persons with an invitation to buy or to return them, have necessitated legislative interference both in England and in Australia. This legislation, which will be discussed later in the present chapter,[3] provides for the passing of title to the recipient on the expiry of a specified period of time. Whereas in England no statutory attempt has yet been made to define the measure of responsibility owed by the recipient before the goods become his own, in Australia such a definition is made under s. 65(1) of the *Trade Practices Act* 1974 and under various State enactments of similar application. Section 65(1) applies only to the supply of unsolicited goods "by a corporation, in trade or commerce"; thus, goods supplied by partnerships, sole traders or private persons are left uncovered by the Act. The equivalent State legislation is not confined to goods sent by corporations, but again requires that the goods be sent in the course of a business. Accordingly, there remains a wide circle of relationships, both in England and Australia, in which one must resort to the slender authority of the Common Law.

It may be argued that the expression "involuntary bailment" is a contradiction in terms. Bailment is generally taken to connote a conscious and willing assumption of the possession of goods, so that without this voluntary element—whether its absence be the result of duress, or concealment, or simple force of circumstance—there can be no true relationship of bailor and bailee. Certainly the approach of the English Courts has been to deny that the involuntary recipient of goods is a bailee.[4] The question is perhaps not very important, but it should be noted that there are arguments to the contrary. Thus William King Laidlaw, writing in the *Cornell Law Quarterly*,[5] considered that involuntary bailments could claim to be classi-

---

[1] Cf. the bailee by concealment, discussed in Chapter 6.
[2] As in *Nicholson* v. *Chapman* (1793) 2 H.Bl. 254; 3 R.R. 374.
[3] See p. 428 et seq., post.
[4] E.g. *Lethbridge* v. *Phillips* (1819) 2 Stark. 478.
[5] (1931) 16 Corn.L.Q. 286, at 306.

fied as bailments proper because of the recipient's duty to redeliver the chattel to the owner:

> The existence of that obligation ought to be enough to shew the existence of some relation. But it does not follow that all the rules governing ordinary bailments should be applied in such cases.[6]

Certainly this analysis is in line with the spacious definition of bailment afforded by some American cases.[7] Historically it enjoys the advantage of equating bailment with detinue, for which there is a plausible if not entirely authentic pedigree.[8] But it seems doubtful whether the mere existence of a duty to redeliver can be taken to connote a bailment. The tort of conversion, for instance, can issue against defendants who were never in possession of the disputed chattel and are not bailees;[9] in theory, it should also be possible to be guilty of detinue without the same element of possession.[10] If liability under these remedies is not conditional upon possession, it is hard to understand why their availability against a defendant who happens to be in possession should automatically make him a bailee. The only reasons why he must redeliver are that he is in control of them and the goods belong to someone else. Possession is unnecessary; the defendant could be a servant, or could be detaining the goods through an independent contractor, and the result would be the same.

But the special nature of the owner's remedies under an involuntary bailment may themselves provide an indication that these relationships are more akin to bailment proper than to the ordinary rules of tort. On conventional theory, an involuntary bailee is not liable for negligence unless it is in the course of misdelivering the goods:[11] careless damage and circumspect, innocent conversions are among the things for which he is exonerated. Admittedly, these principles are in sharp contradiction to those which govern ordinary bailees, as much as they are to the rules which govern defendants who are not in possession. However, it may be no coincidence that the concessions allowed to an involuntary bailee come into effect only when he acquires possession of the goods; and that it is this salient feature which produces not only the peculiar principles of involuntary bailment but also the peculiar principles of bailment generally. Both sets of rules are

---

[6] The learned author's remarks were not confined to true involuntary bailments but were considered to apply "even though the custodian was ignorant that the chattel of another was in his control". In such a case there would be a bailment by concealment of the kind discussed in Chapter 6. It is submitted that however widely bailments are defined, they cannot be taken to include the unwitting possession of goods which belong to another. The only circumstances in which a duty could possibly be owed would be those in which the owner had demanded the return of the goods, in which case the "bailee" would no longer be unwitting. Cf. *Baud Corporation N.V.* v. *Brook* (1974) 40 D.L.R. (3d) 418; (1975) 53 *Can. Bar Rev.* 121.

[7] E.g., *Foulke* v. *New York Consolidated R.R.* (1920) 228 N.Y. 269; 127 N.E. 237: "It is the element of lawful possession, however created, and duty to account for the property of another that creates the bailment, regardless of whether such possession is based upon contract in the ordinary sense or not".

[8] See Fifoot, *History and Sources of the Common Law*, p. 26; Tay (1966) 5 *Sydney Law Review* 239.

[9] See p. 127, ante.

[10] Cf. *Alicia Hosiery Ltd.* v. *Brown Shipley & Co.* [1969] 2 Lloyd's Rep. 187; see also p. 151, ante.

[11] See pp. 384, 387, post.

sui generis and both depend upon possession. Both may therefore indicate the unifying effect of that denominator and the fundamental kinship between ordinary bailments and all other cases in which one man knowingly comes into possession of the chattels of another.

The problem, as Laidlaw pointed out,[12] lies in discerning the extent to which the resemblance can be pushed. Should an involuntary bailee, for instance, be estopped from denying his bailor's title?[13] The temptation is to say no, because the bailee has not bargained for possession and has not induced the bailor to relinquish it. This result would be consonant with policy and justice. There is no conclusive authority for it, but there are very few authorities on involuntary bailment generally. This is, perhaps, one area above all in which it is easier and safer to examine the duties of the parties individually rather than to attempt to deduce them from a general pattern to which they only doubtfully belong.

II. THE DUTIES OF THE BAILEE

The decisions here fall into two main groups.

A. Liability other than for conversion

The involuntary bailee whose conduct does not amount to conversion will only rarely be liable for any loss or damage occurring to the goods. This, at least, is the traditional view, which is embodied in two rather inadequate decisions.

In *Lethbridge* v. *Phillips*[14] one Bernard obtained possession of a miniature belonging to the plaintiff. Without the plaintiff's permission, he sent it to the defendant. While it was in the defendant's possession, it was damaged through being placed near a stove. No request to see the miniature had been made and it seems that the first the defendant knew of its existence was when his son (to whom Bernard had entrusted its delivery) brought it home. The plaintiff's action in assumpsit failed; the defendant could not "without his knowledge and consent, be considered as a bailee of the property".[15] No opinion was offered by the Court as to the sort of conduct for which even an involuntary bailee would be answerable.

A less obvious decision was that of *Howard* v. *Harris*,[16] to which, Beven has remarked, "it is difficult to assign any just principle".[17] A playwright wrote to the manager of Drury Lane Theatre,[18] stating that he had written a play and inviting the manager to help him produce it. The manager asked to see the scene, plot and sketch of the play, which the plaintiff sent to him together with the manuscript itself. The manuscript was lost and the plaintiff sued in trover. Williams J. held that there was no case to go to the jury:

[12] Loc. cit. p. 306.
[13] Something an ordinary bailee can do only in very limited circumstances: see p. 163 et seq., ante and Appendix I, post.
[14] (1819) 2 Stark. 478; 171 E.R. 731.
[15] Ibid.; for a similar American case, see *Houghton* v. *Lynch* (1868) 13 Minn. 85.
[16] (1884) Cababé & Ellis 253.
[17] *Negligence* (2nd ed.), p. 907.
[18] Sir Augustus Harris (1852-1896), knighted 1891, known as Druriolanus in the profession. See *Oxford Companion to the Theatre* (3rd ed.), p. 430.

. . . for the plaintiff had chosen voluntarily to send to the defendant what the defendant had never asked for, and no duty of any sort or kind was cast upon the defendant with regard to what was so sent.[19]

Both of the foregoing decisions have been criticised. Laidlaw[20] contends that *Lethbridge* v. *Phillips*[21] is inadequately reported and fails to shew whether the defendant knew that he had another person's chattel in his possession; if he did not, he was clearly under no duty to use care toward the chattel. Laidlaw concludes that perhaps all that case really decided was that the plaintiff had not made out his alleged case of special assumpsit.

The same author points out that in *Howard* v. *Harris*[22] it was not even certain that the defendant had received the manuscript; and that even if he had, the case decides nothing more than that proof of delivery to an involuntary bailee and his failure to return on demand do not make out a prima facie case for the plaintiff.[23] Beven's criticism of the case is more fundamental and proceeds on the assumption that it involved an ordinary gratuitous deposit. The defendant was therefore under a duty to show slight diligence towards the manuscript and had only himself to blame for being subject to this duty:

> He might have avoided liability by a refusal to accept, by absolutely ignoring the thing sent, or by immediately returning it. In the event of his acquiescing in the receipt, he could not be regarded as in any better position than a finder of the play . . . [24]

Certainly, there are strong reasons for saying that the defendant in *Howard* v. *Harris*[25] had either impliedly invited the sending of the manuscript or had subsequently acquiesced in its acceptance; if it was in his possession it was there for a considerable time and he could easily and safely have rid himself of it if he had chosen to. Moreover, it has since been held that in an action for conversion by misdelivery the involuntary bailee is liable for a want of reasonable care.[26] Since the plaintiff in *Howard* v. *Harris*[27] was suing in trover, it may have been appropriate to apply the same principle to a case of alleged conversion by destruction.

However, the principle that an involuntary bailee is not obliged to treat the unwanted chattel with any amount of care is endorsed by a later decision which was better argued and better reported. In *Neuwith* v. *Over Darwen Co-Operative Society*[28] the lapse of time between delivery and discovery was substantially greater. An orchestra hired the defendants' hall for an evening performance. No arrangements were made about rehearsal, but on the preceding afternoon the orchestra, without objection from the

---

[19] (1884) Cababé & Ellis 253, at 254. cf., *Summers* v. *Challenor* (1926) 70 Sol.J. 745, 760; *Batson* v. *Donovan* (1820) 4 B. & Ald. 21.

[20] (1931) 16 *Cornell Law Quarterly* 286, at 304.

[21] Supra.

[22] Supra. See also (1921-1922) 35 *Harvard Law Review* 873.

[23] See also Beven, at 908, citing *Tobin* v. *Murison* (1845) 5 Moo. P.C. 110; *Tomkins* v. *Saltmarsh* 14 Ser. & Rawle (P.) 275, Cf. p. 390, post.

[24] *Negligence*, p. 908. These criticisms were adopted by Perdue J.A. in his dissenting judgment in *Consentino* v. *Dominion Express* (1906) 4 W.L.R. 498, at 504-505 (Manitoba Court of Appeal).

[25] (1884) Cababé & Ellis 253.

[26] See p. 387 et seq., post.

[27] Ante, n. 19.

[28] (1894) 63 L.J. N.S. 290.

defendants, used the hall for that purpose. When the rehearsal was over the plaintiff left his double-bass violin in an ante-room, where it was later damaged by an attendant who had moved it in order to light the gas-lamp. The plaintiff's action failed because there was no bailment, either in the form of an entrustment of the instrument to the defendants or of an undertaking on their part to be responsible for its safety. Nor was the conduct of the attendant so related to his ordinary duties as to render them liable vicariously for his negligence; a fact which was immaterial in any event, as no duty arose on his part to abstain from negligence in the first place. The judges appear to have largely endorsed the identification of bailment with contract and again offered no opinion as to the sort of conduct for which the defendants would have been liable. *Howard* v. *Harris*[29] was not cited, but Collins J.[30] described the facts of the present case as "extremely analogous" to those in *Lethbridge* v. *Phillips*.[31]

From these decisions the conclusion has been drawn that an involuntary bailee is not liable for mere negligence but must abstain from wilful damage;[32] presumably, recklessness would be included in the latter category of wrong. This principle seems to have been accepted by the Manitoba Court of Appeal in *McCutcheon* v. *Lightfoot*[33] and is generally endorsed by the leading writers on torts.[34] But it is neither as firmly established nor as desirable as this endorsement would lead one to believe.

It must be remembered that the circumstances which place an ordinary bailee in possession can vary tremendously and that one of the most variable factors will be the degree of discredit or demerit attaching to the bailor. Some of these situations are listed by Laidlaw.[35] The owner may have deliberately delivered peas under an order for beans,[36] or he may have sent goods to the defendant's house simply in the hope that he might buy them. He may have left them on the defendant's land because he wanted free storage[37] or may even have forced the defendant to accept them at gun-point. On the other hand, he may have lost them outside the defendant's house and an officious passer-by may have put them through the defendant's letter-box; he may have negligently tied up his boat, which was then carried downstream and washed up on the defendant's land; or he may have employed an apparently competent messenger to deliver the chattel, who delivered it to the wrong person. It would be harsh if the same low standard of recovery should apply in each of these cases. For this reason, it might be equitable to regulate the bailee's duty of care accord-

[29] (1884) Cababé & Ellis 253.
[30] At 293.
[31] (1819) 2 Stark. 478; 171 E.R. 731.
[32] E.g. Winfield and Jolowicz, p. 425; Vaines, *Personal Property*, p. 83.
[33] [1929] 1 D.L.R. 971: affirmed without discussing the point in [1930] 1 D.L.R. 995. Note, however, that one of the judges in the Court of Appeal was Perdue C.J.M. Cf Perdue J.A., had criticised *Lethbridge* v. *Phillips* and *Howard* v. *Harris* in *Consentino* v. *Dominion Express* (1906) 4 W.L.R. 498, at 504-505. See further *Community Life Society* v. *Besel & Simpson & Co.* [1943] 1 W.W.R. 493.
[34] Clerk & Lindsell, pp. 643, 688; Winfield and Jolowicz, pp. 424-425; cf. Paton, p. 117.
[35] (1931) 16 *Corn. L.Q.* 286, at p. 296 et seq.
[36] Cf. *Grimoldby* v. *Wells* (1872) L.R. 10 C.P. 391; Paton, p. 115; p. 393 post.
[37] Cf. *Fong* v. *Tinkess* [1941] 4 D.L.R. 295.

ing to the conduct of the plaintiff. Unfortunately this notion would be of little value in a case where the defendant did not know the full story of how he came into possession. In such a case, he would have no way of judging in advance the degree of care required.

Accordingly, it is suggested that an acceptable compromise would be to exact from the involuntary bailee a variable standard of care according to what is reasonable in all the circumstances of the case. The relevant circumstances would include the nature and value of the goods, the facilities at the defendant's disposal, the readiness with which he could have returned them and (where known to the defendant) the conduct of the owner. In most situations the involuntary nature of the transaction would render this standard very low and possibly no different from that applied in cases like *Lethbridge* v. *Phillips*.[38] But in other cases the nature of the property and the defendant's facilities, coupled even with his previous experience in this regard, might justify a somewhat higher degree of circumspection. If, for instance, a book belonging to A and lent to B is mistakenly returned by B to his local library, it would not seem especially Draconian to expect the library to take reasonable care of the book; likewise where guests leave umbrellas in friends' houses, or where one tenant in a block of flats receives a letter intended for a neighbour.[39]

Of course, an exercise of the degree of care the involuntary bailee normally takes of his own property will generally be sufficient, if not more than enough;[40] for one thing, there is no reliance by the owner upon his being able to manifest anything higher. Again, the likelihood of his being able to notify the owner and to persuade him to retrieve the goods may strongly influence the necessary standard of care; thus, as time goes by, it might often be justifiable for the appropriate standard to diminish.

It must be conceded that there is little authority for such an approach. Involuntary bailees appear generally to enjoy an immunity more fitted to penalising unscrupulous merchandisers than to providing an universally just solution to the problem. But the standard of reasonable care is not without its slender authority. One such case was *Nelson* v. *Mackintosh*,[41] where the captain of a ship was held to owe a duty of reasonable care towards a seaman's chest placed on board by a new recruit, who unbeknown to the captain, had failed to join the ship at the start of the voyage. Involuntary bailment does not appear to have been pleaded.[42]

In *Consentino* v. *Dominion Express Co.*,[43] Perdue J.A. delivered a dissenting judgment in which he, unlike the other members of the Manitoba Court of Appeal, treated the facts before him as disclosing an involuntary

---

[38] (1819) 2 Stark. 478; 171 E.R. 731.
[39] In *Thompson* v. *Starking* [1955] C.L.Y. 149 it was held that a tenant who signed for a fellow-tenant's registered packet in his absence, and left it (in accordance with previous practice) upon a table in the hall of the lodging house, was a gratuitous involuntary bailee and had taken the necessary reasonable care.
[40] But cf. *Consentino* v. *Dominion Express Co.* (1906) 4 W.L.R. 498, at 508.
[41] (1816) 1 Stark. 237.
[42] The actual basis of liability in this case was the enhanced standard of vigilance which the captain was held to owe after he had opened the box and interfered with its contents. Nevertheless, it is clearly stated that before that occasion the captain owed a duty of proper and ordinary care.
[43] (1906) 4 W.L.R. 498; the facts are given at p. 233, ante.

bailment.[44] In his view, the old English cases were unreliable and did not substantiate the view that the involuntary bailee owed no duty at all; a view which, on grounds of common sense, he found wholly unacceptable.[45] He preferred to impose upon the defendants the duties of a gratuitous bailee,[46] and to require them to prove that the loss had occurred without negligence on their part.[47] Admittedly, the learned judge seems to vacillate between ordinary and gross negligence as the criterion of liability, but his judgment provides a clear indication that some degree of circumspection is required, and that even the exercise of such care as the bailee takes of his own goods will not suffice when he is grossly negligent.[48] His reasoning is attractive in the abstract, but clouded by the fact that in the present case the defendants had no reason to know that they were in possession of the plaintiff's goods at all.[49]

Support for the standard of reasonable care can also be collected from two English decisions which are regarded as dealing with the separate issue of the bailee's liability for conversion.[50] In both of these there are generalised statements that the involuntary bailee must take reasonable care; the remarks do not appear to be limited to the immediate context of misdelivery with which they are concerned. On the other hand, in *R. v. Howson*,[51] Laskin J.A. expressed the view that an involuntary bailee is not under the same duty of care as a voluntary bailee, although he confined his expression of the distinction to observing that the former, unlike the latter, is entitled to put unwanted goods off his premises. This right, which may itself depend upon the nature of the goods,[52] is not necessarily inconsistent with a duty of reasonable care.

Of course, it may be objected that it is unfair to compel a custodian to manifest a degree of care to which he would not have bound himself by agreement, and which would have been no greater if he had voluntarily accepted the goods. The duty imposed upon an involuntary bailee should always be a clement one, in which the courts should be ready to find mitigating factors. Indeed, if the gratuitous depository is now liable for want of reasonable care, it may be appropriate to reserve for the involuntary bailee the lighter burden of disproving gross negligence, in the more literal sense of that term.[53]

[44] Ibid., at 503.
[45] Ibid., at 504: "there is surely some duty cast upon him on behalf of the owner."
[46] Ibid., at 506.
[47] Ibid., at 507; a similar approach was taken in *Long* v. *R.* (1922) 63 D.L.R. 134; cf. *Fong* v. *Tinkess* [1941] 4 D.L.R. 295.
[48] Ibid., at 508.
[49] Note, also, that he relied upon *Heugh* v. *L. & N.W. Ry. Co.* (1870) L.R. 5 Ex. 51, which is in a separate category because it involved a carrier who had voluntarily accepted goods and was subsequently unable to deliver them: see p. 393, post.
[50] *Batistoni* v. *Dance*, *The Times*, January 18th, 1908, where the sole ground of action was want of reasonable care; *Elvin and Powell, Ltd.* v. *Plummer Roddis, Ltd.* (1933) 50 T.L.R. 158.
[51] (1966) 55 D.L.R. (2d) 582, at 594.
[52] See p. 391, post.
[53] Cf. Laidlaw (1931) 16 *Cornell L.Q.*, who discusses at 305, the American case of *Hope* v. *Costello* (1927) 222 Mo. App. 187; 297 S.W. 103, and concludes that the defendants would have been liable had they committed "any grossly negligent positive act"; they were not, on the other hand, obliged to take any action to protect the goods. In many cases, a distinction between non-feasance

The circumstances of the delivery may, however, entitle a court to infer consent on the part of the bailee although he has offered no specific invitation or agreement. Certain kinds of enterprise customarily operate on the understanding that goods delivered to them for treatment will, if within the usual sphere of their operations, be dealt with in the ordinary way and handled with reasonable care. Thus, a script submitted to an actor for his perusal, or a manuscript to a publisher or literary agent, may (although not specifically solicited) be deemed to be the subject of a bailment, by virtue of the bailee's having held himself out as open to receiving these or similar articles in the ordinary cause of events.[54] Moreover, even goods which are initially unrequested may become bailed goods when the custodian subsequently acquiesces in their possession or fails to return them through some safe and expeditious method which would cost him minimal trouble and expense: a fortiori perhaps, where he uses the chattel for the purpose for which it was sent.

In one American case,[55] a railroad company were held to be bailees of property mistakenly left by a passenger in one of their compartments. In the opinion of the court, the property had come into:

> . . . the custody and the potential actual possession of the defendant. It was the right of the defendant and its duty to become as to it and its owner a gratuitous bailee. It was its right and duty to possess and use the care of a gratuitous bailee for the safekeeping of the package until the owner called for it.[56]

This decision seems to go rather far, since the defendants could scarcely have known of the presence of the article on their premises at the time when the bailment was supposedly created. Insofar as it suggests that a railway company, department store or other institution to which the public have access should be provided with adequate facilities for the detection and recovery of lost property, it may, however, represent a salutary innovation. Certainly, it is not unlikely that goods may be mislaid in such circumstances and the tenor of the authorities is to treat the finding of goods in a department store by its staff as carrying the same duty as a

---

and misfeasance will possibly provide the most equitable solution. A case in which the involuntary bailee was held liable for lack of reasonable care in performing a positive act (i.e. erasing marks from gauntlets) was *Long* v. *R*. (ante n. 47). Cf. *Grand Trunk Ry. Co.* v. *Frankel* (1903) 33 S.C.R. 115.

[54] In *Summers* v. *Challenor* (1926) 70 Sol. Jo. 745, 760 (Marylebone County Court) the plaintiff sent the defendant (an actor) the manuscript of two plays, after some correspondence had passed between them, in which the defendant, while not requesting to see them, had professed himself willing to peruse them if sent. The judge accepted the principles in *Howard* v. *Harris* (1884) Cababé & Ellis 253 and *Lethbridge* v. *Phillips* (1819) 2 Stark. 544, (see ante p. 381 et seq.) but distinguished them on the question of consent and awarded £3-9-9d damages, to represent the cost of re-typing. The note in Sol. Jo. at 746 suggests that there may occasionally be a general invitation to the public in accordance with the principle in *Carlill* v. *Carbolic Smoke-Ball Co. Ltd.* [1893] 1 Q.B. 256. Note also that the burden of proving a request rests on the owner: *Batistoni* v. *Dance, The Times,* 18 January 1908. It is submitted that where the bailee wilfully takes possession under a mistake of fact (e.g. by taking a suitcase which he thinks is his own) the bailment should not be involuntary unless the mistake was induced by the owner: cf. *McCowan* v. *McCulloch* [1926] 1 D.L.R. 312.

[55] *Foulke* v. *N.Y. Consolidated R.R.* (1920) 228 N.Y. 269; 127 N.E. 237.

[56] Ibid., at 239, 274; cf. *Ridgley Operating Co.* v. *White* (1933) 155 So. 693.

finding whereunder the goods are *for the first time* reduced into the defendant's possession, and to demand from the finder-institution the standard of reasonable care.[57] In any event, it is clear that where mislaid goods are handed in at a department store and accepted for custody, the store becomes a voluntary and not an involuntary bailee.[58]

B. Liability for conversion

The rules here represent a curious modification of the ordinarily strict liability which attaches to one who has committed an act of conversion. Stated briefly, the position appears to be that an involuntary bailee who performs in good faith an act which, taken in the abstract, would amount to a conversion, is liable only if the performance of that act was accompanied by a lack of reasonable care.[59]

Authority for this proposition is slender and rests upon two briefly reported decisions at first instance. In *Batistoni* v. *Dance*[60] the plaintiffs sent the defendant a quantity of clothing on approval, a large proportion of which had not been requested. A rogue purporting to act for the plaintiffs called to collect it from the defendant, claiming that a mistake had been made, and her maidservant handed it over. The Court held that she was not answerable for those articles that had been delivered to her without her consent, but liable for the remainder because, on balance, her maid had shown of lack of reasonable care.

Conversion was not pleaded and the case proceeded solely upon the question whether there was a duty to take reasonable care. It is interesting to note that what amounted to reasonable care in relation to one set of goods was not sufficient in relation to the other, even though both lots were treated in exactly the same way.

---

[57] See e.g. *Newman* v. *Bourne & Hollingsworth Ltd.* (1915) 31 T.L.R. 209; cf. *Helson* v. *McKenzies (Cuba St.) Ltd.* [1950] N.Z.L.R. 818; *Warner* v. *Elizabeth Arden Ltd.* (1939) 83 Sol. Jo. 258. Cf. also the associated but distinguishable problems arising from the duty (if any) owed by an occupier towards goods brought on to his land by a trespasser. In this case there is the additional problem of deciding whether any duty should be owed in the first place by virtue of the occupier's expectation that such goods will be there: this difficulty does not arise in involuntary bailment, where we have assumed, for purposes of definition, that the bailee will know of the presence of the goods. The authors of the recent Law Commission Working Paper on liability to trespassers appear to consider that whatever duties should be owed to goods belonging to a trespasser should apply equally to goods belonging to third parties, which the trespasser has brought on to the land; see W.P. No. 52, paras. 41-44.

[58] *Helson* v. *McKenzies* (ante, n. 57), at 906, 914. The decision is, however, misleading as regards the parties to the bailment, since it relies upon bailment as a consensual, if not a contractual relation: see p. 29, ante.

[59] Of course, the defendant is liable if he deliberately and maliciously converts the chattel, and this would include unequivocally refusing any reasonable demand by the owner to recover it; cf. *Chicago I. & L. Ry. Co.* v. *Pope* (1934) 188 N.E. 594, amusingly criticised in (1933-1934) 9 *Notre Dame Law Review* 333.
In *Foster* v. *Juniata Bridge Co.* (1851) 16 P. St. 393, the defendant was held liable in conversion for using parts of a bridge span (which had been swept up on his land without any fault in the owners) to strengthen some of his buildings, even though the owners had already refused to remove the materials. It was remarked obiter that after giving notice the defendant could legitimately have put the span back into the water.

[60] (1908) *The Times,* 18 January.

In *Elvin and Powell Ltd.* v. *Plummer Roddis Ltd.*,[61] however, the plaintiffs appear to have pleaded both conversion and a failure to take reasonable care. A man had called at their premises, pretending to represent the defendants, and had ordered a number of coats to be sent to the defendants' shop in Brighton. He then telegraphed the defendants stating that the goods had been despatched in error and that a man would be sent to collect them, signing the telegram with the name of the plaintiffs. He or an associate later appeared at the defendants' premises, produced one of the plaintiffs' trade cards and took the goods away. They were never seen again. Hawke J.'s judgment is framed in somewhat general terms and suggests that the duty to take reasonable care (which in the present case had been satisfied) applies not only to acts of conversion but to other conduct, such as carelessness causing loss by theft, on the part of an involuntary bailee:

> If persons were involuntary bailees and had done everything reasonable they were not liable to pay damages if something they did resulted in the loss of the property . . . There was an obligation on the part of an involuntary bailee to do what was right and reasonable . . . .

The defence of reasonable care has been acknowledged in two subsequent cases of wrongful delivery. In *James* v. *Oxley*,[62] Latham C.J. refused to apply it to a case of converted cheques on the ground that the defendants had been manifestly negligent, but did not question its validity: and in *Helson* v. *Mackenzies* (*Cuba St.*) *Ltd.*[63] Hutchinson J. modified it at the extent of saying that the defendants, being gratuitous as well as involuntary bailees, could be liable only for gross negligence in handing over the plaintiff's handbag to someone claiming to be its owner. On appeal, it was held that the bailment was not involuntary and that a gratuitous bailee owed a duty of reasonable care. However, Gresson J. appeared to accept the *Elvin, Powell* decision as correct.[64]

Burnett[65] has suggested that there should be no liability for conversion where the defendant's conduct is intended by him to return the goods to the possession of their rightful owner; and that contributory negligence should be open as a defence to parties who find themselves unwittingly in a situation where some positive act of return is required on their part. The object of these remarks is not so much to mitigate the rigours of the

---

[61] (1933) 50 T.L.R. 158; the case is discussed in [1935] 5 C.L.J. 407.
[62] (1939) 61 C.L.R. 433, at 447; likewise, *Glass* v. *Hollander* (1935) 35 S.R. (N.S.W.) 304.
[63] [1950] N.Z.L.R. 878, at 886-887.
[64] Ibid., at 922. See also *McCowan* v. *McCulloch* [1926] 1 D.L.R. 312 (p. 3, ante) where, however, the bailee's assumption of possession was voluntary but mistaken, since he assumed the property was someone's other than the plaintiff's. He attempted to return the property and was held liable for want of reasonable care when it was lost. In one American case, *Cowen* v. *Pressprich* (1922) 112 N.Y. Supp. 242, the same rule as to negligent misdelivery was applied as in *Elvin, Powell*. But in two earlier decisions, where the facts were almost identical to those in *Elvin, Powell*, the court held that there was no bailment, and therefore no duty, because the parties were not in contract: *Krumsky* v. *Loeser* (1902) 75 N.Y. Supp. 1012; *Wechser* v. *Picard Importing Co.* (1916) 157 N.Y. Supp. 803. These cases are discussed by Tay (1966) 5 *Sydney Law Review* 239, at 247-253. Note, however that in *Wechser's* case the goods were accepted by a co-tenant of the defendant and the defendant never saw them.
[65] (1960) 76 L.Q.R. 364.

liability of an involuntary bailee as to remove the somewhat artificial distinction between the responsibility imposed upon him and that placed upon a "deliveree" of goods who is not placed in possession. As the well-known decision in *Hiort* v. *Bott*[66] shows, the defendant in the latter case may be guilty of conversion notwithstanding that he took reasonable care in performing the act complained of and performed it with the sole object of returning the goods to their rightful owner. As Burnett points out, this distinction can produce anomalies:

> Let us suppose that in *Hiort* v. *Bott* the carriers had by mistake delivered the barley to the defendant's premises without waiting for his order and that at the time he signed the delivery order the barley was, unknown to both him and the rogue who persuaded him to sign, in his own back-yard. We should presumably now have to hold that the defendant was not liable in trover since, at the time when he signed the delivery order, he was an involuntary bailee. The result is that the defendant's liability will often be governed by purely fortuitous circumstances.[67]

This statement, it is submitted, may be open to objection on two levels. First, there is a real difference between the dilemma of the involuntary bailee (who is encumbered with the possession of unwanted goods) and that of a recipient who is merely requested to take possession. The latter need do nothing, apart from telling the messenger to go away, whereas the former has the problem of disposing or taking care of the goods; it is therefore reasonable to exact from him a lesser standard of liability.[68]

Secondly, it may be queried whether the defendant in Burnett's example is genuinely an involuntary bailee. All of the decisions in this area involve persons who, at the material time, know of the existence of the goods and of the fact that those goods are in their possession. Where either of these elements is lacking, it is arguable that the traditional reason for attenuating the strict liability in conversion is again absent because the bailee by concealment is aware of no dilemma and has no immediate reason to act as he does. This position will alter, of course, once he discovers the goods, for then he is faced with the problem, hitherto absent from his mind, of how to rid himself of them.

On the broader issue, it is still uncertain whether conduct of the sort described by Burnett would constitute conversion. Certainly, there are powerful reasons for reducing the operation of this tort upon cases where the act was innocent and assumed to be thoroughly consistent with the rights of the owner.[69] But this is a problem more akin to the general law of tort than to the specialised field of bailments.

The question of contributory negligence, however, clearly affects the position of the involuntary bailee. The problem consists in deciding whether this defence is available in any event to the defendant in an action for conversion. Although isolated decisions in England[70] and New

---

[66] (1874) L.R. 9 Ex. 86; see p. 126, ante.
[67] (1960) 76 L.Q.R. 364, at 368-369.
[68] See (1874) L.R. 9 Ex. 86, at 91, per Cleasby B.
[69] But cf. *Helson* v. *McKenzies* ante; Cmnd. 4774, paras. 46-50.
[70] *Lumsden* v. *London Trustee Savings Bank Ltd.* [1970] 1 Lloyd's Rep. 114.

Zealand[71] have permitted the defence, recent Australian authority points the other way.[72] It is submitted that if an involuntary bailee is indeed liable only for those conversions occasioned by his lack of reasonable care, the action should for these purposes be characterised as one in negligence and the defence should, in appropriate circumstances, be allowed.[73]

Logically, there seems to be no good reason for confining the duty of reasonable care to cases where the involuntary bailee has been guilty of conversion, or to cases of conversion by misdelivery as opposed to conversion by destruction.[74] The only possible justification seems to be that liability in conversion is traditionally strict and that the rules on involuntary bailments are an attenuation of the traditional liability; a proportionate reduction in cases of damage or theft would therefore render the bailee liable only for something less than reasonable care. If it were considered desirable to preserve these distinctions, this could be achieved by making the involuntary bailee liable in all events only for gross negligence.[75] But it may be better to acknowledge, along with Chapman J.,[76] that liability no longer varies between different classes of bailment, even where the bailment in question is only doubtfully classifiable as such at all. Accordingly, the bailee would in all cases be liable for a want of reasonable care, which would vary according to whether the goods were involuntarily accepted or not.[77]

C. The burden of proof

There is little authority on this point, but it is submitted that an involuntary bailee should carry the burden of proving that he exercised the required standard of care. This was the approach favoured by Perdue J.A. in *Consentino* v. *Dominion Express Co.*[78] Although it appears to conflict with some of the other decisions, and with the customary rationalisation of *Howard* v. *Harris*[79] it must be remembered that the ordinary gratuitous bailee's burden of proof was not finally settled in

---

[71] *Helson* v. *McKenzies* ante.

[72] *Wilton* v. *Commonwealth Trading Bank Ltd.* [1973] 2 N.S.W.L.R. 644; see p. 135, ante. Cf. s. 11(1), Torts (Interference with Goods) Act 1977.

[73] In *Batistoni* v. *Dance, The Times,* 18 January (1908) both counsel appeared to accept as relevant the evidence that the plaintiff's servant had been negligent in announcing to a stranger the fact that he was delivering the goods to the defendant. Channell J. did not comment on this evidence, but the treatment of the case suggests that, if established, it may have provided a further ground for exonerating the defendant. Stronger authority for the reduction of the bailor's right of recovery where he has been negligent may perhaps be found in Kelly C.B.'s judgment in *Heugh* v. *L.N.W. Ry. Co.* (1870) 5 Ex. 51, at 57.

[74] Cf. (1921-1922) 6 *Minn. L.R.* 579 where it is suggested that mis-delivery may be a doctrine peculiar to bailments.

[75] The view favoured by Story, loc. cit; and see the *Consentino* case (p. 233, ante) and Beven at 907-908.

[76] In *Griffiths* v. *Arch Engineering Ltd.* [1968] 3 All E.R. 217, at 220.

[77] As seems to have been the accepted rule in *Batistoni* v. *Dance, The Times,* 18 January 1908; see p. 387, ante.

[78] (1906) 4 W.L.R. 498, at 506-507; see also, to similar effect, *Kaufman Metal Co.* v. *R.* [1951] 1 D.L.R. 801, where the involuntary bailee was held to have discharged his burden of proving that the loss was due to an inherent vice in the goods. Cf. Laidlaw, loc. cit., at 309-310.

[79] (1884) Cababé & Ellis 253: see p. 384, ante.

England until around the turn of the century[80] and that in many of these cases the owner was suing in negligence anyway, so that he had in effect assumed the burden of proof.[81] Moreover, to cast the burden upon the involuntary bailee would accord with the philosophy of the burden of proof in bailments generally, under which the person in possession is deemed to be the party who can most probably offer an explanation of the loss.[82] In Australia, it is still uncertain whether a gratuitous, voluntary bailee must prove that he took reasonable care.[83] It is submitted that both here and in the field of involuntary bailments the bailee should be put to proof of his exercise of the appropriate degree of care.

III. REMEDIES OF THE INVOLUNTARY BAILEE

However low the degree of care demanded of him, this will not always suffice to relieve the involuntary bailee of the difficulties of his position. As Winfield and Jolowicz point out, he also has the problem of what to do with the goods:

> It is simple enough with a small and imperishable article like a fountain-pen, but what of a parcel of fish or a piano which is delivered at my house in my absence?[84]

Very little authority exists as to the various courses of action open to someone in this predicament. In *Hiort* v. *Bott*,[85] Bramwell B. remarked that the safest way of dealing with such cases was to wait until they arose. He thought that the involuntary bailee was neither bound to warehouse the goods nor entitled to turn them into the street; if, however, he chose to return them through a trustworthy intermediary, that may or may not be a conversion. In the light of subsequent authority[86] it seems that the involuntary bailee who adopted this expedient would be exonerated. This view draws support from the judgment of Cleasby B. in *Hiort* v. *Bott*,[87] who thought that the owner would have no legitimate complaint if the bailee acts in a manner "which is considered reasonable and proper".

This approach is emphatically to be preferred. It will exonerate the involuntary bailee who conscientiously performs certain acts with the object of returning the goods to their owner[88] or of mitigating his own responsibility towards them. Thus, the redelivery of an unwanted letter to the Post Office, or the placing of valuables in a bank or with the police, would clearly be reasonable acts. Of course, what is reasonable will depend very largely upon the nature of the article. Despite the statement of Bramwell B. it seems clear, for instance, that the owner of a piece

---

[80] Cf. *Powell* v. *Graves* (1886) 2 T.L.R. 663 and see generally p. 311 et seq., ante.
[81] E.g. *Batistoni* v. *Dance, The Times*, 18 January 1908; *Elvin, Powell & Co. Ltd.* v. *Plummer Roddis Ltd.* (1933) 50 T.L.R. 158.
[82] *The Ruapehu* [1925] 21 Lloyd's Rep. 310, at 315 (Atkin L.J.).
[83] See p. 312, ante.
[84] *Torts*, p. 415.
[85] (1874) L.R. 9 Ex. 86, at 90: see also *Heugh* v. *L.N.W.R. Co.* (1870) L.R. 5 Ex. 51, at 56 per Kelly C.B.
[86] See p. 387, ante.
[87] (Ante, n. 85), at 91.
[88] Cf. *McCowan* v. *McCulloch* [1926] 1 D.L.R. 312.

of land upon which the plaintiff has wrongfully parked his car is entitled
to remove it to the roadside:[89]

> I shall not attempt here to speculate on what would be the situation
> if the operator of the lot moved the car to a position of danger from
> traffic or placed it where it would obstruct traffic or exposed it to
> injury by letting it roll down the street . . . I do not think that
> the operator of the lot was under any duty to search out the owner of
> the illegally parked car. If he is not content to let the car remain
> where it is until the owner appears or . . . to remove it to the nearest
> street curb but decides to remove it to an accessible place of safe
> keeping, I would hold that he should be entitled to recover the
> reasonable expenses incurred in doing so.[90]

Nevertheless, between the undesirable alternatives of free custody or
certain liability it remains difficult to chart a middle way. This could be
particularly true in the case of cumbersome or malodorous goods. Winfield and Jolowicz[91] suggest that wherever possible the sender should be
notified and invited to take the goods away; where he declines to do so
(or even in cases of emergency, where he has not been notified) the goods,
if they become a nuisance, could be destroyed.[92] Although no reasonable
judge could object to this expedient in the case of rotting fish, it is harder
to envisage its acceptance in the case of a more valuable or less offensive
nuisance, such as a lorry-load of champagne or a grand piano. It must
also be remembered that the plaintiff may be as innocent as the defendant
of any intention to place the latter in possession. In many cases, if the
owner is untraceable, the obvious solution would be to take the chattel
to the police; they, on the other hand, might be reluctant to accept for
custody such lost property as boxes of mackerel or stray grand pianos.
The difficulties of the involuntary bailee's position remain a blot on the
law, and one which only in Western Australia has been the subject of any
attempt at eradication.[93]

Can the bailee recover any incidental expenses, reasonably arising out
of his disposal or custody of the goods, from the person who deposited
them with him? There are only two recent authorities directly in point. In
R. v. Howson,[94] Laskin J.A. held that such expenses were recoverable
under the law of quasi-contract or restitution.[95] The learned judge went
on to observe that the involuntary bailee could not, however, enforce this

---

[89] In *Fournier* v. *McKenna* [1921] 57 D.L.R. 720, the defendant warned the plaintiff
in advance that he would not be responsible if the plaintiff left a car inside his
garage, and told him to take it away. Later he removed the car into the open,
where it was severely damaged by bad weather. The plaintiff's action failed
because of the disclaimer.
[90] *R.* v. *Howson* (1966) 55 D.L.R. (2d) 582, at 593 (and see further at 594)
per Laskin J.A. See also *Foster* v. *Juniata Bridge Co.* (1851) 16 Pa. St. 393;
Peaslee v. *Wadleight* (1831) 5 N.H. 317.
[91] At 415. See also *Grimoldby* v. *Wells* (1875) L.R. 10 C.P. 391.
[92] But cf. p. 393, post.
[93] *Disposal of Uncollected Goods Act* 1970: see p. 407, post.
[94] (1966) 55 D.L.R. (2d), at 593-594.
[95] Citing *Fibrosa Spolka Akcyjna* v. *Fairbairn Lawson Combe Barbour Ltd.* [1943]
A.C. 32, at 61 and *Deglman* v. *Guaranty Trust Co.* [1954] 3 D.L.R. 785, and
distinguishing *Falcke* v. *Scottish Imperial Insurance Co. Ltd.* (1886) 24 Ch.D.
234, at 248. Cf. *Nicholson* v. *Chapman* (1793) 2 H.Bl. 254; 3 R.R. 374 where
Eyre C.J. also suggests that such expense is recoverable and the note suggests
that this would be by way of implied assumpsit.

right by lien[96] and that he could not detain the goods damage feasant unless there were actual damage and not merely a technical trespass. This approach (which seems unexceptionable) may be contrasted with that in the old Connecticut case of *Leavy* v. *Kinsella*.[97] The purchaser of pigs took them back and left them at the seller's house while the seller was away. The seller fed them and was held entitled to an indemnity:

> The defendant is made a bailee, with the duty of incurring expense, not by his own choice, but by compulsion. Upon these circumstances the plaintiff is liable upon an implied assumpsit to pay the expense of keeping.

In addition, the court held that the defendant was entitled to a lien, which is at variance with the position in English law. Apart from this, however, it seems clear that the courts will find some way of indemnifying the involuntary bailee. The decision in *R.* v. *Howson* may be contrasted with that of Mr J. Newey, Q.C., in *Kolfor Plant Ltd.* v. *Tilbury Plant Ltd.*[97a], who held that there was no authority entitling an involuntary bailee to recover storage charges, but held that such charges could be recovered in the instant case as damages for breach of the defendant's duty to supply goods in accordance with the contract.

Since, therefore, the defendant in such cases seems entitled to do whatever is reasonable, it may be thought that it would be more appropriate to cast his overall duty in relation to the goods as one of reasonable care.

As for the owner, there is no authority concerning his liability for damage or injury by the goods. Logically, he should be in the position of a virtual insurer but it seems likely that unless the bailee can establish trespass to land by virtue of the delivery[97b] the owner will be liable for negligence alone.

IV. Undelivered or Uncollected Goods

In every decision considered so far, it is the defendant's initial reception of goods which has taken place contrary to his wishes and without his consent. Further problems arise when a bailee who has originally consented to the possession of the goods is compelled by circumstances to retain possession longer than he desires. The question here is whether a bailment can become involuntary by lapse of time or other events and whether the bailee in such a position owes any higher duty than the involuntary bailee ab initio. This question really involves two separate issues: (a) What is his duty of care in relation to the goods? (b) What can he do to rid himself of them or otherwise mitigate the effects of his position?

---

[96] *Nicholson* v. *Chapman* ante, is to the same effect.
[97] (1872) 39 Conn. 50; cf. *Binstead* v. *Buck* (1776) 2 Wm. Bl. 1117, where the person caring for an animal was not compelled to take possession and was held unable to recover.
[97a] (1977) *The Times,* May 17th.
[97b] Cf. the *Kolfor* case, supra.

A. Duty of care

As regards the first question, authority is almost non-existent. It seems likely that the bailee's responsibility continues to be one of reasonable care according to all the circumstances of the case. Unfortunately, practically the only decisions in point involve common carriers who, having accepted goods, are unable to effect delivery of them. In relation to such bailees, the courts have logically reduced their responsibility from one which makes them a virtual insurer of the goods to one that obliges them to take reasonable care.[98] Whether a proportionate reduction would apply in the case of an ordinary bailee whose initial duty rose no higher than reasonable care is very much open to question. Of course, the bailment may change from one that is for reward to one that is gratuitous, as in the case of goods sold to a buyer who does not collect them within a reasonable time;[99] here the absence of a continuing reward may in itself affect the bailee's duty of care.[1] On the other hand, the mere fact that the goods are left with a cleaner or repairer for longer than was originally contemplated will not necessarily make the bailee an unrewarded custodian of the goods once the notional collection date has passed;[2] a fortiori, it is submitted, where the relevant *Disposal of Uncollected Goods Act* potentially entitles him to make a reasonable charge for

---

[98] There are three principal authorities. In *Duff* v. *Budd* (1822) 3 B. & B. 177; 129 E.R. 1250, a consignor succeeded in negligence for the carrier's misdelivery to a swindler after the goods had been rejected by the nominal consignee. In *Stephenson* v. *Hart* (1828) 6 L.J.C.P. (O.S.) 97; 130 E.R. 851, the circumstances were similar but the consignor sued on two counts of negligence and one of trover. Park J. held the first two counts to be unsupported by the evidence but considered the action to be maintainable in trover, apparently considering the defendant's lack of care to be relevant in this regard; Burroughs J. favoured the second count, a duty of care being imposed by the implied contract which arose between consignors and carriers when the goods were first found to be undeliverable to the nominal consignee's address; Gaselee J. held against the count in trover since the carriers had delivered to the "right" person, but agreed that the defendants conducted themselves with gross negligence. In *Heugh* v. *L.N.W.R.* (1870) 5 Ex. 51, the carriers stored the goods after being unable to make delivery and invited the consignors to give further instructions. A rogue, formerly in the employment of the nominal consignees, appeared at the defendants' office with the advice note and a further letter requesting the defendants to deliver the goods to him, which they did. The same procedure occurred about a week later. The defendants were exonerated on the ground that, as involuntary bailees, they had taken reasonable care. Kelly C.B. observed that misdelivery in such circumstances is not *per se* a conversion but depends upon whether the defendants have been negligent. This case is criticised by Laidlaw (1930-1931) 16 *Cornell Law Quarterly*, p. 298, who suggests that the defendants should have continued to be subject to the strict liability of a carrier; see to this effect *Security Trust Co.* v. *Wells Fargo & Co.* (1903) 81 N.Y. App. Div. 426, 80 N.Y. Supp. 830: aff'd (1904) 178 N.Y. 620, 70 N.E. 1109. The authority of the *Heugh* case is perhaps weakened by the fact that Martin B. (at p. 55, arguendo) considered the defendants to be bailees for reward since they had warned the consigners that they were storing the goods not as common carriers but as warehousemen, "subject to the usual warehouse charges" (cf. Kelly C.B. at p. 56). Cf. also *Hoare* v. *G.W. Ry. Co.* (1877) 37 L.T.R. 168, which turned on the construction of the consignment contract.

[99] See p. 382, ante.

[1] See generally Chapter 8, ante.

[2] See *Mitchell* v. *Davis* (1920) 37 T.L.R. 68 (plaintiff delayed in Scotland by strike; fur coat stolen from defendant tailor about one month after first ready for redelivery: *held,* defendant retained the coat as a bailee for reward). Cf. *Chapman* v. *G.W. Ry.* (1880) 5 Q.B.D. 278.

storage if and when he becomes entitled to sell the goods.[3] In some cases, the problems of non-delivery or non-collection may be said to be part of the normal hazards of the defendant's operation and there may be an implied understanding that no unintended protraction of the bailee's custody should derogate from his standard of care. Certainly this would in many cases provide the safest solution, at least where the extended period is not excessive or the delay is due to no fault of the bailor. Elsewhere, it is probably best to allow the circumstances (including the conduct of the bailor) to determine the most equitable and appropriate level of safekeeping, whether the plaintiff's complaint be conversion by misdelivery or negligence causing damage or loss by theft. The bailee can always provide in advance for a reduced degree of responsibility once certain events have occurred.[4] In some cases (i.e., where the bailor can still be contacted) such a variation may be imposed after the original period of the bailment has expired. Generally it seems that a reduction in the standard care is not, except in extreme cases, the most appropriate method of dealing with the difficulties that an expired bailment engenders. The real problem is to provide the bailee with effective, positive measures for getting rid of the goods. In this area statute has intervened, but not as decisively as one could wish.

B. Remedies of the bailee

There is at Common Law no general right to dispose of goods which a bailor has refused, or is unable, to collect. In *Sachs* v. *Miklos*,[5] Lord Goddard C.J. suggested that the bailee might place the bailor in a position of having impliedly consented to a sale, by writing to him and warning him that this will take place unless the goods are collected within a specified time. But this raises difficulties, not least in that silence in response to an offer cannot generally be taken to connote consent.[6] Nor will the principle of agency of necessity relieve the bailee, except in very limited circumstances, from the consequences of an unauthorised disposal. As the decision of McCardie J. in *Prager* v. *Blatspiel, Stamp & Heacock*[7] shows, there must be an actual commercial necessity dictating

---

[3] See p. 397 et seq., post.
[4] In *Reeder* v. *Harmeling* (1969) 451 Pa. (2d) 920. (Washington Supreme Court) the defendants were storing seventeen hundred orchids belonging to the plaintiff in one of their plastic greenhouses. They advised him that they would need the space after March 1st. On March 12th, when he had still failed to remove them, they put the orchids outside, where they died from frost. Hill J. held that the defendants were not guilty of conversion and were under no responsibility for the loss: "Reeder could have been intentionally inviting just what did take place". Note, however, that the defendants had proved that the plaintiff could have saved the plants by making reasonable efforts, and thereby mitigated his loss. Quaere whether the same result would have followed if he could not. It is submitted that it should.
[5] [1948] 2 K.B. 23, at 37.
[6] Ibid.; cf. *Fairline Shipping Corporation Ltd.* v. *Adamson* [1974] 2 All E.R. 667. But it seems that if a buyer of goods who has a right to reject them can notify the seller to this effect, the goods thereafter are at the seller's risk: *Grimoldby* v. *Wells* (1875) L.R. 10 C.P. 391. But it is thought that the courts may still exact from the buyer the duties of a gratuitous bailee, on an analogy with the seller of uncollected goods: see p. 282 et seq., ante. It may be that the level of care will depend upon the degree of difference between what was ordered and what was sent. Cf. *Kolfor Plant Hire* v. *Tilbury Plant Hire* (1977) *The Times* May 17th.
[7] [1924] 1 K.B. 566; cf. [1948] 2 K.B. 23, at 24-25.

the disposal before the bailee can evade liability for conversion; in addition, the bailee must have acted prudently and bona fide in the interests of the owner and must have been, for practical purposes, unable to communicate with his bailor prior to the disposal. Although this doctrine may apply where goods are deteriorating or otherwise falling in value (provided the depreciation is sufficiently serious to constitute an emergency) there is little prospect of its acceptance in situations where the disposal or other treatment is for the benefit of the bailee alone.[8] This can be seen from *Sachs* v. *Miklos*,[9] where the first defendant (after a lapse of three years, numerous telephone calls and two unanswered letters) finally sold a quantity of furniture which the plaintiff had stored with him many years before, and which was occupying necessary space. Lord Goddard C.J. acknowledged that what the first defendant did was perfectly natural in the circumstances and observed that in peace-time, with furniture values constant, his action would probably have involved him in no real liability.[10] But in the present case, values had risen and the plaintiff found it worthwhile to sue for conversion. The defendant could not plead agency of necessity because there was no real emergency confronting him; he simply (and quite understandably) wished to be rid of an inconvenience. This was too mild an ambience for the doctrine to apply. Quite apart from the fact that the defence is traditionally confined to shipmasters, acceptors of bills of exchange for the honour of the drawee and carriers by land,[11] it is clear that the act complained of must be in the interests of the principal for the defence to succeed.[12] *Sachs* v. *Miklos* was followed in *Munro* v. *Willmott*,[13] where Lynskey J. doubted whether the doctrine could apply to goods stored in premises[14] and held the defendant liable for disposing of a car which had lain in his yard for nearly three years and which the owner (despite efforts both on the defendant's part personally and through the police to contact her) had failed to collect. Clearly, this is one situation in which the Common Law is incapable of supplying a satisfactory solution. [14a]

Partly to alleviate the problem, the *English Disposal of Uncollected Goods Act* was passed in 1952. This has been complemented by similar legislation in every Australian State, although the statutes are complicated and differ considerably inter se. They will now be considered in turn.

[8] See *Barker* v. *Burns Philp & Co. Ltd.* (1944) 45 S.R. (N.S.W.) 1; *Burns Philp & Co. Ltd.* v. *Gillespie Bros., Ltd.* (1947) 74 C.L.R. 148.

[9] [1948] 2 K.B. 23.

[10] Ibid., at 35.

[11] Cf. Goff and Jones, *The Law of Restitution*, pp. 232-233. Scrutton J. has observed that the courts should be slow to increase the categories of persons who can be regarded as agents of necessity in disposing of goods without authority: *Jebara* v. *Ottoman Bank Ltd.* [1927] 2 K.B. 254, at 270; see also *Gwilliam* v. *Twist* [1895] 2 Q.B. 84.

[12] See the cases cited in n. (8), supra., and *Sachs* v. *Miklos,* supra.

[13] [1948] 2 All E.R. 983: as to the damages awarded in this case, see p. 1023, post.

[14] [1948] 2 All E.R. 983, at 985-986: and see *Sachs* v. *Miklos* [1948] 2 K.B. 23, at 35-36, where Lord Goddard doubts whether it can apply to non-perishable goods.

[14a] Since the ensuing account was written, the 1952 legislation has been replaced, in respect of goods bailed after January 1978, by ss. 12 and 13 of the *Torts (Interference with Goods) Act* 1977. The new provisions are set out in Appendix I, post.

1. *England*: The English Act is confined to those cases where goods are accepted by a bailee[15] "in the course of a business, for repair or other treatment" on the terms that they will be redelivered to the bailor when the treatment is completed and the charges paid.[16] Thus, it would not apply to the situations in *Munro* v. *Willmott*[17] or *Sachs* v. *Miklos*,[18] nor to any bailment entered into between private persons, nor to the storage or carriage of goods as opposed to their cleaning, painting, alteration or repair. The bailee who is within the Act is given a right to sell the goods provided certain conditions are fulfilled:

(i) The goods were ready for redelivery but the bailor has failed both to pay or to tender the relevant charges and to take delivery of the goods or to give directions for their redelivery where the terms of the bailment so provide.[19]

(ii) The bailee's premises[20] displayed at the time of the acceptance a notice, conspicuously placed, indicating that acceptance of such goods is subject to the Act and that the Act confers on the bailee a right of sale exercisable after an interval of not more than twelve months from the time at which the goods are ready for redelivery.[21]

(iii) The bailee (after the goods are ready for redelivery) has given the bailor a notice, conforming with s. 1(7) of the Act, stating that the goods are ready for redelivery, describing the goods, specifying the charges due and warning that if the bailor fails both to pay the charges and collect the goods within 12 months of the giving of the notice the goods may be sold.[22]

(iv) The bailee has given a further notice, 12 months after the first and not less than 14 days before the sale, likewise conforming with s. 1(7) and stating the date on which the redelivery notice was given[23] and the bailee's intention to sell within 14 days if the bailor fails both to retrieve the goods and pay the charges within that time; additionally, the notice must contain the information specified in (iii) above, as to description and charges.[24]

(v) The bailee, when selling the goods, does not include them in a lot containing goods not delivered to him by the bailor and does not sell them otherwise than by public auction.[25]

(vi) Where the bailee's notice of intention to sell states a minimum intended price, he may sell for not less than that price and need not sell by public auction.[26]

---

[15] Whether before or after the commencement of the Act.
[16] Section 1(1): "charges" includes a reasonable sum where none is specifically agreed.
[17] [1949] 1 K.B. 295.
[18] [1948] 2 K.B. 23.
[19] Section 1(2): the right to sell continues for as long as the failure persists.
[20] I.e., all premises used or appropriated by the bailee for accepting for repair or other treatment goods of the class to which the goods accepted belong.
[21] Section 1(3)(a); if the notice is displayed, the section is not offended merely because the goods were accepted elsewhere than at the relevant premises.
[22] Section 1(3)(b).
[23] Or, where there has been a dispute between bailor and bailee (as to which, see infra) the date on which the dispute was determined.
[24] Section 1(3)(c).
[25] Section 1(3).
[26] Section 1(3) proviso (ii).

(vii) Any dispute between the parties concerning the rates of charge or the quality of the work must, if arising before the giving of notice as to the bailee's intention to sell, have already been determined by the time such notice is given; otherwise the right to sell is suspended till determination of the dispute. (See further ss. 1(5) and 1(6) for the circumstances in which a dispute may be deemed to be determined and the consequences thereof.)[27]

Further provisions amplify the requirement of notice. The expression "notice" in the Act always means a notice in writing.[28] A notice of intention to sell must be sent by post in a registered letter.[29] Any other notice required or authorised under the Act may be given by (a) delivering it to the bailor, or (b) leaving it at his proper address,[30] or (c) sending it by post.[31]

After the goods have been sold, the bailee is entitled to recover any difference between the gross proceeds of sale and the aggregate charges owing to him; any excess may be recovered by the bailor.[32] The bailee must, within seven days of the sale, prepare a record setting out a sufficient description of the goods; the place, date and method of sale; the name and principal place of business of the auctioneer where the sale takes place by public auction and, where the sale is not performed by public auction and the gross proceeds are less than £1, the address of the buyer; the amount of gross proceeds of the sale and an itemised statement of the bailee's charges. For the next six years he must keep this record, together with copies of the notice of intention to sell and the certificate of posting such notice, available for reasonable inspection by the bailor.[33] Any failure to comply with this subsection or the furnishing of a document for the purposes of the subsection which is known to be false in a material particular can involve a fine or imprisonment or both.[34]

Supplemental provisions define "goods accepted by the bailee in the cause of a business for repair or other treatment"[35] and amplify the expression "charges of the bailee in relation to any goods" used throughout the Act. Subject to any agreement between bailor and bailee, this expression is to be construed as including the amount agreed between them for the repair or treatment (or reasonable sum where no such charge was agreed) plus, where the goods have been sold, a reasonable storage charge for the period between the giving of the redelivery notice or the determination of the dispute (where there has been one) and the date of sale, sale-expenses and the cost if any of insuring the goods.[36] References in

---

[27] The full text of these subsections corresponds, mutatis mutandis, with ss. 6(3) and 6(6) of the New South Wales *Disposal of Uncollected Goods Act,* set out at p. 402, post.

[28] Section 2(1).

[29] Section 2(3).

[30] I.e., his last known address, or, where a corporation is involved, its registered or principal office: s. 2(5). Delivery in the latter case to the secretary or clerk to the corporation will suffice: s. 2(2).

[31] Section 2(4).

[32] Section 3(1).

[33] Section 3(2).

[34] Section 3(3).

[35] Section 4(1); for the wording of the subsection; see s. 8(1) of the N.S.W. Act of 1966 (set out at p. 403 post) which is identical.

[36] Section 4(2).

the Act to a bailor or bailee includes any other person in whom the rights and obligations of either party in relation to the goods are vested at the relevant time.[37] Section 5 contains special provision for goods accepted before the commencement of the Act.[38]

Finally, it should be noted that nothing in the Act is to derogate from any powers exercisable by the bailee independently thereof.[39] In normal circumstances, such powers would be likely to arise only under the contract or by virtue of any agency of necessity; accordingly, the powers granted by the Act are likely to represent the sole course of action open to the bailee.

Enough has already been said to demonstrate the complications and difficulties inherent in the Act. A bailee of uncollected goods, faced with the morass of details it contains, could almost be pardoned for disregarding it altogether and for taking the risk of an unauthorised disposal, rather than following the procedure laid down by statute. No less serious is the narrowness of the Act: all gratuitous and involuntary bailments are excluded as well as a very high proportion of bailments for reward. In the light of these criticisms, it may be interesting to observe the approach taken by the Law Reform Committee to the general problem.[40] Speaking of the 1952 Act, they said:

> 103 . . . This provision was directed to the case of bailees who are owed money by their bailors and we understand that little use has in fact been made of it, probably in part because of the complicated procedure involved. For both these reasons, we doubt whether it could aptly or with advantage be extended to cover all bailments. But we think that there should be some amelioration in the position of bailees generally in respect of uncollected goods.
>
> 104 . . . It has been suggested to us that this problem might be covered by conferring on bailees a right of prescription, but we consider that such a right would be less than just to bailors in some of the many different circumstances in which the problem may arise. In our opinion, it would be better to make any right of the bailee to dispose of the goods depend, not on the passage of a fixed period of time, but on his having taken reasonable, but unsuccessful, steps to obtain the instructions of his bailor.
>
> 105 . . . It is probably true that in some cases a bailee, faced with the practical need to dispose of the goods and with the impossibility of obtaining his bailor's instructions, will, particularly where the goods are perishable or of little value, "chance his arm" by selling them for the best price obtainable, in the reasonable confidence that, if the bailor does subsequently appear on the scene, the most he can in practice be liable for is the price he has obtained.
>
> 106 . . . This will not, however, always be the case. A bailee who cannot rely on its being necessary (though it may be convenient) for him to sell may not be willing to run the risk of an action by the bailor—or even of the prosecution for theft (although in all proba-

---

[37] Section 4(3).
[38] Now of negligible importance; see also s. 1(3)(b) and proviso (i) to the same subsection.
[39] Section 4(4).
[40] Law Reform Committee, *Eighteenth Report* (*Conversion and Detinue*) Cmnd. 4774, paras. 193-109.

bility he would have a good defence by virtue of section 2 of the *Theft Act* 1968). Moreover, his prospective purchaser may be unwilling to accept a defective title with the possibility of subsequent litigation at the suit of the bailor.

107 . . . To meet these difficulties, we think that the law should confer on a bailee a positive right to sell the goods if he had made reasonable efforts to trace, and obtain instructions from, his bailor, but has not succeeded in doing so within a reasonable time. In these circumstances, provided he obtains a reasonable price for the goods, we think that the bailee's only liability to his bailor should be to account for the price he has obtained (less the costs of the sale) and that, as against the bailor, the purchaser should acquire a good title.

108 . . . A solution on these lines would, we think, meet most of the cases where the goods are of no great value. Its advantage is that it puts the bailee to hardly any trouble or expense. Its disadvantage, on the other hand, is that it gives neither the bailee nor his purchaser complete protection, since, should the bailor ever sue for the conversion of his goods, the court may hold that the bailee's actions have *not* been reasonable.

109 . . . In practice, it is only where the goods are of considerable value that the bailor will sue or the purchaser inquire into (or worry about) the bailee's title to sell. In such a case, it is reasonable that the bailee should be able to safeguard his position with more certainty than he could do under the recommendation in paragraph 107 above. For this purpose, we think that the bailee should be able to apply to the court for directions. If satisfied that the bailee had made reasonable but unsuccessful efforts to trace the bailor, the court should be empowered to give such directions for the disposal of the goods as appeared to be just, including an order that the bailee should bring into court the proceeds, or part of the proceeds, of the sale, less his reasonable costs. The effect of compliance with the directions would be that—

(a) the bailor's only right would be to claim the balance of the purchase price; and

(b) the purchaser would acquire a good title as against the bailor.

This procedure should, in our view, be open to any bailee, whether or not covered by the *Disposal of Uncollected Goods Act* 1952. Accordingly, we recommend the repeal of that Act.

It is interesting to note that some, if not all, of these recommendations had already been implemented in certain Australian States before the Law Reform Committee's Report was published. But the State legislation is still unenviably complicated and, as in England, it is doubtful whether it is very often invoked.

2. *New South Wales*: The *Disposal of Uncollected Goods Act* 1966, enjoys a somewhat wider ambit than the equivalent English statute. It is divided into four parts. Part I deals with preliminary matters; Part II with the disposal of uncollected goods without a court order; Part III with the disposal of uncollected goods pursuant to a court order; and Part IV with general provisions.

The circumstances in which Part II applies are, as with the English Act, defined primarily by reference to the sort of bailment created. Any bailment whereunder goods are accepted by the bailee[41] "in the course of a business, for repair or other treatment on the terms (express or implied) that they will be redelivered to the bailor or in accordance with the bailor's directions when the repair or other treatment has been carried out and on payment to the bailee of such charges as may be agreed between the parties or as may be reasonable" is subject to Part II.[42] Whenever goods delivered under a bailment of this kind are ready for redelivery and the bailor *either* fails to pay or to tender the bailee's charges *or*, having made payment, fails to take delivery of the goods or (if the terms of bailment so provide) to give directions for their delivery,[43] then the bailee may in certain circumstances sell the goods. Many of the restrictions and procedures imposed upon the exercise of this power resemble those laid down in the English Act; for example, the necessity for a warning notice to be conspicuously displayed on the bailee's premises,[44] indicating that goods are bailed subject to the Act and may be sold after an interval of not less than six months from the time they are ready for redelivery;[45] the requirement that, when the goods are thus ready, the bailee should give the bailor a notice containing the information laid down in the Act;[46] the parallel requirement for a notice of intention to sell, to be given no less than six months after the giving of the first notice;[47] and the duty to ensure that "the goods are sold by public auction in a lot in which no other goods are included".[48] But in other respects the New South Wales Act differs considerably from its English equivalent. First, as we have already seen, the bailee need wait only six months before giving notice of an intention to sell; the English Act requires him to wait for a year.

Secondly, both notices must be issued not only to the bailor but also to "every other person, at the time he gives the notice to the bailor, he actually knows has or claims an interest in the goods".[49] Thirdly, the notice of intention to sell must additionally be published in a newspaper published in Sydney and circulating throughout New South Wales;[50] and if the goods are a motor vehicle, notice must also be given in the *Gazette*.[51] Fourthly, it is specifically provided that the right to sell is dependent upon the bailee's lack of knowledge, at the time of carrying out the treatment on the goods, that they were subject to a hire-purchase agreement which prohibited the hirer from creating a lien on the goods.[52]

---

[41] Whether before or after the commencement of the Act.

[42] Section 4.

[43] Sections 5(a), (b); note that under the English Act the two requirements are cumulative; the bailor must *both* have failed to pay *and* have failed to collect the goods, for the bailee to be entitled to sell. The N.S.W. statute is therefore (in this respect) more favourable to bailees. Cf. the Victorian Act, post p. 414, which follows the English model on this point.

[44] I.e., "all premises used or appropriated by the bailee for accepting for repair or other treatment goods of the class to which the goods accepted belong".

[45] Section 6(1)(a).

[46] Section 6(1)(b). The information is listed in s. 6(7) and is broadly similar to that required by the English Act.

[47] Section 6(1)(c).

[48] Section 6(1)(d).

[49] Sections 6(1)(b), 6(1)(c)(ii).

[50] Section 6(1)(c)(iii)(a).

[51] Section 6(1)(c)(iii)(b).

[52] Section 5.

Fifthly, there is more elaborate provision for the determination of disputes relating to charges or the quality of work between bailor and bailee. Section 6(2) provides that if such a dispute arises before the bailor gives notice of intention to sell, the bailee's right of sale shall be suspended until the dispute is determined. Section 6(3) entitles the bailee to treat the dispute as determined if, having given notice that unless the bailor objects within one month the dispute will be so treated, and having fulfilled the requirements of s. 6(7) with regard to such notice, he receives no objection from the bailee within the period of a month. In such a case, the dispute shall be regarded as having been determined on the date upon which the notice to determine was given. In all this, the Act closely resembles the English provisions. But in addition, s. 6(4) empowers the court of petty sessions for the district in which the goods were accepted by the bailee to adjudicate upon the dispute at the instance of either bailor or bailee.[53] This jurisdiction arises if the bailor raises an objection to having the dispute treated as determined within the one-month period. In such a case the court may make an order specifying what it considers to be a reasonable amount for the bailee to charge. Such an order means that the dispute shall be treated as determined for the purposes of the Act;[54] it also fixes the amount of the bailor's liability to the bailee[55] and entitles the bailor to recover the amount of any overpayment previously made[56] in any court of competent jurisdiction. In whatever manner a dispute is determined, the effect is to waive the operation of s. 6(1)(c)(b) —requiring notice that the goods are ready for redelivery—and to cause the six-month period which must elapse before the bailee can give notice of an intention to sell to run from the date of determination of the dispute.[57]

When the goods are sold, s. 7(1) entitles the bailor to recover any amount by which the gross proceeds exceed the charges demanded by the bailee;[58] conversely, the bailee can recover any amount by which the gross proceeds fall short of his charges. As in England, the bailee must prepare a record of the goods within seven days of the sale and must keep it available for inspection by the bailee for the next six years.[59] The information which must be contained in this record is the same as that required by s. 3(2) of the English Act,[60] except that there is no require-

---

[53] The jurisdiction may be exercised only by a stipendiary magistrate: section 6(5).
[54] Section 6(4)(a)(i).
[55] Section 6(4)(a)(ii).
[56] Section 6(4)(a)(iii).
[57] Section 6(6).
[58] The bailee must pay this amount into a special savings bank account opened by him for that purpose within fourteen days of the sale: s. 20(1). If the money is not claimed and paid over within the next twelve months, the seller must (with the following fourteen days) pay both it, and any interest thereon, to the Treasurer to be placed to the credit of the Consolidated Revenue Fund: s. 20(2). He must also give the Treasurer a copy of the record compiled after sale: s. 20(3). Any person entitled to such money may recover it from the Treasurer, provided that the Treasurer shall not already have paid it to some other person "appearing to him to be entitled thereto"; in such a case the claimant shall be entitled to recover it from the first payee: ss. 20(4), (5). Failure to comply with s. 20 is, by subsection (6), an offence.
[59] Section 7(2).
[60] Page 398, ante.

ment as to the address of the buyer and s. 19 lays down special procedures to be followed where the chattel sold is a motor vehicle. Any failure to comply with s. 7(2), or the production or furnishing of a document kept for the purposes of that subsection which is (to the knowledge of the person furnishing or producing it) false in a material particular, is an offence.[61]

Section 8(1) amplifies the expression "goods accepted by the bailee, in the course of a business, for repair or other treatment" used in s. 4 and elsewhere in Part II.[62] Section 8(2) defines charges of the bailee as including the amount agreed between the parties for the repair or other treatment (or, in the absence of agreement, a reasonable charge therefor) and, where the goods have been sold:

(a) a reasonable charge for storing the goods during the period beginning with the date of the giving of the notice that the goods are ready for redelivery, or, where there has been a dispute between the bailor and bailee, the date on which the dispute was determined, and ending with the date of the sale;

(b) any costs of or in connection with the sale; and

(c) the cost, if any, of insuring the goods.

Section 9, which makes provision for goods accepted before the commencement of the Act, will not be discussed because of its decreasing importance. Section 17 ordains that any notice required or authorised by the Act shall be in writing and may be given by delivery to the person to when it is required to be given, by leaving it for him at his last known place of abode or business, with some other person apparently an inmate or employee of the place and apparently over 16, or by posting it addressed to him at his last known place of abode or business. As in England, the Act is not intended to derogate from any power exercisable by a person independently of the Act (s. 16) and applies (where appropriate) to parties other than the original bailor and bailee who enjoy rights and obligations relating to the goods which are the same as those rights and obligations by virtue of which the Act originally took effect: s. 15. But s. 18 contains a provision not explicitly made in the English Act. The buyer of any goods sold under the Act acquires "a good title to them", provided he buys in good faith and without notice of any failure on the seller's part to comply with the Act[63] or of any defect or want of title on the part of the bailor. Accordingly, a sale in pursuance of Part II of the Act has the effect of curing all these defects which prevented the bailor or any predecessor from acquiring title to the goods and of causing a completely fresh title to be engendered in the purchaser.

From the foregoing, it is evident that Part II of the New South Wales Act is modelled broadly upon its English equivalent, but with substantial

---

[61] Section 7(3).

[62] Such references "shall, in relation to goods of any class, be construed as references to goods of that class accepted by him for repair or other treatment in the course of a business consisting of or comprising the acceptance by him of goods of that class for repair or other treatment (whether or not the repair or other treatment is affected by him) wholly or mainly from persons who deliver to him, otherwise than in the course of a business, goods of that class for repair or other treatment".

[63] The onus is always on the seller to establish compliance with the Act: s. 18(2).

modifications and refinements. Part III goes further and covers territory untouched by the English Act. It deals with four distinct matters, each of them having in common the fact that a court order is required before the goods can be sold. The areas in question are:

(a) *Bailments to which Part II of the Act applies*: Instead of waiting for the statutory periods of six months and 14 days to elapse, as required by Part II, a bailee to whom goods are delivered for repair, cleaning, alteration, painting or other treatment may apply to the court for an order authorising him to sell them before that time. The right to do so arises at the same time as the bailee is entitled to despatch a s. 6(1)(b) notice that the goods are ready for redelivery: that is, roughly, when the goods are ready for redelivery and the bailor has failed either to pay for or to collect them.[64] The application to the court may be made although the bailee's right to sell the goods under Part II has not yet come to fruition, but the effect of such application is to cancel and determine the right of sale that would otherwise have arisen under Part II.[65]

(b) *Other bailments for reward*: Many commercial or consumer bailments are not covered by Part II: carriage of goods, warehousing and contracts of hire are all examples. But Part III of the Act applies to every bailment for reward. Section 10(1)(b) makes special provision for the outer circle of bailments for reward that are not covered by s. 10(1)(a) and Part II. The bailee may apply for an order to sell provided he has *either* required the bailor by notice to take delivery of the goods in accordance with the time specified in the contract of bailment,[66] subject to payment of the bailee's charges; *or*, where no such specification has been made, required the bailor by notice to take delivery within such reasonable time as may be specified in the notice itself. Once this has occurred, and the bailor *either* fails to make or tender payment *or* (having made or tendered payment) fails to take, or issue directions for, delivery of the goods at the time specified, application may be made for an order to sell.

(c) *Gratuitous bailments*: Section 10(1)(c) extends the right to apply for an order for sale to unrewarded bailees. This is an important and useful expansion which could be studied with advantage in England. The right to apply arises where:

> . . . the bailee of goods that have been accepted by him (whether before or after the commencement of this Act) pursuant to a bailment not for reward has, by notice in writing given to the bailor, required the bailor to take delivery of the goods at a time specified in or determined in accordance with the contract of bailment or, if the contract of bailment does not specify or make provision for the determination of the time when the goods are to be redelivered to the bailor, within such reasonable time as may be specified in the notice, and the bailor fails, at the time so specified or determined or within such reasonable time, to take delivery of the goods or, if the terms of the bailment so provide, to give directions as to their delivery.

---

[64] Section 10(1)(a).
[65] Section 10(2).
[66] Presumably this expression excludes sub-bailments for reward; in such a case the sub-bailee must deal solely with the median bailee.

Two points call for observation here. First, there is nothing in the subsection to confine it to those gratuitous bailments that are exclusively for the advantage of the bailor; the expression "pursuant to a bailment not for reward" could apply equally to a gratuitous loan. Secondly, the subsection refers to the unrewarded bailment as a contract. This characterisation of gratuitous bailments had been rejected in New South Wales[67] before the Act was passed, so that the use of the term "contract" in this connection really renders the subsection meaningless. It must, however, be assumed that the word will in future be construed loosely, to include any agreement which may or may not be binding on principles other than those of the law of contract. Finally, it should be stressed that s. 10(1)(c) can operate in a purely domestic or private context: for example, where one neighbour fails to collect his dog from another who has agreed to look after it for a specified time. Of course, circumstances may render it difficult to determine whether the bailment is one for reward.

(d) *Tow truck operators*: Persons of this character who, acting in the course of their business as such, and in accordance with lawfully given directions, move motor vehicles from a public place to another place, may apply to the court for an order under Part III once the owner has failed to pay or tender the towing charges.[68]

Likewise, where the operator has, after moving the goods in the manner described, stored them at a place where repairs are ordinarily carried out by himself or another person, and the owner fails to pay or to tender to the person by whom the repairs are carried or his charges for storage, application may be made by the operator or that other person, as the case may be. For these provisions to apply, the vehicle must be in the applicant's possession at the time of application.[69] But where, although a tow truck operator is not in possession, a person carrying on the repair of motor vehicles is, and the circumstances otherwise conform with s. 11(1), the tow truck operator may make a joint application with that person, provided the later is otherwise entitled to apply for an order to sell the goods.[70]

Section 12 lays down the procedure to be followed when applying for an order under Part III and the form of orders to be made. As regards the relevant forum, in applications under s. 10 this is the petty sessions court for the district in which the bailee accepted the goods;[71] under s. 11, the equivalent court for the district in which the goods were situated before being moved has jurisdiction.[72] The form of orders is complicated and will not be considered in any detail;[73] provision is made for their adaptation to particular cases, specifying the amount of costs and charges to be deducted by the bailee or other applicant,[74] and for authorising the sale whenever the applicant (or, in the case of joint applications, one of

---

[67] *Thomas* v. *High* [1960] S.R. (N.S.W.) 401; 76 W.N. 641. See further p. 14 et seq. ante.
[68] Section 11(1).
[69] Section 11(2).
[70] Section 11(3).
[71] Section 12(1)(a).
[72] Section 12(1)(b).
[73] See ss. 12(2) to 12(4).
[74] Sections 12(3) to 12(4).

the applicants) remains in possession of the goods until the order is made.[75]

The power of the court to grant an order is subject to any agreement between the owner and the applicant[76] and does not disentitle any person from recovering the goods within six months of the date of the order.[77] Any action brought for this purpose during the six months suspends the order till the action has been determined: if an order for recovery is made consequently, the applicant's right to sell the goods ceases and determines.[78] The jurisdiction conferred by s. 12 on a court of petty sessions may be exercised only by a stipendiary magistrate.[79]

Section 13 prescribes the procedure to be followed after goods are sold pursuant to s. 12. Any amount by which the gross proceeds exceed the charges specified in the order and any subsidiary charges the applicant is entitled to make under s. 14[80] is recoverable by the owner as a debt from the person authorised to sell; conversely, the grantee of the order may recover any deficiency from the owner.[81] As with sales performed under Part II of the Act, the grantee of the order must prepare a record of the goods within seven days of the sale; but in the present case, the record must *additionally*[82] contain a reference to the order authorising the sale; the method as well as the date and place of the sale, and, where the sale does not take place by public auction, the name and address of the buyer.[83] Within 14 days of the sale, a copy of this record must be lodged for filing with the clerk of the petty sessions court that granted the order.[84] Any person claiming an interest, past or present, in the goods may inspect this copy on payment of 20 cents.[85] There is the usual penalty for non-compliance and false statements.[86] The provisions of ss. 15 (transfer of operation of Act upon persons other than original parties), 16 (non-derogation of other powers), 17 (form of notices), 18 (title). 19 (special provisions for sale of motor vehicles)[87] and 20 (disposal of net proceeds), all of which have been discussed in relation to Part II, apply equally in relation to Part III. Section 21 prescribes the penalties

---

[75] Sections 12(2), 12(6): this provision is subject to the order itself and to the provisions of the Act.
[76] Section 12(5).
[77] Section 12(7).
[78] Section 12(8).
[79] Section 12(10).
[80] Section 14: "Where goods are sold by virtue of the provisions of this Part, the subsidiary charges which a person authorised to sell the goods is entitled to make are — (a) a reasonable charge for storing the goods during the period beginning with the date of the order authorising the sale of the goods and ending with the date of the sale, not exceeding a charge at a rate, if any, specified in the order in accordance with paragraph (f) of subsection three of section twelve of this Act; (b) any costs of or in connection with the sale, not exceeding the cost, if any, specified in the order in accordance with paragraph (f) of that subsection; and (c) the cost, if any, of insuring the goods."
[81] Section 13(1).
[82] For the basic requirements, see p. 401 et seq., ante.
[83] Section 13(2). It follows that sales pursuant to s. 12 need not be by public auction.
[84] Section 13(2).
[85] Section 13(3).
[86] Section 13(4).
[87] See p. 421, post.

imposed under the Act and s. 22 empowers the Governor to make regulations: see also s. 12(9).

3. *Western Australia*: The Western Australian statute[88] differs from its New South Wales counterpart in several significant respects. First, it provides for the disposal of goods by involuntary bailees[89] and other categories of possessor[90] who, not being bailees stricto sensu, are beyond the purview of the New South Wales legislation. Secondly, the Act is arranged not according to the relief which may be granted but according to the nature of the goods in question and, to a lesser extent, the circumstances under which the possessor acquired them. Thirdly, there is more specific provision for certain categories of goods, with varying time-periods and a greater diversity of procedure between these different categories. Fourthly, the Act does not confine itself to disposals by sale at public auction but permits the custodian, in certain circumstances, to dispose of the goods by gift, private sale, destruction or any other method. Fifthly, there is no requirement relating to the display of notices at the bailee's premises. Further differences will become apparent upon a closer examination of its provisions.

Part II of the Act provides for the disposal of those categories of uncollected goods which are prescribed by regulation[91] and have been accepted, before or after the coming into force of the Act, by a bailee in course of business for inspection, custody, storage, repair or other treatment.[92] The relevant period which must expire before the bailee may dispose of the goods commences when they are ready for redelivery[93] and a notice to that effect has been given, and continues for as long as the bailor fails to take redelivery or to give directions to that effect when any agreement between the parties so provides.[94] There is no reference to payment by the bailor as terminating this inchoate right and it must therefore be assumed that the right to sell continues (as in New South Wales) for as long as the goods are uncollected, regardless of whether the bailee has been paid. This is interesting because it suggests that the

---

[88] *Disposal of Uncollected Goods Act* 1970.
[89] See p. 391, ante, for the position at Common Law.
[90] Part VII, ss. 20-21: discussed at p. 410, post.
[91] See s. 4(1); under regulations dated 10th June, 1971, the following goods are prescribed: batteries, bedding (including sleeping bags), bicycle and bicycle parts, books, cooking utensils (including mowers and sprinklers), household appliances (including barbecues, hair clippers, portable hair-dryers, portable electric or gas stoves, shavers), household linen, leather goods, motor vehicle accessories, motor vehicle parts, radiograms, radios, record players, soft furnishings, spectacles, sports equipment, tape recorders, television sets, travel goods, typewriters (non-electric), wearing apparel (except furs). The regulations also prescribe forms for the giving of notices, the making of applications, the keeping of records etc.
[92] Section 7; by s. 4(1), "inspection" includes acceptance of goods for the purpose of submitting a quotation for the repair or other treatment of such goods.
[93] Section 4(2) provides elaborately for the identification of the time at which goods shall be deemed to be ready for delivery. This identification is geared to the completion of the particular service undertaken by the bailee, viz.: *inspection* — where the inspection has been carried out; *custody or storage* — when the agreed period has expired or (when there is no pre-arranged period) after seven days; *repair or other treatment* — when the repair or other treatment has been carried out. Section 4(2) applies generally and not just to goods prescribed within Part II.
[94] Section 8.

primary objective of the relevant provisions is not so much the reimbursement of the bailee as the disposal of abandoned property; contrast the
objective of the English Act, as seen by the Law Reform Committee.[95]

Pre-sale procedure (where the bailee elects to follow this method of
disposal) is closely akin to that required in New South Wales;[96] first, a
notice that the goods are ready for redelivery[97] and, then, a notice of
intention to sell, must be given (in writing) to the bailor. But the second
notice must be given not less than *three* months after the first,[98] and copies
must be sent in addition to every other person who, to the bailee's knowledge at the time of giving notice, has or claims an interest in the goods,
and to the Commissioner of Police.[99] Moreover, the information that must
be contained in these notices is more elaborate than that required in New
South Wales.[1]

More significantly, Part II is not confined to disposal by sale. Section
8 provides that the bailee may:

> . . . subject to the terms of any agreement between him and the bailor
> and to this Act, sell the goods by public auction or private treaty *or
> otherwise dispose of them* unless, the bailee, for any reason, refuses
> to make redelivery to the bailor or prevents him from taking re-
> delivery.

Where any other method is adopted, the bailee must, after giving notice
of his intention to dispose of the goods, have made reasonable efforts to
sell the goods during a period of one month after his right to sell has
arisen.[2] This is the only situation in which the bailee's right of disposal
is suspended beyond the giving of notice of intention to dispose of the
goods; where the method chosen is disposal by sale, it seems that the
sale can take place as soon after the giving of the second notice as the
bailee chooses.

Section 8(3) provides that the general provisions of the Act relating to
the determination of disputes[3] shall apply in relation to Part II.

Part III deals with non-prescribed goods which do not exceed 300
dollars in value and were accepted in circumstances corresponding to
these in Part II.[4] Again, the period runs from the time the goods are
ready for redelivery and the bailee has given notice in writing to that
effect.[5] But in this case the bailee must wait at least six months before
giving notice of intention to sell or otherwise to dispose of the goods[6] and
must delay for a further month before actually attempting to sell; he

---

[95] Cmnd. 4774; p. 399, ante.
[96] Page 401, ante.
[97] Section 9(1)(a).
[98] Section 9(1)(b).
[99] Sections 9(1)(b)(ii); 4(1); no such duplication is required in the case of the first
notice, that the goods are ready for redelivery.
[1] See ss. 26(2) to 26(4), discussed at p. 412 et seq., post. The bailee, when giving
the second notice, must state his intention to sell *or otherwise dispose of* the
goods.
[2] Section 8(2). The rules as to redelivery notices and the time that must elapse
thereafter are the same as in the case of a projected disposal by sale.
[3] Sections 15, 16, 17. The same provisions apply to disposals under Part III.
[4] Section 10; the circumstances are duplicated in s. 7, set out ante.
[5] Sections 11 (identical in effect to s. 8, ante), 12(1)(a).
[6] Section 12(1)(b); the notice must be sent to the same people as laid down in
Part II; see s. 9(1)(b), ante.

must also, at least one month before attempting to sell, publish a *further* notice of intention to sell in both a daily newspaper published in Perth and circulating throughout the State, and the Government *Gazette*.[7] No attempt to dispose of the goods other than by sale at public auction may be made unless he has, after becoming entitled to sell the goods, "in circumstances calculated to offer a reasonable prospect of sale, unsuccessfully offered the goods for sale by public auction on two occasions not less than fourteen days apart".[8]

When goods have been disposed of by sale pursuant to Parts II or III, s. 14(1) makes the usual reciprocal provision for recovery of any excess or deficit.[9] Section 14(2) likewise entitles the bailee to recover as a debt the outstanding charges owed by the bailor when the goods are disposed of by any other method. Section 14(3) defines, in slightly wider terms than the corresponding New South Wales provision,[10] the expression "charges of a bailee". Subject to any agreement and to the terms of the Act, this is to be construed as referring to the amount agreed upon for the service for which the goods were accepted and the cost of transporting the goods to the bailee's premises (or a reasonable sum where none was agreed) *plus* a charge for storage and insurance (if any) between the date of the giving of the redelivery notice and the eventual disposal and the costs of the disposal, including reasonable and necessary expenses arising from the service of notices and the publication of advertisements.

The bailee must prepare within seven days of disposal, and keep available for the following six years, the customary record of the goods.[11] This must contain a sufficient description of the goods, an itemised statement of the bailee's charges, and other details depending upon the method of disposal employed.[12]

The above matters are all contained in Part IV of the Act and apply equally to disposals under Parts II and III. Under Part V, provision is made for the determination of disputes which arise within Parts II and III. Whenever a dispute relating to the charges of the bailee or the quality of the service he performs arises between the giving of the redelivery notice and the giving of the notice of intention to dispose of the goods, and by virtue of this dispute the bailor refuses *in writing* to pay the required sum or to take or give directions for redelivery, the bailee's right of disposal under Part II or Part III of the Act cannot be

---

[7] Section 12(1)(c).
[8] Section 12(2).
[9] See s. 13(1) of the N.S.W. Act, p. 406, ante.
[10] Section 8(2); p. 403, ante.
[11] Section 14(4); s. 14(5) makes the failure to do so a criminal offence, in terms identical to s. 7(3) of the N.S.W. Act; ante, p. 403. The bailee must also keep for the corresponding period a copy of the notice of intention to sell or otherwise dispose of the goods.
[12] If the goods have been sold, the necessary additional details are: the date and place of sale; the name and business address of the person conducting the sale; the amount of the gross proceeds, and the amount of any sum paid to the bailee on account of his charges prior to the sale. If the goods have been disposed of by gift, there must be a record of the name and address of the donee. If destroyed, the name and address of the person by whom they were destroyed must be recorded. Where any other method of disposal has been adopted, details of this method must be given: ss. 14(4)(b) to 14(4)(e).

exercised unless the dispute is determined.[13] When there is a dispute arising between the giving of notice of intention to dispose and the actual disposal, by reason of the bailor's written refusal to accept that the goods prescribed in the notice are prescribed goods or to accept that the assessment of the goods in the notice at a value not exceeding 300 dollars is accurate, the bailee's right to dispose is likewise suspended.[14]

So far as concerns the non-judicial determination of disputes, the procedure is closely comparable to that adopted in New South Wales;[15] the bailee must send a determination notice in prescribed form[16] and the bailor must not have made a written objection within the following month to having the dispute treated as determined. When these conditions are fulfilled, determination shall be deemed to have occurred at the time when the notice was given. When the bailee does object, either party may apply for summary determination of the dispute. In such a case, the court may exercise the powers set out in Part VIII of the Act.[17] An order made under this provision determines the dispute[18] and entitles the party to whom costs are awarded to add that sum to the total of his charges (if he is the bailee) or subtract it from the total of his indebtedness under the bailment (if he is the bailor).[19]

A further category of goods falls to be governed by Part VI of the Act; viz., non-prescribed goods accepted in congruent circumstances to goods within Parts II or III[20] and exceeding 300 dollars in value. Where the goods are ready for redelivery and the bailor has failed to collect them,[21] s. 19(1) empowers the bailee to apply to the court for an order to sell or otherwise dispose of the goods, provided there is no agreement to the contrary and the bailee follows the statutory procedures. As usual, a redelivery notice is required[22] and a notice of intention to apply for an order; the latter must be given not less than six months after the first and must be sent to the Commissioner of Police and to all other parties known to claim or possess an interest in the goods, as well as to the bailor.[23] In addition, the bailee must publish notice of such intention in a state-wide Perth newspaper and in the Government *Gazette* at least a month before making his application.[24] The powers of the court to make an order, and the forms of order available, are set out in s. 22.

Possibly the most ambitious and unusual part of the West Australian statute is Part VII. Its provisions may be invoked by any person who: ". . . without committing a criminal offence, has or acquires possession

---

[13] Section 15.
[14] Section 16.
[15] See ss. 17(1) and (2) of the W.A. Act, which correspond to ss. 6(2) and (3) of the N.S.W. Act, p. 402, ante.
[16] See Part IX of the W.A. Act for the form of the notice; p. 412, post.
[17] Section 17(3). The provisions as to orders in Part VIII are elaborate and will not be examined.
[18] Section 17(4).
[19] Section 17(5).
[20] I.e., accepted (before or after the coming into force of the Act) by the bailee in the course of business for inspection, custody, storage, repair, or other treatment.
[21] Or to give directions for their redelivery, if the terms of any agreement between the parties so provide.
[22] Section 19(2)(a).
[23] Section 19(2)(b).
[24] Section 19(2)(c).

of goods in any way other than under a bailment to which Part II, III or VI apply."[25]

In such a case, the possessor is given the right to apply to the court for an order to sell or otherwise dispose of the goods. But certain conditions, both factual and procedural, must first be satisfied:

(i) *Either* the possessor is unaware of the identity or whereabouts of the person through whom he came into possession, *or* the person through whom he came into possession refuses or fails to relieve him of possession after having been given notice of the possessor's intention to apply for an order to sell or otherwise dispose of the goods.[26]

(ii) At least one month before making his application, the possessor of the goods must give notice of his intention to do so to the usual third-parties[27] and, where appropriate, to the person through whom he came into possession.[28]

The following people appear to be entitled to take advantage of Part VII: finders, hirers, gratuitous bailees, involuntary bailees, all those bailees for reward who do not come within Parts II, III or IV, buyers of goods who are entitled to reject them, bona fide purchasers who have since discovered that they do not have title to the goods, and persons to whom goods have been delivered by mistake. More doubtful is the case of the person who has taken possession of goods under a mistaken assumption that they are his own;[29] here, a court might be reluctant to dilute the possessor's responsibility for returning them to their true owner. Subject to this, the philosophy of this Part of the Western Australian Act is clearly desirable and might with advantage be reciprocated elsewhere.

The forms of order that may be made pursuant to s. 20 are laid down in Part VIII, which applies to all orders that may be awarded under the Act. Provision is made for the adaptation of orders to particular cases[30] and for the addition of certain specified charges by the bailee, such as storage and sale-expenses.[31] The court may impose conditions upon the disposal, such as the form it must take or any period which must elapse beforehand.[32] In every case, the power to make an order is subject to the terms of the bailment agreement[33] and no order can affect the right of any person to recover the goods by an action commenced before the goods are disposed of.[34] If such an action is commenced before disposal of the goods, the right to dispose is suspended until the action is resolved and extinguished if the action is successful.[35]

---

[25] Section 20.
[26] Sections 20(a) and (b). The notice must conform with Part IX of the Act.
[27] I.e. the Commissioner and potential claimants to the goods — ss. 21(b) and (c).
[28] Section 21(a). Again, the notice must conform with Part IX.
[29] Cf. *McCowan* v. *McCulloch* [1926] 1 D.L.R. 312, ante., p. 3.
[30] Section 22.
[31] Sections 22(3)(a), 22(3)(b); see also s. 22(5) (costs). Section 24 provides for the addition by the bailee of certain subsidiary charges arising subsequently to the granting of the order. The provision is in similar form to s. 14 of the N.S.W. Act, discussed at p. 406, ante, except that charges for storage are computed over a slightly different period.
[32] Sections 22(3)(c), 22(3)(d).
[33] Section 22(4).
[34] Section 23(2).
[35] Section 23(3); s. 23(4) deals with the time at which an action shall be deemed to have commenced.

When, pursuant to an order for sale, a bailee or other person in possession sells the goods, he is entitled to recover as a debt the amount by which the gross proceeds of the sale fall short of his authorised charges.[36] Conversely, any surplus may be recovered by the bailor or other person through whom possession was obtained.[37] Whatever the method of disposal, the person authorised to make it must prepare a record within seven days of disposing of the goods and file a copy within a fortnight of the disposal with the court which has made the order.[38] This record is open to inspection by interested parties;[39] non-compliance or false statements are, as usual, an offence.[40] The details that must be included in the record are substantially the same as those required when the goods are disposed of without a court order,[41] except that whereas in the present case no description of the goods is necessary, reference must be made to the order authorising the disposal.[42]

Part IX of the Act prescribes the form which notices must take under the Act. Here again, the rules are substantially similar to those in New South Wales but slightly more detailed. *All* notices must be in writing[43] and must contain the following information:

(a) the names and addresses of bailor and bailee[44]

(b) a sufficient description of the goods and their current situs[45]

(c) a statement indicating the Part of the Act pursuant to which the notice is given.[46] In addition, particular rules are propounded for individual types of notice.

(a) *Notices that goods are ready for redelivery*: These must additionally contain a statement that the goods are available for redelivery, the place at which they are available, the amount and method of calculation of any charges, and an indication that unless the bailor takes, or gives directions for, redelivery of the goods, or notifies the bailee in writing that he disputes any of the matters contained in the notice, the bailee will in accordance with the Act sell or otherwise dispose of the goods.[47]

(b) *Notices of intention to sell or otherwise dispose of goods*: The requisite additional information here consists of a statement that the goods are prescribed goods or are other goods to the value of a stated

---

[36] Defined in s. 25(1) as: (a) the amount specified in any order pursuant to s. 22(2); (b) the amount of any subsidiary charges properly levied in accordance with s. 24; and (c) the amount of any costs awarded to the person authorised to dispose of the goods in respect of the application for the order that are not otherwise recovered or accounted for under any other provisions of this Act. Recovery is from the bailor or other person through whom possession was obtained.

[37] Section 25(1).

[38] Section 25(2).

[39] Section 25(3).

[40] Section 25(4).

[41] See s. 14(4), p. 409, ante.

[42] Section 25(2)(a).

[43] Section 26(2).

[44] In cases falling under Part VII, there may be no true bailment and the possessor may not know the address of the person through whom he acquired possession. Accordingly, it is sufficient in such cases for the possessor to state his own name and address and to give an account of how the goods came into his possession, the place and date of possession and, where possible, the name and address of the person through whom that possession was acquired: s. 26(2)(a).

[45] Section 26(2)(b).

[46] Section 26(2)(c).

[47] Section 26(3).

amount not exceeding $300, the date upon which the bailee gave the bailor a redelivery notice, and an indication that unless the bailor within one month takes, or gives directions for, the redelivery of the goods, nor notifies the bailee in writing that he denies the characterisation of the goods as prescribed goods or as goods not exceeding $300, the bailee intends to sell or otherwise dispose of the goods.[48]

(c) *Notices of intention to apply for order of the court*: These must additionally state: the date on which any redelivery notice was given by the bailee, the manner and date of determination of any dispute between bailor and bailee, and an indication that unless the bailor (within one month of the giving of the present notice) takes, or gives directions for, the redelivery of the goods, the bailee intends to apply to the court for an order to sell or otherwise dispose of the goods in accordance with the Act.[49]

(d) *Notices to treat a dispute as determined*: These must contain the following additional information: the nature of the dispute and the manner in which it arose; the fact that the goods are ready for redelivery by bailee to bailor; the place at which they are so available; and an indication that unless, within a month after the giving of the present notice, the bailor takes, or gives directions for, redelivery of the goods, the bailee will sell or otherwise dispose of them in accordance with the Act.[50]

(e) *Application of surplus proceeds of sale*: Section 28 provides that any sum which has not been recovered within twenty-eight days of becoming recoverable under the Act shall be deposited by the person from whom it is recoverable with the State Treasurer.[51] Along with the surplus itself, there must also be lodged a copy of any record required to have been prepared[52] in connection with the sale and a certificate of the court as to the making and contents of any order that has been made.[53] Depositing the surplus proceeds with the Treasurer extinguishes all rights which any person may have had against the depositor in respect of the sum in question.[54] The Treasurer may pay any such sum to any person who appears to him to be entitled thereto; payment extinguishes the rights of any other person to recover that sum from the Treasurer.[55]

The remainder of Part IX deals with miscellaneous matters; the recovery of charges and expenses from a bailor who retakes possession of his goods after the serving of a redelivery notice but before they have been disposed of;[56] the passing of title to persons who acquire goods disposed of

---

[48] Section 26(4).
[49] Section 26(5).
[50] Section 26(6).
[51] Sections 28(1), 28(5).
[52] Section 28(1)(a); the provisions requiring records are ss. 14(4) and 25(2), discussed at pp. 409, 412, ante.
[53] Section 28(1)(b); such certificate "is evidence of the matters set forth therein"; s. 27.
[54] Section 28(2); failure to comply with the requirement is an offence: s. 28(3), as is the provision of any document for the purposes of s. 28(1) which is known to be false.
[55] Section 28(4).
[56] Section 29: In such a case, ". . . the bailee may in a court of competent jurisdiction, recover as a debt due to him from the bailor the reasonable and necessary expenses incurred by him in serving notices, in publication of advertisements, and in preparing for sale up to the time of payment."

under the Act;[57] the procedure to be followed in applying to the court;[58] the service and summary hearing of applications;[59] penalties;[60] and regulations.[61] In addition, it should be noted that the ambulatory provisions of the New South Wales Act[62] are substantially complemented in the present legislation.[63] On the other hand, the "non-derogation" clause[64] is more cautiously phrased; apart from being made specifically subject to s. 30 (which provides for the passing of title) it places a narrower perspective upon the residual rights of the bailor:

> . . . nothing in this Act shall be construed as derogating in any way from the rights or powers of any person, other than a bailor of goods to which this Act applies, conferred by or under another Act or by the rules of equity or common law, and all such rights and powers may continue to be exercised in the same manner as if this Act had not been passed.[65]

Taken overall, the Western Australian statute emerges as a rather more comprehensive and detailed version of its New South Wales counterpart. But whereas many of the differences are of a purely mechanical character, others transcend mere adaptation and represent significant departures from the scheme and ambit of the earlier legislation. It must, however, be noted that there are substantial areas, ostensibly within the Western Australian Act, from which it is specifically excluded. By virtue of s. 6, it cannot apply to any bailment, possession or other custody of goods to which the Acts mentioned in the Schedule apply. The Acts in question include the *Police Act* 1892, the *Warehousemen's Liens Act* 1952, the *Pawnbrokers Act* 1860, the *City of Perth Parking Facilities Act* 1959, and the *Metropolitan (Perth) Passenger Transport Trust Act* 1957.

4. *Victoria*: The *Disposal of Uncollected Goods Act* 1961, is a composite statute in which the basic legislation[66] has been modified by amendments passed in 1964[67] and 1972.[68] It was in Victoria that the first comprehensive legislation on the English model was passed, and some indications of its influence may be perceived in the New South Wales Act of 1966. There is, however, a much closer resemblance between the Victorian statute and its English ancestor.[69]

---

[57] Section 30(1); the aquisition of good title is conditional upon the disponee having no notice of any failure to comply with the Act or of a lack of title in the bailor or other person who delivered possession to the person making the disposal: ss. 30(1)(a) and (b). See also s. 30(2) (burden of proving compliance with Act upon bailee or equivalent).

[58] Section 31.

[59] Section 32, 33.

[60] Section 34: two hundred dollars or three months imprisonment or both.

[61] Section 35.

[62] Section 15, N.S.W. Act, discussed at p. 406, ante.

[63] Section 4(3): "Any reference in this Act to a bailor or bailee of goods shall, in respect of a period during which his rights and obligations in relation to the goods are vested in any other person, be construed as a reference to that other person."

[64] Section 16, N.S.W. Act, p. 406, ante.

[65] Section 5.

[66] *Disposal of Uncollected Goods Act* 1961.

[67] *Disposal of Uncollected Goods (Damaged Motor Cars) Act* 1964.

[68] *Disposal of Uncollected Goods (Amendment) Act* 1972.

[69] Thus, the bailee's right to sell exists for as long as the bailor has failed *either* to collect the goods *or* to pay the bailee's charges, whereas in N.S.W. the same

The Act is expressed to apply in identical terms, and to the same classes of bailment, as the English legislation;[70] the right to sell the goods arises in the same way as that of the English bailee[71] except that this right is expressly conditional upon the bailee's having no notice, before doing the work on the goods,[72] that they are comprised in a hire-purchase agreement which prohibits the creation of a lien by the hirer over the goods.[73] But the conditions which must be fulfilled before the goods can be sold are slightly different. For instance, there is a requirement as to the display of notices on the bailee's premises,[74] which is identical to the English provision[75] except that the warning contained in the notice must indicate that the Act confers a right of sale over the goods which is exercisable *not* after 12 months from the time when the goods are ready for redelivery but "after an interval of not less than one month from the date on which the goods are ready for redelivery or the date on which the bailor is informed is the date when they will be ready for redelivery (whichever is the later)" (sic).[76] Again, the requirements which relate to notices that the goods are ready for redelivery[77] are more complicated than those in England. When the time referred to in the previous subsection has passed, the bailee must (i) give to the bailor and to every other person actually known to him as having or claiming an interest in the goods a notice that the goods are ready for redelivery[78] and (ii) publish in a newspaper published in Melbourne and circulating throughout Victoria and in the district in which are situated the premises where the goods were accepted for repair or other treatment a notice of his intention to sell the goods. The latter notice may include other goods intended to be sold by the bailee under the Act.[79]

As in England, the bailee is not entitled to sell the goods as part of a lot which includes goods not delivered to him by the bailor.[80] However, he may in limited circumstances sell the goods other than by public auction

right can exist until both of these things have been performed (ante, p. 401); moreover, there is in the Victorian Act no provision for the judicial determination of disputes between bailor and bailee, as is found in s. 6(4) of the N.S.W. Act: ante, p. 402.

[70] Section 2(1) corresponding with s. 1(1) of the English (1952) Act, discussed at p. 397, ante.

[71] Section 2(2), corresponding with s. 1(2) of the English Act, discussed ibid.

[72] Note: "doing" not "performing". Arguably, this provision ceases to apply once the bailee has begun the work; sed quaere.

[73] Section 2(2); reciprocated in the N.S.W. Act; see s. 5, at p. 401, ante.

[74] Section 3(1)(a).

[75] Section 1(3)(a): p. 397, ante.

[76] Section 3(1)(a) of the Victorian Act of 1961, as amended by s. 2(a)(i) of the Act of 1972. Presumably, the amendment *should* read "or the date which the bailor is informed is the date . . .". If the bailee has insufficient particulars of the bailee's address to give the bailor a redelivery notice, he may sell the goods after six months from the date on which the goods are ready for redelivery without complying with the need to give a redelivery notice, provided he complies with the other provisions of s. 3: s. 3B of the 1961 Act, inserted by s. 3 of the Act of 1972.

[77] Section 1(3)(b) of the English Act of 1952.

[78] Section 3(1)(b) of the 1961 Act, as amended by s. 2(a)(ii)(b)(i) of the Act of 1972. The notice must comply with the requirements of s. 3(5) of the 1961 Act: ibid.

[79] Section 3(1)(b) of the 1961 Act, as amended by s. 2(a)(ii)(b)(ii) of the Act of 1972. Again, the notice must comply with s. 3(5) of the 1961 Act.

[80] Section 3(1A)(a) of the 1961 Act, inserted by s. 2(b) of the Act of 1972.

and dispose of them otherwise than by sale. Where such a disposal is *not* authorised by the Act,[81] the bailee must certify that in his opinion the best price cannot be obtained by a sale by public auction, or (according to the circumstances of the disposal) that the goods have no commercial value, and give reasons for that opinion.[82]

Any dispute arising before the goods are sold, involving the rate of the bailee's charges or the standard of his work and a refusal by the bailor to take (or give directions for) redelivery as a consequence thereof suspends the bailee's right of sale until the dispute has been determined.[83] The procedure for determination of such disputes by notice (and the effects of such determination) follow that in the English legislation[84] except that the terms of the necessary notice are slightly more detailed than are required in England.[85] Determination of a dispute causes the period which must elapse before the bailee can sell the goods to run from the date upon which the dispute was determined.[86]

The 1972 statute inserts special provisions relating to the disposal of goods which are certified by the bailee to be worth less than $20. The goods must still have been accepted by him in the course of business for repair or other treatment. In such a case, instead of sending a redelivery notice in accordance with s. 3(1)(b)(i) and publishing the requisite notice of intention to sell required by s. 3(1)(b)(ii), the bailee may send an account for the payment of his charges to the address of the bailor given to him by the bailor,[87] and a second account within not less than 14 days from the first.[88] Once the second account is sent, the bailee may sell the goods in accordance with s. 2, or dispose of them in any other way he considers appropriate, *provided* the bailor fails within six months of the sending of the first account both to pay the charges and to take, or give directions for, the delivery of the goods. Section 3A(3) applies to this modification (mutatis mutandis) the provisions in the principal Act which relate to the determination of disputes.[89]

---

[81] See post, p. 419.

[82] Section 3(1A)(b) of the 1961 Act, inserted by s. 2(b) of the Act of 1972.

[83] Section 3(2) of the 1961 Act, as amended by s. 2(c) of the Act of 1972.

[84] Section 1(5) of the Act of 1952; s. 3(3) of the Act of 1961.

[85] It must contain a sufficient description of the goods; the sum which the bailor claims to be due to way of charges in relation to the goods; and a statement that if the bailor fails within one month of the notice both to pay the said sum and take, or give directions for, delivery of the goods, the bailee is entitled to sell the goods in accordance with the Act without giving the bailor any further notice: s. 2(5) of the 1961 Act, as amended by s. 2(e) of the Act of 1972. This modification governs the form of *all* notices required under the Act, and not merely those relating to determination of disputes. In addition, all notices must be in writing (s. 4(1) of the 1961 Act) and may be given *either* by posting or delivering them personally to the bailor or other person having or claiming an interest in the goods *or* by leaving them at that person's last or most usual place of abode or business with some other person apparently an inmate thereof or employed thereat and apparently not less than sixteen years of age (ibid., s. 4(2)).

[86] Section 3(4) of the 1961 Act, as amended by s. 2(d) of the Act of 1972.

[87] Section 3A(1).

[88] Section 3A(2).

[89] Where at any time before the goods referred to in sub-s. (1) are sold or disposed of a dispute of a nature described in sub-s. (2) of s. 3 arises between the bailor and the bailee, then the provisions of sub-s. (2) and (3) of that section shall with all modifications that are necessary extend and apply to that dispute, and without

Section 5(1) of the principal Act makes the usual surplus/deficit provision[90] and s. 5(2) lays down the details that must be included in the bailee's post-disposal record of the goods. This must be prepared within, and kept available for, the usual seven-day and six-year periods respectively.[91] The relevant details are: (a) a sufficient description of the goods, (b) the date on which they were accepted for treatment, (c) the dates on which either the redelivery notice was given or the two accounts authorised by s.3A were sent, and in the latter case, the name and address of the person to whom they were sent, (d) the method, date and place of sale or disposal, (e) where the goods are sold by public auction, the name and principal place of business of auctioneer, (f) where the goods are disposed of other than by public auction, the reason for the action so taken, the name and address of the person or constitution to whom the goods are disposed of, the market value of the goods and the gross amount which the bailee believes they would have fetched at public auction, (g) the amount of the gross proceeds of the sale and (h) an itemised statement of the bailee's charges.[92]

Section 6(1)(a) of the principal Act embodies the usual amplification of the expression "goods accepted by a bailee in the course of a business for repair or other treatment".[93] Section 6(1)(b) further provides that this expression shall include goods accepted for examination for the purpose of ascertaining and quoting for the cost of repair; in such a case, the goods shall be deemed to be ready for redelivery on the date on which the quotation of the cost of repair is ready to be given to the bailor, or the date which the bailee is informed is the date upon which the quotation will be ready, whichever is the later.[94] Section 6(2) defines the expression "charges of the bailee" in terms identical to those in the New South Wales Act;[95] ss. 6(3) and 6(4) contain the orthodox provisions concerning the ambulatory nature of the Act [96] and its non-derogation of powers exercisable independently thereof.[97]

The 1964 Act adds a further section to the principal Act (s. 6A), dealing with damaged motor cars.[98] A tow-truck operator who lawfully and in the course of his business removes any damaged motor-car[99] shall be deemed to be a bailee of the car for repair or other treatment for the purposes of the Act.[1] This assumption, is, however, conditional upon s. 6A(4), which provides that nothing in s. 6A is to be construed as con-

affecting the generality of the foregoing, in particular with the modification that where the dispute is treated as having been determined the date on which it is so treated as having been determined shall be the date of the sending of the first account.

[90] See s. 7(1) of the N.S.W. Act, p. 402, ante.
[91] See s. 7(2) of the N.S.W. Act, p. 402, ante.
[92] Section 5(2) of the 1961 Act, as amended by s. 4 the Act of 1972.
[93] As modified by s. 5 of the Act of 1972. See s. 8(1) of the N.S.W. Act; p. 403, ante.
[94] Inserted by s. 5 of the Act of 1972.
[95] See s. 8(2) of the N.S.W. Act, p. 403, ante.
[96] See s. 15 of the N.S.W. Act, p. 403, ante.
[97] See s. 16 of the N.S.W. Act, p. 403, ante.
[98] Section 2 of the 1964 Act.
[99] Within the meaning of the *Motor Car Act* 1958.
[1] Section 6A(1).

ferring a right on any person to retain possession of the car for non-payment for repairs if such repairs were carried out without lawful written authority.

Section 6A(2) assimilates the tow-truck operator's position into the general machinery of the principal Act. Any reference in the Act to the date, or to any action taken subsequent to the date, on which goods are ready for redelivery, shall, when used in relation to a damaged motor car accepted in the manner indicated by s. 6A, be construed as a reference to the date etc. on which the car was received by the bailee.[2] The charges due to a bailee under the Act shall in this connection be taken to include reasonable expenses of towage and storage.[3] The relevant date of "commencement of this Act", as used in the principal Act, shall in relation to s. 6A be taken as the commencement of the amending legislation of 1964.[4] It may be suggested that the New South Wales provisions in regard to tow-truck operators,[5] although more abstruse, are probably more adequate and satisfactory than those contained in s. 6A of the Victorian Act.

Section 7 of the principal Act lays down special provisions for goods accepted before the commencement of that Act. Section 8 provides, in almost identical terms to s. 18 of the New South Wales Act,[6] for the passing of title in goods sold by virtue of the Act.[7] Section 9, which attempts to make provision for the owner of goods who is not their bailor, is clearly the forerunner of s. 16 of the Queensland Act, discussed below.[8] Under s. 10, special procedures are created for the sale of motor-cars[9] under the Act. These rules are substantially identical to those in force in Queensland and New South Wales.[10] The Victorian statute does, however, contain an additional subsection (s. 10(4)) which is not present in the New South Wales legislation, but which has been followed in Queensland.[11]

Section 11(1) of the principal Act, which gives directions for the disposal of surplus proceds of a sale by a bailee once he has deducted his charges, is again identical to the rule in the corresponding New South Wales legislation,[12] except that the Victorian statute does not specifically state that these procedures must be adopted within the relevant time "unless (the moneys) have previously been paid by (the bailee) to the person entitled thereto". Under s. 11(2), any such moneys which have not been paid by the bailee to the bailor or to the previous owner of the goods (as the case may be) within 22 months of being credited to a savings bank account under s. 11(1):

---

2 Section 6A(2)(a).
3 Section 6A(2)(b).
4 Section 6A(3).
5 Ante, p. 405.
6 Ante, p. 403.
7 Minimal modifications are made to the N.S.W. Act to cater for the fact that the goods may be sold by persons other than bailees; the Victorian Act applies only to goods "sold by a bailee". See also s. 8(2): burden of proving compliance with Act on seller.
8 Post, p. 423.
9 Within the meaning of the *Motor Vehicles Act* 1958.
10 The text of the Queensland section (s. 19) is set out at p. 421, post.
11 Ibid., s. 19(4).
12 Section 20(1) of the N.S.W. Act; p. 402, ante.

. . . shall within fourteen days after the expiration of such period be paid by the bailee together with any interest thereon to the receiver of revenue in Melbourne to be placed to the credit of the Unclaimed Moneys Fund.

Two further sections are added to the principal Act by s. 6 of the Act of 1972. By virtue of s. 12, the duty to keep a record under s. 5(2), and the penalty provisions of s. 5(3), are made to apply to bailees who dispose of uncollected goods "under an entitlement other than one obtained by virtue of the provisions of this Act": *provided* that the bailment is of the character described in s. 2(1)[13] and the goods are disposed of[14] by the bailee for non-payment of his charges and the failure of the bailor to take or give directions for the delivery of the goods.

Finally, s. 13 empowers the court to re-open a disposal under the Act where it considers that the method of sale or disposal or the price obtained either renders the transaction unfair to the bailor or makes it otherwise of such a kind that a Court of Equity would give relief.[15] The terms of this jurisdiction are amplified by subsections 13(2) and 13(3).

5. *Queensland*: The Queensland *Disposal of Uncollected Goods Act* 1967, is a fairly unambitious example of its type. Like the New South Wales statute,[16] it is divided into four parts, which deal respectively with preliminary matters, disposals other than by court order, disposals by court order and general considerations. But the scope of the Queensland Act is considerably narrower than that of many of its Australian counterparts. There is, for instance, no provision for gratuitous bailees, involuntary bailees or the other categories of unwilling possessor for whom the Western Australian Act lays down specific remedies.[17] The Act applies only to those bailments in which goods have been accepted by a bailee in the course of business[18] "whether before or after the commencement of this Act . . . for inspection, custody, storage, repair or other treatment."[19] The acceptance must, of course, be on the terms, express or implied, that the goods will be redelivered to the bailor or on his directions when they are ready for redelivery and the agreed charges are paid.[20] The Act makes no provision for disposals other than by sale.

---

[13] Page 415, ante.
[14] Note that the section is not confined to disposals by sale.
[15] Quaere whether the section is confined to sales? Section 13(1) begins "where in respect of any *sale of goods* under this Act" etc. but then provides for a re-opening where "because of the method of sale or *disposal*" the transaction is unfair to the bailee etc. Disposals other than by sale are, of course, only permitted under the Act when the bailee certifies the goods to be worth less than $20: see s. 3A, p. 416, ante., or where they have no commercial value: see s. 3(1A)(b), p. 400, ante.
[16] Ante, p. 400.
[17] Ante, p. 410.
[18] Section 3(3) contains the usual amplifying provision with regard to this expression; see s. 8(1) of the N.S.W. Act, discussed at p. 403, ante.
[19] These expressions shall include, where applicable, "the transport or towing of any goods to the premises used or appropriated by the bailee for acceptance for any such inspection, custody, storage, repair or other treatment as the case may be": s. 3(2)(b). The term inspection also includes, where appropriate, the acceptance of goods for the purposes of submitting a quotation for their repair or other treatment: s. 3(2)(c).
[20] Or, where no charge is agreed, a charge that is reasonable: s. 4. As to the identification of the time at which goods shall be deemed to be ready for

(a) *Disposal without court order*: Section 5 of the Act prescribes the circumstances which must exist before the potential right of disposal can come into existence; it is identical to s. 5 of the New South Wales legislation.[21] Section 6 enumerates the requirements that the bailee must himself fulfil before that right crystallises. There must be the usual notice displayed at the bailee's premises at the time when the goods were accepted[22] unless, of course, the goods were accepted before the coming into force of the Act.[23] A redelivery notice must be sent, after the goods are ready for redelivery or after the Act comes into force, whichever is the latter.[24] Again, the provision here is identical to that in New South Wales.[25] The rules relating to the statutory notice of intention to sell substantially follow those laid down in New South Wales,[26] with one significant exception. Where, at the time of giving the redelivery notice (or, if several have been given, at the time of the first) the amount which the bailee claims to be due to him by way of charges in relation to the goods exceeds 100 dollars, the bailee must obtain an order under Part III of the Act.[27] In such a case, s. 6(1)(d) does not apply. In all cases of disposal under Part II the goods must be sold by public auction in a lot in which no other goods are included.[28]

As to the effect and determination of disputes, s. 7(1) of the Queensland Act (suspensory effect) is a copy of s. 6(2) of the New South Wales legislation,[29] except that it applies *either* when a dispute arises before the bailee gives notice of intention to sell *or* when a dispute arises before the giving of notice of intention to apply to the court under Part III; s. 7(2) of the Queensland Act (determination of dispute by notice) corresponds in every material particular with s. 6(3) of the New South Wales Act;[30] s. 7(3) (procedure if bailor objects to having dispute treated as determined) is likewise congruent with the New South Wales s. 6(4);[31] and in subsidiary

redelivery, s. 3(2)(a) makes identical provision to s. 4(2) of the Western Australian statute; see p. 407, ante.

---

[21] *Disposal of Uncollected Goods Act* 1966; ante, p. 401.
[22] Section 6(1)(a), which is in this respect identical to s. 6(1)(a) of the N.S.W. Act, discussed at p. 401, ante.
[23] Like s. 9 of the N.S.W. Act, s. 8 of the Queensland statute provides separately for goods accepted before that time.
[24] Section 6(1)(b). The notice must comply with s. 6(2) of the Act, as to which see p. 421, post.
[25] Section 6(1)(b) of the N.S.W. Act; p. 401, ante.
[26] The relevant subsection in the Queensland Act is s. 6(1)(a), which corresponds with s. 6(1)(c) of the N.S.W. Act. The necessary newspaper notice must of course be published in a newspaper published in Brisbane, not in Sydney: s. 6(1)(d) (iii)(a). In addition, the same notice must be published in a newspaper, if any, published in the district in which are situated the premises where the goods were accepted for inspection, custody, storage, repair or other treatment: s. 6(1)(d) (iii)(b). Note also, that whereas in N.S.W. the notices of intention to sell must be given not less than fourteen days before the sale, in Queensland twenty-eight days must be allowed.
[27] Section 6(1)(c).
[28] Section 6(1)(e).
[29] Page 402, ante.
[30] Page 402, ante.
[31] Page 402, ante.

respects the Queensland statute is derived without material alteration from its New South Wales predecessor.[32]

Redelivery notices, notices of intention to treat a dispute as determined and notices of intention to sell are governed by s. 6(2) of the Queensland statute. This is again identical to s. 6(7) of the New South Wales Act,[33] except that the third of these notices must state that the bailor has 28 days in which to collect the goods and pay the charges, and not merely 14.[34] Post-sale procedure (s. 9) again corresponds closely to that in New South Wales,[35] except that the Queensland Act is adapted to encompass goods sold by order of the court under Part III as well as goods sold, without an order, under Part II. Thus, if the goods are sold by such an order, s. 9(2)(b) requires a reference to that order to be included in the customary record of the goods; and the bailee must lodge a copy of that record within 14 days of the sale with the clerk of the court that made the order,[36] where it may be inspected on payment of 20 cents by any person who had, or claims to have had, an interest in the goods.[37] Non-compliance is, as elsewhere, an offence.[38] It should be noted that, as in New South Wales, special details are required to be contained in the record and special procedures must be followed where the chattel disposed of is a motor-vehicle.[39]

(b) *Disposal by order of the court*: The right to apply for an order to sell the goods is extended to the bailee by s. 10 of the Queensland Act. The bailor must have failed either to pay or to tender the bailee's

---

[32] Thus, s. 7(4) Queensland equals s. 6(5) N.S.W.; s. 7(5) Queensland equals s. 6(6) N.S.W.; see ante, p. 402.

[33] Page 401, ante.

[34] Section 6(2)(b).

[35] Section 7; p. 402, ante.

[36] Section 9(4).

[37] Section 9(5).

[38] Section 9(6); see p. 403, ante.

[39] Section 19 of both Acts. See the extended definition of motor vehicle contained in s. 3(1) of the Queensland Act. Section 19 reads as follows: "*Special provisions applicable to sale of motor vehicles.* (1) Where the bailee of any motor vehicle intends to sell the motor vehicle by virtue of the provisions of this Act, he shall, not less than one month before the sale and before making any application for an order to sell the vehicle under Part III of this Act, give notice to the Commissioner of Police of his intention to sell, or to make application to sell, the vehicle, together with the particulars of the make, model type, colour, registration number, chassis number (if any), body number (if any), and engine number of the vehicle and how and when it came into his possession. Where any part of a motor vehicle is removed pursuant to the contract under which the goods were accepted by the bailee and the number thereof is required to be furnished under this subsection, the notice under this subsection shall include the number of the part so removed. (2) Upon receipt of any such notice and particulars, the Commissioner shall cause a search to be made of the records in his custody and shall forward to the bailee a certificate as to whether or not the motor vehicle referred to is for the time being recorded as stolen. (3) Any bailee who sells a motor vehicle by virtue of the provisions of this Act, or makes an application for an order under Part III of this Act to sell the vehicle, without first having obtained from the Commissioner of Police a certificate that the motor vehicle is not recorded for the time being as stolen, is guilty of an offence against this Act. (4) In any proceedings arising out of the sale of a motor vehicle by virtue of the provisions of this Act, a certificate purporting to be signed by the Commissioner of Police to the effect that any motor vehicle was or was not at any time stated in such certificate recorded as being stolen shall be *prima facie* evidence of the facts stated therein."

charges *or* to take delivery of the goods (or, where the terms of the bailment so provide, to give directions for their delivery).[40] The bailee must *either* have complied with s. 6(1)(b) of the Act (redelivery notice)[41] *or,* where the goods were accepted before the Act came into force and he does not, at the time of its coming into force, know any address of the bailor, have complied with ss. 8(1)(a) and 8(1)(b).[42] Application may be made even though the bailee's charges do not amount to the sum which makes such application compulsory, i.e. in excess of 100 dollars;[43] but no application may be made for as long as a dispute to which s. 7(1) relates is undetermined.[44] The applicant must delay for at least six months from giving the final redelivery notice[45] before making his application, unless he, at least 28 days before the application is made, gives notice of his intention to that effect to the bailor and to every other person who, at the time of giving notice, is known to him to claim or possess an interest in the goods.[46] In addition, the notice must be published in the same places as a notice of intention to sell under Part II.[47] The form of notice is prescribed by s. 10(7). It must contain a sufficient description of the goods (including the details specified in s. 19(1) where the chattel is a motor vehicle), a statement of the sum claimed by the bailee by way of charges, a statement of the date of the redelivery notice or, where appropriate, the date on which any dispute was determined,[48] and a statement that if the bailor fails within 28 days from the date of giving the notice to pay the stated sum or to take, or give directions for, delivery of the goods, application will be made to the court under s. 11 of the Act for an order authorising the bailee to sell the goods.[49]

When all of these requirements have been satisfied, and the relevant periods of six months and 28 days have elapsed, the court may grant an order in the form laid down in s. 11.[50] The powers of the court are broadly equivalent to those in New South Wales[51] and many of the ancillary provisions are identical.[52] But s. 11(b) has no counterpart in the earlier

[40] Sections 10(1)(a), 10(1)(b).
[41] Page 420, ante.
[42] These are not discussed because of their diminishing importance. See ss. 10(1)(c), 10(1)(d).
[43] Section 10(2).
[44] Section 10(3).
[45] He need, of course, give only one. Where a dispute has arisen and been determined, the six months runs from the date on which the dispute was determined: s. 10(b).
[46] Sections 10(4)(a), 10(4)(b).
[47] See s. 10(4)(c), which corresponds with s. 6(1)(d)(iii), p. 420, ante. Section 10(5) deals with goods accepted before the commencement of the Act where the bailee did not know of any address of the bailor.
[48] Section 10 (7)(a).
[49] Section 10(7)(b).
[50] The relevant court is a Magistrates Court held in the Magistrates Courts District in which are situated the premises where the goods were accepted for the relevant treatment: ss. 11(1), 3(1), 11(11).
[51] Sections 12(2) to 12(4), N.S.W.; ss. 11(2) to 11(4), Queensland.
[52] E.g. s. 11(5) Queensland equals s. 12(5) N.S.W. (ante, p. 406); s. 11(7) Queensland equals s. 12(b) N.S.W. (ante, p. 405); s. 11(10) Queensland equals s. 12(10) N.S.W. (ante, p. 406). Note, however, that whereas in N.S.W., the court may order the applicant to delay selling the goods for up to six months, s. 12(3)(g), in Queensland the sale can be delayed by order only for a maximum of twenty-eight days: s. 11(3)(d). Moreover, whereas in N.S.W. an order does

legislation. It provides that where at the time of the giving of the final redelivery notice the amount claimed by the bailee exceeds 100 dollars, the court shall not make an order authorising the sale of the goods unless the bailee has obtained an order in writing for the repair of the goods signed by or an behalf of the bailor or the court is satisfied that it was reasonable in the circumstances that such an order was not obtained. Strangely, this subsection appears to apply only to charges for the *repair* of the goods, and not to charges for other treatment.

Part IV of the Act, which deals with general matters, contains the following provisions which are materially identical to their New South Wales equivalents: s. 12 (ambulatory operation of the Act);[53] s. 13 (non-derogation of other powers);[54] s. 14 (notices);[55] s. 15 (buyer acquires a good title).[56]

But in other respects there is divergence, either because the Queensland provisions are different from their New South Wales counterparts or because they are not complemented in the earlier legislation at all.

An example of the former is s. 20, dealing with the disposal of nett proceeds of the sale. Any surplus remaining after the bailee has deducted his charges[57] must within 14 days, and unless previously handed over to the person entitled thereto, be paid to the Public Curator: s. 20(1). If the surplus is paid by the bailee to the person entitled, the bailee must also provide that person with a copy of the record he has compiled under s. 9(2): s. 20(2). The Curator shall hold the money for the person entitled thereto for six years, after which it becomes unclaimed money, disposable in accordance with the *Public Curator Acts* 1915 to 1957: s. 20(3).

Into the latter category fall a number of sections which serve to tie up loose ends. Section 16 provides that an owner of goods who was not the bailor shall not be entitled to recover the goods once they are sold but shall have the same rights in respect of the proceeds of the sale "as he would have had in respect of the goods if the property had not passed to the buyer" by virtue of the Act. This section is confusing and would appear to disentitle the bailee from deducting his charges before handing the proceeds over.

not prevent a person from recovering the goods by an action brought within six months of the order, s. 12(7), in Queensland the action must be brought before the sale under the order takes place: s. 11(8). If such an action *is* brought, s. 11(9) of the Queensland Act has the same suspensory effect as s. 12(8) of the N.S.W. Act; see p. 406, ante.

[53] Section 15, N.S.W.; p. 403, ante.
[54] Section 16, N.S.W.; p. 403, ante.
[55] Section 17, N.S.W.; p. 403, ante; except that s. 14(2)(c) of the Queensland Act does not include the concluding words "or business".
[56] Section 18, N.S.W.; p. 403, ante; except that whereas the N.S.W. section applies the "goods sold by virtue of the provisions of this Act", the Queensland section applies to goods sold "*by a bailee* in the exercise *or purported exercise* of his powers under this Act". Also the N.S.W. section caters for the fact that the applicant may not be a bailee and that therefore there may be no bailor whose title can be defective: see s. 11 of the N.S.W. Act, p. 405, ante. On the other hand, the Queensland section requires *in all cases* that the purchaser have no knowledge of any defect of title in the bailor, since it applies only to bailees.
[57] As to the definition of charges of the bailee and subsidiary charges, see ss. 3(4) and 3(5) respectively.

Under s. 17(1), any person claiming an interest or right of possession in the goods may pay the bailee (such payment to include reasonable and necessary expenses for notices, advertisements and preparations for sale) before the goods are sold. Upon such payment being made, the bailee seems to be required to exercise a judicial faculty in deciding whether to hand over the goods to the payor. Delivery *must* be made if the person making the payment is the person entitled to the possession of the goods on payment of the bailee's charges thereon. Otherwise, the bailee shall retain possession of the goods according to the contract (express or implied) for the acceptance of the goods: s. 17(2). Not an enviable decision.

Section 18 implies in every bill of sale or other encumbrance in respect of any goods in favour of the grantee or encumbrancee a convenant that any payment made by him in relation to those goods under s. 17 shall be added to or be deemed to be included in the principal moneys secured by the Bill of Sale or other encumbrance.

Further privileges are extended to the owner who is not a bailor by s. 21. At any time after the redelivery notice has been given to the bailor, he may, at a reasonable time and on reasonable notice to the bailee, enter the latter's premises on which "the goods are kept under the bailment" and inspect them: s. 20(1). Failure to acknowledge this rights entitles the court at its discretion to refuse an order under s. 11: s. 20(2).

Section of the Act deals with penalties, s. 23 with regulations to be made thereunder, and s. 24 provides that the *Warehousemen's Liens Act* 1938, and the *Possessory Liens Act* 1942, are henceforth repealed.

6. *Tasmania*: The relevant Tasmanian statute is the *Disposal of Uncollected Goods Act* 1968. It bears a closer resemblance to the New South Wales Act, both in scope and in arrangement, than any other legislation in this field. The following Tasmanian provisions are substantially analogous to those enacted in New South Wales: s. 2(3) (ambulatory nature of the Act);[58] s. 3(1) (class of bailments under which goods may be sold without court order;[59] s. 3(2) (amplification of acceptance "in the course of a business");[60] ss. 4(1) and 4(2) (circumstances which must exist before bailee's entitlement to sell without court order can arise);[61] s. 5 (procedure to be followed by bailee before right to sell without court order can be exercised);[62] ss. 6(1) to 6(3)

[58] See s. 15 of the N.S.W. Act; p. 403, ante.
[59] See s. 4 of the N.S.W. Act, p. 401, ante: other Parts of the N.S.W. Act encompass a wider class of bailment, but the Tasmanian provisions relating to disposals without a court order, like those in N.S.W., are confined exclusively to the sort of bailment to which Part II of the N.S.W. Act applies.
[60] See s. 8(1) of the N.S.W. Act, p. 403, ante.
[61] See s. 5 of the N.S.W. Act, p. 401, ante.
[62] See s. 6(1) of the N.S.W. Act, p. 401, ante. Note, however, that the Tasmanian Act imposes no requirement as to notices displayed on the bailee's premises; that a copy of the redelivery notice must be sent to the Commissioner of Police as well as to the bailor and to other persons claiming an interest in the goods; that the notice of intention to sell must be given not less than *one month* before the sale (as well as not less than six months after the redelivery notice); and that the notice of intention to sell need not be published in a newspaper. As in N.S.W. the bailee may only sell the goods by public auction and must not include with them goods not accepted by the bailee from the bailor: ss. 8(1), 8(3). See further s. 8(3).

(suspensory effect of disputes and determination thereof by notice);[63] s. 9 (procedure after sale);[64] s. 10 (charges of the bailee);[65] s. 12 (circumstances in which bailee for repair or other treatment may apply for an order to sell the goods);[66] s. 13 (circumstances in which other bailees for reward and gratuitous bailees may apply for such an order);[67] s. 14 (powers of court to make orders for sale);[68] s. 15 (effects of order);[69] s. 16 (procedure after sale by order);[70] s. 17 (application of surplus proceeds of sale);[71] s. 18 (title of purchaser);[72] s. 21 (general form and service of notices);[73] s. 22 (non-derogation); s. 23 (penalties) and s. 24 (regulations).[74]

In addition, there is a section which caters for goods accepted before the commencement of the Act[75] and a somewhat lesser degree of special

[63] See ss. 6(2), 6(3) of the N.S.W. Act, p. 402, ante. Under s. 5(3) of the Tasmanian Act, no redelivery notice is needed when there has arisen a dispute of the kind referred to in s. 6(1), and the notice of intention to sell must be given within six months of the determination of the dispute; cf. s. 6(6) of the N.S.W. Act, p. 402, ante.

[64] See s. 7 of the N.S.W. Act, p. 402, ante.

[65] See s. 8 of the N.S.W. Act, p. 403, ante. Note, however, that the Tasmanian Act explicitly confines any recovery for the cost of insuring the goods to the period referred to in s. 10(a).

[66] See ss. 10(1)(a), 10(2) of the N.S.W. Act, p. 404, ante. Note, however, that s. 12(3) of the Tasmanian legislation is not reciprocated in the N.S.W. Act: "The court shall not, on an application under this section, make an order for the sale of goods unless it is satisfied that the goods were ready for redelivery at least six months before the making of the application".

[67] See ss. 10(1)(b), 10(1)(c), and 10(2) of the N.S.W. Act, p. 404. Note that there is no Tasmanian equivalent to s. 10(3) of the N.S.W. Act, p. 404, ante. See also s. 13(4) of the Tasmanian Act (bailor's directions for delivery equivalent to redelivery for purposes of ss. 13(1) and 13(2)).

[68] See s. 12 of the N.S.W. Act, p. 405, ante.

[69] Ibid. and s. 14 (subsidiary charges).

[70] Section 13 of the N.S.W. Act, p. 405, ante. Note that under s. 16(1)(b) of the Tasmanian Act the bailee is entitled to add his costs to the other charges authorised by the section in arriving at the surplus (if any) produced by the gross proceeds of the sale.

[71] Section 20 of the N.S.W. Act, p. 402, ante. Note, however, that there is no Tasmanian equivalent to s. 20(1) of the N.S.W. Act, requiring the bailee to deposit such proceeds in a savings bank account until such time as they are to be delivered to the Treasurer. Moreover, the bailee, when making this delivery, need not include any interest accumulated on the surplus up till that time. Sections 17(3) and 17(4) of the Tasmanian Act also disclose a slightly different approach to the question of recovery from the Treasurer, and the effects of such restitution: "(3) Subject to subsection (4) of this section, a person who is entitled to recover any sum referred to in subsection (1) of this section that is deposited with the Treasurer under that subsection has the like rights against the Treasurer in respect of the recovery of that sum as he had against the person by whom they were so deposited. (4) The Treasurer may pay any sum deposited with him under this section to a person appearing to him to be entitled thereto and if any sum is so paid the rights of any other person in respect of the recovery of that sum from the Treasurer are extinguished."

[72] See s. 18 of the N.S.W. Act, p. 403, ante. The first ten words of s. 18(1)(b) of the Tasmanian Act appear to be based on a misapprehension.

[73] See s. 17 of the N.S.W. Act, p. 403, ante. Note that a notice that is posted must, under the Tasmanian s. 21(c) be sent by registered post; both here and under s. 21(b) a notice may be sent to or left at a last known or *usual* place of abode or business.

[74] See ss. 16, 21 and 22 respectively of the N.S.W. Act; pp. 403, 406-407, ante.

[75] Section 11. Neither this nor the N.S.W. provision (s. 9) will be discussed in this work, but it should be noted that the two sections do not wholly coincide: e.g. s. 9(1)(a) of the N.S.W. Act specifies a period of one month, after the commencement of the Act before the bailee may publish the statutory news-

treatment for the sale of motor vehicles under the Act.[76] Section 5(2) of the Tasmanian Act provides that without prejudice to s. 5(1) (which lays down the requirements of redelivery notices and notices of intention to sell) no bailee is entitled to sell a motor-vehicle under s. 4 of the Act unless, at least six months before giving notice of his intention to sell, he publishes in the *Gazette* a notice containing sufficient particulars to identify the vehicle, and stating that the bailee intends to proceed to exercise his rights under this Act in respect of the vehicle.

In fact, there are only two substantial differences between the Tasmanian and the New South Wales legislation. First, there is no provision in Tasmania for tow-truck operators.[77] Secondly, the Tasmanian statute imposes more individual requirement for particular notices under the Act. All notices to which s. 7 applies (i.e. redelivery notices, notices of intention to sell and notices to treat a dispute as determined)[78] must contain a sufficient description of the goods[79] and (where relevant) a statement of the bailee's charges, specifying the amount of the sum and the manner in which it has been calculated.[80] In addition, the following individual details must be included:

(a) *Notices that goods are ready for redelivery and notices to treat disputes as determined*: The required details are: a statement that the goods are available for collection by the bailor at the place specified in the notice,[81] and a statement that if the bailor fails, within six months of the giving of the notice, both to pay any charges due and to take (or give directions for) the delivery and of the goods, the goods are liable to be sold in accordance with the Act.[82]

(b) *Notices of intention to sell goods*: These must additionally contain: a statement of the date on which the bailor was given notice that the goods were ready for redelivery (or, where there has been a dispute, the date on which the dispute was determined);[83] and a statement that if the bailor fails, within a month of the giving of the notice, both to pay any charges of the bailee and to take, or give directions for, redelivery of the goods, the goods are liable to be sold in accordance with the Act.[84]

Finally, it should be noted that there are slight differences between the Tasmanian machinery for the curial determination of disputes and those which operate in New South Wales. If the bailor objects, within one month of the giving of notice to treat a dispute as determined, to having the dispute so treated, either party may then apply to the court for an order

paper notice, whereas under s. 11(1)(a) of the Tasmanian Act the corresponding period is three months.

---

[76] Cf. s. 19 of the N.S.W. Act, which is identical in all material respects to s. 19 of the Queensland Act, set out at p. 421, ante. In Tasmania, "motor vehicle" means a motor vehicle within the meaning of the *Traffic Act* 1925: s. 2(1).
[77] Cf. ss. 11, 12(1)(b) of the N.S.W. Act, p. 405, ante.
[78] Notices of intention to apply for a court order are dealt with under s. 13(3) of the Tasmanian Act, as to which, see p. 425, ante.
[79] Section 7(2)(a).
[80] Section 7(2)(b).
[81] Section 7(3)(a).
[82] Section 7(3)(b).
[83] Section 7(4)(a).
[84] Section 7(4)(b).

specifying a reasonable amount in respect of the bailee's charges.[85] When such an order has been made, the dispute shall be deemed to have been determined for the purposes of the Act and the amount specified shall be deemed to be the amount of the bailee's charges,[86] subject to the additional amounts empowered by s. 10[87] and to any costs awarded in respect of the application which may be added to or subtracted from the bailee's charges according to the party to whom they are awarded.[88]

Sections 2(1) and 2(2) deal with the interpretation of "hire-purchase agreement" for the purposes of the Act; these provisions are slightly more detailed than those in New South Wales.

7. *South Australia*: South Australia is the only state in which there is no separate legislation dealing with the disposal of uncollected goods. However, provisions to this effect are contained in the *Workmen's Liens Act* 1893. Under s. 41 of this legislation:

> Every person who has bestowed work or materials upon any chattel or thing in altering the condition thereof, or improving the same, and who is entitled to a lien on such chattel or thing at common law, may, while such lien exists, if the amount due to him in respect of such lien remains unpaid for one month after the same has become due, sell such chattel or thing by public auction, upon giving to the owner thereof, or posting to him in his last known place of abode in South Australia fourteen days before such sale, a notice in writing, by registered letter, stating the amount of the debt, a description of the chattel or thing to be sold, the time and place of sale, and the name of the proposed auctioneer.

Section 42 deals with the procedure that must be followed after sale. First, of course, the proceeds must be applied in payment of the sum in relation to which the lien existed and of costs arising from the sale. Any surplus must be paid forthwith to the clerk of the local court nearest to the place of sale, to be held by him for the benefit of the person entitled thereto. Power is given to a special magistrate, on the application of such a person, to order payment of such money to him.

Although the context of the South Australian Act necessarily limits the classes of bailment, and other species of possession, to which it can apply,[89] there is much to be said for the clarity and simplicity of its procedural requirements. At present, most of the state legislation in this field is rather more abstruse and complicated than seems appropriate, in view of the likely frequency of the problem and the likely value of the goods involved; conversely, it seems probable that such legislation is not utilised as often as it should be.

---

[85] Section 6(4); "court" means a court of petty sessions constituted by a police magistrate sitting alone: s. 2(1).
[86] Section 6(5).
[87] Page 425, ante: s. 6(7).
[88] Section 6(6).
[89] Thus, for instance, it would not normally apply to carriers, warehousemen, hirers, recipients of goods sent on approval, gratuitous bailees, involuntary bailees or finders; cf. the West Australian Act, p. 407 et seq., ante.

V. Unsolicited Goods

Substantial legislative machinery now exists to combat the commercial practice of sending unsolicited goods to potential purchasers and requiring the recipients either to purchase or to return them.[90] In Australia, each State possesses legislation dealing with this problem; in addition, the matter is covered by the *Commonwealth Trade Practices Act, 1974.* In England, the matter is dealt with by the *Unsolicited Goods and Services Acts,* 1971 and 1975.

A. Commonwealth

Under s. 65(1) of the *Trade Practices Act,* the recipient's duty is reduced to the barest minimum; provided the goods are unsolicited and have been supplied by a corporation in trade or commerce, he is liable only for loss or damage to the goods which results "from the doing by him of a wilful and unlawful act in relation to the goods". The period of this immunity extends from the time he receives them up until the time when they are either collected by the sender or become the recipient's own property in accordance with the Act. It is difficult to judge what, precisely, amounts to a "wilful and unlawful act"; negligence is obviously excluded by the use of the word "wilful" but conversion of the kind that potentially existed in *Elvin and Powell Ltd.* v. *Plummer Roddis Ltd.*[91] (i.e. by innocent misdelivery) may not be. The result may be a widening of the liability formerly assumed to exist in the case of the involuntary bailee, because a conversion is ex hypothesi wilful although there is no intention to deny the owner's title or to deprive him of the goods.[92] On the other hand, to read the Act as referring only to deliberate (i.e. malicious) damage, destruction or disposal of the goods would mean that even a misdelivery might no longer render the recipient liable. It is probable that the latter interpretation will be preferred.

In addition to defining the recipient's duty of care, s. 65(1) provides that he "is not liable to make any payment for the goods".[93] Section 65 lays down several courses of action for the recipient. He may give notice in writing to the sender,[94] stating his name and address, the address (if different) at which possession may be retaken by the sender, and the fact that the goods are unsolicited.[95] In this event, the sender (or any corporation claiming under the sender) loses the right to recover the goods from the recipient, whose property they become free of all liens and charges, upon the expiration of one month after the giving of notice or three months after the initial receipt of the goods, whichever happens

---

[90] According to one English commentator, the legislation has proved a powerful deterrent in every area except that of the charity Christmas card: see "The Unsolicited" (1973) 138 *Local Government Review,* p. 916.

[91] (1933) 50 T.L.R. 158; ante., p. 388.

[92] Cf. *Arrowsmith* v. *Jenkins* [1963] 2 Q.B. 561; the offence of "wilfully" obstructing the highway is committed by one who intentionally performs the act which in fact amounts to an obstruction, whether he specifically intended the obstruction or not.

[93] Aliter, presumably, if he accepts the transaction and communicates an intention to buy them before the statutory periods have expired.

[94] Section 65(4)(a).

[95] Section 65(5).

sooner.[96] Alternatively, the recipient need do nothing at all; in this event, the goods become his after three months.[97] But whichever course is adopted, the recipient must not during the relevant period have unreasonably prevented the sender or owner from retaking possession.[98] If this has occurred, or if the recipient knew or ought to have known that the goods were not intended for him,[99] or (of course) if the sender has already recouped the goods,[1] then neither the immunity from recovery nor the property in the goods can be enjoyed by the recipient.[2] The moral for recipients is clear; send the notice as soon as possible and keep quiet for the next month. University lecturers and professional practitioners who receive books on approval from publishers are, however, among the many people who may not take advantage of s. 65; for according to subsection (6):

> This section does not apply in relation to a person who receives unsolicited goods if the person ordinarily uses like goods in the course of his profession, business, trade or occupation.

What happens if, before the goods become his property, the recipient wilfully and unlawfully damages them? The position is doubtful, but it seems that the sender's right to sue for the damage will terminate with his property in the goods; and the same rule may apply if he sells goods to a third party before taking action for prior damage.[3] This problem is unlikely to arise in practice.

Under section 64(1), corporations are forbidden from asserting a right to payment for unsolicited goods,[4] unless they have reasonable cause to believe that there is a right to payment,[5] or unless the person against whom the right is asserted ordinarily uses like goods in the course of his profession, business, trade or occupation.[6] Similar provisions exist in respect of unsolicited directory entries.[7]

In dealing with the question of the recipient's title after the relevant periods have expired the Commonwealth Act is somewhat ambivalent. Section 65(2)(a) provides that neither the sender-corporation *nor any person claiming under it* can, after expiry of the relevant period, take action against the recipient for recovery of the goods, thereby suggesting that persons not claiming under the sender may still pursue such action; but s. 65(2)(b) provides that at the same time the goods become "the property" of the recipient "freed and discharged from all liens and charges of any description", which suggests that a further exception to the nemo dat principle is created and that the section operates to extinguish all third-party liens and charges, whether they be asserted under the corporation or not. On the other hand, ownership can scarcely qualify

---

[96] Section 65(4)(a).
[97] Section 65(4)(b).
[98] Section 65(3)(a).
[99] Section 65(3)(c).
[1] Section 65(3)(b).
[2] But it seems that s. 65(1) still applies to govern the recipient's duty of care.
[3] Cf. p. 70 et seq., ante.
[4] Section 64(5) defines what is meant by asserting a right to payment.
[5] The onus of proving this is on the corporation: s. 64(9)(a).
[6] Section 64(2).
[7] See ss. 64(3) to 64(10).

as a lien or charge and it is likely that if, for instance, the sender were a thief, the owner of the goods would not be debarred from recovering them from a recipient who had acquired "property" by virtue of s. 65. It is suggested that s. 65 be read as restrictively as possible on any question which involves its application to third parties, for the essentially deterrent quality of the section can scarcely be relevant to a stranger who neither qualifies as a sender within the Act nor claims under the sender-corporation.

B. Victoria

The Victorian provisions[8] are similar to the Federal legislation, but possess that greater amplitude of detail that is sometimes characteristic of state enactments. Under s. 24, the recipient of unordered goods[9] is not liable to make any payment for them and is not liable for any loss or injury to the goods unless it arises from his wilful and unlawful disposal, destruction or damaging of the goods during the relevant period. The provisions as to time-periods, notices and defeating conditions are broadly the same as in the Commonwealth legislation; thus s. 22(2) (circumstances in which property may not pass), corresponds with s. 65(3) of the Federal Act, s. 22(3) (time which must elapse before the goods become the recipient's) with s. 65(4) of the Federal Act, s. 22(4) (contents of notices) with s. 65(5) of the Federal Act[10] and s. 22(1) (quality of recipient's title) to s. 65(2)(b) of the Federal Act. There is, however, no Victorian equivalent to s. 65(2)(a) of the Federal legislation,[11] disentitling the sender-corporation or anyone claiming under it from taking action, after the expiry of the relevant period, for the recovery of the goods. Assertion of a right to payment is an offence,[12] unless the defendant can prove that he reasonably believed the goods had been required by the recipient, that if such a request had been made the goods actually sent would not have been unordered goods, and that, where he became aware or ought to have become aware, after dispatch, that such a request had not been made, he had informed the recipient that he was not liable to pay for the goods.[13] It is also an offence to perform certain acts directed to the enforcement of any payment for unsolicited goods — viz, asserting an intention to bring legal proceedings, publishing the alleged debtor's name, or invoking any other collection procedure; a

---

[8] Sections 21 to 32 of the *Consumer Protection Act* 1972, as amended by the *Consumer Protection (Unordered Goods and Services Amendment) Act* 1974.
[9] Defined in s. 21(1) as "goods that have been sent whether from a place within or without the state by a person in the course of a trade or business to a person within the State with a view to that person acquiring or hiring those goods or an interest in those goods where that person has not requested that the goods be so sent to him". If the sender sends goods of a kind similar to the goods that a person has requested, with a view to satisfying that request, the goods sent are not (for that reason alone) ordered goods: s. 21(2). For the circumstances in which a person shall not be deemed to have requested goods, see s. 27(3).
[10] Except that under s. 22(4)(d) the notice must additionally contain a description of the goods sufficient to identify them, which is not required under the Federal legislation.
[11] Ante, p. 429.
[12] Section 23(1).
[13] Section 23(3).

defendant may, however, escape liability if he had reasonable cause to believe that he had the right to assert the right to payment.[14] The Act also deals with directory entries, which are not germane to the present discussion. Finally, it should be noted that for the purposes of the Act, the expression "sender" includes a person on whose behalf the goods were sent and any person claiming through or under him or the actual sender;[15] and that there is special provision for offences by corporations.[16]

C. Western Australia

The material portions of the Western Australian *Unsolicited Goods and Services Act* 1973 are substantially similar to those in Victoria. However, the liability of the recipient in relation to the goods during the relevant period is cast in terms identical to that in the Commonwealth statute[17] rather than in the phraseology adopted in Victoria; and s. 7(3)(a) of the Act is the forerunner of s. 65(2)(a) of the Federal legislation.[18] Moreover, there is an additional circumstance (not present in either the Victorian or the Commonwealth legislation) in which the property in the goods is expressed not to pass to the recipient under the Western Australian Act: viz., where "the goods were the subject of a lien or charge of any description at the time when the goods were received by the recipient, in circumstances in which he knew, or might reasonably be expected to have known, that the goods were the subject of such a lien or charge.[19]

On the other hand, there is no equivalent of s. 22(4)(d) of the Victorian Act[20] and s. 11 defines in rather wider terms the circumstances in which a person shall be deemed to have asserted a right to payment for unsolicited goods. Offences by corporations are dealt with by ss. 16 and 17; these also are somewhat more detailed than the relevant Victorian provision. The Western Australian Act also makes provision for the making of charges for directory entries and the rendering of certain unrequested services.

D. New South Wales

The *Unsolicited Goods and Services Act* 1974 is the most recent state enactment in this field and bears a close resemblance both to the *Trade Practices Act* 1974 and the Western Australian *Unsolicited Goods and Services Act* 1973. The correspondence is particularly marked in the section which lays down the recipient's liability for loss of or injury to the goods (s. 4(2)), and in the section which enumerates the circumstances in which the recipient's prescriptive title to the goods may fail to accrue (s. 4(5)); however, it should be noted that the New South Wales legislation has no provision equivalent to the Western Australian s. 7 (4)(d).[21]

14 Section 28. Note that there is no provision here as to the burden of proof.
15 Section 21(1).
16 Section 31.
17 Ante, p. 428.
18 Ante, p. 429.
19 Section 7(4)(d).
20 Ante, p. 430.
21 Ante,

So far as concerns the "relevant period" which must elapse before the goods become the recipient's, s. 4(b) of the New South Wales Act requires notice (in identical terms to that required in Western Australia) to be given within *two months* of the date of receipt of the goods; if this is given, the recipient's right to the goods accrues one month after the date of the giving of that notice. Where no proper notice is given, the relevant period in three months. Finally, it should be noted that some of the definitions in the New South Wales Act are more detailed than those in the Western Australian Statute, and that the Act is not confined (like its federal counterpart) to goods sent by a corporation in trade or commerce.

E. South Australia and Queensland

The relevant statutes are the *Unsolicited Goods and Services Act* 1972, and the *Unsolicited Goods and Services Act* 1973[22] respectively. These again are almost identical to the Victorian Act, the only material difference being that a recipient's notice need not contain a description of the goods. The Acts are therefore far closer to the Victorian statute than to their Western Australian equivalent.

F. Tasmania

The Tasmanian *Unordered Goods and Services Act* 1973 (as amended by the *Unordered Goods and Services Act* (*No. 2*) 1973) is again almost identical to in all material respects the foregoing enactments, except that the "relevant period" which must elapse before the goods become the property of the recipient is only *one* month in the case of a notice given by the recipient to the sender under s. 4(4) of the Act.[23] The notice in question (which must be in writing) need merely "require the sender to take possession of the goods", but it must be sent by certified mail.

G. England

The English *Unsolicited Goods and Services Acts* 1971 and 1975 are of similar effect to the Commonwealth statute, but somewhat broader in scope, since they also make it an offence to send unsolicited material which describes or illustrates human sexual techniques (s. 4)[24] and are not restricted to goods sent by corporations.[25] The periods in question are also somewhat different: six months from receipt of the goods where the recipient does not send the statutory notice[26] or thirty days from the date

---

[22] Minor amendments were made to the Queensland Statute by the *Unordered Goods and Services Act Amendment Act* 1974. They are not relevant to the present discussion.

[23] Section 4(3).

[24] See, on this point, *D.P.P.* v. *Beate Uhse* [1974] 1 All E.R. 753.

[25] The goods must have been sent to the recipient with a view to his acquiring them (and acquire includes hire: s. 6(1); the recipient must have no reasonable cause to believe that they were sent with a view to their being acquired for the purposes of a trade or business; and he must neither have agreed to acquire or return them: s. 1(2).

[26] Section 1(2)(a). For the necessary terms of the notice, (which may be sent by post) see s. 4(3), which requires it to state (a) the recipient's name and address and, if possession of the goods may not be taken by the sender at that address, the address at which possession might be taken; and (b) that the goods are unsolicited. As to the definition of "sender", see s. 4(4).

of giving notice in cases where such notice is given;[27] in both cases providing the sender has not retrieved the goods beforehand. The notice must contain the same information to that laid down by the *Trade Practices Act 1974*. Upon the expiration of the relevant period, the recipient may:

> . . . as between himself and the sender, use, deal with or dispose of them as if they were an unconditional gift to him, and any right of the sender to the goods is hereby extinguished.   (Section 1(1))

There is no definition of the duty owed by the recipient in relation to the goods before the relevant period has expired and it is to be assumed that the Common Law rules continue to apply. Again, the recipient's untrammelled right to deal with the goods does not arise where the recipient has reasonable cause to believe that they were sent with a view to their being acquired for the purposes of a trade or business; or where he has agreed either to acquire or to return them.[28] Sections 1(2)(a) and (b) contain provisions equivalent to s. 65(3)(a) of the *Trade Practices Act* displacing the effect of s. 1 where the recipient has unreasonably refused to permit the sender to retrieve them. The Act also deals with demands for payment for unsolicited goods (which, in certain circumstances, are made an offence under s. 4), unrequested directory entries,[29] and the circumstances in which the members and senior officers of a corporation may be guilty of an offence under the Act.[30]

The cautiously relative wording of s. 1(1) suggests that the Act will not operate to extinguish third-party rights subsisting at the time when the relevant period expires, except insofar as the orthodox exceptions to the nemo dat principle might apply to transmit a good title from sender to recipient; thus, as a general rule, it seems that the recipient will acquire no better title to the goods than the sender himself enjoyed. The recipient may therefore still be liable in detinue or conversion if he acts in contravention of the title of the true owner or other person enjoying the unextinguished right over the goods. The Commonwealth provision, as we have seen, is more ambivalent.

---

[27] Section 1(2)(b).
[28] Supra.
[29] Section 3; this section is substantially remodelled by the *Unsolicited Goods and Services (Amendment) Act* 1975, ss. 1-3.
[30] Section 5.

CHAPTER 13

HIRE OF CUSTODY

Locatio custodiae, or the safekeeping of goods for reward, is in many ways the classic form of bailment. Traditionally, it arises whenever goods are delivered by one party to another to be stored in return for a remuneration and redelivered on demand. The reward will normally be monetary and the delivery will generally be direct, but neither of these features is theoretically essential. Thus, there may be a bailment by way of locatio custodiae when a warehouseman attorns to the purchaser of goods[1], or when a sub-bailee accepts possession of goods belonging to a principal bailor.[2] The bailee's payment may emanate from a third party (such as an intermediate bailee)[3] or may form part of some wider remuneration which he receives from his relationship with the bailor.[4] In most cases, however, the bailment will be contractual in character and the bailee's reward will be identifiable as conventional consideration.

The situations in which the bailment by way of locatio custodiae may arise are multifarious. The underlying factor in all of them is the essential passivity of the bailee's undertaking. This does not mean, of course, that he is free of all obligation to take active or positive measures for the safety of the goods. Rather, it means that he is free of any obligations towards the goods other than those which arise naturally from the discharge of his duty of reasonable care. He is not, unlike the mandatary or hired craftsman, under a duty to improve the goods or to perform any affirmative service upon them; the primary object of the transaction is custody and no more.[5]

---

[1] See p. 13 and Chapter 21, post.

[2] See p. 786 et seq., post. Another example is the seller of goods who remains in possession prior to delivery: *MGonu* v. *Nzekwe* (1977) C.A. Unrep. July 8.

[3] *Morris* v. *C. W. Martin & Sons, Ltd.* [1966] 1 Q.B. 716; or an insurance company, where a car is delivered at its instruction to a garage to be repaired: *Saskatchewan Government Insurance Office* v. *Midwest Motors Ltd.* (1961) 36 W.W.R. 254.

[4] *Andrews* v. *Home Flats Ltd.* [1945] 2 All E.R. 698; *Martin* v. *L.C.C.* [1947] K.B. 628; *MacDonald* v. *Whittaker Textiles (Marysville) Ltd.* (1976) 64 D.L.R. (3d 317; cf. *Houghland* v. *R. R. Low (Luxury) Coaches Ltd.* [1962] 1 Q.B. 694; and see generally Chapter 8 ante.

[5] The distinction is discussed further at p. 329 ante, and p. 503 post. It should be noted, however, that in *Walsh* v. *Palladium Car Park Pty. Ltd.* [1975] V.R. 949 the Victorian Full Supreme Court held that the bailment of a car to a car-park proprietor could be characterised as a "contract for the provision of services" within the Victorian *Small Claims Tribunal Act* 1973. At p. 959 the Court remarked as follows: "If the prosecutor had safe premises which were in existence when the motor vehicle was left at the car-park it might well be said that the contract did not call for any further positive steps for safe custody on the part of the prosecutor or its servants or agents. There is the further aspect that the terms and conditions of the ticket cut down very considerably the obligations of the bailee. None the less, the contract of bailment still remained one for the undertaking of custody and, however much the obligations of the bailee were restricted

Apart from professional wharfingers and warehousemen, the following are likely to represent custodians for reward: banks, when safeguarding customers' valuables,[6] agisters,[7] stable-keepers,[8] car-park operators,[9] cloak-room and left-luggage office proprietors,[10] and even (in appropriate circumstances) hospitals,[11] boarding-houses,[12] and schools.[13] Decisions upon this aspect of bailment are numerous and are almost exclusively concerned with questions of fact.[14] The fundamental rules of liability are well-established and precise.

Broadly, two categories of locatio custodiae can be discovered. The first arises when the storage and safekeeping of goods represent the entire object of the transaction between the parties, such as where A leaves his suitcase at a railway left-luggage office or B stores his car in C's garage while he is abroad. In the second case, the transaction of custody arises collaterally to some other relationship, normally a contract for the provision of services from the bailee to the bailor. Into this category fall the leaving of a car in a restaurant car-park,[15] the depositing of a coat in a restaurant[16] or hair-dressing salon,[17] the special custody of goods by a boarding-house keeper or an hotelier,[18] the storage of a patient's valuables by a hospital[19] or of an employee's work tools by his employer[20] and the custody of a tenant's goods (or of those of his family) by a landlord.[21] No particular importance attaches to the distinction, although it does serve to illustrate the great breadth

---

or limited and however contingent the necessity to take any active steps might be, it seems to us that as a matter of the ordinary use of language a contract for the undertaking of custody of a motor vehicle can appropriately be characterised as a contract for the provision of services."

---

[6] The former notion that the bank was merely a gratuitous bailee unless it charged a separate fee for the service of safekeeping is no longer reliable: see p. 282, ante.

[7] See *Turner* v. *Stallibrass* [1898] 1 Q.B. 56; *Coldman* v. *Hill* [1919] 1 K.B. 443; cf. *Helton* v. *Sullivan* [1968] Qd. R. 562; *Robinson* v. *Waters* (1920) 22 W.A.L.R. 66; *Humphrey* v. *Phipps* [1974] 1 N.Z.L.R. 650; see ante, p. 204.

[8] See *Judson* v. *Etheridge* (1833) 1 Cr. & M. 743; 149 E.R. 598.

[9] *Mendelssohn* v. *Normand Ltd.* [1970] 1 Q.B. 177; *Davis* v. *Pearce Parking Station Pty. Ltd.* (1954) 91 C.L.R. 642; *Penny* v. *Grand Central Car Park Pty. Ltd.* [1965] V.R. 323; *Sydney City Council* v. *West* (1965) 114 C.L.R. 481; *James Buchanan & Co. Ltd.* v. *Hay's Transport Services Ltd.* [1972] 2 Lloyd's Rep. 535; *Walsh* v. *Palladium Car Park Pty. Ltd.* ante, n. 5. But see Chapter 5 ante, as to whether the proprietor is a bailee.

[10] See *Stallard* v. *G. W. Ry. Co.* (1862) 2 B. & S. 419; 121 E.R. 1129; *Alexander* v. *Railway Executive* [1951] 2 K.B. 882; *Aldridge* v. *Franklin* [1953] Scots. C.L.Y. 238; *Vincent* v. *B.T.C.* [1957] Scots. C.L.Y. 186.

[11] See *Martin* v. *L.C.C.* ante, n. 4; and see further ante, p. 205 et seq.

[12] See Chapter 24, post.

[13] See *Poulton* v. *Notre Dame College* (1976) 60 D.L.R. (3d) 501; and see ante, p. 207.

[14] Or with the validity and application of exclusion clauses, as to which see Chapter 25, post.

[15] *Martin* v. *Town 'n' Country Delicatessen Ltd.* (1964) 42 D.L.R. (2d) 449, where, however, it was decided that there was no bailment.

[16] *Ultzen* v. *Nichols* [1894] 1 Q.B. 92; *Murphy* v. *Hart* (1919) 46 D.L.R. 36; ante, p. 204.

[17] *Doyle* v. *Dumaine* (1914) 21 R.L. 44 (Can.).

[18] E.g. *Phipps* v. *New Claridge's Hotel Ltd.* (1905) 22 T.L.R. 49; *Daniel* v. *Hotel Pacific Pty. Ltd.* [1953] V.L.R. 447.

[19] *Martin* v. *L.C.C.* ante, n. 4 and see ante, p. 207.

[20] *MacDonald* v. *Whittaker Textiles (Marysville) Ltd.* ante, n. 4.

[21] *Andrews* v. *Home Flats Ltd.* ante, n. 4.

of this variety of bailment and the different standards of professionalism and responsibility it can impose. Clearly, a greater degree of competence and expertise may be expected of a person who specialises in the safekeeping of clients' property, as compared to the proprietor of a quite different enterprise who merely assumes custody as a favor or as an ancillary service to his customers. Even in the latter event, a high degree of circumspection may be exacted if the bailee's occupation warrants it; thus an hotelier may be expected to show exceptional care towards goods deposited with him and to possess adequate facilities (such as a safe) for their safekeeping.[22]

I. THE DUTIES OF THE BAILOR

In most cases, the bailor's responsibilities are straightforward and easily identified. Case-law has tended to focus for more upon the duties owed to him by the bailee and (in more exceptional cases) upon the extent to which conduct on the part of the bailor can reduce or influence those duties.

A. Payment of charges

When a rate for storage has been determined, the bailor must pay this in the proportions and at the times agreed; when no rate is agreed, he must pay a reasonable charge.[23] In certain circumstances, which are not peculiar to the law of bailment but apply to the law of contract generally, the bailor will be entitled to withold payment; for instance, because of a breach of the terms of the bailment or because of the operation of some external event, such as frustration of the contract.

B. Responsibility for safety of goods

There seems to be no direct authority on the liability of the bailor for defective or dangerous goods. Presumably, as in the case of locatio operis faciendi, the duty is one of reasonable care. There is, however, no reason why the bailor should not enter into a special contract whereunder he warrants absolutely to the bailee the safety of the goods and their fitness for storage. A clause of this kind may well be treated, at least as against the private consumer, as akin to a contract of exclusion, and therefore narrowly construed.

---

[22] Cf. *Daniel* v. *Hotel Pacific Pty. Ltd.* ante, n. 18.

[23] What constitutes a reasonable charge may vary according to whether the bailee is willing to continue warehousing the goods or requires the space for some other purpose: see *Acme Flooring and Paving Co. (1904) Ltd.* v. *S. Spanglett Ltd.* [1959] 2 Lloyd's Rep. 464, where the Court of Appeal held that the bailees were entitled to charge above the market rate. Cf. *Greaves* v. *Ashlin* (1813) 3 Camp. 426 (buyer who does not collect goods within a reasonable time may be charged for storage); *Buxton* v. *Baughan* (1834) 6 C. & P. 674 (no right to charge for storage when chattel placed by bailee on premises of third party without bailor's authority); *Stephen* v. *Costor* (1763) 3 Burr. 1408 (London wharfingers not entitled to wharfage in respect of goods unloaded into lighters from barges moored at their wharves).

C. Collection and re-delivery

The bailor may demand that the goods be made available for him at a particular time or place and can sue for breach of the ensuing obligation.[24] A mere stipulation as to time will not normally oblige him to synchronise his collection of the goods with the stipulated time, however, and will not render him civilly answerable to the bailee for failing to do so. Only if the stipulation amounts to a concurrent promise on his part to collect by a certain date will this result ensue.[25]

Occasionally, a delay in collection will entitle the bailee to employ a lower standard of care in the safekeeping of the goods and may even justify his actual disposal of them.[26] Unless the circumstances of the delay are exceptional, however, and are such as to show an implied agreement to that effect, the bailee's normal responsibility will not abate and he will continue to owe a duty of reasonable care.[27] If he sells the goods without contractual or statutory authority, he will be liable to the bailor in conversion.[28]

The bailor may occasionally be under a duty *not* to demand redelivery before a certain date. This may occur when the bailee, in expectation of a long period of custody, has stored the goods in an inaccessible position and is put to great difficulty in retrieving them before that period has elapsed. In such an event, the finding of a contractual promise by the bailor not to demand delivery before a certain date may either exonerate the bailee in an action for conversion or detinue or entitle him to compensation for the expense and inconvenience of an early redelivery.

D. Observance of lien[29]

If the bailee enjoys a valid and enforceable lien over the goods, the bailor must honour that lien and must not retake the goods without tendering the appropriate charges. A wrongful seizure in contravention of a lien will render him liable for trespass and conversion.[30]

E. Further contractual duties

These are unusual; perhaps the commonest is the standard-form condition in some warehousing contracts that the bailor should indemnify

---

[24] Post, p. 464.
[25] The bailee's action will be for breach of contract. Quaere whether he can sue for trespass: cf. *Westripp* v. *Baldock* [1938] 2 All E.R. 779; *Kolfor Plant Ltd.* v. *Tilbury Plant Ltd.* (1977) *The Times*, May 17th.
[26] Chapter 12, ante.
[27] *Mitchell* v. *Davis* (1920) 37 T.L.R. 68 (ante, p. 394); *Darling Ladies Wear Ltd.* v. *Hickey* [1949] 2 D.L.R. 420, at 423, reversed on other grounds [1950] 1 D.L.R. 720.
[28] *Sachs* v. *Miklos* [1948] 2 K.B. 23. Cf. *Willetts* v. *Chaplin & Co.* (1923) 39 T.L.R. 222, where it was an express condition of the contract that the defendants should be entitled to sell the goods if the warehousing charges became two years in arrears. The defendants were accordingly held not liable for disposing of the goods in order to recoup their charges. The power of a bailee to dispose of uncollected goods is discussed at p. 397 et seq., ante and p. 1029 post.
[29] As to the circumstances in which a lien may arise under this kind of bailment, see p. 493 et seq., post.
[30] Authority is scanty because liens themselves are rare in this context: cf. *Standard Electronic Apparatus Laboratories Pty. Ltd.* v. *Stenner* [1960] N.S.W.R. 447, which involved a bailment for work and labour.

the bailee against all liability to third parties occasioned by the storage
and moving of the goods. A provision of this kind imposes a heavy
burden upon the ordinary consumer and would, no doubt, be narrowly
construed.[31]

Although contracts for storage often seek to impose affirmative duties
upon the bailor, many of these are intended merely as a shield for the
warehouseman and not as the basis of some direct right of action. Thus,
the contract may require disclosure of the value of the goods, or
specification of those articles which exceed a certain value. A failure
to comply with a provision of this kind may result in the qualification
or exclusion of a bailee's conventional duty[32] but it is unlikely to be
directly actionable by him, nor will it per se affect his identity as a
bailee.[33]

The bailor must, of course, comply with all the obligations imposed
upon him by the contract, and may be contractually liable for their
breach. These obligations are potentially so varied and diverse that
little can be gained from any further general discussion.[34]

II. The Duties of the Bailee

The custodian for reward owes certain duties in common with every
category of bailee, such as the duty to account to his bailor for profits
made from the bailment[35] and the duty to refrain from denying his
bailor's title.[36] More especially, he must safeguard the goods with
reasonable care and redeliver them (reasonable wear and tear expected)
in the condition in which they were bailed. It is upon this aspect of
his responsibilities that most decisions centre.

[31] Unreasonable indemnity clauses are rendered inoperative under s. 4 of the
Unfair Contract Terms Act 1977, as against persons dealing as a consumer.

[32] *Van Toll* v. *S. E. Ry. Co.* (1862) 12 C.B.N.S. 76; 142 E.R. 1071; *Pepper* v.
S. E. Ry. Co. (1868) 17 L.T. 149; *Gibaud* v. *G. E. Ry. Co.* [1921] 2 K.B. 426;
Skipwith v. *G. W. Ry. Co.* (1888) 59 L.T. 520; *Newborn* v. *Just* (1825) 2 C. & P.
76; *Handon* v. *Caledonian Ry. Co.* (1880) 7 R. (Ct. of Sess.) 966; *Lyons & Co.* v.
Caledonian Ry. Co. 1909 S.C. 1185. See generally, Chapter 25, post. A similar
provision exonerates the bailee whenever the bailor has personally packaged the
goods; a somewhat unfair rule, not dissimilar to the "non causative exemption"
in a contract of insurance.

[33] See *Parker* v. *S. E. Ry. Co.* (1877) 2 C.P.D. 416; *Williamson* v. *Gray* (1867) 1
I.L.T. Jo. 476; and cf. p. 209 et seq., ante.

[34] An interesting example of an implied contract of indemnity is afforded by
Groves & Sons v. *Webb & Kenward* (1916) 114 L.T. 1082; 32 T.L.R. 424. Here,
the plaintiff wharfingers obeyed a request by the defendant bailors to issue clear
warrants for a quantity of wheat which had not yet been lifted from the lighters.
The warrants enabled the plaintiffs to sell the wheat, which turned out to be
damaged and the wharfinger was made liable to the purchaser for the difference
in value. It was held that there was an implied contract of indemnity between the
wharfinger and the seller, from whom these damages could accordingly be recovered. Cf. *Alicia Hosiery Ltd.* v. *Brown, Shipley & Co.* [1970] 1 Q.B. 195.

[35] Including profits made from enforcing his right of action against a third-party
tortfeasor: *The Winkfield* [1902] P. 42; Chapter 4, ante.

[36] Ante, p. 163 et seq.

A. The duty of care

Although some early authorities suggest a liability based upon gross negligence,[37] the modern duty is clearly established as one of reasonable care.[38] The custodian must accordingly show that any established loss or injury to the chattel did not result from a failure on his part to exercise such care and circumspection as could reasonably have been expected from a bailee of his trade and standing in all the circumstances of the case: "It appears to me that here there was a bailment made to a particular person, a bailment for hire and reward, and the bailee was bound to show that he took reasonable and proper care for the due security and proper delivery of that bailment."[39] This principle, in fact, entitles him to avoid liability by two distinct avenues: either he may show that he has taken reasonable care of the goods, or he may show that his acknowledged or established failure to take reasonable care did not contribute to the loss. In either event, the burden of proof rests upon him.

However, this burden comes into operation only when certain prior conditions have been fulfilled by the bailor. First, he must show that the goods have been "delivered" to the bailee: i.e., that a sequence of events has taken place as a result of which the goods came into the bailee's possession.[40] The bailee cannot normally be required to answer for their safety until they are within his custody and control, unless it is due to his default that they are not.[41] Secondly, the initial burden of establishing loss or injury, and of satisfying the court that these events occurred during the bailment, must likewise be borne by the bailor.[42] In *G. Merel & Co. Ltd.* v. *Chessher*,[43] the plaintiffs failed in their action

[37] E.g., *Finucane* v. *Small* (1795) 1 Esp. 315; *Broadwater* v. Blot (1817) 5 Holt. N.P. 547; but cf. *Coggs.* v. *Bernard* (1703) 2 Ld. Raym. 909; *Cailiff* v. *Danvers* (1792) Peake 114.

[38] *Corbett* v. *Packington* (1827) 6 B. & C. 268 and *Mackenzie* v. *Cox* (1840) 9 C. & P. 632 are early authorities to this effect. The former turned upon a point of pleading.

[39] Per Lord Halsbury in the unreported case of *Morris, Pollexfen & Blair* v. *Walton* (1909); cited by the Court of Appeal in *Joseph Travers & Sons Ltd.* v. *Cooper* [1915] 1 K.B. 73. The principal supporting authorities include *Coldman* v. *Hill* (ante, n. 7) especially per Scrutton L.J. at p. 454; *Paterson* v. *Miller* [1923] V.R. 36; *Brook's Wharf and Bull Wharf Ltd.* v. *Goodman Bros.* [1937] 1 K.B. 534, at 538-540; *Tozer, Kemsley & Millbourn (Australasia) Pty. Ltd.* v. *Collier's Interstate Transport Services Ltd.* (1956) 94 C.L.R. 384, at 397-398, 401; *Fankhauser* v. *Mark Dykes Pty. Ltd.* [1960] V.R. 376; *B.R.S. Ltd.* v. *Arthur V. Crutchley & Co. Ltd.* [1968] 1 All E.R. 811; *Hobbs* v. *Petersham Transport Co. Pty. Ltd.* (1971) 45 A.L.J.R. 356 (obiter, per Windeyer J.); *Re S. Davis Ltd.* [1945] Ch. 402; *Port Swettenham* v. *Wu* (1978) *The Times* June 22 (P.C.).

[40] As to the requirements of delivery, see p. 80 et seq., ante; *Lowenstein & Co. Ltd.* v. *Durable Wharfage Co. Ltd.* [1973] 1 Lloyd's Rep. 221; *Thomas* v. *Day* (1803) Esp. 262.

[41] *Quiggin* v. *Duff* (1836) 1 M. & W. 174; 150 E.R. 394.

[42] *O'Regan* v. *Hui Bros. Transport Pty. Ltd* [1969] P. & N.G.L.R. 261; post, p. 809. It appears sufficient for the bailor to prove that there is "no reasonable prospect of any further recovery" of the goods: *Moukataff* v. *B.O.A.C. Ltd.* [1967] I Lloyd's Rep. 396, at 416; Cf. *Robinson* v. *Waters* ante, n. 7 and see post, p. 464.

[43] [1961] 1 Lloyd's Rep. 534; see also *Tozer, Kemsley & Millbourn (Australasia) Pty. Ltd.* v. *Collier's Interstate Transport Service Ltd.* (ante, n. 39), at 391-394, 400; *Gilbart* v. *Dale* (1836) 5 Ad. & E. 543; 111 E.R. 1270; *Midland Ry. Co.* v. *Bromley* (1856) 17 C.B. 372; 139 E.R. 1116; *Moukataff* v. *B.O.A.C. Ltd.* ante; *Calgary Transport Services Ltd.* v. *Pyramid Management Ltd.* (1977) 71 D.L.R. (3d) 234; cf. *Re S. Davis Ltd.* (ante, n. 39), at 406-407.

for conversion against the defendant wharfinger because they were unable to prove that a quantity of timber had disappeared from the defendant's wharf before the plaintiffs themselves went into possession. Salmon J. agreed that the dating of the loss need be established only upon a balance of probabilities,[44] but refused to attach conclusive weight to the fact that the defendant had already been convicted twice for stealing the plaintiffs' timber. Thirdly, the bailor must "prove his contract";[45] in other words, he must show that the goods were accepted by the defendant as a bailee, rather than that they were cast upon him involuntarily or were harboured by him, for example, under the mistaken impression that they were his own. This burden is normally the easiest of the three to discharge because in many cases there will be a written contract giving rise to the bailment.

Once these three interdependent facts have been established, the defendant bailee must either disprove neglect or must detonate the inference of neglect by demonstrating its irrelevance to the ultimate misadventure. For it is clear, despite suggestions in some of the cases that the bailee can escape only by showing that he took all reasonable care,[46] that a conclusion of negligence against him is not fatal to his defence. This is demonstrated by the decision in *Joseph Travers & Sons Ltd.* v. *Cooper*.[47] In that case, tinned salmon was stored on the Thames in a barge belonging to the defendant. The lighterman placed in charge of the vessel was absent for a long period before and after low tide, and upon his return found the barge in the final stages of submersion. Although his absence was a clear act of negligence, the defendants claimed that they should be exonerated on two grounds: (i) because the plaintiffs had failed to establish any causal connection between the default of the lighterman and the subsequent sinking of the barge; (ii) because in their contention the barge was sunk when it became "mudsucked" while resting on the river bed—a problem which no amount of effort by their servant could have corrected, and a theory which the plaintiffs had failed to controvert. The plaintiffs argued that the effective cause of the loss was the wedging of the barge under the wharfside, which prevented the barge from rising with the tide: a situation which could easily have been rectified by the lighterman if he had been there. Since neither cause could be affirmatively established, the issue resolved itself into one of burden of proof. The Court of Appeal, citing passages from *Morris, Pollexfen & Blair* v. *Walton*,[48] held unanimously that the onus was on the defendant.[49] In so doing, they recognised that a bailee need not necessarily negative a want of reasonable care in order to succeed,

[44] [1961] 1 Lloyd's Rep. 534, at 537.

[45] *Fankhauser* v. *Mark Dykes Pty. Ltd.* (ante, n. 39), at 377.

[46] E.g., *Brook's Wharf and Bull Wharf Ltd.* v. *Goodman Bros.* (ante, n. 39), at 538-540.

[47] [1915] 1 K.B. 73.

[48] (1909), H.L., unreported. An account of the facts is given by Scrutton L.J. (who had been counsel in the case) in *Coldman* v *Hill* [1919] 1 K.B. 443, at 457-458. The primary source of authority was a statement by Lord Loreburn L.C. that the bailee is answerable unless he can satisfy the Court that the loss has occurred "from some cause independent of his own wrongdoing."

[49] [1915] 1 K.B. 73, at 87-88, 90, 97.

but that his only salvation in this event lay in proving on a balance of probabilities that this default had no influence upon the injury or loss, and played no part in its occurrence:

> What did take place it was impossible to prove, and the impossibility arose from the fact that the defendant neglected his obligation to keep a man in charge. The defendant as bailee of the goods is responsible for their return to their owner. If he failed to return them it rested upon him to prove that he did take reasonable and proper care of the goods, and that if he had been there he could have done nothing, and that the loss would still have resulted.[50]

This principle has been consistently acknowledged in many subsequent decisions.[51] The weight of evidence required to satisfy the principle may help to explain why the Courts have tended to look unfavourably upon allegations by warehousemen that no precautions against burglary could possibly have proved availing, so that their own patently inadequate precautions should not be a cause for liability.[52]

The bailee's burden, whether directed to disproving the lack of reasonable care or to showing the ineffectiveness of his negligence as a factor in the bailor's loss, has been described as "the ultimate onus, or 'legal' onus, i.e., the risk of non-persuasion, and not . . . merely the shifting onus, or onus of going forward with evidence. So that, if the plaintiff proves the contract and the non-delivery of the goods, or the delivery in a damaged condition of goods which were not damaged when bailed, and the defendant leaves it in dubio whether or not the non-delivery or the damage was due to his fault, the plaintiff should succeed."[53] It follows that, although this burden has often been equated with the principle res ipsa loquitur, the two are both practically and conceptually quite different; at least under modern Australian analyses of res ipsa loquitur,[54] and quite possibly in England too.[55] It has been stated that the bailee's burden is the same whether the bailor sues in detinue, case or assumpsit.[56]

Even when he has discharged this legal burden, the bailee's difficulties may not be entirely over. It may be that his custodianship of the goods has been impeccable for as long as they were within his protection, but that he has failed to act with reasonable promptitude and care in protecting the owner's interests after an event has occurred, without his default, which jeopardises the goods. The operation of the various

---

[50] Ibid., at 88 per Buckley L.J.
[51] E.g. *Coldman* v. *Hill* ante, at 454; *Paterson* v. *Miller* [1923] V.R. 36 at 46-47; *B.R.S. Ltd.* v. *Arthur V. Crutchley & Co. Ltd.* (ante, n. 39), at 824.
[52] *B.R.S. Ltd* v. *Arthur V. Crutchley & Co. Ltd.* ante; *Petersen* v. *Papakura Motor Sales Ltd.* [1957] N.Z.L.R. 495, at 500-501.
[53] *Fankhauser* v. *Mark Dykes Pty. Ltd.* (ante, n. 39), at 377 per Scholl J.; this statement was approved and applied by Napier C.J. in *A.A. Radio Taxi Trucks Ltd.* v. *Curyer* [1965] S.A.S.R. 110, at 111.
[54] *Fankhauser* v. *Mark Dykes Pty. Ltd.*, at pp. 377-378; *Paterson* v. *Miller* (ante, n. 51), at 40; *Lee & Sons Pty. Ltd* v. *Abood* (1968) 89 W.N. (Pt. 1.) (N.S.W.) 430; *Hobbs* v. *Petersham Transport Co. Pty. Ltd.* (ante, n. 39), at 363-364.
[55] Cross on *Evidence* (4th edn), pp. 131-134; Street on *Torts* (6th edn), pp. 138-141; see ante, p. 40.
[56] *Paterson* v *Miller* at 36, per McArthur J.; cf. Cussen J. at 48-49. As to detinue, see also *Houghland* v. *R. R. Low* (*Luxury Coaches*) *Ltd.* [1962] 1 Q.B. 694; *John F. Goulding Pty. Ltd.* v. *Victorian Railways Commissioners* (1932) 48 C.L.R. 157.

interlocking burdens in this situation is complex. Once the bailee has discharged his conventional burden by establishing reasonable care as against the original event, the bailor may adduce evidence of a subsequent lack of diligence in failing to take effective steps to counter that event. When such evidence has been adduced, the onus again shifts to the bailee to show that the employment of such diligence would not have prevented the injury of which the bailor now complains. Of course, the relevant diligence in the aftermath of an event of this nature need only be such as is reasonable.[57]

On one point the authorities are unanimous. The bailee, confronted by proof of damage or loss, is not bound to establish precisely how those phenomena occurred.[58] Proof of reasonable care or of the irrelevance of its lack will be sufficient: he need not go further (although it may often be helpful for him to do so) and demonstrate the cause of the injury in question.

The discharge of the duty of care depends upon a multitude of factors. The bailee's precautions must be scaled to the value and vulnerability of the goods, the likely hazards, the condition of the goods upon delivery and the professional expertise he has held himself out as possessing. Generally, it will be no defence for him to show that he employed his own resources to the best of his ability, if those resources or facilities are inadequate for the task he has undertaken. Thus, one who receives goods as a warehouseman must show the same degree of care as might be expected from "a skilled storekeeper, acquainted with the risks to be apprehended either from the character of the storehouse itself or of its locality."[59] Although in exceptional cases a knowledge of the bailee's own incompetence may operate to restrict the bailor's rights of action,[60] the general rule is that the bailee, having undertaken to keep the goods according to some objectively ascertained standard of care, must abide by that standard. But lesser precautions may, in appropriate circumstances, be expected of a private bailee than of a professional custodian.[61] It is

---

[57] *Coldman* v. *Hill* discussed in more detail at p. 448 et seq., post.

[58] *Bullen* v. *Swan Electric & Engraving Co. Ltd.* (1906) 22 T.L.R. 275; (1907) 23 T.L.R. 258; *Paterson* v. *Miller*, at 47; *Coldman* v. *Hill*, at 455; *Smith* v. *Taylor*, [1966] 2 Lloyd's Rep. 231; *Northumberland County School Finance Board* v. *Stewart* (1966) 54 D.L.R. (2d) 657; *B.R.S. Ltd.* v. *Arthur V. Crutchley & Co. Ltd.* ante; *Ulster-Swift Ltd.* v. *Taunton Meat Haulage Ltd.* [1977] 3 All E.R. 641, at 650 (semble).

[59] *Brabant & Co.* v. *King* [1895] A.C. 632, at 640. Many of the older authorities favour a standard based upon the care that a reasonably diligent man would exercise "in the custody of his own chattel of the like character and in the like circumstances"; recent Commonwealth decisions adhering to this standard include *Barton, Ginger & Co. Ltd.* v. *Wellington Harbour Board* [1951] N.Z.L.R. 673 and *MacDonald* v. *Whittaker Textiles (Marysville) Ltd.* (1976) 64 D.L.R. (3d) 317. There is little effective difference between this and the more modern standard except that the latter pays closer regard to the professional abilities or pretensions of the defendant. It is preferred by the learned editor of Chitty, *Contracts* (23rd edn), vol. ii, para. 182, cf. *Port Swettenham* v. *Wu* ante.

[60] Post, p. 460.

[61] E.g. *Giles* v. *Carter* (1965) 109 Sol. Jo. 452 where the private pledgee of a mink stole, valued at between £100 and £500, was held not liable for its theft from his flat. There were no burglar alarms or nightwatchmen, but the stole was left in an unlocked wardrobe in the locked flat during the pledgee's absence. In the circumstances, these precautions were held sufficient.

all a question of what, in the final analysis, the custodian has promised to do.

1. *Specific causes of destruction, loss or damage*:

(*a*) *Theft or disappearance*: If goods are expropriated from the bailee's premises, or if animals escape, there is a presumption that their disappearance results from a breach of duty on his part. He will, therefore, be accountable unless he can divorce that disappearance from his own default or neglect. He will not escape merely by demonstrating that the goods have been stolen,[62] nor by pleading simply that they are lost.[63] Conversely, the mere event of theft does not automatically make him liable: for authorities "from the earliest times have laid it down that a bailee is not responsible if the goods in his custody are stolen without any default on his part."[64] The question, therefore, is whether the bailee can provide sufficient and convincing evidence of his having taken reasonable precautions to guard against the disappearance or loss. If he fails to establish reasonable care, the decision will generally fall against him.

Sometimes the sheer paucity of evidence will produce an inference that he has been negligent. Thus bailees have been held answerable, in the absence of more concrete proof of reasonable care, when an overcoat disappeared from a restaurant while its owner was dining there;[65] when a valuable dog disappeared from the custody of a hotel-manager;[66] when a case of silk vanished from a cage in a customs shed despite an apparently effective security system;[67] and when engraving plates went missing (presumed stolen) from a large cabinet in which they had been deposited along with many others.[68] These and many other decisions[69] show that a mere lack of evidence pointing to his neglect will not suffice to exonerate the bailee; for that deficiency is made up by the fact that the goods were lost whilst in his possession. Even when a safe system is established, he may fail on the ground of his inability to show that the loss was not occasioned by the negligence or default of his servants.[70]

In most cases, however, the parties will adduce at least some evidence to support or to diminish the inference of neglect and the courts have,

---

[62] *Barton, Ginger & Co. Ltd.* v. *Wellington Harbour Board* ante, n. 59.

[63] *Houghland* v. *R. R. Low (Luxury Coaches) Ltd.* ante, n. 56; cf. *Rozsasi* v. *Swinton Industries Pty. Ltd.* (1959) 59 S.R. (N.S.W.) 673.

[64] Per Bankes L.J. in *Coldman* v. *Hill*, at 448, cited with approval by McMillan C.J. in the unreported W.A. decision in *Colonial Super Refining Co. Ltd.* v. *Freemantle Harbour Trust Commissioners* (1921) and by Hutchinson J. in *Barton, Ginger & Co. Ltd.* v. *Wellington Harbour Board* ante, at 676.

[65] *Ultzen* v. *Nichols* [1894] 1 Q.B. 92; *Murphy* v. *Hart* (1919) 46 D.L.R. 36; ante, p. 205.

[66] *Phipps* v. *New Claridge's Hotel Ltd.* (1905) 22 T.L.R. 49; cf. *Mackenzie* v. *Cox* (1840) 9 C. & P. 632.

[67] *Makower, McBeath & Co. Pty. Ltd.* v. *Dalgety & Co. Ltd.* [1921] V.L.R. 365.

[68] *Bullen* v. *Swan Electric & Engraving Co. Ltd.* ante, n. 58.

[69] E.g. *Andrews* v. *Home Flats Ltd.* [1945] 2 All E.R. 698; *Woolmer* v. *Delmer Price Ltd.* [1955] 1 Q.B. 291; *Mansfield Exporters & Distributors Ltd.* v. *Casco Terminals Ltd.* [1971] 2 Lloyd's Rep. 73 (British Columbia Supreme Court); *Houghland* v. *R. R. Low (Luxury Coaches) Ltd.* ante, n. 56.

[70] *Makower, McBeath & Co. Pty. Ltd.* v. *Dalgety & Co. Ltd.* ante; *Global Dress Co. Ltd.* v. *W. H. Boase & Co. Ltd.* [1966] 2 Lloyd's Rep. 72; *Hill* v. *J. Crowe Ltd.* [1978] 1 All E.R. 812; *Martin* v. *Thorn* [1978] W.A.R. 10.

therefore, been able to identify specific items of conduct or omission as constituting a breach of the bailee's duty of reasonable care. Of course, individual decisions (involving widely different species of goods and types of bailee) must not be used too liberally as the basis for generalisation; the assessment of reasonable care must be made against the background of the bailee's overall volume of trade and the conditions in which he operates, and no single precaution should be branded as essential or dispensable in every conceivable case.[71] But as between certain types of trade or varieties of goods, most decisions possess a value beyond the circumference of their immediate facts.

If the bailee can prove that his anti-theft precautions are adequate against all but the most intrepid and talented of criminals, he may be absolved from liability when a theft of this exceptional nature occurs.[72] He need only take such precautions as reasonable and prudent care demand, and cannot be held to account if his normally adequate precautions fail to deter thieves who possess an unusually high degree of sophistication and equipment.[73] Thus, when valuables were kept in a locked safe in the locked office of an hotel, the proprietors were held not liable for a theft committed by intruders who entered through the unlocked front door of the hotel in the dead of the night, removed the safe by means of a trolley and took it to a place where it was blown open.[74]

However, the adequacy of a bailee's precautions must be judged against the combined circumstances of the bailment. Especial care must be taken of goods which, because of their value, portability or disposability are especially attractive to thieves.[75] The level of protection against theft must also be related to such factors as the prevalence of crime in the vicinity,[76] the ingenuity of the local criminal population, the degree of public knowledge about the existence of the goods, and the reputation and expensiveness of the bailee himself: a more expensive scale of fees may suggest a more extensive service.[77] Thus even the most insignificant flaw in the bailee's security system may render him liable if it could be exploited by an expert criminal of the sort that is likely to operate in the neighbourhood. One of the factors contributing

---

[71] *B.R.S. Ltd.* v. *Arthur V. Crutchley Ltd.* ante, at 814 per Lord Pearson.
[72] *Brook's Wharf and Bull Wharf Ltd.* v. *Goodman Bros.* [1937] 1 K.B. 534, at 539; *Petersen* v. *Papakura Motor Sales Ltd.* [1957] N.Z.L.R. 495.
[73] Per Lord Wright M.R. in *Brook's Wharf* case, ante. Note the dictum as to the proof of reasonable care provided by Lord Dunedin in *Ballard* v. *North Britain Ry. Co.* 1923 S.C. (H L.) 43, at 54, which Lord Wright claimed to be synonymous with his own formulation: sed quaere. Cf. the observations of Barwick C.J. in *Hobbs* v. *Petersham Transport Co. Pty. Ltd.* (1971) 45 A.L.J.R. 356, at 360.
[74] *Daniel* v. *Hotel Pacific Pty. Ltd.* [1953] V.R. 447. An attempt to establish strict liability against the hotel was unsuccessful because the plaintiffs did not qualify as "travellers"; post, p. 884. Cf. *McCartney-Filgate* v. *Bishop & Sons Depositaries Ltd.* [1964] 2 Lloyd's Rep. 480 (inadequate padlocks).
[75] See, for instance, *Garnham Harris & Elton Ltd.* v. *Alfred W. Ellis (Transport) Ltd.* [1967] 2 All E.R. 940, where carriers were held negligent in delegating performance of contract to carry copper wire ("the gold of thieves"); *B.R.S. Ltd.* v. *Arthur V. Crutchley & Co. Ltd.* (whisky): post, p. 445.
[76] *B.R.S. Ltd.* v. *Arthur V. Crutchley & Co. Ltd.; Saunders (Mayfair) Furs Ltd.* v. *Chas. Wm. Davis Ltd.* [1966] 1 Lloyd's Rep. 78.
[77] See *James Buchanan & Sons Ltd.* v. *Hay's Transport Services Ltd.* [1972] 2 Lloyd's Rep. 535; a right to expect "Rolls-Royce" service.

to the defendants' liability in *B.R.S. Ltd.* v. *Arthur V. Crutchley & Co. Ltd.*, was the vulnerability of the skylight in an otherwise impregnable warehouse. This enabled a thief to enter the building and, by climbing down a crane and across a gantry, to reach the warehouse floor. The defendants were held liable because it was foreseeeable than an intruder of such skill and agility would be employed by the professional thieves that operated in the vicinity and would take advantage of the skylight to facilitate the theft. A warehouse, like a chain, is as strong as its weakest link.

Clearly, when valuable goods are warehoused in an area which is attractive to thieves, the warehouseman should adopt a regular, efficient system of checking the goods and inspecting the premises. This will serve the dual purpose of enabling him to obtain the earliest possible notification of losses and of ensuring that the building remains secure against intruders.[78] It is a precaution which is particularly necessary at times when the warehouse is otherwise unoccupied, when the defendant's organisation is a large one catering for a variety of clients, and when there is a degree of public knowledge as to the presence of valuable merchandise on his premises; indeed, his negligence may sometimes consist in enabling such knowledge to be acquired.[79] Bailees have, therefore, been held negligent in failing to employ a sufficient number of active and reliable watchmen,[80] in failing to properly investigate the honesty of their employees before allowing them to have access to customers' goods,[81] in failing to provide guard-dogs and sufficient fencing,[82]

---

[78] Cf. the *Crutchley* case ante, where the fact that the defendants relied exclusively upon a system of hired patrolmen working a "beat" system, and employed no stationary watchman, was held to be a contributory factor in their failure to take reasonable care.

[79] In the *Crutchley* case, whisky worth £9,000 was delivered to a warehouse situated along a very vulnerable stretch of the Liverpool dockland, much frequented by thieves. The whisky was loaded on to a trailer and left uncovered inside the warehouse for about eight hours, during which time it could be readily observed by passers-by. Sachs L.J. (at 824) seemed to accept the judge's finding that to advertise the consignment in this way was an act of negligence and he pointed out that even if this did not contribute to the ultimate theft of the whisky, this could only be because the contents of the warehouse were observable in some other way. Lord Pearson (at 817) agreed that such conduct was open to criticism but doubted whether it was an effective cause of the loss, or that it was negligent to omit a precaution "which was not likely to do much good." See also *James Buchanan & Co. Ltd.* v. *Hay's Transport Service Ltd.* (ante, n. 77) where the goods were likewise left uncovered on a trailer; *Saunders (Mayfair) Furs Ltd.* v. *Chas. Wm. Davis Ltd.* (ante, n. 76), where a valuable fur coat was left overnight in a lighted and unguarded shop window, and the bailees were held liable; *Giles* v. *Carter* (1965) 109 Sol. Jo. 452.

[80] *Rubery Owen & Co. Ltd.* v. *Rea Ltd.* [1963] 1 Lloyd's Rep. 279; *James Buchanan & Co. Ltd.* v. *Hay's Transport Services Ltd.* ante. In exceptional circumstances, such as in time of war, the shortage of man-power may excuse a lack of sufficient staff: *Edwards* v. *Newland & Co.* [1950] 2 K.B. 534, at 539-540.

[81] *Williams* v. *The Curzon Syndicate Ltd.* (1919) 35 T.L.R. 475; *Adams (Durham) Ltd.* v. *Trust Houses Ltd.* [1960] 1 Lloyd's Rep. 380; *John Carter (Fine Worsteds) Ltd.* v. *Hanson Haulage (Leeds) Ltd.* [1965] 2 Q.B. 495; cf. *Alberta-U-Drive Ltd.* v. *Jack Carter Ltd.* (1972) 28 D.L.R. (3d) 114; *Transmotors Ltd.* v. *Robertson, Buckley & Co. Ltd.* [1970] 1 Lloyd's Rep. 224; *Bamert* v. *Parks* (1965) 50 D.L.R. (2d) 313.

[82] *James Buchanan & Co. Ltd.* v. *Hay's Transport Services Ltd.*, ante.

and in failing to be alerted by suspicious circumstances in the vicinity of the warehouse.[83]

Not all of these duties translate themselves readily into the more modest context of car-parks, cloakrooms, and luggage offices. The obligation to take care in the appointment of staff is probably one which may legitimately be exacted from any organisation which deals in the property of others: how much care is necessary will, of course, depend upon the relative expense of inquiry and the comparative value of the goods. A duty to supervise the bailed property may likewise be exacted from those who are not professional warehousemen, at least in those places (such as a restaurant) where there is regular public access to the place in which it is kept.[84] But the failure to employ night-watchmen is clearly excusable when the premises contain goods of a relatively low value (such as a dry-cleaner's shop) or where other facilities such as an adequate burglar alarm exists to combat the dangers of theft.[85] Likewise, although the lack of a burglar alarm may be deemed negligent in the case of a warehouseman[86] or a bank, it by no means follows that such precautions should be necessary in every case, provided the bailee has done what is reasonable to counteract the risks of intrusion.[87] Similar observations apply to guard-dogs, two-way radios and direct warning devices: their absence may connote neglect on the part of a bailee of goods worth thousands of dollars (particularly when those gooods are stored in a container which can be readily mobilised)[88] but would by no means suggest a breach of duty on the part of a bailee whose operations were more modest. The identification of reasonable care is a cumulative process and no one precaution can be said to be universally vital. Everything depends upon the context in which those precautions are invoked and upon any other precautions with which they are used in conjunction. It is, as Hinchcliffe J. once observed "a matter of impression."[89]

An instructive example of the vigilance that may be exacted from a

---

[83] Cf. *Global Dress Co. Ltd.* v. *W. H. Boase & Co. Ltd.* ante, n. 70; *Coldman* v. *Hill* (see post., p. 448). See further *Lampson & Co. Ltd.* v. *London and India Dock Joint Co. Ltd.* (1901) 17 T.L.R. 663; *London Joint Stock Bank Ltd.* v. *MacMillan & Arthur* [1918] A.C. 777, at 789; *MacCartney-Filgate* v. *Bishop & Sons Depositaries Ltd.* ante, n. 74.

[84] *Ultzen* v. *Nichols* [1894] 1 Q.B. 92; *Murphy* v. *Hart* (1919) 46 D.L.R. 36; *Davis* v. *The Educated Fish Parlour* (1966) *The Guardian*, 26 July; and see Chapter 5, and p. 447, post.

[85] Cf. *Saunders (Mayfair) Furs Ltd.* v. *Chas. Wm. Davis Ltd.* ante, n. 76.

[86] *B.R.S. Ltd.* v. *Arthur V. Crutchley & Co. Ltd.* [1968] 1 All E.R. 811.

[87] See *Jaffa* v. *Waxman* [1966] 2 Lloyd's Rep. 344, at 346, which involved the bailment of furs to a merchant on approval and where the learned judge remarked: "it is going too far to say that everyone must have a burglar alarm. You must have regard to the value of the goods . . . *(and to any other arrangements made)*." It is instructive to compare this decision with the *Mayfair Furs* case (ante), and *Giles* v. *Carter* ante, n. 79. See also, as to the bailee of furs, *Mitchell* v. *Davis* (1920) 37 T.L.R. 68.

[88] *James Buchanan & Co. Ltd.* v. *Hay's Transport Services Ltd.* [1972] 2 Lloyd's Rep. 535.

[89] Ibid., at 543.

warehouseman of valuable goods is provided by the decision of the Court of Appeal in *B.R.S. Ltd.* v. *Arthur V. Crutchley & Co. Ltd.*[90] The warehouse in that case was strongly built and had powerful metal doors, described by a police witness as the best available. Its weaknesses were a reinforced glass skylight which, when used in connection with a crane and gantry, would enable a cat-burglar to get on to the floor of the warehouse, and a system of patrols which involved only four visits to the warehouse within a twelve-hour overnight period. Taking everything into account, the Court held that these precautions were inadequate to satisfy the requirement of reasonable care. In particular it was suggested that a beam alarm trained across the skylight and a regular resident watchman of athletic build would have provided a better system of security and should have been adopted. The defendants had failed to take into proper account the deterrent value of such precautions and had possibly tended to concentrate too much on minimising costs; they could not rely conclusively upon the fact that other warehousing firms had similar security systems to their own, nor upon the "somewhat defeatist" attitude that any precautions which they did adopt would eventually be overcome.[91] These may be factors to be weighed in the balance, but they did not possess an exclusive influence upon the identification of reasonable care.

Lesser precautions may be exacted from the proprietors of such establishments as garages and car parks, but even here the degree of vigilance must take close account of the value of the goods and the likely incidence of theft. Thus, it would probably be negligent for the garage proprietor to leave the keys in a car after parking it,[92] or to allow someone other than the authorised ticket-holder to drive the car away.[93] In *Davis* v. *Pearce Parking Stations Pty. Ltd.*[94] car-park operators were held to be negligent in parking the vehicle near a public street without keeping it under observation or removing the ignition-key, and in failing to notify the police as soon as it became clear that the vehicle had been stolen. Other decisions confirm that the failure to discover a

---

[90] [1968] 1 All E.R. 811; *Royston* v. *Hunslet* (1977) April 19th. Unrep. (C.A.); *The Arawa* [1977] 2 Lloyd's Rep. 416. Cf. *Wallace* v. *Safeway Caravan Mart Pty. Ltd.* [1975] 3 Queensland Lawyer 224, at 232-233; *Halbauer* v. *Brighton Corporation* [1954] 1 W.L.R. 1161, as to the liability of a bailee of caravans.

[91] See also, on this point, *Petersen* v. *Papakura Motor Sales Ltd.* [1957] N.Z.L.R. 495, at 500-501 where Turner J. held that an argument of this kind failed on the burden of proof. He cited with approval a statement by Callan J. in *Fletcher Construction Co. Ltd.* v. *Webster* [1948] N.Z.L.R. 514: "This shed may be burgled again, by the use of saws, gelignite or other means. But the impossibility of providing any shed which can be guaranteed secure does not absolve the employer from doing what is reasonable, nor from liability when the entry has actually been made by means of the respect in which the shed was not . . . properly secure". Cf. *Mitchell* v. *Ealing L.B.C.* (1978) *The Times*, Feb. 21st.

[92] *Cooper* v. *Dempsey* (1961) 105 Sol. Jo. 320; *Mendelssohn* v. *Normand Ltd.* [1970] 1 Q.B. 177; *Minichiello* v. *Devonshire Hotel (1967) Ltd.* (1976) 66 D.L.R. (3d) 619; *Petersen* v. *Papakura Motor Sales Ltd.* ante, n. 91; cf. *Bamert* v. *Parks* ante, n. 81; *British Motor Corporation of Canada Ltd.* v. *Ross E. Judge Auto Transport Ltd.* (1966) 56 D.L.R. (2d) 625; and see further p. 512 et seq., post.

[93] *Penny* v. *Grand Central Car Park Pty. Ltd.* [1965] V.R. 323; cf. *Ashby* v. *Tolhurst* [1937] 2 K.B. 242, where the proprietor was not a bailee.

[94] (1954) 91 C.L.R. 644; cf. *Shorter's Parking Station Ltd.* v. *Johnson* [1963] N.Z.L.R. 135, and see generally Chapter 5.

theft when a reasonably diligent man in the bailee's position would
have done so, or a failure to take reasonable steps for recovering the
goods within a reasonable time of such discovery, may constitute
negligence on the part of the custodian for reward.[95] Indeed, this conclusion may follow although the original theft is not attributable to any
want of reasonable care on the part of the bailee. In *Coldman* v. *Hill*,[96]
the leading authority on this point, the defendant had accepted a number
of cows from the plaintiff for agistment. Two of them were stolen without fault on his part, but he omitted to notify the plaintiff (or anyone
else) until some fifteen or sixteen hours later. The Court of Appeal held
him liable on the principle that when goods are stolen from a bailee
and reasonable diligence on his part could reasonably have been
expected to lead to their recovery he is liable for failing to employ such
diligence although the original misappropriation occurred independently
of his default. As Bankes L.J. pointed out, the defendant had evidently
considered himself under a duty to count the cattle regularly, and this
obligation would have been valueless had he not felt obliged, as a
reasonable man, to act upon his findings.[97] Once the defendant's lack
of diligence in failing to notify the plaintiff had been established (the
burden of which, after discharge of the bailee's conventional burden of
proving reasonable care while the goods were in his possession, fell
upon the plaintiff) the onus again shifted to the defendant to show that
the employment of such diligence could not reasonably have been
expected to result in a recovery of the goods, or of their value from
anyone who dealt in them:

> When, therefore, the respondent established the fact that the cows
> were stolen without any default on his part the onus of proof was
> shifted, and it rested with the appellant (plaintiff) to prove some act
> of negligence connected with the loss of the cows, in the sense that
> the loss may have been occasioned, or contributed to, by that act of
> negligence. That onus the county court judge finds the appellant dis-
> charged. Does the onus again shift, as it undoubtedly would, if the
> act of negligence complained of had occurred while the cows were still
> in the respondent's custody and control: as, for instance, if the com-
> plaint was that no attempt had been made to rescue an animal which
> had got fast in a ditch; or as, for instance, if an animal had been
> injured by some unexplained cause; or as, for instance, if something
> had occurred while the animals were still in the respondent's posses-
> sion, which rendered it reasonable that he should give the appellant
> notice of the facts, as in *Ranson* v. *Platt?*[98] I can see no sound reason
> why the rule should not be the same in one case as in the other. In
> both cases the breach of duty arises directly out of the contract of
> bailment, and the case seems covered by the rule that the bailee must
> show that the loss of the goods was not due to any fault of his own. In

---

[95] See, for instance, *Rubery Owen & Co. Ltd.* v. *Rea Ltd.* (ante, n. 80), where the
delay in discovering and reporting the theft of a number of cases from the
Liverpool docks, stolen over the Christmas holidays, amounted to some two to
four days.

[96] [1919] 1 K.B. 443. See also *Broadwater* v. *Blot* (1817) 5 Holt N.P. 547; 171 E.R.
336; *Edwards* v. *Newland and Co.* [1950] 2 K.B. 534.

[97] See post., 453, and *Leck* v. *Mestaer* (1807) 1 Camp. 138.

[98] [1911] 2 K.B. 291.

such a case as the present it may be said that the goods are not lost in the sense of being completely lost, so long as they are recoverable by any reasonable act on the part of the bailee; and it is, I think in this sense only that a loss without default on his part can be relied on by a bailee as a complete defence to an action for damages for loss of the goods.

Care must, of course, be taken not to extend unduly the duty of a bailee by expecting him to take action which may involve him in unreasonable expense or trouble; but no such question arises in this case.[99]

A similar view was adopted by Scrutton L.J. who inquired whether the bailee who saw a thief leaving his premises, or cattle straying from his field, was relieved of all further responsibility merely because until the point of escape or misappropriation he had guarded the goods with reasonable care. The answer was clearly in the negative; the bailee who found that goods in his control were menaced by a danger which could be averted only by unusual exertions was under a duty to do one of two things—either he must inform the bailor, if he could do so in sufficient time to enable the bailor to act, or he must act as an agent of necessity on the bailor's behalf and take whatever steps are reasonable in order to recover the goods. In the ordinary case, this duty would be most efficiently discharged by informing the police.[1]

Of course, the bailee need generally employ only that degree of care which is appropriate to the apparent value of the goods. He will not be answerable for showing a lower level of precaution than he reasonably believed was necessary. If, however, the circumstances of the deposit should have alerted him to the value of the property, he ignores these circumstances and exercises a lower degree of care than they warrant at his peril. In *Martin* v. *L.C.C.*[2] the defendant hospital authority negligently assumed that a quantity of jewellery taken from a patient admitted under the *Lunacy Act* was of insignificant value. As a result of this misconception, they failed to keep the jewellery in the safe and left it on the floor of a locked room, along with other items of small value. The jewellery was stolen and the defendants were held liable. Henn-Collins J. held that they were bailees for reward and had failed in their duty of care. A number of factors should have alerted them to the value of the jewellery; most notably a letter from the patient's sister inquiring as to its whereabouts and describing it in a manner which gave some intimation of its value.

A recent Canadian case[3] adopts a similar approach, and contains a suggestion that the bailee may owe a collateral duty to inquire into the value of bailed property whenever he is in doubt. The plaintiff, a jeweller, parked his car in the defendants' car park in circumstances

---

[99] [1919] 1 K.B. 443, at 449-450 per Bankes L.J.; see also Warrington L.J. at 452-453 and Scrutton J. at 454 et seq. It should be noted that in the view of Bankes L.J. the circumstances of the loss, while rendering the bailee liable for negligence, were not sufficient to found an action in detinue.

[1] Ibid., at 456-457.

[2] [1947] K.B. 628; for further cases involving hospitals and kindred institutions, see Chapter 5.

[3] *Minichiello* v. *Devonshire Hotel (1967) Ltd.* ante, n. 92; cf. *Mendelssohn* v. *Normand Ltd.*, ibid.

which clearly rendered them bailees for reward of the car. In accordance with practice he handed over the keys, and warned the attendant that there there were valuables in the boot of the car. The car was parked in the plaintiff's absence and the attendant left the keys inside. No further supervision was made of the vehicle and upon the plaintiff's return a case of jewellery (to an alleged value of $17,000) was found to have been stolen from the boot. Rae J. held that the defendants were bailees of the jewellery as well as of the car; that because of the warning he had uttered the plaintiff had not been contributorily negligent; and that the defendants were in breach of their duty of reasonable care:

> The valuables in this case consisted of a valuable quantity of jewellery, but it was open to the defendant through the attendant to inquire further as to the nature and value of the valuables and it did not do so. It was open to it to refuse to take the valuables into its care as distinct from the automobile, and it did not do so . . . Is it sufficient to bring to the attention of the bailee that he is taking into his care what the bailor regards as "valuables" in order to constitute the recipient bailee thereof? In my view it is.[4]

The decision may be regarded as a harsh one, and it may be questioned whether there was sufficient consent to justify implying a bailment of the jewels.[5] It nevertheless shows that liability may often be imposed when the bailee is given an opportunity to ascertain the value of the goods and, by failing to do so, forfeits the occasion to refuse them or to employ the higher and more appropriate standard of precaution. The same principle may be extended to apply to goods which are especially vulnerable to phenomena other than theft.

A redelivery to the bailor will generally exonerate the bailee from all further responsibility for the goods. Sometimes the redelivery may be only partial, and the question may arise as to whether a duty of care extends to parts of the defendant's premises other than those which are specifically set aside for storage. In *Barton, Ginger & Co. Ltd.* v. *Wellington Harbour Board*[6] an employee of the plaintiffs collected a packaged fishing-rod from the defendants' warehouse and left it propped up against a wall while he went in search of other goods. During his absence the fishing-rod was stolen. The defendants were held not liable for its loss because the conduct of the plaintiffs' employee had broken any possible nexus between their negligence (if any) and the theft: it was not their failure to store carefully that caused the loss but the fact that the employee had put the chattel where it was. It will be seen later that a bailor, by insisting upon a particular location for the storage of his goods against the bailee's judgment, may reduce the latter's responsibility.[7] This reduction should apply a fortiori where the bailee does not even know that the goods are left where they are.

If a theft is occasioned by the inadequacy of the bailee's padlocks, or by a failure in his burglar alarms, or by the unfitness of any other security device acquired from a reliable manufacturer, the bailee will

---

[4] *Minichiello's* case, ante, at 624.
[5] See, generally, Chapter 6.
[6] [1951] N.Z.L.R. 673.
[7] See post, p. 460 et seq.

be exonerated provided that he neither made the device unfit personally
nor had reason to suspect its malfunctioning.[8] If, on the other hand, he
delegates the actual duty of safekeeping to a third party, he remains
responsible for the manner in which the goods are guarded and will
be answerable for any default on the part of his delegate, irrespective
of whether the latter is a servant, an independent contractor or a sub-
bailee.[9]

(b) *Fire*: The bailee is not liable for accidental fire[10] unless special
circumstances have made him an insurer of the goods;[11] nor is he bound
to furnish an accurate explanation of how the fire occurred.[12] But the
damage or destruction of the goods by fire casts upon him a duty to
establish, on the balance of probabilities, that this was not caused by
a breach of his duty of care. If he cannot do this, the court will infer
that he has broken that duty and that the breach precipitated the loss.[13]

Combustible goods clearly demand a greater level of precaution
against fire damage, as do premises which are intrinsically prone to
ignition, and labour which involves a particular risk of fire. In *Smith* v.
Taylor[14] a garage-owner was held liable for the destruction of a customer's car by a fire which occurred shortly after an assistant had
negligently spilt petrol. The assistant had under-estimated the quantity
of petrol in the tank and had allowed some to overflow on to the floor
when attempting to drain it off. Blair J. held that although the cause
of destruction had not been positively established, it appeared on the
balance of probabilities that the negligent spillage, and consequent escape
of vapour, were responsible.

In places like garages where hazardous operations are often carried
on, the burden of disproving fault in a case of fire-damage will often be
a very weighty one. This emerges from the decision of the Appellate

---

[8] I.e., the bailee doe not warrant the safety of his premises: see, post, p. 454 et seq.,
and cf. *Riverstone Meat Co. Pty. Ltd.* v. *Lancashire Shipping Co. Ltd.* [1961]
A.C. 807.

[9] (Unless the contract provides otherwise): *Morris* v. *C. W. Martin & Sons Ltd.*
[1966] 1 Q.B. 716; *B.R.S. Ltd.* v. *Arthur V. Crutchley & Co. Ltd.* ante; *Philip
Morris (Australia) Pty. Ltd.* v. *The Transport Commission* [1975] Tas. S.R. 128, at
131.

[10] Cf. *Garside* v. *Trent & Mersey Navigation Proprietors* (1792) 4 Term. Rep. 581;
100 E.R. 1187.

[11] E.g. *North British & Mercantile Insurance Co.* v. *London, Liverpool and Globe
Insurance Co.* (1876) 5 Ch. D. 569 (affirmed (1877) 5 Ch. D. 569, at 578)
(custom); *Shaw & Co. Ltd.* v. *Symmons & Sons Ltd.* [1917] 1 K.B. 799 (deviation);
cf. the liability of the innkeeper, discussed post, at pp. 887-888.

[12] *Paterson* v. *Miller* [1923] V.L.R. 36, at 47; *Smith* v. *Taylor* [1966] 2 Lloyd's Rep.
231; *Thomas National Transport (Melbourne) Pty. Ltd.* v. *May & Baker (Australia) Pty. Ltd.* (1966) 115 C.L.R. 353; *A.A. Radio Taxi Trucks Ltd.* v. *Curyer*
[1965] S.A.S.R. 110 (where Napier C.J. remarked that when the lack of evidence
was so great that one could do no more than hazard a guess as to the cause of
the fire, it is no defence for the bailee merely to show that he did all he could
possibly do (or could do nothing) after it had arisen); *Selig* v. *Greenman* (1966)
51 M.P.R. 381.

[13] See, in addition to the cases cited in the text, *Fairbairn* v. *Miller* [1918] V.L.R.
615 (defendants liable for unexplained fire which broke out in furniture van,
although no employee smoking at the time); *Brunet* v. *Painchaud* (1915) Q.R.
48 s.c. 59; *Walt* v. *Newton Motors Ltd.* [1950] 2 D.L.R. 351; *Short* v. *Deer Lake
Sales & Service Ltd.* (1962) 47 M.P.R. 374; *Evans Products Ltd.* v. *Crest Warehousing Ltd.* (1977) 69 D.L.R. (3d) 575.

[14] [1966] 2 Lloyd's Rep. 231.

Division of the New Brunswick Supreme Court in *Northumberland County School Finance Board* v. *Stewart*,[15] where a school bus was destroyed by fire while parked in the defendant's garage. The defendant brought evidence to show that there were no inflammable liquids or substances on the premises; that no welding had been in progress; that no fire was alight in the furnace; that the garage floor was made of cement and was regularly cleaned with anti-flammable materials; that no-one had been smoking at the appropriate time; and that the garage was equipped with eight fire extinguishers. The Court nevertheless held against him, Bridges C.J. observing that "no evidence of even a possible cause of the fire had been advanced on their behalf." He cited with approval a statement by Harris J., in a case of mandatum that if the evidence be evenly balanced judgment must go against the bailee.[16]

Whether it is reasonable to expect the bailee to install alarms or sprinklers, or to employ watchmen against the risk of fire, depends upon the nature and location of the goods and the character of the bailee's own trade or undertaking. In many cases, an expectation that one or more of these precautions will be adopted will be justified: at least, where the risks are considerable.[17] In *F. & C. Clarke and Pickwick Foods Ltd.* v. *Redburn Wharves Ltd.*,[18] however, the defendant wharfingers were held not liable for failing to employ watchmen to guard against fire, nor for failing to cover a consignment of goods which were aboard a barge in the Thames. The fire risk was low in this setting and both precautions would have been beyond the ordinary contemplation of the reasonable man.

It is, of course, no defence for the bailee to show that the fire was caused by an unauthorised act (e.g., smoking) on the part of his servants, if those servants were acting at the time within the course of their employment or were carrying out the task for which their employer was engaged.[19]

The mere fact that a fire has occurred without fault on the bailee's part will not relieve him from the duty to do whatever is reasonable for the preservation of the goods. At the very least this should involve

---

15 (1966) 54 D.L.R. (2d) 657. Cf. *Romano* v. *Columbia Motors Ltd.* [1930] 1 D.L.R. 815; *Kitchen* v. *Goodspeed & Davidson Ltd.* (1966) 53 D.L.R. (2d) 140; *Selig* v. *Greenman* (1966) 51 M.P.R. 281; *British Motor Corporation of Canada Ltd.* v. *Ross E. Judge Auto Transport Ltd.* (1966) 56 D.L.R. (2d) 625 (lack of care presumed when extensive damage inflicted by juveniles in garage where night-watchman's duty was to make rounds every twenty minutes). For a case in which both principal and subordinate carriers were held liable for a fire caused by defective tyres on the subordinate carrier's lorry, see *Eastman International A.G.* v. *N.M.T. Trading Ltd.* [1972] 2 Lloyd's Rep. 25.

16 *Piper* v. *Geldart* [1954] 2 D.L.R. 97, at 105; see also *A.A. Radio Taxi Trucks Ltd* v. *Curyer* [1965] S.A.S.R. 110, 111. The statement in the text is somewhat similar to the remarks of Asquith L.J. relating to rebuttal of the inference of negligence raised by the principle res ipsa loquitur: *Barkway* v. *South Wales Transport Co. Ltd.* [1948] 2 All E.R. 460, at 471. See generally ante, p. 40 et seq.

17 For example, in timber yards, refineries and aircraft hangars. Aliter, in a private garage in relation to which the burden is probably more easily discharged: see *Thomas National Transport (Melbourne) Pty. Ltd.* v. *May & Baker (Australia) Pty. Ltd.* (1966) 115 C.L.R. 353.

18 [1974] 1 Lloyd's Rep. 52.

19 *Paterson* v. *Miller* [1923] V.L.R. 36; and see *Century Insurance Co. Ltd.* v. *Northern Ireland Road Transport Board* [1942] A.C. 509; post, p. 475.

telephoning the fire brigade and the owner: if the goods are not bulky, it should also include removing them to a place of safety.[20]

(c) *Judicial proceedings*: The bailee must notify the bailor (or at least make reasonable efforts to do so) in the event of any judicial proceedings which threaten to deprive the bailor of his goods. In *Ranson* v. *Platt*[21] the bailee failed to provide such notification and contented himself with a court appearance in which he asserted, without evidence, that the goods belonged to the plaintiff. It was held that this constituted a dereliction of his duty of reasonable care and that he was answerable to the ensuing loss. The magistrate's order depriving the plaintiff of her goods could not be invoked in his defence.[22]

(d) *Temperature changes and deterioration*: Perishable goods demand a more intensive degree of care and attention than most other commodities, and a failure to make regular inspections of such produce as frozen meat or fish will count as a failure to discharge the duty of reasonable care.[23] The goods must be kept at the appropriate temperature[24] and must be kept in a chamber which is designed or adapted for merchandise of that character: it would be negligent, for example, to store meat in a room normally used for storing beer.[25] A temperature change resulting from circumstances beyond the defendant's control will nevertheless result in liability if he fails to discover it within a reasonable period or omits to take steps to preserve the goods subsequent to such discovery.[26] When perishable goods deteriorate for an unexplained reason, the bailee will be answerable unless he can show that the deterioration was unconnected with any breach of his duty of reasonable care.[27]

The peculiar qualities of certain types of merchandise may necessitate specialist treatment. Thus, a bailee for reward was held liable for negligently failing to turn maize, as a result of which the warehouse

---

[20] See *Edwards* v. *Newland & Co.* [1950] 2 K.B. 524; post, p. 458.

[21] [1911] 2 K.B. 291, at 300, 308. Cf. *Baker* v. *Liscoe* (1797) 7 Term. Rep. 171; 101 E.R. 916.

[22] If the bailee cannot notify the bailor, he must do whatever else is reasonable to protect his interests: ibid., at 300, 308.

[23] See *Cordey* v. *Cardiff Pure Ice Co. Ltd.* (1903) 88 L.T. 192; *Fankhauser* v. *Mark Dykes Pty. Ltd.* [1960] V.R. 376; *Adams Bruce Ltd.* v. *Frozen Products Ltd.* [1953] N.Z.L.R. 63; *Geddes Refrigeration Ltd.* v. *Ward* (1962) 4 W.I.R. 170; *Apang Ice Ltd.* v. *Paria Ship Suppliers Ltd.* (1972) 19 W.I.R. 337.

[24] The proper temperature for frozen meat was recognised to be 14° to 16°F maximum by Donaldson J. in *F.M.C. (Meat) Ltd.* v. *Fairfield Cold Stores Ltd.* [1971] 2 Lloyd's Rep. 221 and by Wien J. in *United Fresh Meat Co. Ltd.* v. *Charterhouse Cold Storage Ltd.* [1974] 2 Lloyd's Rep. 286, at 287, although it was deposed in the latter case that general practice favours operating at 0°F. See further *Fankhauser's* case (ante) and, as to the protection of apples from deterioration, *Sharp* v. *Batt* (1930) 25 Tas. L.R. 33; *Aurora Trading Co. Ltd.* v. *Nelson Freezing Co. Ltd.* [1922] N.Z.L.R. 662.

[25] *Rinehard* v. *Inland Ice & Cold Storage Co. Ltd.* [1935] 2 D.L.R. 303. This may also amount to a deviation: see p. 472 et seq., post.

[26] Cf. *Fairline Shipping Corporation Ltd.* v. *Adamson* [1975] Q.B. 180.

[27] See *Gaylord* v. *Milne* [1933] Q.W.N. 47; 28 Q.J.P.R. 1, where the defendant was held liable after he had failed to call any evidence. It is, in fact, uncertain whether there was a bailment in this case. The more probable view is that there was.

became congested, the temperature rose and the plaintiff's wheat over-heated.[28]

(e) *Damage by proximate goods*: The custodian must take care to ensure that the goods are not allowed to come into contact with anything which might destroy or contaminate them, but he is not liable unless it was reasonably foreseeable that such damage or impairment would result. In *Labatt's Saskatchewan Brewery Ltd.* v. *Harrisons & Crosfield (Canada) Ltd.*[29] a warehouseman was sued in third-party proceedings by the manufacturer of a chemical filtering agent. The chemical had been stored in the third party's warehouse and had become contaminated through being near a quantity of herbicide which the third party was storing for another customer. When released from the warehouse and sold to a brewing company the chemical contaminated the purchaser's beer, which had to be destroyed. It was held that the bailors could not recover an indemnity from the warehouseman in respect of damages payable to the purchasers of the chemical because the warehouseman could not reasonably have been expected to possess sufficient chemical knowledge to know that contamination would occur, and because he did not know that the chemical was to be used in making beer. He had satisfied the duty of exercising "that care and diligence which a careful and vigilant owner would exercise in the custody of his own chattels of a similar description"[30]—a standard to which it may perhaps be objected that the ordinary, vigilant owner does not specialise in the storage of chemicals and cannot be taken to know the risks of doing so. At all events, the position may clearly have been different if the warehouseman had specialised in this aspect of his trade and had held himself out as possessing sufficient expertise to judge whether certain goods could safely be left in proximity to others; or if he failed to employ such knowledge as he did possess.

An agister will be liable if he puts an animal in a place inhabited by others of a dangerous disposition, if it is foreseeable that injury will result[31] In a recent case, the Jockey Club were held liable for keeping a racehorse in a box containing straw, as a result of which the horse ate the straw and contracted a cough.[32]

(f) *Defective premises and equipment*: Just as the custodian must take reasonable precautions to ensure that his premises are secure against theft, so he must exercise care to see that their physical condition is not likely to damage the goods or to admit external phenomena

---

[28] *Liverpool Grain Storage & Transit Co. Ltd.* v. *Charlton & Bagshaw* (1918) 146 L.T. Jo. 20; see also *Snodgrass* v. *Ritchie & Lamberton* (1890) 27 Sc. L.R. 546.
[29] (1969) 68 W.W.R. 449 (Saskatchewan Q.B.). Cf. *Evans Products Ltd.* v. *Crest Warehousing Ltd.* (1977) 69 D.L.R. (3d) 575 (goods damaged through being placed too near fire).
[30] Ibid., at 454.
[31] *Smith* v. *Cook* (1875) 1 Q.B.D. 79; *Sanderson* v. *Dunn* (1911) 32 A.L.T. (Supp.) 14; 17 A.L.R. (C.N.) 9. In both cases it was held that liability did not depend upon *scienter*. Cf. *Templeton* v. *Waddington* (1904) 24 C.L.T. Occ. N. 151; 14 Man. L.R. 495, where a stablekeeper was absolved because he did not know of the delinquent animal's disposition. See further *Animals Act* 1971; North, *Liability for Animals*.
[32] *Green* v. *The Jockey Club* (1975) 119 Sol. Jo. 258.

(such as wind, rain or tides) from which damage is likely to result.[33] Thus, the nature of the goods may require him to ensure that the building is free from damp[34] or vermin,[35] or is properly ventilated.[36]

The decision in *Searle* v. *Laverick*,[37] while confirming that a bailee owes a duty of reasonable care to protect the chattel from damage which might result from the condition of his premises, denies that at Common Law he provides any strict warranty of their safety. The defendant stored two carriages belonging to the plaintiff in a shed, which was still in the process of completion.[38] The construction of the shed had been entrusted to competent independent contractors, and the shed itself was, to the best of the defendant's knowledge, a safe and proper place in which to keep the carriages. However, it was blown down in a high wind and the carriages were damaged. In upholding the trial judge's non-suit, Blackburn J. rejected the suggestion that it was negligent of the defendant to store the vehicles in an unfinished building, because there was no evidence that its unfinished condition was the cause of the damage; it might have been otherwise if the carriages had been damaged by workmen dropping materials from aloft. He went on to hold that the custodian's duty is exclusively a duty of reasonable care, which cannot be increased by pleading an absolute warranty as to the safety of his building: partly because there was no authority for such an increase of liability, and partly because it would be unfair:

> The obligation to take reasonable care of the thing entrusted to a bailee of this class involves in it an obligation to take reasonable care that any building in which it is deposited is in a proper state, so that the thing therein deposited may be reasonably safe in it . . . There is, we think, a real difference between the case of one who supplies a carriage, or a seat in a temporary stand, which is in the nature of a chattel,[39] and one who supplies room for goods in a permanent building. We think that we must take notice of the fact that in the general and more ordinary state of things, a warehouseman or livery-stable keeper is tenant of the buildings in which he lodges the goods entrusted to him . . . It is true that, in some cases, the bailee is owner in fee of the building; and in some, as in the present case, he has had it built for him; and even where lessee he might take special covenants.

[33] E.g. *Brabant & Co.* v. *King* [1895] A.C. 632 (post, p. 457). Cf. *Winkworth* v. *Raven* [1931] 1 K.B. 652; *Harper* v. *Jones* (1879) 4 V.L.R. (L) 536; *Leck* v. *Mestaer* (1807) 1 Camp. 138.

[34] See *Mytton* v. *Cock* (1739) 2 Stra. 1099 (ante, p. 292) and *Turner* v. *Merrylees* (1892) 8 T.L.R. 695 (both cases of gratuitous bailment).

[35] *Kenyon, Son & Craven Ltd.* v. *Baxter Hoare & Sons Ltd.* [1971] 1 W.L.R. 519 (post, p. 936). Cf. *British Motor Corporation of Canada Ltd.* v. *Ross E. Judge Auto Transport Ltd.* (1968) 56 D.L.R. (2d) 625 (duty to protect from the depredations of vandals; breach of duty of care presumed in part because of extensiveness of damage).

[36] In *Mears* v. *Sayers* (1974) 41 D.L.R. (3d) 424, a bailee of cattle was held negligent in turning them out in sub-zero conditions after keeping them in a badly ventilated barn. The lack of ventilation increased the risk that pneumonia would develop on a sudden change of temperature.

[37] (1874) L.R. 9 Q.B. 122; cf. *Turner* v. *Merrylees* (1892) 8 T.L.R. 695. (ante, p. 296).

[38] Originally only one carriage was placed in the shed, but upon the complaint (and with the agreement) of the plaintiff, the second carriage was moved there too.

[39] *Readhead* v. *Midland Ry. Co.* (1867) L.R. 2 Q.B. 412; 4 Q.B. 379; *Francis* v. *Cockerell* (1870) L.R. 5 Q.B. 184 and 501.

But these are exceptional cases: and *in ea quae fraequentius accidunt praevenient iura.*[40]

Searle v. *Laverick* has stood without challenge for over a century, and seems unaffected by the *Occupiers' Liability Act* 1957.[41] But in certain instances an absolute obligation may represent the fairer standard of liability. Such an obligation may extend only to a specific part of the bailee's premises. For example, when the bailor insists that the bailee install burglar alarms or other devices for the special protection of the premises, and either contributes towards the cost of their purchase or pays an additional fee for the service, the bailee may be strictly liable for the efficiency of the alarms on a similar basis to any other "supplier".[42]

An agister must take reasonable steps to ensure that his land is safe for animals to roam upon, and will be liable for any direct loss which results from a breach of this duty. Thus he must use ordinary diligence to ensure that there are adequate fences[43] and to see that the place is free from hazardous conditions in which such animals are likely to fall or otherwise become injured.[44] It seems, however that this duty may be varied by an implied agreement based upon the practice in a particular locality, whether or not this practice is sufficiently certain or notorious to be elevated to the status of a custom. Thus in *Humphrey* v. *Phipps*[45] Beattie J. felt able to propound a number of propositions, at possible variance with the ordinary liability of an agister at Common Law, which would apply in the absence of express terms to a contract of agistment in New Zealand. The agister, in his view, must see that the animals roam over the grazing area, must advise the owner if he witnesses anything untoward and must make available for consumption by the animals such feed as there is available on the land. He does not contract to ensure that sufficient feed will be available for them for an undefined period and his duty of surveillance is dependent upon the

---

[40] (1874) L.R. 9 Q.B. 122, at 126-127, 131; cited with approval by Stawell C.J. in *Harper* v. *Jones* (1879) 4 V.L.R. (L.) 536, at 539-540.

[41] Section 5 (1) of the Act, which would normally apply to the situation, imposes upon the occupier only the common duty of care; but in any event the obligations imposed by any contract of bailment are excluded from s. 5(1) by s. 5(3). See North, *Occupier's Liability;* cf. *Defective Premises Act* 1972, ss. 1, 4.

[42] Cf. post, p. 531 et seq.

[43] *Broadwater* v. *Blot* (1817) 5 Holt N.P. 547; 171 E.R. 336 (which confirmed that the agister is not an insurer but is of doubtful wider authority because Gibbs C.J. indicated that the bailor carried the burden of proof); *Rooth* v. *Wilson* (1817) 1 B. & Ald. 59; 106 E.R. 22; *Smith* v. *Cook* (1875) 1 Q.B.D. 79 (bull in inadequately fenced adjoining field).

[44] *Halestrap* v. *Gregory* [1895] 1 Q.B. 561 (defendant's servant negligently left gate open and cow strayed on cricket field; club members tried to force cow back through gate and it fell over the surrounding wire fence: *held* defendant liable for injury); *Turner* v. *Stallibrass* [1898] 1 Q.B. 56 (defendant liable when horse fell over a low wire fence which the defendant had negligently allowed to become concealed and overgrown); *Grubb* v. *Cascade Brewery Co. Ltd.* (1903) 2 N. & S. (Tas.) 133 (defendant liable for death of horse in grassy bog, the existence of which he was unaware). See also *Mears* v. *Sayers* (1974) 41 D.L.R. (3d) 424; *McDermott* v. *Davis and Ross* [1922] G.L.R. 586. The position may differ when the owner of the animal knows of the character of the land: *Reid* v. *Calderwood* (1911) 45 I.L.T. Jo. 139; *Robinson* v. *Waters* (1920) 22 W.A.L.R.

[45] [1974] 1 N.Z.L.R. 650; citing the unreported case of *King and Hollis* v. *Hay* (1964) Unrep. 24th April (Hutchinson J.).
66; post, pp. 460, 468.

fee he is paid; when this is only moderate, the disappearance or death of an animal must be borne by the owner unless he can prove negligence on the part of the agister. Conversely, the owner should inspect the cattle periodically to ensure that they are safe and well. To a large extent, the inconsistency of these duties with those that normally arise upon a bailment of chattels provokes the question whether contracts of agistment in New Zealand do, in general circumstances, give rise to a bailment at all, and it is to be noted that Beattie J. merely "assumed" in the present case that the defendant was a bailee.

It follows from the foregoing that a custodian should make regular inspections of his premises to ensure that they continue to be safe for the storage of goods, and to confirm that appliances (such as heating systems and fire sprinklers) have not degenerated to the stage where they become a danger to the bailed property. If the maintenance of the building or its appliances is delegated to a competent contractor, the bailee will apparently be immune from liability provided that he has not delegated his "primary" duty of safeguarding of the goods[46] and should not reasonably have known of any potential danger.[47] No such exoneration should occur when damage results from negligent maintenance or repair by his own servants or agents.[48]

Often, a selection of locality which is prima facie negligent may be offset by a particular method of keeping the goods within that locality. This is impliedly recognised in the decision of the Privy Council in *Brabant & Co.* v. *King*[49] where, pursuant to a statute requiring that explosives be off-loaded upon entry to a port,[50] the Queensland Government had set up storage sheds close to the water's edge. The sheds were

---

[46] This distinction, which is suggested by a dictum of Lord Radcliffe in *Riverstone Meat Co. Pty. Ltd.* v. *Lancashire Shipping Co. Ltd.* [1961] A.C. 807, at 865-866, may prove difficult to draw. A duty to inspect one aspect of the premises to ensure that they do not constitute a danger seems no more than a part of the larger duty to take reasonable care; a duty which the bailee delegates at his peril. No doubt the terms of the agreement could be invoked in many cases to produce an implied permission to delegate those technical aspects of maintenance of which a bailee could not be expected to have personal knowledge, and an implied absolution of the bailee from further responsibility once such delegation has been properly made.

[47] In *Britain and Overseas Trading (Bristles) Ltd.* v. *Brooks Wharf & Bull Wharf Ltd.* [1967] 2 Lloyd's Rep. 51 bristles bailed by the plaintiffs were damaged by a burst water pipe in the defendants' warehouse. The defendants countered the plaintiffs' assertion that they had been negligent in failing to take precautions against the bursting of pipes in cold weather by contending that they in fact turned the stop-cocks off for the night during which the damage had occurred; that the pipes were lagged; that the injury occurred through the defective sealing of the valves owing to grit upon the stop-cocks; and by denying that the burst pipe had in fact caused damage to the bristles, insofar as the plaintiffs' employee had closed the cases in which the bristles had been contained rather than allowing them to dry. Widgery J. found that the defendants had taken all reasonable precautions to turn off the water overnight and were not in breach of their duty of care. A similar conclusion was reached, on comparable facts, in *Cartlidge* v. *Deboice* (1967) 62 W.W.R. 492.

[48] Post, p. 489.

[49] [1895] A.C. 632; see also *Petersen* v. *Papakura Motor Sales Ltd.* [1957] N.Z.L.R. 495, (bailees of car, whose premises were insufficiently protected from intruders, might nevertheless have escaped liability if they had locked the car and removed the ignition key); *Royston* v. *Hunslet* (1977) Unrep. April 19th (C.A.).

[50] *Queensland Navigation Act* 1876.

flooded and the plaintiff's explosives were rendered valueless. The Privy Council held that the Government were under a duty to preserve the goods with all the care and attention that might be expected from a skilled storekeeper; an obligation wihch involved not only the duty of taking all reasonable precautions to obviate those risks which were inherent in the nature of the goods and of the locality, "but the duty of taking all proper measures for the protection of the goods when such risks were imminent or had actually occurred."[51] The Privy Council felt that while no reasonable complaint could be made about the siting of the warehouses themselves (since this was plainly a matter of necessary convenience), the selection of such a site imposed a duty on the Government to make sufficient arrangements within these warehouses to see that the goods could be placed at a level which would ensure their probable immunity from floods.[52] The case was therefore remitted for trial, to establish whether the defendants had failed in either aspect of their duty of care: to safeguard the goods before the flood or to act promptly and diligently thereafter.

This decision acknowledges, as did *Coldman* v. *Hill*[53] in cases of theft, that the warehouseman may commit a breach of his duty of care by failing to protect the goods from a danger which has arisen independently of his default.[54] In *Edwards* v. *Newland & Co.*[55] a warehouse in which goods were stored was severely damaged by a bomb, and the goods were exposed to thieves. The Court of Appeal, while recognising that this event could scarcely have been induced or prevented by the warehousemen, held that it obliged them to take all reasonable precautions for the protection of the goods in the altered circumstances and Denning L.J. at least, expressed considerable reservations before deciding that this duty had been discharged.

The nature and value of the chattel will normally determine whether the bailee is entitled to leave it in the open air, or must keep in under cover. In most cases, the bailor will be entitled to expect some degree of protection from the elements; thus a bank, repossessing a tractor pursuant to a security agreement, was held to be in breach of its duty as a bailee for reward when it allowed the vehicle to deteriorate by leaving it in the open for three years.[56] It may be that such conduct would amount not merely to negligence but to a deviation from the terms of the bailment.[57]

---

51 [1895] A.C. 632, 640.
52 Ibid., at p. 641.
53 See ante, p. 448.
54 See also *Leck* v. *Mestaer* (1807) 1 Camp. 138; *Canadian Gas Power Launches* v. *Crosby* (1910) 30 C.L.T. 340; 8 E.L.R. 10.
55 [1950] 2 K.B. 534.
56 *Canadian Imperial Bank of Commerce Ltd.* v. *Doucette* (1968) 70 D.L.R. (2d) 657 (P.E.I. Supreme Court). Cf. *Mears* v. *Sayers* (1974) 41 D.L.R. (3d) 424 (cows turned out in snow); *Reid* v. *Canada Bay Lumber Co.* (1964) 51 M.P.R. 397 (tractor abandoned by hirer).
57 Post, p. 472.

Of course, the duty of care extends not only to the bailee's premises, but to any tackle or equipment with which he unloads or moves the goods.[58]

(g) *Other events*: The reports disclose a wide miscellany of events which may indicate a breach of the bailee's duty, or may oblige him to take steps to avoid committing one. Thus, it may be negligent for a warehouseman or carrier to store fragile goods beneath heavy ones;[59] to fail to take possession of the goods from the dockside at an agreed time;[60] to make the goods appear more attractive or easily disposable than they are;[61] to acknowledge receipt of the goods from a carrier "in good order and condition" although their outward appearance suggests otherwise;[62] or to fail to inform the bailor that, since immediate possession cannot be taken of his goods, he should make other arrangements for their safety in the interim.[63] In an old Canadian case[64] the plaintiff returned to the defendant's livery stable to find that the tail and mane of his horse had been cut off. The defendant was held liable because he could not prove that the damage was not due to the neglect or default of his servants.

(h) *The burden of proof in cases involving animals*: Many of the foregoing cases involve bailments of animals and it may be thought that the principles applying to such chattels are no different from the principles that apply to any other. There is, however, one decision which suggests that a shifting burden may operate in the case of animals which die from disease. In *Brazier* v. *Whelan*[65] the plaintiff sued the defendant stable keeper for damages arising from the death of his race-horse. The death was due to disease and Barry J. (after dismissing claims that the horse was ill-treated and that the defendant was guilty of a breach of contract in failing to insure it) held that the burden was on the plaintiff to prove that the disease would not have been contracted if the horse had been properly cared for. Since, however, the defendant had already discharged the burden of proving that the horse had been properly looked after, there seems to be little in this decision that is peculiar to the case of animals. Other authorities

---

[58] *Thomas* v. *Day* (1803) 4 Esp. 262; *Otago Harbour Board* v. *John Lysaght Ltd.* (1901) 20 N.Z.L.R. 541, at 543. Cf. *Richardson* v. *N. E. Ry. Co.* (1872) L.R. 7 C.P. 75, where the loss was caused by the deficiency of the bailor's equipment. A greyhound on a collar and chain was delivered to a railway company to be carried. A member of the railway staff tied the dog to a water pipe, but because of a fault in the collar the dog escaped and was killed. *Held,* the company were not liable. This case may, in turn, be contrasted with *Stuart* v. *Crawley* (1818) 2 Stark. 324, where a common carrier took delivery of a dog with a string around its neck in place of a lead, and tied it in a watch-box. The dog slipped its head through the noose and escaped. The carrier was held liable because he had the means of observing that the bailor's method of securing the dog was insufficient.

[59] *Wellington Harbour Board* v. *Jenkins & Mack Ltd.* [1949] G.L.R. 602; *Elder Dempster & Co. Ltd.* v. *Paterson, Zochonis & Co. Ltd.* [1924] A.C. 522; cf. *Heriteau* v. *W. D. Morris Realty Ltd.* [1944] 1 D.L.R. 28.

[60] *Quiggin* v. *Duff* (1836) 1 M. & W. 174; 150 E.R. 394.

[61] *Barton, Ginger & Co. Ltd.* v. *Wellington Harbour Board* [1951] N.Z.L.R. 673.

[62] Cf. *R.* v. *Whitlock* (1911) 13 W.A.L.R. 160, where the wharfinger was relieved because he had no occasion to suspect that part of the consignment had been stolen.

[63] *O'Neill* v. *McCormack & Co.* (1913) 15 W.A.L.R. 33.

[64] *Durocher* v. *Meunier* (1858) 9 L.C.R. 8; and see, post, p. 475 et seq.

[65] (1960) *The Times,* 21st July.

are equally inconclusive: in *Green* v. *The Jockey Club*[66] the burden of proof was not discussed and negligence was clearly established; while in *Wilson* v. *Dairy Fresh Farms*[67] the court held simply that an allegation that cows had been starved was against the weight of evidence.

2. *The bailor's knowledge, and its effect upon the standard of care:* In *Brabant & Co.* v. *King*[68] the Privy Council rejected the argument that the bailee's liability should be qualified or excluded by the bailor's knowledge of the unsafe conditions of the premises in which the explosives were kept:

> It would be a very dangerous doctrine, for which there is not a vestige of authority, to hold that a depositor of goods for safe custody, who by himself or by his servants, had had an opportunity of observing certain defects in the storehouse, must be taken to have agreed that any risk of injury to his goods which might possibly be occasioned by these defects should be borne by him, and not by his paid bailee. The authorities relating to the vexed maxim "volenti non fit injuria" have no bearing whatever on the point. From the very nature of the transaction the depositor is entitled to rely upon the care and skill of his bailee. The duty is incumbent upon the latter, in the due fulfilment of his contract, of considering whether his premises can be safely used for the storage of explosives or other goods, and, if they cannot, to take immediate steps for placing the goods in a position of safety. If the defects of these Government magazines were as apparent to the servants of the appellant company as the jury have found they were, they ought to have been equally patent to the official storekeeper, with whom the duty of safe custody rested.

This decision is of high authority, and the principle in question was stated in emphatic and general terms. It has been accepted by the majority of modern writers[69] and, on at least one occasion, by the Court of Appeal.[70] But it must be read subject to a number of qualifications.

First, the bailor may have taken upon himself the task of untoward events, by interfering with the bailee's exercise of his own discretion and by insisting that the goods be placed in a particular location. If the selected location is less safe than other parts of the bailee's premises, and if the bailee would not at his sole discretion have stored the goods where they were stored, it would be fair for his customary responsibility to be reduced; at least when his own words, or the circumstances of the deposit, make it clear that the bailor acts on his own initiative and, accordingly, at his own risk.[71]

---

[66] (1975) 119 Sol. Jo. 258.

[67] (1967) 117 New L. Jo. 295.

[68] [1895] A.C. 632, at 641.

[69] E.g. *Chitty on Contracts* (23rd edn.), para. 182.

[70] *Edwards* v. *Newland & Co.* [1950] 2 K.B. 534; but here both the circumstances rendering the goods unsafe and the knowledge thereof arose *after* the bailment was created, so that the bailor had less of an effective option in permitting the bailee to remain in possession.

[71] E.g. *Fournier* v. *McKenna* (1921) 57 D.L.R. 725 (ante, p. 208) which was probably a case of involuntary bailment. Cf. *Talley* v. *G. W. Ry. Co.* (1870) L.R. 6 C.P. 44 (especially at p. 52); *Barton, Ginger & Co. Ltd.* v. *Wellington Harbour Board* ante, p. 459.

The most vivid illustration of this form of exclusion is to be found in *Harper* v. *Jones*.[72] The plaintiffs' manager deposited rice for storage at the defendants' warehouse, and demanded that it be kept on the floor of the building. The defendants wanted to store the rice on a raised platform but the plaintiffs' manager, fearing that other consignments of rice on the same platform might contain weevils, overruled them so emphatically that, against their better judgment, they agreed to keep the rice on the floor. A sudden and extraordinary flooding caused the warehouse to become waterlogged and the plaintiffs' rice was lost, but the water level did not reach the platform and the rice which was stored there was saved. The Victorian Supreme Court held for the defendant, Stawell C.J. observing that:

> . . . the plaintiffs, by their selection of the place of storage, took upon themselves the risks, consistently with reasonable care on the part of the defendant, peculiar to that place; such for instance as would not have arisen had the goods been deposited on the platform, as the defendants advised.[73]

Barry J. concurred, pointing out that the question could be regarded as one of causation: the plaintiffs were the true authors of their own injury, for it flowed "proximately and mediately" from their insistence that the rice be kept on the floor.[74]

The bailee in a case like *Harper* v. *Jones* is faced with something of a dilemma. If he takes it upon himself to override the bailor's instructions and remove the goods to a safer place, he presumably commits a deviation and becomes liable for all ensuing loss, whether due to his default or not. If he keeps the goods in the place demanded, he must continue to take what ever precautions are practicable to preserve them; the defendants in *Harper* v. *Jones,* for example, would have been liable if the warehouse had been carelessly constructed or if it had been ordinarily prone to floods and they had failed to warn the bailor. The difficulty arises when the stipulated place of storage is so unsafe or exposed to hazard that reasonable care, in any meaningful sense, becomes impossible. In cases of locatio operis faciendi a promise to perform the impossible has occasionally been held enforceable, with the result that a bailee may be liable for failing to achieve results which nobody could practically have achieved;[75] it is possible that a similar approach may be taken when a bailee promises to take reasonable care of the goods in an environment in which such care is, objectively, impossible. A more likely interpretation is that the promise to take reasonable care is qualified by the situation in which reasonable care is to be taken. At all events, the bailee should not be exonerated unless the bailor unambiguously agrees that he should be, or demonstrably and exclusively precipitates his own loss. Sometimes the bailor may be bargaining for a service or for advice from the warehouseman and may be relying upon him to discourage the bailor from any notions of his own that are dangerous or impractical.

---

[72] (1879) 4 V.L.R. (L.) 536.
[73] Ibid., at 542.
[74] Ibid., at 543.
[75] Post, p. 518.

A second facet to the problem arises when there is no initial agreement as to the place or manner of storage, and no persuasion of the bailee to adopt a lesser method against his better judgment. In *Brabant & Co.* v. *King,* for instance, both parties had been agreed from the beginning as to where the goods should be kept. Perhaps surprisingly, there is considerable evidence of a tendency to exonerate the defendant in cases of this kind. Thus, in *Mayfair Photographic Supplies (London) Ltd.* v. *Baxter, Hoare & Co. Ltd.*[76] it was held that a carrier was not guilty of a breach of duty in using uncovered vehicles because the bailor knew that he operated exclusively in vehicles of that kind; and in *Reid v. Calderwood*[77] Cherry, L.J., held that where a contract for agistment was made which involved putting the plaintiff's cow in a field which contained an open quarry, the defendant should be exonerated from liability for injuries sustained by the cow in falling into the quarry because the plaintiff knew that the cow was to be put in that field, and knew that there was an unfenced quarry in it. The latter is an extreme case, and must be viewed in the light of Cherry L. J.'s acceptance of the defendant's story that he had warned the plaintiff that the cow would be treated in exactly the same manner as his own.[78]

A Canadian case also provides some recognition of the mitigating effect of a bailor's knowledge of the condition of his bailee's premises. The bailment in *Murphy* v. *Hart,*[79] was created by the leaving of the plaintiff's overcoat upon a rack in the defendant's restaurant, and Harris C.J., rejected the defendant's contention that the plaintiff knew there was no supervision of the rack, on the grounds that there was insufficient evidence of such knowledge. He then cited a passage from an American decision to illustrate the clarity with which any acquiescence to a lower standard of care must be demonstrated:

> Mere knowledge of the mode in which a depository receives and takes care of property entrusted to him will not operate to absolve him from all liability to those who employ him with such knowledge of a want of due care in the keeping of their property. Such knowledge accompanied by evidence of long acquiescence without objection by an employer might be evidence of an agreement as to the nature and degree of care which was to be used by the bailee but beyond this it would not be safe to go.[80]

A reduction in the bailee's liability seems generally fair in cases where there is clear evidence of an agreement to accept a reduced service. A number of factors may help to differentiate between cases in which

---

[76] [1972] 1 Lloyd's Rep. 410; post, p. 937. Cf. *Saunders (Mayfair) Furs Ltd.* v. *Chas. Wm. Davis Ltd.* [1966] 1 Lloyd's Rep. 78, at 83.

[77] (1911) 45 I.L.T. Jo. 139 (Ireland). A somewhat similar case is *Robinson* v. *Waters* (1920) 22 W.A.L.R. 66, where, however, the terrain does not seem to have been a direct cause of the animal's injury and the complaint centred rather upon the bailee's inability to locate and return it: post, p. 468.

[78] Generally, of course, the fact that the bailee took as much care of the bailor's goods as of his own will not discharge him if he failed to take reasonable care: see in this context, *Re United Service Co.* (1870) L.R. 6 Ch. App. 212.

[79] (1919) 46 D.L.R. 36 (Nova Scotia Supreme Court).

[80] *Conway Bank* v. *American Express Co.* (1864) 8 Allen (Mass.) 512, 516, *per* Bigelow, C.J.; cf. *Knowles* v. *Atlantic R. R. Co.* 41 Am. Dec. 234; *Brown* v. *Hitchcock* 28 Vt. 452.

there has been such an agreement and those where there has not: one factor might be the exaction of a lower rate of charges than normal, and another might be the availability of alternative services to the bailor. The latter point was made in a Quebec decision[81] where Andrews J. distinguished *Brabant & Co.* v. *King* on the ground that the plaintiffs there had little option as to where they should leave the explosives:

> Applied to the particular case in which these words [82] appear to have been used the result would work nothing but justice; because in that case the storage was a forced one, the statutory law of the Colony of Queensland compelled the storing of explosive in the particular Government store in which the River Brisbane rose and flooded and ruined them. There could be no question of the doctrine of "volenti non fit injuria", for the owner of the goods could have no will in the matter, he had no choice. But could those ideas be justly applied to the owner of the store who says: "use my store if you like", but who at the same time says "the tide has come into it, and may do so again."[83]

The response in the present case was in the negative, and the warehouseman was relieved of responsibility not only for the initial (and forewarned) flooding of the plaintiff's salt in the lower part of his warehouse, but also for failing to carry them to safety between the first flood and the second; the defendants had provided what they had contracted to provide in the shape of unsafe accommodation at a lower rate.

Three conditions should, however, be fulfilled before the ordinary duty of reasonable care can be overridden in this way. First, that duty should be displaced only by evidence of a free and unequivocal agreement to the contrary; secondly, that agreement should, like the conventional exclusion clause, be construed strictly against the bailee; and thirdly, the burden of proving that such an agreement has superseded the ordinary duty of care should be upon the party alleging it.[84] Since agreements of this kind are almost invariably implicit rather than express, it seems likely that they will remain the exception rather than the rule. But it would be unfortunate if the statements in *Brabant & Co.* v. *King* (having, apparently, been more often distinguished than applied) should, by becoming accepted as a dogmatic principle, be allowed to obscure the exact content of the agreement.[85]

---

[81] *Fry* v. *Quebec Harbour Commissioners* (1896) Q.R. 9 S.C. 14; affirmed (Hall J. dissenting) Q.R. 5 Q.B. 144.

[82] I.e., per Lord Watson at 641; ante, p. 460.

[83] (1896) Q.R. 9 S.C. 14, at 21.

[84] This was apparently accepted by Andrews J. in *Fry* v. *Quebec Harbour Commissioners* (ante) at 23, citing *Brown* v. *Hitchock* 28 Vt. 452.

[85] It should be noted, as a postcript, that the mitigation of the bailee's duty by the bailor's foreknowledge and approval may be considerably harder in the case of a bailment for reward, where there is "ostensibly, a contract for reasonable care to be taken" than in the case of a bailment which is gratuitous. Thus, in *Joyce* v. *Kettle* [1948] St.R.Qd. 139, at 143 (reversed on appeal ibid., at 145 et seq; (1948) 77 C.L.R. 39) Philp J. speaking obiter, confined his remarks to gratuitous bailment: " . . . the matter is somewhat analagous to the acceptance of gratuitous bailment of goods in a store with an obviously leaky roof. I apprehend that in such a case a term of the bailment is the acceptance by the bailor of the risk attendant on the obvious danger". As to the relevance of the defences of volenti

The foregoing observations may be applied mutatis mutandis to cases in which it is not the character of the premises but that of the bailee himself which produces a foreseeable loss of the bailor's goods. There are, as we have seen, occasional statements to the effect that a knowledge of the bailee's character may produce a reduction on the normal standard of competence or care.[86] Although, to date, no decision has turned upon the point,[87] it may be possible, in exceptional cases, for the bailee's duty of safekeeping to be consensually qualified in this way.[88]

3. *Insurers by agreement or custom:* The parties are free to make a special contract placing the entire responsibility for loss or damage upon the bailee, irrespective of fault. Occasionally, such liability may also be imposed by custom. There is a dictum of Sir George Jessel M.R. equating the liability of a wharfinger in the City of London with that of a common carrier,[89] but later decisions do not seem to have turned upon the point. In *Jaffa* v. *Waxman*[90] the plaintiff unsuccessfully alleged a custom in the fur trade whereby traders accepted full responsibility for skins bailed for inspection; a more successful attempt was made in relation to the diamond trade in *Kay* v. *Shuman*,[91] where it was held that there was a custom among dealers and brokers on the London Diamond Bourse that persons taking stones on approval were wholly accountable for their value until they were either paid for or returned. Although the custom was held in the present case not to apply to small retail shops, the defendant wats found liable on the alternative ground of an express oral agreement to be responsible as an insurer.

B. The duty to redeliver

The bailee must return the goods to the bailor or to his appointed agent at the time and place agreed. Care must be taken to distinguish between the various standards of liability and burdens of proof which may arise when a breach of this obligation is alleged.

In most cases, an action for breach of the bailee's duty of care can be alternatively framed as an action for breach of his promise to redeliver.[92] This action is not confined to cases in which the goods have

---

non fit injuria and contributory negligence in this situation, see ante, p. 55 et seq; *A. S. James Pty. Ltd.* v. *C. B. Duncan* [1970] V.R. 705; *Walker* v. Watson [1974] 2 N.Z.L.R. 175; *Minichiello* v. *Devonshire Hotel (1967) Ltd.* (1976) 66 D.L.R. (3d) 619, at 625-626.

[86] See ante, pp. 301, 334; post, p. 520.
[87] Cf. *Walker* v. *Watson* [1974] 2 N.Z.L.R. 175, involving an inebriated borrower, where the question was approached as one of contributory negligence or volenti non fit injuria; ante, pp. 22, 364.
[88] E.g., by exacting a lower standard of care from a private pledgee or custodian than would be expected from someone to whom goods were bailed in the course of a business: cf. *Giles* v. *Carter* (1965) 109 Sol. Jo. 452; *Gutter* v. *Tait* (1947) 177 L.T.I. (post, p. 512).
[89] *North British & Mercantile Insurance Co. Ltd.* v. *London, Liverpool & Globe Insurance Co. Ltd.* (1876) 5 Ch. D. 569 (affirmed (1877) 5 Ch. D. 569, at 578). But cf. *Sidaways* v. *Todd* (1818) 2 Stark. 400, at 401; 171 E.R. 685, at 686 per Abbott C.J.
[90] [1966] 2 Lloyd's Rep. 344 (Bloomsbury County Court).
[91] (1954) *The Times*, 22nd June.
[92] *Paterson* v. *Miller* [1923] V.L.R. 36, at 46 per McArthur J. (who thought that if the plaintiff were suing in assumpsit or case rather than in detinue, both the duty to redeliver and the breach thereof may require to be separately pleaded); *Tozer,*

been destroyed or lost, and in which any form of redelivery is, therefore, impossible; it can equally apply where there is a delay in redelivery, or where the goods are merely damaged, for the essence of the bailee's promise is to return the goods in the condition in which they were bailed.[93]

Generally, there wil be no difficulty in assessing the relationship between this promise and the traditional duty of care. When the bailor complains of destruction, damage or loss, the duty to redeliver is not an absolute one but is qualified by the bailee's central undertaking to exercise reasonable diligence in the management of the chattel.[94] Thus, the bailee, confronted by proof of these events, may escape by establishing that he took proper care, or that any failure to take such care was not an effective cause of the loss.[95] But other aspects of the promise to redeliver may be independent of the duty of reasonable care, and may give rise to liability although due care has been taken.

An obvious example relates to the time of redelivery. The bailee must return the goods to the bailor, or make them available for his collection, either at the agreed or at any reasonable time. Generally, the bailee who fails in this obligation and temporarily delays in redelivering the goods will be liable for a breach of the terms of the bailment,[96] irrespective of whether he has used reasonable care in attempting to fulfil the stated promise. In *Stallard* v. *G. W. Ry. Co.*,[97] for instance, the plaintiff was awarded forty shillings damages for a forty minute delay in redelivery at Paddington left-luggage office. The delay occurred because the office was shut on a Sunday evening, and the plaintiff missed the last train out of town as a result. The Court held that by failing to make it clear that articles would not be retrievable at all times on a Sunday, and by stipulating on its tickets of deposit that luggage would be delivered up only to persons producing such a ticket,[98] the Railway undertook to redeliver within a reasonable period of any demand, which was itself made at a reasonable time. "The proper construction of the bailment evidenced by the ticket is, that the Company undertook to deliver up the portmanteau on a reasonable request and within a reasonable time."[99] However, both Cockburn C.J. and Mellor J. had reservations about the jury's finding that a forty minute delay on a Sunday was unreasonable.[1]

Kemsley & Millbourn (Australasia) Pty. Ltd. v. *Collier's Interstate Transport Service Ltd.* (1956) 94 C.L.R. 384, at 400, per Fullagar J.; *John F. Goulding Pty. Ltd.* v. *Victorian Railways Commissioners* (1932) 48 C.L.R. 157.

[93] Cf., the action in detinue which cannot be founded on more damage: ante., p. 148.
[94] This assumes that the bailee is not guilty of conversion or of a deviation, liability for which is strict: ante., p. 124; post., p. 472.
[95] Ante., p. 440 et seq. The burden stated in the text applies equally to the bailee in an action for detinue: *Reeve* v. *Palmer* (1858) 5 C.B.N.S. 84; *Paterson* v. *Miller,* [1923] V.L.R. 36, 45; *Houghland* v. *R. R. Low (Luxury Coaches) Ltd.,* [1962] 1 Q.B. 694.
[96] And thereupon may become an insurer: see *Shaw & Co., Ltd.* v. *Symmons & Sons, Ltd.,* [1917] 1 K.B. 799; *Mitchell* v. *Ealing* [1978] 2 W.L.R. 999.
[97] (1862) 2 B. & S. 419; 121 E.R. 1129.
[98] Cf. p. 201, ante.
[99] Per Blackburn J. at 425, 1132.
[1] Cf. *Pepper* v. *S. E. Ry Co.* (1868) 17 L.T. 469, where liability for delay was held (perhaps questionably) to have been excluded.

By taking advantage of the fact that the duty to redeliver may be an absolute one, the bailor loses his advantage on the question of proof. If, for example, he wishes to sue for breach of the promise to redeliver *at a certain time,* he must apparently prove both the promise and its breach, because the action is a simple action in contract and the ordinary rules of proof apply.[2] The advantage is that the bailee can no longer evade responsibility by showing that he took all reasonable care. By switching from a simple action on the bailment to a "superadded" action in contract, the bailor both gains and loses.

But what if an action for breach of the promise to redeliver is itself based upon an event (like damage or loss by theft) against which the bailee's liability is not absolute but depends upon the duty of reasonable care? In *Paterson* v. *Miller*[3] McArthur J. tentatively advanced the general rule that the bailee's burden of proof applies whether the bailor's action is founded upon detinue, case or assumpsit. The case in which this observation was made involved the destruction of goods by fire, and the observation must be regarded as confined to cases in which a duty of care is relevant. Clearly, in relation to those aspects of the duty to redeliver that are strict or absolute in character, such as the duty to redeliver at a certain time, or to a certain person, or in a certain place, the bailee's burden of proof is irrelevant. It can hardly be said that the bailor need only allege a breach of such a promise and that the bailee must thereupon rebut it; and if, on the other hand, the bailor must affirmatively prove that the promise has been broken, the bailee has nothing to gain by proving reasonable care in the fulfilment of the promise because this is immaterial to liability.[4]

Even with regard to actions which are founded upon a duty of reasonable care, a strict analysis would suggest that the plaintiff who sues for breach of the promise to redeliver must prove every component of that action. This was the substance of certain doubts entertained by Cussen J. in *Paterson* v. *Miller* as to the validity of McArthur J.'s analysis:

> What, in the absence of any express arrangement in a case like the present, is the implied duty, or in assumpsit, the implied promise — is it a duty or promise to take reasonable care to keep the goods securely, and a separate duty or promise to return the goods unless some excuse is shown? Or is it a duty or promise to take reasonable care both to keep and to deliver goods safely? If the latter is correct, the plaintiff in such a case as this, at any rate where the direct cause of loss is admitted, would have to allege negligence and would have to make out at least a *prime facie* case of negligence.[5]

In fact, it would seem advisable to segregate the two varieties of promise: not merely because of the problems which their conjunction would create as to the burden of proof, but because, as we have seen,

---

[2] Admittedly such obligations might also be superadded to a gratuitous bailment, but the same onus of proof as in an action for breach of contract would apply.

[3] [1923] V.L.R. 36.

[4] Quaere, as to who bears the onus of proving the connection between the breach and the loss: presumably the plaintiffs, although this question will normally be raised by the defendant.

[5] Ante, at 48.

some elements of the promise to redeliver import an absolute duty.[6]
The result would be that when the bailor sues for breach of the duty
of care the onus is on the defendant, but that when he sues for breach
of the promise to redeliver the onus is upon himself. But practically
speaking, such problems are unlikely to trouble the courts in cases where,
whatever the formal character of the action, the essence of the bailor's
complaint of non-delivery is a failure by the bailee to discharge his
obligation of reasonable care. In such a case, the court will probably
look to the substance of the action in determining the location of the
burden of proof. Thus, in *Fankhauser* v. *Mark Dykes Pty. Ltd.*[7]
Scholl J. offered the following observations upon the statement of
Cussen J. cited earlier:

> It would be difficult to suppose the bailee's promise to be (a) to use
> reasonable care to keep safely, plus an independent promise, (b) to
> redeliver, subject only to causes not attributable to his own default;
> for the former obligation would merge in the latter, which would be
> more extensive than it. But it would seem that his real promise must
> now, on the authorities, be taken to be a promise to keep safely and
> to redeliver in good condition, subject only to a discharge from lia-
> bility if he can show that any failure to do either was due to a cause
> not attributable to his own default.

The fact remains that the two promises have often been treated as
separate and that a bailee sued for non-delivery is not always entitled
to escape liability by proving that he took reasonable care. For this
reason, the formulation of his promise by Scholl J. works only if it is
remembered that this formulation is restricted to the fundamental duties
that arise under the bailment, liability for the breach of which is conditional upon lack of care. In other respects, due care and the duty
to redeliver may be entirely separate.

Hitherto, we have assumed that a provision as to the time of redelivery
imposes a strict contractual obligation. In fact, this depends upon the
terms of the contract; and in certain cases a time provision may be
enforceable only when broken through want of reasonable care. This
qualification may exist in the case of temporary delay, and will almost
invariably be implied in the case of delay which is likely to be
permanent. So much may be inferred from a Western Australian case,
where the chattel in question was not definitely known to have been
permanently lost, and may merely havce been mislaid in an area from

---

[6] A number of decisions have held that the duties of redelivery and reasonable
care are entirely separate and can sometimes afford alternative causes of action.
These include *Corbett* v. *Packington* (1827) 6 B. & C. 268; *The Coast Prince*
[1967] 2 Lloyd's Rep. 290 (British Columbia Admiralty Court); *John F. Goulding
Pty. Ltd.* v. *Victorian Railways Commissioners* (1932) 48 C.L.R., at 160 (per
Dixon C.J. arguendo) and 168-169 (High Court of Australia). In the latter case,
the independent character of the promise to redeliver was invoked in order to
allow the bailor to recover in detinue, after a demand for the return of the
goods, although the limitation date for an action for breach of the bailee's duty
of care was statute-barred (see now *Limitation Act* (1939) (U.K.), s. 3(1)). In
the court below, [1932] V.L.R. 243, Cussen A.C.J. had held that *on the facts of
this case* the two duties were compound and indissociable and that the limitation
period could not be surmounted. He cited in this connection *Granger* v. *George*
(1826) 5 B. & C. 149.

[7] [1960] V.R. 376, at 378 (Vic. Full Sup. Ct.).

which it would have been very difficult to retrieve. The bailment (if there was one)[8] in *Robinson* v. *Waters*[9] was by way of agistment, and the place of agistment was a heavily timbered paddock of six thousand acres. The bailor knew this when he handed over his mare to the defendant and seems to have realised that redelivery would be no overnight exercise, because he subsequently gave about two months' notice when he wanted the mare returned. The defendant made intensive efforts to find the mare but saw it only once before the plaintiff sued for damages for its non-delivery. The Full Supreme Court held that the most likely explanation was that the horse had died and that its carcase had escaped detection, and held the defendant not liable because there was no evidence that he had failed to use reasonable care. The case is not free from difficulty because the Court was not convinced that the horse was in the defendant's possession during the agistment; moreover, it declined to offer any guidance as to the burden of proof.[10] It may, nevertheless, provide an illustration of the sort of circumstances in which a bailor, by his knowledge of the enormity of the defendant's premises or of the nature of his organisation, may be deemed to have impliedly agreed that the time of redelivery shall be observed, not strictly, but only by the exercise of reasonable care.

Apart from stipulations as to time, the two aspects of the duty to redeliver that are most likely to provoke litigation are the duty to deliver to a particular person, and the duty to deliver to a particular place. The latter is of little theoretical importance because in the majority of cases the bailee will merely be required to make the goods available for collection at his premises; and fairly strong evidence may be required before the courts would uphold an alleged obligation to transport the goods elsewhere. As a general rule, it may be assumed that promises as to the place of redelivery are strict, and that the bailee cannot evade them merely by proof of reasonable care. Moreover, the burden of establishing breach will presumably rest upon the bailor.[11]

The bailee must deliver only to those persons to whom he is authorised to deliver; if he misdelivers he will be guilty of a breach of the terms of the bailment and again (it seems) cannot escape merely by showing that he was not negligent.[12] Negligence is merely one basis of liability against the bailee for reward, and is not a universal qualification upon his liability. In the absence of express agreement delivery

---

[8] Cf. *Helton* v. *Sullivan* [1968] Qd. R. 562.

[9] (1920) 22 W.A.L.R. 66.

[10] Ibid., at 66-67.

[11] But cf. post., pp. 469, 947 et seq.

[12] Quite apart from liability upon the promise, the bailee who misdelivers will be liable for conversion, even if his conduct was innocent: *Devereux* v. *Barclay* (1819) 2 B. & Ald. 702; 106 E.R. 521; *Helson* v. *McKenzies (Cuba St.)* Ltd. [1950] N.Z.L.R. 878. He may also be guilty of a fundamental breach of contract: *Alexander* v. *Railway Executive* [1951] 2 K.B. 862; *Penny* v. *Grand Central Car Park Pty. Ltd.* [1965] V.R. 323; cf. *Hollins* v. *J. Davy Ltd.* [1963] 1 Q.B. 844. But the warehouseman is not liable for a misdelivery induced by the negligence or default of the bailor or of any person for whom he is responsible: *David Crystal Inc.* v. *Cunard S.S. Co. Ltd.* [1963] 2 Lloyd's Rep. 315 (U.S. District Court).

should be made only to the bailor himself or to any servant or agent having actual, implied or ostensible authority to receive the goods.[13]

Theortically, the burden of proving that delivery has been made to an unauthorised person should rest upon the bailor; he is relying upon a special term of the contract to enforce the obligation and must, therefore, prove both that contract and its breach. This principle was accepted by the High Court of Australia in *Tozer, Kemsley & Millbourn (Australasia) Pty. Ltd.* v. *Collier's Interstate Transport Service Ltd.*[14] where Dixon C.J. phrased the duty in the following way:

> In a bailment of this description the onus lies on a bailor who complains of the loss of the goods through misdelivery to prove by reasonable evidence that the bailee did not perform his undertaking; that is to say that he did not deliver the goods in accordance with the terms of the contract of bailment: cf. *Griffiths* v. *Lee;*[15] *Gilbert* v. *Dale;*[16] *Midland Ry. Co.* v. *Bromley.*[17] To prove so much does not establish conclusively that the bailee is responsible: for the bailee may have some affirmative answer.[18]

In *Tozer, Kemsley's* case, however, special circumstances gave rise to an adaptation of the conventional rule. The defendant warehousemen accepted goods from the plaintiffs on terms that they were to be delivered only by order endorsed on the storage warrant. A quantity of the goods went missing, apparently after the defendants had delivered them without demanding production of the warrant to a person named Cann. It emerged that the plaintiffs had required the defendants to deliver goods to one Duncan, a carrier, and the defendants claimed that Cann was either in Duncan's employment or was in the employment of somebody employed by Duncan. The evidence in the case was obscure and both parties called very few witnesses, but the defendants relied upon an allegation that their delivery to Duncan was to be made without production of the customary warrant. The High Court held that they were liable because they could not prove their allegation. Although in normal circumstances the burden is upon the bailor to prove a misdelivery contrary to his instructions, in the present case the plaintiffs had adequately proved this by production of their *written* contract of bailment requiring delivery upon the production of warrants. If the defendants wished to rely upon a variation of that written contract, they must prove the variation, and in the present case they had failed to do so:

> Once the defendant delivers otherwise than in strict accordance with the terms of the contract of bailment and goes beyond or outside what it is bound to do, it cannot rest simply upon the contract, but must adduce the evidence that what it did was in actual accordance with some request of the plaintiff or was otherwise effectual, authorised or

---

[13] Cf. *Cobban* v. *Downe* (1803) 5 Esp. 41; *Leigh* v. *Smith* (1825) 1 C. & P. 638.
[14] (1956) 94 C.L.R. 384; see especially per Dixon C.J. at 391-392 and per Fullagar J. at 400. Cf. *Levison* v. *Patent Steam etc. Co.* [1978] Q.B. 69.
[15] (1823) 1 Car. & P. 110; 171 E.R. 1123.
[16] (1836) 5 Ad. & E. 543; 111 E.R. 1270.
[17] (1856) 17 C.B. 372; 139 E.R. 1116.
[18] (1956) 94 C.L.R. 384, at 391-392. Cf. *Penny* v. *Grand Central Car Park Pty. Ltd.* [1965] V.R. 323.

justified. The defendant did not offer evidence in support of this position.[19]

Assuming that *Tozer, Kemsley* is an accurate statement of the general burden of proof in cases of alleged unauthorised delivery, the bailor who suspects that misdelivery may be the reason for the disappearance of his goods may find it preferable to invoke their disappearance as the basis of an action for breach of the bailee's duty of reasonable care. Many cases of misdelivery probably arise from a want of care on the part of the bailee, and an action for breach of duty of care would cast upon the bailee the burden of proving that no such want of care was involved in the present disappearance. This burden might well prove difficult to discharge.

In fact, it is not entirely clear that the same conclusion as to the burden of proof on misdelivery would be reached in England as was reached in *Tozer, Kemsley*. The possible divergence originates from a statement by Lord Denning M.R. in *Morris* v. *C. W. Martin & Sons Ltd.*;[20] a case which involved not innocent but theftuous conversion:

> Once a man has taken charge of goods as a bailee for reward, it is his duty to take reasonable care to keep them safe; and he cannot escape that duty by delegating it to his servant. If the goods are lost or damaged, whilst they are in his possession, he is liable unless he can show—and the burden is on him to show—that the loss or damage occurred without any neglect or default or misconduct of himself or any of the servants to whom he delegated this duty.

At first sight, the words "neglect, default or misconduct" appear to cast upon the bailee the burden of disproving any unauthorised act on the part of himself or his organisation. If this were so, he would be liable unless he could prove not only that he had taken reasonable care, but that he was not in breach of any strict contractual promise he had entered into on the creation of the bailment, or that he had not misdelivered the goods however innocently. But it is submitted that Lord Denning, M.R. did not intend to place so comprehensive a burden upon the bailee, and that the foregoing statement was intended to apply only to those acts of default or misconduct which involve a breach of the duty of reasonable care. This seems to emerge from the fact that the three cases cited in support of the above proposition were all cases in which the bailee could only have been liable for negligence:[21]; and from the reformulation of this proposition given by Lord Denning M.R. on the same page of his judgment:

> The bailee, to excuse himself, must show that the loss was without any fault on his part or on the part of his servants. If he shows that he took due care to employ trustworthy servants, and that he and his servants exercised all diligence, and yet the goods were stolen, he will be excused; but not otherwise.

[19] Ante, at 394 per Dixon C.J.; see also Williams and Webb J.J., at 398 and Fullager J. at 400-401, 403.
[20] [1966] 1 Q.B. 716, at 726; and see also at 729.
[21] *Reeve* v. *Palmer* (1858) 5 C.B.N.S. 84; *Coldman* v. *Hill* [1919] 1 K.B. 443; *Building and Civil Engineering Holidays Scheme Management Ltd.* v. *Post Office* [1966] 1 Q.B. 260.

Thus, in an action for negligence the burden of proving reasonable care rests upon the bailee; but in an action alleging breach of a strict contractual obligation, or conversion by innocent misdelivery, the onus of proving the occurrence of the unauthorised act is borne by the bailor. The existence of a bailment can hardly be taken to reverse the burden of proof of every item of misconduct on the part of the bailee, however divorced that misconduct may be from the fundamental obligations of the bailment.

There remains the problem of allocating the burden of proof in cases where the alleged wrong consists in a theft, or wilful conversion, by the bailee or his servant. In *Morris v. C. W. Martin & Sons Ltd.*[22] the bailee was free from personal fault and the theft of the bailed property was *assumed* to have been carried out by the servant whom he put in charge of cleaning it. It is clear from the judgment of Lord Denning M.R. at least that the burden of displacing this assumption was borne by the employer.

The reconciliation (if any is necessary) is to be found in the judgment of Salmon L.J. in the same decision. Salmon L.J. pointed out that the servant's alleged misconduct constituted not only a conversion but "a glaring breach of the duty to take reasonable care to keep it safe—and this is negligence."[23] The bailees had deputed to him the task of taking reasonable care and he had flagrantly violated that duty. Accordingly, there was no purpose in distinguishing between the action for negligence and the action for conversion. On present facts, they were one and the same thing.

This analysis was adopted by Mocatta J. in *Transmotors Ltd. v. Robertson, Buckley & Co. Ltd.*[24] which appears to be the only case in which the burden of proof in cases of alleged fraudulent conversion has been extensively argued. Goods were stolen from the defendants' lorry while their driver was relieving himself in a lay-by, and the bailors claimed that the defendants were answerable unless they could prove that this occurred without the negligence *or complicity* of their servant. This contention was upheld, Mocatta J. remarking:

> Mr. Kidwell submitted that it follows from the language used in *Morris v. C. W. Martin & Sons Ltd.* that in order for a bailee to escape liability for goods stolen in his possession he had, on the balance of probabilities, to prove that he had used all reasonable care in relation to the goods and that this obligation covered proving with the same standard of proof that the goods had not been stolen by his employees. . . . In my judgment it is clear . . . that Mr. Kidwell is right on this matter. . . . After anxious consideration . . . I have come to the conclusion that the defendants have not discharged the burden of proof upon them. It is not necessary for me to make a decision on the evidence that I have listened to whether Davenport (the driver) was or was not an accomplice of the thieves. It is sufficient to say that on the balance of probability I do not feel satisfied that the defendants

---

[22] Ante; see, especially, at 723.
[23] At 738, Cf. *Port Swettenham v. Wu* (1978) *The Times* June 22.
[24] [1970] 1 Lloyd's Rep. 224. See also *Central Motors (Glasgow) Ltd. v. Cessnock Garage and Motor Co.* 1925 S.C. 796, at 798 per Lord Blackburn; *Levison v. Patent Steam Carpet Cleaning Co. Ltd.* [1977] 3 W.L.R. 90.

have discharged the burden of proof which the law placed upon them in circumstances such as the present.[25]

It will be noted that Mocatta J. confined his decision to cases of alleged theft by servants of the bailee. Other decisions in which the principle laid down in *Transmotors* seems to have been accepted were likewise factually confined to instances of theft.[26] It is therefore submitted that the bailee should carry the burden of negativing default only when the default alleged is one which depends upon failure to use reasonable care; that an allegation of theft by the bailee's servant (or of the servant's participating in theft) should be classed for this purpose as an allegation of breach of the ordinary duty of care; and that in all other cases where a breach of obligation is alleged against the bailee, including a conversion by innocent misdelivery, the burden of proving that breach of obligation should rest upon the bailor. On this analysis the burden in respect of theft should apply whether or not the servant of the bailee has, technically, committed a conversion.

C. The duty not to convert[27]

The bailee must, of course, abstain from converting the bailor's goods. This obligation, thereotically quite separate from his duty of reasonable care,[28] extends to conversions committed by his servants or agents, provided they were acting within the scope of their employment when the conversion occurred, or in purported discharge of a duty delegated to them by the bailee involving the safekeping of the goods.[29] When goods disappear while in the bailee's possession, his duty to prove affirmatively that their disappearance was not the result of any negligence *or act of conversion* on the part of himself or his servants depends, as we have seen, upon the nature of the alleged conversion.

D. The duty to observe the terms of the bailment

The bailee must discharge any active obligation which, either from the nature of the goods or from his own express promise, he has lawfully undertaken. Thus, he may be liable for failing to feed an animal,[30] for neglecting to inspect apples,[31] for failing to turn maize[32] or even for omitting to insure the goods.[33] Sometimes a breach of such ancillary

---

[25] Ante, at 227, 231. The learned judge did, however, recommend that when specific allegations of theft are to be made as against a servant of the bailee, it was highly desirable that notice to this effect should be given. The most appropriate place for such notice (which would in no way alter the burden of proof) was in the reply: ibid., at 228. Cf. *Port Swettenham* v. *Wu*, ante.

[26] E.g., *Mendelssohn* v. *Normand Ltd.* [1970] 1 Q.B. 177; *Richmond Metal Co. Ltd.* v. *J. Coales & Son Ltd.* [1970] 1 Lloyds Rep. 423, at 429.

[27] As to the elements of conversion, see p. 126 et seq., ante.

[28] Cf. *Morris* v. *C. W. Martin & Sons Ltd.* [1966] 1 Q.B. 716.

[29] Post., p. 475.

[30] Cf. *Wilson* v. *Dairy Fresh Farms* (1967) 117 New Law Jo. 295.

[31] *Sharp* v. *Batt* (1930) 25 Tas. L.R. 33; and see p. 453, ante.

[32] *Liverpool Grain Storage & Transit Co. Ltd.* v. *Charlton & Bagshaw* (1918) 146 L.T. Jo. 20.

[33] An implied obligation to effect proper insurance was tentatively upheld in *Eastman Chemical International A.G.* v. *N.M.T. Trading Ltd.* [1972] 1 Lloyd's Rep. 25, a case of carriage by road. But it seems that a bailee is not generally bound to insure the goods unless the contract specifically requires him to do so; in any event, many bailees would insure only against their own default. Cf.

obligations will count as a failure to exercise reasonable care, and the burden of disproof will rest with the defendant; in cases where the relevant duty is not part and parcel of the general duty of care, the obligation and its breach must be affirmatively established.

In addition, the bailee must comply with all the limits or restrictions placed upon his right of possession; and a departure from the essential or fundamental limitations will render him strictly liable for all ensuing losses. By deviating from the central terms of the bailment he forfeits his status as a bailee and therefore his right to immunity on proof of reasonable care.[34]

This principle, regarded circumspectly by Abbott C.J. in the old case of *Sidaways* v. *Todd*,[35] derives its main authority from decisions on the carriage of goods by sea.[36] It was specifically applied to the warehousing of goods on land in *Lilley* v. *Doubleday*[37] and has since been regularly acknowledged.[38] In *Lilley* v. *Doubleday* the defendant agreed to warehouse the plaintiff's goods at his own depository but shortly after taking possession moved part of them elsewhere. These were then destroyed (without negligence on his part) and he was held liable for their loss. Grove J. remarked:

> If a bailee elects to deal with the property in a way not authorised by the bailor, he takes upon himself the risks of so doing, except where the risk is independent of his acts and inherent in the property itself.[39]

In this case, the defendant had given an express promise relating to the place of custody, but a later decision of the Court of Appeal[40] shows that in the absence of any agreement to the contrary the bailee is under an implied duty to keep the goods in his own possession and

Brazier v. *Whelan* (1960) *The Times*, July 21st, where the bailor failed to prove an express obligation to insure; *Firmin* v. *Allied Shippers Ltd.* [1967] 1 Lloyds Rep. 633.

---

[34] For other consequences, see pp. 514, 930, post.

[35] (1818) 2 Stark. 400, at 402; 171 E.R. 685, at 686; but cf. *Sleat* v. *Fagg* (1822) 5 B. & Ald. 342; 106 E.R. 1216.

[36] E.g. *Davis* v. *Garrett* (1830) 6 Bing. 716; 130 E.R. 1456; *Hain Steamship Co. Ltd.* v. *Tate & Lyle Ltd.* [1936] 2 All E.R. 597.

[37] (1881) 7 Q.B.D. 510: this case was distinguished by the Supreme Court of Prince Edward Island in *Barbour & Proude* v. *Doucette* [1942] 2 D.L.R. 624 (post, p. 474). See also *G.W. Supply Co.* v. *Grand Trunk Pacific Railway Co.* (1915) 30 W.L.R. 322; 31 W.L.R. 259; *Polish Fraternal Aid Society* v. *Kapusta* [1938] 4 D.L.R. 724, especially per Robson J.A. (dissenting).

[38] E.g. *Edwards* v. *Newland & Co.* [1950] 2 K.B. 534; *Tozer, Kemsley & Millbourn (Australasia) Ltd.* v. *Collier's Interstate Transport Service Pty. Ltd.* (1956) 94 C.L.R. 384, at 393; *Thomas National Transport (Melbourne) Pty. Ltd.* v. *May & Baker (Australia) Pty. Ltd.* (1966) 115 C.L.R. 353; *Hobbs* v. *Petersham Transport Co. Pty. Ltd.* (1971) 45 A.L.J.R. 356, at 362; and see pp. 514, 930, post.

[39] (1881) 7 Q.B.D. 510, at 511. Grove J. further said that the only exception to the rule of strict liability occurs "where the destruction of the goods must take place as inevitably at one place as at the other"; or, presumably, is due to the fault of the bailor. See also *Davies* v. *Garrett* (1830) 6 Bing. 716, at 724; 130 E.R. 1456, at 1459. Insofar as the words of Denning L.J., in *Edwards* v. *Newland & Co.* [1950] 2 K.B. 534, seek to propound a liability wider than this, it is suggested that they are misconceived. Both Grove and Lindley JJ. in *Lilley* v. *Doubleday* (at 512) declined to express an opinion as to whether the defendant was guilty of conversion.

[40] *Edwards* v. *Newland & Co.* [1950] 2 K.B. 534.

not to sub-contract their custody to a third person.[41] A breach of this obligation (which is of the essence of the contract)[42] means that he will be answerable for all loss or damage occurring to the goods while they are out of his possession, irrespective of whether the cause of that loss or injury is within his powers of reasonable prevention. Indeed, Tucker L.J. went so far as to state that someone who was entitled to grant possession to a third party in vicarious discharge of his obligation was not, in strict law, a bailee,[43] and Somervell L.J. held that the obligation of personal custody applies regardless of whether the bailor has shown that he relied on any special or general reputation enjoyed by the bailee.[44] Thus in the present case the defendants, having agreed to warehouse the plaintiff's goods but having immediately delegated the task to third parties without personally gaining possession, were held liable for the loss of the goods by theft after a bomb had partially demolished the third parties' premises. The defendants failed in their attempt to recover against the third parties for breach by the latter of their own duty of care.[45]

Of course, in extreme circumstances (such as the destruction of the building) the bailee may be not merely entitled but obliged to store the goods elsewhere, if to do so would be reasonable.[46]

Although unauthorised delegation of the contract of storage is the primary instance of deviation, other examples can be found. One is the retention of the goods beyond the date of redelivery;[47] others were given by Fraser J. in a recent West Indian decision:[48]

> If he sub-contracted without the bailer's consent and so stored them elsewhere he would have been liable for any ensuing loss; likewise if he stored them in a place other than a cold storage; or in a cold storage which, to his knowledge, because of mechanical defect or otherwise, was incapable of performing the function of a cold storage. In the contract with which we are concerned no such like

---

[41] But cf. Mathieson C.J. in *Barbour and Proude* v. *Doucette* [1942] 2 D.L.R. 624, at 632. "Had this been an ordinary contract to store and keep goods (and if there had *not* been a special term of the contract to store and keep the goods in a particular place) the result in that case (i.e. *Lilley* v. *Doubleday*) would unquestionably have been different." In this case, the court held that (i) the duty to store on the original bailee's own premises arose only during the periods of actual repair for which he had been engaged, and (ii) in any event the car, while in the custody of the second respondent, was as effectively in the possession and under the control of the original bailee as if he had kept it throughout in his own garage. In fact, the bailor seems to have consented to its removal.

[42] [1950] 2 K.B. 534, at 539 per Somervell L.J., 542 per Denning L.J.

[43] Ibid., at 540. But cf. Denning L.J. at 542: "There are many bailments in which a bailee is entitled to make a sub-bailment; the repairer of a motor-car, for instance, can often quite reasonably send away a part of it to another firm of repairers; a carrier of goods may need to entrust them to another carrier for part of the journey; a hirer may himself often, quite lawfully, sub-hire the goods. It all depends on the circumstances of the particular case".

[44] Ibid., at 639; cf. p. 514, post. (locatio operis faciendi).

[45] On this point, see p. 842, et seq., post.

[46] [1950] 2 K.B. 534, at 541.

[47] *Shaw & Co. Ltd* v. *Symmons & Sons Ltd.* [1917] 1 K.B. 799.

[48] *Apang Ice & Storage Ltd.* v. *Paria Ship Suppliers Ltd.* (1972) 19 W.I.R. 337 at 341 (Trinidad and Tobago C.A.) See also *Mendelssohn* v. *Normand Ltd.* [1970] 1 Q.B. 177 (breach of promise to keep car locked held to amount to deviation by Lord Denning M.R.).

breach occurred; and there was no warranty as to temperature or fitness.[49]

It is, of course, central to the concept of locatio custodiae that the **bailee is prohibited from using the goods.** Misconduct of this kind will again render him an insurer during the period of misuse. But in certain cases there will actually be an obligation to use the chattel in order to preserve its efficiency. Examples may be found in the driving of a car, or the exercise of a racehorse, over a prolonged period of safekeping.

Likewise, the bailee may not interfere with the chattel for any purpose other than the discharge of his duty of care or the fulfilment of his other obligations under the bailment. Whether specific acts of interference are to be classed as a deviation must depend upon the gravity of the acts in question, the intention with which they are made and the extent to which they are repugnant to the expressible terms of the bailment.[50]

The burden of proving a deviation rests upon the bailor, unless there is inherent in this allegation an allegation that the bailee has broken his duty of reasonable care.[50a] Normally this dual character will not arise because to constitute a deviation there must be a deliberate act.

E. Liability for acts of servants

1. *Conversion, theft and dishonest misappropriation*: The bailee, like any other employer, is liable for torts committed by his servants when acting in the course of their employment.[51] This form of liability can encompass both the subject-matter of the bailment and any third-party upon whom injury is inflicted while the bailee is performing his duties thereunder. Thus, if a hired motor-car collides with a pedestrian, or if a haulage-vehicle crashes into a stationary bus and overturns it, the hirer of the car or the owner of the haulage-vehicle may be answerable on two levels: to the pedestrian or the bus company for third party injury, and to the lessor of the car, or the consignor of goods in the lorry, for damage inflicted under the bailment. It is no defence for the bailee to show that the collision was caused by his chauffeur or driver and occurred without

---

[49] Quaere as to whether there should not be; ante, p. 454. Cf. *United Fresh Meat Co. Ltd.* v. *Charterhouse Cold Storage Ltd* [1974] 2 Lloyd's Rep. 286, where Wien J. held that the failure to keep the goods at a proper temperature was tantamount to a deliberate breach and thus constituted a deviation; and *Evans Products Ltd.* v. *Crest Warehousing Ltd.* (1977) 69 D.L.R. (3d) 575, where this decision was cited with approval and the same conclusion was reached as to the conduct of the defendants in storing inflammable goods close to a fire. In some cases the separation of the *bailor* from his property might be accounted a deviation: cf. *Martin* v. *L.C.C.* [1947] K.B. 628, where the decision proceeded solely on the question of reasonable care.

[50] Negligence is not generally akin to deviation; per Denning L.J. in *J. Spurling Ltd.* v. *Bradshaw* [1956] 2 All E.R. 121, at 124-125, and Donaldson J. in *Kenyon Son & Craven Ltd.* v. *Baxter Hoare & Co. Ltd.* [1971] 1 W.L.R. 519; but reckless inattention may be equivalent; see the *United Fresh Meat* and *Evans Products* cases, supra.

[50a] But cf. *Levison* v. *Patent Steam Carpet Cleaning Co. Ltd.* [1978] Q.B. 69; post p. 947; *Mitchell* v. *Ealing* [1978] 2 W.L.R. 999.

[51] See generally Street on *Torts* (6th edn), p. 427 et seq. Occasionally the expressions "sphere" or "scope" of employment have been preferred: *Central Motors (Glasgow) Ltd.* v. *Cessnock Garage and Motor Co.* 1925 S.C. 796, at 802; *Cheshire* v. *Bailey* [1905] 1 K.B. 237, at 241; cf. *Lloyd* v. *Grace Smith & Co.* [1912] A.C. 716, at 733, 736.

negligence on his own part. To escape, he must show that the driver was not acting within the course of his employment at the time when the injury was sustained.

But whereas the "course of employment" test works acceptably enough in cases of negligence, in cases which involve more serious torts (such a fraud or dishonesty) it has produced less fortunate results. At one time it gave rise to the conclusion that a bailee whose servant stole the goods entrusted to him (or participated in their theft by a third party) was not answerable for the loss of those goods unless the conversion was for his benefit. How, it was asked, could so violent and fundamental a contravention of the servant's orders be classed as something committed within the course of his employment? "The judges took this simple view: No servant who turns thief and steals is acting in the course of his employment. He is acting outside it altogether."[52] Thus, in *Cheshire* v. *Bailey*[53] the defendant job-master was held not liable for the theft of silver from a carriage hired by him to the plaintiff, the theft having been connived at by the defendant's driver who drove the carriage to a place from which the thieves could unload it.[54] This decision was only faintly distinguishable from others of similar vintage. In *Abraham* v. *Bullock*,[55] where the driver of a chartered carriage was merely negligent in enabling thieves to steal the contents of the carriage, his employer was held liable to the charterer for their loss. In *Coupé Co. Ltd.* v. *Maddick*[56] the hirer of a carriage was held liable to compensate the owner for the conduct of his own coachman in departing from the path he he had been ordered to take and in taking the carriage off on a "frolic of his own"; it was during the coachman's return from this private journey that the vehicle was negligently damaged. In all three cases the misbehaviour of the servant was committed while he was performing, or purporting to perform, the duties for which he had been engaged. Of course, it could be argued that in the last two cases the relevant misconduct was mere negligence, whereas in *Cheshire* v. *Bailey* the servant had engaged in a deliberate fraud. But as Salmon L.J. was later to point out,[57] the servant who converts goods entrusted to him by his master commits a glaring breach of his master's primary obligation to treat those goods with reasonable care; and as Diplock L.J. observed in the same case,[58] a comparison of *Abrahams* v. *Bullock* with *Cheshire* v. *Bailey* showed that the greater the fault of the servant

---

[52] *Morris* v. *C. W. Martin & Sons Ltd.* [1966] 1 Q.B. 716, at 723 per Lord Denning M.R.

[53] [1905] 1 K.B. 237 (C.A.); see also *Mintz* v. *Silverton* (1920) 36 T.L.R. 399, at 400 and cf. *Sanderson* v. *Collins* [1904] 1 K.B. 628; *South Island Motors Ltd.* v. *Thacker* [1931] N.Z.L.R. 1104; *Spencer, Clarke & Co. Ltd.* v. *Goodwill Motors Ltd.* [1939] N.Z.L.R. 493; post, p. 485.

[54] The word "hired" is used colloquially in this context. The plaintiff did not become a bailee of the carriage and the driver remained in the employment of the job-master. See generally, Chapter 7.

[55] (1902) 18 T.L.R. 701 (C.A.); discussed in more detail ante, p. 265.

[56] [1891] 2 Q.B. 413; a similar case is *Aitchison* v. *Page Motors Ltd.* (1936) 154 L.T. 128, except that here the servant was originally making an authorised journey from which he later deviated for a purpose of his own.

[57] *Morris* v. *C. W. Martin & Sons Ltd.* [1966] 1 Q.B. 716, at 738.

[58] Ibid., at 733.

the less the liability of the master. The logic of this equation did not commend itself to either Lord Justice, and the death-knell on *Cheshire v. Bailey* finally sounded.

In fact, the influence of *Cheshire v. Bailey* had been largely emasculated by the decision of the House of Lords in *Lloyd v. Grace, Smith & Co.*[59] This decision neither rejected the "course of employment" test in cases of dishonest misappropriation[60] nor overruled *Cheshire v. Bailey*,[61] but it arrived at a conclusion with which the earlier decision was virtually irreconcilable. In *Lloyd's* case the defendants were a firm of solicitors and the dishonest servant was their managing clerk. He, claiming to act for the benefit of their client, obtained possession of certain title deeds and misapplied them; so that the relevant act of fraud consisted not only in the conversion of the deeds but in his inducing the plaintiff to part with them in the first place. The House of Lords held that the defendants, having clothed their official with apparent authority to take possession of the deeds, became responsible for them as bailees once that possession had been taken. This relationship bound them to deal honestly and diligently with the subject-matter of the bailment, and they were answerable for the failure, through the agency of their official, to do so. Lord Macnaghten[62] adopted with approval a statement of Willes J. in an earlier decision:[63]

> He [the employer] has put the agent in his place to do that class of acts and he must be answerable for the manner in which that agent has conducted himself in doing the business which it was the act of his master to put him in.

The House accordingly discountenanced the view that the master must benefit from an act of dishonesty by his servant in order to be vicariously liable for it.[64] *Lloyd's* case was profoundly at variance with *Cheshire v. Bailey* and it was only a matter of time before the latter decision was overruled.[65] However, this did not finally occur until more than fifty years later. During the interval a somewhat different principle began to be evolved.

This principle gravitated away from the characterisation of the bailee as an ordinary employer and concentrated more upon the *duty* he owed towards the bailor's goods. According to it, whenever a person owes a duty towards goods belonging to another (whether to protect them from theft or injury, or both) he is answerable for the manner in

59 [1912] A.C. 716.
60 Although cf. Lord Macnaughten at 733, 736.
61 An attempt to distinguish *Cheshire v. Bailey* was made by Lord Shaw (ibid., at 739); but this was unconvincing and was dismissed by Diplock and Salmon. L.J.J. in *Morris v. C. W. Martin & Sons Ltd.* [1966] 1 Q.B. 716, at 736, 739-740.
62 [1912] A.C. 716, at 733.
63 *Barwick v. English Joint Stock Bank* (1867) L.R. 2 Exch. 259, at 266.
64 This heresy, which arose from a misunderstanding of the words of Willes J. in *Barwick's* case (supra), had permeated a number of authorities: e.g. *Giblen v. McMullen* (1869) L.R. 2 P.C. 317; *British Mutual Banking Co. Ltd. v. Charnwood Forest Ry. Co.* (1887) 18 Q.B.D. 714, at 718 per Lord Bowen; *Ruben v. Great Fingall Consolidated* [1906] A.C. 439, at 445 per Lord Davey. For a modern acceptance of this now discredited principle, see *Alberta-U-Drive Ltd. v. Jack*
65 A further attempt to accommodate *Cheshire v. Bailey* within existing authority was made by Lord Sands in the *Cessnock* case 1925 S.C. 796, at 805.
Carter Ltd. (1972) 28 D.L.R. (3d) 114.

which that duty is discharged; and if, without negligence, he delegates the performance of any part of that duty to his servant, he is liable for the servant's default is discharging that duty as if the default were his own.[66]

An early application is to be found in the decision of the Court of Session in *Central Motors (Glasgow) Ltd.* v. *Cessnock Garage and Motor Co.*[67] The plaintiffs bailed their car to the defendants for storage overnight in the defendants' garage. The defendants' night watchman took the car without authority and negligently damaged it. In holding the defendants liable for his misconduct Lord Sands said:

> The defenders, having undertaken the safe custody of the car, delegated to . . . their night attendant the fulfilment during the night of this contractual obligation, and they are liable for any failure on his part to fulfil that obligation.[68]

Similar observations were made by Lord Cullen and Lord Clyde.[69] Admittedly the duty test and the "course of employment" test are sometimes used interchangeably in the course of their judgments and Lord Cullen, at least, believed that the master should be answerable only when the breach of a duty entrusted to the servant was committed in the course of that servant's employment.[70] A similar intermixture occurred in the Canadian case of *Van Geel* v. *Warrington*,[71] where the defendant firm of car-washers were held liable for the acts of a servant whom they employed to drive vehicles from one branch of their garage to another; the servant, having gained possession of the plaintiff's car for this purpose, used it to transport his friends on an outing and again the vehicle was negligently damaged.[72] Both cases, nevertheless, suggest an alternative and not merely a synonymous basis of liability to the traditional test of whether the delinquent servant was acting in the course of his employment. In the *Cessnock* case, this is given particular

---

[66] It seems that this principle is not strictly confined to instances of bailment. For example, it may apply as against an employer who is under a duty to safeguard goods from theft without having become a bailee, such as a security contractor: cf. *Morris* v. *C. W. Martin & Sons* Ltd [1966] 1 Q.B. 716, at 726-727 per Lord Denning M.R. and *B.R.S. Ltd.* v. *Arthur V. Crutchley & Co. Ltd.* [1968] 1 All E.R. 811, where the security contractor's employees were merely negligent. It has also been recently suggested that a similar principle may be employed to rationalise the law relating to an employer's liability for his employees' assaults: Rose (1975) 91 L.Q.R. 17, at 18, discussing *Keppel Bus Co. Ltd.* v. *Sa'ad Ahmad* [1974] 2 All E.R. 700 (P.C.).

[67] 1925 S.C. 796.

[68] Ibid., at 804.

[69] Ibid., at 801-803.

[70] Ibid., at 802.

[71] [1929] 1 D.L.R. 94.

[72] See also an almost identical facts, *Aitchison* v. *Page Motors Ltd.* (1935) 154 L.T. 128, where the defendant garage's service manager collected the plaintiff's car from the manufacturers to whom it had been sub-bailed for repair by his employers and negligently wrote if off while on a journey not connected with his duties of employment. Macnaghten J. held that the collection of the car was within the service-manager's authority and that he was acting within the scope of his employment at the time of the destruction. However, he also cited with approval the "delegation" principle advanced in the *Cessnock* case (supra) and held that the ratio of that case accorded with English Law: (1935) 154 L.T., at 131. The principle of these cases was approved as a "modern and sensible" rule by Trueman J.A. in *Webb* v. *Moore's Taxi Co.* [1942] 4 D.L.R. 154, at 164-166.

significance by the suggestion that liability may be contractual and thus need not be founded upon the ordinary rules of vicarious liability at all.

A clearer statement of the independent character of the "duty" principle was given by Mr. Commissioner Fenton Atkinson Q.C. (as he then was) in *Adams (Durham) Ltd.* v. *Trust Houses Ltd.*[73] As the learned Commissioner remarked,[74] the facts of this case were indistinguishable from those in *Central Motors (Glasgow) Ltd.* v. *Cessnock Garage & Motor Co.*[75] The plaintiff's managing-director left his company car overnight in the defendant hotel's garage. The car was wrongfully taken out and driven by the defendants' night porter, who was in charge of the garage during the night and had accordingly been given the garage keys. The learned Commissioner held that the defendants had been negligent in employing the night porter without securing proper references, and that, in any event, they were answerable for his misconduct in taking and damaging the car:

> It seems to me that the duty to take reasonable care to keep the car safe rested on the defendants and they delegated that duty to Atkinson, and they are responsible to the plaintiffs, not so much as being vicariously responsible for the torts of Atkinson driving about the streets, but on the basis that they have entrusted to him the fulfilment of their own contractual duty, and that duty was not performed, and for that breach of contract, apart from any special condition, in my view, they are liable to the plaintiffs.[76]

These three decisions did not, of course, involve a permanent theft of the bailor's property by the servant of the bailee, but merely a dishonest borrowing followed by negligently-inflicted damage. In this they resembled *Coupe Co. Ltd.* v. *Maddick;*[77] and it was this difference that enabled counsel for the defendants in *Morris* v. *C. W. Martin Ltd.*[78] to argue that there was no decision in a superior court in which the ratio decidendi was inconsistent with *Cheshire* v. *Bailey.*[79] But it was evident (despite Lord Sands' contention to the contrary)[80] that there was nothing material in this distinction. If the servant did not cease to act within the sphere of his employment when he dishonestly took the goods for some temporary unauthorised purpose, he clearly did not cease to act when the taking was permanent; and such a taking clearly amounted to a breach of his employer's duty of safekeeping regardless of the period for which that taking was intended to last. Both of these contentions were endorsed by different members of the Court of Appeal in *Morris's* case, the decision in which *Cheshire* v. *Bailey* was finally overruled. The same decision also made it clear that the course of employment test, at one time regarded as too narrow to

---

[73] [1960] 1 Lloyd's Rep. 380.
[74] Ibid., at 386.
[75] 1925 S.C. 796.
[76] [1960] 1 Lloyd's Rep. 380 at 386; approved and applied by the Court of Appeal in *B.R.S. Ltd.* v. *Arthur V. Crutchley & Co. Ltd.* [1968] 1 All E.R. 811, at 820-821, 824.
[77] [1891] 2 Q.B. 413; ante, p. 476.
[78] [1966] 1 Q.B. 716, at 721.
[79] [1905] 1 K.B. 237; ante, p. 476.
[80] In the *Cessnock* case: 1925 S.C. 796, at 804-805.

embrace dishonest conversions by the bailee's servants, could now, if applied without qualification, produce excessively wide results. In this respect, no direct parallel can be drawn from the law relating to vicarious liability for negligence, either in cases of permanent theft or of temporary abstraction. Suppose, for example, that the tea-lady is wheeling her trolley from one end of a warehouse to another. En route, she negligently collides with a pile of crockery, destroying every item except for one, which she dishonestly puts in her pocket. For her negligence in damaging the crockery her employers would undoubtedly be held liable; but for her dishonesty in stealing the surviving item they undoubtedly would not—nor, it is submitted, would they be answerable if she merely decided to borrow it for a few days and during that time negligently broke it. The course of employment test produces acceptable results when applied to cases of dishonest misappropriation only if qualified by the need for some closer relation between the servant and the chattel than that he merely came into contact with it, or was enabled to steal it, by virtue of his duties under the contract of service.[81] As we shall see, the Court of Appeal was not entirely consistent on the question of how close that relationship must be.

In *Morris* v. *C. W. Martin & Sons Ltd.*[82] sub-bailees who were in possession of the plaintiff's stole for cleaning delegated the performance of this task to their servant, Morrissey. Morrissey abstracted the fur and they were held liable for its loss. Lord Denning M.R. rejected the traditional test because of the ambiguity that could arise from an over-literal devotion to the phrase 'course of employment'. He cited the example of the dishonest watchman who takes a car from his employer's garage and negligently causes an accident, injuring a motor-cyclist and damaging the car. The motor-cyclist cannot recover from the employer because the watchman was not, at the material time, acting within the course of his employment; but the owner of the car can recover because, in this context, it would seem that the course of employment test is satisfied and the watchman's misconduct qua the bailor is within the course of his employment:

> I ask myself, how can this be? How can the servant, on one and the same journey, be acting both within and without the course of his employment? Within *qua* the car owner. Without *qua* the motor-cyclist. It is time we got rid of this confusion. And the only way to do it, so far as I can see, is by reference to the duty laid by the law on the master. The duty of the garage proprietor to the owner of the car is very different from his duty to the motor-cyclist. He owes to the owner of the car the duty of a bailee for reward, whereas he owes no such duty to the motor-cyclist on the road. He does not even owe him a duty to use care not to injure him.[83]

[81] Post, p. 484.

[82] [1966] 1 Q.B. 716; the facts are recounted more fully at p. 793, post.

[83] [1966] 1 Q.B. 716, at 724-725. A very similar argument had been unsuccessfully advanced for the plaintiff in the New Zealand case of *South Island Motors Ltd.* v. *Thacker* [1931] N.Z.L.R. 1104, at 1105. Cf. Jolowicz [1965] C.L.J. 200, who claims that the distinction is not confusing at all, and *Coupe Co. Ltd.* v. *Maddick* [1891] 2 Q.B. 413, at 416, where an explanation was advanced by Cave J. "The responsibility of the hirer to the person from whom he hires is a responsibility

After reviewing the different categories of situation in which a person may be under a duty to preserve another person's goods from loss by theft, Lord Denning continued:

> From all these instances we may deduce the general proposition that when a principal has in his charge the goods or belongings of another in such circumstances that he is under a duty to take all reasonable precautions to protect them from theft or depredation, then if he entrusts that duty to a servant or agent, he is answerable for the manner in which that servant or agent carries out his duty. If the servant or agent is careless so that they are stolen by a stranger, the master is liable. So also if the servant or agent himself steals them or makes away with them. It follows that I do not think that *Cheshire* v. *Bailey* can be supported.[84]

Diplock L.J. arrived at the same conclusion by a slightly different route. He regarded Morrissey's misconduct as a wrong committed within the scope or course of his employment, and for which the defendants were liable on ordinary principles of vicarious liability. But he stressed that not every theft committed in the course of a servant's employment would render his master vicariously liable:

> If the principle laid down in *Lloyd* v. *Grace, Smith & Co.* is applied to the facts of the present case, the defendants cannot, in my view, escape liability for the conversion of the plaintiff's fur by their servant Morrissey. They accepted the fur as bailees for reward in order to clean it. They put Morrissey as their agent in their place to clean the fur and take charge of it while doing so. The manner in which he conducted himself in doing that work was to convert it. What he was doing, at best, dishonestly, he was doing in the scope of course of his employment in the technical sense of that infelicitous but time honoured phrase. The defendants as his masters are responsible for his tortious act.
> I should add that we are not concerned . . . with what would have been the liability of the defendants if the fur had been stolen by another servant of theirs who was not employed by them to clean the fur or to have the care and custody of it. The mere fact that his employment by the defendants gave him the opportunity to steal it would not suffice. . . . I base my decision in this case on the ground that the fur was stolen by the very servant whom the defendants as bailees had employed to take care of it and clean it.[86]

A similar qualification was imposed by Salmon L.J. who agreed that the master is liable only for the theft of goods by those of his servants whom he had deputed to discharge some part of his duty of taking reasonable care. "A theft by any servant who is not employed to do anything in relation to the goods is entirely outside the scope of his employment and cannot make the master liable."[87] Salmon L.J. agreed with Diplock L.J. that responsibility for servants' thefts could be accom-

---

arising out of contract, his responsibility to a person run over by the negligent driving of the horse and cart arises out of tort."

[84] [1966] 1 Q.B. 716, at 728.
[85] [1912] A.C. 716.
[86] [1966] 1 Q.B. 716, at 736-737.
[87] Ibid., at 741.

modated within the ordinary rule that the servant must be acting within
the course of his employment.[88] But the substantial limitations which
he and Diplock L.J. imposed upon the class of servants for whom such
liability must be borne reduced considerably the potential differences
between the more conventional "course of employment" basis of liability
and Lord Denning's interpretation of the duty of the bailee.

The fact remains that marginal differences exist between the two. These
differences may be tested by examining the facts of the otherwise
unimportant Canadian decision in *Bamert* v. *Parks*.[89] In this case a car
was stolen after hours from the premises of the Spee-Dee Car Wash.
The culprit was the defendants' car-washer, a youth of low intelligence
who had been able to re-enter the premises by using the key his
employers had given him. This servant was employed solely to wash
cars; he was not allowed to drive them or move them or, indeed, to
assume any control over them at all. The county court judge exonerated
the defendants on two grounds: first, the taking had occurred after
hours, at a time when even the limited range of tasks normally expected
of the servant were no longer entrusted to him; secondly, in any event
he was given no power of control over the vehicle and, therefore, no
duty of safekeeping in respect of it had been delegated to him by his
employers.[90] The learned judge went on to hold that the defendants
had not been negligent in taking him into their service.

Bamert v. *Parks* was decided before *Morris* v. *C. W. Martin & Sons
Ltd.*;[91] both cases concerned servants deputed to clean chattels and it may
be that, but for the time-factor,[92] *Bamert* v. *Parks* would be decided
differently today. But both factually and doctrinally the two cases are
distinguishable. In *Morris's* case the cleaning was performed by Morrissey in a separate room in which no-one else was present; there was
no part of the fur that he was forbidden to touch or to handle and,
therefore, he enjoyed exclusive and total access and control. In *Bamert's*
case, the servant was entrusted with the chattel only for the limited
purpose of external cleaning: the car was continually on public view,
he was not allowed to perform anything but the most menial and
superficial tasks, and he was fairly closely supervised. Thus, if one
applies Lord Denning's criterion that the master must have delegated
to the servant his duty to protect the goods from "theft or depredation"
in order to be answerable for the servant's misappropriation,[93] *Bamert*
v. *Parks* was evidently rightly decided, for no duty remotely as responsible as this was ever entrusted to the delinquent. But if one applies
the apparently different tests of Diplock and Salmon L.J., that the
master must have delegated to the servant *"some part* of his duty of
taking reasonable care" or some part of his wider duty of dealing with

---

[88] Ibid., at 739-740.
[89] (1965) 50 D.L.R. (2d) 313.
[90] Ibid., at 325: "Miller was clearly a car washer and a janitor and was not at any
time charged or entrusted with any responsibility for keeping the plaintiff's car."
[91] [1966] 1 Q.B. 716.
[92] I.e., that the car was taken outside the servant's normal working hours.
[93] [1966] 1 Q.B. 716, at 728; ante, p. 480.

the goods,[94] then the car-washer might well be classified as a servant for whose misconduct his master should be answerable. His master was under a duty to clean the car (a task which required the exercise of reasonable care) and he delegated that task to the servant. He might, therefore, be answerable if the manner in which the servant discharged that duty involved the theft of its subject-matter. *Bamert's* case, therefore, raises the question of responsibility for servants who are given contact with the bailed goods but not control of them; who are employed to discharge some duty which their masters must observe in relation to such goods, but to whom there is no delegation of the responsibility to protect the goods against the very event which (owing to the servant's perfidy) actually occurred.

Occasionally this problem is evaded by means of the simpler general formula that the goods must have been "entrusted" to the servant.[95] The fact that this necessitates some degree of independent and possibly unsupervised control on the servant's part was recognised and amplified by Browne J. in *Moukataff* v. *B.O.A.C.*[96] In this case banknotes had been stolen from a mailbag by a loader in the employment of the defendant airline. The defendants argued that the loader was not acting within the course of his employment, but Browne J. dismissed this contention and held that they were answerable for his misconduct. His grounds for so holding were those pronounced by Salmon and Diplock L.JJ. in *Morris* v. *C. W. Martin & Sons Ltd.*:[97]

> [T]he Post Office handed over possession of the mail bags and their contents to B.O.A.C. for the purpose of being carried by air to Kuwait, and for that purpose they had to be loaded on to an aeroplane. Mr. Ilbury was one of the servants of B.O.A.C. deputed so to load them. It is true that there was a head loader who was in general charge of the loading, but it is clear from the evidence that Mr. Ilbury was in charge of the loading of the forward hold, and that the head loader left all responsibility for the loading of these mailbags to him. It is true that there was also a security officer, but he was outside the aircraft and Mr. Ilbury said "it would be impossible for him to be inside the aircraft".
>
> Applying what Lord Justice Diplock said in the two passages I have quoted . . . Mr. Ilbury was one of B.O.A.C.'s servants to whom they had entrusted the mail bag and its contents for the purpose of loading it, and, B.O.A.C. put Mr. Ilbury as their agent in their place to load this mail bag and to take charge of it while doing so; and applying what Lord Justice Salmon said . . . Mr. Ilbury was one of the servants of B.O.A.C. deputed by them to discharge some part of their duty of taking reasonable care of the plaintiff's property.[98]

Ordinarily, the distinction between servants to whom the goods have

---

[94] This interpretation is drawn from the words of Salmon L.J. [1966] 1 Q.B. at 740-741 and of Diplock L.J. (ibid.), at 733-737.

[95] E.g. *Sanderson* v. *Collins* [1904] 1 K.B. 628, at 632. Cf. *Leesh River Tea Co. Ltd.* v. *British India Steam Navigation Co. Ltd.* [1967] 2 Q.B. 250; post, p. 484. Of course, this test is hardly decisive because the question then remains "entrusted for what purpose?" See *Port Swettenham* v. *Wu,* post. n. 39.

[96] [1967] 1 Lloyd's Rep. 396.

[97] [1966] 1 Q.B. 716, at 733, 737, 741.

[98] [1967] 1 Lloyd's Rep. 396, at 416.

been entrusted or the duties of the bailee have been delegated, and servants to whom they have not, will be a simple one and will be unlikely to give rise to fine conceptual problems. A case which clearly fell upon the other side of the line was *Leesh River Tea Co. Ltd.* v. *British India Steam Navigation Co., Ltd.*[99] where stevedores employed by the defendants stole a brass storm-plate from the ship they were loading. The theft of the plate allowed seawater to enter the hold and a consignment of goods was consequently damaged. The defendants were held not liable for this damage because they had not entrusted the plate to their servants, nor had they delegated to them any duty of dealing with it. The stevedores' employment merely gave them an *opportunity* of stealing the plate, and this alone would not suffice to to render their employers answerable.[1] Similarly, it has been held that a master would not be answerable for the conduct of a clock winder or a window cleaner who takes advantage of his employment to steal articles from the houses he visits;[2] and in *Morris* v. *C. W. Martin & Sons Ltd.*[3] it was stressed that a different result would have followed if the theft had been committed by an employee to whom the custody or cleaning of the fur had not been delegated, such as a clerk in the defendants' office.[4] Of course, liability might be imposed if in the employment or non-supervision of that servant his employers were found to have been negligent.[5]

It is submitted that, for the employer to be liable, the duty entrusted to his servant need not be the duty to guard the goods against theft. Of course, any servant who negligently allows the goods to be stolen may make his master answerable. But in cases of theft by the servant himself liability may clearly be imposed although the security precautions were entrusted to someone other than the immediate delinquent. This is clear from *Moukataff* v. *B.O.A.C.*[6] where there was a sharp division of labour between the work of the airline's security officer and the work of the dishonest loader; it also emerges from the Canadian decision of *Darling Ladies Wear Ltd.* v. *Hickey,*[7] where the plaintiff's car was stolen from a garage by a mechanic employed to repair it. At first instance, Genest J. held the garage owners liable because their mechanic "had work to perform on the car and had the same obligation as his

---

[99] [1967] 2 Q.B. 250; not strictly, a decision at Common Law but one concerning Article IV (2) (q) of the Indian *Carriage of Goods by Sea Act* 1925. However, the principles at stake were substantially congruent.

[1] Ibid., at 276, per Salmon L.J. Cf. Sellers L.J. at 272: "the removal was in no way incidental to or a hazard of the process of discharge and loading . . . The shipowners were liable (for the thief) only when he, as a servant of the stevedores, was acting on behalf of the shipowners in the fulfilment of the work for which the stevedores had been engaged". This and the comparable statement by Danckwerts L.J. at 273 suggest a wider range of liability than the words of Lord Denning M.R. in *Morris's* case (ante), and suggest that the misconduct in *Bamert* v. *Parks* would have fallen within the realm of the master's liability.

[2] *De Parrell* v. *Walker* (1932) 49 T.L.R. 37; aliter, perhaps, if he steals the windows or the clocks.

[3] [1966] 1 Q.B. 716, at 727-728, 737, 741.

[4] Cf. *Makower, McBeath & Co. Pty. Ltd.* v *Dalgety & Co. Ltd.* [1921] V.L.R. 365.

[5] *Morris* v. *C. W. Martin & Sons Ltd.* [1966] 1 Q.B. 716, at 727; *de Parrell* v. *Walker* (1934) 49 T.L.R. 37; ante, p. 445.

[6] [1967] 1 Lloyd's Rep. 396.

[7] [1949] 2 D.L.R. 420.

employer to take care of the chattel in question."[8] Admittedly this decision
was reversed on appeal because the mechanic had not taken the car
during working hours, but after his daily employment had ended.[9] But
there is nothing in the very brief decision of the Appeal Court to suggest
that liability would have been avoided if the car had been taken during
the mechanic's hours of employment.

It is true that whether the course of employment test or the duty test
is applied the master will generally be answerable for his servants'
misconduct only at those times when the servant is "at work" or discharging the duties for which he is engaged. Thus, it has been held that
there is no liability where a coachman, having garaged the coach at
the end of a journey, later returns and takes it out on a spree of his
own devising.[10] Similar decisions have exonerated the garage-owner
where employees (sometimes having deliberately left the garage door
open or dishonestly obtained a key) return to the garage and misappropriate a customer's car after their hours of employment,[11] or even
their entire contract of service with the garage-owner,[12] have ended. At
such a time the employee has no duty to perform in relation to the
vehicle (other than the general duty of all persons to abstain from
conversion)[13] and his employer cannot therefore be held liable for the
manner in which he performs it. But in *South Island Motors Ltd.* v.
Thacker[14] the borrower of a car was exonerated when his chauffer, having been told to garage it at the end of the day, instead took it to
meet a friend and while returning from this journey damaged it. It may
be thought that this was a case in which the chauffeur was still under a
duty to discharge certain acts for the safekeeping of the car and that his
master, having originally delegated that duty to him, should be answerable for its breach.[15] Adam J.'s attempt to distinguish *Central Motors
(Glasgow) Ltd.* v. *Cessnock Garage and Motor Co.*[16] on the ground
that the present case did not involve a contract for safe custody of the
car is, with respect, less than convincing.[17] In other cases the question

---

[8] Ibid., at 423.

[9] "Not being on the premises at the time in connexion with his employment":
[1950] 1 D.L.R. 720. See further (1949) 27 *Canadian Bar Review* 585.

[10] *Sanderson* v. *Collins* [1904] 1 K.B. 628.

[11] *Darling Ladies Wear Ltd.* v. *Hickey* [1950] 1 D.L.R. 720; *Bamert* v. *Parks* (1965)
50 D.L.R. (2d) 213; *Spencer, Clarke & Co. Ltd.* v. *Goodwill Motors Ltd.* [1939]
N.Z.L.R. 493.

[12] *Alberta-U-Drive Ltd.* v. *Jack Carter Ltd.* (1972) 28 D.L.R. 114. This case is
discussed more fully, ante, at p. 221 et seq.

[13] In *Morris* v. *C. W. Martin & Son Ltd.* [1966] 1 Q.B. 716, at 732, Diplock L.J.
especially stressed the duty of the bailee not to convert the chattel. Clearly this is
a duty in relation to which it would be difficult to identify any act of delegation
to the bailee's servants. Even if the duty is rephrased as a promise that the chattel
will not be converted, this undertaking will not be total and must be limited in
the manner suggested above, both as to the time at which the conversion takes
place and as to the persons by whom it is committed.

[14] [1931] N.Z.L.R. 1104.

[15] The bailment was one for reward since the car was lent by a garage while the
defendant's own was under repair: *Sanderson* v. *Collins* (ante); and see generally,
Chapter 8.

[16] 1925 S.C. 796.

[17] The duty of the borrower may be higher than reasonable care: ante, p. 368.

whether a conversion took place within or beyond the hours of employment may nevertheless cause difficult problems.[18]

On balance, it would appear that the bailee's responsibility is best expressed as arising whenever he has delegated any portion or aspect of his several duties under the bailment to his servant, whether this duty is enforceable in tort (such as negligence or conversion) or in contract, or under the special principles of bailment. Thereafter if the servant to whom the duty is delegated purloins or dishonestly borrows the goods, the master's original duty may be broken and he may be liable to the bailor for the ensuing loss. Such responsibility should extend, where appropriate, to malicious damage by the servant as well as to unlawful takings;[19] and to any other conduct as a result of which the bailee's original duty is breached. Admittedly, some of these aspects may be difficult to reconcile with the conventional conception of the bailee's responsibility as vicarious; but it is submitted that in this context the ordinary principles of vicarious liability are both too narrow and substantially otiose.

Professor Atiyah has observed that the liability imposed in *Morris* v. *C. W. Martin & Sons Ltd.*[20] was a form of vicarious liability,[21] and Professor Jolowicz has criticised the notion of the delegated duty, advanced by Lord Denning in that case, as an unnecessary complication.[22] In Professor Jolowicz's view, the problems of *Morris's* case could have been answered by a simple and general test as to whether the servant was acting within the course of his employment. There is no essential confusion in the theory that a servant may be acting both beyond and within his employment on the same sequence of conduct qua different plaintiffs, and Lord Denning's reliance upon the bailee's duty of reasonable care provokes the question why this duty was not discharged by a careful and prudent delegation.

The short answer may be that this would be contrary to the expectations of the parties to the bailment and that it is upon these expectations, and the implied promises arising out of them, that the bailee's liability is most felicitously founded. The issues of ordinary vicarious liability in tort and the bailee's liablity for his servants' misconduct are distinguishable in a number of ways and should be disassociated for a variety of reasons. As regards a dishonest taking, for example, the bailee is clearly not liable for all such torts committed in the course of his servants' employment: something more is required than an opportunity to steal.[23] But in the same context the bailee may be liable although his servant is not, qua the bailor, guilty of a tort at all.[24] Moreover,

---

[18] See generally *Alberta-U-Drive Ltd.* v. *Jack Carter Ltd.* ante.

[19] Cf. an employer's liability for his employee's assaults: *Warren* v. *Henley's Ltd.* [1948] 2 All E.R. 935; *Keppel Bus Co. Ltd.* v. *Sa'ad Ahmad* [1974] 2 All E.R. 700.

[20] [1966] 1 Q.B. 716.

[21] *Vicarious Liability*, pp. 361-362; approved by Windeyer J. in *Hobbs* v. *Petersham Transport Co. Pty. Ltd.* (1971) 45 A.L.J.R. 356, at 365. (H.C.).

[22] [1965] C.L.J. 200, at 202-203.

[23] Ante, p. 479 et seq.

[24] See *Coupé Co. Ltd.* v. *Maddick* [1891] 2 Q.B. 413, at 415-416, where Cave J. advanced this as an additional reason for permitting a remedy against the bailee; and *The Coast Prince* [1967] 2 Lloyd's Rep. 290. Cf. *Smith* v. *Moss,* [1947] 1

the bailee may be liable for the depredations of a non-possessing contractor or of a sub-bailee to whom be has legitimately entrusted the goods;[25] not, in the former case, for all torts committed in the course of the contractor's employment, but only when the contractor has been, for one reason or another, entrusted with the goods.[26] The difficulties of accommodating these aspects within the ordinary principles of vicarious liability in tort suggest that a preferable and more coherent basis of responsibility might be found elsewhere. Such a basis is readily provided by the terms and conditions of the contract.

We have already noted that in *Adams (Durham) Ltd.* v. *Trust Houses Ltd.*, the court discarded ordinary vicarious principles in favour of a contractual form of liability.[27] Much the same approach was tentatively advanced by Lord President Clyde in the *Cessnock*[28] case, who conceded that the question had not been properly argued:

> In an action for a breach of a contract in the nature of a locatio operarum, I am not satisfied that it is any answer for the defenders to say that the cause of the breach was directly traceable to the infidelity of their servant. My present impression is that default by the debtor in fulfilling his obligations under a proper contract of locatio operarum is not met by the explanation that the default was caused by the debtor's servants.

This approach could solve many problems of the bailee's liability for non-personal misconduct and could obviate much of the foregoing confusion. Viewed in its light, his responsibility could be disentangled from such questions as entrustment and the course of his servants' employment and could be resolved into the simple analysis of the duties he has expressly or impliedly undertaken under the bailment. Liability would not, therefore, be vicarious but for breach of a direct consensual undertaking. Of course, vicarious liability in its conventional form would still exist as an alternative ground of action and may be valuable in illuminating the implied undertaking under the bailment. But in many cases it would be a simpler and surer method of establishing the bailee's liability to inquire, not what duty the law of tort imposes upon him, but what duty he has undertaken under the contract.

It is perhaps suprising that in *Morris's* case Lord Denning did not make greater efforts to develop this principle and to explain its relationship with his own interpretation of the bailee's duty of care. Of course,

---

K.B. 424; Jolowicz, loc. cit., ante; *Stavely Iron & Chemical Co. Ltd.* v. *Jones* [1956] A.C. 627; *Broom* v. *Morgan* [1953] 1 Q.B. 597; Street op cit., pp. 427-428.

---

[25] Post, p. 829 et seq.
[26] An obvious example might be the theft of goods from a warehouse by a member of a firm of security patrolmen engaged to guard them. The decision of the Court of Appeal in *B.R.S. Ltd.* v. *Arthur V. Crutchley & Co. Ltd.* [1968] 1 All E.R. 811, while dealing with a theft arising from the security contractor's *negligence*, would nevertheless seem to support a contractual liability on the part of the bailee for malicious as well as negligent depredations.
[27] [1960] 1 Lloyd's Rep. 380, at 386. See also *Coupé Co. Ltd.* v. *Maddick* (ante), at 415-416, where Cave J. based his decision upon the hirer's implied promise to redeliver the carriage in the condition in which he received it, notwithstanding its damage without direct negligence on his part.
[28] 1925 S.C. 796, at 801. See also the *Arthur Crutchley* case (ante), and cf. Hill, *Freight Forwarders*, pp. 157-162.

the two approaches are markedly similar, but *Adams (Durham) Ltd.* v. *Trust Houses Ltd.* was not cited by his Lordship and the impression from his judgment is that the liability under discusson was not liability in contract but in tort. No doubt contractual undertakings may have seemed irrelevant in a case where the relevant relationship was one of sub-bailment and there was no contractual link between the parties. But this appears to be one respect in which non-contractual bailments possess a sufficient affinity with contract to justify the implication into such bailments of undertakings which are broadly based on the more standard contractual model. Certainly an adaptation of this kind should readily and satisfactorily be made in cases of gratuitous bailment.[29] With extended bailments of the kind in *Morris* v. *C. W. Martin & Sons Ltd.*, it should prove no more difficult to imply an undertaking that the goods will not be converted by the bailee's servants and that will be handled with reasonable care. Such bailments normally arise with the consent of both parties and can give rise to obligations which are not identifiable as arising from tort or from contract.[31] There is no reason why an implied term of this nature should not be imported whenever it is necessary to fulfil the expectations of the parties, and to lend commercial efficacy to the relationship of sub-bailment. In many cases such necessity will be self-evident; in some, it may transcend the normal rules of tort.

We conclude with a tabular analysis of the cases in which a bailee's liability for unlawful takings by his servants has been in question.

Cases in which the bailee has been held liable

Article taken	*By whom?*
Banknotes in mailbag	Servant employed to load them[32]
Fur stole	Servant employed to clean it[33]
Car	Servant employed to drive it[34]
Car	Night-watchman employed to guard it[35]
Car	Night-porter in charge of garage where kept[36]
Contents of car	Garage attendant given car keys and ordered to park it[37]
Lorry load of goods	Driver employed to carry them[38]

---

[29] The liability of a gratuitous bailee for his servants' conduct (which is at present in a state of great uncertainty) is discussed ante, at p. 306 et seq.
[30] I.e., they arise with the consent of the parties.
[31] Post, p. 814 et seq.
[32] *Moukataff* v. *B.O.A.C.* [1967] 1 Lloyd's Rep. 396; and see *Leesh River Tea Co. Ltd.* v. *British India Steam Navigation Co. Ltd.* [1967] 2 Q.B. 250, at 276.
[33] *Morris* v. *C. W. Martin & Sons Ltd.* [1966] 1 Q.B. 716.
[34] *Aitchison* v. *Page Motors Ltd.* (1935) 154 L.T. 128; *Van Geel* v. *Warrington* [1929] 1 D.L.R. 94; *Coupé Co. Ltd.* v. *Maddick ante.*
[35] *Central Motors (Glasgow) Ltd.* v. *Cessnock Garage and Motor Co.* 1925 S.C. 796.
[36] *Adams (Durham) Ltd.* v. *Trust Houses Ltd.* [1960] 1 Lloyd's Rep. 380.
[37] *Mendelssohn* v. *Normand Ltd.* [1970] 1 Q.B. 177.
[38] *United Africa Co. Ltd.* v. *Sake Owoade* [1955] A.C. 130 (P.C.); *Transmotors Ltd.* v. *Robertson, Buckley & Co. Ltd.* [1970] 1 Lloyd's Rep. 224; *Richmond Metal Co. Ltd.* v. *J. Coales & Son Ltd.* [1970] 1 Lloyd's Rep. 423. Note that in neither of the last two cases was complicity in the theft actually proved against the servant; it was merely inferred in the absence of proof by his employers to the contrary. See generally, ante, p. 469 et seq.

Six cases of cameras	*Presumably* by servant employed in warehouse[39]
Parcel of diamonds	Customs official in service of the Crown[40]
Car	Mechanic employed to repair it[41]

Cases in which the bailee has been held not liable

Article taken	*By whom?*
Car	Servant employed exclusively to clean it[42]
Coach	Coachman who took it for a private journey and was not under orders to drive it at the time[43]
Car	Employee of bailee returning to steal it after employment terminated or after hours[44]
Car	Chauffeur who misappropriated it instead of putting it away[45]
Brass storm-plate	Stevedore employed to unload ship on which plate formed part of fabric[46]
Jewellery in guest's bedroom	Floor waiter in hotel or boarding house to which innkeeper's strict liability does not apply?[47]

2. *Negligence*: Much of the law relevant to this category of wrong has already been incidentally discussed in the preceding section. Again, it could be argued that the bailee's liability for his servants' negligence depends upon the terms of the bailment, and that the relevant implications are much the same whether that bailment is contractual or non-contractual in character. In practice, however, it is rare for a contract of bailment to specify the circumstances in which a bailee shall be liable for his servants' misconduct, other than in terms of outright exclusion. Accordingly, and because any liability imposed as a term of the bailment is likely (albeit not bound) to correspond with the liability imposed upon the bailee in tort, there must follow an analysis of those decisions in which the possibility of formulating such liability as an undertaking on the bailee's part was not fully considered.

---

[39] *W. Carsen & Co. Ltd.* v. *Eastern Canada Stevedoring Co. Ltd.* (1962) 30 D.L.R. (2d) 18. Cf. *Port Swettenham* v. *Wu* (1978) *The Times*, June 22nd.

[40] *R.* v. *Levy Bros. Co. Ltd.* (1961) 26 D.L.R. (2d) 760.

[41] (Obiter) *Darling Ladies' Wear Ltd.* v. *Hickey* [1949] 2 D.L.R. 420; [1950] 1 D.L.R. 720.

[42] *Bamert* v. *Parks* ante.

[43] *Sanderson* v. *Collins* [1904] 1 K.B. 628 (semble).

[44] *Alberta-U-Drive Ltd.* v. *Jack Carter Ltd.* ante., (not actually a case of bailment); *Bambert* v. *Parks* ante; *Darling Ladies' Wear Ltd.* v. *Hickey* [1949] 2 D.L.R. 420; *Spencer Clarke & Co. Ltd.* v. *Goodwill Motors Ltd.*, [1939] N.Z.L.R. 493.

[45] *South Islands Motors Ltd.* v. *Thacker* [1931] N.Z.L.R. 1104; sed quaere. See ante, p. 485.

[46] *Leesh River Tea Co. Ltd.* v. *British India Steam Navigation Co. Ltd.* [1967] 2 Q.B. 250.

[47] This may be collected by implication from *Kott and Kott* v. *Gordon Hotels Ltd.* [1968] 2 Lloyd's Rep. 228, at 232 (post, p. 894) although it must be conceded that the point was not, and did not require to be, decided. Cf. *David Crystal Inc.* v. *Cunard S.S. Co. Ltd.* [1963] 2 Lloyd's Rep. 315 (U.S. District Ct., Levet J.), where it was held that the theft of documents by the servant of a customs broker employed by the plaintiff bailor was not within the scope of that servant's employment. Accordingly, no wrong had been committed by the customs broker or his employer, the plaintiff, sufficient to enable the defendant warehouseman (whose own employee, a terminal operator, had misdelivered the goods on the strength of a delivery orders forged from use of the stolen documents) to claim that the misdelivery for which he was responsible had been occasioned by the plaintiff's default.

As before, the bailee is traditionally liable for damage inflicted upon the bailor's goods whenever his servants have acted negligently in the course of their employment. The latter requirement is satisfied although the servant may be doing something unauthorised, or expressly forbidden, at the time of the injury or destruction: thus, a carrier may be liable for the destruction of goods caused by his servants' smoking;[48] or for the theft of goods caused by his servants' deliberate disregard of required security precautions.[49] It is no defence to show that the servant was merely performing the authorised task in an unauthorised manner. To escape, the employer must show that the act of negligence was entirely unconnected with the servant's duties under the contract of employment.

In *Morris* v. *C. W. Martin & Sons Ltd.*[50] there is some suggestion that Lord Denning's repudiation of the course of employment test, and his preference for a test which focuses upon the duty undertaken by the bailee, extends beyond cases of dishonest misappropriation to cases of mere negligent damage. On such an approach, the bailee who delegated his duty of care over the goods to his servant would remain liable for the manner in which the servant discharged that duty, irrespective of negligence on his own part. Thus, if the driver of a lorry capsized it and destroyed its contents, his employer would be liable to the bailor for having broken, through his employee, the duty he had originally undertaken that the goods would be transported with reasonable care.

Generally, there will be no practical difference between this foundation of liability and the more usual ground that the bailee's servant was acting in the course of his employment. A bailee's servant will often, if not usually, be acting within the cause of his employment only when performing some part of his master's duty of care. A servant discharging such a duty will usually, if not invariably, be acting within the scope of his employment. Thus the bailee might be held liable for the negligence of a lorry-driver in leaving a valuable load unattended:[51] for the failure of warehouse or restaurant staff to maintain an adequate inspection of bailed property;[52] for the presumed negligence of a driver in causing a fire or in failing to prevent it from spreading;[53] for the omissions of personnel to lock doors or to repair flaws in their employers' security system.[54] In each case the default may be expressly or impliedly pro-

---

[48] *Paterson* v. *Miller* [1923] V.L.R. 36.
[49] *Learoyd & Sons (Huddersfield) Ltd.* v. *Pope & Sons Ltd.* [1966] 2 Lloyd's Rep. 142 (where, in fact, the servant's default did not actually cause the loss).
[50] [1966] 1 Q.B. 716, at 725: "If *(the master)* entrusts that duty (i.e., *the duty to keep the goods safely and protect them from theft and depredation)* to his servant, he is answerable for the way in which the servant conducts himself therein. No matter whether the servant be *negligent,* fraudulent, or dishonest, the master is liable". Admittedly Lord Denning does not explicitly state that in cases of negligence this is the exclusive test, but on one reading of his judgment such an inference is possible.
[51] Cf. *James Buchanan & Co. Ltd.* v. *Hay's Transport Services Ltd.* [1972] 2 Lloyd's Rep. 535.
[52] E.g. *Adams Bruce Ltd.* v. *Frozen Products Ltd.* [1953] N.Z.L.R. 63; *Ultzen* v. *Nichols* [1894] 1 Q.B. 92.
[53] E.g. *A. A. Radio Taxi Trucks Ltd.* v. *Curyer* [1965] S.A.S.R. 110; *Eastman Chemical International A.G.* v. *N.M.T. Trading Ltd.* [1972] 2 Lloyds Rep. 25.
[54] Cf. *Macartney-Filgate* v. *Bishop & Sons Depositaries Ltd.* [1964] 2 Lloyds Rep. 480.

hibited by the employer, but would nevertheless be committed within the course of his servant's employment. In each case the master would be under a duty to take care of the goods and, by delegating that duty in whole or in part of his servant, makes himself responsible for the manner in which that duty is discharged. He need not be negligent in employing the servant, nor in delegating the task to him, nor in failing to supervise him, in order for liability to be imposed. He may have instituted an impeccable system of security and yet be liable if his servants commit a single momentary lapse.[55]

But it seems that the two tests will not always produce commensurate results. An illustration of their potential divergence may be drawn from the case of the warehouse tea-lady cited earlier.[56] She, travelling from one part of the warehouse to another, collides with a stack of goods and negligently demolishes them. Although acting within the course of her employment at the time, she is hardly a person to whom the care of the goods has been entrusted—indeed, no duty in respect of them will have been delegated to her at all. And yet it seems beyond doubt that her employers will be liable, notwithstanding that her employment merely provided her with an opportunity of destroying the goods.

The "course of employment" test would accordingly appear to promote a wider range of liability against the bailee: and it is suggested that, in cases of material difference, this test should be preferred. But in some contexts it must be qualified. For example, it cannot successfully operate without modification where the bailee's liability is for the negligent defaults of his independent contractor. Normally an employer is not liable for the torts of an independent contractor unless he has authorised or ratified them.[57] However, when a bailee delegates his duty of safekeeping to an independent contractor, such as a firm of security guards, he will be answerable if the contractor acts negligently in carrying this duty out. Thus in *B.R.S.* v. *Arthur V. Crutchley & Co. Ltd.*[58] the Court of Appeal held that the defendant warehousemen would have been answerable for the failure of their hired patrolman to make the proper number of visits of inspection had it not been clear that this failure did not contribute to the ultimate theft from the warehouse.[59] Liability, moreover, was based upon an implied term in the contract of bailment;[60] and it is submitted that an equivalent implication should be made whenever a bailment exists between the parties, whether founded on contract or not. But it is not for the acts of *every* independent contractor "acting in the course of his employment" that the bailee is liable, but only for the acts of those to whom he has delegated some part of his general duty of care. In this context, a narrower test than the simple scope of service must accordingly be imposed. Of course, the implied terms of the contract may indicate otherwise: we are dealing only

---

[55] *Global Dress Co. Ltd.* v. *W. H. Boase & Co. Ltd.* [1966] 2 Lloyd's Rep. 72.
[56] Ante, p. 480.
[57] *Jolliffe* v. *Willmett & Co.* [1971] 1 All E.R. 478.
[58] [1968] 1 All E.R. 811.
[59] As it was, the warehousemen were found guilty of personal negligence: ante, p. 447; cf. *Photo Productions* v. *Securicor* (1978) *The Times*, March 16.
[60] See Chapter 20, pp. 829-830.

with the general case. The most appropriate criterion would seem to be a cumulative one: the bailee is liable for any act of negligence committed by his servants or agents while acting within the course of their employment, and for any act of negligence committed by a person to whom he has legitimately delegated part of his duty in relation to the goods. The latter branch of liability might include, where appropriate, these cases in which the bailee has delegated an aspect of his duty which is divorced from the pure obligation of safekeeping or protection against depredation and theft;[61] and it could embrace acts of misconduct by servants and agents as well as by independent contractors. Decisions like *Coupé Co. Ltd.* v. *Maddick*[62] and *Aitchison* v. *Page Motors Ltd.*[63] have always fitted uneasily into the course of employment theory and should preferably be regarded as decisions in which a duty of safekeeping was delegated to the servant and, through his misconduct, broken. It should be noted, moreover, that there is a material distinction between cases in which the sole allegation of misconduct against the servant is his negligence and these in which the relevant act of negligence follows a wrongful misappropriation (or "borrowing") of the goods. In cases of the latter description, which encompasses both the *Coupé* and the *Aitchison* decisions as well as *Central Motors (Glasgow) Ltd.* v. *Cessnock Garage and Motor Co.*[64] there must be some degree of entrustment to the servant, or a delegation of some aspect of the bailee's duty of care to him before liability can be imposed. It should not be sufficient to show that the servant, having borrowed the goods without the necessary element of prior entrustment, subsequently inflicted negligent damage on them "in the course of his employment."[65]

Hitherto we have tended to assume that the negligence of the bailee's servant causes destruction or damage. In cases where his carelessness leads to the loss of the goods by theft, the question is less simple. Must he have been entrusted with the goods before loss of this kind can be brought home to the employer? The answer may depend upon whether the act of carelessness is one of omission or commission. Thus, where a driver employed in the defendants' warehouse negligently backs into a gate, breaks the lock, and drives away without informing his employers, it seems that they should be liable if, as a result of this conduct, the warehouse is entered and the bailor's goods are stolen; likewise if an employee negligently forgets to lock the warehouse when he is the last man to leave the building. More difficult is the case where the servant does nothing, but where his failure to act is foreseeably likely to cause the theft of the goods; such as where the sweeper in a warehouse notices that a cage of valuable goods has been left

---

[61] For example, if the defendants in a case like *Bamert* v. *Parks* (ante, p. 000) had delegated the duty of cleaning the car, on similar terms, to a firm of independent contractors.

[62] [1891] 2 Q.B. 413.

[63] (1935) 154 L.T. 128.

[64] 1925 S.C. 796.

[65] Cases in which this combination of facts are present will naturally be rare. An example might arise where the tea-lady in our earlier example (ante, p. 480), takes an article from its place of custody in the warehouse intending to return it later, but then while going about her ordinary duties negligently damages it (e.g. a watch kept in her pocket).

unlocked by a third party and fails to do anything about it. Although neither the sweeper in this example nor the driver in the preceding one may have been charged with any duty in relation to the goods, it is submitted that on balance it would be appropriate to make their employers liable for an act of inadvertence which, in a loose sense admittedly, occurred in the course of employment.

Again, many of those problems could be solved by a closer regard to the area and content of tthe bailee's undertaking.[66] This approach could apply regardless of whether the servant has committed a tort qua the bailor and regardless of whether he is in breach of a duty imposed by his contract of employment.[67] It should, moreover, operate whether the bailment is contractual, or gratuitous, or of the extended character typefied by the relationship between a principal bailor and his sub-bailee for reward.

3. *Innocent, non-negligent misdelivery*: The bailee is clearly liable for misdelivery, whether effected by his servants or by him in person;[68] the only question is whether such liability should arise *whenever* a servant misde-livers in the course of his employment, or should be confined to cases in which the misdeliveror is entrusted with some duty of dealing with the goods. There is no direct authority on this point and cases will be rare in which the servant does not simultaneously fulfil both of the foregoing require-ments. It is submitted that any misdelivery in the course of the servant's employment, whether arising from his performance of a duty towards the goods or not, should suffice.[69]

III. THE BAILEE'S LIEN[70]

It is extremely doubtful whether at Common Law a mere custodian of goods can assert a particular lien for his storage charges. The tradi-tional attitude is to deny such a lien, largely because the custodian merely preserves the goods in their former condition and expends no labour upon them so as to improve their value.[71] Thus, a garage-keeper has been held not to enjoy a lien when he merely maintains, stores and washes a customer's car,[72] and a keeper of animals has been denied a lien when his sole employment consists in rearing, feed-ing, treating and maintaining them.[73] As a result of this antipathy,

[66] Ante, p. 486 et seq.
[67] If he is, the employer may enjoy a right of contribution or indemnity: see generally, *Street on Torts* (6th edn), pp. 474-481.
[68] Ante, p. 472.
[69] See Chapter 5, p. 220 et seq.
[70] A more detailed discussion of the character of liens and their modes of creation and extinguishment is given in Chapter 14. The present section will confine itself to identifying the circumstances (if any) under which a lien could arise from the relationship of bailor and bailee for safekeeping.
[71] Cf. the workman's lien: post, p. 543 et seq.
[72] *Hatton* v. *Car Maintenance Co. Ltd.* [1915] 1 Ch. 621. There was a further ground for denying the lien in this case, because the bailee allowed the customer to take the vehicle as and when required and, therefore, lacked the continuous right of possession normally requisite to the establishment of a lien.
[73] *Re Southern Livestock Producers Ltd.* [1964] 1 W.L.R. 24; see further, p. 544 post, and, as to the inability of the finder to assert a lien, p. 877, post.

custodians have sought other derivations for their contended right of lien, and have been compelled to rely upon three principal sources: special agreement, general or local custom applying to their particular trade, and statute. It is the second of these categories which necessitates the closest examination. This will be conducted in the context of individual trades.

A. Wharfingers

Most writers assume that the wharfinger has a customary, general lien upon goods deposited with him.[74] In fact, the authorities which are relied upon to establish this lien are of somewhat doubtful persuasion; not only because they are old, but because it is possible to view them as establishing a customary lien only in a particular locality rather than some universal custom peculiar to the trade in question.[75] Certainly, the wharfinger's lien may still be refuted in relation to a particular region,[76] even if it can now be considered to be one of general acceptance. The burden of establishing a general customary lien is a heavy one[77] and it may be that outside the City of London the wharfinger cannot rely upon automatic judicial recognition of the relevant custom but must establish it independently in relation to his particular port or locality.[78] Of course, a lien may be conferred by express contract[79] or, in special cases, by statute.[80]

B. Warehousemen

Although it has recently been stated that precedents favour the granting of a particular lien to the warehouseman,[81] the tide of authority seems more generally opposed to a lien of this character.[82] Such opposition is

---

[74] E.g. Halsbury, *Laws of England* (4th edn), Vol. ii, para. 1549; Bowstead, *Agency* (13th edn), 220; Hall, *Possessory Liens* p. 38. As to the meaning of general liens, see post, p. 550.

[75] Thus both *Naylor* v. *Mangles* (1794) 1 Esp. 109; 170 E.R. 295, and *Spears* v. *Hartley* (1800) 3 Esp. 81; 170 E.R. 545, were regarded by Chancellor Spragge in the Ontario case of *Gills* v. *Bickford* (1879) 26 Gr. 512, at 513-514 as limited to the City of London; an interpretation which has recently been approved by Stephen J. in the Australian High Court in *Majeau Carrying Co. Pty. Ltd.* v. *Coastal Rutile Ltd.* (1973) 1 A.L.R. 1, at 6, although neither of the older cases is expressly limited in its effect to the City of London and in each decision the wharfinger's lien is quite emphatically upheld. Other English decisions acknowledging the wharfinger's general lien include *R.* v. *Humphrey* (1825) M'cle & Yo. 173, at 188; 148 E.R. 371, at 377, per Graham B. (in which Garrow and Hullock B.B. concurred); *Bock* v. *Gorrissen* (1860) 2 De G. F. & J. 434, at 443; 45 E.R. 689, at 693 per Lord Campbell L.C.; *Moet* v. *Pickering* (1878) 8 Ch. D. 372.

[76] E.g. *Holderness & Collinson* (1827) 7 B. & C. 212; 108 E.R. 702—a decision relating to the port of Hull. This case shows that the onus of proving the local custom as to a general lien is upon the party asserting it.

[77] Post, p. 550.

[78] See, to this effect, Vaines, *Personal Property* (5th edn), 139, where it is remarked that "Wharfingers and warehousemen apparently may claim a general lien only as arising by express agreement or local usage."

[79] This possibility is recognised by Parke B. in *Bowman* v. *Malcolm* (1843) 11 M. & W. 833, at 844; 152 E.R. 1042, at 1047, cited by Stephen J. in the *Majeau* case (1973) 1 A.L.R. 1, at 8.

[80] For example, under the *Merchant Shipping Act* 1894, s. 499.

[81] Hill, *Freight Forwarders*, p. 216.

[82] *Hatton* v. *Car Maintenance Co. Ltd.* [1915] 1 Ch. 621; *Kilner's Ltd.* v. *The John Dawson Investment Trust Ltd.* (1935) 35 S.R. (N.S.W.) 274, at 279-280;

consistent with the normal requirement that a bailee should improve or, at least, alter goods before he can claim to retain them as security for his charges.

The warehouseman's right to a customary *general* lien has recently been examined by the High Court of Australia. In *Majeau Carrying Co. Pty. Ltd.* v. *Coastal Rutile Ltd.*[83], Stephen J. reviewed the relevant English authorities and concluded that, at Common Law, no such right could be sustained. He pointed out that the older cases suffered from a number of weaknesses from the warehouseman's point of view: some were ambiguous,[84] some were against the lien,[85] and some could be otherwise explained.[86] In his view, the appellants had failed to establish either a universal custom sufficiently notorious to be judicially noticeable without specific proof (as in the case of bankers)[87] or a particular custom operating locally within their own state of Queenlsand. Speaking of the first limb of their argument, and of the cases cited in support, he said:

> These authorities do not, I think, support the view that any judicial recognition has been accorded to any general right of warehousemen to a possessory lien. Such decisions as may be said to lend some support to the appellant's contentions are, at most, instances confined to particular localities and do not even appear to have reached that stage at which, without evidence of custom and usage, even a local right to such a lien has been accorded judicial notice.[88]

As regards their second contention, he stressed the jealousy with which the courts regard general liens and the judicial reluctance to allow them to proliferate.[89] The weight of evidence required to counter-

---

Majeau Carrying Co. Pty. Ltd. v. *Coastal Rutile Ltd.* ante, at 9. See further, post. But in Australia warehousemen in all states except Tasmania may have a particular *statutory* lien: post, p. 497.

---

[83] (1973) 1 A.L.R. 1 (Menzies J. concurring).

[84] E.g. *R.* v. *Humphery* (1825) M'cle & Yo. 173; 148 E.R. 371 (where the judges disagreed and the question was eventually left undecided: see especially per Garrow and Hullock BB. at 195, 380); *Buxton* v. *Baughan* (1834) 6 C. & P. 674; 172 E.R. 1414 (where the point was not argued because the decision revolved around the consent of the owner); *Moet* v. *Pickering* (1878) 8 Ch. D. 372 (where the judges appear to have used the words warehouseman and wharfinger interchangeably but James L.J. at 375 seemed opposed to a warehouseman's lien); *Nicholson* v. *Harper* [1895] 2 Ch. 415 (where North J. assumed the existence of the lien without discussion).

[85] E.g. *Bowman* v. *Malcolm* (1843) 11 M.L.W. 833, at 844; 152 E.R. 1042, at 1047 per Parke, B., Gurney and Rolfe BB. concurring: "as a shipping agent, or warehousekeeper, he could have no general lien unless by contract".

[86] E.g. *Ex. p. Ludlow* [1879] W.N. 65; *Re Catford* (1894) 71 L.T. 584 (which dealt merely with the custom in favour of Bristol warehousemen); *Hill* v. *London Central Markets Cold Storage Co. Ltd.* (1910) 102 I.T. 715 (where the lien was admitted and where there may in any event have been a purely local custom to that effect: see *Jowitt & Sons* v. *Union Cold Storage Co. Ltd.* [1913] 3 K.B. 1, at 10 per Scrutton J.); *Singer Manufacturing Co. Ltd.* v. *L. & S.W. Ry. Co.* [1894] 1 Q.B. 833 (where the lien seems to have been statutory in character).

[87] Post, p. 498.

[88] (1973) 1 A.L.R. 1, at 8.

[89] E.g. *Rushforth* v. *Hadfield* (1806) 7 East 224, at 228; 103 E.R. 86, at 88 per Lord Ellenborough C.J.; *Bock* v. *Gorrissen* (1860) 2 De G. F. & J. 434, at 443; 45 E.R. E.R. 689, at 693, per Lord Campbell L.C.

act this antipathy was considerable and the defendants had failed to adduce it.[90]

Whereas Menzies J. concurred with Stephen J. in the *Majeau* case, the third member of the High Court took a different approach. In the view of Gibbs J. it was unnecessary to decide whether at Common Law the warehouseman enjoyed a general lien because any such right would have been permanently extinguished by the *Warehousemen's Liens Act* 1938 (Qld.). The repeal of that Act by s. 24 of the *Disposal of Uncollected Goods Act* 1967 (Qld.) could not serve to revive any former right to a general lien;[91] and accordingly the learned judge declined to consider whether this right had ever, in fact, existed.[92]

In England, the question may be regarded as open. Halsbury[93] goes no further than to admit the possibility of a general lien for warehousemen and Chitty[94] does not advert to the question at all. In view of the condition of the authorities, it seem unlikely that courts would accept the assertion of a general lien unless cogent and unambiguous evidence of its existence within the relevant locality were provided.[95]

In the United States, there has been a greater willingness to extend the power of lien to bailees whose duties of safekeeping are substantially passive and do not involve adding to or benefitting the chattel. Thus, in contrast to *Hatton* v. *Car Maintenance Co. Ltd.*[96], it has been held that garage-keepers who have kept and cared for a motor vehicle may have a lien against the bailor[97] and it has also been held that at common Law a warehouseman enjoys a particular lien in respect of his storage charges.[98] The latter decision was referred to by Stephen J. in the *Majeau case,*[99] where the learned judge appeared to regard the doctrine as one peculiar to the United States. But although it is true that no particular lien was pleaded in the *Majeau* case and that the decision cannot be taken as conclusive on that point, the prospects of its successful assertion in England or Australia must be regarded as remote. There is, among the authorities, occasional evidence of an assumption

---

[90] (1973) 1 A.L.R. 1, at 9-10; see also *Protean Enterprises (Newmarket) Pty. Ltd.* v. *Randal* [1975] V.R. 327, and, for discussion of the rules as to proof of custom, post, p. 550.

[91] Cf. the discussion as to the wife's agency of necessity in (1973) 36 M.L.R. 638, 642; (1974) 37 M.L.R. 240, 360, 480; and see now *Warehousemen's Liens Act* 1973 (Qld): post, p. 497.

[92] (1973) 1 A.L.R. 1, at 2-3; Gibbs J. did, however, remark that there were no grounds for impugning the trial judge's decision that no local custom had been adequately made out: ibid.

[93] Op cit., para. 1549.

[94] See 23rd edn, para. 186, where other types of bailee enjoying a general lien by custom are enumerated but the warehouseman is not specifically mentioned.

[95] Vaines, *Personal Property* (5th edn), p. 139.

[96] [1915] 1 Ch. 621.

[97] E.g. *Diamond Service Station* v. *Broadway Motor Co.* (1929) 158 Tenn. 258; 12 S.W. 2d. 705; *Gem Motor Co.* v. *Security Investment Co.* (1933) 16 Tenn. App. 608; 65 S.W. (2d) 590. Cf. *R.* v. *Howson* (1966) 55 D.L.R. (2d) 582 (no lien to person upon whose land car parked without his consent: ante., p. 392).

[98] *Jewett* v. *City Transfer and Storage Co.* (1933) 18 P. (2d) 351.

[99] (1973) 1 A.L.R. 1, at 9; see also at 5, citing *Steinman* v. *Wilkins* Am. Dec. 254.

that a particular lien may arise in favour of the warehouseman,[1] but
the influence of the American cases is unlikely to be strong in this area
and the warehouseman (a fortiori the car-park and cloak-room
operator)[2] would be better advised to rely upon an express agreement
empowering him to detain the goods.[3]

In certain instances, however, a statutory lien is granted to the
warehouseman. This is conferred in England under the *Merchant Shipping Act 1894*[4] and in Australia under various State enactments which,
to some extent, render redundant any speculation as to whether the
warehouseman has a lien at Common Law.[5] Unfortunately, space does
not permit discussion of the Australian legislation in detail.

C. Agisters

The Common Law rule that an agister has no particular lien over
animals bailed to him is upheld by substantial authority in England,[6]
Australia[7] and New Zealand.[8] The justification is that "unless the bailee
can establish improvement he has no lien";[9] an agister does not normally
improve the animals agisted to him but merely provides for their day-
to-day maintenance and survival.[10] There may be another reason in

---

[1] One case which appears to assume this is *Vacha* v. *Gillett* (1934) 50 Ll.L.R.
67 ("a case of repulsive complexity") where, however, there was no evidence
that a lien was ever asserted and the point did not fall to be decided. The
decision is interesting because Mackinnon J. remarks obiter (at 76) that the
doctrine laid down in *Somes* v. *British Empire Shipping Co.* (1860) 8 H.L.
Cas. 338, whereunder the person asserting a lien is disabled from claiming
charges for storing the goods after the lien has been asserted, should not
apply when the contract is exclusively for storage in the first place and the
charges are therefore no more than "the contractual cost of storage". This
distinction seems, with respect, to be a sensible one. See also *R.* v. *Humphery*
(1825) M'cle & Jo. 173; 148 E.R. 371.

[2] Cf. *Singer Manufacuring Co. Ltd.* v. *L. & S.W. Ry. Co.* [1894] 1 Q.B. 833

[3] Such an agreement existed in *Jowitt & Sons* v. *Union Cold Storage Co.* [1913]
3 K.B. 1, where the lien created was a general one. See also *United States Steel
Products Co.* v. *G.W. Ry. Co.* [1916] 1 A.C. 189.

[4] Section 499, which is confined to cases in which goods are delivered to a
wharfinger or warehouseman under the authority conferred by Part VII of the
Act.

[5] The lien is a *particular* lien to cover storage, preservation, transportation and
certain other specified expenses incurred with regard to the goods. It exists, in
varying forms, in all States except Tasmania. See *Warehousemen's Liens Act
1935* (N.S.W.); *Warehousemen's Liens Act 1958* (Vic.); *Warehousemen's Liens
Act 1941-1974* (S.A.); *Warehousemen's Liens Act 1952-1954* (W.A.); *Warehousemen's Act 1973* (Qld.); *Warehousemen's Liens Ordinance 1969* (N. Territory);
Mercantile Law Ordinance 1962, ss. 17-32 (A.C.T.).

[6] *Chapman* v. *Allen* (1632) Cro. Car. 271; 79 E.R. 836; *Jackson* v. *Cummins*
(1839) 5 M. & W. 342, at 349-350; 151 E.R. 145, at 148 per Parke B.; *Richards*
v. *Symons* (1845) 8 Q.B. 90; *Hatton* v. *Car Maintenance Co. Ltd.* [1915] 1 Ch.
621, at 624; Halsbury, op. cit., vol. i., para. 216.

[7] *Helton* v. *Sullivan* [1968] Qd. R. 562.

[8] *Grazing & Export Meat Co. Ltd.* v. *Anderson* [1976] 1 N.Z.L.R. 187.

[9] *Re Southern Livestock Producers Ltd.* [1964] 1 W.L.R. 24, at 28 per Pennycuick J.

[10] See *Helton* v. *Sullivan* (ante) where Matthews J. held that the mustering, tagging
and branding of cattle did not take the case outside the general rule, but
conceded that the castration of bulls might objectively be deemed a sufficient
improvement to justify the assertion of a lien.

that the size of the land upon which the animals are agisted prevents the agister from acquiring possession of them.[11]

Consistently with this, livery-stable keepers have been held to enjoy no lien upon animals deposited with them for feeding and stabling;[12] and in *Re Southern Livestock Producers Ltd.*[13] a farmer who had, in accordance with his agreement, housed, fed, cared for and arranged for the proper servicing and farrowing of a quantity of pigs was held not to be entitled to claim priority in the bailor's bankruptcy by virtue of a possessory Common Law lien. Pennycuick J. conceded that if the farmer himself had been bound to supply the boars for servicing, he would have had a lien for that part of the labour;[14] but he held that there was no authority for permitting the lien where the bailee merely supervises the production of litters. In any event, the separation of this aspect of the work from those aspects which did not warrant the imposition of a lien was an impossible task and effectively operated to make the claim inseverable.

The position as regards a custodian of animals is inequitable and beset with over-refined distinctions, as a passage from this decision shows:

> If this matter were free from authority it would, I think, be tempting to draw the line in rather a different place so as to cover the case where a person by the exercise of labour and skill prevents a chattel from deteriorating in contradistinction to improving it. The obvious example is feeding of animals which would otherwise die; but other examples come to mind. It seems to me illogical that a kennel-keeper should have a lien for the expense of stripping a dog, but not for that of boarding it. However, it is quite impossible for me at this time of day to introduce that sort of modification into a well-established principle.[15]

No case is reported in which the agister has sought to prove a customary general lien. Although theoretically such a lien might be established in relation to particular areas, the prospects of its successful assertion must be regarded as negligible.

D. Bankers

The position with regard to bankers was succinctly stated by Lord Campbell L.C. in *Brandao* v. *Barnett*;[16]

> Bankers most undoubtedly have a general lien on all securities deposited with them as bankers by a customer, unless there be an express contract, or circumstances that show an implied contract, inconsistent with lien.

---

[11] *Helton* v. *Sullivan*; cf. *Robinson* v. *Waters* (1920) 22 W.A.L.R. 66. In *Helton's* case, the lien was also negatived by the lack of a continuing power of possession in the agister; cf. the case of the race-horse trainer, post, p. 545.

[12] *Wallace* v. *Woodgate* (1824) 1 C. & P. 575; 171 E.R. 1323 (where the need for a special agreement was recognised); *Judson* v. *Etheridge* (1833) 1 Cr. & M. 743; 149 E.R. 598; *Binns* v. *Pigot* (1840) 9 C. & P. 208; 173 E.R. 804; *Armstrong* v. *Sutherland* (1857) *Argus Newspaper*, 23 November (N.S.W.); cf. *White* v. *Crozier* (1886) 20 S.A.L.R. 44.

[13] [1964] 1 W.L.R. 24.

[14] *Scarfe* v. *Morgan* (1838) 4 M. & W. 270; 150 E.R. 1430.

[15] [1964] 1 W.L.R. 24, at 28.

[16] (1846) 12 A. & Fin. 787, at 806; 8 E.R. 1622, at 1630; and see Buckley J. in *Re London & Globe Finance Corporation* [1902] 2 Ch. 416.

The lien is based upon commercial custom which is part of the law merchant, and need not be specifically proved.[17] It is doubtful, however, whether it would extend to articles deposited with a bank for safe-keeping.[18] The reader is referred to more specialist works for amplification of this variety of lien.[19]

E. Other cases

The remaining cases fall into two main categories: those in which a general lien is conferred by custom and those in which no lien, general or particular, can probably be sustained without express agreement. In to the first category fall packers,[20] factors,[21] insurance brokers,[22] stock-brokers[23] and solicitors.[24] In to the second, a host of miscellaneous bailees for safekeeping such as car-park operators, landlords who take custody of tenants' trunks, restaurant keepers and private warehouse-men. It is surprising, perhaps, that car park operators in particular do not seem to have included a right of lien within their extensive conditions of exclusion; no doubt the construction and organisation of the modern car-park confers sufficient practical ability to detain vehicles without the need to invoke any legal right to do so.

IV. Exclusion Clauses[25]

In Australia, it seems that the warehouseman or "bare" custodian of goods is not prohibited from restricting or excluding the obligations that would otherwise arise at Common Law. Section 74(1) of the *Trade Practices Act* 1974 (Cth.) imposes obligatons of due care and skill upon any corporation which, in the course of a business, supplies services to a consumer; and s. 68 of the Act prohibits any attempt to qualify or exclude liability for breach of these obligations.[26] There is authority for the view that a contract for storage or safekeeping may qualify as a contract for the supply of services,[27] but s. 74(3) of the *Trade Practices Act* defines so narrowly the types of service contract that are included within the statutory entrenchment that mere bailments by way of custody appear to be excluded.[28]

In England, however, the *Unfair Contract Terms Act* Bill 1977 con-

---

17 *Majeau Carrying Co. Pty. Ltd.* v. *Coastal Rutile Ltd.* (1973) 1 A.L.R. 1 5.
18 This is not one of the species of property listed by Paget, *Law of Banking* (8th edn), pp. 498-501, as falling within the field of the lien; and it is difficult to see how such property would qualify as "security".
19 E g. Paget, op. cit., pp. 498 507.
20 *Re Witt, Ex parte Shubrook* (1876) 2 Ch. D. 489; and see post, p. 552.
21 *Kruger* v. *Wilcox* (1755) Amb. 252; 27 E.R. 168; *Baring* v. *Corrie* (1818) 2 B. & Ald. 137, at 148; 109 E.R. 317, at 321; *Godin* v. *London Assurance Co.* (758) 1 W. Bl. 103; 96 E.R. 58.
22 *Mann* v. *Forrester* (1814) 4 Camp. 60; 171 E.R. 20; *Westwood* v. *Bell* (1815) 4 Camp. 349; 171 E.R. 111; *Fisher* v. *Smith* (1878) 4 App. Cas. 1.
23 *Jones* v. *Peppercorne* (1858) Johns 430; 70 E.R. 490; *Hope & Co.* v. *Glendinning* [1911] A.C. 419.
24 See generally, Bowstead, op. cit., p. 220 et seq.
25 See, generally, Chapter 25.
26 See also s. 74(2) and generally, p. 527 and Appendix II, post.
27 *Walsh* v. *Palladium Car Park Pty. Ltd.* [1975] V.R. 949; ante, p. 434.
28 For a list of the relevant services falling within s. 74 see p. 527, post.

tains a substantial measure of prohibition upon the insertion of exclusion clauses within contracts for the storage of safekeepng of goods. The Act applies mainly to "business liability", which means liability for a breach of obligation arising from something done or to be done in the course of a business, or from the occupation of premises used for business purposes.[29] Business liability for negligence (which includes breach of a contractual obligation to take reasonable care) can be restricted or excluded only so far as is reasonable.[30] Further restrictions are imposed under s. 3, which prohibits unreasonable attempts to exclude liability for breach of contract,[31] when one party deals as a consumer on the other's written standard terms of business; and s. 4, which prohibits unreasonable indemnity clauses.

V Carriers as Warehousemen

The liability of the carrier, who warehouses goods as an incidental part of his performance of the contract of carriage, is discussed in Chapter 15.[32]

---

[29] Section 1(3).
[30] Section 2(2): for criteria see Schedule 2. The onus is on the party alleging that the clause is not reasonable: s. 10(3).
[31] Defined by s. 11.
[32] Post, p. 572 et seq.

CHAPTER 14

HIRE OF WORK AND LABOUR

INTRODUCTION

This variety of bailment, known to the Roman lawyers as "locatio operis faciendi",[1] was defined by Holt C.J. as arising "when goods or chattels are delivered to be carried, or something is to be done about them, for a reward to be paid by the person who delivers them to the bailee, who is to do the thing about them."[2] Locatio operis faciendi therefore contains two elements: a contract for services, coupled with a bailment of the article upon which those services are to be performed.[3] The goods will remain in the bailee's possession until the work is completed and will then be returned to the bailor, or delivered to a third party, in accordance with his instructions. A wide range of everyday commercial activity, including dry-cleaning, laundering, repair, valuation, auctioneering, alteration and the treatment of sick animals, may therefore fall within this category of bailment.[4]

A number of preliminary observations should be made. The first is that not all contracts of work and labour will give rise to a bailment. A workman may be engaged, for instance, to repaint a house or to repair a television on the owner's premises. The following analysis will confine itself to those contracts for services which involve a delivery of goods. Nevertheless, in many respects the obligations of the parties will coincide, whether or not possession in the subject-matter has passed to the workman.

This introduces the second point. Bailments by way of work and labour are essentially contractual phenomena, and to a great extent the duties of the parties will depend upon the general law of contract rather than the specialised rules of bailment. This is not a book on contract, and it is not proposed to discuss in detail the contractual obligations of the parties. Most of these exist quite independently of bailment and are unaffected by its creation. The ensuing chapter will concentrate upon those rights and duties which flow directly from the

---

[1] Jones, *An Essay on Bailments,* p. 104 et seq.
[2] *Coogs* v. *Bernard* (1703) 2 Ld. Raym. 909, at 913; 92 E.R. 107, at 109.
[3] Occasionally, the work will be performed not upon but *with* the chattel. For illustrations, see post.
[4] Assuming, of course, that possession of the chattel is given to the workman. Contracts of carriage represent a special case and are dealt with independently: see Chapters 15-18, post. The preparation of a corpse for burial by an undertaker probably involves a bailment locatio operis faciendi, insofar as it is possible to become a bailee of human tissue: ante, p. 7.

bailment relationship, to the exclusion (as far as possible) of any contractual modification imposed by the parties or by Common Law.[5]

Although many definitions of bailment (particularly the older ones) stress the need for the chattel to be returned in specie at the end of the bailment, it is clear that re-delivery in the altered or modified form contemplated by a contract of work and labour does not prevent the original transfer of possession from giving rise to a bailment. This is made clear in a passage from an American decision,[6] where it was held that the delivery of seeds, to be planted and raised on the defendant's land, gave rise to a bailment locatio operis faciendi:

> In principle, the transaction between the parties to the present action is not different from that involved where the owner of leather delivers it to a manufacturer to be made into shoes (*Mansfield* v. *Converse,* 8 Allen [Mass.] 182); or where the owner of logs delivers them to a miller to be sawed into lumber (*Gleeson* v. *Beers,* 59 Vt. 581, 10 Atl. 86, 59 Am. Rep. 757); or where the owner of milk delivers it to a factory to be made into butter or cheese (*Bank* v. *Schween,* 127 Ill. 573, 20 N.E. 681, 11 Am. St. Rep. 174); or where the owner of live animals delivers them to another to be kept for compensation. . . . In any of these cases the transaction is a bailment, and it is altogether immaterial whether the compensation of the bailee is fixed at a definite sum in money or is a share of the product itself, a share of the net proceeds of the adventure, a share of the increase, or is computed upon the product of the undertaking.

The identity of the transaction as a bailment will accordingly survive, irrespective of whether the labour in question merely alters the goods in some minor degree or totally transforms them. Thus where grapes are delivered to be pressed into wine, there is a bailment of the grapes until they are pressed and a bailment of the wine thereafter. Similar principles apply to the progeny of animals delivered pursuant to contracts of work and labour; the deliveree will owe the duties of a bailee not only towards the original or parent chattel but towards its produce, or end-product, as well.[7] An example is the delivery to a veterinary surgeon of an animal which is about to give birth, or the delivery of a bull to a laboratory farmer for the extraction of semen.[8]

---

[5] Exclusion clauses in these and other bailments are considered in Chapter 25. It should be noted that occasionally the bailee's duties as a workman and a bailor's responsibility for payment may arise under a *collateral* contract, the principal agreement being one between the artificer and the bailor's insurance company. This is especially common, of course, in cases which involve the bailment of cars for repair: see *Charnock* v. *Liverpool Corporation* [1968] 1 W.L.R. 1498; *Brown & Davis Ltd.* v. *Galbraith* [1972] 1 W.L.R. 997: post, p. 968 et seq.

[6] *D. M. Ferry & Co.* v. *Forquer* (1921) 202 P. 193; 29 A.L.R. 642.

[7] At least, where the produce was contemplated by the parties as a partial subject-matter of the bailment. If it were not, the result may be somewhat different. A slaughterer, for instance, who took possession of a sow without knowing that it was pregnant and later found himself in possession of a litter of 8 piglets might conceivably be held to owe to their owner the duties of a mere involuntary bailee. Cf. *Re Rauf* (1974) 40 D.L.R. (3d) 362; (1975) 49 D.L.R. (3d) 345.

[8] Cf. *Anselmi* v. *Animal Breeding Services* (1975) Unrep. N.Z. Sup. Ct. (August 8th), where the bull itself was injured; *Mitchell* v. *Davis* (1920) 37 T.L.R. 68 (coat made from customer's fur skins).

Equally it seems that a bailment locatio operis faciendi will arise when the chattel or its ultimate product are not to be restored to the bailor but are to be sold or delivered to a third party. An auctioneer or factor is clearly a bailee[9] and it seems that the bailment is most appropriately classified as one of work and labour, although he does nothing to alter the intrinsic value or character of the goods themselves.

As with gratuitous bailments by way of depositum and mandatum, there is some difficulty in differentiating between mere custody for reward and bailments locatio operis faciendi. Often, acceptance of the chattel will create not only a duty to safeguard or warehouse it for the owner but to provide additional services for its support or preservation. One example is the bailment by way of agistment; another might be the bailment entered into with the proprietor of a boarding kennel, who undertakes not merely to protect the animal from theft or escape but to feed, exercise and examine it for infection. It seems that the test laid down by Story for cases of mandatum[10] should apply equally in the context of bailments for reward and that a bailment will be deemed to be by way of custody alone when custody is the primary object of the transaction and the service and labour are merely accessorial. Thus, whereas bailments for agistment (which involve very few active duties on the part of the agister) seem to have been traditionally classified as bailments locatio custodiae,[11] the case of the boarding kennel proprietor may fall on the other side of the line.[12]

Where frozen meat is bailed for storage and the contract demands that it be kept at a certain temperature, this special obligation alone should not transform the bailment into one of work and labour.[13] Such affirmative duties as are owed by the warehouseman would be incidental to the central duty of safekeeping and a breach of them (e.g. by failing to check and maintain the temperature) could be subsumed within the general duty to take what, in all the circumstances, amounts to reasonable care.[14]

A somewhat different problem of classification concerns chattels which are delivered in order to facilitate the performance of work but

---

[9] E.g. *Gutter* v. *Tait* (1947) 177 L.T.1; *Biddle* v. *Bond* (1865) 6 B. & S. 225; *Williams* v. *Millington* (1785) 1 H. Bl. 85; *Harding* v. *Commissioner of Inland Revenue* [1977] 1 N.Z.L.R. 337. Cf. *R.* v. *Prince* (1827) 2 C. & P. 517; Pollock & Wright, *Possession in the Common Law*, pp. 161-162.

[10] Story, *Bailment*, § 140; ante, p. 329.

[11] At least, insofar as this is relevant to deciding that the bailee has no lien: see *Re Southern Livestock Producers Ltd.* [1964] 1 W.L.R. 24; *Grazing and Export Meat Co. Ltd.* v. *Anderson* [1976] 1 N.Z.L.R. 187; ante, p. 497.

[12] Although it is still doubtful whether this would entitle him to a particular lien for improving the value of the goods: post, p. 544. The processing of turkeys by a bailee would clearly involve a bailment by way of locatio operis faciendi: see *Grenn* v. *Brampton Poultry Co.* (1958) 13 D.L.R. (2d) 279, where the point was not material.

[13] *Gaylard* v. *Milne* [1933] Q.W.N. 47; 28 Q.J.P.R.I.; *United Fresh Meat Co. Ltd.* v. *Charterhouse Cold Storage Ltd.* [1974] 2 Lloyd's Rep. 286; *Fankhauser* v. *Mark Dykes Pty. Ltd.* [1960] V.R. 376. See also *Aurora Trading Co. Ltd.* v. *Nelson Freezing Co. Ltd.* [1922] N.Z.L.R. 662; *Adams Bruce Ltd.* v. *Frozen Products Ltd.* [1953] N.Z.L.R. 63; *Geddes Refrigeration Ltd.* v. *Ward* (1962) 4 W.I.R. 170.

[14] It may even amount to a deviation: see *United Fresh Meat Co. Ltd.* v. *Charterhouse Cold Storage Ltd.* ante.

upon which no labour is expended.[15] In discussing the gratuitous equivalent of this type of transaction, we have observed that at least one decision favours classification of the bailment as mandatum.[16] Logically, the same principle should apply in cases of bailment for reward, so that the delivery (for instance) of ledgers and account-books to an accountant for compilation of a tax-return should give rise to a bailment locatio operis faciendi.[17] In fact, it is difficult to envisage circumstances in which the distinction would possess any importance.[18] Whatever classification is adopted, the bailee would be under a duty to take reasonable care of the chattel, to deliver it up in accordance with the agreement, to supply fit and suitable materials in the performance of the work and to perform that work with proper care and skill. The primary importance of locatio operis faciendi, as distinct from other bailments, seems to lie in its separation of those aspects of the transaction which relate to mere safekeeping from those which relate to the work to be performed. A breach of the latter duty may not be held established in the absence of affirmative proof by the bailor.[19] But with bailments of the kind under discussion this dichotomy can scarcely arise since the workman will merely be a bailee of the instrument with which the work is to be performed and not of the chattel upon which it is to be carried out.[20]

To a lesser extent, the same legal indifference attaches to the distinction between a contract for work and materials and a contract for the sale of goods. This distinction can impinge upon a bailment locatio operis faciendi only when the workman is bound to ally or intermix property of his own with the bailor's goods or chattels, and when property in those goods is thereupon intended to pass to the bailor; for instance, when connecting rods are to be attached to a car bailed for repairs.[21] The question whether the materials used in performance of such a contract pass to the bailor under a contract of sale or under a mixed contract for the supply of work and materials is of diminishing importance because both at Common Law and, in Australia, under the *Trade Practices Act* 1974, similar terms as to fitness for purpose and merchantable quality are implied.[22] The distinction is not entirely redundant, however, because in England the customer under a contract for the provision of work and materials will not enjoy the rights conferred by the *Sale of Goods Act* 1893, or the *Supply of Goods (Implied*

---

[15] As to the duty of the bailor in this situation, see *Derbyshire Building Co. Pty. Ltd.* v. *Becker* (1962) 107 C.L.R. 633; post, p. 739.

[16] Ante, p. 327.

[17] Certainly the accountant in such cases has a lien: *Woodworth* v. *Conroy* [1976] 1 All E.R. 107. So, of course, does a solicitor in equivalent circumstances: *Caldwell* v. *Sumpters* [1972] Ch. 478; post, p. 545.

[18] Cf. the case of *mandatum*, where it could be relevant to establish the obligation to perform the work; ante, p. 339.

[19] Ante, p. 343.

[20] The question may be decisive, however, in deciding whether the bailee enjoys a lien. See post, p. 545 et seq.

[21] *G. H. Myers & Co. Ltd.* v. *Brent Cross Service Co. Ltd.* [1934] 1 K.B. 46; and see *Stewart* v. *Reavell's Garage Ltd.* [1952] 2 Q.B. 545 (*held*: contracts for work and labour).

[22] Post, p. 531 et seq.

Terms) *Act* 1973.[23] Moreover, other statutes still refer exclusively to contracts for the sale of goods.[24]

Unless the contract provides a specific definition of its nature, the question as to whether it creates a sale of goods or a supply of work and materials will normally be resolved by looking to the "substance" of the agreement:

> If the substance of the contract is the production of something to be sold, and the exercise of skill, though high, is primarily for the purpose of producing goods for delivery at a price, then the contract is one for the sale of goods. But if the contract is one for skill and labour to be exercised, and the article which results is merely a vehicle to record the maker's skill, it is one for work done and materials supplied.[25]

This criterion, although frequently criticised,[26] seems to be supported by most of the decisions. On the one hand, it has been held that contracts for the installation of machinery[27] or security devices[28] on the customer's premises, or for the tiling of roofs,[29] the renovation of equipment,[30] the installation of spare parts in a vehicle[31] and the fitting of a built-in cocktail-cabinet in the customer's home,[32] are all contracts for the supply of work and materials.[33] Conversely, it has been held that the following are contracts for the sale of goods: the making-up, from the tradesman's own materials, of a fur-jacket,[34] a tombstone,[35]

---

23 Cf. *Law Com., No. 69 and Scottish Law Com. No. 39* (1975), paras 12-28, and *Working Paper No. 71 (Implied Terms in Contracts for the Supply of Goods)* (1977) paras 24 et seq.
24 A modern example is *Lyle* v. *Ajax Distribution Agency Pty. Ltd.* [1974] 11 S.A.S.R. 9, a case arising under the *Book Purchasers Protection Act, 1963-1972* (S.A.). See also *R.* v. *Wood Green Profiteering Committee* (1919) 89 L.J. K.B. 55 and, for further examples of the relevance of the distinction, Sutton, *Sale of Goods* (2nd edn), p. 29 et seq.; Benjamin, *Sale of Goods* (1974), p. 28.
25 Sutton, op. cit., p. 40. Cf. *Atkinson* v. *Bell* (1828) 8 B. & C. 277; 108 E.R. 1046.
26 *Lee* v. *Griffin* (1861) 1 B. & S. 272; Bartholomew (1961) 35 A.L.J. 65; Benjamin, op. cit.
27 *Buxton* v. *Bedall* (1803) 3 East. 308; *Clark* v. *Bulmer* (1843) 11 M. & W. 243; *Sydney Hydraulic and General Engineering Co. Ltd.* v. *Blackwood and Son* (1908) 8 S.R. (N.S.W.) 10. Cf. *H. Parsons (Livestock) Ltd.* v. *Uttley Ingham & Co. Ltd.* [1978] 1 All E.R. 525.
28 *Reginald Glass Pty. Ltd.* v. *River's Locking Systems Pty. Ltd.* (1968) 120 C.L.R. 516; cf. *Davis & Co. (Wines) Ltd.* v. *Afa-Minerva (E.M.I.) Ltd.* [1974] 2 Lloyd's Rep. 27.
29 *Young & Marten Ltd.* v. *McManus Childs Ltd.* [1969] 1 A.C. 454. See also *Gloucestershire County Council* v. *Richardson* [1969] 1 A.C. 480 (supply and erection of concrete columns); *Greaves & Co. Ltd.* v. *Baynham Meikle & Partners* [1975] 1 W.L.R. 1095.
30 *Anglo-Egyptian Navigation Co. Ltd* v. *Rennie* (1875) L.R. 10 C.P. 271.
31 *G. H. Myers & Co. Ltd.* v. *Brent Cross Service Co. Ltd.* [1934] 1 K.B. 46; *Stewart* v. *Reavell's Garage Ltd.* [1952] 2 Q.B. 545; *Helicopter Sales (Australia) Pty. Ltd.* v. *Rotor Work Pty. Ltd.* (1974) 132 C.L.R. 1 (contract for servicing of helicopter and supply of spare parts).
32 *Brooks Robinson Pty. Ltd.* v. *Rothfield* [1951] V.L.R. 405; cf. *Collins Trading Co. Pty. Ltd.* v. *Maher* [1969] V.R. 20, where the contract was for the sale of an oil heater coupled with an ancillary incentive agreement to install it; *Love* v. *Norman Wright (Builders) Ltd.* [1944] K.B. 484.
33 See also *Robinson* v. *Graves* [1935] 1 K.B. 579 (contract to paint a portrait *held* not a sale of goods); cf. *Isaacs* v. *Hardy* (1884) Cab. & El. 287, where the commissioned painting seems to have been regarded by the parties primarily as a merchantable item.
34 *Marcel (Furriers) Ltd.* v. *Tapper* [1953] 1 W.L.R. 49.
35 *Wolfenden* v. *Wilson* (1873) 33 U.C.R. 442.

a ship's propellor according to specification[36] and a set of false teeth:[37] the preparation and supply of a meal in a restaurant;[38] and the taking and selling of a photograph.[39] But the supply of architects' plans do not fall within the concept of sale because the primary objective is the exercise of specialised skills[40] and not the provision of a tangible commodity.

Two facts emerge from the foregoing summary. The first is that the distinction is largely an intuitive one: the second, that it is impossible to divorce it from the circumstances or location in which the work is to be performed. Thus, whereas contracts for the installation of goods on the customer's premises will almost invariably be classed as contracts for work and materials, contracts for the manufacture of goods with materials not supplied by the customer will normally be classed as contracts of sale. A statement from Benjamin[41] is useful in relating this dichotomy to bailments locatio operis faciendi:

> . . . if the contract is intended to result in transferring for a price from A to B a chattel *in which A had no previous property,* it is a contract for the sale of the chattel.

Bailments locatio operis faciendi fall into four potential categories: (i) those in which a chattel is supplied in order to enable the performance of work for the bailor; (ii) those in which a chattel is supplied for the purpose of labour which is intended to involve the supply of materials not previously owned by the bailor; (iii) those in which the work to be performed (e.g. sale or valuation) involves no addition or passing of property in materials not previously owned by the bailor; (iv) those in which the bailor supplies materials which are to be made into some finished artefact by the bailee. Of these four categories, the first and third can be dismissed as bearing no relationship to the distinction between sale and supply of work and materials, because no property is intended to pass from bailee to bailor. Much the same observation applies to the fourth category, although the true analysis of the transaction may be in terms of a sale to the workman of the raw materials and a resale to the customer of the finished product[42] and it will be unusual for the contract not to involve some minor addition to those materials by the workman, such as buttons and thread. Never-

---

[36] *Cammell Laird & Co. Ltd.* v. *Manganese Bronze & Brass Co. Ltd.* [1934] A.C. 402.

[37] *Lee* v. *Griffin* (1881) 1 B. & S. 272; *Wansborough* v. *Edwards* [1941] Tas. S.R. 1; cf. *Samuels* v. *Davis* [1943] K.B. 526.

[38] *Lockett* v. *A. & M. Charles Ltd.* [1938] 4 All E.R. 170; cf. Benjamin, *op. cit.*, pp. 30-31.

[39] *Rider* v. *Ogden* (1894) 16 A.L.T. 256; *Newman* v. *Lipman* [1951] 1 K.B. 333, at 336. Contra: *Lyle* v. *Ajax Distribution Agency Pty. Ltd.* [1974] 11 S.A.S.R. 9.

[40] *Vautier* v. *Fear* [1916] G.L.R. 524.

[41] *Op cit.,* p. 31; italics supplied.

[42] *Dixon* v. *London Small Arms Co. Ltd.* (1876) 1 App. Cas. 632; here the client (the Crown) supplied steel barrels and stocks in the rough to be made into rifles by the defendants. The materials thus supplied were assessed at a figure which, it was agreed, should be deducted from the final price. *Semble,* this involved a contract for the sale of goods. But note that the defendants in this case partly used and supplied their own materials in performance of the work.

theless, contracts of this kind will almost invariably be characterised as contracts for the hire of work and labour.[43]

So far as concerns the third category, it seems in some respects the antithesis of the situation described by Benjamin. Where, for instance, a contract for the repair of a car or the servicing of a helicopter[44] necessitates the replacement of defective parts, there will very rarely be a separate "price" for the replacment and the part installed is not, when the vehicle is redelivered, so much a chattel in its own right as something incorporated into a larger chattel already owned by the bailor. In fact, the great majority of repair and renovation contracts will constitute transactions of work and labour, in which the supply of parts is ancillary to the substance or main object of the agreement. Theoretically, the supply of the spare part could constitute a sale, as where the customer agrees to buy the part and the garage-owner offers to instal it as an incentive or as a favour, or where the two aspects of the arrangement—repair and replacement—are treated as entirely separate transactions by the parties. Generally, however, the supply aspect will be subordinated to the agreement for work and labour and will not give rise to a separate contract of sale.[45] From the point of view of implied conditions and warranties, this could have unfortunate results. It may be preferable, despite the difficulty of determining an individual price, to treat materials supplied under such contracts as supplied under separate contracts of sale.

I. The Duties of the Bailor

These are few and almost exclusively contractual. The locator's primary obligation is, of course, to pay the price of the work, provided it complies with the necessary standards and no other event (such as frustration or misrepresentation) has occurred to release him.[46] Where no price is agreed, the courts will generally impose a reasonable price.[47]

---

[43] A typical case is *Mitchell* v. *Davis* (1920) 37 T.L.R. 68: post., p. 512.
[44] See n. 31, ante.
[45] *G. H. Myers & Co. Ltd.* v. *Brent Cross Service Co. Ltd.* [1934] 1 K.B. 46. Cf. *Charles Rickards Ltd.* v. *Oppenhaim* [1950] 1 K.B. 616, where under an agreement for the building of a vehicle body on to a chassis supplied by the defendant, the Court of Appeal found it unnecessary to express an opinion upon Finnemore J.'s finding that this was a contract for the sale of goods: see Denning L.J. at 624. However, Singleton L.J. (at 628) entertained doubts as to whether this was a proper classification. See further *H. Parsons (Livestock) Ltd.* v. *Uttley Ingham & Co. Ltd.* [1978] 1 All E.R. 525, where an agreement for the sale and installation of a ready-made storage-hopper was treated as two separate contracts by Lord Denning, M.R., but as a single indivisible contract (apparently of sale) by Scarman and Orr, L.JJ.
[46] E.g. *Farnsworth* v. *Garrard* (1807) 1 Camp. 38; 170 E.R. 867; *Basten* v. *Butter* (1806) 7 East 479; 103 E.R. 185; cf. *Parkes* v. *G. W. Ry. Co.* (1842) 3 Ry. & Can. Cas. 17; 6 Jur. 628; *Menetone* v. *Athawes* (1764) 3 Burr. 1592; 97 E.R. 998; *Gillett* v. *Mawman* (1808) 1 Taunt. 137; 127 E.R. 784.
[47] *Jewry* v. *Busk* (1814) 5 Taunt 302; *Brown* v. *Nairne* (1839) C. & P. 204; *Hughes* v. *Lenny* (1839) 5 M. & W. 183; cf. *Watson* v. *Pearson* (1863) 8 L.T. 395; 9 Jur. N.S. 501. Sometimes the rate that is accepted as reasonable for the work will be that which is customary in the particular trade (although mere custom will not suffice as against a rate that is not just and reasonable): see on this point *Brown* v. *Nairne* (ante); *Price* v. *Hong Kong Tea Co.* (1861) 2 F. & F.

Where the work is not completed and the non-completion goes to the root of the contract, the bailee will generally be precluded from claiming anything. Although in exceptional circumstances, there may be a quantum meruit, the general rule under a contract for work and labour is that failure to complete does not entitle the workman to charge for that part of the work he has completed.[48]

If the bailor retakes the goods in breach of the bailee's lien,[49] he will be liable for trespass or conversion.

There seems to be no direct authority on the bailor's liability for injuries or losses caused by the defective condition of his chattel. It seems that he will be liable only for a breach of the duty of reasonable care and will not be deemed (unless the agreement provides to the contrary) to have warranted the safety or fitness of the goods.

II. THE DUTIES OF THE BAILEE

These have been summarised by Jordan C.J.[50] as follows:

. . . to do the stipulated work on the bailed chattels, to do it

466 N.P.; *Debenham* v. *King's College Cambridge* (1884) Cab. & E. 438; *A.G.* v. *Draper's Co.* (1869) L.R. 9 Eq. 69; *Faraday* v. *Tamworth Union* (1916) 86 L.J. Ch. 436. The obligation to pay does not arise until the hirer has had a reasonable time for inspection of the work: *Hughes* v. *Lenny* (ante). It may, in exceptional cases, be rebutted by the circumstances of the transaction: *Cannon* v. *Miles* [1974] 2 Lloyd's Rep. 129 (where a term was implied that repairs should not be effected to a car unless they would make the car saleable for more than the cost of the repairs themselves). *Manson* v. *Bailey* (1885) 2 Macq. 80; 26 L.T.O.S. 24 (H.L.); cf. *Hingeston* v. *Kelly* (1849) 18 L.J. Ex 360; and cannot, of course, arise when the work in question has not been authorised: *Lovelock* v. *King* (1831) 9 L.J. (O.S.) K.B. 179; *Whitaker* v. *Dunn* (1887) 3 T.L.R. 602; cf. *Robson* v. *Godfrey* (1816) 1 Stark. 285; *Burn* v. *Miller* (1813) 4 Taunt. 745; *Parmeter* v. *Burrell* (1827) 3 C. & P. 144.

[48] See *Sinclair* v. *Bowles* (1829) 9 B. & C. 92; *Sumpter* v. *Hedges* [1898] 1 Q.B. 673; *Bolton* v. *Mahadeva* [1972] 1 W.L.R. 1009; *Veregen* v. *Red Maple Farms Ltd.* (1976) 59 D.L.R. (3d) 221 and, for further authority, *Halsbury's Laws,* vol. ii, para. 1564. The general rule that the employer is not liable for payment if there has been substantial non-completion of the work may be displaced (inter alia) by proof of agreement or custom to contrary effect; by the fact that the hirer takes the benefit of the partially completed performance (see *Hoenig* v. *Isaacs* [1952] 2 All E.R. 176); by frustration or impossibility of performance (see *Hoenig* v. *Isaacs* (ante) at 181, 182; *Appleby* v. *Myers* (1867) L.R. 2 C.P. 651, at 661); or by proof that the failure to complete resulted from the locator's own default: *Planche* v. *Colburn* (1831) 8 Bing 14; *Craven-Ellis* v. *Canons Ltd.* [1936] 2 K.B.; cf. *Kewley* v. *Stokes* (1846) 2 Cas. & Kir. 435; and see further Halsbury, loc. cit. ante. When non-completion does not affect the essence of the contract and does not therefore entitle the hirer to repudiate, the rate recoverable will generally represent the original price of the work minus a deduction in respect of the non-completed portion thereof: *Appleby* v. *Myers* (1867) L.R. 2 C.P. 651, at 660; *Hoenig* v. *Isaacs* [1952] 2 All E.R. 176; and see *Chapel* v. *Hicks* (1833) 2 Cr. & M. 214; *Cousins* v. *Paddon* (1835) 2 Cr., M. & R. 547; *Baithe* v. *Kell* (1838) 4 Bing. N.C. 638; *Stegmann* v. *O'Connor* (1899) 80 L.T. 234; 81 L.T. 627. As to the proper defendant in an action for non-payment, see inter alia *Churchill d. Thomas* v. *Day* (1828) 3 Man. & Ry. K.B. 71; *Leggat* v. *Reed* (1823) 1 C. & P. 176; *Chidley* v. *Norris* (1862) 3 F. & F. 228; *Mountstephen* v. *Lakeman* (1871) L.R. 7 Q.B. 196.
[49] Post, p. 543.
[50] *Crouch* v. *Jeeves (1938) Pty. Ltd.* (1946) 46 S.R. (N.S.W.) 242, at 244-245: see also *Causer* v. *Browne* [1952] V.L.R. 1, at 4; *XYZ Ltd.* v. *Kennedy* 1946 S.L.T. (Sh. Ct.) 31; *Fankhauser* v. *Mark Dykes Pty. Ltd.* [1960] V.R. 376, at 379.

within a reasonable time, to do it properly, and to take reasonable care of the chattels whilst in its custody.

Each of these duties will now be considered. It should be remembered (as Jordan C.J. pointed out) that they are subject to any contractual provision to the contrary. In Australia, they may also be subject to the *Trade Practices Act* 1974.

A. Duty of safe-keeping

Although custody of the chattel is not the primary object of the bailment locatio operis faciendi, it is clear that while the chattel remains in his possession[51] the workman is a bailee for reward[52] and must exercise reasonable care in its safekeeping. The contrary argument was repudiated in a Scottish case,[53] where the Lord President observed:

> In my opinion, every contract of locatio operis faciendi which entails, as this contract did, that the subject on which the work is to be done is to be left in the premises of the tradesman and in his possession must normally be presumed to include as an inherent ingredient an element of locatio custodiae, the charge for which, like other overhead charges, is covered by the price of the work done. The opposite view . . . would involve that the tradesman with whom goods are left to have repairs or other work performed upon them, and who does not stipulate for, or charge, ex nomine a sum to cover the storage, would owe no duty as an onerous custodian to preserve the goods from loss or damage.[54]

Whether the bailee has taken reasonable care of the goods is a question of fact; in answering it the court will pay regard to such factors as the value of the goods, the prevalence of crime in the vicinity and the nature of the services which are to be provided.[55] Clearly, a greater degree of circumspection is expected from those who perform work upon valuable articles than from those trade is normally in items of small value. A furrier or silversmith may well be negligent in failing to instal a burglar-alarm whereas a dry-cleaner may not.[56]

In deciding whether there has been a failure to take reasonable care, the burden of proof rests upon the bailee.[57] Admittedly, the bailor must

---

[51] This includes a reasonable period (and perhaps even longer) after the work has been completed: *Mitchell* v. *Davis* (1920) 37 T.L.R. 68; e.g. *Chown and Son* v. *Moreland* (1975) N.Z. Sup. Ct. Unrep., November 17th; post, p. 512.

[52] Cf. *Price* v. *Le Blanc* (1957) 7 D.L.R. (2d) 716, which seems to be wrong in holding the garage proprietor a mere gratuitous bailee.

[53] *Sinclair* v. *Juner* 1952 S.C. 35, at 43. See also *Alderslade* v. *Hendon Laundry Ltd.* [1945] K.B. 189, at 193.

[54] Sed quaere: at Common Law he would be a gratuitous bailee and would probably owe a similar duty of reasonable care; cf. p. 288. et seq., ante.

[55] *Saunders (Mayfair) Furs Ltd.* v. *Chas. Wm. Davis Ltd.* [1966] 1 Lloyd's Rep. 78, 83; and see generally ante, p. 439 et seq., where the custodian's duty of care is discussed in detail.

[56] It depends, in part, upon his alternative arrangements; cf. ante, p. 444; *Jaffa* v. *Waxman* [1966] 2 Lloyd's Rep. 344.

[57] *Crouch* v. *Jeeves* (1938) *Pty. Ltd.* (ante, n. 50), at 245 (cf. *Alderslade* v. *Hendon Laundry Ltd.* (ante, n. 53) at 193); *Sinclair* v. *Juner* 1952 S.C. 35; *Fankhauser* v. *Mark Dykes Pty. Ltd.* [1960] V.R. 376, at 377; *Hollier* v. *Rambler Motors (A.M.C.) Ltd.* [1972] 2 Q.B. 71; *Cooper* v. *Dempsey* (1961) 105 Sol. Jo. 320; *Stewart* v. *Batson* [1948] Q.W.N. 20; 42 Q.J.P.R. 108; *Gutter* v. *Tait* (1947) 177 L.T.I. The foregoing list is not exhaustive but, because the principle is established beyond question, further authority is considered un-

show that there was a delivery of the goods and (where they are alleged to be damaged) that their condition upon delivery was superior to that on re-delivery.[58] Once these facts are established, however, and the goods are shown to have been lost or damaged while in the bailee's possession,[59] the bailee can escape only by proving that he took reasonable care of the goods, or that his failure to take reasonable care was not connected with the loss.[60] In this respect there is no material difference betwen the position of the bailee under a bailment locatio operis faciendi and that of his counterpart under a simple locatio custodiae. Of course, the professional warehouseman may be expected to possess a greater degree of expertise in the safekeeping of customers' goods and a greater alertness, for instance, to the perils of professional crime; but in abstract terms the duty is the same.[61]

As in the case of locatio custodiae, it is generally no defence for the bailee to show that the loss or damage resulted from a defect in his premises which was self-evident to the bailor at the time of contracting.[62] The bailee prima facie contracts to safeguard the goods with reasonable care and cannot evade this obligation except by clear disclaimer or

necessary. The same rule applies whether the bailor sues in detinue, negligence or breach of bailment. But when the alleged breach relates to a positive, super-added obligation not inherent in the fundamental duty of care, the onus of proving the breach rests upon the bailor: *Fankhauser* v. *Mark Dykes Pty. Ltd.*, at 377-378, discussed ante, pp. 343, 468. Moreover, it has been held that when a vehicle sent for repair is returned to the bailor and breaks down several days and about a hundred miles later through loss of oil, the onus was upon the bailor to establish negligence and unless he could do so affirmatively his action should fail: *Krieger* v. *Bell* [1943] S.A.S.R. 153, at 168. This case was argued on the doctrine of res ipsa loquitur and the bailee's peculiar burden of proof does not seem to have been discussed. See further *The Schipol* [1977] 1 Lloyd's Rep. 114.

[58] *Fankhauser* v. *Mark Dykes Pty. Ltd.* ante. This issue does not seem to have loomed very large in bailments locatio operis faciendi, probably because the occurrence of the damage is usually conceded by the bailee, although a recent Canadian decision on this species of bailment affirms the rule: *Calgary Transport Services Ltd.* v. *Pyramid Management Ltd.* (1977) 71 D.L.R. 3d) 234. It has, however, assumed some importance in relation to sub-bailments for reward, because the principal bailor who is unable to show that the goods were not damaged *before* delivery to the sub-bailee may be prevented from recovering: see *O'Regan* v. *Hui Bros. Transport Pty. Ltd.* [1969] P. & N.G.R. 261 (post, p. 809) and, more generally, ante p. 439 et seq. It may be fairer to require the bailee to prove that the goods as redelivered are in no worse a condition than when originally bailed to him.

[59] Cf. *Rozsasi* v. *Swinton Industries Pty. Ltd.* (1959) 59 S.R. (N.S.W.) 375, where the bailees (dry cleaners) claimed that the goods had been sold pursuant to a term on the docket entitling them to dispose of goods not claimed within three months. The trial judge held that they had failed to prove this and that the goods were lost. Since the clauses on the docket were not incorporated in the contract, they could not protect the defendants. This decision was upheld on appeal. It seems that failure to redeliver will be prima facie evidence of loss, requiring rebuttal by the bailee.

[60] Ante, p. 440.

[61] Conventionally, to take as much care of the property as a reasonable person would take of his own: *Becker* v. *Lavender Ltd.* (1946) 62 T.L.R. 504; *Gutter* v. *Tait* ante. A preferable formulation might emphasise the care a reasonable man takes of the property of others, but there is little practical difference between these standards and they are normally used interchangeably. See further *Port Swettenham* v. *Wu* (1978) *The Times*, June 22nd.

[62] *Brabant & Co.* v. *King* [1895] A.C. 632; ante, p. 460; and see *Saunders (Mayfair) Furs Ltd.* v. *Chas. Wm. Davies Ltd.* [1966] 2 Lloyd's Rep. 78, at 83.

contractual variation. To some extent, this may be illustrative of the insufficiency of the defences of contributory negligence or volenti non fit injuria to an action for breach of contract.[63] But the duty may be waived or varied impliedly, as where the bailor insists that the goods be kept in a particular part of the bailee's premises which is less safe than elsewhere and is not a place in which the bailee would ordinarily have kept them.[64] Even in this event, the courts will require strong evidence that the direction amounted to an agreement to exonerate the bailee from his duty to take reasonable care. The prudent bailee will either refuse to execute the labour in a manner contrary to his judgment, or will extract an express exemption from the bailor before so doing.[65]

Bailees have been held liable for loss or damage to customers' goods in the following circumstances: where a car slips from a hoist at a garage without proof that the misadventure arose from extraneous causes or inherent vice;[66] where a vehicle bailed to a garage for repairs is damaged by an unexplained fire,[67] or by one which is caused by an employee's spillage of petrol;[68] where handkerchiefs sent to a laundry[69] or clothes to a dry-cleaner[70] are returned in a damaged condition without proof, by the launderer, of reasonable care; where a watchmaker takes less care in the custody of a watch bailed for repair than he does of his own property;[71] where a boat bailed to a builder for modifications breaks away from its moorings;[72] where furs disappear from a repairer's

[63] Ante, p. 55.
[64] *Harper* v. *Jones* (1879) 4 V.L.R. (L.) 536; and cf. *Sanders* v. *Spencer* (1566) 3 Dyer 266b; 73 E.R. 591.
[65] Cf. the provision in many removalists' standard form contracts that the bailees will not accept liability for goods packed by the householder personally: ante, p. 438.
[66] *Stewart* v. *Batson* [1945] Q.W.N. 20; 42 Q.J.P.R. 108.
[67] See in conjunction with the cases cited ante, at p. 451 et seq: *Sinclair* v. *Juner* ante.; *Selig* v. *Greenman* (1966) 51 M.P.R. 381; *Marleau* v. *Clark* [1946] O.W.N. 623; *Karn* v. *Ontario Garage Ltd.* (1919) 16 O.W.N. 31; *Stables* v. *Bois* (1956) 3 D.L.R. (2d) 701 (a divergent authority); *Short* v. *Deer Lake Sales and Services Ltd.* (1962) 47 M.P.R. 374; *Caplan* v. *Honey Harbour Boats Ltd.* [1951] 1 D.L.R. 710. Cf. *Hollier* v. *Rambler Motors (A.M.C.) Ltd.* ante, n. 57. *Macrae* v. *Swindells* [1954] 2 All E.R. 260 (where negligence was admitted); *Rutter* v. *Palmer* [1922] 2 K.B. 87; *Johnson* v. *Cenrow* [1951] 4 D.L.R. 710.
[68] *Smith* v. *Taylor* [1966] 2 Lloyd's Rep. 231.
[69] *Alderslade* v. *Hendon Laundry Ltd.* ante.
[70] *Causer* v. *Browne* [1952] V.L.R. 1, at 8; *Curtis* v. *Chemical Cleaning and Dyeing Co. Ltd.* [1951] 1 K.B. 805; see also *Davies* v. *Collins* [1945] 1 All E.R. 247; *Martin* v. *H. Negin Ltd.* (1945) 172 L.T. 275; *Crouch* v. *Jeeves (1938) Pty. Ltd.* (1946) 46 S.R. (N.S.W.) 242; *Rozsasi* v. *Swinton Industries Pty. Ltd.* (1959) 59 S.R. (N.S.W.) 375; cf. *Cartlidge* v. *Deboice* (1967) 62 W.W.R. 492 (burst water-pipe: bailees held not liable); *Scottish Dyers and Cleaners (London) Ltd.* v. *Manheimer* (1942) 166 L.H. 368 (where garment lost by burglary from dry-cleaner's shop, magistrate held not entitled to make summary order for delivery to the owner under s. 40 *Metropolitan Police Courts Act* 1839, by virtue of goods being "detained without just cause": this decision was without prejudice to any civil action for recovery in another court).
[71] *Clarke* v. *Earnshaw* (1818) Gow. 30 N.P. (where the watch was stolen by a servant who was allowed to sleep in the shop). Note, however, that merely to fail to take the care of a customer's goods that one takes for one's own will not *necessarily* amount to the failure to take reasonable care, any more than to take no more care of one's own goods than one does of the customer's will automatically indicate that this standard has been attained: *Doorman* v. *Jenkins* (1834) 2 Ad. & E. 256.
[72] *Polson Iron Works Ltd.* v. *Laurie* (1911) 3 O.W.N. 213; see also *Porter* v. *Muir Bros. Dry Dock Co., Ltd.* [1929] 2 D.L.R. 561.

workshop without evidence as to the cause of their disappearance;[73] where a mink coat is exhibited in a shop window overnight without effective anti-burglar precautions;[74] and where a bailee for sale unnecessarily keeps valuable jewellery in a wallet in his pocket and allows a stranger (whom he has admitted to his house without inquiry as to his credentials) to see it.[75]

The bailee's duty to take reasonable care does not automatically terminate when he has completed the work for which he was engaged. As a general rule, he continues to owe this duty until the goods are delivered to the bailor or his authorised agent. Although in exceptional cases the period of delay in collection may be deemed to have reduced the bailee's obligation (e.g. where the goods are cumbersome and are occupying much needed space) the normal rule is that the bailee continues to be a bailee for reward until redelivery and is liable for any lack of reasonable care until that event occurs.[76] Thus, in *Mitchell* v. *Davis*[77] a tailor was held liable when, having made the plaintiff's marten skins into a coat, he left the coat in an unlocked glass-fronted case in the showroom, whence it was stolen during his absence. Swift J. held that the delay in collecting the goods (which had been caused by a strike) did not relieve the defendant of the duty to take reasonable care of the coat until its owner called for it. "Until the parties had shown either by express words or by conduct that they intended to alter the relationship between them that relationship continued." The defendant's liability was unaffected by the fact that he had only put the coat in the case when the plaintiff had said she would be calling for it, and had until then kept it in his safe.

Likewise, in *Cooper* v. *Dempsey*[78] garage proprietors were held liable for damage to a vehicle stolen from their car-park, because the car had been left in the park unlocked with the ignition key in the dashboard and no supervision. There is a Canadian decision which holds that the relationship between a customer and the proprietor of a car-wash, when the car has been washed and is standing on the forecourt awaiting collection by its owner, was no longer one of bailor and bailee but (at least after the lapse of a reasonable time) one of licensor and licensee.[79] However, the better view is that the bailee's

---

[73] *Woolmer* v. *Delmer Price Ltd.* [1955] 1 Q.B. 291; *Pearlman* v. *Silverberg Bros.* (1921) 21 O.W.N. 74; cf. *Becker* v. *Lavender Ltd.* (1946) 62 T.L.R. 504; *Levison v. Patent Steam Carpet Cleaning Co. Ltd.* [1978] Q.B. 69.

[74] *Saunders (Mayfair) Furs Ltd.* v. *Chas. Wm. Davies Ltd.* ante, n. 62.

[75] *Gutter* v. *Tait* ante (a somewhat harsh decision).

[76] Of course, the contract may provide for disposal of the goods or for a reduced standard of care, in the event of non-collection: cf. *Rozsasi* v. *Swinton Industries Pty. Ltd.* ante, n. 59, (and see post, p. 1030), where the term was not incorporated according to Else-Mitchell J.

[77] (1920) 37 T.L.R. 68; *E. G. Chown & Son* v. *Moreland* (1975) Unrep N.Z. Sup. Ct. (November 17th); *Darling Ladies' Wear Ltd.* v. *Hickey* [1949] 2 D.L.R. 420; reversed on different grounds [1950] 1 D.L.R. 720; and see Chapter 12, ante.

[78] (1961) 105 Sol. Jo. 320 (C.A.) See further ante, p. 86 and cf. *Saskatchewan Government Insurance Office* v. *Midwest Motors Ltd.* (1961) 36 W.W.R. 254; *Gavin* v. *Douglas Securities Ltd.* (1958) 25 W.W.R. 408; *Wallace* v. *Safeway Caravan Pty. Ltd.* (1975) 3 Qld. Lawyer 224.

[79] *Furbank* v. *Andersen* (1966) 57 W.W.R. 647. (B.C. County Court). In this case, as in many others, the keys had been left by the workman in the ignition

status does not ipso facto determine upon completion of the labour but survives until re-delivery of the goods to the bailor, unless clear evidence of an express or implied agreement to the contrary is given. Certainly, a repairer or car-wash operator may be liable if, on completion of the work, he leaves the vehicle unlocked in the street;[80] or where, having agreed with the owner of a car to leave it in the open car-park of an hotel, he leaves the ignition keys in the vehicle and fails to lock it, rather than delivering them to the porter of the hotel, in accordance with his usual practice.[81] Lord Guthrie remarked in the latter case[82] that:

> It will not do for the defenders to submit that, because no agreement was proved as to what was to be done with the keys, their servants could legally do nothing else than leave them in the unlocked car. Since a duty of care rested on them arising out of the contract, they were bound to consider the likely consequences of leaving the car unlocked and with the keys inside it. The duty continued until the moment when their servants could leave the car in a safe condition. If the likely result of leaving the keys in it when it was unlocked was to incur the risk of theft, then they had a duty not to do so.

It may be otherwise, of course, where the bailor explicitly instructs the bailee to leave the chattel in a particular place or manner, or where his directions as to procedure for redelivery render the exercise of reasonable care repugnant or impossible.[83]

The bailee's duty of care extends, therefore, to the conduct whereby re-delivery is effected. In *Becker* v. *Lavender Ltd.*[84] the plaintiff had bailed her mink coat to the defendant furriers for alterations. The shop was about to close for a holiday and the plaintiff agreed that it would be safer for the coat to be redelivered to her until the holiday was over. Accordingly, the defendant proprietor (Madame Lavender) arrived with the coat at the block of flats in which the plaintiff lived. Instead of taking the coat up to the plaintiff's flat, however, she handed it in the entrance hall to a man dressed as a hall porter, and told him to deliver it to the plaintiff. The man and the coat both disappeared and the plaintiff sued for breach of bailment, negligence and conversion. Her action succeeded on the ground that the defendant had failed to take such care of the property as a reasonable woman would take of her own. It may be questioned, however, whether this was not a simple case of conversion by misdelivery to which notions of care were irrelevant.

---

switch of the car. The decision was acknowledged as correct in *Valley Auto Wrecking & Demolition Ltd.* v. *Colonial Motors Ltd.* [1977] 1 W.W.R. 759.

[80] *Edelson* v. *Musty's Service Station and Garage* [1956] O.W.N. 848; cf. *Shorter's Parking Station Ltd.* v. *Johnson* [1963] N.Z.L.R. 135.
[81] *Forbes* v. *Aberdeen Motors Ltd.* 1965 S.C. 193.
[82] Ibid., at 202.
[83] But see post, p. 518. Although *Price* v. *Le Blanc* (1957) 7 D.L.R. (2d) 716 suggests to the contrary, it would seem that even where the method of redelivery is at the bailor's request the bailee is not, during the period of redelivery, a merely gratuitous bailee.
[84] (1946) 62 T.L.R. 504.

Certainly, the bailee must abstain from converting the chattel and will be liable for any unauthorised delivery or disposition, whether innocently intended or not.[85] This liability includes not only personal acts of conversion but those committed by his servants, at least where the latter are acting within the course of their employment or the chattel has been entrusted to them. Thus, if a furrier's servant steals the mink stole which he is employed to clean, the furrier will be liable for the loss.[86] There have been numerous cases in which bailees such as carriers and car-park proprietors have been held liable because they could not prove that the loss was not caused by the negligence or complicity of their servants.[87] The same onus extends to all bailees by way of locatio operis faciendi. But there is no liability for conversion where the servant was not entrusted with some task relating to the chattel, unless the conversion was authorised by the bailee, or (perhaps) unless the conversion was an innocent one committed within the apparent scope of the servant's authority (e.g. redelivery by unauthorised personnel.)[88] Nor, it seems, will the bailee be liable if a servant normally entrusted with the chattel returns to steal it out of hours[89] unless of course the bailee has conduced to this theft by his own negligence.[90] In such a case the conversion is entirely divorced from the master-servant relationship and the servant's employment merely affords him the opportunity to steal the chattel. If, on the other hand, the servant has been entrusted with the chattel at the material time, the fact that he was using it in an unauthorised manner (e.g. by taking a car for a joy-ride) will not relieve his employer, who will be liable for the manner in which the task entrusted to the servant is conducted and answerable for the safety of the chattel throughout.[91]

B. Breach of bailment

The bailee must comply with the terms of bailment. A departure from its essential terms involves three main consequences. First, the bailor will be entitled to reject the contract and take immediate possession of the chattel. Secondly, the bailee ceases to be liable merely for negligence and becomes an insurer of the chattel. Thirdly, any exclusion clauses in the contract of bailment will normally cease to protect him.[92]

The commonest manifestation of this forfeiture occurs when the bailee unlawfully delegates the work and hands over possession of the chattel

---

[85] *Wilson* v. *Powis* (1826) 3 Bing. 633; *Booth* v. *Wellby* (1928) 165 L.T. Jo. 213; ante, p. 132.
[86] *Morris* v. *C. W. Martin & Sons Ltd.* [1966] 1 Q.B. 716.
[87] Ante, p. 464 et seq.
[88] Ante, p. 479.
[89] *Darling Ladies Wear Ltd.* v. *Hickey*, ante, n. 77; *Spencer, Clarke & Co. Ltd.* v. *Goodwill Motors Ltd.* [1939] N.Z.L.R. 493; cf. *Alberta-U-Drive Ltd.* v. *Jack Carter Ltd.* (1972) 28 D.L.R. (3d) 114; ante, p. 221.
[90] *Bamert* v. *Parks* (1965) 50 D.L.R. (2d) 313 (not negligent to give untestimonialled servant a key to the premises and to leave keys in cars overnight).
[91] *Van Geel* v. *Warrington* [1929] 1 D.L.R. 94; *Morris* v. *C. W. Martin & Sons Ltd.* [1966] 1 Q.B. 716, explaining *Aitchison* v. *Page Motors Ltd.* (1935) 154 T.R. 128; *Central Motors (Glasgow) Ltd.* v. *Cessnock Garage and Motor Co. Ltd.* 1925 S.C. 796; cf. *South Island Motors Ltd.* v. *Thacker* [1931] N.Z.L.R. 1104; *Everett's Blinds Ltd.* v. *Thomas Ballinger Ltd.* [1965] N.Z.L.R. 266.
[92] This aspect of the bailee's liability is discussed in Chapter 25, post.

to a third party. Generally, the duty imposed by a bailment locatio operis faciendi is a personal one which the bailee delegates at his risk. The bailor will be deemed to have selected him for his personal skill and ability and, in the absence of agreement to the contrary, is entitled to expect that the work will be performed by the defendant in person. Normally, this will include a duty to execute the work of his own premises and not on those of a third party, but will include permission to delegate to a servant.

The foregoing principle has been applied to prohibit delegation under contracts of warehousing,[93] bleaching,[94] tailoring,[95] carriage,[96] and repair.[97] In a Scottish case,[98] however, it was held than an agreement by a firm of upholsterers to remove, beat and relay a carpet was not one which imposed a mandatory duty of personal performance. Accordingly, the defendants were not liable for the accidental destruction of the carpet on the premises of a firm of carpet-beaters, to whom they had deputed part of the labour. The Court of Session placed some emphasis on the fact that the plaintiff had specifically asked that his carpet should not be vacuum-cleaned, which was the only form of cleaning carried on by the defendants personally, and on the fact that he had admitted that he would not have objected to the delegation had he known of it. The defendants merely engaged in usual trade practice and this, coupled with the everyday nature of the labour, was sufficient to absolve them.[99]

> Here the carpet was an ordinary carpet. It was to be subjected to work of a character that could be done by ordinary housemaids. The pursuer . . . nowhere suggests in his evidence that, in sending his carpet to the defenders to be cleaned, he relied on their personal skill and experience as carpet beaters. . . . It appears to me that the pursuer's case which depends on delectus personae is lacking in the first essential element.[1]

It may be questioned whether it should be incumbent upon the bailor, even in the case of everyday goods or labour, to make it plain that he was relying on the bailee's personal skill and judgment. The need for such an expression of reliance was expressly repudiated in *Edwards*

---

[93] *Edwards* v. *Newland & Co.* [1950] 2 K.B. 534.
[94] *Cassils & Co.* v. *Holden Wood Bleaching Co. Ltd.* (1915) 112 L.T. 373, at 378 per Phillimore L.J.; cf. Pickford and Buckley L.JJ. at 377, 379.
[95] *Gadbois* v. *Lauzon* (1915) Q.R. 47 S.C. 276.
[96] *Hobbs* v. *Petersham Transport Co. Pty. Ltd.* (1971) 45 A.L.J.R. 356, at 362 per Windeyer J.; *Garnham, Harris & Elton Ltd.* v. *Alfred W. Ellis (Transport) Ltd.* [1967] 2 Lloyd's Rep. 22 (where the particular value of the load made personal performance essential).
[97] *Morgan* v. *Maurer & Son* (1964) 30 Ir. Jur. Rep. 31; cf. *Stewart* v. *Reavell's Garage Ltd.* [1952] 2 Q.B. 545; *Robson* v. *Drummond* (1831) 2 B. & Ad. 303; *British Wagon Co. Ltd.* v. *Lea* (1880) 5 Q.B.D. 149; *Edwards* v. *Newland & Co.* [1950] 2 K.B. 534, at 539, 542 (ante, p. 473). In *Krieger* v. *Bell* [1943] S.A.S.R. 153 and 168, an agreement to rebore a truck was held on the facts to be one which the repairer could delegate: "By the course of dealing between the parties it is clear personal performance by the respondent was not of the essence of the contract, and it could properly be carried out, at least in part, by his nominee" per Mayo J., at 172.
[98] *Stevenson & Sons, Ltd.* v. *Maule & Son* 1920 S.C. 335.
[99] Ibid., at 338-339 per Lord Ormidale, approved by the majority in the Court of Session at 343 et seq.
[1] Ibid., at 344 per Lord Mackenzie.

v. *Newland & Co.*[2] (a case of warehousing) and it may be that the
Scottish case would be decided differently today.[3] A recent decision
from Ireland shows that the onus of proving permission to delegate
is upon the bailee, and that this onus will not lightly be discharged. In
Morgan v. *Maurer & Son*[4] the plaintiff sent a Longine watch to the
defendants to be repaired. The defendants ("quite reasonably", according to the judge) sent the watch to the Longine agent in Dublin for
advice. The agent returned it by registered post but it was stolen in
transit. The court held that although their parting with possession was
without negligence the defendants had failed to prove that the plaintiff
had authorised them to do so, and were liable for the loss.

The value of the goods in question may be as relevant an indication of
any permission to delegate as the specialised nature of the work to be
performed. Another important factor, which Lord Skerrington stressed
in his dissenting judgment in *Stevenson & Sons Ltd.* v. *Maule & Son Ltd.*,[5]
is the amount of care which the bailee is known to exercise in the selection of his servants; for this too could produce a powerful influence upon
the customer's decision to employ him. In Lord Skerrington's opinion
most customers would prefer to avoid the use of sub-contractors because
such arrangements tend to increase costs, cause delay and give rise to
misunderstandings. Unless, therefore, the work is necessarily work which
could only be performed by a sub-contractor, "it is wholly fallacious to
argue . . . that, because [it] may be described as 'of an ordinary kind'
it necessarily follows that the employer has no interest in having it
performed by the particular tradesman whom he selected for that purpose."[6]

---

[2] [1950] 2 K.B. 534, at 539 per Somervell L.J.

[3] It is to be contrasted with two English decisions in which the express terms of
the contract were held to prohibit a dry-cleaner from sending garments to a sub-
contractor to be cleaned: *Davies* v. *Collins* [1945] 1 All E.R. 247; *Martin* v.
H. Negin Ltd. (1945) 172 L.T. 275 (both decisions of the Court of Appeal).
In *Davies* v. *Collins* (at 248) Mackinnon L.J. observed: "If it was simply the
case of a man bringing clothes to a dyer and cleaner, asking to have them
cleaned, and the shopman acceding to his request, I think that would be work
which the shopman could carry out vicariously within the principle laid down in
the case of the *British Waggon Co.* v. *Lea* (1880) 5 Q.B.D. 149, 153". This
statement was described at "surprising" by Somervell L.J. arguendo in *Edwards* v.
Newland & Co. [1950] 2 K.B. 534, at 536 and seems, with respect, to be too
widely stated. The Scottish decision must also be read in the light of the strong
dissent by Lord Skerrington, 1920 S.C. 335 at 345 et seq. who thought that
good faith required the bailee to obtain the customer's specific assent before
delegating the work and depriving him of the power to elect a substitute. Such
an assent was clearly obtained by Beder in *Morris* v. *C. W. Martin & Sons Ltd.*
[1966] 1 Q.B. 716. Cf. the inability of an estate agent appointed as "sole agent"
to delegate: *John McCann & Co.* v. *Pow* [1974] 1 W.L.R. 1643.

[4] (1964) 30 Ir. Jur. Rep. 31, following *Edwards* v. *Newland & Co.* [1950] 2 K.B. 534.

[5] 1920 S.C. 335, at 348-349.

[6] Different considerations might apply to goods that are bailed for sale or approval.
In this event, the bailee may well enjoy (by trade custom or implied agreement)
a right to grant custody and perhaps possession to a third party for trial or
inspection: *Camoys* v. *Scurr* (1840) 9 Car. & P. 383; *Von Minden* v. *Pyke* (1863)
4 F. & F. 533; *Genn* v. *Winkel* (1912) 107 L.T. 434. Of course, the sub-bailment
or grant of custody must not be executed negligently: *Gutter* v. *Tait* (ante, p. 000).
For cases in which custom was alleged to make the bailee of goods for sale or
approval an insurer see ante, p. 464.

Occasionally, the terms of an exclusion clause will cast some light upon whether the bailee has permission to delegate. In *Davies* v. *Collins*[7] the Court of Appeal held that a clause in a dry-cleaning docket which began: "Whilst every care is taken in cleaning and dyeing garments . . ." constituted a promise to take proper care which carried, inferentially, an undertaking by the defendants not to put the exercise of such care beyond their control by employing sub-contractors. The same conclusion was reached in *Martin* v. *H. Negin Ltd.*[8] where the defendants' dockets carried the legend "Personal service and individual attention" amidst a plethora of exclusion clauses. The defendants were held liable for the loss of a coat while wrongfully sub-bailed to another firm of cleaners, notwithstanding the attempted exclusion.

Even where the work to be performed is of an essentially personal character, the bailee may be entitled to delegate certain non-personal aspects of his performance, such as delivering the goods to the Post Office or to a carrier for redelivery to the customer.[9] Again, such entitlement is a question of fact to be inferred from the parties' agreement, but it should be emphasised that even a legitimate delegation must be made with reasonable care.

A lawful delegation does not relieve the bailee from all liability for loss or damage while the chattel is in the possession of the deputed performer. Regardless of the power to delegate, he will normally have contracted that reasonable care shall be taken of the chattel and that it will not be converted. Accordingly, he must answer for the defaults of the sub-bailee as well as for his own,[10] unless it can be shown that he contracted merely as agent and not as principal.[11]

Unlawful delegation is not the only way in which the bailee may forfeit the protection of the bailment. He may also do so by misusing the goods, by keeping them in a place other than that authorised[12] or

---

[7] [1945] 1 All E.R. 247.

[8] (1945) 172 L.T. 275 (C.A.).

[9] See the learned editorial note in *Davies* v. *Collins* [1945] 1 All E.R. 247, at 248.

[10] *Stevenson & Sons Ltd.* v. *Maule & Son Ltd.* (ante, n. 98), at 347 (Lord Skerrington); *Genn* v. *Winkel* (1912) 107 L.T. 434, at 437; *B.R.S. Ltd.* v. *Arthur V. Crutchley & Co. Ltd.* [1968] 1 All E.R. 811; *Krieger* v. *Bell* ante, n. 97, and see p. 475 et seq., ante, p. 829 et seq., post.

[11] Post, p. 834 et seq. A passage in the judgment of Fletcher Moulton L.J. in *Genn* v. *Winkel* (1912) 107 L.T. 434, at 437, suggests that the bailee's liability for the chattel while it is in the possession of the sub-bailee (or, as in this case, of a sub-sub-bailee) is absolute and independent of any fault on the part of that sub-bailee himself. However, it seems that this inference must be qualified in the light of two facts. First, it seems that the head bailee in *Genn* v. *Winkel* was unable to offer any explanation for the loss of the goods, other than that he was unable to recover them from the sub-bailee; and clearly the onus of proving non-fault is upon the bailee, whether he has sub-bailed or not. Secondly, the terms of the agreement between the bailor and the head bailee may well have enlarged the head bailee's responsibility for the goods and made his liability strict, at least during those occasions when the goods were out of his possession. Moreover the issue in the case was not whether the head bailee had been guilty of a breach of bailment but whether he had performed an act "adopting the transaction" within the meaning of s. 18 r. 4(a) of the *Sale of Goods Act* 1893, the diamonds having originally been delivered to him on sale or return. This question the C.A. answered in the affirmative. Contrast a dictum of Denning L.J. in *Edwards* v. *Newland & Co.* [1950] 2 K.B. 534, at 542.

[12] *Edwards* v. *Newland & Co.* [1950] 2 K.B. 534: ante, p. 473.

by failing to redeliver them at the appointed time. In *Shaw & Co. Ltd.* v. *Symmons & Sons Ltd.*[13] the plaintiffs bailed books to the defendants for binding, the contract requiring that the defendants should redeliver them bound within a reasonable time, as and when required. A demand was made but no redelivery occurred within a reasonable time; and while the books were still on the defendants' premises they were destroyed by an accidental fire. Their endeavour to escape liability on the grounds of the *Fires Prevention (Metropolis) Act* 1774 failed because their detention was a breach of bailment and the goods were at their own risk. Avory J. dismissed the contention that the principle in *Lilley* v. *Doubleday*[14] should be confined to positive acts and should not extend to mere omissions.

C. Standard of workmanship

The bailee must perform the work for which he is engaged, and must bring to it the same degree of proficiency as he has expressly or impliedly undertaken. Both of these duties are absolute; questions of reasonable endeavour are immaterial if there is a departure from the agreed standard of performance, whether the lapse consists in the manner of that performance or its final result:

> What I may call the hard core of the contract . . . is the obligation of the defendants to launder. It is the contractual obligation which must be performed according to its terms, and no question of taking due care enters into it. The defendants undertake, not to exercise due care in laundering the customer's goods, but to launder them, and if they fail to launder them it is no use their saying, "We did our best, we exercised due care and took reasonable precautions, and we are very sorry if as a result the linen is not properly laundered". That is the essence of the contract . . .[15]

Therefore, unless the performance of the labour is frustrated by an event such as the death of the bailee (where his personality is an essential factor) or by the destruction of the subject-matter without default on his part,[16] the bailee will be bound, irrespective of notions of relative care, to a strict performance of its terms. It follows that if the bailee undertakes a task without disclosing to the bailor that it is impossible, he will not be entitled to evade his promise merely by proving that he used his best endeavour to perform it. In *Pearce* v. *Tucker*[17] the defendant agreed to install a kitchen-range in front of the plaintiff's boiler. The object of the installation was to allow the range to be fed by the boiler, but because there were insufficient flues the arrangement failed to work. The defendant brought evidence to show that he had made the flues as large as the situation of the boiler permitted and claimed that, since he could not possibly have done more towards achieving the desired result, he

[13] [1917] 1 K.B. 799: see also *Genn* v. *Winkel* ante, n. 11.
[14] (1881) 7 Q.B.D. 510.
[15] *Alderslade* v. *Hendon Laundry Ltd.* [1945] K.B. 189, 193 per Lord Greene M.R. It is interesting to compare these observations with the approach taken by English authorities to the lessor's duty to supply a fit chattel: post, p. 724 et seq.
[16] Cf. *XYZ Ltd.* v. *Kennedy* 1946 S.L.T. (Sh. Ct.) 31.
[17] (1862) 3 F. & F. 136, N.P.; 176 E.R. 61.

should be released. This plea was dismissed and the defendant was held to the strict letter of his promise:

> Was it not the duty of the defendant to tell the plaintiff that he could not do the work in a workmanlike manner and that in fact it would be throwing away money to have it done at all, as it must have been obvious to any competent workman that it could not be done. If so, it is no excuse to the defendant that he could not do the work properly; prima facie, it must be taken that a workman undertakes to do his work in a workmanlike manner. If the plaintiff had been told that it was impossible to do it, he might not have sustained the action. But non constat that he knew it, whereas the defendant must be taken to have known it.[18]

An interesting modern variation of this principle is to be found in a decision of the Supreme Court of Canada. In *Brunswick Construction Ltd.* v. *Nowlan*[19] a building contractor was held liable for breach of contract although he followed the architect's plans carefully in constructing the plaintiff's house. The plans were obviously defective and the house suffered from leaking, rotting and condensation. The Court found that an experienced contractor should have realised the inadequacy of the plans and should have drawn this to the plaintiff's attention, rather than follow them slavishly. The plaintiff had relied upon the contractor's skill and judgment and this had not been properly exercised.[20]

Both of these decisions proceeded on the assumption that the contractor knew, or should have known, of the circumstances which made satisfactory completion of the work on the given instructions impossible. Where no such knowledge can be inferred, the contractor may well be entitled to a release from his undertaking if circumstances subsequently appear which make performance impossible or radically different from that originally contemplated.[21] Indeed, he may be under a duty to cease performance of the work and to obtain the employer's further instructions before proceeding, at least where performance according to his original directions now threatens to harm the chattel.

Numerous expressions of the degree of skill and expertise to be demanded of the contractor have been given over the years. Many of these arise in decisions that are not concerned with bailment, but the general duty of proficiency is not affected by the fact of that relation. The commonest formulation of the duty is that which requires "due" (or

---

[18] Ibid, at 137-138 and 62 per Erle C.J.

[19] (1974) 49 D.L.R. (3d) 93. Cf. *Batty* v. *M.P.R.* [1978] 2 All E.R. 445.

[20] Quaere whether the contractor impliedly warranted that the house would be fit for human habitation. The majority of the Supreme Court did not specifically answer this point, but it had constituted one of the grounds of judgment in the Appeal Division of the New Brunswick Supreme Court (1973) 34 D.L.R. (3d) 422. Dickson J. dissenting, denied that there was such a warranty in this case, but his judgment seems, with respect, to overlook the possibility of a partial reliance upon the contractor's skill and judgment: cf. *Cammell Laird & Co. Ltd.* v. *Manganese Bronze & Brass Co. Ltd.* [1934] A.C. 402; *Manawatu Asphalts Ltd.* v. *Rae* [1950] N.Z.L.R. 709, at 711-712; post, p. 524.

[21] Treitel, *Law of Contract* (4th edn), p. 590. Generally, of course, a contract is not frustrated merely because its performance is less profitable than originally contemplated: *Davis Contractors Ltd.* v. *Fareham U.D.C.* [1956] A.C. 696.

"proper") care and skill.[22] A more specific description was offered by Willes J. in a case which concerned some incompetent scene-painters:[23]

> Where a skilled labourer, artisan or artist is employed, there is on his part an implied warranty that he is of a skill reasonably competent to the task he undertakes—spondes peritiam artis: Thus, if an apothecary, a watchmaker, or an attorney be employed for reward, they each impliedly undertake to possess and exercise reasonable skill in their respective arts. The public profession of an art is a representation and undertaking to all the world that the professor possesses the requisite ability and skill.[24] An express promise or express representation in the particular case is not necessary.

Thus, whereas the workman does not impliedly promise that his skill and ability are equal to those of the finest practitioner of his art,[25] he does undertake that those talents are such as may reasonably be considered equal, in the light of current practice and experience, to the satisfactory performance of the work he has undertaken.[26] A man without proficiency or experience in a particular trade professes that trade at his peril. Unless the contract indicates otherwise, he must show that degree of expertise or aptitude that would normally be found in a competent practitioner of that trade; for this will be the level of proficiency which he has held himself out as possessing and which the other party will reasonably expect. Occasionally, this rule is expressed in terms that the work must be performed in a "workmanlike" manner.[27]

In *Harmer* v. *Cornelius*[28] there are suggestions that the necessary duties of care and skill may be extenuated or qualified by the known incompetence or inexperience of the workman. Certainly these qualities are irrelevant if they are unknown to the employer and he is given no

---

[22] E.g. *Kimber* v. *William Willett Ltd.* [1947] K.B. 570; *Mayne* v. *Silvermere Cleaners Ltd.* [1939] 1 All E.R. 693; *Peters* v. *C. W. McFarling Floor Surfacing Ltd.* [1959] S.A.S.R. 261; and see *Trade Practices Act* 1974 s. 74 (1) (Cth); post, p. 527.

[23] *Harmer* v. *Cornelius* (1858) 5 C.B.N.S. 236, at 246; 141 E.R. 94, at 98.

[24] The authority cited is *Jenkins* v. *Betham* (1855) 15 C.B. 168.

[25] Cf. *Roe* v. *Minister of Health* [1954] 2 Q.B. 66; *Tiesmaki* v. *Wilson* (1976) 60 D.L.R. (3d) 19 (medical practitioners); *Greaves & Co. (Contractors) Ltd.* v. *Baynham Meikle & Partners* [1975] 1 W.L.R. 1095 (structural engineers).

[26] Cf. *Cousens* v. *Paddon* (1836) 2 C.M. & R. 547: ". . . the labour shall be of the quality which would be bestowed by a workman of ordinary skill in his trade"; *Bolam* v. *Friern Hospital Management Committee* [1957] 1 W.L.R. 582, at 586: ". . . it is sufficient if he exercises the ordinary skill of an ordinary competent man exercising that particular art"; *Krieger* v. *Bell* [1943] S.A.S.R. 153, at 168, 172: "Where a person undertakes work upon the property of another he is deemed to warrant by implication, unless, of course, the terms of the agreement exclude any such intendment, that he will exercise reasonable care, and a reasonable degree of skill, and knowledge in the work, and, if any work be delegated, he will select persons of skill and competence to carry it out. Unless so excluded, there is such an implication in every case in which skill is required" (per Mayo J.); *Brown & Davis Ltd.* v. *Galbraith* [1972] 1 W.L.R. 997, at 1006: ". . . the work should be done with reasonable skill and within 'a reasonable time' " (per Buckley L.J.).

[27] E.g. *Manawatu Asphalts Ltd.* v. *Rae*, ante, n. 20; and see *Pearce* v. *Tucker* (1862) 3 F. & F. 136; N.P. 137; 176 E.R. 61, at 62 (ante, p. 518).

[28] (1858) 5 C.B.N.S. 236, at 246; 141 E.R. 94, at 98.

reasonable cause to suspect them.[29] But is it said that to entrust a watch for repair to a roadsweeper[30] or to a blacksmith,[31] or to solicit medical attention from a farrier,[32] is to demand of the party entrusted with the labour no more than the degree of ability that could normally be expected from a person of his calling. These observations may be useful in helping to delineate the scope of the defendant's promise but should not be permitted to obscure the primacy which must be granted to the expression of that promise itself. If, for instance, the road-sweeper freely and unambiguously undertakes for reward to put a watch in going order, a court should be reluctant to hold that either his incom-petence or the owner's imputed suspicions thereof should absolve the roadsweeper from liability for breach of that undertaking. For all the owner of the watch may know, the roadsweeper may be a skilled amateur watchmaker, or even a professional one down on his luck. It has been held that an employer is not prevented from recovering for faulty workmanship by the fact that he knew the contractor had never performed work of that particular kind before.[33] It is submitted that the defendant's personal ineptitude should provide a defence only when the employer's knowledge and acceptance of it can be clearly construed as an agreement to demand no more than that the defendant do his incompetent best, and to exonerate him for failing to do more.[34] To do otherwise seems to move close to making contributory negligence or volenti non fit injuria a defence to an action for breach of contract when the undertaking itself may be a strict one.[35]

Nevertheless, there is at least one decision which indicates that the duty to perform in a proper and workmanlike manner may be qualified by the facilities which the bailor knows to be at the bailee's disposal; in any event, where it is contemplated that those facilities and none other are to be employed. In *Kufeke* v. *Gilchrist Bros.*[36] the plaintiff sent Indian wheat to the defendants' mill to be ground. To be efficiently pro-cessed, the wheat needed to be washed and dried before grinding. The defendants attempted to wash the wheat but their facilities were not adapted to this process and a quantity of the wheat was lost. The plaintiff had inspected the mill before entering into the contract and had, apparently, stipulated that the wheat should be ground at that mill and nowhere else. The Court held that the defendants had merely undertaken to process the wheat according to the facilities at their disposal and had not undertaken to adapt their mill to cater for the special needs of the plaintiff's consignment. In carrying out this undertaking they had

---

[29] See *Low* v. *Foss* [1845] Res. & Eq. J. 40 (Sup. Ct. N.S.W.), where the ability of a surgeon was exacted from one who was not practising, but was retained, as such; *M.L.C. Ltd.* v. *Evatt* [1971] A.C. 793, especially at 803-806.

[30] *Harmer* v. *Cornelius* ante, n. 23.

[31] *Insurance Commissioner* v. *Joyce* (1948) 77 C.L.R. 39, at 46.

[32] Jones, *Bailments*, p. 100. Cf. *Wells* v. *Cooper* [1958] 2 Q.B. 265.

[33] *Hall* v. *Burke* (1886) 3 T.L.R. 165 (construction of machine); *Manawatu Asphalts Ltd.* v. *Rae*, ante (installation of floor on skating-rink).

[34] The defence may be stronger in cases of mandatum: ante, p. 463 et seq.

[35] Cf. ante, p. 460 et seq; *Adams* v. *Richardson & Starling* [1969] 1 W.L.R. 1645.

[36] (1888) 4 T.L.R. 326; cf. *Helicopter Sales Pty. Ltd.* v. *Rotor Work Pty. Ltd.* (1974) 132 C.L.R. 1; post, p. 533.

acted with reasonable care and skill and their appeal was accordingly allowed.[37]

Whereas the workman normally promises that the work will be performed in a competent and acceptable manner, he does not necessarily guarantee the suitability of the finished product for any particular purpose, or its ability to achieve any particular effect. As Lord Denning M.R. has said:[38]

> The surgeon does not warrant that he will cure the patient. Nor does the solicitor warrant that he will win the case. But when a dentist agrees to make a set of false teeth for a patient, there is an implied warranty that they will fit his gums.[39]

Whether such further guarantee is to be inferred will depend upon any communication (express or implied) of the contemplated purpose and upon the terms and efficacy of the contract. In many cases, the common intention of the parties will give rise to an undertaking that the finished article is competent to attain a required objective. Thus, consultant structural engineers have been held answerable for the failure of a warehouse to meet the demands required of it, notwithstanding that the plans they drew up were drafted with all proper and reasonable skill, because they knew the purpose for which it was to be used and had clearly undertaken to provide a plan that would accommodate that purpose.[40] Likewise, building contractors have been liable upon a warranty that a house built for a customer is reasonably fit for human habitation[41] and flooring specialists upon a warranty that a floor is reasonably fit for rollerskating.[42]

In fact, contracts for work and labour seem capable of producing three different obligations each dependent upon the nature of the task and the degree of reliance placed upon the workman. These obligations are: first, a warranty that the labour will be performed with due care and skill; secondly, a warranty that the labour will be reasonably fit for its purpose; and thirdly, a warranty that the finished artefact will be fit for its purpose.

The first warranty is the commonest and will almost invariably be implied. The second warranty will generally be indistinguishable from

---

[37] Cf. *New Brunswick Construction Ltd.* v. *Nowlan* (1974) 49 D.L.R. (3d) 93; ante, p. 519; s. 13, *Unfair Contract Terms Act, 1977.*

[38] *Greaves & Co. (Contractors) Ltd.* v. *Baynham Meikle & Partners* (ante, n. 25), at 1100.

[39] *Samuels* v. *Davis* [1943] K.B. 526.

[40] *Greaves & Co. (Contractors) Ltd.* v. *Baynham Meikle & Partners* (ante).

[41] E.g. *Miller* v. *Cannon Hill Estates Ltd.* [1931] 2 K.B. 113; *Hancock* v. *B. W. Brazier (Anerley) Ltd.* [1966] 1 W.L.R. 1317; cf. ante, p. 519.

[42] *Manawatu Asphalts Ltd.* v. *Rae,* ante; cf. *Peters* v. *C. W. McFarling Floor Surfacing Ltd.* [1959] S.A.S.R. 261, where the flooring proved inadequate because of excess water in the wood of the underlying floor. This fact was unknown to either party and the work was conducted with reasonable care and skill. Reed J. held that although the general purpose of the installation had been made known and although the respondent, as a specialist, would have known of the dangers of dampness there was no specific notification to the respondent that he was regarded as guaranteeing the sufficiency of the under-floor ventilation, and thus no communication of the particular purpose alleged by the appellant. His duty had been adequately discharged by his inspection of the floor before commencing work and his competent performance of the work thereafter. This was a case involving an abnormal sensitivity in the subject matter, akin to *Griffiths* v. *Peter Conway Ltd.* [1939] 1 All E.R. 685 and *Ingham* v. *Emes* [1955] 2 Q.B. 366.

the first, but it may enjoy an independent existence and produce a different result. Thus, a workman may, while exercising proper expertise and care, nevertheless pursue a course of treatment which is grossly unsuitable for the chattel upon which he is working. In such a case the relevant question is whether the contractor merely undertook to show a proper degree of competence for his task or went further and guaranteed the efficacy of his treatment. Generally, it may be thought that the peculiar sensitivities of a chattel, or the lack of any general professional knowledge about its proper treatment, would carry such treatment beyond the normal expectations of the parties.[43] Conversely, compliance with the implied warranty of ordinary care and skill is clearly valueless if the work is not performed. If the promise to execute the task overrides the promise to use reasonable care and skill, it will of course prevail.

Ultimately, the question resolves itself into one of common sense. The degree of scientific knowledge involved in the performance of the work and the dependence of its ultimate success upon chance or extraneous circumstances will often be material, and even decisive, in this inquiry. In such professions as law and medicine the incidence of these factors is high and clearly militates against a contractual guarantee of the success of the work or the efficacy of the treatment employed. The same can probably be said of veterinary surgery, subject to the possibility that the practitioner may warrant the suitability of drugs or other substances employed in the course of his treatment.[44] But in the case of less esoteric professions such as laundering or dry-cleaning, it seems fairer to bind the contractor to a more total guarantee of efficacy and success. As Lord Greene M.R. remarked,[45] the essence of a contract for laundering is to launder; either the labour attains that objective or it does not. The absolute nature of this undertaking renders irrelevant the cause of its breach. It may be, in any event, that the cleaner will be held to have warranted the fitness and quality of his materials.[46]

The foregoing analysis produces an acceptable result when the only consequence of the inadequate treatment is the non-performance of the work. The contractor can always try again, and unless the task is practically impossible he will be bound to do so.[47] When, on the other hand, the inadequate treatment leads to the destruction of the chattel the position is more ambiguous. If the bailor sues for breach of the workman's ordinary duty of reasonable care he will fail, for the foregoing discussion assumes that the bailee has at all times exercised reasonable care and skill. If he sues on the warranty of adequate treatment, he will apparently succeed. It may be thought unfair that the ordinary liability for damage or destruction could be circumvented in this way. One solution might be to hold that the action for breach of warranty can give rise to damages only for the failure of the particular event contemplated by that warranty, viz. the cleaning of goods which have subsequently been destroyed. But on

---

[43] Cf. n. 42, ante.
[44] Cf. *Dodd* v. *Wilson* [1946] 2 All E.R. 691.
[45] *Alderslade* v. *Hendon Laundry Ltd.* [1945] K.B. 189 at 193.
[46] *Ingham* v. *Emes* [1955] 2 Q.B. 366.
[47] Even when it *is* impossible, he may be liable for non-performance: see ante, p. 518. et seq.

balance it seems that the bailor's damages should not be limited in this way.

Individual circumstances may, of course, displace a warranty of this character. Examples might be the insistence of the bailor upon a mode of treatment of his own devising, the failure to disclose any abnormal sensitivity in the article, or any event which either indicates that the bailor is not relying upon the bailee's skill and judgment or prevents the bailee from exercising those qualities.

In those cases in which the warranty *is* implied, there will generally be no necessity to consider whether the bailee has additionally warranted that the services will achieve a particular result.[48] If the treatment is reasonably fit for its purposes it will generally produce any reasonable effect demanded of it; conversely, the desired result will generally be a chattel that is fit for its purpose. It is at this stage that the second potential warranty begins to merge into the third.

So far as concerns the latter warranty (that the finished product should be reasonably fit for the bailor's purpose) it seems that its implication may be dependent upon the type of bailment in question. In many cases it will be justly and legitimately implied. This is particularly so where the bailor is an ordinary consumer and the bailee a professional craftsman, and the labour is intended to produce something substantially different from the chattel as originally bailed. In such a case, the purpose in engaging the bailee's services will normally be self-evident and will not require specific communication. Of course, the warranty may be excluded where the failure to serve the customer's purpose is due to an undiscoverable defect in his chattel[49] or where the purpose contemplated by the bailor is too specialised or remote to be warranted without express communication or agreement.[50] But often its implication will be equitable and will form part of the consideration for which the customer bargained. Thus, Sellers L.J. has recognised that in a contract for the service and repair of a car the repairer warrants not only that the work be performed in a "suitable and efficient manner" but that the chattel will function in the manner which the repairs contemplate: for instance, that the new brakes will work.[51]

However, it is submitted that both the warranty itself and the relevant purpose upon which it operates should be restrictively construed. Generally, the warranty will become important only when there has been no breach of the more commonplace warranty of reasonable care and skill. In cases like repair, where the bailee is allying or intermixing materials of his own with the principal chattel, it is fair to assume that he guarantees the fitness of that chattel in its repaired state to perform the ordinary functions of a chattel of that kind, because he has some

---

[48] A warranty similar to this is implied in certain circumstances by s. 74 (2) of the *Trade Practices Act* 1974 (Cth). See post, p. 527 et seq.

[49] Cf. *Peters* v. *C. W. McFarling Floor Surfacing Ltd.* [1959] S.A.S.R. 261, ante, n. 42.

[50] Or where the employer has produced a specification which he requires to be followed at all events: *Manawatu Asphalts Ltd.* v. *Rae* [1950] N.Z.L.R. 709 at 711-712. Cf. ante, p. 519.

[51] *Stewart* v. *Reavell's Garage Ltd.* [1952] 2 Q.B. 545, at 551.

influence over its final constitution. But where the chattel and all its accessories or components belong throughout to the bailor and nothing is added by the bailee, closer regard must be paid to the nature of the service and its likely impact upon the functional efficiency of the chattel. In the case of the repairer, the warranty may well survive, albeit confined to those particular areas of repair to which the bailee was assigned: a man who is ordered to repair the brakes on a car can hardly be expected to warrant the windscreen, because there will have been no reliance upon his skill or competence to do so. But with services like laundering, dry-cleaning and (perhaps) veterinary treatment, the case against implying the warranty is considerably stronger. The dry-cleaner (as we have seen) will be liable for a failure to treat the garment with proper care and skill[52] and may be held to have warranted the suitability of chemicals used in the cleaning process.[53] If these duties have been met it seems inapposite to hold him additionally liable because the garment does not answer the customer's particular purpose, unless that purpose has been clearly communicated and bargained for.

Where, however, the bailee's task is to produce some finished artefact from raw materials supplied entirely (or almost entirely) by the bailor, the case is strong for implying analogous obligations to those implied into contracts for the sale of goods. The finished product should conform with any sample or description furnished by the artificer and should, at least where the bailor relies on the bailee's skill and judgment, be reasonably fit for its intended use. In appropriate cases, the bailee may also be taken to have warranted that the product will be of good or merchantable quality. And whereas considerations of title are irrelevant if the materials belong throughout to the bailor,[54] the bailee may nevertheless be held liable for any charge or encumbrance or any disturbance of the bailor's quiet possession which arises from his dealing in the goods.

Curiously enough, this question does not seem to have directly arisen. The nearest analogy is perhaps to be found in those bailments locatio operis faciendi which involve the acquisition and supply of materials or parts by the bailee as an ancilliary to the performance of labour.[55] Both at Common Law and (in Australia) by statute there is authority for implying into such contracts warranties of quality and fitness analogous to those implied in case of sale. The case for making such implications in the present case may well be stronger, for the bailee is not dependent upon materials supplied or manufactured by third parties. If the contractor who manufactures a chattel for his customer from materials supplied by a third party can be liable for its functional deficiency,[56] so should the artificer whose work is from materials supplied entirely by the customer. There seems little doubt that similar terms would be implied, subject to the greater reliance which the bailor who supplies his own materials may place upon his own skill and judgment as opposed to that of the bailee.

---

[52] Mayne v. Silvermere Cleaners, Ltd. [1939] 1 All E.R. 693.
[53] Ingham v. Emes, ante, n. 42.
[54] Cf. Dixon v. London Small Arms Co. Ltd. (1876) 1 App. Cas. 632; ante, p. 506.
[55] Post, p. 531 et seq.
[56] Cf. Ashington Piggeries Ltd. v. Christopher Hill Ltd. [1971] 1 All E.R. 847.

The bailee's liability for breach of his duties of care and skill can extend not only to the impairment of the chattel itself but to injury or damage to persons or other property. Again, many of the decisions are of general application and are not peculiar to the relationship of bailor and bailee. In *Kimber* v. *William Willett Ltd.*[57] the defendants agreed to remove and clean the plaintiff's carpet. They left one end of the adjoining carpet untacked, with the result that the plaintiff tripped and was injured. She sued for breach of their implied undertaking that the work should be performed in a proper and workmanlike manner and succeeded both at first instance and on appeal. Tucker L.J. remarked[58] that it would be a clear breach of this obligation to perform the work in a manner which was likely to injure persons in the vicinity. The same observations may be applied, mutatis mutandis, to the likely threat of injury to property.[59]

In *Mayne* v. *Silvermere Ltd.*[60] the plaintiff contracted dermatitis after wearing a suit which had been cleaned by the defendants. After receiving the suit back from the defendants he had not worn it for six months but had left it wrapped in tissue paper in a wardrobe. He sued in contract, alleging breach of their obligation to exercise due care and skill. This was approached not as a simple action in negligence but as an action for breach of warranty. Croom-Johnson J. concluded that the illness was something which ought not to have happened without a failure to take reasonable care. The onus was on the plaintiff to satisfy the court that his illness was caused by defective cleaning.[61] By showing that the suit had never caused discomfort before it was cleaned by the defendants and that he had done nothing since its return which was likely to precipitate the illness, the plaintiff enabled the court to infer that the irritant substance was introduced into the cloth by the defendants. This conclusion rendered the defendants liable irrespective of the fact that they successfully cleaned two thousand suits per week and their plant was "the best possible".[62] Since no evidence had been adduced that the plaintiff was a man of abnormal or allergic sensivitity to the defendants' cleaning materials, this defence could not succeed. The case may be taken as suggesting that the workman's liability for personal injuries may be stricter than in simple negligence, but there is little in Croom-Johnson J.'s statements of this liability that justifies this conclusion and the case seems to have been generally approached upon the issue of burden of proof.

---

[57] [1947] K.B. 570. See also *Schmitz* v. *Stoveld* (1976) 64 D.L.R. (3d) 615 (floor surfacers liable for injury caused to plaintiff through their failure to apply the surfacing material according to instructions).

[58] Ibid, at 574.

[59] Cf. *Stansbie* v. *Troman* [1948] 2 K.B. 48; *Petrovich* v. *Callingham's Ltd.* [1969] 2 Lloyd's Rep. 386; *H. Parsons* (*Livestock*) *Ltd.* v. *Uttley Ingham & Co. Ltd.* [1978] 1 All E.R. 525 (suppliers of storage hopper liable for death of pigs resulting from contamination of feed, which in turn resulted from supplier's negligent failure to open a ventilator prior to delivery).

[60] [1939] 1 All E.R. 693 (Liverpool Assize).

[61] Ibid, at 697, 698.

[62] Cf. *Daniels & Daniels* v. *R. White & Sons, Ltd.* [1938] 4 All E.R. 258. This decision was recently disapproved by MacKenna J. in *Hill* v. *J. Crowe Ltd.* [1978] 1 All E.R. 812; *Martin* v. *Thorn* [1978] W.A.R. 10.

D. The Trade Practices Act 1974 (Cth)

To a large and perhaps uncertain extent the workman's Common Law duties have been modified in Australia by s. 74 of the *Trade Practices Act* 1974.[63] This section governs contracts for the supply of services, to a consumer, by a corporation in the course of business.[64] However, only a limited range of services fall within its provisions. These services are: the construction, maintenance, repair, treatment, processing, cleaning or alteration of goods or of fixtures to land; the alteration of physical state of land; and the distribution or transportation of goods.[65]

Therefore, provided the necessary relationship is established,[66] section 74 will now apply to the great majority of bailments locatio operis faciendi. Garage repairs, dry-cleaning and laundering, painting, servicing, veterinary treatment, the alteration of garments and the fabrication of articles from the customer's own materials are among the transactions affected. Into all these transactions (which need not necessarily arise by way of bailment) the Act implies two concurrent obligations:

(1) an implied warranty that the services will be rendered with due care and skill;[67] and

(2) where the consumer, expressly or by implication, makes known to the corporation any particular purpose for which the services are required or the result that he desires to achieve—an implied warranty that the services supplied under the contract will be reasonably fit for that purpose, or are of such a nature and quality that they might reasonably be expected to achieve that result. Such warranty does not apply, however, where the circumstances show that the consumer does not rely, or that it unreasonable for him to rely, on the corporation's skill and judgment.[68]

Section 74(1) is really bifurcal in nature. On the one hand, it binds the corporation to exercise "due care" in the performance of the work, the adjective "due" in such circumstances presumably meaning "such as is reasonable in the circumstances" or "such as is demanded by the contract". This would be the provision under which liability for "collateral" negligence, not directly affecting the standard of craftsmanship or the quality of the end-product, would be imposed: such defaults as negligently leaving the door unlocked and enabling thieves to enter[69] or injuring the customer by the negligent performance of the labour.[70] The same provision would also encompass the bailee's duty of care as a custodian,[71] but it is submitted that this inclusion should not be regarded as altering the bailee's burden of proof. Whereas the onus of proof under an action

---

[63] No. 51 of 1974. A comparable provision, which will not be separately discussed, is to be found in s. 9 of the *Consumer Transactions Act* 1972-1973 (South Australia).

[64] Sections 74 (1), (2).

[65] Section 74 (3).

[66] I.e., that the transaction is between a corporation and a consumer. The supply of services by way of competitive tender is also excluded from s. 74.

[67] Section 74 (1).

[68] Section 74 (2).

[69] *Stansbie* v. *Troman* [1949] K.B. 48.

[70] *Mayne* v. *Silvermere Cleaners Ltd.* [1939] 1 All E.R. 393; *Kimber* v. *William Willett Ltd.* [1947] K.B. 570.

[71] Ante, p. 509 et seq.

for breach of warranty rests upon the party alleging the warranty, the onus of proof under an action for breach of the bailee's duty of reasonable care rests squarely on the bailee. It is clearly desirable that the latter rule be preserved and that s. 74(1) should not be regarded as reversing the traditional burden.[72]

Apart from this, the due care provision of s. 74(1) would seem to add little to the position at Common Law. The real value of this provision, and indeed of s. 74 generally, is that liability for its breach can no longer be restricted or excluded.[73]

The requirement of due skill, on the other hand, seems prima facie to relate to the essential service to be provided under the contract, and to be entirely divorced from notions of relative care. The corporation must possess and employ the skill demanded of the job; a skill which, by undertaking the job originally, it has represented itself as possessing.[74] This part of s. 74(1) would therefore encompass such defaults as incompetent workmanship or professional ignorance, whether arising from negligence on the part of the corporation or not. But of course the two segments of s. 74(1) are closely interrelated. In the majority of cases a breach of the warranty of due care will also amount to a failure to render the services with due skill, and vice versa. The difficulty arises when it is uncertain whether the complaint is founded upon a lack of care or a want of skill. In such an event it may be possible for the corporation to escape liability merely by proving that it took reasonable care of the goods, and by requiring the consumer to prove that loss was due to the corporation's failure in its stricter duty to exercise due skill; for prima facie the "due care" provision of s. 74(1) would penalise only those corporations which should have known better, whereas the "due skill" provision would extend to those who represented that they did. For this reason, it is suggested[75] that the former provision should be construed in appropriate cases as imposing a heavier liability than in simple negligence and a stricter degree of care than that which is merely reasonable.

Greater problems of overlap and interrelationship arise from s. 74(2) This is an interesting and intelligent subsection because it recognises the possibility (recently endorsed by Lord Denning M.R.)[76] that a contractor may promise something more than reasonable skill in the performance of his engagement. But the obligation as enshrined in s. 74(2) is not an absolute one for several reasons. First, of course, it depends upon an express or implied communication of the purpose or result intended; this communication is not, however, specifically required to be made "so as to show" that the consumer relied on the contractor's skill and judgment, because the rebuttal of such reliance (or proof that it was unreasonable) must be shown by the circumstances and there

---

[72] Cf. the observations by Dr. North on s. 5 (3), *Occupiers' Liability Act* 1957; North, *Occupiers' Liability*, pp. 157-158; ante, p. 218.

[73] Section 68, *Trade Practices Act* 1974.

[74] Ante, p. 518 et seq.

[75] Palmer and Rose (1977) 26 I.C.L.Q., at 187, 188.

[76] *Greaves & Co. (Contractors) Ltd.* v. *Baynham Meikle & Partners* ante, p. 522. Section 74 (2) would not have applied to this contract as it was not inter alia one between a corporation (as supplier) and a consumer.

fore presumably borne by the contractor. Secondly, s. 74(2) proceeds upon a peculiar dichotomy between the purpose of the services and their intended result. Whereas the subsection does not demand that the pro- jected result should actually be attained by the services rendered, but merely that those services should be of a kind that could reasonably be expected to attain that result, the requirement that the services be reason- ably fit for their purpose is a total one, to which reasonable expectation is irrelevant. This disparity of treatment raises questions as to the dif- ference between purpose and result. It has been suggested that the dichotomy could give rise to complicated disputes:

> A builder who contracts to erect a building designed for a particular purpose, and or from whose construction the consumer expects a particular result to follow, is given a curiously ambivalent opportunity to evade liability on the latter ground by proving that the construc- tion might reasonably have been expected to achieve that result. If, however, the building is merely unsuitable for its purpose, he has no such escape. The "reasonable expectation" clause may represent a well-meaning attempt to restrict the corporation's liability in those cases where the consumer's objectives are eccentric, or beyond the supplier's field of experience, but the distinction it proceeds upon is difficult to prove in practice. Very often, "purpose" and "desired result" will prove synonymous.[77]

At first sight, the distinction would appear to be redundant. The normal result desired by the consumer is the fitness of the services for their purpose; and services which are fit for their purpose will generally be capable of satisfying any result the consumer has demanded. Of course, the latter proposition is not necessarily true and s. 74(2) may be influenced by a conviction that projected results are more dependent for their satisfaction upon external vicissitudes, or the peculiar whims of the employer, than is the fitness of labour for its purpose. On the other hand, the supplier who has undertaken to accommodate such whims should be strictly liable for failing to fulfil them. Where the customer's desired result has been communicated and the corporation has led him to believe that it will be attained, there is no reason for limiting the corporation's liability to cases in which the result could not reasonably have been expected to follow the services. The corporation can always disclaim any guarantee of attainment, or make it clear than in expecting such attainment the consumer either relies upon his individual skill and judgment or relies unreasonably upon that of the corporation. There would seem to be no need for the further qualification that the services need only be of a nature and quality that might reasonably be expected to attain the expressed result. Indeed, this qualification would seem repugnant to the absolute nature of most contractual undertakings.

One of the more undesirable consequences of the "reasonable expecta- tion" part of s. 74(2) would be its capacity to override the stricter war- ranty that the services are fit for their purpose. It would be absurd, for instance, if a corporation could argue that since the desired result of its services was that these services should be reasonably fit for their

77 Palmer and Rose, op. cit., at 188.

purpose, and since those services were of a kind that could reasonably have been expected to be fit for their purpose, it should be exonerated from liability notwithstanding that the services rendered actually proved inadequate. To this extent, it must be assumed that the word "result" in s. 74(2) connotes any result other than the general one that the services be fit for their purpose.

Many of the foregoing difficulties might have been avoided if, instead of implying an attenuated warranty that the desired result should be achieved, the draftsman had inserted a warranty that the finished product (as well as the services which created it) should be reasonably fit for its purpose. A warranty of this kind was recognised by the Court of Appeal in *Greaves & Co. (Contractors) Ltd.* v. *Baynham, Meikle & Partners*[78] and has been described by Henry J., in the New Zealand Supreme Court, as a term of general implication.[79] In the present state of s. 74(2), it is to be hoped that care will be taken to avoid drafting all but the most exceptional cases into the "result" portion of that subsection, and that the courts will sustain so far as possible the doctrine that, if a supplier has promised to perform or achieve something, no amount of reasonable expectation should absolve him if he fails.

Further difficulty may be occasioned by the need to reconcile the warranty of due care and skill in s. 74(1) with the apparently more exceptional warranty contained in s. 74(2). Again, these sections will often overlap and a particular dispute will be answerable according to either. Unfortunately, the drafting of these subsections suggests that the answer in each case may be different. Where, for instance, the alteration of a coat by a bailor is so incompetently performed that the coat cannot be worn and the result or object of the transaction is not achieved, s. 74(1) would appear to allow immediate recovery on the basis of a failure to use reasonable care and skill, whereas s. 74(2) would make recovery dependent upon the customer's communication of his particular purpose or intended result. In many cases it may be possible to resolve the conflict by emphasising the formula "any particular purpose" in s. 74(2).[80] The latter subsection could then be read as a rider to s. 74(1), catering for those situations in which services might be provided for more than one purpose and the consumer has either designated one particular or specialised purpose as his own (e.g. wearing the coat for a special occasion) or has stipulated, from the fulfilment of that purpose, a result peculiar to himself (e.g. to look like someone else). This interpretation would not cut down any right of action he may have for general ineptitude under s. 74(1), but it would make the possibly higher level of damages recoverable under s. 74(2) (e.g. for loss of enjoyment) subject to the more restrictive requirements contained in that subsection. Against this it may be pointed out that s. 74(2) does not (as with the case of "purpose") refer to "any particular" result, but merely to the result that the consumer has expressly or impliedly made known to the contractor as the one which he desires the services to achieve. Thus,

---

[78] [1975] 1 W.L.R. 1095; ante, p. 522.
[79] *Batchelers Pram House Ltd.* v. *McKenzie Bros. Electrical Ltd.* [1962] N.Z.L.R. 545, at 547. Cf. p. 522 et seq., ante.
[80] Palmer and Rose, op cit.

quite everyday results could fall within the narrower ambit of s. 74(2) and could bring that subsection both closer to s. 74(1) and more difficult to dissociate from it.

An alternative or supplementary method of reconciliation lies in the suggestion that whereas s. 74(1) governs the manner in which the services are performed, s. 74(2) governs the standard of the finished product.[81] But again, the distinction is a misleading one because a complaint may be attributable to either of these elements. The standard of services is dependent upon the manner of their performance and their manner of performance is evidence of their standard. From these and other difficulties, it may follow that s. 74(2) should be sparingly applied. But there are many everyday cases (not involving especially eccentric purposes) in which a warranty as to result would be desirable and a warranty as to the aptitude of the services for their purpose commonplace. Thus, although the distinction between the method of performance and standard of product is (like that between purpose and result) somewhat superficial and inadequate, the very vagueness of their interrelationship may allow sufficient judicial discretion to attain a just result.

Section 68 of the *Trade Practices Act* prohibits any attempt by the supplier-corporation to exclude, restrict or modify the obligations imposed by ss. 74(1) and (2). By confining itself to "(a)ny term of contract for the supply by a corporation of . . . services to a consumer", s. 68(1) would appear to leave intact any exclusion clause incorporated (otherwise than by contract) within the relationship between a bailor and a sub-bailee.[82]

Finally, it should be noted that expression "consumer", in relation to the supply of services within the Act, is defined by s. 4(3)(b) of that Act as follows:

[A] person who acquires services shall be taken to be a consumer of the services if the services are of a kind ordinarily acquired for private use or consumption and the person does not acquire the services for the purposes of, or in the course of, a profession, business, trade or occupation or for a public purpose.[83]

E. Quality and fitness of materials[83a]

1. *At Common Law*: The courts have been willing to imply into contracts of work and labour a warranty that any materials supplied by the workman in the performance of the labour will be reasonably fit for their purpose and will be of good or merchantable quality.[84] Such an under-

---

81 Ibid.
82 Post, p. 1000; *Morris* v. *C. W. Martin & Sons Ltd.* [1966] 1 Q.B. 716; *Johnson, Matthey & Co. Ltd.* v. *Constantine Terminals Ltd.* [1976] 2 Lloyd's Rep. 215; cf. s. 3(2) *Unfair Contract Terms Act*, 1977.
83 The burden of proof is upon the supplier to show that the customer was not a consumer: s. 4 (4). But see now App. II *post*.
83a See Law Commission W.P. No. 71, *Implied Terms in Contracts for the Supply of Goods* (1977).
84 *G. H. Myers & Co.* v. *Brent Cross Service Co.* [1934] 1 K.B. 46 (citing *Francis* v. *Cockrell* (1870) L.R. 5 Q.B. 501); *Stewart* v. *Reavell's Garage Ltd.* [1952] 2 Q.B. 545; *Young & Marten Ltd.* v. *McManus Childs Ltd.* [1969] 1 A.C. 454; *Helicopter Sales Pty. Ltd.* v. *Rotor Work Pty. Ltd.* (1974) 132 C.L.R. 1; *Batcheler's Pram House* case, *ante*; and, for further authorities, see *post*. The separate identity of these two undertakings was stressed, especially by Lord Reid, in

taking would arise, for instance, where a mechanic contracts to replace worn-out parts in a car or a tailor contracts to make up a suit from the customer's own material, supplying the buttons, lining and thread. Agreements of this kind do not normally qualify as contracts for the sale of goods[85] and are not therefore subject to the terms implied by the *Sale of Goods Act* 1893.[86] Nevertheless, similar terms are normally implied at Common Law.

Thus, in *G. H. Myers & Co.* v. *Brent Cross Service Co.*,[87] where a car was bailed to the defendant garage-company for correction of an engine defect, the Court of Appeal held that unless the customer had relied upon his own skill and judgment in selecting the source from which spare parts were to be obtained there was an absolute warranty on the part of the repairers that connecting-rods installed in pursuance of the contract were of good quality and reasonably fit for their purpose. It made no difference that the rods had been acquired from a reputable manufacturer and suffered from a latent defect which the defendants could not have discovered by the exercise of reasonable care and skill. To hold otherwise would create, in the Court's opinion, an unjustifiable distinction between contracts for the supply of work and materials and contracts for the sale of goods.[88]

In accordance with this approach, it has been held that strict warranties of fitness and quality are impliable against such craftsmen as a dentist making a set of false teeth for a customer,[89] a repairer fitting a new braking system to a car,[90] an engineering company installing an anti-burglar device,[91] a roofing contractor laying a new roof[92] and a veterinary surgeon innoculating an animal with toxin.[93] Admittedly, the equation with the sale of goods is not absolute, because with few exceptions the authorities treat these undertakings as warranties and not conditions.[94] The distinction may not be particularly important in this context because in many cases the incorporation of the materials into the customer's chattel or premises will render him unwilling or unable to exercise a

---

Young & Marten Ltd. v. *McManus Childs Ltd.* (ante, at 468), and was recognised by the majority of the High Court of Australia in *Helicopter Sales Pty. Ltd.* v. *Rotor Work Pty. Ltd.* (ante, cf. Jacobs J. dissenting, at 16).

[85] Ante, p. 504.
[86] As amended by the *Supply of Goods (Implied Terms) Act* 1973.
[87] [1934] 1 K.B. 46.
[88] For a stronger expression of the same opinion see *Young & Marten Ltd.* v. *McManus Childs Ltd.* (ante, n. 84), at 473 (Lord Upjohn).
[89] *Samuels* v. *Davis* [1943] K.B. 526.
[90] *Stewart* v. *Reavell's Garage Ltd.* ante, n. 84; see also *Krieger* v. *Bell* [1943] S.A.S.R. 168, at 173.
[91] *Reg. Glass Pty. Ltd.* v. *River's Locking Systems Pty. Ltd.* (1968) 120 C.L.R. 516.
[92] *Young & Marten Ltd.* v. *McManus Childs Ltd.*, ante; *Martin* v. *McNamara* [1951] Q.S.R. 225; cf. *Manawatu Asphalts Ltd.* v. *Rae* [1950] N.Z.L.R. 709; *Peters* v. *C. W. McFarling Floor Surfacing Ltd.* [1959] S.A.S.R. 261 (flooring); *Batcheler's Pram House* case, ante (electrical installations).
[93] *Dodd* v. *Wilson* [1946] 2 All E.R. 691. In the *Helicopter Sales* case (a decision in which neither warranty was admitted on the facts), Jacobs J. said at 16: "I do not think the question of using reasonable care arises. Proof that reasonable care was used will not absolve from liability. Therefore I do not think it is necessary to distinguish between latent defects and patent defects".
[94] Cf. *Martin* v. *McNamara* ante, n. 92 ("warranty or condition"); *Dodd* v. *Wilson* ante ("condition").

right of rescission. It is submitted, however, that if a breach of these terms goes to the root of the contract the customer should be entitled to reject the services and rescind. The obligations of fitness and quality should not therefore be regarded as warranties in the literal sense[95] but as conditions or innominate terms.[96]

The obligation as to reasonable fitness may be displaced if it can be shown that in selecting the materials or directing their installation the customer relied upon his own skill and judgment to the exclusion of that of the contractor.[97] However, the mere fact that he has nominated a particular brand of materials to be used in the performance of the labour will not necessarily exonerate the contractor,[98] for as in the sale of goods[99] this is merely one factor to be considered in answering the overall question of reliance.[1] It is quite consistent with this requirement for the consumer to select a particular type or manufacture of materials and yet rely upon the contractor's judgment in accepting the specification.

Even when reliance is negatived in this manner, and the warranty as to fitness for purpose is accordingly excluded, the contractor may be liable under the second implied warranty if the materials are not of adequate quality. This was the situation in *Young & Marten Ltd.* v. *McManus Childs Ltd.,* where the plaintiffs had specified both the manufacturer and the particular brand of tile to be used by the defendants in roofing their houses. The defect complained of was not a functional defect common to every specimen of that brand of tile but a defect, caused by faulty manufacturing, peculiar to that particular consignment. The House of Lords, while agreeing that no warranty as to fitness for purpose could be implied,[2] held nevertheless that the contractors had warranted that the tiles would be of good or merchantable quality. Lord Reid pointed out that in normal circumstances this conclusion would not penalise the contractor, for he could recover damages in turn from the party who sold the goods to him.[3]

A different conclusion was reached in *Helicopter Sales Pty. Ltd.* v. *Rotor-Work Pty. Ltd.,*[4] where the High Court of Australia held by a majority that neither a warranty of reasonable fitness nor a warranty as to quality should be imported. The contract in this case, which was for the servicing of a helicopter, bound the defendants to acquire all necessary spare parts from a certain manufacturer. Further terms provided that the

---

[95] I.e., as terms which can only engender a right to damages: see generally p. 733 et seq., post.

[96] Cf. sections 74 (1) and (2), *Trade Practices Act* 1974: post, p. 537.

[97] A merely partial reliance upon the customer's own skill and judgment will not necessarily absolve the contractor: cf. *Cammell Laird & Co. Ltd.* v. *Manganese Bronze and Brass Co. Ltd.* [1934] A.C. 402; *Ashington Piggeries Ltd.* v. *Christopher Hill Ltd.* [1972] A.C. 441, at 490.

[98] Cf. the observations of du Parcq J. in *G. H. Myers & Co.* v. *Brent Cross Service Co.* [1934] 1 K.B. 46, at 55, discussed critically by the House of Lords in *Young & Marten Ltd.* v. *McManus Childs Ltd.,* ante, at 468, 471, 475.

[99] *Baldry* v. *Marshall* [1925] 1 K.B. 260.

[1] *Martin* v. *McNamara*, ante. Cf. *Young & Marten Ltd.* v. *McManus Childs Ltd.,* ante, at 475 (Lord Upjohn).

[2] Ibid., at 465, 468-469, 474-476.

[3] Ibid., at 466. This was not possible in the present case because the limitation period had expired.

[4] (1974) 132 C.L.R.I.

servicing should comply with Department of Civil Aviation and manufacturers' requirements, and that the defendants should obtain a release-
note from the manufacturers' agent in respect of all replacement parts.
It was held that these provisions, coupled with the plaintiffs' knowledge
that the defendants had no facilities for testing replacement parts, were
inconsistent with the alleged warranties of quality or reasonable fitness
for use. Accordingly, the defendants were not liable for the loss of the
helicopter, occasioned by the installation of a bolt which suffered from
a latent defect:

> The defendant, as the plaintiff well knew, was in no position to
> give such a warranty. It did not have the specifications according
> to which the bolt was made: it had not means of testing the bolt:
> it had no expertise to determine whether or not it was suitable
> for the purpose for which it was being used. Both the plaintiff
> and the defendant plainly enough were relying upon the manu-
> facturer to have a bolt made suitable for the purpose for which
> is was to be used and of airworthy quality.[5]

Stephen J. did, however, acknowledge that the warrantor's own inability
to comply with quality standards will not of itself necessarily exclude
the warranty as to quality. For this to occur, it appears that the facts
must generally go further and establish that positive reliance is being
placed elsewhere, whether upon the customer's own discrimination or
(as in the present case) upon that of a third party.[6] In the absence of
such proof, assuming that all other circumstances are consistent with
the conclusion, the warranty will be implied.

The decision in *Helicopter Sales Pty. Ltd.* v. *Rotor-Work Pty. Ltd.* may
itself be compared with that of the House of Lords in *Gloucestershire
County Council* v. *Richardson*.[7] Under a building contract the builder
was required to obtain concrete columns from a supplier nominated by
the Council. The columns suffered from latent defects which became
evident only after they had been incorporated into the building. The
contractors purported to terminate the contract under a clause which
entitled them to do so if the work was delayed for more than one month
by reason of architects' instructions. The House of Lords, deciding that
the contract was properly determined, held that any warranty as to the
quality or fitness of the pillars was displaced by the facts of the case.
Lords Pearce and Wilberforce reach this conclusion on the ground that
the contract itself did not contemplate such reliance, the plaintiffs
evidently preferring to put their faith in the nominated supplier. Lord
Upjohn held that although the contract itself did not exclude the warranty, any such implication was inconsistent with the secondary contract
imposed by the Council between the builder and the supplier. This contract, to the knowledge of the Council, excluded all liability for deficiency
or lack of quality unless a claim was made within twenty-four hours.
Accordingly, it could hardly be claimed that the Council, having made
entry into such a contract mandatory by its nomination of the supplier,

---

[5] Ibid., at 5 per Menzies J.; see also Stephen J. at 11, and Jacobs J. (dissenting)
at 19-20.
[6] Ibid, at 12; and see [1969] 1 A.C. 454, at 466 per Lord Reid.
[7] [1969] 1 A.C. 480.

should be entitled to ignore it and to allege that the contractor never-theless warranted the fitness of the columns.[8] As Lord Wilberforce pointed out,[9] this case was distinguishable from *Young & Marten's* case because there the builders were free to enter into their own contract with the nominated supplier: here, on the other hand, the entire inventory of specifications, design, price etc. had been pre-arranged between employer and supplier. This clearly left no room for the extraction of any war-ranty as to quality by the contract or from the supplier, and made it fanciful to expect the contractor to pass such a warranty along to the employer himself. Nemo dat quod non habet.

Support for this conclusion was, in fact, derived from dicta in *Young & Marten's* case itself. Lord Reid, in particular, had expressed the view that the relevant warranties might more readily be discounted where the party engaging the labour knows that the supplier whom he has nominated customarily refuses to give any warranty as to the fitness or quality of his merchandise.[10] Lord Pearce, on the other hand, remarked that the warranty would not necessarily be excluded merely because the materials required were manufactured by one company alone;[11] and Lord Reid himself stressed that the contractor for whom a supplier was not expressly nominated would not be exonerated simply because the sup-plier whom he chose in fact imposed onerous exclusions.[12] The cases vary enormously and the question must, in every case, rest ultimately upon the facts and intentions of the parties.[13]

A number of further guidelines were also given by the House of Lords in *Young & Marten's case*. Lord Reid, in particular, suggested that the relevant warranties might more readily be excluded when the customer knows that only the manufacturer produces the necessary replacement parts and that he gives no warranty;[14] a situation commoner today than when du Parq J. delivered his judgment in *G. H. Myers & Co.* v. *Brent Cross Service Co.*[15] Again, both Lord Reid and Lord Wilberforce favoured a possible relaxing of the strictness of the warranties when the supply of goods represented only a minimal part of the transaction;[16] this may be contrasted with the views of Lord Upjohn,[17] who thought that in all cases of work and labour the warranties imposed as to materials should, if anything, be stronger. Thirdly, of course, the fact that the con-tractor advises against a particular material may operate to displace any warranty,[18] as may the fact that he uses the chattel negligently or before it is ready for use.[19]

---

8 Ibid., at 504.
9 At 507.
10 [1969] 1 A.C. 454, at 467; see also Lord Pearce at 471 and Lord Wilberforce at 479.
11 Ibid, at 471.
12 Ibid., at 466.
13 See, in particular, Lord Wilberforce at 476.
14 Ibid., at 468. See also Lord Pearce at 471.
15 [1934] 1 K.B. 46, at 55; see ante, p. 532. The dictum bears an interesting resemblance to the facts in the *Helicopter* case: ante, p. 533.
16 Ibid., at 468, 476-477, 479.
17 At 473-474.
18 Ibid., at 471 (Lord Pearce).
19 *Manawatu Asphalts Ltd.* v. *Rae* [1950] N.Z.L.R. 709; cf. *Heil* v. *Hedges* [1951] 1 T.L.R. 512.

The contractor may also be relieved where the bailed chattel suffers from a latent defect or abnormal sensitivity which renders the materials used for the performance of the labour unsuitable for their purpose. In such a case, there may be no reliance upon his skill and judgment or there may be insufficient communication of the purpose and nature of the transaction to enable him to exercise those qualities to the full.[20] It may nevertheless be possible for the warranties of quality and fitness to be implied in these circumstances, even where the defect or sensitivity was not one which the contractor could have discovered by exercising care and skill. The question is one of fact, depending upon the extent of the contractor's undertaking and the degree of reliance placed upon him, to his knowledge and with his consent, by the other party.

In *Ingham* v. *Emes*[21] the plaintiff sought to recover damages for dermatitis, contracted through the use of a hair dye called Inecto. The dye had been applied to her hair by an assistant employed by the defendant hairdresser, after performing the test suggested by the manufacturers of the dye and obtaining a favourable result. The Court of Appeal held that normally a warranty as to the reasonable fitness of the dye would be implied, similar to that contained in s. 14(1) of the *Sale of Goods Act* 1893.[22] However, in the present case the plaintiff had failed to inform the defendants that some four years earlier she had become ill after the application of Inecto and that her doctor had, on that occasion, told her that he suspected she was allergic to the dye. Accordingly, the warranty was excluded because it "is dependent upon proper disclosure by the customer of any relevant peculiarities known to her."[23] Denning L.J, treating the case as a simple contract for the supply of work and materials, drew a direct parallel between such contracts and contracts for the sale of goods:

> In order for the implied term to arise . . . the customer must make known to the contractor either expressly or by implication the "particular purpose" for which the materials are required so as to show that he relies on the contractor's skill or judgment. The particular purpose in this case was to dye the hair, not of a normal person, but of a person known to be allergic to Inecto. Mrs. Ingham did not make that particular purpose known to the assistant. She cannot therefore recover on the implied term.[24]

On the assumption that this decision could apply by analogy to cases of chattels bailed for dyeing or cleaning, interesting questions are raised as to the range of materials which may be warranted and the boundaries of the word "supply". In its loosest sense, this expression might include any application or consumption of materials for the customer's benefit, even though no property in them passes to him. Such a construction

---

[20] Cf. *Peter* v. *C. W. McFarling Floor Surfacing Ltd.* [1959] S.A.S.R. 261 (ante, p. 522); *Griffiths* v. *Peter Conway Ltd.* [1939] 1 All E.R. 366; *Mayne* v. *Silvermere Cleaners Ltd.* [1939] 1 All E.R. 693; *Ingham* v. *Emes* [1955] 2 Q.B. 366; *Henry Kendall & Sons* v. *William Lillico & Sons, Ltd.* [1969] 2 A.C. 31.
[21] Ante. See also *Parker* v. *Oloxo Ltd.* [1937] 3 All E.R. 524; *Watson* v. *Buckley Osborne, Garrett & Co.* [1940] 1 All E.R. 174.
[22] Now s. 14 (3).
[23] [1955] 2 Q.B. 366, at 374.
[24] Ibid.

may seem fanciful, but seems to follow from *Ingham* v. *Emes*. Thus, a dyer of garments may be held to warrant the quality and fitness of his dye, a cleaner that of his cleaning-chemicals and a veterinary surgeon that of his ointments or lotions. None of these commodities may be, strictly speaking, "supplied" to the customer but there seems no reason why the warranty should not exist. Admittedly, there must be limits to its implication, for otherwise a warehouseman might be held to strictly warrant the fitness of his premises and padlocks, whereas it is clear in ordinary circumstances that he is liable only for want of reasonable care.[25]

In *Young & Marten Ltd.* v. *McManus Childs Ltd.*[26] Lord Pearce discussed the possibility that a consumer might recover in tort from a manufacturer for substandard materials, supplied by an intermediate contractor. Such an action would necessitate, as his Lordship recognised, an extension of the principle in *Donoghue* v. *Stevenson*[27] to cases of purely economic loss caused by substandard workmanship. Lord Pearce thought that this extension was prone to great difficulty, and could not justifiably be made. More recently, however, Lord Denning M.R. in *Dutton* v. *Bognor Regis Urban District Council*[28] has remarked that the manufacturer should be liable in negligence for the cost of repair, and in *Rivtow Marine Ltd.* v. *Washington Iron Works and Walkem Machinery & Equipment Ltd.*[29] this dictum was upheld by Laskin, C.J. (dissenting) in the Canadian Supreme Court. In England and Australia, the question remains an open one; but recent developments in the law of negligence suggest that it cannot be discounted entirely.[29a]

2. *The Trade Practices Act 1974 (Cth)*: Statutory warranties as to fitness for purpose are implied by ss. 74(1) and (2) of the Act. Section 74(1) enacts as follows:

> 74.(1) In every contract for the supply (otherwise than by way of competitive tender) by a corporation in the course of a business of services to a consumer there is an implied warranty . . . that any materials supplied in connexion with those services[30] will be reasonably fit for the purpose for which they are supplied.

Section 74(2) is more specialised and applies only to those cases in which the consumer has communicated any particular purpose or result which he desires to be fulfilled:

> 74.(2) Where a corporation supplies (otherwise than by way of competitive tender) services to a consumer in the course of a business and the consumer, expressly or by implication, makes known to the corporation any particular purpose for which the services are

---

[25] Ante, p. 454.
[26] [1969] 1 A.C. 454, at 469.
[27] [1932] A.C. 562.
[28] [1972] 1 Q.B. 373, at 396. Cf. *Sparham-Souter & Anor.* v. *Town and Country Developments (Essex) Ltd.* [1976] 2 W.L.R. 493.
[29] (1974) 40 D.L.R. (3d) 530; Harvey (1974) 37 M.L.R. 320. See also *The Diamantis Pateras* [1966] 1 Lloyd's Rep. 179; *Anns* v. *Merton London Borough Council* [1977] 2 W.L.R. 1024; *Batty* v. *M.P.R. Ltd.* [1978] 2 All E.R. 445.
[29a] E.g. *Caltex Oil (Aust.) Pty. Ltd.* v. *The "Willemstad"*, (1976) 11 A.L.R. 227.
[30] I.e. "the services supplied under the contract for the supply of the services". For the limited range of services governed by ss. 74 (1) and (2), see ante, p. 527; s. 74. (3).

required or the result that he desires the services to achieve, there is an implied warranty that . . . any materials supplied in connexion with those services will be reasonably fit for that purpose or are of such a nature and quality that they might reasonably be expected to achieve that result, except where the circumstances show that the consumer does not rely, or that it is unreasonable for him to rely, on the corporation's skill or judgment.

A number of difficulties are created by these subsections. First, they imply warranties only as to fitness for purpose and not as to quality;[31] the latter obligation presumably remains to be implied at Common Law,[32] although in this event s. 68 would not appear (as it does in the case of the warranties as to fitness) to prohibit its exclusion. Secondly, the Act speaks only of warranties, and not of conditions or innominate terms: presumably, therefore, a breach of ss. 74(1) or (2) may generate only a right to damages and not per se a right to rescind.[33] Thirdly, s. 74(1) requires the materials merely to be suitable for the purpose for which they were supplied and not (which may be different) for the purpose for which they were intended to be used; in many cases this will not prove troublesome because the two purposes will coincide or because any specialised purpose contemplated by the consumer will fall within s. 74(2). Nevertheless, the form of words employed by s. 74(1) could prove undesirable and it may be thought that a clearer emphasis should have been placed upon the purpose of the consumer rather than that of the supplier.

A fourth and more serious difficulty concerns the interrelationship between s. 74 and ss. 69-72. The latter sections imply a wide range of obligations into every contract for the supply of goods from a corporation (acting in the course of a business) to a consumer.[34] These terms include conditions as to title,[35] fitness for purpose,[36] merchantable quality,[37] correspondence with description[38] and correspondence with sample,[39] and warranties as to quiet possession[40] and freedom from encumbrance.[41] "Supply", in relation to goods, is defined by s. 4(1) of the Act to include supply (including re-supply) by way of sale, exchange, lease, hire or hire-purchase. Assuming that these categories of supply are not exhaustive, the question arises as to whether materials supplied under a contract for the supply of services within s. 74 can alternatively be

---

[31] Ante, pp. 524, 532.
[32] But cf. post.
[33] Cf. *Cehave N.V.* v. *Bremer Handelsgesellshaft M.F.H.* [1976] Q.B. 44; *Reardon Smith Line Ltd.* v. *Yngvar Hansen-Tangen* [1976] 1 WL.R. 989.
[34] "Consumer", in relation to the supply of goods, was defined by s. 4 (3) (a) as follows: "A person who acquires goods shall be taken to be a consumer of the goods if the goods are of a kind ordinarily acquired for private use or consumption and the person does not acquire the goods or hold himself out as acquiring the goods for the purpose of re-supply". But see now App. II, post.
[35] Limited to contracts of sale and hire-purchase: s. 69 (1) (a).
[36] Section 71 (2).
[37] Section 71 (1).
[38] Section 70.
[39] Section 72.
[40] Section 69 (1) (b).
[41] Section 69 (1) (c): limited to those contracts under which property "is to or may pass to the consumer".

characterised as goods supplied under a contract for the supply of goods within ss. 69-72. If so, the consumer can discard the generally more limited remedies under ss. 74(1) and (2) of the *Trade Practices Act* and avail himself of the wider redress contained in ss. 69-72. It could follow that, for most practical purposes, those parts of ss. 74(1) and (2) which deal with supply of materials under service contracts are otiose.

Certainly, ss. 69-72 present a more attractive range of remedies to the consumer than ss. 74(1) and (2). With the exception of the warranties as to quiet possession and freedom from encumbrance, the terms implied are all conditions, and of course they are more extensive than the warranties of fitness for purpose implied under ss. 74(1) and (2). The draftsman seems to have overlooked the fact that whereas there is an established and fairly well-defined distinction between contracts for the supply of work and materials and contracts for the sale of goods,[42] no such distinction has hitherto been made between contracts for the supply of work and materials and contracts for the *supply* of goods. The statute itself fails to differentiate between the two species of contract and makes it difficult for them to be sharply and exclusively defined. Goods may be supplied without being "sold", even when property in them is to pass from the supplier to the consumer; one example would be the installation of connecting-rods in a car bailed for repairs, as in *G. H. Myers & Co.* v. *Brent Cross Service Co.*[43] Semantically at least, there seems no reason why the contract under which they are supplied should not constitute a contract for the supply of goods within the meaning of ss. 69-72.

Various reconciliations of the two varieties of contract have been suggested, in an effort to avoid duplication and to allot to each category an exclusive field of operation.[44] The likeliest solution is that the courts will apply some kind of "main purpose" test to the transaction and will hold that if the principal objective is the performance of services the standard of any material supplied in connexion therewith will be governed exclusively by s. 74.[45] But this approach, although superficially logical, could have unfortunate results. It would mean that the majority of work and materials contracts disclose no implied terms as to title, quiet possession, freedom from encumbrance, description, merchantable

---

[42] Discussed ante, at p. 504 et seq.
[43] [1934] 1 K.B. 46: ante, p. 532.
[44] Palmer & Rose (1977) 26 I.C.L.Q. 169, 174-175.
[45] Other possible interpretations are: (a) that the courts will distinguish between "goods" as employed in ss. 69-72 and "materials" in ss. 74 (1) and (2); (b) that the courts will look to the services set out in s. 74 (3) and will hold that any materials supplied in connection with such services are supplied under a contract for the supply of services and therefore fall within ss. 74 (1) and (2). Neither of these explanations is satisfactory. The first is untenable because the Act itself makes no distinction between "goods" and "materials" (although the former are defined by s. 4 (1)) and because materials per se are indisputably identifiable as goods. The second has no logical justification and could mean that even where the supply of goods in connection with the supply of a service enumerated by s. 74 (3) is the paramount feature of the transaction, that transaction must nevertheless be classified as a contract for the provision of services and thus governed solely by ss. 74 (1) and (2).

quality and sample but are left to "the ambivalent and generally inferior mercies of s. 74."[46] Such a result seems unjustifiable.[47]

It is therefore submitted that contracts for work and materials should be recognised as contracts for the supply of goods within ss 69-72 and that the consumer under such a contract should enjoy the same remedies as any other consumer who is party to a contract for the supply of goods. It would(as Lord Upjohn has recently observed)[48] be "most unsatisfactory, illogical and indeed a severe blow to any idea of a coherent system of common law" to discriminate against contracts for work and materials in this respect. The suggested approach would not prevent a consumer from proceeding, in appropriate circumstances, under ss. 74(1) and (2); and there may well be cases in which he finds that these provisions confer a more convenient remedy.[49] It would, however, mean that he is given substantial parity of redress with other consumers under contracts for the supply of goods.[50]

A further point of difficulty concerns the relationship between ss. 74(1) and (2). To some extent, this issue has already been examined in the discusion of the supplier's duty of good workmanship.[51] In the case of materials, s. 74(1) is a somewhat Draconian provision, for it applies irrespective of whether the consumer has communicated the purpose for which the materials are required or has relied upon the supplier's skill and judgment.[52] Thus it has been suggested that it could apply to a situation similar to that in *Helicopter Sales Pty. Ltd.* v. *Rotor-Work Pty. Ltd.*,[53] where the customer (not, in this case, a consumer within the meaning of the Act) had insisted that only materials supplied by one manufacturer should be employed.[54] Conversely, such a contract would not fail within s. 74(2) because the consumer would clearly be relying upon skills or judgment other than that of the supplier. The difference between the two subsections is great, and it is unfortunate that no more effective means of delimiting their respective spheres of operation has been given than the confusing distinction between, on the one hand, the purpose for which the materials are supplied[55] and, on the other, any particular purpose for which the integral services are required or the result which the consumer desires those services to achieve.[56] Section 74(1) merely requires that the former criterion be satisfied by the materials; s. 74(2) demands the latter:

> One can foresee complicated disputes in which the parties may argue lengthily and expensively about whether theirs is a "purpose"

---

[46] Palmer & Rose, op. cit.
[47] Cf. the observations of Lords Reid and Wilberforce in *Young & Marten's* case, [1969] I A.C. at 465-468, 475-479, with those of Lord Upjohn at 473-474.
[48] At 473; cf. Law Com. No. 69 and Sc. Law Com. No. 39, para. 20.
[49] Post.
[50] Substantial but not total; he would still have no implied condition as to title because s. 69 (1) (a) is unnecessarily limited to contracts of sale or hire-purchase: Palmer & Rose, loc. cit.
[51] Ante, p. 522.
[52] Both qualifications are inherent in s. 74 (2).
[53] (1974) 132 C.L.R. I (ante, p. 533): Palmer & Rose, loc. cit. at 176.
[54] Likewise, the consumer-corporation equivalent of *Gloucestershire County Council Ltd.* v. *Richardson* [1969] 1 A.C. 480; ante, p. 534.
[55] Section 74 (1).
[56] Section 74 (2).

or a "result" case and whether the more liberal sub-section (1) is ousted by the restrictively obscure sub-section (2).[57]

It may be useful, by way of conclusion, to consider the operation of the Trade Practices Act upon two particular kinds of bailment locatio operis faciendi. The first of these is the transaction which arises when raw materials supplied entirely by the bailor are made into a finished article by the bailee.[58] Logically, the bailee should be answerable at least for the fitness of the artefact and for its compliance with any description; and there may well be cases in which he should be held to have undertaken that it will be of good or merchantable quality and that the bailee will have quiet possession. It is difficult to see how he can be deemed to have supplied "any materials" in connexion with his services[59] and it would seem preferable, in any event, that his liability for the quality of the article itself should be governed by the wider provisions of ss. 69-72. The problem consists in ascertaining whether he has "supplied" the goods within the meaning of those sections.[60] It is submitted that a chattel could be deemed to have been supplied for these purposes although both the chattel itself and its component parts belong, throughout performance of the contract, to the consumer. Of course, the bailor will continue to enjoy his remedies in respect of quality of workmanship under ss. 74(1) and (2).

The second case involves bailments for cleaning or other treatment whereunder no materials are to be added permanently to the bailed chattel but certain materials (e.g. cleaning fluid) are to be applied in the performance of the labour. The decision of the Court of Appeal in *Ingham* v. *Emes*[61] suggests that at Common Law the bailee may be deemed to have warranted the fitness of such materials. While it would seem unnecessary, if not impossible, to apply to such materials the gamut of obligations imposed by ss. 69-72, it may well be desirable that their fitness should be warrantable under ss. 74(1) and (2). Again, the problem is whether such materials are "supplied" for the purpose of that section. It is submitted that a liberal reading of that word, encompassing those cases in which materials are applied or expended for the performance of the work, might be preferable to a more restrictive interpretation.

F. Redelivery

The bailee must complete the work and redeliver the chattel at the appointed time. Where no date is fixed, a reasonable period will be allowed, having regard to such factors as the nature of the work, the availability of any necessary materials and the general conditions or customs of the trade.[62] Where a date is specified and the bailor himself

---

[57] Palmer & Rose, op. cit. at 176.
[58] The position at Common Law is discussed ante, p. 525.
[59] Cf. *Dixon* v. *London Small Arms Co.* (1876) I App. Cas. 632.
[60] "Supply" in this context is defined (but not, it seems, exhaustively) by s. 4 (1) of the Act; but see now App. II post.
[61] [1955] 2 Q.B. 366.
[62] The test is an objective one, based upon the normal time it would take a reasonably competent workman to complete the task in question: *Charnock* v. *Liverpool Corporation* [1968] 1 W.L.R. 1499, at 1506, 1507. Thus in *Charnock's* case it

is not materially at fault, the bailee who fails to deliver at that time is in breach of contract and will henceforth become an insurer of the goods.[63] Whether time is of the essence of the contract, thereby enabling the bailor to rescind if an appointed completion date is not met, depends upon the terms of that agreement.[64] Clearly the parties may stipulate to that effect, as where the owner of a coat tells a cleaner that it must be returned before a certain date because she wishes to wear it for a particular occasion. Whereas there is no general rule that time is an essential element in contracts of work and labour, so that the bailor who wishes to rescind for delay must make clear provision to that effect a persistent or protracted failure to redeliver may entitle him to introduce a subsequent provision into the contract requiring the bailee to complete performance by a certain time and indicating his refusal to accept performance thereafter.[65] His right to do so may depend, however, upon the cause of the delay itself; a failure to complete arising from a strike within the bailee's organisation or from general trade conditions beyond the bailee's control, for instance, will be weaker evidence of an intention on his part to repudiate the contract than mere laziness or inefficiency. No such difficulty arises when the stipulation as to time was originally essential.[66]

The manner of redelivery is likewise a question to be determined by the terms of the bailment. As a general rule, responsibility for collecting the goods will rest upon the bailor. This rule may be varied when the nature of the original delivery (e.g. sending the goods by post) or the normal practice adopted by the bailee (e.g. a collection and delivery round operated by a laundry) suggest that the parties expect a similar process to be adopted in returning the goods to the bailor. In this event, it seems that the bailee who adopts an unauthorised method of redelivery will be strictly liable for losses occurring from its adoption, whether due to his negligence or not. There may even be circumstances in which the bailee is bound, by virtue of his ordinary duty of care, not to employ the agreed method or redelivery. Such an occasion might arise when urgently-needed goods are to be returned by post and the bailee knows that there is a postal strike, or when the chattel is to be collected at

---

was held to be no excuse that the defendant motor-repairer took the goods at a time when (a) he knew that the summer holidays were approaching; (b) he was under-staffed in any event and (c) he was heavily engaged in "warranty work" for a leading manufacturer. It may have been otherwise if he had communicated these facts to the plaintiff beforehand and obtained his consent to a longer delay than was normal, or if the delay had been caused by unforeseen events occurring *after* the vehicle had been bailed to the repairer, such as a strike. See *Hick* v. *Raymond & Reid* [1893] A.C. 22; cf. *Dash* v. *Faulkner* (1886) 2 T.L.R. 255.

[63] Ante, p. 518.
[64] See generally, Lindgren, *Time in the Performance of Contracts;* Treitel, *Law of Contract* (4th edn), p. 566.
[65] Cf. *Charles Rickards Ltd.* v. *Oppenhaim* [1950] 1 K.B. 616, where time was originally an essential provision of the contract but the defendant continued to press for delivery after the date appointed for completion. The Court of Appeal held that he could, on giving reasonable notice, re-introduce the essential term as to time of performance and require delivery by a final, extended date.
[66] Ibid.

the bailee's premises and circumstances beyond his control have subsequently made those premises unsafe.

Where there is a failure to redeliver, this will generally have arisen because the goods are lost, or have been damaged to such a degree that the bailee refuses to accept them. In this event, the bailee's liability will be answered according to his exercise of the proper standard of care. It may be, however, that the goods are capable of redelivery but that this will involve the bailee in greater expense than was originally contemplated. Such an occasion might arise where part of his building has collapsed and the chattel is buried beneath it, or where the goods have been stolen without negligence on his part and have been recovered by the police hundreds of miles away. Prima facie the duty to redeliver is an absolute one which, unless rendered impossible by circumstances equivalent to frustration, remains incumbent upon the bailee regardless of changed events.[67] Occasionally, the contract might be construed as relieving the bailee in the specific circumstances, but as a general rule he carries the burden of increased expense or difficulty in the performance of the labour, whether precipitated by his own default or not. There are few decisions specifically in point and it may be that the courts would impose a reasonableness test in asceretaining the party who is to bear the increased cost of redelivering the goods.[68]

III. THE WORKMAN'S LIEN[69]

A. Particular liens

"A lien" said Grose J. in *Hammonds* v. *Barclay*[70] "is a right in one man to retain that which is in his possession belonging to another until certain demands on him, the person in possession, are satisfied". At Common Law the bailee who has performed work upon a chattel will generally be entitled to a particular lien. This does not entitle him to sell the goods in order to recoup his expenditure[71] unless a special right of sale be conferred by statute, custom or agreement.[72] It merely empowers him to retain them until all obligations "incurred in respect of the goods and chattels subject to the right"[73] are discharged. A particular lien cannot extend to debts that were not incurred in relation to the goods detained.

---

[67] This is particularly evident from those decisions concerned with the duties of the hirer: post, p. 756 et seq.

[68] *British Crane Hire Corporation Ltd.* v. *Ipswich Plant Hire Ltd.* [1975] 1 Q.B. 303; cf. *Percy Bros.* v. *Fly & Young* [1916] N.Z.L.R. 837; [1917] N.Z.L.R. 461; ante, p. 87.

[69] See generally, Vaines, *Personal Property* (5th edn), Chap. 7; Hall, *Possessory Liens; Bowstead on Agency* (13th edn), pp. 217-238; Elliott, *The Artificer's Lien.*

[70] (1802) 2 East. 227, at 235; 102 E.R. 356, at 359.

[71] *Thames Iron Works Co.* v. *Patent Derrick Co.* (1860) 1 John & H. 93. A sale will destroy the lien and render him liable in conversion: *Siebel* v. *Springfield* (1863) 8 New Rep. 36; *Mulliner* v. *Florence* (1878) 3 Q.B.D. 484.

[72] *Thames Iron Works Co.* v. *Patent Derrick Co.* (ante) (shipbuilders: no right to sell merely because chattel causing considerable expense); *Smart* v. *Sanders* (1848) 5 C.B. 895 (factor has no general authority to sell goods in his hands to repay unsatisfied advances made to him principal). For the statutory power to dispose of uncollected goods see ante, p. 396 et seq. and App. I, post.

[73] Bowstead, op cit., p. 217.

There can be no lien without possession of the chattel over which it is asserted.[74] In *Protean Enterprises (Newmarket) Pty. Ltd.* v. *Randall*[75] animal carcasses were seized by the appellant company to secure payment of sums owed to them by Randall. The appellants were lessees of an abattoir from the Melbourne City Council and Randall was a slaughterer whom the appellants, under a licence for reward, permitted to use their slaughtering and storage facilities. Randall, like other operators in a similar position, was allotted a specified area within the abattoir for his own use, and was given the right to use certain refrigeration chambers and pens for purposes of storage. The carcasses seized by the appellants were not the property of Randall but belonged to a third party who had bailed them to Randall for slaughtering. The Court held that, irrespective of other considerations, the appellants could have no lien because they were never in possession of the carcasses until they wrongfully seized them.[76]

Assuming, however, that the bailee acquires and retains possession of the chattel upon which he has expended his labour, it is clear that, in all but exceptional cases, he will enjoy a particular lien. The general rule was upheld by Lord Ellenborough in *Chase* v. *Westmore*,[77] and has since been regularly acknowledged. Lord Ellenborough's decision makes it plain that there is no distinction for the purposes of lien between a contract to pay a stipulated price for labour and an agreement to pay a reasonable sum.

It is established that for a possessory lien to take effect the labour or skill of the artificer must improve the condition of the chattel.[78] Clearly

---

[74] *Kinloch* v. *Craig* (1790) 3 T.R. 783; *Nichols* v. *Clent* (1817) 3 Price 547; *Taylor* v. *Robinson* (1818) 8 Taunt 648; *Sunbolf* v. *Alford* (1838) 3 M. & W. 248; *Re Adams* (1855) 26 L.T.O.S. 96; *Shaw* v. *Neale* (1858) 6 H.L.C. 581, at 601; *Bristow* v. *Whitemore* (1861) 9 H.L.C. 391, at 407; *James Bibby Ltd.* v. *Woods* [1949] 2 K.B. 481, at 499; *Langley, Beldon & Gaunt Ltd.* v. *Morley* [1965] 1 Lloyd's Rep. 297 (which involved a forwarding agent); *The Narada* [1977] 1 Lloyd's Rep. 256; cf. *Wilson* v. *Lombank Ltd.* [1963] 1 All E.R. 740. The original possession must be lawful: *Madden* v. *Kempster* (1807) 1 Camp. 12 N.P.; *Wickens* v. *Townshend* (1830) 1 Russ. & M. 361; *Bernal* v. *Pim* (1835) 1 Gale 17; *Pocock* v. *Novitz* [1912] 4 D.L.R. 105.

[75] [1975] V.R. 327 (Vic. Full Sup. Ct.).

[76] Ibid., at 334, following *Dinmore Meatworks Pty. Ltd.* v. *Kerr* (1963) 108 C.L.R. 628, at 632. Cf. on the question of possession, *Wilmers & Gladwin Pty. Ltd.* v. *W.A.L. Building Supplies Ltd.* (1955) 55 S.R. (N.S.W.) 442; *Fairline Shipping Corporation Ltd.* v. *Adamson* [1975] 1 Q.B. 180; *Gaylard* v. *Milne* [1933] Q.W.N. 47; 28 Q.J.P.R. 1; *G. E. Ry* v. *Lord's Trustee* [1909] A.C. 109.

[77] (1816) 5 M. & S. 180; the workman in this case was a miller. See also *Bleaden* v. *Hancock* (1829) 4 C. & P. 152.

[78] *Judson* v. *Etheridge* (1833) 1 Cromp. & M. 743; *Jackson* v. *Cummins* (1839) 5 M. & W. 342; *Scarfe* v. *Morgan* (1838) 4 M. & W. 270, at 283; *Re Southern Livestock Producers Ltd.* [1964] 1 W.L.R. 24; Paton, *Bailment in the Common Law*, pp. 344-345. The work must also be completed (*Pinnock* v. *Harrison* (1838) 3 M & W. 532) unless the bailor countermands it before completion, in which event the bailee has a lien only for that part which is, in fact, completed: *Lilley* v. *Barnsley* (1844) 1 Car. & Kir. 344. Cf. on the latter point Scrutton L.J. in *Albermarle Supply Co. Ltd.* v. *Hind & Co. Ltd.* [1928] I K.B. 307.

the repair of a car[79] or a ship,[80] or the mending,[81] dyeing[82] or printing[83] of textiles or garments, all fall within the necessary description of improvement: and in such cases a lien has been implied at Common Law.[84] Other examples include the packing of goods,[85] the breaking of horses[86] and (semble) the treatment of sick animals.[87] The owner of a stallion, to whom a mare is sent to be served, has also been held to enjoy a lien at Common Law,[88] and it seems that a similar right may extend to the race-horse trainer[89] and the castrator of bulls.[90] It has been suggested obiter that a right of lien should also apply to a jeweller weighing a diamond or a goldsmith assaying gold.[91]

Conversely, there will be no lien where a garage-owner merely stores, washes and maintains a car[92] or where the bailee of an animal merely feeds and takes care of it.[93] In such a case, the necessary element of improvement is lacking. The same observation is probably true of the factor or bailee for sale, although the factor apparently has a general lien and may well enjoy a lien in any event by virtue of express agreement.[94]

In 1952 Paton stated[95] that a conveyancer has no lien upon deeds

[79] *Tappenden* v. *Artus* [1964] 2 Q.B. 185.
[80] *Franklin* v. *Hosier* (1821) 4 B. & Ald. 341; *Thames Iron Works* case, ante; *The Narada* [1977] 1 Lloyd's Rep. 256; cf. *T. D. Keegan Ltd.* v. *Palmer* [1961] 2 Lloyd's Rep. 449 (repair of aircraft: no lien asserted).
[81] *Hussey* v. *Christie* (1809) 9 East. 426, at 433.
[82] *Bennett* v. *Johnson* (1784) 3 Doug. 387; *Kirkman* v. *Shawcross* (1794) 6 Term. Rep. 14; cf. *Close* v. *Waterhouse* (1802) 6 East. 524n (general lien).
[83] *Webb* v. *Fox* (1797) Peak Add. Cas. 167; and see post, (general lien).
[84] The fuller has a particular lien: *Rose* v. *Hart* (1818) 2 Moore C.P. 547, except in Exeter where it may be general: post, p. 552.
[85] *Ex parte Deeze* (1748) 1 Atk. 228; *In re Witt, Ex parte Shubrook* (1876) 2 Ch. D. 489 (general lien).
[86] *Scarfe* v. *Morgan* (1838) 4 M. & W. 270, at 283.
[87] *Scarfe* v. *Morgan*, ante: cf. *Rushworth* v. *Hadfield* (1806) 7 East. 224, at 229 (in which the lien claimed was a general one and which Paton, p. 344, states on this point to be wrong); *Orchard* v. *Rackstraw* (1850) 9 C.B. 698.
[88] *Scarfe* v. *Morgan*, at 283; *Fly & Young* v. *Percy Bros.* [1916] N.Z.L.R. 837, at 840 (obiter); affirmed on other grounds [1917] N.Z.L.R. 451; *Re Rauf* (1975) 49 D.L.R. (3d) 345 (where the lien was held to extend to the foals). Aliter, where the stallion is not the bailee's own but belongs to a third party: *Re Southern Livestock Producers Ltd.* [1964] 1 W.L.R. 24.
[89] The trainer was held to enjoy a lien in *Green* v. *The Jockey Club* (1975) 119 Sol. Jo. 258, where he recovered from the defendants for negligent injury to a horse while in the latter's custody. Other decisions also accept in principle that a lien should be allowed in this situation, subject to the possibility that the owner's contractual right to call for possession of the animal at any time may be repugnant to the nature of a lien: see *Bevan* v. *Waters* (1828) M. & M. 235; *Scarfe* v. *Morgan*, at 283; *Forth* v. *Simpson* (1849) 13 Q.B. 680; cf. *Jacobs* v. *Latour* (1828) 5 Bing. 130; *Jackson* v. *Cummins* (1839) 5 M. & W. 342; *Malone* v. *Ivey* (1890) 16 V.L.R. 192.
[90] *Helton* v. *Sullivan* [1968] Qd. R. 562; ante, p. 497.
[91] *Steadman* v. *Hockley* (1846) 15 M. & W. 553, at 557 per Pollock C.B.; cf. the judgment of Rolfe B. loc. cit., where this was doubted. For further examples see *Standard Electronic Apparatus Laboratories Ltd.* v. *Stenner*, [1960] N.S.W.R. 447; *Doulton Potteries Ltd.* v. *Bronotte* [1971] 1 N.S.W.L.R. 591.
[92] *Hatton* v. *Car Maintenance Co. Ltd.* [1915] 1 Ch. 621, at 624.
[93] *Re Southern Livestock Producers Ltd.* ante, p. 497. The agister has no lien, neither does the livery-stable keeper: ante, p. 498.
[94] Paton, op. cit., p. 345; ante, p. 499.
[95] *Op. cit.*, pp. 344-345; *Steadman* v. *Hockley* (1846) 15 M. & W. 553, where it was held that a lien could not arise if a certificated conveyancer claimed to retain the deeds on the ground that he had performed work "with respect of" them.

merely because he has performed work for which they are necessary, if he has not expended labour upon the deeds themselves. In modern times, however, it may be that a solicitor may assume a *general* lien over a client's papers irrespective of whether they are the subject-matter of the work or merely an aid to it.[96] Nevertheless, it has been held that this lien does not extend to documents merely deposited with him for safe custody.[97]

It has also been held that an accountant has at least a particular lien over files and account-books delivered to him by a client in the course of his ordinary professional work, including documents which come into the accountant's possession while acting as his client's agent in the course of such work.[98] On a somewhat different level, brokers have been held to possess a lien over insurance policies upon which they have paid premiums on the insured's behalf;[99] and a lien was held to exist in favour of the bailee of manuscripts whose task included the writing of notes upon them.[1]

American authority adheres to the view that the instrument with which work is to be performed, but upon which no labour is to be expended, cannot itself be made the subject of a lien.[2] It seems indisputable that the same rule would be upheld by a modern court in England or Australia,[3] although some of the foregoing decisions involving documents bailed to professional persons might suggest a contrary result.

The parties' agreement may be inconsistent with the existence of a particular lien, in which event no lien can come into being. This may occur, for instance, when the bailor of a chattel for repair has a

---

[96] Cf. *Caldwell* v. *Sumpters* [1972] Ch. 478, where the deeds retained related to a property which the solicitors had been conveying for the plaintiff, and the original existence of a lien was not contested.

[97] *Re Long, Ex. p. Fuller* (1881) 16 Ch. D. 617. See generally, Bowstead, op. cit., p. 220 et seq.; *Conquest* v. *Maffey* (1900) 22 V.L.R. 616; *In re a Solicitor* [1968] 3 N.S.W.R. 404; *Bolster* v. *McCallum* [1966] 2 N.S.W.R. 660.

[98] *Woodworth* v. *Conroy* [1976] 1 All E.R. 107 (C.A.); *John Penman* v. *MacDonald* 1953 S.L.T. (Sh. Ct.) 81; *Re Hill, Ex Parte Southall* (1848) 17 L.J. Bcy. 21 (obiter); *Stuart* v. *Stevenson* (1828) 6 Sh. (Ct. of Sess.) 591; *Findlay* v. *Wadall* 1910 1 S.L.T. 315; *Compass Mapping Corporation of Canada Ltd.* v. *Maw, Devonshire & Co.* ((1954) 11 W.W.R. (N.S.) 108; See also *Raymer & Co.* v. *Goldberg* [1912] S.R. 147; *Spurrier* v. *Coxwell* [1914] C.P.D. 83 (S. Africa); *Anon.* (1830) 1 Russ. & M. 330.

[99] *Levy* v. *Barnard* (1818) 8 Taunt. 149; *Fisher* v. *Smith* (1878) 4 App. Cas. 1.

[1] *Lord Brougham* v. *Cauvin* (1868) 18 L.T. 281.

[2] E.g. *Jeanette Doll Co.* v. *Cusmano* (1923) 120 Misc. 782; 199 N.Y.S. 751: "The law is well settled that, when an article or instrument is delivered by the owner thereof to another, with which instrument the latter is to perform work for the former, the person now using it is not, at Common Law, entitled to a lien on the instrument itself . . . Undoubtedly a lien would exist on the work resulting from the use of the article or instrument referred to, but not on the article or instrument itself".

[3] It is supported by *Steadman* v. *Hockley* (1846) 15 M. & W. 553 ante, and by *Bleaden* v. *Hancock* (1829) 4 C. & P. 152 (no lien over "stereotype plates" bailed to defendant so that he could print from them). See also *Frew* v. *Burnside* (1925) 42 W.N. (N.S.W.) 111, where there was held to be no lien over a tracing which had been used by the artificer to make helio prints. On this principle a printer would not have a lien over a manuscript, although he may well have one upon the proofs. The rule is accepted by Halsbury, *Laws*, vol. ii, para 1571.

regular, periodic account with the repairer[4] or where it is clearly contemplated that the chattel shall be readily available for use by the bailor through the period of work and labour.[5] In each case the question is whether the terms of the bailment are consonant with the exercise of a lien or are calculated to prevent or exclude it.[6]

Normally, a lien is forfeited when the party asserting it loses or transfers possession of the chattel.[7] The loss of possession is a question of fact[8] but the effect this has upon the lien itself is one of law. Again, the question is whether the change of circumstances, and the intentions accompanying it, are inconsistent with the further continuance of the lien,[9] and although in the great majority of cases a loss of possession will permit no other conclusion than that the lien has been extinguished, in exceptional cases it may be deemed to continue. Thus it may be preserved where a solicitor, having a lien over his client's documents, delivers them at his client's request to a third party with a specific reservation that the third party shall hold them to the solicitor's order.[10] Likewise, a solicitor's lien has been held to continue though one of his partners wrongfully removes the relevant documents upon leaving the firm,[11] and a broker's lien has been held to survive although, in accordance with Stock Exchange custom, the broker returned the share certificates in question to the owner on the day the moneys became payable.[12] Where possession is regained by the bailor through a misrepresentation, it seems that the lienee may, by retaking the goods without the use of force, cause the lien to revive.[13]

A lien will be extinguished by payment of the amount due for the labour performed, or by tender of the same amount if such tender is then unreasonably refused.[14] In this regard, it is important to note that

---

[4] *Wilson* v. *Lombank Ltd.* [1963] 1 All E.R. 740, at 743; *Raitt* v. *Mitchell* (1815) 4 Camp. 146 N.P.; *Crawshay* v. *Homfray* (1820) 4 B. & Ald. 50; *Chase* v. *Westmore* (1816) M. & S. 180.

[5] *Hatton* v. *Car Maintenance Co. Ltd.* [1915] 1 Ch. 621; *Scarfe* v. *Morgan* (1838) 4 M. & W. 270, at 284; *Jackson* v. *Cummins* (1839) 5 M. & W. 342; *Hartley* v. *Hitchcock* (1816) 1 Stark. 408, N.P.; *Albermarle Supply Co. Ltd.* v. *Hind & Co.* [1928] 1 K.B. 307. Cf. *James Bibby Ltd.* v. *Woods* [1949] 2 K.B. 449.

[6] *Chase* v. *Westmore* (1816) 5 M. & S. 180.

[7] *Lickbarrow* v. *Mason* (1793) 6 East. 20n; *Kruger* v. *Wilcox* (1755) Amb. 252; *Hathesing* v. *Laing* (1873) L.R. 17 Eq. 92: and see post.

[8] *Bernal* v. *Pim* (1835) 1 Gale 17.

[9] *Hill & Sons Ltd.* v. *London Central Markets Cold Storage Co. Ltd.* (1910) 26 T.L.R. 397 (Hamilton L.J.).

[10] *Caldwell* v. *Sumpters* [1972] Ch. 478. Megarry J. held that this condition was a clear expression of intention not to abandon the lien, and that the third party's possession was that of the solicitor himself for the purposes of the lien.

[11] *Re Carter, Carter* v. *Carter* (1885) L.J. Ch. 230.

[12] *Burra* v. *Ricardo* (1885) Cab. & El. 478; 1 T.L.R. 230.

[13] *Wallace* v. *Woodgate* (1824) 1 C. & P. 575; cf. *Levy* v. *Barnard* (1818) 8 Taunt. 149; *Millburn* v. *Millburn* (1848) 4 U.C.R. 179 (Canada).

[14] *Caunce* v. *Spanton* (1844) 7 Man. & G. 903; 135 E.R. 367; cf. *Hardingham* v. *Allen* (1848) 5 C.B. 793; 136 E.R. 1091 (where the tender was of a lesser amount and the party tendering it did not state which part of the total debt was to be discharged by the sum tendered: *held* the lien was not lost); *Jenkyns* v. *Brown* (1849) 14 Q.B. 496; 117 E.R. 193 (where the tender was abortive because certain bills could not be found at the time and the party making the tender was instructed to return later: *held* the lien survived); *Gamblings Ltd.* v. *Westons* [1933] S.A.S.R. 26 (where, upon an offer of payment being made, the lienee further claimed certain additional sums not covered by the lien: *held* the lien was

a refusal to pay or to tender sums with respect to which no lien can be asserted, such sums being simply aggregated to the bailee into one general debt due from the bailor, does not by itself prevent an extinguishment of the lien if payment or tender of those amounts for which the lien *is* legitimately exerted has been made.[15] Moreover, the bailee's own response to a claim for redelivery, or to a payment or tender of payment, may preclude his subsequent exercise of the lien. This may occur when he takes additional security[16] or claims an excessive or different amount from that owing to him.[17] In the latter respect, it may be that there is a distinction between the bailee who merely groups all charges into a general debt and claims a lien for them, and a lienee who claims to exercise his lien for specific items.[18] In the former case, the lien is said to be destroyed, while in the latter it survives in relation to those items for which it can legitimately be claimed. Possibly this distinction is no longer valid and the lien would subsist upon those charges for which it is properly exercised, irrespective of the generality of the claim.[19]

The bailee may also lose his lien if, having been asked to deliver the goods, he claims to retain them upon a different ground from that conferred by the lien.[20] A wrongful sale or other act of conversion will likewise terminate the lien,[21] as will an express waiver thereof or any sequence of conduct from which a waiver can be implied.[22]

---

discharged because it had been shown that the lienee would not have released the goods upon tender of the proper amount); a similar case is *Ayling* v. *Williams* (1832) 5 C. & P. 399 N.P. See further, p. 901 post, (innkeeper's lien).

[15] *Gambling's Ltd.* v. *Westons* [1933] S.A.S.R. 26.
[16] *Cowell* v. *Simpson* (1809) 16 Ves. 275; *Hewison* v. *Guthrie* (1836) 2 Bing. N.C. 755; *Mason* v. *Morley (No. 1)* (1863) 34 Beav. 471. But the effect of alternative security is a question of intention and not a rule of law. Thus the taking of security may be quite consistent with the continuance of the lien, as recognised in *Solarte* v. *Hilbers* (1832) 1 L.J.K.B. 196; *Re Taylor* [1891] 1 Ch. 590; *Re Westlake* (1881) 16 Ch. D. 604. See further the cases concerning innkeepers discussed at p. 900 et seq., post.
[17] *Ayling* v. *Williams* (1832) 5 C. & P. 399, N.P.; *Jones* v. *Tarleton* (1842) 9 M. & W. 675; 152 E.R. 285 (where a tender was deemed to be waived by the making of such a demand).
[18] *Scarfe* v. *Morgan* (1838) 4 M. & W. 270, at 283.
[19] Cf. *Park* v. *Berkery* (1930) 25 Tas. S.R. 67; post, p. 901.
[20] *Boardman* v. *Sill* (1808) 1 Camp. 410n; *Skinner* v. *Lambert* (1850) 16 L.T.O.S. 244; *Weekes* v. *Goode* (1859) 6 C.B.N.S. 367; cf. *Kerford* v. *Mondel* (1859) 28 L.J. Ex. 303; *White* v. *Gainer* (1824) 2 Bing. 21; 130 E.R. 212. In the latter case, the party possessing the lien purchased the goods in question from the bailor after the latter's bankruptcy. When approached by the bailor's assignees, he replied "I may as well give up every transaction of my life". It was held that these words did not disentitle him from relying upon the lien. The Court agreed that if he had explicitly relied upon his purchase of the goods as a defence to the assignees the lien would have been extinguished; but his actual reply was perfectly consistent with a reliance upon the lien itself and there was no such inconsistency of claim as would defeat it. The case illustrates the principle that a lien may be enforced although, at the time of the demand, no specific reliance upon the lien itself was manifested.
[21] *Gurr* v. *Cuthbert* (1843) 12 L.J. Ex. 309 (lienee cutting up and using hay); *Mulliner* v. *Florence* (1878) 3 Q.B.D. 484 (sale). See further *Clark* v. *Gilbert* (1835) 2 Bing. N.C. 343; 132 E.R. 135, as to the attachment of a lien to the proceeds of a wrongful sale; *Barry* v. *Longmore* (1840) 4 Per. & Day. 344.
[22] See generally *Morley* v. *Hay* (1828) 3 Man. & Ry. K.B. 396; *Re Noble* (1833) 3 Deac. & Ch. 310; *Harrison* v. *Scott* (1846) 4 Moo. P.C.C. 357; *Re Aubusson*

The bailee must take reasonable care of the goods throughout the period of the lien.[23] He is not entitled to add storage or maintenance charges in respect of the period after which the lien was asserted to the amount due under the lien.[24] Nor is he entitled to sell the chattel in order to avert the expense of keeping and maintaining it.[25] He is further prohibited from using the chattel.[26]

Occasionally an artificer who has redelivered part of the subject-matter to the bailor will seek to claim a lien over the remainder of the goods to the extent of his entire charges, and not merely for the cost of his work upon those items that actually remain in his possession. Whether the bailee can legitimately do this depends upon whether the subject-matter of the work was treated as an entirety by the contracting parties or merely as a collection of separate units. The latter conclusion was reached in *Dinmore Meatworks Pty. Ltd.* v. *Kerr*,[27] where a slaughterer was held not to be entitled to a lien upon meat in his possession for the whole amount of the bailor's indebtedness but merely for those charges which related to the preparation of the meat still in his possession.[28]

alone (ante, p. 000); and see further *Doulton Potteries Ltd.* v. *Bronotte* [1971]

The bailor who seeks to repossess goods in violation of a legitimate lien will be liable in trepass or conversion.[29]

In South Australia certain classes of artificer enjoy a specific statutory lien by virtue of the *Workmen's Liens Act* 1893-1964;[30] but this is confined to work relating to land and does not (except insofar as there is a statutory power of sale under s. 41 of the Act) affect the law of bailment.

(1821) 1 Gl. & J. 25; *Buck* v. *Shippam* (1846) 1 Ph. 694; *Jacobs* v. *Latour* (1828) 5 Bing. 130. Cf. *Farmeloe* v. *Bain* (1876) 1 C.P.D. 445.

---

[23] *G. W. Ry. & Co.* v. *Crouch* (1858) 3 H. & N. 83; Hall, *Possessory Liens*, pp. 62-64. See further, p. 900 post, (innkeepers).

[24] *Somes* v. *British Empire Shipping Co.* (1860) 8 H.L.C. 338; *Bruce* v. *Everson* 5 D.L.R. (2d) 46, at 56. The position may differ when the bailment was for custody (1883) 1 Cab. & El. 18; *General Securities Ltd.* v. *Brett's (Lillooet) Ltd.* (1956) 1 N.S.W.L.R. 591 (declaration that locator should pay a reasonable price for repairs and storage costs whereupon injunction would issue restraining artificer from preventing locator from removing the chattel from its place of safekeeping in a bank).

[25] *Thames Iron Works Co.* v. *Patent Derrick Co.* ante, p. 543.

[26] *Cooke* v. *Haddon* (1862) 3 F. & F. 173. Aliter if this is necessary to its preservation or safekeeping.

[27] (1963) 108 C.L.R. 628.

[28] Cf. *Blake* v. *Nicholson* (1814) 3 M. & S. 167 (tailor held to have particular lien for price of entire suit upon any part thereof; a similar principle would probably apply to the printer).

[29] *Standard Electronic Apparatus Laboratories Pty. Ltd.* v. *Stenner* [1960] N.S.W.R. 447.

[30] As to the degree of territorial connection that must be existent between the State of South Australia and the debt sought to be enforced by way of charge by a builder under the statute, see *W. Cure & Sons, Regd.* v. *Buck Industries Pty. Ltd.* [1972] 2 S.A.S.R. 335.

B. General lien

A general lien may be created by custom or by agreement.[31] When effectively asserted, it entitles the workman to retain goods as security for debts which have been incurred not only in relation to the goods themselves but for other purposes: e.g., for a general balance of account between himself and the bailor.[32] "Where an individual is permitted to retain the goods of another, which are in his possession, until all claims against the owner in respect of a general balance of account are satisfied, whether such claims arise in respect of the particular goods or not, the person in possession is said to have a general lien."[33] General liens offer manifest advantages to the bailee, and the circumstances in which they are deemed to arise are correspondingly limited. The law does not favour them[34] and they must be strictly proved. Hall[35] defines the three requirements of a customary general lien as follows:

> . . . each must be demonstrated as a matter of law by the party asserting the lien.
> (1) The usage must be certain;
> (2) It must be reasonable and not inconsistent with the general law;[36]
> (3) It must be so universally acquiesced in that everybody involved in the relevant trade must be taken to have known of it, or must be taken to be capable of ascertaining it upon enquiry.

The latter requirement has been recently examined in two Australian decisions. In *Majeau Carrying Co., Pty. Ltd.* v. *Coastal Rutile Ltd.*[37] Stephen J. stressed that the standard of proof is a high one and cited with approval a passage from Brown on Custom and Usage:[38]

> Seeing that custom is only to be inferred from a large number of individual acts, it is evident that the only proof of the existence of a usage must be by the multiplication or aggregation of a great number of particular instances: but these instances must not

---

[31] For cases involving an implied agreement to this effect, see *Aspinall* v. *Pickford* (1802) 3 Bos. & P. 44n. (carrier); *Demainbray* v. *Metcalf* (1715) 2 Vern. 691, 698 (S.C.). Sometimes this agreement may be created by a general notice to that effect given out by bodies of tradesmen: e.g., *Kirkman* v. *Shawcross* (1794) 6 T.R. 14, where the dyers of Manchester passed resolutions that they would accept goods only on the basis of a general lien, and published their resolutions. Cf. *Oppenheim* v. *Russell* (1802) 3 Bos. & P. 42.

[32] Bowstead, *op cit.*, p. 217.

[33] Hall, *Possessory Liens*, pp. 22-23. For the distinction between general and particular liens, see further *Dinmore Meat Works Pty. Ltd.* v. *Kerr* (1963) 108 C.L.R. 628, at 632-633.

[34] Ante, p. 495. See especially per Le Blanc J. in *Rushford* v. *Hadfield* (1805) 6 East. 519, at 528: ". . . general liens are a great inconvenience to the bulk of the generality of traders, because they give a particular advantage to certain individuals who claim to themselves a special privilege against the body of creditors at large, instead of coming in with them for an equal share of the insolvent estate".

[35] Op. cit., p. 34.

[36] As to reasonableness, see *Leuckhart* v. *Cooper* (1836) 3 Bing. N.C. 99. A further requirement is that the custom should be uniform in its operation: *Majeau Carrying Co. Pty. Ltd.* v. *Coastal Rutile Ltd.* (1973) 1 A.L.R. 1, at 10; *Nelson* v. *Dahl* (1879) 12 Ch. D. 568, at 575.

[37] (1973) 1 A.L.R. 1 (H.C.). The decision is also discussed ante, p. 495 et seq.

[38] Adopted by Darley C.J. in *Anderson* v. *Wadey* (1899) 20 L.R. (N.S.W.) 412, at 417-418.

be miscellaneous in character, but must have a principle of unity running through their variety, and that unity must show a certain course of business and an established understanding respecting it.[39]

Accordingly no lien could be asserted by the appellants in the present case, notwithstanding that they produced evidence of its successful assertion by fellow warehousemen in the same State over the previous five or six years; and that these latter warehousemen included such a right in their standard printed forms of contract.

Similar principles were invoked to reject the appellants' assertion of a general lien in *Protean Enterprises (Newmarket) Pty. Ltd.* v. *Randall*.[40] In this case the lien was alleged to extend to animal carcasses belonging to parties other than the debtor.[41] This contention was repudiated, inter alia, on the grounds that insufficient proof had been adduced of the alleged custom, or of the owner's knowledge thereof.

> In order to establish a usage at the abattoirs there must be evidence of a repetitive course of conduct and general acceptance of that conduct by all persons involved in and affected in their business dealings by the conduct of operations at the abattoirs. Mr. Berkeley submitted that although there were only a few incidents of enforcing or attempting to enforce the lien, nevertheless to justify a finding of the existence of a possessory lien by trade, custom or usage in the abattoirs, it was not necessary to prove that the lien had been enforced on many occasions, but rather it was necessary to look at the repetitive creation of the lien by the conduct of the operators and their general acceptance of such condition. To say the least, there was little or no evidence to support any such findings. In substance there was nothing further proved than appeared in the evidence of the manager . . . This might have been interpreted as *Protean* laying down conditions for operators using the facilities of the abattoirs and thereby forming part of the contract between *Randall (the debtor)* and *Protean* but it could not form the basis of a finding of a usage or trade custom at the abattoirs or a repetitious course of conduct of creating liens to the knowledge of the defendant butchers.[42]

Most of the situations in which a general lien has been judicially recognised involve old-established trades or callings; often, the right will be confined to a particular locality. In addition to those professions and trades set out in Chapter 13,[43] general liens have been successfully asserted

---

[39] (1973) 1 A.L.R. 1, at 10; see also Gibbs J. at 3, who described the custom as "So notorious that everybody in the trade contracts on the basis that it forms a term of the contract."

[40] [1975] V.R. 327 (Vic. Full Supreme Court). The facts are set out at p. 544, ante.

[41] As to the validity of such liens generally, see p. 1008 et seq., post.

[42] [1975] V.R. 327, at 332-333.

[43] Ante, p. 494.

by:—packers;[44] calico printers;[45] the fullers of Exeter;[46] the dyers of Manchester;[47] and the bleachers of Nottingham;[48] whereas the following have failed to establish customary general liens:—the dyers of Halifax;[49] dyers generally;[50] forwarding agents in the West Riding;[51] slaughterers at Melbourne;[52] warehousemen in Queensland or Brisbane;[53] engravers as against calico printers.[54]

The methods by which a general lien may be waived or extinguished are equivalent to those in the case of particular liens.

---

[44] *Ex parte Deeze* (1748) 1 Atk. 228; *Green* v. *Farmer* (1768) 4 Burr. 2214, at 2222 (obiter); *Re Witt, Ex parte Shubrook* (1876) 2 Ch. D. 489. This lien extends to money lent to the bailor because, as Lord Mansfield and Mellish L.J. observed respectively in the last two cases, the packer generally acted as a factor.

[45] *Webb* v. *Fox* (1797) Peake Add. Cas. 167, N.P.; *Weldon* v. *Gould* (1801) 3 *Esp.* 268: "but . . . it must be for work done in the course of that business, for which the lien was claimed:— they could not have a lien for money lent, or for any collateral matter: it should be confined to work done in that particular business", per Lord Kenyon.

[46] *Sweet* v. *Pym* (1800) 1 East 4: semble, although the point seems to have been assumed rather than decided.

[47] *Kirkman* v. *Shawcross* (1794) 6 Term. Rep. 14 ante, p. 550: the resolution also included dressers, whisters, printers, calenderers and bleachers. As to dyers generally, see post.

[48] (1866) 4 F. & F. 1074, where Willes J. held that evidence of practice and custom in adjoining localities may be relevant. But cf. *Cassils & Co.* v. *Holden Wood Bleaching Co. Ltd.* (1915) 112 L.T. 373, where the bleaching was sub-contracted by calico-printers and no lien, particular or general, was upheld; see further, post, p. 1008.

[49] *Close* v. *Waterhouse* (1802) 6 East. 524n.

[50] *Green* v. *Farmer* ante, n. 44; *Bennett* v. *Johnson* (1784) 3 Doug. 387; Hall, *op cit.*, p. 47; but cf. *Savill* v. *Barchard* (1801) 4 Esp. 53; *Humphreys* v. *Partridge* (1803) Unrep. (cited by Hall, *op. cit.*, p. 47) where the dyers' lien was upheld.

[51] *Langley, Beldon & Gaunt Ltd.* v. *Morley* [1965] 1 Lloyd's Rep. 297; see generally, Hill, *Freight Forwarders*, p. 212 et seq., and cf. *Societa Anonima Angelo Castelletti* v. *Transmaritime Ltd.* [1953] 2 Lloyd's Rep. 440, at 449 (particular lien).

[52] *Protean Enterprises (Newmarket) Pty. Ltd.* v. *Randall* [1975] V.R. 327.

[53] *Majeau Carrying Co.'s case*, ante.

[54] *Lilley* v. *Barnsley* (1844) 1 Car. & Kir. 344.

CHAPTER 15

CARRIAGE OF GOODS BY ROAD

The principles that govern the carriage of goods by road are, like the rules applying to carriage generally, based upon wide historical foundations. The duty of a common carrier to carry and deliver goods entrusted to him safely, and to answer for any loss of or damage to those goods, developed as part of the law of bailment well before greater stress was laid upon its contractual element.[1] The duty of a carrier to safeguard the goods is considered at common law to exist apart from contract and is laid upon him not as a consequence of the contract of carriage but because he has been put in possession of another's goods. One of the consequences of this is that the owner of goods may successfully sue a carrier for loss or damage to goods even though no contract of carriage can be proved.[2] Despite the virtual extinction of the common carrier for the purposes of English law the position of the common carrier is still of considerable relevance in Australia.[3] Even so, the present law relating to carriage of goods can be made comprehensible only by understanding the distinction between common and private carriers.

I. COMMON CARRIERS

A common carrier is one who undertakes for reward[4] to transport the goods of any who wish to employ his services. Even though a carrier limits the kind of goods he is prepared to carry and/or the route on which they are carried, he may still remain a common carrier.[5] Likewise, his status as such is not lost if he holds himself as ready to carry goods between two fixed termini[6] or even where the termini are not fixed[7] or where one lies outside the jurisdiction.[8]

A carrier will not be a common carrier if he holds himself out as ready to carry goods for the general public in connection only with another business to which the carriage of goods is ancillary.[9] A common carrier

---

[1] See Kahn-Freund, *The Law of Carriage by Inland Transport*, p. 194.
[2] Ibid., and see ante, p. 14.
[3] See Chapter 18.
[4] He must perform the service for reward; *Bennett* v. *Peninsular Steamboat Co. Ltd.* (1848) 6 C.B. 775, at 787 per Wilde C.J. A gratuitous carrier is not a common carrier: *Tyly* v. *Morrice* (1699) Carth 485. Consideration need not, however, be furnished by the person suing the common carrier; see Paton, *Bailment in the Common Law*, pp. 238-239.
[5] *Johnson* v. *Midland Railway* (1849) 4 Exch. 367, at 373.
[6] Ibid.
[7] *Belfast Ropework Co.* v. *Bushell* [1918] 1 K.B. 210, at 214.
[8] *Crouch* v. *L.N.W. Railway* (1854) 14 C.B. 255, at 289; *Pianciani* v. *L.S.W. Railway* (1856) 18 C.B. 226.
[9] *Consolidated Tea and Lands Co. Ltd.* v. *Oliver's Wharf* [1910] 2 K.B. 395.

who represents himself as prepared to allow all passengers to carry a given amount of personal luggage free of charge with them is a common carrier of such luggage. Accompaniment of the luggage by a passenger does not prevent the carrier from being a common carrier to the same extent as if they had not been so accompanied.[10] The above rule does not apply unless the public carrier of passengers is also a common carrier of goods; to be a common carrier the carrier must hold himself out as ready to carry goods for the public whether accompanied by the passenger or not.[11]

The way a carrier describes himself is not decisive of his status; this is for the court to judge according to the facts of each case.[12] Thus if a carrier reserves the right to refuse to carry goods and exercises that right in each case he is not a common carrier. Thus a carrier holding himself out as ready to carry goods for the public but who gives an estimate and negotiates the price of particular goods to be carried, e.g. furniture, is not a common carrier in respect of those goods, though he is for other goods where he does not require such a procedure.[13] Nor will a carrier be a common carrier if he carries only for particular persons.[14] The fact that a carrier is a common carrier at some times does not make this so at all times.[15]

There has been a demonstrable tendency on the part of the courts during the last hundred years not to attach the liability of common carriers to carriers by road.[16] Nevertheless, the fact that a road carrier habitually enters into special contracts does not ipso facto make him a private carrier. For instance, in *Hunt & Winterbotham (West of England) Ltd.* v. *B.R.S. (Parcels) Ltd.*[17] the defendants admitted that they were common carriers.

---

[10] *Munster* v. *S.E. Railway* (1858) 4 C.B. (N.S.) 676, at 703.

[11] *Rosenthal* v. *London County Council* (1924) 131 L.T. 563. See Kahn-Freund, op. cit., pp. 598-609.

[12] *Belfast Ropework Co.* v. *Bushell* [1918] 1 K.B. 210, at 212; *Eastman Chemical International A.G.* v. *N.M.T. Trading Ltd.* [1972] 2 Lloyd's Rep. 25. See also *Dar es Salaam Motor Transport Co. Ltd.* v. *Mehta and Others* [1970] H.C.D. (Tanz.) 179, at 180 per Georges C.J. applying dicta of Bailhache J. in the *Belfast Ropework* case: "A transporter who behaves like a common carrier cannot remove himself from that category by stating that in fact he is not a common carrier. The conduct of his business must be consistent with his description of himself." (at 210). In the Tanzanian case a condition in a notice on a carrier's premises which reserved the right to refuse dangerous goods was held not to have been communicated to the plaintiff or their agents, although receipts specified that parcels were accepted and carried subject to conditions of carriage, but without reference to the exhibition of notices on the carrier's premises. No instance was given by the carriers of their having refused to carry a parcel. In *Siohn* v. *R. H. Hagland & Sons (Transport) Ltd.* [1976] 2 Lloyd's Rep. 428 the defendants were held to be common carriers. They were road carriers who specialized in the carriage of hanging garments and occasionally transported other light, clean loads. Circulars were issued by the defendants detailing their services directed to persons not already customers, inviting them to use their services. Cusack J. (at 429) particularly noted the cases cited to him of *Ingate & Anor* v. *Christie* (1850) 3 C. & K. 61 and *Belfast Ropework Co. Ltd.* v. *Bushell* [1918] 1 K.B. 210, at 215.

[13] *Electric Supply Stores* v. *Gaywood* (1909) 100 L.T. 855.

[14] *Re Oxlade and N. E. Railway* (1864) 15 C.B. (N.S.) 680.

[15] See *R. M. Griffiths & Co. Ltd.* v. *Armstrong & Springhall Ltd.* [1975] 1 N.Z.L.R. 115, at 116; and see post.

[16] See Kahn-Freund at 204 et seq., citing *Brind* v. *Dale* (1837) 8 Car. & P. 207; *Belfast Ropework Co.* v. *Bushell* (ante); *Watkins* v. *Cottell* [1916] 1 K.B. 10; *Electric Supply Stores* v. *Gaywood* (ante).

[17] [1962] 1 Q.B. 617; see also *G.N. Railway* v. *L.E.P. Transport Co.* [1922] 2 K.B. 742 where a similar admission was made.

This case illustrates the point that a carrier can publicly withdraw from such profession and can either announce the cessation of his operations or their continuation by him as a private carrier; but he must in this event leave no doubt that he is not to be regarded as a common carrier. It will not be sufficient for this purpose that he is known to limit his liability by contract. By omitting to enter into a special contract on one occasion such a carrier will then be liable as a common carrier.[18]

In practice carriers by road, in common with other carriers, contract out of their common law liability. Therefore if a carrier is unable for economic reasons to choose the type of consignment he wishes to carry he can avoid becoming a common carrier by a safeguarding contractual provision such as that included in the Road Haulage Association's conditions of carriage.[19]

A. The contract of carriage

Normally there will be no difficulty in identifying the person with whom the contract of carriage is made. When the consignor remains the owner of the goods throughout the period of transit, he alone can be sued for freight and he alone may sue upon the carrier's contractual undertakings. Difficulties arise, however, when the goods have been sold to a consignee and when the passing of property to the buyer either precedes or is itself effected by the delivery of the goods to the carrier, or occurs during the course of transit. In such a case, the general rule is that the consignor enters into the contract of carriage as agent for the buyer (consignee), and accordingly that it is the consignee alone who can sue and be sued upon the contract. He is deemed to be the bailor of the carrier, and it is his title (and his alone) that the carrier is estopped from disputing.[20]

In limited cases, however, it may be possible to establish a special agreement by the carrier to answer to the consignor for the full extent of any loss or damage to the goods, notwithstanding that the consignor no longer owns the goods and is not answerable for their impairment to the consignee. The circumstances in which this special right to extra-compensatory damages may be enforced are discussed elsewhere in the present work.[21]

Moreover, an action against the carrier need not be based upon any contractual obligation; the mere fact that he is in possession of goods which belong to another will generally entitle that other person to proceed against him as a bailee.[22] Thus, even where there exists a special contract of the kind indicated in the preceding paragraph, this will not disable the consignee from proceeding against the carrier; and when goods are sub-

---

18 Op. cit., Kahn-Freund, p. 197. The position of British Rail is discussed in Chapter 18; see *Transport Act* 1962 s. 43(6).
19 See condition 2, discussed below. The position in Australia is discussed later in this chapter.
20 *The Albazero* [1976] 3 All E.R. 129, at 132-133 per Lord Diplock; *Dawes* v. *Peck* (1799) 8 T.R. 330. Cf. now s. 8, *Torts (Interference with Goods) Act*, 1977.
21 *The Albazero;* see p. 187 ante.
22 In exceptional cases the carrier may be excused on the ground that he did not consent to stand as bailee to anyone other than the person delivering the goods to him: Chapter 20, post. Note that for certain purposes the action against a carrier may be characterised as one in tort: ante, p. 54.

bailed to a carrier, either the original or the intermediate bailor will normally be entitled to proceed against him for loss or damage to the goods.[23] Similarly, when goods belong both prior to the contract of carriage and throughout the period of transit to someone other than the consignor, that other party will be entitled to proceed against the carrier for breach of his Common Law duties as a bailee but the contract of carriage will generally be deemed to be between the carrier and the consignor. An example of this situation might arise when a bailee (such as a launderer) delivers goods to a carrier for transportation to their owner. The carrier will be deemed to be the bailee of the deliveror (or consignor) and will evidently be estopped from disputing the latter's title,[24] but he may be concurrently liable to the owner of the goods,[25] provided the owner can establish either an immediate right to possess,[26] or damage to his reversionary interest.[26a]

Where neither the consignor nor the consignee are owners of the goods, the contract is deemed to have been made on behalf of the owner by consignor. But if a consignor as agent sends goods owned by his principal to another agent the consignor in his capacity as bailee may be entitled to claim damages for loss or injury from the carrier.

The general principle is that servants of a carrier and any contractors or agents he employs in the carrying out of the contract are not normally parties to it. However, where the carrier clearly establishes in making the contract that he acts as agents for those whom he employs they will be parties to the contract and may be able to rely on the exemption clauses in the contract. This matter is discussed later and in detail elsewhere in the work.[27]

B. Liability of a common carrier

A common carrier is under three special obligations at common law. These are: (a) to accept for carriage goods delivered to him provided he has space to carry them on his vehicle,[28] (b) to charge only a reasonable rate for carriage,[29] (c) to be strictly answerable for all loss or damage that occurs during the course of carriage. Each will be dealt with in turn.

1. *Duty of acceptance*: If a common carrier refuses to accept goods for carriage without lawful justification he is liable in damages for tort on the basis of wrongful refusal.[30] He will, however, be justified in refusing in the following circumstances:—

---

[23] E.g. *Philip Morris (Australia) Ltd.* v. *The Transport Commission* [1975] Tas. S.R. 128; and see generally Chapter 20, post.

[24] *Freeman* v. *Birch* (1833) 3 Q.B. 492.

[25] Cf. *Gwyatt* v. *Hayes* (1871) 2 A.J.R. 107.

[26] Cf. *Kahler* v. *Midland Bank Ltd.* [1950] A.C. 24.

[26a] *Moukataff* v. *B.O.A.C. Ltd.* [1967] 1 Lloyd's Rep. 396.

[27] Chapter 26, post.

[28] *Jackson* v. *Rogers* (1683) 2 Show. 327; *Lane* v. *Cotton* (1701) 12 Mod. 472, at 484; *Riley* v. *Horne* (1828) 5 Bing. 217, at 224.

[29] *Pickford* v. *Grand Junction Railway* (1841) 8 M. & W. 372, at 377; *G.W. Railway* v. *Sutton* (1869) L.R. 4 H.L. 226, at 237.

[30] A carrier who unjustifiably refused to carry was stated also to be guilty of a common law misdemeanour in *Pozzi* v. *Shipton* (1838) 1 Per. & Dav. 4, at 12 per Patterson J. There is no reported case of such an indictment so the liability is probably obsolete; Ridley, op. cit., p. 13.

(i) Where his vehicle is full.[31] The carrier is not bound to run a special vehicle in such circumstances or to operate one outside his normal schedule;

(ii) Where the goods are not of the class he usually carries, either because they are outside those specified by him or because, in the absence of such specification, it would be unreasonable to expect him to carry them;[32]

(iii) Where the goods are dangerous[33] or their size is exceptional,[34] or they would expose the carrier to undue risk,[35] or their value is disproportionate to his safety measures;[36]

(iv) Where the goods are not properly packed;[37]

(v) Where the consignor refuses to inform the carrier, at his request, as to the nature of the goods carried;[38]

(vi) Where the goods were tendered at an unreasonable time before the carrier was ready for his journey;[39]

(vii) Where the consignor fails to pay freight on request when the goods are delivered to the carrier for carriage.[40] If, however, the carrier refuses to carry goods for a consignor who is apparently solvent, unless the consignor pays in legal tender *before* delivery to the carrier, then the carrier is liable for unlawful refusal to carry.[41]

Goods accepted by the carrier, which he could justifiably have refused, are then carried in his capacity as a common carrier, subject to any special contract he may make.[42]

2. *Reasonable charges*: If the carrier demands an unreasonably high freight rate this constitutes a refusal to carry and the carrier is liable accordingly.[43] A common carrier is not liable to charge all consignors the same freight; there is nothing to prevent him from charging an unreasonably low rate or none at all. The only requirement is that the charge should be reasonable.[44] What is a reasonable charge is determined by the circumstances. A common carrier can demand a higher rate for delivering two parcels to different consignees than for the same number to one consignee. Similarly a higher rate can be demanded for goods to be

---

[31] *Jackson* v. *Rogers*, ante.
[32] See Leslie, op. cit., p. 8.
[33] *Bamfield* v. *Goole and Sheffield Transport Co. Ltd.* [1910] 2 K.B. 94, at 115.
[34] *Date* v. *Sheldon* (1921) 7 Ll.L.R. 53, at 54.
[35] *Edwards* v. *Sherratt* (1801) 1 East 604 (district unsafe on account of riot).
[36] *Batson* v. *Donovan* (1820) 4 B. & Ald. 21, at 32.
[37] *Munster* v. *S.E. Railway Co.* (1858) 4 C.B. (N.S.) 676, at 701.
[38] *Riley* v. *Horne*, ante.
[39] *Lane* v. *Cotton* (1701) 12 Mod. 472, at 481.
[40] *Wyld* v. *Pickford* (1841) 8 M. & W. 443.
[41] *Pickford* v. *Grand Junction Railway Co.* (1841) 8 M. & W. 372 (semble).
[42] As to entitlement to exclusion of liability by a common carrier by means of a special contract where under a duty to carry, see *G.N. Railway Co. Ltd.* v. *L.E.P. Transport and Depository Ltd.* [1922] 2 K.B. 742.
[43] *Harris* v. *Packwood* (1810) 3 Taunt. 264, at 272; *Garton* v. *Bristol and Exeter Railway Co.* (1861) 1 B. & S. 112, at 162 per Cockburn C.J.
[44] *G.W. Railway* v. *Sutton* (1869) L.R. 4 H.L. 226, 237, per Blackburn J. Where an unreasonable charge is levied the difference may be recovered on an action for money had and received; *Baxendale* v. *L.S.W. Railway* (1866) L.R. 1 Ex. 137. Where a carrier usually charges less than a reasonable rate, he can make a particular consignor pay more than the usual rate provided it does not amount to more than a reasonable rate; *Baxendale's* case, ante.

carried through an area where they are especially liable to theft, where the carrier will be liable for loss.[45]

3. *Liability for loss or damage of goods in transit*: A common carrier is liable for any loss or damage to goods while in possession of them as a carrier. He is, prima facie, strictly liable for all loss and damage that occurs in transit.[46] This is described in various texts as an "insurer's liability"[47] although this is strictly inaccurate.[48] Such liability arises where goods are lost or damaged by wrongful acts of third parties,[49] such as robbery,[50] accidental fire,[51] riot,[52] or other inevitable accident.[53] The liability can be traced to the early eighteenth century where in *Coggs* v. *Bernard*,[54] Holt C.J. justified it on the grounds of policy.[55] It is for the carrier to prove that the damage to the goods was caused by one of those causes for which he, as a common carrier, is not liable. These, the four excepted perils, are as follows:

(i) Act of God: This constitutes any operation of natural forces which it is not reasonably possible to anticipate or to guard against.[56] The carrier has only to establish that it was sufficiently unusual that he could not reasonably be expected to guard against it.[57]

(ii) Act of the Queen's enemies: For practical purposes an act of the Queen's enemies is restricted to acts of armed forces with which the country is at war. The acts of bandits, armed robbers, rioters and strikers are not within this category.[58] It has been claimed that the term would apply to rebels fighting against the Crown under the orders of a de facto rebel government in a civil war; but this has been criticized as not representing a true exception.[59]

---

[45] *Gibbon* v. *Paynton* (1869) 4 Burr. 229 per Lord Mansfield. At common law the carrier was entitled to higher freight for the carriage of valuables, a point last decided in *Riley* v. *Horne*, ante. Ridley's view is that the rule was abrogated by provisions relating to the carriage of valuables in the *Carriers Act* 1830; see post.

[46] As to transit, see post.

[47] E.g. Ridley, p. 15.

[48] Chitty, op. cit., p. 267.

[49] *Gosling* v. *Higgins* (1808) 1 Camp. 451.

[50] *Gibbon* v. *Paynton* (1769) 4 Burr. 2298.

[51] *Forward* v. *Pittard* (1785) 1 T.R. 27.

[52] *Hyde* v. *Trent & Mersey Navigation Co.* (1793) 5 T.R. 389.

[53] *Forward* v. *Pittard*, ante.

[54] (1703) 2 Ld. Raym. 909.

[55] Particularly at 918; one argument used by the Chief Justice was that the absence of such liability would encourage the carrier to combine with thieves in plundering goods given to his care.

[56] *Forward* v. *Pittard* (lightning); *Ryan* v. *Youngs* [1938] 1 All E.R. 522 (heart attack); *Blyth* v. *Birmingham Waterworks Co.* (1856) 11 Ex. 781 (frost); *Nugent* v. *Smith* (1876) 1 C.P.D. 423 (storm); *Makins* v. *L.N.E. Railway* [1943] K.B. 467 (flood).

[57] *Nugent* v. *Smith* (ante) at 434-438, per Cockburn J.

[58] *The Marshal of Marshalsea's Case* (1455) Y.B. 33 Hen VI; 1 p. 3. See further *Richmond Metal Co. Ltd.* v. *J. Coales & Son Ltd.* [1970] 1 Lloyd's Rep. 423.

[59] Ridley, *The Law of Carriage of Goods by Land, Sea and Air*, at p. 16, cites *Secretary of State for War* v. *Midland G.W. Railway Co. of Ireland* [1923] 2 I.R. (where the Irish Courts held the acts of rebels during the 1916 Easter Rising in Dublin to be acts of the King's Enemies) and *Curtis and Sons* v. *Mathews* [1919] 1 K.B. 425 (where the English Courts held such activity to be an act of war for the purpose of an express term in a contract of insurance). Kahn-Freund claims that the exception covers the decision in *Curtis*, op. cit., p. 247. Contra Chitty, op. cit., p. 267n. The views of Ridley and Kahn-Freund are felt to be more

(iii) Inherent vice: The common carrier is not liable where damage is caused by an inherent defect in the goods themselves, including their containers. In the case of animals the carrier will not be liable for injury caused by their attacking one another or by their own violent natures, or due to fright in transit which it was not reasonable for the carrier to foresee or guard against.[60] The same rule has been applied to fruit rotting due to a latent defect within it.[61] The other group of cases are typified by those involving the explosion of fermented wine,[62] inadequate gin casks[63] and a carriage coupling that broke due to an inherent defect while being loaded onto a railway truck.[64]

(iv) Fault of the owner or consignor of the goods: The carrier will not incur liability where the loss, damage or destruction is solely due to the fault of the consignor or the owner or their servants or agents. This usually occurs where goods are defectively packed;[65] and even where the carrier is aware of such a defect, and is not liable to accept goods in this state, he is still not liable for damage if he does so accept them.[66] Also included in this defence are misleading packing[67] and insufficient or misleading addressing.[68] However, the carrier will incur liability where damage is caused by faulty covering on the carrier's vehicle even if placed there by the consignor.[69] Where the owner or consignor or their agents are guilty of fraud the carrier will not be liable. Thus where a consignor makes an untrue statement concerning the nature and value of the goods to the carrier and does not reveal the fact that the goods are valuables on enquiry by the carrier then the carrier will not be liable at common law.[70]

In all these four excepted perils the burden of proof is on the carrier to show that true facts bring him within them.[71]

4. *Liability for negligence*: Even though the goods carried by the carrier are damaged or lost due to one of the excepted perils discussed above the common carrier will be liable if he has caused or contributed to such loss or damage by his negligence, and the onus is on the carrier to show that neither he nor his servants contributed to the loss or injury by their own negligence.[72] The common carrier will be liable where damage caused by an excepted peril is aggravated by his negligence.[73] In such cases the duty to mitigate such loss on the part of a common carrier

in accord with modern commercial practice and the realities of present day hostilities against civil governments.

---

[60] *Blower* v. *G.W. Railway Co.* (1872) L.R. 7 C.P. 655.
[61] *Bradley* v. *Federal Steam Navigation Co.* (1927) 137 L.T. 266 (H.L.).
[62] *Farrow* v. *Adams* (1711) Buller N.P. 69(c).
[63] *Hudson* v. *Baxendale* (1857) 2 H. & N. 575.
[64] *Lister* v. *L. & Y. Railway* (1885) 2 T.L.R. 89.
[65] *Barbour* v. *S.E. Railway* (1876) 34 L.T. 67.
[66] *Gould* v. *S.E. & C. Railway* [1920] 2 K.B. 186. A limitation of liability for loss of, as distinct from damage to, damageable goods packed improperly, was held unreasonable in *Simons* v. *G.W. Railway* (1856) 18 C.B. 805.
[67] *Barbour* v. *S.E. Railway*, ante.
[68] *Bradley* v. *Waterhouse* (1823) 3 C. & P. 318.
[69] *London & N.W. Railway Co.* v. *Hudson & Sons* [1920] A.C. 324.
[70] *Tichburne* v. *White* (1719) 1 Stra. 145, per Lord King L.C. But see the *Carriers Act* 1830 s. 1, post.
[71] See Kahn-Freund, p. 200.
[72] Ibid.
[73] *Cox* v. *L.N.W. Railway* (1862) 3 F. & F. 77; *Amies* v. *Stevens* (1718) 1 Stra. 127.

is not absolute. He is only under a duty to take reasonable steps to do so and is liable only in negligence.[74]

C. The Carrier's Act of 1830

The strict liability imposed on the common carrier by the common law was not balanced by any right of the carrier to check packets presented for carriage or obtain information as to their contents; nor did the common law distinguish between different kinds of goods. *The Carrier's Act* of 1830 was passed partly to remedy the anomalous position of carriers who would be strictly liable for goods stolen in transit yet had no means of discovering their value.[75] Generally the Act relieved the carrier of liability for particular goods of an especially valuable or fragile nature, worth more than £10, unless the consignor made a special declaration of value. The other reason for the passing of the *Carrier's Act* was that the courts had come to presume generally that notices excluding or limiting the carrier's liability, provided they were conspicuously placed in the carrier's receiving office where the consignor had an opportunity of reading them, had a binding effect on the consignor. The Act thus gave a remedy to the carrier in relation to liability for valuables and dealt with the public dissatisfaction with unilateral notices.[76]

The Act provides that no common carrier by land for hire shall be liable for the loss of or injury to a parcel or package containing certain articles of a valuable or breakable nature listed in s. 1[77] totalling over £10 unless their value is declared at the time of delivery to the carrier and an increased charge paid.[78] Clear and public notice of such an increased charge must be given by the carrier on his premises[79] who must give a signed receipt on request for a parcel or package.[80] If either notice or receipt are not given the carrier is liable as a common carrier for loss or damage.[81] Where the consignor makes no declaration of value or does not pay or promise to pay the increased charge the carrier is only liable for injury to, or loss of, the goods if this occurs as a result of theft, forgery or embezzlement by his employees.[82] Where the mandatory requirements of the Act are not met the value of the goods, in the event of loss or injury, plus the increased charge may be recovered by the owner.[83]

Section 1 of the *Carrier's Act* refers only to loss and damage to the goods, and not to delay. Thus if the consignor does not make a declaration of the nature and value of the goods he can still recover damages for delay to valuables exceeding £10 in value in a package.[84] Section 1 has been held

---

[74] *Nugent* v. *Smith* (1867) 1 C.P.D. 423.
[75] On the background to, and scope of, the *Carriers Act* 1830 see Kahn-Freund, pp. 218-222.
[76] Kahn-Freund, p. 220.
[77] Kahn-Freund, pp. 348-350; amended marginally by the *Carriers Act* 1865.
[78] If demanded; see *Behrens* v. *G.N. Railway* (1861) 6 H. & N. 950.
[79] *Carriers Act* s. 2.
[80] Ibid., s. 3.
[81] Ibid., s. 3.
[82] Ibid., ss. 1, 8. The onus of proving that the goods were stolen by a servant rests on the plaintiff; *Vaughton* v. *L.N.W. Railway* (1886) 18 Q.B.D. 121; *M'Queen* v. *G.W. Railway* (1875) L.R. 10 Q.B. 569. For definition of "servant" see *Stephens* v. *L.S.W. Railway* (1886) 18 Q.B.D. 121.
[83] *Carriers Act* s. 7.
[84] *Hearn* v. *L.S.W. Railway Co.* (1855) 10 Exch. 793.

to apply to temporary as well as to permanent loss.[85] A carrier who has deviated from his route thereby repudiating the contract, and possesses the goods as a wrongful possessor, can rely on the Act and the owner of goods within s. 1 cannot recover if the consignor failed to make the declaration of nature and value.[86]

The most important application of *Carrier's Act* in modern commerce, where its practical importance is small, is probably to the carriage of passenger's luggage in public service vehicles.[87] The Act applies to passenger's luggage in such vehicles even though it is carried "free of charge" as the fare paid by the passenger is construed as including freight for his luggage.[88]

D. The freight forwarder as a common carrier

The liability of a forwarder as an intermediary between consignor and carrier would appear to turn on whether the forwarder is regarded as a common or private carrier for any transit he carries out himself for a client with or without the employment of another independent carrier.[89] In *Hellaby* v. *Weaver*[90] the defendant forwarders were held to be common carriers. There the defendants collected and forwarded goods by rail, sometimes collecting all freight charges and sometimes only those for carriage to the station. In the case at issue, when goods were lost en route to the station, they were held to be common carriers as they had on this occasion collected the total charge. In similar cases, it may be presumed that the defendants would be regarded as mere forwarders by the courts, certainly in respect of the carriage forwarded by rail.[91] The conclusion that may be made with respect to forwarders is that their normal capacity is that of private, rather than a common, carrier[92] based on the fact that forwarders normally reserve the right to accept or reject shipments as opposed to holding themselves out as ready to accept any goods offered to them for collection and delivery in their own vehicles. Two Australian decisions, which support this contention, involved clearing agents which the courts held were not common carriers when moving inward shipments, and so not liable for any loss or damage without negligence on their part.[93]

---

[85] *Miller* v. *Brasch and Co.* (1882) 10 Q.B.D. 142.

[86] *Walker* v. *York* and *N.M. Railway Co.* (1853) 2 E. & B. 750.

[87] Kahn-Freund, op. cit., p. 221. See Paton, pp. 228, 598. Note that the Road

[88] *Le Conteur* v. *L.S.W. Railway* (1865) L.R. 1 Q.B. 54; *Casswell* v. *Cheshire Lines Committee* [1907] 2 K.B. 499. But see now *Carriage of Passengers by Road Act 1974* (U.K.).
Haulage Association's "Conditions of Carriage" (U.K.) whilst stipulating that "the contractor (carrier) is not a common carrier" (cond. 2) provides that "the contractor shall have in every event the protection of the Carriers Act, 1830"; (cond. 7). (Revision of April 1967 as amended December, 1971).

[89] For a recent authoritative discussion of this problem see Hill, *Freight Forwarders*, pp. 18-20.

[90] (1851) 17 L.T. (O.S.) 271.

[91] Hill, op. cit., p. 18. The case cited above is brief and does not deal with the situation where the forwarder does not collect the whole charge for carriage.

[92] Hill, op. cit., p. 19; there appears no direct authority on this point.

[93] *O'Neill* v. *McCormack & Co.* (1913) 15 W.A.L.R. 33; *Hyland* v. *Mullaly & Byrne Pty. Ltd.* [1923] V.L.R. 193. See also *New Zealand Express Co.* v. *Pemberton* (1915) 17 G.L.R. 524; *Wilson* v. *New Zealand Express Co.* [1923]

The forwarder's method of operation may determine whether he is a common carrier. In *Date & Cocke* v. *G. W. Sheldon & Co. (London) Ltd.*[94] the defendant forwarders had a smaller ancillary business as carriers. The court decided the case against them (an action for loss of goods due to the driver leaving his vehicle unattended) on the basis of the driver's negligence; the defendants thus being liable whether or not they were common carriers. However, Bailhache J. observed[95] that he had not been satisfied by the defendants that they were not common carriers in respect of carrying goods around London. It was not necessary that they should carry from one particular destination to another and the view taken was that at the time in question the defendants were operating as common carriers in regard to the business distinct from their work as forwarders. The view expressed above is important as such short haul business to and from docks is a common feature of forwarding businesses whether or not the forwarder deals with any other additional part of the carriage.[96]

II. PRIVATE CARRIERS

A. General position

The majority of carriers by road are private carriers and as such are liable for careless acts of their servants in the course of their employment, but not for the acts of strangers over whom they have no control. Unlike the common carrier the private carrier is liable only for negligence.[97] The onus is on the carrier to show that his servants exercised reasonable care in relation to the consignor's property. If goods are lost or damaged in transit it is for the carrier to show either that he or his servants were not negligent or that such negligence did not contribute to the loss.[98] This principle was laid down in *Joseph Travers & Sons Ltd.* v. *Cooper.*[99] In that case goods loaded onto a barge at the barge-owner's wharf were damaged, after being left unattended at night, by rising tide. The barge-owner was protected from liability from negligence by the clause in the contract but the Court of Appeal held unanimously the burden of proof was on the defendant.[1] Whether the carrier's servants have been negligent

N.Z.L.R. 201; *R. M. Griffiths & Co. Ltd.* v. *Armstrong & Springhall Ltd.* [1975] 1 N.Z.L.R. 115; post

---

[94] (1921) 7 Ll.L. Rep. 53.
[95] Ibid., at 54.
[96] Hill, op. cit., p. 20.
[97] *Whalley* v. *Wray* (1799) 3 Esp. 74; or, of course, for breach of any express or implied contractual term.
[98] See generally p. 475 et seq., ante.
[99] [1915] 1 K.B. 73. Regarded by Kahn-Freund as simply a special application of the doctrine of res ipsa loquitur, citing Goddard L.J. in *Easson* v. *L.N.E. Railway* [1944] 1 K.B. 421, op. cit., p. 267; see also Ridley, p. 20; but cf. ante p. 40.
[1] See also *Coldman* v. *Hill* [1919] 1 K.B. 443, at 450; *Brook's Wharf and Bull Wharf Ltd.* v. *Goodman Bros.* [1937] 1 K.B. 534; *James Buchanan & Co. Ltd.* v. *Babco Forwarding & Shipping (U.K.) Ltd.* [1977] 2 W.L.R. 107; [1977] 3 W.L.R. 907 (H.L.). The principles in *Joseph Travers* apply to cases of loss as well as damage; per Denning L.J. in *Spurling Ltd.* v. *Bradshaw* [1956] 1 W.L.R. 461, at 466. In *Hunt* v. *Winterbotham (West of England) Ltd.* v. *B.R.S. (Parcels) Ltd.* [1962] 1 Q.B. 617, Donovan L.J. stated (at 626) that a carrier who failed to deliver the goods or some of the goods had to establish he was not negligent, but

is essentially a question of fact. It is clear, however, that the carrier's duty with regard to the fitness of his vehicle for carriage is a heavy one. Thus when the carrier breaches any statutory provisions relating to fitness of vehicle for carriage this raises a strong presumption of negligence.[2]

The private carrier will be liable if his servant, having been entrusted with the goods, steals or commits any intentional or negligent harm to them, whether such servant is acting for the carrier's benefit or not. Thus the carrier is answerable not only where goods are stolen by his servant at his own instigation,[3] but where the servant steals them independently and for personal gain alone;[4] likewise where the servant, by his negligence, makes it possible for some third party to abstract the goods.[5]

The carrier and his servants are under a duty to ensure that goods entrusted to them for carriage are saved in the event of fire, breakage or theft, whether or not caused by the negligence of either the carrier or his servants; a carrier will be liable to pay the owner of goods damages if he does not do all he can to mitigate damage to such goods.[6]

The obligations outlined above can be varied or modified and abrogated by contract. As will be seen, a road carrier operating under the Conditions of Carriage of the Road Haulage Association (U.K.) limits his

---

did not have to prove absence of fundamental breach. On the last point, see post p. 947.

[2] Kahn-Freund, op. cit., pp. 268-269. See Cresswell J. in *Austin v. Manchester, Sheffield and Lincolnshire Railway* (1852) 10 C.B. 454 at 473-474 and Lord Watson in *Brabant & Co. v. King* [1895] A.C. 632, at 640. There is no absolute warranty of roadworthiness akin to the common law warranty of seaworthiness imposed on a ship owner; see the refusal of the Privy Council to assimilate the position of a ship at sea with that of a motor-car on land in *Tricket v. Queensland Insurance* [1936] A.C. 159, at 165 et. seq. For recent decisions in which the carrier was held or presumed to be negligent, see further *Pye Ltd. v. B.G. Transport Service Ltd.* [1966] 2 Lloyd's Rep. 300 (carrier failing to immobilize the lorry while it was left locked but unattended for half an hour, with the result that radio sets worth over £5000 were stolen: cf. *Mayfair Photographic Supplies (London) Ltd. v. Baxter Hoare & Co. Ltd.* [1972] 1 Lloyd's Rep. 410, where it was held that it was unnecessary in 1965 for a lorry carrying cameras to be fitted with an immobilizer); *Arcweld Constructions Pty. Ltd. v. Smith* (1968) Unrep. Vic. Sup. Ct. Sept. 18th (carrier transporting heavy tower crane under low bridge); *Lee & Sons Pty. Ltd. v. Abood* (1968) 89 W.N. (N.S.W.) (Pt. 1) 430 (vehicle capsizing for unexplained reason); *A. F. Colverd & Co. Ltd. v. Anglo Overseas Transport Co. Ltd.* [1961] 2 Lloyd's Rep. 352 (driver leaving body of van unlocked and removing ignition key but leaving cab unlocked). Contrast three cases in which a carrier was held not to have been negligent: *Hobbs v. Petersham Transport Co. Pty. Ltd.* (1971) 45 A.L.J.R. 356; *Thomas National Transport (Melbourne) Pty. Ltd. v. May & Baker (Australia) Pty. Ltd.* (1966) 115 C.L.R. 353; *Presvale Trading Co. Ltd. v. Sutch & Searle* [1967] 1 Lloyd's Rep. 131; and see further *Gallaher Ltd. v. B.R.S. Ltd.* [1974] 2 Lloyd's Rep. 440; *Eastman Chemical International A.G. v. N.M.T. Trading Ltd.* [1972] 2 Lloyd's Rep. 25. Other authorities relating to the bailee's general duty of care and his liability for the negligence or dishonesty of his servants are discussed at length in Chapter 13, ante.

[3] *Barwick v. English Joint Stock Bank* (1867) L.R. 2 Ex. 259.

[4] *Morris v. C. W. Martin & Sons Ltd.* [1966] 1 Q.B. 716; *Moukataff v. B.O.A.C.* [1967] 1 Lloyd's Rep. 396; ante, p. 475.

[5] *Abraham v. Bullock* (1902) 86 L.T. 796. As to the liability where two or more carriers are used see post and Hill, op. cit., p. 269 et seq.

[6] *Notara v. Henderson* (1872) L.R. 7 Q.B. 255; *G.N. Railway v. Swaffield* (1874) L.R. 9 Ex. 132.

liability for loss or damage and failure of the consignee to take delivery within a reasonable time.[7]

B. Road Haulage Association conditions of carriage

Although there are no standard conditions that apply to the road haulage industry the conditions of carriage issued by the Road Haulage Association Ltd. are used by most road carriers.[8] These conditions of carriage (referred to subsequently as the Conditions) have been modelled upon the former Standard Terms and Conditions used by the railways and the former now tend to closely resemble the present Railway Board conditions of carriage.[9] However, the Road Haulage Association conditions do not have provisions similar to those of the Rail Board's owner's risk conditions of carriage nor allow for "a fair alternative rate"[10] and different degrees of liability are allowed to the carrier.

Under the Conditions the carrier states that he is "not a common carrier and accepts goods for carriage only on these conditions."[11] If the Conditions have been incorporated in the contract either expressly or impliedly, the general principles of law that apply to private carriers also apply to the liability of the carrier. However, the Conditions exempt the carrier from liability for loss or damage arising from the excepted perils, act or omission of the trader or owner of the goods or agents or servants of either, riots, civil commotion, lockouts, general or partial stoppage or restraint of labour from whatever cause.[12] Similarly, liability is exempted due to insufficient or improper labelling addressing or packing, seizure under legal process or where the consignee does not take or accept delivery within a reasonable time.[13] The carrier, under the Conditions, does not accept liability of any kind where, in respect of a consignment, there has been fraud on the part of the trader or owner or the servants or agents of either. Liability of the carrier in respect of one consignment is limited to £800 per ton, unless the total value is less than £10. The carrier is entitled to require proof of the value of the whole consignment and is

---

[7] See Road Haulage Association Conditions of Carriage (1967 Revision as amended December, 1971); conditions 8, 11, 12 discussed below.

[8] The text of these Conditions is reproduced in Ridley, p. 241. See also Hill, pp. 154, 157, 165; Kahn-Freund, pp. 271, 280, 288 and Hill [1969] J.B.L. 100. The current Conditions of Carriage are as follows: (i) Conditions of Carriage (April, 1967 revision, as amended December, 1971); (ii) Conditions of Sub-Contracting (April, 1967 revision); (iii) Special Conditions for Carriage of Abnormal, Indivisible Loads (adopted April, 1970); (iv) Conditions of Carriage of Livestock (other than Wild Animals), (January, 1962 revision); (v) Special Conditions for Carriage or Towing of Caravans and Mobile Units (June 1971, revision).

[9] See Chapter 18. Under the R.H.A.'s General Conditions liability for loss or damage is the same as that of the Railways Board although there is no provision in the R.H.A.'s General Conditions that the carrier is liable, even in the case of an excepted peril, if he fails to prove he used all reasonable foresight and care; see condition 11. For livestock see Livestock Conditions, condition 25.

[10] General Conditions, condition 2; the stipulation that "the contractor shall in every event have the protection of the *Carriers' Act* 1830" (condition 7 of the 1967 edition of the General Conditions) does not appear in the 1971 revision.

[11] General Conditions, condition 2.

[12] General Conditions, condition 11.

[13] Ibid. Special aspects of these conditions such as liability for delay, etc., will be discussed later.

not liable for indirect or consequential loss or for the loss of a particular market.[14] The Conditions take their effect solely from their incorporation into the individual contracts of carriage and cease to have effect when that contract loses its force so that a carrier cannot rely upon them in a situation where they no longer operate. In the case of deviation, for example, such action amounts to repudiation of the contract by the carrier. Since all contractual terms of carriage have been repudiated with the contract itself the carrier can no longer rely on terms of the contract by which he sought to limit his common law liability, including the Condition.[15] It is not obligatory for members of the Road Haulage Association to adhere to these Conditions and individual variations of them may apply.[16] It has been held that even where a contract of carriage has not been expressly made subject to the Conditions the contract at issue may be brought under them by a previous course of dealings.[17] In *Eastman Chemical International A.G.* v. *N.M.T. Trading Ltd.*[18] the plaintiffs contracted with the first defendants, who were haulage contractors, to carry a quantity of synthetic resin by road from London to Wellerbone, Warwickshire. The first defendants employed the second defendants, also haulage contractors and carriers, to carry the goods for them. While in charge of a driver employed by the second defendants the goods were destroyed when the tyres of the lorry caught fire. The plaintiffs claimed the value of the goods from both defendants on the grounds that they were common carriers; from the first defendants on the basis of contract and negligence, and from the second defendants on grounds of negligence only. The first defendants denied liability and argued that the contract with the plaintiffs was subject to R.H.A. Conditions, condition 2 of which stated that the first defendants were not common carriers and could rely on condition 8[19] and claimed that there had been no breach of contract or negligence. The rulings of this case in relation to fundamental breach and exemption clauses will be shortly considered. On the question of the contract of carriage the court held that, although not made expressly subject to the R.H.A. Conditions, a previous course of dealing between the parties made it so, based on a continuity of invoices tendered to the plaintiffs specifically referring to the application of conditions.[20] The court also found that the first defendants were common carriers. It was shown that the first defendants did not choose customers but carried goods for anyone without selection, provided they could

---

[14] General Conditions, condition 12.

[15] *London & N.W. Railway* v. *Neilson* [1922] 2 A.C. 263; see post.

[16] Member-carriers may use the 1961 Conditions of Carriage which are more restrictive of the carrier's liability although those carriers who do so will be in the minority. For an interesting example of a dispute as to which set of conditions governed the relevant contract of carriage, see *Charles Davis (Metal Brokers) Ltd.* v. *Gilyott & Scott Ltd.* [1975] 2 Lloyd's Rep. 422.

[17] As to the incorporation of exculpatory clauses, see generally p. 919 et seq., post.

[18] [1972] 2 Lloyd's Rep. 25.

[19] This stated:
"The contractor shall not be liable for delay or detention of goods or any loss, damage or deterioration arising therefrom except upon proof that the delay, detention, loss, damage or deterioration was solely due to the wilful negligence of the contract or the contractor's servants." But now see the 1967 R.H.A. Conditions, condition 10(b). See also Hill, p. 118 and Kahn-Freund, pp. 289-290; liability for delay is separately considered below.

[20] [1972] 2 Lloyd's Rep. 25, at 32.

pay, save only that they would not carry explosives or certain goods such as wines or tobaccos which were particularly liable to theft. Similarly, on the basis that the second defendants did not limit the goods carried, they too were held to be common carriers.[21]

The circumstances of the revision of the Conditions in 1971 is worthy of note. The apparent need for this arose from the Queen's Bench decision in *Gillespie Bros. Ltd.* v. *Roy Bowles Transport Ltd.*[22] The facts of the case basically were that watches belonging to the plaintiffs were stolen from a van at London Airport after a driver employed by the defendants had left the van unattended. The defendants were acting on the instructions of a third party who were arranging the carriage of the watches for the plaintiff. The plaintiffs sued the defendants for the value of the watches, claiming that the defendants were common law bailees and under a duty to take all reasonable care. The defendants, on their part, argued that there had been no breach of this duty and that in any event they were entitled to limit their liability under condition 12 of the Road Haulage Association's Conditions of Carriage (1967).[23] The defendants failed to prove that they had taken reasonable care and, further, were disabled from relying on condition 12 as there was no contractual relationship between themselves and the plaintiffs. In the third party proceedings, the defendants claimed indemnity from the third party under condition 3(4) of the R.H.A. Conditions which provided:

> The Trader shall save harmless and keep the Carrier indemnified against all claims or demands whatsoever by whomsoever made in excess of the liability of the carrier under these conditions.

The defendants claimed that those conditions of carriage were implied in the contract of carriage as the third party knew or had notice that the defendants carried goods only on R.H.A. Conditions in the absence of any special agreement to the contrary. There had been previous agreements between the parties in which the R.H.A. Conditions had been incorporated. The third party argued that these conditions could only apply to a contract of carriage and not, as in this case, to a contract of hire. It was held that the R.H.A. Conditions were incorporated in the contract and were not inconsistent with the terms of that contract. It followed that clause 3(4) did apply to the agreement but that, on its true construction, the clause did not expressly or impliedly extend to cover claims arising from the defendant's own negligence, as clause 3(4) did not contain any express reference to negligence nor any phrases which had been held judicially to exclude negligence.[24] The principle thus applied to construing clause

---

[21] Ibid., at p. 31.

[22] [1971] 2 Lloyd's Rep. 521.

[23] See ante.

[24] Browne J. cited the use of such words as "however caused", "however arising" or "sole risk" as "enough to exclude in the case of an exemption clause (and I think therefore to include in the case of an indemnity) the negligence of the proferens himself" (at 538). The learned judge also referred to the anthology of such phrases in Chitty (23rd edition) at para. 728; but cf. now *Smith* v. *South Wales Switchgear Ltd.* [1978] 1 All E.R. 18, where the House of Lords held that similar words did *not* exclude liability for negligence. See also the cases quoted by Kahn-Freund at pp. 233-234. On the situation where there is no express cover for negligence Browne J. cited the Privy Council case of *Canada Steamship*

3(4) was that since it did not expressly cover the carrier's own negligence, their claim against the third party could only succeed if the sub-clause extended, by implication to their own negligence. The carriers were indemnified against claims or demands on grounds other than negligence and so were not indemnified against a claim and demand based on their own negligence.

On appeal the Court of Appeal reversed the earlier decision.[25] It was held that the words "all claims and demands", strengthened by the additional word "whatsoever" in clause 3(4), amounted to an agreement in express terms that the trader would indemnify the carrier against all claims without exception, including a claim arising from the negligence of the carrier or his servant.[26] It followed that the carriers were entitled to be indemnified by the trader in excess of £10 on any one consignment under the proviso to clause 12 of the conditions.[27]

C. Interpretation of limitation and exemption clauses in private contracts of carriage

The problems of interpretation of limitation and exemption clauses generally are dealt with in detail elsewhere.[28] Certain aspects relating to private contracts of carriage should be noted however. With regard to the construction of exemption clauses there is an important difference between common and private carriers. Where a clause purports to exempt a carrier for loss or damage due to fire this does not cover him in the event of fire caused by his servant's negligence if he is a common carrier, as the courts regard this general clause as not relieving him of liability for negligence but having the restricted effect of reducing that liability to that of a private carrier.[29] In the case of a private carrier, however, he is only liable for his own and his servants' negligence. The same words which leave the common carrier with liability for negligence may therefore exempt a private carrier from that liability.[30] A common carrier may also by the

---

Lines Ltd. v. *The King* [1952] A.C. 192, at 208; [1952] Lloyd's Rep. 1, at 8. The Privy Council ruling was based on Lord Greene M.R.'s statement in *Alderslade* v. *Hendon Laundry Ltd.* [1945] K.B. 189, at 192. But see n.(26) post.

[25] [1973] Q.B. 400.

[26] Lord Denning suggesting that the ruling in *Canada Steamship Lines Ltd.* v. *The King* (ante) should not be applied in full force: "The correct proposition, as I have always understood it, is this. Even though the words of a clause are wide enough in their ordinary meaning to exclude liability for negligence, nevertheless if it is apparent that sufficient content can be given to them without doing so (as in the case of a common carrier) then they will be give that content only. They will not be held to cover negligence. So stated, however, the forwarding agents may still rely on it. Condition 11 puts a liability on the carrier equivalent to a common carrier. So they may still say that the indemnity clause should not be held to cover negligence of the carrier himself"; at 1012-1013 Buckley L.J. regarded the decision as turning on the proper interpretation of "whatsoever" in clause 3(4) of the R.H.A. Conditions. See generally Chapter 25.

[27] For construction of a similar provision to cl.3(4) of the 1967 Conditions namely cl.20 of the R.H.A. 1961 Conditions see *Hair and Skin Trading Co. Ltd.* v. *Norman Airfreight Carriers Ltd.* [1974] 1 Lloyd's Rep. 443.

[28] See Chapter 25.

[29] *Price & Co.* v. *Union Lighterage Co.* [1903] 1 K.B. 750, at 752; affirmed [1904] 1 K.B. 412; *Beaumont Thomas* v. *Blue Star Line Ltd.* [1939] 3 All E.R. 127; see Kahn-Freund, pp. 230-234.

[30] *Rutter* v. *Palmer* [1922] 2 K.B. 87, at 90 per Bankes L.J. See Lord Denning's remarks in *Gillespie Bros. and Co. Ltd.* v. *Roy Bowles Transport Ltd.* [1973]

use of clear and unambiguous language contract out of liability for negligence;[31] even to the extent of theft by his servants.[32]

The carrier may not be able to rely on exemption clauses in the contract where he commits a fundamental breach.[33] In the case of *Eastman Chemical International A.G.* v. *N.M.T. Trading Ltd.*,[34] the facts of which have been given above, it was held inter alia that the destruction of the lorry and its load brought the contract and a condition exempting liability of both defendants as common carriers to an end.[35] On the facts, the lorry used for transportation was equipped with poor tyres, one of which burst and caught fire, no fire extinguisher being provided. The lorry was subsequently abandoned by the driver; no arrangement had been made by either of the defendants to insure the load. A carrier may be unable to rely on an exemption clause in a contract of carriage where the carrier unjustifiably deviates from his usual or agreed route,[36] delivers to the wrong person[37] or sub-contracts to a carrier of whom he knew or should have known his client would not approve.[38] It had been held that a carrier may be liable for fundamental breach where a driver employed by him leaves his lorry unattended while he has a meal and the lorry's contents are stolen,[39] but the reverse may apply if the driver steals the goods himself.[40] It has been decided, however, that an employee who steals goods bailed to the employer may be acting within the scope of his employment,[41] and that the carrier bears the onus of showing that the loss of the goods did not result from such theft.[42] It has also been made clear that a driver leaving his loaded lorry for a short period will not necessarily of itself constitute fundamental breach.[43] Similarly, where a carrier is tricked into sub-contracting a contract by a thief posing as a representative of a fictitious firm of carriers, his negligence in not checking on the thief's standing may amount to a fundamental breach,[44] but this will not be the case where a

---

Q.B. 400 on the statement of Green M.R. in *Alderslade* v. *Hendon Laundry Ltd.* [1945] K.B. 189, at 192 regarding construction of claims exempting solely for negligence and see note (26) ante.

[31] *Price & Co.* v. *Union Lighterage Co.* [1903] 1 K.B. 750.
[32] *Shaw* v. *G.W. Railway* [1894] 1 Q.B. 373; and see *Metrotex Pty. Ltd.* v. *Freight Investments Pty. Ltd.* [1969] V.R. 9.
[33] See Chapter 25
[34] [1972] 2 Lloyd's Rep. 25.
[35] Ibid., at 32 per Tudor Evans D.J. Counsel for the plaintiffs relied on *Harbutts Plasticine Ltd.* v. *Wayne Tank and Pump Co.* [1970] 1 Lloyd's Rep. 15 particularly at 464-465, 472 and 475; Lord Cross was cited by Tudor Evans D.J. at 475. The decision is criticised post, p. 935.
[36] *L.N.W. Ry.* v. *Neilson* [1922] 2 A.C. 263.
[37] *Alexander* v. *Railway Executive* [1951] 2 K.B. 882.
[38] *Garnham, Harris & Elton Ltd.* v. *Alfred Ellis (Transport) Ltd.* [1967] 1 W.L.R. 940; and see post.
[39] *Bontex Knitting Works Ltd.* v. *St. John's Garage* [1943] 2 All E.R. 690.
[40] *Carter (Fine Worsteds) Ltd.* v. *Hanson Haulage Ltd.* [1965] 2 Q.B. 495; cf. *Metrotex Pty. Ltd.* v. *Freight Investments Pty. Ltd.* [1969] V.R. 9.
[41] See *Morris* v. *C. W. Martin & Sons Ltd.* [1966] 1 Q.B. 716.
[42] Ante, p. 471.
[43] See *Harris Ltd.* v. *Continental Express Ltd.* [1961] 1 Lloyd's Rep. 251, at 260; *Colverd & Co. Ltd.* v. *Anglo-Overseas Transport Co. Ltd.* [1961] 2 Lloyd's Rep. 352; *Mayfair Photographic Supplies (London) Ltd.* v. *Baxter, Hoare and Co. Ltd.* [1972] 1 Lloyd's Rep. 410.
[44] *Garnham, Harris & Elton Ltd.* v. *Alfred W. Ellis (Transport) Ltd.* [1967] 1 W.L.R. 940; and see post.

carrier is deceived by forged references proffered by a thief to get employment as the carrier's driver, and the thief then steals the goods.[45] Such cases appear to be anomalous.[46]

As has already been noted earlier, alternative remedies based on tort, bailment or breach of contract lie against a carrier by a person whose goods have been lost or damaged in transit.[47] However, it does not follow that the plaintiff can disregard a contract containing an exemption clause: for as has already been shown, an exemption clause may be construed as wide enough to indemnify a carrier against liability in tort, both his own and that of his employees.[48] Where there is no privity of contract between parties the ability of the plaintiff to sue in tort is important. This may arise where the plaintiff is outside the contract of carriage as in the case where his goods are borrowed, hired or stolen from him and then given by the borrower, hirer or thief to be carried to a consignee. It will also occur where the defendant is not a party to the contract of carriage where the contract of carriage is between the owner of the goods and the carrier and the owner sues the carrier's employee or another carrier to whom the carriage was sub-contracted.[49]

In a claim for loss or damage to goods the plaintiff will base his claim for damages in tort on either conversion or detinue or negligence. If he claims on conversion or detinue he will have to prove an immediate right to possession;[50] if he sues in negligence, he must establish a permanent injury to his reversionary interest by the loss or destruction of the goods.[51] If negligence is relied on by the plaintiff he will have to prove the defendant owed him a duty of care which was breached and, at the time of the negligent act or omission, the plaintiff was owner of, or entitled to possession of, the goods.[52] Where the contract of carriage has been sub-contracted with the owner's actual or ostensible authority the plaintiff and defendant may be in the relationship of head-bailor and sub-bailee. If the plaintiff then sues for negligence there will be no need to prove that a duty of care was owed to him by the defendant as it arises from the nature of the relationship between them and it will be for the defendant

---

[45] Carter (Fine Worsteds) Ltd. v. Hanson Haulage Ltd. [1965] 2 Q.B. 495.

[46] See Kahn-Freund, p. 239. "The borderline between mere negligence which may be within the terms of an exceptions clause and a fundamental breach which is not, is often difficult to find." See also his criticism, also at p. 239, of Hunt and Winterbotham (West of England) Ltd. v. B.R.S. (Parcels) Ltd. [1962] 2 Q.B. 617 and Note by Ms. O. Aikin (1963) 26 M.L.R. 98.

[47] Ante; see also Harris Ltd. v. Continental Express Ltd. [1961] 1 Lloyd's Rep. 251; Lee Cooper Ltd. v. C. H. Jeakins & Sons Ltd. [1967] 2 Q.B. 1; Morris v. C. W. Martin & Sons Ltd. [1966] 1 Q.B. 716; Moukataff v. B.O.A.C. [1967] 1 Lloyd's Rep. 396 (see Chapters 17 and 20); Transmotors Ltd. v. Robertson, Buckley & Co. Ltd. [1970] 1 Lloyd's Rep. 224; James Buchanan v. Hay's Transport Services [1972] 2 Lloyd's Rep. 535; Gillespie Bros. Ltd. v. Roy Bowles Transport Ltd. [1973] Q.B. 400.

[48] The Gillespie case, ibid.; cf. Allan J. Panozza & Co. Pty. Ltd. v. Allied Interstate (Qld.) Pty. Ltd. [1976] 2 N.S.W.R. 192.

[49] Philip Morris Ltd. v. Transport Commission [1975] Tas. S.R. 128; on sub-contracting see post.

[50] Kahler v. Midland Bank Ltd. [1950] A.C. 24.

[51] Mears v. L.S.W. Railway (1862) 11 C.B. (N.S.) 850; Moukataff v. B.O.A.C. [1967] 1 Lloyd's Rep. 396; ante, p. 153.

[52] Margarine Union GmbH. v. Cambay Prince Steamship Co. Ltd. [1969] 1 Q.B. 219.

to disprove negligence.[53] Similarly, given the same relationship, where a plaintiff sues for either conversion or detinue, he will not have to prove a better right to title as the defendant will probably be estopped from denying his head bailor's title.[54]

D. Sub-contracting and successive carriers

The duty of the carrier is to deliver the goods to the consignee in the absence of any contrary agreement. He does not carry out this duty if the goods are misdelivered, lost or damaged while in the possession of a second carrier and is liable as if he were still undertaking the contract of carriage.[55] It will be a breach of contract by the first carrier if he delivers the goods to a second carrier where the contract of carriage provides that the first carrier shall carry the goods throughout the entire journey. But if the consignor has expressly or impliedly authorized the carrier to deliver goods to a second carrier the carrier may discharge his duty simply by delivering the goods to the second carrier[56] and having done that the first carrier will have no liability for loss, misdelivery or damage to the goods while in possession of the second carrier. The onus of proving that the carrier may discharge his liabilities by delivering the goods to another carrier rests on the first carrier himself.

Standard form contracts, such as the R.H.A. Conditions of Carriage, expressly authorize the carrier to employ another carrier to perform the contract and give such another carrier similar powers to sub-contract.[57] The R.H.A. Conditions of Sub-Contracting re-inforce these provisions by requiring the carrier to "do all such things as may be reasonable to secure to the sub-contractor the benefit of the contract."[58] These conditions also require the sub-contractor to indemnify the carrier against liability arising where the goods are in transit (see below) and that of any failure by the

---

[53] Chapter 20, post.
[54] Ante, p. 163. But see *Torts (Interference with Goods) Act,* 1977, ss. 7, 8.
[55] *Hyde* v. *Trent & Mersey Navigation Co.* (1793) 5 T.R. 389; see generally Chapter 20.
[56] *Muschamp* v. *Lancaster & Preston Junction Railway* (1841) 8 M. & W. 421. The second carrier may still be liable to the owner in tort; see *McEachern Ltd.* v. *McKenzie Barge & Marine Ways Ltd. & Others* (1963) 40 D.L.R. (2d) 444, at 421, 453. See Kahn-Freund, pp. 354-334; Chapter 20, post.
[57] Clause 3 of the 1967 Conditions of Carriage (as amended) provides:—
(1) Where the Trader is not the owner of some or all of the goods in any consignment he shall be deemed for all purposes to be the agent of the owner or owners.
(2) The Carrier may employ the services of any other carrier for the purpose of fulfilling the Contract. Any such other carrier shall have the like power to sub-contract on like terms.
(3) The Carrier enters into the Contract for and on behalf of himself and his servants, agents and sub-contracts and his sub-contractors' servants, agents and sub-contractors; all of whom shall be entitled to the benefit of the Contract and shall be under no liability whatsoever to the Trader or anyone claiming through him in respect of the goods in addition to or separately from that of the Carrier under the Contract.
(4) The Trader shall save harmless and keep the carrier indemnified against all claims or demands whatsover by whomsover made in excess of the liability of the Carrier under these conditions in respect of any loss, damage or injury however caused, whether or not by the negligence of the Carrier, his servants, agents or sub-contractors.
For similar Conditions issued by the Railways Board see Chapter 18.
[58] R.H.A. Conditions of Sub-Contracting Clause 3(2).

sub-contractor to collect the goods within a reasonable time.[59] The sub-contractor is also required to take out policies of insurance which are acceptable to the carrier against liabilities arising under the Conditions of Sub-Contracting.[60]

Such agency devices would appear to be highly artificial in nature in that carriers contract with carriers as agents for their own employees and agents, as well as agents for the consignor. The effectiveness of this agency device is discussed fully elsewhere,[61] particularly in the light of recent cases.[62] The wording of clause 3(3) of the R.H.A. General Conditions it has been suggested[63] has the effect of establishing an agency relationship for the benefit of third parties. It is clear that a second carrier can act as agent of either the owner of the goods or of the first carrier.[64] This can be done by inserting an express clause into the contract of carriage. Another possibility is that an owner will be bound by the terms of a sub-contract where the owner has impliedly or expressly consented to the bailee making a sub-bailment containing these conditions.[65] In the absence of express consent the problem remains of deciding in what circumstances consent will be deemed to have been implied. On one authority it is suggested that due to the independent nature of transport operations it will be difficult to prove that a carrier is contracting on behalf of another. Thus a court will not be easily persuaded that where a carrier employs a sub-contractor he intends to lessen his status to that of a mere agent.[66]

In *Garnham, Harris & Elton Ltd.* v. *Alfred W. Ellis (Transport) Ltd.*[67] the definition of a "Contractor" in clause 1(a) of the R.H.A. Conditions 1961 as including "any . . . person carrying goods under a sub-contract with the Contractor", was considered as to whether it gave a carrier authority to sub-contract to another carrier without further authorization. In *Garnham's* case the defendant carrier sub-contracted carriage of a load of copper wire to third parties without checking on their honesty, and gave them a delivery order to collect the wire, whereupon the third party disappeared with the load. The plaintiff was held, on the facts, not to have been aware that the load of wire or any previously carried by the defendants for him had been sub-contracted. The court decided that the carrier had no right to sub-contract without the consent of the owner.[68] Even if such authority did

---

[59] Ibid., clause 8.
[60] Ibid., clause 9.
[61] See Chapter 26.
[62] *New Zealand Shipping Co. Ltd.* v. *A. M. Satterthwaite & Co. Ltd.* [1975] A.C. 154 is probably the most important.
[63] See Hill, op. cit., p. 166 on the basis that the wording of clause 3(3) is very close to those used in the British Rail and British Road Services Conditions which Kahn-Freund considers to establish an agency relationship; op. cit., p. 329. See B.R.S. Conditions, Clause 2(2) and British Rail General Conditions of Carriage of Goods, Clause 2(2); see also Chapter 18.
[64] Hill, op. cit., citing *Lee Cooper Ltd.* v. *C. H. Jeakins & Sons Ltd.* [1964] 1 Lloyd's Rep. 300.
[65] *Morris* v. *C. W. Martin & Sons Ltd.* [1966] 1 Q.B. 716 at 729-730 per Lord Denning M.R. See generally p. 1000 et seq., post.
[66] Hill, op. cit., p. 166. See Chapter 26.
[67] [1967] 1 W.L.R. 940.
[68] In doing so the court disapproved earlier dicta that the clause gave a general right to sub-contract; *John Carter Ltd.* v. *Hanson Haulage Ltd.* [1965] 1 Lloyd's Rep. 49, at 60 per Davies L.J. Paull J. was "prepared to hold that in any contract for the carriage of such [valuable] goods there must be some express

exist without the need for express consent the question was, was the carrier aware, or should he be, that such a method of sub-contracting was not in the view of the parties bearing in mind the value of the consignment. Both the lack of a right to sub-contract together with the way in which the sub-contracting was carried was held by the court to be a fundamental breach ruling out reliance on the R.H.A. Conditions.[69]

To overcome the implications of *Garnham's* case clause 3(2) was drafted into the 1967 R.H.A. Conditions.[70] This, it is suggested, overcomes the problem of express authority to contract absent in *Garnham's* case. Clause 3(2) does not relieve the carrier of his duty to exercise care in sub-contracting in that reckless behaviour on the lines of *Garnham's* case will not protect a carrier who commits a fundamental breach of the contract of carriage.[71]

E. The liability of the carrier as a warehouseman

A carrier's liability lasts only for the period of the carriage; where he holds goods prior to, or subsequent to, their carriage, he holds them as a warehouseman and not a carrier.[72] The liability of a warehouseman is that of a bailee and, as such, the carrier is only liable for his negligence. The carrier becomes an involuntary bailee where he remains in possession of the goods at the end of the carriage due to failure by the consignee to take delivery of the goods within a reasonable time.[73] Both private and common carriers have the same liability as warehousemen. A common carrier is liable only for negligence when in possession of goods as a warehouseman as a voluntary bailee. Thus, where goods are stolen from a carrier's warehouse when the transit is at an end or destroyed by fire without negligence on the part of his servants, the carrier is not liable.[74] If a road carrier who had no proper storage informed the consignee of the fact and disclaimed responsibility for damage arising from such lack of proper storage, the court would probably hold that the carrier was not a warehouseman (provided no rent was charged) but an involuntary bailee whose liability, if any, was less extensive than that of a bailee for reward. The liability of a carrier here is not clear and the authorities appear confused.[75] It is even suggested that an involuntary bailee would not be generally held liable by the court save in the case of intentional recklessness,[76] but this rule, if it exists at all, would probably be confined

---

words, preferably in the body of the contract, giving a carrier the right to sub-contract."

[69] Particularly Clause 12(a) R.H.A. Conditions 1961; see Hill, op. cit., pp. 287-288.
[70] See n. 57 ante.
[71] Hill, op. cit., p. 288; the carrier is still left with the question raised by Paull J. in *Garnham's* case as to whether the actual giving of authority to the sub-contractor to collect the goods is itself outside the scope of his own authority.
[72] *Chapman* v. *G.W. Railway & L.N.W. Railway* (1880) 5 Q.B.D. 278, at 281 per Cockburn C.J. See also *Mitchell* v. *L. & Y. Railway* (1875) L.R. 10 Q.B. 256. The liabilities of the warehouseman are discussed in Chapter 13.
[73] See below; see also Kahn-Freund, p. 322 et. seq.
[74] See *Brook's Wharf and Bull Wharf Ltd.* v. *Goodman Bros.* [1937] 1 K.B. 534; *J. Spurling Ltd.* v. *Bradshaw* [1956] 1 W.L.R. 461.
[75] Paton, op. cit., pp. 114-117; Chapter 12, ante.
[76] Kahn-Freund, op. cit., p. 323 suggests the carrier's liability would be similar to that under the Railway's Board at owner's risk; see also R.H.A. Conditions of

to bailees who were involuntary ab initio. Unless the carrier holds the goods expressly or impliedly as a warehouseman before carriage commences, transit begins, and he possesses the goods as carrier, when the goods are delivered to the carrier and accepted by him or by his actually or ostensibly authorized agents or employees.[77] Where there is acceptance by a third party or employee without the express or implied authority of the carrier, the goods are not regarded as having been delivered to the carrier.[78] Under the R.H.A. conditions transit is stated as commencing when the consignment is handed to the carrier or contractor either at the point of collection or at either's premises.[79] Transit ends at common law when the goods, whether accepted or not, are tendered to the consignee.[80] In the case of goods not to be delivered at the consignee's premises transit ends at a reasonable time after their arrival at their destination.[81]

F. Delay

Unless protected by an express term in the contract the carrier is under a duty to use all reasonable care to deliver goods within a reasonable time.[82] For a carrier to be liable in damages for delay the plaintiff must show a failure to deliver within a reasonable time and negligence on the part of the carrier or his employees.[83] A carrier will not be liable for delay for a cause beyond his reasonable foreseeability and control, such as the act of a third party,[84] the imperfect addressing of goods by the consignor,[85] a strike by the carrier's employees,[86] or an act of God.[87] But liability will follow where the carrier negligently either fails to send goods on or holds

Carriage 1967 (as amended) condition 7(2)(b) below. Kahn-Freund regards the situation of an involuntary bailee in a case such as *Heugh* v. *L. &. N.W. Railway* as exceptional; op. cit., p. 323 and see also pp. 300-301.

[77] *Soanes Bros.* v. *Meredith* [1963] 2 Lloyd's Rep. 293, at 307; *Rigby (Haulage) Ltd.* v. *Reliance Marine Insurance Co. Ltd.* [1956] 2 Q.B. 468.
[78] *Slim* v. *G.N. Railway* (1854) 14 C.B. 647; *Crows Transport Ltd.* v. *Phoenix Assurance Co. Ltd.* [1965] 1 W.L.R. 383.
[79] R.H.A. Conditions, 7(1). See Kahn-Freund, pp. 312-321.
[80] R.H.A. Conditions, 7(2) provide:—
"Transit shall (unless otherwise previously determined) end when the consignment is tendered at the usual place of delivery at the consignee's address within the customary cartage hours of the district.
Provided:
(a) that if no safe and adequate access or no adequate unloading facilities there exist then transit shall be deemed to end at the expiry of one clear day after notice in writing (or by telephone if so previously agreed in writing) of the arrival of the consignment at the Carrier/Contractor's premises has been sent to the consignee; and
(b) that when for any other reason whatsoever a consignment is held by the Carrier/Contractor 'to await order' or 'to be kept till called for' or upon any like instructions and such instructions are not given, or the consignment is not called for and removed, within a reasonable time, the transit shall be deemed to end."
[81] *Chapman* v. *G.W. Railway* (1880) 5 Q.B.D. 278.
[82] *Raphael* v. *Pickford* (1843) 5 Man. & G. 551.
[83] *Taylor* v. *G.N. Railway* (1866) L.R. 1 C.P. 385.
[84] Ibid.
[85] *Briddon* v. *G.N. Railway* (1858) 28 L.J. Ex. 51.
[86] *Sims* v. *Midland Railway* [1913] 1 K.B. 103.
[87] *Briddon* v. *G.N. Railway* (1858) 28 L.J. Ex. 51. See Chapter 18.

them beyond a reasonable time at their destination;[88] this constitutes detention which is an aspect of delay.

G. Deviation

No carrier at common law, private or common, must deviate from his usual or agreed route.[89] When a carrier is entitled to deviate from his route is not clear, but such entitlement seems to exist where it is necessary to keep the goods carried safe.[90] Where deviation results in delay the carrier is liable to compensate the owner of the goods for the financial loss caused by the delay. A private road carrier will be liable for negligence in such circumstances where no special contract exists; where he is a common carrier he will be liable only for negligence.[91] The R.H.A. Conditions provide that the carrier will not be liable for damage, deviation, misdelivery, delay or detention unless he is so advised in writing within three days and the claim made in writing within seven days after the end of transit.[92] The R.H.A. Conditions also state that the carrier will not be liable for indirect or consequential damages or for the loss of a particular market.[93] As has been noted, unjustifiable deviation by the carrier from his usual or agreed route may amount to a fundamental breach and, depending on their construction, may mean that the carrier cannot rely on exemption clauses within that contract.[94]

H. Misdelivery

Where a carrier delivers the goods to any other person than the consignee he is liable for breach of contract and conversion on the basis of misdelivery.[95] However, if the carrier obeys the consignor's instructions and the goods are delivered to a person who commits a fraud on the consignor the carrier will not be liable for misdelivery.[96] Similarly, if the carrier delivers the goods to the consignee's address the duty to deliver has been duly performed and the carrier will not be liable for misdelivery if the person who takes delivery of the goods at the consignor's address is not so authorized by the consignee.[97] But the carrier will be liable for breach of contract and conversion if he is duped into delivering to the wrong person when the circumstances should have made him suspicious that the

---

[88] *Gordon* v. *G.W. Railway* (1881) 8 Q.B.D. 44. See R.H.A. Conditions, condition 10 (1)(b).
[89] *Taylor* v. *G.N. Railway* (1880) 5 Q.B.D. 278.
[90] Ibid. Ridley sugegsts that a carrier is entitled to deviate in order to avoid travelling through a district made unsafe due to war, civil war, riot or flood; op. cit., p. 25. For the position in carriage by sea see Chapter 16.
[91] Kahn-Freund, op. cit., p. 285.
[92] R.H.A. Conditions, 10 (1)(b). Advice in writing must be other than on a consignment note or delivery document; ibid.
[93] R.H.A. Conditions, 12 (2)(b); whether the market is held daily or at intervals.
[94] See above; *Mallet* v. *G.E. Railway* (1899) 1 Q.B. 309; *L. & N.W. Railway* v. *Neilson* [1922] 2 A.C. 263; and see Chapter 25. The question of measure of damages *inter alia* for delay is dealt with below.
[95] *Stephenson* v. *Hart* (1828) 4 Bing. 476.
[96] *McKean* v. *McIvor* (1870) L.R. 6 Ex. 36; *British Traders Ltd.* v. *Ubique Transport Ltd.* [1952] 2 Lloyd's Rep. 236.
[97] *Heugh* v. *L. & N.W. Railway* (1870) L.R. 5 Ex. 51.

person purporting to be the consignee was not lawfully entitled to the goods.[98]

Where the carrier has tried unsuccessfully to deliver goods to the address indicated he becomes an involuntary bailee who is apparently liable for negligence alone, even in the case of misdelivery. Provided the goods are properly tendered even where they are given to a person for whom they are not intended liability will not be absolute.[99]

The R.H.A. Conditions make it clear that the carrier is not liable in respect of a consignment, including liability for misdelivery, where there has been fraud on the part of the trader or owner or servants or agents of either.[1] The limitations regarding liability for loss, damage and misdelivery of goods under the R.H.A. Conditions have already been dealt with.[2]

I. Transit and stoppage in transitu

The question of transit has already been considered when discussing the carrier's liability as warehouseman.[3] The R.H.A. Conditions provide that transit begins when the consignment is handed in at the carrier's place of business or point of collection and ends when the consignment is tendered at the usual place of delivery at the consignee's address within the usual cartage hours of the district.[4] Where no safe and adequate unloading facilities exist, transit is deemed to end one day after notice in writing has been sent to the consignee (or telephone if written prior arrangement has been made) of the arrival of the consignment at the carrier's premises. Transit will also end when a consignment cannot be delivered for any other reason or if it is held by the carrier "to await order" or "to be kept until called for" and instructions to this effect are not given, or the consignment is not called for and removed within a reasonable time.[5]

The right of the unpaid seller of goods to stop the goods in transitu is equally important to the carrier. If the owner of the goods alters the carrier's instructions then the carrier must follow these new directions if he is satisfied that the person giving them is the owner when the orders are given.[6] As it is the consignee who normally has the right to change the place of destination, the carrier (provided there is no notice to the contrary) is justified in assuming the consignee is owner and following his instructions. Thus under s. 32 of the *Sale of Goods Act* 1893 the rule that delivery to the carrier is deemed to be delivery to the buyer is qualified by any contrary agreement made by the parties to the contract of sale.[7]

---

[98] *Duff* v. *Budd* (1822) 3 Brod. & Bing. 177; *Stephenson* v. *Hart* (1828) 4 Bing. 476. Kahn-Freund op. cit. suggests that the circumstances in *Stephenson* v. *Hart* are such as should have alerted the carrier to the fact that the person claiming the goods was neither the consignee nor one acting with his authority while in *McKean* v. *McIvor* these circumstances were lacking; at pp. 299-300.

[99] Kahn-Freund op. cit. at p. 300. As to proper tender see *Heugh* v. *L. & N.W. Railway*, ante which is also cited by Kahn-Freund as illustrating the situation of an involuntary bailee; and see also note 75, above.

[1] Ibid. clause 11.

[2] See above. For a discussion of misdelivery in relation to fundamental breach see above and, generally, Chapter 25.

[3] See above.

[4] Ibid. clauses 7 (1), (2), and see above.

[5] Ibid. clauses 7 (2)(a), (b).

[6] *Scothorn* v. *South Staffordshire Railway* (1853) 3 Ex. 269.

[7] *Cork Distilleries Co.* v. *G.S. & W. Railway* (1874) L.R. 7 H.L. 269.

Fresh directions to the carrier must be given by the owner before the goods have reached their destination so the carrier has a reasonable time to make the necessary provisions. Under the *Sale of Goods Act*[8] where the buyer becomes insolvent the seller can exercise his right of stopping the goods in transit and requesting the carrier to redeliver them to the seller. For this right to be exercised the following conditions must apply: first, the seller must be either partly or wholly unpaid. Secondly, the buyer must be insolvent, i.e. unable to pay his debts. Thirdly, the goods must be in transit. In the context of the *Sale of Goods Act* "transit" is not the meaning used in relation to the carrier's own liability.[9] For the purpose of exercising the right of stoppage in transitu transit begins when the goods are delivered to the carrier and ends when the goods are delivered to the buyer or his agent, either at the original destination or at another later indicated by the buyer[10] or when the carrier agrees to hold the goods as the buyer's bailee. Transit will also be at an end where the carrier wrongfully refuses to hand over the goods to the buyer for the purposes of exercise of the right of stoppage in transitu[11] but the transit will continue as far as the carrier's own liability is concerned. Where the buyer rejects the goods and they remain in the carrier's possession transit continues as far as the exercise of stoppage in transitu is concerned but transit ceases with regard to the carrier's liability.[12] Fourthly, the seller in exercising the right of stoppage in transitu must either take actual possession of the goods or give notice of the claim to the carrier. Such notice is not required in any particular form and may be given to the carrier's employee who at the time is in control of the goods, or to the carrier.

Where notice of stoppage in transitu is given by the seller the carrier is under a duty to redeliver the goods to the seller at the latter's expense. If the carrier refuses or fails to do so he will be liable to an action for conversion,[13] as he will if he obeys an invalid notice. This will be so where the transit has ended and the seller gives notice to the carrier to stop the goods in transitu and the carrier redelivers the goods to the seller; here the buyer may sue the carrier for conversion.[14]

J. The carrier's lien

The common carrier has a right at common law to hold goods against payment of his freight.[15] This is not a right available to the private

---

[8] *Sale of Goods Act* 1893 ss. 44-46; and see Ridley at pp. 34-36.
[9] See above in connection with the carrier's liability as a warehouseman.
[10] See *Plischke* v. *Allisons Bros. Ltd.* [1936] 2 All E.R. 1009.
[11] S.G.A. s. 45(6).
[12] S.G.A. s. 45(4).
[13] *Litt* v. *Cowley* (1816) 7 Taunt. 169.
[14] *Taylor* v. *G.E. Railway* (1901) 70 L.J. (K.B.) 499.
[15] *Skinner* v. *Upshaw* (1702) 2 Ld. Raym. 752. In *Goldsbrough* v. *McCulloch* (1868) 5 W.W. & A'B.(L.) 154 the defendant carried a quantity of wool under contract with the lienor of the wool, and delivered it to the lienees, who did not pay him his freight. The defendant claimed a lien over the remainder of the wool for a general balance owing to him and for his freight. The Full Court of the Supreme Court of Victoria held that although the defendant had not got a lien for his general balance and that a contract with the lienees would not, in the circumstances, be implied, the defendant did have a lien at common law on the remainder of the wool which was undelivered, for its carriage. A carrier

carrier.[16] Such a lien is a particular lien in that the carrier may hold a consignment of goods solely for charges relating to that consignment and for no other goods or services.[17] A carrier by common law may acquire the right to sell the goods after a reasonable time (termed an active lien) and additionally a right to hold goods against freight due for other goods termed a general lien. Both these liens may be acquired by agreement express or implied between the parties or by clearly established and strongly evidenced trade custom.

Under standard form contracts such as the R.H.A. Conditions the common law lien is extended to make it active and general, so that a

had no right of lien for the carriage of goods, given to him to be carried, when they were so given without the consent of the true owner.

A lien was also held to arise in *Gallimore* v. *Moore* (1867) 6 S.C.R. (N.S.W.) 388 where the plaintiff had ordered goods from his agent to be forwarded to him at Black Rock. The agent instructed a carrying agent to forward them. The carrying agent agreed with a carrier to take the goods if he could find a mate going that road, and a way-bill signed by the carrier undertaking to deliver at Black Rock was forwarded to the plaintiff. As the carrier was unable to find a mate he agreed with the carrying agent to take the goods to Wellington. On delivery of the goods by the carrier at Wellington the plaintiff refused to pay the freight. The Supreme Court of New South Wales held, on an action by the plaintiff for the conversion of the goods, with a plea setting up a lien for carriage, that although the carrying agent was not authorized to make a second contract so as to bind the plaintiff, yet the carrier was bound to take the goods under the new contract, they being tendered to him by the agent to be carried, and that therefore he had a lien for the carriage.

In *Kilners Ltd.* v. *John Dawson Investment Trust Ltd.* (1935) 35 S.R. (N.S.W.) 274 furniture on certain premises became subject to a bill of sale which contained a covenant against its removal from the premises without the consent of the bill of sale holder. Without such consent the grantor of the bill of sale, who remained in possession of the furniture, employed a company engaged as storers and carriers to remove and store the furniture in its warehouse. The removal contract provided that the removal charge was payable on demand, and gave the removers a lien for its charges. A second contract was then entered into for removing and storing the furniture, which specified the charge for storage and contained a similar term to that in the former contract, giving a lien for all moneys payable to the company. Subsequently the holder of the bill of sale demanded the furniture which the company refused to deliver, claiming a lien for its charges. This claim was disallowed in the District Court and the company appealed. The Supreme Court of New South Wales, dismissing the appeal, held (1) that the contract was not a contract of common carriage but a composite special agreement to carry and store the furniture, and no common carrier's lien attached for the carrying charges; and (2) that the company could not maintain any claim to a special lien or contractual lien for the removal and storage charges since the holder of the bill of sale had not expressly authorized the removal and storage, and no implied authority arose from the fact that the grantor of the bill of sale had been left in possession of the furniture. (See *A.L.J.* 199, n.9).

It follows that carriers and removalists who are not common carriers do not have a specific lien on the goods that they carry unless there is a specific agreement to that effect with the owner of the goods. Nor do such carriers have an artificer's lien on goods which they carry or transport as their carrying work is not work improves or increases the value of the goods in question; *Hirst* v. *Page & Co.* (1891) T.L.R. 537; see Elliott, *The Artificer's Lien*, p. 20.

In *Brilawsky* v. *Robertson & Cannell* (1916) 10 Q.J.P.R. 113 the defendants, who were common carriers, were held to have wrongly detained, in the purported exercise of a carrier's lien, a box of artist's materials which they had agreed to carry for hire. The damages were assessed by the Supreme Court of Queensland on the basis of the plaintiff's average profits as an artist in Queensland, and the return of a sum of money paid under protest to release the box.

---

[16] *Electric Supply Stores* v. *Gaywood* (1909) 100 L.T. 855.
[17] *Prenty* v. *M.G.W. Railway* (1866) 14 W.R. 314.

general lien is available against the owner of the goods and enforceable by sale of such goods if charges are not met within a reasonable time after the carrier first gave notice to the owner of the goods of exercise of the lien.[18] The carrier's right under a standard form contract to exercise a general lien may arise when the contract is made even though it cannot be exercised when a particular event occurs, such as the carrying of the goods. A lien does not depend on permission being given for it to come into existence. In the case of *George Barker (Transport) Ltd.* v. *Eynon*[19] the plaintiffs were transport contractors regularly trading with a meat exporting company whose indebtedness to a bank was secured by mortgage debenture creating a floating charge. All transport transactions between the parties were subject to the R.H.A. Conditions,[20] and payments were made by the company to the plaintiffs four to six weeks after deliveries. On August 23, 1971, the company, who then owed the plaintiffs over £3,000, sent them two delivery orders to collect and deliver cartons of meat from a ship, one order being carried out. On August 31, the defendant was appointed receiver of the company under the terms of the mortgage debenture and the plaintiffs obtained this information on September 2, while collecting the second order. It was orally agreed between the plaintiffs and defendant that the former would deliver this second order without prejudice to any general lien they might have on the goods. It was further agreed that the defendant would pay for the second delivery and clear the outstanding freight if the plaintiffs could later establish under the claimed lien entitlement to refuse delivery of the second order. Delivery having been made the defendant then was prepared to pay only for that delivery and not the balance owed. The plaintiff's claim for a declaration that the lien was enforceable was dismissed at first instance on the grounds that they had no lien on the goods as these were not in their possession when the defendant was appointed receiver. The Court of Appeal held, in allowing the appeal by the plaintiffs, that the contract of August 23 gave them a contractual right to exercise a general lien on the happening of certain events, i.e. the carrying of the goods. After this date the plaintiffs were entitled to exercise the lien even though a receiver was appointed subsequently as the rights of the debenture holders arising when the floating charge crystallized were subject to the prior rights of the plaintiffs.[21]

A general lien cannot be exercised until the goods reach their destination or the unpaid seller stops them in transitu.[22] This right of the unpaid seller has priority over the carrier's general, but not his particular lien.[23]

---

[18] R.H.A. Conditions cl. 13; which states: "The carrier shall have a general lien against the owner of any goods for any moneys whatsoever due from such owner to the Carrier. If any lien is not satisfied within a reasonable time the Carrier may at his absolute discretion sell the goods as agents for the owner and apply the proceeds towards the moneys due and the expenses of the sale, and shall upon accounting to the Trader for the balance remaining, if any, be discharged from all liability whatsoever in respect of the goods."
[19] [1974] 1 W.L.R. 462.
[20] Which included cl. 13 above.
[21] Decision of Mocatta J. [1973] 1 W.L.R. 146 reversed; *Parsons* v. *Sovereign Bank of Canada* [1913] A.C. 160 applied.
[22] See ante.
[23] *U.S. Steel Products Co.* v. *G.W. Railway* [1916] 1 A.C. 189.

Thus the carrier is not justified in detaining the goods at the commencement of transit and refusing to give them up until his general account is paid.[24] If the carrier remains in possession of the goods at the end of transit as a warehouseman his lien continues. The carrier must take reasonable care of goods held under the exercise of his lien and keep them where they can be conveniently repossessed by the consignor or consignee on payment of the debt due under the lien. Such expenses as have been incurred by the carrier in taking care of the goods are recoverable from the owner[25] but the carrier has no right to charge for warehousing goods he detains in exercise of his lien as such detention is for his own benefit and interest.[26]

K. Dangerous goods

The consignor is liable to a carrier for all damage caused by dangerous goods that have been delivered to the carrier by the consignor unless the nature of the goods has been declared to the carrier on delivery for carriage and these were accepted by the carrier in full knowledge of their dangerous attributes.[27] Under common law a common carrier is not obliged to carry dangerous goods.[28] If goods are damaged by dangerous goods of another owner carried in the same vehicle a common carrier is liable to the owner of the damaged goods unless this has been excluded by special contract; the owner of the dangerous goods is liable to compensate the carrier in this case.

The common law principle that the consignor impliedly warrants that goods are suitable for carriage and not dangerous probably applies to all carriers, whether or not they are under a duty to carry the goods and whether or not the consignor knows of the danger.[29] The carrier's right to damages in this case includes those for injury to himself or his employees[30] and his own property or goods of other consignors.[31]

In the case where goods are delivered to a private carrier under no common law or statutory duty to carry, the consignor is liable for damage caused by dangerous goods not so declared to the carrier, if the consignor knew or should have known them to be dangerous.[32] Under the R.H.A. Conditions[33] dangerous goods accepted by the carrier must be accompanied by a full declaration of their nature and contents. They must also be properly and safely packed in accordance with any statutory regulations relating to road transport currently in force. It is also provided that the trader shall indemnify the carrier against all loss, damage or injury arising from the carriage of any dangerous goods, whether declared or not.[34]

---

[24] *Wiltshire Iron Co* v. *G.W. Railway* (1871) L.R. 7 Q.B. 776.
[25] *G.N. Railway* v. *Swaffield* (1874) L.R. 9 Ex. 132.
[26] *Somes* v. *British Empire Shipping Co.* (1860) 8 H.L. Cas. 338; but cf. ante, p. 497.
[27] *Bamfield* v. *Goole & Sheffield Transport Co.* (1910) 2 K.B. 94; *Brass* v. *Maitland* (1856) 6 E. & B. 470.
[28] *Bamfield* v. *Goole* ante, see generally Kahn-Freund, p. 386 et. seq.
[29] *Burley* v. *Stepney Corporation* [1947] 1 All E.R. 507, at 510.
[30] *Bamfield* v. *Goole* ante.
[31] *The Winkfield* [1902] P. 42; see generally Chapter 4, ante.
[32] *G.N. Railway* v. *L.E.P. Transport and Depository Ltd.* [1922] 2 K.B. 742.
[33] R.H.A. Conditions, cl. 4.
[34] Ibid., cl. 4(2).

Under the R.H.A. Special Conditions for Carriage[35] the trader is required
to supply the carrier inter alia with full information regarding dimensions
and weight of the goods and the route to be followed.[36] The carrier is
entitled to an indemnity from the trader for damage caused by the goods
in transit and any costs involved in the removal of obstructions in the
way of the passage of the load.[37]

L. Measure of damages

A carrier who is responsible for loss or injury to goods arising naturally
from his default must compensate their owner.[38] The measure of damages
as a general rule is the difference in the market value of the goods at the
time and place at which they were due to be delivered and when they were
delivered.[39] A carrier is not liable for indirect or consequential damages
or loss of a particular market,[40] unless there is a special contract to this
effect. Similarly, a carrier cannot be made liable for any loss of profits or
damages incurred by the owner due to the latter's inability to carry out
a contract of sale.[41] A carrier will only be liable for loss of exceptional
profits if it can be proved that he was aware of facts which would result
in such a loss if he were guilty of delay.[42]

III. INTERNATIONAL CARRIAGE OF GOODS BY ROAD

The international carriage of goods by road is governed in the United
Kingdom by the *Carriage of Goods by Road Act* 1965,[43] which puts into
legislative effect the Geneva Convention on the Contract of International

---

[35] Special Conditions for Carriage of Abnormal, Indivisible Loads (adopted
April 1970).
[36] Abnormal Load Conditions, cl. 2.
[37] Ibid., cl. 6. Dangerous goods are defined in the R.H.A. Conditions as follows
by cl. 1:—
"(a) goods which are specified in the special classification of dangerous goods
issued by the British Railways Board or which, although not specified therein,
are not acceptable to the British Railways Board for conveyance on the ground
of their dangerous or hazardous nature; or
(b) goods which though not included in (a) above are of a kindred nature."
In respect of the carriage of nuclear material special provision is made by the
Nuclear Installations Act 1965 (U.K.). The Act places all liability upon the
operator of the nuclear plant concerned so that that operator is absolutely liable
for injury to any person or damage to any property to the exclusion of anyone
else even if the damage or injury occurs when the nuclear material is being
carried on his behalf (s. 7(2)(b)). The Act does not affect the operation of
inter alia the *Carriage of Goods by Road Act* 1965 in relation to exoneration
of the carrier (s. 12(4) as amended by the *Nuclear Installations Act* 1969 s. 1).
[38] *Hadley* v. *Baxendale* (1854) 9 Exch. 341, at 345-355; *Victoria Laundry (Windsor)
Ltd.* v. *Newman Industries Ltd.* [1949] 2 K.B. 528.
[39] *The Heron II* [1969] 1 A.C. 351.
[40] R.H.A. Conditions cl. 12(2); see above.
[41] See *Heskell* v. *Continental Express Ltd.* [1950] 1 All E.R. 1033 per Devlin J.,
at 1048; cited by Kahn-Freund, pp. 275-276.
[42] *Simpson* v. *L.N.W. Railway* (1876) 1 W.B.D. 274; contrast *Horne* v. *Midland
Railway* (1873) L.R. 8 C.P. 131.
[43] No. 37 of 1965; the Act does not apply to carriage between the United Kingdom
and the Irish Republic; see end of Schedule, below.

Carriage of Goods by Road (C.M.R.) of 1956 (hereinafter referred to as the Convention).[44]

The Convention applies to every contract for carriage by road in vehicles[45] for reward, when the place for taking over the goods and the place designated for delivery, as specified in the contract, are situated in two different countries, one of which is a party to the Convention, irrespective of the place of residence and the nationality of the parties.[46] The Convention applies where goods from a vehicle are not unloaded and that vehicle is carried over part of the journey by sea, road, rail, inland waterways or air.[47] Where any loss, damage or delay in delivery occurs driving the carriage by such other means of transport the Convention does not govern the road carrier's liability but this is determined by the law of carriage relating to that particular mode of transport. The Convention will govern if no conditions apply to the method of transport in question.[48]

A. Consignment note

The consignor and the carrier are required to make out a consignment note, in three parts, one of which is given to the consignor, one held by the carrier, and one which has to accompany the goods. The Convention provides[49] that the consignment shall contain:—

(a) the date of the consignment note and the place at which is is made out;

(b) the name and address of the sender;

(c) the name and address of the carrier;

(d) the place and the date of taking over of the goods and the place designated for delivery;

(e) the name and address of the consignee;

(f) the description in common use of the nature of the goods and the method of packing, and, in the case of dangerous goods, their generally recognised description;

(g) the number of packages and their special marks and numbers;

(h) the gross weight of the goods or their quantity otherwise expressed;

(i) charges relating to the carriage (carriage charges, supplementary charges, customs duties and other charges incurred from the making of the contract to the time of delivery);

(j) the requisite instructions for Customs and other formalities;

(k) a statement that the carriage is subject, notwithstanding any clause to the contrary, to the provisions of the Convention. Where applicable the note shall contain the following additional particulars:—

(a) a statement that transhipment is not allowed;

---

[44] See *Carriage of Goods by Road Act 1965* (No. 37 of 1965); the Convention is reproduced in substance in the Schedule to the Act. See also Hill, op. cit., p. 615 et seq. See generally D. J. Hill [1975] Lloyd's M.L.Q. 303; A. E. Donald [1975] Lloyd's M.L.Q. 420; O. C. Giles (1975) 24 I.C.L.Q. 379. The other parties to the Convention besides the U.K. are Austria, Belgium, Denmark, France, West Germany, Gibraltar, Guernsey, Holland, Hungary, Isle of Man, Italy, Luxembourg, Norway, Portland, Portugal, Sweden, Switzerland and Yugoslavia.
[45] See *Carriage of Goods by Road Act 1965*, Sched. Art. 1(2).
[46] C.M.R. Art. 1.
[47] Ibid., Art. 2(1).
[48] Ibid., Art. 2(1) see Chapter 17.
[49] Ibid., Art. 6.

(b) the charges which the sender undertakes to pay;

(c) the amount of 'cash on delivery' charges;

(d) a declaration of the value of the goods and the amount representing special interest in delivery;[50]

(e) the sender's instructions to the carrier regarding the insurance of the goods;

(f) the agreed time-limit within which the carriage is to be carried out;

(g) a list of the documents handed to the carrier.

The consignor is responsible for all expenses, loss and damage the carrier sustains due to the insufficiency or inaccuracy of particulars detailed in (b), (d), (e), (f), (g) and (j) in the first list and of all particulars in the second list, and of any other particulars or instructions given by the consignor so that the consignment note can be made out.[51]

The validity of the carriage is unaffected by the irregularity, loss or lack of the consignment note but if it does not contain the required statement under (k) in the first list the carrier is liable for all expenses, loss or damage that the person entitled to dispose of the goods sustains as a result of such omission.

B. Carrier's liability

The carrier is liable for any loss or damage to the goods from when he accepts the goods for carriage to the time of delivery. Under Article 17 the carrier is not liable if the loss, damage or delay is caused by the wrongful act or neglect of the claimant, by his instructions given other than as a result of a wrongful act or neglect of the carrier or by inherent vice of the goods or through circumstances which the carrier could not avoid and the consequences of which he could not prevent.

It is for the carrier to prove that he is exempt from liability on the grounds stated above and when he has so succeeded, it is for the plaintiff to prove that the loss, damage, or delay was not, either wholly or partly, the result of one of the causes.[52] The carrier will not escape liability due to the defective condition of the vehicle used for the carriage because of the wrongful act or neglect of the person from whom the carrier hired the vehicle or of the former's agents or servants.[53]

The carrier will not be liable when loss or inherent damage is a result of the special risks in:—

(a) use of open sheeted vehicles, when their use has been expressly agreed and specified in the consignment note; or

(b) the lack of, or defective condition of, packing in the case of goods which by their nature, are liable to wastage or to be damaged when not packed or when not properly packed; or

(c) handling, loading, storage or unloading of the goods by the sender, the consignee or persons acting on behalf of the sendere or the consignee; or

(d) the nature of certain kinds of goods which particularly exposes them to total or partial loss or to damage, especially through breakage,

---

[50] See post.
[51] Ibid., Art. 7.
[52] Ibid., Art. 18.
[53] Ibid., Art. 17(3).

rust, decay, dessication, leakage, normal wastage, or the action of moth or vermin;

   (e) insufficiency or inadequacy of marks or numbers on the packages;

   (f) the carriage of livestock.[54]

The position of the carrier inter alia under Art. 17 is examined in a later discussion of recent decisions;[55] it has been suggested that the carrier's position here is weaker than that of a private carrier, but stronger than that of a common carrier in that in the present context the carrier will be exempted from liability if he can prove, not only the fault of the plaintiff or inherent vice of the goods, but additionally that the damage was caused by circumstances that the carrier was unable to prevent.[56]

C. Consignor's right of disposal

The consignor has the right to dispose of the goods; for example by requesting the carrier to stop them in transitu, to change the delivery destination or substitute another consignee.[57] This right is not dependent on the consignee being an insolvent buyer or on the seller being an unpaid seller and does not, presumably, apply between the seller and the consignee but only between the consignor and the carrier. The consignor's right of disposal ends when the second copy of the consignment note is handed to the consignee[58] or when the goods reach their designated destination for delivery and the carrier is required by the consignee to deliver the goods and the second copy of the consignment note.[59]

D. Delay

The carrier will be liable for delay if the goods are not delivered within the agreed time-limit, or where there is none, within a reasonable time.[60] Liability for delay is governed by Art. 17(2)[61] and would seem to approximate to that applying under the common law. Where there is an agreed time-limit within which the carriage is to be carried out it must be stated in the consignment note.[62]

---

[54] Ibid., Art. 17(4) subject to Art. 18(4), (2). Under Art. 17(4)(f) and Art. 18(5) the carrier is not liable for loss or damage caused by special risks involved in the carriage of livestock provided he can prove he took all steps normally incumbent upon him and complied with any special instructions issued to him. The carrier under Art. 18(4) is not entitled to exemption under Art. 17(4)(d) where carriage is undertaken in a specially equipped vehicle. See *Ulster-Swift Ltd.* v. *Taunton Meat Haulage Ltd.* [1975] 2 Lloyd's Rep. 502; [1977] 3 All E.R. 641.

[55] See post; *James Buchanan & Co. Ltd.* v. *Babco Forwarding & Shipping (U.K.) Ltd.* [1977] 2 W.L.R. 107; [1977] 3 W.L.R. 907; *Ulster-Swift Ltd.* v. *Taunton Meat Haulage Ltd.; Fransen Transport N/V (Third Party)* [1977] 3 All E.R. 641; *Muller Batavia Ltd.* v. *Laurent Transport Co. Ltd.* [1977] 1 Lloyd's Rep. 411.

[56] Op. cit., Ridley at p. 61.

[57] Ibid., Art. 12(1).

[58] Ibid., Art. 12(2).

[59] Ibid., Art. 13(1).

[60] Ibid., Art. 19.

[61] See ante.

[62] Ibid., Art. 6(2)(f); Art. 17(1)(b) above. Quaere whether these provisions exempt a carrier from liability for damages for delay when agreement on a time limit has not been included in the consignment note and the carrier does not deliver the goods within the agreed time limit, and yet within a reasonable time; see Ridley, p. 62.

Where goods are not delivered within thirty days of the agreed time-limit or, where there is none, within sixty days of the carrier taking over the goods, it will be conclusively presumed that the goods are lost.[63]

E. Dangerous goods

The consignee is under a duty to inform the carrier of the exact nature of any dangerous goods which he delivers to him, and if he does not so inform the carrier the latter may unload or destroy the goods, or render them harmless, without being liable for compensation.[64] Where the nature of the goods is not stated in the consignment note, the consignee bears the burden of proof that he informed the carrier.

F. Limitation of damages

Damages recoverable for total or partial loss of the goods are calculated by reference to the value of the goods at the place and time when they were accepted for carriage.[65] Such damages are limited to twenty five gold francs per kilogram of gross weight short,[66] unless the consignee in the consignment note declared a higher value[67] or a special interest in delivery[68] against an agreed surcharge. The carrier is additionally liable to refund all carriage and other charges and customs duties.

Carriage here refers only to the carriage dealt with under the contract and does not include return carriage charges and storage costs on goods damaged during the period of carriage covered by the contract. In the case of total destruction the full amount of the carriage and other charges and customs duties are refunded but in the case of damage short of total destruction this is only in proportion to the actual damage.[69] Compensation recoverable for damaged goods are subject to the maximum sum laid down.[70] The limitation on the amount recoverable as damages for goods which are lost, damaged or delayed, does not apply if the carrier or his employees or agents in the course of their employment have been guilty of misconduct.

The carrier's liability for delay is limited to the carriage charges[71] and his liability for damage is the amount by which the goods have diminished in value but is limited to the amount payable in respect of loss.[72]

---

[63] Ibid., Art. 20(1). See *William Tatton & Co. Ltd.* v. *Ferrymasters Ltd.* [1974] 1 Lloyd's Rep. 203, at 206; *Ulster-Swift Ltd.* v. *Taunton Meat Haulage Ltd.* [1975] 2 Lloyd's Rep. 502; [1977] 3 All E.R. 641.

[64] Ibid., Art. 22.

[65] Ibid., Art. 23.

[66] Ibid., Art. 23(3). The gold franc being the gold franc weighing 10/31 of a gramme, of millesimal fineness 900, the value of which is laid down periodically in Sterling Equivalent Orders. Where amounts on which compensation under the Convention is based are not expressed in the currency of the country in which payment is claimed, conversion is at the rate of exchange applying on the day and at the place of payment of compensation; ibid., Art. 27(2).

[67] Ibid., Art. 24.

[68] Ibid., Art. 26.

[69] *William Tatton and Co. Ltd.* v. *Ferrymasters Ltd.* [1974] 1 Lloyd's Rep. 203 disapproved in *James Buchanan* v. *Babco Forwarding & Shipping (U.K.) Ltd.* [1977] 2 W.L.R. 107. Cf. the decision of the House of Lords in the latter case on appeal in [1977] 3 W.L.R. 907.

[70] Ibid., Art. 25(2); see generally *William Tatton and Co. Ltd.* ibid.

[71] Ibid., Art. 25.

[72] Ibid., Art. 25.

At any stage of proceedings the court is empowered to make such order as is just and equitable if the carrier's liability is limited and may take note of proceedings begun or likely to be begun in the U.K. or elsewhere.[73]

G. Subcontractors and successive carriers

Under the *Carriage of Goods by Road Act* 1965 a successive carrier and his employees and agents as well as the consignee and the carrier are parties to the contract of carriage[74] and this enables sub-contractors to benefit from exemption clauses in the main contract; the carrier being responsible for the acts and omissions of his employees and agents acting within the scope of their employment.[75] The latter are entitled to rely on provisions within the Convention that exclude or limit the carrier's liability[76] and become party to the original contract of carriage.

Where a second carrier takes over the goods from the first carrier during the carriage he must give a dated and signed receipt for the goods to the first carrier and put his name and address on the second copy of the consignment note;[77] this will also apply if the goods are delivered to subsequent carriers during the carriage. Legal proceedings for loss, damage or delay to the goods may only be brought against the first carrier, the last carrier, or the carrier who was carrying the goods when the loss, damage or delay occurred[78] except in the case of a counter-claim or set-off. An action may also be brought at the same time against several of such carriers. The various carriers have the right to claim contribution or indemnity from other carriers responsible for the damage.[79] Where one of the carriers is insolvent, the share of the compensation due from, and unpaid by, him will be divided among the other carriers in proportion to the share of the payment for the carriage due to them.[80] When a carrier has been given notice of proceedings being brought against another carrier he cannot afterwards dispute the validity of any judgement given against the other carrier in this case.[81]

H. Recent cases on carrier's liability under the Convention

In *Ulster-Swift Ltd.* v. *Taunton Meat Haulage Ltd.*[82] the defendant carriers agreed to transport three hundred pork carcases, the property of the plaintiffs, from Enniskillen to Basle. It was agreed that the carriage should take place in a refrigerated vehicle, and the contract was subject to the Convention as set out in the schedule to the 1965 Act. Upon arrival the pork was found to be unfit for human consumption and was destroyed by

---

[73] *Carriage of Goods by Road Act* 1965 s. 3.
[74] Ibid., s. 14(2); see also Arts. 3, 28(2) and 34.
[75] Ibid., Art. 3.
[76] Ibid., Art. 34; see *Ulster-Swift Ltd.* v. *Taunton Meat Haulage Co. Ltd.* [1975] 2 Lloyd's Rep. 502; [1977] 3 All E.R. 641; *SGS-Ates Componenti Elettronici S.p.A.* v. *Grappo* [1977] R.T.R. 442.
[77] Ibid., Art. 35.
[78] Ibid., Art. 36.
[79] Ibid., Art. 37; but not under s. 6(1)(c) of the *Law Reform (Married Women and Tortfeasors) Act* 1935 by s. 5 of the 1965 Act.
[80] Ibid., Art. 38.
[81] Ibid., Art. 39.
[82] [1977] 3 All E.R. 641; affirming the decision of Donaldson J., reported at [1975] 2 Lloyd's Rep. 502.

the Swiss authorities. In an action by the plaintiff owners, the carriers sought exemption under Art. 17. Para. 2, of the Convention, arguing that the deterioration of the pork had been caused by "inherent vice". Alternatively, they contended that they were entitled to the protection of Art. 17, Paras. 4 (d) and 18, Para. 4, of the Convention: viz. that the deterioration was occasioned by "risks inherent in . . . the nature of" the pork and that they (the defendants) had taken all steps incumbent on them in the circumstances, with respect to the choice, maintenance and use of the refrigerated vehicle, in order to protect the pork. The Court of Appeal[83] held against them on both defences. It relied upon (and upheld) the trial judge's finding that, on all the evidence, the balance of probabilities favoured the conclusion that the carriers had failed to take some step incumbent upon them for the protection of the goods. In the Court of Appeal's opinion it was not necessary to identify exactly what the relevant step was in order to arrive at that conclusion. The Court accordingly adopted Donaldson J.'s conclusion that ". . . the sole cause of the damage was excessive temperature which, as I find on the balance of probabilities, occurred during the transit and it could not be ascribed to inherent vice."[84] As a result of this, it was no longer open to the defendants to rely upon Art. 17, Para. 4 (d). In order to do so, they would have had to discharge the burden, imposed upon them under Art. 18, Para. 4, of proving that all steps incumbent on them in the circumstances with respect to the choice, maintenance and use of the (refrigerated vehicle) had been taken, and that they complied with any special instructions issued to them. This they had failed to do; and the inability or refusal of the trial judge to pin-point the precise regard in which they had failed to comply with Art. 18, Para. 4, did not invalidate his conclusion, based on the balance of probability, that it had not been complied with. The Court of Appeal referred, by way of analogy, to the shipowner's duty to exercise diligence in order to comply with the implied undertaking as to seaworthiness in contracts for the carriage of goods by sea.[85]

Megaw L.J., went on to consider a defence raised by the carriers under Art. 18, Para. 2, of the Convention. This provided that:

> When the carrier establishes that in the circumstances of the case, the loss or damage could be attributed to one or more of the special risks referred to in Article 17, Paragraph 4, it shall be presumed that it was so caused. The claimant shall however be entitled to prove that the loss or damage was not, in fact, attributable either wholly or partly to one of these risks.

---

[83] Judgement delivered by Megaw L.J.

[84] [1977] 3 All E.R. at 645. The burden of proving inherent vice lay upon the carrier by virtue of art. 18, para. 1, but Donaldson J. was able, on all the evidence, to hold affirmatively that no such vice had been in existence: [1977] 3 All E.R. at 647.

[85] *Riverstone Meat Co. Pty. Ltd.* v. *Lancashire Shipping Co. Ltd.* [1961] A.C. 807; and see *Carriage of Goods by Sea Act,* 1971, Schedule Art. IV, para. 1 (post. p. 622). The reference by Megaw L.J. to *Houghland* v. *R.R. Low (Luxury Coaches) Ltd.* [1962] 1 Q.B. 694 at [1977] 3 All E.R. 650 is presumably misprinted and should read "it is *unnecessary* for a plaintiff to prove what was the precise, specific event by reason of which his goods were lost while in the custody of the carrier."

It was held that this provision could have no impact upon the defendants' liability in the light of the findings of fact already reached by Donaldson J. Even if they were able to satisfy the court as to the facts demanded by the first sentence of Art. 18 Para. 2, the defendants fell down on the second sentence because of the affirmative conclusion that no inherent vice had existed at the time of delivery. This finding involved the conclusion that the plaintiff *had* proved the facts demanded by the second sentence to Para. 2, which therefore put the defendants back where they had started. The plaintiff had only to establish such facts upon the balance of probability,[86] and even if, as the defendants had contended, some higher standard such as the criminal standard had to be fulfilled, it would seem equally proper to apply that same standard to the carrier's exemption under Art. 18, Para. 4.[87] As Megaw, L.J., observed:

> It would seem absurd to suggest that the intention of the Convention is that, although it expressly provides for the possible disproof of the presumption (*raised by Art. 18, Para. 2*), nevertheless, when that disproof is achieved, it produces no result, for the claimant's claim still fails![88]

The carriers were accordingly held liable to the consignors for the value of the pork and for certain associated expenses.[89] They were, however, permitted to recover this amount by way of an indemnity from the third parties to whom they had delegated the actual carriage of the pork. The third parties' contention that there was only one contract of carriage, between themselves and the plaintiff and that any claim against them by the defendants was accordingly time-barred under Art. 32 of the Convention, was dismissed by the Court of Appeal, further upholding on this point the decision of Donaldson J.[90]

The decision contains some valuable reflections on the part of Megaw L.J., as to the approach to be adopted by an English court in interpreting the Convention. Referring to the suggestion by Lord Denning M.R., in an earlier decision[91] that international conventions should be interpreted in a 'Continental' or more intuitive manner by asking "what is the sensible way of dealing with this situation so as to give effect to the presumed purpose of the legislation?", the learned Lord Justice observed:

> We shall, as we say, seek to follow the approach indicated by Lord Denning in the *Buchanan* case. But a possible danger of that approach, of which an example is to be found in the judicial decisions to which we have referred,[92] is not, indeed, that the judges become legislators,

---

[86] [1977] 3 All E.R. at 648-649.
[87] Ibid., at 650.
[88] Ibid., at 648.
[89] Viz., the cost of carriage and destruction and veterinary expenses. The disallowance of damages at first instance for survey fees was made the subject of a cross-appeal by the plaintiffs, but was not pursued: see [1977] 3 All E.R. 641 at 651.
[90] Ibid.
[91] *James Buchanan & Co. Ltd.* v. *Babco Forwarding & Shipping (U.K.) Ltd.* [1977] 2 W.L.R. 107; subsequently affirmed on different grounds [1977] 3 W.L.R. 907 (infra).
[92] Megaw L.J. was referring to the fact that some thirty decisions of European courts had given rise to no fewer than twelve differing interpretations of arts. 17, para. 4, and 18 para. 2. See Wijffels, *European Transport Law* C.M.R. 1976,

but that they may become legislators with a widely differing, and perhaps unduly legalistic, views of the policy which is, or ought to be, behind the legislation. Hence the law, whatever it may gain in other respects, may in some cases suffer a loss of what has always been regarded as one of the essential features of the law—uniformity; or, at least, predictability. Sometimes, in relation to the judicial view of 'the presumed purpose of the legislation', it may be a case of quot judices, tot sententiae: whereas, in relation to what the legislation has actually said, it is unlikely that judicial opinion would vary so widely. The danger of lack of predictability, or uniformity, is of course much less serious in a legal system where the doctrine of precedent is an important element, or where there is one supreme court whose decision will be accepted as binding by all other courts concerned in the interpretation of the law in question. That, one hopes, will apply in general to European Community matters, but it does not apply in respect of this convention.[93]

These "wise words" were cited with approval by Lord Edmund-Davies in his dissenting speech in *James Buchanan & Co. Ltd.* v. *Babco Forwarding & Shipping (U.K.) Ltd.*[94] In that case, the defendants had agreed to carry whisky from the plaintiffs' bonded warehouse in Glasgow to Teheran. The contract was subject to the Convention and, because the whisky was intended for export, the plaintiffs paid no excise duty on it. The goods were delivered to the defendants in Glasgow but were stolen en route from a lorry park in London. There was no doubt that the defendants were liable for this loss under Art. 17, Para. 1, of the Convention, but there was considerable dispute as to how that loss should be quantified. This dispute involved the House in a consideration of Art. 23, which (so far as is material) provided that:

1. When, under the provisions of this Convention, a carrier is liable for compensation in respect of total or partial loss of goods, such compensation shall be calculated by reference to the value of the goods at the place and time at which they were accepted for carriage.
2. The value of the goods shall be fixed according to the commodity exchange price or, if there is no such price, according to the current market price or, if there is no commodity exchange price or current market price, by reference to the normal value of goods of the same kind and quality.
. . .
4. In addition, the carriage charges, Customs duties and other charges incurred in respect of the carriage of the goods shall be refunded in full in case of total loss and in proportion to the loss sustained in case of partial loss, but no further damages shall be payable.

The dispute arose because the theft of the whisky prior to export made it dutiable under s. 85 of the *Customs and Excise Act* 1952. The plaintiffs were accordingly obliged to pay over a sum of £30,000 to the Customs authorities. They claimed that this sum should be recoverable, together

Pt. 1, p. 208 (vol. XI, no. 2, 1976): *Legal Interpretations of C.M.R.: the Continental Viewpoint.*

---

[93] [1977] 3 All E.R. 641 at 646-647.
[94] [1977] 3 W.L.R. 907 at 927 (H.L.(E.)).

with the ex duty value of the whisky, from the defendants: *either* because it was a component in the market value of the goods under Art. 23, Paras. 1 and 2, *or* because the £30,000 duty fell within the category of "other charges incurred in respect of the carriage of the goods" as specified in Art. 23, Para. 4. The defendants resisted, contending that the relevant value was the ex duty value, that the £30,000 duty was not a charge within the contemplation of Para. 4, and that they should accordingly be liable only for the export value of the whisky, some £7,000.

The House of Lords held for the defendants on the first point but against them on the second. Applying the decision of the House in *Charrington & Co. Ltd.* v. *Wooder,*[95] their Lordships recognised that it is possible for there to be more than one market for a commodity and unanimously held that the only logical market upon which an assessment could be made under Art. 23, Para. 1 was the export market for the goods. Were the alternative accepted, the bizarre consequence might follow that the plaintiffs could recover the dutiable value of the goods even if they had been lost in circumstances in which no duty would be attracted; for example, if the bottles had been negligently broken and the whisky lost through spillage.[96]

> 'The current market price' can surely, in its context, refer only to the current export market price, and this according to the respondents' own invoices and the evidence of their own financial director is the net value of the goods exclusive of excise duty, i.e. . . . about £7,000 . . . In these circumstances, the current price of the goods in home market of the country where the carrier takes delivery is, in my view, irrelevant.[96a]

Upon Art. 23, Para. 4, the House of Lords came to the conclusion (Lords Edmund-Davies and Fraser of Tullybelton dissenting) that the £30,000 excise duty did constitute a charge "incurred in respect of the carriage of the goods" and was accordingly recoverable from the carriers. In so concluding, they specifically repudiated the assertion by Lord Denning M.R. in the Court of Appeal that there was a gap in the Convention on this point which could be filled (in favour of the plaintiffs) by looking to the presumed but unarticulated intention of the legislators. Paragraph 4 could legitimately be read in such a way as to accommodate the present form of liability by substituting the words "in consequence of the way in which the goods were carried" for the original "in respect of carriage"; a process which Lord Salmon evidently regarded as a mere exchange of synonyms,[96b] and which was endorsed by both Lord Wilberforce and Viscount Dilhorne.[96c] In the view of the majority, there was no hiatus in the legislation because that legislation itself should be construed "not . . . pedantically or rigidly but sensibly and broadly".[96d] Lord Wilberforce agreed with Lawton and Roskill JJ. in the Court of Appeal that it would be permissible to consult the French text of the Convention

95 [1914] A.C. 71.
96 [1977] 3 W.L.R. 907 at 910 per Lord Wilberforce.
96a Ibid. at 918-919 per Lord Salmon.
96b Ibid. at 919.
96c Ibid. at 913-914 and 916-917.
96d Ibid. at 919 per Lord Salmon.

in order to lend clarity to the English translation, even when the English text was not on its surface ambiguous; but he observed that in the present case the words of the French version ("frais encourus a l'occasion du transport") were no less widely-drawn than their English equivalent and therefore provided little aid or advancement in the interpretation of the statute.

> I think that the correct approach is to interpret the English text, which after all is likely to be used by many others than British businessmen, in a normal manner, appropriate for the interpretation of an international convention, unconstrained by technical rules of English law, or by English legal precedent, but on broad principles of general acceptation: *Stag Line Ltd.* v. *Foscolo, Mango & Co. Ltd.* [1932] A.C. 328, per Lord Macmillan, at p. 350. Moreover, it is perfectly legitimate in my opinion to look for assistance, if assistance is needed, to the French text. This is often put in the form that resort may be had to the foreign text if (and only if) the English text is ambiguous, but I think this states the rule too technically . . . There is no need to impose a preliminary test of ambiguity.[96e]

Although Lords Edmund-Davies and Fraser of Tullybelton disagreed with the majority on the question whether excise duty counted in the present case as a charge incurred in respect of carriage, they did so in terms which, no less than those of the majority, discountenanced the opinion of Lord Denning M.R. that a more intuitive or innovative method of interpretation could satisfy any deficiencies in the language of the Act itself.[96f] In this respect attention was drawn to the Continental authorities which, on broadly comparable facts, had taken quite different approaches to the question at issue, and which were regarded as refuting any notion that some more generalised but ascertainable and uniform Continental system of interpretation lay waiting to be utilised by an English Court.[96g]

I. Carrier's right to sell goods

The carrier has a right to sell the goods without waiting on instructions from the person entitled to dispose of them if the goods are perishable and their condition requires sale, where cost of storage is disproportionate to the goods' value and if the carrier has not received, after a reasonable time, contrary instructions from the person entitled to dispose of the goods.[97] The latter is entitled to the proceeds of the sale, after deduction of expenses chargeable against the goods.[98]

[96e] Ibid. at 911-912; and see Lord Salmon at 920. Cf. Lord Edmund-Davies at 925, who had misgivings on this question but agreed on balance that a foreign text might legitimately be consulted.

[96f] See especially Lord Edmund-Davies at 924-925; and further at 927.

[96g] *British American Tobacco Co. (Nederland) B.V.* v. *van Swieten B.V.* (Unreported, March 30, 1977, Amsterdam Arrondissementsrechtsbank 3rd Chamber A); *L'Helvetia (Cie)* v. *Cie Seine & Rhone* (1973) Bulletin des Transports (Paris), 1973, p. 195, Court of Appeal of Paris (5th Chamber). The latter decision accords with that in the case discussed in the text. For further recent decisions on specific provisions in the Act, see *Muller Batavier* v. *Laurent Transport Co.* [1977] R.T.R. 499; *SGS-Ates Componenti Elettronici S.p.A.* v. *Grappo* [1977] R.T.R. 442.

[97] Art. 16(3).

[98] Art. 16(4).

J. Time limit for claims and limitation of actions

If the consignee has inspected the goods before taking delivery of them where loss or damage is not apparent evidence contradicting the result of such inspection is admissible only if the consignee has sent notification of this in writing to the carrier within seven days of the inspection.[99] Failure to notify the carrier on this basis will extinguish all claims for loss or damage by the consignee. Such claims will be similarly extinguished by the consignee taking delivery. Unless a written reservation is sent to the carrier within twenty-one days from the time when the goods were placed at the disposal of the consignee no compensation is payable for delay.[1]

All actions arising from the contract of carriage are time-barred after one year; in the case of wilful misconduct three years. The limitation period, in the case of partial loss, damage or delay in delivery, runs from the date of delivery. In the case of total loss it runs from the thirteenth day after the end of the agreed time limit, or where there is none, from the sixtieth day from the date when the goods were taken over by the carrier. In all other cases the period of limitation runs after the expiry of three months after the making of the contract of carriage.[2]

K. Contracting out

The parties are not entitled to contract out of the terms of the Convention and any contract purporting to do so is void to the extent that it is repugnant to those terms.[3] Exceptionally, where there are two or more carriers, they are entitled to make a special contract to vary the provisions of the Convention in respect of contribution and indemnify against each other regarding their liability under the contract of carriage.[4]

IV. CARRIAGE OF GOODS BY ROAD IN AUSTRALIA

The law of carriage of goods by road in Australia derives generally from English case law and early statute. The Carrier's Acts of each State will be examined together with relevant case law and, in conclusion, the position of standard conditions of road transport in Australia will be discussed.

A. New South Wales

The *Common Carriers Act* 1902 provides that no common carrier for hire shall be liable for the loss of, or injury to, any articles or other property falling within the Second Schedule to the Act when the value of such articles exceeds $20 unless the sender or deliverer declares their value and nature at the time of delivery and the person receiving them on the carrier's behalf accepts the appropriate increased charge.[5] The articles specified in the Second Schedule are:

[99] Art. 30(1), (2).
[1] Art. 30(3).
[2] Art. 32(1). See *Muller Batavier* v. *Laurent Transport Co.*, ante.
[3] Art. 41(1).
[4] Art. 40.
[5] Section 4. By s. 3, "common carrier" means a common carrier by land.

Gold or silver coin of the realm or of any foreign State or any gold or silver in a manufactured or unmanufactured state or any precious stones jewellery watches clocks or time-pieces of any description trinkets gold or silver ores bills notes of any bank orders notes or securities for the payment of money English colonial or foreign stamps maps writings title-deeds paintings engravings pictures gold or silver plate or plated articles glass china silks in a manufactured or unmanufactured state and whether wrought up or not wrought up with other materials furs lace or opium or any of them.

In the event of a declaration that goods are of a value exceeding the aforementioned sum, the carrier may demand an increased rate of charge,[6] provided that such rate is stated and notified by a legible notice affixed in some conspicuous part of the office, warehouse or receiving-house where the carrier receives such goods.[7] The object of the increased rate is expressed to be "as a compensation for the greater risk and care to be taken for the safe conveyance of such valuable articles."[8] A receipt must be given on demand,[9] and the failure to comply with such a demand (or to affix the statutory notice of increased charges upon the relevant premises) will deprive the carrier of the protection of the Act, reduce his responsibility for the goods to that imposed at Common Law, and render him liable to refund the increased rate of charge.[10] However, a declaration of the value of articles delivered for carriage is not conclusive evidence of their value; the carrier may require the deliveror to prove the declared value and shall be liable only for such damage (not exceeding the declared value) as is proved by the "ordinary legal evidence."[11]

A notice in the form prescribed by s. 5(2) binds all persons sending or delivering parcels or packages containing the valuable articles in question without further proof of its having come to their knowledge.[12] Conversely, no other public notice or declaration made by the carrier shall be deemed to limit or affect his common law liability for goods carried by him;[13] in the words of s. 7(2), "all common carriers shall be liable as at the Common Law to answer for the loss or injury to any articles and goods in respect whereof they are not entitled to the benefit of this Act, any public notice or declaration by them made and given contrary thereto or in anywise limiting such liability notwithstanding."

Section 8(1) provides that, for the purposes of the Act, every office, warehouse or receiving-house used or appointed by any common carrier for the receiving of parcels to be conveyed shall be deemed to be his office, warehouse or receiving-house. Any one or more of such common carriers shall be liable to be sued by his or their name or names only;[14] and no action to recover damages shall abate for failure to join any co-partner or co-proprietor in the relevant conveyance by land for hire.[15]

---

6 Section 5(1).
7 Section 5(2).
8 Ibid.
9 Section 6(1).
10 Section 6(2).
11 Section 11.
12 Section 5(3).
13 Section 7(1).
14 Section 8(2).
15 Section 8(3).

Section 9 defines (in terms which are expressly made subject to the special liability for articles contained in the Second Schedule)[16] the general responsibility of the common carrier for neglect or default. Every such carrier is liable for loss of or injury to goods (including animals) if such loss or injury occurs in the receiving, forwarding or delivering thereof, and is occasioned by the neglect or default of himself or his servants. Such liability cannot be excluded by any "notice, condition or declaration made", and provisions to this effect are declared null and void. But the foregoing liability is subject to three major qualifications:

(a) the carrier may impose conditions which are just and reasonable;[17]

(b) the plaintiff cannot recover (without declaration of their higher value) damages for animals greater that the sums specified in the Third Schedule to the Act.[18] If declaration of such higher value is made, the carrier is entitled to demand an increased rate, provided that this represents a reasonable percentage of the excess upon such value and is publicised by notice in the manner prescribed in s. 5.[19]

(c) no special contract for the receiving, forwarding or delivering of goods (including animals) shall affect any party other than the carrier unless signed by him or by the person delivering the goods for carriage.[20]

Finally, s. 10 provides that nothing in the Act shall be deemed to protect any common carrier for hire from liability arising from the felonious or fraudulent act of any servant in his employ: nor shall it protect any such servant from liability for any loss or injury occasioned by his personal neglect or misconduct.

B. Queensland

The carriage of goods by land is governed in Queensland by the *Carriage of Goods by Land (Carriers' Liabilities) Act* 1967, which is the most modern and radical of all the State enactments in its field.[21] It amounts to a substantial (if not complete) codification of the duties of private and common carriers alike. It must, however, be read subject to the overriding effect of ss. 69 and 74 of the *Trade Practices Act* 1974 (Cwth.) which apply to every contract entered into by a corporation for the supply to a consumer of services involving the transportation and distribution of

---

[16] Section 9(d); ante.
[17] Section 9(a).
[18] The Third Schedule reads as follows:
Scale of Damages for Loss or of Injury to Animals.
For any horse $100
For any meat cattle per head $30
For any sheep or pigs per head $4
[19] Section 9(b).
[20] Section 9(c).
[21] The expression "carriage by land" within the Act applies to the carriage of goods by railway as well as by road (s. 2); but the expression "carrier" as used in the Act does not include the Commissioner for Railways "or any other person or authority, in his or its conduct of a railway or tramway within the State": ibid. As to the liability of the Commissioner of Railways in Queensland, see post, p. 000 et seq.

goods.[22] Moreover, the 1967 Act does not, except in very limited circumstances,[23] extend to the carriage of goods by sea or by air.[24]

1. *Duty to deliver*: Section 4(1) requires every carrier to take all reasonable steps to ensure delivery of goods entrusted to him. This obligation applies whether the contract is a simple contract for the transportation of goods or a contract for the carriage of a passenger for reward, to which the carriage of goods is incidental.[25] In either event, delivery must be in accordance with the relevant contract of carriage.

Section 4(2) endorses the general Common Law rule that a bailee's duties are not discharged merely upon his exercising (with reasonable care) an authority to engage a substitute party to perform the work for which he was retained.[26] It provides that the carrier shall not be deemed to have performed the duty imposed upon him by s. 4(1) by reason only of the fact that he engages another person to deliver the goods. Section 4(3), however, enables the carrier to obtain release by agreement with the other party from the duty imposed by s. 4(1), in the event of an occurrence which reasonably affects the delivery of goods as prescribed by that subsection.

2. *Liability for loss of or injury to goods*: Section 5(1) places the carrier's liability for loss or injury exclusively upon "the unlawful act or the negligence of the carrier or any of his agents."[27] In so doing, it abolishes the special status and responsibilities of the common carrier by road within the State of Queensland. The liability in question is stated to commence upon receipt of the goods by the carrier for the purpose of carriage and to continue for as long as they remain in the carrier's custody.[28] The latter expression is amplified by s. 5(2), whereunder goods entrusted to a carrier[29] shall be deemed to remain in his custody until he delivers them—

(a) in accordance with the contract of carriage in question or a subsequent agreement lawfully entered into by him with the other party to such contract or with the owner of such goods; or

(b) where such goods are carried as incidental to the carriage by land

---

[22] Post, p. 527.

[23] Defined in s. 3(1)(b).

[24] Section 3(2)(a). Transitional provisions detailing the commencement of the operation of the Act, and its effect upon contracts already entered into before the Act came into force, are contained in ss. 3(1)(a) and 3(2)(b).

[25] Section 4(1): ibid. The application of s. 4(1), and indeed the whole of the provisions of the Act, to both types of carriage of goods is emphasised by s. 2, which defines "carrier" for the purposes of the Act as a person "who holds himself out for hire for reward for the carriage by land of goods as a common carrier or otherwise", and specifically includes within this definition "a person who carries by land (whether for reward or not) luggage as incidental to his carriage by land of a passenger for reward."

[26] Post, p. 829 et seq. (Chapter 20); *B.R.S. Ltd.* v. *Arthur V. Crutchley & Co. Ltd.* [1968] 1 All E.R. 811; *Philip Morris (Australia) Ltd.* v. *The Transport Commission* [1975] Tas. S.R. 128, at 131.

[27] Agent includes "any servant" and "unlawful act" means any crime or misdemeanour: s. 2. Again, s. 5(1) endorses the Common Law rule that a mere delegation of the task of carriage does not per se exonerate the carrier.

[28] Section 5(1).

[29] This expression includes goods in the personal custody of a passenger being carried under a contract of carriage for reward: s. 5(4).

of a passenger for reward, in accordance with his contract with such passenger; or

(c) to any person or authority to whom or to which he is required by or under any Act or other enactment or any order of a court of competent jurisdiction to deliver or to relinquish possession of such goods.

Other than in limited circumstances involving the death of the consignor or other customer of the carrier by land,[30] a claim against a carrier in respect of loss of, or injury to, goods shall not be enforceable unless the claimant gives notice in writing, within the specified period, of such loss or injury to the carrier.[31] When the goods have been delivered at the place contracted for, such notice must be given within five days of the date of that delivery;[32] when the goods have not been thus delivered, notice must be given within five days after the claimant has become aware of the loss or injury in question.[33]

3. *Limitation of liability*: A statutory ceiling upon liability for goods of an undeclared value (corresponding to that in the more traditional common carriers' Acts) is imposed by s. 6 of the Queensland Act. By virtue of s. 6(1), special procedures must be followed to render a carrier liable for the loss of, or injury to, goods entrusted to him under a contract of carriage, or entrusted to him as incidental to the carriage by land of a passenger by reward, in an amount greater than $20 per package or, in the case of unpacked goods, $20 per item of goods or $200 per consignment, whichever is the less.[34] To recover damages in excess of this amount the consignor must, at or before the time when the goods were delivered to the carrier, have given to him a statement in writing declaring the nature and value of such goods; and he must have received from the carrier the latter's acceptance in writing of the consignment, specifying the nature and value so declared and his acceptance

---

[30] Detailed in s. 5(3).

[31] This requirement was held to be merely procedural and not a matter of substantive law, with the result that it was not applied by the forum, in the decision of the New South Wales Court of Appeal in *Allan J. Panozza & Co. Pty. Ltd.* v. *Allied Interstate (Qld.) Pty. Ltd.* [1976] 2 N.S.W.R. 192.

[32] Section 5(3)(a).

[33] Section 5(3)(b). The coda to s. 5(3) provides that in calculating the five days no account is to be taken of any Saturday or Sunday or of any day on which the premises of the carrier concerned, at the address at which such notice is given, were closed to business during the whole of his usual business hours.

[34] By section 2, "consignment" means the quantity of goods carried at one and the same time in or on any one vehicle for any one consignor: and this term includes the quantity of goods so carried as incidental to the carriage by land of any one person for reward. In *Penn Elastic Co. Pty. Ltd.* v. *Sadler's Transport Co. (Vic.) Pty. Ltd.* (1976) 10 A.L.R. 185, the High Court held that the statutory limitation of liability operates as a modification upon the contract of carriage, with the result that it attaches independently to each separate contract and governs the carrier's liability only for the packets or units comprised within the particular contract in question. Thus where a consignor consigned goods under twenty separate consignment notes he was held entitled to recover, in aggregate, the statutory limit in respect of each distinct contract, and not a single overall sum of $200. "A coincidental identity of consignor under a number of contracts of carriage does not make the goods a single consignment simply because they happen to be carried at one and the same time in or on a vehicle. There remain as many different consignments as there are contracts of carriage provided all the goods consigned under a contract of carriage are carried in or on one vehicle at one and the same time", per Jacobs J. at 189.

of the increased risk in respect of the same. Moreover, if the carrier has so required, the consignor must have paid or agreed to pay to him an amount in addition to the ordinary rate of charge for carriage of such goods, by way of compensation for the increased risk and care expected of the carrier in cases of this kind.

A carrier who holds himself out as ready to accept liability in excess of the statutory maximum laid down by s. 6(1) must exhibit a notice, in legible print, stating the substance of s. 6(1) and setting out any additional charges which are payable in the event of the carrier's accepting liability in excess of that subsection.[35] But even where such liability is properly accepted the carrier shall not be liable for loss or injury to a greater amount than the actual value of the goods or their declared value (whichever is the less) plus the amount of any additional charge paid, as required by the carrier, in respect of the carriage of those goods.[36]

4. *Remedies for delay*: A person who alleges that a carrier has delayed unreasonably and without lawful excuse in the delivery of goods may complain to this effect to a Magistrate's Court having jurisdiction at the place of the carrier's principal place of business. The Court may then, under s. 7, order that the goods be delivered to the person who appears to be entitled to their possession, and that the carrier shall pay a just amount by way of compensation, to the person to whom such payment appears just. Such order shall be without prejudice to any other remedy which a person may have against the carrier by virtue of the latter's delay in the delivery of the goods.

5. *Carrier's indemnity*: Section 8 requires any consignor to compensate the carrier for additional charges, expenses, and liabilities (including liability in damages) incurred by the carrier in connection with the carriage by reason of "false or inaccurate particulars furnished by the consignor to the carrier" in respect of goods consigned for carriage by land, or in respect of the carriage of such goods.

6. *Contractual modification*: Section 9 of the Queensland Act provides as follows:

> 9. (1) *Provisions of Act incorporated in contracts.* There shall be deemed to be incorporated in every contract of carriage and in every other contract under which is to be performed a carriage of goods to which this Act applies the provisions of sections four, five and eight and of subsections (1) and (3) of section six of this Act.
>
> (2) *Contracting out prohibited.* Save as is prescribed by this Act, a contract made by a carrier which purports to exclude, modify, alter or avoid any provision of this Act or directly or indirectly has the effect of such an exclusion, modification, alteration or avoidance shall, to that extent, be void except in the case of a contract made,

---

[35] Section 6(2). As to the requisite siting of such notices, see ss. 6(2)(a) and (b) and the coda to s. 6(2).

[36] Section 6(3). By s. 11(a), in any proceedings brought for loss or injury in respect of goods, the plaintiff "shall be required to prove the value of the goods or, as the case may require, the quantum of damage occasioned by the loss or injury in question."

in the event of loss of or injury to goods, with a claimant for damages in respect thereof in settlement of the claim in question.[37]

7. *Servants and agents*: In any action brought against the servant of a carrier in respect of loss or injury occasioned to goods which have been entrusted to the carrier for carriage by land, such a servant shall be entitled to avail himself of sections 5, 6 and 8 of the 1967 Act as could the carrier himself; provided that, at the time of the loss or injury, that servant was acting within the course of his employment.[38] Moreover, it is provided that the aggregate of amounts recovered from a carrier and his agents in respect of loss of or injury to goods shall not exceed the statutory maxima prescribed by s. 6.[39]

8. *Non-reversal of bailee's burden of proof*: Carriers are bailees, and s. 11(b) of the Queensland Act preserves the carrier's common law obligation to prove the absence of fault on his part. It provides, therefore, that in any proceeding brought in respect of loss of, or injury to, goods which have been entrusted to a carrier for carriage by land.

> The plaintiff shall not be required to prove the cause of such loss or injury but the defendant, if he seeks to avoid liability, shall be required to prove that such loss or injury was not occasioned by such cause as would render him liable therefor.

9. *Regulations*: Section 12 empowers the Governor in Council to make regulations for giving effect to the objects and purposes of the Act, and lays down rules for the propounding of such regulations.

C. Victoria

The *Carriers and Innkeepers Act* 1958 as amended by the *Carriers and Innkeepers Amendment Act* 1974[40] provides that no mail contractor, stage coach proprietor, or common carrier by land for hire shall be liable for the loss or injury to articles or property described in the Act when the value of such articles or property exceeds $20;[41] unless the sender or deliveror declares their value and nature at the time of delivery and the person receiving them on the carrier's behalf accepts the appropriate increased charge or an undertaking to pay the same.[42] Where a declaration that goods are of a value exceeding $20 has been made, the carrier may demand an increased rate of charge.[43] A receipt is required to be given on

---

[37] In the case of a contract of carriage to which s. 9 applies, the consignor cannot apparently avoid the contract and allege a wider liability in tort or bailment: *Allan J. Panozza & Co. Pty. Ltd.* v. *Allied Interstate (Qld.) Pty. Ltd.* [1976] 2 N.S.W.R. 192. But see the comment on this ruling at p. 595, n 31, ante.

[38] Section 10(1). For a discussion of the general common law rules regarding third-party protection under contracts of exclusion (to which s. 10(1) represents an exception) see p. 986 et seq., post.

[39] Ante; s. 10(2).

[40] No. 6214 of 1958 amended by No. 8534 of 1974 repealing ss. 13-25 of the principal Act and Third Schedule. The 1958 Act repealed the *Carriers and Innkeepers Act* 1928 (insofar as those parts not then repealed), the *Carriers and Innkeepers Act* 1948 in its entirety and an item in a Schedule to the *Statute Law Revision Act* 1939 referring to the *Carriers and Innkeepers Act* 1928; see First Schedule *Carriers and Innkeepers Act* 1958.

[41] Section 3; the articles or property are described in terms similar to the Second Schedule of the New South Wales Act; ante.

[42] Section 3.

[43] Section 4; on terms similar to s. 5(2) of the New South Wales Act.

demand and failure to do so, or to affix the statutory notice of increased charges upon the premises, removes the protection of the Act from the carrier and makes him liable on the basis of common law and additionally liable to refund the increased rate of charge.[44] No other public notice or declaration made by the carrier shall be deemed to limit or affect his common law liability for goods carried by him.[45] Every office, warehouse or receiving house used or appointed by any common carrier is deemed to be his office, warehouse or receiving house.[46] Any one or more of such common carriers shall be liable to be sued by his or their name or names only;[47] and no action to recover damages shall abate for failure to join any co-partner or co-proprietor in the relevant conveyance by land for hire.[48]

In the case of loss of or damage to a package or parcel the value and contents of which have been declared and the increased rate of charge paid, the party entitled to recover damages in respect of such parcel or package is entitled to recover the extra charge in addition to the value of the parcel or package.[49] A declaration of the value of articles delivered for carriage is not conclusive evidence of their value; proof of the declared value may be required from the deliveror by the carrier and the carrier shall be liable only for such damage (not exceeding the declared value) as is proved by the ordinary legal evidence.[50] Nothing in the Act protects any common carrier for hire from liability arising from the felonious act of any servant in his employ; nor does it protect any such servant from liability for any loss or injury occasioned by his personal neglect or conduct.[51]

Additionally, the Act by s. 12 provides that any carriers' agent, for-warding agent or other person undertaking for reward to deliver any goods to a carrier by land for hire for the purpose of carriage or procuring any such carrier to carry such goods shall be deemed to have received such goods to be carried by himself and is liable to be sued as if he had actually undertaken to carry such goods as a common carrier. This is sub-ject to the qualification that such a person will not be liable if it has been expressly agreed in writing between him and the person employing him that he will not be so liable and that his liability shall end on his delivering the goods to any licensed carrier or, alternatively, on his procuring a licensed carrier to carry the goods and informing his employer of this fact, or mutually agreeing on such other conditions with his employer.[52]

Nothing in the Act shall affect or annul any special contract for the conveyance of goods and merchandises; but no special contract shall be

---

[44] Section 5.
[45] Section 6; the wording is similar to s. 7(2) of the New South Wales Act.
[46] Section 7.
[47] Ibid.
[48] Ibid.
[49] Section 9.
[50] Section 11.
[51] Section 10; the equivalent s. 10 of the New South Wales Act includes "fraudulent" act.
[52] Section 12 also provides that the carriers' agent, forwarding agent or other person must enter in a book the name and licence number of the carrier to whom the goods are passed in order to avoid the liability mentioned at the beginning of the section. Apart from s. 11 of the *Carriers Act* 1891 of South Australia, s. 12 appears to have no counterpart either in other Australian States or in England.

binding on or affect any party unless signed by him or by the sender or deliveror of such goods and merchandises.[53]

In *Arcweld Constructions Pty. Ltd.* v. *Smith and others*[54] the plaintiff claimed to be entitled to succeed against the defendant on the basis of s. 12. McInerney J. was disposed to accept the argument advanced by defendants' counsel that the words of s. 12, "or other person" were to be construed eiusdem generis with the words "carriers agent" and "forwarding agent" as indicating a person who does not himself carry the goods but who arranges for or procures a carrier by land for hire to carry the goods, including a person who receives the goods for a limited purpose such as delivery of them to a carrier for carriage. The words "other person undertaking for reward" were viewed by the learned judge (although not finally so determined by him) as referring to a person who holds himself out as ready, willing and able to carry out such an undertaking on a regular basis and that the words quoted had no application to a person who did not undertake to procure another person to carry the goods as a regular part of his business.[55] On this construction neither of the defendants were held to come within s. 12.

The liability of common carriers under a special contract was considered in *Renwick* v. *McCulloch*.[56] In an action for the value of work and labour done in the carriage and delivery of goods, the defendant pleaded that the work and labour was done by the plaintiff "as a carrier by land for hire within the colony of Victoria", and that the plaintiff had not a licence to carry on business as a carrier under the *Innkeepers and Carriers Act* 1859.[57] The plaintiff pleaded that the work was done under a special contract. The Supreme Court of Victoria held that the Act was not limited to common carriers and that though a common carrier who enters a special contract for the carriage of goods ceases to be a common carrier quoad that contract a carrier within the meaning of the Act could enter into a special contract and continue as a carrier quoad the subject matter of that contract. Therefore the plaintiff could not recover. In *Hyland* v. *Mullaly & Byrne Pty. Ltd.*[58] the defendants were customs agents whose ordinary course of business was to proceed to the wharf where goods were located, to clear those goods from the Customs Department, paying the duty, if any, payable on such goods, and then delivering them as indicated by the customer. They reserved the right to refuse to do business for any customer. It was held that, on the facts, the defendants were not common carriers.[59]

Negligence on the part of the carrier's servants was considered in

---

[53] Section 8. There is no stipulation that the carrier must impose conditions which are just and reasonable (see s. 9(a) New South Wales Act) nor are there provisions relating to limitation or damages recoverable for injury to or loss of animals (see Third Schedule New South Wales Act).
[54] Unreported judgement of McInerney J., Supreme Court of Victoria, 17 September 1968. For the facts of this case see Chapter 20.
[55] At p. 43.
[56] (1864) 1 W.W. & A'B(L.) 48.
[57] Now repealed; the licensing provisions were repealed by the *Carriers and Innkeepers Amendment Act* 1974.
[58] [1923] V.L.R. 193.
[59] See ante.

Paterson v. *Miller*[60] and *Hyland's*[61] case already noted. In *Hyland's* case the defendants were employed by the plaintiff to deliver forty bales of kapok at the plaintiff's factory. A servant of the defendant drove a lorry containing the goods up to the door of the plaintiff's factory at which delivery was to be made. The lorry driver commenced unloading, but after a few bales had been unloaded, fire was discovered to have broken out in the plaintiff's factory and unloading stopped. The place where the lorry stood was blocked by lumber and before the vehicle could be moved the load caught fire and was destroyed. It was held that the driver of the lorry had not acted negligently and that the defendant was not liable for the loss of the goods. In *Paterson* v. *Miller*[62] it was held to be no defence to an action for damages for loss of goods bailed that the loss resulted by fire due to smoking and related acts on the part of the bailee's servant who had custody of the goods at the time of the loss.

D. Tasmania

The *Common Carriers Act* 1874 closely resembles the New South Wales *Common Carriers Act* 1902 but the definition in the Tasmanian Act of "common carrier" is wider than that given in the New South Wales Act. By s. 2 a common carrier includes mail contractors, stage coach proprietors, railway companies, and carriers by railway or tramway.[63]

Section 3 of the *Common Carriers Act* provides for exemption of the carrier from liability for undeclared goods of specified value in terms similar to s. 4 of the New South Wales Act and s. 4 in the Tasmanian Act which entitles the carrier to demand an increased rate of charge for declared goods in excess of $20 and s. 5 dealing with carriers' receipts for increased charges are couched in identical terms to ss. 5 and 6 of the New South Wales Act. The same rules apply regarding prohibition on other types of notice limiting or affecting the liability of a common carrier;[64] as to the definition of the office of a carrier;[65] as to the inability of a carrier to object to a plaintiff's failure to join any other co-partner of the carrier in any suit and action;[66] as to liability based on misconduct of the carrier's servants with the addition in the Tasmanian Act of liability for their criminal acts.[67] The carrier's right to require the other party to prove the actual value of declared goods is also in terms similar to the New South Wales Act.[68] Where any parcel or package whose value has been declared has been lost or damaged and an increased charge paid, the party entitled to recover damages for the loss or damage shall be entitled to recover the increased charge paid, in addition to the value of the parcel or package.[69] By s. 13 every railway company shall be liable, notwithstanding any

---

[60] [1923] V.L.R. 36.
[61] Ante, p. 599.
[62] Ante.
[63] For the position of the Transport Commission as a common carrier in respect of the operation of railways in Tasmania, a function now taken over by the Federal Government, see *Railway Management Act* 1935 s. 15 and Chapter 18.
[64] Section 6 Tasmania; s. 7(1) N.S.W.
[65] Section 7(a) Tasmania; s. 8(1) N.S.W.
[66] Section 7(c) Tasmania; s. 8(3) N.S.W.
[67] Section 10 Tasmania; s. 10 N.S.W.
[68] Section 11 Tasmania; s. 11 N.S.W.
[69] Section 9.

notice to the contrary, for loss of or injury to any horses, cattle, or other animals, or any articles, goods or things resulting from neglect or default by the company or its servants. Damages recoverable from a railway company for injury to any horse, cattle, sheep or pigs is limited to $100 for a horse, $30 for neat cattle per head and $2 for sheep and pigs unless a higher value was declared at the time of delivery.[70] Nothing in the Act annuls or otherwise affects any special contract between a common carrier, as defined, and any other party for the conveyance of goods and merchandise.[71]

E. Western Australia

The *Carriers Act* 1920, bears a close resemblance to the New South Wales *Common Carriers Act* 1902. It is, like its New South Wales counterpart, confined to common carriers by land for hire, and it contains the same provision for exempting the carrier from liability for undeclared goods of specified value as is contained in s. 4 of the New South Wales Act.[72] However, the specification of such valuables differs slightly from that in the New South Wales statute. The Schedule to the Western Australian Act prescribes them as follows:

> Australian Notes, Bank Notes issued in any country, Bills of Exchange, cheques or promissory notes, China, Certificates of title or other documents of title, Clocks, watches, or timepieces of any description, Coins (gold or silver) of any country, Deeds, Engravings, Furs, Glass, Gold or silver in a manufactured or unmanufactured state, Gold or silver plate or plated articles, Jewellery or trinkets, Lace (not being machine made), Maps, Notes, orders, or securities for the payment of money, Pictures or paintings, Precious stones, Silks in a manufactured or unmanufactured state, and whether wrought up or not wrought up with other materials, Stamps of any country, Writings.

Section 3 of the Act entitles the carrier, in terms which correspond to those in s. 5 of the New South Wales Act, to demand an increased rate of charge for declared goods in excess of $20; and the same provisions exist as to receipts[73] as in s. 6 of the counterpart statute.[74] Likewise, the same rules exist as to the prohibition upon other types of notice limiting or affecting the common carrier's liability;[75] as to the definition of a carrier's office, warehouse or receiving-house;[76] as to the inability of a carrier to

---

[70] Section 14(1) Tasmania; s. 9(6) and Schedule 3 N.S.W.; and see Chapter 18.
[71] Section 8. In *Baily* v. *Thompson* (1914) 10 Tas. L.R. 33 the plaintiff, a merchant, wrote to the defendant, a coach proprietor, asking for terms of conveyance of a traveller with samples who had travelled in the defendant's vehicles on other occasions. The defendant replied, quoting terms by "special" or by "ordinary mail vehicle", and the terms by "special" were accepted; the only difference between the two being price. On the journey, on which other passengers were carried without reference to the plaintiff's traveller, the brakes of the motor vehicle failed and it, with the passengers and goods, went into a river. The Supreme Court of Tasmania held that the terms of the contract did not relieve the defendant from liability as a common carrier.
[72] Ante; Western Australia *Carrier's Act* 1920, s. 2.
[73] Section 4.
[74] Ante, p. 592.
[75] Section 5 of the W.A. Act; see s. 7(1) of the N.S.W. Act, ante, p. 592.
[76] Section 6 of the W.A. Act; see s. 8(1) of the N.S.W. Act, ante, p. 592.

raise any objection based upon the plaintiffs' failure to join any other co-partner of the carrier in any suit or action;[77] as to liability founded upon the misconduct of servants;[78] and as to the carrier's power to require the other party to prove the actual value of declared goods.[79] However, the Western Australian Statute contains no separate schedule limiting liability for loss or injury occasioned to animals[80] and the provision as to special contracts is less restrictively phrased. It provides merely that:

> Nothing in this Act contained shall extend or be construed to annul or in anywise affect any special contract between any common carrier and any other parties for the conveyance of goods or merchandises.[81]

Moreover, s. 8 provides that when loss or damage occurs to a parcel or package the value of which has been declared under s. 2, and an increased charge in respect of which has been exacted under s. 3, the party entitled to recover damages for the loss or damage shall also be entitled to recover the increased charge so paid.

Under section 11, the Western Australian Act does not bind or apply to the Commissioner of Railways, but is otherwise binding upon the Crown and upon all State Government departments and agencies.

F. South Australia

The *Carriers Act* 1891, is closely similar to the Western Australian Act of 1920.[82] The principal differences are as follows.

(i) The articles specified in s. 2 of the South Australian Act, for which the carrier is not liable if they are valued in excess of $20 and if a special declaration has not been made at the time of delivery, differ in some detail from those set out in the Western Australian statute. The material portion of the South Australian Act reads as follows:

> . . . gold or silver in a manufactured or unmanufactured state, or any precious stones, jewellery, watches, clocks, or timepieces of any description, trinkets, bills, notes of any bank in His Majesty's dominions or of any foreign bank, orders, notes or securities for payment of money whether foreign or otherwise, stamps, maps, writings, title deeds, paintings, engravings, pictures, gold or silver plate or plated articles, glass, china, silks in a manufactured or unmanufactured state and whether wrought up or not wrought up with other materials, furs or lace, or any of them . . .

(ii) The South Australian Act applies to mail contractors and stage coach proprietors as well as to common carriers by land for hire.[83]

(iii) Section 3 of the South Australian Act (increased rates of charge) makes no provision for the exhibition of the necessary notice to that effect upon the vehicle into which the parcel or package is received.[84]

---

[77] Section 6 of the W.A. Act; see s. 8(3) of the N.S.W. Act, ante, p. 592, and note that there is no Western Australian equivalent of the New South Wales s. 8(2).
[78] Section 9 of the W.A. Act; see s. 10 of the N.S.W. Act, ante, p. 000, and note that the words "or fraudulent" do not appear in the Western Australian provision.
[79] Section 10 of the W.A. Act; see s. 11 of the N.S.W. Act, ante, p. 592.
[80] Cf. s. 9(b) of the N.S.W. Act and Schedule 3; ante, p. 593.
[81] Section 7.
[82] Ante, p. 601 et seq.
[83] Section 2.
[84] Cf. s. 3 of the W.A. Act: ante, p. 601.

(iv) Section 7 of the South Australian Act requires that any special contract abrogating the effect of the Act shall be signed by the non-carrying party to the contract, or by the person sending, delivering or bringing the goods, as the case may be.

(v) Section 9 of the South Australian Act, which deals with the liability of the carrier for the felonious acts of his servants, provides a slightly more amplified description of that word than s. 9 of the Western Australian Act, and refers specifically to "any coachman, guard, book-keeper, porter or other servant" of the carrier.

(vi) Section 11 of the South Australian Act is not complemented in the Western Australian enactment. It seeks to impose the liabilities of a common carrier upon carriers' and forwarding agents unless there is specific agreement to the contrary

> 11. Any carrier's agent, forwarding agent, or other person undertaking for reward to deliver any goods to a carrier by land for hire for the purpose of carriage, or to procure any carrier by land for hire to carry such goods, shall be deemed to have received such goods to be carried by himself, and may be sued in like manner as if he had actually undertaken to carry such goods as a common carrier for hire, unless before or at the time at which he shall have so undertaken it shall have been expressly agreed in writing between him and the person by whom he shall be employed that he shall not be so liable, and that his liability shall cease upon his delivering such goods to any carrier, or upon his procuring a carrier to carry such goods and making the same known to the person by whom he shall have been employed as the case may be, or upon the performance of such other conditions as shall be mutually agreed upon in writing between him and the person by whom he shall have been so employed, and unless he shall have truly entered in a book to be kept by him the name of such carrier.

(vii) Likewise, the South Australian Act contains a further section[85] which has no equivalent in the Western Australian Act. This provides that a receipt given by any person to whom any parcel or package shall have been delivered,[86] acknowledging that the parcel or package has been received in good order and condition, shall exonerate the carrier (or mail contractor or stage-coach proprietor) from any liability for loss or damage to property contained therein. This immunity may, however, be displaced if "some evidence shall be given to show, or from which it may reasonably be inferred, that the damage to any such property, or loss of any such property, occurred while the parcel or package containing such property was in the possession of the carrier in question."

The 1891 Act is expressed not to apply to the South Australian Railways Commissioners.[87]

G. Standard conditions of road carriage in Australia

Prior to the introduction of the *Trade Practices Act* 1974 the various state road transport associations who were members of the Australian Road Transport Federation sought to control competition in the industry

---

[85] Section 12.
[86] Or by his duly authorised agent.
[87] Section 13.

by laying down minimum freight rates and providing for market-sharing through "no poaching" arrangements. Although there were sanctions for failure to observe Association rate schedules, some discounting from the schedules occurred chiefly in respect of large customers. However, the market sharing scheme had the effect of restricting vigorous price competition between the main freight companies.

The *Trade Practices Act* 1974 provides by s. 68 for certain conditions and warranties be implied into contracts for the supply of goods or services to a consumer by a corporation.[88] Any attempt to exclude, limit or modify the effect of these implied conditions and warranties is declared void.[89] Further, by s. 74 services are so defined as to include the transportation of goods.[90]

Following the Act the various road transport associations moved to delete the "no poaching" rules and the sanctions for non-adherence to rate scales for cartage. The Associations adopted "recommended" rate scales and sought Trade Practices Commission authorization of these in terms similar to the application put before the Commission by the New South Wales Road Transport Association.[91] The application by the above Association related inter alia to authorization of the recommended rates and conditions of cartage by members. The Commission was not satisfied that the public benefit test under s. 90(5) of the Act was met regarding recommended rates and conditions and dismissed that part of the application, but granted the arrangement interim authorization.[92]

An application by the National Freight Forwarders Association was also dismissed by the Commission.[93] This application sought authorization of an agreement on a common rate chargeable for normal freight transport and the dissemination of such information to industry and to statutory

---

[88] Section 68(1). See s. 69. See the definition of consumer under the *Trade Practices Amendment Act* 1977 s. 4B(1) and (2). See Appendix II, post.

[89] Section 68(1).

[90] Section 74(1) reads:
"In every contract for the supply (otherwise than by way of competitive tender) by a corporation in the course of a business of services to a consumer there is an implied warranty that the services will be rendered with due care and skill and that any materials supplied in connexion with those services will be reasonably fit for the purpose for which they are supplied."
Section 74(3) reads:
"In this section, 'services' means services by way of—
    (a) the construction, maintenance, repair, treatment, processing, cleaning or alteration of goods or of fixtures on land;
    (b) the alteration of the physical state of land;
    (c) the distribution of goods; or
    (d) the transportation of goods.

[91] Application A 3027 of January 1, 1977 *C.C.H. Trade Practices Reporter* 16598. The Tasmanian Road Transport Federation made no such application and no longer recommends cartage rates but publishes a "Cost Movement Index" which charts increases in the costs associated with road transport. According to their secretary the Association, following the Act, no longer recommends standard conditions to their members.

[92] *C.C.H. Trade Practices Reporter* at para. 36, 16605. The New South Wales Road Transport Federation have appealed to the Tribunal but that body has not yet handed down its determination. Currently (September, 1977) the Tribunal has adjourned consideration of the Federation's appeal who have stated that they will seek a declaratory judgement from the Federal Court on the application.

[93] A.3019.

bodies. The application was dismissed by the Commission on the ground that the agreement would clearly restrict competition between the companies and pricing would be on an industry basis instead of on a company basis except to the extent that large customers could force prices below the agreed common schedule.

The current legal position of standard conditions in the road transport industry is therefore in something of a limbo and its resolution will depend on the confirmation or otherwise of the Commission's decision in the *New South Wales Transport Federation Case.*

Despite the fact that the combined effect of ss. 68 and 74 of the *Trade Practices Act* strike down exemption and limitation clauses in standard conditions of contract hitherto currently used by the road transport industry and the *New South Wales Road Transport Federation* decision further underlines the likelihood that such conditions are likely to have no legal sanction behind them, a typical set of such conditions[94] can be briefly reviewed, bearing in mind the above qualifications.

A general lien on all property received for all moneys owing to or liabilities incurred by the carrier is stipulated, to be unaffected by delivery or sale of any part of such property. Entitlement to charge storage and incidental expenses is claimed by the carrier during the duration of their assertion of the lien.[95]

The carrier reserves complete discretion as to routes to be travelled and methods and time of removal of goods. Liability for delay loss or damage arising from exercise of this discretion is expressly excluded[96] and the carrier accepts no liability for deviation from any route.[97] The carrier stipulates the right to enter into any contract with any third party to carry out his obligations and the conditions of the contract under consideration are stated to apply to storage or transport by such a third party.[98] No article or substance which is, or is likely to be of a dangerous, corrosive, inflammable, explosive or damaging nature, nor anything likely to encourage vermin, borer or other pest shall be sent or given to the carrier for packing, removal or storage, or any contained in any article sent or given to the carrier for such purpose. The customer, by this stipulation, releases and indemnifies the carrier from and against all claims arising out of the handling, storage or carriage of such articles. The customer also undertakes to make good any loss or damage suffered by the carrier and arising from the handling, storage or carriage of such articles. If any such articles are discovered the carrier is given a right to dispose of them in any manner and is not responsible or accountable to any person for them or their value.[99] The carrier accepts no liability for any article not specified in the inventory.[1] The carrier declares himself

---

[94] I am grateful to Mr. L. Bell of Green's Transport Pty. Ltd., Hobart, for a set of conditions of contract used by his firm and also a set of those used by the Australian National Line.

[95] Condition 6, Conditions of Contract, ibid. The term "company" is used instead of "carrier" in the original document.

[96] Condition 9.

[97] Condition 18.

[98] Condition 11.

[99] Condition 14.

[1] Condition 17.

not to be a common carrier and states that he does not undertake the obligations or liabilities of such a carrier. The carrier thus reserves the right to refuse to accept goods for carriage or storage and does so only on the terms and conditions of the contract.[2] The carrier does not accept liability for any loss of or damage to any goods whatsoever and howsoever arising or caused whether by or through the negligence of the carrier or its agents or servant. Nor is liability on such terms accepted if caused or arising through fire howsoever caused, or water, strikes, labour troubles, riots, civil commotion, war, invasion, act of God, flood, stress of weather, moths, borers, vermin, insects (damp, mildew, rot, rust) burglary, house breaking, explosion, accident, mechanical breakdown or any other event happening act or thing except as may be agreed in writing.[3] Such liability as is caused or arises from negligence by the carrier, his servants or agents, in carrying out the contract of road carriage cannot be excluded by virtue of ss. 68 and 74 of the *Trade Practices Act* 1974.[4] The carrier also stipulates that he will not be liable upon any claim under the contract or otherwise or in respect of any goods unless notice of such claim is made in writing to the carrier within seven days after delivery of the goods or after failure to so deliver.[5]

Lastly certain aspects of the Australian National Lines (A.N.L.) conditions of contract may be noted in the integrated nature of transport in Australia. A.N.L. states that it is not a common carrier and reserves the right to refuse or carry articles at its discretion.[6] The A.N.L. reserves the right to contract or arrange, on any terms, for the whole or part or parts of the carriage to be performed by any other person or persons termed a "contractor" in the A.N.L. conditions.[7] A.N.L. declares itself to have a general lien over cargo for all amounts payable to it by any owner.[8] At all times and under all circumstances cargo shall be and remains for all purposes and in all respects at the sole risk of the owners and neither the A.N.L. nor their representatives are stated to be under any liability whatsoever and no claim shall be made or brought by any owner against A.N.L. or their representative for loss or damage.[9]

---

[2] Condition 19.

[3] Condition 20.

[4] Ante.

[5] Condition 22. The carrier additionally states that he will not be liable on such a claim unless legal proceedings are begun within three months of delivery or of failure to do so.

[6] Condition 2; reference P.T. 13. Revision of April 1975.

[7] Condition 3.

[8] Condition 8; owner is defined in Condition 1.

[9] Condition 13. The condition has not been quoted in full; it includes disclaimer for liability for inter alia deterioration, misdelivery, non-delivery and delay as well as negligence, including a breach going to the root of the contract. These last two aspects of the condition would appear to be made invalid by ss. 68 and 74 of the *Trade Practices Act* as s. 74(3)(d) defines services as expressly including the transportation of goods.

CHAPTER 16

CARRIAGE OF GOODS BY SEA

I. INTRODUCTION

The arrangements involved in the carriage of goods by sea are many and varied and the resulting problems can be particularly complex. Basically, however, the owner of goods who wishes them to be carried overseas has two courses open to him.

First, he may charter the services of a ship and its crew for a specified time or voyage[1] and arrange himself for the carriage of his goods by that ship. Indeed, it is possible, in the less usual case where the master and crew are to be the agents of the charterer,[2] to contract for the hire or demise of the ship itself (as opposed to its services only). In that case the charterer, and not (as in the previous cases) the shipowner, will be the carrier of the goods and the relationship between the shipowner and the charterer so far as the ship is concerned will be that of the owner and hirer of a chattel.[3]

Secondly, and this is more common, the cargo owner may look for space in a general ship (that is, one which will carry the goods of all who so wish) and he will generally employ a forwarding agent to find the space.[4] The forwarding agent will arrange this with a loading broker acting on behalf of a shipowner or, where the ship is under charter, on behalf of charterer.[5] Although not normally in possession of the goods, the forwarding agent will often arrange for them to be placed on board the ship, taking in return from the master a mate's receipt, which will subsequently be exchanged for the document of title, again issued by the master, a bill of lading.[6] The bill of lading, as a document of title, may be sold several times over while the goods are in transit thus altering the relationship of the various parties concerned in the transaction under consideration. Careful attention must therefore be paid to the times of passing of property and of risk and the need to insure goods.

---

[1] This hire of services is often loosely called the hire of the ship, which expression is more accurately confined to demise charterparties. See *Tankexpress A/S* v. *Compagnie Financiere Belge des Petroles S.A.* [1949] A.C. 76, at 90 per Lord Porter; *Mardorf Peach & Co. Ltd.* v. *Attica Sea Carriers Corporation of Liberia, The Lanconia* [1977] 2 W.L.R. 286, at 291-292 per Lord Wilberforce.
[2] *Baumwoll Manufactur von Carl Scheibler* v. *Furness* [1893] A.C. 8; *Manchester Trust* v. *Furness* [1895] 2 Q.B. 282, and 539; *Weir* v. *Union Steamship Co. Ltd.* [1900] A.C. 525.
[3] *Reed* v. *Dean* [1949] 1 K.B. 188.
[4] Hill, *Freight Forwarders* (1972).
[5] *Heskell* v. *Continental Express Ltd.* (1950) 83 Ll. L.R. 438, at 449. See *Texada Mines Pty. Ltd.* v. *The Ship "Afovos"* (1972) 46 A.L.J.R. 476.
[6] Post, p. 609.

The above picture can be greatly complicated by multiplication of the relevant arrangements, by the differing degrees of involvement of the interested parties and their agents and by new forms of commercial practice (such as containerisation of cargoes and roll-on/roll-off shipping) and the increasing impact of modern developments in the law. For example, an increasingly common practice is the use of through bills of lading which may evidence a contract for carriage by land or air as well as by sea. The extent to which they share the characteristics of the conventional bill of lading is not clear. A detailed exposition is neither possible nor desirable in a book of this nature or size.[7] A brief and to some extent generalised account may, however, be given. We shall look in turn at some of the principal documents used in the international carriage of goods, some aspects of the commercial context of such carriage, then the rights and obligations under carriage agreements.

II. THE DOCUMENTS INVOLVED

A. Mate's receipt

Subject to contrary custom at the port of loading, a mate's receipt will be issued when the goods have been received for shipment.[8] This will be either "clean" or, if qualified by adverse comments as to the condition of the goods, "foul". The document is an acknowledgment that the goods have been received in the condition stated therein. The qualification it contains will generally, although not necessarily, be embodied in the subsequently issued bill of lading, which will be accordingly "clean" or "claused".[9] The mate's receipt itself acknowledges that the goods are in the possession and at the risk[10] of the shipowner, who will generally hold them on the terms of the usual bill of lading.[11] Until shipment, the liability of the carrier will only be that of an ordinary bailee.[12]

The person in possession of the mate's receipt is generally entitled to receive the bill of lading[13] and to sue for any wrongful dealing with the goods but, except where local custom provides otherwise,[14] the mate's receipt is not a document of title and only prima facie evidences ownership of the goods. Thus mere endorsement and transfer, without notice to the shipowner or his agent, does not pass the property in the goods[15]

---

[7] See Carver's *Carriage by Sea* (12th ed. 1971); *Scrutton on Charterparties* (18th ed. 1974).

[8] *Nippon Yusen Kaisha* v. *Ramjiban Serowgee* [1938] A.C. 429, at 445.

[9] See *Cremer* v. *General Carriers S.A., The Donna Mari* [1974] 1 W.L.R. 341.

[10] *British Columbia Saw-Mill Co.* v. *Nettleship* (1868) L.R. 3 C.P. 499; *Cobban* v. *Downe* (1803) 5 Esp. 41.

[11] See *De Clermont and Donner* v. *General Steam Navigation Co.* (1891) 7 T.L.R. 187.

[12] *Nottebohn* v. *Richter* (1886) 18 Q.B.D. 63. c.f. *Dampskebsselskabet Skjoldborg and C. K. Hansen* v. *Charles Calder & Co.* (1911) 12 Asp. M.L.C. 156.

[13] *Craven* v. *Ryder* (1816) 6 Taunt. 433; *Thompson* v. *Trail* (1826) 6 B. & C. 36; *Falk* v. *Fletcher* (1865) 18 C.B. (N.S.) 403.

[14] See *Kum* v. *Wah Tat Bank* [1971] 1 Lloyd's Rep. 439, at 443, where the words "non-negotiable" prevented it from being so.

[15] *Hathesing* v. *Laing* (1873) L.R. 17 Eq. 92; *Nippon Yusen Kaisha* v. *Ramjiban Serowgee* (supra, n. 8); *Kum* v. *Wah Tat Bank* [1971] 1 Lloyd's Rep. 439.

and retention of a mate's receipt for a disputed account by, for example, a lighterman will not prevent the issue of the bill of lading to the shipper. Usually no person is named in the mate's receipt as owner but where someone is so named the mate's receipt acts as a recognition of property in that person and an acknowledgment that the goods are held to his account; thus, the shipowner may safely deliver them to that person.[16] Where the mate's receipt is not produced and there is only one claimant who proves to be the true owner, the shipowner is entitled to deliver the goods to that person.[17]

B. Bill of lading

The most important document used in the sea carriage of goods is the bill of lading.[18] This is in practice a standard form document which the shipper (traditionally) completes and hands to the shipowner's agent. When the latter agrees its accuracy, he signs it, generally in triplicate. Where possible, the shipper should try to obviate disputes in dealing with it, particularly where goods are shipped as part of a transaction financed by a banker's documentary letter of credit,[19] by securing "clean" bills of lading. In a simple situation, two copies of the bill of lading are sent by air mail and by different posts to the consignee and the third one is despatched to him on board the vessel carrying the goods. Since the bill of lading is a document of title,[20] the goods may be dealt with several times by its transfer while they are afloat. Where a transaction is financed by letter of credit, the bank will generally insist on obtaining the complete set of bills.[21]

The bill of lading has three functions. First, it is evidence of the previously concluded contract of carriage and of its terms.[22] The contract will in fact normally be concluded on the usual bill of lading terms and this may be important where goods have been damaged before actually being loaded on board.[23] Since the bill of lading only *evidences* the contract of carriage, it is possible for the shipper to adduce external

[16] *Evans* v. *Nichol* (1841) 3 Man & G. 614; *Craven* v. *Ryder* (supra, n. 13).
[17] *Cowas-Jee* v. *Thompson* (1845) 5 Moo. 165; and cases cited supra, n. 15.
[18] Where goods are carried by sea for only part of a contracted journey a "through bill of lading" may be issued. This is particularly so where containers are used for combined transport. See Scrutton, op. cit., chapter XVII.
[19] Purvis and Darvas, *The Law and Practice of Commercial Letters of Credit, Shipping Documents and Termination of Disputes in International Trade* (1975 Butterworths, Sydney); Ellinger, *Documentary Letters of Credit—A Comparative Study, Singapore* (1970); *Benjamin's Sale of Goods* (1974), Chapter 23; Gutteridge and Megrah, *The Law of Bankers' Commercial Credits* (5th ed., 1976).
[20] See post, p. 610.
[21] See *Donald H. Scott & Co.* v. *Barclays Bank Ltd.* [1923] 2 K.B. 1.
[22] *Sewell* v. *Burdick* (1884) 10 App. Cas. 74, at 105 per Lord Bramwell; *S.S. Ardennes (Cargo Owners)* v. *S.S. Ardennes (Owners), The Ardennes* [1951] 1 K.B. 55; *Heskell* v. *Continental Express Ltd.* (1950) 83 Ll. L.R. 438, at 449, 453, 455 per Devlin J. In some cases particularly in that of f.o.b. contracts, it may be difficult to decide who made the contract of carriage with the shipowner: see post, p. 610. Moreover, there may be a collateral contract in addition to the main contract of carriage: see *President of India* v *Metcalfe Shipping Co. Ltd.* [1970] 1 Q.B. 289. See also *Ross* v. *Orient Steam Navigation Co.* (1884) 5 L.R. (N.S.W.) 30; *Parbury* v. *Purdy* (1876) 14 S.C.R. (N.S.W.) 207.
[23] *Pyrene Co. Ltd.* v. *Scindia Navigation Co. Ltd.* [1954] 2 Q.B. 402. Cf. *Waters Trading Co. Ltd.* v. *Dalgety & Co. Ltd.* (1951) 52 S.R. (N.S.W.) 4.

evidence of the real terms of the contract, if different,[24] although, as far as an endorsee is concerned, the bill of lading generally offers the only evidence of that contract. Thus, although carriage is ostensibly under the same contract, the rights and duties of the shipper and of an endorsee of the bill of lading in relation to the shipowner may differ.[25]

Secondly, the bill of lading acts as a receipt for the goods described therein, reference generally being made to their nature, quantity, quality,[26] marks,[27] packing and condition.[28] As far as statements as to quantity are concerned, the bill of lading is prima facie evidence that goods of that quantity have been shipped, so the carrier is liable for any short delivery.[29] However, the shipowner is free to demonstrate that they were never in fact shipped.[30] Where the bill of lading has been endorsed to a third party, the latter may receive additional protection if the Hague-Visby Rules[31] apply, for they provide that proof to the contrary will be inadmissible.[32] Where goods are shipped other than by a charterer,[33] the bill of lading provides some evidence of their condition on shipment. This will not, without more, suffice to make the shipowner liable where the goods delivered fail to answer that description,[34] although he may be estopped from adducing evidence to contradict the bill of lading as against an endorsee of it.[35]

Thirdly, the bill of lading operates as a document of title to the goods, thus, possession of it is generally equivalent to possession of the goods. Furthermore, if intended, endorsement and delivery of the bill of lading will operate to transfer both possession and ownership of the goods[36] and the endorsee shall have transferred to and vested in him all rights of suit and be subject to the same liabilities in respect of such goods as if the contract contained in the bill of lading had been made with himself.[37]

---

[24] *S.S. Ardennes (Cargo Owners)* v. *S.S. Ardennes (Owners), The Ardennes* [1951] 1 K.B. 55.

[25] See *Leduc* v. *Ward* (1888) 20 Q.B.D. 475; *Hain Steamship Co. Ltd.* v. *Tate & Lyle Ltd.* (1936) 41 Com. Cas. 350.

[26] See *Cox, Patterson & Co.* v. *Bruce & Co.* (1886) 18 Q.B.D. 147.

[27] See *Parsons* v. *New Zealand Shipping Co.* [1901] 1 K.B. 548.

[28] See *Sea-Carriage of Goods Act* 1924, Sched., Art. III, rr.3-5; cf. *N.T.I. Ltd.* v. *Queensland Insurance Co. Ltd.* [1962] S.A.S.R. 51.

[29] *Sea-Carriage of Goods Act* 1924, Sched., Art. III, r.5. See also *H. Jones & Co. Ltd.* v. *N.Z. Shipping Co. Ltd.* (1916) 12 Tas. L.R. 112; *The Ship "Marlborough Hill"* v. *Alexander Cowan & Sons Ltd.* [1921] 1 A.C. 444; *Bank of Australasia* v. *Blyth* (1874) 5 A.J.R. 166.

[30] *Smith & Co.* v. *Bedouin Steam Navigation Co. Ltd.* [1896] A.C. 70; *Grant* v. *Norway* (1851) 10 C.B. 665; *Sea-Carriage of Goods Act* 1924, Sched., Art. III, r.4; *Rosenfield Hillas & Co. Pty. Ltd.* v. *The Ship "Fort Laramie"* (1923) 32 C.L.R. 23.

[31] Post, p. 625.

[32] *U.K. Carriage of Goods by Sea Act* 1971, Sched., Art. III, r.4.

[33] *Rodocanachi, Sons & Co.* v. *Milburn Brothers* (1886) 18 Q.B.D. 67.

[34] *The Peter der Grosse* (1875) 1 P.D. 414; affirmed (1876) 34 L.T. 749.

[35] *Compania Naviera Vasconzada* v. *Churchill & Sim* [1906] 1 K.B. 237; *Silver* v. *Ocean Steamship Co. Ltd.* [1930] 1 K.B. 416; *The Skarp* [1935] P. 134. See also *Sea-Carriage of Goods Act* 1924, Sched., Art. III, r.5; (U.K.) *Carriage of Goods by Sea Act* 1971, Sched., Art. III, r.4. Cf. *Australian General Electric Pty. Ltd.* v. *A.V.S.N. Co. Ltd.* [1946] S.A.S.R. 278

[36] *Sewell* v *Burdick* (1884) 10 App. Cas. 74.

[37] (N.S.W.) *Usury, Bills of Lading and Written Memoranda Act* 1902, s. 5; (Vic.) *Goods Act* 1958, s. 73; (Qld.) *Mercantile Acts* 1867-96, s. 5; (Tas.) *Bills of*

Where a bill of lading is issued for goods on a chartered ship, it almost invariably contains words which contradict the terms of the charterparty. The effect of this conflict is considered below.[38]

When the ship arrives at its destination, the master, if unaware of any contrary claim to the goods,[39] is justified in delivering them to the first person presenting a bill of lading making the goods deliverable to that person.[40] He delivers to someone else at his peril[41] but does not transfer to that person any better right to the goods than the latter already has.[42]

It has recently become not uncommon to use non-negotiable receipts called "ocean waybills" rather than bills of lading. Ocean waybills may be all that are necessary where a shipper of goods consigns them to himself or a specific consignee and the parties do not contemplate any dealing with the goods while in transit, for the waybills are not documents of title and will not operate to pass any property in the goods. They may, however, provide that they are to be governed by the Hague-Visby Rules.[43]

C. Delivery order

It is common practice when a ship arrives at its destination for the bill of lading to be presented to the shipowner's agent in return for a delivery order. This document is essentially an order given by the owner of the goods to the person in possession of them directing that person to deliver the goods to the person named in the order. Two types of delivery order may be distinguished.[44]

First, a ship's delivery order, that is, one addressed to the carrier, although not necessarily of the same order and quality as a bill of lading,[45] may give the holder a direct course of action, against the shipowner where the latter attorns to him. Delivery orders are not generally, however, documents of title at common law.[46]

Secondly, a delivery order may be directed to an agent of the owner (or seller) of goods directing delivery of the consignment (or of part of it) to the person named therein.[47] In this respect, it is a particularly useful document where the holder of the bill of lading wishes to sell different

---

Lading Act 1857, s. 1; (S.A.) *Mercantile Law Act* 1936, s. 14(1); (W.A.) by Adoption 20 Vict. No. 7 (1856); (U.K.) *Bills of Lading Act* 1855, s. 1.

---

[38] See p. 620.

[39] *Alexander Cross & Sons Ltd.* v. *Hasell* [1908] V.L.R. 194; cf. *Hamilton* v. *Ritchie* (1876) 14 S.C.R. (N.S.W.) 274. *Glyn Mills & Co.* v. *East and West India Dock Co.* (1882) 7 App. Cas. 591. If he has any suspicions of contrary claims, he should either ensure he delivers to the actual owner or interplead.

[40] For this reason, a bank financing a transaction by letter of credit will wish to protect its interest by obtaining all three bills of lading. See ante, p. 609. See also *Levi* v. *Learmonth* (1862) 1 W. & W. (L) 283.

[41] *The Stettin* (1889) 14 P.D. 142; *London Joint Stock Bank Ltd.* v. *British Amsterdam Maritime Agency Ltd.* (1910) 16 Com. Cas. 102; *Sze Hai Tong Bank Ltd.* v. *Rambler Cycle Co. Ltd.* [1959] A.C. 576, at 586.

[42] *Barber* v. *Meyerstein* (1870) L.R. 4 H.L. 317.

[43] See (U.K.) *Carriage of Goods by Sea Act* 1971, s. 1(6) and Sched. See post, p. 625.

[44] See also *Cremer* v. *General Carriers S.A.* [1974] 1 W.L.R. 341, at 349.

[45] *Colin & Shields* v. *W. Weddel & Co. Ltd.* [1952] 2 All E.R. 337, at 343.

[46] *Comptoir d'Achat* v. *Luis de Ridder, The Julia* [1949] A.C. 293, at 316.

[47] See, e.g., *The Julia* (supra).

portions of the cargo named therein. Property will generally pass when the relevant goods are ascertained and appropriated to the contract[48] and this will often be simultaneous with attornment by the person in possession of them to the person named in the delivery order, which will amount to constructive delivery and a transfer of possession to the latter.[49]

If the goods are not delivered to the person in whose name the delivery order is made out, he may have an action for damages for breach of contract against the person in possession of them. Often, there will be breach of a contract of sale but even when the person giving the delivery order is not a seller there may still be a contract if the issue of the delivery order is intended to constitute a promise which is to be legally binding and is supported by consideration and not merely an authority given by the bailee of the goods to deliver them.[50] If the holder of the delivery order has not been in possession of a bill of lading he will not have rights against and obligations to the carrier under the contract of carriage.[51] But if attornment by the latter constitutes a promise to deliver, this may, if supported by consideration, be turned into a binding contractual obligation. Moreover, if the bailee, when attorning, makes statements about the goods (for example, as to their condition) and the person presenting the delivery order acts upon those statements, it seems the former may be estopped from denying their truth and so be liable for the consequences.[52]

III. INTERNATIONAL SALES OF GOODS

A sale of goods is, of course, different from a bailment of them[53] and the law relating to international sales is best dealt with in specialised works on the subject.[54] Since, however, many shipments of goods are made in pursuance of a contract of sale, it is useful to consider shortly the transactions under which ownership of the goods may change. There are several different types of international sale contracts, of which the most common are c.i.f. and f.o.b. contracts.[55]

Under a c.i.f. contract, it is the duty of the seller to arrange for conveyance of the goods to a named port of destination in return for a unified price which combines the *cost* of the goods under the contract of sale, the premium for a policy of marine *insurance* covering them

---

48 *Sale of Goods Act* (N.S.W.) 1923-1953, ss. 21, 23 r. 5(i); S.G.A. (U.K.) 1893, ss. 16, 18 r. 5(i); *Margarine Union G.m.b.H.* v. *Cambay Prince Steamship Co. Ltd.* [1969] 1 Q.B. 219. Cf. *Tradax Export S.A.* v. *Andre & Cie S.A.* (1977) *The Times* 11 July.
49 See *Sterns Ltd.* v. *Vickers Ltd.* [1923] 1 K.B. 78.
50 *Alicia Hosiery Ltd.* v. *Brown Shipley & Co. Ltd.* [1970] 1 Q.B. 195.
51 *Heilbert, Symons & Co. Ltd.* v. *Harvey, Christie-Miller & Co.* (1922) 12 Ll. L.R. 455, at 457.
52 *Coventry, Sheppard & Co.* v. *G.E. Ry. Co.* (1883) 11 Q.B.D. 776; *Laurie and Morewood* v. *Dudin & Sons* [1926] 1 K.B. 223; *Alicia Hosiery Ltd.* v. *Brown Shipley & Co. Ltd.* [1970] 1 Q.B. 195. See generally Ch. 21, post.
53 Ante, p. 96.
54 E.g. *Benjamin's Sale of Goods* (1974).
55 Sassoon, *C.I.F. and F.O.B. Contracts* (2nd ed. 1974).

during transit and the remuneration due under the contract of carriage with the shipowner, the *freight*. He must then deliver the documents (invoice, insurance policy and bill of lading) to the buyer, who becomes the owner when the property in the goods passes to him.[56] The buyer must collect the goods on arrival. He may transfer his rights and liabilities under the contract of carriage by endorsement and delivery of the bill of lading to another party.[57] Furthermore, an endorsee, even if he has not acquired property in the goods, can obtain delivery of them on presenting the bill of lading and paying the freight.[58] Where the seller's obligation is to secure delivery of the goods (as opposed to the documents representing them), it will be an *ex ship* or *arrival* contract and he will generally be liable to the buyer for their non-delivery.

The seller's duties are less onerous in the case of f.o.b. contracts although the precise nature of the duties to these "flexible instruments"[59] cannot be stated with certainty. It is a common feature of them that the seller has to ensure that the goods are placed *free on board* a vessel nominated by the buyer, the seller thus paying for the cost of loading but leaving the freight to be paid by the buyer. In practice the cost of loading is often borne by the buyer as part of the freight. A significant feature of f.o.b. contracts is that the risk generally passes on shipment,[60] although, as Devlin J. noted sardonically in *Pyrene Co. Ltd.* v. *Scindia Navigation Co. Ltd.*,[61] "only the most enthusiastic lawyer could watch with satisfaction the spectacle of liabilities shifting uneasily as the cargo sways at the end of a derrick across a notional perpendicular projecting from the ship's rail."

His Lordship distinguished between three types of f.o.b. contract.[62] His second category is similar to a c.i.f. contract, the contract of sale providing that the seller, rather than the buyer, is to make the necessary shipping arrangements, taking the bill of lading in his own name and obtaining payment against its transfer. He called his first type of "classic" f.o.b. contract. Under it, the seller places the goods on board a ship nominated by the buyer and procures a bill of lading, the seller being directly a party to the contract of carriage, at least until he takes out a bill of lading in the buyer's name. The third type, which Dixon C.J. in *Saffron* v. *Société Minière Cafrika*[63] called a "classic" f.o.b. contract and which may have become the most common type,[64] should be carefully distinguished. Here the buyer himself or his forwarding agent books space on the ship. The seller puts the goods on board and obtains a

---

56 If the goods fail to arrive, the buyer must have recourse to the insurer: *Manbre Saccharine Co. Ltd.* v. *Corn Products Co. Ltd.* [1919] 1 K.B. 198.
57 See the provisions cited supra, n. 37. See also *Lickbarrow* v. *Mason* (1974) 5 T.R. 683; *Fowler* v. *Knoop* (1878) 4 Q.B.D. 299.
58 *Brandt* v. *Liverpool, Brazil and River Plate Steam Navigation Co. Ltd.* [1924] 1 K.B. 575.
59 *Pyrene Co. Ltd.* v. *Scindia Navigation Co. Ltd.* [1954] 2 Q.B. 402, at 424 per Devlin J.
60 *Carlos Federspiel & Co. S.A.* v. *Charles Twigg & Co. Ltd.* [1957] 1 Lloyd's Rep. 240.
61 [1954] 2 Q.B. 402.
62 Ibid., at 424.
63 (1958) 100 C.L.R. 231, at 241.
64 *Benjamin's Sale of Goods* (supra), para 1644.

mate's receipt which he hands to the forwarding agent for the latter to obtain the bill of lading. Thus the seller will not be a party to the contract of carriage and will not normally obtain a bill of lading himself.[65] This would not ordinarily mean that the shipowner becomes a bailee vis-à-vis the seller since the goods will have been accepted in pursuance of a previously concluded contract with the buyer and the risk (and often the property) will pass to the latter on shipment.

A distinction which must be kept clear is that between the f.o.b. contract, as such, and the bill of lading issued on it. Provisions of the Hague Rules[66] do not have effect on terms of the contract of sale but on the contract of carriage, whether or not it happens to answer the description of a bill of lading. The f.o.b. contract is a contract which anticipates the sea carriage of goods but it imposes no obligation with respect to the carriage itself.[67]

Despite the preceding generalisations, it is important to note that c.i.f. and f.o.b. contracts may appear in various and not necessarily distinct forms. Thus, a common variant of the former is the c. and f. contract, under which the seller's duties are identical to those under the c.i.f. contract except that it is incumbent on the buyer to arrange insurance, the seller being obliged to furnish the necessary information as under an f.o.b. contract.

Furthermore, just as the arrangements under an international contract of sale may extend to or beyond the end of the sea voyage, as in ex ship or arrival contracts, they may not even extend as far as shipment. For instance, under an f.o.b. contract, the seller may be obliged to place the goods in possession of the shipowner by delivering them *free alongside* a ship nominated by the buyer.[68] At that time property and risk will, subject to any reserved right of disposal, pass to the buyer and he must bear the expenses of loading and any subsequent expenses. Less significant, in relation to the particular area of carriage by sea, are ex works and ex warehouse (or ex store) contracts. Under the former, an overseas buyer may take delivery at the seller's place of business and property and risk will normally pass at that time. Under the latter, delivery may take place at premises where a third person is in possession of the goods at the moment that person acknowledges that he holds the goods on the buyer's behalf.[69] He may deliver to the first person presenting a bill of lading without incurring liability in tort to a previous endorsee of a different bill of lading from the same set,[70] although for wrongful or non-delivery he may be liable for conversion or, possible, breach of contract. The holder of a bill of lading or delivery warrant may be obliged to pay the warehouseman's charges before he can obtain delivery of the goods.

[65] Cf. *Brown* v. *Hare* (1859) 4 H. & N. 822; *The Tromp* [1921] P. 337; *President of India* v. *Metcalf Shipping Co. Ltd.* [1970] 1 Q.B. 289.

[66] See p. 621, post.

[67] *John Churcher Pty. Ltd.* v. *Mitsui & Co. (Australia) Ltd.* [1974] 2 N.S.W.L.R. 179.

[68] *Nippon Yusen Kaisha* v. *Ramjiban Serowgee* [1938] A.C. 429.

[69] *Sale of Goods Act* (N.S.W.) 1923-1953, s. 32(3); *Sale of Goods Act* (U.K.) s. 29(3).

[70] *Glyn, Mills & Co.* v. *East and West India Dock Co.* (1882) 7 App. Cas. 591.

IV. LIABILITY OF ANCILLARY PARTIES

The position at law of intermediaries in contracts for the carriage of goods, such as forwarding agents, is discussed in Chapter 20 but it is proposed that some points be noted here with respect to agents' liability in a sea carriage of goods context. There is a custom in sea carriage relationships that the forwarding agent incurs a personal liability to the carrier in respect of freight. It has been said that this custom receives effect in the form of a term implied into an agreement made by the agent with the carrier.[71] Whether the custom has this weight or not, because of the reasons outlined by Barry J. in *Anglo Overseas Transport Ltd.* v. *Titan Industrial Corpn.*,[72] it seems that there must always be a presumption that the forwarding agent incurs a personal liability for freight.

As a parallel to this liability, the forwarding agent probably has a lien over goods or documents relating thereto in respect of lawful claims arising in connection with the goods.[73] As the lien is only possessory, the forwarding agent's right expires on the placing of the goods in the possession of the carrier.[74] However, if the documents are retained, the agent can endeavour to prevent a consignee from taking delivery of the goods by virtue of the agent's lien on the documents.[75]

The carrier may employ a loading broker to accept goods for sea carriage. In such case it will probably be the broker, rather than the master, who signs the bill of lading. What is of importance here is the extent of the broker's usual authority. Where freight is payable at the loading port, the loading broker has a usual authority to receive same. Therefore, in the absence of notice, payment of freight to a broker will be a proper discharge of that burden. It follows that the loading broker owes a duty to his principal not to release bills of lading except against payment of freight. The extent of the broker's usual authority in signing the bill of lading is to make acknowledgments as to the date of shipment and the external condition and quantity of goods shipped. Usual authority does not extend to the signing of a bill of lading for goods that have never been shipped at all.[76] However, where a broker goes beyond this limitation, he will of course be personally liable for breach of his implied warranty of authority. The loading broker's principal will be

---

[71] See Barry J. in *Anglo-Overseas Transport* v. *Titan Industrial Corpn.* [1959] 2 Lloyds Rep. 152; *Perishables Transport Co.* v. *N. Spyropoulos (London)* [1964] 2 Lloyds Rep. 379, at 382 per Salmon L.J.; cf. *Longley, Beldon & Gaunt* v. *Morley* [1965] 1 Lloyds Rep. 297, at 306 per Mocatta J.

[72] [1959] 2 Lloyds Rep. 152.

[73] *Edwards* v. *Southgate* (1862) 10 W.R. 528; *Soc. Anon. Angelo Castalletti* v. *Transmaritime Ltd.* [1953] 2 Lloyds Rep. 440, at 449 per Devlin J.

[74] *Longley, Beldon & Gaunt* v. *Morley* [1965] 1 Lloyds Rep. 297. In fact, it would appear as a general rule that the forwarding agent does not acquire possession of the goods and cannot therefore be considered a bailee: see post, p. 834 and in particular *Evans* v. *Merzario* [1975] 1 Lloyds Rep. 162 (not apparently disapproved on this point on the subsequent appeal) [1976] 2 All E.R. 930. Of course, the foregoing is merely a general rule and in any event a forwarding agent will normally gain possession of the relevant documents, if not of the goods themselves.

[75] *Edwards* v. *Southgate* (1862) 10 W.R. 528.

[76] *Heskell* v. *Continental Express Ltd.* (1950) 83 Ll. L.R. 38, per Devlin J.

liable vicariously in respect of torts committed by the broker acting within the ambit of his authority.

V. Liability of The Carrier By Sea

A. At common Law

Most questions concerning the liability of the carrier by sea fall in practice to be resolved by the rules outlined in paragraphs B. and C. of this section. For that reason, and partly because of ambiguous judicial dicta and disagreements between members of the judiciary, the common law rules are notoriously uncertain.

It has at least been settled that a shipowner who carries goods is absolutely bound to provide a seaworthy ship at the beginning of the voyage[77] and to proceed on the voyage with reasonable despatch[78] and without unreasonable deviation.[79] What is not clear is whether the carrier by sea is absolutely liable to deliver goods at the port of destination in exactly the condition in which he received them (subject to the defences recognised at common law[80]) or whether he is liable only to exercise due care and diligence. Much may depend on whether or not the shipowner is a common carrier.[81]

If he is, his liability is absolute. To be a common carrier it appears that he must regularly engage in the carriage trade for reward, employing his ship (or at least part of it[82]) as a general ship. It is not clear whether he must regularly ply between fixed places or whether he should habitually carry for the public. A common carrier who refuses to take goods offered to him will be liable to suit. Part of the difficulty in ascertaining the nature of the sea carrier's liability originates in, first, doubt as to whether a carrier by sea can be sued for such a refusal and, secondly, whether in the absence of such liability to suit a shipowner's liability for carriage is similar to that of a common carrier or not.[83] A further difficulty lies in whether the shipowner's liability varies according to whether he is carrying the goods of several persons (as a common carrier often does) or of a single person (in which case there is usually a special contract).

It was Lord Esher's view that the shipowner's liability for carriage, being at least akin to that of a common carrier, was that of an insurer.[84]

---

[77] *Steel v. State Line Steamship Co.* (1878) 3 App. Cas. 72; *Hyman v. Nye* (1881) 6 Q.B.D. 685, at 690 per Mathews J. As to the legal character of this obligation see *Hong Kong Fir Shipping Co. v. Kawasaki Kisen Kaisha Ltd.* [1962] 2 Q.B. 26, at 71 per Diplock L.J.

[78] *Anglo-Saxon Petroleum Co. Ltd. v. Adamasto Shipping Co. Ltd.* [1957] 2 Q.B. 255 (reversed on other grounds [1959] A.C. 133); *Universal Cargo Carriers Corporation v. Citati* [1957] 2 Q.B. 401.

[79] *Scaramanga & Co. v. Stamp* (1880) 5 C.P.D. 295.

[80] Post, p. 618.

[81] Cf. ante, p. 553 et seq.

[82] Payne & Ivamy's *Carriage of Goods by Sea* (10th ed.), p. 145.

[83] See *Belfast Ropework Co. Ltd. v. Bushell* [1918] 1 K.B. 210, at 212; *Hill v. Scott* [1895] 2 Q.B. 371, at 376. See generally, as to the identification of a common carrier, Ch. 15.

[84] *Liver Alkali Co. v. Johnson* (1874) L.R. 9 Ex. 338, at 344; *Nugent v. Smith* (1876) 1 C.P.D. 19, at 33.

This view conforms with the old case of *Morse* v. *Slue,*[85] in which it was held that the master of a ship had the same strict liability with respect to the goods carried as a common carrier. It is at least arguable that his principal's liability should be identical.[86]

The more recent authorities regarding the master's liability, to the effect that he is merely bound to take reasonable care of the goods entrusted to him,[87] are inconclusive as they are not concerned with the common law position. Nevertheless, despite Lord Esher's great authority on commercial matters, his view has been vigorously dissented from,[88] although there is no definite decision to confirm that he is wrong.

The problem arises most conspicuously where the whole of a vessel is used for the goods of one shipper without any express stipulations in the contract. This would be unusual in the case of the charter of a ship but common in the hire of lighters. In such a case the position is similar to where goods are carried under a special contract and it is arguable that a shipowner should suffer the whole of his potential common law liability unless he were prudent enough to qualify it by contract.

In fact, there appears to be no distinction at common law between cases where goods of one or several persons are carried and there is much sense in the view[89] that even if the shipowner is not trading as a common carrier the reasons for the particular liability of the common carrier[90] are equally applicable, so that liability of the carrier by sea at common law should be uniformly strict.

Not surprisingly, the common law saw fit not merely to impose liability but also recognise certain defences which, it seems, may be pleaded whether or not the shipowner is a common carrier.[91]

First, he is not liable for loss caused by Act of God, that is, any accident "due to natural causes, directly and exclusively, without human intervention, that could not have been prevented by any amount of foresight and pains and care reasonably to be expected from him."[92] Similarly, his liability is excluded for loss caused by the Queen's enemies, which expression includes states or peoples with which the flag state is at war[93] and possibly pirates or robbers on the high seas.[94]

The carrier is further not liable where the goods are lost or damaged as a result of inherent vice (that is, where the cause is an inherent defect

---

[85] (1671) 1 Ventris 190, 238; *Barclay* v. *Cuculla y Gana* (1984) 3 Dough, 389; *Nugent* v. *Smith* (1876) 1 C.P.D. 19, at 423; *Hill* v. *Scott* [1895] 2 Q.B. 371, at 713; cf. Holmes, *The Common Law*, at 192-195.

[86] *Priestley* v. *Fernie* (1863) 3 H. & C. 977.

[87] *Notara* v. *Henderson* (1872) L.R. 7 Q.B. 225.

[88] In particular by Cockburn C.J. in *Nugent* v. *Smith* (1876) 1 C.P.D. 423, at 433.

[89] Carver, op. cit., p. 7.

[90] *Coggs* v. *Bernard* (1703) 2 Ld. Raym. 909, at 918 per Holt C.J.; *Forward* v. *Pittard* (1785) 1 T.R. 27, at 34 per Lord Mansfield; *Riley* v. *Horne* (1828) 5 Bing. 217, at 220 per Best C.J.

[91] Cf. *F. C. Bradley & Sons Ltd.* v. *Federal Steam Navigation Co. Ltd.* (1927) 27 Ll. L.R. 395, at 396 per Viscount Sumner.

[92] *Nugent* v. *Smith* (1876) 1 C.P.D. 423, at 444 per James L.J.

[93] *Southcote's Case* (1601) 4 Co. Rep. 83b; *Russell* v. *Niemann* (1864) 34 L.J.C.P. 10; *The Teutonia* (1872) L.R. 4 P.C. 171.

[94] Cf. *Russell* v. *Niemann* (1864) 34 L.J.C.P. 10, at 14 per Byles J.; *Semper* v. *Australian United Steam Navigation Co.* (1904) 6 W.A.I.R. 63.

in or quality of the goods)[95] unless he has contributed to it.[96] Similarly, the shipowner is excused liability for loss or damage caused by defective packing of the goods unless he was aware of it or neglected to take account of it.[97] Finally, he may be protected where loss is caused due to an intentional act on his part when a sacrifice, in particular a jettison, is made of properly stowed goods for the safety of the common venture.[98] The parties to that venture[99] are bound to contribute to the loss.[1]

Where there has been such a loss and the adjustment of contributions is likely to occupy a long period, it has been held[2] that the consignees are entitled to delivery of their goods on executing bonds for contributions. However, in *Shaw & Co* v. *Houston*[3] it was held that the master of a vessel is not bound to accept in lieu of his lien for general average upon goods carried by him the bond of the consignee of such goods, or to accept any other security except such as he thinks reasonable and proper upon the statement of adjustment to be payable by the consignees or owner. The earlier decision[4] was expressly differed from.

The common law defences were limited and could be denied altogether if the shipowner contributed to the loss or damage by negligence,[5] or by having deviated[6] or provided an unseaworthy ship.[7] In most cases, however, the shipowner's liability is qualified by express contractual provisions or by statute. We must, therefore, consider these two cases in turn.

B. By contract

It has been said that where the law imposes a duty upon a man he will be excused non-performance which is not due to his own default but where the man voluntarily takes this duty upon himself he is absolutely bound to perform subject only to any contrary stipulations he has expressly made.[8] It would appear to follow that where a shipowner's liability is to be judged by obligations he has assumed by contract rather

---

95 *Albacora S.R.L.* v. *Westcott & Laurance Line Ltd.* [1966] 2 Lloyd's Rep. 53.
96 *Internationale Guano* v. *Macandrew* [1909] 2 K.B. 360; *The Freedom* (1869) L.R. 3 P.C. 594; *Hutchinson* v. *Guion* (1858) 5 C.B₄ (N.S.) 149.
97 *Hudson* v. *Baxendale* (1857) 2 H. & N. 575; *Richardson* v. *North Easton Ry. Co.* (1872) L.R. 7 C.P. 75; *Goodwin Ferreira & Co. Ltd.* v. *Lamport and Holt Ltd.* (1929) L1.L.R. 192; *Silver* v. *Ocean Steamship Co. Ltd.* [1930] 1 K.B. 416.
98 *Royal Exchange Shipping Co. Ltd.* v. *Dixon* (1886) 12 App. Cas. 11; see also (1884) 1 T.L.R. 178, and 490.
99 The ship, the freight and the cargo owners. Cf. *Burns Philp & Co. Ltd.* v. *Gillespie Brothers Pty. Ltd.* (1947) 74 C.L.R. 148.
1 See Lowndes and Rudolf, *The Law of General Average and the York-Antwerp Rules* (10th ed. 1974).
2 *M'Lean and others* v. *The Liverpool Association* (1883) 9 V.L.R. 93.
3 (1883) 1 Q.L.J. 182.
4 *M'Lean and others* v. *The Liverpool Association* (1883) 9 V.L.R₄ 93.
5 *The Freedom* (1869) L.R. 3 P.C. 594; *Notara* v. *Henderson* (1872) L.R. 7 Q.B. 225.
6 *Internationale Guano* v. *Macandrew* [1903] 2 K.B. 360; *Morrison* v. *Shaw, Savill* [1916] 2 K.B. 783; *Davis* v. *Garrett* (1830) 6 Bing. 716. Cf. *Hain Steamship Co. Ltd.* v. *Tate & Lyle Ltd.* (1936) 41 Com. Cas. 350; *The Angelia* [1973] 1 W.L.R. 210.
7 *Lyon* v. *Mells* (1804) 5 East 428; *Steel* v. *State Line Steamship Co.* (1877) 3 App. Cas. 72.
8 *Lloyd* v. *Guibert* (1865) L.R. 1 Q.B. 115, at 121 per Willes J.; *Nichols* v. *Marsland* (1876) 2 Ex. D. 1 at 4, per Mellish L.J. See also *Connor* v. *Spare* (1878) 4 V.L.R. (L) 243.

than by those existing at common law he should not even obtain the benefit of the common law defences discussed in paragraph A. above, unless he expressly provides for them. It is submitted that this should not be so, particularly in view of the uncertainty surrounding the liabilities of carriers at common law who may not be classifiable as common carriers and so not entitled to the defences allowed to complement the duties imposed on them by law.

The problem is of little practical importance, for the shipowner's duties will usually be lessened by contract. Not only is it customary for him to expressly include the common law defences but the standard range of contractual exceptions is so great[9] that the shipowner's obligation has been said to have been reduced to merely receive the freight.[10] Thus, for example, he may exclude liability for loss or damage caused by strikes,[11] perils of the sea (accidents peculiarly incident to navigating the sea which could not have been foreseen or guarded against by the carrier or his servants,[12]) and even by the negligence of himself or his crew (although such an exception is construed strictly).[13] Nonetheless, the carrier may lose the benefit of the exceptions where he is in breach of his implied duties under the contract of affreightment to provide a seaworthy ship,[14] to proceed without unreasonable delay[15] and not to deviate.[16] Furthermore it was argued in the *Vita Food Case*[17] for the shipper that if the bills of lading were illegal in that their issue did not comply with the laws of the issuing country, ". . . no Court would enforce their terms and exceptions and the carriage would therefore be upon the terms implied where goods are taken for carriage by a common

[9] See e.g. the list in Scrutton, op. cit., pp. 208-215.
[10] But see *Empresa Cubana de Fletes* v. *Lagonisi Shipping Co. Ltd., The Georgios C.* [1971] 1 Q.B. 488, at 494D per Donaldson J.
[11] See *Williams Brothers (Hull) Ltd.* v. *Naamlooze Vennootschap W.H. Berghuys Kolenhandel* (1915) 21 Com. Cas. 253, at 257 per Sankey J.; *J. Vermaas' Scheepvaartbedr ijf N.V.* v. *Association Technique de L'Importation Charbonniere, The Laga* [1966] 1 Lloyd's Rep. 582. Cf. *Caltex Oil (Australia) Pty. Ltd.* v. *Howard Smith Industries Ltd.* [1973] 2 N.S.W.L.R. 89.
[12] *The Xantho* (1887) 12 App. Cas. 503; *Charles Goodfellow Lumber Sales Ltd.* v. *Verreault, Hovington and Verreault Navigation Inc.* [1971] 1 Lloyd's Rep. 185.
[13] *The Glenfruin* (1885) 10 P.D. 103; *Brooks, Robinson & Co.* v. *Howard Smith & Sons* (1890) 16 V.L.R. 245; *Henty* v. *Orient Steam Navigation Co. Ltd.* (1907) 29 A.L.T. 48; *Elderslie Steamship Co. Ltd.* v. *Borthwick* [1905] A.C. 93; *Briscoe & Co.* v. *Powell & Co.* (1905) 22 T.L.R. 128; *Elder, Dempster & Co.* v. *Paterson, Zochonis & Co.* [1924] A.C. 522. As to the ability of a contracting party to secure protection from suit in favour of strangers to the contract, see generally Ch. 26.
[14] Supra., p. 618, note 7; *Connor* v. *Spence* (1878) 4 V.L.R. (L.) 243; *Peyton, Dowling & Co.* v. *Houlder Bros.* (1890) 16 V.L.R. 812.
[15] *M'Andrew* v. *Adams* (1834) 1 Bing. N.C. 29; *Anglo-Saxon Petroleum Co. Ltd.* v. *Adamastos Shipping Co. Ltd.* [1957] 2 Q.B. 255 (reversed on other grounds [1959] A.C. 133); *Suisse Atlantique Société d'Armement Maritime S.A.* v. *N.V. Rotterdamsche Kolen Centrale* [1967] 1 A.C. 361. See also *Sea-Carriage of Goods Act* 1924, Sched. Art. IV, r. 4; *Thiess Bros. (Queensland) Pty. Ltd.* v. *Australian Steamships Pty. Ltd.* [1955] 1 Lloyd's Rep. 459.
[16] Supra, n. 93. It seems that the shipowner who has deviated becomes thereafter subject to the rights and liabilities of a carrier at common law; *Internationale Guano* v. *Macandrew* [1909] 2 K.B. 360; *Morrison* v. *Shaw, Savill* [1916] 2 K.B. 783.
[17] [1939] A.C. 277.

carrier . . ."[18] As the bills of lading were held to be legal, this argument was not canvassed.[19]

Except where the Hague Rules govern the contract,[20] or where there exists some other statutory prohibition upon the operation of exculpatory provisions in the contract,[21] the shipowner is free to *limit* his liability to any amount he stipulates by a clause expressly having that effect. The cargo owner may, however, still be able to recover from persons carrying out the duties of the carrier but not parties to the contract and so unable to take advantage of the limitation clause.[22]

It has been pointed out above that a bill of lading may be issued for goods carried on a chartered ship. In such a case, it may appear that there is a conflict between obligations attached by the contracts. However, although new obligations may be created by the bill of lading, the obligations under the charterparty subsist.[23] If such a bill of lading is in the hands of the charterer, it will be prima facie taken as only an acknowledgment of receipt of the goods.[24] But if the bill of lading is endorsed over, as between the shipowner and the endorsee, the bill of lading must be considered to contain the contract.[25] In the event of inconsistency between express terms of that contract contained in the bill of lading and provisions purported to be incorporated from the charterparty, the provisions will be rejected.[26] On the other hand, the master or broker has no authority by signing bills of lading differing from the charter to vary the contract the owner has already made.[27] Furthermore, it is now common to provide that "the master is to sign bills of lading as presented by the charterer without prejudice to the

---

[18] See Lord Wright at 295.
[19] Cf. *Regazzoni* v. *K. C. Sethia (1944) Ltd.* [1956] 2 Q.B. 490 and *Dicey & Morris on the Conflict of Laws* (9th ed.) pp. 748-765.
    pp. 748-765.
[20] Post, p. 621.
[21] See e.g. *Trade Practices Act* 1974 (Cwth), s. 74, and Unfair Contract Terms Act 1977 (U.K.).
[22] See *Elder, Dempster & Co.* v. *Paterson, Zochonis & Co.* [1924] A.C. 522; *Gilbert, Stokes & Kerr Pty. Ltd.* v. *Dalgety & Co. Ltd.* (1948) 48 S.R. (N.S.W.) 435; *Waters Trading Co. Ltd.* v. *Dalgety & Co Ltd.* (1951) 52 S.R. (N.S.W.) 4; *Wilson* v. *Darling Island Stevedoring & Lighterage Co. Ltd.* (1956) 95 C.L.R. 43; *Scruttons Ltd.* v. *Midland Silicones Ltd.* [1962] A.C. 446; *Gilchrist Watt and Sanderson Pty. Ltd.* v. *York Products Pty. Ltd.* (1970) 44 A.L.J.R. 268; *New Zealand Shipping Co. Ltd.* v. *A. M Satterthwaite & Co Ltd., The Eurymedon* [1975] A.C. 154; *Palmer* [1974] J.B.L. 101, at 220; *Rose*, 4 Anglo-Am L.R. 7; *Herrick* v. *Leonard & Dingley Ltd.* [1975] 2 N.Z.L.R. 566; *Rose & Palmer* 39 M.L.R. 466; *Johnson Matthey Ltd.* v. *Constantine Terminals Ltd.* [1976] 2 Lloyd's Rep. 215; *The Suleyman Stalskiy* [1976] 2 Lloyd's Rep. 609; *Salmond & Spraggon (Australia) Pty. Ltd.* v. *Joint Cargo Services Pty. Ltd., The New York Star* [1977] 1 Lloyd's Rep. 445; and see generally, Ch. 26.
[23] *Den of Airlie S.S. Co.* v. *Mitsui* (1912) 17 Com. Cas. 116; *Hogarth S.S. Co.* v. *Blyth* [1917] 2 K.B. 534, at 550 per Scrutton L.J.; *Gardano and Giampieri* v. *Greek Petroleum* [1961] 2 Lloyd's Rep. 259.
[24] *Rodocanachi* v. *Milburn* (1886) 18 Q.B.D. 67, at 75 per Lord Esher, 78 per Lindley L.J.; *Wagstaff* v. *Anderson* (1880) 5 C.P.D. 171, at 177 per Lord Bramwell.
[25] *Leduc* v. *Ward* (1888) 20 Q.B.D. 475, at 479 per Lord Esher.
[26] *Gardner* v. *Trechmann* (1884) 15 Q.B.D. 154, at 157 per Brett M.R.; *Akt. Ocean* v. *Harding* [1928] 2 K.B. 371, at 384 per Scrutton L.J.
[27] *Grant* v. *Norway* (1851) 10 C.B. 665, at 687; *Margaronis* v. *Peabody* [1964] 1 Lloyd's Rep. 172, at 181; *President of India* v. *Metcalfe Shipping Co.* [1970] 1 Q.B. 289, at 305; *R.* v. *Roach* (1879) 13 S.A.L.R. 96.

charter." This, a fortiori, establishes the paramouncy of the terms of the charterparty over the bill of lading as between shipowner and charterer.

In a recent decision[28] the House of Lords considered the position of a charterer who sought to claim on the charterparty for loss of goods subject to a bill of lading which had been endorsed over to a third party. There was no action available on the bill of lading because of the expiry of the one year prescription period provided for by the Hague Rules. It was held that the charterers were not able to claim more than nominal damages.[29]

C. By statute

The most significant way in which the sea carrier's liability has been modified is by statute.[30] By virtue of his superior bargaining position, the shipowner was often able, as we have noted, to reduce his liabilities dramatically and virtually to reverse the common law relationship between shipper and carrier. The former could either ship goods on the terms offered or not at all. A further problem was that the usefulness of bills of lading was reduced by, first, their varied and complex characters and, secondly, by their consequent restricted utility so far as third parties were concerned.

An attempt to overcome these difficulties resulted in the recommendation by an international conference held at Brussels in 1924 of a uniform set of rules for the carriage of goods by sea, commonly known as the Hague Rules. These Rules were given effect (occasionally with minor divergences) by municipal legislation. In Australia, the Rules appear in the Schedule of the *Sea-Carriage of Goods Act* 1924.[31] Australia was thus one of the first nations to enact the Convention and acceded to the Convention on July 4, 1955. It is provided in the Australian Act that any clause in bills of lading which would oust the Australian Courts is invalid. The purpose of the Hague Rules is to establish a balance between the shipper and shipowner, the latter being obliged to accept certain listed liabilities in return for enumerated qualifications on his liability.[32] In this sense, the Rules represent a compromise between the positions at common law and under contract.

Under the Act, no absolute warranty of seaworthiness is implied[33] but the carrier[34] is bound before and at the beginning of the voyage[35] to exercise due diligence to make the ship seaworthy.[36] This undertaking is

---

[28] *The Albazero* [1976] 3 All E.R. 129.
[29] See further, Ch. 4 ante.
[30] The most important instance of statutory intervention is the imposition of the Hague Rules: see post.
[31] See also (U.K.) *Carriage of Goods by Sea Act* 1924; Colinvaux, *The Carriage of Goods by Sea Act 1924* (1954); (Canada) *Water-Carriage of Goods Act* 1936; (U.S.) *Carriage of Goods by Sea Act* 1936; (New Zealand) *Sea-Carriage of Goods Act* 1940.
[32] *Gosse Millard Ltd.* v. *Canadian Government Merchant Marine* [1929] A.C. 223, at 236 per Viscount Sumner.
[33] Section 5.
[34] See also *Riverstone Meat Co. Pty. Ltd.* v. *Lancashire Shipping Co. Ltd.* [1961] A.C. 807 (liability extends to the defaults of an independant contractor).
[35] *Maxine Footwear Co. Ltd.* v. *Canadian Merchant Marine Ltd.* [1959] A.C. 589.
[36] *Commonwealth* v. *Burns Philp & Co. Ltd.* (1946) 46 S.R. (N.S.W.) 307.

neither a condition nor a warranty but an "innominate obligation". As such, a breach entitles the charterer to treat the contract as discharged only if it goes to the "root of the contract".[37] The seaworthiness required is relative to the nature of the ship, the cargo and the voyage contracted for.[38] The obligation to exercise due diligence has long been established to be non-delegable and personal to the carrier but the full extent of that duty was not realised before the decision of the House of Lords in *Riverstone Meat Co.* v. *Lancashire Shipping Co. (The Muncaster Castle).*[39] It was there held that the obligation could not be discharged by evidence of due diligence in the selection of an independent contractor if damage is caused as a result of negligence on the part of an employee of that independent contractor. The duty of the carrier is to exercise due diligence in repair work even when this work requires technical or special knowledge and is delegated to an independent contractor of standing. The Act stipulates that the carrier impliedly undertakes that the vessel shall be ready to commence the voyage, to load the cargo and to proceed upon and complete the voyage with all reasonable dispatch. A breach of this undertaking, if such as to deprive the shipper of the whole benefit of the contract, may entitle a shipper to refuse to perform his part of the contract.[40] If the breach is not so serious, the carrier will be liable for damages if the loss incurred could be reasonably anticipated as the result of delay.[41] Circumstances which delay performance may discharge the parties, in the absence of breach of contract, if amounting to frustration.[42]

The carrier must properly man, equip and supply the ship and make the holds, refrigerating and cool chambers and all other parts of it in which goods are carried fit and safe for their reception, carriage and preservation.[43] The carrier is further obliged, subject to the immunities contained in Article IV of the Rules,[44] to properly and carefully load, handle, stow, carry, keep, care for and discharge the goods carried.[45] Where goods are lost or damaged, the carrier or other person claiming

---

[37] *Hong Kong Fir Shipping Co.* v. *Kawasaki Kisen Kaisha (The Hong Kong Fir)* [1962] 2 Q.B. 26; *The Mihalis Angelos* [1971] 1 Q.B. 164; *Reardon Smith Line Ltd.* v. *Hansen-Tangen* [1976] 3 All E.R. 570.

[38] *Burges* v. *Wickham* (1863) 3 B. & S. 669; *Stanton* v. *Richardson* (1874) L.R. 9 C.P. 390; *Queensland Bank* v. *P. & O. Co.* [1898] 1 Q.B. 567.

[39] [1961] A.C. 807. Cf. the position of the warehouseman at Common Law, as discussed in *B.R.S. Ltd.* v. *Arthur V. Crutchley Ltd.* [1968] 1 All E.R. 811.

[40] *Freeman* v. *Taylor* (1831) 8 Bing. 124; *Universal Cargo Carriers* v. *Citati* [1957] 2 Q.B. 401.

[41] *The Wilhelm* (1866) 14 L.T. 636; cf. *Associated Portland Cement Co.* v. *Houlder* (1917) 22 Com. Cas. 279; *Monarch S.S. Co.* v. *Karlshamns* [1949] A.C. 196.

[42] *Taylor* v. *Caldwell* (1863) 3 B. & S. 826; *Port Line* v. *Ben Line* [1958] 2 Q.B. 146, at 162 per Diplock L.J.; *The Angelia* [1973] 1 W.L.R. 210; cf. *The Eugenia* [1964] 2 Q.B. 226.

[43] *Sea-Carriage of Goods Act* 1924, Sched., Art. III, r.1. See also *McGregor* v. *Huddart Parker Ltd.* (1919) 26 C.L.R. 336.

[44] Infra.

[45] *Sea-Carriage of Goods Act* 1924, Sched., Art. III, r.2. Cf. *McEwan & Co.* v. *Brabender* (1895) 16 L.R. (N.S.W.) 200; *Dimond* v. *William Collin & Sons Ltd.* [1912] Q.W.N. 1.

immunity will be liable unless he satisfies the burden of proving the exercise of due diligence.[46]

In return for fulfilling these obligatory minimum obligations, from the time when the goods are loaded on to the time when they are discharged from the ship,[47] the carrier is permitted certain immunities. Thus Article IV, Rule 2 of the Hague Rules provides that neither the carrier nor the ship shall be responsible for loss or damage arising or resulting from an exhaustive list of excepted perils, including act, neglect or default of the master, mariner, pilot or the servants of the carrier in the navigation or in the management of the ship.[48] If loss or damage is caused partly by the unseaworthiness of the ship and partly by negligent management of the ship by its officers and crew, the carrier gains no protection from Rule 2 in the absence of proof of how much of the damage was due to the negligent management.[49] The carrier and ship are further exempted from liability for loss or damage caused by fire, unless caused by the actual fault or privity of the carrier; perils, dangers and accidents of the sea or other navigable waters;[50] Act of God; act of war; act of public enemies; arrest or restraint of princes, rulers or people, or seizure under legal process; quarantine restrictions; act or omission of the shipper or owner of the goods, his agent or representative; strikes or lock-outs or stoppage or restraint of labour from whatever cause, whether partial or general; riots and civil commotions; saving or attempting to save life or property at sea; wastage in bulk or weight or any other loss or damage arising from inherent defect, quality or vice of the goods; insufficiency of packing;[51] insufficiency or inadequacy of marks; latent defects not discoverable by due diligence; any other cause arising without the actual fault or privity of the carrier, or without the fault or neglect of the agents or servants of the carrier, but the burden of proof is on the person claiming the benefit of this exception to show that neither the actual fault or privity of the carrier nor the fault or neglect of the agents or servants of the carrier contributed to the loss or damage. The carrier's reliance on the excepted perils is subject to his exercising his duty of diligence under Article III Rule 1 of the Rules[52] where breach of that duty causes the loss or damage and to his not making an unpermitted deviation.[53] If deviation is voluntary, for the benefit of the shipowners and the consequent delay was to the detriment of the cargo, the deviation will not be such as excused by the Rules.[54] The carrier will not escape

---

[46] *Sea-Carriage of Goods Act* 1924, Sched., Art. IV, r.1. Cf. *Colonial Sugar Refining Co. Ltd.* v. *British India Steam Navigation Co. Ltd.* (1931) 32 S.R. (N.S.W.) 245.

[47] *Sea-Carriage of Goods Act* 1924, Sched., Art. I(e).

[48] *Chubu Asahi Cotton Spinning Co. Ltd.* v. *The Ship "Tenos"* (1968) 12 F.L.R. 291; *Minnesota Mining* v. *The Ship "Novoaltaisk"* [1972] 2 N.S.W.L.R. 476; 1 A.B.L.R. 356.

[49] *Commonwealth* v. *Burns Philp & Co. Ltd.* (1946) 46 S.R. (N.S.W.) 307.

[50] See *Vacuum Oil Co. Pty. Ltd.* v. *Commonwealth & Dominion Line Ltd.* [1922] V.L.R. 693.

[51] *Parke, Lacey, Hardie Ltd.* v. *The Ship "Clan MacFadyen"* (1930) 30 S.R. (N.S.W.) 438.

[52] Supra.

[53] *Sea-Carriage of Goods Act* 1924, Sched., Art. IV, r.4.

[54] *Thiess Bros. (Qld.) P/L* v. *Australian Steamships Pty. Ltd.* [1955] 1 Lloyds Rep. 459.

liability unless he can show that loss or damage was occasioned either by an Act of God, or by the Queen's enemies, or as the result of inherent vice in the goods and, in addition, that such loss or damage would have occurred if there had been no deviation.[55]

Where goods of an inflammable, explosive or dangerous nature are shipped without the carrier or his agent consenting, with knowledge of their nature and character, they may at any time before discharge be landed at any place or destroyed or rendered innocuous by the carrier without compensation and the shipper of such goods shall be liable for all damages and expenses directly or indirectly arising out of or resulting from such shipment.[56] If any such goods are shipped with the knowledge and consent of the carrier or his agent and become a danger to the ship or cargo, they may similarly be landed at any place or destroyed or rendered innocuous by the carrier without liability on his part except to general average, if any.[57]

In return for the increased liabilities under the Hague Rules, it is further provided that an action must be brought within one year from when the goods were or should have been delivered[58] and that the carrier shall not be liable for loss or damage to or in connexion with the goods for an amount exceeding £100 gold value[59] or its equivalent per package or unit,[60] unless the nature and value of the goods has been declared by the shipper before shipment and inserted in the bill of lading.[61] If the nature or value of the goods has been knowingly misstated by the shipper in the bill of lading, the carrier shall not be responsible in any event for loss or damage.[62] It is possible, however, for him to increase (but not to decrease) his liability[63] by agreeing a higher maximum with the shipper;[64] indeed, it is possible for shipowners and their insurers to agree that liability will be accepted for a higher amount.[65] In any event the distribution of risks by the Hague Rules should go a long way towards assisting the determination of how insurance should be arranged.[66] The Rules state little as to when a bill of lading is null. Apart from a misrepresentation by the shipper, the effect of a major breach of

---

[55] *F. Kanematsu & Co. Ltd.* v. *The Shahzada* (1956) 96 C.L.R. 477.
[56] At common law, the shipper impliedly warrants that he will not ship dangerous goods without notifying the shipowner unless the latter is or should be conversant with the facts. See *Mitchell, Cotts & Co.* v. *Steel Brothers & Co.* [1916] 2 K.B. 610, at 614 per Atkin L.J.
[57] *Sea-Carriage of Goods Act* 1924, Sched., Art. IV, r. 6.
[58] Ibid., Art. III, r.6; *Colonial Sugar Refining Co.* v. *British India Steam Navigation Co. Ltd.* (1931) 32 S.R. (N.S.W.) 245; *Automatic Tube Co. Pty. Ltd.* v. *Adelaide Steamship (Operations) Ltd.* (1966) 9 F.L.R. 130.
[59] *Sea-Carriage of Goods Act* 1924, Sched., Art. IX.
[60] On the meaning of "per package or unit", see *Scrutton*, op. cit., pp. 441-444.
[61] See *Parke, Lacey, Hardie Ltd.* v. *The Ship "Clan MacFadyen"* (1930) 30 S.R. (N.S.W.) 438; *William Holyman & Sons Pty. Ltd.* v. *Foy & Gibson Pty. Ltd.* (1945) 73 C.L.R. 622; cf. *Australasian United Steam Navigation Co. Ltd.* v. *Hiskens* (1914) 18 C.L.R. 646.
[62] *Frank Hammond Pty. Ltd.* v. *Huddart Parker Ltd.* [1956] V.L.R. 496.
[63] See *Sea-Carriage of Goods Act* 1924, Sched., Art. V; *William Holyman & Sons Pty. Ltd.* v. *Foy & Gibson Pty. Ltd.* (1946) 73 C.L.R. 622.
[64] Ibid., Art. IV, r.5.
[65] See The British Maritime Law Association Agreement 1950, reproduced in *Carver*, op. cit., Appendix 6.
[66] See Ivamy, *Marine Insurance* (2nd ed. 1974); *Marine Insurance Act* 1909.

contract is not clear. In the Australian context, a condition in a bill of lading that all legal actions arising out of its interpretation or performance should be determined by courts other than Commonwealth or State is made illegal, null and void, and of no effect by the Rules.[67]

The Rules apply to the carriage of goods by sea[68] from any port in Australia to any other port except one in the same State as the first[69] and every bill of lading or similar document of title containing or evidencing a contract to which the Rules apply should contain an express statement (commonly known as a "clause paramount") that the Rules apply,[70] although such a contract is not invalidated by omission of the clause paramount.[71] In view of the number of countries that have adopted the Rules their effect is widespread. Moreover, there is no reason why parties should not agree to incorporate the Rules into contracts not otherwise governed by them, and this they frequently do.

It should be noted that the Rules do not apply to charterparties as such.[72] However, if the charterparty specifically incorporates the Rules[73] or if a bill of lading issued under a charterparty regulates the relations between the carrier and the holder of the bill of lading (that is, when the bill of lading is in the hands of a person not a party to the charterparty) the Rules apply. The effect of this is that certain clauses, normally valid in a charterparty, will be rendered invalid.

The Rules are subject to certain general restrictions. For example, they are inapplicable to the carriage of live animals or to cargo which by the contract of carriage is stated as being carried on deck and is so carried.[74] Also the immunities provided by the Rules do not protect the servants, agents or independent contractors of the carrier unless this is expressly provided by a clause having that effect.[75]

An attempt to update the Rules resulted in a protocol signed at Brussels in 1968, the effect of which is to replace them by an amended set of rules, sometimes referred to as the Hague-Visby Rules.[76] These have not proved as popular as the 1924 Rules and have not, so far, been embodied in the domestic legislation of a large number of countries, including Australia. They were enacted in the United Kingdom in the Schedule to the *Carriage of Goods by Sea Act* 1971 which has recently been brought into force.[77] It looked at first as if the Act might never come into effect, particularly in view of the preparation by UNCITRAL of a Draft Convention with the effect of more radically altering the

---

[67] *Compagnie Des Messageries Maritimes* v. *Wilson* (1954) 95 C.L.R. 577.

[68] *Sea-Carriage of Goods Act* 1924, Sched., Art. I(b) and (c).

[69] Ibid., s. 4; cf. *John Churcher Pty. Ltd.* v. *Mitsui & Co.* [1974] 2 N.S.W.L.R. 179.

[70] *Sea-Carriage of Goods Act* 1924, s. 6.

[71] *Vita Food Products Incorporated* v. *Unus Shipping Co.* [1939] A.C. 277. Cf. *Sea-Carriage of Goods Act* 1924, s. 9(2); *Cie. des Messageries Maritimes* v. *Wilson* (1954) 94 C.L.R. 577.

[72] See Article 5.

[73] *J. B. Effenson Co.* v. *Three Bays Corp. (The Church Bay)* (1957) A.M.C. 16.

[74] *Sea-Carriage of Goods Act* 1924, Sched., Art. I(c).

[75] Known as a Himalaya clause after the ship in *Adler* v. *Dickson* [1955] 1 K.B. 158. See also the cases cited supra, p. 620, n. 22.

[76] See Gronfors [1968] J.B.L. 201.

[77] On 23 June 1977, the same day the Brussels Protocol came into force.

relationship between carrier and cargo-owner.[78] This has not proved to be the case and it is therefore worth noting briefly the amendments contained in the Hague-Visby Rules.

The Hague-Visby Rules are to apply to more voyages than were covered by the Hague Rules. They are to apply to every bill of lading relating to the carriage of goods between ports in two different States if: (a) the bill of lading is issued in a contracting State;[79] or (b) the carriage is from a port in a contracting State; or (c) the contract contained in or evidenced by the bill of lading provides that the Rules or legislation of any State giving effect to them are to govern the contract.[80] This provision was included because of the decision in the *Vita Food Case*.[81] The Privy Council there believed that the Rules were not mandatory and effect was given to a statement in the bill of lading that the contract was to be governed by English law. As the goods carried under the contract were not shipped from an English port, the Rules were held inapplicable. The decision has been criticised[82] and, outside Great Britain, has not been followed. The Rules have, however, been altered in an attempt to have them regarded as mandatory.

Section 1(3) of the U.K. Act further extends the application of the Rules to coastal trade within the U.K. where carried out under bills of lading. Moreover, Section 1(6) provides that the Rules may[83] apply to any bill of lading if the contract contained in or evidenced by it expressly provides that the Rules shall govern the contract and to any receipt which is a non-negotiable document marked as such if the contract contained in or evidenced by it is a contract for the carriage of goods by sea which expressly provides that the Rules are to govern the contract as if the receipt were a bill of lading.

The new Rules provide that where carriage is to take place using containers, the items packed in the container may be separately listed as packages or units if expressly provided[84] and, except where the nature and value of goods shipped has been declared and inserted in the bill of lading, an increased maximum amount of liability on the carrier's part is stipulated.[85] Article IV BIS extends the protection of the carrier under the rules in actions in contract and tort to his servants or agents (but not to his independent contractors).[86]

The Hague-Visby Rules are an amended form of the Hague Rules. They will most likely be superseded by the more radical set of reforms contained in the UNCITRAL[87] Draft Convention on the Carriage of Goods by Sea[88] if and when that comes into force. The range of the

---

[78] Infra.
[79] I.e. one that is a party to the Brussels Protocol.
[80] (U.K.) *Carriage of Goods by Sea Act* 1971, Sched., Art. X.
[81] [1939] A.C. 277.
[82] Falconbridge, *Conflict of Laws* (2nd ed. 1954), p. 406 et. seq.
[83] See s. 1(3).
[84] (U.K.) *Carriage of Goods by Sea Act* 1971, Sched., Art. IV, r.5(c).
[85] Ibid., Art. IV, r.5(a).
[86] Cf. cases cited supra, p. 620, n. 22.
[87] United Nations Commission on International Trade Law.
[88] U.N. General Assembly Official Records: Thirty-First Session, Supplement No. 17 (A/31/17). See Sweeney (1975) 7 J.M.L.C. 69, at 327; O'Hare (1976) 10 M.U.L.R. 527; O'Keefe (1977) 8 Sydney L.R. 68.

UNCITRAL rules is more extensive than that of the Hague Rules. They are applicable to all contracts of carriage by sea other than charter-parties (although they will apply to a bill of lading issued under a charterparty where the bill governs the relationship of parties other than the owner or charterer)[89] and are not limited to contracts governed by a bill of lading or other similar document of title.[90] Moreover the UNCITRAL rules will apply to the carriage of deck cargo and live animals.[91] They go beyond the provisions of the Hague Rules and the Hague-Visby Rules and apply to the whole of the period during which the goods are in the hands of the carrier.[92] His liability is greatly increased. Not only is most of the protection provided by the Hague Rules eradicated, in particular the exemption from liability for nautical fault, but there is wider prohibition on clauses designed to escape the impact of the Convention.[93]

Australia has supported the elimination of the exception of error of navigation but, in an attempt at compromise with carrier countries, has also supported retention of the exception of fire. The argument for the carrier countries—U.K., Federal Republic of Germany, Japan and the Soviet Union—against removing nautical error as an exception is that it would result in considerably higher liability insurance premiums for carriers without a corresponding decrease in cargo insurance rates. It is said that shippers would continue to take out cargo insurance as they would prefer to continue dealing with their own insurers and being reimbursed by them; further, that such insurance would be needed in order to preserve complete protection "warehouse to warehouse". A further argument is that removal of the error of navigation exception would lead to no greater care in the handling of cargo. Norway, the United States, Hungary, Kenya and France have joined with Australia in arguing that there is a lack of data or statistics to support these allegations and that the simplification of the liability regime would diminish litigation and overlapping insurance.[94]

D. Other Australian statutes

The New South Wales *Sea-Carriage of Goods (State) Act* 1921 applies in relation to ships carrying goods from any one place in New South Wales to any other place in that state, and in relation to goods so carried or received to be so carried in those ships. The substantial difference between this Act and the Commonwealth statute is that it is not possible to contract out of rights and immunities[95] in interstate shipping. Cl. 5 of the New South Wales Act declares illegal, null and void any part of a bill of lading whereby the carrier is relieved from liabilities such as Article III of the Commonwealth Act would impose. Furthermore, the New South Wales Act does not impose the £100 limitation to

---

[89] Article 2, cl. 3.
[90] Article 2, cl. 1.
[91] Article 5, cl. 5.
[92] Articles 10-11.
[93] Article 8.
[94] See generally, *Report*, International Trade Law Meeting, Australian Academy of Science, Canberra, June 1976.
[95] As in Article V, Schedule, Commonwealth *Sea-Carriage of Goods Act* 1924.

liability. Again, whereas interstate carriers are not responsible for loss or damage resulting from fire unless caused by their actual fault or privity, there is no waiver of such liability to be implied in case of New South Wales intrastate carriage of goods by sea.

Similar provisions form part of the Western Australian internal shipping law by virtue of the *Sea-Carriage of Goods Act* 1909, and part of the Tasmanian internal shipping law by virtue of the *Water Carriage Act* 1918. The New South Wales, Western Australian and Tasmanian Acts are, in effect, adoptions of the 1904 Commonwealth *Sea-Carriage of Goods Act*—the Act to be later replaced by adoption of the Hague Rules. The 1904 Act was, in turn, founded upon a law of the United States of America, commonly known as the *Harter Act*. The provisions of these Acts are discussed by the High Court in *Australasian United Steam Navigation Co. Ltd.* v. *Hiskens*.[96] It was there pointed out that the legislation was a codification of the obligations of a shipper as common carrier. Thus goods shipped between ports in New South Wales, between ports in Western Australia and between ports in Tasmania bear considerably more protection than goods shipped elsewhere. Queensland's internal shipping is governed by the *Sea Carriage of Goods (State) Act* of 1930 which is, in effect, an application of the Hague Rules. Victoria and South Australia have no equivalent legislation.

VI. Compensation for Loss or Damage to Goods

A. Insurance

In Australia this aspect of carriage of goods by sea is governed by provisions of the Commonwealth *Marine Insurance Act* 1909-1973. This Act substantially reproduces the provisions of the United Kingdom *Marine Insurance Act* of 1906. The Commonwealth Act applies to marine insurance other than State marine insurance, and to State marine insurance extending beyond the limits of the State concerned. In view of the limitations to State territory, as clarified in the *Sea-Bed Case*,[97] the Commonwealth Act is of general scope. The perils to which the Act is addressed include those consequent on, or incidental to, sea navigation including perils of the seas, fire, war, pirates, thieves, captures, seizures, restraints and detainments of princes and peoples, jettisons, barratry and any other perils of like kind or which may be designated by the policy.

Unless an insurer has an insurable interest, a contract of marine insurance may be deemed to be a gaming or wagering contract and so void. The Act sets out the requirements which limit insurable interest but in the most general of terms. A person is interested in a marine adventure where he stands in any legal or equitable relation to the adventure or to any insurable property at risk therein, in consequence of which he may benefit by the safety or due arrival of insurable property, or may be prejudiced by its loss, or by damage thereto, or by the detention thereof, or may incur liability in respect thereof.

[96] (1914) 18 C.L.R. 646.
[97] *New South Wales* v. *Commonwealth* (1975) 8 A.L.R. 1.

By virtue of Rule 17, Schedule 2 of the Act, the term "goods" means "goods in the nature of merchandise and does not include personal effects or provisions and stores for use on board". Thus a shipper need only give a general description of his merchandise as "goods". Whether a policy also covers the material in which the goods are packed is a question of construction, or of fact.

Expected freight is a lawful subject of marine insurance, as is expected profit. Although, generally, the shipowner alone has an insurable interest in freight, sometimes shippers protect against sea-damage loss by a policy on "contingency freight". This is prima facie the freight payable on delivery of the goods but, in such cases, the insurance is not really one on freight. It is rather an insurance on an interest in the goods akin to an insurance on profits. With regard to the insurable interest in goods, sale of goods law is generally applicable alongside provisions of the Act. However an insurable interest in profit on goods may exist although the goods are not, at the time of the loss, the property of the assured. Consignees of goods, being in advance to the consignors, may insure in their own name to the full value of the goods provided the proceeds are applied to their own benefit only to the extent of their claims in respect of such advances.

Several points may be noted in respect of the role of insurance agents who act on the behalf of the assured to effect policies. The liability of such agents to their employers for negligence is determined by general principles of agency. A person who accepts instructions to procure an insurance for another is bound to use reasonable care and skill to effect the policy. A person who voluntarily and without consideration undertakes to effect insurance for another is liable for any negligence in doing so if he takes any steps towards performance of his undertaking. Every insurance broker is bound to know all the ordinary and formal details necessary to be complied with in order to make a marine policy a legally valid instrument and, further, is bound, without any express directions, to insert in the policy all the ordinary risks and customary clauses which are usual and proper in respect of the contemplated voyage.[98]

B. Litigation

Various parties are entitled to claim under the bill of lading. In tort, the owner of the goods or the person entitled to their possession at the time of the tort may sue whether or not such person is a party to the bill of lading.[99] The consignee is deemed to have a prima facie interest in the goods.[1] An action in tort is not available to a normal shipper who acts merely as agent for the true owner.[2] Parties with a merely equitable or contractual right or licence to possession cannot sue for conversion of

---

[98] See e.g. *Mallough* v. *Barber* (1814) 4 Camp. 150.
[99] *Margarine Union G.m.b.H.* v. *Cambay Prince Steamship Co. Ltd.* [1969] 1 Q.B. 219; *The Arpad* [1934] P. 189, at 231 per Maugham L.J. See also the *Caltex Oil Case* (1976) 11 A.L.R. 227.
[1] *Coleman* v. *Lambert* (1839) 5 M. & W. 502; *Tronson* v. *Dent* (1853) 8 Moore P.C. 419.
[2] *Moores* v. *Hopper* (1807) 2 B. & P.N.R. 411.

the goods.[3] In contract, the shipper can sue only if he has acted as principal[4] except where, although an agent, he makes a special contract in his own name with the shipowner.[5] Any person can sue if in receipt of absolute property in the goods or if in receipt of the goods by presenting the bill of lading.

The shipowner is liable in tort if he is, or was, in possession of the goods by his agents; in contract to any claimant with whom he has contracted or to the assignees of such person. The charterer is similarly liable. The master is liable in tort if he is, or was, in possession of the goods or if the goods were lost or damaged by his negligence.[6] He is, of course, liable in contract to any person with whom he has personally contracted but is not liable if he has signed a bill of lading as agent for the charterers.[7] Members of the crew are liable for negligent handling or care of the goods resulting in loss or damage, and an independent contractor may be liable if employed by someone in contractual relationship with the owner of the goods.[8]

In an action under the Rules, the claimant first bears a burden of proving that he is owner of the goods and/or is entitled to claim, that the contract was breached or the tort was committed, that the person claimed against is the responsible person, that the loss or damage took place in his hands and the extent of the loss or damage. The carrier must then prove the cause of the loss, that he took due diligence to make the vessel seaworthy at the beginning of the voyage and that the loss is excluded under one of the above-mentioned heads.[9] If the loss has not been excluded, the claimant must then show that there was negligence at loading, in stowage or at discharge, or that there was no care of the cargo.

[3] *Nippon Yusen Kaisha* v. *Ramjiban Serowgee* [1938] A.C. 429; cf. Ch. 4 ante.
[4] *Moores* v. *Hopper* (1807) 2 B. & P.N.R. 411.
[5] *Joseph* v. *Knox* (1813) 3 Camp. 320; *Dunlop* v. *Lambert* (1839) 6 Cl. & Fin. 600, explained in *The Albazero* [1976] 3 All E.R. 129.
[6] *Midland Scruttons* v. *Silicones* [1962] A.C. 445.
[7] *Repetto* v. *Millar's Karri and Jarrah Forests* (1901) 6 Com. Cas. 129, at 135 per Bigham J.; *Lee Cooper* v. *Jeakins* [1967] 2 Q.B. 1.
[8] *Mayfair Photographic* v. *Baxter Hoare* [1972] 1 Lloyd's Rep. 410.
[9] See p. 623, ante.

CHAPTER 17

CARRIAGE BY AIR

International air transport operates within an extremely complex legal network. This is based upon rules and regulations made by the International Civil Aviation Organization (ICAO) and the International Air Transport Association (IATA) and on international conventions such as the Warsaw Convention of 1929 as amended by the Hague Protocol of 1955 and the Guadalajara Convention of 1961 (supplementary to the Warsaw Convention).

Scheduled air services are determined by multilateral exchange or rights across international frontiers which rights in turn are founded upon a matrix of bilateral international treaties concluded after long bargaining by individual states. These bilateral treaties have been described by one authority as precarious since they are terminable at very short notice although this apparent vulnerability is tempered by the common interest shared by nations in keeping their international air services intact.[1]

In order to appraise concisely this field of transportation law the main conventions affecting carriage of goods and passengers by air will be considered first, followed by a review of related ICAO and IATA regulations. Lastly, the domestic legislation of Australia and relevant case law will be dealt with.

I. INTERNATIONAL CONVENTIONS

The law relating to carriage by air is principally governed by the following conventions:

(a) the original Warsaw Convention of 1929 which controls international air carriage between two states, both of which have ratified the 1929 Convention but only one of which (or neither of which) has ratified the Convention as amended by the 1955 Hague Protocol.

---

[1] Cheng, *The Law of International Air Transport* (1962); see Preface, pp. vi, vii. However, as an Australian commentator has observed: "The I.C.A.O. has never been able to gain sufficient support to successfully sponsor a multilateral Convention for the exchange of commercial rights in air navigation. Instead, States have had to base their dealings on bi-lateral agreements between them. These treaties are a problem in international law because they serve as instruments of economic discrimination. It has been said that bilateral agreements in this field sectionalize the world and make air transport both more expensive and less convenient than it should be" (citing Billyou, *Air Law* (2nd ed. 1964), p. 271); M. Sassella, "The International Civil Aviation Organisation: Its Contribution to International Law" (1971) 8 Melbourne University Law Review, p. 90.

(b) the Warsaw Convention (as amended in 1955) which governs all cases of international carriage by air between two states both of which have ratified the amended Convention.[2]

A. The Original Warsaw Convention of 1929

This Convention applies to international carriage of passengers, luggage or goods by air for reward as well as to air carriage performed gratuitously. For the purpose of the Convention, international carriage occurs where both the places of departure and destination are in states parties to the Convention even if there is an agreed stopping place in a third state not a party to Convention. Similarly, carriage is deemed to be international where the destination and arrival point are in the territory of the same state but there is an agreed stopping point in the territory of another state (whether a party to the Convention or not). Thus a flight between Brisbane and Melbourne is non-international if direct, but it is international for the purposes of the Convention if there is a scheduled stop in Auckland. Article 1(1) of the the Convention lays down that the Convention applies to all international carriage of persons, luggage or goods performed by an aircraft for reward and equally applies to gratuitous carriage by aircraft carried out by an air transport undertaking ("air transport undertaking" not being given definition).

International Carriage is defined by Articles 1(2) and (3) as follows:

(2) For the purposes of this Convention the expression "international carriage" means any carriage in which, according to the contract made by the parties, the place of departure and the place of destination, whether or not there be a break in the carriage or a transhipment, are situated either within the territories of two High Contracting Parties, or within the territory of a single High Contracting Party, if there is an agreed stopping place within a territory subject to the sovereignty, suzerainty, mandate or authority of another Power, even though that Power is not a party to this Convention. A carriage without such an agreed stopping place between territories subject to the sovereignty, suzerainty, mandate or authority of the same High Contracting Party is not deemed to be international for the purposes of this Convention.

(3) A carriage to be performed by several successive air carriers is deemed, for the purposes of this Convention, to be one undivided carriage, if it has been regarded by the parties as a single operation,

[2] The 1929 Warsaw Convention was implemented in Australia by the *Carriage by Air Act* 1935 (No. 18 of 1935). The *Civil Aviation (Carrier's Liability) Act* 1959 incorporates the Warsaw Convention and approves ratification given to the 1955 Hague Protocol read and interpreted with the Convention as one instrument in accordance with Article 19 of the Hague Protocol (s. 10 of the above Act). The provisions of the Guadalajara Convention (subject to Parts II and III of the above Act) are also included (ss. 25A-25C inclusive). (For the Guadalajara Convention, see below.)

In the United Kingdom the Warsaw Convention as amended by the 1955 Hague Protocol was given effect by the *Carriage by Air Act* 1961 brought into force by Order in Council (s. 1 1967, No. 480). This order also applied the original Warsaw Convention of 1929 to cases of international carriage still governed by that Convention. This was necessary as the 1961 Act repealed the legislation which had previously given force of law to the 1929 Convention, namely the *Carriage by Air Act* 1932. On both Convention and the Protocol *see* McNair, *The Law of the Air* (3rd ed.), pp. 240-250.

whether it had been agreed upon under the form of a single contract or of a series of conttracts, and it does not lose its international character merely because one contract or a series of contracts is to be performed entirely within a territory subject to the sovereignty, suzerainty, mandate, or authority of the same High Contracting Party.

Despite the difficulties that may arise in deciding whether or not a contract of carriage by air is one of international carriage, an important factor in determining this may be the common practice of travelling on a return ticket. In *Grein* v. *Imperial Airways Ltd.*,[3] Mr Grein took a return ticket from London to Antwerp, with an agreed stopping place at Brussels. On the return flight the plane crashed due to the pilot's negligence and Mr Grein was killed. The Court of Appeal (Greer L.J., dissenting) took the view that the carriage was international although Belgium, having signed but not yet ratified the Warsaw Convention, was not regarded as a High Contracting Party—the court treating the contract as being in respect of one carriage only, namely, London-Antwerp and return. Thus the damages to the plaintiff were limited to the amount laid down by the *Carriage by Air Act* 1932.

1. *Liability of Carrier for Goods*: Every carrier of goods has the right to require that the consignor supply a document designated an "air consignment note" (air way-bill) and every consignor has a right to require acceptance of this document by the carrier. The air way-bill has three parts; one signed by the consignor and marked "for the carrier", a second signed by both carrier and consignor marked "for the consignee" intended to accompany the goods, and a third part signed by the carrier and handed back to the consignor after the goods have been accepted. Where there is more than one package one air way-bill may be used to cover them.

By Article 8 of the Convention the air consignment note should contain the following details:
   (a) the place and date of its execution;
   (b) the place of departure and destination;
   (c) the agreed stopping places (which can be altered by the carrier in necessity);
   (d) the name and address of the consignor;
   (e) the name and address of the first carrier;
   (f) the name and address of the consignee if the circumstances require it;
   (g) the nature of the goods;

---

[3] [1937] 1 K.B. 50. See also (1936) 7 *Air Law Review*, at 447-448. On the problem of what constitutes a High Contracting Party see generally McNair, op. cit., pp. 171-172 and in particular *Philippson and Others* v. *Imperial Airways Ltd.* [1939] A.C. 332. The House of Lords in that case held that for the purposes of the contract of carriage at issue it was necessary to decide the meaning of "High Contracting Party" in the Convention. By a majority their Lordships decided that the terms included states which had signed but not ratified the Convention. This decision is reflected in Article 40A(1) of the Warsaw Convention as amended by the Hague Protocol of 1955 (see below) which defines "states" for the purposes of Article 37(2) and Article 40(1), and as meaning in all other cases a state "whose ratification of or adherence to the Convention has become effective and whose denunciation thereof has not become effective". McNair, op. cit., p. 251.

(h) the number of the packages, the method of packing and the particular marks or numbers on them;

(i) the weight, quantity and volume or dimensions of the goods;

(j) the apparent condition of the goods and of the packing;

(k) the freight, if it has been agreed upon, the date and place of payment, and the person who is to pay for it;

(l) the price of the goods if they are sent for payment on delivery, and the amount of the expenses incurred if the circumstances require it;

(m) the amount of the value declared under Article 22(2), (3);

(n) the number of parts of the air way-bill;

(o) the documents handed to the carrier to accompany the air way-bill;

(p) the time fixed for the completion of the carriage and a brief note of the route to be followed, if these matters have been agreed upon;

(q) a statement that the carriage is subject to the rules relating to liability established by the Convention.

Under Article 9, if the carrier accepts goods without an air way-bill or if that document does not contain all the provisions set out in (a) to (i) inclusive and (q) then the carrier will not be able to claim the protection of the provisions of the Convention which either exclude or limit his liability. The carrier will thus be liable for all damage howsoever caused unless he can prove that it did not occur during the carriage by air.[4]

---

[4] The view has been taken that carriers by air may be regarded as common carriers; see *Luddit* v. *Ginger Coote Airways Ltd.* [1942] 2 D.L.R. 29 where the case was disposed of on a narrow ground. In *Nysted and Anson* v. *Wings Ltd.* [1942] 3 D.L.R., the King's Bench Court of Manitoba held that the defendant was a common carrier, the law governing carriers by air being the same as that governing carriers by land or sea. It asserted that the position is similar in the United States, citing *Kilberg* v. *North East Airlines Inc.* [1961] 2 Lloyd's Rep. 406, at 407; McNair, op. cit., p. 140. Ibid., p. 139: "If air carriers have invariably chosen to employ written notices and contracts limiting their liability, this surely shows, if anything, that they are concerned to escape the duties which might otherwise be imposed upon them as common carriers. It is certainly not indicative of the conclusion that they cannot be so regarded. And while it is true that the strict liability of the common carrier and innkeeper is not found today in the case of other bailees for reward, this does not advance the argument materially. It may be answered that the air carrier who otherwise fulfils the necessary requirements of a common carrier, does not represent a completely new genus of bailee for reward. He is rather a species belonging to the genus common carrier."

Although there is no direct English authority on this point it was referred to in *Aslan* v. *Imperial Airways Ltd.* (1933) 45 Ll.L.R. 322. In that case gold was sent by air from Baghdad to London. It was alleged that the plane supplied for the purpose by the defendants contained no strong-room or suitable compartment for bullion. The gold was stolen and it was held in the subsequent action that the defendants escaped liability under the express protective provisions in the consignment note. MacKinnon J. (as he then was) observed at p. 322 (obiter): "I see no reason why a man who carries goods by a machine that travels through the air should not be a common carrier if he acts in a certain way . . . If a man who owned an aeroplane or a seaplane chose to engage in the trade of carrying goods as a regular business and to hold himself out ready to carry for any who wished to employ him so far as he had room in his airship or aeroplane for their goods, very likely he would become a common carrier or be under the various liabilities of a common carrier."

In respect of adequate packaging in the carriage of animals the Divisional Court of Queen's Bench held in *British Airways Board* v. *Wiggins* (1977) *The Times* 29 March that the Board had a duty to ensure that animals carried on their aircraft were correctly packed, although they had no control over packing which had taken place abroad. This decision was made in dismissing an appeal by the

In the case of *Westminster Bank Ltd.* v. *Imperial Airways Ltd*[5] the plaintiffs delivered gold bars valued at £9,138 to be carried from London to Paris. The gold was placed in a strong-room at Croydon airport, but on the following day the room was found open and the gold stolen. The back of the consignment note contained the following statement:

> Carriage by Air: The general conditions of carriage of goods are applicable to both internal and international carriage. These general conditions are based upon the Convention of Warsaw of October 12, 1929, in so far as concerns international carriage within the meaning of the said convention.

Upon an action to recover the value of the gold by the plaintiffs the court held:

(i) the carriage had commenced (Article 18 of the Convention);

(ii) the statement on the consignment note should have been that the carriage is *subject* to the rules relating to liability established by this Convention. To say that the conditions were *based upon* the Convention was not enough. The Act required a simple, clear statement and there was a statutory duty to incorporate it without variation.

(iii) Although the Bank had declared the value of the gold at £9,000 and had paid a higher rate than for other types of merchandise, it was a rate appropriate to gold bars and the valuation was needed to calculate the ad valorem rate. The payment of their higher rate was not, however, the payment of a supplementary sum since this should be something over and above the normal rate for that type of merchandise. If, therefore, the statement on the consignment note had complied with the Act, the liability

---

Board against a conviction by Uxbridge justices of an offence contrary to regulation 8(1)(b) of the *Transit of Animals (General) Order* 1973 (made under the *Diseases of Animals Act* 1950) in that being the carrier in charge of animals, namely tortoises, they failed to ensure that they were provided with a receptacle suitable for carrying the species.

---

5 [1936] 2 All E.R. 890; followed in *Philippson* v. *Imperial Airways Ltd.* (see ante, n. 3.) See McNair, pp. 184-189. *Seth* v. *B.O.A.C.* [1964] 1 Lloyd's Rep. 268 is consistent with the *Westminster Bank* and *Philippson* cases. In *Seth's* case the U.S. Circuit Court of Appeals upheld a standard provision used in most air consignment notes and passenger and luggage tickets as complying with Article (3)(h) of the Warsaw Convention, i.e. "Carriage hereunder is subject to [the Convention] unless such carriage is not international carriage as defined by the Convention". The court held that this statement gave the passenger clear notice that limitations are provided under the Convention and the carrier will avail himself of these limitations if he can. McNair, op. cit., 543-544.

In the United Kingdom non-international carriage is governed by the Non-International Carriage Rules 1967 which apply in every case of carriage by air not governed by the original Warsaw Convention or the Convention as amended by the Hague Protocol. However, the Non-International Carriage Rules do not include the Articles of the amended Convention, or any other provisions, in respect of the air-way bill or baggage check; this is not required by the Rules and there are no legal consequences if a carrier fails to issue either an air-way bill or baggage check or fails to include any particular statement in these documents if issued. Thus the Rules have no provision equivalent to Article 9, nor are Articles 12 and 13 included (delivery and stoppage of goods in transit); Articles 28 (dealing with questions of jurisdiction) and 34 are also absent. The Rules apply the same maximum limits with regard to death or injury to passengers and loss or damage to goods and passengers' baggage. With these exceptions the provisions of the Warsaw Convention, as amended, apply to non-international carriage in the United Kingdom.

of Imperial Airways would have been subject to the limits of the Convention.[6]

A later decision by the English Court of Appeal, *Samuel Montague and Co. Ltd.* v. *Swiss Air Transport Co. Ltd.*[7] held that the insertion after the words required by Article 8(9) of the additional words "unless such carriage is not 'international carriage' as defined by the Convention" did not contravene the provisions of Article 9 since the parties to a contract of carriage by air must be deemed to know what constitutes "international carriage" under the Convention.

2. *Liabilities of Carriers for Loss or Damage*: By Article 18 the carrier is liable for the loss of, or damage to, any registered luggage or any goods during the carriage by air, and this includes any period during which the goods or luggage are in charge of the carrier, whether in the aerodrome, or on board an aircraft, or, in the case of a landing outside an aerodrome, in any place whatsoever. Under Article 19 the carrier is liable for damages occasioned by delay in the carriage by air of passengers, luggage or goods. Delay arises after the agreed time for carriage has expired, or, where no such time is laid down, after a reasonable time has passed without delivery.

In *Bart* v. *British West Indian Airways Ltd.*[8] the Guyana Court of Appeal had to consider *inter alia* the question of delay in air carriage. In that case the plaintiff sent his football coupon, distributed on behalf of Sherman Pools Ltd., via one L., who then sent the completed coupons with the stake money to Sherman Pools, Ltd. in London on the basis that if coupons left Guyana on Thursday before the Saturday on which the matches were played and were received by Shermans on the following Sunday, they would be honoured by the firm. L used B.W.I.A., the defendants, for the carriage of coupons from Georgetown to Trinidad where they would be transhipped on to a B.O.A.C. aircraft leaving Trinidad on Saturdays, arriving at London on Sundays. The B.W.I.A. flights from Georgetown on Thursdays and Fridays would be in time to catch the

---

[6] In *Corocraft Ltd and Another* v. *Pan American Airways Inc.* [1969] 1 All E.R. 82, a package of jewellery was consigned from the United States to England via the defendant's airline but the package was stolen by one of the defendant's servants before it could be delivered to the second plaintiffs. The defendant's liability was limited under Article 22 of the Warsaw Convention. By Article 9 of the same Convention the defendants were not entitled to any limitation of liability if the air consignment note did not contain, *inter alia*, the particulars set out in Article 8 of the Convention (see text above). The senders had completed an air consignment note (including the weight) in respect of the package but had not included particulars relating to the quantity, the volume or the dimensions of the package although it was admitted that the volume and dimensions were known to the plaintiffs at all material times and to the defendants as soon as the package was received for carriage. It was held, on the question as to whether the defendant's right to limit their liability was excluded by any omission from the air consignment note, that on the true construction of the French text of Article 8 the weight should be given when appropriate, the volume and dimensions need not be given except when they were necessary or useful, and the quantity need not be stated except where it was applicable. Alternatively, on the true construction of the English text of Article 8 the particulars referred to were required to be given only so far as applicable or necessary or useful. Thus the defendants had complied with Article 8 and were entitled to limitation of liability.
[7] [1966] 1 All E.R. 814.
[8] [1967] Lloyd's Rep. 239.

B.O.A.C. aircraft in Trinidad. The plaintiff sent his coupon to L for transmission to Sherman's Pools in time to catch a Thursday B.W.I.A. flight, but due to that airline's negligence, L's package was mislaid at the Georgetown terminal office until Saturday when it was too late to catch the B.O.A.C. flight at Trinidad. The plaintiff's coupon was a winning coupon. L cabled Sherman's Pools asking them to honour coupons which had been delayed. This Sherman's refused to do as these arrived on Thursday, together with the plaintiff's coupon. Had this been honoured it would have entitled him to a dividend of £20,457 10s.

The plaintiff claimed against B.W.I.A., alleging:

(i) negligence and/or breach of contract in delaying delivering the coupon;

(ii) that although not a party to the contract, he was a person interested and entitled to sue upon it; or that L. was acting as agent of an undisclosed principal (the plaintiff) when contracting with B.W.I.A.;

(iii) that B.W.I.A. were in fundamental breach of contract and could not rely on exemption clauses in the contract;

(iv) that B.W.I.A. were, in any event, liable in negligence and/or in breach of duty as bailees.

B.W.I.A. denied liability, contending that only the consignor and consignee had a right to sue the carrier as the *Carriage of Goods by Air Act* 1932 (which contained the Warsaw Convention) had been applied to Guyana by Order in Council.

Article 13 of the Carriage by Air (Non-international Carriage) (Colonies, Protectorates and Trust Territories) Order 1953 (No. 1206) provided (inter alia):

(3) If the carrier admits the loss of the cargo, or if the cargo has not arrived at the expiration of seven days after the date on which it ought to have arrived, the consignee is entitled to put into force against the carrier the rights which flow from the contract of carriage.

B.W.I.A. claimed that their liability was limited; and there was no cause of action for delay in tort, and that the plaintiff had suffered no loss as Sherman's Pools would not have accepted the coupon even if it had arrived on Sunday, owing to suspicious circumstances.

In the lower court the plaintiff was awarded the equivalent of £10,000 damages for the loss of the chance of the coupon being honoured. B.W.I.A. then appealed to the Guyana Court of Appeal. The Chancellor, Sir Kenneth Stoby, in a detailed judgment, allowing the appeal, held *inter alia* that the plaintiff was not a party to the agreement between L and B.W.I.A.; that delivery on the Thursday was not within a reasonable time; that under Article 19 the carrier was liable for unreasonable delay although less than seven days in length (notwithstanding Article 13) and that the intention was not to give the carrier seven days' grace to cure his negligence, but to place the onus on the carrier to prove that the cargo was not lost:

The words in Art. 13(3), "if the cargo has not arrived at the expiration of seven days after the date on which it ought to have arrived" do not mean that the carrier incurs no liability for delay until seven days have elapsed. The date on which the cargo ought to have arrived has to be ascertained, and to ascertain that date the test is a reasonable time in all the circumstances. Once that date is ascertained an arrival after such date makes the carrier liable (and absolutely liable in international carriage) for delay. In legislating that the consignee is entitled to put into force against the carrier the rights which flow from the contract seven days after the ascertained date of arrival, the intention was not to give the carrier a period of seven days' grace to cure his negligence, but to place the onus on the carrier to prove that the cargo is not lost. To interpret the Article otherwise would mean that the carrier is not liable for delay unless the delay extends for seven days.[9]

This argument was not accepted by Bollers C.J., who argued that in the absence of a fixed time there would be an implied agreement between the shipper and carrier that the goods would be conveyed by air within a reasonable time but that under the air consignment note issued by the defendants, it was agreed that no time was fixed for completion of the carriage and no obligation was assumed by the carrier to carry the goods by any specific aircraft or over any particular route or to make any connection at any point according to any particular schedule. Further, Bollers C.J. observed that under the general conditions of carriage for cargo no time was fixed for the commencement or completion of the carriage; time tables were to be regarded as approximate only, were not guaranteed and formed no part of the contract of carriage.

Bollers C.J. stated " . . . it would be surprising to me to find an airline company willing to bind itself to deliver goods within a fixed time when weather conditions, aircraft worthiness and expected or unexpected eventu-

---

[9] Ibid. p. 252. On the question of who could sue under the Convention his Lordship quoted with respect to Article 19 this extract from Drion, *Limitations of Liabilities in International Air Law*, p. 135, part of which reads; "As to loss, damage or delay of goods, the better view would seem to be that only the consignor or the consignee has a right of action. With respect to loss, damage or delay of baggage, and delay of passengers, the person contemplated as entitled to an action for damages was no doubt the passenger, *though especially in the case of delay the person with whom the carrier contracted—assuming him to be other than the passenger—should be considered a good plaintiff*" (italics supplied).
His Lordship also cited earlier the following extract from Shawcross and Beaumont on *Air Law*: "In some cases the passenger or consignor (or consignee) may have two alternative courses open to him: either (i) to sue the carrier for delay under art. 19 . . or (ii) to sue for damages due to non-performance in which case the action would not, it seems, be subject to the provisions of the Act" (3rd ed. 1966), p. 435. Since all three judges in *Bart's* case agreed that the plaintiff was outside the contract between L. and B.W.I.A., Sir Kenneth Stoby's remarks must be considered obiter. In addition, Drion's remarks quoted above expressly state that in respect of goods (which the coupons manifestly were, being in a registered parcel) being delayed the better view is that only the consignor and the consignee have a right of action. In respect of the Shawcross and Beaumont extract cited, non-performance was not at issue in *Bart's* case and, with respect, there seems no support for his Lordship's view that the plaintiff was entitled to bring his action on the basis of the extracts quoted above. In addition his Lordship himself noted that the American cases quoted indicated a uniform stand in New York Courts to confine a carrier's liability to the consignor or consignee, ibid., p. 248; *Manhattan Novelty Corp.* v. *Seaboard & Western Airlines Inc.* [1958] U.S. & Can. Av. Rep. 311, followed in *Holzer Watch Co. Inc.* v. *Seaboard & Western Airlines Inc.* [1958] U.S. & Can. Av. Rep. 142; *Pilgrim Apparel Inc.* v. *National Union Fire Insurance Company & Ors.* [1960] U.S. & Can. Av. Rep. 373. See also the South African case of similar conclusion, *Pan American World Airways Incorporated* v. *S.A. Fire and Accident Insurance Co. Ltd.* [1965] 3 App. Div. 150. It is submitted that the views of Bollers C.J. and Lucklee J.A. are to be preferred to those of Sir Kenneth Stoby on this point.

alities may intervene to render futile their most earnest intention."[10] Luckhoo J.A. was in agreement with Bollers C.J. in his general view that under the Order-in-Council none other than the consignor or consignee could sue the carrier and if a different result were required a special contract would need to be made for that purpose under Article 15(2).[11]

A related issue is that of deviation, i.e. a voluntary or negligent departure from the journey that the carrier has agreed to perform. In *Lichten v. Eastern Airlines Inc.*[12] the alleged deviation took the form of an over-carriage of goods beyond the correct destination. The majority of the court held that this did not deprive the carrier of the benefit of an exclusionary tariff. Assistance may be gained by analogy with the effect of contracts of carriage by sea subject to the Hague Rules.[13] Another case which dealt briefly with the argument of whether over-carriage or miscarriage of the goods in question amounted to a deviation depriving the carriage of its international character and put it outside the Warsaw Convention was *Rotterdamsche Bank N.V.* v. *British Overseas Airways Corporation.*[14]

Pilcher J. observed:

> Even assuming that the doctrine of deviation, as known in maritime law, applies to air carriage, and assuming that the over-carriage or miscarriage, which here occurred . . . amounted to an unjustifiable deviation from the contractual voyage, I can find nothing in the 1932 Act or the Convention which justifies the conclusion that what occurred in this case served to remove the carriage from the ambit of the Convention.

As the learned judge expressed no view as to whether or not the doctrine of deviation applied to air carriage, the case would not be conslusive on this point. It may be that logically aerial deviation should deprive a carrier of such provisions in the Warsaw Convention that he might otherwise rely on but this point still awaits clear judicial pronouncement.[15]

---

[10] at 275.

[11] at 287, 285.

[12] [1951] U.S. Av.R. 310. See McNair, op. cit., p. 157 et seq. where the decision is strongly criticized, and the dissenting judgment of Frank J. (who held that the deviation prevented the carrier from relying on the exemptions) is preferred.

[13] McNair, op. cit., pp. 214-215. This view has been strongly criticised by Drion in *Limitation of Liabilities in Air Law*, pp. 60-62, where the learned writer makes a distinction between the expression in Article II of the Rules of the *Carriage of Goods by Sea Act* 1924 providing that *"under every contract of carriage* of goods by sea the carrier [. . .] shall be subject to the responsibilities and liabilities and entitled to the rights and immunities hereinafter set forth" and the Warsaw Convention which by Article 1(1) provides that it "applies to all international carriage of persons, luggage or goods, performed by aircraft for reward;" additionally that by Article 24 the Convention deals with any action for damages however founded in cases covered by Articles 18 and 19 respectively. Drion further argues that the deviation rule in English law has been developed as a rule of interpretation of contractual clauses (ibid., p. 62). McNair, ibid., at p. 215 in footnote 6 submits that the Warsaw Convention applies equally to contracts of carriage, and in a common law jurisdiction the doctrine of deviation would displace the statutory restrictions upon the carrier's liability. The learned authors cite Article 33 as indicating that "the Convention applies only to contracts, which the carrier has agreed to make, and the definition of 'international carriage' in Art. 1(2) refers expressly to the contract between the parties."

[14] [1953] 1 W.L.R. 493.

[15] McNair, op. cit., p. 216.

3. *Avoidance and Limitation of Liability*: Article 20 provides that the carrier can avoid his liability as follows:

(i) If he proves that he and his agents have taken all necessary measures to avoid the damage, or that it was impossible for him or them to take such measures;

(ii) If, in the case of the carriage of goods or luggage, he proves that the damage was caused by negligent pilotage or negligence in the handling of the aircraft or in navigation, and that, in all other respects, he and his agents have taken all necessary measures to avoid the damage.[16]

By Article 25 the carrier cannot protect himself by the provisions of the Convention which exclude or limit his liability in the following cases:

(i) if the damage is caused by wilful misconduct, or default equivalent to misconduct;

(ii) if the damage is caused by the wilful misconduct, or default equivalent to misconduct, of his servants or agents acting within the scope of their employment.[17]

---

[16] The carrier may in appropriate cases raise the defence of contributory negligence against the person whose goods were damaged. See *Civil Aviation (Carrier's Liability) Act* 1959, s. 39, below. See generally, McNair, ibid, pp. 74, 117, 187-188, 290, 498 and Drion, ibid., pp. 123-125.

[17] In *Horabin* v. *British Overseas Airways Corporation* [1952] 2 All E.R. 1016 "wilful misconduct" was held to be a term that might include even a comparatively minor breach of safety regulations or a minor lapse from comparative standards of safety. However, the mere fact that an act was done contrary to a plan or to instructions, or even to the standards of safe flying, to the knowledge of the person doing it, does not establish wilful misconduct on his part, unless it is shown that he knew that he was doing something contrary to the best interests of the passengers and of his employers or involving them in a greater risk than if he had not done it. A grave error of judgment, particularly one apparent as such in the light of after events, is not wilful misconduct if the person responsible thought he was acting in the best interests of the passengers and of the aircraft. Per Barry J., at 1019:

"Wilful misconduct to which the will is a party; and it is wholly different in kind from mere negligence or carelessness, however gross that negligence or carelessness may be. The will must be a party to the misconduct, and not merely a party to the conduct of which the complaint is made. As an example, if the pilot of an aircraft knowingly does something which subsequently a jury find amounted to misconduct, that fact alone does not show that he was guilty of wilful misconduct. To establish wilful misconduct on the part of this imaginary pilot, it must be shown, not only that he knowingly (and in that sense wilfully did the wrongful act, but also that, when he did it, he was aware that it was a wrongful act, i.e., that he was aware that he was committing misconduct."

This view of wilful misconduct was applied by Webb J. in *Royal Victorian Aero Club* v. *Commonwealth* (1954) 92 C.L.R. 236. *Horabin's* case was considered recently in *Rustenburg Platinum Mines Ltd. and others* v. *South African Airways and Pan American World Airways Inc.* [1977] 1 Lloyd's Rep. 564 where it was decided inter alia that the theft of a box of platinum at Heathrow Airport presumably by a Pan Am loader was within the scope of his employment and that there was no wilful misconduct by any servant other than in that theft. Judgement was given for the plaintiffs as it was held that Pan Am had not taken all measures to avoid the damage to the plaintiffs as they could have instructed their loaders not to leave an aircraft hold with valuable cargo unsupervised until closed or ought not to have despatched the cargo when, due to a security emergency at the airport, there were few security guards available. See also *American Airlines* v. *Ulen* [1949] U.S. Av. R. 338; *Ritts* v. *American Overseas Airlines Inc.* [1949] U.S. Av. R. 65, 68; *Rashap* v. *American Airlines* (1955) U.S.C. Av. R. 593 (N.Y. Southern District Court).

See generally, on this topic of wilful misconduct, Drion, op. cit., Chapter 12.

The onus of proof under Article 25 rests, it appears, on the plaintiff, although wilful but minor acts of misconduct will be sufficient in view of the greater risks involved in carriage by air.[18]

By Article 26(2) in the case of damage the person entitled to delivery must complain to the carrier forthwith after the discovery of the damage, and, at the latest, within seven days from the date of receipt in the case of baggage.[18a]

B. The Amended Convention of 1955[19]

The main changes brought about by the amended Convention relate to the contents of the air way-bill and the carrier's liability.

1. *The Air Way-bill*: Article 8 of the Warsaw Convention is amended to provide as follows:

The air way-bill shall contain:

(a) an indication of the places of departure and destination;

(b) if the place of departure and destination are within the territory of a single High Contracting Party, one or more agreed stopping places being within the territory of another State, an indication of at least one such stopping place;

(c) a notice to the consignor to the effect that if the carriage involves an ultimate destination or stop in a country other than the country of departure, the Warsaw Convention may be applicable, and that the Convention governs and in most cases limits the liability of carriers in respect of loss of or damage to cargo.

Article 9 of the Amended Convention modifies the otherwise strict provisions of Article 9 of the Warsaw Convention by providing as follows:

If with the consent of the carrier, cargo is loaded on board the aircraft without an air way-bill having been made out, or if the air way-bill does not include the notice required by Article 8, paragraph (c), the carrier shall not be entitled to avoid himself of the provisions of article 22, paragraph (2).

The carrier, therefore, may rely on all the other provisions limiting his liability except Article 22(2) which limits his liability to 250 francs per kilogram. These provisions apply also to the "baggage check" issued in connection with the passenger's baggage.[20]

---

[18] Both Articles 20 and 25 have been changed in the amended Convention of 1955, (see below). Article 21 of the Convention relating to contributory negligence in respect of liability for passenger injury is given effect to by the *Civil Aviation (Carriers' Liability) Act* 1959-1973, s. 16. See also *Horabin* v. *British Overseas Airways Corporation* [1952] 2 All E.R. 1016.

[18a] In *Fothergill* v. *Monarch Airlines Ltd.*, (1977) *The Times* 18 March, the Divisional Court of Queen's Bench decided, in allowing a claim by the plaintiff for a declaration against the defendants that under Article 26 no complaint lay in respect of partial loss, that loss of part of the contents of an airline passenger's suitcase is not "damage" to baggage within the meaning of Article 26(2) and an airline can therefore be made liable for such loss even if the passenger does not notify the airline within seven days; *Stag Line Ltd.* v. *Foscolo, Mango & Co.* [1932] A.C. 328 and *Schwimmer* v. *Air France* (1976) Av. Cas. No. 17/46 on the question of construction of the term "damage" applied.

[19] See *Civil Aviation (Carriers' Liability) Act* 1959 and see ante, n.2. For a description of establishment and operation of air transport services and international law of carriage by air in general see Shawcross and Beaumont, pp. 275-291 and pp. 333-349 respectively.

[20] See post.

2. *Carrier's liability*: Article 20 of the Warsaw Convention exempting the carrier from liability in respect of damage caused by negligent pilotage or negligence in handling or navigation is abolished by Article 20 of the 1955 Convention which provides the only defence open to the carrier in the following terms:

> The carrier is not liable if he proves that he and his agents have taken all necessary measures to avoid the damage or that it was impossible for him or them to take such measures.

Similarly Article 25 of the Warsaw Convention by which the carrier was not entitled to use the provisions of the Convention which excluded or limited his liability where he was guilty of wilful misconduct has been superseded by Article 20 of the 1955 Convention which provides:

> The limits of liability specified in Article 22 shall not apply if it is proved that the damage resulted from an act or omission of the carrier, his servant or agents, done with intent to cause damage or recklessly and with knowledge that damage would probably result; provided that, in the case of such act or omission of a servant or agent, it is also proved that he was acting within the scope of his employment.[21]

Article 23 of the Warsaw Convention is retained as Article 23(1) of the 1955 Convention, but a new provision is added as Article 23(2). Article 23 (as extended) reads:

> (1) Any provision tending to relieve the carrier of liability or to fix a lower limit than that which is laid down in the Convention shall be null and void, but the nullity of any such provision does not involve the nullity of the whole contract, which shall remain subject to the provisions of this Convention.
> (2) Paragraph (1) of this Article shall not apply to provisions governing loss or damage resulting from the inherent defect, quality or vice of the cargo carried.[22]

The Hague Protocol thus has simplified the requirement relating to documents of carriage (i.e. passenger ticket, luggage ticket, air consignment note). All these documents need now show is an indication of the points of departure and destination, and, if they are in the same State, an indication of at least one of these stopping places, and notice to the effect that if the passenger's journey crosses an international boundary the Warsaw Convention applies. As noted, under the Warsaw Convention the sanction for failure by the carrier to comply was unlimited liability under the Warsaw Convention but this now applies under the Protocol only if the passenger embarks without delivery of a ticket and the carrier consents, or if the ticket does not contain the required notice. The carrier's

---

[21] If an agent or servant of the carrier is sued personally he can rely on Article 22 so long as he was acting within the scope of employment.

[22] Article 23(2) would appear to be unnecessary in view of the provisions of Article 20 (see ante). The Warsaw Convention did not apply to experimental flights and certain other flights in extraordinary circumstances beyond the scope of the air carrier's business. A similar provision in the 1955 Convention, Article 34, provides:

"Articles 3 to 9 relating to documents of carriage shall not apply to carriage performed in extraordinary circumstances outside the normal scope of an air carrier's business."

defences are uniform under the Protocol for passengers, luggage and cargo, with the carrier unable to plead negligent pilotage or negligent handling of aircraft where luggage or cargo are lost or damaged.[23]

The Protocol has raised the limit of liability for death or injury to 250,000 gold francs while the limits for luggage remain as before.[24] The carrier's limited liability ends if it is shown that the damage resulted from an act done "with intent to cause damage or recklessly and with knowledge that damage would probably result".[25] This does away with the old formula of "wilful misconduct or such default as is considered equivalent to wilful misconduct"[26] which has been given different interpretations in different national courts.[27] The carrier, although deprived of limited liability still has the defences recognized by the Convention open to him. Carriers' servants are now entitled to recourse to the limits of liability of the carrier and amounts won against both carrier and servant must not exceed in total the maximum available to the plaintiff.[28]

The relationship between parties to the Warsaw Convention and parties to the Hague Protocol poses certain problems. Although at the time it was suggested that parties to the Hague Protocol should denounce the Warsaw Convention this was not provided for in the Protocol itself. The Protocol has taken effect and, although parties to both the Protocol and Convention could be said to have assumed inconsistent obligations, most States are bound by at least one agreement, and if a dispute arose the claimant could act under either in an action for damages.[29]

C. The Guadalajara Convention 1961[30]

The Warsaw Convention while providing for liability for damage by successive carriers (each compensating for the damage occurring during his part of the carriage) did not cover "sub-contracting" by the agreed carrier to a second carrier. As hire and charter of aircraft increased, the need to cover this type of operation became urgent and under pressure from the I.C.A.O. the above Convention was drafted and presented for signature.

The Guadalajara Convention by Article 1 defines "contracting" and "actual" carriers:

> "Contracting carrier" means a person who as a principal makes an agreement for carriage governed by the Warsaw Convention with a passenger or consignor or with a person acting on behalf of the passenger or consignor (Article 1 (b)).

---

[23] See Article 25, ante.
[24] See Hague Protocol (1955) Articles 10 and 11 respectively.
[25] Ibid., Article 13.
[26] Warsaw Convention, Article 25 (see ante).
[27] Pyman, "Australia and International Air Law" in O'Connell, *International Law in Australia* (1965), pp. 141, 172.
[28] Hague Protocol (1955), Article 14.
[29] Sassella, op. cit., p. 69.
[30] The provisions of the Guadalajara Convention (subject to Parts II and III of the Act referred to below) are included in the *Civil Aviation (Carriers' Liability) Act* 1959 (ss. 25A-25C) effective 1st May, 1964. Section 25A states:
"The provisions of the Guadalajara Convention have, subject to Parts II and III of this Act as affected by the next succeeding section, the force of law in Australia in relation to any carriage by air to which that Convention applies" (see post). For details of Conventions currently in force see Shawcross and Beaumont, pp. 38-49.

"Actual carrier" means a person other than a contracting carrier
who, by virtue of authority from the contracting carrier, performs
the whole or part of the carriage contemplated in [Article] 1 (b)
but who is not with respect to such part a successive carrier within
the meaning of the Warsaw Convention. Such authority is presumed
in the absence of proof to the contrary.[31]

Where the contracting carrier makes an agreement with a passenger or
consignor for carriage governed by the Warsaw Convention (with or without the Hague Protocol) which is performed by another carrier (the actual
carrier) in whole or part, both the contracting carrier and the actual
carrier are subject to the Warsaw Convention (and the Hague Protocol,
if applicable), the contracting carrier for the *whole* of the carriage the
actual carrier for the *part* he performs.[32]

The acts and omissions of one carrier are deemed to be those of the
other.[33] The plaintiff has an option whether to sue the contracting carrier,
or actual carrier who performed the relevant part of the carriage, or both,
either together or separately and either carrier, if sued alone can require
that the other be made a party to the proceedings.[34] However, an action
must be brought either in a court where the contracting carrier may be
sued in accordance with Article 28 of the Warsaw Convention or before
a court having jurisdiction at the place where the actual carrier is
ordinarily resident or has his principal place of business.[35] Before any
action for damage to baggage or goods is commenced the consignor is
required by the Warsaw Convention (Article 26) to make a complaint in
writing within the specified time limit and by the Guadalajara Convention
such complaints can be made either to the contracting carrier or actual
carrier.[36]

---

[31] A contract for international carriage may be, however, partly performed by an
actual carrier who is not a "successive carrier", or performed wholly by carriers
or a carrier other than the contracting carrier; e.g. where the contracting carrier
charters aircraft from another operator to perform all, of the flight. In such
instances opinion is divided as to whether the contracting carrier is "the
carrier" for the purposes of the Warsaw Convention, or in respect of such part
of the carriage as he performs. The better view would appear to be that "carrier"
refers to the contracting carrier, but English courts would be ready to hold that
an implied contract arises, in the absence of an express contract, between the
passenger (or, perhaps, consignor) and the actual carrier, and that the carriage
is performed on the terms of the original contract made with the contracting
Carrier. McNair, op. cit., p. 229. See also *Fosbroke Hobbes* v. *Airwork Ltd. and
British American Air Services Ltd* [1937] 1 All E.R. 108. In that case the pilot
of an aircraft handed an envelope to a passenger immediately before take-off.
This contained a variety of terms and conditions, and contemplated signature by
the passenger as well as eventual return to the company's officials. The plane
crashed causing the passenger's death before he had any opportunity of examining the contents of the envelope. It was held that the deceased was not bound by
the conditions and they had not been communicated to him before the journey
commenced. Thus it has been suggested if, as in *Fosbroke Hobbes*, the contract
of carriage is made between one passenger and the company, then there will be
no contractual nexus between guests of the passenger contracting as agent for
each and everyone of his guests: McNair, p. 155. See also, on the interpretation
of "carrier", Drion, op. cit., p. 133 et seq.
[32] Ibid., Article 2.
[33] Ibid., Article 3.
[34] Ibid., Article 7.
[35] Ibid., Article 8.
[36] Ibid., Article 4. Orders required under the Warsaw Convention to be given to the
"carrier" can be given to either the actual or contracting carrier but by Article 4

In certain circumstances the contracting carrier and the actual carrier are each vicariously liable for the acts and omissions of the servants and agents of the other.[37] Such liability can arise only when the servant or agent is acting within the scope of his employment and when the act or omission relates to the carriage performed by the actual carrier. Subject to these limitations, both the contracting carrier and the actual carrier incur liability, apart from the provision that each servant or agent can avail himself of the limits or liability applicable to his employer unless he acted in such a way so as to deprive himself of this right.[38] If the actual carrier is liable on the ground of vicarious liability solely his liability never exceeds the limits laid down in Article 22 of the Warsaw Convention.[39] But where the damage is caused by a servant or agent of the actual carrier and the circumstances are such that the limited liability provisions do not apply, both the liability of the actual carrier and contractual carrier is *unlimited*.[40]

The possibility of proceedings against one or more defendants is provided for in the Guadelajara Convention.[41]

If a servant or agent of *either* carrier is liable for the damage and is not entitled to limit his liability[42] because at the material time he was acting outside the scope of his employment, his unlimited liability does not increase the limit of liability under Article 7 as is regulated by the maximum liability or either the actual carrier or the contracting carrier.

D. The Rome Convention 1952[43]

The purpose of the Rome Convention was to ensure adequate compensation for persons who suffer damage caused on the surface by foreign air-

(*ibid.*) orders regarding the disposition of goods which the consignor is entitled to give by Article 12 of the Warsaw Convention until they arrive at their destination must always be given to the contracting carrier.

---

[37] Ibid., Article 3.
[38] Ibid., Article 5 and see below.
[39] See ante.
[40] Article 3(2) of the Guadalajara Convention. The Article further provides that any special agreement whereby the contracting carrier has assumed additional obligations or waived any of the carrier's rights under the Warsaw Convention does not affect the actual carrier unless he agrees to this assumption or waiver. Even if the responsibility lay with a servant or agent of the actual carrier, it appears that the actual carrier would incur no liability to the consignor, and the contracting carrier would be solely responsible to the consignor. McNair, op. cit., p. 232.
[41] Ibid., Article 6.
[42] Under Article 25 of the Warsaw Convention (as amended by the Hague Protocol) which provides that the aggregate of amounts recoverable from the carrier and his servants shall not, in such circumstances, exceed the limits laid down in Article 22 of the Warsaw Convention.
    Article 9 of Guadalajara Convention precludes attempts to relieve the liabilities of the contracting and actual carrier or avoid the application of the Convention but the actual carrier is given the right to exclude liability for loss or damage resulting from inherent defect, quality or vice of the cargo carried. Ibid., Article 9(2).
[43] There were only five initial ratifications and the U.K. and U.S. have never ratified the Rome Convention. See McNair, ibid., pp. 121, 356-357; Pyman, ibid., pp. 179-181; Sassella ibid., pp. 71-72. Australia ratified the Rome Convention and gave effect to its terms in the *Civil Aviation (Damage by Aircraft) Act 1958* (No. 81 of 1958); now see *Civil Aviation (Damage by Aircraft) Act 1958*, s. 7. See also Professor J. E. Richardson, *Aviation Law in Australia*,

craft, while limiting operators' liability. It also set out to unify the rules applying in different countries to liability for such damage.

The basis of the Convention is that of strict or absolute liability, the sole exceptions being where damage is the result of civil disturbance or armed conflict or contributory negligence on the part of the person suffering the damage.[44] The Convention also covers damage resulting from actual contact, explosion or fire, including damage caused by a person or thing falling from an aircraft and applies to damage directly resulting from flight which interferes with the use of land or causes damage (other than that occasioned by mere passage in compliance with current air traffic regulations) directly resulting from flight which interferes with the use of land or injures livestock by way of noise, vibration, slip-stream or air disturbance. Under the Convention the operator, that is the person making use of the aircraft at the time the damage was caused, is liable; in the case where control of the aircraft is retained by a person from whom the aircraft is chartered, that person is considered liable.[45]

Liability is limited; with regard to accidents the limit increases with the weight of the aircraft but the rate of increase becomes progressively lower with the increase in weight. In respect of death or personal injury of any one person there is a limit of 500,000 gold francs per person in addition to the overall limit. One half of this overall limit is set aside for claims for loss of life or injury; to the extent it is not absorbed it is available for property claims.[46]

Each state is left to decide whether it wishes to impose an obligation to insure in respect to surface damage on foreign aircraft entering its territory. If it does decide to do so then it is obliged to accept the insurance if certain specified conditions are met.[47]

---

pp. 277-279; *Federal Law Review* Vol. 1, 1964-65; L. P. Edwards, "Some Aspects of the Liabilities of Airline operators in Australia", A.L.J. Vol. 34, at pp. 147-149.

[44] Ibid., Article 6.
[45] Ibid., Article 2.
[46] Under Article 11 a limit is imposed on the liability of the operator for damages "for each aircraft and incident" according to the weight of the aircraft. This varies from 500,000 gold francs ($A1,500,000) for an aircraft weighing 1,000 kilogrammes or less to twenty-one times that amount for an aircraft weighing 50,000 kilogrammes. Maximum liability increases at the rate of 100 francs for every kilogramme over 50,000 kilogrammes. Weight is defined as the maximum weight of the aircraft authorized by the certificate of airworthiness for take-off (Article 11(2)). Liability in respect of loss of life or personal injury shall not exceed 500,000 francs per person killed or injured. Additionally, under Article 14, ibid., if the total amount of claims are exclusively in respect of loss of life or personal injury or damage to property such claims will be reduced in proportion to their respective amounts. If the claims are both in respect of loss of life or personal injury and damage to property, one half of the total sum distributable shall be appropriated preferentially to meet claims in respect of loss of life and personal injury and, if insufficient, shall be distributed proportionately between the claims concerned. The remainder of the total sum distributable shall be distributed proportionately among the claims in respect of damage to property and that portion not already covered of the claims in respect of loss of life and personal injury.
[47] Ibid., Part III. Articles 15-18 inclusive. The key conditions are (a) that the insurer is authorized to effect insurance under the law of the State where the aircraft is registered or the insurer has his principal place of business, and (b) that the final responsibility of the insurer has been certified by either of those States.

Actions under the Rome Convention can only be brought in a "single forum", i.e. the courts of the place where the damage occurred. Normally, as the party injured would be a national of the State where the damage occurred it would be more to his advantage to bring an action in that State's courts.[48]

II. THE MONTREAL DIPLOMATIC CONFERENCE[49]

The above conference sponsored by the I.C.A.O. added four new Protocols to international air transport law in September 1975.[50] The first three dealt with the problems raised by the monetary limits to carrier's liability in air conventions being expressed in gold francs (an increasingly obsolescent and uncertain unit of account). The fourth dealt with amendments to existing liability for carriage of cargo and baggage by air.

The Conference agreed to replace the gold franc by the Special Drawing Right (SDR) as defined by the International Monetary Fund. The SDR is a weighted unit of account reflecting a spread of 16 major world currencies. However, although altering the means of expressing the limits the Conference did not increase the monetary amounts. The new Warsaw limit of 8,300 SDR's is intended to be as faithful a translation as possible of 125,000 poincaré francs at the "old" official price for gold.[51]

With respect to the air carrier's liability for cargo the Montreal Conference made minor changes in the nature of that liability, as well as dealing with airmail carriage and documentation. The United States favoured a more direct level of liability being imposed on the carrier, a view opposed by the U.K., U.S.S.R. and Scandinavian countries. The compromise new rule states:

> (2) The carrier is liable for damage sustained in the event of the destruction or loss of, or damage to, cargo upon condition only that the occurrence which caused the damage so sustained took place during the carriage by air.

The effect of (b) is that the State overflown cannot claim the right to verify for itself whether the insurers of foreign aircraft are "financially responsible" but have to accept a certificate on this matter from another State. However, if a State overflown has reasonable grounds for doubting the insurer's financial responsibility, that State may request additional evidence of this and in the event of a dispute between States on this evidence the dispute can be referred to an arbitral tribunal, either the Council of the International Civil Aviation Organization or a person mutually agreed on by the parties (Article 15(7)(a).

---

48 Ibid., Article 20.
49 On this topic see "Four New Protocols to the Warsaw Convention", N. R. Gilchrist, *Lloyd's Maritime and Commercial Law Quarterly*, May 1976, p. 186 et seq. The Conference was attended by Australia.
50 They were:
  (a) Additional Protocol No. 1 amending the 1929 Warsaw Convention.
  (b) Additional Protocol No. 2 amending the 1929 Warsaw Convention as amend- by the 1955 Hague Protocol.
  (c) Additional Protocol No. 3 amending the Warsaw Convention 1929 as amended by the Hague Protocol 1955 and the Guatemala City Protocol, 1971.
  (d) Additional Protocol No. 4 amending the Warsaw Convention 1929 as amended by the Hague Protocol 1955.
51 Gilchrist, op. cit., p. 187.

(3) However, the carrier is not liable if he proves that the destruction, loss of, or damage to the cargo resulted solely from one or more of the following:

(a) inherent defect quality or vice of that cargo;
(b) defective packing of that cargo performed by a person other than the carrier or servants or agents;
(c) an act of war or an armed conflict;
(d) an act of public authority carried out in connexion with the entry, exit or transit of the cargo.[52]

With respect to documentation, I.A.T.A. had been long pressing for reduction of formal documentary requirements for cargo movements imposed by the Warsaw Convention and also for the making of the air way-bill an optional document to facilitate electronic data processing methods. The new rule in Article 3 of the Protocol provides as follows:

(1) In respect of the cargo of carriage an air way-bill shall be delivered.
(2) Any other means which would preserve a record of the carriage to be performed may, with the consent of the consignor, be substituted for the delivery of the air way-bill. If such other means are used, the carrier shall, if so requested by the consignor, deliver to the consignor a receipt for the cargo, permitting identification of the consignment and access to the information contained in the record preserved by such other means.
(3) The impossibility of using, at points of transit and destination, the other means which would preserve the record of carriage referred to in paragraph 2 of this Article does not entitle the carrier to refuse to accept the cargo for carriage.

Even if the consignor consents to the use of alternative means of preserving the record of carriage he can still demand a cargo receipt from the carrier.

Finally, Article 2(2) of the Warsaw Convention is replaced by a new provision (Article 2 of the Protocol) that prevents users of the postal system from claiming directly against the air carrier.[53]

Liability for passenger injury and death

The problem of compensation of victims of international air disasters has become one of extreme legal complexity and exemplified in the litigation and claims resultant on the Turkish Airlines DC 10 crash near Paris in March 1974.[54] Before this issue is dealt with however, it is salutary to

---

[52] As one writer has observed it is arguable that the new principles of liability hardly satisfy those who seek a regime of strict liability in order to reduce litigation; "At the very least, the most committed supporter of the amendments can hardly argue that they substantially alter the allocation of risk as between carrier and cargo owner. That being the case, those to benefit most from the new provisions may well prove to be the lawyers whose involvement the amendments were in fact designed by their supporters to reduce." Gilchrist, loc. cit.

[53] See *Moukataff* v. *B.O.A.C.* [1967] 1 Lloyd's Rep. 396. Neither the Warsaw Convention nor the Hague Protocol in that case was held to apply to air mail carriage so that the carrier could limit his liability.

[54] See, in particular, W. A. Rawley, "Whose Law is best for the D.C. 10 victims?" *The Times*, 11 March 1976. See also on the question compensation Heller, P.P. "Accident Compensation in New Zealand", *Air Law* 11 (2) 1977 62 where the *Accident Compensation Act* 1972 (NZ) has substantially changed the law in that country relating to the air carrier's liability to passengers; see also

look at one important Canadian case which dealt with the limitation of liability under Articles 3 and 4 of the Warsaw Convention.

1. *The Ludecke case*: In *Dame Rita Hildegarde Aranka Ludecke* v. *Canadian Pacific Airlines*[55] the plaintiff's husband was killed when a airliner of the defendant company crashed at Tokyo on 4 March 1966. The defendants admitted liability for the death of the plaintiff's husband (and for loss of baggage) but claimed limitation of liability under Articles 3 and 4 of the Warsaw Convention. (Schedule 1 of the *Carriage by Air Act* (Canada)). The Supreme Court of Canada held that the defendants were entitled to limit their liability with respect to the passenger claim but not with respect to the claim in connection with the loss of baggage. On appeal to the Canadian Court of Appeal it was there held that:

(i) with regard to the passenger claim the ticket on which the plaintiff's husband travelled contained the "statements" required by Article 3(2) in reasonably readable type; and that the content satisfied the requirements of the Convention and the claim therefore failed;

(ii) with regard to the baggage claim, the ticket covered both passenger and luggage and was sufficiently legible and comprehensible to satisfy Articles 3 and 4 and the defendants were entitled to the baggage limitation. Mr Justice Casey in dealing with the passenger claim argued that while Article 3(1) of the Convention called for the delivery of a ticket which must contain a statement that the carriage was subject to the rules relating to liability established by the Convention there was no sanction if the duty was not discharged.[56] The trial judge had further reasoned that the sanction of Article 3(2) applied only when the carrier "accepts a passenger without a passenger ticket having been delivered" and this sanction could not be involved if a ticket had been delivered (as in the present case) even though the ticket did not contain the statement of article 3(1)(e).[57] Mr Justice Casey observed: "This reasoning is not acceptable. The limitation contemplated by the Convention must be earned: the Carrier must deliver a ticket which satisfies the mandatory requirements of 3(1) which Article is in effect a definition. If the ticket delivered does satisfy these requirements it is not a ticket within the meaning of that article and the sanction of Article 3(2) will apply. However, the appellant has two other hurdles; she must establish either that the ticket does not contain 'a statement that the carriage is subject to the rules relating to liability established by this Convention' or that statement, if there is one, is not legible."[58]

Appellant's counsel had contended that it was not sufficient that the Court be able to read the document but that the ticket must satisfy the standards

Camarda, G. "Liability of carriers for damages of passengers on charter flights", *Air Law* 11 (2) 1977 96.

[55] [1975] 2 Lloyd's Rep. 87.
[56] Ibid., at 89.
[57] Article 3(1)(e) states (when read together):
"1. For the carriage of passengers the carrier must deliver a passenger ticket which shall contain the following particulars:
... (e) a statement that the carriage is subject to the rules relating to liability established by this Convention."
[58] Ibid., at 89.

of legibility which she submitted had been established by the courts of the countries in which the Convention applied.[59] Mr Justice Casey was not prepared to accept these decisions as a basis for judging ticket legibility:

> What I cannot concede is that we must accept the decisions cited by the appellant as establishing the standards by which the legibility of the "statement" must be judged. My view is that on this matter of fact the Convention should contain its own criteria. I see no reason why we should treat this case differently from the others that come before this Court. Proceeding from this premise and having examined the relevant documents I conclude that the carrier did print these statements in reasonable type.
>
> Nor do I regard the essential matter as being "hidden in a ticket" or "artfully camouflaged". The fact that it is there draws attention to its presence and the reason for its doing so is that it be read. That the passenger fails or is unable to read or to understand are matters beyond the control of the carrier.[60]

With respect to the content of the ticket it had been argued by the appellant that the ticket issued did not clearly and unequivocally state that the journey was subject to limitation of liability under Article 3(e). Further, to comply with the meaning of "notice" the carrier had to deliver to the passenger a ticket containing a readable and unqualified notice to the effect that the carriage was international and subject to the liability under the Convention, which was accordingly limited in respect of death or injury of each passenger. Mr Justice Casey was unable to share the views above and held that the content of the ticket satisfied the Convention and

---

[59] Decisions cited included the following terms: unnoticeable and unreadable; camouflaged in Lilliputian print in a thicket of conditions of contract; ineffectively positioned, diminutively sized; unemphasized by bold face type; contrasting colour; so artfully camouflaged that their presence is concealed.

[60] Ibid., at 89. Appellant's counsel in *Ludecke* relied upon *Lisi and Others* v. *Alitalia —Linee Aeree Italiane, S.P.A.* [1967] Lloyd's Rep. 140, where the notification of limitation of liability under the Warsaw Convention was virtually invisible due to the small type on the passenger tickets and baggage checks. By a majority, Lumbard Ct.J., Kaufman Ct.J. (Moore Ct.J., dissenting) confirmed the judgment of the District Court of the Southern District of New York in dismissing an appeal by Alitalia. Kaufman Ct.J. citing *Warren* v. *Flying Tiger Lines Inc.* (1965) 352 F (2d) 494 and *Mertens* v. *Flying Tiger Lines Inc.* (1965) 341 F (2d) 851 (2nd Cir.), argued that the question at issue was whether the ticket had been delivered to the passenger in such a manner as to afford him a reasonable opportunity to take self-protective measures; such an inquiry was necessary in order to give the Convention's Article meaning; ibid. at 143. Moore Ct.J., dissenting, was of the opinion that since his brother judges did not approve of the terms of the treaty they were rewriting it by judicial fiat. In the context of the two decisions cited above he stated "To support their argument they refer, quite illogically in my opinion, to cases in which the courts have held that there was no real delivery of a ticket to passengers as contemplated by the treaty. Cases based upon facts tantamount to no effective pre-flight delivery, are scarcely relevant to this case where the passengers had their tickets from three to 36 days before departure. Were actual notice to be the requirement, every airline would have to have its agents explain to every passenger the legal effect of the treaty" (at p. 144).

The *Ludecke* and *Lisi* decisions are clearly in conflict; if a doctrine of equality of bargaining power were of obvious application to this area of aviation law then the *Lisi* decision would be preferable to that of *Ludecke*. For a recent Australian case involving the question of notice of terms contained in an air ticket see *Miller Airline Services* v. *Commissioner of State Taxation of the State of Western Australia* (1975) A.L.J.R. 348.

on that basis together with his views already given, dismissed the appeal.[61]

2. *The DC 10 Paris aircrash*: In March 1974, a Turkish Airlines operated DC 10 crashed north of Paris.[61a] The ensuing legal claims raised and continue to raise important questions concerning the lex fori.[62] The insurance

[61] On the incidental appeal relating to the baggage claim Mr Justice Casey observed " . . . we are dealing with one ticket which covered both the passenger and luggage and was sufficiently legible and comprehensible to satisfy Articles 3 and 4."

Ludecke was followed in *Canadian Pacific Airlines Ltd.* v. *Montreal Trust and Others* [1975] Lloyd's Rep. 90; a suit arising from the Tokyo aircrash of 4 March 1966. For comment on special contractual terms and, in particular the English law relating to tickets, see Shawcross and Beaumont, pp. 478-482. For I.A.T.A. conditions of carriage, see below. See also *Preston Hunting Air Transport* [1956] 1 All E.R. 443; *M'Kay* v. *Scottish Airways* 1948 S. C. 254.

[61a] The question of selection of the forum and rights of the passengers against the airlines and manufacturers are dealt with by S. J. Levy, "The rights of the International Airlines Passenger," in *Air Law* Vol. 1 No. 5 1976, p. 275 et seq., where the Turkish Airlines DC-10 crash is used as an instance of the complexity of the issues that can arise. France, Great Britain and Japan were parties to both the Warsaw Convention and the Hague Protocol with $10,000 and $20,000 U.S. limitations respectively; the United States was a party to the Warsaw Convention but had refused to ratify the Hague Protocol and Turkey was a party to neither treaty. While most airlines had signed the 1966 Montreal Agreement which raised the damage limitation to $75,000 U.S. Turkish Airlines had not. Some of the passengers on the Turkish Airlines DC-10 had Turkish Airlines tickets and others had Montreal or BEA tickets although they were on a non-Montreal carrier. BEA, although not a Montreal signatory had agreed, as a matter of policy, to raise its liability to $75,000 U.S. on all flights. Under existing treaties a passenger with an Istanbul—Paris—London ticket would not be involved in international transportation as the point of departure was a non-signatory country, Turkey; thus neither the Warsaw Convention nor the Hague Protocol apply and common law rules of negligence apply without any limitation of damages. The rights of passenger with a New York—Istanbul—London ticket would be determined by the Warsaw Convention as their flight began and ended in a Warsaw country (the United States) and damages would be limited to $10,000 U.S. unless wilful misconduct could be proved. If, as would be the likely case, the passenger were flying on a Montreal ticket, they would be entitled to the $75,000 U.S. Montreal limit. A passenger with a London—Istanbul—Paris—London ticket would have his rights governed by the Hague Protocol and damages would be limited to $20,000 U.S. as the flight began and ended in a Hague country (England). A passenger, additionally, would be entitled to $75,000 U.S. if flying on a BEA ticket. See also *Day* v. *Trans World Airlines* 528 F. (2d) 31 (2nd) Cir. 1975), *Reed* v. *Wiser* (S.D.N.Y. April 19 1976) and, on class actions see *Causey* v. *Pan American World Airways Inc.* 66 F.R.D. 329 (E.D.Va. 1975).

It should be noted that in 1975 and 1976 the scheduled air carriers of most West European countries and Japan, under Art. 22(1) of the Warsaw Convention undertook to raise the limit of their liability for death or injury suffered by a passenger to U.S. $58,000 (or equivalent in national currency) where accidents occur on board an aircraft in the service of the carriers concerned or in the course of embarkation on, or disembarkation from an aircraft in such service. The limit agreed equals that specified in the 1966 Montreal Agreement (exclusive of legal fees and costs) in respect of international transportation including a point in the United States as point of origin, point of destination or agreed stopping place. Most carriers did not waive defences under Art. 20(1) of the Warsaw Convention as to transportation not covered by the Montreal Agreement, although those from Great Britain did. Scheduled air carriers from the following countries are involved: Austria, Belgium, France, Great Britain, Greece, Ireland, Japan, Holland, Scandinavian countries, Switzerland, Western Germany. Several non-scheduled air carriers followed and raised the limit of their liability accordingly.

[62] See the *Fatal Accidents Act* 1846 (as amended by the *Law Reform* (*Limitation of Actions*) *Act* 1954 and *The Law Reform* (*Miscellaneous Provisions*) *Act* 1934); for corresponding Australian legislation see relevant State Acts.

interests, with whom McDonnell Douglas, the plane's manufacturers, had insured the DC 10 under product liability and Turkish Airlines under carrier's liability, wished to settle quickly to minimise the effect of inflation upon claims. A few of the 200 United Kingdom plaintiffs agreed to take non-dependency awards[63] but there was no settlement with the remainder. The reluctance to settle was partly due to the fact that plaintiffs' lawyers from the United States or their agents were contacting claimants' lawyers in other countries inviting them to go to California in the hope that, although the 346 victims of the crash were mainly non-American, California would accept them on the basis that McDonnell Douglas was domiciled there and in expectation of higher compensation. This development has to be seen in the context of the contingent legal fee system which operates in America but is contrary to laws of other common law countries such as England, New Zealand and Australia on grounds that it constitutes champerty, or its equivalent.

In July 1975, the defendants [64] in the DC 10 case reached a joint agreement whereby they would all contribute towards the damages to be awarded, on the basis of an undisclosed proportional contribution. By admitting liability it was hoped to proceed to have the damages agreed or settled by the courts. Turkish Airlines were prepared to join in the agreement partly as a result of the fact that they were not a party to the Warsaw Convention and the Hague Protocol which limits total compensation payable by a carrier in the event of an air crash.[65]

The key development was the decision of the Court of the Southern District of California; Judge Pierson Hall ruled that Californian law should be applied in the assessment of damages for British and other foreign nationals involved in the DC 10 crash. Californian law does not provide for an interim appeal against a ruling of this kind but there can be an appeal against a specific judgment. Such a judgment was given this year in the *Kween* case by the Los Angeles District Court. In that case damages of approximately $1.5m U.S. were awarded to two sisters living in Washington, Oregon, whose father was English and whose mother was American. This decision clearly affects the status of claims of other British and foreign plaintiffs since the damages awarded in the *Kween* case were based on Californian law and living standards. One source has even stated that some Japanese plaintiffs were claiming damages in California in accordance with Japanese law, which damages could be potentially higher than those awarded under the *Kween* decision.[66]

---

[63] See 61a.

[64] See now the Montreal Agreement, ante.

[65] *The Times,* n. 54 (supra). The defendants' lawyers are currently discussing an appeal in the *Kween* case which, if lodged, would go to the Ninth Circuit, below the United States Supreme Court. Another unresolved aspect of this issue is that some plaintiffs are claiming punitive damages as well as compensatory damages against the defendants. Californian law does not recognize punitive damages, and to proceed with these claims would require a trial of liability. See Drion, op. cit., in particular Chapter 8 and p. 334 et seq.

[66] See generally Buergenthal, *Law-Making in the International Civil Aviation Organization* 1969. McNair, op. cit., pp. 413-420; Sassella, op. cit.; Pyman, op. cit., pp. 161-183.

III. The International Civil Aviation Organisation: I.C.A.O.[67]

The I.C.A.O., set up under the Chicago Convention 1944,[68] and arising out of the International Civil Aviation Conference held in that city, began functioning in 1947. It followed earlier attempts at international organisation and since its inception has been instrumental in sponsoring multilateral conventions, some of which have already been considered, and other treaties which represent a major contribution to international law in general and the law of international air carriage in particular.[69] As a detailed description of the I.C.A.O. and its functions are beyond the bounds of this study[70] it is proposed to firstly deal with the Chicago Convention with special reference to the International Air Services Transit and the International Air Transport Agreements then, secondly, to consider the important distinction between scheduled and non-scheduled air services and the guidance the I.C.A.O. has given in interpreting these terms.[71]

[67] Convention on International Civil Aviation (1944) ratified in Australia by the *Air Navigation Act* 1947 (No. 6 of 1947).

[68] For details of its functions and contributions see above and especially Sassella, op. cit., p. 6.

[69] Sassella, op. cit., pp. 77-79 and see Chicago Convention, Articles 6 and 7, post. The functions and activities of the I.C.A.O. derive from the objectives of the organization as listed in Article 44 of the Chicago Convention:

> The aims and objectives of the Organization are to develop the principles and techniques of international air navigation and to foster the planning and development of international air transport so as to:
> (a) Ensure the safe and orderly growth of international civil aviation throughout the world;
> (b) Encourage the arts of aircraft design and operation for peaceful purposes;
> (c) Encourage the development of airways, airports, air navigational facilities for international civil aviation;
> (d) Meet the needs of the peoples of the world for safe, regular, efficient and economical air transport;
> (e) Prevent economic waste caused by unreasonable competition;
> (f) Ensure that the rights of contracting States are fully respected and that every contracting State has a fair opportunity to operate international airlines;
> (g) Avoid discrimination between contracting States;
> (h) Promote safety of flight in international air navigation;
> (i) Promote generally the development of all aspects of international civil aeronautics.

[70] Australia's attitude at the Chicago Convention is chronicled in Pyman, op. cit., pp. 143-144; Sassella, op. cit., p. 51. Briefly, the U.S.A. favoured an international body with executive functions in the technical field of civil aviation and advisory functions in the economic field; the U.K. wanted the I.C.A.O. (when formed) to be empowered to fix rates, frequencies and rates of flights, the Canadian proposal being essentially similar; Australia and New Zealand wanted international ownership and operation of all international air services. This proposal gained little support and was rejected in early discussions. Ultimately a joint U.S.-U.K.-Canadian plan was agreed and the proposals of other states were incorporated into it which then became the basis for the Chicago Convention. See *Current Notes on International Affairs* Vol. 5 No. 1 (Jan. 1944), pp. 4-5; Pyman, op. cit., 143.

[71] Like the International Air Services Agreement 1944, the International Air Transport Agreement was an Appendix to the Final Act of the Chicago Conference (Cmd. 6614); the other Appendices were the Interim Agreement on International Civil Aviation, the Convention on International Civil Aviation (The Chicago Convention) and Drafts of the Technical Annexes.
The First Freedom (i) raises discussion on the common law position relating to use by aircraft of airspace.
See McNair, op. cit., Chapter 3; also see *Kelsen* v. *Imperial Tobacco Co.* [1957] 2 Q.B. 334; *Pickering* v. *Rudd* (1815) 4 Camp. 219, at 220; contra *Wandsworth*

The International Air Transport Agreement (1944)[72] attempted to provide for a mutual exchange of freedoms of flight between the parties to the Agreement, to cover scheduled services. The 1944 Agreement (also known as the "Five Freedoms Agreement") sought the exchange of five reciprocal freedoms:

(i)   the privilege to fly over the territory of other parties without landing;

(ii)   the privilege to land for non-traffic purposes;

(iii) the privilege to put down passengers, mail and cargo on the territory of the State whose nationality the aircraft possesses;

(iv) the privilege to take on passengers, mail and cargo destined for the territory of the State whose nationality the aircraft possesses;

(v)   the privilege to take on passengers, mail and cargo destined for the territory of any other party and the privilege to put down passengers, mail and cargo coming from any such territory.

Few states ratified this agreement and it has little practical significance.[73]

The less ambitious International Air Services Transit Agreement (1944) which provides for a similar exchange of the First and Second Freedoms listed above in relation to scheduled services has had much greater acceptance than the Agreement just noted. Despite this limitation to transit without landing and landing for non-traffic purposes such a multilateral arrangement has wrought an advance in substantive air law.[74]

The right of aircraft to fly across the territory of another State in transit and non stop, and to make stops for non-traffic purposes while not on scheduled operations, that is a "non-scheduled" flight, is provided

---

Board of Works v. *United Telephone Co.* (1884) 13 Q.B.D. 904; *Kelsen and the* latter two authorities would support the view that at common law an act performed in the airspace above another's land constitutes trespass to land; see also the Tasmanian case of *Davies* v. *Bennison* (1927) 22 Tas. L.R. 52. As the learned authors of McNair (op. cit., p. 47) point out, the maxim *cujus est solum, ejus est usque ad coelum et ad inferos* in itself has no authority in English law; see also Richardson, op. cit. on this maxim, p. 243 and H. D. Klein, "Cujus Est solum Ejus Est . . . Quo usque Tandem?" (1959) 26 *Journal of Air Law and Commerce* 237. See *Bernstein* v. *Skyviews and General, Ltd.* (1977) *The Times* 11 February and see also note in *J.B.L.* April 1977 at pp. 146-148. As there is no common law applicable directly to aircraft, statute has been enacted to deal with the matter; see the *Civil Aviation Act* 1949 (U.K.) s. 40(1) and *The Wrongs Act* 1958 (Victoria) s. 30 and s. 31, of similar effect to the U.K., legislation; s. 30 reads: "No action for trespass shall lie in respect of trespass or nuisance by reason only of the flight of an aircraft over any property at a height above the ground which having regard to the wind, the weather and all the circumstances is reasonable, or the ordinary incidents of such flights, so long as the provisions of the Air Navigation Regulations are duly complied with." See also, *Damage by Aircraft Act* 1964 (W.A.) s. 4; *Damage by Aircraft Act* 1963 (Tas.) s. 3.

---

[72] As at 1 January 1969, twelve states had satisfied the Agreement; Shawcross and Beaumont, op. cit., Appendix A. 12-7. There were 74 ratifications to the Agreement on 1st January, 1969; Shawcross & Beaumont, ante.

[73] Pyman, op. cit., p. 146 and see note, ibid. Since the 1944 Chicago Conference the I.C.A.O. has failed to successfully sponsor a multilateral Convention for the exchange of the five freedoms. Instead States have regulated their scheduled services on the basis of bilateral agreements. For comment on the pattern of bilateral agreements similar to those negotiated by Australia see Pyman, pp. 147-156.

[74] Ibid., Article 5.

under the Chicago Convention.[75] All members of the I.C.A.O. have granted this right to each other. However, each contracting State has a right, for safety reasons, to require aircraft exercising this privilege to follow prescribed routes or obtain special permission when the region over which it is desired to fly is inaccessible or without adequate air navigation facilities. It is provided that where such non-scheduled aircraft wish to exercise the right to embark passengers, cargo or mail in another State, the latter State can impose such regulations, conditions or limitations as it may consider desirable.[76] The Convention further provided that no scheduled international air service may be operated over or into the territory of a contracting State, except with its special permission or other authorization, and in accordance with such terms.[77]

While "international air service" is defined as "an air service which passes over a territory of more than one State" and an "air service defined as "any scheduled air service performed by an aircraft for the public transport of passengers, mail or cargo"[78] the term "scheduled" remains undefined by the Convention. Such a clarification is essential as Article 5 parties have mutually granted one another ostensibly far reaching rights in respect of non-scheduled flights. The I.C.A.O. itself in 1952 provided a definition[78] of an international air service together with "notes" on the application of the definition. The definition is as follows:

A scheduled international air service is a service of flights that possesses all the following characteristics:

(a) It passes through the airspace above the territory of more than one State;

(b) it is performed by aircraft for the transport of passengers, mail or cargo for remuneration in such a manner that each flight is open to use by members of the public;

(c) it is operated so as to serve traffic between the same two or more points, either

(i) according to a published timetable, or

(ii) with flights so regular or frequent that they constitute a recognisable systematic series.

[75] Under the *Air Navigation Act* (C'mwth) 1920, s. 14(4), the Director-General of Civil Aviation, in considering an application for approval in the case of commercial non-scheduled flight of an aircraft possessing the nationality of a contracting State of the Chicago Convention, shall have regard to the public interest, the need to provide reasonable protection for regular international airline operators serving Australia and any resolutions or decisions of I.C.A.O., or I.A.T.A., approved by the Minister for Civil Aviation and relevant to the substance of the application under consideration. In the case of non-scheduled flights over or into Australia by a foreign aircraft that does not possess the nationality of a contracting State of the Chicago Convention whether or not a commercial flight needs the approval of the Minister who may impose such conditions and requirements as he considers necessary to ensure compliance with the general principles contained in the Chicago Convention, s. 15. See also Article 7 which gives each State the right to refuse permission to aircraft of their States to take on in its territory passengers, mail and cargo destined for another point within its territory. This is the right to reserve cabotage. See Wassenbergh, *Post War International Civil Aviation Policy and the Law of the Air*, p. 69 et seq.
[76] See Article 6; this sector of air transportation regulation has been determined by bi-lateral negotiation and treaty. See Pyman, p. 183, Annex A.
[77] Article 96.
[78] I.C.A.O. Document 7278C/841 (1952), 3-6.

The "notes" state that all the elements of (a) to (c) of the above definition must be present before a service is a scheduled service; the meanings of a "series" of flights, a "transport" service, "remuneration", flights being "open to use by members of the public", and a "systematic" series are clarified.

As the I.C.A.O. definition is close to a similar section in the *Air Corporations Act* (U.K.) the construction placed upon this section by the English courts is relevant to the definition of a scheduled air service.[79]

In *D.P.P.* v. *Ackroyd's Air Travel Ltd.*,[80] the defendants were convicted of aiding and abetting a breach of s. 24(2) of the *Air Corporations Act*. The agency had arranged with a South African airline operating a regular air service between Paris and South Africa to charter aircraft on various occasions from different operators to carry passengers from London to Paris who had made reservations on the Paris to South Africa Service. Tickets for the London-Paris flight were issued by the charter company at no charge. The defendant agency paid the charter company and reimbursed themselves by charging the South African airline which included a small profit margin. In *D.P.P.* v. *Millbank Tours Ltd.*[81] the magistrates dismissed a number of summonses against a travel agency under s. 24(2). The agency had been charged with a breach of the Act as, not being an air corporation or associate under the statute, Millbank had carried passengers for reward on a scheduled flight between London-Palma and Majorca and other flights of a similar nature between London-Nice and London-Perpignan. Hunting Clan Air Services Ltd., an independent airline, had applied to the Ministry of Transport and Civil Aviation on behalf of Millbank for permission to run tours, which was refused. Millbank then wrote their clients informing them of the refusal and suggesting that if they joined the "International English Language Association" they could take an identical holiday, it being explained that Millbank were official travel agents for the I.E.L.A. The prosecution claimed that the letter was an outward symbol of what was nothing more than a device to avoid the restrictions under s. 24(2) of the Act while the defence pleaded that the I.L.E.A. was bona fide and that Hunting Clan Ltd. had performed the actual carriage of passengers. The magistrates in the case agreed that the passengers were bona fide members of the I.L.E.A. and that Hunting Clan Ltd. were entitled to carry them.

---

[79] Section 24(2) of the *Air Corporations Act* 1949; although the Act itself was partly repealed by the Air Navigation Order 1960, s. 24(2) was not. Section 24(2) of the *Air Corporations Act* reads: "In this Act the expression 'scheduled journey' means one of a series of journeys which are undertaken between the same two places and which together amount to a systematic service operated in such a manner that the benefits thereof are available to members of the public from time to time seeking to take advantage of it."

[80] [1950] 1 All E.R. 933. Cheng, op. cit., p. 179 remarks that if the I.C.A.O. definition is applied to *Ackroyd's* case it is doubtful whether the flights organized by the agency could be regarded as scheduled international air services as definition (b) was lacking.

[81] (1959) *The Times*, 10 April, decision of Feltham (London) magistrates; Cheng, op. cit., p. 181-182, appeal dismissed [1960] 1 W.L.R. 630 (see also *D.P.P.* v. *Fairway (Jersey) Ltd.* reported in the *Times*, 1 May and 4 June 1956; Cheng, op. cit., p. 180).

IV. The International Air Transport Association (I.A.T.A.)

The International Air Transport Association succeeded the earlier body known as the International Air Traffic Association in 1945. In 1949 I.A.T.A. adopted a series of "Conditions of Contract" which have since been replaced.[82] These Conditions are compulsory for "interline carriage", that is, where members are operating services in which more than one carrier is to take part and these conditions must appear on the passenger ticket or consignment note; these documents refer expressly to the Conditions of Carriage of the carrier in question. I.A.T.A. has also drafted a standard form of General Conditions of Carriage but unlike the Conditions of Contract have not been made compulsory for, or finally accepted by, carriers who are I.A.T.A. members. However, many statutory air corporations in common with other carriers, have adopted a series of Conditions of Carriage based upon them. The net result is that conditions of air carriage undertaken by the main airline companies, irrespective of whether such carriage is national or international, are based on the Warsaw Convention as amended by the Hague Protocol and one set of contracts governs many carriages without distinction of place or territory.[83]

As indicated above the freight forwarder has come under the control of I.A.T.A. and member airlines have agreed upon uniform conditions governing freight forwarders wishing to forward and consolidate shipments on their behalf in return for commission paid by the airline concerned. A forwarder who is not an I.A.T.A. sales agent cannot claim commission for the business obtained and will be treated as any other consignor. However, such a forwarder will benefit from bulk rates and to some extent forwarders have continued to function as non-I.A.T.A. consolidators, their profits arising from the difference between the rates charged to their customers and those paid to the carrier, as in the case of domestic freight forwarding in the United States, Australia and other countries.

In the situation where a freight forwarder is an I.A.T.A. approved cargo sales agent, his relationship with the air carrier is governed by the relevant I.A.T.A. resolutions. These put him in the position of an agent for the carrier, his principal, and lay down defined duties.[84] The position of the I.A.T.A. freight forwarded was stated as follows in *Perishables Transport Co. Ltd.* v. *N. Spyropoulos Ltd.*:[85]

> It is quite plain that air agents are in the same position as shipping agents: if they arrange for the shipment or air passage, even though they disclose that they are doing so for a principal; even for a named principal, they incur a personal liability to the shipping company or the air company for the freight. This has been so for many years in shipping, it has been so for quite a long time so far as air

---

[82] See *General Conditions of Carriage (Passenger)*, I.A.T.A., issued 1 September 1974. The main office of the organization is in Montreal. For comment on I.A.T.A. conditions of carriage see Shawcross & Beaumont, op. cit., pp. 482-495.
[83] McNair, op cit., p. 164.
For details of Standard Conditions (1970) Governing F.I.A.T.A. Combined Transport Bills of Lading see Hill, *Freight Forwarders* 1972, Appendices, pp. 362-366.
[84] Ibid.
[85] [1964] 2 Lloyd's Rep. 379, per Salmond L.J. 382.

transport is concerned. The Cargo Sales Agency Rules of the International Air Transport Association . . . apply to all countries in Europe and many parts of the world. I have no doubt that they incorporate the usual practice of the trade among airlines, agents and the merchants in various parts of the world who make use of these transport facilities.

The forwarder may also act as agent for the shipper and thus in many cases be an agent for both carrier and shipper.

There are no circumstances where the forwarder will carry out the function of an air carrier himself, while operating under I.A.T.A. Resolutions.[86]

V. Australian Domestic Legislation
relating to Carriage by Air[87]

In 1945 the Labour post war government secured the passing of the *Australian National Airlines Act*[88] setting up an Australian National Airlines Commission empowered to establish airline services between any place in another State, "between any place in any Territory of the Commonwealth and any other place in that Territory." The Act also gave power to the Commission to acquire property, aircraft and equipment either by purchase or by compulsory acquisition. The Act also attempted to make inoperative the licence of an established operator on any interstate or Territorial route once the Commission had established an adequate service to meet the needs of the public either itself or through a contractor. The Act prohibited the Director-General of Civil Aviation from issuing any new licences on interstate and Territorial routes served by the Commission unless he was satisfied the licence was necessary to meet the needs of the public. The Commission might issue a licence to a private operator if the Commission failed to maintain a service on the above-mentoned routes. The use of the phrase "adequate airline service" indicates that the draftsmen of the Act were conscious of s. 92 of the Constitution in that it might be construed to be an interference with the freedom of interstate trade if private airlines were abolished by the Commonwealth before its own services were set up and operating adequately. By the same token if the abolition of private airlines did not diminish the volume of trade between the States then s. 92 would not be infringed.[89]

In *James* v. *The Commonwealth*[90] the Judicial Committee of the Privy

---

[86] Under rule 810b(K) of the Cargo Sales Agency Rules of I.A.T.A. there are special provisions for appointment of non-I.A.T.A. air carriers as cargo sales agents; see Sundberg, *Air Charter* 1962 for a discussion of the problem raised in the United States due to the attempts of the Civil Aeronautics Board to give the forwarder the status of an indirect carrier. The problem of deciding whether an air carrier is acting as a mere forwarder or as a carrier himself no longer arises as this has been settled by the Guadalajara Convention, see above.

[87] See generally Pyman, Richardson, Edwards, *op. cit.*

[88] No. 31 of 1945.

[89] S. 92 reads: "On the imposition of uniform duties of customs, trade, commerce, and intercourse among the States, whether by means of internal carriage or ocean navigation, shall be absolutely free."

[90] (1936) 55 C.L.R. 1.

Council[91] had decided that although the Commonwealth had power to legislate with respect to trade and commerce among the States under s. 51(1) of the Constitution, this power could only be used subject to the restriction of s. 92. The phrase trade and commerce including the business of carrying goods and passengers for reward meant that although the Commonwealth could regulate interstate transport it could not restrict or prohibit it.

In the challenge by Australian National Airlines in the High Court in *Australian National Airways Pty. Ltd.* v. *The Commonwealth*[92] counsel for ANA, Garfield Barwick, K.C. (as he then was), argued that freedom of trade between the States referred not only to a free flow of goods and services but also to freedom of individual traders to participate in interstate trade. To eliminate a private airline therefore from interstate operations was un-constitutional as it interfered with his freedom of interstate trade. It was also argued inter alia that the whole Act was ultra vires s. 51(1) of the Constitution as the latter is a power to regulate and not engage in trade. The Act if invalid in part was also invalid in toto as its parts were inseparable. The *Air Navigation Regulations* 1940, s. 79(3) were attacked as going beyond the constitutional power as they purported to give the Director-General of Civil Aviation a discretionary power to withold a licence and this discretion could be used to prohibit interstate trade and thus contravene s. 92.

Counsel for the Commonwealth argued that in refusing or issuing a licence the Director-General could have regard to (safety matters apart) whether unlimited competition between airlines is in the public interest. In refusing a licence this would be an exercise of a power consistent with s. 92 as interpreted in *James* v. *Commonwealth* as the power was one of refusing licences for the purpose of controlling, regulating, promoting and facilitating air navigation.

It was also contended inter alia that s. 51(1) of the constitution authorized the Commonwealth not only to regulate and control but also to engage in interstate trade and commerce. Finally, it was put that the invalid parts were severable from the Act without impairment as it had been so designed if the need arose.

The High Court ruled that parts of the Act attempting to establish a monopoly for the publicly-owned airline were unconstitutional. "The exclusion of competition with the Commonwealth is not a system of regulation and is, in my opinion, a violation of s. 92."[93] Williams, J., explicitly stated that freedom of trade between the States included freedom for individuals to engage in that trade, citing with approval Isaacs, J., in *James* v. *Cowan*[94] where he said, "The right of inter-state trade and commerce protected by s. 92 from State interference and regulation is a *personal right attaching to the individual and not attaching to the goods* . . . The right of passing from one State to another, of transporting goods

---

[91] This empowers Commonwealth Parliament, subject to the Constitution to make laws for the 'peace, order and good government of the Commonwealth' with respect to (i) trade and commerce with other countries and among the States.
[92] (1945) 71 C.L.R. 39.
[93] Per Sir John Latham. C.J., 71 C.L.R. 1 at p. 52.
[94] (1930) 43 C.L.R. 386 at 418, cited by Williams, J., at p. 107.

from one to another and dealing with them in the second State cannot be conferred by either State solely. And so s. 92 must be understood. The right is not an adjunct of the goods: it is the possession of the individual Australian, protected from State interference by s. 92."[95]

The Court held that the unconstitutional parts of the Act purporting to set up a government-owned monopoly were severable from the rest, and so the remaining part of the Act was valid. The Commonwealth was empowered under s. 51(1) to establish an interstate trading corporation such as the Australian National Airlines Commission. Under s. 122 it was also held valid for the Commonwealth to operate a government-owned monopoly of airlines in the Territories. However, Reg. 79(3) of the *Air Navigation Regulations* was struck down as, in the Court's view, such a power could lead to a breach of s. 92 as the Director-General might use his unlimited powers to eradicate private airlines. Thus the case determined that, under the Constitution, the Commonwealth could set up an airline, but could not grant itself a monopoly of interstate air services.

The legal right of the Commonwealth to exercise general control over civil air carriage was firmly established in *Airline of New South Wales Pty. Ltd.* v. *New South Wales*.[96] In 1963, Airlines of New South Wales Pty. Ltd. (a subsidiary of Ansett Transport Industries Ltd.) challenged the validity of the *State Transport (Co-ordination) Act* 1931 (N.S.W.) in relation to the provisions governing State licensing of aircraft engaging in intrastate air flights.[97] The New South Wales Commissioner for Transport had decided to cancel licences held by the plaintiff company for particular

---

[95] *James* v. *The Commonwealth* (1936) 55 C.L.R. 1 at p. 33.
[96] (1964) 37 A.L.J.R. 399; [1964] Argus L.R. 876. The first Commonwealth aviation statute, the *Air Navigation Act* 1920, empowered the Governor-General to make regulations to give effect to the Paris Convention of 1919 and further, to make regulations providing for the control of air navigation throughout the Commonwealth and Territories. The Act was passed on the assumption that the Commonwealth Parliament possessed three main sources of primary power; (a) interstate and overseas trade and commerce power under s. 51(1) of the Constitution, (b) the external affairs power in s. 51 (xxix) and (c) the power to make laws for the Territories under s. 122.
   In *R.* v. *Burgess; ex p. Henry* (1936) 55 C.L.R. 605 the High Court held that (i) the Commonwealth could not exercise control over civil aviation in the Commonwealth, including intrastate legislation and (ii) in respect of the *Air Navigation Act* empowering the Governor-General to make regulations for the carrying out of the Paris Convention, it was a valid exercise of the external affairs power. Subsequent to this case the Commonwealth withdrew from attempted regulation of intrastate air navigation and the new *Air Navigation Act* as redrafted was upheld in *R.* v. *Poole; ex p. Henry* (No. 2) (1938) 61 C.L.R. 634. An attempt by the Commonwealth in 1937 to add "air navigation and aircraft" to the powers in s. 51 of the Constitution was defeated in a referendum under s. 128 of the Constitution. See *'The Airlines' Case'*, P. H. Lane 39 A.L.J. p. 17 et seq.
[97] Under State Air Navigation Acts the Regulations provide for Federal licensing of intrastate commercial services; most States, however, in addition to Federal licences required State issued licences to conduct intrastate air operations; *Air Transport Act* 1964 (N.S.W.); *State Transport Act* 1960 (Queensland); *State Transport Co-ordination Act* 1933 (W.A.); *Traffic Act* 1925 (Tas.); *Traffic Act* 1961 (Tas.); *Transport Act* 1938 (Tas.) as amended. No State administered licensing system exists in South Australia.
   See also, (below) *R.* v. *Public Vehicles Licensing Appeal Tribunal of Tasmania, ex p. Australian National Airways Pty. Ltd.* (1964) 37 A.L.J.R. 503; [1964] A.L.R. 918.

intrastate services and reallocate these to a rival company, East-West Airlines; in return the plaintiff company were granted some of the unprofitable routes operated by East-West Airlines. Airlines of New South Wales Ltd. claimed that the *Commonwealth Air Navigation Act* and *Regulations,* including the Federal licensing of air transport services, covered all air navigation within the Commonwealth and the additional licensing system set up by New South Wales was inconsistent with Commonwealth law and thus invalid under s. 109 of the Constitution.[98]

The High Court held that the provisions of the State Act were not inconsistent with the Federal law and that Airlines of New South Wales Pty. Ltd. were not entitled to use aircraft within New South Wales without a licence under the State Act.[99] The decision contained important dicta suggesting that Commonwealth power to control air navigation extended into the area of intrastate commerce. The most forceful view in this respect was that of Windeyer J.:

> As to the constitutional power: In my opinion the powers with respect to trade and commerce with other countries and among the States (s.51(1)), external affairs (s.51(xxix)), and incidental matters as described in s.51(xxxix), are ample to give the Commonwealth Parliament complete power over all air navigation in Australia.
>
> . . . I see no reasons for confining the interests and concern of the Commonwealth with air navigation to areas of the superincumbent air that have been declared to be controlled air space. As I see it, Commonwealth power extends to the control of the movement of all aircraft in all air space above Australia and its territories. It extends too, I consider, to all such incidental matters as the control of airports and airfields, the take-off and landing of aircraft, and the prescribing and policing of safety precautions. I do not overlook, indeed, I respectfully adopt, the observation of Dixon J., as he then was, in *R. v. Burgess*; *ex P. Henry* (1936) 55 C.L.R. 608, at p. 674, that "under colour of carrying out an external obligation the Commonwealth cannot undertake the general regulation of the subject matter to which it relates". But in carrying out an obligation, measures that at one time might have been unnecessary may, with changing circumstances, become necessary. It is not that the nature of the power changes. What changes are the conditions and circumstances within which the power is exercisable, and in consequence the particular aspects of the subject-matter that can be regulated. The great development in recent times of air traffic of all kinds in Australia, including overseas and interstate air traffic, has created a situation today that is very different from that of thirty years ago. The proper regulation in the interests of safety of the

---

[98] Section 109 reads: "When a Law of a State is inconsistent with a law of the Commonwealth, the latter shall prevail, and the former shall, to the extent of the inconsistency, be valid."

[99] Dixon C.J. stated there was no reason why State legislation should not operate in respect of allocation of air routes consistently with Commonwealth law, whereas Taylor J. viewed the Commonwealth Regulations restricted to the safety of air traffic and did not deal with co-ordination of intrastate transport, a matter dealt with under the State Act. Menzies J. thought that the Federal Regulations were not intended to be exclusive and exhaustive and did not purport to extend to intrastate air navigation except within controlled airspace; ibid., at 402-403, 880-891, 410-411 respectively. See generally, Richardson, op. cit., at 255-257.

operations of interstate and overseas airlines, and the due execution by Australia of the international obligations it has accepted, may well make it desirable that the one authority should exercise sole control of all movement of aircraft in the air and of matters connected with such movement, that is to say of all matters connected with how aircraft may be used.[1]

Following this case the *Air Navigation Regulations* were amended as a result of declared Commonwealth government policy to assume comprehensive legal control over civil aviation in place of the existing divided system. In retaliation the New South Wales Parliament passed the *Air Transport Act* 1964 making it an offence for a person to carry passengers or goods by aircraft between places in New South Wales without a State licence covering him, the aircraft and the route. The conflict took an interesting turn when Airlines of New South Wales applied to the New South Wales Commissioner for Motor Transport, the licensing authority under the State Act, for a licence to conduct commercial air transport operations between Sydney and Dubbo. This was refused and the rival airline, East-West Airlines were allocated the service but the Commonwealth would not grant them a licence to operate it. Proceedings were then commenced by Airlines of New South Wales challenging the validity of the State Act culminating in the High Court case of *Airlines of New South Wales Pty. Ltd.* v. *New South Wales* [No. 2].[2] The High Court upheld the Federal Regulations providing a licensing system for all commercial airline systems in Australia by a six to one majority[3] and a clear majority held that the licensing regulations were valid under the trade and commerce power.[4] In making their decision the Court followed the principle enunciated in *R.* v. *Burgess; ex p. Henry* (*The Goya Henry Case*) that while the constitutional division of power of trade and commerce had to be observed a new and complicated situation had developed in national and international air transport since that case. Therefore, in the present context, a licensing law applying to intrastate flights could be justified in order to protect both interstate and overseas aviation against potential physical hazards. However, it was proper for a State to prohibit intrastate air transport operations for non-navigational reasons and thus it was beyond the powers of the Federal Parliament to take over sole authority to initiate air transport operations within a State and thus the regulation purporting to do this was invalid.[5] The licencing provisions[6] of the *Air Navigation Regulations* were valid and there was no conflict between the Commonwealth law and the State Act as the Commonwealth

---

[1] Ibid., 411-412.
[2] (1965) 38 A.L.J.R. 388. For further detailed comment upon this case see under *Case Notes*, P. Armstrong, *Federal Law Review* Vol. 1 (1964-5), at 348-358.
[3] Barwick C.J., McTiernan, Kitto, Menzies, Windeyer and Owen JJ.; Taylor J. dissenting.
[4] The licensing regulations were held to be valid by the external affairs powers by McTiernan J.; Kitto and Windeyer JJ. thought the regulations were not authorised by the external affairs power, but by the trade and commerce power; Menzies and Owen JJ. held them to be within both powers. Opinion was divided as to whether the scheme could also be sustained under the external affairs power as a law to give effect to the Chicago Convention.
[5] Regulation 200B.
[6] Regulation 198, 199.

licensing regulations dealt with matters of safety, regularity and efficiency and the State Act was based on public needs and other such policy considerations. Therefore, there was no inconsistency for the purposes of s.109.[7]

The decision discussed above clearly established the right of the Commonwealth to make navigational laws applicable to all flying operations in Australia. The States, however, may still exercise licensing control for non-navigational reasons.[8]

The question of licensing also arose in *R. v. Public Vehicles Licensing Appeal Tribunal of Tasmania; ex p. Australian National Airways Pty. Ltd.*[9] The *Traffic Act* 1925-1961 (Tas.) provided the issue of aircraft licences by the Transport Commission and prohibited the use of aircraft without licence. The Act provided that any person who, being the holder of a licence, was aggrieved by the grant of a licence to any other person, might appeal from the decision of the Commission granting the licence to the Public Vehicles Licensing Tribunal.[10] The matter of air transport in Tasmania was referred to the Commonwealth Parliament by the *Commonwealth Powers (Air Transport) Act* 1952 (Tas.).[11] Trans-Australia Airlines (hereinafter referred to as T.A.A.) operating on intrastate air routes[12] was granted aircraft licences by the Transport Commission to operate within Tasmania. Ansett-A.N.A. then appealed to the Public Vehicles Licensing Appeal Tribunal from the decision and argued, inter alia, that the Commonwealth Act (ibid.) did not effectively refer the matter of air transport to the Commonwealth Parliament. The Tribunal dismissed the appeal on the grounds that there was a valid reference under s. 51 (xxxvii) of the Constitution and that under the Commonwealth Act (*ibid.*) T.A.A. did not need a licence under the State Act.[13] Following upon this Ansett-A.N.A. obtained orders nisi for certiorari and mandamus in the High Court against the decision of the Tribunal arguing (i) that the relevant section of the Commonwealth Act only gave a power to T.A.A. to conduct its air

---

[7] Ibid., see ante. The High Court unanimously upheld the permit regulations requiring Federal permits to use Commonwealth aerodromes and fly in controlled airspace.

[8] Richardson, op. cit., p. 259.
Thus, in New South Wales an air transport operator wishing to engage in intrastate carriage must hold both Federal and State licences. Federal covering permits must additionally be held if such flights involve the use of a Commonwealth aerodrome or controlled airspace.

[9] (1964) 37 A.L.J.R. 503 [1964] A.L.R. 918. High Court of Australia; Dixon C.J., Kitto, Taylor, Menzies, Windeyer and Owen JJ. See P. Buchanan, Case Note, F.L.R., at 324-327. This case was applied in the recent case of *Minister for Justice for Western Australia (Ex. p. Ansett Airlines)* v. *Australian National Airlines Commission and the Commonwealth* (1977) 12 A.L.R. 17.

[10] *Traffic Act* 1925 (Tas.) s. 30B; as amended by s. 27 of the *Traffic Act* (1961).

[11] Under s. 2 of the Act: "The matter of air transport is referred to the Parliament of of the Commonwealth for a period commencing on the date on which this Act commences and ending on the date fixed, pursuant to section three, as the date on which this Act shall cease to be in force, but no longer."
Section 3 provides: "The Governor may at any time, by proclamation, fix a date on which this Act shall cease to be in force, and this Act shall cease to be in force accordingly on the date so fixed." For similar provisions see *Commonwealth Powers (Air Transport) Act* 1952 (Qld.) and *Commonwealth Powers (Air Navigation) Act* 1921 (Sth. Australia).

[12] Under the *Australian National Airlines Act* 1945 (Cth.), s. 19A.

[13] Section 19A.

services within Tasmania and (ii) the section required T.A.A. to hold a
State licence and be subject to State regulation in respect of its air services
in Tasmania and (iii) the section was ultra vires the Commonwealth
Parliament as there had been no reference of power within the meaning
of s. 51 (xxxiii) of the Constitution.

The High Court held that an interpretation of the relevant section of
the Commonwealth Act did authorise T.A.A. to operate airline services
within a State without a State licence. A reference for a determinable period
in the State Act was held valid by the Court; the words of the Constitution
were to be read without imposing limitations or implications which were
not found in the express words.[14]

In this general context of Federal-State relations s. 92 of the Constitution
deserves to be mentioned. Section 92 guarantees the right of the individual
to trade freely between the States and a refusal to issue a licence for an
interstate cargo or passenger service where the operator can show he is
capable of complying with the Regulations would be contrary to s. 92 as
a restraint on interstate trade as well as being ultra vires the powers given
to the Director-General of Civil Aviation under the Regulations.[15] Using
the trade and commerce power the Commonwealth has prohibited the
importation of aircraft unless the Director-General grants permission, so
that a potential interstate operator may not be able to obtain aircraft with
which to operate his service. In the I.P.E.C. case[16] this situation arose and

---

[14] Ibid., at 507. See also on the point of whether a State can revoke or amend
a reference, Professor Sawyer (1957) 4 *University of Western Australia Annual
Law Review*, p. 1.
[15] Ibid., at 199.
[16] *The Queen* v. *Anderson; ex p. I.P.E.C.-Air Pty. Ltd.* (1965) 39 A.L.J.R. 66.
In February 1977 Ansett Industries Ltd. obtained two temporary High Court
orders to prevent Ipec Co. Pty. Ltd. and Air Express Ltd. from importing two
aircraft each for a projected air freight service between Melbourne and Tasmania.
The orders were directed to the Commonwealth Government and to the secretary
of the Department of Transport. The injunctions were granted on the grounds that
the issue of import permits would contravene the two airline agreement of 1952.
This agreement was made between Australian National Airlines (subsequently
taken over by Ansett), the government airline Trans-Australia Airlines and the
Menzies government. Essentially, the agreement gave each operator a substantial
share of airmail and equal access to government business and guaranteed government aid in paying for new aircraft. There was also a rebate on air charges already
paid and the two airlines were charged with consulting each other on the sharing
of routes, on timetables, freight rates and fares in order to avoid what was termed
unnecessary overlapping of services and wasteful competition. In the event of
failure to agree on the matters outlined an impartial Chairman would be appointed by the Government with the agreement of TAA and ANA with power to
make a binding decision if the parties could not agree to a settlement. The
agreement was enshrined in the *Civil Aviation Agreement Act* 1952, now re-
enacted and extended as the *Airlines Agreements Act* 1952-73 (*see* First, Second,
Third and Fourth Schedules). The rationalization of operations by the two main
airlines was taken a step further with the *Airlines Equipment Act* 1958 (now the
Airlines Equipment Act 1958-73), which prevented the two operators from
effective competition with each other by the purchase of new and expensive planes.
Under the Act the Minister of Civil Aviation was empowered to determine the
size of the fleet TAA and Ansett-ANA required for their individual non-com-
petitive routes plus one half of the traffic on the routes where they competed.
Once this was determined, TAA and Ansett-ANA had to conform by fleet reduction if necessary and not purchasing or renting aircraft. The *Airline Equipment Act* prohibited TAA and Ansett-ANA from buying new planes without a
certificate from the Minister to the effect that the purchase was not detrimental to
the domestic air transport industry.

I.P.E.C. sought writs of mandamus in the High Court to compel the Director-General to issue a charter licence and grant permission to it to import five aircraft. The Court by a majority held that a writ of mandamus should be granted to compel issue of a charter licence but that the Director-General had acted within his powers in refusing an import permit. With reference to s. 92 the act of refusal did not have any legal operation on interstate carriage nor did it have effect upon anything which formed part of interstate commerce; therefore s. 92 was not infringed.

Imposition of air navigation charges upon aircraft engaged in interstate commerce raises the question whether s. 92 applies as it does in respect of charges made for the use of roads by interstate commercial road transport vehicles. In *Hughes and Vale Pty. Ltd.* v. *New South Wales* (No. 2)[17] a charge requiring interstate road traffic to pay more than a reasonable sum for the use of the roads was held to infringe s. 92. The joint judgments of Dixon C.J., McTiernan and Webb JJ., in that case strongly hint that charges imposed by a State for the use of a wharf or a government aerodrome indispensable to interstate air or sea navigation may be within s. 92 so that the charges should be no more than a reasonable cover for the use of facilities.[18]

VI. AIRPORT LEGISLATION

The Commonwealth can rely on the interstate and overseas and commerce powers to support its ownership, maintenance, and control of airports, including those it owns in State capital cities and any traffic.[19]

Under the *Airports (Business Concessions) Act* 1959 which binds the Crown of a State, the Minister of Civil Aviation is empowered to grant leases and licences for business purposes in respect of land within an airport on such terms and conditions as he thinks fit and a person may not trade within an airport without authority of the Minister.[20] Thus the Commonwealth may grant a person a right to trade within a Commonwealth

The current issue concerning Ipec, now awaiting the decision of the High Court, may well lay open the question as to whether the two airline agreement contravenes s. 92 of the Constitution. Interestingly, one of the agreements is terminable on 31 December 1977, and another ends on 30 June 1978. *(See* Schedules to the *Airlines Agreement Act* 1952-1973.) Such is the interest of the Tasmanian community in an increase in air freight facilities that the Tasmanian Government intervened when the High Court considered the constitutional question. The High Court has not yet handed down its decision. *See* D. Corbett; *Politics and the Airlines* (1965), pp. 122-137; this work provides an excellent background to domestic air line policy in Australia. See also H. W. Poulton, "Legal and Policy Aspects of Air Transport in Australia" *Journal of Air Law and Commerce* Vol. 26, 1959, p. 27.

17 (1955) 93 C.L.R. 127.
18 Section 92 probably applies to air navigation charges and thus the Commonwealth would have to show that these were reasonable. There appears little danger that, in this context the Commonwealth is infringing s. 92; Richardson op. cit., p. 262
19 Other powers are the defence power (Constitution, s. 51(vi)), territories power (Constitution, s. 122) and the incidental power (Constitution, s. 51 (xxxix)). Power also is provided by s. 52 of the Constitution; but see Richardson, op. cit., p. 262 and *Kingsford Smith Air Services* v. *Garrison* (1938) 55 W.N. (N.S.W.) 122.
20 Section 6 and ss. 7-8.

airport in a State disregarding, for example, a State liquor licensing law. The *Airports (Surface Traffic) Act* 1960 as amended by the *Airport (Surface Traffic) Amendment Act* 1976 binding on both Commonwealth and State Crowns, empowers the Director-General of Civil Aviation to provide for the control of surface traffic including parking.

VII. IMPLEMENTATION OF INTERNATIONAL CONVENTIONS

The main Conventions affecting Australia have already been dealt with; in this context they are only considered where their implementation in Australia has been subject to modification, clarification or amplification and, in certain instances, separate enactment by the States.

A. Damage by Aircraft Legislation

Legislative action was not necessary in order to apply the Convention to Australian registered aircraft operating abroad, but Part II of the *Civil Aviation (Damage by Aircraft) Act* 1958, besides approving ratification by Australia, gives the provisions of the Convention force of law in Australia.[21] Part III of the Act extends the operation of the main provisions of the Convention to Australian registered aircraft in flight in Australia in the course of trade and commerce between Australia and another country and to foreign aircraft of countries who are not parties to the Convention in the course of flight in Australia during international carriage. The limits of liability laid down in the Rome Convention do not apply to foreign aircraft.

New South Wales, Victoria, Western Australia and Tasmania have Acts dealing with damage by aircraft based on the *Civil Aviation Act* 1949 (U.K.) s. 40.[22] The State Acts cannot apply to cases of damage within the purview of the Federal Act but this Act does not cover instances of damage caused by aircraft engaged in interstate flights the State Acts mentioned apply to most aircraft operations in Australia.

B. Carrier's Liability Legislation

The *Civil Aviation (Carriers' Liability) Act* 1959 now amended by the *Civil Aviation (Carriers' Liability) Amendment Act* 1976 repealed the earlier 1935 Act and approved ratification by Australia of the Hague Protocol which is set out in the Second Schedule to the Act.[23] The present Act deals with various matters which neither the Warsaw Convention nor the Hague Protocol adequately cover. For instance the Act provides that payments under insurance policies, superannuation schemes and the like, are not to be taken into account when assessing damages in respect of liability under the Convention.[24] Similarly, the Act provides for apportionment of contributory negligence by regard to the plaintiff's share in the responsibility for the damage and then determining the net amount, if

[21] Section 8. The text of the Rome Convention is set out in the Schedule to the Act.
[22] See ante.
[23] *Civil Aviation (Carriers' Liability) Act* 1959, Part III.
[24] Section 15.

any, which the carrier should pay before the limits laid down by the Convention apply.[25]

Under Part IV of the Act the Warsaw Convention provisions as amended by the Hague Protocol are part of Australian domestic legislation. Part IV applies to contracts for interstate and territorial carriage by commercial airlines, also to carriage by T.A.A. whether intrastate or commercial airlines, also to carriage by T.A.A. whether intrastate or not and to overseas carriage outside either the Warsaw or Hague rules.[26] Liability to a passenger under Part IV is stated to be in substitution for civil liability under any other law.[27] Part IV has been implemented in all States by Acts modelled on the Federal legislation so that there are now uniform rules governing the liability of air carriers throughout the Commonwealth.[28]

The Guadalajara Convention was ratified by Australia and given legislative force by amendment of the *Civil Aviation (Carriers' Liability) Act* 1959 effective from 1st May, 1964.[29]

VIII. AIR ACCIDENTS (AUSTRALIAN GOVERNMENT LIABILITY) ACT 1963

The above Act applies Part IV of the *Civil Aviation (Carriers' Liability) Act* (ibid.) to the carriage of passengers in aircraft operated by the Commonwealth or a Commonwealth authority not covered by Part IV.[30] The *Air Accidents Act* as amended by the *Air Accidents (Commonwealth Government Liability) Amendment Act* 1976 applies mainly to Commonwealth employees required to travel by air on duty and persons travelling for Commonwealth purposes. The Act does not apply to members of the defence forces or persons carried to perform duties in the aircraft or

---

[25] Section 16. In *Saunders* v. *Ansett Industries* (1975) 5 ALR 1975 509, Ansett admitted liability to the plaintiff in an action for damages under the *Civil Aviation (Carriers' Liability) Act* 1959 (Com) as incorporated into the *Civil Aviation (Carriers' Liability) Act* 1962 (S.A.) but claimed that s. 31 of the Commonwealth Act limited its total liability for damages to $30,000. The plaintiff, whose damages were assessed at $30,000 argued that the limitation in s. 31 related only to Ansett's liability in respect of actual damage and that the plaintiff would be entitled to seek and obtain an order for interest under s. 30c of the *Supreme Court Act* 1935 (SA) on the amount claimed as damages. The Supreme Court of South Australia in the exercise of Federal jurisdiction held (Wells J.) that ss. 28 and 31 of the Commonwealth Act limited the liability of the carrier only as to damage caused by him. Section 30c of the *Supreme Court Act* gave the court a supplemental power to award interest on the judgment. This power was an incident not of the cause of action but of the judgment that takes the form or an award of money for a wrong committed to the plaintiff.

[26] Section 27.

[27] Section 35. The *Civil Aviation (Carriers' Liability) Amendment Act* 1976 by s. 3 amends. 31 of the *Principal Act* by raising the limit of liability from $30,000 to $45,000. This amendment is stated by s. 3 (2) of the amending Act not to apply in relation to an accident or occurrence that took place before the commencement of the amending Act.

[28] *Civil Aviation (Carriers' Liability) Act:* 1961 (Victoria) (No. 6808); N.S.W. 1967 (No. 64 of 1967); Tasmania 1963 (No. 6 of 1963); West. Australia 1961 (No. 69 of 1961) as amended by No. 52 of 1970; Queensland 1964 (No. 24 of 1964); South Australia 1962 (No. 11 of 1962) as amended by the *Civil Aviation (Carriers' Liability) Act Amendment Act* 1970-1971 (No. 4 of 1971).

[29] Part III and see ante, "Guadalajara Convention".

[30] The Australian National Airlines Commission is regulated by Pt. IV of the *Civil Aviation (Carriers' Liability) Act* 1959, ss. 26-27.

persons not lawfully entitled to be on board the aircraft.[31] The Act does cover persons travelling for the purposes of, or in the course of their employment by, the Commonwealth or Commonwealth authority in an aircraft not operated by these two bodies and to which Part IV does not apply.[32] The maximum liability of Commonwealth or a Commonwealth authority in respect of any one person by reason of death or injury within the above category is limited to $45,000.

IX. CRIMES ABOARD AIRCRAFT[34]

Essentially criminal law is a State matter and the general assumption in the States is that jurisdiction depends upon the crime being committed in the territory of the State.[35] There are problems in determining over which State a crime on board an aircraft has been committed. In *R.* v. *Hildebrandt*,[36] a case involving a charge under the Criminal Code of Queensland, s. 12 of intent to destroy an aircraft by putting an explosive in it,[37] the Queensland Court of Criminal Appeal held that where a person is charged in Queensland with intent to destroy an aircraft by putting an explosive substance in it, or is charged with depositing an explosive substance in it, wilfully and without reasonable cause or excuse, under such circumstances that it might cause injury to persons in the aircraft, or damage to the aircraft, the onus was upon the Crown to prove the jurisdiction of the Queensland Court. On the facts the bomb had not been deposited in Queensland but had been connected together when the aircraft was out of Queensland, then the charge failed for lack of jurisdiction. If, however, the fabrication of the bomb had taken place when the aircraft was in flight over Queensland, then there would be jurisdiction.[38]

Crimes (Aircraft) Act 1963-1973: By legislation the Commonwealth Government has dealt with crimes on board aircraft and affecting aircraft in the *Crimes (Aircraft) Act* 1963. In view of the discussion above the Act does not extend to all Australian aviation.

Part II of the Act (ibid.) deals with crimes on board aircraft and applies to any aircraft engaged in interstate and territorial flights or in

---

[31] Part I, s. 4.

[32] Part II, s. 11.

[33] Part II, s. 8, as amended by s. 1 of the *Air Accidents (Commonwealth Government Liability) Amendment Act* 1976.

[34] See *Crimes (Aircraft) Act* 1963; *Crimes (Hijacking of Aircraft) Act* 1972, giving effect to the Hague Convention, 1970; *Crimes (Protection of Aircraft) Act* 1973, giving effect to the Montreal Convention 1971.

[35] *Macleod* v. *A.G. for New South Wales* [1891] A.C. 455; *Ex p. Iskra* (1962) 63 S.R. (N.S.W.) 538.

[36] [1964] Qd. R. 43, and see *R.* v. *Hildebrandt* [1963] 81 W.N. (N.S.W.) 143.

[37] Section 12 reads: "This Code applies to every person who is in Queensland at the time of his doing any act or making any omission which constitutes an offence."

[38] Per Stanley J.: If the bomb, although completely fabricated outside Queensland was "deposited" by the accused at some other place within the aircraft when in flight over Queensland, there would be jurisdiction to lay a charge in relation to any of the places in the aircraft in which the accused deposited the fabricated bomb during the time when the aircraft was in flight over Queensland. The actual depositing of the bomb took place between Sydney and Casino in New South Wales; see *R.* v. *Hildebrandt* (1963) 81 W.N. (N.S.W.) 143.

flights between Australia and an outside place.[39] It also applies to registered Australian aircraft engaged in a flight wholly outside Australia[40] and to all flights of defence and Commonwealth aircraft. The Act does not have general application to intrastate flights, but does apply to intrastate flights by Commonwealth and defence aircraft. Both State and Federal courts are vested with jurisdiction under the Act[41] but the Act does not exclude any existing State or territorial law. State and Territorial courts retain their existing criminal jurisdiction[42] save that a person cannot be convicted twice for the same conduct.[43] Legislation has been enacted in some States to incorporate specific offences in relation to aircraft.[44]

Part III of the Commonwealth Act deals with crimes affecting aircraft. It applies to Australian registered aircraft engaged in or used mainly for "prescribed flights" which definition includes interstate flights, flights within or to or from a territory of the Commonwealth and flights to, from or completely outside Australia, and applies also to any foreign aircraft flight that is in Australia or is intended to end in Australia.[45] Additionally Part III applies generally to Commonwealth and defence aircraft but, like Part II, has no general application to intrastate flights.[46]

Crimes (Hijacking of Aircraft) Act 1972-1973 and the *Crimes (Protection of Aircraft) Act* 1973[47]: The *Crimes (Hijacking Aircraft) Act* 1972 gives approval to the Convention for the Suppression of Unlawful Seizure of Aircraft signed at the Hague in 1970,[48] the text of the Convention being given in the Schedule to the Act. Under the Act a person commits hijacking, if while on board the aircraft he unlawfully, by force or threat of force, or any form of intimidation, seizes or exercises control of the aircraft, or attempts to do so, or is an accomplice of a person who performs or attempts to perform any such act.[49] The hijacking, for the purposes of the offence, must be committed on board an aircraft that is in flight, i.e. when moving off for takeoff or when the last door of the aircraft is closed preparatory to take-off;[50] and engaged in a prescribed flight. Hijacking on board a Commonwealth aircraft is included; as is

[39] The view the Act adopts is that Australian laws are in force on board an aircraft registered in Australia while it is outside Australia even if the law of some other country also applies because of the aircraft's presence over or in that country.
[40] Sections 3(1), 6(2); registered as to nationality under the Air Navigation Regulations.
[41] Section 22.
[42] Section 27.
[43] See *R. v. Hildebrandt* [1963] 81 W.N. (N.S.W.) 143.
[44] *Crimes (Aircraft) Act* 1963 (Victoria) (No. 7088); *Aircraft Offences Act* 1971 (Sth Australia) (No. 1 of 1971); *Criminal Code Amendment Act* 1904 (Queensland) (No. 14 of 1964); *Criminal Code Amendment Act* 1964 (West. Australia) (No. 53 of 1964).
[45] Section 10(2), 10(1).
[46] Part III specifies various offences such as taking control of an aircraft without lawful excuse (s. 11), wilful destruction of an aircraft (s. 12), destruction of an aircraft with intent to kill (s. 13), prejudicing the safe operation of an aircraft with intent to kill (s. 15), assaulting crew members on board an aircraft (s. 16), and taking and sending dangerous goods on aircraft (s. 18). For penalties see Part III, ss. 10-19 inclusive.
[47] For the Tokyo Convention on Inflight Offences 1963 which has been overtaken by the legislation listed here see Sassella, op. cit., pp. 72-76.
[48] Section 6.
[49] Section 7.
[50] Section 8(2), s. 3(2) (a).

where the hijacking is committed on board an aircraft that is owned or operated by a government other than Australia, and the aircraft is in Australia or in a flight starting in Australia or ending in Australia or in the case where hijacking was committed by an Australian citizen or an aircraft which would be considered to be in flight if the Convention applied.[51]

The *Crimes (Protection of Aircraft) Act* 1973 approves the ratification by Australia of the Convention for the Suppression of Unlawful Acts against the Safety of Civil Aviation signed at Montreal in 1971 and here-inafter referred to as the Montreal Convention.[52] A person is guilty of an offence against the Act (ibid.) if he unlawfully and intentionally performs an act of violence against a person on board an aircraft in flight if that act is likely to endanger the safety of that aircraft; destroys an aircraft in service or causes such damage to it as to render it either incapable of flight or endangering flight safety. An offence is similarly committed if such a person places or causes to be placed a device or substance on an aircraft by any means which is likely to destroy, damage or incapacitate the aircraft. It is also an offence under this section to destroy, damage or interfere with navigational facilities if this is likely to endanger an aircraft in flight. Attempts to perform the above acts are unlawful and accomplices to such acts or attempts are in like manner offenders against the section.[53] Powers of arrest without warrant are given to the person in command of an aircraft including placing in custody of a person committing or being reasonably suspected of having committed an offence under the Act.[54] These powers apply to an Australian aircraft either inside or outside Australia or any other aircraft while in Australia or engaged in a prescribed flight.[55]

[51] Section 8(2), s. 9(1) provides, additionally: "A person who, on board an aircraft, does an act of violence against all or any of the passengers or crew the doing of which, if it took place in the Australian Capital Territory, would be an offence against a law in force in that Territory, other than this Act or the *Crimes (Aircraft) Act* 1963, is . . . guilty of an offence against this section and punishable by the same penalty as that by which he would have been punishable. For s. 9(1) to apply the act must be one over which Australia is required to establish its jurisdiction by Article 1 of the Convention or where the act is committed on prescribed flight subject to the provisions listed in the main text prior to this note."
[52] Section 6; the Schedule to the Act contains the English text of the Montreal Convention.
[53] Section 7(1).
[54] Section 9(2).
[55] Section 9(1).

CHAPTER 18

CARRIAGE BY RAIL

I. INTRODUCTION

The carriage of goods and passengers by rail in the United Kingdom is the responsibility of the British Railways Board, which by the *Transport Act* 1962 is not a common carrier.[1] The legal background to this Act, which still has relevance, particularly in the Australian context, will be dealt with as a preliminary to examining the current standard conditions governing the carriage of goods and passengers' luggage laid down by the British Railways Board. In contrast the Australian Commonwealth Commissioners for Railways and the States' Boards and Commissioners responsible for the operation for their respective railway networks are declared common carriers by statute.[2] Although the economic conditions surrounding the growth and running of the railway systems in each country have been different, much of the early English case law has been used as the basis of Australian judicial decisions. Similarly the legislation of nineteenth century England has been adopted in Australia to strike a balance between the authorities in whom the responsibilities for the railways are vested and their customers.

II. CARRIAGE BY RAIL: THE ENGLISH LEGAL BACKGROUND

Rail transport was in its infancy when the *Carriers' Act* 1830 was passed and railways per se only came within the ambit of that statute by use of the terms "other public conveyances by land for hire" and "other common carriers". Within a short space of time, however, the railways acquired a monopoly position in inland transport and began to insist on making special contracts with consignors to limit their own responsibilities as common carriers, notice of which terms (as a set of printed conditions) were normally contained in a note or ticket given to the consignor. The courts tended to take the line that the consignor had notice of these conditions when these were placed in his hand.[3] As a result of the general public reacting to what no doubt in modern judicial terms would be expressed as a gross inequality of bargaining power, the *Railways and Canal Traffic Act* 1854 was passed. This Act imposed upon

---

[1] *Transport Act* 1962, ss. 43(6), 52(2).
[2] *Commonwealth Railways Act* 1917-1973, s. 34; *Government Railways Act* 1912-1957, s. 33 (New South Wales); *Railways Act* 1914-1964, s. 101(4) (Queensland); *South Australian Railways Commissioners Act* 1936, s. 100 (South Australia); *Common Carriers' Act* 1974, ss. 13 and 14 (Tasmania); *Railways Act* 1958, s. 4 (Victoria); *Government Railways Act* 1904-1972, s. 37(3) (Western Australia).
[3] O. Kahn Freund, *The Law of Inland Transport* (1963), p. 222.

railway carriers the duty to carry any goods which they were able to carry for anyone who wished them to do so.[4] However, the Act did not debar the railway companies from contracting out from their liability as common carriers. Even so, the railway carrier was made statutorily liable for the loss of or damage to any goods they carried due to the negligence or default by their servants or themselves.[5] Any special contracts made with the consignors purporting to limit such liability with regard to receipt, forwarding and delivery of goods to be valid had to be just and reasonable.[6] The powers of the railway (and canal) carriers were constrained in the making of contracts limiting their liability for the negligence or default of their servants (i.e. committed within the scope of the servant's authority). Although in circumstances outside the above the Act left railway and canal carriers free to reduce their common carrier's liability to that of a bailee in any form they chose and under conditions not necessarily just or reasonable,[7] once an act occurred due to the negligence of the carrier or his servants, then any limitation on liability for such loss had to conform to the statutory provision if the carrier were to be relieved of his liability.

In *Peek* v. *North Staffordshire Railway*,[8] the House of Lords laid down bases for assessing the reasonableness of a contract of carriage under the 1854 Act. Following the provision that a carrier had to carry for a reasonable remuneration[9] their Lordships noted that in offering to carry at "owner's risk" a railway carrier could alternatively offer to carry on terms that excluded or limited his liability. Such an alternative was neither just nor reasonable unless the carrier offered a reduction in price below what would have been reasonable remuneration if the goods had been carried at "owners' risk" or the carrier in question offered any other advantage he was not bound to give. Thus once the court was satisfied that the railway carrier had offered what came to be known as a "fair alternative" it was presumed that the arrangement was just and reasonable, the onus of demonstrating that the conditions were so being borne by the carrier.[10]

The doctrine of the fair alternative laid down in *Peek's* case was elaborated in later decisions[11] and set a limit to the freedom of carriers by rail to restrict their own liability. As a result the railway companies developed alternative consignment rates governing carriage at owner's and carrier's risk. The owner's risk conditions were those by which the rail carriers restricted their liability and had to be part of a

---

[4] Now repealed: *Transport Act* 1962, Schedule XII, Pt. 1.
[5] *Railway and Canal Traffic Act* s. 7.
[6] Ibid.
[7] *Shaw* v. *Great Western Railway* [1894] 1 Q.B. 373; see, in particular, Wright J. at 382, 383.
[8] (1863) 10 H.L. 473.
[9] Ibid., s. 2.
[10] *Brown* v. *Manchester, Sheffield and Lincolnshire Railway* (1883) 8 App. Cas. 703, at 716.
[11] See principally; *Glenister* v. *G.W. Railway* (1873) 29 L.T. 423; *Lewis* v. *G.W Railway* (1877) 3 Q.B.D. 195; *Dickson* v. *G.N. Railway* (1886) 18 Q.B.D. 197; *G.W. Railway* v. *McCarthy* (1887) 12 App. Cas. 218; *Williams* v. *Midland Railway* [1908] 1 K.B. 252; and see *Gregory* v. *Commonwealth Railways Commissioner* (1941) 66 C.L.R. 50.

contract signed by the consignor or his agent to be valid. These "owner's risk" conditions were not usually relied on by the railway companies to absolve themselves totally from liability for the safety of goods carried. In practice the companies accepted, even at owner's risk, liability for the wilful misconduct of themselves and their servants since the courts were reluctant to hold conditions of carriage as reasonable if they excluded such liability. Thus an attempt by companies to contract out of this liability ran the risk that the courts would not uphold the conditions.[12]

By contrast the carrier's risk conditions eventually were the common law rules governing common carriers' liability slightly modified, in other words the fair alternative which the company had to offer the consignor.[13] Special conditions were provided for perishables and fragile goods as well as livestock and eventually conditions used by the companies were virtually in standard form.

In 1921 the *Railways Act* was passed to produce complete uniformity in contract terms for carriage of goods by rail which would have statutory authority. The new "Standard Terms and Conditions" applied automatically in the absence of contrary agreement and were deemed to be reasonable and ipso facto not capable of being invalidated by the *Railway and Canal Traffic Act* 1854.[14] From 1, January 1928 until 31 December, 1962 ordinary goods carried by rail were governed by "Standard Terms and Conditions" A and B, which themselves constituted two out of fourteen sets of Standard Terms and Conditions agreed to by the railway companies and the Railway Rates Tribunal. Conditions A governed the carriage of ordinary goods by rail without special contract and took the place of the common law rules. Conditions B applied if an owner's risk rate operated and the consignor requested that the goods should travel at owner's risk, the carrier only being liable on wilful misconduct being proved.

The Standard Terms and Conditions no longer applied after 1 January, 1963, as a result of the *Transport Act* 1962,[15] and full freedom of contract was given to the various Transport Boards, including the British Railway Board[16]; the 1854 Act was also repealed. This freedom of contract applies in relation to exemption from liability as in other matters and there are no statutory standard terms remaining; carriers by rail in the United Kingdom are no longer common carriers. However, sweeping as this legal change may appear, it is not, in practice, as fundamental as it seems. The "General Conditions of Carriage for the Carriage of Merchandise" (other than Dangerous Goods) and Merchandise for which conditions are specially provided issued by the Board constitute the most important of the standard contract forms governing carriage by rail. Although these sets of conditions have no legal effect

---

[12] See *Brown* v. *Manchester, Sheffield and Lincolnshire Railway* (1883) 8 App. Cas. 703 and *Smith (H.C.)* v. *S.W. Railway* [1922] 1 A.C. 178; *W. Young and Son (Wholesale Fish Merchants)* v. *British Transport Commission* [1955] 2 Q.B. 177 per McNair J., at 193.
[13] Kahn Freund, op. cit.
[14] *Railways Act* 1921, s. 43(2).
[15] Ibid., s. 43(3).
[16] Hereinafter referred to as "the Board".

per se they derive legal force solely from express or implicit incorporation in contracts of carriage made between the Board and their customers. As a learned author on this subject has noted:

> The sets of conditions used by the Railways Board which are in fact bound to dominate the majority of the relationships between the Board and its customers reflect in their content the result of four hundred years of development; the common carrier's liability, the "excepted perils", "wilful misconduct" at owner's risk and many other things besides. These principles are no longer rules of law or statute, but simply typical terms of contracts. That which in the past was imposed from above has continued to exist as a voluntary arrangement.[17]

III. British Railways Board: General Conditions of Carriage of Goods

The General Conditions of Carriage of Goods (hereinafter referred to as the General Conditions) issued by the British Railways Board provide the following definitions at the outset:[18]

> "The Board" means the British Railways Board and includes, unless the context otherwise requires, their sub-contractors and agents;
> "trader" means any person sending or receiving goods by the Board's services and includes, unless the context otherwise requires, his servants and agents;
> "sender" and "consignee" include, unless the context otherwise requires, their respective servants and agents;
> "consignment" means goods accepted by the Board at one time from one sender at one address for carriage to one consignee at one address;
> "sub-contractor" means any carrier engaged by the Board to carry goods on their behalf;
> "private siding" means a railway or siding not belonging to the Board or their sub-contractor;
> "dangerous goods" means goods included in the list of dangerous goods published by the Board or goods which present a comparable hazard.[19]

A. Parties and sub-contracting

The Board may engage sub-contractors to perform the contract of carriage or any part of the same on their behalf. The Board enter into the contract of carriage for themselves and on behalf of their sub-contractors, agents and servants. All of these shall have the benefit of the contract and shall be under no liability to the trader in respect of the goods greater than or in addition to that of the Board under the contract.[20] The carrier's servants and any contractors or other agents employed by the carrier to carry out the contract are not normally parties

---

[17] Kahn Freund, op. cit., p. 230.
[18] General Conditions of Carriage of Goods (other than goods for which Conditions are specially provided) (B.R. 18793/1) issued by the British Railways Board and dated 1st July, 1974.
[19] Ibid., Condition 1.
[20] Ibid., Condition 2(2). As to the efficacy of such clauses, see p. 986 et seq., post.

to it. Thus if goods are lost or damaged due to the negligence of those employed by the carrier, such persons may be liable to the owner of the goods but on the basis of tort (or as bailees) and not in contract.

It is a general principle of law that no one can be a party to, or derive a benefit from, a contract not made by himself or by a person or persons acting as his agent or agents. It is uncertain, in fact, whether reliance can be placed, by those employed by the carrier when made liable for their negligence in dealing with goods, upon any contractual clauses whereby the liability of the carrier has been excluded or restricted.[21] However, the effect of the Board's condition is to clearly establish the carrier (the Board) as agent for those whom he employs; in this case they will also be party to the contract and can rely upon exemption clauses in that contract.[22]

B. Warranties

The General Conditions provide that all goods are warranted by the sender to be fit to be carried or stored. The trader is also required to keep the Board, harmless from, and indemnified against, all claims, demands and expenses irrespective of their origin so far as they result from the trader under declaring the actual weight of the goods concerned and/or an incorrect description of all or any part of a consignment. The sender also warrants that if the goods are not his own unencumbered property he has the authority of all persons owning or interested in the goods to enter into the contract and contracts on their behalf.[23]

C. Liability for loss, damage or delay

As has already been noted the Board is not a common carrier but when it carries goods at its own risk it takes on common carrier's liability.[24] Therefore an owner whose goods have been carried at Board's risk and which have been either lost or damaged in transit need only prove that loss or damage and financial loss as a consequence to himself. This right to compensation does not depend on proving that the loss or damage was due to a particular event nor on whether the loss or damage was contributed to by negligence on the part of the carrier's servants. The General Conditions state that the Board will be liable for loss, misdelivery of or damage to goods occuring during transit as defined by the Conditions unless the Board can prove that in the event of such liability the loss, misdelivery or damage has arisen from:

    (a) Act of God;

    (b) any consequence of war, invasion, act of foreign enemy, hostili-

---

[21] See *Scruttons Ltd.* v. *Midland Silicones* [1962] A.C. 446; but contrast *New Zealand Shipping Co. Ltd.* v. *A. M. Satterthwaite & Co. Ltd.* *(The Eurymedon)* [1974] 1 All E.R. 1015, and see Palmer, "The Stevedores Dilemma: Exemption Clauses and Third Parties", *Journal of Business Law* 1974, p. 101 et seq.; for general comment on exemption clauses, contracts of carriage and third parties, see Crossley Vaines, *Personal Property* (4th ed. 1-973), pp. 110-112; see post, p. 986 et seq.

[22] Kahn Freund, op. cit., pp. 212-213; see also Conditions of Carriage for the Carriage of Coal, Coke and Patent Fuel (B.R. 18793/3—1st April, 1965); Condition 2(2), Conditions of Carriage by Water (B.R. 18793/4—1st April, 1965); Condition 2(2), Conditions of Carriage of Livestock (B.R. 18793/2—1st March, 1970).

[23] Ibid.

[24] Kahn Freund, op. cit., p. 242.

ties, insurrection, military or usurped power or confiscation, requisition, destruction of or damage to property by or under the order of any government or public or local authority;

(c) seizure under legal process;

(d) act or omission of the Trader;

(e) inherent liability to wastage in bulk or weight, latent defect or inherent defect, vice or natural deterioration of the goods;

(f) insufficient or improper packing;

(g) insufficient or improper labelling or addressing;

(h) riot, civil commotion, strikes, lockouts, stoppage or restraint of labour from whatever cause;

(i) consignee not taking or accepting delivery within a reasonable time.[25]

These exceptions are governed by a rider in the Conditions that where the Board fails to prove that they used all reasonable foresight and care in the carriage of goods they will incur liability for loss, misdelivery or damage. Additionally the Board will be liable where the trader can prove in the case of goods consigned as damageable goods not properly protected by packing that loss, misdelivery or damage was caused by the Board's wilful misconduct or it would have been suffered even if the goods had been properly protected by packing. The Board, however, is not liable in respect of goods where there has been fraud on the part of the trader. The Board is liable for loss proved by the trader to have been caused by delay in the carriage of goods unless the Board on their part are able to prove that such delay has arisen without negligence by them.[26]

In respect of the exceptions (a) to (i) inclusive, the scope of the four excepted perils is much wider than at common law, and it is these that can now be examined in more detail, drawing as they do, for their explanation, upon judicial decisions.[27]

D. Act of God

Act of God, despite its theological overtones, means an elemental natural force which directly causes the injury, unforeseen, or incapable of being reasonably guarded against if foreseen. Thus the carrier is not liable for any accident where he can show that it was due to entirely natural causes and could not have been prevented by reasonable foresight and care on his part. It is the extraordinary forces against which the carrier is not bound to take precautions. In the case of *Nugent* v. *Smith*[28] the duty of the carrier in this context was stated as follows:

> All that can be required of the carrier is that he shall do all that is reasonably and practically possible to insure the safety of the goods. If he uses all the known means to which prudent and experienced carriers ordinarily have recourse, he does all that can be reasonably required of him, and if, under such circumstances, he is overpowered

[25] Ibid., Condition 5A(1).
[26] Ibid., Condition 5A(2), and see below.
[27] They are: act of God, act of foreign enemy, etc., act or omission of trader, his servants or agents, inherent liability to wastage, etc., inherent vice, etc.
[28] (1876) 1 C.P.D. 423.

by storm or other natural agency, he is within the rule which gives immunity from the effects of such *vis major* as the act of God.[29]

In *Briddan* v. *Great Northern Railway*[30] an unusually heavy fall of snow blocked a railway line and a goods train was used to assist a passenger train to get through, as a consequence of which cattle in goods vans were left on a siding for thirty hours and suffered due to lack of food and intense cold. The railway company, on being sued for injury to the cattle and loss of market, pleaded that the damage was caused by the act of God, i.e. the heavy snowfall. On the facts it was found delay was caused by the state of the line and not due to any fault of the company. The court held that the company were not bound to give the assistance to the goods train that they had to the passenger train and were not liable.[31]

The General Conditions in their earlier form included casualty (including fire and explosion) in their list of expected perils; this no longer appears in the current issue. This would mean, it is submitted, that the Board are liable for the consequences of major accidents where these do not fall within the judicial construction given to the term "act of God".[32]

E. Consequence of war, etc.

The common law exception "act of the Queen's enemies" has been extended by the General Conditions to include "any consequence of war, invasion, act of foreign enemy".[33] Thus the exception applies if the act is one of the British government or one of its allies performed during a war and where an armed conflict exists (as opposed to a state of war within the meaning of international law); this is covered by the term "hostilities". Consequences of civil war, rebellion and so forth in the terms of the General Conditions include acts carried out by internal forces hostile to the Crown such as I.R.A. terrorists. The term "consequences of war" would cover damage resulting from explosion of mines or bombs laid during wartime.[34] Executive action is an exception to liability as in the case of confiscation, requisition of or damage to property under government, public or local authority direction, which may cover such destruction or confiscation for health reasons.[35]

F. Riots, civil commotion, strikes, etc.

At common law a carrier was liable for damage done by a group of rioters. The grouping of riot with "strikes, lockouts, stoppage or restraint

---

[29] Ibid., per Cockburn C.J., at 437.

[30] (1858) 28 L.J. Ex. 51.

[31] It is suggested that where a driver of a vehicle suffers a heart attack which the company could not be expected to have foreseen in the circumstances of the driver's clean bill of health, any accident resulting from such cardiac arrest can be attributed to an act of God; see Kahn Freund, op. cit., citing *Ryan* v. *Youngs* [1938] 1 All E.R. 522.

[32] This would appear to be a correct interpretation in view of the construction put upon the earlier wording by Kahn Freund, op. cit., p. 245.

[33] Ibid., 5A(1).

[34] Kahn Freund, op. cit., p. 247.

[35] Judicial action is covered under (c), seizure under legal process; this would occur where a bailiff seized goods in a purported execution of a court judgment which had been delivered to the Board for carriage in the mistaken belief that such goods belonged to the judgement debtor; Kahn Freund, op. cit., at 248.

of labour from whatever cause" may seem unusual but is in fact common with many types of contract.[36] On construction of the section dealing with strikes it has been suggested that what would be tantamount to an "unofficial" strike by a group of men, within the ordinarily used terminology of "walk-out" or "lightning strike" would fall within the exception.[37] The use of the words, "from whatever cause" suggests that in this instance the Board is not liable for its own or its servants' negligence. This outcome has been decried by one authority on the ground that "it appears to be contrary to the whole scheme of carriers' risk conditions and to its common law basis that in this isolated case the carrier is not even liable for negligence".[38]

G. Inherent liability to waste, etc., inherent vice etc.

The traditional common law exception, loss or injury caused by "inherent vice" in the thing carried, is extended in the Board's Conditions by including "inherent liability to wastage in bulk or weight" and "latent defect". These terms can best be regarded as a clarification of inherent vice. The phrase itself can be translated as a default or defect latent in the thing itself which tends to the injury or destruction of the thing carried.[39] Thus a carrier is not liable for injury to perishable goods, such as fruit, vegetables or grain due to fermentation or natural decay provided these were properly stored and ventilated. Neither will the carrier be liable for evaporation or leakage of liquids if this were not reasonably preventable, nor for destruction by spontaneous combustion. Similarly there will be no responsibility on the carrier's part, if, using reasonable care, goods are injured simply by being moved. This latter example, as inherent vice generally, can best be illustrated in relation to carriage of animals and livestock. Carriers are bound to take reasonable precautions to guard against animals taking fright, but if an animal is unusually sensitive and becomes injured while unmanageable the carrier is not liable as long as reasonable care has been taken.

An example is provided in *Blower* v. *Great Western Railway*[40] where a bullock was loaded properly into a standard livestock van. During carriage the bullock broke out and was found dead on the track. On an action for damages against the company it was found as fact that the bullock had been entirely responsible for its own escape and neither the

---

[36] Seen as a standard clause in insurance contracts.

[37] Kahn Freund, op. cit., pp. 248-249. Such a construction in the view of Professor Kahn Freund would be doubtful where only one man was concerned. See the view taken by McNair J. in *W. Young & Son (Wholesale Fish Merchants) Ltd.* v. *B.T.C.* [1955] 2 Q.B. 177, at 194. In that case, if the railway authorities had tried to deliver the consignment of fish to the plaintiffs under the contract Bishopsgate station staff would have stopped work or the Billingsgate porters would have stopped handling Danish fish. McNair J. obiter stated that "an act of insubordination" by a particular group of men "unless approved by the union representatives would not amount to a partial stoppage or restraint of labour." See also, post.

[38] Kahn Freund, op. cit., p. 249, who later (at p. 250) refers to this as a "deplorable conclusion. Cf. now *Smith* v. *S. Wales Switchgear* [1978] 1 All E.R. 18.

[39] Kahn Freund, op. cit., p. 250.

[40] (1872) L.R. 7 C.P. 655; see also *Kendall* v. *London and South-Western Railway* (1872) L.R. 7 Ex. 373, *Lister* v. *Lancashire and Yorkshire Railway* [1903] 1 K.B. 878.

escape nor death were attributable to any negligence on the part of the company and that the van used was reasonably satisfactory for the purpose of carrying livestock. The company were therefore not liable, having only a duty to provide vans reasonably sufficient to hold cattle on a normal journey The general rule can be expressed as follows; that if the cause or injury arises from something in the goods themselves which the carrier cannot be reasonably expected to forsee or guard against, or from the ordinary wear and tear of the goods, which cannot be avoided if the goods are carried in the ordinary way, and which is in no way due to negligence on the carrier's part, the carrier will not be responsible for the injury.[41]

H. Fault of consignor or consignee

Where goods are lost or injured due to the consignor's own fault, at common law the carrier has no liability, as it would be unreasonable for a blameless carrier to have to pay compensation for loss caused by the consignor's fault. Thus it is the duty of a consignor to pack goods properly where goods are liable to injury in transit unless packed properly.[42] The Board is protected by the General Conditions against claims arising from the carriage of goods which do not require special packing; in the case of damageable goods not properly packed, the owner has to prove that the lack of adequate packing was not the cause of the loss or injury. The Board can be made liable, however, in two instances. First, if the owner can prove wilful misconduct the carrier is liable even though his servants' wilful misconduct may have been facilitated by the improper packing; by placing himself in the position he would have been if the goods were carried at owner's risk, the owner prevents the Board from relying on improper packing as a defence. Secondly, if the owner cannot prove misconduct he must show that the loss or damage would have been suffered even if the goods had been properly packed and that the Board would have been liable if the goods had been carried under standard conditions applicable to ordinary merchandise at carrier's risk rates.[43]

The Conditions also provide, as is the case at common law, that the Board will not be liable for loss, misdelivery or damage to goods that have been improperly addressed and labelled. If the consignor fails to address goods plainly and legibly and with an easily identifiable address of the consignee, the Board will not be responsible for loss of goods as the result of an insufficient address provided that Board's servants have done all that could be reasonably done in the circumstances to prevent loss.

Where the Board carries at its own risk it is liable for delay, deviation and detention as in the case or ordinary goods, as the issue of improper packing has no relation to the route on which the goods are sent nor speed of dispatch. In the case of addressing and labelling, the Board, as much as the common carrier, is only liable for negligence in connection

---

[41] Kahn Freund, op. cit., p. 252.
[42] Condition 5A(1)(f); see, generally, Kahn Freund, op. cit., pp. 373-374.
[43] Kahn Freund, ibid, at pp. 373-374.

with delay. Thus if goods do not arrive at their destinations on time due to faulty or insufficient addressing by the consignor, the carrier bears no responsibility.

In the Scottish case of *Caledonian Railway* v. *Hunter*[44] a parcel of goods was delivered to the railway company at Glasgow, labelled, "Wm. Rae, draper, Sudbury". In fact there are three places in England called Sudbury and the company sent the parcel to Sudbury in Derbyshire but on arrival the consignor could not be found. After a month after the parcel had been consigned for delivery the true destination was found to be Sudbury, Suffolk. Due the delay the consignee refused delivery, and the goods were returned to the consignor, who sued the company for the delay. The court held him primarily responsible for the delay in addressing the parcel ambiguously and further held that the company had acted reasonably in sending it to the nearest town called Sudbury and they were not responsible in the circumstances.

The Board is not liable for any loss or damage caused by the consignee not taking delivery within a reasonable time.[45] In this instance the Board is under no legal obligation to give notice to the consignor of the consignee's refusal to accept the consignment; but the Board must do what is reasonable in the circumstances.[46] If the consignee refuses to pay carriage and on that basis the Board refuses to deliver, the goods should be held for a reasonable time at the destination station.[47]

Under the General Conditions the Board undertakes to sign a document prepared by the sender acknowledging receipt of the consignment but no such document shall be evidence of the condition or of the correctness of the declared nature, quantity and weight of the consignment at the time it is received by the Board.[48]

I. Owner's risk conditions

Owner's risk conditions appear in the General Conditions as a single paragraph[49] as a footnote to the Board's Risk Conditions. The owner's risk conditions simply state that where goods are accepted by the Board for carriage at owner's risk, the Board shall not be liable for any loss, misdelivery, damage or delay to the goods except where the trader can prove this was caused by wilful misconduct of the Board. The Board's liability for non-delivery of a consignment or of any separate package forming part of a consignment (not being attributable to fire or to an accident to a train or vehicle) shall be determined as if the goods had been accepted for carriage at Board's risk. Thus Board's risk and owner's risk conditions are identical except for the key point relating to general liability. As the Board is no longer a common carrier it can refuse to carry any consignment nor can it be compelled to quote an owner's risk rate.[50]

---

44 (1858) 20 Sessions' Cases (2nd Series) 1097.
45 Ibid., Condition (i).
46 *Hudson* v. *Baxendale* (1857) 2 H. & N. 575.
47 *Crouch* v. *Great Western Railway* (1858) 27 L.J. Ex. 345.
48 Ibid., Condition 3(2).
49 Ibid., Condition 5B.
50 Kahn Freund, op. cit., p. 256.

The basis of liability under the owner's risk conditions is that the Board undertakes to compensate the owner for the consequences of the wilful misconduct of its own servants if the owner can prove it. Where there has been a misdelivery the Board takes on full liability at owner's risk. Thus in the context of owner's risk the onus is on the trader to prove the Board responsible. Wilful misconduct has been considered elsewhere and in *Horabin* v. *B.O.A.C.*[51] was defined as the doing of something which it is wrong to do or to omit, and which the person answerable does or omits intentionally, knowing that his act or omission is wrong. Wilful misconduct includes the doing of an act with reckless indifference, not caring what the result may be. Such an act goes beyond the limits of the grossest negligence; at best the wrongdoer forsees that his act may cause injury but is indifferent to such an occurrence resulting.

In *W. Young & Son (Wholesale Fish Merchants) Ltd.* v. *B.T.C.*[52] railwaymen at Bishopsgate Station in London acting in concert with Billingsgate fish porters refused to handle consignments of Danish fish consigned to the plaintiff's business premises. This was done so that the consignments would have to go through Billingsgate and the porters there would get their customary porterage charges. The Transport Commission then sold the fish by virtue of a power under the then current Standard Terms and Conditions enabling them to sell perishable merchandise.[53] The plaintiffs, owners of the consignment, sued the Commission for the difference between the full value of the fish and the price obtained by the Commission. The action was dismissed on the grounds that although the Bishopsgate men had been guilty of wilful misconduct, the defendants were protected by the clause by which payment of the proceeds of sale fully relieved them of liability for the goods. The Commission had also relied on the strike clause which protected the carrier from liability for loss damage or delay, the terms of which differ from the present strike clause earlier considered in that loss, misdelivery or damage are mentioned in the current Conditions but not delay.[54] Although the point was not decided by the learned judge as to whether the strike clause relieved the Commission of liability for misconduct he was clearly of the opinion that it did, although he said that he would have had difficulty in deciding for the defendants on this ground because he was inclined to interpret the word 'loss' as referable to physical and financial loss.[55]

---

[51] [1952] 2 All E.R. 1016, at 1019 per Barry J., see also Kahn Freund, op. cit., pp. 257-259, citing *Graham* v. *Belfast and Northern Counties Railway* [1901] 2 I.R. approved and adopted by Hallet J. in *Hartstroke Fruiterers* v. *London Midland and Scottish Railway* [1942] 2 All E.R. 488, at 490; affirmed Court of Appeal [1943] K.B. 362. See Chapter 17, "Carriage by Air".

[52] [1955] 2 Q.B. 177.

[53] See Condition 9(a), although the sale of perishable goods per se is not expressly mentioned.

[54] Ibid., 5A(1)(f), read together.

[55] [1955] 2 Q.B. 177, at 192. See also Kahn Freund ibid. on the interpretation of the strike clause. *Young's* case is sufficiently authoritative on the facts. The omission of the word "delay" in the current strike clause would not seem to debar the Board from relying on it in addition to their powers of sale under Condition 9(a) should a case similar to *Young's* arise, given Professor Kahn-Freund's interpretation of what constitutes a strike i.e., including unofficial action; see above.

In the case of *Forder* v. *Great Western Railway*[56] a fellmonger delivered a parcel of sheepskins to be carried by the company at owner's risk between London (Paddington) and Winchester, the company undertaking no liability save on proof of wilful misconduct on the part of its servants. The skins were injured in transit by being carried on a bedding of wood chips, which got into the wool. On complaint by the owner at Winchester he was told that the Paddington officials had been requested not to use such bedding again. In a similar contract a second consigment suffered identical injury for the same reasons. On a claim for damages for injury to both consignments the court found that there was no evidence that the loaders or those superintending them at Paddington had been informed of the likelihood of the bedding being harmful; thus wilful misconduct had not been proved and the company were not liable. By contrast in *Bastable* v. *North British Railway*[57] a switchback plant was sent by rail, the contract exempting the company from damage unless arising from wilful misconduct. The company's regulations required a load should be gauged to see if it was within proper limits for loading height. The load was not gauged, eye estimation being relied upon and the plant was damaged while being taken under a bridge in transit. The court held that failure by the company's servants to check the load by gauge amounted to wilful misconduct.[58]

At owner's risk the trader must prove, where claiming damages for misdelivery, that it arose from the wilful misconduct of the Board or their servants. But the Board does not intend in these circumstances, to contract out of its normal liability in the event of non-delivery of a whole consignment or of any separate packages forming part.[59] In *Hoare* v. *Great Western Railway*[60] sixty cases of pollard were sent by rail at owner's risk to a Mr Jeeves at Pewsey, Hampshire. The address was given in mistake and as Mr Jeeves was not expecting such goods he refused delivery. A few days later a person called Jarvis applied to the station master for sixty cases of pollard he expected from another place. The station master handed over the cases and when the consignor sued the company the court found against them on the grounds of wilful misconduct, despite the company's plea that their servant had been guilty only of negligence. The court ruled that deliberate delivery of goods to a person with a name other than that of the consignee was a wilful act, known to be wrong.

In *Stevens* v. *Great Western Railway*[61] goods were handed to the defendants on 27 October to be carried at owner's risk, and to be delivered to a particular firm. They were, in fact, delivered to another

[56] [1905] 2 K.B. 532.
[57] 1912 S.C. 555.
[58] See also *Lewis* v. *Great Western Railway*, (1877) 3 Q.B.D. 195; *Hartstroke Fruiterers Ltd.* v. *L. M. S. Railway* [1942] 2 All E.R. 488; [1943] K.B. 362; *H. C. Smith Ltd.* v. *Great Western Railway* [1922] 1 A.C. 178.
[59] See Condition 7, ibid.
[60] (1877) 37 L.T. 186.
[61] (1885) 52 L.T. 324. As to what constitutes proper delivery see Kahn Freund., op. cit., pp. 298-301 and see also *Stephenson* v. *Hart* (1828) 4 Bing. 476; *M'Kean* v. *M'Ivor* (1870) L.R. 6 Ex. 36; *Heugh* v. *London and North Western Railway* (1870) L.R. 5 Ex. 51.

firm by mistake and were not found by the defendants until 9 December. They were then tendered to the consignees who refused delivery. At the end of January next year the defendants informed the consignors of the facts. The defendants were held not liable to the consignors as, although misdelivery and delay had occurred, this could have been caused as much by negligence as wilful misconduct and as the plaintiff had not proved misconduct their action would fail.

Thus delivery to the wrong person will not be presumed to be misconduct. The cases of misdelivery where the Board is liable when it carries at owner's risk are (non-delivery apart) arguably instances where the Board could not have validly excluded or restricted liability on the basis of fundamental breach of contract.[62]

In cases of deviation, as distinct from misdelivery and delay, it has long been established in the law of carriage by sea that the carrier cannot claim the protection of common law excepted perils if loss or injury occurred during deviation.[63] Similarly a carrier by rail in such circumstances cannot rely on the terms of the contract. In *Mallet* v. *Great Eastern Railway*[64] a consignment of fish were delivered to the defendants at Lowestoft to go to Jersey via the Great Western Railway and Weymouth, the plaintiffs signing an owner's risk contract making the defendants free of liability save on proof of wilful misconduct. By mistake the defendants sent the consignment via London and the South Western Railway and Southampton, a longer route. The connecting steamer was delayed by storms and the fish arrived late for the Jersey market and an action for damages was brought against the company. The English High Court held the company liable; the deviation from the route agreed on was not covered by a delay clause in the consignment note as this was referable to a delay in performance not a delay, as here, which was due to action outside the contract.[65] In *Gunyan* v. *South Eastern and Chatham Railway*[66] a consignment of fruit was sent by the plaintiff from Sittingbourne to Glasgow on terms of a consignment note which specified carriage of perishable and other merchandise by passenger train or other similar service at owner's risk. The goods reached London on a passenger train but were sent to Glasgow on a goods train. As a result delivery was considerably delayed at Glasgow and the fruit deteriorated. The court held that the company was not protected by the consignment note terms at it was essential to the contract that the fruit be carried by passenger train and forwarding from London by goods train amounted to a departure from the agreement, so that the goods were not carried at owner's risk.

---

[62] Kahn Freund, op. cit., p. 297; but cf. p. 920 et seq., post.
[63] See *James Morrison & Co. Ltd.* v. *Shaw, Savill & Albion Ltd.* [1916] 2 K.B. 783; *Davis* v. *Garrett* (1830) 6 Bing. 716.
[64] [1899] 1 Q.B. 309.
[65] The principle of *Mallet* was confirmed by the House of Lords in *London and North Western Railway* v. *Neilsen* [1922] A.C. 263; see also *Swan Hunter and Wigham Richardson Ltd.* v. *France Fenwick Tyne and Wear Co. Ltd., The Albion* [1953] 1 W.L.R. 1026, at 1031. *Foster* v. *Great Western Railway* [1904] 2 K.B. 306, similar on facts to *Mallet's* case, appears irreconcilible with it. Judgment in *Foster* was to the defendant railway company. See further, Ch. 25 post (exclusion clauses).
[66] [1915] 2 K.B. 370.

Although the General Conditions state that "goods accepted by the Board for carriage may be carried by such means of transport and by such route as the Board think fit and these conditions shall apply by whatever means or route the goods are carried",[67] these General Conditions take their effect from incorporation into individual contracts of carriage, so that once the contract loses its force the Conditions cease to operate; it follows then that a term in the General Conditions cannot enable the carrier to rely on the Conditions in circumstances when they no longer have any force. Thus the Condition quoted above cannot enable the carrier to rely on the Conditions once he, without excuse, has deviated from the ordinary and agreed route.[68]

J. The carrier's right to sell the goods

The right of the carrier to sell perishable goods where these are not accepted or other circumstances prevent delivery has already been noted under the General Conditions.[69] In general the carrier's position has to be examined in the context of the carrier acting as an agent of necessity for the owner.

Where no special contract exists at common law the carrier may sell perishable goods and pay the proceeds to the owner after deduction of charges and expenses. Such a power must only be exercised in cases of real business necessity and it must be practically impossible to obtain instructions from the owner.

In *Sims & Co.* v. *Midland Railway*[70] butter was accepted by the defendants for delivery. Shortly afterwards a general strike of the company's employees occurred and the goods in question were not forwarded. The butter began to deteriorate rapidly in the hot weather and to avoid loss it was sold by the defendants. On an action for damages for failure to deliver the butter the court held the company to have acted rightly in selling. In the case of *Springer* v. *Great Western Railway*[71] tomatoes were delivered to the defendant at St Helier, Jersey for carriage to Covent Garden. En route to Weymouth the ship carrying the tomatoes was held up by bad weather and on arrival in Weymouth the consignment was further delayed by a strike by the defendants' employees. When unloaded at Weymouth the tomatoes were found to be in a poor state and a company official, in view of the strike continuing, decided to sell them. The court held, in an action for damages by the owner, that the company were liable as before sale the company's agent should have communicated with the owner to obtain instructions.

In common law the carrier only has a right to sell goods where they are perishable or in a similar category, such as livestock which have to be fed and looked after. In *Great Northern Railway* v. *Swaffield*[72] a railway company delivering a horse on behalf of the plaintiffs encountered delays for which they were not responsible so that the horse could

---

[67] Condition 12(1).
[68] Kahn Freund, op. cit., p. 289.
[69] See ante, p. 681; *Young's* case.
[70] [1913] 1 K.B. 103.
[71] [1921] 1 K.B. 257.
[72] (1874) L.R. 9 Exch. 132.

not be delivered to the consignee. As nowhere on the railway premises was suitable to keep the horse until delivered, the company kept it in livery stables. On an action for recovery of the costs of feeding and shelter by the company the court found the defendants liable to pay the charges. Both this case and *Sim's* case are regarded by an eminent writer on the law of agency as instances of breach of the contract of carriage rather than cases of agency; further it is contended that in both what was involved was a determination of the scope of authority given to a carrier of goods where the goods are in danger of perishing, thus limiting the liability of the carrier for failure to deliver, or for expenses incurred in the course of delivery.[73] However, as far as questions of rights and liabilities arising from acts of carriers are concerned, it would seem to be of little practical importance whether their position is regarded as that of agents of necessity, or, as in the case of medical attendance, their rights and duties under the contract of carriage are looked upon at as including the right (or duty) to care for perishable goods, or, in extreme circumstances, to sell them on the owner's behalf.[74]

The General Conditions of the Board extend the common law right of the carrier to sell goods.[75] The Conditions do not specifically mention perishable goods as such. The Board may sell goods held after transit or whilst transit is suspended and payment on tender of the proceeds of such sale after deducting the expenses of the sale and all other charges due shall discharge the Board from all liability in respect of the goods. This is without prejudice to any outstanding claim the trader may have against the Board. This right of sale is subject to the following conditions; first, the goods shall not be sold unless the Board have done what is reasonable in the circumstances to notify the sender or the consignee that the goods will be sold unless within a reasonable time of the giving of the notice the goods are removed or instructions are given for their disposal. Secondly, the Board shall do what is reasonable to obtain the value of the goods. Therefore to exercise the right of sale the Board, as distinct from common law, do not have to be able to communicate with the owner. Where the name and address of the sender is not known, but that of the consignee is, notice must be given to him. Where neither is known, no notice need be given. Deduction is permitted of all proper charges and expenses include those paid relating to carriage and warehousing of the goods, but if they were not carried through to their destination charges for the journey actually completed only are payable. The view has been taken that the Board is free from liability for the event

---

[73] Fridman, *The Law of Agency* (4th ed., 1976), p. 75. Professor Fridman would appear to regard the cases of agency of necessity quoted in connection with the liability of railway companies not so much cases of agency of necessity as "the implied extension of what is undoubtedly the authority of certain railway agents"; op. cit., p. 73. In *Sachs* v. *Miklos* [1948] 1 All E.R. 67 Lord Goddard accepted such cases as an extension to the agency of necessity of a shipmaster in respect of perishable goods, at p. 68; cited by Kahn Freund, op. cit., p. 308. See further Chapter 12, post (involuntary bailment).

[74] Fridman, op. cit., p. 74.

[75] Condition 9.

which gave rise to the need for the goods to be sold, even where this was an act of their own employees, e.g. a refusal to handle goods.[76]

K. Transit

Transit begins when the goods are delivered to the carrier and are in transit when awaiting despatch.[77] As the Boards' General Conditions put it transit begins when the goods are handed to or collected by the Board for carriage.[78] Any person who seeks to make the carrier responsible for goods given to his care must prove, unless this is admitted, that he delivered the goods to the carrier and that the carrier accepted them. Delivery to the carrier's servant or agent with authority to accept delivery on the carrier's behalf is deemed to be delivery to the carrier. If a parcel is handed to a servant of the carrier who was not authorised to receive it the carrier is not liable.[79] However, if a person is justified in the circumstances in believing that a servant of the carrier to whom he gives care of his goods is authorised to receive them, the carrier is liable for the goods and may not be allowed to prove that in fact the servant had no such authority.[80]

Where goods are delivered at an office of a carrier used for receiving such goods and accepted by a person who appears to be the carrier's servant then delivery and acceptance are completed. A carrier who allows another to receive goods on his behalf is responsible for the goods as soon as they are delivered to that person even if where such person is a thief.[81]

Under the Board's General Conditions transit is suspended when goods are held by the Board at some place other than the destination at the request or for the convenience of the trader or because he refuses or is unable to take delivery at the destination; alternatively where the goods are detained for certain purposes. Transit is resumed when the Board resumes the carriage of the goods.[82]

At common law the end of transit does not of necessity coincide with the end of the actual journey; this can be seen in cases where a carrier by rail undertakes to deliver the goods. Thus transit may end where there has been no delivery in the case where the consignee refuses to accept the goods tendered by the carrier or where the consignee refuses to pay carriage and the carrier refuses to deliver. As a basic principle

---

[76] This is the interpretation adopted by McNair J. in *Young's* case [1955] 2 Q.B. 177. Professor Kahn Freund states that the right to sell could be exercised even if the goods were held up by acts which amounted to wilful misconduct; op. cit., p. 310.

[77] Condition 10(1).

[78] The same principle applies to carriage of goods by air; *Westminster Bank Ltd.* v. *Imperial Airways Ltd.* [1936] 2 All E.R. 890; bars of gold stolen from defendants' strong room at an airport deemed to be a loss occurring during carriage by air. See Chapter 17, "Carriage by Air".

[79] *Slim* v. *London and South Western Railway* (1919) 120 L.T. 598. See further, Chapter 7, ante.

[80] *Sloane* v. *London and South Western Railway* (1919) 120 L.T. 598. See further, Chapter 7 ante.

[81] *John Rigby (Haulage) Ltd.* v. *Reliance Marine Insurance Ltd.* [1956] 2 Q.B. 468 (C.A.); swindler persuading carrier he is a servant of one of the carrier's subcontractors.

[82] Condition 10(2).

transit ends when the goods have been tendered to the consignee, whether he has accepted them or not. In the instance of goods not to be delivered at the consignee's premises, transit ends a reasonable time after arrival at the station or destination.[83]

The General Conditions stipulate that transit shall end (unless otherwise previously determined) in the following circumstances; in the case of goods delivered by the Board, when they are tendered at the usual place of delivery within the customary cartage hours of the delivery district, or at such other times or places as may be agreed between the Board and the trader. In the case of goods not to be delivered by the Board or to be retained by the Board waiting instructions, transit ends at the expiration of one clear day after notice of arrival has been given either orally or in writing to the consignee or, to the sender, where the consignee's address is not known or where the address of neither is known or in cases of goods to be called for at the expiration of one clear day after the goods arrive at the place where they are consigned. Transit will end, lastly, where goods consigned to a private siding are delivered there or at a place where the trader has agreed with the Board to take delivery. If the Board through no fault of theirs are unable to deliver the goods at such siding or place, transit shall end at the expiration of one clear day after notice has been given (orally or in writing) by the Board to the consignee that they are ready and willing to deliver.[84]

L. Limitation of damages and claims

Liability of British Rail is limited by the General Conditions in respect of any one consignment to the following extent. Where monetary loss is caused in any way in respect of the whole consignment liability is limited to £1,000 per metric tonne on the gross weight of the consignment; in the case of monetary loss in respect of part of the consignment the proportion of liability is calculated in accordance with the value which that part consignment bears to the value of the whole consignment. The Board's lower limit of liability is set at not below £10 in respect of any one consignment and the Board is entitled to require proof of the value of the whole consignment. The Board state they will not be liable for indirect or consequential damages or for loss of a particular market whether held daily or at intervals.[85]

The General Conditions also provide that the Board will not be liable unless they are advised of the loss from a package or from an unpacked consignment, or for damage, misdelivery or delay in writing within three clear days and the claim is made within seven clear days at the end of transit of the consignment or part. Nor will the Board be liable for the non-delivery of the whole of a consignment or any entire wagon load or separate package forming part of the consignment unless they are advised of the non-delivery in writing within twenty-eight days and the claim is made in writing within forty-two days after the transit began. The Board will not be protected by the above if the trader can prove that it was not reasonably possible for the trader to advise the Board in writing

---

[83] See *Chapman* v. *Great Western Railway* (1880) 5 Q.B.D. 278.
[84] Condition 10(3).
[85] Conditions 6(1), 6(2).

in the time limits laid down and such advice or claim was given or made within a reasonable time.

These limitations of the Board's liability have no effect on the principles of liability already discussed. Thus, in the event of delay, the rules against liability for consequential damages before calculating the amount that can be claimed and these rules must first be applied in order to determine if the amount to be claimed exceeds the limits laid down by the General Conditions.

M. Carrier's liability for passenger's luggage

At common law a passenger carrier was a common carrier of their luggage. This is no longer the case with British Railways Board under the *Transport Act* 1962. However, as all carriers by rail, whether under States or Commonwealth systems are common carriers such liability at common law is relevant to the Australian jurisdiction.

The common law rules that apply to the carriage of passengers' luggage are those that have been considered in relation to carriage of goods.[86] *The Carriers Act* 1830 applies to the carriage of passengers' luggage by common carriers.[87] Thus no passenger can recover damages for any money, jewellery or any other articles covered by the Act, unless he has declared it under its provisions. In respect of other articles the carrier is absolutely liable unless he has restricted his liability by contract. Thus where an accident causes luggage carried to be destroyed the carrier would be liable for the loss even where no negligence on his part or that of his servants could be proved. However, the carrier does not insure against the four excepted perils, act of God, act of Queen's enemies, inherent vice and consignor's fault[88] or additionally, the passengers' own fault. In the last instance where, for example, the luggage is stored in a van the carrier is liable in the ordinary way but where the passenger has assumed partial or entire custody of the luggage then the carrier is not liable for any of loss or injury to the luggage.[89] But in the case of luggage carried outside the control of the passenger the carrier has no liability if the luggage is wrongly labelled, addressed or badly packed and injury results. It may be lawful for a common carrier to refuse luggage that is not properly labelled and packed, and the fact that luggage accepted is unlabelled or faultily packed will be no defence to an action for damages unless the lack of labelling or faulty packing can be shown to have caused the loss.[90]

Liability of British Railways Board: The Railways Board is a private carrier, thus a bailee for reward, of passengers' luggage and their common law liability is that of a prvate carrier of goods.[91] Of paramount importance are the "Conditions of Carriage of Passengers and their Luggage"[92] (hereinafter referred to as the Conditions) which govern the Board's liability. Luggage is defined as:

---

86 See above.
87 *Caswell* v. *Cheshire Lines Committee* [1907] 2 K.B. 499.
88 See ante.
89 See post.
90 Kahn Freund, op. cit., p. 611.
91 See ante.
92 BR 25833/2 issued by the British Railways Board on June, 1974.

. . . articles (including animals) and any trunk, suitcases, travelling bag, box or similar receptacle in which they may be contained which passengers are permitted to take with them and which can be taken into the passenger carriage and cause no inconvenience to other passengers or the condition, size and weight of which are such that they can be readily loaded and accommodated in the guard's or luggage van.[93]

Subject to exemptions to be considered later the Board are liable for loss of or from or for damage or delay to luggage brought onto the Board premises or trains on proof that such loss, damage or delay was caused by the neglect or default of the Board, their servants or agents.

In the case of luggage carried in the guard's or luggage van the Board are similarly liable unless the Board can prove that such loss damage or delay was *not* caused by the neglect or default of the Board, their servants or agents.[94] It is assumed that in order to shift the burden of proof on to the Board the passenger must prove that the luggage in fact got into the guard's or luggage van.[95]

The liability of Board is limited to £50 per passenger[96] and the Board disclaims liability in the following circumstances:

(a) for loss of or from or for damage or delay to any luggage caused by:

(i) its being improperly or insufficiently packed or labelled, or

(ii) its comprising or containing any fragile or brittle article or any article liable to be broken and to damage any other article;

(b) loss, as under (a) caused by the act, neglect or default of the passenger;

(c) loss, as under (a) where the passenger does not travel in the same train as his luggage unless the Board would apart from this paragraph of this Condition be liable and either —

(i) such luggage is carried on terms that the passenger is not required to accompany it, or

(ii) the passenger's failure to accompany it is due to the neglect or default of a servant or agent of the Board;

(d) loss, as under (a) due to the failure of the passenger to comply with any of the Board's Conditions;

(e) loss, as under (a) not occurring in or on the Board's trains, road vehicles or premises;

(f) for indirect or consequential loss or damage.[97]

Clause (b) is similar to the common law rule that a common carrier of passenger's luggage can rely on passenger's fault as an excepted peril. The current position can be clarified by reference to decided cases.

In *Talley* v. *Great Western Railway Co.*[98] a passenger got out of his compartment on a way station and leaving his case in the train went into

---

[93] Condition 1(d).
[94] Condition 5(1).
[95] The Board probably bears the burden of proof with regard to unaccompanied luggage; Kahn Freund, op. cit., p. 613.
[96] Condition 5(2).
[97] Condition 5(3).
[98] (1870) L.R. 6 C.P. 44.

the station refreshment room. On return, as the train had moved, he could not find his original carriage and got into another for the remainder of the journey. On arrival at his destination he rediscovered his case which had been cut open and some of its contents stolen. The court held the company not liable as the passenger had taken control of his own luggage and was bound to look after it as an ordinarily careful person. This would be similar to passengers' own fault under current Board Conditions.[99] In *Vosper* v. *Great Western Railway Co.*[1] the passenger spent almost the entire journey outside his own compartment, part of it in the restaurant car. On returning to his own compartment he could not find his suitcase. The court held the company liable for the loss as the passenger was under no duty to remain in his own compartment all the time, particularly when the company had invited him to spend part of his journey in the restaurant car. In other cases it has been held that a passenger is not negligent by the mere fact that he goes to buy a newspaper at a station bookstall or by going to the telephone.[2] It is considered that *Vosper's* case would no longer be followed in view of the current Conditions and the purchase of a newspaper would probably go against a passenger claiming for loss of luggage; in the case of the phone call the luggage had been left with a porter so it might be deemed to be in control of the Board and thus they would be liable for loss.[3]

Under the Conditions if a passenger does not travel in the same train as his luggage the Board disclaims all liability for such luggage unless it was agreed that the passenger was not required to accompany it, or failure to do so was due to the neglect of one of the servants or agents of the Board.[4]

Transit begins when the luggage is handed to a servant of the carrier to be placed in the train. The porter at the departure station is under an ordinary duty to take charge of a passenger's luggage while the passenger acquires his ticket at the booking office and the Board is responsible for the luggage.[5] The commencement of transit can be illustrated by a case which is still valid.

In *Steers* v. *Midland Railway Co.*[6] luggage was taken to a sleeping compartment over one hour before the train left; the passenger being assured by a company inspector that it would be safe. While having a meal outside the station, the luggage was stolen from the train, and the company were held liable for the loss.

Under the Conditions the transit of luggage is at end (unless otherwise previously determined) when it has been removed at the termination of the journey from the compartment or has been unloaded from the Board's luggage vehicle on to the platform and the passenger has claimed it or has had a reasonable opportunity of claiming it. If assistance is given

---

[99] Kahn Freund, op. cit., p. 615.
[1] [1928] 1 K.B. 340.
[2] See *Carr* v. *London, Midland and Scottish Railway Co.* [1931] K.B. N1 94; *Henderson* v. *London, Midland and Scottish Railway Co.* 1930 S.C. 822.
[3] Kahn Freund, op. cit., p. 616.
[4] See ante, Condition 5(3)(c).
[5] *Lovell* v. *London, Chatham & Dover Railway* (1876) 34 L.T. 127.
[6] (1920) 36 T.L.R. 703; see also *Great Western Railway Co.* v. *Bunch* (1888) 13 App. Cas. 31.

at the end of transit by the Board's servants in removing accompanied luggage from the station platform to a vehicle or otherwise on the Board's premises at that station the Board are liable for any loss or damage to the luggage caused by the neglect or default of the Board or their servants during removal. Such liability is subject to any exclusion or limitation of the Board's liability for the luggage applicable during transit under the Conditions. The Board also state that they may refuse to deliver any luggage at any station other than that to which it is labelled by the Board's servants.[7]

The Conditions provide that the Board's servants are prohibited from taking charge of luggage for the purposes of custody except for deposit at a left luggage office (which includes left luggage lockers). The Board are not to be responsible for luggage or other property left at their stations or delivered to one of their servants for the purpose of being left at a left luggage office unless it is personally deposited by the passenger with the left luggage office attendant and a left luggage ticket is issued and accepted by the passenger. The luggage or other property is then held subject to ticket conditions either on the ticket or incorporated by reference.[8]

Subject to the foregoing Conditions porters have no general authority to take charge of luggage after the journey is ended, and if a porter does take charge of it, he is acting outside the scope of his employment and the Board is not responsible for negligence or misconduct. This can be illustrated by the case of *Hodkinson* v. *London and North-Western Railway Co.*;[9] a woman passenger refused a porter's offer to put her luggage in to a cab at the arrival station. The porter put it aside and promised to look after it until the passenger returned. After an hour and half she returned and found one of the bags had gone, the porter's explanation being that he had given it to another woman believing it to be hers. The company were held not liable as their responsibility ended when the luggage was taken from the van and placed at the owner's disposal on the platform and the porter was not acting within his authority as the company's agent in taking charge of the luggage.

N. Cloakroom tickets

When a passenger leaves property at a railway station by depositing it at a left luggage office and obtaining a cloakroom ticket he enters into a cloakroom contract; one which is essentially outside the scope of a commentary upon carriage of goods by rail, as it is basically a warehousing agreement. As a warehouseman at common law the keeper of a cloakroom is a bailee and as such is liable for loss, injury or unreasonable delay in redelivery caused by negligence. He is not liable for any loss or injury not caused by negligence on his part or by his servant. This rule does not apply to cloakroom contracts governed by the Conditions. Under these the Board is only liable for loss or detention of or damage to any articles deposited when caused by negligence of the Board or their

---

[7] Conditions 9(1), (3) and (4), respectively.
[8] Condition 10.
[9] (1884) 14 Q.B.D. 228; see also *Firth* v. *North Eastern Railway Co.* (1888) 36 W.R. 467.

servants or agents.[10] When an article is put into a cloakroom the Board's servants are under a duty to hand the depositor a printed ticket purporting to contain or refer to the Conditions. The depositor is bound by these provided reasonable notice is given.[11] Conditions laid down by the Board are similar to previous rules governing cloakroom deposit and have been validated by decided cases.[12]

The Board limits its liability to £25 for any articles deposited at any one time by one depositor. It also disclaims liability for loss of or damage to articles of a fragile or perishable nature whether or not caused by the negligence of the Board their servants or agents. No liability either is accepted for indirect or consequential loss or damage or loss or detention of or damage to articles deposited contrary to the Board's regulations and the Conditions.[13] The Board will deliver the articles deposited to a person producing the ticket issued in respect of them on payment of all charges. Alternatively the articles will be delivered to a person who does not produce such a ticket on evidence of loss of the ticket or authority to receive the articles which the Board's servants may consider satisfactory, in which case an indemnity must be signed by the person to whom the articles are delivered.[14] This clause protects the Board from claims for misdelivery, e.g. a thief, but it does not necessarily protect the Board in all cases of delivery to the wrong person. In *Alexander* v. *Railway Executive*[15] the plaintiff, A, accompanied by one C, deposited a number of trunks in a station cloakroom. A then paid the charges and received the ticket but ten days later C persuaded cloakroom staff to allow him to open the trunks without producing the ticket. Over a few weeks C managed to get the entire baggage handed over or sent to him. C had no authority from A and was later convicted of larceny. The court found the defendants liable; they were unable to rely on the exemption clause in the contract relieving them from liability since allowing an unauthorized third party to have access to goods deposited in the cloakroom meant the defendants had broken a fundamental term of the contract.[16]

---

[10] Section V, Conditions relating to Miscellaneous Facilities; A2(1).

[11] On the question of notice in relation to passenger tickets which is relevant to the topic under consideration see Kahn Freund, op. cit., at Chapter 26 generally, and in particular pp. 556-560 and the cases there cited.

[12] See *Pratt* v. *South Eastern Railway* [1897] 1 Q.B. 718; *Skipwith* v. *Great Western Railway* (1888) 59 L.T. 520; *Lyons* v. *Caledonian Railway* 1909 S.C. 1185.

[13] Condition 2(3).

[14] Condition 3.

[15] [1951] 2 K.B. 882.

[16] On this issue see Kahn Freund, op. cit., pp. 236, 238, 286, 297 and also see *Hunt* v. *Winterbotham (West England) Ltd.* v. *British Road Services (Parcels) Ltd.* [1962] 1 Q.B. 617 and Note by Ms. O. Aikin (1963) 26 M.L.R. 98. International carriage, which is outside the scope of this study is governed by the International Convention Concerning the Carriage of Passengers and Luggage by Rail (CIV) 1961. See *Carriage by Railway Act* 1972, s. 1(1), s. 1(5) and The International Convention concerning the Carriage of Goods by Rail (CIM) 1961; both signed at Berne 25 February 1961 and published prior to ratification (Cmnd. 2186 and Cmnd. 2810 respectively). See Kahn Freund, op. cit. at Chapters 20, 29.

IV. INTERNATIONAL CONVENTIONS GOVERNING CARRIAGE BY RAIL

The United Kingdom is a party to two major multi-lateral treaties on international carriage by rail and to an additional supplementary treaty. The two treaties are the revised International Convention dealing with the carriage of Goods by Rail (CIM) and the revised International Convention dealing with the Carriage of Passengers and Luggage by Rail (CIV) both signed at Berne on February 7, 1970.[17] An Additional Convention to the 1961 C.I.V. in the form of a supplementary treaty was signed at Berne on February 26, 1966.[18]

Although all three Conventions are in force in United Kingdom only the Additional Convention has been expressly made part of English law by enactment, the text of the Convention being a schedule to the *Carriage by Railway Act* 1972.[19] However the Act provides that where passengers and goods are carried in accordance with the "Railway Passenger Convention" (CIV) or the "Railway Freight Convention" (CIM) all rights of action against the railway in respect of English law will be governed by the appropriate Convention.[20] The terms of the CIM and CIV Conventions have been incorporated in passenger tickets, consignment notes and luggage registration vouchers issued by British Railways since 1965.

A CIM

The Convention, which came into force on January 1, 1975, governs carriage of goods consigned under a through consignment note for carriage over territories of at least two contracting states, including regular road or shipping services complementing rail services.[21] The Convention determines the form and conditions of the contract of carriage, performance, modification, liability for loss, damage and delay, enforcement of claims and the right and liabilities inter se of the railway authorities dealing with a through consignment.

The railway is obliged under the Convention to carry any goods that do not come within the specified categories of unacceptable articles[22] (such as goods too large or heavy for rolling stock) but may lay down

---

[17] Cmnd. 5210. The original C.I.M. was signed on February 25, 1961 and abrogated on December 31, 1974 as was the C.I.V. of 1970.

[18] A Protocol was adopted by a Diplomatic Conference convened in 1973 which extended the operation of the Additional Convention after the 1961 C.I.V. was abrogated, and made it supplementary to the C.I.V. of 1970.

[19] 1972 c. 33. The Schedule was amended under s. 9(1) of the Act to take account of the Additional Convention supplementing the 1970 C.I.V.; see Carriage by Railway (Revision of Conventions) Order 1974.

[20] Sections 1(4), 6, 7 and 8.

[21] Art. 1(1). Carriage must be solely over listed railway lines. The Convention is examined in detail by Kahn Freund, op. cit., pp. 408-445. For comment on combined transport provisions see F.J.J. Cadwallander *Uniformity in the Regulation of Combined Transport* J.B.L. 193 July 1974; see also *Uniform Rules for a Combined Transport Document* International Chamber of Commerce, Brochure 273, November 1973. This was adopted in 1974 by the Joint Committee on Containerisation of the International Chamber of Commerce (ICC).

[22] Art. 5(1); Art. 3.

conditions for the carriage of dangerous goods and livestock or similar consignments.[23]

The through consignment notes are in two forms;[24] one for fast carriage (grande vitesse) and slow carriage (petite vitesse). Goods under fast carriage, unless a different period applies in the railway regulations, must be despatched within 24 hours of being received and travel in "transit periods" in general at a minimum speed of 300 kilometres (186 miles) every 24 hours. A similar despatch period operates in respect of slow carriage, but the speed of transit is a minimum of 200 kilometres (124 miles) every 24 hours.[25] As soon as the consignment note and goods for carriage have been accepted by the forwarding railway the contract of carriage comes into existence.[26]

The rights of the sender and the consignee to vary the contract by issued instructions to the railway are dealt with in detail in the Convention,[27] and are wider than those of stoppage in transitu in English law as they do not rest on the sender being an unpaid seller or the consignee being an insolvent buyer. The sender, apart from stoppage in transitu can alter the destination station, substitute another consignee, order return of the goods to the station from which they were sent and alter the carriage from fast to slow[28] (see above). The right to vary the contract on the part of the sender ends when the consignee's right to do so begins, either when the consignee accepts the goods, or the consignment note is handed to him, or when the goods arrive at the destination station and the railway is required to deliver the goods and the consignment note.[29]

The railway is liable for total or partial loss of goods and for damage and delay,[30] and for its own servants and others it employs in carrying out the contract of carriage.[31] Liability for loss or damage is subject to two types of excepted perils, the first similar to those of the General Conditions of the Railway Board,[32] the second are different.

The first include (a) wrongful act or neglect of the claimant; (b) instructions of the claimant given other than as a result of the railway's wrongful act or neglect; (c) inherent vice; (d) circumstances that the rail carrier could not avoid and the consequences of which it could not prevent.[33] The second type covers situations when loss or damage arises from special risks inherent in (a) the carriage in open wagons when this has been agreed; (b) lack or inadequacy of packing; (c) loading by sender or unloading by consignee (d) failure to comply with customs requirements; (e) the nature of goods that specially expose them to loss or damage; (f) irregular, incorrect or incomplete description of articles not accepted for carriage or accepted only under certain conditions; (g) the carriage of

[23] Art. 4(1).
[24] Art. 6 deals with form and content of consignment notes generally.
[25] Art. 11(2).
[26] Art. 8(1); the sender bears all the consequences of irregularities in entries in the consignment note made by, or on behalf of, him; Art. 7(1).
[27] Arts. 21-25.
[28] Art. 21.
[29] Art. 21(4) (a), (b), (c) and see 21(4)(d) and 22(1).
[30] Art. 27(1).
[31] Art. 39.
[32] See above.
[33] Art. 27(2); 28(1).

livestock; (h) the carriage of consignments which have to be accompanied by an attendant.[34] If loss or damage is established by the rail carrier as attributable to one or more of the excepted perils this is a rebuttable presumption unless there is an abnormal shortage or an entire package is lost.[35] Loss is presumed in the case where the goods are not delivered to the consignee or held at his disposal within thirty days after the end of the transit period.[36] The railway may exempt itself from liability for loss, damage and delay in the cases of combined rail and sea transport covered by the Convention while goods were on board in respect to the acts or omissions of the master and other of the carrier's employees in the operation of the vessel. The railway may also exempt for fire and perils of the sea and, if the carrier can prove that there was no lack of care by him, unseaworthiness.[37]

The liability of the railway for total or partial loss is limited to fifty francs per kilogram of gross weight short unless a special declaration of interest in delivery is made in the consignment note by the sender and he pays an increased charge. In this case a claim can be made up to the total amount of interest declared. Carriage charges, customs duties and other expenses paid in relation to the missing goods must be paid by the railway.[38] Where a claimant can prove actual loss or damage resulting from the delay the compensation is limited to a ceiling of double the amount of carriage charges.[39] Where actual loss or damage cannot be proved and the transit period is exceeded by more than forty-eight hours the amount payable is one-tenth of the carriage charges with a fifty francs per consignment ceiling.[40] Liability for damage is on the basis of the amount by which the goods have fallen in value, but may not go beyond the amount payable for loss.[41] There can only be a reduction in the amount payable for loss, damage or delay unless the carriage charges are also reduced.[42] There is no limit to compensation where loss, damage or delay was caused by wilful misconduct by the railway; in the case of gross negligence by the railway, the maximum limits are doubled.[43]

The forwarding railway and the railway of destination are liable in the case of loss, damage or delay; only if the cause of action arose on its system is an intermediate railway liable.[44]

Only the sender can claim for loss, damage or delay unless the consignee has asserted his rights under the contract of carriage as when he takes possession of the consignment note, or accepts the goods, or when the goods arrive at the destination station and he requires delivery

---

[34] Art. 27(3).
[35] Art. 28(2).
[36] Art. 30(1). The railway is not liable for loss or damage caused by nuclear accidents; Art. 64.
[37] Art. 63(1). See note 21, above.
[38] Art. 31(1).
[39] Art. 34(2).
[40] Art. 34(1); but see s. 8(2) *Carriage by Railway Act* 1972.
[41] Art. 33.
[42] Arts. 6(6)(b), 35.
[43] Art. 37.
[44] Art. 43(3). This defines the rights of the sender or consignee against the various railways; for rights of the railways inter se see Arts. 48-53.

of the consignment note by the railway, or when he exercises his right to modify the contract.[45] The consignee is treated as if he were a party to the contract of carriage from its inception and is subject to the provisions of the Convention.[46] Generally actions arising from claims under the Convention can only be brought in the competent court of the state in which the defendant railway operates.[47]

All rights of action for partial loss, delay or damage are lost once the person entitled to them has accepted the goods. However, this will not be so if wilful misconduct or gross negligence can be proved. Claims for delay can also be made within sixty days of acceptance. Claims for partial loss or damage can be made if discovered before acceptance and for loss or damage not apparent or discovered until after acceptance can be made if the claimant requests a report within seven days of acceptance from the railway and proves that the loss or damage occurred between the time of acceptance and delivery.[48] No action can be brought on the contract of carriage after one year, or two years where the grounds include wilful misconduct or fraud.[49] The limitation period runs from the date of delivery in the case of partial loss, damage or delay and from the thirtieth day after the end of the transit period in the case of total loss.[50]

B C.I.V.

The C.I.V. Convention applies to the carriage of passengers and registered luggage under international transport documents over territories of two or more contracting states where carriage is solely over listed railway lines.[51] Here only the provisions in respect of registered luggage will be referred to in brief. The rail carrier is under a general obligation to carry luggage (and passengers) if they comply with the Convention's provisions and carriage can be undertaken by ordinary transport facilities and carriage is not prevented by unavoidable circumstances.[52] The railway is liable for damage or total or partial loss of any articles a passenger had as hand luggage who has sustained an accident[53] unless the cause of the accident was not connected with the operation of the railway, or which it could not avoid or prevent the consequences. The railway will not be liable either if the accident was the result of the passenger's wrongful act or omission or abnormal conduct as a passenger, or if caused by the action of a third party which the railway could not avoid or prevent the consequences.[54]

Compensation for loss of, or damage to, hand luggage is limited to two thousand francs per passenger but in the case of wilful misconduct

45 Arts. 42(3)(a), 42(3)(b).
46 *Carriage by Railway Act* 1972 s. 7(2).
47 Art. 44. All actions against railways are subject to Convention provisions; *Carriage by Railway Act* 1972 ss. 6(1) and 7(1).
48 Arts. 46(1), 46(2).
49 Art. 47(1).
50 Arts. 47(2)(a)(b), 47(3).
51 C.I.V. Art. 1(1); the Convention came into force on January 1, 1975.
52 Art. 3(1).
53 Art. 2(1).
54 Arts. 2(2), 2(3), 2(4).

or gross negligence by the railway there is no limit to liability.[55] Actions arising from the contract of carriage can only be brought by a person producing a ticket or providing other proof of a right to sue.[56]

Registered luggage by contrast to passenger luggage is widely defined.[57] Anything is accepted as registered luggage which is contained in trunks, baskets, suitcases, travelling bags, hatboxes and similar receptacles.[58] Luggage may be refused for carriage if inadequately packed, clearly damaged or in a defective state.[59] When luggage is registered a passenger must be issued with a luggage registration voucher.[60] Liability of the railway for partial or total loss, damage or delay in respect of registered luggage is similar to that in the C.I.M. and there is a similar burden of proof.[61] There is a presumption that missing articles are lost if not delivered within fourteen days after a request to the railway for delivery.[62] Liability depends on the passenger proving the amount of loss or damage suffered. Where he can do this compensation is limited to forty gold francs per kilogram; where he cannot the limit is twenty gold francs per kilogram.[63] Liability for damage is the amount by which the luggage has diminished in value but may not exceed forty gold francs per kilogram.[64] In the case of delay where a passenger can prove loss or damage suffered compensation is limited to eighty gold centimes per kilogram for every twenty-four hours up to a maximum of fourteen days; where he cannot the limit is twenty gold centimes per kilogram.[65] In the case of gross negligence the limits for loss, damage or delay are doubled, there are no limits if due to the railway's wilful misconduct.[66]

V. AUSTRALIAN RAILWAYS: FEDERAL RESPONSIBILITIES

The responsibility for the operation of railways under the control of the Commonwealth is vested in the Commonwealth Railways Commissioner by the *Commonwealth Railways Act* 1917-1973 and detailed operation of the federal network is governed by this statute and by-laws made thereunder.[67] The Trans-Australian Railway and the Central Australian

[55] *Carriage by Railway Act,* 1972 Schedule Pt. 1, Art. 7; Art. 8. Under s. 4(1) of the 1972 Act a court dealing with an action to enforce liability in relation to hand luggage limited under Art. 7 may take account of other proceedings begun to enforce the same liability. See also s. 6(1).
[56] Art. 38.
[57] See above and see British Railway Board's Conditions; *Conditions of Carriage of Passengers and their Luggage* s. 1.
[58] Art. 14(1); unless it is dangerous or its carriage infringes the postal monopoly of any territory or is prohibited in any territory in which it is to be carried, Art. 15.
[59] Art. 17(1). Luggage may be examined by the railway if it is likely it would breach the provisions of the C.I.V. as to acceptable articles.
[60] Art. 19.
[61] See above.
[62] Art. 29(1).
[63] Carriage charges must also be refunded by the railway; Art. 29(1).
[64] Art. 31.
[65] Arts. 32(2), 32(1).
[66] Art. 33.
[67] The *Commonwealth Railways Act* 1917-1973 provides inter alia as follows: Section 29(1): "The Commissioner may carry and convey upon the railways all such passengers and goods as are offered for that purpose, . . . and impose

Railway are the property of the Commonwealth and are ordinarily operated as two separate and distinct systems.[68] The Commonwealth government in pursuance of its constitutional powers in the field of communications[69] has, under the *Appropriation (Urban Public Transport) Act* 1974, taken steps to enter agreement with the States to acquire their railway systems. At the time of writing only two States, South Australia and Tasmania respectively, have passed the necessary legislation to bring about a handing over of their separate railway networks to the Commonwealth.[70]

The liability of the Commonwealth Railways Commissioner as a carrier of goods and as a common carrier was considered (inter alia) in *Gregory* v. *Commonwealth Railways Commissioner* by the High Court.[71] In that case a by-law purported to have been made under the *Commonwealth Railways Act* 1917-1936[72] provided as follows:

> The Commissioner will not be liable for the loss or damage to goods at Darwin occurring while the goods are: (a) Being received into trucks from any vessel at the Jetty or unloaded from a truck into any vessel at the Jetty; (b) on the Jetty or being conveyed between a sorting shed and the Jetty in either direction; (c) stored on the Jetty or in a sorting shed; (d) in the process of receipt or delivery at a sorting shed; or (e) left in trucks standing in the station yard.

Additionally, the Commonwealth Railways Goods and Livestock Rates made the following provisions (under Part 6, 1. General, clause 12):

> The Commissioner will not be responsible for damage from whatever cause arising done to goods lying or adjacent to the wharf (including shed), nor will he be liable for goods stolen therefrom while under storage or otherwise.

such conditions in respect thereof as are, upon the recommendation of the Commissioner, approved by the Minister." Section 34: "For the purpose of this Act the Commissioner shall be deemed to be a common carrier, and (except as by this Act otherwise provided) shall be subject to the obligations and entitled to the privileges of common carriers."
Section 36: "The Commissioner shall maintain the railways and all works in connexion therewith in a state of efficiency, and shall carry persons and goods without negligence or delay."
Section 88(1): "The Commissioner may make by-laws not inconsistent with this Act, prescribing all matters which by this Act are required or permitted to be prescribed, or which are necessary or convenient to be prescribed for carrying out or giving effect to this Act, and in particular the following . . . (h) the limitation of the liability of, and the conditions governing the making of claims upon the Commissioner in respect of any damage to or loss of any goods."

[68] By the *Seat of Government Railway Act* 1928-1973 the operation of railways in Canberra are placed under the jurisdiction of the Commonwealth Railways Commissioner. The Northern Railway (Darwin-Harrimah) in the Northern Territory is under the Commissioner's ownership and control by virtue of the *Commonwealth Railways Act* 1917-1973.
[69] Principally the *Commonwealth Constitution Act* 1901 s. 51 (paras. 32-34 specifically, in relation to railways, para. 33), s. 98, s. 104; *Post and Telegraph Act* 1901-1974 ss. 17 and 18.
[70] Under the *Railways (Transfer to Commonwealth) Act* 1975 (Tasmania) the Tasmanian Railways passed under Federal control on 1 July 1975. By the *Railways (South Australia) Act* 1975 the South Australian railways were similarly transferred; see below.
[71] (1941) 66 C.L.R. 50 reversing the decision of the Supreme Court of the Northern Territory (Bathgate A.J.).
[72] Ibid., s. 88.

The plaintiff alleged that the Commonwealth Railways Commissioner had received at the Darwin Jetty 350 tons of cement, the property of the plaintiff, and had delivered only 342 tons. The plaintiff claimed the return of the remaining eight tons of cement and damages for its detention, or alternatively damages for its conversion.

In his defence the Commissioner denied the receipt or loss of the cement. Additionally, or alternatively, he set up and relied upon the provisions of the *Commonwealth Railways Act* 1917-1925 and the by-laws thereunder; in particular the one cited above. He also alleged that the clause in the Commonwealth Railway Goods and Livestock Rates (also quoted above) was a term of the contract made between the plaintiff and the Commissioner for the delivery of the cement. As a further or alternative defence he set up that if he received the cement and/or failed to deliver it (which was denied) the failure to deliver was because the cement was stolen whilst lying on or adjacent to the wharf or in a sorting shed or whilst under storage or otherwise on the wharf or in the shed, again relying on the Rates clause. In reply the plaintiff inter alia alleged that both the by-law and condition were invalid.

It was held by Rich, Starke and Williams JJ. (McTiernan J. dissenting) that the by-law excluded a liability imposed on the Commissioner by the Act to a person injured by the damage to or loss of goods and was therefore beyond the by-law making power conferred on the Commission by s.88 of the *Commonwealth Railways Act* and thus was invalid and so incapable of affording the Commissioner any defence to the plaintiff's claim. It was also held by Rich, Starke and McTiernan JJ. (Williams J. dissenting) that the Commissioner might validly impose such a condition as contained in the Goods and Livestock Rates in respect of carriage of goods. Thus the condition would form a valid term of the contract.

Rich J., in examining the provisions of the Act noted that s.88(1)(h) spoke of "the limitation of the liability of, and the conditions governing the making of claims upon, the Commissioner in respect of any damage to or loss of any goods." Such a limitation of liability did not justify a total exclusion, which appeared to be the effect of the by-law.

> It would be anomalous if the Commissioner were enabled to prescribe conditions upon which claims were to be made and at the same time were enabled to prescribe that no claim whatever may be made for such loss or damage. So that, although s.34 confers on the Commissioner a wide power of altering a common carrier's obligation for the safety of the goods entrusted to him, it does not enable him to obliterate and destroy all responsibility during the period which the contract of carriage covers. It is this respect that the by-law exceeds the power conferred upon the Commissioner and extends to the services performed by the Commissioner in other capacities which are so interwoven into the services performed *qua* common carrier as not to be severable. I think, therefore, the by-law is *ultra vires* and invalid.[73]

In respect of the condition, Rich J. observed:

> There is no principle which prevents a common carrier who in his contract undertakes to do more than "commonly carry" or who by

[73] Ibid., at 59.

the nature of things becomes a bailee from contracting to fix the conditions of liability (if any) he is prepared to assume in respect of these additional functions. The condition seems reasonably to meet the circumstances of railway transit at its beginning or end of carriage to or from abroad at Darwin. The circumstances of carriage of goods in the more remote districts to fixed yet inadequately protected points will afford illustrations of the necessity of such conditions in the contracts of common carriers.[74]

In a judgement noteworthy for the examination of the background to the position of the Commonwealth Railways Commissioner as a common carrier, Starke J. observed that apart from statutory provisions a common carrier could limit his liability by notice brought home to the consignor or by special contract, whether reasonable or not, for loss arising from negligence however great, even, apparently, from gross negligence or misconduct or fraud on the part of his servants.[75] A carrier of passengers, however, was only liable for negligence, but not as an insurer. Statute apart, such a carrier could limit his liability by notice brought home to the passenger or by special contract.[76]

Starke J. held the by-law in the case under consideration to be consistent with s.34 of the Act as the section reserved to the Commissioner the privileges of common carriers, which included the right to limit stability. Section 36, however, was not a similar provision to the *Railway and Canal Traffic Act* 1854, s.7.[77] The first limb of s.36, which requires the Commissioner to maintain the railways and all works in connection therewith in a state of efficiency, creates a public duty and is more or less a counsel of perfection enforceable possibly by means of the writ of mandamus but conferring no civil rights upon anyone. So also the other provision that the Commissioner shall carry passengers and goods without negligence or delay imposes a public duty upon him and according to the doctrine illustrated in *Graves* v. *Wimborne (Lord)*[78] creates a right in the individuals for whose protection and benefit the duty has been imposed.[79] Starke J. also held that the duty of the Commissioner under the Act was to carry goods in the capacity of carrier and whilst the

---

[74] Ibid., at 60. Rich J. also stated that it was established beyond question that the reasonableness or unreasonableness of a by-law or a condition made under statutory powers was not a separate and distinct ground of invalidity; at p. 60 citing *Williams* v. *Melbourne Corporation* (1933) 49 C.L.R. 142.

[75] At 62, citing *Peek* v. *North Staffordshire Railway Co.* (1863) 10 H.L. 473 per Blackburn J., and *Shaw* v. *Great Western Railway Co.* (1894) 1 Q.B. 373.

[76] At 62, citing *Duckworth* v. *Lancashire and Yorkshire Railway Co.* (1901) 84 L.T. 774.

[77] "The provision that the railway authority shall be deemed a common carrier goes back a long way in railway administration in Australia" per Starke J., ibid.
Section 7 reads: "Every such company as aforesaid shall be liable for the loss of or for any injury done to any . . . goods . . . in the receiving, forwarding, or delivery thereof, occasioned by the neglect or default of such company or its servants, notwithstanding any notice, condition or declaration made and given by such company contrary thereto, or in any wise limiting such liability."

[78] (1898) 2 Q.B. 402.

[79] (1941) 66 C.L.R. 50, at 64.

goods were in itinere.[80] The Act applied only to loss or injury caused by the negligence or delay of the Commissioner or his servants. It imposed no duty in respect of accidental injuries and loss by theft of strangers or the Commissioner's servants as that was not occasioned by negligence or delay within the meaning of the section.[81] As a result, by-laws limiting liability in such cases would not be inconsistent with s.36. Similarly, nor would by-laws limiting the amount of liability for negligence and delay, nor would they go beyond the powers in s. 88 so long as such by-laws did not exempt the Commissioner from liability for negligence or delay and were reasonable in the relevant sense.

> The provisions of s.36 impose a duty to take care, but not an unlimited liability in respect of amount in case of breach of that duty. In my opinion, it is not inconsistent with the provision of that section if the amount of liability be regulated by by-law made under s.88 so long as the by-law be reasonable[82] . . . Still in my opinion, the by-law No. 21 as amended by by-law No. 60, transcends the authority given by s.88 of the Commonwealth Railways Act 1917-1925. It exempts the Commissioner from loss or damage to goods at Darwin, howsoever caused. It is not confined to accidental injuries or to theft or other loss without negligence on the part of the Commissioner. It extends to loss or damage to goods due to the negligence or delay of the Commissioner or his servants and the exemption is not limited in amount. It is unnecessary, therefore, to consider in this case whether the by-law as amended is or is not reasonable . . . a by-law is not unreasonable unless it be such that no responsible man exercising in good faith the powers conferred by the Statute could pass such a by-law[83] . . . It is enough to say that the by-law as amended is beyond power, without determining whether it is beyond power because it is unreasonable.[84] . . . The Commissioner enjoys a monopoly under the Commonwealth Railways Act, but it is a monopoly regulated by the Act itself. He can only demand tolls, fares, charges and impose conditions in respect of the carriage of the passengers or goods on the railways as the Minister approves, and the provisions of s. 29(2) allow. But I find nothing in the Act which prevents the Commissioner from making agreements with his customers limiting his liability, either by public notice brought home to them or by special contract, or makes such agreements inconsistent with the Act itself, so long as they be reasonable. I say so long as they be reasonable, for the Commissioner has a monopoly and has a duty to serve the public at large in the matter of carriage. He cannot refuse to perform his duty by imposing arbitrary and capricious conditions upon the public desirous of using the railways. At the common law, as we have seen carriers could have so limited their liability by special contracts whether reasonable or not. Again there is nothing

---

[80] Ibid., at 64, citing *Van Toll* v. *South Eastern Railway* (1862) 31 L.J.C.P. 241; *Hyde* v. *Trent and Mersey Navigation Company* (1793) 5 T.R. 389 [101 E.R. 218]; *Chapman* v. *Great Western Railway Co.* (1880) 5 Q.B.D. 278.

[81] Ibid., at 64, citing *Peek* v. *North Staffordshire Railway Company* (1863) 10 H.L. 473; *Shaw* v. *Great Western Railway Co.* [1894] 1 Q.B. 373; *Duckham Brothers* v. *Great Western Railway Co.* (1899) 80 L.T. 774.

[82] Ibid., at 64. See *Weir* v. *Victorian Railways Commission* (1919) V.L.R. 454.

[83] Ibid., at 65, citing *Widgee Shire Council* v. *Bonney* (1901) 4 C.L.R., at 983; *Jones* v. *Metropolitan Meat Industry Board* (1923) 37 C.L.R., at 260-262.

[84] Ibid., at 65.

in the Act which prevents members of the public from relieving the
Commissioner of the duty of care imposed upon him by the provisions
of s. 36. The duty is imposed for the benefit of such persons, but it
is not an absolute duty. But the Commissioner, I would again say,
cannot refuse to perform his duty under the Act by insisting upon a
limitation of liability in the matter of carriage that is unreasonable
in the sense that it is arbitrary and capricious. And it is for the Court
to determine whether the contract or condition imposed is or is not
reasonable.[85]

Commonwealth railways: general provisions

Since the Commonwealth and States' Railway Commissioners (or Boards)
are common carriers it follows that what has been said earlier about the
common law duties and liabilities of common carriers applies to the
carriage of goods (including luggage) by rail in Australia. All the States
have their own Common Carriers and Railways Acts[86] which will be
discussed, together with the relevant regulations, at a later point. It is
useful, at this juncture, to look at the legislation and conditions governing
the carriage of goods (and luggage) by rail on the Commonwealth system.

The *Commonwealth Railways Act* 1917-1973[87] governs the construction
and management of Commonwealth railways and provision is made for
the Commissioner by arrangement with any State to connect the Commonwealth railways with any State railway or vice versa and to arrange
the running of Commonwealth or State trains or rolling stock over the
respective systems.[88] The Commissioner is deemed to be a common carrier
for the purposes of the Act[89] and is subject to their obligations and
privileges. However, the Commissioner may, with a view to preventing a
decrease of income by reason of loss of traffic on the railway, enter into a
contract with any person for the conveyance for a specified contractual
period of a proportion of goods of that person at a special rate or fixed
charge subject to a rebate or concession.[90] The Commissioner is also
empowered to make by-laws, not inconsistent with the Act governing,
inter alia, the working of the railways, the maintenance of order, the
disposal of unclaimed goods and the limitation of the liability of, and
the conditions governing the making of claims upon, the Commissioner

---

85 At 66-67. Starke J. held the clause in question to be a valid condition of the
contract between the appellant and the Commissioner. The provision incorporated
in the contract that the Commissioner would not be liable for goods stolen from
or adjacent to the wharf was valid and not inconsistent with s. 36 as
the fault was neither negligence nor delay on the part of the Commissioner.
Starke J. also stated he assumed that the provision in clause 12 related to the
carriage of goods within the meaning of s. 36. However, the book of conditions, Part 6, suggested that goods lying on or adjacent to the wharf were
not received by the Commissioner as a carrier, but rather as a wharfinger; if
this were so all possible inconsistency between cl. 12 and s. 36 disappeared.
86 *Commonwealth Railways Act* 1917-1973, s. 34; *Government Railways Act*
1912-1957, s. 33 (New South Wales); *Railways Act* 1914-1964, s. 101(4)
(Queensland); *South Australian Railways Commissioner's Act* 1936, s. 100
(South Australia); *Railway Management Act* 1935-1955, s. 15 (Tasmania);
Railways Act 1958, s. 4 (Victoria); *Government Railways Act* 1904-1972, s.
37(3) (Western Australia); *Seat of Government Railway Act* 1928-1973 (A.C.T.)
87 Ibid.
88 Ibid., s. 32.
89 Ibid., s. 34.
90 Ibid., s. 30A.

in respect of loss or damage to goods.[91] Such by-laws have no force until approval by the Governor-General, and published in the *Gazette*; such by-laws are not deemed to be Statutory Rules within the meaning of the *Rules Publication Act* 1903-1916.[92] No person is allowed to send, or offer for conveyance on any railway, goods which are of a dangerous nature in the judgement of the Commissioner or his officers without either marking the goods on the outside of the package or giving notice to the employee to whom the goods are delivered.[93]

The Commonwealth Railways conditions for the carriage of goods lay down the rules governing carriage of goods on interstate railways (referred to as the inter-system).[94] All inter-system traffic is carried subject to the Commonwealth goods rates book and the Railways Acts and by-laws in force on each system to which carriage extends. Each of the Commissioners (that it, of each State) contracts on its own behalf for carriage on the system which it operates and in respect of carriage beyond that system, as an agent for the Commissioners of the other States operating each other system to which the carriage will extend. Every contract for inter-system carriage of goods, including any contract covered by special arrangement to which the Railways Act and by-laws apply, is deemed to be entered into on the basis that each of the Commissioners its servants and agents, shall have the benefit of the provisions of such contract for inter-system carriage and they will have no lesser or greater liability to any person claiming in respect of a consignment than that which the Commissioner who accepted it for carriage would have.[95]

All traffic for interstate destinations, charged at goods rates, are carried at the risk of the Commissioners provided it is tendered in good order and condition, checked at originating and destination stations by the Commissioners' employees, legibly and clearly addressed[96] and conforming to regulation packing requirements.[97] Otherwise traffic is accepted for carriage at owner's risk whereby the sender undertakes or agrees to relieve the Commissioners from all liability in respect of loss, detention, injury, delay or damage even if this occurs before, during or after carriage except on proof of wilful misconduct of the Commissioners or their employees.[98] However, goods classified as "explosives" and "goods of a dangerous nature" are accepted only at owner's risk and subject to the conditions for such goods as published in each system's goods rates book.[99] The Commissioners are not liable for injury to or loss of specified articles of over $50 in value unless at the time of delivery to the station or warehouse for carriage the value and nature of the articles or property

[91] Ibid., s. 88(1).
[92] Ibid., ss. 88(2), 88(3).
[93] Ibid., s. 70; penalty for breach, $100.
[94] Goods Rates Book (Uniform Classification, Rates and Conditions for Inter-system Goods Traffic) effective from 1 July 1973.
[95] Ibid., Condition 1.
[96] See Condition 10.
[97] See pp. 7-11 of the Goods Rates Book.
[98] Condition 2(a), and see above regarding wilful misconduct.
[99] Condition 2(b).

is declared by the person sending or delivering them and the increased rate payable has been paid to and accepted by an authorised employee.[1]

The interstate system raises questions of special liability which have been considered in the English cases. In *White* v. *South Eastern Railway*,[2] it was held that if a person books goods through by one railway company for a journey over more than one line of railway, he may, in a case of damage to the goods on any part of the journey, sue the company that booked the goods. Additionally, he may also sue the other company concerned if the damage occurs upon their line and due to their negligence, but not otherwise.

The liability of the South Australian Railways Commissioner for misconduct was considered in *White* v. *South Australian Railways Commissioner*.[3] In that case goods were delivered to the defendant to be consigned to the plaintiff "care A. H. Landseer, Morgan". Landseer had a river steamship which traded to Morgan. The clerk of the defendants in making out the consignment note omitted the above words. The goods on arrival at Morgan, because of this omission, were handed to a steamship belonging to a different owner. This ship was sunk and part of the goods were lost. The goods were carried at "owner's risk", which relieved the defendant from liability for loss or damage unless this arose through misconduct.[4] In applying *Forder's* case, Murray C.J. held that the defendants' clerk made an unintentional slip and there was no indication of conscious wrongdoing.[5] Liability for loss in respect of goods caused at owner's risk arose in *A. Abrahams & Sons Pty. Ltd.* v. *Commissioner for Railways*[6] and an interesting point of alternative remedy in tort was dealt with by the Supreme Court of New South Wales. In *Abrahams'* case the plaintiff consigned certain goods under a contract of carriage with the defendant company in 1952. In June 1953 a notice was served on the defendant by the plaintiff giving notice of intention to sue for damages of breach of contract on the grounds that the goods did not arrive at their destination. An action was commenced in the Supreme Court in July 1953 and almost a year later the plaintiff sought to amend the declaration, but leave was refused. The action was discontinued in February 1955 which was out of time in any case under s.143 of the *Government Railways Act* (*N.S.W.*) 1912-1951. By letter of August 1954 the plaintiff demanded the return of certain goods (some of which were referred to in the first action). In September 1954 he then gave notice to the defendants of an intention to commence an action in detinue, and a writ was issued accordingly in March 1954. On the hearing of the case stated, the Court was asked whether the plaintiff was prevented

---

[1] Condition 2(c); the list includes inter alia, coins of the realm or any foreign state, precious stones, jewellery, watches, clocks, bank notes, title deeds, gold and silver plate, television sets, china, furs, lace and opium; tin trays are not expressly included.
[2] (1885) 1 T.L.R. 391 (D.C.); see also *Coxan* v. *Great Western Railway Co.* (1860) L.J. Ex. 165. See generally *English & Empire Digest*, pp. 30-32.
[3] [1919] S.A.L.R. 44.
[4] Ibid., see above.
[5] Ibid., p. 50.
[6] [1958] S.R. (N.S.W.) 134; 75 W.N. (N.S.W.) 41; *United Australia Ltd.* v. *Barclays Bank Ltd.* [1941] A.C. 1, p. 30, applied.

by the original notice and commencement of the first action from bringing the action in detinue. It was held by Roper C.J. and Clancy J. (Owen J. dissenting) that on the breach of contract the plaintiff did not have to elect between inconsistent rights, but could properly treat the breach as bringing the contract to an end and then had alternative remedies in respect of it: i.e. to sue for damages or for detention. The action in detinue depended on wrongful detention by the defendant, not upon the construed operation of any terms of the contract of carriage. Detention is a wrong that is independent of contract and the remedies are alternative; no question of election arises until one or the other claim has been brought to judgement.

Delivery of goods will entitle the carrier to payment and in *Hunt* v. *Barber*[7] the consignee requested delivery at an intermediate place. In this case goods had been shipped to Wagga Wagga from Echuca but the barge on which the goods were shipped went aground at Narandera and on notice from the plaintiff that they could not move the goods until the river rose the defendants took the goods at Narandera and carried them by land to Wagga Wagga, signing the bill of lading of the plaintiff without protest. The defendants claimed they were not bound to pay the plaintiff in full as he had not been prevented from delivering to Wagga Wagga by any of the excepted perils and was not entitled to full freight. On appeal from Melbourne County Court the Victorian Supreme Court held that as the defendants had chosen to take the goods at Narandera and signed the unconditional bill of lading then once that receipt had been given the carrier was entitled to recover the freight, as the return of the receipted bill of lading was evidence of due delivery under the contract.[8]

The question of notice in special contracts has arisen in Australian carriage cases although in *McWhinnie* v. *Union Steamship Company of New Zealand*[9] the liability at issue was not that of a rail carrier but a shipowner. Briefly, in *McWhinnies* case the plaintiff made an oral arrangement with the defendant company for the shipping of three horses from Sydney to New Zealand with nothing said about conditions limiting the defendant's liability. Due to defects in the defendant's lifting tackle one horse was killed. The receipt when given stated the horses were to be carried at owner's risk and on the reverse that shipping, carrying and landing of livestock was at owner's risk. It was held that the terms of this contract were not binding on the plaintiff as they were not entered into until after the horse was killed.

The issue of fundamental breach has not been raised specifically in any case dealing with carriage by rail as such, but judicial decisions in Australia are elsewhere considered and thus, apart from what has been said earlier in this study touching the carrier operating within the four corners of the contract, reference may be made to this topic dealt with separately.[10]

---

[7] (1887) 3 V.L.R. (L) 189.
[8] Ibid., per Stawell C.J. at 193.
[9] (1887) 9 N.S.W.R. L.R. 1.
[10] See Chapter 25 (Exclusion Clauses) and in particular *Thomas Nationwide Transport (Melbourne) Pty. Ltd. and Pay* v. *May & Baker (Australia) Pty.*

The question of reasonableness in a contract of carriage by rail has been extensively explored in the Australian High Court decision in *Commissioner for Railways (N.S.W.)* v. *Quinn.*[11] It has been suggested in English courts that as a matter of common law a judge might delete a wholly unreasonable term from a contract[12] although there is no authority directly in point and the weight of judicial opinion is against such a contention.[13] In *Quinn's* case power to delete an unreasonable clause from a contract of carriage was expressly given by statute to the judiciary, and duly exercised. A contract between the appellant and the respondent, Mrs. Quinn, for the carriage of her goods from Coolah Railway station to St Leonard's railway was made subject to the *Government Railways Act* 1912 as amended, and the provisions of by-laws, regulations and conditions published under the Act and to the terms and consignment note signed by Mrs. Quinn. A by-law incorporated contained (inter alia) two conditions: (1) that a claim for loss or damage to goods tendered for conveyance by rail would not be allowed unless lodged in writing with the Commissioner within fourteen days after the date when delivery was or should have been given; (2) that the Commissioner did not guarantee the arrival or delivery of any goods at any particular time and that he did not undertake to advise the consignor of the arrival of the goods or that delivery had not been taken. The goods were consigned at "Commissioner's risk" rates, were lost and Mrs Quinn failed to lodge her claim in writing within fourteen days.

On appeal from the Supreme Court of New South Wales the High Court held that the by-law containing the condition requiring claims for loss or damage to be lodged within fourteen days was not invalidated through the failure of the Commissioner to exhibit it on railway stations and other places in accordance with ss.66 and 67 of the *Government Railways Act.* It was further held that the condition was not just and reasonable and therefore contrary to the provisions of s.9(a) of the *Common Carriers' Act* 1902 (N.S.W.) and thus invalid.[14] Additionally the Court ruled that despite the fact that the goods were tendered to the owner's agent the Commissioner, in the circumstances of the case, remained a common carrier in respect of the goods of which delivery had not been taken and was not a bailee for their safekeeping.[15] The judgment of Dixon J. is of particular interest and his arguments are

---

Ltd. [1967] A.L.R. 3; [1966] 2 Lloyd's Rep. 347; *Bergl (Australia) Ltd.* v. *Moxon Lighterage Co. Ltd.* (1920) 28 C.L.R. 194.

11 (1946) 72 C.L.R. 345.
12 See the views of Bramwell L.J. in *Parker* v. *South Eastern Railway Co.* (1887) 2 C.P.D. 416, at 428; *John Lee & Son (Grantham) Ltd.* v. *Railway Executive,* [1949] 2 All E.R. 581, at 584; Lord Denning's observations in *Bonsor* v. *Musicians' Union* [1954] Ch. 479 at p. 485; on deletion of unreasonable terms from a contract see generally, Cheshire and Fifoot, *Law of Contract* (3rd Australian ed. 1974), pp. 139-140; but cf. p. 928 et seq., post (exclusion clauses); *Unfair Contract Terms Act* 1977.
13 See in particular the observations of Lord Haldane V.C., in the Privy Council case of *Grand Rail Truck Co. of Canada* v. *Robinson* [1915], at 747-748; Barton J. in *Hirsh* v. *Zinc Corporation Ltd.* (1917), 24 C.L.R. 34, at 52.
14 (1946) 72 C.L.R. 345, per Rich, Starke, Dixon and McTiernan JJ., Williams J. dissenting.
15 Ibid., per Rich, Starke, Dixon and McTiernan JJ., Williams J. dissenting.

worth reproducing fully.[16] In the learned judge's view the considerations which told against the justice and reasonableness of the limitation were as follows:

1. It requires the claim to be in writing and treats an oral claim as useless, even though it had been entertained and investigated by the Commissioner. Many consignees, expecting the arrival of articles despatched by railway, would be likely to make inquiries and then complain at the railway station, but it would not occur to them to reduce a claim to writing until the station staff had rejected it.

2. There was no definite time from which the period of fourteen days limited in the case of loss in transit begins to run. The long distances over which goods may be conveyed and the variable Conditions affecting railway transportation in Australia make it very difficult for a consignee to make up his mind when he should treat failure of the goods to arrive as a reason for inferring their loss. The consignors may not advise the consignees promptly or at all of the despatch of goods. Much of the goods traffic carried is for consignors and consignees outside the course of routine and organized business. The difficulty of being sure either of the meaning or the application of the expression "fourteen days after that date when delivery should have been given" led the respondent to contend that the provision was void for uncertainty, at all events if considered as a by-law. That it is an extreme contention, but the difficulty has a real bearing on the reasonableness and justice of the clause in the conditions prevailing in Australia.

3. The necessity of giving notice is a thing of which many consignees would be unaware. The voluminous pamphlet in which it is contained would be in the hands of relatively few and of these not many could be expected to discover the clause. Non-fulfilment of the condition is fatal, and the ordinary man would not give notice in writing instinctively unless he knew that he was required to do so.

4. The condition forms part of the Commissioner's risk contract. It is not part of the protection for which the Commissioner bargains in consideration of giving a reduced rate. There is no alternative offered. The consignor paying the higher rate in order to secure the greatest protection he can for the goods can obtain no better contract and finds that the Commissioner escapes liability unless notice in writing is given within fourteen days of a hypothetically ascertained date. The fact that the clause forms part of the Commissioner's risk conditions is perhaps the most important consideration.

These arguments grounded not on a theoretical view of contract but on a practical analysis of the real problems raised would serve, it is submitted, as an admirable basis of assessing contracts where the parties are not of equal bargaining power; it is to the railway carriage cases dealing with a common carrier's liability to his customers that one can profitably look for the source of an evolving doctrine of contractual equality.

Finally, in dealing with the role of the Commonwealth in rail carriage it should be noted that the Commonwealth has entered into various statutory agreements with the States for the financing and operating of State railway systems. One example is the *Railway Agreement (Queensland) Act* 1961 which provides for financial advances to that

[16] Ibid., at 376-377.

State for specific line improvement;[17] similar agreements have been made for the construction of new lines within States and for the standardization of rail gauges.[18] The most significant development recently has been the enactment of Commonwealth and State legislation to secure the taking over the Tasmanian and South Australian railways by the Commonwealth.[19] It remains to be seen whether this policy will be extended.

In concluding this part of the study dealing with carriage of goods by rail in Australia it is necessary to look at the individual States' legislation and the regulations made thereunder governing each railway system. Although the bulk of goods carried by rail in Australia are carried by the inter-system discussed above the picture would be incomplete without a consideration of the relevant law in each State of the Commonwealth.

VI. New South Wales

The general conditions for the carriage of goods by rail in New South Wales are set out in the Merchandise and Livestock Rates book[20] which are adopted by by-laws made under the *Government Railways Act 1912-1957* by virtue of the *Public Transport Commission Act, 1972.*[21]

Under the *Government Railways Act* the Commissioners are given the duty of carrying persons, animals and goods without negligence or delay and in respect of such carriage are common carriers.[22] The Commissioners are not permitted to afford or give any undue or unreasonable preference or advantage to any particular person, or to any particular description of traffic; similarly they must not subject any person or traffic to any undue or unreasonable prejudice or advantage[23] and must provide reasonable proper and equal facilities for the interchange of traffic between the lines under their control and receiving, forwarding and delivering of goods and passengers, subject to the provisions of the Act.[24] The Commissioners are also empowered to make by-laws[25] and expressly for fixing fares and charges for goods, livestock, passengers and parcels and regulating the terms and conditions on which goods, livestock,

---

17 See also the *Railway Agreement (Queensland) Act* 1968; the *Railway Agreement (Tasmania) Act* 1971; the *Railway Agreement (Western Australia) Act* 1961-1971; the *Railway Equipment (South Australia) Act* 1961; *Railways (South Australia) Agreement Act* 1926.

18 See the *Railway Agreement (New South Wales and South Australia) Act* 1968; *Railway Standardisation (New South Wales and Victoria) Agreement Act* 1958 (Sydney-Melbourne line); *Railway Standardization (South Australia) Agreement Act* 1949.

19 *Railways (Tasmania) Act* (Cmwlth) (No. 70 of 1975); *Railways (Transfer to Commonwealth) Act* 1975 (Tasmania) (No. 35 of 1975); *Railways (South Australia) Act* 1975 (Cmwlth) (No. 60 of 1975); *Railway (Transfer Agreement) Act* (South Australia) 1975 (No. 60 of 1975).

20 Issued by the Public Transport Commission of New South Wales Rail Division effective from 1st July, 1973; a Passenger Fares and Coaching Rates Book was issued at the same time.

21 Ibid., by-law 1, 273.

22 Ibid., s. 33.

23 Ibid., s. 35.

24 Ibid., s. 36.

25 Ibid., s. 64(1).

parcels or passengers' luggage will be collected, received or delivered.[26] *Quinn's* case has already been discussed in relation to the reasonableness of a by-law made under the Act.[27]

The General Conditions for the Carriage of Merchandise (hereinafter referred to as the General Conditions) provide that all traffic is carried under the legislation and by-laws mentioned in the introductory paragraph and that in the case of any traffic consigned to or from any place outside New South Wales this shall be carried under and subject to the inter-system traffic rates and conditions which may be applied,[28] in other circumstances the railway Acts and by-laws of each system apply. In the event of conflict between the inter-system traffic rates and conditions and similar State provision the inter-system rates and conditions will prevail.

The General Conditions reproduce the corresponding sections of the Commonwealth Conditions for inter-system carriage concerning benefit by the Commissioners from inter-system contracts of carriage and the Commission disclaimer of liability conforms to that already noted under the inter-system carriage regulations.[29]

The Commission states it will not be liable, without negligence on its part, for:

(a) Loss or misdelivery of any goods improperly or insufficiently marked, directed or described, nor for loss of, or damage to, any goods which are insufficiently or improperly packed or secured; nor will it be responsible for any loss or damage occurring to goods consisting of a variety of articles in the same package liable by breakage to damage each other or other articles, or arising from leakage due to bad vessels or bad cooperage, or to fermentation.

(b) Damage to any articles of a fragile or brittle nature, such as marble ornaments or statuary, musical instruments, furniture or toys, which are more than ordinarily hazardous, unless properly packed and protected. Furniture and fragile articles simply covered with canvas, etc., or if in frail skeleton frames, will be regarded as unprotected. Except where specially authorised, parcels packed in paper will not be accepted for transit by goods trains.

(c) Damage to fruit, fish, meat, poultry, game and other perishable articles arising from the perishable nature of such articles, or from the same not being taken away forthwith on notice to consignees of arrival at the destination station.

(d) The quantity or condition of goods loaded or unloaded by the consignor or consignee at private sidings, unattended stations or sidings, or stations or sidings in charge of women.

(e) Any loss, damage, injury, misdelivery or delay in the delivery of goods which may have been occasioned by flood, storm, tempest, strikes, lock-outs or industrial disputes or other unforeseen cause; nor will it be liable for any loss, damage, injury, misdelivery or delay in

---

26 Ibid., s. 64(1), (1a).
27 See ante; see also *Chief Commissioner for Railways* v. *Great Cobar Ltd.* (1911) 11 S.R. 65; 28 W.N. 21; regarding by-law dealing with application for trucks; owner's risk rate, see *Hicks* v. *Commissioner for Railways* (1957) S.R. (N.S.W.) 449; 74 W.N. 230.
28 Ibid. Condition 1; Railways of Australia Uniform Classification, Rates and Conditions; s. 24A of the *Government Railways Act,* ibid. See ante.
29 See ante.

connection with the receipt, carriage or delivery of goods unless occasioned by the neglect or default of the Commission.

(f) Any loss or injury to any articles, goods, or things put into wrappers, boxes, packages, cases, or baskets, marked, described, returned, delivered or represented as "Empties".[30]

Where goods are carried at the Commission's risk rate the Commission, subject to the *Government Railway Act,* as amended, and the by-laws, regulations and conditions published thereunder, takes the ordinary risk and liability of a common carrier; where goods are carried at the owner's risk rate, the Commission takes no liability or responsibility for loss, detention, damage, injury, misdelivery or delay whatsoever and howsoever caused. Alternative rates for carriage at owner's risk are laid down in the General Conditions and items specified that will be carried at Commission's risk, all other goods being carried at owner's risk.[31] The Commission does not guarantee time of arrival or delivery of any goods (perishable or otherwise) on any particular train or for any particular market nor undertakes to advise consignees of arrival of goods nor that consignor's delivery of goods has not been taken. In consequence of non-receipt of notice no exemption from demurrage, storage or risk of loss or damage will be allowed.[32]

In the case of consignees refusing to receive goods these will not be returned to the sending station until instructions have been received from the consignor, who will, if possible, be advised of the refusal. If such goods are likely to deteriorate, or it is considered that their value is less than the freight and other charges, such charges must be prepaid before the goods will be accepted for return transit.[33] The Commission has power of sale of goods not claimed or removed by owners; in the case of agricultural produce and goods likely to deteriorate these may be sold immediately; for other goods, except empties, these may be sold after two calendar months.[34]

VII. QUEENSLAND

Carriage of goods by rail in Queensland in subject to the *Railways Act* (1914-1972) and the Railways Goods Traffic By-laws issued under the Act.[35] The Commissioner of Railways is entitled to the protection and privilege of a common carrier;[36] he is entitled in the making of special contracts to limit his liability to any extent and manner.[37] Liability of the Commissioner is limited similarly as in New South Wales with an added qualification that the Commissioner shall not be liable if the neglect or

---

[30] Ibid., Condition 3.
[31] Including goods classified under manure, coal, miscellaneous, A. B and C classes and agricultural produce of all kinds; see General Conditions, Condition 4.
[32] Condition 6.
[33] Condition 9.
[34] Condition 29.
[35] By-law No. 1038, issued by Queensland Railways under s. 133 of Act; effective 1st July, 1973.
[36] Section 120.
[37] Section 101(4).

default of an officer or officers of the Department is associated with any strike or industrial dispute.[38] Claims for detention, loss of or damage to or non-delivery of any consignment of goods, parcels, traffic, livestock or passengers' luggage offered for conveyance will not be allowed unless lodged in writing within thirty days after the date when the consignment was offered.[39] Goods carried at owner's risk are indicated[40] and the usual provisions apply. Under the by-law relating to goods and livestock, additionally, the Commissioner is not liable for loss of, or injury to, goods safely carried to the place consigned after notice of arrival has been given to the consignee; no undertaking is given to advise consignees of arrival except to suit the Department's convenience.[41] Unclaimed goods (except dangerous or perishable goods) may be sold by the Commissioner, if unclaimed by the owner, in such manner as the Commissioner thinks fit three months after arrival. In the case of livestock, where the consignee has refused delivery, or other causes, the Commissioner may sell twenty-four hours after arrival.[42] All perishable goods not removed within twelve working hours after arrival at the station to which they are consigned, or refused by consignee, may be sold by auction or otherwise. The Commissioner may destroy goods which become offensive or dangerous to health.[43] Carriage of luggage is dealt with in great detail and conveyed on condition that it is open to inspection by any duly authorised employee of the Commissioner.[44]

VIII. SOUTH AUSTRALIA

The *South Australian Railways Commissioner's Act* 1936-1974 governs the carriage of goods within that State; by the Act the Commissioner for Railways has no greater liability than that of a common carrier and is subject to the *Carriers Act (South Australia)* 1891 and any by-law governing conditions of carriage of goods.[45] The Commissioner is empowered to make special conditions for receiving, forwarding, or delivering any horse, cattle, or other animals, and any articles, goods or things.[46] Disclaimer of liability is similar to that appertaining in New South Wales and alternative rates are offered at Commissioner's or owner's risk.[47] Time of arrival and delivery of goods is not guaranteed in terms similar to those already noted in respect of New South Wales.[48]

38 Condition 7; Goods and Livestock Rates.
39 Condition 9; but see *Quinn's* case, ante.
40 Condition 18; subject to Condition 12 and 59(a) of the Goods and Livestock Rates all goods of classes M, AP, A and B in Schedule 1 of the Rates, and all goods lower than Class 1 are carried at owner's risk.
41 Condition 30.
42 Condition 32.
43 Condition 41.
44 Perusal of this section of the Goods and Livestock Rates Book gives great insight into the minds of those who draft such regulations; within the free luggage allowance is included, inter alia dentists' equipment, masonic regalia and drovers' gear (provided this does not exceed the luggage allowance).
45 Section 100. Power to make by-laws is given under s. 133.
46 Section 98(1).
47 See Conditions 5(a) and (b).
48 See *White's* case above regarding delivery; the court approved a definition of misconduct cited in Vol. 7 of the *South Australian Statutes*, p. 692.

As already noted the South Australian government has enacted legislation transferring the administration and financial running of railways in the State to the Commonwealth government. The *Railways (Transfer Agreement) Act* 1975 provides for the acquisition of the administration, maintainence and operation of the railways services vested in the South Australia Railways Commission to be transferred to Commonwealth Parliament.[49]

IX. TASMANIA

Carriage of goods by rail in Tasmania is governed by the *Railways Management Act* 1935, the *Common Carriers Act* 1874 and by-laws and regulations made under the former statute. The *Common Carriers Act* states that every railway company shall be liable for loss or injury to horses, cattle or other animals, articles, goods or things in receiving, forwarding or delivering them caused by the neglect or fault of the company or its servants and such liability cannot be validly contracted out it. However, conditions for the receiving, forwarding and delivering of such items can be made provided these are found just and reasonable by the Court or judge before whom any question concerning them is brought.[50] The Act limits damages recoverable for loss or injury to any horse, cattle, sheep or pigs unless a value has been declared above the statutory limit.[51] By the *Railways Management Act* the Commissioner is deemed to be a common carrier[52] but is empowered to fix higher rates for the carriage of certain goods at the Commission's risk than for carriage of such goods at owner's risk and may determine that certain goods shall be carried at owner's risk only.[53] Where goods are carried without charge, the Commission take no liability or responsibility for any loss, detention, injury, damage, non-delivery, misdelivery, or delay, whatsoever, and however occasioned. The Commission is empowered to make by-laws for the management of the railways and to enter into any special contract with any person for the custody, carriage, or delivery of goods upon such conditions as it thinks fit.[54] All claims for loss or damage in respect of custody, carriage or delivery of goods must be made in writing to the Commission within twenty-one days of such loss or damage.[55]

Where any goods delivered to be carried along or upon the railway have been carried to their agreed destination the Commission is only liable as a bailee for custody in respect of any loss or damage to the goods after eight hours from their arrival.[56] The Commission will not be

---

[49] Section 10; construction of new railways by either the State Commission or the Commonwealth are limited by s. 11.

[50] Section 13.

[51] The limits under the Act are: a horse, $100, neat cattle, $30, sheep and pigs, per head $4.

[52] Section 15.

[53] Sections 19(2), 19(1).

[54] Sections 22(1), 23; see General Conditions of Carriage Transport Commission at p. 34, cl. 26.

[55] Section 25.

[56] Section 89.

liable for loss or injury to articles declared special goods exceeding $20 unless the value has been declared and the charges paid and accepted.[57]

The Commission is given power of sale of goods in default of payment of rates or charges demanded after fourteen days and goods left by the owner (or where the person liable for charges is not known) may be sold within one month of the Commissioner giving public notification of sale.[58]

General conditions for the carriage of goods at inter-system distance rates between Melbourne and Tasmania are laid down in the Railways of Australia Goods Rates Book.[59] All inter-system traffic to Tasmania (except from Victorian stations) is carried subject to the conditions already outlined as applicable to the mainland systems. In respect of such traffic from Tasmania to mainland destinations this will be covered by insurance subject to exceptions listed.[60] All goods subject to the *Railway Management Act* and the *Transport Act* 1938 (Tasmania) are governed by the following conditions. The Transport Commission gives notice that all goods are consigned at Commission's risk with a limit of $20,000 per consignment recoverable; this is subject to the provisions of the two State Acts above and with the exception of dangerous goods, explosives and special goods. Such goods are carried at owner's risk and the Commission accepts no liability for loss, injury, damage, non-delivery, delay, detention or other happening whatsoever, other than that caused by wilful misconduct on the part of servants of the Commission.

Goods not properly packed in accordance with trade conditions or Transport Commission requirements are consigned and carried at owner's risk. The Commission disclaims liability for (a) any loss or damage of the goods; and (b) for inherent vice or loss or damage consequent on delay or loss of market; and (c) for loss or damage directly or indirectly resulting from war, invasion, acts of foreign enemies, hostilities, etc., confiscation, nationalization, requisition or destruction of or damage to by property by or under government or local authority order.

As in the case of South Australia responsibility for running and managing railways in Tasmania has now been passed to the Commonwealth government under the *Railways (Transfer to Commonwealth) Act* 1975.

A recent Tasmanian case should be noted. In *Phillip Morris (Australia) Ltd. v. Transport Commission*[61] a cigarette maker wishing to send cigarettes from Melbourne to Burnie employed Ansett Freight Express for this purpose. That organization employed the Transport Commission to carry the goods from Devonport, as they were entitled to do under their contract. The Commission placed the goods in a shed at Burnie railway station, into which thieves broke at night and the cigarettes were stolen. The contract between Ansett Freight Express and Phillip Morris

---

[57] Sections 27(1), 28.
[58] See Part II of the General Conditions of Carriage: Transport Commission, p. 31, cl. 4.
[59] See above; specifically p. 31 of the Rates Book.
[60] See Rates Book, p. 43.
[61] [1975] Tas. S.R. 128; Tasmanian Supreme Court (Serial No. 66/1975) before Nettlefold J.

protected Ansett from liability for any damage including injury, delay or
loss of any kind arising out of or incidental to the carriage or ancillary
services occurring after delivery to the carrier and before delivery to the
consignee; this would apply whether due to misconduct or negligence on
the part of the carrier. By the last section the contract attempted to
protect the Transport Commission. The Supreme Court of Tasmania held,
on an action by Phillip Morris against the Transport Commission, that:
(a) the plaintiff was not a party to the Commission's contract of carriage
at owner's risk; (b) the Commission was bailee for reward for the
plaintiff's goods; (c) having lost the goods it was liable unless it showed
that the loss occurred without its fault and it had not been able to do so;
(d) it could not be implied for the Commission's benefit that Phillip
Morris had impliedly consented to Ansett Freight Express' contract with
it.[62]

X. VICTORIA

By the *Railways Act* 1958 the Victorian Railways Board is deemed to be
a common carrier.[63] Accordingly, the carriage of goods is effected on the
basis of the ordinary liability of a common carrier and carriage is at
Board's risk. The Board has power to make conditions for receiving,
forwarding and delivering any horses, cattle, sheep or pigs or other
animals or any goods; these conditions are subject to a just and reasonable test similar to that in the Tasmanian legislation.[64] The Board also
has power to make special contracts for the carriage inter alia of goods
and livestock;[65] as well as by-laws under the Act.[66] Where goods are
carried at owner's risk; where the consignor prefers a lower rate or where
goods are not properly packed, the Board is only liable for wilful
misconduct on the part of its servants. The Act also provides for
arrangements to be made with the Commissioner for Railways in New
South Wales for reciprocal running of trains and rolling stock of either
State over each States' rail system.[67] Liability for loss after transit is

---

[62] The decision of Nettlefold J. followed *Cosgrove* v. *Horsfall* (1945) 62 T.L.R.
140; *L. Harris (Harella) Ltd.* v. *Continental Express Ltd.* 1961, 1 Lloyd's Rep.
251 and *Lee Cooper Ltd.* v. *C. M. Jeakins & Sons Ltd.* (1964) 1 Lloyd's L.R.
300 but declined to follow the dictum of Denning M.R., in *Morris* v. *C. W.
Martin & Sons* [1966] 1 Q.B. 716, at 729-730. *Satterthwaite's* case, ibid., was
not cited to the learned judge by counsel; *Wilson* v. *Darling Island Stevedoring
& Lighterage Co. Ltd.* (1956) 95 C.L.R. 43; particularly, Fullagar J. at 66 67,
70, was cited with *Scruttons Ltd.* v. *Midland Silicones Ltd.* [1962] A.C. 46;
Gillespie Bros. & Co. Ltd. v. *Bowles Transport* [1973] 1 Lloyd's L.R. 10 at
p. 14 and *Jeakin's* case as authorities for upholding the doctrine of privity of
contract thus barring the attempt of Ansett Freight Express from conferring
the benefit of the exemptions on its servants and sub-contractors including the
Transport Commission. With respect, the decision of Nettlefold J. does little to
assist sound commercial practice and valid business considerations; a more
detailed criticism is offered at p. 1005 et seq., post.
[63] Section 4. By the *Carriers and Innkeepers' Act* a common carrier shall not be
liable for loss of enumerated articles which exceed $20.00 in value unless
their value is declared and an increased charge paid.
[64] Section 7.
[65] Section 83(3).
[66] Section 137; see by-law No. 351; see also *Weir* v. *Railways Commissioner*
[1919] V.L.R. 459; *Lang* v. *Thomson* (1890) 16 V.L.R. 655.
[67] Section 82.

restricted in that once goods have been conveyed and unloaded at their destination the Board is only liable as a bailee for custody in respect of any damage or loss to the goods.[68] Power of sale and detention of animals and goods arises on failure by any person to pay rates or charges on demand; no time limit is set, nor any limitation placed on notice and manner of sale.[69] A limit of $50 is set on the Board's liability in respect of passenger's luggage unless a higher value is declared.

In *John F. Goulding Pty. Ltd.* v. *Victorian Railway Commissioners*[70] the plaintiff delivered corn sacks to be carried by rail by the defendants and then be redelivered on the plaintiff's order. The goods were safely carried to their destination, but after discharge they were removed or delivered by persons, none of whom was the owner or authorized by him to receive them. The plaintiff demanded the goods and as the defendants had parted with them, effectively the demand was refused. Six months after the loss the plaintiff brought an action in detinue. The defendants relied on the *Railways Act* 1928 which provided that all actions brought against the Commissioners should be commenced within six months after the act complained of was committed.[71] The High Court, on appeal from the Supreme Court of Victoria, held that the act complained of in the Act referred to the cause of action sued upon; more importantly, that, notwithstanding the previous loss of the goods by the defendants, a new cause of action in detinue arose on their failure to deliver the goods at the request of the plaintiff.

XI. Western Australia

Carriage of goods in Western Australia is governed by the *Government Railways Act* 1904-1972 under which the Commission is a common carrier.[72] Power is given to the Commission to make by-laws and such by-laws are deemed to be part of the contract between the Commission and the consignor or owner of the goods.[73] Special agreements may be made insuring the Commission against all liability for all loss and damage from any cause and special contracts may[74] also be made in respect of carriage of goods or livestock. The Commission accepts no liability in respect of any goods left on railway premises before or after transit if they are left or deemed to be left at the risk of the person leaving them or by the owner or consignee.[75]

In the event of a person failing or refusing to pay charges for goods,

---

[68] Section 6(1).
[69] Section 12.
[70] (1932) 48 C.L.R. 157; *Wilkinson* v. *Verity* (1871) L.R. 6 C.P. 206 approved and applied. Cf. s. 3(1), *Limitation Act* 1939 (U.K.).
[71] Section 200, now repealed by the *Railways Act* 1958 (No. 6355) see *Victorian Statutes* 1958, Vol. VII, First Schedule, p. 511.
[72] Section 37(3).
[73] Sections 23, 24(6); see generally the General Conditions for Conveyance of Passengers, Parcels and Livestock, Local and Inter-system issued by the Western Australian Government Railways Commission, effective 1 July 1973.
[74] Sections 26-26A.
[75] Section 27.

these may be ordered to be sold after public notice, or, in case such goods have been delivered, any other goods on railway premises belonging to the same person may be ordered to be sold. A similar power of sale arises in the case of goods left on a railway and the owner or the person liable for the charges is not known. Perishable goods may be sold without notice and such goods causing an offence or creating a nuisance may be destroyed at the owner's expense.[76]

No liability will attach to the Commission for loss or damage to goods which are left at or consigned to any station, siding or stopping place marked in timetables on rates books as places where no officer is in charge.[77]

[76] Sections 31-32.
[77] Section 40.

CHAPTER 19

HIRE OF CHATTELS

The modern contract of hire is probably the most important and certainly the most versatile of contemporary bailments.[1] In its short-term aspect, it embraces almost every kind of chattel, from sun-lamps, deck-chairs, builders' requisites and cars, to clothing, taped music, films, books, glass-ware and even paintings or prints. On a long-term basis, it represents a valuable method of avoiding the legal consequences of sale, or credit-purchasing, while producing broadly similiar commercial effects; the hirer enjoys the indefinite use of the chattel for an instalment charge which is roughly scaled to the value of the goods and their expected life-span.[2] This aspect of hire is particularly prominent in the case of vehicles and other expensive equipment such as computers, television sets, fruit machines, juke boxes, neon-signs, industrial plant and photocopying devices. Its ultimate rationalisation is to be found in the finance lease,[3] which unquestionably constitutes a sale in all but name. In fact, the idea of using the contract of hire as a disguised contract of sale is not entirely novel; the practice (or an early version of it) was common among coster-mongers in the East End of London, who would hire their barrows on a weekly basis extending over many years.[4] Nowadays the bailment will often be accompanied by an agreement for ancillary services on the part of the bailor, such as maintenance, servicing and inspection.[5]

In view of the modern diversity of contracts of hire, it is unfortunate that in England neither the *Supply of Goods (Implied Terms) Act* 1973 nor the *Consumer Credit Act* 1974 attempts to clarify or strengthen the terms to be implied in such agreements. The *Unfair Contract* Terms Act 1977[6] aims to provide a substantial measure of control over exclusion clauses in contracts of hiring, but even here the opportunity to put the necessary terms in statutory language seems to have been beyond the

---

[1] For a useful account of the development and significance of chattel-hiring, see the Crowther Report on Consumer Credit (1971) Cmnd. 4596, para. 2.4.56 et seq.

[2] See Turner, "Avoidance of the Operation of the Australian Hire-Purchase Legislation and the Development of Alternative Instalment Credit Contracts" (1974) 48 A.L.J. 63 and 134.

[3] Defined by Crowther, op. cit., para. 1.2.14, as: "one in which the lessor recovers the total cost of the leased asset (including interest on capital) over the period of the lease, or rather, over that period for which a substantial rent is charged"; see further para. 5.2.7. Para. 1.2.14 of the Report also contains a useful description of the types of rental or hiring agreement currently in use in the commercial world.

[4] See Charles Booth, *London* (1971 edn.).

[5] An obvious example being the television rental, as to which see Crowther, op. cit. See also *Western Electric Co. (Australia) Ltd.* v. *Adams* (1933) 50 W.N. (N.S.W.) 197.

[6] Post, p. 952.

respective Law Commissions' acknowledged terms of reference.[7] It seems extraordinary that the implied terms in contracts of hire should be left to the operation of the Common Law, while in cases of sale, hire-purchase and instalment-buying generally there are sophisticated and progressive statutory definitions of the duties owed by the supplier. In this respect, both the Commonwealth *Trade Practices Act* 1974 and the South Australian *Consumer Transactions Act* 1972-1973[8] are a welcome development, which could be studied with advantage in England.

I. DEFINITION

Four principal qualities distinguish contracts of hire: the transfer of possession in a chattel, an authority in the bailee to use it for his benefit, an advantage or reward accruing to the bailor in return for this permission, and a promise by the hirer to redeliver the chattel at a stated or determinable time. From the first requirement it follows that there may be no bailment by way of hire where the chattel is leased with a servant who retains custody on behalf of his general employer,[9] or where it remains attached to the owner's premises in a place frequented by his servants.[10] Conversely, the fact that the chattel is subsequently attached to the bailee's land (or that the bailor's servants are bound to inspect or regulate it on occasions) does not necessarily negate the creation of a bailment. It has been held in New South Wales that the lease of furnished premises does not produce, with regard to the furniture, the relationship of lessor and hirer.[11] However, the tenant undoubtedly obtains possession of the furniture and, upon proof of damage, should carry the bailees normal burden of proof.

The bailor's reward need not be monetary; any mutual advantage in the use or delivery of the chattel can give rise to a transaction of hire. Thus, the bailor may owe the duties of a lessor for reward when he delivers a machine to expedite work for which he has engaged the bailee.[12] Indeed, it is in regard to the bailor's responsibilities that the question of reward is primarily important, for it may mark the difference between an absolute duty and a duty of reasonable care.

---

[7] Law Comm. No. 69; Scot. Law Comm. No. 39, para. 25. But see now W.P. No. 71 (1977).

[8] Post, pp. 722, 736.

[9] Ante, p. 246 et seq.

[10] *Southland Harbour Board* v. *Vella* [1974] 1 N.Z.L.R. 526; ante, p. 83; cf. *Washwell Inc.* v. *Morejon* (1974) 294 So. (2d.) 30, where a washing machine in a laundromat was held to be leased to the plaintiff customer for the purpose of implying a warranty as to reasonable fitness for use. The subject matter of the contract must be a chattel; there could be no bailment, for instance, of the rights comprised by a taxi meter licence: *Sexton* v. *King* [1957] Q.S.R. 355.

[11] *Pampris* v. *Thanos* (1967) 69 S.R. (N.S.W.) 226; cf. *Australian Provincial Assurance Co. Ltd.* v. *Coroneo* (1938) 38 S.R. (N.S.W.) 700; *McKenzie* v. *Ocean Accident & Guarantee Corporation Ltd.* (1921) 20 O.W.N. 406.

[12] *Derbyshire Building Co. Pty. Ltd.* v. *Becker* (1962) 107 C.L.R. 633; Chapter 8, ante. The fact that money changes hands will not necessarily create a hiring; e.g., where the borrower of a car pays for the petrol he consumes: *McCarthy* v. *British Oak Insurance Co. Ltd.* [1938] 3 All. E.R. 1; cf. *Rainsbury* v. *Ross* (1843) 4 N.B.R. 179.

Theoretically, it should be possible to create a lessor-hirer relationship without a contract between the parties. By analogy with the sub-bailment cases[13] the source of the lessor's reward would seem to be immaterial. There is, as we have seen, an American decision which impliedly supports this result[14] but the issue does not appear to have been raised in any Commonwealth Court. Of course, most hirings will be the product of contract and it is with these that the present chapter is primarily concerned.

The permission given to the hirer may be a personal one, or it may include an authority to grant the use of the chattel to a third person. Whether this permission can be inferred will depend upon the nature and terms of the contract. The latter will often be elaborate and comprehensive and it is uncertain how many contracts of hire now fall to be regulated solely according to the Common Law.

The hirer obtains a possessory interest which he may enforce against third parties; he may also sue the bailor for any unwarranted incursion upon his possession during the period of hire.[15] It is generally assumed that the lessor is not liable for torts committed by the hirer while the chattel is in his possession.[16] In most cases this is the obvious conclusion, but the circumstances may occasionally point to a dual relationship of master and servant and bailor and bailee, if the bailor enjoys a sufficient interest in the purpose for which the chattel is employed.[17]

In some respects, it should be possible to create an enforceable contract of hire although the bailor has no authority from the owner to transfer possession. The unauthorised bailee will owe a duty of care and will be estopped from denying his bailor's title; the bailor must, in turn, answer for the state of the chattel and honour the agreement for the period of the lease. It has, however, been suggested that the lessor cannot recover hiring charges if he is not entitled to lease the chattel, even though the hirer may have suffered no real detriment from that fact.[18] This seems exceptionally harsh and would appear to conflict with the bailee's estoppel. Of course, an illegal contract will be unenforceable, but it could be unjust to extend the prohibition to cases where both parties were innocent of the claims of the third party at the time when the contract was made.

II. The Duties of the Bailor

Often, the contract will contain a comprehensive account of the parties' obligations and the answer to any dispute will be reached upon the express terms of their agreement. In other cases, the general law of contract will

---

[13] See especially *Morris* v. *C. W. Martin & Sons Ltd.* [1966] 1 Q.B. 716, and Chapter 20, post.
[14] *Lovely* v. *Burroughs Corporation Inc.* (1974) 527 P (2d.) 557.
[15] See, for instance, *Lee* v. *Atkinson* (1609) Yelv. 172; *Holmes* v. *Clarke* (1835) 2 N.B.R. 167; *Turner* v. *Hardcastle* (1862) 11 C.B.N.S. 683; cf. *Leader* v. *Rhys* (1861) 2 F. & F. 399.
[16] Post, p. 961 et seq.
[17] For the distinction between lessor and hirer and master and servant, see ante, p. 109; for the distinction between sale, hire and loan in cases involving returnable bottles, see ante, p. 96.
[18] *Warman* v. *Southern Counties Motors Ltd.* [1949] 2 K.B. 576, at 582-583; cf. *Park* v. *Berkery* (1930) 25 Tas. L.R. 67, at 78-79.

provide a solution. Thus contracts of hire may be unenforceable by either party if illegal or contrary to public policy;[19] they may be frustrated by destruction of the subject-matter[20] or (if his personality is a material factor) by the death of either party;[21] and they will be unenforceable against an infant or other party suffering from a recognised incapacity to contract.[22] Likewise, the rules of agreement, consideration, privity and intention to create legal relations may (to a lesser extent) render the alleged contract of hire unenforceable.[23]

A promise given by either party may amount to a condition, breach of which will entitle the other party to rescind; it would seem that the hirer's acceptance of the goods does not (as in cases of sale)[24] convert the condition into a warranty,[25] although in appropriate cases he may be held to have affirmed.[26] Whether a particular promise amounts to a condition is a matter of construction. In *Quickmaid Rental Services Ltd.* v. *Reece*[27] a garage-proprietor entered into written agreements for the installation, on a five-year lease, of a beverage vending machine upon his premises. He stipulated that the suppliers should not instal a similiar machine in the same road and an oral assurance to this effect was given before the contracts were signed. The promise was broken and the Court of Appeal held that the hirer was entitled to rescind. Lord

---

[19] *Pearce* v. *Brooks* (1866) L.R. 1 Ex. 213; *J. M. Allan (Merchandising) Ltd.* v. *Cloke* [1963] 2 Q.B. 340; cf. *Upfill* v. *Wright* [1911] 1 K.B. 506. The illegality will not generally prevent the bailor from recovering the goods (or damages for their conversion) by virtue of his independent title: see *Bowmakers Ltd.* v. *Barnett Instruments Ltd.* [1945] K.B. 65; *Belvoir Finance Co. Ltd.* v. *Harold G. Cole & Co. Ltd.* [1969] 1 W.L.R. 1877; *Evans* v. *Credit Services Investments Ltd.* [1975] 2 N.Z.L.R. 560; cf. *Belvoir Finance Co. Ltd.* v. *Stapleton* [1971] 1 Q.B. 201; *N.Z. Securities & Finance Ltd.* v. *Wrightcars, Ltd.* [1976] 1 N.Z.L.R. 77; *Bigos* v. *Bousted* [1951] 1 All E.R. 92; *Thomas Brown* v. *Deen* (1962) 108 C.L.R. 391; *Swiss Bank* v. *Lloyd's Bank* (1978) *The Times*, May 16th.

[20] *Taylor* v. *Caldwell* (1863) 3 B. & S. 826; see generally Treitel, op. cit., Chapter 20.

[21] *Newell* v. *Moulden* (1911) 11 S.R. (N.S.W.) 539 (lease of racehorses, to be trained by the hirer, frustrated by latter's death); *Shepherd* v. *Ready Mixed Concrete (London) Ltd.* (1968) 112 Sol. Jo. 518; cf. H.P. Act 1965, s.30; Consumer Credit Act 1974 (U.K.), ss. 86, 128. As to whether contracts for the lease of neon signs were frustrated by war-time regulations prohibiting the external use of lighting, see *Scanlon's New Neon Ltd.* v. *Toohey's Ltd.* (1943) 67 C.L.R. 169, disapproving in part *Consolidated Neon (Phillips System) Pty. Ltd.* v. *Toohey's Ltd.* (1942) 42 S.R. (N.S.W.) 152.

[22] *Fawcett* v. *Smethurst* (1914) 84 L.J.K.B. 473; *Jennings* v. *Rundall* (1799) 8 T.R. 335. But an infant may be liable in tort if he steps outside the bailment: see *Walley* v. *Holt* (1876) 35 L.T. 631; *Burnard* v. *Haggis* (1863) 14 C.B.N.S. 45; *Burton* v. *Levey* (1891) 7 T.L.R. 248; *Ballett* v. *Mingay* [1943] K.B. 281; cf. p. 752 post.

[23] The qualification is necessary because (a) the obligations that arise under a naked bailment can exist irrespective of contract; (b) to some extent, privity and consideration may be immaterial to the validity of additional promissory obligations undertaken by either party; see generally ante p. 313 et seq. The presence of a vitiating factor within the contract of bailment will not, in most cases, exonerate the bailee from the duty to exercise reasonable care, nor preclude him from defending his possession against third parties.

[24] *Sale of Goods Act* 1893, s.11(1)(c); *Misrepresentation Act* 1967 (U.K.), s.4(1).

[25] (1975) 4, *Anglo-American Law Review* 207, at 233.

[26] *Arrow Transfer Co. Ltd.* v. *Fleetwood Logging Co. Ltd.* (1961) 30 D.L.R. (2d) 631, at 646. For the effect of affirmation upon liability for a fundamental breach, see p. 935 et seq., post.

[27] (1970) 114 Sol. Jo. 372; cf. *Doobay* v. *Mohabeer* [1967] 2 A.C. 278; *Costigan* v. *Johnson* (1897) Q.R. 6 Q.B. 308; *Howard* v. *Ogden* [1978] 2 W.L.R. 515.

Denning M.R. held that the oral term had been incorporated into the agreement as a condition, breach of which went to the root of the contract. Megaw L.J., thought that the same result could be reached on the ground that the promise gave rise to a collateral contract which, when broken, entitled the defendant to regard the whole transaction as repudiated.[28]

This case may be contrasted with *Hope* v. *R.C.A. Photophone of Australia Ltd.*,[29] where the High Court refused to infer, from an agreement that the suppliers would manufacture and hire goods to the defendants, any condition or warranty that the equipment should be new. The court was assisted in this conclusion by a widely-drawn exclusion clause, which declared that all express or implied warranties or representations were excluded and that the written document contained the entire understanding of the parties.[30] Similarly, in *Western Electric Co. (Australia) Ltd.* v. *Adams*,[31] the New South Wales Full Supreme Court refused to hold that a promise by the hirer to allow the owner to make periodic inspections of the equipment imposed a duty on the owner to make such inspections at the rate of one a week. In all of these decisions (and in many others) the court applied ordinary contractual principles and nothing revolved around the fact that the contract was one of hire.[32]

A question of more general importance concerns the nature and extent of the terms that a court will imply in the hirer's favour. Here, the nature of hire as a contract for the supply of goods, resembling in some respects the contract of sale, allows some generalisations to be made.

III. Implied Terms[32a]

1. *Quiet possession*: The lessor impliedly warrants that the hirer will enjoy uninterrupted use and enjoyment of the goods for the period of hire. Thus, if the hirer's possession is disturbed, whether by conduct on the part of the bailor or through an assertion of title by a third party, the bailor will be liable in damages for the resulting loss.[33] In fact, there are

---

[28] Cf. *J. J. Savage & Sons Pty. Ltd.* v. *Blakney* (1970) 44 A.L.J.R. 123; *Academy of Health and Fitness* v. *Power* [1973] V.R. 254; *J. Evans & Co. (Portsmouth) Ltd.* v. *Andrea Merzario Ltd.* [1976] 2 All E.R. 903; *Johnson Matthey & Co. Ltd.* v. *Constantine Terminals Ltd.* [1976] 2 Lloyd's Rep. 215.

[29] (1937) 50 C.L.R. 348 (H.C.).

[30] *L'Estrange* v. *F. Graucob Ltd.* [1934] 2 K.B. 394 applied; post., p. 924.

[31] (1933) 50 W.N. (N.S.W.) 197.

[32] Questions of construction may be particularly important in determining the length of the period of hire: see, for instance, *Tilling* v. *James* (1906) 94 L.T. 823, where the agreement provided that "after the expiration of the first year the hiring can be terminated by either party giving one quarter's written notice from a quarter day". It was held that this produced a hiring for one year certain and a right to terminate by quarterly notice thereafter. See also *Hutton* v. *Brown* (1881) 45 L.T. 343.

[32a] Law Commission Working Paper No. 71 (1977), *Implied Terms in Contracts for the Supply of Goods*.

[33] Which may presumably include damages for loss of enjoyment: cf. *Jarvis* v. *Swan Tours Ltd.* [1973] 2 Q.B. 233; *Jackson* v. *Horizon Holidays Ltd.* [1975] 3 All E.R. 92; *Harris* v. *Lombard New Zealand Ltd.* [1974] 2 N.Z.L.R. 161; *Heywood* v. *Wellers* [1976] 1 All E.R. 300; *Cook* v. *Swinfen* [1967] 1 W.L.R. 457; *Diesen* v. *Samson* 1971 S.L.T. (Sh. Ct.) 49. In *Howe* v. *Teefy* (1927) 27 S.R. (N.S.W.) 301 the owner of a racehorse wrongfully repossessed it from the plaintiff, a

very few decisions which apply this principle to cases of simple hire. One of the earliest, *Lee* v. *Atkinson*,[34] involved an action against the owner, who had objected to his horse being used for an unauthorised journey and had resumed possession by assaulting the hirer. The hirer was granted an action for assault and it was held that the proper remedy for the owner was an action on the case. So far as concerns interference by third parties, the warranty seems only to have arisen in bailments by way of hire-purchase, and even here it has been overshadowed by the implied condition as to title.[35] The hirer's object is the uninterrupted use and enjoyment of the chattel; if this is guaranteed by a warranty of quiet possession, any further requirement as to the lessor's own title might be superfluous and could produce undesirable results. This policy seems to have been tacitly approved by the Commonwealth *Trade Practices Act* 1974, which implies into every contract of lease or hire between a corporation (as supplier) and a consumer:

> an implied warranty that the consumer will enjoy quiet possession of the goods except so far as it may lawfully be disturbed by the supplier or by another person who is entitled to the benefit of any charge or encumbrance disclosed or known to the consumer before the contract is made.[36]

It will be observed that the Act implies neither a condition that the supplier has a right to supply the goods,[37] nor a warranty that the goods are free from any charge or encumbrance.[38]

It must be conceded, however, that in unusual circumstances a warranty of quiet possession could prove inadequate for the protection of the hirer. If the lessor has no right to lease the goods, a delivery of them under an unauthorised contract of hire (or their use or redelivery pursuant to such a contract) may amount to conversion on the part of the hirer. If action is brought by the true owner after the hiring term has expired, it might prove difficult to establish that such action creates an incursion upon the hirer's quiet possession; he will have had untrammelled use and enjoyment of the goods for the period for which he has contracted. In such a case, the Courts might be willing to extend the concept of quiet possession to include any later derogation from the hirer's enjoyment (or economic

---

trainer. The trainer was allowed to recover damages inter alia for betting prize money and "stable information" emoluments he would have received had the horse remained in his possession.

[34] (1609) Yelv. 172.
[35] *Karflex Ltd.* v. *Poole* [1933] 2 K.B. 251; *Warman* v. *Southern Counties Motors Ltd.* [1949] 2 K.B. 576; *Butterworth* v. *Kingsway Motors Ltd.* [1954] 1 W.L.R. 1286; and see generally Sutton, *Sale of Goods* (2nd ed.), p. 197 et seq. In contracts of hire-purchase, both implied terms have now received statutory formulation: see *Supply of Goods (Implied Terms) Act 1973*, ss. 8(1)(a) and 8(1)(b)(ii) as amended by Schedule 4 para. 35. *Consumer Credit Act* 1974 (U.K.), and for Australian references, Else-Mitchell and Parsons, *Hire-Purchase Law* (4th ed.), p. 60 et seq.
[36] Section 69(1)(b). See also South Australia's *Consumer Transactions Act* 1972-1973, s.8(2).
[37] Section 69(1)(a): this is limited to sales and hire-purchase agreements.
[38] Section 69(1)(c): this is limited to cases where property "is to or may pass to the consumer." The obligations imposed by the foregoing subsections may be qualified under s.69(3). As to the implication of equivalent terms under South Australian law, see *Consumer Transactions Act* 1972-1973, s.8(2).

immunity) in using the chattel. Such a solution could prove more satisfactory than the universal implication of a condition that the lessor has the right to hire the goods, which would lead to difficulty in determining whether the hirer has a right to reject if he discovers the absence of this right in the lessor at the time when the period of hire has substantially or completely elapsed.[39] Alternatively, the problem could be solved by implying a mere warranty as to title, complementary to the warranty of quiet possession. In the event of breach, the hirer's remedy would be an action for damages and he could recover no more than the fact of his loss.

The precise ambit of the warranty of quiet possession will of course depend upon the individual facts of the case. Normally, the hirer will have no complaint if an independent and wrongful act by a third-party deprives him of possession, as where the goods are stolen by a thief. The position may differ, of course, when the lessor connives at the disturbance or negligently permits it to occur. Moreover, fault on the part of the lessor is irrelevant when it is the nature or identity of the goods themselves that provokes the disturbance, as where they belong to a third person, or are liable to seizure by customs, or infringe some patent or copyright enjoyed by a stranger to the transaction.[40]

Further, it would appear under both the *Trade Practices Act* and at Common Law, that the lessor's liability for breach of the implied warranty of quiet possession is not confined to disturbances which arise from some quality inherent in the goods, or from third-party rights which are already in existence, when the contract is made; nor is it liable to displacement in cases where the hirer has been evicted by title paramount. Both conclusions follow from a recent decision of the Court of Appeal dealing with a contract of sale;[41] in cases of hiring the necessity for an enduring warranty of quiet possession is, if anything, more pronounced.[42]

Although liability for breach of s.69(1)(b) of the *Trade Practices Act* cannot (except by disclosure of the relevant charge or encumbrance) be excluded,[43] there seems no reason why such exclusion should not operate at Common Law, even extending to any implied warranty that the bailor has the right to lease the goods. Certainly the supplier's title is less important to the hirer than to the purchaser of goods, for hirings do not contemplate that title will be transferred. But an exclusion clause which attempted to deprive the hirer of a remedy for loss of what was sub-

---

[39] A statement by Finnemore J. in *Warman* v. *Southern Countries Motors Ltd.* [1949] 2 K.B. 576, at pp. 582-583, suggests that the charges are always unenforceable in such an event.

[40] See, for instance, *Niblett* v. *Confectioners' Materials Ltd.* [1921] 3 K.B. 387; *Sumner Permain & Co.* v. *Webb* [1922] 1 K.B. 55; *Phoenix Distributors Ltd.* v. *L. B. Clarke (London) Ltd.* [1966] 2 Lloyd's Rep. 285; *Rowland v. Divall* [1923] 2 K.B. 500; *Margolin* v. *Wright Pty. Ltd.* [1959] A.L.R. 988; *Microbeads A.C.* v. *Vinhurst Road Markings Ltd.* [1975] 1 All E.R. 529; [1975] C.L.J. 199; (1975) 5 *Tas. U.L.R.* 77.

[41] *Microbeads A.C.* v. *Vinhurst Road Markings Ltd.*, ante.

[42] Quaere, however, whether s.69(1)(b) is not in any event confined to disturbances which arise from any charge or encumbrance; see generally (1975) 5 *Tas. U.L.R.* 77.

[43] Section 68; see also the *Consumer Transactions Act* 1972-1973 (S.A.) and cf. *Unfair Contract Terms Act* 1977, p. 954, post.

stantially the essence of the agreement would be very narrowly construed.[44]

Because of the uncertainty which surrounds the scope of "safety and fitness for use" we shall deal separately with its operation in England and Australia.

2. *Safety and fitness for use in England*:[45] The lessor of goods impliedly contracts that the chattel is both reasonably safe, and reasonably suitable in a functional sense, for the purpose for which it was hired. At one time it was thought that no such obligation arose where the hire was of a specific chattel which the hirer had seen and inspected beforehand.[46] Now it is recognised that these facts no longer defeat the hirer's claim[47] except insofar as they may demonstrate that the hirer preferred to rely on his own skill and judgment rather than that of the owner, or agreed to take the chattel with all defects that were apparent or liable to discovery upon such inspection.

The standard of liability for breach of this undertaking is in a much less settled question. English authority has wavered between strict liability (as in the case of sale), liability for want of reasonable care, and liability for those defects which "any amount" of care and skill could guard against. The first standard is impliedly supported by many of the older authorities[48] and (as regards functional suitability at least) by several more recent decisions predominantly concerned with hire-purchase.[49] The standard of reasonable care enjoys the support of a number of older authorities,[50] and perhaps of a majority of those modern deci-

---

[44] Post, p. 924 et seq.

[45] Paton, op. cit., pp. 289-298; Goode, *Hire-Purchase Law and Practice* (2nd ed.), pp. 885 et seq.; Palmer (1975) 4 *Anglo-American Law Review,* 207; Law Com. No. 69 and Scot. Law Com. No. 39, *Exemption Clauses, Second Report* (1975), para 19; W.P. No. 71 (1977).

[46] *Robertson* v. *Amazon Tug and Lighterage Co. Ltd.* (1881) 7 Q.B.D. 598 (obiter); see also *Sutton* v. *Temple* (1843) 12 M. & W. 52; 152 E.R. 1108; *Fowler* v. *Lock* (1872) L.R. 7 C.P. 272, at 281 per Grove J.

[47] *Reed* v. *Dean* [1949] 1 K.B. 188, at pp. 192-193; *Yeoman Credit Ltd.* v. *Apps* [1961] 2 All E.R. 281; and see *Jones* v. *Page* (1867) 15 L.T. 619, where the hirer inspected the carriage merely for its capacity and not to see whether it was safe; the Court held that the implied term as to safety continued to operate.

[48] *Sutton* v. *Temple* (1843) 12 M. & W. 52; 152 E.R. 1108; *Chew* v. *Jones* (1847) 10 L.T.O.S. 231; *Gibbons* v. *Standon* (1867) 16 L.T. 497; *Fowler* v. *Lock* (1872) L.R. 7 C.P. 272, at 280 (but cf. Willes J. at 286); *Bentley Bros.* v. *Metcalfe & Co. Ltd.* (1906) 75 L.J. K.B. 891; *Scott* v. *Foley, Aikman & Co.* (1899) 5 Comm. Cas. 53; *Mowbray* v. *Merryweather* [1895] 2 Q.B. 640 (but cf. Rigby L.J. at 646); *Vogan & Co. Ltd.* v. *Oulton* (1899) 79 L.T. 384; 81 L.T. 435; *Dare* v. *Bognor Regis U.D.C.* (1912) 76 J.P. 174, and 425.

[49] *Karsales (Harrow) Ltd.* v. *Wallis* [1956] 2 All E.R. 866, at 870 per Parker L.J.; *Yeoman Credit Ltd.* v. *Apps.* ante, n.47 at 286, 287 per Pearce L.J. and at 291 per Harman L.J.; *Charterhouse Credit Ltd.* v. *Tolly* [1963] 2 All E.R. 432, at 437 per Donovan L.J. and at 444 per Ormerod L.J.; *Astley Industrial Trust Ltd.* v. *Grimley* [1963] 1 W.L.R. 584, at 590 per Pearson L.J.; *Farnworth Finance Facilities Ltd.* v. *Attryde* [1970] 1 W.L.R. 1053; cf. *Guarantee Trust of Jersey Ltd.* v. *Gardner* (1973) 117 Sol. Jo. 564 (a case of simple hire where there was found have been a fundamental breach of the term).

[50] *Mowbray* v. *Merryweather* [1895] 2 Q.B. 640, at 646 per Rigby, L.J.; *Jones* v. *Page* (1867) 15 L.T. 619, at 621 per Pigott B.; cf. p. 620 per Kelly C.B. whose judgment is ambiguous on this point; see (1975) 4 *Anglo-American Law Review* 207, at 216.

sions which are directly in point.[51] To a lesser extent, it is reinforced by a number of cases in which the hirer has chosen to frame his action in negligence without relying upon a stricter contractual undertaking.[52] Moreover, some of the decisions cited in *Hyman* v. *Nye*[53] (as case which ostensibly imposed a more onerous duty) are consistent with the duty of reasonable care.[54] This level of responsibility seems well entrenched and is endorsed by the latest edition of Halsbury.[55]

Support for the intermediate standard is considerably more ambivalent. Its primary source is the judgment of Lindley J. in *Hyman* v. *Nye*,[56] a decision which probably did not involve a bailment at all but an ordinary contract of carriage. A carriage and driver had been hired for a journey from Brighton to Shoreham and back. The lessor's servant remained in charge of the carriage throughout and the "hirer" was confined to the role of passenger.[57] While travelling in the carriage, he was injured through the breaking of an under-bolt. Lindley J. conceded that the lessor was not liable for latent defects but rejected the trial judge's direction that he should be liable only upon proof of a want of reasonable care. In Lindley J.'s view the lessor was responsible for ensuring that the chattel was free from ". . . all defects which care and skill can guard against"[58] and was liable for failing to correct deficiencies that could be discovered by "any care and skill". The judgement of Mathew J. seems to go further and to impose a strict duty upon the lessor, since he remarked that there is apparently "no distinction in this respect between contracts for the sale and contracts for the hire of an article for a specific purpose."[59]

On the other hand, Mathew J. remarks that the lessor is not an insurer. The strength of his judgment (as authority for an absolute duty) is further reduced by the fact that the learned judge explicitly charac-

---

[51] *Reed* v. *Dean* [1949] 1 K.B. 188; *O'Brien* v. *Bridge Marine Works Ltd.* [1954] 2 Lloyd's Rep. 79; *Vendair (London) Ltd.* v. *Giro Aviation Co. Ltd.* [1961] 1 Lloyd's Rep. 283, 287 (Veale J.); *Hadley* v. *Droitwich Construction Co. Ltd.* [1967] 3 All E.R. 911, 913 (Sellers L.J.); cf. *Ludgate* v. *Lovett* [1969] 1 W.L.R. 1016, where the hirer's counterclaim seems to have been based upon negligence but there are grounds for believing that the lessor did not hire out goods in the ordinary course of business; *Oliver (or Chapman)* v. *Saddler & Co. Ltd.* [1929] A.C. 584, where there was a loan of equipment for the mutual benefit of two groups of employee, but probably no bailment, and the House of Lords held that the special circumstances created a duty of reasonable care; *Griffiths* v. *Arch Engineering Ltd.* [1968] 3 All E.R. 217, where the facts were similar and the relevant standard was again one of reasonable care. Statements to similar effect in hire-purchase cases include *Felston Tile Co. Ltd.* v. *Winget Ltd.* [1936] 3 All E.R. 473, at 477 per Greer L.J.; *Charterhouse Credit Ltd.* v. *Tolly* [1963] 2 All E.R. 432, at 441 and *Astley Industrial Trust Ltd.* v. *Grimley* [1963] 1 W.L.R. 584, at 498 per Upjohn L.J.

[52] *Chapelton* v. *Barry U.D.C.* [1940] 1 K.B. 532; *White* v. *Steadman* [1913] 3 K.B. 340; and see *Ludgate* v. *Lovett*, ante.

[53] (1881) 6 Q.B.D. 685; post.

[54] *Christie* v. *Griggs* (1809) 2 Camp. 89; *Readhead* v. *Midland Ry. Co.* (1869) L.R. 4 Q.B. 379 (neither of them cases of bailment).

[55] (4th ed.), vol. 2, para. 1554.

[56] Ante.

[57] See Chapter 7, ante.

[58] At 687.

[59] At 690; cited with approval by Wright J., in *Vogan & Co. Ltd.* v. *Oulton* (1898) 79 L.T. 384, at 385 and by Blair Co. Ct. J. in *Burlington Leasing Ltd.* v. *De Moura* (1976) 60 D.L.R. (3d) 71, at 74.

terised the lessor's obligations as less onerous than the shipowner's duty to supply a seaworthy ship.[60] In *Geddling* v. *Marsh*[61] both Bray and Bailhache JJ. refused to regard *Hyman* v. *Nye* as authority for the wholesale equation of implied terms as to reasonable fitness in hirings and in sales.[62] Despite its frequent acceptance,[63] *Hyman* v. *Nye* cannot be regarded as a strong authority.[64]

Nevertheless, it was upon this decision that Pearce L.J. relied in stating his unqualified version of the lessor's duty in *Yeoman Credit Ltd.* v. *Apps.*[65] The same authority also formed the basis of Denning L.J.'s assertion in *White* v. *John Warwick Cycle Co. Ltd.*[66] that the obligation went beyond a simple duty of reasonable care. The question in the latter case was whether a clause in a contract for the hire of a bicycle, purporting to exclude liability for personal injuries, could apply to injuries caused by the negligence of the supplier. The Court of Appeal, relying on *Rutter* v. *Palmer*[67] held that the clause was competent to protect the supplier only against breach of his stricter duty to provide a safe and adequate machine; it did not extend to tortious liability and the case was remitted to ascertain whether the delinquent defect had arisen from a want of reasonable care. Since it was unnecessary in *Warwick's* case to specify how far above that level the lessor's contractual duty lay, the decision can be regarded either as an authority for the absolute liability of the lessor or as a confirmation of his lighter responsibility to take "any amount" of care and skill.

In the absence of any concrete judicial or statutory definition, it is suggested that the opportunity still exists for an English court to dissociate the lessor's undertaking from notions of care or relative skill and to formulate it in strict and unqualified terms Almost every judicial statement in point has been by way of dictum.[68] There is no reason why the hirer's rights should be inferior to those of a purchaser and it may be that the test of reasonable care is particularly ill-suited to cases of functional efficiency as opposed to cases of injury to the person.[69] The

---

[60] This duty is absolute at Common Law. See generally *Hong Kong Fir Shipping Co. Ltd.* v. *Kawasaki Kisen Kaisha* [1962] 2 Q.B. 26; and cf. *Astley Industrial Trust Ltd.* v. *Grimley* [1963] 1 W.L.R. 584, at 598 per Upjohn L.J.; *Carriage of Goods by Sea Act* 1971, Art. III, r. 1.

[61] [1920] 1 K.B. 668, at 672.

[62] This denial was itself doubted by Charlesworth, *Negligence* (4th ed.), p. 375.

[63] The decision is cited with apparent approval by North, *Occupier's Liability,* p. 155 and has been applied in several Canadian cases, e.g. *Boorman* v. *Morris* [1944] 3 D.L.R. 382; *Crawford* v. *Ferris* [1953] O.W.N. 713; *Coleshaw* v. *Lipsett* (1973) 33 D.L.R. (3d) 382 (where it was regarded as authority for a duty of "due care"); cf. *Burlington Leasing Ltd.* v. *De Moura* (ante n.59) at p. 74..

[64] Possibly because it did not involve a bailment by way of hire at all. In *Hyman* v. *Nye* there were no citations from *Sutton* v. *Temple* (1843) 12 M. & W. 52 (152 E.R. 1108), *Jones* v. *Page* (1867) 15 L.T. 619, or *Chew* v. *Jones* (1847) 10 L.T.O.S. 231.

[65] [1961] 2 All E.R. 281, at 286-287.

[66] [1953] 1 W.L.R. 1285, at 1293. See also *Collins* v. *Richmond Rodeo Riding Ltd.* (1966) 55 W.L.R. 289.

[67] [1922] 2 K.B. 87; see p. 926 et seq., post.

[68] The most obvious exceptions are *Hyman* v. *Nye* (ante, n.53) and *White* v. *John Warwick & Co. Ltd.* ante, both of which are inconclusive but favour a stronger duty than that of reasonable care; cf. *Jones* v. *Page* (1867) 15 L.T. 619, where there was "abundant evidence" of negligence.

[69] (1975) 4 *Anglo-American Law Review* 207, at 222-225.

great preponderance of Australian authority favours an unqualified duty[70] and at least one American court has declared that public policy demands the extension to the consumer-hirer of duties and undertakings equivalent to those enjoyed by a consumer-buyer.[71] It is within the power of the English Courts to bring about this extension.

The duty to supply a suitable chattel will extend, of course, to such ancillary equipment as the hirer could reasonably expect to accompany the principal chattel. Thus the absence of a fire-extinguisher on a rented motor-cruiser,[72] or the failure to provide operating instructions for a leased sprinkler system,[73] may constitute a breach of lessor's obligation. Whether the lessor is under a contractual duty to provide a particular item of equipment will, of course, depend upon the agreement, the nature of the chattel and the ordinary range of secondary aids that are necessary for its efficient employment.

It has been stated on several occasions that the occurrence of damage or injury while the chattel is being used by the hirer is prima facie evidence of a breach of the lessor's obligation of reasonable fitness.[74] Normally, this would seem to amount to no more than an invocation of res ipsa loquitur as a means to establishing what may in fact be a strict liability. The presumption encounters difficulties when the lessor counter-claims for damage to the chattel and thereby casts upon the hirer the duty of establishing reasonable care.[75] It is suggested that in cases of this

---

[70] Post, p. 736 et seq. Canadian authority seems divided on this point. *Coleshaw* v. *Lipsett* (1973) 33 D.L.R. (3d) 382, holds that the hirer of a chattel "warrants only that it is free from defects which are known or which could be discovered by the exercise of due care"; see further, and to similar effect, *Boorman* v. *Morris* [1944] 3 D.L.R. 382; *Crawford* v. *Ferris* [1953] O.W.N. 713. On the other hand, *Burlington Leasing Ltd.* v. *De Moura* quite clearly favours an absolute standard; see further *Canadian Dominion Leasing Corporation Ltd.* v. *Suburban Superdrug Ltd.* (1966) 56 D.L.R. (2d) 43; *Arrow Transfer Co. Ltd.* v. *Fleetwood Logging Co. Ltd.* ante, n.26.

[71] *W. E. Johnson Equipment Co.* v. *United Airlines Inc.* (1970) 238 So. (2d) 98 (Sup. Ct. Florida), where Drew J. points out that there may be as much reliance upon the expertise of a lessor as upon that of a vendor. cf. *Sleeskin* v. *Grant Food Inc.* (1974) 318 A. (2d) 874, which rejects the implication of a warranty of merchantable quality in contracts of hire, and *Reader* v. *General Motors Corporation* (1971) 475 P. (2d) 497, which retains the standard of reasonable care. Other decisions favouring a strict obligation are *Penton* v. *Budget Rent-a-Car* (1973) 304 So. (2d) 410 and *Equilease Corporation* v. *Hill* (1974) 290 So. (2d) 423. In addition, some American courts have extended the doctrine of manufacturers' or retailers' strict liability in tort to the commercial lessor of goods: an example is *Price* v. *Shell Oil Co.* (1970) 466 P. (2d) 722, a decision of the Supreme Court of California where (at p. 725) Sullivan J. remarks: ". . . we can perceive no substantial difference between *sellers* of personal property and *non-sellers*, such as bailors and lessors. In each instance, the seller or non-seller places [an article] on the market, knowing that it is to be used without inspection for defects. . . . In the light of the policy to be subserved, it should make no difference that the party distributing the article has retained title to it. Nor can we see how the risk of harm associated with the use of the chattel can vary with the legal form under which it is held."

[72] *Reed* v. *Dean* ante, n.47.

[73] *Imperial Furniture Pty. Ltd.* v. *Automatic Fire Sprinkler Pty. Ltd.* [1967] 1 N.S.W.R. 29. Quaere whether the failure to supply a competent driver could qualify as a breach of the accompanying contract of hire; cf. *Abraham* v. *Bullock* (1902) 18 T.L.R. 701.

[74] *Reed* v. *Dean*; *Hyman* v. *Nye* (1881) 6 Q.B.D. 685, at 687-688; Wyatt Paine, *Bailments*, pp. 105-106; cf. *O'Brien* v. *Bridge Marine Works Ltd.* [1954] 2 Lloyd's Rep. 79.

[75] Cf. *Ludgate* v. *Lovett* [1969] 1 W.L.R. 1016; post., p. 749.

kind the bailee's burden (being probably the stronger)[76] will prevail. The practical consequence may be that the hirer will be required to establish that he was using the chattel properly and safely before his action for breach of contract can succeed. When no counterclaim exists, the question is a simple one of ascertaining whether on a balance of probabilities the lessor's obligation has been broken; ultimately, therefore, the hirer's success will depend upon the attractiveness of this theory of causation.

(a) *Circumstantial exclusion*: Occasionally, the implied term as to fitness may be excluded, not by express agreement, but by the circumstances in which the contract of hire is formed or carried out. There are three principal ways in which this may occur:[77]

1. Obvious non-reliance, by the hirer, upon the lessor's skill and judgment.
2. The existence of defects which must have been evident to the hirer at the time of contracting.
3. The use of the chattel for a purpose not specifically communicated to the lessor and not contemplated by him in the ordinary course of events.

So far as concerns the first of these events, it is uncertain whether the hirer bears the burden of establishing his reliance or the owner bears the burden of refuting it. An analogy from the law relating to sales would indicate the former. Section 14(1) of the original *Sales of Goods Act* 1893, implied a condition of reasonable fitness into every contract of sale in which the goods were of a description which it was in the seller's course of business to supply and the buyer had, expressly or impliedly, made known to the seller and the particular purpose for which the goods were required, so as to show that he relied upon the seller's skill and judgment. Although this ostensibly placed the burden upon the buyer, the courts were not slow to infer reliance in appropriate cases; particularly those that involved a private customer dealing with an established supplier or manufacturer,[78] or a purchaser of tender years.[79] The revisions to s.14(1), which occurred by virtue of s.3 of the *Supply of Goods (Implied Terms) Act* 1973[80] altered this nominal burden of proof but provided an additional method of escape for the supplier; the implied condition was expressed to apply whenever ". . . the buyer, expressly or by implication, makes known to the seller any particular purpose for which the goods are being bought . . . *except* where the circumstances show that the buyer does not rely, or that it is unreasonable for him to rely, on the seller's skill and judgement." A similar renovation took place in contracts of hire purchase.[81]

[76] Ante, p. 40 et seq.
[77] (1975) 4 *Anglo-American Law Review* 207, at 234.
[78] See e.g., *Wallis* v. *Russell* [1902] I.R. 585; *Preist* v. *Last* [1903] 2 K.B. 148; *Henry Kendall & Sons Ltd.* v. *William Lillico & Sons Ltd.* [1969] 2 A.C. 31 (especially per Lord Reid at 81-82 and Lord Pearce at 115-116); *Vacwell Engineering Co. Ltd.* v. *B.D.H. Chemicals Ltd.* [1971] 1 Q.B. 88.
[79] *Godley* v. *Perry* [1960] 1 All E.R. 36.
[80] Under the 1973 Act, the section numbers of the old *Sale of Goods Act* were rearranged and the section dealing with reasonable fitness for use became s. 14(3).
[81] See *H.P. Act* 1965, s. 17(4); *Supply of Goods (Implied Terms) Act* 1973, s. 10(2); *Consumer Credit Act 1974*, Fourth Schedule, para. 35.

In view of the acknowledged desirability of treating sales and hirings (for this purpose) as substantially identical[82] it would seem both symmetrical and equitable to confine the lessor's liability to those instances in which the hirer has expressly or impliedly made known the purpose for which the chattel is required, so as to show that he is relying upon the lessor's skill and judgement. This seems to have been the rule in cases of sale, both at Common Law and under the *Sale of Goods Act,* until the modification of that Act in 1973. Admittedly, it would be hard to justify importing the latter amendments into a relationship which remains entirely regulated by the rules of Common Law, but, as we have seen, the courts were willing to waive express communication of the intended purpose of an everyday chattel put to its ordinary use,[83] and (in normal consumer-retailer relationships at least) regularly took for granted the buyer's reliance upon the seller's expertise.

Accordingly, it is submitted that little would be lost by framing the lessor's obligation in terms more akin to those of 1893 than those of 1973. The latter formulation would no doubt be preferable, but there are limits to the extent to which statute can influence the residual Common Law.[84]

In fact, there are very few cases of simple hire which deal with this specific question. A recent Canadian case (where the owner did not purchase the chattel until four days after the contract of hire was executed) suggests that the onus is on the hirer to demonstrate the necessary reliance[85] and a simliar warning is sounded by Pearson L.J. in a hire-purchase case, *Astley Industrial Trust Ltd.* v. *Grimley.*[86] Referring to a statement of Parker L.J. in *Karsales (Harrow) Ltd.* v. *Wallis,*[87] that it is the duty of a finance company to ascertain that the chattel it lets is reasonably fit for the purpose for which it is hired, Pearson L.J. remarked:

> In my view, that sentence should be understood as stating a general proposition not necessarily applying to every case. For instance, it cannot apply if (as in the present case) the evident contractual intention of the parties is that the finance company shall not have an opportunity of ascertaining the fitness of the chattel before the hiring begins . . . Presumably, the finance company had never seen the vehicle and had no previous knowledge of it. The first defendant obviously was not relying on the skill or judgment of the finance

---

[82] *W.E. Johnson Equipment Co.* v. *United Airlines Inc.* (1970) 238 So. (2d.) 98; ante, p. 726; cf. *Geddling* v. *Marsh* [1920] 1 K.B. 688; post, p. 738 (the position in Australian law).

[83] Likewise in contracts of hire: see *Vogan & Co. Ltd.* v. *Oulton* (1899) 81 L.T. 435.

[84] Cf. *Gillespie Bros. Ltd.* v. *Roy Bowles Transport Ltd.* [1973] Q.B. 400, at p. 416; *Cehave N.V.* v. *Bremer Handelsgesellschaft* [1975] 3 All E.R. 739, at p. 748, per Lord Denning M.R.

[85] *Burlington Leasing Ltd.* v. *De Moura* (1976) 60 D.L.R. (3d) 71, at 74. The relationship was not an ordinary consumer-supplier relationship since the hirer was an estate-agent and the equipment (an automatic telephone answering service) was for use in business; nor, on the other hand, does it appear to have been a contract between corporations dealing at arms' length. Nevertheless it may be a reliable authority on the ordinary consumer-lessor situation.

[86] [1963] 2 All E.R. 33, at 42, 44.

[87] [1956] 2 All E.R. 866, at 870.

company to choose a suitable vehicle for his purpose, or to give him any advice as to his choice.

These statements suggest a serious weakness in the position of the hirer. It is by no means uncommon in Australia for leasing arrangements to take the same tripartite form as contracts of hire-purchase, and for the lessor to be a finance company which has never seen the chattel beforehand. In the case of hire-purchase and other varieties of deferred purchasing, most consumers are now protected by ss.56(1) and (2) of the *Consumer Credit Act* 1974, which provide that the dealer (or "negotiator", to place him within the wider identity prescribed by the Act) shall be deemed to be acting in the capacity of agent for the finance company (or creditor) throughout any antecedent negotiations.[88] Hirers do not seem to enjoy this protection, and are therefore obliged to fall back on the collateral liability of the dealer[89] or the possibility of proving that he was the agent of the finance company at Common Law. The latter is especially difficult since the House of Lords have denied the existence of a general agency between dealer and finance company in hire-purchase transactions.[90] It would seem to follow that any reliance communicated to the dealer under such an arrangement could not generally be imported into the hirer-owner relationship for the purpose of engendering an implied obligation of reasonable fitness.

So far as concerns the ordinary, bipartite contract of hire, the nature of the chattel and the relative standing of the parties will usually enable the necessary reliance to be inferred. The lack of authority on this question, and the disputed affinity between hire and sale, may further justify the conclusion that the reliance requirement is less rigorous in cases of simple hire, and that reliance is in every case a matter for the lessor to rebut. In this regard, it should be recalled that *Astley's* case involved hire purchase; and that the greater proximity of such transactions to sales than to simple hirings may reduce its influence upon the latter form of agreement. On the other hand, the Court in *Astley* were dealing with the Common Law obligations of a lessor on hire-purchase and clearly drew support from the equivalent duties of an ordinary lessor of goods. Regrettably, the question remains unresolved.

The fact that the hirer has inspected the chattel beforehand may be relevant for two associated reasons: it may show that he did not rely upon the lessor's skill and judgement and it may indicate that the agreement was to hire a chattel subject to all those defects and characteristics that were evident upon an inspection of the kind that has been made. Again, there are few authorities in point, but the analogy with sale of goods is both a helpful and (it is submitted) a desirable one.[91] The

---

[88] Goode, *The Consumer Credit Act 1974*, p. 89 et seq. The Act is confined in most respects to agreements under which the credit to be provided does not exceed £5,000.

[89] Cf. *Andrews* v. *Hopkinson* [1957] 1 Q.B. 229; *Drury* v. *Victor Buckland Ltd.* [1941] 1 All E.R. 269; *Brown* v. *Sheen and Richmond Car Sales Ltd.* [1950] 1 All E.R. 1102; *Weidemann* v. *Dawson* [1929] V.L.R. 35.

[90] *Branwhite* v. *Worcester Works Finance Ltd.* [1968] 3 All E.R. 104; cf. *St Margaret's Trust Ltd.* v. *Byrne* (1976) *The Times*, 22 January; *Credit Services Investments Ltd.* v. *Evans* [1974] 2 N.Z.L.R. 683.

[91] See generally, Atiyah, *Sale of Goods* (5th ed.) pp. 92-96.

emphasis in *Jones* v. *Page*[92] upon the purpose for which inspection was made clearly indicates that if the hirer had made his examination with a view to discovering the actual defect in question, and should reasonably have discovered it upon such examination, the warranty may have been displaced.[93] Likewise, in *Charterhouse Credit Ltd.* v. *Tolly*[94] Upjohn L.J. observed that the failure to equip the vehicle with satisfactory tyres did not constitute a breach of the lessor's obligation, because the hirer had an opportunity inspecting the vehicle beforehand, and a reasonable examination would have brought the defect to light.[95] But perhaps the clearest acknowledgement that an inspection by the hirer can deprive him of the benefit of any implied term as to fitness is given by Pearson L.J. in *Astley Industrial Trust Ltd.* v. *Grimley*[96]:

> Suppose that a customer, proud of his skill as a mechanic, hired or took on hire-purchase a dilapidated and immobile vehicle, hoping to be able by his own efforts to put it into good repair and working order, and making it clear to the persons letting it out on hire to him that he would not hold them responsible either for the existing state of disrepair or for the success or otherwise of his attempts to rectify it. In such a case, no rule of law would compel the court to defeat the contractual intention of the parties by imposing on the persons letting the vehicle on hire an obligation as to the fitness of the vehicle for the hirer's purpose.

Accordingly, if the hirer can be said to have agreed to take the chattel in its actual condition (or if the lessor is entitled to assume such agreement in the light of the hirer's opportunities to make examination) there can be no liability for breach of the duty to supply a fit and suitable chattel. But the lessor will not readily be relieved on this ground and there will be many cases in which the hirer is entitled to rely upon the description or outward appearance of the chattel, without verifying every detail. Moreover, it is submitted that the duty to supply a reasonably fit chattel should not (except in extreme cases) be eliminated by some more specific description accorded to the goods by the owner,[97] unless the description is itself so comprehensive or revealing as to render the other obligation entirely repugnant or otiose.

---

[92] (1867) 15 L.T. 619.

[93] A similar inference can be drawn from the observations of Grove J. in *Fowler* v. *Lock* (1872) L.R. 7 C.P. 272, at 281: ". . . I am consequently of opinion that, where there is a hiring of goods, not agreed to as specific chattels, and where, as here, the person hiring has no means of ascertaining their quality, the hirer is bound to supply such as are reasonably fit for the purpose". The "specific chattel" exception has, of course, now been expunged; see *ante*, p. 724.

[94] [1963] 2 All E.R. 432, at 444. See also *Tetreault* v. *Simonean* (1941) 47 Rev. Leg. 218.

[95] Cf. *Karsales (Harrow) Ltd.* v. *Wallis* [1956] 2 All E.R. 866, at 868 where Denning L.J. held that when the hirer, under a hire-purchase agreement, has seen and inspected the chattel beforehand, an obligation arises on the part of the lessor to deliver the car in substantially the same condition as when it was seen and to keep it in suitable order and repair till that time. The same rule will presumably apply to contracts of simple hire, whether its effect be (as in *Karsales*) to establish the owner's liability or to absolve him from failure to attain any higher standard.

[96] [1963] 1 W.L.R. 584, at 590; see also Upjohn L.J. at 599·600 and Ormerod L.J. at 601.

[97] As suggested by Pearson L.J. in *Astley Industrial Trust Ltd.* v. *Grimley* [1963] 1 W.L.R. 584, at 595; cf. at 597-598 per Upjohn L.J. who discerned two separate

The lessor does not, of course, guarantee the adequacy of his chattel under all conditions and for every kind of use. If the hirer employs it for an abnormal purpose, (at least, if it is a purpose which has not been communicated to the lessor at the time of contracting) he loses the protection of the obligation of reasonable fitness. Thus, to stand upon a hired deckchair, to drive a hired car at a speed greater than its known capacity, to use a hired ladder as a trestle from which to work,[98] or to disobey the standard instructions for using the chattel at any time, would normally amount to an improper user and would result in the forfeiture of the owner's obligation. Few cases on hire deal with this problem,[99] but the principles stated follow naturally from the resemblance to contracts of sale. From this resemblance, it may further be assumed that if the hirer is expected to do something to the chattel in order to make it workable, the owner's liability for injury or loss resulting from the use of the thing may take effect only from the time when this intervening act has been performed.[1]

The lessor is under no duty (unless the contract otherwise provides)[2] to service and maintain the chattel during the period of hire.[3] Accordingly, the further this period progresses, the harder it may become to attribute the defective state of the chattel to the default of the lessor at the time of delivery. However, this is a question of proof, and the owner will be liable if the court is satisfied, on a balance of probabilities, that the loss or injury emanates from a defect inherent in the chattel at the time of contracting.[4] No doubt the length of the expired period of hire will be a material factor in deciding whether the occurrence of the injury or loss raises a presumption as to the defectiveness of the chattel at the time of contracting.

It is submitted, however, that the fact that the hirer has agreed to service and maintain the chattel during the contract-period does not by itself exonerate the owner from all responsibility for its condition at the time of delivery,[5] unless he issues a warning which indicates the likely defects and emphasises that the hirer takes it 'warts and all'. Occasionally, it is true, the agreement will have an exclusory effect without particularising the defects in the chattel; but generally this will be due to some defect developing after delivery, combined with a refusal by the owner to maintain it or to be responsible for its operation unless certain

duties of reasonable fitness and compliance with description, and arrived at what is considered (with respect) to be the preferable result.

---

[98] *Campbell* v. *O'Donnell* [1967] I.R. 226 (a case of loan).
[99] An exception is *Vogan & Co. Ltd.* v. *Oulton* (1899) 81 L.T. 435.
[1] Cf. *Heil* v. *Hedges* [1951] T.L.R. 512.
[2] As with the ordinary television rental.
[3] See *Hadley* v. *Droitwich Construction Co. Ltd.* [1967] 3 All E.R. 911; cf. *Pomfret* v. *Ricroft* (1968) 1 Wms. Saund. 321 (a case of loan). Nor is he under a duty to ensure that the goods remain merchantable: Goode, op. cit., 457; Borrie, *Commercial Law* (4th ed.), p. 150. cf. *Reading* v. *Menham* (1832) 1 M. & Rob. 234; 174 E.R. 80; post, p. 758.
[4] See, for instance, *Guarantee Trust of Jersey Ltd.* v. *Gardner* (1973) 117 Sol. Jo. 564; cf. *Crowther* v. *Shannon Motor Co. Ltd.* [1975] 1 All E.R. 139 (a case of sale).
[5] Cf. **Hadley v. Droitwich Construction Co. Ltd.** [1967] 3 All E.R. 911, at 914 per Harman L.J.

procedures are observed.[6] On the other hand, it may be that a chattel which was reasonably fit at the time of delivery has ceased to be so, not through any deterioration in the chattel itself, but from extraneous circumstances.[7] In general, it will be the hirer who bears the risk of such vicissitudes, but it may be otherwise where the change was within the lessor's contemplation, or was the subject of an express guarantee on his part, at the time of contracting.[8]

Where the chattel is supplied with a servant who remains throughout in the employment of the owner, it is the owner (and not the hirer) who bears responsibility for the servant's negligence In such a case there will be a strong presumption that the servant continues in the service of his general employer, although this has not prevented the courts from holding on occasions that the "hirer" acquires possession of the machine and, thus, becomes a bailee.[9] Where no bailment exists because of the intervening custody of the lessor's servant the courts may nevertheless construe the contract as imposing strict liability upon the owner for the inadequacy or unsafety of the machine;[10] but much will depend upon the real nature of the relationship between the parties. It may be one of occupier and contractee, in which case the liability of the defendant will depend upon whether the relevant jurisdiction is one in which the *Occupiers' Liability Act* 1957, or its equivalent, applies. If so, the occupier will generally be liable for breach of the common duty of care; if not, there will be a Common Law warranty of fitness which, (insofar as the contract was directly related to the defective structure) traditionally binds the occupier to such safety as reasonable care and skill on the part of anyone could achieve.[11] Alternatively, the appropriate relationship may be one of carrier and passenger; generally, this gives rise to a Common Law duty of reasonable care, but liability may be enhanced by statute or when the use of a particular conveyance is set aside for the plaintiff.[12] All these are questions beyond the immediate scope of this book.[13]

(b) *The nature of the term*: In contracts of sale, the seller's obligation of reasonable fitness is a condition[14] and, subject to the operation of s.11(1)(c) of the *Sale of Goods Act* 1893,[15] the buyer can automatically reject for breach. Most of the older decisions on contracts of simple hire speak of the lessor's obligation as a warranty, suggesting that the hirer is confined to an action for damages if the chattel falls below the

---

[6] Ibid.

[7] Cf. *Reed* v. *Dean* [1949] 1 K.B. 188, where the absence of an extinguisher contributed to the inadequacy of the motor launch in the particular event (viz. fire); but this event was itself presumed to have resulted from the defective state of the engine.

[8] Cf. *Quickmaid Rental Services Ltd.* v. *Reece* (1970) 114 Sol. Jo. 372.

[9] See Chapter 7, ante.

[10] A probable example is *Mowbray* v. *Merryweather* [1895] 2 Q.B. 640; cf. *Trade Practices Act* 1974 (Commonwealth); ss. 69-72, 74, post, p. 736 et seq.

[11] *Francis* v. *Cockerell* (1870) L.R. 5 Q.B.D. 501; cf. *Southland Harbour Board* v. *Vella* [1974] 1 N.Z.L.R. 526.

[12] *Hyman* v. *Nye* ante, n. 53.

[13] As to the duty of a ship owner to supply a seaworthy ship, see post, Chapter 16.

[14] *Sale of Goods* Act 1893, s. 14(3) (as amended by *Supply of Goods (Implied Terms) Act* 1973, s. 3).

[15] As amended by *Misrepresentation Act* 1967, s. 4.

standard of reasonable fitness. However, this conclusion is anachronistic for two reasons. First, it was not until the enactment of the *Sale of Goods Act* that the courts began to make any coherent and systematic distinction between warranties and conditions,[16] and to attach independent consequences to the breach of each variety of term;[17] accordingly, the use of the term "warranty" in the nineteenth-century cases is neither a conclusive guide to the character of the term according to modern classifications, nor a conclusive argument against the hirer's right to repudiate for breach of that term. This is particularly so since, in the great majority of these cases, the status of the term was not in question at all.

Secondly, there is an increasing judicial recognition that the abstract character or magnitude of a given term is less important than the consequences of its breach; and that a breach which renders performance of the contract radically different from the performance which would have followed upon a proper observance of its terms will in many cases engender a right to rescind.[18] Consistently with this theory, it has been held that there exists a large class of innominate terms which cannot be characterised for all purposes as warranties or conditions, but in which the consequences of the breach alone are determinative of the right to rescind; that the language of condition and warranty (except insofar as the parties may consensually characterise a term as such) is irrelevant to most contracts not involving the Sale of Goods; and that the principle allowing rescission for a total deprivation of the benefits expected to accrue under a contract can apply even within the partially definitive ambit of the *Sale of Goods Act* 1893.[19] This approach is, of course, without prejudice to the legal consequences that flow from an acknowledged breach of condition, and when a given term has been characterised as such the courts will generally endeavour to adhere to this identification;[20] but it does, to a very large degree, subordinate the status of a term to the consequences of its breach and endow the courts with a substantial discretion as to whether they will allow the innocent party to rescind.

If this approach is applicable to contracts of simple hire, the question whether the lessor's duty possesses the status of a condition is clearly reduced in importance. The hirer will be entitled to reject if (and only

---

[16] See for instance, *Re Lees, ex p. Collins* (1875) 10 Ch. App. 367, at p. 372; Cheshire & Fifoot, *Law of Contract* (8th ed.), p. 118.

[17] The most influential analysis after 1893 was probably that of Fletcher Moulton L.J. in *Wallis, Son & Wells Ltd.* v. *Pratt & Haynes Ltd.* [1910] 2 K.B. 1003, at 1012 et seq.; his dissenting judgment in this case was upheld by the House of Lords on appeal: [1911] A.C. 394. Although the immediate dispute involved a contract for the sale of goods (and was therefore subject to the 1893 Act) the learned judge emphasised that his division of terms into conditions and warranties applied throughout the law of contract.

[18] *Hong Kong Fir Shipping Co. Ltd.* v. *Kawasaki Kisen Kaisha* [1962] 2 Q.B. 26; *Astley Industrial Trust Ltd.* v. *Grimley* (per Upjohn L.J.); *The Mihalis Angelos* [1971] 1 Q.B. 164; *L.G. Schuler A.G.* v. *Wickman Machine Tool Sales Ltd.* [1974] A.C. 235; *Cehave N.V.* v. *Bremer Handelsgesellschaft m.b.H.* [1975] 3 All E.R. 739.

[19] *Cehave N.V.* v. *Bremer Handelsgesellchaft m.b.H.* (ante.)

[20] *L.G. Schuler A.G.* v *Wickman Machine Tool Sales Ltd.* ante; *The Mihalis Angelos* ante.

if) the effect of a failure to supply a suitable chattel is to frustrate the contract. Such an approach was specifically advocated by Upjohn L.J. in a case involving a contract of hire-purchase at Common Law:[21]

> Suppose that a vehicle which is to be let on hire or hire-purchase over a period of two years is at the moment when it ought to be delivered minus four tyres and all its sparking plugs and the carburettor is unserviceable; that would not, I think, entitle the hirer to treat the contract as repudiated; not at all events if the lender offers to put on four tyres, the necessary number of sparking plugs and fit a new carburettor, all of which could be done within a day; no doubt the hirer would be entitled to sue for damages for one day's delay of delivery. On the other hand, if a car which is to be hired at 9 a.m. sharp for the express purpose known to the lender of carrying the hirer 150 miles to lunch in the country and back that same afternoon, is at 9 a.m. in the defective condition to which I have just referred, in my judgment the defects would go to the root of the contract and would clearly frustrate it, for the defects could not be put right in time to permit the hirer to reach his luncheon engagement in time. He would be entitled therefore to treat the contract as repudiated if he so desired.

This reasoning is attractive for a number of reasons It has the advantage of flexibility and, by appearing to discourage an unjustified rescission, promises to do greater justice between the parties than a universal commitment to the theory that the lessor's obligation is a condition. Conversely, it possesses disadvantages; it makes for a greater uncertainty[22] and it further accentuates the disparity (which has never been convincingly justified) between contracts of hire and sale. There may be cases in which the hirer, upon delivery of a deficient chattel, will reasonably wish to reject it without waiting to ascertain whether the defects can be rectified; his rejection may be reasonable even though (as it later transpires) the chattel could have been rendered reasonably fit for its purpose soon enough to avoid defeating the main purpose of the contract. The characterisation of the owner's obligation as an innominate term would preclude this result and would impose upon the hirer a duty to "wait and see". This could prove to be a mixed blessing, particularly in consumer transactions.

The foregoing discussion assumes (as did Upjohn L.J. in *Astley Industrial Trust Ltd.* v. *Grimley*) that the relevant duty has not been elevated to the status of a condition at Common Law. In fact, there are a number of cases which seem to favour this classification, but they represent the minority and cannot be regarded as conclusive.[23] A recent decision in the Court of Appeal is too briefly reported to be useful on this point, but seems if anything to favour the approach sanctioned by Upjohn L.J., by speaking of the relevant defects as

---

[21] *Astley Industrial Trust Ltd.* v. *Grimley* (ante, n. 18) at 598-599.
[22] See the observations in *The Mihalis Angelos.*
[23] *Geddling* v. *Marsh* [1920] 1 K.B. 668, at 672 (Bailhache J.); *Vendair (London) Ltd.* v. *Giro Aviation Co. Ltd.* [1961] 1 Lloyd's Rep. 283, at 287 per Veale J.; *Charterhouse Credit Ltd.* v. *Tolly* [1963] 2 All E.R. 432, at 437-438 per Donovan L. J. (a case of hire-purchase); cf. *Yeoman Credit Ltd.* v. *Apps.* [1961] 2 All E.R. 281, at 287 per Holroyd Pearce L.J.

creating a fundamental breach rather than the breach of a fundamental term.[24] Accordingly, it would seem that the hirer can generally rescind for a failure to supply a fit and suitable chattel only when this event goes to the root of the contract and constitutes a fundamental breach.[25] Of course, the agreement may enhance the status of the lessor's obligation to that of a condition, and so confer upon the hirer the right to reject for any failure to supply a reasonably fit chattel, however minimal the consequences; but the courts will not readily interpret a contract as expressing this intention and even the express designation of the term as a condition may not be conclusive if the Court considers there to be a difference between the colloquial employment of the word and its orthodox legal effect.[26] Therefore, it is only to a very limited practical extent that the precise status of the term will depend upon "the circumstances of the case".[27] The characterisation of the lessor's obligation as an innominate term does, however, possess a further advantage in that it may be difficult for a lessor to show that the breach of such a term was contemplated by an exclusion clause which referred merely to "all conditions and warranties, express or implied".[28]

3. *Safety and fitness for use in Australia*: The owner's duty has been largely clarified and formalised by statute. The most important enactment in this area is the *Trade Practices Act* 1974,[29] which deals with contracts of hire within the broader framework of contracts for the supply of goods. Section 71(2) provides as follows:

> Where a corporation supplies (otherwise than by way of sale by auction or sale by competitive tender) goods to a consumer in the course of a business and the consumer, expressly or by implication, makes known to the corporation or to the person by whom any

---

[24] *Guarantee Trust of Jersey Ltd.* v. *Gardner* (1973) 117 Sol. Jo. 564.
[25] For a recent Canadian decision which seems to adopt this characterisation see *Davidson* v. *North America Business Equipment Ltd.* (1975) 49 D.L.R. (3d) 533. Gould D.C.J. invoked *Karsales (Harrow) Ltd.* v. *Wallis* [1956] 2 All E.R. 866 ("as qualified" by the *Suisse Atlantique* case [1967] 1 A.C. 361) to de-activate certain exclusion clauses in the lease of a cash register which was unusable for a substantial part of the period of hire. However, this decision can equally be explained on the ground that there was a total difference of identity between what was promised and what was supplied, a difference to which the unsuitability of the chattel was merely a contributory factor. In this event, the case was presumably concerned not with the implied term of reasonable fitness but with the more fundamental term that the chattel should comply with its described identity. See also *Burlington Leasing Ltd.* v. *De Moura*, (1976) 60 D.L.R. (3d) 71, where the term of reasonable fitness was excluded because the hirer had not relied upon the owner's skill and judgment, but the hirer succeeded upon the grounds of an essential difference between the contractual chattel and the chattel that had been supplied; "it is not a case of equipment not being reasonably fit but rather that it was totally unfit;" *Canadian Dominion Leasing Corp. Ltd.* v. *Suburban Superdrug Ltd.* (1966) 56 D.L.R. (2d) 43; *Inelco Industries Ltd.* v. *Venture Well Services Ltd.* (1975) 59 D.L.R. (3d) 458.
[26] *L.G. Schuler A.G.* v. *Wickman Machine Tool Sales Ltd.* [1974] A.C. 235; cf. *Sale of Goods Act* 1893, s. 11(1)(b).
[27] *Halsbury's Laws* (4th ed.) Vol. 2, para. 1554.
[28] Cf. *Guarantee Trust of Jersey Ltd.* v. *Gardner* (1973) 117 Sol. Jo. 564, where the exclusion was in similar vein but reliance upon it was held to be precluded by the decision in *Farnworth Finance Facilities Ltd.* v. *Attryde* [1970] 1 W.L.R. 1053; post, p. 936 et seq.
[29] No. 51 of 1974 (Commonwealth). See also *Consumer Transactions Act* 1972-1973 (S. Australia), s. 8(6).

antecedent negotiations are conducted any particular purpose for which the goods are being acquired, there is an implied condition that the goods supplied under the contract for the supply of the goods are reasonably fit for that purpose, whether or not that is a purpose for which such goods are commonly supplied, except where the circumstances show that the consumer does not rely, or that it it unreasonable for him to rely, on the skill or judgment of the corporation or of that person.[30]

Under this provision, reliance becomes a matter to be rebutted by the lessor rather than to be established positively by the hirer. It should be observed, however, that the lessor may escape liability by proving that any reliance (however genuine) upon his skill and judgement was unreasonable. Of course, the more unreasonable the reliance, the easier it will be for the lessor to refute its existence.

The problems of identifying a "consumer" are clarified by s.4(3)(a), which provides that in the absence of contrary intention:

[A] person who acquires goods shall be taken to be a consumer of the goods if the goods are of a kind ordinarily acquired for private use or consumption and the person does not acquire the goods or hold himself out as acquiring the goods for the purposes of re-supply.

There is, of course, a close resemblance between s.71(2) of the *Trade Practices Act* and s.14(3) of the *English Sale of Goods Act* 1893. Presumably, many of the decisions relative to contracts of sale in this area will now (with appropriate modifications) become relevant to contracts for the supply of goods generally, and contracts of hire in particular. "Supply" (in relation to goods) is defined by s.4(1) of the Act to include "Supply (including re-supply) by way of sale, exchange, lease, hire or hire-purchase". Presumably this definition is wide enough to encompass the several kinds of "hiring" under which, for various reasons, possession does not pass to the consumer;[31] the supply of furniture in connexion with the lease of premises;[32] and those arrangements which, although for the mutual advantage of the parties, may not technically qualify as contracts of hire.[33] It is unfortunate that the Act is

---

[30] See also s. 71(3), whereunder s. 71(2) is expressed to apply "to a contract for the supply of goods made by a person who in the course of a business is acting as agent for a corporation as they apply to a contract for the supply of goods made by a corporation in the course of a business, except where that corporation is not supplying in the course of a business and either the consumer knows that fact or reasonable steps are taken to bring it to the notice of the consumer before the contract is made." Combined with that segment of s. 71(2) which relates to antecedent negotiations, this goes some way towards alleviating the difficulties envisaged by Pearson L.J. in *Astley Industrial Trust Ltd.* v. *Grimley* [1963] 2 All E.R. 33, at 42-44; ante, p. 729.

[31] E.g. because the chattel is supplied with a custodian employed by the owner (ante, Chapter 7) or because it remains attached to the owner's premises in a place frequented by his servants: *Southland Harbour Board* v. *Vella* [1974] 1 N.Z.L.R. 526; *A.S. James Pty. Ltd.* v. *C.B. Duncan* [1970] V.R. 705. Cf. s. 74 of the *Trade Practices Act,* which deals, inter alia, with the terms implied into contracts for the supply of services involving the auxiliary supply of "materials".

[32] Held not to give rise to a contract of hire in *Pampris* v. *Thanos* (1967) 69 S.R. (N.S.W.) 226; and see ante, p. 718.

[33] See generally Paton op. cit., pp. 305-307; Palmer and Rose, (1977) 26 I.C.L.Q. 169.

necessarily confined to contracts between a corporation and a consumer.
Partnerships and sole traders escape its provisions entirely, and its
valuable assistance is withheld from most inter-corporate contracts, which
are still governed (in the case of hiring) by the uncertainties of the
Common Law.[34]

Section 71(2) characterises the lessor's obligation as a condition, so
that (short of affirmation) the hirer is given an unfettered prerogative to
reject substandard goods. This means that there is no room for the
application to s.71(2) of the more pragmatic approach advocated by
Upjohn L.J. in *Astley Industrial Trust Ltd.* v. *Grimley*.[35]

At Common Law, the picture is more confused,[36] although the question
whether the lessor can escape liability by showing that he took reasonable
care is readily answered. It is clearly established that the lessor's
undertaking is an absolute one and is not dependent upon gradations of
care or the detectability of the defect.[37] The only modern dissentient
appears to be Crisp J. who, speaking obiter in an unreported Tasmanian
decision,[38] expressly preferred the formulation of the lessor's duty as one
of reasonable care in *Reed* v. *Dean*[39] to the absolute standard adopted by
Jordan C.J. in *Gemmell Power Farming Co. Ltd.* v. *Nies*.[40] There can be
little doubt that the absolute standard is now authoritative and that the
lessor's liability extends to latent defects which no amount of care and
skill could detect.[41]

Whether the hirer must demonstrate reliance upon the seller's skill
and judgement will depend, in some degree at least, upon the measure of

---

[34] As to the implied terms of reasonable fitness in South Australia, see the *S.A.
Consumer Transactions Act* 1972-1973, s. 8(6).
[35] [1963] 1 W.L.R. 584, 598-599; ante, p. 235.
[36] Davies (1964) 38 A.L.J. 277; Turner (1972) 46 A.L.J. 560, and 619.
[37] *Derbyshire Building Co. Pty. Ltd.* v. *Becker* (1962) 107 C.L.R. 633, at 645
(McTiernan J.), 649 (Kitto J.), 656 (Taylor J.) and 659-660 per Windeyer J.,
affirming *Becker* v. *Derbyshire Building Co. Pty. Ltd.* [1961] N.S.W.R. 864. See
also *Gemmell Power Farming Co. Ltd.* v. *Nies* (1935) 35 S.R. (N.S.W.) 469,
at 475; *Woods Radio Exchange Ltd.* v. *Marriott* [1939] V.L.R. 309, at 317;
Beaton v. *Moore Acceptance Corporation Pty. Ltd.* (1959) 104 C.L.R. 107, at
119; *Criss* v. *Alexander* (1928) 28 S.R. (N.S.W.) 297, at 300-301; *Star Express
Merchandising Co. Pty. Ltd.* v. *V.G. McGrath Pty. Ltd.* [1959] V.R. 443; *Pampris*
v. *Thanos* (1967) 69 S.R. (N.S.W.) 226, at 228-229; *A.S. James Pty. Ltd.* v. *C.B.
Duncan* [1970] V.R. 705, at 715-717.
[38] *Smith* v. *Caltex Oil (Australia) Pty. Ltd.* (1962) Tas. Unrep. 50/1962; see, to
similar effect, *Roach* v. *Roberts* (1924) 26 W.A.L.R. 110, at 112 per McMillan
C.J.; *Klose* v. *Duncan & Fraser Ltd.* [1928] S.A.S.R. 139, at 146 per Angas
Parsons J.
[39] [1949] 1 K.B. 188.
[40] (1935) 35 S.R. (N.S.W.) 469, at 475; Crisp, J. does not appear to have expressed
an opinion upon the more recent decisions in the *Becker* and *Star Express* cases,
ante.
[41] Cf. *Southland Harbour Board* v. *Vella* [1974] 1 N.Z.L.R. 526, at 530-531, where
McCarthy P. was prepared to exempt from the operation of the warranty implied
by *Francis* v. *Cockerell* (1870) L.R. 5 Q.B. 501 those "unseen or unknown defects
which there were no means of discovering or ascertaining under ordinary or
reasonable modes of enquiry or examination", but cited by way of analogy the
Becker case ante and the judgement of Holroyd Pearce L.J. in *Yeoman Credit
Ltd.* v. *Apps* [1962] 2 Q.B. 508, neither of which endorses the test of reasonable
care. Richmond J. at 533 cited with apparent approval the statement of Kitto
J. in *Becker's* case, i.e. that the lessor's duty extends to latent defects, while
Beattie J. at 541 cited the same decision without specifically adverting to this point.
The overall result of these dicta seems to be support for the absolute standard in
cases of hire.

identity that Australian courts are prepared to discern between contracts of sale and hire. At Common Law, the buyer's remedy seems to have required some manifestation of reliance[42] and there are Australian cases which specifically extend this requirement to the hirer. Thus, in *Criss* v. *Alexander*[43] Campbell J. suggested that it was immaterial whether the lessor of a lorry on hire-purchase owed a duty under the *Sale of Goods Act*,[44] to supply a reasonably fit chattel:

> . . . because whether the transaction comes within the language and intention of s.19 or not, it is quite clear that at common law, a similar implication of a condition of reasonable fitness would arise where a person desiring to buy or to hire a particular article for a certain purpose goes to another person whose business it is to supply such articles and makes known to him the purpose for which the article is required, so as to show that the person proposing to buy or take on hire relies on the skill or judgement of the person proposing to sell or let on hire.[45]

A less orthodox approach was adopted by Dean J., in the *Star Express* case, who observed that prima facie an ordinary hirer would rely upon a professional lessor to supply him with a suitable chattel, and that "the onus of showing that the hirer had taken upon himself the risk as to its suitability so as to exonerate the supplier should be on the supplier."[46] This accords with the normal tenor of English authorities on the sale of goods, which have waived the need for express communication of purpose or reliance in transactions (such as those involving a private consumer and a reputable supplier) from which it can readily be inferred.[47] For this reason, of course, the disputed identity between sale and hire[48] would in many cases be immaterial. Thus, whereas in the *Becker* case there are some fairly strong statements of the conventional view, appearing at first

---

[42] *Brown* v. *Edgington* (1841) 2 Man. & G. 279; *Bigge* v. *Parkinson* (1862) 7 H. & N. 955, at 961; *Jones* v. *Just* (1868) L.R. 3 Q.B. 197, at 202-203; *Drummond* v. *Van Ingen* (1887) 12 App. Cas. 284, at 293-294, 297.

[43] (1928) 28 S.R. (N.S.W.) 297, at 300-301.

[44] *Sale of Goods Act* 1923 (N.S.W.), s. 19 the equivalent to s. 14(1) of the unrevised *English Sale of Goods Act* 1893, before modification under the *Supply of Goods (Implied Terms) Act* 1973.

[45] See further *Beaton* v. *Moore Acceptance Corporation Pty. Ltd.* (1959) 104 C.L.R. 106, at 119-121 (High Court of Australia), citing *Gemmell Power Farming Co. Ltd.* v. *Nies* (1935) 35 S.R. (N.S.W.) 469-475 and *Woods Radio Exchange Ltd.* v. *Marriott* [1939] V.L.R. 309; *Traders Finance Corporation Ltd.* v. *Rourke* (1966) 85 W.N. (Pt. 1) (N.S.W.) 739. The decision in *Woods Radio Exchange* does not totally discount a differentiation between sale and hire for the purposes of reliance, nor does it necessarily preclude a greater latitude in this respect to the hirer; but Lowe J. did observe that it would be hard to suppose that the parties to a business transaction would harbour such an intention. See also *Klose* v. *Duncan & Fraser Ltd.* [1928] S.A.S.R. 139, at 145, where Angas Parsons J. cited with approval the decision in *Geddling* v. *Marsh* [1920] 1 K.B. 688, to the effect that the terms implied into contracts of bailment are not identical to those implied in contracts of sale; and see *Roach* v. *Roberts* (1924) 26 W.A.L.R. 110, at 112.

[46] [1959] V.R. 443, at 446; cf. Smith J. at 454 with O'Bryan J. at p. 443, whose judgment favours the need for positive communication of the *purpose* for which the goods are required but is less specific upon the question whether this communication must be made "so as to show" reliance.

[47] Ante, p. 728; and see *Derbyshire Building Co. Pty. Ltd.* v. *Becker* (1962) 107 C.L.R. 633, at 652 per Kitto J.

[48] This controversy is very closely analysed by Dr. Turner in (1972) 46 A.L.J. 560, at 566, 619.

sight to impose a heavy onus upon the hirer, it is clear that this burden will often be lightened, and the conclusion that the hirer relied upon the lessor's skill and judgement accelerated, by the circumstances of the delivery and the relative standing or experience of the parties:

> The necessary foundation for implying a condition as to fitness is proof that the person to whom the chattels are supplied brought home to the mind of the supplier that he was relying on him in such a way that the supplier can be taken to have contracted on that footing.[49]
>
> We have held[50] . . . that the common law rules relating to the implication in a contract for the sale of goods of a general condition that the goods shall be reasonably fit for a specified purpose apply with equal force to a hire purchase agreement . . . and we have pointed out that it was a pre-requisite to the implication of such a general condition at common law that it should appear, in effect, that the buyer had bought on the seller's judgement that the subject goods would answer a particular purpose. Likewise, I see no reason why the same rules should not apply with equal force to an agreement for the hire of a chattel for a particular purpose.[51]

Recent authority has to some extent favoured a closer equation between the implied term of reasonable fitness in contracts of hire and its *statutory* equivalent in contracts of sale. This equation was explicitly endorsed by Kitto J. in *Becker's* case,[52] in a statement which was approved obiter by the New South Wales Court of Appeal in *Pampris* v. *Thanos*.[53] Dr Turner has contended that this approach is without foundation and should be discarded in favour of that "the broad common law principle" espoused by McTiernan J.[54] The principle is somewhat difficult to elicit. At first sight, McTiernan J. seems to envisage the need for clear evidence indicating that the hirer trusted solely to his own judgement before the lessor will be entitled to escape. He cites with approval the statement of Jordan C.J. in *Gemmell Power Farming Co. Ltd* v. *Nies*[55] that "when one person, for value, supplies a chattel to another to be used for an agreed or stated purpose, or for a purpose indicated by the nature of the chattel,

---

49 (1962) 107 C.L.R. 633, at 650 per Kitto J.

50 *Beaton* v. *Moore Acceptance Corporation Pty. Ltd.* (1959) 104 C.L.R. 107, at p. 119.

51 (1962) 107 C.L.R. 633, at 656-657 per Taylor J., criticised by Turner (1972) 46 A.L.J. 619, at 623; cf. McTiernan J. at 646 and the decision of the N.S.W. Full Supreme Court [1961] N.S.W.R. 864, which denied that it was necessary for the hirer to show that he had relied upon the lessor's skill and judgment. The need for reliance was taken in *Beaton's* case (1959) 104 C.L.R. 107 to be a ground for assuming that many hirers under contracts of hire-purchase would be unable to proceed for breach of this term against a finance company (cf. p. 729, ante) although it was conceded that this requirement did not operate to prevent the implication of a condition that the chattel would be free from those defects that rendered it fundamentally different from what the finance-company had contracted to supply, as opposed to defects which merely rendered it functionally unsuitable for the particular class of work for which it had been acquired.

52 (1962) 107 C.L.R. 633, at 649, criticised by Turner, (ante, n. 50) at 621-623; see also Windeyer J. (1962) 107 C.L.R., at 659.

53 (1967) 69 S.R. (N.S.W.) 226, at 229. Cf. *A.S. James Pty. Ltd.* v. *C.B. Duncan* [1970] V.R. 705, at 715-716, which is more ambivalent on this point, but seems to recognise at least a prima facie requirement that the hirer's purpose and his reliance be made evident to the owner.

54 (1962) 107 C.L.R. 633, at 646; see Turner, at 621.

55 (1935) 35 S.R. (N.S.W.) 469, at 475.

he impliedly promises, in the absence of some provision to the contrary, that it is reasonably fit for such use"; he also places considerable emphasis on the old case of *Jones* v. *Page*[56] which at no point specifically mentions the need for a hirer to have manifested his reliance upon the seller's skill and judgement. However, *Jones* v. *Page* was a case in which both the nature of the chattel and the parties' relationship enabled such reliance to be readily inferred. Nor can there be any doubt that if the vehicle in *Jones* v. *Page* had transpired to be unsuitable from the point of capacity (which was the object of the hirer's examination) the action would have been dismissed without any need on the part of the lessor to disprove reliance. Taken in its entirety, there is little in McTiernan's J.'s judgment to support the view that a term of reasonable fitness will necessarily be implied "unless it can be firmly established that the hirer had taken upon himself the 'risk' of its being defective for the specified purpose, or for the purpose indicated by its nature."[57] Whether reliance is to be inferred depends upon the nature of the chattel, the particular purpose for which it is hired, its evident condition at the time of contracting, and the character and relationship of the parties. Similarly, the fact that the hirer has specifically indicated his purpose in requiring the goods, or has made an inspection, or is hiring a specific ascertained chattel, are merely elements in the general inquiry as to whether in the circumstances the fitness of the chattel was being guaranteed.[58] Whether there is total identity between sales and hirings is therefore largely academic because as a matter of commonsense the results will generally be the same.

Admittedly, it might be inconvenient if the common law term of fitness in contracts of hire were to be geared to the haphazard operation of statutory changes in the case of sale of goods. This problem is perhaps accentuated by s.74 of the *Trade Practices Act* 1974, which applies only to those contracts of hire between a corporation (as supplier) and a consumer, and upon one argument brings the hirer's position back full circle by requiring the supplier to refute reliance.[59]

(a) *Warranty, condition or innominate term?* At Common Law,[60] Australian authority appears to be tilted in favour of a condition that the chattel

---

[56] (1867) 15 L.T. 619.

[57] Turner, ante.

[58] The theory that no implication as to fitness can arise on the hire of a specific and ascertained chattel (a theory which formerly drew its inspiration from *Robertson* v. *Amazon Tug & Lighterage Co. Ltd.* ante, p. 724) was rejected by the N.S.W. Full Supreme Court in *Becker* v. *Derbyshire Building Co. Pty. Ltd.* [1961] N.S.W.R. 864, at 869. Cf. McTiernan and Kitto JJ. in the High Court (1962) 107 C.L.R. 633, at 645, 652, who do not appear to dispute the decision, while arriving at a result with which it is not easy to reconcile. In *Star Express Merchandising Co. Pty. Ltd.* v. *V.G. McGrath Pty. Ltd.* [1959] V.R. 443, at 445, both O'Bryan and Dean JJ. adopted the *Robertson* doctrine (cf. Smith J. at 450) but in *A.S. James Pty. Ltd.* v. *C.B. Duncan* [1970] V.R. 705, at 716, McInerney J. seemed, without expressly saying so, to associate himself with its repudiation in *Reed* v. *Dean* at 193 and in *Yeoman Credit Ltd.* v. *Apps* at 516. The doctrine is obsolete and should undoubtedly be discarded, since it is merely one facet of the broader question of reliance: see further (1975) 4 *Anglo-American Law Review* 207, at 209-210.

[59] Cf. *Cehave N.V.* v. *Bremer Handelsgesellschaft* [1975] 3 All E.R. 739, at 748.

[60] For the status of the term under statutory definitions, see ante, p. 736 et seq.

shall be reasonably fit for use. Certainly, this characterisation of the lessor's duty is favoured by several of the Common Law decisions relating to hire-purchase,[61] although authorities can be cited to the contrary, both in hire-purchase cases[62] and in those which concern simple hire.[63] The question has never arisen for direct decision and the parallel with cases of sale seems to justify importing the larger variety of term, particularly since this is the species adopted by the *Trade Practices Act* 1974, and the *Consumer Transactions Act* 1972-1973 (S.A.).[64] On the other hand, Australian courts may be influenced by the judgment of Upjohn L.J. in *Astley Industrial Trust Ltd.* v. *Grimley*[65] and may prefer to classify the lessor's obligation as an innominate term. It is submitted that considerations of certainty make the former approach marginally to be preferred.

(b) *Hiring in the course of business*: Again, there is little direct authority, but it would seem reasonable that the lessor's strict obligation should generally be confined to those cases in which the chattel is let as part of a commercial operation. This requirement (which corresponds with the analogous duty upon a seller of goods) could be construed quite liberally so as to include, for instance, a garage which normally only sells or repairs cars but on an isolated occasion leases one to a customer,[66] or a private citizen who has a part-time hobby of renovating and renting out vehicles.[67] In fact, the only immediate statement upon this requirement has been non-committal; in *Star Express Merchandising Co. Pty. Ltd.* v. *V. G. McGrath Pty. Ltd.*[68] Dean J. contented himself with observing that if it were necessary that the bailor should habitually hire out chattels of the kind in question, in the present case this requirement had been fulfilled. In the *Becker*[69] case the facts were held to give rise to a duty to provide a properly maintained chattel where the plaintiff, working as an independent contractor for the defendant, had been loaned a saw

---

[61] *Criss* v. *Alexander* (1928) 28 S.R. (N.S.W.) 297, at 300-301; *Beaton* v. *Moore Acceptance Corporation Pty. Ltd.* (1959) 104 C.L.R. 107, at 119-121 (although the identification is not wholly consistent and the Court occasionally refers to a "condition or term"); *Gemmell Power Farming Co. Ltd.* v. *Nies* (1935) 35 S.R. (N.S.W.) 469, at 476; *Woods Radio Exchange Led.* v. *Marriott* [1939] V.L.R. 309, at 317-318.

[62] E.g. *Klose* v. *Duncan & Fraser Ltd.* [1928] S.A.S.R. 139, at 146; *Roach* v. *Roberts* (1924) 26 W.A.L.R. 110, at 112.

[63] *Star Express Merchandising Co. Pty. Ltd.* v. *V.G. McGrath & Co. Pty. Ltd.; Smith* v. *Caltex (Australasia) Pty. Ltd.* (1962) Tas. Unrep. 50/1962. See also *Pampris* v. *Thanos* (1967) 69 S.R. (N.S.W.) 226; *A.S. James Pty. Ltd.* v. *C.B. Duncan* [1970] V.R. 705.

[64] Ante, p. 736 et seq. The High Court's decision in *Derbyshire Building Co. Pty. Ltd.* v. *Becker* is inconclusive on this point, since the character of the term was not in issue; the plaintiff had, in fact, alleged a "term or condition" that the saw would be maintained safe and fit for use. Taylor J. at 656-657 seems to favour a condition. Windeyer J. at 659-660 speaks in terms of a warranty, though he favours a closer equation with the sale of goods.

[65] [1963] 1 W.L.R. 584, at 598-599; ante, p. 735.

[66] Cf. *Havering London Borough Council* v. *Stevenson* [1970] 1 W.L.R. 1375.

[67] Cf. *Ludgate* v. *Lovett* [1969] 1 W.L.R. 1016.

[68] [1959] V.R. 443, at 446.

[69] (1962) 107 C.L.R. 633.

from their joinery shop for the purpose of carrying out his work. In all the remaining Australian decisions the lessor seems to have been professionally engaged in leasing chattels of the kind in question, and clearly the element of reliance is easier to infer when the parties stand in the relation of consumer and supplier. Such a restriction does not prevent the implication in exceptional cases of a term of reasonable fitness against a private supplier, but it does avoid the possible charge of imposing strict liability upon ordinary lenders of domestic articles who make the loan in return for a small or indirect consideration: e.g. an academic who lends his car to a neighbour while on study leave because he wants it to be regularly used. In cases of this kind, liability in negligence would appear to meet the demands of justice.

4. *Description, sample and merchantable quality*: Both Pearson and Upjohn LJJ., discussing the terms implied into contracts of hire-purchase at Common Law, have favoured the implication of a term that the goods should correspond with their description.[70] This obligation has been described by Upjohn L.J.[71] as a fundamental term, breach of which automatically gives the hirer the right to treat the contract as repudiated. The question whether a chattel complies with its description is one of fact, involving such factors as its apparent condition upon ordinary inspection, the extent of any defects that were unknown to the hirer at the time of delivery, their impact upon its safety and ability to fulfil its intended purpose, the likely cost of repairs and the probable period of delay.[72] Presumably the same requirements as govern the implication of the equivalent condition in sale of goods cases[73] apply to contracts of hire, and the description must be one which identifies the goods.[74] The implication of this condition in cases of simple hire is assumed by the English Law Commission,[75] which also favours a term relating to correspondence with sample. In Australia, there is no decision directly in point,[76] but conditions as to correspondence with description are implied by the *South Australian Consumer Transactions Act* 1972-1973[77] and by s.70 of the *Commonwealth Trade Practices Act* 1974. The latter section enacts as follows:

1. Where there is a contract for the supply (otherwise than by way of sale by auction or sale by competitive tender) by a corporation in the course of a business of goods to a consumer by description, there is an implied condition that the goods will correspond with the description, and, if the supply is by reference to a sample as well as by description,

---

[70] *Astley Industrial Trust Ltd.* v. *Grimley* [1963] 1 W.L.R. 584, at 595 per Pearson L.J., at 597-598 per Upjohn, L.J.

[71] Ibid.

[72] Ibid., per Upjohn L.J.

[73] *Sale of Goods Act* 1893, s. 13.

[74] *Ashington Piggeries Ltd.* v. *Christopher Hill Ltd.* [1972] A.C. 441 (esp. at p. 470, per Lord Hodson); cf. *Beale* v. *Taylor* [1967] 3 All E.R. 253 and see Coote (1976) 50 A.L.J. 17; (1977) 51 A.L.J. 44.

[75] *Law Com. No. 69; Scot. Law Com. No. 39* (1975) para. 19.

[76] Cf. *Beaton* v. *Moore Acceptance Corporation Ltd.* (1959) 104 C.L.R. 107; ante., p. 740, n. 51.

[77] Section 8(3).

it is not sufficient that the bulk of the goods corresponds with the sample if the goods do not also correspond with the description.
2. A supply of goods is not prevented from being a supply by description for the purposes of sub-section (1) by reason only that, being exposed for sale or hire, they are selected by the consumer.

Both statutes also imply conditions of merchantable quality,[78] and the *Trade Practices Act* additionally implies a condition as to correspondence with sample.[79] Probably, such conditions would be held to exist both in England and in Australia at Common Law.[80]

IV. THE DUTIES OF THE HIRER

The hirer owes four principal duties: to pay the agreed rental, to take proper care of the chattel, to comply with the limitations upon his use of it and to restore it to the owner at the end of the hiring. These duties may, of course, be modified by agreement.

A. Payment of rental

A failure to pay the agreed rental is a breach of contract which entitles the owner to sue for damages. Normally, a single lapse in payment will not amount to a repudiation by the hirer and will not entitle the owner to recover the goods; aliter, where the failure to pay is a persistent one or where the agreement specifically provides for termination in this event.[81] If the hirer resumes payments after a temporary lapse, and the lessor does not exercise any right to rescind, his damages are limited to the arrears under the contract, plus any additional loss he may have suffered by reason of the delay.[82] Where, on the other hand, the hirer under a fixed term rental repudiates the contract and there is no ready market for the goods elsewhere, he becomes liable for the full amount of unpaid rentals, minus a sum for accelerated payment.[83] If, however, the owner sells the chattel before the period has ended, this operates as a rescission of the contract; the owner cannot therefore recover the projected amount of rentals but is reduced to an ordinary action for damages.[84] Of course, the owner is bound to take reasonable steps to mitigate his loss, and in appropriate cases a sale may represent reasonable mitigation. It will be unusual for an owner to be able to show loss if he has sold the chattel to a third party, but in cases where this can be

---

[78] *Consumer Transactions Act* 1972-1973 (S.A.) ss. 8(4) and (5); T.P.A. 1974 (Com.) s. 71(1). These obligations cannot be excluded: see ibid., ss. 10(1) and 68 respectively.

[79] T.P.A. 1974, s. 72. Again s. 68 prohibits exclusion of liability for breach.

[80] Cf. *Sleeskin* v. *Grant Food Inc.* (1974) 318 A. 2d. 874; ante, p. 727.

[81] *Bowmakers Ltd.* v. *Barnet Instruments Ltd.* [1945] 1 K.B. 65.

[82] Generally the lessor will suffer no recoverable loss under this head.

[83] *Interoffice Telephones Ltd.* v. *Robert Freeman Ltd.* [1958] 1 Q.B. 190, overruling *British Automatic Co. Ltd.* v. *Haynes* [1921] 1 K.B. 377; *Robophone Facilities Ltd.* v. *Blank* [1966] 3 All E.R. 128; cf. *Bentworth Finance Ltd.* v. *Jennings* (1961) 111 Law Jo. 488; *Karsales (Harrow) Ltd.* v. *Wallis* [1956] 2 All E.R. 866, at 869 per Denning, L.J.

[84] *Wright* v. *Melville* (1828) 3 Car. & P. 542 N.P. (Best C.J.); cf. *Bentworth Finance Ltd.* v. *Reeder* [1961] C.L.Y. 491; *R. V. Ward Ltd.* v. *Bignall* [1967] 1 Q.B. 534.

shown there will be grounds for permitting him to recover this loss from the hirer.

The terms of the contract may, as we have seen, grant the owner the right to retake the chattel upon a single failure in payment; at Common Law he then acquires an immediate right of possession and may bring the bailment to an end.[85] It seems, however, that without an express agreement to this effect, an isolated lapse or delay in payment does not entitle the owner to repudiate, and does not constitute a fundamental breach on the part of the hirer.[86] If, on the other hand, the hirer declares his refusal or inability to pay any further instalments, or if his failure to pay is a substantial one, the lessor may be entitled to rescind the contract and recover the goods.[87] Whether this right exists will depend upon the construction of the contract and the nature of the hirer's breach. Of course, there may be other conduct on the part of the hirer, such as an unauthorised disposition, which justifies the owner's claim to repudiate. Again, this will be a matter of construction.

In many cases, lessors have endeavoured to protect themselves by providing for the payment of specific sums by the hirer upon default. Great difficulty has been caused by the necessity to decide whether such a provision represents a genuine attempt to pre-estimate the owner's damages or a penalty, and therefore unenforceable.[88] Occasionally, the agreement will represent neither;[89] particularly since both English and Australian courts have affirmed that a term will not be characterised as a penalty clause if it is expressed to take effect upon an event other than a breach of contract by the hirer.[90]

The owner's remedies for default in payment have been substantially modified by statute in England[91] and South Australia,[92] in cases of consumer hiring. These and associated reforms will be discussed at the end of the present chapter.[93]

---

[85] E.g., *Wertheim* v. *Virtue* (1890) 16 V.L.R. 369.

[86] *Ex p. Marks* (1902) 19 W.N. (N.S.W.) 151; cf. *Bowmakers Ltd.* v. *Barnett Instruments Ltd.* [1945] 1 K.B. 65. See also *Healing (Sales) Pty. Ltd.* v. *Inglis Electrix Pty. Ltd.* (1968) 42 A.L.J.R. 280; *Healy* v. *Tait* [1954] S.A.S.R. 56, both of which concerned convenants for repossession on the levy of distress against the hirer. As to relief in equity, see ante, p. 68.

[87] *International Leasing Corporation Ltd.* v. *Aiken* [1967] 2 N.S.W.R. 427.

[88] See *Lamson Store Service Co. Ltd.* v. *Weidenbach & Co's Trustees* (1904) 7 W.A.R. 166; *Lamson Store Service Co. Ltd.* v. *Russell Wilkins & Sons Ltd.* (1906) 4 C.L.R. 672; *Western Electric Co. (Australasia) Ltd.* v. *Ward* (1933) 51 W.N. (N.S.W.) 19; *International Leasing Corporation Ltd.* v. *Aiken* (ante); *Re Mutual (Queensland) Knitting Mills* [1959] Qd. R. 357; *Claud Neon Lights (Victoria) Ltd.* v. *Gorham* [1962] V.R. 493; *Lessors Ltd.* v. *Westley* [1964-1965] N.S.W.R. 2091; *I.A.C. (Leasing) Ltd.* v. *Humphrey* (1972) 126 C.L.R. 131.

[89] E.g., *Metro-Goldwyn-Mayer Pty. Ltd.* v. *Greenham* [1966] 2 N.S.W.R. 717; 41 A.L.J. 508.

[90] *Associated Distributors Ltd.* v. *Hall* [1938] 2 K.B. 83; *Bridge* v. *Campbell Discount Co. Ltd.* [1962] A.C. 600; *United Dominions Trust (Commercial) Ltd.* v. *Ennis* [1968] 1 Q.B. 54; *Granor Finance Ltd.* v. *Liquidator of Eastore Ltd.* 1974 S.L.T. 296; *I.A.C. (Leasing) Ltd.* v. *Humphrey* (1972) 126 C.L.R. 131, at 143; cf. *United Dominions Trust (Commercial) Ltd.* v. *Patterson* [1973] N.I.R. 142.

[91] *Consumer Credit Act* 1974.

[92] *Consumer Transactions Act* 1972-1973.

[93] Post, p. 760 et seq.

B. Duty of care

The hirer, as an ordinary bailee for mutual advantage, must take reasonable care of the chattel and must use reasonable skill in its management. This rule is supported by authority in every major Commonwealth jurisdiction.[94]

The burden of proving that the appropriate degree of care has been taken rests, of course, upon the bailee. He is not bound to establish the precise cause of the loss,[95] however, and may escape even on proof of negligence if he can show that it was not his neglect or mismanagement that caused or contributed to the loss.[96] The Supreme Court of Canada have further held that the ordinary burden of proof may be displaced when the chattel is lost and the hirer disappears or is killed.[97] In the instant case, the hirer of an aircraft disappeared while flying it over Lake Ontario and neither he nor the machine was ever recovered. The Court emphasised the injustice of requiring his estate to give positive evidence of the deceased's care and skill, and invoked the reasons given by Atkin L.J. in *The Ruapehu*[98] as grounds for discarding the traditional burden of proof. In their view, when the bailee is dead and the chattel is lost (and perhaps in other cases where the bailee does not or could not know of the circumstances surrounding the loss) the general burden should be displaced in favour of the rule appropriate to cases in which one party is alleged to have induced the frustration of the contract. That rule requires the person alleging fault to prove it directly, unless the circumstances are such as to raise a prima facie case, in which event the doctrine

---

[94] England: *Dollar* v. *Greenfield* (1905) *The Times*, May 18th (H.L.): *Dean* v. *Keate* (1811) 3 Camp. 4; *Arbon* v. *Fussell* (1862) 3 F. & F. 152; *Tilling* v. *Balmain* (1892) 8 T.L.R. 517; *Brice & Sons Ltd.* v. *Christiani & Nielsen* (1928) 44 T.L.R. 335; *Ludgate* v. *Lovett* [1969] 1 W.L.R. 1106; *British Crane Hire Corporation Ltd.* v. *Ipswich Plant Hire Ltd.* [1975] 1 Q.B. 303, at 311-312; cf. *Coggs* v. *Bernard* (1703) 2 Ld. Raym. 909, at 916; 92 E.R. 107, at 111; Australia: *Bell* v. *Walker* (1856) 1 V.L.T. 63: *Watts* v. *Cuthbert* (1912) 14 W.A.L.R. 205; *Hughes* v. *Rooke* [1954] Q.S.R. 45; *Smith* v. *Caltex Oil (Australia) Pty. Ltd.* (1962) Tas. Unrep. 50/1962; *A.S. James Pty. Ltd.* v. *C.B. Duncan* [1970] V.R. 705: New Zealand: *Oldham* v. *Lyons Ltd.* (1908) 27 N.Z.L.R. 535; *Manchester* v. *Glenie* (1890) 28 N.Z.L.R. 123; *Smith* v. *Blower* (1882) N.Z.L.R. 1 S.C. 329; *Sumich* v. *Auckland Rental Cars Ltd.* [1955] N.Z.L.R. 1131; *Otago Aero Club Inc.* v. *John H. Stevenson Ltd.* [1957] N.Z.L.R. 471. Canada: *Reynolds* v. *Roxburgh* (1886) 10 O.R. 649; *Lang* v *Brown* (1898) 34 N.B.R. 492; *Gremley* v. *Stubbs* (1908) 39 N.B.R. 21; *Hearle* v. *Vanwest Logging Co. Ltd.* (1951) 4 W.W.R. 246, 252; *Murray* v. *Collins* (1920) 53 D.L.R. 120; *Gray* v. *Steeves* (1914) 42 N.B.R. 676; *Aseltine* v. *McAnally* [1950] O.W.N. 229; *Coast Crane Co. Ltd.* v. *Dominion Bridge Co. Ltd.* (1961) 28 D.L.R. (2d) 295; *Arrow Transfer Co. Ltd.* v. *Fleetwood Logging Co. Ltd.* (1961) 30 D.L.R. (2d) 631: *A-1 Rentals Sales & Service Ltd.* v. *Alberta Arches and Beams Ltd.* (1966) 60 D.L.R. (2d) 4; *Allison Concrete Ltd.* v. *Canadian Pacific Ltd.* (1973) 40 D.L.R. (3d) 237. For Scottish decisions, see Beven, *Negligence in the Modern Law* (2nd ed.) 961-963; *Jackson's (Edinburgh) Ltd.* v. *Constructors John Brown Ltd.* 1965 S.L.T. 37. For a recent South African decision, see *Niekirk* v. *Assegai* (1977) 2 S.A.L.R. 416.

[95] *Sumich* v. *Auckland Rental Cars Ltd.* (ante).

[96] See ante, p. 440 et seq. (hire of custody).

[97] *National Trust Co. Ltd.* v. *Wong* (1969) 3 D.L.R. (3d) 55. Cf. *Huard* v. *Feiczewicz* (1911) Q.R. 40 S.C. 385.

[98] "The bailee knows all about it; he must explain": (1925) 21 Lloyd's Rep. 310, at 315.

of res ipsa loquitur may apply.[99] In the present case, the hirer's estate had put forward an explanation of the loss[1] which was acceptable on the evidence and consistent with the hirer's exercise of reasonable care; accordingly, it was entitled to be discharged.

The decision is interesting for a number of reasons. It confirms that the doctrine of res ipsa loquitur may (in Canada at least) operate by way of long-stop in bailment actions, where the traditional bailee's onus of proof has been ousted by special circumstances.[2] It also suggests that the circumstances in which this displacement may occur are wider than was traditionally thought. In this respect the decision is open to question. It could be argued that the whole purpose of the bailee's burden of proof is to supply an assumed or inferred conclusion as to liability when the facts cannot speak decisively for themselves. Whatever the injustice of requiring a man's estate to prove that he was not negligent on a given occasion, it seems no less harsh to expect a bailor to demonstrate the contrary proposition in relation to an event which is as far beyond his observation at the material time as in the case of any other bailor. While, therefore, it is tempting to envisage extensions of *National Trust Co.* v. *Wong* to such phenoma as amnaesiac bailees, it seems that the principle laid down in that decision will be sparingly applied.[3]

Most of the decisions in this area are of a factual nature, involving questions as to what amounts to negligence on the part of the hirer and the circumstances in which it will be inferred. It has been held negligent for a hirer to continue to exercise a horse after it has refused its feed because of exhaustion;[4] to order the manoeuvring of a crane over a marshy piece of ground without the protection of navimats[5] or of a pay loader over a frozen lake when coal has caused the ice to melt in places;[6] to take a car out in severely hazardous conditions;[7] to exercise a horse in a place from which it is likely to take fright and bolt;[8] or to leave a boat unguarded in a place from which it can readily be stolen.[9] Likewise,

---

[99] (1969) 3 D.L.R. (3d), at 63-64, citing the statement by Lord Wright in *Joseph Constantine S.S. Co. Ltd.* v. *Imperial Smelting Corporation Ltd.* [1941] 2 All E.R. 165, at 181. See further p. 749, post.

[1] Viz., bad weather conditions; it being considered sufficient under Canadian law for a defendant to adduce a convincing alternative explanation in order to rebut the presumption of res ipsa loquitur.

[2] Cf. Laskin J., in the Ontario Court of Appeal, (1966) 56 D.L.R. (2d) 228, at 232, who had remarked "I do not agree that res ipsa loquitur has any place in our law of bailment"; and *Ludgate* v. *Lovett* [1969] 1 W.L.R. 1016, where the two doctrines appear to have been equated.

[3] A further notable feature of this authority is its assumption that the bailee's burden of proof can operate only within contractual bailments. or at least within those that arise by direct delivery inter partes. See further p. 40 et seq., ante, and Chapter 20 post (sub-bailments), for criticism of this view.

[4] *Bray* v. *Mayne* (1818) Gow I. N.P.; *Manchester* v. *Glenie* (1908) 28 N.Z.L.R. 123 (where the animal twice refused its feed and on the second occasion the hirer did not trouble to verify the fact).

[5] *British Crane Hire Corporation Ltd.* v. *Ipswich Plant Hire Ltd.* [1975] 1 Q.B. 303.

[6] *Allison Concrete Ltd.* v. *Canadian Pacific Ltd.* (1973) 40 D.L.R. (3d) 237.

[7] *Fairley & Stevens (1966) Ltd.* v. *Goldsworthy* (1973) 34 D.L.R. (3d) 554 (car on approval, *held* to be bailed for mutual advantage).

[8] *Smith* v. *Blower* (1882) N.Z.L.R. 1 S.C. 329; *Oldham* v. *Lyons Ltd.* (1908) 27 N.Z.L.R. 535.

[9] *Truesdell* v. *Holden* (1913) 4 O.W.N. 1138; 5 O.W.N. 58.

the hirer will be liable if he negligently entrusts the chattel to a dishonest or incompetent third-party,[10] or continues to use it after it has become apparent that it is suffering from a serious defect.[11] What constitutes reasonable care on the part of the hirer will depend upon the value and character of the chattel, the purpose for which it is hired, the general circumstances of the delivery and (in occasional cases) the character of the bailee. The circumstantial permutations are endless and each case must be judged according to its peculiar facts.

Negligence has been inferred, in the absence of positive evidence, when a hired animal dies without explanation or apparent cause while in the possession of the hirer;[12] when the chattel is returned damaged or mutilated in a manner which could not have resulted from ordinary wear and tear;[13] when goods are destroyed by fire;[14] when a hired vehicle is damaged in a totally unexplained road accident;[15] and when a horse bolts for no apparent reason from its stable.[16] But the burden of proof has on occasions been discharged. One such case was *Watts* v. *Cuthbert*,[17] where a horse sustained a fractured hip while being driven along a rutted and unmade road. The owner adduced veterinary evidence to show that the fracture could not have occurred through the animal's merely slipping in a rut. The court nevertheless held, on a balance of probabilities, that the injury was consistent with the defendant's theory of accident and with the exercise of reasonable care and skill on his part. The burden of proof was accordingly discharged. Similarly, in *Tilling* v. *Balmain*[18] the hirer of a horse was exonerated when the cause of injury was shown to be weakness of a theatre stage. The hirer had taken the horse for the purpose of using it in a play and appears generally to have exercised reasonable care in its management. The court held that he was not, in the circumstances, bound to examine the flooring for structural weakness before he took the horse on stage. But of course the deliberate use of an animal or a piece of equipment for a venture which is known to be hazardous may (unless the owner has consented to the venture) produce a different result.[19]

Difficulties may arise when a hired vehicle is involved in an unexplained accident and the hirer counterclaims for injuries resulting from a breach of the owner's warranty of reasonable fitness for use. As we have seen, a number of decisions[20] suggest that the occurrence of a collision

---

[10] Including, of course, a servant: *Arbon* v. *Fussell* (1862) 3 F. & F. 152.

[11] Cf. *Wiebe* v. *Lepp* (1974) 46 D.L.R. (3d) 441.

[12] *Murray* v. *Collins* (1920) 53 D.L.R. 120; Cf. *Williams* v. *Lloyd* (1628) Palm. 548; 82 E.R. 95, where default was negatived.

[13] *Gremley* v. *Stubbs* (1908) 39 N.B.R. 21; *Taylor* v. *Carnell* (1909) 2 Atla. L.R. 237; *Fick* v. *de Klerk* (1907) E.D.C. 294; Cf. *Cooper* v. *Barton* (1810) 3 Camp. 5n. N.P.

[14] *McCreary* v. *Therrien Construction Co. Ltd.* [1952] 1 D.L.R. 153; see also *Huard* v. *Feiczewicz* (1911) Q.R. 40 S.C. 385; *Longman* v. *Gallini* (unreported) 1790.

[15] *Ludgate* v. *Lovett* [1969] 1 W.L.R. 1106.

[16] *Dollar* v. *Greenfield* (1905) *The Times*, 19 May.

[17] (1912) 14 W.A.L.R. 205.

[18] (1892) 8 T.L.R. 517; cf. *Smith* v. *Caltex Oil (Australia) Pty. Ltd.* (1962) Tas. Unrep. 50/1962.

[19] Contrast *Tilling* v. *Balmain* with *Wiehe* v. *Dennis Bros. Ltd.* (1913) 29 T.L.R. 250 (ante, p. 296) and *British Crane Hire Corporation Ltd.* v. *Ipswich Plant Hire Ltd.* [1975] 1 Q.B. 303 (ante, p. 251).

[20] Most notably, *Hyman* v. *Nye* (1881) 6 Q.B.D. 685; see further, p. 725 et seq., ante.

or similar mishap may give rise to a presumption that the injury occurred through a failure to supply an adequate or safe machine. In such a case, the co-existence of a claim by the lessor for breach of bailment would seem to generate conflicting presumptions, which could prove difficult to resolve.

Such a problem arose in *Ludgate* v. *Lovett*,[21] the facts of which have been recounted.[22] The Court of Appeal dismissed the hirer's counter-claim because he had failed to establish the necessary cause of injury, and held him liable on the principle of res ipsa loquitur for the damage to the van. Although some of the assumptions in this case are open to criticism, it does appear that the safest method of approaching the question is to segregate (so far as possible) the relevant actions and to deal with each independently. In cases where the absence of concrete proof of causation threatens to produce different conclusions as to responsibility according to the duty involved, the presumption against the bailee will presumably prevail.[23]

Nor can the hirer evade his traditional burden of proof by pleading frustration of the contract of hire. In *Taylor* v. *Caldwell*[24] Blackburn J. remarked that if redelivery of the chattel became impossible through the loss or destruction of the chattel, the bailee would be excused from performing that obligation. He qualified this statement by stressing that the bailee would continue to be liable if the loss occurred through fault on his part, or from some event of which he had assumed the risk. Later authority has confirmed that, in cases of contract generally, the *onus* of proving that a frustrating event was induced by the fault of one party rests upon the party alleging that such fault has occurred.[25] If this principle were extended to contracts of hire (or indeed to bailments generally) it could entitle the bailee to reverse the usual burden of proof merely by proving that the chattel had perished. It must be assumed, therefore, that the bailee's duty of proving reasonable care will prevail, and that a failure to discharge this burden will render the bailee liable for loss or destruction of the chattel as well as for lesser impairments.

---

[21] [1969] 1 W.L.R. 1106.

[22] Ante, p. 41.

[23] This seems to draw support from the judgment of Crisp J., in *Smith* v. *Caltex Oil (Australia) Pty. Ltd.* (1962) Tas. Unrep. 50/1962, where (at p. 2) the learned judge remarked: "At a late stage — a very late stage indeed — the defendants produced a counterclaim based on an alleged breach of the implied warranty *(as to reasonable fitness)* by which the defendants sought to recover as damages the value of the cargo carried in the tanker at the time, and which was consumed in the fire. But in regard to this claim . . . the onus is on the defendants to establish affirmatively the greater probability of their allegations. Should they fail to do so, either because it is established that the loss was due to some fault or neglect on their part or because the matter is left in such a state of doubt that the court cannot affirmatively resolve the issue either way, both the defence and the counterclaim must fail".

[24] (1863) 3 B. & S. 826, at 838-839; 122 E.R. 309, at 314 (obiter, since the contract involved a lease of premises). See also *Walker* v. *British Guarantee Association* (1852) 18 Q.B. 277; 118 E.R. 104.

[25] *Joseph Constantine S.S. Co. Ltd.* v. *Imperial Smelting Corporation Ltd.* [1942] A.C. 154; see further Treitel, *Law of Contract* (4th ed.), pp. 600-601, who assumes that fault includes negligence; *Financings Ltd.* v. *Stimson* [1962] 3 All E.R. 386; *Goulston Discount Co. Ltd.* v. *Sims* (1967) 111 Sol. Jo. 682.

This conclusion is endorsed by *National Trust Co. Ltd.* v. *Wong*[26] which clearly envisages that the bailor must establish that the bailee had induced the frustration only in those cases (admittedly rare) in which the ordinary bailee's burden of proof has ceased to take effect.

1. *Liability for acts of servants*: The hirer is answerable not only for any personal failure to deal with the chattel as demanded by the terms of the bailment, but also for any lapse below that standard on the part of his servants; provided, of course, that they were acting in the course of their employment at the relative time, or in discharge of a duty imposed upon the hirer and delegated to them.[27] Thus if a chauffeur steals a hired vehicle while driving it to meet his master, or if a jockey negligently over-taxes a leased racehorse, or if a workman negligently damages a hired machine, the hirer who employs him will be answerable for the loss.[28]

If a machine is hired with an operator, there is a strong presumption that the operator remains in the service of his general employer.[29] Thus, even in cases where the hirer becomes a bailee of the accompanying machine, he may escape by showing that the loss or injury was due to the negligence of the servant, for whom he would not of course be responsible.[30] However, the onus would be upon the hirer, as bailee of the chattel, to identify, allocate and establish the default.

2. *Special contracts*: The terms of the agreement may enlarge or reduce the hirer's Common Law Liability for loss or damage to the chattel. Generally, such agreements take the form of an undertaking by the hirer to restore the chattel in a certain condition, irrespective of whether he has been at fault in permitting it to fall below that condition.[31] Less commonly, the contract will place the risk of deterioration, even that arising from the default of the hirer, upon the owner of the goods. One such case was *Brice & Sons* v. *Christiani & Neilsen*.[32] The plaintiffs rented a crane-barge to the defendants and undertook to insure it against all risks, the defendants paying the premium. A policy was taken out which failed to cover the machine against certain risks, one of which inevitably occurred, damaging the machine. The defendants, although unable to prove that the injury did not result from any default on the part of their servants, were relieved because the contract clearly indicated that they had declined to assume liability for risks to the machine.

---

[26] (1969) 3 D.L.R. (3d) 55; *Jackson's (Edinburgh) Ltd.* v. *Constructors John Brown Ltd.* 1965 S.L.T. 37, at 38-39. See further *British Crane Hire Corporation Ltd.* v. *Ipswich Plant Hire* [1975] 1 Q.B. 303, discussed at p. 756, post.

[27] *Morris* v. *C.W. Martin & Sons Ltd.* [1966] 1 Q.B. 716. cf. *Arbon* v. *Fussell* (1862) 3 F. & F. 152, N.P.; *Sanderson* v. *Collins* [1904] 1 K.B. 628; *South Island Motors Ltd.* v. *Thacker* [1931] N.Z.L.R. 1104.

[28] See *Coupe Co. Ltd.* v. *Maddick* [1891] 2 Q.B. 413; *Stead* v. *Bligh* (1893) 62 J.P. 458; *Dollar* v. *Greenfield* (1905) *The Times,* 19 May; *Brice & Sons* v. *Christiani & Neilsen* (1928) 44 T.L.R. 335.

[29] Ante, p. 246.

[30] This was the position with regard to the first disaster in *British Crane Hire Corporation Ltd.* v. *Ipswich Plant Hire Ltd.* [1975] 1 Q.B. 303. cf. *Great Lakes Steel Products Ltd.* v. *M.E. Doyle Ltd.* (1969) 1 D.L.R. (3d) 349.

[31] Such contracts are discussed post, p. 758.

[32] (1928) 44 T.L.R. 335. cf. *Moons Motors Ltd.* v. *Kiuan Wou* [1952] 2 Lloyd's Rep. 80.

Even more rarely, the hirer's common law duty of care may be squeezed out of existence by more specific covenants, which delineate every aspect of his responsibility and leave nothing to the implications of Common Law. In *Bell* v. *Walker*[33] the hirers of a steam-engine and quartz-crushing machine were alleged to have covenanted, *inter alia,* to erect the equipment in suitable buildings; to devote all reasonable time to its proper working; not to leave such working to other persons, but to keep the machinery under their immediate command; *to take reasonable, due and proper care thereof and to use the same in a careful and reasonable manner.* However, the latter covenant was not expressly recorded in the memorandum of agreement. The machinery was destroyed in an explosion and the plaintiffs claimed that, irrespective of whether the agreement incorporated the disputed covenant expressly, a covenant to like effect should be implied by law. The Victoria Supreme Court dismissed their contention on the ground that the alleged covenant did not arise necessarily from the covenants expressed and was too general and indefinite to be implied.

C. Compliance with terms of the bailment

The hirer must observe the restrictions imposed upon his right of possession by the contract of hire. Any departure from the conditions, expressed or implied, upon which he has assumed the position of bailee will render him strictly liable for ensuing losses and will often (though not necessarily) constitute a conversion. For this result to follow, however, the limitation transgressed must be central to the bailment, rather than merely peripheral or incidental: "the position can never be maintained that all departure from a bailor's instructions is such neglect as gives him a right to cast the loss of his goods on the bailee."[34] Whether a particular instruction is sufficiently material to produce this result depends upon the intention that can be gathered from the language of the parties and the contract as a whole. Generally, the nearer an act of disobedience approaches to a conversion of the chattel, the more probable it is that the parties intended to accompany its commission with an insurer's liability on the part of the bailee.

In *Roberts* v. *McDougall*[35] the hirer of a cart left it overnight on a quay-side, in which position it was accidentally destroyed by fire. It was found by the jury that the contract of hire did not entitle the hirer to leave the cart in the open but required him to garage it upon his own premises overnight. He was accordingly held liable for the value of the vehicle, even though the risk of fire was no greater in the unauthorised *situs* and he had not been negligent in leaving it there. Likewise, in *Hughes* v. *Rooke*[36] it was held that a departure by the hirer of an aircraft from the agreed flight-route made him liable for the destruction of the aircraft which occurred during the deviation. It was during this deviation that the hirer was forced to land by smoke from bushfires; upon

---

[33] (1856) 1 V.L.T. 63; cf. *Arrow Transfer Co. Ltd.* v. *Fleetwood Logging Co. Ltd.* (1961) 30 D.L.R. (2d) 631.
[34] *Tobin* v. *Murison* (1845) 5 Moore 110, at 128 per Lord Brougham.
[35] (1887) 3 T.L.R. 666.
[36] [1954] Q.S.R. 45; 48 Q.J.P.R. 138; 28 A.L.J. 159.

his attempting to take off again, the engine failed from an unforeseeable cause and the plane crashed, becoming a total loss. Although in the present case the original deviation seems to have been negligent rather than intentional, it is clear that a deliberate departure from the agreed itinerary, albeit unaccompanied by negligence and based upon a careful calculation of the risks involved, would make the hirer answerable for all consequent injury, whether foreseeable or not. Certainly in *Hughes* v. *Rooke* the immediate causes of the hirer's predicament (bush-fires and an unexpected engine-failure) were beyond his control and were not attributable to any neglect on his part; nevertheless, the court had no difficulty in discerning the necessary connexion between his original contravention of the bailment and the loss which ultimately occurred. Only where the deviation is unavoidable, or the loss would have occurred regardless, or the bailor is to blame for the departure from his instructions, will be hirer be excused.

Departure from the agreed route is perhaps the commonest method of making the bailee an insurer; its effect in contracts of hire was recognised by Holt C.J. in *Coggs* v. *Bernard*[37] and was probably implicit in *Lee* v. *Atkinson*,[38] almost a century earlier. In *Fawcett* v. *Smethurst*,[39] however, Atkin J. declined to hold that an infant who had driven a hired car further than was allowed under the agreement was liable for damage sustained as a result. Such liability could, in the learned judge's view, have arisen only ex contractu, and in the present case the contract was clearly unenforceable; it would have been otherwise if the infant had committed an independent tort, such as negligence or conversion, upon the chattel.[40] We have already suggested that since bailments need not be contractual, and since an infant can undoubtedly be made as a bailee, it is perhaps unnecessarily restrictive to regard all limitations upon an infant bailee's right of possession as essentially or exclusively contractual.[41] If an infant hirer fails to return goods after the bailment has expired, he may be liable for detinue,[42] but there is no reason why he should not also be liable as an insurer for all risks to the goods during his extended period of possession. Such liability, if it exists, does not fit into any recognised category of tort but seems to be implicit in the infant's promise to restore the goods at a certain time. Promises which form the essence of a bailee's possession, and indicate the conditions upon which his right to occupy the character of bailee depends, can exist without a contract between the parties[43] even in the case of bailees who enjoy full capacity to contract. It is only the failure to recognise the independent character of bailment that prevents a court from identifying what appear to be

---

[37] (1703) 2 Ld. Raym. 909; 92 E.R. 107.
[38] (1609) Cro. Jac. 236; Yelv. 172; 79 E.R. 204.
[39] (1914) 31 T.L.R. 85.
[40] See generally, p. 16 ante.
[41] In *Fawcett* v. *Smethurst* (ante) Atkin J. held that the plaintiff had failed to establish the incorporation of a condition that the infant be liable for all damage to the car, and that such a term would in any event be unenforceable since it could not satisfy the requirement of relating to necessaries.
[43] As in the case of an augmented degree of care on a gratuitous deposit: ante, p. 313.
[42] *Ballett* v. *Mingay* [1943] K.B. 281.

contractual limits upon an infant's right to possession as boundary stones around the totally different relationship of bailor and bailee.

Apart from keeping the goods in an unauthorised place, using them for an unauthorised purpose, and retaining them beyond the period of hire,[44] the hirer may become an insurer of the goods by wrongfully allowing a third-party to use or acquire possession of them.[45] Whether such permission is inherent in the agreement is a matter of construction. Certainly, in cases of hire involving industrial plant or machinery it would be absurd to insist that the hirer alone, and not his employers, should operate the machine.[46] In Canada, it has been held that the client of a garage, who borrowed a car from them while on his own was being repaired, was not limited to using the car personally but could allow his fiancee to drive.[47] In New South Wales, Jordan C.J., has observed that the hirer of chattels has an interest which he may assign to third-parties, provided the bailment involves no personal element and does not prohibit the disposition;[48] even if the bailment contains no such prohibition, the chattel must continue to be used only for the purpose for which it was originally hired. In many cases, such as the hire of a car from a rental company by a private consumer, it seems that the hirer's right will be a personal one and incapable of alienation, especially perhaps where questions of insurance are involved. The opposite result must follow when the whole object of the hiring is for the hirer to sub-lease the goods to third parties (as in the case of a rental company which holds its fleet of vehicles upon lease from another company) or where the identity of ultimate consumer is a matter of indifference to the owner, so long as he is paid (as may be the case with a rented deckchair or a suit of clothes). In each case, the question must be answered by the terms, express and implied, of the agreement and the intentions of the parties as expressed therein. Even where the hirer is entitled to allow a third-party to use the chattel he must show in his selection of that user the same amount of care and skill as if he were continuing to use the chattel personally.

There has been, in the past, some confusion about the relationship between those departures from the terms of the bailment which are sufficient to visit the bailee with liability as an insurer and the quite separate question of liability for conversion.[49] This confusion was particularly evident in some of the older American cases, which held, for instance, that the taking of a horse beyond an agreed destination was a

---

[44] But cf. *Leggo* v. *Welland Vale Manufacturing Co.* (1901) 21 C.L.T. Occ. N. 374; 2 O.L.R. 45, which seems to be wrong on this point.

[45] This was the nature of the infant's misconduct in *Ballett* v. *Mingay* [1943] K.B. 281.

[46] For an express contract to this effect, see *Healy* v. *Tait* [1954] S.A.S.R. 56; post, p. 759. Aliter, of course, when it is supplied with an operator who has the exclusive right to handle the machine.

[47] *Queens Sales & Service Ltd.* v. *Smith* (1963) 48 M.P.R. 364; the loan was characterised as one for mutual advantage, and thus analogous to a contract of hire, by the majority of the Nova Scotian Supreme Court, Bissett J. dissenting.

[48] *Australian Provincial Assurance Co. Ltd.* v. *Coroneo* (1938) 38 S.R. (N.S.W.) 700, at pp. 715-716; noted, 12 A.L.J. 384.

[49] See the excellent discussion by Paton, op cit., 303-304.

conversion on the part of the hirer;[50] but the principle was not always consistently applied[51] and provoked the criticism of authors, including Street in his Foundations of Legal Liability.[52] In fact, the two forms of liability are quite distinct, although they may often coalesce within a single situation. A conversion requires some degree of denial of title; a mere misuse, without an intention to gainsay the owner's right or to act adversely to his ownership, cannot therefore amount to conversion.[53] The liability of a bailee who deviates from the conditions of his tenure is both wider and narrower than his liability for conversion; wider in that it need not be accompanied by any denial of title, but narrower in that he need account only for the actual loss that has been sustained.[54] It therefore represents a more flexible remedy, which neither makes the bailee indiscriminately liable for the full value of the chattel nor places upon him the risk of events occurring after the deviation has been corrected.[55]

Later American authority has to some extent, perpetuated the confusion. In *Vermont Acceptance Corporation* v. *Wiltshire*[56] the bailee of a car under a conditional sales agreement was held liable for conversion when, without causing any damage, he used it without authority for an illegal purpose. This seems consistent with the English decision in *Moorgate Mercantile Co. Ltd.* v. *Finch*,[57] for the mere risk of confiscation may be serious enough to justify an interference that the owner's title is being abrogated or impaired.[58] In *E. J. Caron Enterprises Inc.* v. *State Operating Co.*,[59] however, the Supreme Court of New Hampshire, while apparently conceding that the unauthorised use of personal property by one who has a limited right to its possession does not necessarily amount to a conversion, held the defendant liable in conversion although he had merely shifted the goods from an authorised site to an unauthorised one

---

[50] *Wheelock* v. *Wheelwright* (1809) 5 Mass. 104; cf. *Spooner* v. *Manchester* (1882) 133 Mass. 270; *Mortimer* v. *Otto* 206 N.Y. 89; 99 N.E. 189; and see *Fawcett* v. *Smethurst* (1914) 31 T.L.R. 85.

[51] See *Doolittle* v. *Shaw* (1894) 60 N.W. 621; *Harvey* v. *Epes* (1855) 12 Gratt. (Va.) 153.

[52] Vol. II, p. 287.

[53] *Penfolds Wines Pty. Ltd.* v. *Elliott* (1946) 74 C.L.R. 204, at 229 per Dixon J.; *McKenna & Armistead Ltd.* v. *Excavators Pty. Ltd.* [1957] S.R. (N.S.W.) 515; ante., p. 129 et seq.

[54] The traditional level of damages in conversion is the value of the chattel, which the defendant in a successful action for conversion is accordingly compelled to buy. But recent authority has stressed that the plaintiff cannot recover more than this material loss. In (1913-1914) 27 *Harvard Law Review* 195, it is pointed out that the difference between a deviation which amounts to a conversion and one that does not may often depend upon the bailee's state of mind: he is more likely to be guilty of conversion if he deviates intentionally than if he does so from negligence. But even a deviation of the former character may not necessarily be a conversion (see ante), and if the deviation is of the latter character the bailee will often be answerable in negligence anyway.

[55] See *Daugherty* v. *Reveal* (1913) 102 N.E. 381; *Farkas* v. *Powell* (1891) 13 S.E. 200; (1894-1895) 8 *Harvard Law Review* 280.

[56] (1931) 102 Vt. 219; 153 Atl. 199; 73 A.L.R. 792; cf. *Donovan* v. *Barkhausen Oil Co.* (1929) 200 Wis. 194; 227 N.W. 940.

[57] [1962] 1 Q.B. 701.

[58] Note, however, that in this case the vehicle was actually seized and forfeited by the customs. Cf. *Union T'port Finance* v. *B.C.A.* (1977) 245 E.G. 131.

[59] (1935) 179 Atl. 665; cf. *Scott-Mayer Commission Co.* v. *Merchants Grocer Co.* (1921) 226 S.W. 1060.

and had done them no physical harm. This decision was criticised by Blaugrund,[60] who pointed out that there was an essential difference between a mere breach of contract (or of bailment) and an act of conversion; the latter, in his view, should be confined to those acts which interfere with "a substantial and material portion" of the owner's legal rights and interests. Of course the two wrongs will frequently coincide, but this does not mean that they should be completely assimilated.[61]

There can be no doubt that conversion is a blunt instrument in cases of deviation and is capable of perpetrating a rather rough brand of justice. For this reason, it is desirable to preserve the separate identity of a remedy which pays a more sensitive regard to the quantum of the owner's loss. Undoubtedly there will continue to be marginal cases, for a departure from the terms of the bailment is a serious wrong which represents nothing less than a repudiation by the bailee of his personal status as well as of the agreement itself. Indeed, there is very little authority on the identity of hazardous but actually harmless acts of disobedence as acts of conversion: conduct such as deliberately using the chattel for a dangerous and unauthorised venture, or sub-bailing it to a party without checking his honesty and in contravention to the owners instructions.[62] On the one hand, it can be argued that mere creation of the hazard, in violation of the owner's trust, connotes a denial of his title; conversely, it seems unduly harsh to compel the bailee to pay for a chattel which he does not want and to which he has done no actual harm. In *Kelly* v. *White*[63] it was held that a bailee of slaves, who puts them to work in a more perilous place than was authorised, was liable (and liable only) for any loss that might occur. Adapted to modern circumstances, this seems the preferable approach, at least until the damages obtainable in conversion become universally established as comprising no more than the fact of the plaintiff's loss.

The fact remains that the damages payable by a bailee upon deviation include all losses occurring to the chattel, whether foreseeable or preventable or not. In this respect, deviation seems to be treated in a manner akin to fraud;[64] in fact, some of the older authorities speak of it as a fraud upon the owner's confidence or trust. Moreover, the owner has the right to terminate the bailment and to recover possession of the chattel. In *Lee* v. *Atkinson*[65] the owner was held liable for assault when he attempted to take back his horse after finding that the hirer was riding it in an unauthorised direction; the court remarked that he should have contented himself with an action on the case. It seems, however, that a bailor who is entitled to the immediate possession of his chattel is

---

[60] (1935-1936) 21 *Cornell Law Quarterly* 112.

[61] "At some point the deviation is so marked, so serious that the only reasonable inference is that (the bailee) intends to assume dominion. But to hold the mere slight deviation a conversion seems utterly contrary to sound legal theory and common sense": ibid.

[62] Cf. *Garnham, Harris & Elton Ltd.* v. *Alfred W. Ellis (Transport) Ltd.* [1967] 2 All E.R. 940, where the goods were actually stolen by the sub-bailee; see further, p. 125 et seq. ante.

[63] (1856) 56 Ky. 124; see also *Harvey* v. *Epes* (1855) 12 Gratt. (Va.) 153.

[64] Cf. *Doyle* v. *Olby (Ironmongers) Ltd.* [1969] 2 Q.B. 158 (measure of damages for fraudulent misrepresentation).

[65] (1609) Cro. Jac. 236; Yelv. 172; 79 E.R. 204; ante, p. 722.

entitled to use such reasonable measures as are necessary for its retrieval; possibly one of the reasons for the decision in *Lee* v. *Atkinson* was the violence of the assault.[66]

When the hirer is in breach of a minor term of the bailment, and commits a wrong falling short of deviation, the owner is limited to recovering damages for the breach and cannot ipso facto claim to terminate the bailment; he may become entitled to rescind, however, if the consequences of the breach are such as to destroy the whole identity of the contract, and to render performance a different thing from what it would otherwise have been.[67] His damages will nevertheless continue to be assessed on contractual principles and not upon the wider level of liability that attends a deviation.

D. The duty to return the chattel

There is inherent in every contract of hire a promise by the hirer to return the goods when the purpose or the period for which they were bailed has expired. This promise will generally (but not necessarily) be an express one. It may be frustrated by supervening events or enlarged by agreement between the parties.

1. *Release from the promise*: If performance of the promise is rendered impossible by events beyond the hirer's control, that promise will be deemed frustrated and he will be released. This result is part of the general theory of frustration of contract and is dependent upon an absence of fault on the hirer's part.[68] Sometimes it is expressed in the terms that the hirer is relieved by an act of God,[69] but it is clear that the foregoing defence embraces a wider circle of events than are comprehended by that expression.

Generally, it will be insufficient for the hirer merely to show that the return of the chattel has been made more costly or inconvenient by events beyond his control. However, the express or implied terms of the agreement may indicate the contrary result. Such terms will be exceptional, as the recent observations in *British Crane Hire Corporation Ltd.* v. *Ipswich Plant Hire Ltd.*[70] suggest. In this case, a dragline crane became embedded in marshy ground in circumstances not involving negligence on the part of the hirer. The owners of the crane, relying upon their standard conditions of hire,[71] successfully contended that the responsibility of retrieving the crane lay with the hirer. Two members of the Court of Appeal went on to hold that, irrespective of the incorporated conditions, the cost of extracting the crane would have fallen upon the hirers at Common Law. Lord Denning M.R., commenting on the implied term that the hirer must return the chattel at the end of the hiring, pointed out that this duty was quite separate from the hirer's duty of reasonable care

[66] Cf. Paton, op. cit., p. 16. The various Hire Purchase Acts and the *Consumer Credit Act* 1974, place stringent limitations upon the lessor's right to enter private premises to recover his goods.
[67] See ante p. 733 (lessor's duty of reasonable fitness).
[68] *Taylor* v. *Caldwell* (1863) 3 B. & S. 826; 122 E.R. 309; and see ante., p. 749.
[69] Paton, op. cit., pp. 302-303; *Williams* v. *Lloyd* (1628) Palm. 548; 82 E.R. 95 (hirer relieved by death of horse without negligence on his part).
[70] [1975] Q.B. 303.
[71] Ante, p. 247.

in the keeping of the chattel; whether or not the hirer was at fault in relation to the event which renders its return more difficult, he must do whatever is reasonable to effect that return. Thus, neither illness on his part, nor gales, nor perilous road conditions are occurrences which would normally relieve him from his responsibility to restore the chattel, however expensive it may be for him to salvage that chattel from the aftermath of these phenomena.[72] Sir Eric Sachs agreed substantially with these observations, and added two further events — the embedding of a vehicle in a snowdrift or its skidding into a ditch — which would not relieve the hirer. However, he conjectured that "if some great boulder descended on the vehicle and damaged it beyond repair, that might well be good cause for not returning it."[73] While the precise extent of this duty will of course depend upon construction of the contract (and the courts will try to avoid arriving at an unreasonable result) it may, however, be speculated that an unconditional promise to return the chattel to a particular place would not in many cases be frustrated by the mere damaging of the vehicle beyond repair; indeed this may be the very event (or one of the events) in contemplation of which the clause was originally inserted.

Sir Eric Sachs further indicated[74] that his remarks were confined to the situation where the owner and the hirer are in similar "walks of life". Insofar as this qualification suggests that an inequality of bargaining-power between the parties can attenuate the operation of the Common Law obligation to restore goods at the expiration of the bailment, it lacks authority and should, perhaps, be treated with caution. It is true that English courts have recently begun to favour the judicial mitigation of unconscionable terms in contracts between parties of significantly different bargaining-power[75] but it is rather a far cry from this to the release of an ordinary hirer from a duty of restoration implied under the principles of Common Law.

There can be no doubt, however, as further stated by Sir Eric Sachs, that if the misadventure is caused by the lessor's own negligence the hirer will (subject, again, to the contract) be excused. The same result should follow if the cause of the misadventure is a breach of the lessor's strict liability under an implied warranty of reasonable fitness for use.[76]

The use of the word "return" in the foregoing discussion may perhaps have suggested that it is invariably the duty of the hirer to deliver the chattel to the lessor's place of business and not the duty of the lessor to collect it. In fact, many commercial contracts now make elaborate provision for this aspect of the agreement and many hirers would either refuse, or would not be trusted, to undertake responsibility for the safe delivery and re-delivery of the goods. So far as concerns those contracts of hire which are silent upon this point, it may be hazarded that the duty of redelivery is generally upon the hirer but that the general rule

---

[72] [1975] Q.B. 303, 311-312.
[73] Ibid., at 313.
[74] Ibid.
[75] *Lloyd's Bank Ltd.* v. *Bundy* [1975] Q.B. 326; *A Schroder Music Publishing Co. Ltd.* v. *Macaulay* [1974] 1 W.L.R. 1308; *Clifford Davis Management Ltd.* v. *W.E.A. Records Ltd.* [1975] 1 W.L.R. 61.
[76] Cf. *Arrow Transfer Co. Ltd.* v. *Fleetwood Logging Co. Ltd.* (1961) 30 C.L.R. (2d) 631; *Pearce* v. *Brain*, [1929] 2 K.B. 310.

may be varied when the original delivery has been effected by the owner. However, it is impossible to be dogmatic in this area and each case must ultimately depend upon its own facts.[77]

The chattel must be returned properly assembled and in as near a condition to its state upon original delivery as is consistent with the hirer's duty of care.

2. *Special contracts*: At Common Law, the hirer is not liable for depreciation of the chattel resulting from ordinary wear and tear, or for damage or destruction which do not result from a lack of reasonable care on his part. It is, however, possible for the contract to impose a heavier liability upon the bailee and to render him responsible, for instance, for all injuries to the chattel, whether arising from a breach of his Common Law duty or not.[78] Generally, this will be effected by a phrasing of the duty to redeliver in strict or absolute terms.[79] The decisions in this area are of little conceptual value, since they turn upon the construction of particular terms. In *Reading* v. *Menham*[80] the relevant term was imposed not upon the hirer but upon the owner of the chattel. A contract for the hire of a gig bound the owner to keep the vehicle "in perfect repair without any further charges whatever." While in the hirer's possession, it was damaged, apparently without negligence on the hirer's part, and in a manner which did not result from ordinary wear and tear. The bailor pleaded a custom in the carriage trade that lessors were liable only to repair defects arising from ordinary wear and tear, but Denman C.J. held that this was displaced by the "clear and unequivocal" language of the agreement. The effect of this agreement was to render the lessor wholly responsible for the cost of repairs, even, perhaps, where the damage had been caused by the default of the hirer.[81]

A more clement approach was taken in *Schroder* v. *Ward*.[82] Here a contract for the renting of a barge provided that "fair wear and tear were to be allowed by the owner" but demanded that the barge be re-delivered "in good working order, with all her rigging, gear and implements complete". Both Erle C.J., and Willes J., agreed that this did not amount to an absolute undertaking by the hirer to deliver the barge up in what would, in the abstract sense, constitute good working order. Rather, the promise was to be construed relatively, and the expression 'good working order' was to be qualified in the light of the purpose for which a barge of the same age and condition as the plaintiffs' could be used. Willes J.

---

[77] See further p. 377, ante (commodatum).

[78] For a term of similar effect in a bailment by way of loan, see *A.R. Williams Machinery Co. Ltd.* v. *Muttart Builders Supply (Winnipeg) Ltd.* (1961) 30 D.L.R. (2d) 339; (1961) 31 D.L.R. (2d) 187; ante, p. 370. It seems that clauses of this kind, being akin to indemnity clauses, will be construed fairly strictly against the bailor: see for instance, *Ritchie's Car Hire Ltd.* v. *Bailey* (1958) 108 L. Jo. 348; cf. *Etudes et Enterprises* v. *Snowy Mountains Hydro-Electric Authority* [1962] N.S.W.R. 204.

[79] Cf. the relevant clauses in *British Crane Hire Corporation Ltd.* v. *Ipswich Plant Hire Ltd.* [1975] Q.B. 303; ante, p. 247.

[80] (1832) 1 M. & Rob. 234; 174 E.R. 80.

[81] Ibid., at pp. 236-237; 81. It seems that in this event the promise to repair would be treated as an exclusion clause and therefore subject to the rules laid down in Chapter 25, post.

[82] (1863) 13 C.B.N.S. 410; 143 E.R. 162. cf. *Danks* v. *Farley* (1853) 1 C.L.R.; 95 N.P.

conceded that the result may have been different if the barge had been damaged by overloading and the case was remitted for trial.[83] But in *Vendair (London) Ltd.* v. *Giro Aviation Co. Ltd.*[84] Veale J. held that a provision requiring the hirers of an aircraft to return it "in condition equivalent to when supplied" rendered them liable for fair wear and tear, and not merely for deterioration caused by a breach of their duty as bailees.[85] Both in this decision and in that of the British Columbia Court of Appeal in *Arrow Transfer Co. Ltd.* v. *Fleetwood Logging Co. Ltd.*[86] it is acknowledged that an undertaking of this kind may be displaced when the deterioration results from a breach of the lessor's implied obligation of reasonable fitness, or of any express warranty given in relation to the goods.[87] The application of the redelivery clause in such circumstances may be likened to the validity of an exclusion clause when the *proferens* has stepped outside the four corners of the contract. In theory, it should be possible for the redelivery clause to govern notwithstanding a breach of any warranty as to fitness or condition, but for this to occur express language would probably be required.

3. *Ownership of progeny*: Offspring born during the subsistence of a lease of animals belong, as a general rule, to the hirer and not to the owner of the parent animal. This rule is laid down in a recent decision of the Court of Appeal, dealing with a contract for the hire-purchase of ewes;[88] and it is clear from that decision that the same principle applies

---

[83] This decision should be contrasted with two Australian cases dealing with the lease of race-horses. In *Wilding* v. *Kelly* (1921) 24 W.A.L.R. 58 the lease contained two apparently conflicting provisions, which stated respectively that (i) the hirer should be liable only for those injuries which resulted from neglect or default of himself and his servants, and (ii) that he should keep the horse at all times in a proper condition and return it at the termination of the lease in a good racing condition to the owner. The W.A. Full Supreme Court held that the latter obligation was absolute and justified the owner's repossession of the horse when it fell below a proper racing condition, regardless of whether this deterioration was the result of any default by the lessee. In *Healy* v. *Tait* [1954] S.A.S.R. 56 a promise to keep the horse in a proper condition was similarly interpreted by Mayo J. The contract additionally forbade the lessee to part with possession and personal control of the horse. The horse contracted a bowed tendon and, on the advice of a veterinary surgeon, the lessee sent it to rest in a paddock about thirty miles away. Mayo J. held that both the malady and the parting with possession entitled the owner to repossess the horse.

[84] [1961] 1 Lloyd's Rep. 283; cf. *Jackson's (Edinburgh) Ltd.* v. *Constructors John Brown Ltd.* 1965 S.L.T. 37; *Oke* v. *Great Northern Oil etc. Co.* (1905) 5 O.W.R. 429.

[85] The defendants were in fact held to be in breach of this duty, through their failure to carry out reasonable maintenance.

[86] (1961) 30 D.L.R. (2d) 631. cf. *Inelco Industries Ltd.* v. *Venture Well Services Ltd.* (1975) 59 D.L.R. (3d) 458. There are many Canadian cases concerned with the construction of clauses whereby the hirer ostensibly undertakes a greater liability for the return of the goods than would be imposed at Common Law. See, inter alia, *Grant* v. *Armour* (1893) 25 O.R. 7; *Chamberlen* v. *Trenouth* (1874) 23 U.C.C.P. 497; *Oke* v. *Great Northern Oil etc. Co.* (ante.)

[87] Occasionally, too, the duty of redelivery may be qualified by a promise on the lessor's part to insure the goods in which event the bailee's liability will be mitigated to the extent of the warranted level of insurance: see *Moons Motors Ltd.* v. *Kiuan Wou* [1952] 2 Lloyd's Rep. 80. For a decision in which this was successfully achieved, see *Inelco Industries Ltd.* v. *Venture Well Services Ltd.* (1975) 59 D.L.R. (3d) 458.

[88] *Tucker* v. *Farm & General Investment Trust Ltd.* [1966] 2 Q. B. 421; following *Wood* v. *Ash and Foster* (1586) Owen 139; 1 Leon. 42 and *Morket* v. *Malan* [1933] S.C.R. C.P.D. (S.A.) 370 (Cape Province Supreme Court). Cf. *Re Rauf*

(subject to any contrary intention) in the case of a simple lease. Presumably the length and purpose of the lease would be important factors in establishing an intention to preclude the operation of the rule that produce follows possession. This rule would also apply to other produce-bearing things such as plants,[89] although instances of such chattels being bailed by way of lease would be extremely rare.

V. THE CONSUMER CREDIT ACT 1974 (U.K.)[90]

Until 1974, the position of the simple hirer was grossly inferior to that of his companion consumers, the outright purchaser, the hirer under a contract of hire-purchase and the purchaser under a conditional or credit sale. The ordinary hirer's rights were governed exclusively by the Common Law and this allowed the owner an almost unlimited latitude to impose his own terms upon the consumer. The disparity was vividly accentuated by the decision in *Galbraith* v. *Mitchenall Estates Ltd.*,[91] where the hirer under a long-term lease of a caravan had not even realised that the vehicle would never become his own property. Sachs J., commented harshly upon the propensity of finance companies to evade the Hire-Purchase Acts by phrasing their agreements in the terms of a simple lease, without option to purchase:

> It is becoming increasingly apparent from cases which come before the courts that there is a tendency on the part of some finance companies to try to use contracts of what I have referred to as simple hire in order to ensure that the hirer does not have the protection of the Hire-Purchase Acts. These contracts of hire to which finance companies are inclined are simple only in the sense that they are not technically contracts of hire-purchase. One has but to look at the contract in this particular case to see in its small print how far from simple it is, either from the layman's or indeed the lawyer's point of view. The sooner the legislature is apprised of this tendency and the sooner it takes in hand the problem, the fewer will be the occasions when finance companies are able to inflict on an unwary hirer hardships of the type that have become manifest in the present case.[92]

Reform had become necessary because in many cases traders and finance companies were employing the ordinary contract of hire as a substitute for hire-purchase or other deferred-payment systems. The contract of hire had financial advantages for the hirer as well as for the owner, but from a legal standpoint the advantage was almost exclusively with the latter. He was not bound by the Hire Purchase Acts and was therefore free to

(1975) 49 D.L.R. (3d) 345 (bailee receiving mares for stallion services has a lien on both the mares and their foals); *Harding* v. *Commissioner of Inland Revenue* (1974) N.Z. Sup. Ct. Unrep. 26th July; *Horne* v. *Richardson* (1970) 64 Q.J.P. 47.

---

[89] Cf. Harman L.J. [1966] 2 Q.B. 421, at 429.
[90] Goode, *The Consumer Credit Act 1974;* Guest & Lloyd, *The Consumer Credit Act 1974;* Goode [1975] C.L.J. 79.
[91] [1965] 2 Q.B. 473. cf. *Credit Services Investments Ltd.* v. *Evans* [1974] 2 N.Z.L.R. 683; subsequent proceedings [1975] 2 N.Z.L.R. 560.
[92] Ibid., at 485.

impose his own terms as to repossession, liability on default and termination of the agreement; and he stood substantially less chance of losing his investment under one of the exceptions to the rule nemo dat quod non habet. The Report of the Crowther Committee on Consumer Credit[93] readily acknowledged the need for reform in this area, particularly in the zone of consumer hirings. Three factors in particular led them to this conclusion: the fact that many consumers taking out long-term contracts of hire genuinely believe that they are engaging in what will ultimately become a contract of purchase; the ready and extensive employment of minimum payment clauses in such transactions; and the logical unsoundness of discriminating in favour of consumer hire agreements by excluding them from legislation which encompassed conditional sale and hire-purchase, when in all but name the long-term consumer hire agreement was itself a credit transaction. These observations were endorsed in general terms by the ensuing Government White Paper[94] and have been largely translated into legislative reform by the *Consumer Credit Act* 1974.

A. The boundaries of the Act

It may be useful to begin with an outline of what the Act does not do. First, it does not apply to all hire agreements, but only to those which fall within the wider definition of a regulated agreement. A regulated agreement is defined by s.189(1) as comprising two alternative elements: it means a consumer credit agreement, or a consumer hire agreement, other than an exempt agreement. A consumer hire agreement is itself defined by s.15 of the Act:[95]

15(1) A consumer hire agreement is an agreement made by a person with an individual (the "hirer") for the bailment or (in Scotland) the hiring of goods to the hirer, being an agreement which

   (a) is not a hire-purchase agreement, and
   (b) is capable of subsisting for more than three months, and
   (c) does not require the hirer to make payments exceeding £5000.

(2) A consumer hire agreement is a regulated agreement if it is not an exempt agreement.

"Person" can of course include a limited company; "individual" is defined by s.189(1) as including a partnership or other unincorporated body of persons[96] not consisting entirely of bodies corporate. Thus, the lease of a photocopying machine to a firm of solicitors or a television set to an unincorporated hotelier for use by his guests could qualify as a consumer hire agreement. It will be noted that the purpose or use to which the hired goods are to be put (or are customarily put) is no relevance to the identity of the transaction as a consumer hire agreement. The goods may be leased for private enjoyment, for personal use in a business or even for re-lease to the hirer's customers, and the result would be the same.

---

[93] Cmnd. 4597 (1971), paras. 6.2.53-6.2.58.
[94] *Reform of the Law on Consumer Credit,* Cmnd. 5427 (1973); see pp. 5-8 passim.
[95] See also s. 189(1).
[96] But not a corporation: Goode [1975] C.L.J. 79, 87n.

Hire purchase contracts[97] are of course excluded from s.15, as are agreements which are not capable of subsisting for three months. Thus, the hire of a car for a fixed term of three weeks, or of a deck-chair for charges computed by the hour but bound to terminate at the end of the day, are among the many varieties of hiring which fall beyond the purview of the Act. But if a periodic hiring (e.g. one that is by the week or by the month) contains no provision that it must terminate before three months have elapsed, it will satisfy the requirements of s.15(1)(b) and will qualify as a consumer hire agreement. No doubt in appropriate cases such a provision may be implied.

A hire agreement will exceed the financial ceiling laid down by s.15(1)(c) only if the hirer is contractually committed to paying more than £5000 under the agreement. The mere fact that he "is capable" of doing so, insofar as the agreement may subsist (if the hirer so chooses) beyond a time at which his instalments would total £5000, is insufficient to carry the agreement beyond the purview of the Act if the hirer can in fact bring it to an end before that point is reached.[98]

So far as concerns exempt agreements, the only provision relevant to contracts of hire is s.16(6), which is self-explanatory:

16(6) The Secretary of State may by order provide that this Act shall not regulate consumer hire agreements of a description specified in the order where

(a) the owner is a body corporate authorised by or under any enactment to supply electricity, gas or water, and

(b) the subject of the agreement is a meter or metering equipment, or where the owner is the Post Office or the Kingston-upon-Hull City Council.[99]

The use of the word bailment in s.15 presumably excludes from the definition of consumer hire agreement those transactions (commonly called contracts of hire) in which the presence of the lessor's servants precludes a transfer of possession.[1] Certainly, the renting of furniture as a concomitant to a lease of premises is excluded;[2] it is less certain whether the lease of a chattel for a non-monetary consideration would qualify as a contract of hire for the purpose of s.15.[3] Ostensibly, there seems no reason why the latter should not count as regulated agreements but the position is uncertain. It is, perhaps, unfortunate that the Act provides no definition of the root concept of hiring. "Hirer" is defined by s.189(1);[4] but this is merely a relative definition to be used in the secondary context of s.15, which itself fails to delineate the necessary constituents for a Common Law contract of hire. Indeed, it is possible to

---

[97] Defined by s. 189(1).

[98] In making this computation, the statutory power of termination conferred by s. 101 is to be disregarded.

[99] Kingston-upon-Hull runs its own telephone system.

[1] See Chapter 7, ante, and *Southland Harbour Board* v. *Vella* [1974] 1 N.Z.L.R. 526.

[2] S. 18(b); Goode, op. cit., 25, 40. cf. *Pampris* v. *Thanos* (1967) 69 S.R. (N.S.W.) 226.

[3] Quaere how the financial commitment would be computed.

[4] It means "the individual to whom goods are bailed or (in Scotland) hired under a consumer hire agreement, or the person to whom his rights and duties under the agreement have passed by assignment or operation of law, and in relation to a prospective consumer hire agreement includes the prospective hirer."

interpret s.15 as applying to all bailments and not merely to those contracts which at Common Law would be considered contracts of hire, for rather than requiring that the bailee should be a hirer in the Common Law sense it seems to merely use the expression hirer as a synonym, or shorthand symbol, for all bailees, for the purposes of the Act. Any agreement made for the bailment of goods (if Scotland be excluded) can qualify as a consumer hire agreement and be treated as such under the act whether or not it amounts at Common Law to a bailment *by way of hire* or not. No doubt this is an interpretation which an English court would vehemently resist.

In addition to excluding a large proportion of hire agreements (including most finance leases) from its area of control, the *Consumer Credit Act* leaves untouched certain regions of transactional obligation, even those arising under consumer hire agreements. Most notable of these abstentions is the failure to redefine in statutory language the implied obligations of title, quality and fitness for use that appear to be owed by the lessor at Common Law; and the concommitant failure to prohibit any exclusion of these obligations under consumer hire agreements.[5]

Despite these lacunae, the impact of the Act upon the field of hiring agreements (and upon the operation of leasing concerns) is profound. The foregoing analysis will attempt to give a condensed account of the changes made by the Act within its peculiar area of operation.

B. Conduct of business

The whole spectrum of supervisory controls and penal prohibitions imposed by the Act applies with roughly equal force to those who carry on consumer hire and consumer credit businesses. Thus, operators of consumer hire businesses[6] fall within the licensing provisions of Part III of the Act[7] and a failure to obtain a licence where necessary will render any regulated agreement (i.e., in our present context, any consumer hire agreement) unenforceable against the hirer unless the Director-General of Fair Trading has made an order to contrary effect.[8] The general restrictions on seeking business likewise apply to persons carrying on consumer hire businesses, who accordingly must observe the mandatory form and content of advertisements,[9] must abstain from the use of false or misleading advertisements[10] and are bound to comply with such orders as are made concerning the giving of quotations,[11] the display of informa-

---

[5] Arguably beyond the draftsman's terms of reference, though cf. Schedule 4; and see now *Unfair Contract Terms Act,* 1977; post, p. 954.
[6] Note the amplification of the word "business" contained in ss. 189(1) and (2): (1) "business" includes profession or trade, and references to a business apply subject to subsection (2); (2) A person is not to be treated as carrying on a particular type of business merely because occasionally he enters into transactions belonging to a business of that type.
[7] Sections 21-42.
[8] Section 40(1); the non-enforcement rule for unlicensed operators does not apply to non-commercial agreements, which are consumer credit or consumer hire agreements not made by the creditor or owner in the course of a business carried on by him: s. 189(1).
[9] Section 44. For the advertisements to which this and succeeding provisions apply, see s. 43.
[10] Section 46; see further s. 47.
[11] Section 52.

tion[12] and the seeking of business generally.[13] In addition, it is an offence to send to any minor (with a view to financial gain) any document inviting him to obtain goods on hire or to apply for information or advice on hiring goods.[14]

C. Negotiations for, and entry into, consumer hire agreements

The Act imposes equally heavy duties upon the owner during the period between initial acquaintance or introduction to the customer and the time of contracting with him. A consumer hire agreement will be improperly executed if the owner has failed:

(i) to comply before the agreement was made with regulations specifying information to be disclosed to the hirer;[15]

(ii) to comply with regulations as to the form and content of documents embodying the consumer hire agreement.[16] A regulated agreement is not properly executed unless a document in the prescribed form is signed in the prescribed manner both by the hirer and by or on behalf of the owner.[17] In addition, the document must embody all the terms of the agreement, other than implied terms;[18] and must be sent or presented to the hirer in such a state that all its terms are readily legible.[19]

The consequences of improper execution are set out in s.65(1). An improperly executed agreement is enforceable[20] against the debtor or hirer only upon an order of the court.[21] Section 127 outlines the circumstances in which an order to this effect may be made.

The *Consumer Credit Act* makes careful provision for ensuring that hirers under prospective consumer hire agreements have adequate information, and adequate time for reflection, before they are finally committed. Thus, ss. 62-63 promulgate strict rules requiring the owner to supply copies of unexecuted and executed agreements[22] in appropriate circumstances, and s.64 requires notice to be given, in the case of cancellable agreements, of cancellation rights. Failure to comply with any of these sections makes the agreement improperly executed.

So far as concerns withdrawal, the ordinary common law rules are supplemented by a provision that any agreement is void insofar as it purports to bind a person to enter as hirer into a prospective regulated

---

[12] Section 53.
[13] Section 54.
[14] Sections 50(1)(b), (d); see further ss. 50(2), (3).
[15] Sections 55(1), (2).
[16] As to the factors to which the Secretary of State shall have regard in making such regulations, see ss. 60(1), (2).
[17] Section 61(1)(a).
[18] Section 61(1)(b).
[19] Section 61(1)(c): see further s. 61(4). Under s. 60(3), power is given to the Director-General of Fair Trading to direct (subject to any conditions he thinks fit) that compliance with the form and content rules (s. 60(1)) be waived or varied, if it appears to him impracticable for the applicant to comply with them. Such a notice of waiver or variation shall be given only if the Director is satisfied that to do so would not prejudice the interests of debtors or hirers: s. 60(4).
[20] By s. 65(2), enforcement includes a retaking of goods to which a regulated agreement relates.
[21] But cf. s. 173.
[22] Both expressions are defined in s. 189(1).

agreement;[23] and the potential hirer is given an opportunity to withdraw from a prospective regulated agreement by giving any notice, written or oral, which indicates this intention.[24] By ss.57(1) and (4) the effects of a withdrawal under s.57(2) are equated with that of cancellation under s.69. The latter phenomenon is elaborately dealt with under ss.67-73. Section 67 provides as follows:

> A regulated agreement may be cancelled by the debtor or hirer in accordance with this Part if the antecedent negotiations included oral representations made when in the presence of the debtor or hirer by an individual acting as, or on behalf of, the negotiator, unless,
> (a) the agreement is secured on land, or is a restricted-use credit agreement to finance the purchase of land or is an agreement for a bridging loan in connection with the purchase of land, or
> (b) the unexecuted agreement is signed by the debtor or hirer at premises at which any of the following is carrying on any business (whether on a permanent or temporary basis)
> (i) the creditor or owner;
> (ii) any party to a linked transaction (other than the debtor or hirer or a relative of his);
> (iii) the negotiator in any antecedent negotiations.

A cancellation notice must be served between the hirer's signing of the unexecuted agreement and the end of the fifth day following the day on which he received a copy of the executed agreement under s.63(2) or a notice of cancellation rights under s.64(1)(b).[25] If, however, regulations made under s.64(4) make s.64(1)(b) inapplicable, the hirer shall have till the end of the 14th day following the day on which he signed the unexecuted agreement.[26] Once a notice is given within the statutory period,[27] it operates:
1. to cancel the agreement, and any linked transaction, and
2. to withdraw any offer by the . . . hirer, or his relative, to enter into a linked transaction.[28]
Cancelled agreements are, moreover, to be treated (subject to the provisions of the Act) as if they had never been entered into.[29]

---

[23] Section 59(1); unless regulations exclude particular agreements from the operation of the rule: s. 59(2).

[24] Section 57(2); the following are to be deemed to be the agent of the owner for the purpose of receiving a notice under s. 57(2): Section 57(3) "(a) a credit-broker or supplier who is the negotiator in antecedent negotiations, and (b) any person who, in the course of a business carried on by him, acts on behalf of the debtor or hirer in any negotiations for the agreement.": See further, s. 175. The expressions "credit-broker" and "supplier" are defined by s. 189(1); "antecedent negotiations" is defined by s. 56: see post.

[25] Section 68(a).

[26] Section 68(b).

[27] As to parties who shall be deemed to be agents for the purpose of accepting cancellation notices, see s. 69(1). The remarkable width of this subsection is commented upon by Goode, *The Consumer Credit Act 1974*, at 92-93; and Guest & Lloyd, op. cit. in their note to s. 69(1). The notice may be one "however expressed . . . (which) . . . indicates the intention of the . . . hirer to withdraw from the agreement": s. 69(1). It is effective even though it does not make use of the information contained in the notice of cancellation rights given by the owner under s. 64(1): ibid.

[28] Section 69(1)(i) and (ii). Linked transactions are defined by ss. 19(1) and 189(1). By s. 69(5), regulations may exclude linked transactions of the prescribed description from the operation of s. 69(1)(i) and (ii).

[29] Section 69(4).

Once a cancellation has been effected, the hirer (or his relative) is entitled to recover any sums paid in contemplation of the agreement, including any item in the total charges for credit;[30] and any sum which might, apart from the cancellation, have become payable by the hirer or his relative (including any item in the total charge for credit) ceases to be payable.[31] A hirer or his relative in possession of the goods under the terms of the agreement has a lien for sums repayable on cancellation.[32] These provisions are further amplified by ss.70(3) to 70(8).[33]

Section 72 is concerned with the return of goods held by the hirer upon cancellation of a consumer hire agreement, or upon withdrawal from it under s.57. Subject to his lien,[34] the hirer who has acquired possession of goods to which the agreement relates is under a duty to return them to the person from whom he received them.[35] Throughout the pre-cancellation period,[36] and after cancellation,[37] the hirer shall be under a duty (or shall be treated as having been under a duty) to retain these goods and to take reasonable care of them; but he is under no duty to deliver the goods otherwise than at his own premises and upon a written request signed by or on behalf of the person from whom he has acquired possession. This request must be served upon the possessor either before, or at the time when, the goods are collected from his premises.[38] Section 72(6) provides the hirer in possession with the alternative of delivering the goods (at any place) to a person upon whom a notice of cancellation could have been served,[39] or of sending them at his own expense to such a person. Upon doing so, provided that in sending the goods he takes reasonable care to ensure that they reach the other party and are not damaged in transit, the hirer ceases to be responsible for them.[40] Breach of a duty imposed by s.72 is actionable as a breach of statutory duty.[41]

At Common Law, the person who retains unwanted goods may (even where there are simple mechanisms for disposing of them) become an involuntary bailee. The duties of such a person are uncertain,[42] but s.72(8) replaces the Common Law in cases of cancelled consumer hire agreements by provisions of its own. Unreasonable refusal of a request, made within 21 days of cancellation, and in the terms laid down by s.72(5), will oblige the hirer to contrive to take reasonable care of the goods until he has despatched or delivered the goods in accordance with s.72(6). If, however, *no* such request is made within 21 days of cancellation, the hirer's duty in respect of the goods shall cease at the end of that period. Of course, if the initial delivery of the goods to the

---

[30] Section 70(1)(a).
[31] Section 70(1)(b).
[32] Section 70(2).
[33] See Goode, *The Consumer Credit Act 1974,* pp. 94 et seq. Section 71, which deals with the repayment of credit under regulated agreements, is not relevant to contracts of hire.
[34] Ante: s. 70(2).
[35] Sections 70(1), (2) and (4).
[36] Section 70(3).
[37] Section 70(4).
[38] Section 70(5).
[39] Other than a person referred to in s. 69(a) or (b).
[40] Sections 72(6), (7).
[41] Section 72(11).
[42] Ch. 12, ante.

hirer took place at his request, he will not acquire a title to them by virtue of the *Unsolicited Goods and Services Act* 1971. The duty referred to is the duty to take reasonable care, and there would seem to be nothing in s.72(8) justifying a conversion, detinue or trespass to the goods on the part of the hirer before the owner has retrieved them.

Section 72 does not apply to perishable goods, goods which by their nature are consumed and were in fact consumed before the cancellation, goods supplied to meet an emergency[43] or goods which had before the cancellation become incorporated in any land or thing not comprised in the cancelled agreement or a linked transaction.[44] Thus it would seem that if a hired television set were incorporated into a built-in wall cabinet, s.22 would not apply; but s.72(9) will probably be construed restrictively and therefore may not include goods such as televisions and refrigerators which, in ordinary circumstances at least, are merely attached to land.[45]

Section 73, which deals with the recovery, upon cancellation, of goods given in part-exchange, will not be discussed in detail because in most cases part-exchange does not take place under consumer hire agreements. It should be noted that none of the foregoing provisions[46] applies inter alia to non-commercial agreements: that is, in the present context, consumer hire agreements which are not made by the owner in the course of a business carried on by him.[47] The reader is referred to the decision in *Ludgate* v. *Lovett*[48] for a possible illustration of the sort of circumstances which may give rise to a non-commercial hire agreement.

D. The remedies of the owner

The *Consumer Credit Act* severely circumscribes the lessor's exercise of his customary Common Law remedies, such as repossession, termination and acceleration of payments, against the hirer. Section 76(1) provides that he is not entitled to enforce any term of a consumer hire agreement by demanding earlier payment of any sum, recovering possession of any goods or treating any right conferred on the hirer by the agreement as terminated, restricted or deferred, *unless* he has given the hirer at least seven days' notice of his intention to do so. Such notices must be in the prescribed form.[49] Section 76(1) applies only, however, to right of enforcement which do *not* arise by reason of any breach of the agreement by the hirer; the owner's rights on default are dealt with under Part VII of the Act.[50] Section 76(1) is subject to two further exceptions; it does not apply to agreements excluded by regulation[51] and is confined to agreements where:

---

[43] A vague and potentially wide exception.
[44] Section 72(9)(a)-(d).
[45] Note s. 16; ante., p. 762.
[46] Viz., Part V, ss. 55-73.
[47] Section 189(1).
[48] [1969] 1 W.L.R. 1016. (Owner renovating and leasing out van as a spare-time occupation). In fact, the duration of this particular contract of hire would have excluded it from the definition in s. 15 of a consumer hire agreement.
[49] Section 76(3).
[50] Post.
[51] Section 75(6).

(a) the period for the duration of the agreement is specified in the agreement, and

(b) that period has not ended when the owner performs the act of enforcement specified in s.76(1).[52]

If, however, these conditions are satisfied, s.76(1) is not displaced by the fact that, under the agreement, any party is entitled to terminate the agreement before the end of the period so specified.[53]

Section 87 is the "default" counterpart of s.76. Again, it requires notice to be given to the hirer under a consumer hire agreement before the owner may perform one of a specified series of acts by way of enforcement by reason of a breach by the hirer. The acts which must be prefaced by notice are:[54]

termination of the agreement;
demanding earlier payment of any sum;
recovery of possession of goods;
treating any right conferred on the hirer by the agreement as terminated, restricted or deferred; or
enforcing any security.

Section 87(1) may, however, be excluded from agreements described by regulation.[55] The required contents of the default notice are outlined in s.88 and are to be amplified by regulation. The notice must be in the prescribed form and must specify the nature of the alleged breach, the action required to remedy that breach and the date before which such action must be taken; or, if the breach is not capable of remedy, the sum required as compensation for the breach and the date before which it must be paid.[56] Such dates must be not less than seven days after service of the default notice, and until they fall due the owner is prohibited from taking the enforcement action specified in s.87(1). If not date is specified, the restraint period is seven days.[57] In addition, the default notice must contain information in the prescribed terms about the consequences of non-compliance with it.[58] Upon compliance by the hirer with the requirements laid down in the notice, the breach shall be treated as never having occurred.[59]

The acts of enforcement specified in s.87(1) as being beyond the owner's power to perform without a default notice are likewise provided, by s.86(1), to be acts which he may not perform by reason of the death of the hirer,[60] if at the time of death the agreement is fully

---

[52] Section 76(2).
[53] Ibid.
[54] Section 87(1)(a)-(e).
[55] Section 87(4).
[56] Sections 88(1)(a)-(c).
[57] Section 88(2); see also ss. 88(3) (breaches arising from failure to comply with provisions which become operative only upon breach of other provisions not generally to be treated as breaches in the default notice); 88(5) (default notices making requirements under s. 88(1) may provide for taking of enforcement action as specified in s. 87(1) at any time after the restriction imposed by s. 88(2) will cease, and may include a statement that the provision will be ineffective if the breach is duly remedied or the compensation duly paid).
[58] Section 88(4).
[59] Section 89.
[60] For the meaning of "by reason of the death of the hirer", see further s. 86(6).

secured. Where, on the other hand, the agreement is at the relevant time unsecured or merely partly secured, his right to perform one or more of the specified acts of enforcement is dependent upon his obtaining an order of the court.[61] The operation of s.86 is however, subject to a number of limitations. It applies to inhibit the owner from *terminating* an agreement only where the agreement itself specifies a period for its duration and that period has not ended when the owner purports to terminate,[62] but it so applies notwithstanding that, under the agreement, any party is entitled to terminate it before the end of the period so specified. Nor does s.86 affect the operation of any agreement providing for the payment of sums due under the consumer hire agreement, or becoming due under it on the death of the hirer, out of the proceeds of a policy of assurance on his life.[63]

The foregoing provisions are further fortified by s.92(1) of the Act, which prohibits the owner from entering any premises to take possession of goods subject to a regulated consumer hire agreement unless he does so under an order of the court. Breach of this provision is actionable as a breach of statutory duty.[64]

Section 98 completes the trinity of major inhibitions imposed upon the owner during the currency of the agreement. Whereas ss.76 and 87 deal with enforcement otherwise than upon default, and enforcement upon default, respectively, s.98 restricts the owner's right to *terminate* a consumer hire agreement other than by reason of a breach by the hirer.[65] Such right shall only be exercised after giving the hirer not less than seven days' notice of the termination,[66] the notice to be in the prescribed form and ineffective if not.[67] This restriction is confined to set-period agreements in terms identical to ss.76(2) and 86(3),[68] and may be excluded from such agreements as are described by regulation.[69]

E. Duties of information under consumer hire agreements

These may exist on both sides of the agreement, but the duties of the owner are (as may be expected) more extensive. If the agreement is a regulated consumer hire agreement (other than a non-commercial agreement)[70] the owner must give the hirer a copy of the executed agreement and of any other agreement referred to in it, together with a statement by him or on his behalf showing (according to the information to which it is practicable for him to refer) the total sum payable and unpaid by the hirer under the agreement, and the various amounts comprised in that total sum, together with the date when each became due.[71] This duty arises only, of course, upon the making of a request

---

[61] Section 86(2); see further s. 128.
[62] Section 86(3).
[63] Section 86(5).
[64] Section 92(3); but see s. 173(3), which creates an exception where the entry or repossession takes place with the consent of the hirer.
[65] Section 98(1).
[66] This limitation is imposed by s. 98(6).
[67] Section 98(3).
[68] Section 98(2); see ante, pp. 744, 751 et seq.
[69] Section 98(5).
[70] Section 79(4); see s. 189(1); ante., p. 763.
[71] Section 79(1).

to that effect by the hirer; such request must be in writing and must be accompanied by payment of a fee of 15 new pence.[72] Further, the owner is under no duty to comply where the agreement is one under which no sum is, or will or may become, payable by the hirer; or where the hirer has already within the previous month made a previous request under s.79(1) and the owner has complied with that earlier request. In those cases where a duty to respond *is* imposed, however, the response must be within the prescribed period[73] and failure precipitates the following consequences:

(a) the owner is not entitled, while the default continues, to enforce the agreement; and

(b) if the default continues for one month he commits an offence.[74]

Under s.172, a statement given by virtue of s.79(1) is binding on the owner, subject to relief by the court in any proceedings before it wherein it is sought to rely on the statement and such statement is shown to be incorrect.[75]

The hirer under a regulated consumer hire agreement (other than a non-commercial agreement), which requires him to keep goods to which the agreement relates in his possession and control, must, within seven working days of receiving a request in writing from the owner, tell the owner where the goods are. If his failure to do so persists for fourteen days, he commits an offence.[76]

F. Appropriation of payments

Where the debtor or hirer is liable to make payments to the same person in respect of two or more regulated agreements, s.81(1) gives him a power to appropriate any payment he makes which is not sufficient to discharge all the agreements. If the debtor or hirer fails to appropriate, and one or more of the agreements is a consumer hire agreement, or an agreement in relation to which any security is provided, or a hire-purchase agreement or conditional sale agreement, the payment will be divided, and appropriated towards the sums due under the several agreements respectively, in a manner rateable with these sums themselves.[77]

G. Variation of agreements

Section 82(1) requires the owner who wishes to use his power under a regulated consumer hire agreement to vary that agreement to give the prescribed notice before making the variation. This power is further amplified by ss. 81(2) - (6) and does not apply to non-commercial agreements.[78]

H. The hirer's right to terminate

A general statutory power of termination is conferred by s.101(1), which provides that the hirer under a regulated consumer hire agreement may

---

[72] Ibid., and see s. 181.
[73] Section 79(1).
[74] Sections 79(3)(a), (b). For penalty under the latter sub-sub-section, see s. 167 and Sched. I.
[75] Sections 172(1) and (3). See also s. 180 (power to prescribe form etc. of copies).
[76] Sections 80(1) and (2). For penalty, see above; for "working days", see s. 189(1).
[77] Section 81(2).
[78] Section 82(7).

do so "by giving notice to any person entitled or authorised to receive the sums payable under the agreement".[79] This power is indefeasible,[80] but is liable to be displaced in certain circumstances and must be carefully exercised. Section 101 does not apply to any agreement which provides for the making by the hirer of payments which in total (and without breach of the agreement) exceed £300 p.a.;[81] nor does it apply, by virtue of s.101(7)(b), to any agreement where:

(i) goods are bailed or (in Scotland) hired to the hirer for the purposes of a business carried on by him, or the hirer holds himself out as requiring the goods for those purposes, and

(ii) the goods are selected by the hirer, and acquired by the owner for the purposes of the agreement at the request of the hirer from any person other than the owner's associate.[82]

A further line of exclusion is provided by s.101(7)(c), whereunder s.101 is prevented from applying to any agreement where the hirer requires, or holds himself out as requiring, the goods for the purpose of bailing or hiring them to other persons in the course of a business carried on by him. The expression "bailing or hiring" is presumably inserted to accommodate the Scottish lack of a concept of bailment, but it could produce wider results than were intended; for instance, where the hirer wishes to lend the goods to a third party or to keep them stored, for reason best known to himself, with such a person. Admittedly, this problem would arise only in very unusual circumstances.

Under s.101(8), a person carrying on a consumer hire business may apply to the Director and invite him to direct that s.101 shall not apply to consumer hire agreements carried on by the applicant. Such a direction may be made subject to conditions and shall issue only if it appears to the Director to be in the interests of hirers to do so.

Termination of an agreement under s.101(1) does not affect any liability under the agreement accruing before termination.[83] No hirer may exercise this right if the notice is to expire earlier than eighteen months

---

[79] Cf. s. 102, which provides as follows:
"(1) Where the debtor or hirer under a regulated agreement claims to have a right to rescind the agreement, each of the following shall be deemed to be the agent of the creditor or owner for the purpose of receiving any notice rescinding the agreement which is served by the debtor or hirer —
(a) a credit-broker or supplier who was the negotiator in antecedent negotiations, and
(b) any person who, in the course of a business carried on by him, acted on behalf of the debtor in any negotiations for the agreement.
(2) In subsection (1) "rescind" does not include —
(a) service of a notice of cancellation, or
(b) termination of an agreement under section 99 or 101, or by the exercise of a right or power in that behalf expressly conferred by the agreement."
Guest & Lloyd, *The Consumer Credit Act 1974,* note to s. 102, suggest that the word rescind should be construed liberally so as to include not merely rescission for fraud, misrepresentation etc. in the equitable sense, but rescission consequent upon an election by the hirer to treat the agreement as repudiated, as where, for instance, there has been a breach of an implied term as to fitness.
[80] Guest & Lloyd, op. cit., note to s. 101.
[81] Section 101(7)(a); cf. s. 181 (power to alter financial ceiling).
[82] "Associate" is defined by ss. 184, 189(1).
[83] Section 101(2).

after the making of the agreement.[84] If this requirement is satisfied, the minimum permissible period of notice is as follows:

1. For agreements which provide for the making of payments by the hirer to the owner at equal intervals — the length of one such interval or three months, whichever is the less.[85]

2. For agreements which provide for the making of such payments at differing intervals — the length of the shortest interval or three months, whichever is the less.[86]

3. In any other case — three months.[87]

Section 103 deals with the right of the hirer to obtain a termination statement from the owner. To obtain such a statement, he must serve a notice of "the trader" stating that he (the hirer) was a hirer under a regulated agreement described in the notice, and that the trader was the owner under that agreement, that the hirer has discharged his indebtedness to the owner thereunder; and that the agreement has ceased to have any operation.[88] Further, he must require the owner to give him a notice, signed by the owner or on his behalf, confirming that the foregoing statements are correct.[89] When these requirements are fulfilled, the owner shall, within the prescribed period, either send the requested statement or serve on the customer a counter-notice stating that, as the case may be, he disputes the correctness of the notice or asserts that the customer is not indebted to him under the agreement.[90] If he disputes the correctness of the hirer's notice, he must give details of the alleged incorrectness;[91] if he fails to comply with s.103(1), and this default continues for a month, the owner commits an offence.[92] The duty to supply termination statements does not apply in cases of non-commercial agreements,[93] nor does it apply where the owner has already complied with an earlier notice demanding such a statement in relation to the same agreement.[94] But where this duty does obtain, the owner is bound (unless relieved by the court) by the ensuing statement.[95]

I. Liability for acts and statements during antecedent negotiations

Under s.56(3), an agreement which, in relation to a consumer hire (or any other regulated) agreement, purports (a) to provide that a person acting as, or on behalf of, a negotiator is to be treated as the agent of the the hirer; or (b) to relieve a person from liability for acts or omissions of any person acting as, or on behalf of, a negotiator, is void that extent.[96]

---

[84] Section 101(3); as to modifying agreements (dealt with in s. 82 — variation); see s. 101(9).
[85] Section 101(4).
[86] Section 101(5).
[87] Section 101(6).
[88] Section 103(1)(a)(i)-(iii).
[89] Section 103(1)(b).
[90] Section 103(1): ibid.
[91] Section 103(2).
[92] Section 103(5); for penalty, see s. 167 and Sched.1.
[93] Section 103(4).
[94] Section 103(3).
[95] Section 172; see ante., p. 000.
[96] "Negotiator" is limited by s. 56(1) in this context to owners who conduct negotiations with hirers in relation to making of consumer hire agreements: there is no provision for including credit-brokers who introduce potential hirers

The reforms effected by this section are necessary ones; indeed, the type of provision referred to in s.56(3)(a) has recently caused concern in the superficially disparate field of insurance and undoubtedly presents wide potential for abuse. Nevertheless, it is unfortunate that s.56 does not go further and acknowledge that in cases of long-term hiring agreements there may be a tripartite arrangement, involving the hirer, the original owner and a finance company to whom the goods are sold in order to be leased. Although it is uncertain how far this practice has developed in England, it would seem to have acquired some foothold in Australia and would seem, in some respects, to be ripe for export: for whereas s.56(2) imposes upon the creditor under certain types of debtor-creditor-supplier agreement (e.g. the orthodox triangular hire-purchase contract) a notional liability for the acts of his negotiator (e.g. a dealer) as his agent,[97] no such rule would appear to assist the simple hirer under a similar tripartite system. In the light of observations made earlier[98] about the difficulty experienced by hirers in proving reliance upon the owner's skill and judgment, this omission would appear to be a matter for regret.

J. Security

The giving of security[99] in relation to regulated agreements is covered by Part VIII. Any such security must be in writing;[1] the security instrument must comply with regulations[2] and be signed in the prescribed manner, in order to be properly executed.[3] In addition, no security instrument shall be properly executed unless it embodies all the terms (other than implied terms) of the security;[4] is readily legible at the time of presentation or sending for signature by or on behalf of the surety;[5] and is accompanied at such time by a duplicate copy.[6] In addition, s.105(5) provides two further grounds of improper execution, by requiring that:

(a) where the security is provided after, or at the time when, the regulated agreement is made, a copy of the executed agreement, together with a copy of any other document referred to in it, is given to the surety at the time the security is provided, or
(b) where the security is provided before the regulated agreement is made, a copy of the executed agreement, together with a copy of any other document referred to in it, is given to the surety within seven days after the regulated agreement is made.

Where a security instrument is not expressed in writing or is improperly executed on the foregoing grounds, the security (so far as provided in

to owners with the ambit of s. 56(3). As to the commencement of antecedent negotiations, s. 56(4) states that they are to be taken to begin when the negotiator and the hirer first enter into communication, including communication by advertisement. They include any representations made by the negotiator to the hirer and any other dealings between them: ibid.

[97] See further, s. 75.
[98] Ante, p. 729.
[99] Defined by s. 189(1).
[1] Section 105(1); unless provided by the debtor or hirer: s. 105(6).
[2] Section 105(2); for guidelines as to the content of such regulations, see Sections 105(3), and see further s. 105(9).
[3] Sections 105(2), 105(4)(a).
[4] Section 105(4)(b).
[5] Section 105(4)(c).
[6] Section 105(4)(d).

relation to a regulated agreement) shall be enforceable only upon an order of the court.[7] Dismissal of an application for such an order (unless the dismissal be purely on technical grounds) means that s.106 shall apply to the security.[8] This section provides as follows:

(a) the security, so far as it is so provided, shall be treated as never having effect;

(b) any property lodged with the creditor or owner solely for the purposes of the security as so provided shall be returned by him forthwith;

(c) the creditor or owner shall take any necessary action to remove or cancel an entry in any register, so far as the entry relates to the security as so provided; and

(d) any amount received by the creditor or owner on realisation of the security shall, so far as it is referable to the agreement, be repaid to the surety.

Supplementary provisions are contained in s.109 (which imposes a duty to give information on request to sureties under consumer hire agreements) and s.110 (imposing an analogous duty to give the hirer, on request, a copy of any security instrument executed in relation to the regulated agreement after that agreement was made). These rules are similar in content and effect to s.79.[9] In addition, s.111(1) obliges the owner to serve upon any surety a copy of any default notice served by him on the hirer under ss.76(1) or 98(1). Failure to comply means that, in respect of the breach or other matter to which the default notice relates, the security is enforceable against the surety only upon an order of the court.[10]

A general power to make regulations governing the sale or other realisation of property provided by way of security in relation to regulated agreements (other than non-commercial agreements) is conferred by s.112; and ss.113(1) and (2) make elaborate provision for ensuring that the terms of the Act are not evaded by the use of security devices.[11] The remainder of s.113[12] deals with the impact of cancellation, determination, failure by the owner to obtain a necessary enforcement order, and the making of a declaration under s.142(1) of the Act,[13] upon the security (in this event, s.106 shall apply) and with ancillary questions of which space does not permit discussion.

Negotiable instruments: One of the abuses to which the Crowther Committee drew particular attention was the practice whereby certain traders (notably, perhaps, building, double-glazing and central-heating contractors) would extract from the consumer a promissory note or bill of exchange which was payable by instalments covering the entire cost of

---

[7] Section 105(7).
[8] Section 105(8).
[9] Ante, p. 769.
[10] Section 111(2); cf. s. 173(3).
[11] For the interpretation and effect of this section, which will not be discussed in the present account, see Goode, *The Consumer Credit Act 1974*, pp. 139-140, 146-147; [1975] C.L.J. 79, at 111-115.
[12] Sections 13(3)-(8).
[13] Declaration of non-entitlement on part of owner to perform acts permissible only upon obtaining an order of the court.

work done, and then discount this to a finance-house.[14] This introduced an undesirable element of third-party immunity into consumer transactions, for the consumer had no remedy against the finance-company for defective workmanship and the latter took free from defences that would have availed against the supplier.[15]

To combat the practice, s.123(1) provides flatly that no creditor or owner shall take any negotiable instrument[16] other than a bank-note or a cheque, in discharge of any sum payable by the debtor or hirer under a regulated agreement, or by any person as surety in relation to the agreement. Further, the creditor or owner is forbidden from negotiating a cheque taken in these circumstances unless he does so to a banker within the meaning of the *Bills of Exchange Act* 1882,[17] and from taking a negotiable instrument as security for the discharge of any sum specified in s.123(1).[18] The foregoing provisions do not apply to non-commercial agreements[19] and may excluded by regulation from applying to regulated agreements which have a connection with a country outside the United Kingdom.[20]

Breach of s.123 makes the relevant agreement or security (as the case may be) unenforceable except by order of the court.[21] S.106[22] is made to apply whenever an application to enforce a security under the preceeding sub-section is dismissed other than on technical grounds.[23] Section 125(1) provides that no person who has taken a negotiable instrument in contravention of ss.123(1) or (3) is a holder in due course, or is entitled to enforce the instrument: and ss.125(2) to (4) make consequential amendments to the position of others who are affected by the effect of s.123.

K. Judicial control of consumer hire agreements

Part IX of the *Consumer Credit Act* contains a variety of measures enabling the court to exercise a close supervisory and modifying power over regulated agreements. These measures come into effect through a number of different media and on a series of different occasions. Only the briefest outline will be possible in the ensuing account.

1. *Granting of enforcement orders*: An application for an order for enforcement under ss.65(1), 105(7)(a) or (b), 111(2) or 124(1) or (2) shall be refused if (and only if) the court considers it just and equitable to do so, having regard to the prejudice and culpability involved

---

[14] Cmnd. 4597 (1971), paras 6.6.35 et. seq.
[15] Goode [1975] C.L.J. 79, at 114.
[16] As to the problems of defining a negotiable instrument, see Guest & Lloyd, op. cit. note to s. 123.
[17] Section 123(2). If a person breaches this sub-section, his doing so constitutes a defect in his title within the meaning of the Bills of Exchange Act 1882.
[18] Section 123(3); the taking of a negotiable instrument as security for the discharge of a sum is defined by s. 123(4) as where "the sum is intended to be paid in some other way, and the negotiable instrument is to be presented for payment only if the sum is not paid in that way."
[19] Section 123(5).
[20] Section 123(6).
[21] Sections 124(1) and (2).
[22] Ante, p. 774.
[23] Section 124(3).

in the contravention and powers conferred on the court by ss.127(2), 135 and 136.[24]

Upon making an enforcement order, the court may (by way of compensation for prejudice suffered by the relevant contravention) reduce or discharge any sum payable by the hirer or any surety.[25] Further conditions attend the making of enforcement orders under s.65(1)[26] (improperly executed agreements) and s.86(2) (acts of enforcement by owner on death of hirer under unsecured or partially secured consumer hire agreements).[27] No order shall be made under the latter section unless the owner proves that he has been unable to satisfy himself that the hirer's present and future obligations under the agreement are likely to be discharged.[28]

2. *Time orders*: Section 129 empowers the court to order the payment of sums owed by hirers or sureties by way of instalments.[29] This may be coupled with a provision that the hirer remedy any breach of the agreement (other than a failure to pay money) within a specified time.[30] Time order may be made in the following circumstances:

(i) on an application for an enforcement order; or

(ii) on an application by the hirer (under this paragraph) after service upon him of a default notice or a notice under ss.76(1) or 98(1); or

(iii) in an action brought by the owner to enforce a regulated agreement or any security, or to recover possession of any goods or land to which such agreement relates.[31]

Supplemental provisions concerning time orders are set out in s.130.

3. *Protection of property pending proceedings*: The court has a discretion to make orders (on the application of the owner) for protecting his property (or property subject to any security) from damage or depreciation pending proceedings. Such orders may inter alia restrict or prohibit the use of the property or give directions as to its custody.[32]

4. *Financial relief for hirer on repossession*: This important power is contained in s.132, which deserves to be set out verbatim:

> (1) Where the owner under a regulated consumer hire agreement recovers possession of goods to which the agreement relates otherwise than by action, the hirer may apply to the court for an order that,
>
> (a) the whole or part of any sum paid by the hirer to the owner in respect of the goods shall be repaid, and
>
> (b) the obligation to pay the whole or part of any sum owed by the hirer to the owner in respect of the goods shall cease.
>
> And if it appears to the court just to do so, having regard to the

---

[24] Section 127(1); see post.

[25] Section 127(2).

[26] See ss. 127(3)-(5) and, for s. 65(1), ante, p. 764. The agreement must, in general terms, comply with form and content regulations, be properly signed and be accompanied by a copy and a notice of cancellation rights.

[27] Ante, p. 769.

[28] Section 128.

[29] Provided that such order is considered reasonable having regard to the means of the hirer and any surety: ibid.

[30] Sections 129(2)(a) and (b).

[31] Section 129(1).

[32] Section 131.

extent of the enjoyment of the goods by the hirer, the court shall grant the application in full or in part.

(2) Where in proceedings relating to a regulated consumer hire agreement the court makes an order for the delivery to the owner of goods to which the agreement relates the court may include in the order the like provision as may be made in an order under subsection(1).

5. *Miscellaneous powers*: In making an order in relation to a consumer hire agreement, the court has a general discretion to impose certain conditions. Thus, it may make the operation of any term of the order contingent upon the performance, by any party to the proceedings, of certain specified acts,[33] or may suspend the operation of any term of the order, *either* until a time subsequently directed by the court *or* until the occurrence of a specified act or omission.[34] However, the power of suspension shall not be used so as to extend the period for which, under the terms of the agreement, the hirer is entitled to possession of the goods.[35] Finally, the court has a blanket jurisdiction to include, in orders made under the Act, any such provision as it considers just for amending any agreement or security in consequence of a term of the order.[36] This is as near as the Act approaches to an extension to the hirer of the power to re-open extortionate *credit* bargains contained in ss.137-140.[37]

L. Residual provisions

The remainder of the Act deals with an assortment of duties and prohibitions which will be mentioned only in the briefest possible terms. Part X of the Act regulates the operation of ancillary credit businesses[38] and is of fairly marginal importance to the majority of consumer hire agreements,[39] although it should be noted that the failure of a credit-broker to obtain a licence can render unenforceable any subsequent consumer hire agreement effected on his introduction.[40] Part XI lays down the various agencies charged with the enforcement of the Act and the powers and duties to which those agencies are subject. Specific attention is drawn to ss.168 and 169 (defences and offences),[41] 171 (onus of proof in proceedings under the Act) and 173, which prohibits any 'contracting out' of the protection afforded by the Act, but provides that notwithstanding this:

> 173(3) . . . a provision of this Act under which a thing may be done in relation to any person on an order of the court or the Director only shall not be taken to prevent its being done at any time with

[33] Section 135(1)(a).
[34] Sections 135(1)(b)(i) and (ii). But see ss. 135(2) (no suspension of order for delivery up of goods unless court satisfied that such goods are in that person's possession and control) and 135(4) (power to vary).
[35] Section 135(3).
[36] Section 136.
[37] Note also s. 142 (power to declare rights of parties).
[38] Defined by s. 145.
[39] But note the definition of credit brokerage in s. 145(2)(b) and (c), which brings the introduction of potential hirers to potential lessors within the ambit of that term.
[40] Section 149.
[41] As to s. 168, cf. *Tesco Supermarkets Ltd.* v. *Nattrass* [1972] A.C. 153.

that person's consent given at that time, but the refusal of such consent shall not give rise to any liability.

Finally, Part XII contains a range of supplemental provisions covering such questions as the duties of persons deemed to be agents under the Act,[42] the service of documents[43] and the legal effects of a series of agreements with more than one hirer:

> 185(1) Where an actual or prospective regulated agreement has two or more debtors or hirers (not being a partnership or an unincorporated body of persons) —
> (a) anything required by or under this Act to be done to or in relation to the debtor or hirer shall be done to or in relation to each of them; and
> (b) anything done under this Act by or on behalf of one of them shall have effect as if done by or on behalf of all of them.

Part XII also contains various definition sections[44] and incorporates the examples propounded in Schedule 2 into the Act.[45]

VI. THE CONSUMER TRANSACTIONS ACT 1972-1973 (SOUTH AUSTRALIA)

South Australia is the first state to have attempted to deal comprehensively with consumer credit and allied transactions. It operates upon contracts of hire via the concept of the 'consumer lease'. The definition of this concept lacks some of the precision of s.15 of the *Consumer Credit Act*.[46] The following are the essential components of a consumer lease:[47]

(i) It must be a consumer contract; *i.e.,* in the present context, a contract or agreement under which a person who is not a body corporate takes any goods on hire.[48] A contract may fulfil the description of a consumer contract irrespective of whether the contract purports to confer upon the consumer a power to purchase the goods. However, in order to qualify as a consumer *lease* the agreement must not confer any right or option to purchase upon the consumer and the consideration to be paid or provided by the consumer in money or money's worth must not exceed (excluding any credit charge) ten thousand dollars. Moreover, contracts or agreements for the bailment or disposition of goods to persons who trade in goods of that description[49] are excluded from this definition, as are other agreements specified by regulation.[50]

(ii) The goods must be let on hire to a "consumer". For present purposes, a consumer is a person who is not a body corporate and who

---

[42] Section 175.
[43] Section 176.
[44] Sections 184 ("associates"); 189 (definitions generally).
[45] Section 188.
[46] Ante, p. 761.
[47] C.T.A., 1972-1973, s. 5.
[48] The letting on hire must be by a "supplier", viz a person carrying on a business in the course of which he enters into the consumer contract. For certain purposes, supplier has a wider connotation: ante, p.000.
[49] Quaere whether using the goods in the course of a business (e.g. putting rented television sets in hotel bedrooms) necessarily amounts to trading; presumably not.
[50] See Consumer Transactions Regulations 1973, First Schedule, which exempts contracts or agreements for the sale or lease (i) of any goods by tender; (ii) of antiques other than antique furniture; and (iii) of works of art.

enters into a consumer contract "with a view to — acquiring the use or benefit of goods . . .". This definition includes a person to whom the rights interest or liability of a consumer under the consumer lease are assigned.

(iii) The goods must be let "for a period exceeding four months".

While it is welcome to note that s.5 caters for the lease that does not involve monetary consideration (or, possibly, a strict transfer of possession) it seems that the methods for computing the necessary financial and time-limits are somewhat blunt and inadequate compared to those employed under the U.K. legislation.

A. Formal validity

Under s.20(1), a consumer lease must be in writing and must contain certain information:

(a) a brief description or identification of the goods to which the lease applies;

(b) the amount or value of any consideration to be paid or provided by the consumer prior to the delivery of the goods subject to the lease;

(c) the amount of any stamp duty or other impost payable in respect of the lease;

(d) the amount of any other charges not included in the rental payable under the lease, and a brief description of those charges;

(e) the amount of each payment to be made by the consumer under the lease, the date on which the first payment is due and either —

(i) the dates upon which the subsequent payments are due; or

(ii) the interval between payments;

(f) the number of periodic payments to be made by the consumer, and the total amount payable under the lease;

(g) a statement of the conditions upon which the consumer may terminate the lease; and

(h) a statement of the liabilities (if any) of the consumer upon termination of the lease.

Failure to comply with the requirements constitutes an offence on the part of the supplier;[51] and if the agreement is not in writing, renders the lease unenforceable by the supplier against the consumer.[52] It is also a criminal offence[53] for the supplier to fail to serve upon the consumer, within fourteen days of the formation of the consumer lease, a copy of that lease and a notice in the prescribed form setting out the provisions of the Act which afforded protection to the consumer.[54] If a failure to comply with the formal requirements of s.20(1) is shown to the satisfaction of the Credit Tribunal[55] not to operate so as to mislead the consumer to his prejudice or disadvantage, the Tribunal may deem that those requirements have been complied with.[56]

---

[51] The penalty is $500: s. 20(3).
[52] Section 20(5).
[53] And one carrying the same penalty.
[54] Section 20(2). See Consumer Transactions Regulations 1973, Fourth Schedule.
[55] Constituted under the *Consumer Credit Act* 1972 (S.A.).
[56] Section 20(4).

B. Repossession

No supplier with whom a consumer has entered into a consumer lease may exercise any right under the lease to take possession of goods subject to the lease unless he has served upon the consumer, at least seven days before taking possession of the goods, a written notice in the prescribed form indicating his intention to exercise that right.[57] This requirement does not obtain, however, when the right to repossess arises under a lease granted for a fixed term and at the expiration of that term;[58] or where there are reasonable grounds for believing that the goods comprised in the lease will be (or have been) removed or concealed by the consumer contrary to the provisions of the lease;[59] or where the supplier has been authorised by the Tribunal to take possession of the goods, notwithstanding the failure to comply with s.21(1).[60]

C. Avoidance or modification of consumer leases

Section 22(1) of the Act confers a blanket jurisdiction upon the Tribunal to avoid or modify, upon the application of a consumer, "any term or condition of a consumer lease that is harsh or unconscionable, or such that a Court of Equity would give relief." This provision is conspicuously bald and may perhaps be criticised for failing to provide more specific indicators as to the circumstances in which this jurisdiction is to be exercised.[61]

D. Termination by the consumer

Section 22(2), which is a rough equivalent to s.132 of the *Consumer Credit Act* 1974,[62] allows the consumer under a consumer lease which has been granted for a fixed term to terminate the lease, at any time before the expiration of that term, by returning the goods that are the subject-matter of the lease "to the supplier at his place of business or[63] at any place fixed by the agreement between the consumer and the supplier" or fixed on application by the consumer to the Tribunal. In the latter regard, there is no appeal from a determination by the Tribunal.[64] Whenever *any* termination has occurred prior to the expiry of the lease (be it by reason of breach of the provisions of the lease or otherwise) the amount payable by the consumer is to be:

(a) the amount that is in accordance with the terms of the lease to be paid in that event; or

(b) the amount arrived at by the application of the principles established by regulation for this purpose, whichever is the lesser.[65]

---

[57] Section 21(1). See Consumer Transactions Regulations 1973, Fifth Schedule.
[58] Ibid.
[59] Section 21(2)(a).
[60] Section 21(2)(b). And see Consumer Transactions Regulations 1973, Fourteenth Schedule.
[61] See further s. 38, post, and Consumer Transactions Regulations 1973, Eleventh Schedule.
[62] Ante, p. 776.
[63] The word "or" was omitted from the text of the 1973 Act and was added by s. 8 of the *Consumer Transactions Act Amendment Act* 1973.
[64] Section 22(3), added by s. 8, C.T.A.A.A., 1973 (ante) and see Consumer Transactions Regulations 1973, Twelfth Schedule.
[65] Section 23.

E. Variation notices

Section 20(6) of the Act[66] requires that whenever the terms or conditions of a consumer lease are varied in any manner, the lessor shall within fourteen days from the date of variation serve a notice upon the consumer that sets out "in a clear and concise manner" the nature of the variation to the consumer's rights under the lease and the nature and extent of his obligations under the lease as varied. Such notice shall further contain such other information as is prescribed by regulation, and failure to comply can involve a penalty of $500.

The foregoing are the only provisions of the 1972-1973 Act that apply exclusively to consumer leases, but there are a number of other sections which affect such leases through the medium of consumer transactions generally. Examples are the conditions and warranties of fitness etc. implied by ss.8-10,[67] the scope of liability for misrepresentations,[68] and the consumer's power to rescind.[69] Further examples include:

1. *The right to know where the goods are situate*: Section 31(1) entitles the lessor under a consumer lease to serve upon the lessee at any time a written notice requiring him to state in writing where the goods are, and (if the goods are not in the lessee's possession), requiring him either to take reasonable steps to ascertain their whereabouts and inform the lessor accordingly, or to state to whom he delivered the goods or the circumstances in which he lost possession of them. Failure to comply with such a requirement, or to knowingly supply a false statement in response thereto, is an offence.[70]

2. *Removal of goods by lessee*: Frequently, contracts of hire oblige the hirer to keep the goods in his possession or control at a particular place, or not to remove them from a specified location. Section 32(1) provides in such an event that the Credit Tribunal may, on the application of the consumer under a consumer lease, authorize the removal of the goods to some other place, subject to such conditions as the Tribunal thinks fit to impose.[71] A removal pursuant to such an order shall not be deemed a breach of the lease.[72]

3. *Fixtures*: Goods subject to a consumer lease, which were not at the time of the creation of the lease fixtures to land, shall not (in respect of the period for which the lease remains in force) be treated as fixtures to land for the purposes of any Act or law.[73]

4. *Power to order delivery of goods unlawfully detained*: Section 34(1) strengthens the lessor's powers of repossession by providing that where he is entitled to take possession of the goods under a consumer lease and satisfies the tribunal both that the detention is without just cause and that

---

[66] Added by s. 7 of the amending Act of 1973.
[67] Ante, p. 736 et seq.
[68] Sections 11-14.
[69] Section 15-18.
[70] Section 31(2).
[71] There is no appeal from such an order: s. 32(3). See further Consumer Transactions Regulations, Sixteenth Schedule.
[72] Section 32(2).
[73] Section 33.

the consumer's failure to deliver up the goods has occurred after written notice of demand, the Tribunal may order delivery subject to such terms as it thinks fit. Failure to comply with such an order is an offence.[74]

5. *Misdealings with subject-matter of the lease*: Not content with allowing the lessor his Common Law action for conversion, s.35(1) makes it a criminal offence for any person to defraud or attempt to defraud the supplier under a consumer lease by the disposal, sale, removal or otherwise of the goods comprised in the lease. This provision is in addition to any other criminal liability incurred by the defendant.[75]

6. *Consumer leases and the nemo dat rule*: One possible criticism of the *English Consumer Credit Act* 1974, is that it makes no attempt to unify or re-define the circumstances in which title can be conferred by one who is not the owner of goods. Section 36(1) of the South Australian Act makes some modest provision to this end in the context of consumer leases,[76] by providing that where a person, in good faith and for valuable consideration, purports to acquire title to goods subject to a consumer lease, without actual notice[77] of the lessor's interest, from the lessee or a person in possession with the lessee's consent and in circumstances in which he appears to be the owner, then the person acquiring the goods shall acquire a good title in defeasance of the lessor's interest. This provision does not apply, however, to acquisitions by persons who carry on a trade or business in which they trade in goods of the kind acquired.[78] The onus of proof in proceedings arising under this section is upon the party alleging that title has been acquired.[79]

7. *Liens*: Sections 37(1) and (2) permit the acquisition of a lien over goods comprised in a consumer lease by a workman who performs work upon them, unless the lease contains a prohibition upon the creation of liens and the workman has knowledge of that prohibition before commencing the work.

8. *Relief against consequences of breach*: Section 38 allows for the supervision, variation and mitigation of consumer leases under which the consumer finds himself temporarily unable to discharge his obligations. Section 38(1) provides as follows:

> Where by reason of any circumstances that were not reasonably foreseeable by a consumer at the time of entering into a consumer credit contract, consumer lease, or a consumer mortgage, he is temporarily unable to discharge his obligations under the contract, lease, or mortgage, the consumer may make an application under this section for relief against the consequences of breach of the contract, lease or mortgage.

Such application may be made prior to re-possession[80] and shall be made in the first instance to the Commissioner for Prices and Consumer

---

[74] Section 34(2). See further Consumer Transactions Regulations 1973, Fourteenth Schedule.
[75] Section 35(2).
[76] And consumer mortgages, with which the present work is not concerned.
[77] Cf. *Barker* v. *Bell* [1971] 2 All E.R. 867.
[78] Section 36(2); *Stevenson* v. *Beverley Bentinck Ltd.* [1976] 2 All E.R. 606.
[79] Section 36(3).
[80] Section 38(2).

Affairs.[81] If the latter officer is satisfied that the application has been made on proper grounds, he must attempt to obtain, by negotiation with the supplier, a consensual variation of the lease, by virtue of which the consumer may be enabled to comply with the lease.[82] Failing such variation, the application will be referred to the Credit Tribunal,[83] who may grant the relief sought subject to such terms and conditions as will, in the Tribunal's opinion, do justice between the parties.[84] Such order is non-appealable.[85] In granting relief, the Tribunal may both extend the time allowed for payment of any instalment under the lease and (where the consumer has committed any breach of the lease) order that he be re-instated in the lease in all other respects as if no breach had occurred.[86]

9. *Other provisions*: Parts VII and VIII of the Act[87] deal with contracts of insurance relating to consumer transactions, and guarantees. They will not be examined in any detail.

Part IX contains a variety of miscellaneous or supplemental provisions designed to further the enforcement of the Act. Of particular note are ss.46 (which grants the Tribunal power to extend the times laid down for service of notices or documents as required by the Act);[88] 47 (which avoids any provision in any agreement which purports to exclude, modify or restrict the operation of the Act, except as provided for in the Act itself); 49 (service of documents or notices) and 48, which provides as follows:

48(1) Subject to subsection (3) of this section, any provision of a written consumer contract, consumer credit contract, or consumer mortgage —
> (a) that is in handwriting that is not clear and legible; or
> (b) that is printed in type the dimensions of which do not comply with the regulations

shall not be enforceable against the consumer by the supplier, credit provider, or mortgagee as the case may be.

(2) Where a consumer has been supplied with a copy of a consumer contract, consumer credit contract or consumer mortgage, the contract or mortgage shall not be regarded as being in conformity with subsection (1) of this section unless that copy is in conformity with that subsection.

(3) The provisions of subsection (1) of this section shall not prevent a credit provider from enforcing a consumer credit contract or consumer mortgage in so far as it provides for the repayment of principal.

(4) Any notice or other document that is required or permitted by this Act to be served on a consumer shall not be regarded as having been duly given if any part thereof —

---

[81] Sections 38(3), (5).
[82] Sections 38(4).
[83] Section 38(5). And see Consumer Transactions Regulations 1973, Seventeenth Schedule.
[84] Section 38(6).
[85] Section 38(9).
[86] Section 38(7).
[87] Sections 39-42, 43-44, respectively, as amended by ss. 11-12 of the C.T.A.A.A. 1973.
[88] And see Consumer Transactions Regulations 1973, Nineteenth Schedule.

Section 50[89] sets out the power of the Governor to make regulations under the Act and s.6[90] makes provision for transactions involving a foreign element. The amendments to the latter section may perhaps symbolise the haste with which the Act as a whole was drafted.

> (a) is in handwriting that is not clear and legible; or
> (b) is printed in type the dimensions of which do not comply with the regulations.

---

[89] As amended by s. 13, C.T.A.A.A., 1973.
[90] As amended by s. 6, C.T.A.A.A., 1973.

CHAPTER 20

EXTENDED OR CONSTRUCTIVE BAILMENTS

I. INTRODUCTION

In 1927, an American judge remarked:

> Bailment is bottomed in contract, express or implied, excepting in case of constructive bailment, in which case it is not necessary that there be either an actual or constructive delivery. A constructive bailment arises where the person having possession of a chattel holds it under such circumstances that the law imposes upon him the obligation of delivering it to another.[1]

Disregarding the suggestion that all bailments by direct delivery are necessarily contractual (which seems to be an inadequate rationalisation of the gratuitous deposit or loan), it is clear there are many situations in which a bailee will enjoy neither a contractual relationship with, nor an immediate delivery from, the person to whom he owes his obligations as bailee. These situations may, for convenience, be grouped together under the heading of constructive bailment, although in fact they are multifarious. A primary example is that of the finder,[2] who, although possessing goods without the knowledge or consent of the owner, is deemed to owe him a duty of reasonable care and a duty not to convert the chattel. Further illustrations are manifold. There may be no physical transfer at all, as where a carrier collects goods from the dockside for delivery to a consignee, or a warehouseman agrees to hold property currently in his possession for a purchaser from the original bailor. Alternatively, the person granting possession may not be the owner but himself a mere bailee, as where the hirer of a car leaves it at a garage for repairs or the borrower of a dinner jacket sends it to be cleaned. Indeed, the chain of possession may extend further than that, for the garage may send a component away to be reconditioned and the cleaner may sub-contract the work out to a fourth party. In all of these cases, and in the multiple variations upon them, it will be necessary to establish the precise rights and duties of the parties and the persons to whom they are owed. At the outset, it should be observed that the powers of remedy and enforcement in this area are not always purely horizontal; the legal translation of this series of relationships may represent a web rather than a chain. Thus, a given party in the sequence of possession may be liable at the behest of more than one of his predecessors, and may share with more than one prior recipient his right of action against successive holders. It is this, and the uncertain

---

[1] *Hope* v. *Costello* (1927) 297 S.W. 199, at 103 per Arnold J.; see also *Berglund* v. *Roosevelt University* (1974) 310 N.E. (2d) 773.

[2] Chapter 22, post.

equation between possession and liability, that renders the law in this area so variable and complex.

Not every bailee who grants control to another will be authorised or entitled to do so; nor will he necessarily make the person to whom he grants control a bailee, for control is dissociable from possession, and the existence of a bailment demands the latter. Each of these elements may or may not affect the inter-related duties of the parties; for everything depends upon which permutation of relationships is in issue at the time. Broadly, it may be said that whereas the lack of authority to create a subsidiary bailment is irrelevant to the ultimate, and affects only the original, bailee, the question whether possession has passed from one bailee to another is material only to the liability of the ultimate bailee. However, these are matters which can only be coherently explained by systematic analysis, and after a clear definition of the terms involved.

Although the relationships we have outlined are often widely different, no comprehensive classification or analysis has hitherto been attempted by the courts. In part, this may be due to a former judicial adherence to the identification of bailment with contract in part to a tendency to take too much for granted. To a large extent, therefore, the writer in this area is free to define his own terms, provided that they do not offend authority and are consistently applied. However, it must be stressed that questions of nomenclature are important only insofar as they indicate, or aid the exposition of, different obligations. Indeed, this is an observation which may be applied to the definition of bailment generally, and not merely to its sub-divisions.

Leaving aside the case of the finder, it is submitted that four main categories of constructive bailment can be discovered.

II. Sub-bailment

A true sub-bailment may be defined as that relationship which arises whenever a bailee of goods, with or without the authority of his bailor[3] transfers possession to a third party for a limited period or a specific purpose, on the understanding (express or implied) that his own position as bailee is to persist throughout the subsidiary disposition. The third party, by taking possession and by consenting to the limits set upon it, assumes the role of a special class of bailee. He will owe to the original bailor all the Common Law duties which would traditionally arise upon a direct bailment of the kind in question. In addition, he will owe these duties to the principal bailee, except insofar as they are modified by the

[3] In at least two authorities, *Chapman* v. *Robinson and Ferguson* (1969) 71 W.W.R. 515 and *Roufos* v. *Brewster and Brewster* [1971] 2 S.A.S.R. 218, 234, there are clear suggestions that a transaction should be characterised as one of sub-bailment only when the secondary disposition is authorised by the principal bailor. There seems to be little value in limiting the concept of sub-bailment in this way, because the cardinal object of identifying such a bailment is to assess the responsibilities of the ultimate bailee, and so far as he is concerned these are substantially similar whether or not the sub-bailment is authorised. Of course, the lack of authority to sub-bail may significantly affect the intermediate party and may, if known to the ultimate bailee, make his reception of the goods a conversion: ante, p. 146.

terms of any contract between them. To this extent, both bailor and principal bailee may be said to enjoy concurrently the rights of a bailor against the sub-bailee; the former although he possesses no direct contract with the sub-bailee, and the latter notwithstanding that he does not own the goods and cannot be made liable for their loss to the bailor. Thus the principal bailee's rights are comparable to those of an ordinary bailee where the goods are damaged by a third party who does not acquire possession; except that in the latter case the bailee would enjoy no advantage as to burden of proof and the tortfeasor would not be subjected to further potential duties peculiar to bailment. Both situations, incidentally, represent exceptions to that general rule that, in order to sue for negligent damage to goods, a plaintiff must prove himself their owner[4] or must be in possession at the time of injury.[5]

III. BAILMENT BY ATTORNMENT

This species of bailment possesses both a wider and narrower meaning. In its broader sense, it signifies the direct substitution of one bailee for another and the complete withdrawal of an antecedent bailee from his relationship with the bailor.[6] If, for instance, a bailor instructs his original bailee to deliver the goods to a third person, on the understanding that the principal bailee's responsibility shall determine from the moment he relinquishes possession, the third person will (upon taking delivery) occupy directly the relationship of bailee with the owner and the preceding bailee will simultaneously retire from the chain altogether. In its narrower sense, bailment by attornment serves to denote the obligation which arises whenever a seller of goods continues in possession on behalf of the new owner, or a bailee who holds for their owner is informed by him that they have been sold and agrees henceforth to hold them for the purchaser.[7] This engenders important legal consequences other than the duty of care and may often raise very technical issues as to the time of passing of property.[8]

In both cases, the bailee will normally advise his bailor that he now holds possession on the latter's behalf. This communication, and the fact

---

[4] *Margarine Union* v. *S. S. Cambay Prince* [1969] 1 Q.B. 219; *The Albazero* [1976] 3 All E.R. 129.

[5] Chapter 4, ante.

[6] Goodeve, *Personal Property* (9th edn) p. 48: "The bailee may do that which amounts to returning the goods to the bailor, without making actual redelivery to the bailor, by redelivering the goods, with the consent of the bailor, to a third person who consents to hold them as the bailee of the original bailor. This is called 'bailment by attornment'." The case cited in this connection, *Godts* v. *Rose* (1855) 17 C.B. 229, in fact concerned a bailee who continued in possession throughout an alleged change of ownership.

[7] Paton, *Bailment in the Common Law*, p. 15; Pollock & Wright, *Possession in the Common Law*, p. 134; *Rogers, Son & Co. Ltd.* v. *Lambert & Co. Ltd.* [1891] 1 Q.B. 318; *Dublin City Distillery Ltd.* v. *Doherty* [1914] A.C. 823, at 847; Goodeve, op. cit., p. 44: "A bailment may arise from a mere change in the character of the possession, without any change in the possession itself. Thus, A, being in possession of the goods, either as owner or as bailee for B, may (in the latter case with B's consent) agree with C to hold them as his bailee. This is called 'bailment by attornment'."

[8] Discussed in Chapter 21, post.

that the bailor will be expected to pay the bailee before retrieving the goods, will generally make their relationship a contractual one; the bailee continues to safeguard the property in consideration for the bailor's express or implied promise to reimburse him when it is restored. But it is clear that neither contract or direct communication inter partes is essential to cast the possessor in the position of bailee. In *Makower, McBeath & Co. Pty. Ltd.* v. *Dalgety & Co. Ltd.,*[9] McArthur J. held that licensed wharfingers who took delivery of goods from alongside a ship became bailees, in the literal sense of the word, as soon as they acknowledged to the consignee that they held the goods for him. However, the learned judge went on to remark that the same duty of care, whether it could be described as the duty of a bailee or not, was owed to the consignee from the moment the wharfingers took possession. The bailee's position is not, therefore, improved by direct communication, except insofar as he may prospectively impose modifications upon his general liability for default.[10] The important question is not the literal meaning of bailment but the circle of relationship in which its chacteristic duties will apply. For most practical purposes, any person who comes knowingly into the possession of another's goods is, prima facie, a bailee.

Bailments by attornment are a fairly orthodox and well-established variety of bailment, differing from more common-place bailments only in that no positive physical transfer occurs between bailor and bailee. Practically the only area in which they give rise to special difficulty is that which concerns the passing of property.[11] For most other purposes, (at least after attornment has occurred) the bailee by attornment stands in the position of an ordinary bailee for reward. His liability for loss or damage to the goods will not, therefore, be separately considered since it corresponds substantially with that of any other custodian.

IV. THE SPRINGING OR SUBSTITUTIONAL BAILMENT

Frequently, a secondary bailee will take possession of goods with the consent of the principal bailor but without entering into a contract with him, and without any attornment. If the intermediate bailee remains responsible for the goods while they are in the secondary bailee's possession, the transaction is one of sub-bailment.[12] Occasionally, however, the terms of the arrangement will exonerate the middle-man once he has handed over the goods. An obvious example is that of someone who agrees to arrange for the transportation of a friend's goods. Provided he takes reasonable care of them and delivers them to a reputable carrier, his liability for the goods will normally cease as soon as they leave his possession.

---

[9] [1921] V.L.R. 365.
[10] It seems that where a warehouseman attorns to a purchaser, the purchaser becomes an assignee of the original contract of bailment and must abide by the conditions thereof: *H.M.F. Humphrey Ltd.* v. *Baxter, Hoare & Co. Ltd.* (1933) 149 L.T. 603; *Britain & Overseas Trading (Bristles) Ltd.* v. *Brooks Wharf & Bull Wharf Ltd.* [1967] 2 Lloyd's Rep. 51, at 60.
[11] Chapter 21.
[12] Ante, p. 786.

Generally, the facts will render it easy to differentiate between a 'springing' bailment of this kind and a genuine sub-bailment. The primary question is: did the bailor and the principal bailee intend that the latter's duties should continue to be owed throught the subsequent bailment? One significant element in establishing this intention will be the complexion of the ultimate bailment and the proposed manner of its determination. If, for instance, the parties have agreed that when the second bailment ends the goods shall be restored to the owner via the first bailee, who shall resume possession for that purpose, it may often be legitimate to infer that their relationship is one of sub-bailment and that the first bailee remains liable throughout. It, on the other hand, redelivery is to be effected through some other medium, it may be easier to infer that the first bailee's responsibilities are circumscribed by the period of his own possession. A shopkeeper who sends away goods to be repaired will normally be a bailee under a sub-bailment, whereas a carrier who transports goods to a third person for purposes of, say, hire, deposit or pledge, will cease to be liable upon delivery. However, this criterion will not suffice for all cases. It may be agreed that a carrier shall transport goods to a repairer and then retransport them back to the owner when repaired. In such a case it would be unfair to hold him responsible for the goods while they are in the possession of the repairer. Alternatively, there may be no redelivery at all. The carrier may be authorised to transfer the goods to another carrier for delivery to a purchaser. In this case the terms of the original bailment will often dictate that the first bailee remains responsible for the goods until they have safely arrived at their destination.

Equally material, therefore, will be the nature of the services undertaken by each succeeding bailee, their similarity, the destination and division of the overall reward, and the general function the principal bailee has assumed. If, on a proper analysis, he has accepted overall responsibility for the performance of a task, albeit with a power to delegate it wholly or in part to another, the mere fact of delegation will not exonerate him if, as a result, the goods are wrongfully lost or damaged.[13] Indeed, this may be so even where he delegates the task in its entirety and never takes possession from first to last; although in such circumstances the delegate would not, strictly speaking, be a bailee under a sub-bailment but what we should call a quasi-bailee. If, on the other hand, the original bailee was agreed only to perform and to be responsible for one link in a chain of successive services, albeit a link which may recur before the full circle of obligations is complete, he will be liable only for these services he has undertaken personally and (excluding unauthorised dispositions) will not be answerable for anything happening to the goods while they are out of his possession.

Roufos v. *Brewster and Brewster*[14] illustrates the distinction. The appellant damaged the respondents' truck and agreed to transport it to Adelaide for repairs. Subsequently he agreed to arrange for its return to the respondents and was given their permission to load some of his own goods on to it for the return journey. On his instructions, the truck was

---

[13] Post, p. 829.
[14] [1971] 2 S.A.S.R. 218.

collected from the repairers and located and loaded at his depot. On the return journey, the truck was driven by one Joanni, who was not, at that time, his servant. The truck overturned and was damaged and the respondents sought to recover their loss from the appellant. The South Australian Full Supreme Court held that the appellant was a bailee of the truck only during the original journey to Adelaide and until delivery to the repairers; and subsequently, when the truck was being loaded at his premises. From the moment it set out on the return journey it was either in the possession of the respondents through their servant pro hac vice, or was in the possession of the driver himself as a bailee; the court strongly preferring the first of these analyses but agreeing that the choice was immaterial. Thus, the appellant was not a bailee under a sub-bailment but a mere 'springing' bailee whose responsibility for the goods coincided only with his actual possession of them. The action was therefore dismissed and his appeal allowed.[15]

Two further points should be mentioned. The distinction between sub-bailments and springing bailments has little practical effect upon the position of a succeeding or ultimate bailee. Generally, he remains liable to the owner of the goods for any failure to take reasonable care of the goods, or any conversion, on the part of himself or his servants. On the other hand, it would appear that if the principal bailee's responsibility ceases upon delivery over, so should his right to proceed "concurrently" against the secondary bailee. Authority on this point is scarce, but this is one area at least where it seems reasonable to make the (ex-) bailee's rights of action conditional upon his liability to the bailor.[16] In *B.R.S.* v. *Arthur V. Crutchley Ltd.,*[17] the plaintiffs were carriers who had engaged to transport whisky for a consignor; the defendants were warehousemen with whom they had deposited the goods. The whisky was stolen and the plaintiffs, having compensated the owners, now sought to recover this amount from the secondary bailees. It appears from the report at first instance that the goods were eventually to be loaded on board two ships lying at Merseyside Docks and that "it was convenient to the plaintiffs for the final stage of transport to be handled by other carriers". In other words, this was a "block" contract of carriage between the owners and the plaintiffs whereunder the latter were entitled , at their own risk, to delegate part of their overall performance. In such a case, the secondary bailment clearly took the form of a sub-bailment and the plaintiff's concurrent action

---

[15] For a similar case, see *E.A. Marr (Contracting) Pty. Ltd.* v. *Broken Hill Pty. Ltd.* [1970] 3 N.S.W.R. 206, which concerned a sub-contract of hire. This case is discussed post, at pp. 805, 829. Cf. *Gallaher Ltd.* v. *British Road Services Ltd.* [1974] 2 Lloyd's Rep. 440, where the first defendant, having contracted to carry the plaintiff's goods from Belfast to Outer London, engaged the second defendant to perform the Belfast-Preston part of the journey. The crossing was made and the change-over was effected at Preston but the goods were subsequently stolen from the first defendants in St. John's Wood. It was held that sub-contractors, having performed their own part of the operation successfully, ceased to be liable for the safety of the goods once they delivered them over to their principal contractors. See further: *Valley Auto Wrecking & Demolition Ltd.* v. *Colonial Motors Ltd.* [1977] 1 W.W.R. 759; *E.M.I. (New Zealand) Ltd.* v. *W. N. Holyman & Sons Pty. Ltd.* [1976] 2 N.Z.L.R. 567.

[16] Cf. *The Winkfield* [1902] P. 42; Chapter 4, ante.

[17] [1968] 1 All E.R. 811.

against the sub-bailee was properly allowed. It is suggested, however, that if by the terms of the principal bailment the plaintiff's Common Law responsibility had ceased from the time of delivery over, and if there had been no provision in the contract obliging them to compensate the owner, the only proper plaintiff would have been that owner himself: even if the principal bailee had, unnecessarily, taken it upon himself to reimburse the bailor. The position might differ, of course, if the secondary bailment had been unauthorised or if the principal bailor had been negligent in his selection of the secondary bailee, for in these circumstances his liability would have continued beyond the period of his possession.

V. QUASI-BAILMENT

Quasi-bailment is a loose and indefinite term, which has occasionally been used as a repository for all kinds of bailment arising otherwise than upon a direct delivery. For present purposes it may be defined as any bailment which fulfils this description but does not fall within the preceding categories. Thus, it will include (a) bailments which arise by theft, fraud or finding; and (b) all those cases in which a person, other than by direct delivery from an antecedent bailee, takes possession of goods upon the instructions or at the request of an intermediary. The commonest example of a commercial quasi-bailment occurs when a forwarding-agent (without acquiring possession of the goods) arranges for delivery to be taken by a third-party, for the purposes of carriage to a consignee.[18] The quasi-bailee owes the owner the traditional duties associated with a bailment of the kind he has undertaken, viz. to take care of the goods, and to abstain from converting them, whether personally or through the instrumentality of any servant or deputed performer.

As with the sub-bailee, the quasi-bailee enjoys no direct contract with the bailor. But whereas in the case of a sub-bailment or a springing bailment there is an intervening possessor, in the quasi-bailment there is none; the quasi-bailee will not, in other words, receive possession direct from the intermediary himself. Although it would appear that the quasi-bailee owes the same duties to the owner as does his counterpart under a sub-bailment stricto sensu, the distinction remains important for two reasons. First, the existence of a quasi-bailment may affect the liability of the intermediary, who will not have acquired possession but who may nevertheless be answerable for the defaults of his sub-contractor. Whether this result follows will depend upon a multiplicity of factors, including the contract the intermediary has made with the owner. However, it may not be irrelevent that the intermediary has never been, personally, a bailee of the property in question. With this in mind, it may aid the clarity of our exposition if we provisionally designate him the "quasi-bailor".

Secondly, if there be no intervening possessor with a 'projecting' liability it would seem to follow that there can be no concurrent right of recovery against the quasi-bailee, as there would be under an ordinary sub-bailment. The quasi-bailor will almost invariably pursue contractual remedies

---

[18] As to the position of the forwarding-agent himself, see p. 831 et. seq., post.

against him in the event of his default but it would seem that the only person to whom the quasi-bailee is liable *as a bailee* is the owner. This curious consequence is based more upon logic than authority; indeed, in at least one case it would appear to have been disregarded completely.[19]

Whatever classification is adopted, the categories cannot be water-tight; the residual nature of quasi-bailment inevitably makes its boundaries rather elusive and amorphous. It may be argued that there is little difference between a quasi-bailment and a springing bailment, or a bailment by attornment, where the ultimate bailee takes possession of goods on terms (arranged between the prior bailee and the owner) that the former's obligation are to cease upon delivery. The distinction lies in the degree of independence with which the ultimate bailee is acting. On a pure springing bailment, there is no ulterior party organising and taking overall responsibility for the employment of subsequent possessors; even the seller who instructs his present bailee to hold for the buyer does so on the understanding that his own duties in relation to the uncollected goods are thereupon discharged. Under a quasi-bailment, such a party will exist. It will be at his behest (albeit not directly from him) that the quasi-bailee takes possession and it is in establishing his responsibility for the defaults of his employees that the distinction possesses its practical value. Moreover, the bailment by attornment will generally be contractual, whereas under a quasi-bailment there will be no direct privity between the owner and the person in possession. The importance of these distinctions will be understood later. For the present, it should be remarked that the courts have sometimes confused the issue of the quasi-bailor's responsibilities by attributing him, through his sub-contractor, with possession of the goods.[20] This is questionable, but it does at least enable them to impose the heavy duties of a bailee upon one who, on a more technical analysis, would appear to lack the salient quality of every bailee—viz., possession.

The following are examples, from decided cases, of the ordinary form quasi-bailment. In each case the bailee enjoyed no contractual relations with the owner of the goods and assumed possession of them at the direction of an intermediary. In each case, that intermediary did not take personal possession of the goods prior to the quasi-bailee, but remained contractually responsible for the performance of the quasi-bailee's duties.

In *Thomas National Transport (Melbourne) Pty. Ltd.* v. *May & Baker (Australasia) Pty. Ltd.*[21] T.N.T., having arranged for the collection and delivery of May & Baker's goods, delegated the collection part of the contract to Pay, the quasi-bailee. T.N.T. were held liable when the goods were destroyed in Pay's possession although Pay himself was not at fault. T.N.T. had contracted that the goods would be stored on their own

---

[19] *Edwards* v. *Newland & Co. Ltd.* [1950] 2 K.B. 534; post, p. 842 et seq.
[20] Authorities include *Hobbs* v. *Petersham Transport Co. Pty. Ltd.* (1971) 45 A.L.J.R. 356, at 361 per Menzies J. (cf. Barwick C.J. at 359 and Windeyer J. at 362-363, both of whom deny this conclusion); *Thomas National Transport (Melbourne) Pty. Ltd.* v. *May & Baker (Australasia) Pty. Ltd.* (1966) 115 C.L.R. 353, at 369 per Windeyer J.; cf. *Eastman Chemical A. G.* v. *N.M.T. Trading Ltd.* [1972] 2 Lloyd's Rep. 25; *Edwards* v. *Newland & Co. Ltd.* [1950] 2 K.B. 534; *Arcweld Constructions Pty. Ltd.* v. *Smith* (1968) Unrep. Sept. 17th (Victoria Supreme Court).
[21] Ante.

premises overnight and not (as happened) upon those of Pay. Accordingly they were responsible for any loss befalling the goods and were not protected by the exclusion clauses in their contract of carriage.[22] In *Gallaher Ltd.* v. *B.R.S. Ltd.*[23] B.R.S. agreed to carry a consignment of cigarettes from Ireland to London. They engaged Containerway (the quasi-bailee) to transport the cigarettes as far as Preston, and took possession of them there. After delivery to B.R.S. the lorry was hijacked. B.R.S. were held liable for the loss but Containerway were exonerated, their responsibility being coterminous with their possession.

VI. Duties of the Constructive Bailee

Having regard to the frequency with which sub-bailments arise, and the even greater frequency with which contracts between bailors and principal bailees contain exclusion clauses, it is remarkable that it was not until 1965 that the relationship between the owner and the sub-bailee was authoritatively discussed by the courts. The decision in question is probably the most important case on bailment this century, although other facets of the case have attracted a greater attention (and been a more prominent case of its application) than the point with which we are presently concerned.

In *Morris* v. *C. W. Martin & Sons Ltd.*[24] the plaintiff sent her mink stole to a furrier named Beder for cleaning. Beder explained that he did not provide this service and, with the plaintiff's consent, forwarded the stole to the defendants. Whilst in their possession it was stolen by the servant entrusted with the cleaning operation, in circumstances which did not establish negligence on their part. The Court of Appeal's primary concern was whether any bailee (sub or otherwise) could be made liable for an unauthorised theft or conversion by his servant when this expropriation could not be traced to any negligent default on the part of the bailee himself. The Court unanimously agreed (overruling *Cheshire* v. *Bailey*)[25] that in the circumstances such liability should accrue: Lord Denning M.R., by virtue of the rule that a bailee could not escape liability by delegating his task, or entrusting the goods, to another; Diplock and Salmon L.JJ., on the more traditional ground that since the servant had, at the time of the theft, been performing one of that class of acts for which he was

---

[22] See further post, p. 925. Cases which, upon their material facts, are almost identical include *Hobbs* v. *Petersham Transport Co. Pty. Ltd.* (1971) 45 A.L.J.R. 356; *Eastman Chemical A.G.* v. *N.M.T. Trading Ltd.* [1972] 2 Lloyd's Rep. 25; *Lee Cooper Ltd.* v. *C.H. Jeakins & Sons Ltd.* [1964] 1 Lloyd's Rep. 300; *W.L.R. Traders (London) Ltd.* v. *British & Northern Shipping Agency Ltd.* [1955] 1 Lloyd's Rep. 554. Most of these decisions involved the tripartite relationship of consignor, forwarding agent and carrier, but the quasi-bailment is not limited to such situations because the quasi-bailor will often intend to perform a subsequent part of the carriage personally.

[23] [1974] 2 Lloyd's Rep. 440.

[24] [1966] 1 Q.B. 716. Cf. the New York decision in *Halbren* v. *Goldberg* (1919) 175 N.Y. Supp. 474, which on very similar facts, substantially anticipated the right of action discussed in the text.

[25] [1905] 1 K.B. 237.

employed, his employers should, on the principle laid down in *Lloyd* v. *Grace, Smith & Co.,*[26] be vicariously answerable for his misconduct.

Having so decided, the Court went on to apply this liability to the sub-bailee, holding it immaterial that he possessed no contract with the owner of the garment and had not received it directly from him. In other words, they permitted the owner to leap-frog over the intermediate bailee and proceed directly against the sub-contractor. This was the first case in which the possibility of converting the chain of sub-bailment into a triangle, with the bailor-sub-bailee relationship as its base, had been explicitly acknowledged and approved. Each member of the Court of Appeal accepted it as logical result of the fact that a bailment need not be created by contract.

A. The Common Law background

To some extent, this was a radical decision. Although sub-bailment was an accepted phenomenon long before *Morris* v. *C. W. Martin & Sons,* earlier analysis had tended to concentrate upon the position of the first bailee and his relationship with the bailor: in particular, whether an unauthorised sub-bailment constituted conversion on the part of the bailee and whether the latter remained answerable for the goods when they were in the hands of the sub-bailee.[27] An exception was the Treatise on Possession by Pollock and Wright in 1888, wherein it was observed:

> If the bailee of a thing sub-bails it by authority, there may be a difference according as it is intended that the bailee's bailment is to determine and the third person is to hold as the immediate bailee of the owner, in which case the third person really becomes a first bailee directly from the owner and the case passes back into a simple case of bailment, or that the first bailee is to retain (so to speak) a reversionary interest and there is no direct privity of contract between the third person and the owner, in which case it would seem that both the owner and the first bailee have concurrently the rights of a bailor against the third person according to the nature of the sub-bailment.[28]

Part of this passage was cited with approval by Lord Denning M.R. in the Court of Appeal.[29] Unfortunately, there was very little judicial authority in point and the Court were driven to rely upon two rather ambiguous decisions to support their conclusion. The cases invoked were *Meux* v. *G.E. Ry. Co.*[30] and *Kahler* v. *Midland Bank, Ltd.*[31] As Professor Carnegie has pointed out,[32] neither is authority for the proposition stated.

Meux's case was a simple one. The plaintiff's servant took a ticket at the defendants' railway station. His personal luggage consisted of a portmanteau which contained, inter alia, a livery owned and supplied by the plaintiff. A porter dropped the portmanteau on the line and both it

26 [1911] 2 K.B. 489.
27 E.g. *Genn* v. *Winkel* (1912) 107 L.T. 434.
28 Pollock & Wright, *Possession in the Common Law,* p. 169.
29 [1966] 1 Q.B. 716, at 729.
30 [1895] 2 Q.B. 387.
31 [1950] A.C. 24.
32 *Bailment and Contract in English Law Today* (1966) 3 *Adelaide Law Review* 7, at 12.

and its contents were destroyed by a train. The plaintiff was held entitled to recover from the defendants despite the absence of any contract between her and the railway company. The goods were lawfully on the latter's premises and "were injured by an act of misfeasance"; or, in the words of A. L. Smith L.J. "she has incurred loss by reason of her property having been destroyed by the active negligence of the servants of the company while it was lawfully on the premises of the company; she has therefore a right of action in tort, irrespective of contract.[33]

It has been suggested that this case "must, if anything, be sub silentio authority for the view that a sub-bailee, although liable to the owner for the loss of the owner's goods, is not liable as a bailee, but by virtue of a duty of care arising otherwise.[34] The reason given is that the case was decided without reference to the peculiar principles of bailment. Even if this were so, the omission might have been made per incuriam, as the result of a failure on counsel's part to adduce those principles, in which event it could hardly be said that the Court's silence on this point constituted a rejection of it. In fact, there is considerable evidence that the rules of bailment were present in at least one judge's mind at the time of judgment. Counsel for the plaintiff is recorded as having argued[35] that whether or not the decision in *Claridge* v. *South Staffordshire Tramway Co.*[36] was correctly decided, the result must be that an owner whose goods are damaged during a bailment is entitled to sue the wrongdoer; and A. L. Smith L.J., delivering judgment, remarked with some prescience that *Claridge's* case "may possibly require at some future time further consideration".[37] Now *Claridge's* case was undoubtedly a case of bailment, as was *G.W. Ry. Co.* v. *Bunch*,[38] cited by counsel for the railway;[39] but they were not cases of *sub*-bailment. Rather, they concerned the liability of a non-possessing third party for torts committed to property while in the hands of a bailee; or, as in *Bunch's* case, the liability of the bailee for such torts when the perpetrator is his servant. Nor, for that matter, was *Meux's* case itself a case of sub-bailment; first, because in order to have a sub-bailment one must have an original bailee, and a servant receiving goods from his master would only rarely (and perhaps even more rarely in 1895) acquire the necessary element of possession;[40] secondly, because it is by no means clear that the porter himself had sufficient control of the portmanteau to render his employer a bailee.[41] If either of these objections be well-founded, *Meux's* case emerges as one in which it would have been positively wrong to found the defendants' liability on the principles (if any then existed) relating to sub-bailment. Whilst, therefore, it is beyond dispute that the decision was an inadequate foundation for the rule

---

[33] [1895] 2 Q.B. 387. Cf. *Walton Stores Ltd.* v. *Sydney City Council* [1968] 2 N.S.W.R. 109.
[34] Carnegie, op. cit., p. 13.
[35] [1895] 2 Q.B. 387, at 388.
[36] [1892] 1 Q.B. 422; ante, p. 179.
[37] [1895] 2 Q.B. 387, at 394. *Claridge's* case was in fact overruled in *The Winkfield* [1902] P. 42; ante, p. 179.
[38] (1888) 13 A.C. 31.
[39] [1895] 2 Q.B. 387.
[40] See generally Chapter 7, ante; cf. *Becher* v. *G.E. Ry. Co.* (1870) L.R. 5 Q.B. 241.
[41] Cf. *Richards* v. *London, Brighton & South Coast Ry. Co.* (1849) 7 C.B. 839.

adduced in *Morris* v. *C. W. Martin & Sons Ltd.*,[42] it can hardly be advanced as an authority contrary to that rule. It seems to have little more than a simple case of negligent misfeasance in a non-contractual context.[43]

In *Morris* v. *C. W. Martin & Sons Ltd.*,[44] both Diplock and Salmond L.JJ. appear to refer to *Meux's* case as an authority on sub-bailment. It may be thought that since the rule in *Claridge* v. *South Staffordshire Tramway Co.*[45] has, in accordance with A. L. Smith L.J.'s prognosis, been reconsidered and reversed,[46] and since it is now clear that the bailee does not generally evade his duty of care by delegating the task to another (be he a non-bailee[47] or a sub-bailee[48]), any rule providing for direct recovery by the bailor against the sub-bailee would be redundant; the bailor could sue the bailee and the bailee could recover in turn from the sub-bailee. Lord Denning M.R. remarked obiter[49] that on the authority of *The Winkfield* Beder could clearly have sued the defendants for the value of the stole "unless the cleaners were protected by some exempting conditions."[50] This latter qualification may indeed have something to do with the Court of Appeal's readiness to permit the bailor a direct right of recovery, since it allowed him to surmount the conditions contained in the contract between Beder and the defendants, and which would have prevented the former from recovering.[51] A more general advantage of the rule in *Morris* v. *C. W. Martin & Sons Ltd.* is that it avoids circuity of litigation.

Kahler v. *Midland Bank Ltd.*[52] is a much more complicated decision, the facts of which have already been presented elsewhere.[53] It is impossible to see how the Court of Appeal could have considered it authority for clothing a sub-bailee with direct responsibility to the owner of a kind normally arising on a delivery inter partes. The variance between this decision and the interpretation put upon it by the Court of Appeal is cogently summarised by Professor Carnegie:

> Had the majority, who dismissed the plaintiff's appeal, considered the defendants to be the plaintiff's bailees, it would surely have been necessary for them to consider whether the proper law of the extended bailment between the parties to the action might not have been different from the proper law of the head bailment, which was

[42] [1966] 1 Q.B. 716.
[43] Although several writers have chosen to regard *Meux's* case as a case of bailment (e.g. Fifoot, *History and Sources of the Common Law*, p. 25n.), in *Lee & Sons Pty. Ltd.* v. *Abood* (1968) 89 W.N. (Pt.1) (N.S.W.) 430, at 432, Goran D.C.J. treated it as a non-bailment case. The same judge also treated *Lee Cooper Ltd.* v. *C.H. Jeakins & Sons Ltd.* [1967] 2 Q.B. 1 (post) as a case of sub-bailment; sed quaere.
[44] [1966] 1 Q.B. 716, at 732, 737.
[45] [1892] 1 Q.B. 422.
[46] *The Winkfield* [1902] P. 42.
[47] *B.R.S. Ltd.* v. *Arthur V. Crutchley Ltd.* [1968] 1 All E.R. 811.
[48] *Philip Morris (Australia) Ltd.* v. *The Transport Commission* [1975] Tas. S.R. 128, at 131; and, for further authority, p. 829, post.
[49] [1966] 1 Q.B. 716, at 728.
[50] This does not seem quite exact, since Beder was out of possession at the material time. Rather, he could have recovered under the sub-bailment, relying upon defendant's inability to plead jus tertii: ante, p. 186.
[51] See, on this point, post, p. 924.
[52] [1950] A.C. 24.
[53] Ante, p. 57.

held to be decisive. But the fundamental inconsistency of *Kahler* v. *Midland Bank Ltd.* with the *Morris'* case concept of extended bailment appears most clearly from the dissenting judgments. If there had been such a bailment, Lord Macdermott and Lord Reid, who dissented in the plaintiff's favour would have been only too anxious to discover its existence. However, they both expressly denied the existence of such a bailment; and Lord Reid regarded his conclusion on this point as being in agreement with that of the majority.[54]

Other authority seems equally inconclusive. In *Edwards* v. *Newland,*[55] where a storage contractor wrongfully delegated performance to a third party and the goods were subsequently stolen, Somervell L.J. cited with apparent approval the opinion of Humphreys J. at first instance that the plaintiff could not have brought an action against the third party because he had no contract with him.[56] Denning L.J. made no comment on this observation, which was not material to the decision. In fact, this would appear not to have been a true case of sub-bailment because, at least according to Tucker L.J.,[57] the defendants never took possession of the goods. It is interesting to note, however, that although the defendant had at no stage acquired possession or ownership of the goods, the Court of Appeal nevertheless considered that the third party owed the defendant the duty of displacing the bailee' characteristic onus of proof.

Similarly, in *Lee Cooper Ltd.* v. *C. H. Jeakins & Sons Ltd.*[58] a delegation of the contract of carriage appears to have occurred without the head contractors' gaining possession, although there was no suggestion that, in the circumstances, this delegation was wrongful. The consignors sued the sub-contractors for the negligence of their servant in leaving their vehicle unattended. After remarking that there was no contract between the parties and that the defendants were bailees for reward of the plaintiffs' goods (albeit that their contractual duty was owed to their employers) the learned judge found for the plaintiffs, basing his decision upon the simple principle of negligence as formulated in *Donoghue* v. *Stevenson:*

> Have the plaintiffs satisfied me that they are able to bring themselves within Lord Atkin's famous dictum in *Donoghue's* case? I think they have . . . Whilst it may be that there is no previous decision exactly fitting the facts of this case, that it no answer, and in Lord Macmillan's words, "the categories of negligence are never closed".[59]

This decision (which was cited to the Court in *Morris* v. *C. W. Martin & Sons*[60] but not referred to in the judgments) has a rather ambiguous flavour. On the one hand it may be seen as a tentative approach to the position later adopted by the Court of Appeal, but inhibited by a reluctance

---

[54] (1966) 3 *Adelaide Review* 7, at 13.
[55] [1950] 1 All E.R. 1072.
[56] Ibid., at 1074-1075.
[57] Ibid., at 1080.
[58] [1967] 2 Q.B. 1; judgment delivered 24 April 1964. The case is more fully reported in [1964] 1 Lloyd's Rep. 300.
[59] [1967] 2 Q.B. 1, at 8. But cf *W.L.R. Traders* v. *B. & N. Shipping Agency Ltd.* [1955] 1 Lloyd's Rep. 554, at 561, where in broadly similar circumstances Pilcher, J. held that the carriers (who had no contractual relationship with the plaintiff consignor) bore the onus of proving that they had taken reasonable care.
[60] [1966] 1 Q.B. 716, at 721.

to impose the full rigours of a bailee's duties upon a party who already owes a contractual obligation of similar weight elsewhere. Certainly the decision would have lost much of its self-confessed uniqueness if Marshall J. had been prepared to cast plaintiff and defendant unequivocally in the roles of bailor and bailee, for it has been established for centuries that even a gratuitous bailee may be liable for loss by theft resulting from his own negligence.[61] Indeed, is is unfortunate that the decision of McArthur J. in *Makower, McBeath & Co. Pty. Ltd.* v. *Dalgety & Co. Ltd.*[62] was not urged upon the Court in support of this conclusion. Others may see the *Jeakins* case as one which merely made "unnecessarily heavy weather" of the issues involved.[63] Certainly, it is difficult to construe it as positive authority against the direct and total duplication of a bailor-bailee relationship against a sub- or secondary bailee, as adopted in *Morris* v. *C. W. Martin & Sons Ltd.*[64] At worst it is distinguishable from, and at best compatible with, the later decision; a decision which may now be taken to have enveloped it completely.

Certain Australasian decisions present a less conciliatory picture. In *Gwyatt* v. *Hayes*[65] a tailor entrusted the plaintiff's goods to the defendant carrier for delivery to the plaintiff. The goods were lost and the plaintiff was held unable to recover from the carrier because she had no contract with him. In *Helson* v. *McKenzies (Cuba St.) Ltd.*[66] the plaintiff left her bag on a counter in the defendants store and another woman handed it to one of their assistants. A third woman claimed the bag and the defendants, without conducting a proper check upon her ownership, delivered it to her. The plaintiff succeeded in conversion against the defendants[67] but failed on her allegation of a bailment. Finlay J. was clearly of the opinion that the only bailment was one between the finder and the defendants; the plaintiff had not delivered the bag to them and the finder could not be considered as her agent for doing so.[68] A similar view was taken by Gresson J.,[69] both judges apparently considering that no bailment can arise without a direct delivery and a resulting contract between the parties.[70]

It has been suggested[71] that the decision of the House of Lords in *Elder, Dempster & Co. Ltd.* v. *Paterson Zochonis & Co. Ltd.*[72] affords some

[61] *Coggs* v. *Bernard* (1703) 2 Ld. Raym. 909; 92 E.R. 107.
[62] [1921] V.L.R. 365; ante, pp. 13, 788. Cf. the criticisms advanced in *Johnson Matthey & Co. Ltd.* v. *Constantine Terminals Ltd.* [1976] 2 Lloyd's Rep. 215, at 221-222.
[63] Carnegie, (1966) 3 *Adelaide Law Review* 7, at 15. Cf. Weir [1965] C.L.J. 186, who castigates the decision. Its correctness has more recently been acknowledged, however, by Lord Denning M.R. in *Gillespie Bros. Ltd.* v. *Roy Bowles Transport Ltd.* [1973] Q.B. 400, at 412.
[64] [1966] 1 Q.B. 716.
[65] (1871) 2 A.J.R. 107.
[66] [1950] N.Z.L.R. 878. (N.Z.C.A.).
[67] Although her damages were reduced by three-fourths on the grounds of contributory negligence: ante, p. 135.
[68] [1950] N.Z.L.R. 878, at 905-905. Cf. *Chapman* v. *Robinson and Ferguson* (1969) 71 W.W.R. 515.
[69] [1950] N.Z.L.R. 878, at 914.
[70] Cf. *Beauchamp* v. *Powley* (1831) 1 M. & Rob. 38 (ante, p. 332); *Lethbridge* v. *Phillips* (1819) 2 Stark. 544 (ante, p. 384) both of which arguably provide recognition of the principal bailor's right to sue a sub-bailee.
[71] Carnegie, op. cit., at 13-14.
[72] [1924] A.C. 522.

authority for the principle expressed in *Morris* v. *C. W. Martin & Sons Ltd.* Certainly this was a case in which the owner of goods was allowed to proceed directly against a wrongdoer, despite the apparent absence of any privity of contract. But of course there was no novelty in this. As early as 1778, Lord Mansfield is recorded as having held that any person to whom a contractor delegates a task or duty will be directly liable to the injured party if he performs that task negligently:

> As to the action on the case lying against the party really offending, there can be no doubt of it; for whoever does an act by which another person receives an injury, is liable in action for the injury, sustained. If the man who receives a penny to carry the letters to the Post-office, loses any of them, he is answerable; so is the sorter in the business of his department. So is the Post-master for any fault of his own . . .[73]

Since then, it has frequently been recognised that the victim of a tort committed by an employee of the contracting party may proceed directly against that employee in tort although precluded from suing his master on the contract. This has been allowed in the field of personal injuries[74] as well as damage to goods; and against any such employee, whether a servant, agent or independent contractor.

However, to make an employee liable for his own defaults in damaging customers' chattels is not synonymous with making him a bailee; there is more to bailment than custody and more to its obligations than a responsibility to take care. *Elder, Dempster* is in fact a most unreliable authority for the existence of a doctrine of extended bailment. Only Lord Sumner specifically mentioned the question of bailment, and he did so merely as an alternative (albeit "preferable") basis for his decision that the shipowners were protected by the terms of the bill of lading between shippers and charterers.[75] Viscount Cave, on the other hand, cited with approval a statement by Scrutton L.J. in the Court of Appeal that the shipowners "took possession of the goods on behalf of and as agents for the charterers"[76]: a statement which, when seen in its original context, unequivocally denies that the shipowner was a bailee:

> But it was argued that the (ship) owner was liable in tort because he was not a party to the bill of lading and therefore could not claim the benefit of the exceptions contained in it, but was a bailee liable for negligence . . . The real answer to the claim is in my view that the shipowner is not in possession as a bailee, but as the agent of a

---

[73] *Whitfield* v. *Lord Le Despencer et al.* (1778) 2 Cowp. 754, at 765, cited by Browne J., in *Moukataff* v. *B.O.A.C. Ltd.* [1967] 1 Lloyd's Rep. 396, at 413. Cf. *Govett* v. *Radnidge* (1802) 3 East 62.

[74] E.g. *Adler* v. *Dickson* [1955] 1 Q.B. 158; *Cosgrove* v. *Horsfall* (1945) 62 T.L.R. 140. Cf. *The Coast Prince* [1967] 2 Lloyd's Rep. 290.

[75] [1924] A.C. 522, at 564-565: "It may be, that in the circumstances of this case the obligations to be inferred from the reception of the cargo for carriage . . . amount to a bailment upon terms, which include the exceptions and limitations of liability stipulated in the known and contemplated form of bill of lading . . . but, be this as it may, I cannot find here any such bald bailment with unrestricted liability as would be necessary to support the (*plaintiffs'*) contention." Lord Dunedin concurred with Lord Sumner; Lord Carson concurred with both Lord Sumner and Viscount Cave.

[76] [1924] A.C. 522, at 534.

person, the charterer, with whom the owner of the goods has made a contract defining his liability, and that the owner as servant or agent of the charterer can claim the same protection as the charterer.[77]

This is, in fact, almost identical to the alternative ground advanced by Lord Sumner for allowing the shipowners' immunity.[78]

Earlier rationalisations of *Elder, Dempster* seem to have accepted it as a simple illustration of the liability of a negligent employee, qualified by the doctrine of vicarious immunity, whereby any servant or agent 'acting under' a contract was entitled to the limitations and immunities contained therein.[79] It was only in later decisions that the alternative theory more strongly emerged that the shipowner in that case was a bailee, and that the delivery constituted a bailment upon terms.[80] Even then, the acceptance of this theory was far from unequivocal, although it is hard to dissociate the expressions of doubt upon the "bailment upon terms" theory from the expressions of doubt (if any) upon the broader question of the liability of a sub-bailee. The decision which appears at first sight to have tipped the balance in favour of a doctrine of extended bailment was that of the House of Lords in *Scruttons Ltd.* v. *Midland Silicones Ltd.*,[81] where two (and possibly three) of the five Law Lords, by acknowledging that *Elder, Dempster* was a case of bailment, impliedly recognised that a party who lacks direct contractual relations with the owner of goods could nevertheless owe him duties of a bailee.[82] But even here the identification was made solely for the purpose of circumscribing the doctrine of vicarious immunity. In fact, it is doubtful whether *Elder, Dempster* was not a case of non-contractual bailment by direct delivery inter partes rather than of bailment between a principal bailor and a sub- or extended bailee.[83] Certainly, the burden of proof was not an issue.

In spite of the wide and unqualified acceptance which the rule in *Morris* v. *C. W. Martin & Sons Ltd.*[84] has found in later decisions, the foregoing discussion is not entirely academic. Hitherto, the application of the rule in England and Australia has been confined to the primary instances of a bailee's Common Law duty: viz., to guard against negligence or conversion and, in unexplained cases, to prove that the necessary duty has been discharged. As to what would be the position if some other

---

[77] [1923] 1 K.B. 420, at 421-422 per Scrutton L.J. See also *Wilson* v. *Darling Island Stevedoring & Lighterage Co. Ltd.* (1956) 95 C.L.R. 43, at 68-69 per Fullager J.; at 84 per Kitto J.

[78] [1924] A.C. 522, at 564-565.

[79] E.g. *Mersey Shipping & Transport Co. Ltd.* v. *Rea Ltd.* (1925) 29 LL.L.R. 375, at 378 per Scrutton L.J.; and see Lord Finlay in the *Elder, Dempter* case [1924] A.C. 522, at 547-548.

[80] E.g. Pilcher J. in *Adler* v. *Dickson* [1955] 1 Q.B. 158, at 169-170 (and on appeal ibid.); Williams, Fullager and Taylor, JJJ., in *Wilson* v. *Darling Island Stevedoring & Lighterage Co. Ltd.* (1956) 95 C.L.R. 43, at 60, 69-72, 74, 78, 91, 93.

[81] [1962] A.C. 446.

[82] Ibid., at 470 per Viscount Simonds at 487, 489-490 (Lord Denning, dissenting). Cf. Lord Keith of Avonholm at 480 and Lord Morris of Borth-y-Gest at 494; and see the decision of the trial judge (Diplock J.) [1959] 2 Q.B. 171, at 189.

[83] It appears from the Report that the goods were loaded directly by the respondents on to the owners' ship and that no intervening possession was assumed by the charterer.

[84] [1966] 1 Q.B. 716.

facet of the relationship were in issue (for instance, the sub-bailee's inability to deny the bailor's title, the variation of the ordinary duty by a consent to take greater or lesser care or the existence of a warranty of fitness for carriage) there is a marked lack of authority. In this regard, the ancestry of *Morris* v. *C. W. Martin & Sons Ltd.* may still be of considerable importance as a means of assessing the extent to which a sub-bailment enjoys all the traditional legal properties that arise upon a more conventional bailment, be it gratuitous or for reward.

B. The ambit of the rule

However anaemic the precedents upon which it was based, the decision in *Morris* v. *C. W. Martin & Sons Ltd.* has gained widespread acceptance throughout the Commonwealth. It has been recognised in jurisdictions as far apart as Guyana[85] and Papua and New Guinea[86] as well as in Canada,[87] England and Australia.[88] It is interesting to compare this acceptance with Professor Carnegie's speculation that the difficulty of reconciling *Morris* v. *C. W. Martin & Sons Ltd.* with authority might prove fatal to its development.[89] Not all of these cases involved a sub-bailment stricto sensu and it may safely be assumed that the principal in question applies equally to subsitutional bailees, quasi-bailees and bailees by attornment. The decision in *Morris* v. *C. W. Martin & Sons Ltd.* marks the final stage in the emancipation of bailment from contract, for it enables the former relation to arise not only without consideration but without communication or agreement of any kind.

Admittedly, English and Australian authority was not entirely consistent, in the early years after *Morris* v. *C. W. Martin & Sons Ltd.,* as to the duties of the sub-bailee. In *Moukataff* v. *B.O.A.C. Ltd.*[90] the plaintiff, who was resident in Kuwait, ordered his London bank to transmit £20,000

---

[85] *British West Indian Airways Ltd.* v. *Bart* (1966) 11 W.I.R. 378 (Guyana C.A.).
[86] *O'Regan* v. *Hui Bros. Transport Pty. Ltd.* [1969] P. & N.G.L.R. 261.
[87] *Chapman* v. *Robinson and Ferguson* (1969) 71 W.W.R. 515; *Seaspan International Ltd.* v. *The Kostis Prois* (1973) 33 D.L.R. (3d) 1, at 5-6 (Ritchie J., Can. Sup. Ct.). See also *Jenkins* v. *Smith* (1969) 6 D.L.R. (3d) 309; *The Suleyman Stalskiy* [1976] 2 Lloyd's Rep. 609; *Eisen und Metall* v. *Ceres* [1977] 1 Lloyd's Rep. 665. Unfortunately, the acceptance of the rule in Canada is somewhat clouded by the reasoning of the Canadian Supreme Court in *Wong* v. *National Trust Corporation Ltd.* (1969) 3 D.L.R. (3d) 55, at 57. In this case, the owner of a light aeroplane bailed it to a company, authorising the company to let the plane on hire. A hirer disappeared while on a flight over Lake Ontario and neither he nor the plane was ever found. The Supreme Court of Canada seemed to accept that whereas the normal onus of proof would (but for special circumstances) have applied between the company and the hirer, the owner himself must rely upon the inferior plea of res ipsa loquitur to sustain what could only, in effect, be a simple action in negligence. The reason for this discrimination between the duty owed to an owner and the duty owed to a sub-bailor under an extended bailment was, apparently, the absence of any privity between the parties at each extremity; the owner and the sub-hirer were joined by no contractual link. But if it be true, as *Morris* v. *C.W. Martin & Sons Ltd.* affirms, that one may be liable as a bailee in the absence of contract, there is no reason why the owner in this case should not have enjoyed the same advantages as to proof as the second (contractual) bailor. It may be that a hirer should not in any event be liable as bailee to an owner of whose existence and ownership he is entirely unaware, but this is a very different thing from reducing the bailor to a mere action in negligence, unassisted by the conventional advantages as to proof.
[88] The English and Australian cases are discussed post.
[89] (1966) 3 *Adelaide Law Review* 7, at 15.
[90] [1967] 1 Lloyd's Rep. 396.

in banknotes by post to his Kuwait address. The bank delivered the package to the Post Office who in turn delivered it to B.O.A.C. for onward flight to Kuwait. The contents were stolen by a B.O.A.C. loader and the plaintiff sued his employers. Although it was specifically held that the plaintiff became the owner of the notes before their despatch (and therefore could presumably satisfy the role of bailor by "remote control") Browne J. twice implied that under that part of the pleadings which alleged a failure by B.O.A.C. to take proper security precautions it was the plaintiff who carried the burden of providing negligence.[91] If, however, their relationship were one of bailor and sub-bailee the burden would more properly have rested upon the defendants. No such difficulty attended the alternative plea, which alleged liability for the employee's conversion, because this was a form of liability independent of negligence.

Learoyd Bros. Ltd. v. *Pope & Sons Ltd.*[92] was a more everyday case, similar in its facts to *Lee Cooper & Co. Ltd.* v. *C. H. Jeakins, Ltd.*[93] except that in this case the intermediaries had already acquired and transferred possession to the ultimate bailees before the loss occurred. A haulage company, engaged by the plaintiffs to carry goods from Huddersfield to London docks, delegated part of the work to the defendants. The defendants' driver left his vehicle unattended and the goods were stolen. The plaintiffs alleged breach of the defendants' duty as a bailee, and/or negligence. Sach J. found for them on both counts:

> [I]t is to my mind clear that where the vehicle is one which remains with its driver under the general control of the sub-contractor, that sub-contractor . . . is in the position of bailee to the owner of the load on the vehicle. To use current legal language, these sub-contractors can conveniently be described as sub-bailees: but I should add that if technically it could be said that "bailment" is not the correct terminology to apply to such cases (where there is this particular combination of physical possession and control taken for reward by a servant of the defendants on one of their vehicles) yet that combination is such that my judgment would be no different if some other terminology were used to describe its effect.[94]

Two further points may be noted about this case. First the learned judge found negligence both on the part of the driver (who had failed to report a broken lock to his employers and had retired to a position from which he could not observe the lorry) and on the part of the defendants themselves (for failing to fit brake-locking devices to all their lorries working in the dockyard area). As regards the driver's negligence, this was held to be directly attributable to the defendants, either because he was acting under their orders at the material time (and was, therefore, within the course of his employment) or because the defendants had failed, through his default, to discharge their general responsibility of safeguarding the load from theft.[95] Thus, whether one applies the reasoning of Diplock and Salmon

91 Ibid., at 412, at 416.
92 [1966] 2 Lloyd's Rep. 142.
93 [1967] 2 Q.B. 1; [1964] 1 Lloyd's Rep. 300; ante, p. 797.
94 [1966] 2 Lloyd's Rep. 142, at 148.
95 Ibid., at 149.

L.JJ. in *Morris* v. *C. W. Martin & Sons Ltd.*[96] or that of Lord Denning M.R., the resultant liability is the same; not only where a servant of the sub-bailee converts the chattel personally, but also where his negligence facilitates the conversion (or, presumably, damage or destruction) by an outsider. In the event, the learned judge went on to hold that the driver's negligence probably did not cause the loss; he might also have mentioned that the onus of disproving that the bailee's negligence did not cause the loss rests upon the bailee himself.[97] He also expressed the view that the line of authority most prominently represented by *Deyong* v. *Shenburn*[98] (holding that a master does not contract for the safe-keeping of a servant's chattels deposited on the master's premises during the period of employment) was wholly inapplicable here.

Sachs J. also considered that it would have made no difference if the relationship between the head contractors and the defendants had disclosed a contract of hire rather than a contract of carriage.[99] This remark, which requires amplification, is discussed elsewhere.[1] For the present it need only be noted that if the arrangement betweeen principal and subsidiary carrier does amount to a lease of the sub-contractor's vehicle and a transfer of his servant into the temporary service of the principal carrier, the sub-contractor cannot in ordinary circumstances be held liable as a bailee.

Stripped of these complications, however, *Learoyd* v. *Pope* emerges as clear authority for the rule that the duties of a bailee may be owed by one who holds goods other than by direct delivery from the owner. Nor is it surprising that, in this case as in *Jeakins* and *Moukataff*, the plaintiffs elected to plead negligence in the alternative rather than to rely solely upon the traditional onus of proof. This is a feature common to most cases of bailment. Obviously it is a wise precaution to anticipate the rebutting evidence and, if possible, to establish breach of bailee's duty by affirmative evidence of one's own.[2]

The acid test of whether a sub-bailee carries the same burden as under an ordinary bailment will most prominently be seen in those cases where the immediate cause of the loss or injury is unexplained. The conventional bailee, while not encumbered with establishing the precise cause, must show that (however it happened) the loss was not due to his negligence. No such case involving a sub-bailment has hitherto arisen in English Law, but there are two decisions in which there was grave uncertainty as to whether the immediate cause (in both cases, theft) was occasioned by

---

[96] [1966] 1 Q.B. 716.
[97] *Ante,* p. 439.
[98] [1946] 1 K.B. 227; see also the observations of Marshall J. in the *Lee Cooper* case [1967] 2 Q.B. 1, at 7, where it was stated that it is impossible to distil from *Deyong* v. *Shenburn* and similar decisions the general rule that a defendant has no duty to guard another's goods from theft. But cf. *Johnson Matthey & Co. Ltd.* v. *Constantine Terminals Ltd.* [1976] 2 Lloyd's Rep. 215, at 221-222.
[99] [1966] 2 Lloyd's Rep. 142, at 148-149.
[1] *Ante,* p. 264, *et seq.*
[2] See, on this point, the observations of McArthur J. in *Paterson* v. *Miller* [1923] V.L.R. 36, at 42: "The mere fact that the pleader, perhaps from abundance of caution, adds an allegation of negligence, should not, I think, carry much weight in support of an argument that it is necessary for the plaintiff to allege and prove negligence".

the sub-bailee's default. In each case the onus was held to be upon the sub-bailee to prove either that he had attained the necessary standard of care or that, if he had failed to do so, there was no connexion between the loss and his default; and in each case the defendant failed to do so. In *British Road Services Ltd.* v. *Arthur V. Crutchley Ltd.*[3] the plaintiff was a sub-bailor who had already compensated the owners within the limits of their contract. In *James Buchanan & Co. Ltd.* v. *Hay's Transport Services Ltd.*[4] the owner himself was the plaintiff. A consignor of whisky had entrusted it to the second defendants for transportation from Glasgow to Tilbury. The lorry developed mechanical trouble and the consignment missed the boat. The carriers' driver therefore left the trailer and its contents with the first defendants, who were a sister company of the carriers and owned a compound at Dagenham, wherein the lorry was deposited. The driver stayed in the cab for the first night and, during the day, used the tractor for private purposes. On the second day, the entire trailer was stolen. Hinchcliffe J. held that the yard-owners were bailees rather than licensees and had failed to discharge the onus of satisfying the court that they had, in all the circumstances, taken reasonable care of the consignment.

> It is, I suppose, a matter of impression . . . The first defendants knew that the trailer had upon it a valuable load of whiskey, that such a load was valuable to thieves, that the trailer was to be in their compound over the weekend, that the goods had been entrusted to them for safe custody, and for this purpose were in their possession, as were the trailer and its load, that they were in control of the lorry and load in that the gates were opened for their entry, and it was placed where it was thought it would be safe—it could be moved by the first defendants had they so wished—that at night there was only one guard, and he was on duty without a guard dog, and there was no system of alarms.[5]

The decision is interesting, among other reasons, because Hinchliffe J. found that the bailment between the plaintiffs and the first defendants was a gratuitous one. However, in his view ". . . the standard of care is the same. It is that which a reasonable man would take of his own goods in similar circumstances."[6]

Recent English authority has emphatically confirmed that both a sub-bailee (who receives possession directly from an intermediate bailee) and a quasi-bailee (who assumes possession at the behest of an intermediary who was not personally in possession) is answerable to the principal bailor for any failure to take reasonable care of the goods, and must prove, in the event of loss or damage, that such care has been taken.[7] This liability

---

[3] [1968] 1 All E.R. 811; ante, pp. 445, 790.
[4] [1972] 2 Lloyd's Rep. 535.
[5] Ibid., at 543.
[6] Ibid. This aspect of the decision is questionable; see generally, Chapter 8.
[7] As to sub-bailees, see *Charles Davis (Metal Brokers) Ltd.* v. *Gilyott & Scott Ltd.* [1975] 2 Lloyd's Rep. 422; *Green* v. *The Jockey Club* (1975) 119 Sol. Jo. 258. As to quasi-bailees, see *Mayfair Photographic Supplies (London) Ltd.* v. *Baxter Hoare & Co. Ltd.* [1972] 1 Lloyd's Rep. 410; *Eastman Chemical International A.G.* v. *N.M.T. Trading Ltd.* [1972] 2 Lloyd's Rep. 25; *Hair and Skin Trading Co. Ltd.* v. *Norman Airfreight Carriers Ltd.* [1974] 1 Lloyd's Rep. 433; *Gallaher, Ltd.* v.

extends to any conversion of the goods committed by a servant of the sub- or quasi-bailee, provided the servant was one to whom the goods were entrusted or who dealt with them in the course of his employment. Thus, both as to the relevant Common Law duties of safekeeping and as to the burden of proof, there is now no material difference between the direct and the ultimate bailee.

In Australia, the same broad pattern has been adopted, although not without some initial prevarication. Three areas of doubt appear to have arisen: first, whether a sub-bailee should owe to the original bailor the duties of a bailee for reward when the reward he receives emanates not from that bailor but from another source; secondly, assuming the sub-bailment to be (vis-a-vis the owner) a gratuitous one, whether the onus of proof rests upon the bailor or the bailee;[8] and thirdly, whether in any event the sub- (as opposed to the ordinary) bailee carries the burden of negativing his own default. In *Thomas National Transport (Melbourne) Pty. Ltd.* v. *May & Baker (Australasia) Pty. Ltd.*[9] the alleged sub-bailee had voluntarily assumed the burden of disproving fault. Barwick C.J. seemed to think this was a proper concession—"Pay's liability is as a bailee of goods"[10]—as did McTiernan, Owen and Taylor JJJ., who remarked in their joint judgment that it was made "no doubt on the strength of *Morris* v. *C. W. Martin & Sons Ltd.*"[11] Windeyer J. remarked that since no contract or reward between the consignors and the ultimate bailee had been asserted, the latter's obligations seemed to be those of a depositary or mandatary;[12] he then went on to observe that even assuming the sub-bailee's assumption of the burden of proof to be a correct one, he had not in any event been careless.[13] However, the learned judge had already expressed the view that possession of the goods was in the principal contractors;[14] a debatable inference, but one which may at least explain any apparent doubts as to whether the sub-contractor carried the ordinary burden of a bailee.[15] It is difficult to see how this case could have been one of sub-bailment, when the supposed sub-bailee took delivery direct from the owner and the intermediary party never took possession at all. Little may revolve around the point, but it seeems more probably a case of quasi-bailment.

E. A. Marr (Contracting) Pty. Ltd. v. *Broken Hill Pty. Ltd. and I.P.I. Pty. Ltd.*[16] is an even more inconclusive case. Here it was specifically held that the relationship created when hirers of a crane loaned it to independent contractors was not a sub-bailment but one whereunder the owners and the independent contractors occupied directly the positions of

---

British Road Services, Ltd. [1974] 2 Lloyd's Rep. 440; *Johnson, Matthey & Co. Ltd.* v. *Constantine Terminals Ltd.* [1976] 2 Lloyd's Rep. 215.

[8] As to the burden of proof under conventional gratuitous bailments in Australia, see ante, p. 311 et seq.
[9] (1966) 115 C.L.R. 353.
[10] Ibid., at 360.
[11] Ibid., at 366.
[12] Ibid., at 375.
[13] Ibid., at 387.
[14] Ibid., at 383.
[15] Windeyer J. considered that Pay was a sub-bailee: ibid.
[16] [1970] 3 N.S.W.L.R. 306.

bailor and bailee. Thus, there was a substitutional bailment similar in effect, if not in character, to that in *Makower, McBeath & Co. Pty. Ltd. v. Dalgety & Co. Ltd.*[17] fifty years earlier. There was some difficulty with the pleadings and it is not clear whether the plaintiffs actually alleged a bailment. The judgment of Meares J. does not specifically state where he considered the burden to lie and negligence was found to have been positively proved. His caveat as to what would have been the position if the facts had disclosed a true sub-bailment is confined to an assessment of the effect this would have had upon the position of the intervening bailee.

An earlier New South Wales decision, not cited in the *Marr* case, was that of Goran D.C.J. in *Lee & Sons Pty. Ltd. v. Abood.*[18] Here, the hirer of two air compressors engaged the defendants to transport them from Sydney to Port Macquarie. The lorry overturned and the compressors were damaged. The plaintiffs (owners of the compressor) alleged negligent driving and the defendants countered with an assertion that their vehicle capsized because of a pot-hole in the road. The learned judge held that while the plaintiffs had failed to substantiate the plea of negligence, the defendants had likewise failed to discharge their onus of proving that the accident occurred otherwise than through their default; accordingly, judgment was entered for the plaintiffs.

The case is interesting not only in that it assumes a sub-bailment and places the burden of proof decisively on the sub-bailee. The learned judge was clearly concerned by the fact that the defendants, although paid by the hirer for the service they were performing, had received no benefit from the plaintiffs who were now seeking to charge them with the liability of a bailee for reward. In arriving at the apparent conclusion that the source of reward was immaterial, he therefore rejected the contention (already dismissed as "unrealistic" by Browne J. in *Moukataff v. B.O.A.C.*[19]) that a sub-bailee who is not paid by the owner owes only the duties of a gratuitous bailee towards him. It may be added that to some extent this conclusion had been impliedly endorsed, thirty years earlier, by the Court of Appeal in *Andrews v. Home Flats Ltd.*[20] The decision in *Lee v. Abood* is consistent with English authority and is to be welcomed for its refusal to evade the several difficulties that arise when one attempts to assess the similarity between a sub-bailee and a "proper" or "ordinary" bailee.

At the time of this decision, the question of the sub-bailee's burden of proof could still have been regarded as undecided in Australia. However, it is submitted that after the unreported decision of McInerney J. in *Arcweld Constructions Pty. Ltd. v. C. E. Smith and others,*[21] and the Privy Council's decision in *Gilchrist Watt & Sanderson Pty. Ltd. v. York Products Pty. Ltd.*[22] the equation of burdens enjoyed by sub- and ordinary bailees should be assumed (at least where the sub-bailee is rewarded) to be complete. In *Gilchrist's* case, admittedly, negligence had been affirma-

---

[17] [1921] V.L.R. 365.
[18] (1968) 89 W.N. (Pt. 1) (N.S.W.) 430.
[19] [1967] 1 Lloyd's Rep. 396, at 415-416.
[20] [1945] 2 All E.R. 698.
[21] Victorian Supreme Court; 17 September 1968.
[22] [1970] 3 All E.R. 825.

tively established. The defendants came into possession of two cases of clocks when they were discharged by ship-owners at Sydney. They carried on business as ships' agents and stevedores and had, on arrival of the ship, unloaded and stored the clocks in their warehouse, whence one of the cases was stolen. The Privy Council were prepared to assume in their favour that the initial bailment to the ship-owner continued throughout, despite a clause in the bill of lading whereby:

> The carrier shall not be liable in any capacity whatsoever for any delay, loss or damage occurring . . . after the goods leave ship's tackle to be discharged transhipped or forwarded.

But this assumption merely meant that there was a sub-bailment between the consignees and the defendants; a relationship which cast upon the latter the duty of exercising due care for the safety of the goods, which duty they had admittedly failed to discharge. In the words of Lord Pearson:

> Both on principle, and on old as well as recent authority, it is clear that although there was no contract or attornment between the plaintiffs and the defendants, the defendants by voluntarily taking possession of the plaintiffs' goods, assumed an obligation to take care of them and are liable to the plaintiffs for the failure to do so (as found by the trial judge). The obligation is at any rate *the same as that of a bailee,* whether or not it can with strict accuracy be described as the obligation of a bailee.[23]

The foundation for Lord Pearson's semantic qualms appears to have been the fact that the plaintiffs in this case had not specifically alleged a bailment and that this word could only literally apply where one person had *"baillé"* (i.e. delivered) goods to another. He observed: "In the English Courts the word 'bailment' has acquired a meaning wide enough to include this case. It may not have acquired such a meaning in the Australian Courts."[24]

However, as his Lordship had already stressed, the important factor is not the etymological ancestry of bailment but whether its traditional incidents apply with equal effect to the sub- or quasi-bailee. That this is so may now be regarded, in England and Australia at least, as established beyond reasonable doubt.

Further authority for this view, showing that, at least in a dispute with the owner of the goods, there is no significant difference between the positions of the sub- and (as in the present case) the quasi-bailee, can be found in certain dicta of Windeyer J. in *Hobbs* v. *Petersham Transport Co. Pty. Ltd.*[25] In this case, the defendants were private carriers engaged by the plaintiffs to transport a machine from Sydney to Ashford. Without acquiring possession of the machine, they sub-contracted the work to a third party, who collected the equipment and undertook delivery throughout. The lorry carrying the machine overturned because of a broken axle, and the machine was damaged. In the ensuing action against the defen-

---

[23] Ibid., at 832; citing inter alia *Hooper* v. *L. & N.W. Ry. Co.* (1880) 43 L.T. 570. The facts of this case were very similar to those in *Makower, McBeath & Co. Pty. Ltd.* v. *Dalgety & Co. Pty. Ltd.* [1921] V.L.R. 365; ante, p. 788. See also *Global Dress Co. Ltd.* v. *W.H. Boase & Co. Ltd.* [1966] 2 Lloyd's Rep. 72.
[24] [1970] 3 All E.R. 825, at 832.
[25] (1971) 45 A.L.J.R. 356; Proksch [1973] A.B.L.R. 266.

dants, two members of the High Court[26] held that the plaintiffs had failed
to sustain their assertion that the accident occurred through the neglect of
the defendants or their sub-contractors, an assertion which did not by
itself cast a burden of disproving negligence upon the non-bailee; the
remaining three members[27] held (on the assumption that the defendants
were bailees) that they had proved that the accident had occurred without
the default of themselves or of their sub-contractors. The decision is
marred by the confusion as to whether the defendants were bailees; the
pleadings alleged that they were but the fact suggested otherwise and
the court was divided on this issue to the ratio of three or two respectively.
Nor was this a case where the bailor was proceeding against the ultimate
bailee directly: perhaps because the circumstances giving rise to the action
took place in 1957, long before such a claim was generally thought
possible; perhaps because, in the words of Windeyer J., the claim had
become "stale and statute barred". The same judge distinguished *Lilley*
v. *Doubleday*[28] and *Edwards* v. *Newland*[29] on the ground that these were
cases of unauthorised sub-bailment by a bailee. He then observed:

> The Hobbs brothers were sub-contractors of the defendant to per-
> form its contract with the plaintiff. They were strangers to that
> contract. They had no contract with the plaintiff. But the Common
> Law, deriving its concept of bailment largely from the Civil Law,
> has never subsumed bailment under the general law of contract. It
> is now beyond dispute that the relationship of bailor and bailee can
> arise and exist independently of contract. By taking the plaintiff's
> goods into their physical possession when they were loaded on to their
> lorry the Hobbs brothers undertook the obligations and duties of
> a bailee for reward. Whether or not a sub-contractor of a bailee
> is himself properly called a bailee is a debatable question of
> terminology . . . However, whether that were so or not, the Hobbs
> brothers unquestionably became directly liable to the plaintiff if they,
> by their servants and agents, failed to take due care of the goods.[30]

Finally, in *Philip Morris (Australia) Ltd.* v. *The Transport Commission*[31]
Nettlefold J. unequivocally stated that the defendant carriers, to whom
Ansett Airlines had delegated part of a larger contract of carriage and
who took possession of the plaintiffs' goods as sub-contractors from
Ansett, owed to the owners of the goods the duties of a bailee for reward
and bore the traditional onus of proof common to every bailee.

It follows from the foregoing decisions that the sub-bailee owes the same
Common Law duties towards his principal bailor as are owed by the bailee
under a conventional, bilateral bailment. No better judical summary of
these duties can be found than that given by Browne J. in *Moukataff* v.
B.O.A.C.[32] In the learned judge's view, *Morris* v. *C. W. Martin & Sons
Ltd.*[33] established the following propositions:

[26] Barwick C.J. and Windeyer J.
[27] McTiernan, Menzies and Owen JJJ.
[28] (1881) 7 Q.B.D. 510.
[29] [1950] 2 K.B. 534.
[30] (1971) 45 A.L.J.R. 356, at 363.
[31] [1975] Tas. S.R. 128; and *The New York Star* (1978) 18 A.L.R. 335.
[32] [1967] 1 Lloyd's Rep. 396, at 414-415.
[33] [1966] 1 Q.B. 716.

1. Where a bailee, with the consent of the bailor, hands over goods of the bailor to a sub-bailee for reward as between the bailee and the sub-bailee, the sub-bailee owes to the original bailor the duties of a bailee for reward, including the duty to take reasonable care for the safety of the goods.

2. The sub-bailee is under a double duty to the original bailor (a) to take reasonable care to keep goods safe; and (b) not to do any intentional act inconsistent with the bailor's right,[34] such as converting the goods. The sub-bailee is liable for any breach of these duties on his own part as well as for breaches committed vicariously.

3. If the goods are stolen by a servant of the sub-bailee, the bailee is vicariously liable to the original bailor if (and only if) the servant by whom the goods were stolen was one of the servants to whom the sub-bailee had deputed some part of his duty to take reasonable care of the goods while they were in his possession.[35]

4. The original bailor has a right of action against the sub-bailee for breach of the latter's duty if the original bailor has the right to immediate possession of the goods of if they are permanently lost or injured. It remains to be established whether misadventures which are incapable of classification as "loss or damage", such as the prolonged delay and consequent fall in economic value of the goods, are actionable by the principal bailor against a sub-bailee.[36]

In addition, of course, the sub-bailee carries the burden of proving that he took the proper degree of care of the goods. However, this rule comes into operation only when the principal bailor has affirmatively demonstrated that the goods were lost or damaged while in the sub-bailee's possession. In cases of sub-bailment this rule can cause hardship, because a principal bailor may be incapable of knowing the exact point at which the goods were damaged or lost. Thus, the intermediate bailee may claim that the goods were in excellent condition when he delivered them over to the sub-bailee and the sub-bailee may claim that they were already damaged when he received them. In each case, the onus of pin-pointing the time of damage rests with the principal bailor, and until he accomplishes this the bailee's burden of proof cannot take effect. In one decision the learned judge, finding himself unable to reach a specific conclusion on this point, reduced the plaintiff's damages by fifty per cent.[37] There was no doubt that the sub-bailee had been negligent and the only doubt concerned the extent to which this negligence was the effective cause of the relevant damage; the sub-bailees claiming that it had already substantially occurred before they came into possession. The award in this case seems to have been little more than an equitable guess, for which there was little, if any, supporting evidence. It would surely be fairer in a case of this kind to hold the bailee fully responsible unless he can positively identify both the cause of the injury and the extent to which that cause affected the

---

[34] The Report actually says "bailee's right", but it is submitted that this is a misprint. The expression bailor as used in the text would embrace both original and intermediate bailors, whereas 'bailee' would be confined to the intermediate party.

[35] *Morris* v. *C.W. Martin & Sons Ltd.* [1966] 1 Q.B. 716, at 728, 732-733, 736-737, 740-741.

[36] Post, p. 822.

[37] *O'Regan* v. *Hui Bros. Transport Pty. Ltd.* [1969] P. & N.G.L.R. 261.

ultimate condition of the goods. In cases where the bailee's proof falls
short of this the plaintiff should recover in toto, leaving any apportionment to be decided in a contest between successive bailees.

Although the preceeding discussion has been phrased in terms of the
sub-bailment, it seems clear that identical duties should attend the
relationship between a principal bailor and a quasi- or substitutional bailee.
Indeed, many of the decisions cited above have involved the latter forms
of bailment; the principal value to be derived from distinguishing them
rests in the different effects each may have upon the intermediate party.

C. The relevance of knowledge as to the owner's identity

Not every bailee is readily indentifiable as such. Often, he will be superficially indistinguishable from the owner and the subsidiary bailee will
not know with which of these parties he is dealing. Should it affect the
liability of a secondary bailee that he was unaware of the real owner's
existence and had assumed that property, as well as possession, resided
in the party who bailed the goods to him?

The answer depends to some extent upon whether one regards bailment
as a consent-based relationship or as a duty-structure within which the
ordinary rules of tort apply. Clearly it is no defence for a negligent tortfeasor to say that although he should have foreseen the damage in question
he could not foresee that the particular plaintiff would be affected. In
most cases he will not know the identity of the victim until after the
event and his duty to him depends upon proximities rather than questions
of identity. Likewise, one could argue that under a sub-bailment it is
completely irrelevant for the sub-bailee to plead his ignorance of the
owner in his defence; the sub-bailee has negligently damaged goods and
should pay for them, as he would have to if he were a non-bailee who
collided, for example, with a hired car, or an occupier whose breach of
duty caused the damage to a chattel borrowed, and brought on to the
premises, by a lawful visitor.[38]

The reverse argument would emphasise that at the heart of every
bailment there lies, if not consensus, at least consent; an undertaking
(express or implied, assumed or imposed) to take care of and be
responsible for another's goods. Admittedly, the "bailor" himself may
not consent to the bailment and there will be occasions (one would
suspect the majority) on which the identity of the owner will be a matter
of indifference to the sub-bailee. Nevertheless, bailment connotes for
the most part a voluntary assumption of duty, and it may be thought that
the bailee has a right to know when he may be liable to more than one
plaintiff; especially as one of those plaintiffs may not be bound by the
terms of the sub-bailee's contract.

What little authority there is seems divided. In two English cases, *Lee
Cooper Ltd.* v. *C. H. Jeakins Ltd.*[39] and *Morris* v. *C. W. Martin & Sons*

---

[38] *Drive-Yourself Lessey's Pty. Ltd.* v. *Burnside* [1959] S.R. (N.S.W.) 390.
[39] [1967] 2 Q.B. 1, at 8.

Ltd.[40] the point was made, apparently as justification for the bailee's direct liability, that he knew that the goods belonged to someone other than the immediate bailor. In a third, *Meux* v. *G.E. Ry,*[41] where the defendants did not know the precise nature of the goods or that they belonged to another, the Court stressed that the goods were lawfully on the defendants premises and that they could not lawfully have refused to carry them. But of course, the latter decision may have nothing to do with the principles of bailment.

In *Lee & Sons Pty. Ltd.* v. *Abood,* on the other hand, Goran D.C.J. held after careful reflection that sub-bailee's ignorance of the fact that the sub-bailor was not the owner did not absolve him from liability. His grounds were interesting:

> I am not considering a new category of negligence: I am rather deciding a principle for which there is little authority. But it appears to me that if I decide that the sub-bailee's lack of knowledge as to the real ownership of the compressors is a material factor, then I am importing into the doctrine of liability for negligence a concept derived from the doctrine which Denning L.J. in *Green* v. *Chelsea Borough Council*[42] called the "privity of contract" doctrine which, he said, "received its quietus" by the decision of the House of Lords in *Donoghue* v. *Stevenson*[43] . . . When all questions of a contractual nature are set aside, since they are being paid to carry the goods with care, is their duty any the less because those paying them are not the owners of the goods? It must be remembered that the authorities are clear that they owe such a duty in respect of the goods to the real owners. I feel that the nature of this duty and the standard of care that they must employ while the goods are in their custody is not affected by the question of who owns the goods.[44]

This reasoning is persuasive, but it seems to involve an unqualified recognition of total identity between actions for breach of bailment and actions in tort. In fact, as we have already attempted to demonstrate, significant differences exist between the two.[45] *Lee & Sons Pty. Ltd.* v. *Abood* itself indicates one of the major distinctions, for the judge himself conceded that a simple action in negligence (even presumably, assisted by the doctrine of res ipsa loquitur), would have failed on the facts before him. This is one area where the rules of bailment should, perhaps, be encouraged to develop independently and without the restrictions imposed by subsumption under other heads of liability. In some circumstances it would operate harshly against a sub-bailee that he did not know his bailor was not the owner. He may have lost the opportunity of stipulating for an indemnity from the intermediate bailee; he may be subjected to a wider liability than he would, with full knowledge of the divided interest, have consented to assume. If bailment be truly dependent upon consent,[46] it might

---

[40] [1966] 1 Q.B. 716, at 731. See also *B.W.I.A. Ltd.* v. *Bart* (1966) 11 W.I.R. 378. In every English case on the question, the sub- or quasi-bailee seems to have known that the intermediate party was not the owner of the goods.

[41] [1895] 2 Q.B. 387.

[42] [1954] 2 Q.B. 127, at 138.

[43] [1932] A.C. 562.

[44] (1968) 89 W.N. (Pt. 1) (N.S.W.) 430, at 436-437.

[45] Ante, p. 36 et. seq.

[46] Ante, p. 30.

be arguable that certain contractual phenomena should find an analogous existence in the field of non-contractual bailment. In certain regards the law of tort is an inadequate basis for full rationalisation of the bailee's liability. As Winfield says:

> Liability in tort is primarily fixed by the law itself, irrespective of the assent of the persons bound but in bailment it is primarily fixed by the parties themselves. When once they have entered into the relation, a good many legal consequences follow and some of them were probably never contemplated by either bailor or bailee . . . A bailee, like a contractor, may protest against some of them as harsh and not contemplated by him when he became a bailee, but that does not alter the fact that primarily it was he, not the law, that brought into being the legal relation to which these consequences are attached. Bailment originates in an agreement, express or implied, and tortious liability does not—and, though it is possible, according to the balance of opinion, to have a bailment without a contract, it is not possible to have it without agreement. A man cannot without his knowledge and consent be considered as a bailee of property.[47]

Since contract is the primary model (in the commercial context) of a consent-based relationship, it might be argued that certain of its elements could provide an appropriate foundation for the establishment of other consensual relationships such as bailment. In particular, those factors which seek to answer the question of consent—fraud, misrepresentation, duress, offer and acceptance, mistake—and even perhaps those which elaborate the ambit of agreement—such as deviation, frustration, and repudiation—might justifiably be imported, in a modified form, into the non-contractual bailment. To some extent, as we shall see, this has already been done.[48] To what extent it *should* be done is a matter of very great difficulty, for clearly there is more to the varied forms of non-contractual bailment than the absence of consideration. For the present, two observations may be offered. First, of course, the presence of a consent-vitiating factor may entitle the bailee to relief under his immediate contract with the sub-bailor. Thus, for instance, if the sub-bailee is induced to assume possession by a misrepresentation that the goods belong to the sub-bailor, he will, in appropriate circumstances, be able to repudiate the arrangement and, by so doing, to determine forwith his duties as bailee. Secondly, it might be legitimate to hold that a sub-bailee whose reception of goods was induced in such a manner that he would not, had he known the truth, have accepted them, and would not (had his relationship with the owner been contractual) have been bound to do so, should owe to that owner only the duties an involuntary bailee; just as would be the case, for example, with a person who was compelled to assume possession of the goods gratuitously by virtue of the bailor's duress. When questions of consent are involved, the absence of privity of contract should not necessarily debar the adaptation of contractual notions in an attempt to elucidate the existence of such consent, provided that the individuality of the bailment relation, and its special needs, are not obscured thereby.

Admittedly, an approach of this kind would be viable only in extreme

---

[47] *Province of the Law of Tort,* pp. 99-100.
[48] Post, p. 821 et. seq.

cases. On most occasions the sub-bailee will either not have objected, or will not have attached sufficient importance, to the location of title in the goods as to entitle him to abdicate his normal duty of care. As Owen J. remarked in 1959, discussing the case of the hirer of a car who left it in a car-park wherein it was damaged:

> It is a matter of common knowledge, at the present day, that a large number of cars belong to hire-purchase companies and not to those who drive them, and that many cars are driven by hirers under a contract such as here existed . . . It was submitted that, in the light of modern conditions, those who conduct car-parks, "drive-in" theatres and the like places and invite persons to use them offer that invitation or licence to the owner of a car which is lawfully in the custody of the person to whom personally the invitation or licence is given . . . I am of opinion that the occupier of premises who invites or licenses car drivers to leave their cars on his premises should be regarded as extending that invitation or licence to the owner of the car.[49]

This was a case in which the existence of a bailment had been negatived and the plaintiff was relying on an alternative plea, alleging breach of the defendant's duty as an occupier or breach of a general duty of care. However, it seems that the same principles should obtain in cases of bailment, with the result that if the bailee knew or ought to have known that the goods customarily bailed to him did not belong to the immediate bailor, but to a third party, and did not customarily object to them for that reason, his consent to safeguard them should be deemed to extend to the owner as well as to the intermediary. It is suggested that the presence of an exclusion of or indemnity clause in the contract of sub-bailment, purporting to relieve the sub-bailee from liability to his immediate bailor or any other person possessing an interest in the goods, would be prima facie evidence that the sub-bailee acknowledged or assumed a duty in relation to third parties, whether or not that duty had been successfully excluded.

If an exceptional case arose and it were held that the sub-bailee were, vis-a-vis the owner, an involuntary bailee, the question would then arise as to whether the owner could succeed alternatively on a simple action in negligence. Presumably, the quality of the bailment would determine the total scope of the defendant's obligation as it would in the case of a bilateral involuntary bailment of the kind in *Howard* v. *Harris*.[50] A person should not be forced to assume the onerous duties of a bailee against his will, whether the relevant lack of consent relate to the assumption of a duty of care or to the person to whom it is owed.

---

49 *Drive-Yourself Lessey's Pty. Ltd.* v. *Burnside* [1959] S.R. (N.S.W.) 390, at 401-402.
50 (1884) 1 Cab. & E1. 253; cf. *Lethbridge* v. *Phillips* (1819) 2 Stark. 544, which obliquely supports this proposition, and see *Johnson Matthey & Co. Ltd.* v. *Constantine Terminals Ltd.* [1976] 2 Lloyd's Rep. 215.

VII. The Degree of Identity between Extended
and Ordinary Bailments

With few exceptions,[51] all the decisions applying *Morris* v. *C. W. Martin &
Sons Ltd.* have raised straightforward issues as to liability for negligence
or conversion and the location of the burden of proof. It is therefore
uncertain whether the extended bailment is in other respects a replica of
its bipartite equivalent. The degree of identity seems to depend upon two
principal factors: first, the extent to which the courts would be willing to
transplant certain contractual models or concepts into the field of extended
bailment, and secondly the relationship between the action against an
extended bailee and the parallel but distinct action in negligence which
eevery owner of goods ostensibly enjoys against a person who carelessly
damages them. The only generalisation that can safely be made is that
there will come a point at which the element of privity creates insuperable
distinctions between an ordinary bailment, where the parties will at least
have been in direct communication, and an extended bailment, where they
will almost invariably be strangers.

A. Diversity of duty between owner-intermediate bailee relationship and owner-extended bailee relationship

Clearly the duty owed by the ultimate bailee to the owner may be
greater or lesser than the duty owed by the intermediary. It has been
established[52], for instance, that if a sub-bailee receives payment or other
reward from his sub-bailor, the duty he owes to the original bailor will
be that of a bailee for reward. There is also authority for the proposition
that if the sub-bailment is gratuitous the sub-bailee owes to the original
bailor only the duty of a gratuitous bailee.[53] Accordingly, it would follow
that if a gratuitous bailee (such as a depositary) redeposits the chattel
with a third person and pays him for taking care of it, the sub-depositary
may be under a greater liability to the owner than the original bailee. Of
course, if the sub-deposit is unlawful the principal depositary will probably
be guilty of conversion and will become an insurer of the goods in any
event. But if the foregoing analysis is correct, it should make no difference
to the liability of the ultimate bailee that his reward under the sub-
bailment took the form of something prohibited by the original bailor. Thus,
if A gratuitously deposits his bicycle with B, forbidding B to ride it, and
B asks C to undertake custody of the machine in return for B's permission
to ride it, C would appear to owe to A the duties of a bailee for reward.

Of course, if C knew that B was not entitled to part with the bicycle
it would be entirely reasonable to impose upon him the duties of a bailee
for reward. He will not be guilty of trespass because there has been no

---

51 *B.W.I.A. Ltd.* v. *Bart* (1966) 11 W.I.R. 378; *Chapman* v. *Robinson and Ferguson*
(1969) 71 W.W.R. 515; *post,* p. 822.
52 *Ante.*
53 *James Buchanan Ltd.* v. *Hay's Transport Services Ltd.* [1972] 2 Lloyd's Rep. 535.
Admittedly, Hinchcliffe J. held in this case that the absence of reward made no
difference to the sub-bailee's duty, but Australian authority may favour some
variation: see generally Chapters 9, 10, ante. Cf. *Thomas National Transport
(Melbourne) Pty. Ltd.* v. *May & Baker (Australia) Pty. Ltd.* (1966) 115 C.L.R.
353, at 375 per Windeyer J.

violation of the bailee's possession[54] and he may not be guilty of conversion.[55] But the policy of the law may well be better served by making him an insurer of the goods. If an original bailee contravenes a fundamental restriction upon his use of the chattel, he is strictly liable to the owner for all ensuing losses. The same liability should be imposed under an owner—sub-bailee relationship, provided that the restriction was one which was imposed originally by the owner and which has been knowingly contravened. Unfortunately, in the only decision in which this problem has arisen the court appears to have thought that an insurer's liability could be imposed only if there were a contract between the owner and the sub-bailee.[56] The fictitious method by which such a contract was implied in this case argues strongly in favour of an extra-contractual liability, based upon the terms of the bailment.[57]

Hitherto, we have assumed the sub-bailee is aware that his use of the chattel is wrongful. It may be, however, that the sub-bailor has told the sub-bailee that the owner has given permission for the sub-bailee to use the chattel. Although the sub-bailee should not in this event be liable as an insurer, he can have no legitimate complaint against being made liable as a bailee for reward. He has impliedly agreed to assume such liability towards the sub-bailor and he should realise that this liability may be enforced by more than one plaintiff.

The situation may be entirely different if the ultimate bailee is unaware of the owner's interest: for instance, where the sub-bailor tells him that he (the sub-bailor) is the owner. In this event, we have already suggested[58] that the sub-bailee should be entitled to relief if he can show (i) that he would not have taken possession with full knowledge of the ulterior interest, and (ii) that his assumption of possession was induced by conduct (such as misrepresentation, mistake or duress) which would have entitled him to withdraw from his immediate contract and which effectively rendered him an involuntary bailee. The practical effect of such a rule would be that the relationship between an owner and a sub-bailee, although based neither upon contract or direct agreeement, could give rise to certain rights and immunities comparable to those which normally arise in contract.

Certainly it is not difficult to envisage circumstances arising *after* the creation of the owner-sub-bailee relationship in which it would be desirable to recruit and modify contractual principles to establish the rights of the parties. Thus, the relationship should be capable of supporting a defence of promissory estoppel and should be capable of variation. If, for example, the sub-bailee warns the owner that he can no longer guarantee to keep the goods with reasonable care,[59] and the owner agrees only to demand a lesser standard, the owner might legitimately be pre-

---

[54] *Penfolds Wines Pty. Ltd.* v. *Elliott* (1946) 74 C.L.R. 204; ante p. 000.
[55] Ante, pp. 127, 753. Cf. *Chapman* v. *Robinson and Ferguson* (1969) 71 W.W.R. 515, at 519; *Penfolds Wines Pty. Ltd.* v. *Elliott* ante.
[56] *Chapman* v. *Robinson and Ferguson* ante, p. 375 et seq.
[57] Post, p. 821 et seq.
[58] Ante, p. 812.
[59] Cf. *Edwards* v. *Newland & Co.* [1950] 2 K.B. 534.

cluded from enforcing the original duty.[60] Likewise, the sub-bailee's right to
hold the goods may be forfeited by conduct which amounts to a fundamental
breach of the sub-bailment.[61] Even the doctrine of affirmation may have a
role to play in the context of the sub-bailment. The owner who, knowing
of a fundamental breach by the sub-bailee (for instance, a misuse under
a sub-lease) elects not to exercise a right of re-possession, may be deemed
to have affirmed the sub-bailment and will accordingly be restricted, for
the period of the sub-lease, to a remedy in damages. Other principles,
such as deviation and frustration, might also be invoked to elaborate
the rights and duties of the parties. There can be little doubt that similar
doctrines are applicable in cases of gratuitous bailment and modern view
that such bailments are non-contractual[62] would seem to justify importing
the same principles into cases of extended bailment. Two factors in
particular militate in favour of this extension: the foundation of all
varieties of bailment upon consent and the inadequacy of conventional
tortious remedies to provide a complete or satisfactory theory of extended
bailment.[63]

The circumstances of the secondary transaction may limit the sub-
bailee's duty to the owner in other ways than by reward or non-consent.
The sub-bailor may entrust the goods to a sub-bailee whom he knows to
be drunk, or who is notoriously incompetent. It is clearly established that
the responsibilities of a bailee may be regulated by his known abilities or
reputation. Thus: "If you confide a casket of jewels to the custody of a
yokel, you cannot expect him to take the same care of it that a banker
would."[64] Here again, it would be contrary to principle to allow the owner
a greater right of recovery against the sub-bailee than the sub-bailor could
have pursued in person. The sub-bailee will have impliedly agreed to
accept the goods only upon the terms engendered by the sub-bailment. He
will have assumed no greater duty towards the owner than he has assumed
towards the sub-bailee, and the definition of that duty, as contained in the
terms of the sub-bailment, should be exclusive.

If (as seems likely) the method by which the sub-bailee is induced to
assume possession can indeed provide a universal definition of the sub-
bailee's responsibility, a similar weight might legitimately be accorded
to the express terms of the sub-bailment itself. In many cases, a provision
in the contract of sub-bailment which appears to exclude liability for a
breach of duty by the sub-bailee will in fact perform the prior function
of enumerating or delineating his duties *ab initio*. As Windeyer J. pointed

---

60 It seems well established that the pre-existing legal relations which are conventionally necessary for the defence of promissory estoppel to operate need not
be contractual in character: *Robinson* v. *Minister of Pensions* [1949] 1 K.B. 227;
Durham Fancy Goods Ltd. v. *Michael Jackson (Fancy Goods) Ltd.* [1968] 2 Q.B.
839. In *Evenden* v. *Guildford City Association Football Club Ltd.* [1975] I.C.R.
367, at 374 Lord Denning M.R. went so far as to say that *no* pre-existing legal
relations were necessary. Whether or not this is true, it seems entirely reasonable
that the owner-sub-bailee relationship should satisfy the requirement.
61 This question is discussed in more detail post, p. 824.
62 Ante, pp. 20, 314.
63 See further post, p. 821 et seq.
64 *Halsbury's Laws* (4th edn) Vol. ii, para 1503.

out in *Thomas National Transport (Melbourne) Pty. Ltd.* v. *May & Baker (Australia) Pty. Ltd.*:[65]

> The question is whether the effect of an exception clause is a contract as to absolve a party from liability for the consequences of a breach of duty, or whether its effect is to define substantively the limits of his duty by negativing obligations that the law would otherwise impose and undertakings that it would otherwise imply. The answer in any given case may, I think, depend upon the actual words of the contract.

Therefore it should be possible to argue that if the sub-bailee's contract contains clauses of a defining rather than an absolving character, his entire responsibility towards both the owner and the sub-bailor is to be judged by the limits of that contract. He has consented to hold the chattel only upon these terms and the contract of sub-bailment contains an exclusive definition of his liability, just as it would if he were drunk at the time of the sub-bailment or had been forced to accept the goods under duress.

The difficulty of this approach lies in the doctrine of privity of contract and the traditional theory that only a party to a contract is bound by the terms therein. Admittedly, this doctrine is of doubtful influence in the field of sub-bailment because it seems that an owner who consents to a sub-bailment on terms will be bound by those terms although he and the sub-bailee are joined by no contractual relation.[66] Nevertheless, to allow the subsidiary bailment to provide an exclusive definition of the sub-bailee's duty towards a party who is stranger to that agreement might seem to involve diluting the doctrine out of existence.

In fact, the cases in which this problem is likely to occur will represent the exception rather than the rule. The circumstances in which a sub-bailee's terms will be of a defining character will probably be rare, and it may always be open to the owner to prove that since the sub-bailee regularly accepted goods belonging to third parties his ignorance on this occasion is not sufficiently material to negate the conventional duty imposed at Common Law. Moreover, delineating clauses will, like excluding or exempting clauses, be strictly construed,[67] so that in many cases the clause will fail upon ordinary principles of construction, whether it is in fact capable of applying between the owner and the sub-bailee or not. Nevertheless, if bailment is a relationship conferring status and is founded upon consent, the bailee should be protected against unconsented extensions of that status. Not every provision in the contract of sub-bailment will be central or essential to the relationship between the owner and the sub-bailee; but those that are, and represent an exhaustive definition of the sub-bailee's duties under this relationship, should be enforced in his favour.

Surprisingly, authority can be cited in favour of this proposition. In *Mayfair Photographic Supplies (London) Ltd.* v. *Baxter Hoare & Co. Ltd.*[68] the second defendant was a quasi-bailee who had been employed by

---

[65] (1966) 115 C.L.R. 353, at 385; see further, p. 918 et seq., post.
[66] Post, p. 1000 et seq.
[67] Post, p. 918 et seq.
[68] [1972] 1 Lloyd's Rep. 410.

the first defendant forwarding agents to transport a consignment of cameras belonging to the plaintiffs. The cameras were stolen in transit and the second defendant was sued for the loss. MacKenna J. found it unnecessary to determine whether he could claim the protection of the principal contract between plaintiffs and first defendants, because his own contract with the first defendants afforded him relief against the plaintiffs. This contract entitled the second defendant to adopt a certain itinerary while transporting the goods, and was subject to implied terms that the lorry in which the cameras were transported need be neither enclosed nor fitted with an immobilizer. Both of these were terms based upon the forwarding agents' knowledge of the second defendant's facilities. It was held sufficient for his defence against the owners that he had done all that his own contract with the forwarders required of him. The owner could not, in other words, outflank these duties and enforce a superior level of responsibility by suing in negligence:

> The authorities recognise that a person in Mr. Stembridge's position (*the quasi-bailee*) . . . owes an independent duty to the owner which may be enforced in an action in tort. But that is not to say that the contract of carriage is irrelevant. If the contract is within the apparent authority of the (*forwarding agent*) and the carrier obeys the (*forwarding agent's*) instructions under the contract and commits no breach of its terms, he owes no liability to anyone—none to the (*forwarding agent*) because he has fulfilled his contract, and none to the owner because he cannot owe him any higher duty than that imposed by the contract. In other words, if the carrier does what the contract obliges or entitles him to do, he cannot be found guilty of negligence against the owner of the goods. He is not obliged to sit in judgment on any orders he receives from the (*forwarding agent*) and to obey them only if he considers them to be in the owner's interests.[69]

This method of approach seems eminently sensible. It would be absurd if the sub-bailee, having performed to the letter his contract with the intermediary, should be additionally bound to ensure that this contract is consistent with a duty of care to third parties, or to do more than that contract necessitates so as to ensure that such a duty is discharged. Where the contract is thus consistent (and the mere presence of exclusion clauses obviously does not make it otherwise) the duty can properly be enforced. Where it is not, the contract should be given precedence, for it is a definition of the sub-bailee's duty to anybody with an interest in the goods; and having made his acceptance of the goods conditional upon that definition, he should be entitled to enforce it. Thus, if the contract of sub-bailment provides that the sub-bailee should adopt certain specified security procedures and, having done so, should be under no further duty of precaution or care, the question whether he had additionally taken reasonable care of the goods should be quite irrelevant. Likewise, as in the *Mayfair* case, where the sub-contract provides for a particular itinerary or for the use of specific, known facilities in the custody of the goods, the

---

[69] Ibid, at 416. At 417 the learned judge found that Stembridge had not, in fact, been negligent. Cf. *W.L.R. Traders Ltd.* v. *B. & N. Shipping Agency Ltd.* [1955] 1 Lloyds Rep. 554, at 561; *Batty* v. *M.P.R.* [1978] 2 All E.R. 445.

compliance with these terms should be sufficient as against third-parties. For this reason, MacKenna J.'s suggestion that the owner's action against the sub-bailee is a simple action in tort is, with respect, an over-simplification.

A more recent decision endorses the theory that the sub-bailment may provide a universal definition of the sub-bailee's liability. In *Johnson, Matthey & Co. Ltd.* v. *Constantine Terminals Ltd.*[70] a consignment of silver was bailed by the plaintiffs to N and sub-bailed by N to C. Neither N nor C were in contract with the plaintiffs, the whole operation being performed on the instructions of I, a forwarding agent. The silver was stolen while on C's premises and the plaintiffs brought an action against both I and C. C were held to be protected by their contract with I. Donaldson J. held that the terms of this contract were "an essential part of the consideration for which they took possession of the silver." Their liability for its loss could only be assessed by reference to the bailment whereunder they acquired it,[71] and this transaction was a total one, negating any responsibility for the loss by theft of the goods. The plaintiffs could not pick and choose between these parts of the sub-bailment which they would rely upon and these which they wished to disregard; instead, they must take it or leave it:

> . . . the plaintiffs cannot prove the bailment upon which . . . they must rely, without referring to terms upon which the silver was received by C . . . from I . . . These terms establish (a) that C were bailees for reward but also (b) that the implied duties of such a bailee were qualified by exceptions. And . . . I really do not see how the plaintiffs can rely upon one part of the contract while ignoring the other.[72]

Again, the rule seems sensible because, in the absence of bailment, there is generally no duty to protect the goods by another person from theft;[73] any person who enters into that relationship should therefore be entitled to stipulate the terms upon which he does so, and should not be debarred from doing so by the absence of direct communication between himself and the owner. A person who has agreed to take possession *only* on the understanding that he is not liable for loss to the owner is (if such liability can be exacted) an involuntary bailee. It would be unfair to penalise him for the breach of a duty he had expressly declined to undertake.

If the terms of the sub-bailment are capable of providing a conclusive picture of the sub-bailee's relationship with the owner, it would seem to follow that the consent of the owner to the terms of the sub-bailment is immaterial to that resultant definition. This is one of the points of

---

[70] [1976] 2 Lloyd's Rep. 215, disapproving *Lee Cooper Ltd.* v. *C.H. Jeakins & Sons Ltd.* [1967] 2 Q.B. 1; [1964] 1 Lloyd's Rep. 300. Cf. *U.S. Fire Insurance Co.* v. *Paramount Fire Service Inc.* (1959) 156 N.E. (2d) 121.

[71] Cf. *Thomas Brown & Sons Ltd.* v. *Fazal Deen* (1962) 108 C.L.R. 391.

[72] [1976] 2 Lloyd's Rep. 215, at 222; cf. *Philip Morris (Australia) Ltd.* v. *The Transport Commission* [1975] Tas. S.R. 128, at 136 where Nettlefold J. treated the question as a simple one of privity of contract. This decision, by concentrating upon contractual and tortious bases of exemption, ignores completely the special character of the bailment relation: see further, p. 1000 et seq.

[73] See Chapter 5 ante; cf. Chapter 24, post.

difference between MacKenna J.'s judgment in the *Mayfair Photographic*[74] case and the judgment of Donaldson J. in *Johnson, Matthey*.[75] In the former case, MacKenna J. thought that the sub-bailee should be protected by the terms of his contract with the intermediary, provided that the intermediary enjoyed the owner's apparent authority to enter into a contract of that kind.[76] In *Johnson, Matthey* Donaldson J. took a contrary view, considering that questions of authority or consent as between owner and head bailee were immaterial:

> Consent seems to me relevant only between the bailor and head bailee. If the sub-bailment is on terms to which the bailor consented, he has no cause of action against the head bailee. If it was not, the sub-bailee is still protected, but if the bailor is damnified by the terms of the sub-bailment he has a cause of action against the head bailee.[77]

Logically, this conclusion seems correct. If the head bailee compelled the sub-bailee to accept the goods under duress, the sub-bailee's duty would be correspondingly modified regardless of whether the duress was authorised by the owner.[78] Much the same result should follow where other circumstances, such as reward or agreement, exist to delineate the status and responsibilities of the sub-bailee.

The approach advocated by Donaldson J. is a radical one, which may not meet with universal approval. The present writer submits that it is legitimate and should be sustained, provided that the terms of the secondary bailment are invoked only when they clearly amount to a proclamation of the sub-bailee's *duty* towards the owner of the goods. They should constitute the essential or indispensable terms upon which the sub-bailee took possession. They should, in Donaldson J.'s own words, represent an essential part of the sub-bailee's consideration; for not every provision in the contract of sub-bailment will necessarily be central to the separate relationship between owner and sub-bailee. In *Johnson, Matthey* the terms were of this character because they provided, in effect, that the ultimate bailees should be under no duty to the goods unless they were in their custody at the material time. This delineation of their duty was essential, and without it they would presumably not have taken possession of the silver. But in some cases the mere presence of exclusion clauses within the sub-bailment may actually be consistent with the existence of a duty towards the owner; they will not purport to exclude that duty but merely to mitigate the effects of its breach. In such a case it should by no means follow that the contract of sub-bailment provides a shield against the owner. If it does have this effect, it will be by virtue of the somewhat

---

[74] [1972] 1 Lloyd's Rep. 410.
[75] [1976] 2 Lloyd's Rep. 215.
[76] [1972] 1 Lloyd's Rep. 410, at 416.
[77] [1976] 2 Lloyd's Rep. 215, at 222.
[78] Quaere as to the position where the sub-bailment is illegal. If the owner is unable to rely upon his independent title to the goods (ante, p. 18) he would presumably be unable to enforce the sub-bailment: again, irrespective of whether the illegality was authorised or not. Cf. *Thomas Brown & Sons Ltd.* v. *Deen* (1962) 108 C.L.R. 391. Of course, the fact that he was not implicated in the illegality might justify enforcement, but this would not alter the characterisation of the sub-bailment as illegal.

different principle that an owner who has consented to the sub-bailment of his goods on particular terms is bound by that consent.[79] This is distinguishable from the notions advanced by Donaldson J. because it is conditional upon the owner's authority or consent. Again, however, it provides an illustration of the incapacity of the owner-sub-bailee relationship to be rationalised exclusively in terms of contract or of tort.

A final point to be noted about the *Johnson, Matthey* case is that Donaldson J. considered that a different result might have followed if the defendants had negligently damaged the plaintiffs' goods. His reason for this view (which was not a concluded one) was that negligent damage represents a form of liability existing independently of bailment, so that the plaintiffs would not have been forced to rely upon the bailment to recover for such damage.[80] Although this is true, it does not appear that the sub-bailee's power to delimit his duties towards the owner should be confined to those types of duty which would not have arisen without the creation of the bailment. The sub-bailee would not, in most cases, have entered into a sufficiently proximate relation with the goods to be capable of damaging them if he had not accepted them under the sub-bailment. Moreover, the existence of the sub-bailment confers advantages upon the owner even in relation to negligent damage; the sub-bailee bears the burden of proving that he was not negligent and seems to be estopped from denying the owner's title.[81] Certainly it may be rarer for a dispensation against negligent damage to form a central part of the owner-sub-bailee relationship, but this does not mean that it is impossible. Donaldson J. himself conceded that the point was one of "some nicety, to be tackled only when it arises."

B. The imposition of additional duties upon the ultimate bailee

Occasionally, the terms of the sub-bailment will cast upon the sub-bailee a greater responsibility for the safety of the goods than would exist at Common Law. These terms are clearly enforceable by the intermediate party since he will enjoy a contractual relationship with the sub-bailee. Even if the sub-bailment is gratuitous the sub-bailee will apparently be bound by his promise to the intermediary because a gratuitous bailee seems capable of enlarging his duty at Common Law.[82]

The more immediate question is whether such additional duties are directly enforceable by the owner against the sub-bailee. In certain

---

[79] This doctrine (which is discussed in more detail post, at p. 1000 et seq.) was advanced by Lord Denning M.R. in *Morris* v. *C.W. Martin & Sons Pty. Ltd.* [1966] 1 Q.B. 716, at 729-730 (cf. Diplock L.J., at 731 and Salmon L.J. at 741) and reiterated by him in *Gillespie Bros Ltd.* v. *Roy Bowles Transport Ltd.* [1973] Q.B. 400, at 412. It draws some support from the speech of Lord Sumner in *Elder, Dempter & Co. Ltd.* v. *Paterson, Zochonis & Co. Ltd.* [1924] A.C. 522, at 564 and has been recognised in several more recent decisions: see for instance, *Moukataff* v. *B.O.A.C. Ltd.* [1967] 1 Lloyd's Rep. 396, at 416-418; *B.W.I.A. Ltd.* v. *Bart* (1966) 11 W.I.R. 378; cf. *Philip Morris (Australia) Ltd.* v. *The Transport Commission* [1975] Tas. S.R. 128, where Nettlefold J. emphatically (and, it is suggested, wrongly) rejected the doctrine.

[80] [1976] 2 Lloyd's Rep. 215, at 222.

[81] Ante, p. 175. But see now s. 8, *Torts (Interference with Goods) Act* 1977.

[82] Ante, p. 313 et seq.; Carnegie (1966) 3 *Adelaide Law Review* 7, at 10-11. The head-bailee who recovers in this manner will hold the proceeds, after deduction of any personal loss, on trust for the owner: ante p. 190.

circumstances such enforcement should be possible. If the terms of a
sub-bailment can be invoked to reduce the Common Law duties that are
owed by the sub-bailee to the owner, they should be relevant to establish
a responsibility that is greater. The criterion would be whether such
additional duties were an integral part of the owner-sub-bailee relationship, and essential to its efficacy, or were merely incidental. The sub-
bailee should therefore be liable to the owner for the non-performance of
any duty which represents one of the central terms or understandings upon
which he was allowed to assume possession.

Admittedly, this definition of the sub-bailee's responsibility would be
difficult to establish if the owner himself had not seen fit to impose analogous terms in his contract with the sub-bailor. In such a case, it is the
owner's definition of his interests (and the acceptance of this definition
by the sub-bailee) which is paramount; and the owner can have little
complaint if the sub-bailee has failed to discharge a duty which he himself has not demanded. Thus, if the sub-bailee promises the sub-bailor
that he will keep the goods in a particular warehouse, and no equivalent
promise has been extracted from the sub-bailor himself, the sub-bailor
may be entitled to cast the sub-bailee in the position of an insurer but
the owner probably cannot. Even here, the position may differ if a change
in circumstance renders the promise essential to the continuing efficacy
of the relationship between owner and sub-bailee.

The corollary would be that a sub-bailee who had knowledge of extra
conditions imposed by the owner upon the head-bailment, and who had
agreed in turn with the sub-bailor to observe the same or similar conditions,
might be bound thereby. In these circumstances, provided the owner knew
of the sub-bailment and had demanded that similar conditions be imposed,
there will be an implied agreement between the parties and there is no
reason why the Courts should not enforce it. Suppose that A stores his
paintings with B, with permission to sub-bail. The contract contains a
stipulation that B will not on any account use guard-dogs, because of A's
unreasonable fear they may damage the goods; and that if B sub-bails to C
he will do so on these terms, giving him full information as to the origin of
the goods and the nature of his contract with A. C breaks the condition and,
entirely without his negligence, the guard-dogs eat the paintings. It is
suggested that C should be liable to A, either because the contract with
B has necessarily defined his scope of duty to A or because the whole
spectrum of facts reveals an implied agreement between A and C from
which C deviates at his peril. If such agreement (or mutual understanding) is not dependent upon consideration for its efficacy, it is hard to
see why it should be made dependent upon express communication, provided all the elements of consensuality are present.

There is only one case in which this sort of problem has fallen to be
seriously considered. In *B.W.I.A.* v. *Bart*[83] a football punter delivered his
coupon to the area distributor who despatched it on the defendants' aircraft
to England. The plane was delayed and the coupon arrived too late for the
plaintiff's winning entry to be accepted. The contract of carriage was between the area distributor and the defendants and most of the discussion

[83] (1966) 11 W.I.R. 378.

turned upon two points: whether a non-party to this contract could sue upon it, and whether the terms of the contract excluded liability for delay which did not physically damage the goods. Stoby, C. acknowledged that *Morris* v. *C. W. Martin & Sons Ltd.*[84] now gave the owner of goods a direct right of action against a sub-bailee, regardless of the lack of privity between them, but he held that the sub-bailee owed only the Common Law obligations of (i) protecting the goods against negligent loss or damage; (ii) refraining from converting them. He was not, therefore, liable for delay, the duty to guard against which was not something imposed upon all bailees but the mere result of a contract to which the plaintiff was not a party. However, his Lordship appeared to concede that the situation might have been different had the defendants specifically promised the plaintiff more than their Common Law duties obliged them to do. He said:

> The respondent placed considerable reliance upon *Hedley Bryne & Co. Ltd.* v. *Heller & Partners Ltd.*[85] In a very interesting argument he said that the fact of bailment brought the parties together into a relationship of proximity and that such proximity imposed a bailment obligation similar to a contractual obligation; the contractual obligation owed to Lee, he said, is to send the package within a specified time or within a reasonable time and the bailment was to do the same thing to the package.
> As I understand the submission, Counsel, relying on *Hedley Bryne,* is contending that while Bart could not sue B.W.I.A. for breach of contract, yet if B.W.I.A. undertook with Lee to send the package to London within a reasonable time and did not do so through negligence, they are liable for economic loss to Bart.
> The great weakness of this argument, if I may say so, is that B.W.I.A. did not give any undertaking to Bart. Without any undertaking whatsoever B.W.I.A. would be liable to Bart if they destroyed or lost his coupon; this is not because of a proximity relationship but from a bailor/bailee relationship . . . (But)   . B.W.I.A. had a specific contractual obligation to Lee and a common law tortious liability to Bart and no amount of proximity between B.W.I.A. and Bart can enable Bart to sue on Lee's contract.[86]

This implies that such an undertaking, even though unsupported by consideration, might have sufficed to oblige B.W.I.A. to perform within a reasonable time. But little support for this contention can be found elsewhere. The judgment of Bollers C.J. adopts the same general approach to that of Stoby C. and relies upon the same distinction between those aspects of a bailee's duty that are basic and tortious and those that are superimposed by contract. Speaking of *Morris* v. *C. W. Martin & Sons Ltd.,* he said:

> The breach of the common law duty was the failure to take reasonable care to keep the goods and not to convert them. Nowhere was it suggested that the action which the plaintiff could maintain against defendants as bailees for loss or damage to the goods included loss by delay in delivery, or consequential loss.[87]

[84] [1966] 1 Q.B. 716.
[85] [1964] 1 A.C. 465.
[86] (1966) 11 W.I.R. 378, at 398.
[87] Ibid., at 406.

Moreover, like Stoby C. he did not consider that this was a relationship of sufficient proximity for the defendants to owe the plaintiffs a duty to guard against the instant kind of economic loss.[87a] There is no suggestion that some species of direct undertaking on the part of B.W.I.A. would, of itself, have altered the position.

The question of purely economic loss, (i.e. loss which does not arise out of damage to goods) again raises the dilemma as to whether the action on an extended bailment is to be contractual or tortious in character. Even if the courts consider themselves committed to the view that a gratuitous bailee is not liable for such loss because the bailor's action sounds only in tort, this need not be so with regard to the rewarded sub-bailee. In many cases he will know that a failure to perform his duties will produce loss of profits and other expenses and should be liable, on broadly contractual principles, for such loss.

As to the broader issue, the decision in *B.W.I.A.* v. *Bart* may be criticised on two grounds. First, delay may be akin to loss or destruction, such as where the goods are perishable or where the delay otherwise renders them valueless.[88] Secondly, the whole question should have been decided by reference to the duty (if any) which the sub-bailee assumed *towards the owner.*[89] In this case, the overall undertaking by B.W.I.A. was one which vitally affected, and was clearly known to affect, someone other than the party supplying the reward. It was for the discharge of this undertaking that they were being paid and without it their consideration totally failed. If Bart were entitled to treat Lee's consideration as his own for the purposes of rendering B.W.I.A. a bailee for reward, it would seem logical that Bart should be able to sue, if not for all breaches of the sub-bailment contract, at least for those which rendered that consideration nugatory. To say that at Common Law a bailee owes no duty not to delay goods which, if delayed, are patently valueless, seems restrictive in the extreme. And yet even Stoby C., who was prepared to hold that the delay produced a fundamental breach of the consignor-carrier contract, did not think that this amounted equally to a fundamental breach of the extended bailment between Bart and B.W.I.A. Indeed, the possibility of fundamental breach in the owner/sub-bailee context was not discussed at all.[90]

[87a] But cf. now *Caltex Oil (Aust.) Pty. Ltd.* v. *The Tug "Willemstad"* (1976) 11 A.L.R. 227; *The Albazero* [1977] A.C. 774 at 846-847.

[88] For an interesting example, see *Miner* v. *Canadian Pacific Railway Co.* (1910) 15 W.L.R. 160; (1911) 18 W.L.R. 476, where a mother recovered against the defendant railroad for losses incurred through the delay of her son's corpse in transit. In this case, the mother was a contracting party, but the action was brought in negligence.

[89] As was allowed to occur, in a negative sense, in *Johnson, Matthey & Co. Ltd.* v. *Constantine Terminals Ltd.* [1976] 2 Lloyd's Rep. 215; ante, p. 820 et seq.

[90] (1966) 11 W.I.R. 378, at 402. Cf. *Thomas National Transport (Melbourne) Pty. Ltd.* v. *May & Baker (Australia) Pty. Ltd.* (1966) 115 C.L.R. 353, where it was assumed without discussion that a deviation by the intermediary from his contract with the owner automatically precluded the ultimate bailee from relying upon terms within that contract in defence to a direct action by the owner. It is questionable whether the ultimate bailee, having broken no duty personally towards the owner, should necessarily forfeit the protection of such terms solely on the strength of a breach of duty by his superior. The problem raised in this decision accentuates the necessity for separating the two relationships which an owner enjoys with ultimate bailees. Conduct which constitutes a fundamental breach of one relation-

Even if the goods are not rendered valueless there may be strong reasons for discovering a duty to avoid delay. Suppose that A, the owner of candles, requests his bailee B to engage a carrier to deliver them by express rate to England in time for the forthcoming power strike, C. who is paid accordingly by B, knows who owns the candles and why they are wanted; but his contract is solely with B. If the candles are delayed by C's negligence and arrive months after the strike is settled, the decision in *B.W.I.A.* v. *Bart* would appear to exonerate C almost completely; as against B, because B has lost nothing[90a]; as against A, because he owed him only a duty not to convert or destroy.[91] But if both owner and sub-bailee are agreed that the whole efficacy of the sub-bailment rests upon certain duties, for the discharge of which the sub-bailee is being paid, these duties should form the foundation of their relationship and should be enforceable against the sub-bailee; regardless of privity (for bailment can exist without it) or consideration (which need not issue from the owner at all).

It is therefore submitted that the duty of a sub-bailee should be determined by all the circumstances of the case: the nature of the goods, his degree of knowledge as to both the identity and intentions of the owner, the existence and rate of his reward, his normal commercial experience, etc. Obviously not every special condition in his contract with the sub-bailor will be fundamental to his relationship with the owner; even a fundamental breach vis-à-vis the former will not necessarily amount to one vis-à-vis the latter, and where certain obligations are commonly fundamental different degrees of conduct may be required before each is fundamentally breached. But if, by common consent and mutual understanding, certain portions of the sub-bailment contract are made central to the owner/sub-bailee relationship as well, these elements should not be ignored, merely because they originated in a contract, in assessing the full scope of the sub-bailee's obligations towards the owner. The duties of a bailee at Common Law are, ex hypothesi, those which he has undertaken or agreed to assume; they cannot be definitively enumerated in advance for every case. The courts should not be straitened by the presence of a contract of sub-bailment into assuming that the duties and thereunder cannot conscionably be owed by the sub-bailee elsewhere.

It must be conceded that there is little present authority for this approach. The courts, chary of incursions upon the doctrine of privity of contract, have tended to segregate the contractual and tortious aspects of bailment with a resultant obscuring of the full extent of the concept of privity of bailment. The fact that bailment is a relationship needing neither

---

ship will not necessarily have the same effect upon the other. The foregoing decision does, however, provide some tenuous recognition of the fact that concepts of deviation or fundamental breach may operate as between owner and sub-bailee. This principle is clearly of importance if the sub-bailee can claim the protection of exclusion clauses, either by virtue of a sub-bailment on terms (as in *Morris* v. *C.W. Martin & Sons Ltd.* [1966] 1 Q.B. 716, 729-730) or by virtue of the definition of his responsibility as contained in the sub-bailment contract (as in *Johnson, Matthey & Co. Ltd.* v. *Constantine Terminals Ltd.* [1976] 2 Lloyd's Rep. 215, at 222). See further Carnegie (1966) 3 *Adelaide Law Review* 7, at 11.

[90a] This assumes that there is no continuing relationship of bailor and bailee between B and C; ante, p. 788.

[91] Cf. *The Albazero* [1976] 3 All E.R. 129; ante, p. 186 (Chapter 4).

consideration nor direct agreement may supply the key to this hitherto unexplored province of the law, but it is a key that has become mislaid among the crevices of a restrictive modern compartmentalisation of the forms of action.

A possible model for future development may, however, be found in a recent decision of Judge Tudor Evans, Q.C. in the English Commercial Court. It seems to have been long accepted that a common carrier may be liable as such even though his reward did not emanate from the consignee or other owner but from a third party.[92] In *Eastman Chemical International A.G.* v. *N.M.T. Trading Ltd.*[93] this principle was applied (without discussion) so as to render a quasi-bailee directly liable to the consignor for breach of the strict liability duties of a common carrier. The quasi-bailee had no contract with the consignor and was employed (and rewarded) throughout by an intermediary, who never took possession of the goods. The question was not argued and the status of the defendant as a common carrier seems to have been decided entirely by default. But by recognising the "status" quality of a constructive bailee's obligation it provides a valuable precedent; for it might enable the owner under an ordinary contract of carriage to adduce general evidence of the degree and nature of the bailee's undertaking (albeit expressed only to the intermediary) as a foundation for the synthesis of a general duty owed to non-contracting parties.

Taken to its logical extreme, the implication of additional duties within an extended bailment could produce a system of transmissible covenants not dissimilar to those evolved in consumer-manufacturer contests under American law.[94] Whenever a particular term was deemed to be central to the relationship between the parties at each extremity of an extended bailment, or essential to its efficacy, that term could be implied. Normally, the sub-bailee would carry the burden of the covenant. Thus, it might be central to the relationship between the owner and a sub-bailee for work and labour that the sub-bailee should warrant the fitness of his materials or the ability of his labour to produce a required result; or it might be essential to the relationship between a lender and a sub-borrower that the sub-borrower should observe the limits imposed upon his use of the chattel under the sub-loan.[95] However, there is no reason why the burden of the undertaking should not operate in a reverse direction and be imposed upon the owner. For example, it may be possible to extend the warranty of fitness or safety, implied against a lessor of goods or a consignor by common carrier, in favour of any sub-carrier or sub-lessee.[96] Of course, implications of this kind would not be made automatically, but only when

---

[92] Paton, *Bailment in the Common Law*, p. 239; ante, p. 555.
[93] [1972] 2 Lloyd's Rep. 25.
[94] See, for instance, *Escola* v. *Coca-Cola Bottling Co. of Fresno* (1944) 150 Pac. (2d) 436; *Henningsen* v. *Bloomfield Motors Inc.* (1960) 161 A. (2d) 69; 32 N.J. 358; *Greenman* v. *Yuba Power Products Inc.* (1963) 377 P. (2d) 897; 59 Col. (2d) 57; Greig, *Sale of Goods*, pp. 257-258.
[95] Cf. *Chapman* v. *Robinson and Ferguson* (1969) 71 W.W.R. 515 (ante, p. 000) where the opportunity to imply such a term was missed and the problem was evaded by means of a contractual fiction.
[96] For an illustration of this principle in a leasing context, see *Lovely* v. *Burroughs Corporation* (1974) 527 P. (2d) 557; ante p. 48.

they are essential, on the common understanding of the parties, to the efficacy of the extended relationship. The principles of implication should (like the terms themselves) be broadly similar to those which would obtain under a contractual relationship.[97]

To some extent, it is already possible to discern the transmission of covenants from intermediate to ultimate bailee. Thus, it has been generally assumed that an owner who bails on certain terms and consents to a sub-bailment upon similar terms (or who bails on no additional terms but agrees to their inclusion within the sub-bailment) may be bound by the terms of the subsidiary relationship although they are not the product of any contract between himself and the sub-bailee.[98] Similarly, a bailee may create a valid lien against the owner by depositing the goods, with the owner's actual or apparent authority, in the possession of a sub-bailee for the performance of work and labour; again, the owner may be bound by the lien although there is no contract between him and the sub-bailee.[99] Finally, it has never been expressly decided that a covenant between the owner of goods and a bailee cannot run in favour of that bailee against any subsequent purchaser who takes with actual notice of the covenant.[1] Clearly this is a distinguishable question, but its openness does suggest the continued possibility that undertakings may be binding between bailor and bailee although there has been neither a direct exchange of promises nor a supporting contract between them.

It is impossible to rationalise the foregoing characteristics of an extended bailment relationship exclusively in terms of contract or of tort. There is no contract between the parties and no tortious remedy or defence is capable of explaining satisfactorily the immunity of the sub-bailee on terms or the lienee's rights of tenure under an extended lien.[2] The difficulty in this regard lies not in establishing that bailment is a separate legal relation but in deciding whether its incidents and character should be closer to those which arise in contract or in tort. It is suggested that although the fundamental duties are clearly expressible in terms of tortious liability, the approximate model for any additional duties is contract rather than tort.

---

[97] An interesting modern discussion of the principles of implication in contracts is to be found in Lord Pearson's speech in *Trollope & Colls Ltd.* v. *N.W. Metropolitan Regional Hospital Board* [1973] 1 W.L.R. 601, at 609; and in the decision of the House of Lords in *Liverpool City Council* v. *Irwin* [1976] 2 All E.R. 39.

[98] This authority is listed at p. 821, at n. 79, and discussed in more detail post, p. 1000 et seq. Note also the somewhat different principle enunciated by Donaldson J. in *Johnson, Matthey & Co. Ltd.* v. *Constantine Terminals Ltd.* [1976] 2 Lloyd's Rep. 215, at 222; ante, p. 819.

[99] See, for instance, *Tappenden* v. *Artus* [1964] 2 Q.B. 185; *Protean Enterprises (Newmarket) Pty Ltd.* v. *Randall* [1975] V.R. 327; *K. Chellaram & Sons (London) Ltd.* v. *Butlers Warehousing & Distribution* [1977] 2 Lloyd's Rep. 192. post, p. 1008.

[1] See *Port Line Ltd.* v. *Ben Line Steamers Ltd.* [1958] 2 Q.B. 146, at 163-164; discussed more fully post, p. 973 et seq.

[2] The sub-bailee's immunity has occasionally been described as an illustration of the defence volenti non fit injuria (see post, p. 1000 et seq.) but this characterisation seems inexact because the latter defence may require knowledge of the circumstances giving rise to the risk: see, on this point, *Phillip Morris (Australia) Ltd.* v. *The Transport Commission* [1975] Tas. S.R. 128, following *Morrison* v. *Union Steamship Co. of New Zealand Ltd.* [1964] N.Z.L.R. 468.

The closest analogy from the field of non-contractual bailment is the gratuitous deposit or loan. The belief that such bailments are a form of contract has long been reviled as an anachronism, with the result that the responsibilities of the parties are assumed to rest solely and exclusively in tort.[3] But this is an oversimplification. It leaves unexplained certain cases which recognise the ability of the parties to vary their primary obligations and to undertake heavier duties than the law of tort would impose. Thus a gratuitous bailee may be guilty of deviation if he radically departs from an agreed route or place of custody, and may be bound by a promise to exercise greater care than would otherwise have been incumbent on him.[4] Admittedly, most of the decisions in point date from the time of the contract-fallacy, but it does not follow that a modern court would willingly resile from them. One judge at least has recently supported the idea that superimposed promises issuing from a gratuitous bailee should, once possession has been taken, be held binding. Bray C.J. was in favour of attaining this result by means of the theory that such bailments are, despite the lack of consideration, contracts.[5] Since this analysis has been widely contested elsewhere, it may be preferable to explain the anomaly (if it exists) by reference to the peculiar character of bailment. This may be one of the dimensions of that relationship which cannot be explained purely in terms of other forms of action. Since consent and not consideration is the key, a consensual variation of the Common Law duty may be acceptable under a bailment while being ineffective elsewhere. The duty owed by the bailee is the duty he voluntarily undertakes, whether or not he is rewarded for doing so.

The relevance of this to extended bailments is not immediately clear, because the gratuitous bailment contains one element that the owner/sub-bailee relationship lacks. This may be termed privity of agreement. More specifically, the gratuitous bailee will have been in direct communication with the bailor and, through such communication, may have purported to modify his normal obligations. But in other respects the extended bailment seems closer to a contractual relationship than the gratuitous deposit or loan. In most cases, the sub-bailee will receive a consideration for his services; the parties will possess complementary commercial interests and an identity of intention.[6] It would be remarkable if a sub-bailee for reward, who has so much in common both with the gratuitous and the contractual bailee, were unable to increase his obligations towards the owner by agreement, undertaking or mutual understanding, in cases where it is equitable and commercially desirable that he should do so. If he can reduce his liability in this direction he should be able to augment it. The methods of establishing such variation may be borrowed, broadly from the law of contract; but this does not predicate a wholesale assimilation between that concept and bailment.

---

[3] Ante, p. 313 et seq.; *Walker* v. *Watson* [1974] 2 N.Z.L.R. 175.

[4] Ibid.; (1966) 3 *Adelaide Law Review* 7, at 10-11.

[5] *Roufos* v. *Brewster and Brewster* [1971] 2 S.A.S.R. 218, at 223-224.

[6] Other questions may also pivot upon whether the relationship is tortious or quasi-contractual: for instance, whether contributory negligence or volenti non fit injuria are available as a defence. See generally ante, p. 55 et seq.

VIII. THE LIABILITY OF THE INTERMEDIARY

Liability in this context varies according to two principal factors: whether the intermediary has received possession, and whether the subsidiary bailment is authorised.

A. The substitutional bailment

If the intermediate party under a substitutional bailment[7] properly delivers possession to a secondary bailee, his duty is discharged and he is under no further liability for the goods.[8] The disposition must be authorised by the principal bailor and the secondary bailee must be chosen with reasonable care.[9] If unauthorised, the delegation amounts to a deviation by the intermediary and renders him liable for all ensuing losses.[10] He will probably also be guilty of conversion.[11]

B. The sub-bailment

The essence of a true sub-bailment is the continuation of the liability of the sub-bailor throughout the subsidiary disposition.[12] The measure of that liability is, however, dependent upon the legitimacy of the sub-bailment.

An unauthorised sub-bailment constitutes a deviation. The intermediary forfeits his ordinary status as a bailee and becomes liable for all loss or injury suffered as a result of the deviation. This rule is illustrated by numerous decisions[13] and is discussed more fully within the appropriate chapters.[14] Again, the sub-bailor will probably be guilty of conversion.[15]

If the sub-bailment is authorised, the intermediate bailee will be liable only for losses or injuries which result from a breach of duty on the part of the ultimate bailee. Some decisions go so far as to suggest that, without personal negligence, there can be no liability on the part of the prior bailee.[16] However, the better view is undoubtedly that the first bailee,

---

[7] Ante, p. 788.

[8] *Roufos* v. *Brewster and Brewster* [1971] 2 S.A.S.R. 218; ante, p. 789; *E.A. Marr (Contracting) Pty. Ltd.* v. *Broken Hill Pty. Ltd.* [1970] 3 N.S.W.L.R. 306; ante, p. 805; cf. *Gallaher Ltd.* v. *B.R.S. Ltd.* [1974] 2 Lloyd's Rep. 440 and other recent cases, ante, p. 790.

[9] Cf. *Garnham, Harris & Elton Ltd.* v. *Alfred W. Ellis Ltd.* [1967] 2 Lloyd's Rep. 22; *James Buchanan & Co. Ltd.* v. *Hay's Transport Services Ltd.* [1972] 2 Lloyd's Rep. 535 (reasonable care extends to the premises as well as to the honesty of the sub-bailee). If a particular secondary bailee is selected by the principal bailor, the lack of discretion on the part of the intermediary will normally relieve him of any duty to inquire into the bona fides of the party thus chosen.

[10] Ante, pp. 473, 570-574.

[11] Ante, p. 127.

[12] Ante, p. 786.

[13] E.g. *Lilley* v. *Doubleday* (1881) 7 Q.B.D. 510; *Edwards* v. *Newland & Co.* [1950] 2 K.B. 534; *Morgan* v. *Maurer & Sons* (1964) 30 Ir. Jur. Rep. 31; cf. *Barbour and Proude* v. *Doucette* [1942] 2 D.L.R. 624 (ante, p. 474).

[14] Ante, p. 514, et seq; post; p. 930 et seq.

[15] But note that this question was explicitly left open by Grove and Lindley JJ. in *Lilley* v. *Doubleday* (ante); and cf. *Garnham, Harris & Elton Ltd.* v. *Alfred W. Ellis Ltd.* [1967] 2 Lloyd's Rep. 22.

[16] *E.A. Marr (Contracting) Pty. Ltd.* v. *Broken Hill Pty. Ltd.* [1970] 3 N.S.W.L.R. 306, at 312; *James Buchanan & Co. Ltd.* v. *Hay's Transport Services Ltd.* ante, at 543 (where an inquiry as to personal fault was necessary for the purposes of apportionment between principal and secondary bailee); and cf. *Eastman Chemical International A.G.* v. *N.M.T. Trading Ltd.* [1912] 2 Lloyd's Rep. 25. The learned judge in *Marr's* case cited *Edwards* v. *Newland & Co.* ante, at 1081, in support, but this does not seem to sustain the proposition stated.

having undertaken responsibility for the performance of a task, remains answerable for the manner in which that task is executed. This view has been adopted in decisions where the duty was delegated by a bailee to his servant[17] and by a bailee to an independent contractor.[18] In the latter decision, Lord Pearson explained the rule as follows:

> The bailor could not reasonably be expected to be content with a contractual promise of the bailee to take proper care of the goods or engage a competent contractor to do so. If that were the contractual promise, then in the event of default by a competent contractor duly selected by the bailee, the bailor would have no remedy against the bailee and would have to rely on the possibility of an action of tort against the contractor. To give business efficacy to the contract, the bailee's implied promise should be that he will himself or through his servants or agents take proper care of the goods.[19]

If anything, this reasoning is stronger in the context of a sub-bailment, where the intermediate party is not merely delegating performance but is allowing the goods to leave his possession. It is now recognised that the bailee who exercises an authority to sub-bail remains accountable for the goods while they are in the possession of the sub-bailee. To absolve himself, he must show that the relevant harm did not result from a want of care on his own part, or on the part of the sub-bailee and his servants or agents.[20] As counsel aptly remarked in *Morris* v. *C. W. Martin & Sons, Ltd.*,[21] "a master cannot delegate responsibility, he can delegate performance". The same is true, in general circumstances, of the relationship between prior and succeeding bailees.

The distinction between a sub-bailment and a substitutional bailment has already been discussed.[22] Whether the intermediate bailee ceases to be liable upon a transfer of the goods, or remains liable for the defaults of the secondary bailee, is a question of fact to be answered from the intention of the parties and the circumstances of the agreement. When the intermediate bailee is in business to provide a service for his customers (such as the operation of a dry-cleaning business or an electrical repair shop),

---

[17] *Morris* v. *C.W. Martin & Sons Ltd.* ante; *Mendelssohn* v. *Normand Ltd.* [1970] 1 Q.B. 177.

[18] *B.R.S. Ltd.* v. *Arthur V. Crutchley & Co. Ltd.* [1968] 1 All E.R. 811.

[19] Ibid, at 820, citing *Adams (Durham) Ltd.* v. *Trust Houses Ltd.* [1960] 1 Lloyd's Rep. 380, at 386 per Fenton Atkinson Q.C. See also Sachs L.J. [1968] 1 All E.R., 811, at 821.

[20] *Hobbs* v. *Petersham Transport Co. Pty. Ltd.* [1971] 45 A.L.J.R. 356, at 359, 364-365; *Philip Morris (Australia) Ltd.* v. *The Transport Commission* [1975] Tas. S.R. 128, at 131; *Thomas National Transport (Melbourne) Pty. Ltd.* v. *May & Baker (Australia) Pty. Ltd.* [1966] 115 C.L.R. 353; *Gilchrist, Watt & Sanderson Pty. Ltd.* v. *York Products Pty. Ltd.* [1970] 3 All E.R. 825; *Arcweld Constructions Pty. Ltd.* v. *Smith,* Unrep., 17th September 1968 (Vic. Sup. Ct.: McInerney, J.); *Colverd & Co. Ltd.* v. *Anglo Overseas Transport Co. Ltd.* [1961] 2 Lloyd's Rep. 352, at 263; *Charles Davis (Metal Brokers) Ltd.* v. *Gilyott & Scott, Ltd.* [1975] 2 Lloyd's Rep. 422; *Doolan* v. *Midland Ry. Co.* (1877) 2 App. Cas. 792; *John* v. *Bacon* (1870) L.R. 5 C.P. 437; *Machu* v. *L. & S.W. Ry. Co.* (1848) 2 Ex. 415; *Wilson* v. *New Zealand Express Co. Ltd.* (No. 2) [1924] N.Z.L.R. 465; *(No. 3)* [1924] N.Z.L.R. 890; *Joseph Abrams Ltd.* v. *Coady and Vint* (1962) 37 D.L.R. (2d) 587, at 590-591; *A.C. McEachern Ltd.* v. *McKenzie Barge & Marine Ways Ltd.* (1963) 40 D.L.R. (2d) 444; *Riverstone Meat Co. Pty. Ltd.* v. *Lancashire Shipping Co. Ltd.* [1961] A.C. 807, at 865-866.

[21] [1966] 1 Q.B. 716, at 719 (E. Eveleigh Q.C.).

[22] Ante, p. 789.

and normally performs that service by engaging sub-contractors, the interests of his customers and the demands of business efficacy will generally dictate that he should answer for the faults of such sub-contractors. The absence of a contract between the customer and the sub-contractor, and the fact that the principal bailee will receive his reward directly from the customer, militate in favour of this conclusion. He will accordingly be liable for any negligently occasioned injury to the goods, or for any conversion, on the part of the subsidiary bailee or his servants or agents;[23] in addition, he must answer for any failure on the part of the sub-contractor to carry out the work contracted for, and (presumably) for any deviation from the authorised terms of the sub-bailment which results in damage or loss.

In exceptional cases, however, the principal contractor will be liable for the goods only when they are immediately in his possession. Thus, a carrier or forwarding agent may contract to carry a consignment of goods for a part of a given journey and to arrange a substitute carrier for the remaining distance on the terms that he, the principal carrier, should cease to be liable for the goods upon delivery to the sub-contractor.[24] Again, a furrier to whom a stole is delivered for cleaning, but who explains to the customer that he does not provide this service and offers to send the garment on to someone who does, may be deemed to be no more than a go-between with no responsibility for the manner in which the task of cleaning is performed; although if he exacts an overall fee from the customer and passes part of this on to the cleaner, there may well be room for the inference that he is contracting as a principal and is answerable for the latter's defaults.[25]

C. The quasi-bailment

The essence of a quasi-bailment is that the intermediate party does not obtain possession of the goods but merely arranges for possession to be taken by a third party.[26] Since he does not obtain possession, he would appear to lack the one element which is commonly agreed to be necessary to the existence of a bailment between himself and the owner, and would therefore seem incapable of becoming a bailee.[27] Furthermore, if he is not

---

[23] Assuming, generally, that the fault is one for which the sub-contractor himself would be answerable: in other words, that the servant stole the goods in the course of his employment or whilst in the process of discharging a duty delegated to him, by the sub-contractor, in respect of the goods.

[24] L.R. Harris (Harella) Ltd. v. Continental Express Ltd. [1961] 1 Lloyd's Rep. 251 (ante, p. 269). Roufos v. Brewster and Brewster [1971] 2 S.A.S.R. 218 (ante, p. 271) is not a dissimilar case.

[25] Cf. Morris v. C.W. Martin & Sons Ltd. [1966] 1 Q.B. 716, where the facts were broadly as stated but the liability of the principal bailee did not arise for decision. However, Lord Denning M.R. did remark at 728 that the principal bailee could have recovered the quantum of loss from the sub-bailees under the sub-bailment, which supports a continuing rather than oscillating liability on the part of the principal bailee. See further Charles Davis (Metal Brokers) Ltd. v. Gilyott & Scott Ltd. [1975] 2 Lloyd's Rep. 442; post, p. 836.

[26] Ante, p. 791. The third-party will be an independent contractor and it is misleading to regard his possession as that of his employer: however, a number of decisions do support this conclusion: see ante, p. 245.

[27] See per Windeyer J. in Hobbs v. Petersham Transport Co. Pty. Ltd. [1971] 45 A.L.J.R. 356, at 363: "But a person who undertakes that he will carry goods is not a bailee of them unless they be actually delivered to and received by him".

a bailee he would appear to be unable to enter into a bailment with the third party, and is thus disqualified from occupying the role of bailor towards him. There is no authority for the proposition that a person who has neither transferred his own possession in goods to another, nor is the owner of those goods, can be his bailor. It would seem to follow that both his liability to the owner of the goods and his rights of action against the quasi- or non-contractual bailee are exclusively contractual, and cannot be founded upon the principles of bailment. However, authority is not consistent on this question and the law is correspondingly obscure.

1. *Unauthorised delegation of possession*: The first problem likely to arise in this context concerns a party who has agreed to take possession of the owner's goods but wrongfully procures someone else to discharge this duty and never assumes possession of the goods in person. The goods are then stolen or damaged while in the third party's possession and the owner wishes to make the intermediate party accountable for the loss. What are the principles upon which such accountability can be founded?

The simple answer is that the intermediary is guilty of a breach of contract and will be liable on contractual principles for the resultant loss. To some extent, this was the approach adopted in *Lilley* v. *Doubleday*.[28] In that case, the defendant had originally taken possession of the plaintiff's goods before breaking an express term of the agreement and moving them elsewhere; the Court seems to have decided the question of liability on principles of bailment but to have regarded the assessment of damages as something to be determined on established principles of contract. On this approach, the defendant was held accountable for all losses ensuing from his breach of the agreement, irrespective of default on his part: and some reservations were entertained before the Court reached the conclusion that the proper contractual measure of damages was the full value of the goods.

In fact, *Lilley* v. *Doubleday* was an undoubted case of bailment and the measure of damages, like the fact of liability itself, could have been decided equally satisfactorily on the basis of a liability peculiar to all bailees, both contractual and non-contractual. A bailee (i.e. a party who has knowingly and voluntarily assumed possession of another's goods) becomes an insurer of those goods if he transfers possession to a third party without the permission of the owner. The fact that this brand of liability is not essentially contractual may be demonstrated by reference to the gratuitous bailment. Where A deposits his goods with B for no reward, and B is expressly or impliedly forbidden to delegate the task of safekeeping, any attempt by B to break this prohibition will make him an insurer of the goods. This result will follow although on a modern analysis of the gratuitous bailment there is no contract under which he could be liable to A.

The crucial question arises when the party who is alleged to have deviated from the bailment never assumes possession of the goods from first to last. Again, he may be liable for breach of contract, but this remedy

For authority to the effect that forwarding agents are not, in ordinary circumstances, bailees, see post, p. 836.

---

[28] (1881) 7 Q.B.D. 510; ante, p. 473.

is imperfect for two reasons: first, because it is by no means clear that the level of damages obtainable in such an action is necessarily as extensive as the liability imposed upon a deviating bailee; secondly, because such a remedy would be inappropriate if the intended bailee were unrewarded. Can he, instead, be made liable as a bailee?

What little authority there is suggests that he may. Thus, in *Edwards* v. *Newland & Co.*[29] the defendant was held to become an insurer of the plaintiff's goods when he arranged for them to be warehoused by a third party, having never taken possession of the goods in person but having represented throughout to the plaintiff that the goods were in his hands. The Court of Appeal invoked two decisions relating to unauthorised sub-bailment (one of them *Lilley* v. *Doubleday*[30] itself) to justify imposing upon the defendant the strict responsibility of a deviating bailee.[31] No significance appears to have been attached to the fact that (unlike the bailees in all the preceding cases) the defendant had never been in possession.[32]

A comparable conclusion was reached by the High Court of Australia in *Thomas National Transport (Melbourne) Pty. Ltd.* v. *May & Baker (Australia) Pty. Ltd.*[33] Here, the delegation to Pay (a sub-contractor) was originally legitimate but involved the intermediate carriers in a breach of contract when Pay failed to deliver the goods for storage in their depot overnight. Most of the discussion in this case centred around the application of the intermediaries' exclusion clauses, but both McTiernan, Taylor and Owen, JJJ, (for the majority) and Windeyer J. (who dissented on the construction of the relevant clauses) relied both upon *Lilley* v. *Doubleday* and the principles of contract to establish the intermediaries' original liability, even though they were never technically in possession and were therefore, perhaps, not bailees.[34]

> . . . T.N.T. cannot protect itself by seeking to rely upon the exemption clauses and . . . must be held liable for the damage which occurred whether or not it can be said to have resulted from lack of care or to have been directly caused by T.N.T's. unauthorised departure from the terms of the contract.[35]

---

[29] [1950] 2 K.B. 534; ante, p. 473.
[30] (1881) 7 Q.B.D. 510.
[31] The other decision was *Davies* v. *Collins* [1945] 1 All E.R. 247.
[32] Note that *Edwards* v. *Newland & Co.* (ante) seems to have been accepted as correct by Windeyer J. in *Hobbs* v. *Petersham Transport Co. Pty. Ltd.* (ante) at 362, who described both *Edwards* v. *Newland* and *Lilley* v. *Doubleday* (ante) as "cases of sub-bailment by a bailee": sed quaere as to the former.
[33] (1966) 115 C.L.R. 353; post, p. 925.
[34] But cf. Windeyer J. ibid.
[35] Ibid., at 366; cf. Windeyer J. at 388. Both of the foregoing cases should be contrasted with *Garnham, Harris & Elton Ltd.* v. *Alfred W. Ellis (Transport) Ltd.* [1967] 2 Lloyd's Rep. 22, where, again, the defendants wrongfully delegated without acquiring possession. Paull J. confined his attention to three issues (whether there had been authority to delegate, whether the defendants were guilty of conversion, and whether their standard trading conditions protected them) and did not venture any opinion as to the burden of proof or as to whether the defendants were liable qua bailees (although he did cite in this context the decision in *Morris* v. *C.W. Martin & Sons Ltd.* [1966] 1 Q.B. 716). Note, moreover, that the defendants *had* been put in possession of the delivery order: thus, their liability in the present case could be viewed alternatively as a simple breach of contract or as a deviation from the bailment of the delivery order, from which the loss of the goods was the direct and natural consequence.

The results produced by these two decisions are reasonable, and the decisions themselves are of high authority. It is submitted that they justify an extension of the conventional rules of bailment, so as to impose a bailee's liability upon any party who has agreed to take possession of another's goods but has failed, through his own default, to do so. In such a case, an agreement for a bailment should be as good as a bailment; and a party who misleads the owner of goods into thinking that he will take, or has taken, possession of these goods should not be allowed to rely upon his own wrongdoing (i.e. his failure to assume possession) to evade the traditional duties of a bailee. One of these duties is to refrain from parting with the goods unless authorised to do so. A breach of this duty should be followed by strict liability for succeeding losses, irrespective of whether the defendant has assumed a prior possession.[36]

2. *Authorised delegation of possession*: Most forwarding agents, and other contracting parties whose business consists in arranging for the storage or transportation of goods, will insert in their agreement a power to discharge their duty by means of sub-contractors. Indeed, the contract may specifically contemplate that only third-party performers are to take possession of the goods: in such a case, the immediate contractor who assumes possession personally may be guilty of a breach of contract or liable as upon a deviation.

Assuming that a power to delegate can be inferred from the agreement, two questions then arise: is the primary contracting party answerable for the defaults of his sub-contractor, and if so, what is the basis of his liability—contract or bailment? Clearly there is no *automatic* liability for misadventures which occur to the goods while they are in the hands of the sub-contractor, because the primary contractor has broken neither contract nor bailment in allowing them so to reside. In the absence of a contract to contrary effect, his responsibility comes into operation only (if at all) when the sub-contractor is in breach of his own duties as an extended or constructive bailee.

The first question may be answered in much the same way as that relating to the intermediate party under a normal sub-bailment.[37] In order to escape liability, the quasi-bailor must show that he entered into the relationship with the owner not as a principal but as an agent for the ultimate parties. If his task is the purely ministerial one of arranging for a service to be undertaken, or of putting the owner and the third party in contact with one another, his responsibility should cease upon delivery of the goods to a competent and carefully selected 'sub-contractor'. Broadly, the distinction is between a party who positively undertakes to secure the performance of a given service for the owner, albeit with a discretion to delegate, and a party who merely undertakes to find someone to perform it, or to arrange that it shall be performed.[38] But it is

---

[36] Quaere whether a mere failure to take possession at the appointed time should not likewise be accounted a deviation: cf. *Quiggin v. Duff* (1836) 1 M. & W. 174, and p. 831, n. 27, ante.
[37] Ante, p. 829.
[38] Hill, *Freight Forwarders*, p. 159; and see Proksch [1973] A.B.L.R. 266, at 267. The distinction is illustrated by a comparison of *Colverd & Co. Ltd. v. Anglo-Overseas Transport Co. Ltd.* [1961] 2 Lloyd's Rep. 352 with *L. R. Harris*

difficult to state the principles of differentiation with any exactitude; the classification of individual agreements will depend upon the terms of that agreement, the intention that can be inferred from it and the conduct (where appropriate) by which it is evidenced. When there is a positive commitment by the first bailee that the service will be performed, "business efficacy"[39] clearly demands that he should be liable for non-existent or defective performance. When such a commitment is lacking, and the intermediate party's function is purely introductory, his duty to the bailor will normally be discharged upon his discovering and engaging a reliable carrier.[40] Certainly, this result should follow when the result of the intermediary's exertions is the formation of a contract between the owner and the ultimate bailee. The intermediary's responsibilities are adequately enforced by means of his contract of agency and the defaults of the secondary party may be remediable in contract, bailment or tort. Whether the intermediary should be exonerated from further liability *without* the existence of such a contract is a more unsettled question, the answer to which can only be discovered by close attention to the character of his original undertaking. Theoretically, there is no reason why continuing liability for the faults of a sub-contractor and the existence of a contract between the owner and the sub-contractor should be exclusive alternatives;[41] conversely, it may be possible to have neither, although the circumstances in which this conclusion would be justified must admittedly be rare.

Much of the difficulty in this area concerns the responsibility of forwarding-agents for the defaults of persons whom they engage to carry or to warehouse goods. In principle, the case of the forwarding-agent is no different from that of any other intervening party. His profession alone does not confer any special obligations or immunities and he is capable of contracting upon either of the aforementioned bases. However, Professor Hill has argued that a blanket liability should, in the present context, represent the exception rather than the rule:

> Although Lord Pearson is probably correct in stating that warehouse keepers and certain other bailees should be subject to an implied promise to take proper care of the goods through their "servants and agents", from the very nature of the forwarding-trade it is far from essential for such an implied promise to be read into a forwarding contract.[42]

As a generalisation, this seems reasonable. The fundamental inquiry must focus upon what the intermediate party has promised, and it is likely that in a majority of cases the forwarding agent will have promised

---

(Harella) Ltd. v. *Continental Express Ltd.* [1961] 1 Lloyd's Rep. 251 (ante, p. 266 et seq.); see also *W.L.R. Traders (London) Ltd.* v. *B. & N. Shipping Agency Ltd.* [1955] 1 Lloyd's Rep. 554 and post p. 836 et seq.

---

[39] Per Lord Pearson in the *Crutchley* case [1968] 1 All E.R. 811, at 820; ante p. 830.
[40] All of the relevant cases concern contracts of carriage: in theory, of course, the above principles can apply to any variety of bailment.
[41] Cf. *Charles Davis (Metal Brokers) Ltd.* v. Gilyott & Scott Ltd. [1975] 2 Lloyd's Rep. 422, where this assumption seems to have been justified: and see further Proksch [1973] A.B.L.R. 266, at 267.
[42] Hill, op. cit., p. 159.

merely to act as a go-between for the owner and to arrange with a third party for the carriage of his goods.[43] Of course, such arrangements must be effected bona fide, with the proper degree of prudence and in conformity with the owner's instructions. There remains a substantial difference between an undertaking of this kind and an overall guarantee that, irrespective of whether they are in the forwarder's possession or someone else's, the goods always will be handled and guarded with reasonable care.

Of course, the forwarding-agent may enter into a transaction which represents a compound of the foregoing elements. Thus, he may undertake part of the work personally while merely promising to make arrangements for the performance of the remainder. In such a case, his liability for default or non-performance may be limited to the period of his personal undertaking and in relation to the residual period he may disappear from the picture completely.[44]

The fact remains that many defendants who have merely 'farmed out' carrying work to selected contractors have been held liable as principals vis-à-vis both owner and carrier, and have failed to satisfy the requirements of being a mere agent inter partes. This conclusion may be easier to draw, perhaps, when the defendant has received possession of the goods prior to the misadventure,[45] because an earlier, immediate physical control suggests a service and a responsibility that are continuing until the goods are re-delivered to their owner.[46] Two recent decisions illustrate the process of differentiation between a primary contracting party and a mere agent or procurer of transportation.

In *Charles Davies (Metal Brokers) Ltd.* v. *Gilyott & Scott, Ltd.*[47] the first defendant warehousemen were in possession of a quantity of tin belonging to the plaintiffs. The plaintiffs sold the tin and asked the first defendants to "deliver" it to London, requesting that "All charges for

---

[43] Cases illustrative of this conclusion include *Marston Excelsior Ltd.* v. *Arbuckle Smith & Co. Ltd.* [1971] 2 Lloyd's Rep. 306; *Hair & Skin Trading Co. Ltd.* v. *Norman Airfreight Carriers Ltd.* [1974] 1 Lloyd's Rep. 443. At p. 445 of the latter decision, Bean J. cited with approval the classic statement of the forwarder's conventional position by Rowlatt J. in *Jones* v. *European and General Express Co. Ltd.* (1920) 4 Lloyd's L. Rep. 127: "It must be clearly understood that a forwarding agent is not a carrier; he does not obtain the possession of the goods; he does not undertake the delivery of them at the other end, unless prevented by some expected cause of loss or something which affords an excuse. All that he does is to act as agent for the owner of the goods, to make arrangements with the people who do carry . . . steamships, railways and so on . . . and to make arrangements, so far as they are necessary, for the intermediate steps between the ship and the rail, the Customs, or anything else".

[44] As in *L.R. Harris (Harella) Ltd.* v. *Continental Express Ltd.* [1961] 1 Lloyd's Rep, 251; see *Hill* op. cit.; Proksch [1973] A.B.L.R. 266, at 267.

[45] Ante, p. 789.

[46] Of course, it is impossible to state this feature dogmatically, as the preceding footnote shows: but a "personalised service" is perhaps more likely when there has been a "personal" possession.

[47] [1975] 2 Lloyd's Rep. 422. See also *Eastman Chemical International A.G.* v. *N.M.T. Trading Ltd.* [1972] 1 Lloyd's Rep. 25; *E.M.I. (New Zealand) Ltd.* v. *W. N. Holyman & Sons Pty. Ltd.* [1976] 2 N.Z.L.R. 567. In the latter case it was held that the forwarding agent owes no duty to supervise the actions of his carriers, but that where he undertakes part of the carriage himself and cannot identify the precise time of theft he must discharge the burden of proving that he took all reasonable precautions Cf. p. 809, ante.

this delivery are to be rendered to us". The first defendants engaged the second defendant carriers to effect the delivery and the tin was stolen in transit through the negligence of the second defendant's driver. Donaldson J. held that the first defendants undertook the task of carriage as principals and were answerable for the defaults of their sub-contractor. Three factors militated in favour of this conclusion: the fact that the first defendants twice referred, in letters to the plaintiffs, to their reliance upon the conditions of the Road Haulage Association as governing the projected carriage of the goods; the fact that their consignment note described the second defendants as sub-contractors; and the fact that they charged the plaintiffs for "delivery to" the instructed address and not merely for "arranging delivery".[48] In view of these indications, the fact that the original letter requested charges to be rendered to the plaintiffs could not be taken to mean that the plaintiffs proposed to engage and to pay the second defendants through the medium of a direct and independent contract.

There is, in fact, a strong tendency to hold the intermediate party directly liable as a principal contractor whenever payment is intended to be directly enforceable by him against the owner and against him (with appropriate reductions) by the sub-contractor.[49] In *Arcweld Constructions Pty. Ltd.* v. *Smith*[50] the plaintiffs engaged the defendant Smith to transport two cranes from Victoria to South Australia. The task of carrying the first crane was delegated by Smith to Barker, who collected and carried it without incident. The task of carrying the second crane was delegated by Smith to Opperman's, who delegated it to Metelmann's, who delegated it to Obst. Obst drove the carrier under a low bridge, in circumstances which clearly allowed an inference of negligence against him, and the crane was badly damaged. McInerney J. held that Smith was answerable for this default because he had contracted as a principal and not merely as an agent for Opperman's or for any of the subsidiary parties. In other words, he had promised the plaintiffs not merely that arrangements would be made for transporting the crane but that it would actually be transported, and that reasonable care would be used in its handling and delivery. This undertaking rendered him accountable for the manner in which the transportation was carried out by any person to whom the task was legitimately delegated; a liability which extended along the chain of command to cover the defaults of further subsidiary carriers at the second or third remove from his original captaincy.[51] Among the reasons for reaching this conclusion on the present facts were:

[48] Ibid, at 424-425.
[49] But cf. *Marston Excelsior Ltd.* v. *Arbuckle Smith & Co. Ltd.* [1971] 2 Lloyd's Rep. 306; *Hair & Skin Trading Co. Ltd.* v. *Norman Airfreight Carriers Ltd.* [1974] 1 Lloyd's Rep. 443, at 445.
[50] (1968) Unreported; judgment delivered 17th September, 1968 (Vic. Sup. Ct.)
[51] See p. 22 of the transcript: ". . . the arrangement for the carriage of the goods . . . was one whereby a contract was brought into existence under which Smith was to procure the goods to be carried to Adelaide . . . and undertook responsibility to the plaintiff company to have the goods carried . . . It was within the contemplation of both parties at the time of making the contract, and it was a term of the contract, that Smith was not bound to carry these goods personally but that he could comply with his contract by procuring a sub-contractor to carry the goods". At p. 28 it is further said to have been a term of the contract

1. The parties (Arcweld and Smith) clearly contemplated that Arcweld would be directly and contractually liable to Smith for the overall cost of transportation, and that this would be charged by means of a single fee. (In fact, this was a regular feature of Smith's trading pattern over the years, and one which he had already adopted in the transaction involving Barker).

2. Smith's practice was to assume personal responsibility for paying his sub-contractors, rather than leaving them free to pursue claims against the party who had engaged him; moreover, Smith spoke of himself as allowing roughly the same period of credit to Arcweld as his own sub-contractors allowed to him;

3. Smith exhibited great personal concern about the plight of the crane after he had discovered the accident; a concern which extended even to telephoning the original sub-contractors to inquire about their arrangements for its recovery, and to telephoning the plaintiffs to apologise for what had happened;

4. Smith's general occupation was (in his own words) that of a "low-loader cartage contractor", and in this capacity he had personally carried goods for the plaintiff over the past two years.

In view of these circumstances, and of the correlative fact that no contractual relationships arose between Arcweld and any of the secondary carriers, it was clearly essential to the plaintiff's interests and to the efficacy of their contract with Smith that they should be entitled to look to Smith for compensation against any damage or loss which resulted from a breach of the duty of care by those sub-contractors.

It should be noted that at least two of the intermediate parties in the *Arcweld* case—Metelmann's and Smith—never acquired possession of the crane in the course of its journey. It was driven by the plaintiff's manager to a place where there was a suitable loading ramp, and there delivered to Obst.[52] McInerney's judgment provides important acknowledgment that liability of the kind discussed in *B.R.S. Ltd.* v. *Arthur V. Crutchley & Co. Ltd.*[53] is not confined to cases where an existing bailee, such as a warehouseman, delegates the various duties which arise out of the bailment, but may arise whenever any contracting party who is given the option of becoming a bailee elects to renounce that status completely and (without ever gaining possession personally) to depute a third person to discharge those duties ab initio:

> Although the views of Cairns J. and of Lord Pearson, Sachs L.J. and Danckwertz L.J. (in the *Crutchley case*) were expressed in relation to a case of bailment they are, in my opinion, equally applicable to

that "if Smith procured some other carrier to carry the goods . . ., payment for the carriage was to be made by the plaintiff to Smith and the plaintiff was not to be liable to the sub-contractor for payment for the carriage done".

---

[52] It is uncertain whether the first sub-contractors (Opperman's) acquired possession of the crane. Presumably they did because, as McInerney J. remarks at p. 14 of the transcript, Obst appears to have taken the crane to Opperman's depot before setting out for South Australia. McInerney J. was clearly disposed to treat Opperman's as a sub-bailee rather than as a quasi-bailor: post, p. 844.

[53] [1968] 1 All E.R. 811; ante, p. 830.

Further recognition of this principle is afforded by the judgments of the case of a contract for carriage in which the carrier does not obtain actual possession of the goods simply because he sub-lets or delegates the duty of carriage to a sub-contracting carrier.[54] Barwick C.J. and Windeyer J. in the more recent High Court decision of *Hobbs* v. *Petersham Transport Co. Pty. Ltd.*[55]

The conceptual foundation for this form of liability is not bailment, because the defendant is never a bailee. Rather, his liabiilty is a contractual one, arising from the terms and necessary implications of his promise to the original bailor. This provides him with an advantage in the context of proof because the onus is upon the plaintiff to establish a breach of the relevant undertaking, rather than upon the principal contractor to prove that the person to whom he delegated the work took reasonable care.

The foregoing analysis, although colourably in conflict with the approach taken by the Court of Appeal to unauthorised delegations in *Edwards* v. *Newland & Co.,* is supported by the judgments of Barwick C.J., and Windeyer J., in the *Petersham Transport* case. Every other judge in that case assumed that the principal contracting carriers were bailees; a conclusion which was clearly misconceived, but which does at least mean that their judgments are irrelevant to the position of the contracting *non*-bailee.[56]

Both Barwick C.J. and Windeyer J. conceded that the plaintiff could invoke the doctrine of res ipsa loquitur against the defendant forwarder. Non-delivery of the goods did no more than afford prima facie evidence of the breach of the defendant's promise; it did not place the legal onus upon him to show that reasonable care was taken and that the promise was accordingly discharged. Provided the defendant could adduce an explanation for the misadventure which contradicted or destroyed that original inference, and which was consistent with the taking of reasonable care by the parties for whose conduct he was responsible, he would be relieved.

> So here it seems to me that once the non-delivery of the goods is explained as it was explained, there is no room for an inference from the fact of non-delivery of the goods that the defendant had failed to take due care of the goods. In my opinion, once such an explanation is given and accepted, the defendant is not required to go further and establish that he could not have prevented the road accident which happened by any exercise of due care in the maintenance of the vehicle. To require the defendant to do so would, in my opinion, be pressing the evidentiary consequence of the non-delivery too far. To so require proof by the defendant would shift the onus to the defendant to disprove an absence of breach. That, in my opinion, is an unwarranted step. The onus of proving breach of the promise is always with the plaintiff. The matter would be otherwise in an action founded on a bailment of the goods.[57]

The conclusion pronounced in this decision rests upon two assumptions: the essential difference between the doctrine res ipsa loquitur and the

[54] At pp. 35-36 of the transcript.
[55] (1971) 45 A.L.J.R. 356; see especially per Windeyer J. at 364-365.
[56] Proksch [1973] A.B.L.R. 266, at 270-271.
[57] (1971) 45 A.L.J.R. 356, at 359 per Barwick C.J.; see also Windeyer J. at 364-365.

bailee's burden of proof,[58] and the adequacy of an acceptable or credible explanation to discharge the prima facie inference that a case of res ipsa loquitur engenders.[59] In England, the operation of the latter rule seems to enjoy a more persuasive effect and (on some authorities at least) to place a heavier burden upon the defendant.[60] It appears, nevertheless, that the two principles are quite separate and distinguishable, because whereas in an ordinary action for negligence the relevant lack of care must, at the end of the day, be unambiguously established, an action against a bailee may succeed upon a total lack of evidence one way or the other.[61] Accordingly, the forwarder non-bailee who is sued for an alleged breach of his promise that reasonable care shall be taken may still enjoy, in England, an advantage over the forwarder who received possession and subsequently passed it to a sub-bailee. It seems peculiar that a difference in result should depend upon so narrow and technical a question as the existence of a prior possession, but as Windeyer J. has remarked this seems to flow from the especial character of the action on the bailment.[62]

It is instructive to examine briefly the evidence upon which the defendants in the *Petersham Transport* case succeeded in avoiding liability for damage to the plaintiff's goods. The vehicle upon which these goods were being carried suffered a broken axle, as a consequence of which it overturned. The defendants showed that the vehicle was travelling at a moderate speed; that it was suitable for its task; that it was not overloaded; and that it had been proficiently maintained. They further established that the breaking of the axle was sudden and without warning; that the axle had not suffered from any signs of incipient weakness; and that the fracture itself was a clean one; facts which excited Barwick C.J. to observe that even if they had occupied the role of bailees, he would have found that the defendants had satisfied the relevant onus.[63] But the central element in the decision was the fact that the defendants had been able to indicate the *cause* of the accident and to convince the Court that this was the sort of event that could happen without fault on their part. They were not bound to establish their own exercise of reasonable care, provided they could produce a convincing explanation of the accident which was not, by its nature, repugnant to the taking of such care.

> . . . the plaintiff could claim that the fact that the vehicle ran off the road spoke for itself as negligence, and called for an explanation. But the explanation of the accident is a broken axle and left it upon the plaintiff to prove that this was the result of negligence. The mere

---

[58] This is explained at some length by Windeyer J. at 363-364; it is endorsed by other Australian decisions (e.g. *Paterson* v. *Miller* [1923] V.L.R. 36, at 42; *Fankhauser* v. *Mark Dykes Pty. Ltd.* [1960] V.L.R. 376, at 377) and by the Supreme Court of Canada in *Wong* v. *National Trust Corporation* (1969) 3 D.L.R. (3d) 55. See generally ante, p. 40.

[59] Australian decisions in point are *Mummery* v. *Irvings Pty. Ltd.* (1956) 96 C.L.R. 99; *Anchor Products Ltd.* v. *Hedges* (1966) 115 C.L.R. 493; *Nominal Defendant* v. *Haslbauer* (1967) 117 C.L.R. 448; *Piening* v. *Wanless* (1968) 117 C.L.R. 498.

[60] Ante, pp. 43, 441.

[61] Ante, p. 441.

[62] (1971) 45 A.L.J.R. 356, at 363-364.

[63] Ibid, at 360. In this the majority (Menzies, McTiernan and Owen, JJJ.) concurred.

fact that the mechanism of a vehicle fails does not itself show that the owner or driver was negligent.[64]

The principles laid down by Barwick C.J. and Windeyer J. in this decision show that it could be more advantageous for a consignor to proceed directly against the ultimate carrier than against the intermediate principal. The carrier (with whom the consignor has no contracual relationship) will be accountable as a bailee for the safety of the goods and must demonstrate that any loss or damage occurred without negligence on his part. The intermediary is liable only for breach of contract and such a breach must be affirmatively proved. Thus there may be circumstances in which the carrier is accountable whereas the intermediary is not; for a failure by the carrier to discharge the necessary onus of proof in individual proceedings against him will not necessarily justify an affirmative finding of negligence so as to inculpate the party who employed him. No doubt in cases of this kind the courts would be tempted to equate the two conclusions, but this would mean that the intermediary could be exonerated only if the carrier himself had shown that he was not negligent. Such an approach would erode the intermediary's right to have the alleged breach of contract affirmatively established and to escape liability unless this can be achieved. It seems to follow that a judgment against the carrier does not necessarily predicate a judgment against his principal.

For these and associated reasons, it is clearly advisable for the subcontracting carrier to stipulate for an indemnity within the subsidiary contract of carriage. Such a provision is a common feature of commercial transportation and is included within the Road Haulage Association's General Conditions of Carriage. An indemnity clause will, it seems, be treated in much the same way as an exclusion clause. It must be clearly incorporated, it must unambiguously cover the loss sustained and it must, in the opinion of Lord Denning M.R. at least, be reasonable between the parties.[65]

---

[64] Ibid., at 365 per Windeyer J. See also *Eastman Chemical International A.G.* v. *N.M.T. Trading Ltd.* [1972] 1 Lloyd's Rep. 25 where, on very similar facts, the first defendant forwarders were held liable as common carriers. Deputy Judge Tudor Evans Q.C. went on to remark obiter that the first defendants were also guilty of personal negligence (in failing to insure the goods while in the hands of the sub-contractor) and of a breach of contract, in so far as the vehicle in which the goods were carried suffered from faulty tyres, and they had promised as principals that the goods would be carried with reasonable care. No differentiation seems to have been made between the burdens of proof in each limb of the proceedings, but it would appear that the carriers' negligence was in any event affirmatively established.

[65] *Gillespie Bros. Ltd.* v. *Roy Bowles Transport Ltd.* [1973] Q.B. 400; *British Crane Hire Corporation Ltd.* v. *Ipswich Plant Hire Ltd.* [1975] 1 Q.B. 303; *Levison* v. *Patent Steam Carpet Cleaning Co. Ltd.* [1977] 3 W.L.R. 90; *Hair & Skin Trading Co. Ltd.* v. *Norman Airfreight Carriers Ltd.* [1974] 1 Lloyd's Rep. 443; *Charles Davis (Metal Brokers) Ltd.* v. *Gilyott & Scott, Ltd.* [1975] 2 Lloyd's Rep. 422. If no such provision is inserted in the sub-contract of carriage it seems that any liability on the part of the principal contractor for the defaults of the carrier will normally be recoverable by him by way of reverse indemnity from the carrier: see for instance, *Eastman Chemical International A.G.* v. *N.M.T. Trading Ltd.* [1972] 1 Lloyd's Rep. 25, at 35. If the principal contract contains an undertaking by the consignor not to proceed against the subsidiary carrier, judgment in contravention of this undertaking may entitle the intermediate contractor to an indemnity from the consignor to the level of any indemnity he has had to pay to the sub-contractor: *Charles Davis (Metal Brokers) Ltd.* v.

The restriction of the consignor-intermediary relationship to one of contract and not bailment appears to be predicated in the relationship between the intermediary and the carrier. The intermediary is, as we have attempted to explain earlier,[66] a mere "quasi-bailor"; he never obtains possession of the goods and therefore never transfers possession to the carrying party. Admittedly, it is not always necessary for a person to have acquired a prior possession of goods in order to stand as a bailor of those goods towards some other person. Thus, the purchaser of goods held by a warehouseman becomes a bailor of them to the warehouseman once the latter has attorned;[67] and a finance company may be the bailor of a vehicle to a hirer on hire-purchase although both the transaction and the transfer of possession were handled throughout by the dealer (or prior owner) and the finance company never saw or gained possession of the vehicle.[68] But in these instances, of course, the party alleged to represent the bailor enjoys the ownership of the goods, and it is logical that the bailee, who holds them with his consent, should owe to him the ordinary duties that arise from the bailment relationship. Where there is neither ownership nor prior possession, there can in general circumstances be no sufficient interest to entitle the party who lacks these accoutrements to enforce the current possessor's obligations as bailee.[69] An associated principle may be seen in contracts of carriage; apart from exceptional circumstances, nobody but the owner of goods or the person who has bailed them to the carrier can sue for their loss or destruction.[70]

It would follow that when the sub-contractor under a tripartite consignor-forwarder-carrier situation is in breach of his duty of care, the consignor may proceed against the carrier under the principles of bailment but the forwarder (assuming that he has acquired no prior possession) cannot. As with the consignor's action against him, his action against the carrier is in contract alone. Thus, he must affirmatively prove that the carrier has broken the relevant duty and cannot rely upon any duty on the carrier's part to prove that reasonable care has been taken.

Again, however, the decision in *Edwards* v. *Newland & Co.* would appear to confute this conclusion; for in that case the defendants (who had undertaken to warehouse the plaintiff's goods personally but had delegated the task ab initio to third parties) were allowed to proceed against the third parties *as bailees* from them. The result was a very heavy onus of proof upon the ultimate bailees in the third party proceedings, which they only narrowly managed to discharge. But if, as seeems clear, the defendants never gained possession of the goods before allowing the third parties to do so, it is difficult to see how their relationship could have been one of bailor and bailee. It might be argued that the traditional rules of bailment could be extended in a case of this kind because a similar extension appears to

Gilyott & Scott (ante). An undertaking of this kind may entitle the intermediary to demand the stay of any action against the carrier, post, p. 1007.

[66] Ante, p. 791.
[67] Post, Chapter 21.
[68] *Belvoir Finance Co. Ltd.* v. *Stapleton* [1971] 2 Q.B. 710.
[69] See *Arcweld Constructions Pty. Ltd.* v. *Smith* (ante) at p. 62 of the transcript; post, p. 844.
[70] Ante, p. 186.

have been made as against those parties (like the defendant in *Edwards* v. *Newland & Co.*) who have contracted to assume possession but fail, in the event, to do so. In such a case the defendant appears to be accountable as if he were a deviant bailee; and it may seem reasonable to allow him to project this fictional relationship of bailment upon his own relations with the party who eventually assumes possession. But whereas this result may seem reasonable if the ultimate bailee himself is guilty of a deviation (or where, for instance, he also breaches his contract to assume possession in person and delegates instead to a fourth party) it is rather less satisfactory when the only default alleged against him is a breach of his duty of care. To expand the traditional rules which govern the creation of the relationship of bailor and bailee so as to cater for a situation of this kind, thereby imposing a much heavier burden of proof upon the party in possession in an action by the intermediary, would be to allow the intermediary to invoke an original and fundamental breach of contract on his part as the basis of an augmented liability on the part of the third party: in short, it would allow him to profit from his own wrong.[70a]

Thus, in all but the most unusual cases, a quasi-bailor will be reduced to suing the quasi-bailee in contract. Normally this will be for an indemnity against his own liability to the original bailor;[71] if the quasi-bailor attempts to sue before such liability has been established, he will presumably fail because he cannot establish loss. If he were a conventional bailor (for instance, under a sub-bailment) he would be entitled to recover the value of the goods (or damages for their impairment) without a corresponding liability on his own part,[72] although he would, of course, be accountable to the bailor for the proceeds of such action, over and above his immediate interest.

It would also seem to follow, from the peculiar structure of the relationships under discussion, that (a) the non-possessing intermediary, or quasi-bailor, is not estopped from denying the original bailor's title and (b) that the ultimate or quasi-bailee may likewise raise the jus tertii in any proceedings against him by the quasi-bailor. Both conclusions result from the absence of any bridging or intermediate bailment: the latter, of course, affords a supplementary reason why the quasi-bailor cannot sue the quasi-bailee for loss or damage to the goods without some

---

[70a] It might be argued in appropriate circumstances that the intermediary has, as against the ultimate possessor, a superior or reversionary right to possession which, even though he does not exercise it, is sufficient to entitle him to claim as the ultimate party's bailor. This argument would appear to be capable of advancement even where the intermediary's delegation is unauthorised and therefore leads to the forfeiture of his own right to possession as against the original bailor, because it is his rights as against *the ultimate party* that are relevant; but it would appear inapplicable if (as with the ordinary case of the forwarding agent) the subsidiary contract creates no such right.

[71] Quaere whether he can claim contribution under the *Law Reform (Married Women and Tortfeasors) Act* 1935. The weight of authority suggests that he cannot because the statute cannot apply against a party who is merely guilty of breach of contract: *McConnell* v. *Lynch-Robinson* [1957] N.I. 70; *Street, Torts* (6th edn) p. 446; see *Arcweld Constructions Pty. Ltd.* v. *Smith* (1968) at p. 62 of the transcript. But in *Eastman Chemical International A.G.* v. *N.M.T. Trading Ltd.* [1972] 1 Lloyd's Rep. 25, at 35, it seems to have been accepted (without discussion) that the Act might apply in this situation.

[72] *Morris* v. *C.W. Martin & Sons Ltd.* [1966] 1 Q.B. 716, at 728.

concrete resultant injury (i.e. in normal circumstances, liability to the original bailor) on his part.

IX. COMPOUND OR MULTIPLE EXTENDED BAILMENTS

In theory, an extended bailment may involve any number of parties, each of them interrelated by some contractual or possessory link. Moreover, the individual character of such parties and their relationships inter se may differ within the compass of a single extended bailment. Thus, the chain of command may include both sub-bailees and substitutional bailees, or it may involve both sub-bailors and quasi-bailors, according to the traceable path of possession. Very often this path will diverge from the sequence and direction of the relevant contractual network, so that the two are not parallel but intermeshed.

The first-mentioned type of extended bailment (involving both sub- and substitutional bailees) is probably illustrated by the facts of *Mouka-toff* v. *B.O.A.C.*[73] In that case, the Common Law responsibility of the second and third bailees (i.e. the Post Office and the airline) was presumably a continuing or projecting one, which did not terminate when the goods left their possession but survived throughout the entire contract of carriage. On the other hand, it is likely that the status of the first bailee (i.e. the bank, which originally withdrew and appropriated the banknotes for the plaintiff's use and therefore held them as bailees from him prior to their despatch) terminated as soon as the notes left their possession.

The second type of extended bailment is represented by the unreported Victorian case of *Arcweld Constructions Pty. Ltd.* v. *Smith*,[74] where the following conclusions were reached as to the relationship of the parties:

1. Arcweld were not bailors to Smith because Smith never got possession; their relationship was purely contractual, but Smith was a 'quasi-bailor' to Opperman's and to Obst.[75] Smith could recover a *contractual* indemnity from Opperman's but, being neither his bailor nor in any contractual relationship with him, he lacked a sufficient interest in the goods to recover an indemnity from Obst. Smith was, in other words, neither bailee nor bailor: his rights and liabilities were exclusively contractual and as such were circumscribed by the limits of privity of contract.

2. Opperman's were entitled to an indemnity from Metelmann's "on the same basis and according to the same principles as Smith's entitlement to contribution and indemnity from Operman's". In other words, the right was purely contractual. Although Operman's may briefly have gained possession, they neither took that possession from Smith nor conferred it upon Metelmann's, so that no bailment claim could exist in either direction. Smith could claim no indemnity from Metelmann's because there was neither contract nor bailment between them.

---

[73] [1967] 1 Lloyd's Rep. 396; ante, p. 801.
[74] (1968), 17 September; ante, p. 837.
[75] Both of whom, presumably, got possession: Obst because he collected the goods from Arcweld and Opperman's because Obst drove them to their premises for checking in before setting off for South Australia.

3. Opperman's could, however, obtain an indemnity from Obst; *not* by way of contract but because they had sub-bailed to him. For much the same reason (i.e. the path of possession) Arcweld could have claimed as bailors from both Opperman's and Obst (both being non-contractual bailees).

4. Metelmann's could only have claimed against Obst in contract; and as they had failed to do so, such claim did not call for consideration.

Thus, whereas the path of contract ran from Arcweld to Smith to Opperman's to Metelmann's to Obst, the path of possession (and thus the bailment) ran more modestly from Arcweld to Obst to Opperman's to Obst. The decision, for all its complexity, does at least illustrate two important principles: first, that if there is a chain of forwarders and sub-forwarders none of whom acquires an intervening possession of the goods, the principal bailor's rights of action are confined to the primary contracting forwarder and to anyone who takes possession, whereas the non-possessing forwarders' own rights of action are confined to their immediate contractual neighbours; secondly, that a non-possessing forwarder or quasi-bailor may, by acquiring a possession subsequent to that of the carrier junior to himself, thereafter render himself liable as a bailee not only for as long as he retains that possession[76] but during any subsequent transfer of possession to another, whether to the carrier from whom he received it or to anybody else.

---

[76] As in *Gallaher Ltd.* v. *B.R.S. Ltd.* [1974] 2 Lloyd's Rep. 440; ante, p. 790.

CHAPTER 21

BAILMENT BY ATTORNMENT

I. INTRODUCTION

Attornment represents a method by which the relationship of bailor and bailee can arise without any form of physical transfer or delivery.[1] In commercial transactions, the ownership of goods will often be transmitted along a chain of successive vendors and purchasers without any corresponding transmission of possession; the goods may be on board a ship, in transit from one point to another, or they may be stored with a wharfinger or warehouseman.[2] In this chapter we discuss, not the general liability of the bailee, but the identity of the party to whom at any given time his duties as bailee are owed.

It could clearly be inequitable to make the bailee liable as such to anyone who happened to be the owner of the goods at the material time. The change in ownership may occur without the bailee's prior knowledge, or he may be uncertain whether a purported sale actually affects the title to the goods; moreover, having received them from one person he may consider it inconsistent with his position as that person's bailee to acknowledge title in another. A bailee is estopped from denying his bailor's title[3] and clear rules are necessary to establish the identity of that party.

In answer to this problem the law has devised the doctrine of attornment. Basically, an attornment is an overt or positive acknowledgment by a bailee that he now holds goods as bailee for someone other than the party who originally bailed them to him. Thus, in the case of goods which are sold to a purchaser while stored in a warehouse:

> The warehouseman holds the goods as the agent of the owner until he has attorned in some way to this person, and agreed to hold the goods for him; then, and not until then, does the warehouseman become a bailee for the latter.[4]

[1] An equivalent doctrine developed under the law of landlord and tenant: see Pollock & Wright, *Possession in the Common Law*, pp. 52-53.

[2] For variations on the conventional form of bailment by attornment, see ante, p. 787. Occasionally, the seller himself may become the bailee by continuing in possession of the goods after property has passed to the buyer or after he has attorned; for an example, see *Knights* v. *Wiffen* (1870) L.R.5.Q.B. 660.

[3] Ante, p. 163 et seq. But see now s. 8, *Torts (Interference with Goods) Act* 1977.

[4] *Dublin City Distillery Ltd.* v. *Doherty* [1914] A.C. 823, at 847 per Lord Atkinson; see also *Farina* v. *Home* (1846) 16 M. & W. 119, at 123 per Parke B.

846

II. The Manner of Attornment

An attornment gives rise to a form of estoppel[5] and cannot subsequently be denied or qualified by the attornor. Accordingly, it requires a concrete expression of fact by the bailee, directed to the alleged attornee or his servant or agent,[6] to the effect that the goods are now held as that person's and that the attornor is now his bailee. Subject to this, the forms which a valid attornment may take are various:

> I think, myself, that very little will suffice to create an attornment. If the warehouseman writes on the order in the presence of the messenger the word "accepted", so that he sees it; if he makes delivery of part of the goods, as in the case of *Gillett* v. *Hill*[7], where a delivery of five sacks of flour in compliance with an order to deliver "5 sacks ex 20" was held to be an admission of the possession of twenty sacks; if he makes a claim for charges on the person presenting the delivery order[8]; or if he tells him he has entered his right. In each of these cases I think it ought to be found that the warehouseman had attorned.[9]

In the case in which this statement was uttered, the warehousemen were in possession of six hundred and eighteen quarters of maize, deposited with them by the original owner, A. A sold two hundred quarters to W, and gave W a delivery order addressed to the warehousemen in the following form: "Please deliver to bearer for Messrs. John Wilkes & Son 200 quarters of maize *ex. ss. Harperley.*" W then endorsed the order "Please hold against our sub-orders" and lodged it with the defendants, who received it without objection but (other than making an entry in their books acknowledging its receipt) did nothing by way of response. W subsequently sold the two hundred quarters to the plaintiffs and gave them a delivery order addressed to the warehousemen which read "Deliver to Messrs. Laurie & Morewood 200 quarters Plate maize *ex* delivery order lodged." This order was also lodged with the defendants without their objection, but this time their response did not even extend to entering it in their books; and when the plaintiffs subsequently applied to them for a delivery warrant, they refused to deliver on the grounds that the original vendor A had put a stop on delivery for non-payment. The Court of Appeal held that the warehousemen had not, merely by receiving the delivery orders without objection, attorned as bailees to the sub-purchaser and were not therefore estopped from denying the plaintiff's title. There was held to be no custom in the corn trade whereby the mere receipt of a delivery order could be deemed after a reasonable time to make the person to whom the goods were deliverable under the

---

[5] Post, p. 848.

[6] For an example of attornment to an agent of the attornee, see *Knights* v. *Wiffen* (1870) L.R.5.Q.B. 660.

[7] (1834) 2 C. & M. 530.

[8] As in *Gosling* v. *Birnie* (1831) 7 Bing. 339, a very clear case of attornment; and see *Seton, Laing & Co.* v. *Lafone* (1887) 19 Q.B.D. 68.
Scrutton L.J. See further *Remnant* v. *Savoy Estate Ltd.* [1949] 1 Ch. 622; ante, p. 168.

[9] *Laurie & Morewood* v. *Dudin & Sons* [1926] 1 K.B. 223, at 237 per

order their owner;[10] and mere silence alone did not constitute an attornment:[11]

> I do not see how it is possible to get an attornment or recognition of the title of the person named in the order out of the mere fact that an order is brought by a messenger and given to a clerk, where nothing is done which is communicated to the other party. To raise an estoppel there must be something of which the party setting up the estoppel has notice, and which influences his conduct, but here the plaintiffs had no notice of anything at all.[12]

In this case the plaintiff's own delivery order was never entered in the defendants' books. In discussing whether such entry alone would suffice to create an attornment, Bankes L.J. apparently thought that the answer depended upon whether the goods in question were specific or unascertained. If, as in the present case, they were unascertained, the mere entry of the order without communication thereof to the person in whose favour it was made would be insufficient evidence of an attornment.[13] But if the goods were specific the question of attornment could be irrelevant for most practical purposes because property would normally have passed to the purchaser and he could recover them on the strength of his title.[14]

III. The Consequences of Attornment

Once the bailee has attorned to someone other than his original bailor, the attornment operates as an estoppel and he may not subsequently deny the attornee's title to the goods comprised in the attornment. Accordingly, the goods or their value may be recovered in an action for detinue or conversion if the bailee is later unable or unwilling to surrender them, and damages may be recovered by the attornee for any negligent injury which occurs through the bailee's default. The rule is supported by a long sequence of authority.[15] In one case, Bosanquet J. observed that any other principle would run counter to the general understanding "by which a large portion of the trade of London is regulated."[16]

---

[10] Scrutton L.J., did, however, concede (see ante) that such a custom would not be unreasonable.

[11] Distinguishing *Woodley* v. *Coventry* (1863) 2 H. & C. 164 and *Knights* v. *Wiffen* (1870) L.R. 5 Q.B. 660, both of which involved an acceptance of the delivery order by the warehouseman "in the sense that an intimation was given to the person presenting it that goods of the quantity specified in the order were being held by the warehouseman at his disposal", per Bankes L.J. [1926] 1 K.B. 223, at 230.

[12] Per Scrutton, L.J. at 237-238 (see ante). See further *Seton, Laing & Co.* v. *Lafone* (1887) 19 Q.B.D. 68, especially per Lord Esher M.R.

[13] [1926] 1 K.B. 223, at 230-231, thus distinguishing *Gillett* v. *Hill* (1834) 2 C. & M. 530 and a statement by Lord Ellenborough in *Harman* v. *Anderson* (1809) 2 Comp. 243, as to the "transfer in the books being in itself decisive". See also Scrutton L.J. at 233, who likewise thought that communication of the entry would be necessary in a case like the present.

[14] Post, p. 850.

[15] *Stonard* v. *Dunkin* (1809) 2 Comp. 344, N.P.; *Hawes* v. *Watson* (1842) 2 B. & C. 540; *Gosling* v. *Birnie* (1831) 7 Bing. 339; *Holl* v. *Griffin* (1833) 10 Bing. 898; *Gillett* v. *Hill* (1934) 2 C. & M. 530; *Henderson & Co.* v. *Williams* [1895] 1 Q.B. 521.

[16] *Gosling* v. *Birnie* ante, at 345.

In such an event it becomes irrelevant whether the attornee is the owner of the goods or whether the attornor is capable of delivering them. They may have been sold to the attornee by a fraudulent intermediary with no authority to pass title;[17] the time for the passing of property to the attornee may not yet have occurred; the bailee may have mistakenly attorned for a greater amount than was currently in his possession;[18] or he may already have mistakenly delivered the goods to someone else.[19] Neither of these events affords a defence if the bailee has attorned to the plaintiff as owner of the goods, for their relationship is thereafter one of bailor and bailee and no jus tertii can be pleaded. Some authorities do, it is true, impose the further requirement that the attornee should have acted on the attornment,[20] but it is clear that the act of reliance need not be substantial or extreme and that it is not ncessary to prove that the attornor intended it.[21] Conduct which has been held to satisfy this requirement includes the purchase of the delivery order by the attornee[22] and the refraining by him of redeeming his price from an intermediate vendor on the ground that title in the goods has vested in him.[23]

It follows from the foregoing that an attornment precludes the attornor from pleading that the sale to the attornee was a sale of unascertained goods forming part of a general bulk in the warehouse and that no appropriation in the purchaser's favour, sufficient to pass title in any part of the goods to him, has yet taken place.[24] As Blackburn J. remarked in the leading case, "The plaintiff did rest satisfied in the belief as a reasonable man that the property had been passed to him".[25] Therefore when the bailee's conduct leads the attornee to believe that he is now the owner, and thus by implication that the goods have been appropriated to him, the bailee should be estopped from denying the appropriation, at least when the attornee has altered his position in reliance upon the attornment.

When a bailee agrees to attorn before the chattel has come into his possesion, the attornment takes effect as soon as he takes possession thereof.[26]

---

[17] *Henderson & Co.* v. *Williams* (1895) 1 Q.B. 521.

[18] *Gillett* v. *Hill* (1834) 2 C. & M. 530.

[19] *Seton, Laing & Co.* v. *Lafone* (1887) 19 Q.B.D. 68.

[20] E.g. *Seton, Laing & Co.* v. *Lafone* (1887) 19 Q.B.D. 68; *Knights* v. *Wiffen* 1870) L.R. 5 Q.B. 660.

[21] *Seton, Laing & Co.* v. *Lafone* ante, at 72 per Lord Esher M.R.

[22] *Seton, Laing & Co.* v. *Lafone* ante.

[23] *Knights* v. *Wiffen* (1870) L.R. 5 Q.B. 660.

[24] *Knights* v. *Wiffen* (where the seller himself was bailee), following *Woodley* v. *Coventry* (1863) 2 H. & C. 164; contra, *Unwin* v. *Adams* (1858) 1 F. & F. 312, an Assize decision of Bramwell B., which was not cited in *Knights* v. *Wiffen*

[25] *Knights* v. *Wiffen* (ante), at 665.

[26] *Holl* v. *Griffin* (1833) 10. Bing. 246, at 248, per Tindal C.J.
   and may be misreported; and possibly certain dicta in *Gillett* v. *Hill* (1834) 2 C. & M. 530. The rule is also recognised in *Laurie & Morewood* v. *Dudin & Sons* [1926] 1 K.B. 223. Cf. *Evans* v. *Nichol* (1841) 3 Man. & G. 1286; Chitty, *Contracts* (23rd ed.), vol. ii, para. 163.

IV. SUPERIORITY OF TITLE

A bailee has no better title to the goods in his possession than his bailor,[27] and if some third party can establish a superior right to those goods the fact that the bailee has not attorned to him will, in an action for their non-delivery, prove unavailing.[28] Normally this situation will be confined to the sale of specific goods lodged with a bailee for safekeeping, but the problem can arise with unascertained goods if the bailee performs an act amounting to an appropriation and thus causes title to pass to someone other than his original bailor. The appropriation may in fact amount to an attornment, or it may operate without this aspect at all; once property has passed to the plaintiff, the goods are his to demand irrespective of whether the person to whom the demand is made is, technically, his bailee.

The part delivery by a warehouseman of goods comprised in a delivery order will constitute a constructive delivery of the whole when this is the intention of the parties. If this intention is apparent, property in the entire parcel will pass to the purchaser and the warehouseman cannot dispute his right to the remainder.[29] If, however, the vendee takes possession of part of the goods "not meaning thereby to take possession of the whole, but to separate that part, and to take possession of that part only, it puts an end to the transitus only with respect to that part, and no more: the right of lien and the right of stoppage in transitu on the remainder still continue."[30]

The mere receipt without objection, by a bailee, of a delivery order for goods which still form part of a given bulk lodged within the warehouse does not per se constitute an appropriation of the goods comprised in the order so as to pass title to the person named in the order; and neither does the mere entry of the receipt of the order in the bailee's books.[31]

Whereas, however, a full right of property should be exercisable against the bailee irrespective of attornment in an action based upon the conversion or detention of the goods, it is submitted that other aspects of the bailee's duty should not apply in favour of the purchaser until the bailee has attorned. Thus, unless there is strong evidence of an intention to the contrary, the bailee should not generally be answerable to the purchaser for any negligent loss of the goods occasioned prior to attornment; the remedy for such loss should rest instead with the original and currently-subsisting bailor.[32] To some extent, this may raise problems akin

---

[27] Ante, p. 164.
[28] See *Batut* v. *Hartley* (1872) 26 L.T. 968, where the plaintiff was the original vendor in whom property had revested after a dispute with the vendee as to the correspondence of the goods with their sample. The defendant was the bailee of the purchaser, and was held liable to the vendor in detinue for refusing to deliver up the goods.
[29] *Gillett* v. *Hill* (1834) 2 C. & M. 530.
[30] *Tanner* v. *Scovell* (1845) 14 M. & W. 27, at 38 per Pollock C.B.
[31] *Laurie & Morewood* v. *Dudin & Sons* [1926] 1 K.B. 223, disapproving *Whitehouse* v. *Frost* (1810) 12 East. 614; see also *Godts* v. *Rose* (1855) 17 C.B. 229.
[32] See Pollock & Wright, *op. cit.*, p. 189. Cf. *Makower, McBeath & Co. Pty. Ltd.* v. *Dalgety & Co. Ltd.* [1921] V.L.R. 365, where there was no change of ownership between the bailee's taking possession of the goods and his subsequent

to those discussed in the previous chapter, relating to the sub-bailee's knowledge of the existence of the original bailor.[33]

V. Other Obligations Arising Upon An Attornment

There is Canadian authority for the view that a bailor by attornment is liable to pay all reasonable warehousing charges arising subsequently to the attornment.[34] Such a principle is clearly equitable and may be based alternatively upon an implied contract between attornor and attornee or upon a term implied into their relationship of bailment. In fact, it seems likely that most bailments by attornment will be contractual in character, although an attornment is equally possible within the context of a gratuitous bailment.[35] Accordingly, the courts should be free to make such implications as are necessary to give efficacy to the bailment and to satisfy the intentions of the parties.

Consistently with the foregoing, it has been held that the purchaser of goods, to whom their current bailee has attorned, is subject to the same exclusions of liability as are contained in the original bailment between the vendor and the attorning bailee.[36] Again, this principle may be regarded in several ways: as an informal assignment of the original contract, as the incorporation by reference of certain terms within the implied contract between bailee and attornee, or as a bailment upon terms. Again, it would not seem essential that the bailment be contractual in character for this principle to apply.

---

attornment, and he was held to owe to the owner the normal duty of care arising from a bailment for reward even before he had attorned.

[33] Ante, p. 810 et seq.
[34] *Howland* v. *Brown* (1855) 13 U.C.R. 199.
[35] E.g. where the gratuitous depositary of goods, after receiving information of a sale of these goods by the depositor, advises the purchaser that he now holds the goods to his order and on his behalf.
[36] *H. M. F. Humphrey Ltd.* v. *Baxter, Hoare & Co. Ltd.* (1933) 149 L.T. 603; *Britain & Overseas Trading (Bristles) Ltd.* v. *Brooks Wharf & Bull Wharf Ltd.* [1967] 2 Lloyd's Rep. 51, at 60 (obiter); Weir [1977] 36 C.L.J. 24, at 27.

CHAPTER 22

FINDERS AND OTHER UNREQUESTED KEEPERS*

I. INTRODUCTION

Finding represents one of the more questionable forms of bailment, for it involves neither contract, delivery nor agreement between the loser and the finder. Even the congruence of intention that may exist between a principal bailor and his authorised sub-bailee is absent. It is for this reason that the assimilation of findings into the orthodox rules of bailment is partial and imperfect.

For certain purposes, the responsibilities of a finder have been successfully equated with those that are owed by an orthodox bailee.[1] One commentator at least has utilised this conclusion to argue that bailment is a non-consensual relation.[2] But in other respects the equation between findings and ordinary bailments is more difficult to sustain. A bailee stricto sensu (whether he takes by direct delivery or holds under an attornment) cannot deny his bailor's title.[3] A finder has no bailor in the literal sense[4] and is entitled to require any claimant to substantiate his claim.[5] Of course, the claimant need not be the owner; most of the problems of title in cases of finding involve questions as to whether an occupier of premises enjoyed an immediate possession prior to that of the finder.[6] But the absence of any relation, direct or indirect, to identify the terms upon which the finder assumes possession suggests that finders are bailees only to the limited extent that the custodial duties of both classes of possessor are the same.[7]

There are obvious similarities between a finder and any other person who takes goods without the owner's consent: the thief, the confidence trickster, the person who seizes property under the mistaken impression that it is own[8] and the person who takes possession of goods to save them

---

* See, generally, Torts (Interference with Goods) Act 1977; Appendix I, post.
[1] Post, p. 873 (finder's duty of care).
[2] Tay (1966) 5 Sydney Law Review 239, at 243 et seq.; cf. Stoljar (1955) 7 Res Judicatae 160, at 169; Laidlaw (1930-1931) 16 Cornell Law Quarterly at 293, et seq.
[3] Ante, p. 163. But see now s. 8, Torts (Interference with Goods) Act 1977.
[4] I.e. someone who has "baille" (delivered) the goods to him; Gilchrist Watt & Sanderson Pty. Ltd. v. York Products Pty. Ltd. [1970] 3 All E.R. 825, at 830-831; Makower, McBeath & Co. Pty. Ltd. v. Dalgety & Co. Ltd. [1921] V.L.R. 365, at 373-374.
[5] Ante, p. 172; post, p. 858.
[6] Bridges v. Hawkesworth (1851) 21 L.J.Q.B. 75; 15 Jur. 1079; post, p. 865.
[7] cf. Thompson v. Nixon [1966] 1 Q.B. 103; [1965] C.L.J. 173 (finder not a bailee for the purposes of the Larceny Act 1916); Zuppa v. Hertz Corporation (1970) 268 A. (2d) 364.
[8] Held to owe the duties of a gratuitous bailee in McCowan v. McCulloch [1926] 1 D.L.R. 312.

from a sudden emergency.[9] In each case the assumption of possession takes place without the permission of the owner and the person assuming possession (irrespective of whether he has committed conversion) must treat the goods with reasonable care. But the position of the finder differs in one material respect. Whether he is an occupier of land upon which the goods have been lost or a chance wayfarer who picks them up in a public street, there will be something in the nature of a possessory vacuum; the loser will either have ceased to possess the goods before the finder takes possession[10] or will have lost his possession to someone who (because of his control over the premises upon which they are situate) obtains an immediate, succeeding possession otherwise than as a bailee. Accordingly, the finder is not depriving the loser of possession and is unaffected by the traditional rule that, as against a wrongdoer, possession qualifies as title.[11] It follows that the loser's right of recovery is conditional upon his proving either that he is the owner of the goods or that he enjoys some other immediate right of possession. If a thief steals goods and loses them in a public place, he has no remedy against a finder who subsequently possesses them;[12] likewise, perhaps, where a bailee loses goods through a fundamental departure from the terms of the bailment and thereby forfeits his right to possess.[13] But the negotiorum gestor who seizes goods to save them from a fire, or the thief who steals them from under the plaintiff's bed, will have violated an immediate, prior possession and is answerable to the person from whom he took them, irrespective of whether that person held by authority of the owner or not.[14]

The problems of jus tertii represent one of the few areas of the civil law in which it may be necessary to define the circumstances in which goods are lost, and to identify who is a finder. In contests between the finder and a third party non-owner (e.g., the occupier of land upon which the goods are found) this question is, for the most part, immaterial. Such a situation presupposes the absence of the true owner; and whether the finder may retain against the occupier becomes simply a question of whose was the earlier possession. If the finder was first in possession, this possession will normally be good against everyone except the true owner. Where the finder fails to establish a prior possession, this failure

---

[9] Held to be bailee for the purpose of the criminal law in *Leigh's* case (1800) 1 Leach. 411, n. 9; see Pollock & Wright, pp. 143, 163. In the instant case the seizure was with the knowledge and assent of the owner, but there is no reason to suppose that a different result would follow if it had taken place in his absence; cf. *R.* v. *Reeves* (1841) 5 Jur. 716, where a person who took a watch from a drunken and apparently assenting man was held to take as a bailee.

[10] cf. *Minigall* v. *McCammon* [1970] S.A.S.R. 82, at 92, where Wells J. took the view (at least for the purposes of the criminal law) that the loser of a chattel in a public place or on land occupied by a person whose mere occupancy does not give him possession of the chattel continues in possession until the finder takes the goods. See further, Bray C.J. at 87.

[11] Ante, Chapter 4.

[12] cf. *Buell* v. *Foley* (1913) 25 O.W.R. 177; *Buckley* v. *Gross* (1963) 3 B. & S. 566; 122 E.R. 213.

[13] Aliter, of course, where the bailor's right to possession has revived but the bailee remains in possession: cf. *Miles* v. *Cattle* (1830) 8 L.J. (O.S.) (C.P.) 271.

[14] *Amory* v. *Delamirie* (1722) 1 Stra. 505; 92 E.R. 644; *Jeffries* v. *G.W. Ry. Co.* (1856) 5 E. & B. 202; 119 E.R. 680; *Bird* v. *Fort Frances* [1949] 2 D.L.R. 791; *Chapman* v. *Robinson* (1969) 71 W.W.R. 515, at 522; cf. *Buckley* v. *Gross* (1863) 3 B. & S. 566; 122 E.R. 213.

will in most cases be the result of some closer, antecedent relationship between the occupier and the chattel, or some special relationship between the occupier and the finder. Whether the loser had possession immediately beforehand is, from the very nature of the dispute, immaterial, and the same applies to any contest between the finder of goods in a public place and anyone who seeks to retain the goods against him.

In contests between a loser non-owner and a finder, however, the question whether the goods were genuinely lost may assume a greater significance because it may serve to answer whether the loser enjoyed an immediate prior possession. Such a question might arise when A, having found a suitcase by the roadside in circumstances which clearly indicate that it has fallen from a passing car, picks it up and carries it into a park, where he sits down on a bench for a sleep, leaving the suitcase beside him. When he wakes up he forgets about the case and walks away without it. Three minutes later he remembers his find and returns in haste to the bench only to see B walking off with the case. The true owner is untraceable and the sole contest is between A and B. Who should succeed?

There can be no doubt that if B had taken the case while A was asleep, A would be entitled to recover it on the grounds of his possession.[15] The difficulty lies in establishing the point at which A's possession came to an end. On the rare occasions upon which this question has arisen, the courts seem to have been generous in their assumption that the first finder's possession continued until the second finder dispossessed him; at the same time must be conceded that their reasoning is not always conclusively in favour of this requirement in any event. In the Tennessee case of *Deaderick* v. *Oulds*[16] the defendant found a walnut log floating in a stream and reduced it into his possession. The log was subsequently lost by the breaking of the defendant's boom and floated downstream to the plaintiff's land, whence the defendant recovered it. It was held that he was entitled to do so. Although the judgment of Lurton J. arguably supports the view that even a loss of possession by an earlier finder will not divest him of his right to the goods[17] it is by no means clear that the court considered such possession to have been lost: the first finder had "the superior right . . . growing out of his prior possession and earlier finding of the log", and a possession which is apparently equated with a right to possess.[18] Certainly, in two subsequent decisions the courts appear to have considered a continuing possession to be necessary and have been prepared to find it in circumstances which involved considerable geographical separation from the chattel or an apparent intervening bailment to a third-party on the part of the finder.[19] It is

---

15 Post, p. 869.
16 (1887) 5 S.W. 487. Cf. *Sutton* v. *Buck* (1810) 2 Taunt. 302.
17 This is the interpretation favoured in *Corpus Juris Secundum*, Vol. 36A, p. 424.
18 (1887) 5 S.W. at 488; see also *Clark* v. *Maloney*, 3 Harrington (Del.) 68.
19 *McFadyen* v. *Wineti* (1908) 11 G.L.R. 345 (Supreme Court of New Zealand); *Bird* v. *Fort Frances* [1949] 2 D.L.R. 791 (Ontario High Court); cf. *Minigall* v. *McCammon* [1970] S.A.S.R. 82. In the *McFadyen* case, a Maori found a totara log on the banks of the Wanguanui River. He marked it with his initials and departed for the Christchurch Exhibition of 1906-1907, leaving the log where it was. It was proved that the natives in these parts customarily respected such

difficult to envisage any right, other than one arising from his possession, which a finder can ever enjoy in lost goods; or how any remedy can consequently lie once that possession has been lost.[20]

In this respect, it is interesting to consider the distinction made in some United States jurisdictions between goods that are lost and goods that are merely mislaid. A recent commentator[21] has epitomised this distinction as one between "objects parted with deliberately and forgotten unintentionally" (such as a handbag left on a cinema floor by a departing customer) and "objects parted with unintentionally" (such as a wallet which falls on to the floor from the customer's pocket). More specifically, goods are mislaid rather than lost when the following conditions are satisfied:

> An individual enters premises to transact business, lays the res with care on the appropriate surface, has every intention of retaining possession and control of the res, intends to pick it up as soon as the purpose for laying it down has been accomplished, forgets to do so, leaves the premises never intending to relinquish possession and control, and will be able to recall these events and return to the premises to retrieve his property.[22]

In America the distinction is invoked for the purpose of determining disputes between occupiers and finders. When the goods can be characterised as mislaid, possession will be awarded to the occupier, usually on the grounds that they have been left in his custody or impliedly entrusted to him.[23] This approach is strongly influenced by the assumption that an owner of goods will enjoy a better chance of recovering them from the occupier than from the more transient finder.[24] But as Professor Cohen has pointed out, this assumption is no more justified in cases of mislaid than in cases of lost property;[25] indeed it is unlikely that any loser who

---

identification as conveying a superior claim to goods. The appellant (who was not the occupier of the land) took possession of the log in the Maori's absence and cut it into posts, which the Maori, on his return, seized and refused to redeliver. Chapman J. held that the Maori had assumed possession and that there was nothing in his absence to suggest any abandonment of that possession. Note, however, that the log was res nullius so that ownership as well as possession presumably vested in the Maori by earmarking the log. *Bird* v. *Fort Frances* is set out at p. 870, post; see also Holmes. *The Common Law*, pp. 236-238.

---

[20] cf. Holmes, op. cit., p. 238: "It is conceivable that the common law should go so far as to deal with possession in the same way as a title, and should hold that, when it has once been acquired, rights are acquired which continue to prevail against all the world but one, until something has happened sufficient to divest ownership."

[21] Professor E. R. Cohen (1970) 48 *Texas Law Review* 1001, at 1006; see further *Cohen* v. *Manufacturers' Deposit Co.* 116 *N.Y. Law Jo.* 1521; (1946) 21 *St. John's Law Review* 58; Paton, op. cit., p. 126.

[22] Cohen, op. cit., p. 1004; the classic case is *McAvoy* v. *Medina* (1866) 93 Mass. (11 Allen) 548.

[23] See the authorities discussed by Riesman (1939) 52 *Harvard Law Review* 1105, at 1117-1125, and by Cohen, loc. cit. Riesman observes that neither the distinction nor its conclusion has found universal acceptance. Sometimes, however, the courts have gone so far as to characterise the occupier as a bailee: *Foulke* v. *New York Consolidated R.R.* (1920) 228 N.Y. 269: ante, p. 380.

[24] *McAvoy* v. *Medina*, ante; *Loucks* v. *Gallogly* (1892) 1 Misc. 22, at 26; 23 N.Y. Supp. 126; Riesman, op. cit., p. 1122.

[25] See pp. 1006-1007.

has not returned to claim the goods before the dispute between finder and occupier is litigated—a process which inevitably takes a considerable time—will appear and demand them afterwards.[26] Clearly, a rule which relies so heavily upon the loser's state of mind is an unsatisfactory basis for resolving disputes to which he is not a party. For these and other reasons, the lost-mislaid distinction has been condemned by American writers[27] and, in the context of finders and occupiers, is entirely without foundation in English law.[28]

It is suggested, however, that a similar distinction might occasionally prove useful in deciding whether the "loser" of goods in a public place has actually lost possession before they are taken into the custody of a finder. It would be undesirable, for instance, if the man who temporarily forgets where his car is parked should be held to have lost possession until he remembers where it is. Likewise, the man who mistakenly leaves his umbrella on a park bench, or his bicycle outside a shop, will probably remember where he has left it and will eventually return to retrieve it. In these and other cases, there is some justification for saying that one does not lose possession merely by intentionally placing the goods in a particular place and departing from that place while temporarily forgetting that they are there.[29] If, however, the goods are not intended to be there in the first place, possession can more readily be assumed to have lapsed. So far as concerns the intention to control the goods, to exclude strangers from them, and to exercise the necessary dominion, there is a clear difference between these cases and some justification for looking to the state of mind of the loser at the time when he first became separated from his chattel.

Of course, it may be thought that the existing rules on possession are sufficiently ductile to produce a satisfactory solution without resort to the lost-mislaid distinction. At best, it represents no more than a general guide, and there will come a time when the distance between the mislayer and his chattel, or the period that has elapsed since he mislaid it, point in any event to a loss of possession on his part. Each case must depend upon its facts and no amount of illustration can en-

---

[26] Cohen, p. 1003.

[27] Riesman described it as "inexplicable, if not contradictory": (1939) 52 *Harvard Law Review* 1105, at 1121. See also Cohen op. cit.; Holmes, *The Common Law*, pp. 22-225; cf. Aigler (1923) 21 *Michigan Law Review*, at 664; Moreland (1927) 15 *Kentucky Law Journal* 225.

[28] See Cohen (op. cit., p. 1013, n. 21), who cites *Hannah* v. *Peel* [1945] 1 K.B. 509 as evidence of the "utter contempt" held by English Courts for the lost-mislaid distinction, and remarks that "If ever a piece of property was *mislaid* this brooch was". Although the distinction has occasionally found acceptance in some of the older Canadian decisions; e.g. *Heddle* v. *Bank of Hamilton* (1912) 5 D.L.R. 11, *Haynen* v. *Mundle* (1902) 22 C.L.T. 152; it was criticised by Dixon J. in *Willey* v. *Synan* (1937) 57 C.L.R. 200, at 219-220. Cf. *Minigall* v. *McCammon* [1970] S.A.S.R. 82, at 87-88 (a case of larceny) where Bray C.J. was prepared to uphold it for the purpose of establishing that a finder of goods acquired a possession superior to that of the occupier, but found it unnecessary to invoke the doctrine.

[29] This approach is favoured by certain decisions in the criminal law, e.g. *R.* v. *Wynne* (1786) 1 Leach 413; 168 E.R. 308; *R.* v. *Pierce* (1852) 6 Cox C. C. 117; *R.* v. *West* (1845) Dears. 402; 169 E.R. 780; *Minigall* v. *McCammon* [1970] S.A.S.R. 82, at 87-88.

compass the many forms these facts may take. But as elements to be considered in any allocation of possession between loser and finder, the intention of the loser to place the goods where they were, and the likelihood that he would remember their location, have considerable importance and should not be disregarded.

The relevance of this question is not confined to disputes between finders and losers who have no independent right to possess. Where the chattel is not genuinely lost, but remains in the owner's possession, there may well be a remedy in trespass against a finder who (even innocently) violates that possession.[30] Where, on the other hand, the chattel is lost, the honest finder is said to commit no trespass because he is deemed to take by the implied consent of the owner.[31]

Normally, a finder does not commit conversion merely by taking lost goods into his custody;[32] again, he will be deemed to do so on the owner's behalf. Arguably, the same result should follow where the goods are not lost but the finder honestly and reasonably assumes that they are. But where the taking in this case results in the loss of the goods to the owner, or in his being deprived of them for a substantial period, it is submitted that the putative finder should be answerable irrespective of his own negligence or of any dishonest intention on his part. Although the policy of the law should be to encourage acts of philanthropy by finders and comparable persons, this encouragement should not be at the expense of an owner who would not have lost his chattel if the finder had not, unnecessarily, interfered.

Sometimes the identity of the finder may arise independently of any consideration of the rights of the owner. There may be several competing finders, each of whom claims that he saw the goods first and is entitled to keep them until the owner appears. Here, it is a simple matter of identifying the party who first came into possession; but the facts of the case may make this task more difficult than it appears. In one American case the court decided upon a pragmatic, equitable approach.[33] Several boys were playing by a railroad track when one of them picked up an old

---

[30] For the elements of trespass, see p. 117 et seq., ante. A mere asportation, without physical damage, will suffice, but the finder may have a defence in that he reasonably believed his conduct to be necessary for the protection of the chattel: *Kirk* v. *Gregory* (1976) 1 Ex. D. 55; *Proudman* v. *Allen* [1954] S.A.S.R. 336; Pollock & Wright, p. 172. But cf. post.

[31] Pollock & Wright, pp. 171-172. It would seem to follow that the *dishonest* finder does commit trespass by taking the chattel into his possession. But trespass is an offence to possession and if the owner has lost this prior to the misappropriation, there can surely be no trespass. In fact, Wright concedes that the authorities upon which he based his view that every finder (except he who takes a thing really lost in charity to save it for its owner) is civilly a trespasser are not wholly reliable. Wright was, in any event, discussing the application of these authorities to the criminal law, as was Bray C.J. in *Minigall* v. *McCammon*, ante.

[32] *Chowne* v. *Baylis* (1862) 31 Beav. 361; 54 E.R. 1174; *Hollins* v. *Fowler* (1875) L.R. 7 H.L. 757, at 766, per Blackburn J.; aliter, of course, if he intends to steal them or to conceal them from the owner.

[33] *Keron* v. *Cashman* (1896) 33 All 1055; noted in (1896-1897) 10 *Harvard Law Review* 63. See also *Cummings* v. *Stone* (1864) 13 Mich. 80; Aigler, "Rights of Finders" (1922-1923) *Michigan Law Review* 664, at 681; Holmes, *The Common Law*, pp. 234-235; Riesman (1939) 52 *Harvard Law Review* 1105, at 1110-1111; *Ranger* v. *Giffin* (1968) 89 W.N. (N.S.W.) 531, at 538.

stocking which was fastened at the neck. He played with it until a second boy decided that he wanted a turn and either snatched it from him or picked it up from where the first boy had left it. One by one the boys all played with the stocking and then, when the second boy was swinging it again, it burst open to reveal a sum of money. The boys all examined the money and eventually handed it to a policeman. The owner was never traced and the court awarded the money to the boys jointly, to be divided equally between them. The property was not found until the stocking burst open; when this occurred the boys were engaged in a joint enterprise and the money came into the possession of all.

In this situation, it was probably correct to say that none of the boys had exerted sufficient control over the stocking to acquire (or to retain) possession of it before the money came to light.[34] But the decision of the Supreme Court of Rhode Island in *Durfee* v. *Jones*[35] cannot be rationalised in the same way and seems to be palpably misconceived. The plaintiff bought a safe which was handed to the defendant with orders to sell it for ten dollars. The defendant, while examining the safe, found a roll of bills concealed in the lining, and was held entitled to retain this money as against the plaintiff. The court, citing *Bridges* v. *Hawkesworth*,[36] held that the only prior possession enjoyed by the plaintiff was an unwitting one, and: "Such possession, if possession it can be called, does not of itself confer a right." It went on to reject the idea that the money was mislaid rather than lost[37] and to dismiss the plaintiff's contention that the finding was a wrongful act on the part of the defendant. But there is a world of difference between money left on the floor of a shop[38] and money concealed in a portable container over which one has (either personally or through one's agent) undoubted possession and physical control. Possession of a container will, for the purposes of the civil law, almost invariably impart possession of its contents,[39] irrespective of whether one knows of the existence of those contents or can be made liable as their bailee There is no reason why one should not be a finder for the purposes of the civil law without even knowing that one has found anything at all.[40]

II. TITLE TO LOST GOODS[41]

When goods are found, and there is a dispute as to who should be allowed to keep them, the court is in one sense deciding who should occupy the

---

[34] Quaere, however, whether a dispersal of the subject-matter is in the best interests of the owner.

[35] (1877) 11 R.I. 588; 23 Am. Rep. 528; criticised by Aigler, op. cit., at 670. See further *Bowen* v. *Sullivan* (1878) 62 Ind. 281.

[36] (1851) 21 L.J.Q.B. 75; 15 Jur. 1079; post, p. 866.

[37] Ante, p. 855.

[38] As in *Bridges* v. *Hawkesworth* (ante), which has itself been criticised.

[39] See Chapter 6, ante.

[40] Any objection that the owner of the safe was no longer in possession of its contents could, it is submitted, be countered by arguing that the defendant was in an analogous position to a bailee of both the safe and its contents and thus was estopped from denying his bailor's title. See p. 000, post.

[41] The literature on this topic is vast, and has been described as bearing to the case-law much the same ration as the literature on Hamlet does to the play

position of bailee. The owner's title continues paramount and no lapse of time, however great, will by itself extinguish that title.[42] Thus, whoever acquires possession of the goods becomes responsible for their safe-keeping until the owner reappears. Most finders are willing enough to accept this responsibility because the chances are that he will not.

The question of title to lost property is a vexed and variable one, in which certain aspects have achieved excessive prominence while others remain virtually untouched. Clearly, the solutions differ according to the circumstances of the finding and the character of the contestants. For this reason, the major permutations will now be considered individually.

A. Owner versus finder

We have already seen that the owner of goods continues as owner although he may no longer enjoy possession.[43] This continuation could have undesirable results, particularly, perhaps, in cases of lost money, where the honest finder who waits for a substantial period after adver-tising his find will probably assume that he can eventually spend it. Legis-lation could solve this problem by defining the procedures to be followed by the finder and by granting an indefeasible title after a certain period has elapsed.[44]

In *Moffatt* v. *Kazana*[45] a biscuit tin containing banknotes was dis-covered by a workman while installing a boiler in the defendant's bunga-low. It was established that the previous owner of the bungalow had possessed a biscuit tin to which he attached abnormal importance, and that he had once visited the loft of the bungalow in order to obtain money to lend to his son; an excursion from which he had returned clutching

---

itself: Riesman (1939) 52 *Harvard Law Review* 1105. Among the most important contributions are Goodhart, "Three Cases on Possession" (1928) 3 C.L.J. 195; Francis, "Three Cases on Possession — Some Further Observations" (1928) 14 *St. Louis Law Review* 11; Harris, "The Concept of Possession in English Law", *Oxford Essays in Jurisprudence* (1st ed.), Chapter IV; Aigler, "Rights of Finders" (1922-1923) 21 *Michigan Law Review* 664; Tay, "Possession and the Modern Law of Finding" (1964) 4 *Sydney Law Review* 383; Cohen, "The Finders Cases Revisited" (1970) 48 *Texas Law Review* 1001; Riesman, op. cit. See also Vaines *Personal Property* (5th ed.), Chapter 17; Cmnd. 4774 App. I (proposals for reform).

[42] See Harris, op. cit., p. 81, who points out that unless the finder commits a tort in relation to the chattel he can acquire no title as against the owner, for there is no event from which the relevant limitation period can run. Riesman, op. cit., pp. 1108-1109, compares this result unfavourably with the continental law, whereunder a finder who publicises his find will acquire title by affirmative prescription after a stated period; in Riesman's view, "Anglo-American courts, preoccupied with possession, have been incapable of making the finder an independent source of title". But since Riesman wrote, many American states have introduced legislation affecting this problem; Cohen (1970) 48 *Texas Law Review* 1001, at 1003. cf. *Elwes* v. *Brigg Gas Co.* (1886) 33 Ch. D. 562, at 568-569.

[43] Even, according to some authorities, when he has abandoned the goods: *Haynes'* case (1614) 12 Co. Rep. 113; *R.* v. *Edwards and Stacey* (1877) 36 L.T. 30; *Johnstone & Wilmot Pty. Ltd.* v. *Kaine* (1928) 23 Tas. L.R. 43; cf. *Elwes* v. *Brigg Gas Co.* (1886) 33 Ch. D 562, at 568-569; *The Crystal* [1896] A.C. 508, at 532; *The Tubantia* [1924] P. 78; *McFadyen* v. *Wineti* (1908) 11 G.L.R. 345.

[44] At present, the only state which appears to possess relevant legislation is Wes-tern Australia: see *Disposal of Uncollected Goods Act* 1970, ss. 20, 21; p. 407 et seq., ante.

[45] [1969] 2 Q.B. 152.

ninety-eight £1 notes. Wrangham J. found that the tin and its contents were the property of the previous owner, and awarded them to his executors. There had been no abandonment and s. 62 of the *Law of Property Act* 1925, did not operate to effect a conveyance of the money when the bungalow itself was conveyed.

Although no specific guidance is given in *Moffatt* v. *Kazana*,[46] it is clear that the onus of establishing ownership rests upon the party who asserts it.[47] In *Ranger* v. *Giffin*[48] the plaintiff claimed that £8,500, found buried beneath the soil of a house she and her husband had sold to the present incumbents some 12 months earlier, represented her winnings on various horses during the 1945 season. Her silence and concealment were explained on the grounds that she did not want her husband (a bookmaker) to know. McClemens J. found against her on the balance of probabilities.

The only serious problems that are likely to arise in this area involve goods which cannot be retrieved without expense. Such a situation might arise when A, having bricked up valuables in his house, sells the house to B and then wants to demolish B's chimney-breast in order to retrieve them; or where C leaves goods on D's land and D unwittingly builds over them. This point was raised by counsel for the defendants in *Moffatt* v. *Kazana*,[49] but, because of the circumstances of the discovery, it was not directly material. Wrangham J. was content to leave it open until such a case actually arose. It seems that a refusal to allow the owner to interfere seriously with the land upon which his goods are concealed is reasonable and should not per se render the occupier guilty of detinue or conversion.[50] If the owner promises to compensate for inconvenience and expense in retrieving the property a different result might apply; but this is an area in which the solution must depend upon the particular facts of the case.

B. Owner of land versus occupier of land upon which goods are found

Where the occupier holds under a lease, the question of title will often be answered by the express terms of the instrument itself.[51] Thus, in

---

[46] Ibid.

[47] Wrangham J. cited with approval the statement of Vaisey J. in *In re Cohen, National Provincial Bank Ltd.* v. *Katz* [1953] Ch. 88 to the effect that where no trustworthy evidence of ownership exists there is a presumption that an owner of land is the owner of chattels found thereon; cf. Riesman, op. cit. pp. 1107-1108.

[48] (1968) 87 W.N. (N.S.W.) 531.

[49] [1969] 2 Q.B. 152, at 156-157.

[50] See *Wilde* v. *Waters* (1855) 24 L.J.C.P. 193, at 195, per Maule J.: "Where an outgoing tenant leaves a picture hanging on a wall, the new tenant may refuse to admit the owner of the picture to take it, and may not choose to put himself to the trouble of giving it, but the picture is still the owner's chattel. The question in such a case, would be whether the jury could infer from the refusal that the new tenant exercised any dominion over the chattel. It appeared that he had merely said: I don't want your chattel, but I shall not give myself any trouble over it; that would not give the owner an action of trover." cf. Clerk & Lindsell, *Torts* (14th ed.), para. 109.

[51] Cf. *Elwes* v. *Brigg Gas Co.* (1886) 33 Ch. DD. 562, where Chitty, J. found it unnecessary to decide whether a lease which reserved "all mines and minerals" to the tenant for life encompassed a preserved but non-petrified prehistoric boat. He did, however, express the view that the boat was not a mineral: ibid. at 567, 570.

Corporation of London v. *Appleyard*[52] it was held that a reservation to the freeholders of "every relic or article of antiquity or value which may be found in or under any part of the site" entitled them to retain, as against the leaseholders and a sister company for whom the lease was held in trust, a box containing banknotes which had been found in an old wall-safe.

Where no specific agreement exists, it seems that the courts will generally resort to the notion that possession of land carries with it possession of everything lying beneath the surface, "down to the centre of the earth." In *Elwes* v. *Brigg Gas Co.*[53] the result was the award of a prehistoric boat, submerged beneath the land, to the tenant for life in possession, as against a lessee for ninety-nine years. Two facts assisted this conclusion: first, the original owner of the boat has been dead for centuries, so that property as well as possession was vested in the landowner;[54] secondly, the lease could not be construed as granting permission to the lessees to excavate and remove the boat, of the existence of which neither party had any inkling before it was discovered.[55]

If the possession of land imparts possession of everything beneath it, it may be thought that the occupancy of a tenant would give him a superior title to that of a reversioner out of possession. Much will depend, of course, upon the nature of the lease: whether it gives the tenant the power to disturb the soil and whether any reservation of possession in lost chattels can be implied in favour of the landlord notwithstanding such a power. In cases of ordinary residential tenancies or building leases, *Elwes* v. *Brigg Gas Co.*[56] could possibly represent the exception rather than the rule. In *Corporation of London* v. *Appleyard*,[57] McNair J. was clearly of the opinion that possession of the banknotes resided in the leaseholders (or their sister company) as against the freeholder. The freeholder recovered solely on the strength of a specific term in the lease, which had nothing to do with the question of possession at all.[58]

In many ways, this problem resembles the situation in *Durfee* v. *Jones*,[59] for in both cases an unwitting possessor of a chattel transfers possession to somebody who then discovers its existence. If the prior possessor is not the owner, a loss of possession would prima facie suggest that he loses all right to the chattel. He might rely upon the bailment and argue that the second possessor is estopped from denying his title; likewise in cases of leaseholds, he may argue that the lessee of land is in an analogous position to a bailee vis-à-vis things beneath the soil. But it is

[52] [1963] 2 All E.R. 834.
[53] (1886) 33 Ch. D. 562, at 568.
[54] (1886) 33 Ch. D., at 568-569; the boat may also have been abandoned; but see n. 43, ante.
[55] (1886) 3 Ch. D. at 569-570; see the discussion by Harris, *Oxford Essays in Jurisprudence*, pp. 87-89, and cf. *Ferguson* v. *Ray* (1904) 44 Or. 557; 77 P. 603.
[56] (1886) 33 Ch. D. 562.
[57] [1963] 2 All E.R. 834, at 837-838.
[58] In the absence of any claim by the freeholder, the courts would almost certainly prefer the claim of a lessee to that of a third-party finder on the ground that the lessee was in possession of the goods. Of course if the goods come on to the land after the lessee goes into possession the landlord will generally have no right; cf. Aigler, op. cit., at 678-680.
[59] (1877) 11 R.I. 588; 23 Am. Rep. 528; ante, p. 858.

hard to see how there can be a bailment of something of which the bailee is entirely unaware.[60] Possibly the courts would invoke an analogous principle to the bailee's estoppel, based upon the second possessor's promise to return the property in the condition in which he received it. Alternatively it may be held that, for the purposes of such actions, the owner remains in possession of the concealed goods[61] or that the bailee is under a duty to account for profits made from the bailment. Any one of these approaches may provide a solution where the bailment or lease is revocable at will or involves some act of service on the part of the tenant or bailee. They are, however, less likely to assist the lessor of land for a specific term.[62]

It would seem that the principles governing concealed, attached or buried goods in landlord and tenant contests should prima facie apply to goods that are merely lying on the land. But contests involving finders and occupiers have shown that mere occupancy does not necessarily impart possession of goods that are on the surface of the land without the occupier's knowledge. In such cases it may be possible to argue that the land-owner's original possession continues as against the occupier; but of course this original possession may be correspondingly harder to establish.[63]

C. Master versus servant

There is a general rule that a servant who obtains custody of goods as the result of his employment holds them for his master and does not acquire any independent possession.[64] If there exists between the finding and the servant's employment a close enough relationship for this rule to apply, no subsequent detention or acquisition of the goods by the master will constitute an actionable wrong, for he has violated no possession enjoyed by his employee.

South Staffordshire Water Co. v. *Sharman*[65] offered an ideal opportunity for the operation of this principle, but the case was decided on different grounds. However, in *Hannah* v. *Peel,*[66] Birkett J. conceded that the master-servant theory "seems to afford a sufficient explanation" of the earlier case. Other decisions have endorsed the view that a servant-finder may acquire no independent possession but may hold solely for his master.[67] Often, this view is supplemented by reliance upon the servant's

---

[60] Ante, p. 225.
[61] Cf. *Deaderick* v. *Oulds* (1887) 5 S.W. 487; *Bird* v. *Fort Frances* [1949] 2 D.L.R. 791, at 800; ante, p. 854.
[62] See *Tucker* v. *Farm and General Investment Trust Ltd.* [1966] 2 Q.B. 421, and p. 869, post.
[63] Cf. *Hannah* v. *Peel* [1949] 1 K.B. 509; post, p. 869.
[64] Chapter 7, ante.
[65] [1896] 2 Q.B. 44: post, p. 865.
[66] [1949] 1 K.B. 509, at 519. The explanation was previously put forward by Salmond, *Jurisprudence* (7th ed.), p. 307.
[67] See e.g. *Willey* v. *Synan* (1937) 57 C.L.R. 200, at 216-217 per Dixon J. (boatswain, ordered to search ship for stowaways, acquired no independent possession of coins hidden in forepeak, even assuming that he took "manual custody" thereof); *McDowell* v. *Ulster Bank Ltd.* (1899) 33 Ir.L.T.Jo. 223 (the possession gained by a porter sweeping out a bank and finding lost notes on the floor was "the possession of the Bank itself"); *Corporation of London* v. *Appleyard* [1963] 2 All E.R. 834, at 838-839 (workmen finding money concealed in wall on build-

fiduciary duty to account for profits made as the result of his employment.[68] Clearly, this reasoning is strongest when the finding takes place
on the master's premises, for here it is reinforced by the possibility that
the master was in possession of the goods before the finding occurred.[69]
On the other hand, there seems no reason why it should be confined to
such situations.[70] Roadsweepers, dustmen, police officers and workmen
put to work on premises occupied by third parties[71] are all examples of
employees against whom their masters might claim a superior right of
retention and a supervening possession of goods that are found in the
course of the servant's duties. The difficulty lies in determining whether
the act of finding is sufficiently related to the servant's employment to
justify imposing the rule of vicarious possession. Should the chimney-
sweep's boy in *Armory* v. *Delamirie*[72] have been liable, assuming that
he found the jewel up a chimney, to account for it to his master? Should
a milkman be similarly accountable for valuables he finds in the gutter
on his rounds,[73] or a taxi-driver for a banknote left in his cab by a fare?[74]
In *Byrne* v. *Hoare*[75] a gold ingot was found near the approach-road of a
drive-in cinema, on land occupied by the cinema company. The finder
was a police constable, who had been walking from the cinema towards
the main highway in order to direct traffic that would shortly be coming
from the cinema egress road. At the time he was on special duty for the
cinema company, who paid the relevant police district for his services
while he remained under the control of the regular force. The majority
of the Queensland Full Supreme Court held that he was entitled to keep
the ingot as against the Crown. This was not a case of a finder being
instructed by his master to search for lost or stolen goods, but a case of
purely fortuitous and incidental finding: his employment was merely the
occasion of the discovery, or merely afforded the opportunity for it, rather

ing site would, if entitled to the goods as finders, have been liable to account
to their employer, an independent contractor engaged by the occupier, rather
than to the occupiers themselves); *Crinion* v. *Minister for Justice* [1959] Ir. Jur.
15 (member of Civic Guard finding £184 on public footpath while on duty not
entitled to retain as against the State); *White* v. *Alton-Lewis Ltd.* (1975) 49
D.L.R. (3d) 189 (shop assistant, picking up a lost jewel from the shop-floor, held
thereby to have reduced it into employer's possession); *Ranger* v. *Giffin* (1968)
87 W.N. (N.S.W.) 531, at 538. Cf. *Grafstein* v. *Holme and Freeman* (1958) 12
D.L.R. (2d) 727, at 740; *Haynen* v. *Mundle* (1902) 22 C.L.T. 189; *Heddle* v.
Bank of Hamilton (1912) 5 D.L.R. 11.

[68] In most of the cases in the preceding footnote there was reference to this principle,
generally citing *Parker* v. *McKenna* (1874) 10 Ch. App. 96; *Attorney-General* v.
Goddard (1929) L.J.K.B. 743; *Reading* v. *Attorney-General* [1951] A.C. 507.
[69] Cf. *White* v. *Alton-Lewis Ltd.* (1975) 49 D.L.R. (3d) 189.
[70] Cf. Riesman (1939) 52 *Harvard Law Review* 1105, at 1117, who argues that in
America at least the question of possession is irrelevant in this context: "the
cases are only sensibly approached by reference to tort and contract questions
as to the scope of the employment."
[71] As in *Corporation of London* v. Appleyard [1963] 2 All E.R. 824.
[72] (1722) 1 Stra. 505; 92 E.R. 664.
[73] Evidently not, per Stable and Gibbs JJ. in *Byrne* v. *Hoare* [1965] Qd.R. 135
at 140, 148-149; and see *Hume* v. *Elder* (1917) 178 App. Div. 652 (N.Y.).
[74] No, according to a dictum in *In re Savarino* (1932) 1 F. Supp. 331, at 334.
[75] [1965] Qd. R. 135.

than constituting the "real"[76] or "effective"[77] cause. Hart J. delivered a strong dissent[78] in which he equated the constable's position with that of the boatswain in *Willey* v. *Synan*.[79]

The facts of *Byrne* v. *Hoare* accentuate the problems that can arise from an application of the master-servant relationship to cases of off-premises finding. The decision is at variance with *Crinion* v. *Minister for Justice*,[80] and it is possible that stricter rules will be applied to police-officers than to other classes of employee.[81] Nor is it easy to appreciate, in the abstract, the distinction between an employment which provides the cause of the finding, and one which merely affords the occasion or opportunity for it. But the result adopted by the Queensland court seems to be one with which future courts will generally endeavour to conform. As a general rule, the servant will not acquire possession of (i) goods lost on his master's premises;[82] (ii) goods found while conducting a search for his master, whether the search be for those goods, similar goods or something different; and (iii) goods concealed within real or personal property upon which the servant is working or with which he is dealing in the course of his employment.[83] Whether the necessary degree of proximity exists between that employment and the discovery must, however, be answered by all the facts of the particular case.

The terms of the servant's contract of employment may vary or amplify his employer's right to retain chattels found in the course of the servant's duty. In the absence of such provision, the general rule seems to apply not only to those who are servants stricto sensu, but to others, such as police-officers and company directors,[84] who are in a substantially analogous position. On the other hand, it seems to have no operation between independent contractors and those who engage them.[85] Where a workman on loan from one company to another finds a lost chattel, difficult questions may arise as to the identity of his master at the relevant time.[86] The principle of a master's supervening possession has not generally commended itself to American judges.[87]

---

[76] Ibid., at 141-142 per Stable J., citing Denning J in *Reading* v. *Reginam* [1949] L.J.R. 280; approved by Lord Porter in *Reading* v. *Attorney General* [1951] 1 All E.R. 617, at 619.

[77] [1965] Qd. R., at 149 per Gibbs J.

[78] Ibid, at 158-160.

[79] (1937) 57 C.L.R. 200.

[80] [1959] Ir. Jur. 15.

[81] In *Majewski* v. *Farley* 196 N.Y.S. 508; 203 App. Div. 77, a policeman was held unable to retain against his police district property which he found while off-duty; cf. *Noble* v. *City of Palo Alto* (1928) 264 P. 529; *Carr* v. *Summers* 59 Pa. Dist. 2 Co. 6.

[82] Arguably because the terms of his employment will oblige him to hand them to the master for collection by the loser.

[83] Cf. *Burns* v. *Clark* 133 Cal. 634; 66 P. 12.

[84] Cf. *Scobie* v. *Steele & Wilson Ltd.* 1963 S.L.T. 45.

[85] *Corporation of London* v. *Appleyard* [1963] 2 All E.R. 834; sed quaere. See further *Hurley* v. *City of Niagara Falls* (1969) 25 N.Y. (2d) 687; 254 N.E. (2d) 917; 306 N.Y.S. (2d) 6891.

[86] See p. 246, ante.

[87] See for instance *Tatum* v *Sharpless* (1865) 6 Phila. 18; *Danielson* v. *Roberts* (1904) 44 Or. 108; 74 P. 913; *McDonald* v. *Railway Express Agency* 81 S.E. (2d) 525; *Toledo Trust Co.* v. *Simmons* (1935) 3 N.E. (2d) 661; *Burnley* v. *First National Bank of Delaware Co.* 87 Pa. Dist. & Co. 433; 41 Del. Co. 8; cf. *Jackson* v. *Steinberg* (1949) 186 Or. 129; 205 P. (2d) 562; *Roberson*

D. Finder versus occupier

The finder is said, as a general rule, to enjoy a good title against every-one except the true owner;[88] but where goods are found upon land occupied by another, the majority of decisions have preferred the claims of the occupier to those of the finder, even where the latter is not in the employment of the former. The question to be decided in such cases is whether the occupier was in possession of the goods before the finder appeared. Knowledge of the existence of a chattel is not an essential condition of possession[89] and in most cases the possession of land, coupled with a presumed intention to exclude marauders, will be suffi-cient to give the occupier possession of chattels attached to or concealed under that land. Thus, in *South Staffordshire Water Co.* v. *Sharman*[90] the occupiers were held entitled to two gold rings found in the mud at the bottom of a pool, which was situated on their land and which the finders had been employed by them to clean; in *Hibbert* v. *Mackiernan*[91] a golf-club were held to be in possession (for the purposes of the criminal law) of golf-balls lost on their course by members; in *Ranger* v. *Giffin*[92] the owners of a house were entitled to recover a tin of banknotes found beneath the soil by excavating workmen about a year after the owners moved in; and in the American decision of *Allred* v. *Biegal*[93] the land-owner was awarded an ancient canoe which had been discovered sub-merged in a river bank on his land and was removed by two swimmers.[94]

In *Sharman's* case, Lord Russell C.J. based his decision on the fact that the defendants had "actual control" over the pool, and he cited with approval the passage in Pollock & Wright[95] to the effect that possession of land generally carries with it possession of everything attached to or under that land.[96] This reasoning illuminates the two central difficulties of occupier-finder contests. First, it is uncertain whether the conventional doctrine applies to chattels which are merely lying on the land. Logically these should attract no different principle from goods that are buried or affixed to the realty; the only practical difference is that the finder is less likely to do damage when he removes them. In *Grafstein* v. *Holme and Freeman*,[97] Le Bel J.A. pointed out that Lord Russell had not limited himself to buried or attached chattels but had spoken of the general presumption of possession applying whenever goods were "upon

v. *Ellis* 58 Or. 219; 114 P. 100; Riesman (1939) 52 *Harvard Law Review* 1105, at 1116-1117.

---

[88] *Armory* v. *Delamirie* (1722) 1 Stra. 505; 92 E.R. 664; *Bridges* v. *Hawkesworth* (1851) 15 Jur. 1079; 21 L.J.O.B. 75; Salmond, *Torts* (15th ed.), p. 109.
[89] Chapter 6, ante.
[90] [1896] 2 Q.B. 44.
[91] [1948] 2 K.B. 142. Cf. Parry, *What the Judge Thought,* Chapter 2.
[92] (1968) 87 W.N. (N.S.W.) 531; *Corporation of London* v. *Appleyard* [1963] 2 All E.R. 824; *Kowal* v. *Ellis* (1977) 76 D.L.R. (3d) 546.
[93] (1949) 240 Mo. App. 818; 219 S.W. 665; [1950] *Washington University Law Review* 272; cf. *McFadyen* v. *Wineti* (1908) 11 G.L.R. 345.
[94] Cf. *Hurley* v. *City of Niagara Falls* (1969) 25 N.Y. (2d.) 687; 254 N.E. (2d.) 917; 306 N.Y.S. (2d.) 289.
[95] Op. cit. p. 41.
[96] [1896] 2 Q.B., at 47.
[97] (1958) 12 D.L.R. (2d) 727 (Ontario C.A.); Todd (1957) 35 *Can. Bar Rev.* 962; Sommerfield (1958) 36 *Can. Bar Rev.* 558.

or in" the land or house occupied by a landowner.[98] Le Bel J.A. went on to observe[99] that in his view Lord Russell's extension of the principle to unattached chattels was acceptable, provided it could be established that the occupier was in fact in possession of the premises with a clear intention to exercise control over them and over things in or upon them. In the instant case, this conclusion was assisted by the fact that one of the occupier's servants had drawn his attention to the container (a box containing banknotes) more than two years before the servant and colleague forced it open and discovered the contents. The box had been lying undisturbed in the basement of the occupier's premises ever since he moved in some two years before the servant pointed it out to him and the occupier claimed that he had noticed it shortly after moving in. When his attention was drawn to it, he told the servant to put it on a shelf. The court held that the occupier came into possession of the box and its contents at that time[1] and was accordingly entitled to retain it against the servants, even though the nature of its contents was not discovered until they broke it open. The difficult case of *Bridges* v. *Hawkesworth*[2] was distinguished on the ground that the occupier in that case was unaware of the existence of the lost article before it was taken up by the finder. This suggests that if the inquisitive servant in *Grafstein* v. *Holme and Freeman* had removed the box before pointing it out to his master, the latter would have no remedy. But such a conclusion disregards the master's own assertion that he saw the box before the servant entered his employment and overlooks the fact (which may or may not be relevant) that the place of concealment in the instant case was not one to which the public had access, whereas in *Bridges* v. *Hawkesworth* it probably was.

The second difficulty raised by Lord Russell's decision therefore concerns the extent to which public access over the occupier's land affects his prior possession. In *Bridges* v. *Hawkesworth,* the plaintiff, a traveller, found a parcel of banknotes on the floor of a shop occupied by the defendant. The owner never came forward and several years later the plaintiff sought to recover the money from the defendant, with whom he had left it pending the arrival of a claimant. His action succeeded,[3] but the grounds of Patteson J.'s decision are somewhat obscure. Parts of it suggest an affinity with the American distinction between goods that are lost and goods that are mislaid;[4] others indicate that the defendant could only have gained the necessary custody prior to the finding if he became, by virtue thereof, responsible as a bailee.[5]

---

[98] [1896] 2 Q.B., at 47.
[99] (1958) 12 D.L.R. (2d) at 734.
[1] Ibid., at 734.
[2] (1851) 15 Jur. 1079; 21 L.J.Q.B. 75.
[3] For a similar American case, see *In re Savarino* (1932) 1 F. Supp. 331: cf. *Flax* v. *Monticello Realty Co.* (1946) 185 Va. 474: 39 S.E. (2d) 308.
[4] Ante, p. 855.
[5] Or was an innkeeper. At one point Patteson J. implies (21 L.J.Q.B. at 78) that the position may have differed if the goods had been *intentionally* deposited in the shop; he does not make any reference to this being done with the knowledge of the occupier. But in the preceding sentence he distinctly postulates this requirement and his later remarks must be read subject to the qualification. Of course

The tenor of the judgment (and the fact that the only case mentioned, apart from *Armory* v. *Delamirie,*[6] was *Merry* v. *Green*)[7] suggests that no antecedent possession could have existed without the defendant's knowledge of what he was possessing. If this is a correct rationalisation of *Bridges* v. *Hawkesworth* (and it is one strongly supported by the plaintiff's argument) later authority would suggest that the decision is misconceived.

Professor Goodhart has summarised the various explanations of *Bridges* v. *Hawkesworth*[8] and has added one of his own, viz. that the case was wrongly decided.[9] Certainly it is difficult to extract any ratio which is simultaneously coherent and convincing. It is of course arguable that the occupation of land does not necessarily impart possession of goods that are lying upon it; but any distinction between these and buried or attached chattels is difficult to justify, and the circumstances in which this conclusion is merited must surely represent the exception rather than the rule. A more likely explanation, as Lord Russell pointed out in *South Staffordshire Water Co.* v. *Sharman,*[10] is that the occupier of a place which is open to the public (such as a pleasure-ground,[11] a cinema[12] or a department store) will find it harder to establish the elements of dominion and control over the land which are necessary to justify an inference that he is in possession of chattels lying on its surface.[13] But it is not the intention to exclude visitors from the land, so much as the intention to exclude them from articles dropped or mislaid on the land, that is relevant in this connection.[14] If this exists, and it is clearly manifested, it should make no difference whether the premises in question are a place of public resort or a private house. Much may depend, of course, upon the size of the premises and the volume of people passing through them.[15] Nevertheless, it is submitted that neither the public nature of the land nor the fact that the goods are unattached

---

knowledge is different from consent and the absence of the latter may have made the defendant no more than an involuntary bailee.

---

6 (1722) 1 Stra. 505; 92 E.R. 664.
7 (1841) 7 M. & W. 623.
8 (1851) 15 Jur. 1079; 21 L.J.Q.B. 75.
9 (1928) 3 C.L.J. 195, at 202-203. The same view is taken by Hart J. in *Byrne* v. *Hoare* [1965] Qd. R. 135, at 168-169; see also the observations of Wells J. in *Minigall* v. *McCammon* [1970] S.A.S.R. 82, at 93. But cf. *McFadyen* v. *Wineti* (1908) 11 G.L.R. 345, *Byrne* v. *Hoare* [1965] Qd. R. 135 (per Stable and Gibbs JJ.) *Kowal* v. *Ellis* (1977) 76 D.L.R. (3d) 546 and *Minigall* v. *McCammon* (ante), at 88, where *Bridges* v. *Hawkesworth* was accepted or approved.
10 [1896] 2 Q.B. 44, at 47.
11 *Hoagland* v. *F.P.H. Amusement Co.* (1902) 170 Mo. 335; 70 S.W. 878.
12 *Byrne* v. *Hoare* [1965] Qd. R. 135.
13 This was the ground upon which Lord Russell distinguished *Bridges* v. *Hawkesworth* despite Patteson J.'s denial that the place in which the goods were found "makes any legal difference" (21 L.J.Q.B., at 78); a denial which is clearly too broadly stated.
14 (1928) 3 C.L.J., at 199-200.
15 In *Helson* v. *McKenzies (Cuba St.) Ltd.* [1950] N.Z.L.R. 878 it was held that a handbag mistakenly left on the counter of a department store did not come into the possession of the proprietors until another customer handed it to them for safe-keeping. *Bridges* v. *Hawkesworth* seems to have been approved both here and by Stable J. in *Byrne* v. *Hoare* [1965] Qd. R. 135, at 139; see also *White* v. *Alton-Lewis Ltd.* (1975) 49 D.L.R. (3d) 189; *Newman* v. *Bourne & Hollingsworth Ltd.* (1915) 31 T.L.R. 209.

to that land should, by themselves, inhibit the conclusion that the occupier was in possession.[16] A decision in favour of the occupier has the advantage of discountenancing trespassers and fortune hunters[17] and (in most cases) of giving the owner a better chance of recovering his property.[18] Nor is it difficult to envisage circumstances in which a court may wish to grant the owner of goods a remedy against the proprietor of a shop or similar institution who permits the finder of goods on his premises to take them away without inquiry as to his title or bona fides. Such a remedy is clearly assisted by the principle that an occupier is presumed to possess everything that is lying upon his land. There is, in any event, no justification for applying different rules as to possession according to whether or not the chattel is buried on the land. In each case the question is wholly one of fact and the same general considerations apply. Public access (or the lack of it) is merely one of those considerations.

Occasionally the terms upon which the finder has entered the occupier's premises will provide an answer to this problem irrespective of the issue of possession.[19] It may therefore be open to the proprietor of a department store or similar institution, by means of a carefully drafted notice, to acquire a superior right to lost articles over the immediate finder.[20] Indeed, it may be possible to argue that in most cases the finder's permission to enter the premises is subject to the condition that he will not appropriate anything he finds thereon.[21]

---

[16] *Flax* v. *Monticello Realty Co.* (1946) 185 Va. 474; 39 S.E. (2d) 308 (Innkeeper entitled to brooch found by a guest in his room: "the presumption is that the possessor of the thing is the owner of the locus in quo"). See further *Foulke* v. *N.Y. Consolidated Railroad* (1920) 228 N.Y. 269; 127 N.E. 237; *Hannah* v. *Peel* [1945] 1 K.B. 509, at 517.

[17] Goodhart (1928) 3 C.L.J., at 207 contends that there is a distinction between attached or buried goods and goods lying on the surface, because in removing the former the finder must interfere with the land, whereas with the latter he may simply pick them up. With trespassing finders this is by no means always true; broken fences, trodden crops and frightened babies may all occur regardless of the exact location of the goods. But with trespassers the courts may invoke the principle that no man shall profit from his wrong, which would presumably apply irrespective of whether the occupier was in possession: see Salmond, *Jurisprudence* (7th ed.), misleadingly explaining *Elwes* v. *Brigg Gas Co. Ltd.* (1886) 33 Ch. D. 562; *Byrne* v. *Hoare* [1965] Qd. R. 135, at 166, per Hart J. (dissenting). So far as concerns non-trespassers, Goodhart's distinction is sounder but overlooks the prospect of recovery discussed in the following footnote. Cf. *Kowal* v. *Ellis,* ante, n. 9.

[18] Especially with institutions like department stores and restaurants: Riesman (1939) 52 *Harvard Law Review* 1105, at 1125-1126; although in such places it may be harder to make the initial assumption that the occupier is in possession. The problem could perhaps be solved by regarding such occupiers as constructive bailees of lost property and by obliging them to take reasonable steps for its detection and retrieval.

[19] *Ranger* v. *Giffin* (1968) 87 W.N. (N.S.W.) 531 (contractors entitled to remove "debris"; *held* this did not include biscuit-tins of cash); *Byrne* v. *Hoare* [1965] Qd. R. 135, at 169, where such an implied prohibition was utilised by Hart J. to characterise the finder in *Bridges* v. *Hawkesworth* as a trespasser: "He was a trespasser but for the permission to enter and that permission was not shewn to entail any right to make finds for his own benefit as against the plaintiff's".

[20] See British Rail's "Conditions of Carriage of Passengers and their Luggage" which provide, inter alia, that all goods found upon the British Railways Board's premises or trains shall, as between the finder and the Board, be deemed to be in the possession of the latter; Cmnd. 4774 App. I, para. 7.

[21] But cf. Cmnd. 4774 App. I, para. 2.

E. Owner non-occupier versus finder non-occupier

The only English decision in point is *Hannah* v. *Peel*,[22] where judgment was given for the finder on the grounds that the owner of the premises "was never physically in possession (of them) at any time" and accordingly enjoyed no prior possession of the article itself.[23] The decision suggests that the same result would have followed if the chattel had been concealed under, or attached to, the land rather than merely hidden in a crevice in a wall. It further suggests that any period of prior occupation by the freeholder, even one that had ceased at the time of the finding, would have entitled him to retain the chattel provided it had been on the premises at the time of such occupation. The latter conclusion raises problems as to the enduring character of an earlier possession which has, to all appearances, lapsed at the time of finding. If the freeholder does not own the chattel, and has not parted with it to the finder in circumstances equivalent to a bailment, he is compelled to rely upon his possession alone. When he parts with the premises he presumably loses that possession. Such a result could be undesirable, especially where, as in *Hannah* v. *Peel* itself, the freeholder has no choice about surrendering the land.[24] It could be averted by holding that the freeholder has merely yielded possession of the land and not of its contents or of things on its surface,[25] but this is unsatisfactory in the context of the occupier's rights against the finder. Alternatively it could be argued that possession of the chattel has merely passed to the present occupier under a relationship which is analogous to a bailment[26] or that the freeholder's right to recover the chattel from the present occupier gives him that "power of resuming effective control" which is regarded as equivalent to possession.[27] If this is so (and clearly there are difficulties about applying such a rule to freeholders who have surrendered their premises for a fixed period) there is a clear distinction between occupiers who were never in possession and those who were; for although modern authority countenances the status of bailor in one who never possessed the goods in question,[28] generally this will apply only to owners, and with lost goods the owner is ex hypothesi someone other than the parties to the dispute.

F. Finder versus non-owner

Subject to the foregoing, the finder is said to be entitled to retain the goods against anyone who neither owns them nor enjoys a better right of possession.[29] Practically every case on finding reiterates this principle and at least one of them, viz., *Bridges* v. *Hawkesworth*,[30] seems to have

---

22 [1945] 1 K.B. 509.
23 Ibid, at 521; *Bridges* v. *Hawkesworth* (1851) 21 L.J.Q.B. 75; 15 Jur. 1079, followed.
24 It was requisitioned by the War Office.
25 Cf. *Elwes* v. *Briggs Gas Co.* (1886) 33 Ch. D. 562.
26 See p. 862, ante.
27 *Bird* v. *Fort Frances* [1949] 2 D.L.R. 791, at 800 per McRuer C.J.
28 *Belvoir Finance Ltd.* v. *Stapleton* [1971] 1 Q.B. 210.
29 E.g. a hirer who loses them and sues for their recovery during the currency of the bailment.
30 (1851) 15 Jur. 1079; 21 L.J.Q.B. 75.

accentuated it at the expense of a prior possessor. The rule applies not only to finders from whom the goods are stolen or otherwise taken without permission, but to finder-bailors as well. Thus if A finds a watch and takes it to B to be repaired, B (subject to any lien he may enjoy) has no right to retain the watch against A unless he does so under one of the exceptions to the bailee's estoppel.[31]

A more difficult question may arise when B dishonestly sells the article to C, or when C breaks into B's shop and steals it. Here there is no bailment between A and C, and A appears unable to rely upon an existing possession at the time of the offence. Of course, in the first case he may proceed against B and in the second B may proceed against C,[32] but neither of these prospects affords a clue to A's right of action against C on his own account. The only recent decision in which this question even remotely arose was *Bird* v. *Fort Frances*.[33] There, a boy found a can of money on the understructure of a billiard-hall and handed most of it to his mother. The police took it from her and, upon the owner's failing to reappear, refused to return it.[34] The boy sued and was held entitled to recover. McRuer C.J. held that it was immaterial whether the plaintiff was a true finder or whether he had been trespassing at the time and was guilty of felony in taking the money. Nor did the fact that the plaintiff's possession had been interrupted by the handing of the goods to his mother necessarily deprive him of the right to sue for its recovery.[35] Although the finder must, at the time of suing, "actually have possession", a greater degree of control is needed to acquire possession than to retain it; for the latter purpose a mere "power of resuming effective control" will be enough.[36]

It is not easy to predicate upon this decision the theory that a finder-bailor will always be entitled to recover the goods from a third party. McRuer C.J. clearly thought that the boy remained in possession until the police took the money away: indeed, he added that if the plaintiff were out of possession the difficulty could be surmounted by adding his mother as a party to the proceedings. It is uncertain whether every bailor has this right. The proper solution may be to recognise that possession is a variable thing and that different people can be in possession of the same chattel for different purposes at any given time. As between the finder and his bailee, or between that bailee and a third party, the bailee would undoubtedly have possession. In the context of finder and third party, however, it may be permissible to contend that the bailee's possession is that of his bailor and that the finder, having the power of

---

[31] Ante, p. 163; *Armory* v. *Delamirie* (1722) 1 Stra. 505; 92 E.R. 664 is possibly such a case.

[32] *The Winkfield* [1902] P. 42.

[33] [1949] 2 D.L.R. 791 (Ontario H.C.).

[34] The occupier made no claim.

[35] [1949] 2 D.L.R. 791, at 799; and see *Deaderick* v. *Oulds* (1887) 5 S.W. 487; *Sutton* v. *Buck* (1810) 2 Taunt. 302; 127 E.R. 1094. Cf. *Barker* v. *Furlong* [1891] 2 Ch. 172.

[36] Ibid., at 800.

resuming effective control, has sufficient locus standi to bring an action to vindicate his possession.[37]

To some extent this question is immaterial because the bailor under a revocable bailment enjoys an acknowledged right to sue third parties for trespass: in this area at least, the fiction that the bailor enjoys "vicarious" possession[38] is sustained. Moreover, a bailee who commits a fundamental breach of the bailment necessarily causes his bailor's right of possession to revive, so that even the bailee for a term holds under a revocable bailment once he has purported to sell the goods to a third party. But trespass can be brought by a bailor only when the defendant has violated the bailee's possession.[39] If, in our earlier example, B sells and delivers the watch to C, A has no right of trespass against C. The immediate right to possess which would be necessary to sue in conversion exists only in the relationship between A and B: as against C, A has nothing upon which to ground it. Possibly this right alone would be sufficient, so that any succeeding possessor would be deemed to inherit the duties and limitations of the original bailee.[40] A less precarious solution, however, may be to say that A for present purposes continued in possession of the goods until they were misappropriated by C. If this fiction is good enough for trespass, it should be good enough for conversion and detinue as well.

A further problem arises, however, when the finder leases the goods to a bailee for a fixed term. If the finder were the owner, or held by his authority (e.g. as principal bailee), proof of damage to his reversionary interest would entitle him to recover against a third party who interfered with the goods.[41] It is difficult to see what reversionary interest of a universal nature the finder would enjoy in such a case. All he has is a postponed right of possession against a non-tortfeasor who is estopped from denying his title. No similar prohibition governs the third party, whose primary liability is obviously to the bailee. The one lesson that may be learnt from these difficulties is the need for a bailor to be able, in necessary circumstances, to compel his bailee to sue a third party. Even a right to sue on his own account without proof of reversionary damage, as is proposed by the Law Reform Committee,[42] would seem to be valueless to the bailor who enjoys no independent title to the goods.[43] Unless the courts are prepared to hold that the finder's reversionary interest as against his bailee is good, without more, against the whole world,[44] there is only the forlorn hope that he may succeed on the

---

[37] Cf. *Byrne* v. *Hoare* [1965] Qd. R. 135, at 144 per Stable J. The view stated in the text is supported by *Wilson* v. *Lombank Ltd.* [1963] 1 W.L.R. 1294; 1 All E.R. 740 and *U.S.A.* v. *Dollfus Mieg & Cie.* [1952] A.C. 582, at 611; cf. Paton, *Preface* and ante p. 85.

[38] Ante, p. 121.

[39] Ibid.

[40] Of course, no immediate right to possess will suffice to ground an action for detinue unless it arises from some proprietary right: ante, p. 150.

[41] Ante, p. 000.

[42] Cmnd. 4774, para. 34 et seq.

[43] Ibid., para. 53.

[44] Thereby flouting the long-established rule that "a plaintiff who was not in actual possession of the goods but who relies upon a right to possess, can be met by the defence of jus tertii": loc. cit., ante.

grounds of bad faith or negligence against his own bailee; or the equally forlorn hope that he may pray in aid the decision of the Australian High Court in *Beaudesert Shire Council* v. *Smith*;[45] or the prospect of attempting to persuade the bailee to bring an action in a matter in which he may have no more than a negligible interest.

If a court, in valid exercise of its jurisdiction, makes an order that the goods be detained by the police, it seems that any person later deriving title from the police obtains a superior title to a prior thief or finder from whom the order divested the goods. Certainly, this result has been sustained in cases of thieves or suspected thieves.[46] In *Byrne* v. *Hoare*,[47] however, the majority held that an order made under the Justices Acts[48] could not deprive a genuine finder of his right to recover possession against the person holding by virtue of the order. Their ground for so deciding was the somewhat loose one that a finder has not merely "bare naked possession" but "such a property as will enable him to keep (the chattel found) against all but the true owner."[49] In so far as this principle is capable of transcending the limitations attendant upon individual remedies, it suggests both a peculiar body of law relating to finders and some support for the collective uniqueness of bailments as a whole; it may also provide a convenient foundation for the solution of those difficulties previously under discussion. But it is unlikely that *Armory* v. *Delamirie* can be so widely construed as to endow finders with a right of property capable of surviving every lapse or interruption in their possession. If this were so, a finder who lost the goods might be able to reclaim them from a second finder; this, we have already suggested, seems out of the question.[50] The rights of the finder must stand or fall, in the ultimate analysis, upon the traditional remedies which protect all interests in chattels; it is within the framework of those remedies, and the notions of possession, that the true equivalence between finders and owners must eventually be sought. A finder's sole claim to paramountcy seems to consist in his bare possession. Once this is lost, unless violated by a wrongdoer or by a bailee who is estopped from denying the finder's title, the very foundation of his so-called property seems to disappear.[51]

45 (1966) 120 C.L.R. 145; 40 A.L.J.R. 211.
46 *Buckley* v. *Gross* (1863) 3 B.&S. 566; 122 E.R. 213; *Irving* v. *National Provincial Bank Ltd.* [1962] 2 Q.B. 73. See the comments on *Buckley* v. *Gross* in (1974) 37 M.L.R. 213 (D. G. Powles); (1975) 38 M.L.R. 77, at 80 (G. Battersby, A. D. Preston) and cf. *Bird* v. *Fort Frances* [1949] 2 D.L.R. (2d) 791, at 800.
47 [1965] Qd. R. 135, at 144-145, 151-152; and see Hart J. at 175-176.
48 Equivalent to the *Police (Property) Act* 1897 (U.K.); as to which, see *Raymond Lyons & Co. Ltd.* v. *Metropolitan Police Commissioner* [1975] 1 All E.R. 335.
49 Citing *Armory* v. *Delamirie* (1722) 1 Str. 505; 93 E.R. 664.
50 Ante, p. 853; and see *Buckley* v. *Gross* (1863) 3 B.&S. 566, at 572; 122 E.R. 213, at 215 per Crompton J. In his dissenting judgment in *Byrne* v. *Hoare* [1965] Qd. R., at 171-172, Hart J. observed that: " . . . the whole basis of the rule that the possessor of goods has a good title against one that takes them from him is that the defendant is a wrongdoer and this basis drops away when the defendant is in lawful possession under an Order of the Court." In his view the plaintiff had acquired possession by trespass and his bare possession was accordingly lost when the Order was made. It is difficult to see how the circumstances of the acquisition could be relevant, except to show that the finder was not a bailee. Cf. Shartel (1932) 16 *Minn. L. Rev.* 611.
51 See further Atiyah (1955) 18 M.L.R. 97, at 102-104, Jolly, ibid., at 371.

III. The Duties of the Finder

A person discovering goods that are apparently lost is under no duty to take them into his custody or possession.[52] He may even examine them briefly and cast them aside without attracting the duties of a constructive bailee.[53] Once he finally reduces them into his possession, however, he becomes responsible for their safe-keeping and liable to prove that he took the appropriate amount of care.[54]

Most authorities concur in equating the duties of the finder with those of a gratuitous bailee.[55] In some cases this has led to the conclusion that a finder is liable only for gross negligence;[56] in others that he owes a duty of reasonable care.[57] Insofar as the question of reward remains material to standards of care in bailment, it is submitted that the finder should not be regarded as a gratuitous bailee. Although he may not be able to recover his expenses in salvaging the goods, he takes them through his own volition and with the prospect that their owner may never return to claim them. Even where the finder is acting from motives of the purest unselfishness and the chattel is unattractive or of no use to him, an obligation to treat it with reasonable care would seem to provide the fairest result.[58]

The finder is not an involuntary bailee,[59] except insofar as an occupier of land or the bailee of a container, discovering chattels concealed therein, comes into possession of them without his initial knowledge or consent.[60] Where there is no alternative claimant and no procedure for disposing of the goods, it is hard to see how the finder is anything but an involuntary bailee. If, on the other hand, the chattels are valuable, his subsequent retention of them might cancel any inference drawn from the circumstances in which he originally acquired possession. A continuing possession is scarcely involuntary when the occupier might hand the goods to the police but fails to do so, or where he contests and defeats a claim to the goods on the part of a third-party finder. In any event, it is

---

52 *Vandrink & Archer's* case (1590) 1 Leon 221, at 223; 74 E.R. 203, at 204; Wyatt Paine, at 28.

53 Vaines, *Personal Property* (5th ed.), p. 83.

54 Contra, *Vandrink & Archer's* case (1590) 1 Leon 221; 74 E.R. 203.

55 *Newman* v. *Bourne & Hollingsworth Ltd.* (1915) 31 T.L.R. 209; *Helson* v. *McKenzies (Cuba St.) Ltd.* [1950] N.Z.L.R. 878; *Grafstein* v. *Holme and Freeman* (1958) 12 D.L.R. (2d) 727, at 738-739; Story, s. 87: Street, *Foundations of Legal Liability,* Vol. II, p. 278; *Kowal* v. *Ellis* (1977) 76 D.L.R. (3d) 546.

56 E.g. *Grafstein* v. *Holme and Freeman, ante;* Beven, *Negligence* (2nd ed.); *Ramsay* v. *Bell* (1872) 1 P.E.1. 417. Cf. *Mosgrave* v. *Agden* (1591) Owen, 141; 74 E.R. 960; *Johnson* v. *Jones* (1626) Benl. 170; 73 E.R. 1032, both of which involved actions in conversion.

57 *Newman* v. *Bourne & Hollingworth Ltd., ante,* where it is suggested that there is no difference between the two standards anyway: cf. *Helson* v. *McKenzies (Cuba St.) Ltd., ante.*

58 In America, authority is divided upon whether the finder is a gratuitous bailee: Riesmann (1939) 52 *Harvard Law Review* 1105, at 1109; *Corpus Juris Secundum,* Vol. 36A, 425. Although American authorities are much more liberal in granting the finder his expenses, this fact alone does not clearly assist the conclusion that he is a bailee for reward.

59 *Helson* v. *McKenzies (Cuba St.) Ltd.* [1950] N.Z.L.R. 878.

60 Cf. *Warner* v. *Elizabeth Arden Ltd.* (1939) 83 Sol.Jo. 258.

possible that even an involuntary bailee must treat the goods with such care as is reasonable in all the circumstances of the case.[61]

There are few cases in which a finder has been found liable on the basis of a lack of reasonable care. In *Helson* v. *McKenzies (Cuba St.) Ltd.*[62] the question did not fall to be decided because the court discovered no bailment between the owner of the handbag and the owners of the department-store where it was lost and subsequently handed in. The decision on this point seems to rely upon an outmoded conception of bailment as a consensual, if not contractual, relation. There is, in fact, a strong modern authority for the view that a finder occupies for most civil purposes the position of a bailee.[63] When, therefore, a finder delivers the goods to a third party for redelivery to their owner, the third party should owe both to the original finder and to the owner, the duties of a bailee.[64] Of course, he will not be expected to make double restitution.

The onus of proving that he took reasonable care of the goods must be assumed to rest, as in the case of ordinary bailments, upon the finder-bailee. Thus, where jewellery is mislaid in a department store and picked up by a shopwalker who, disobeying house instructions, puts it in his desk, the owners of the store must show that any disappearance from his custody occurred without negligence on the part of their staff.[65]

The finder will, moreover, be liable for the acts or omissions of his servants in performing any duty which he has delegated to them in relation to the goods, or which occur in the ordinary course of their employment.[66] He is liable in conversion when the goods are delivered to someone other than their owner or his authorised representative;[67] in this respect negligence is immaterial because the finder is not an involuntary bailee.[68] He is also answerable for any misappropriation of the goods by a servant whom he has charged with their custody.[69]

The mere possession of lost chattels does not per se amount to a conversion, although it will be otherwise if the finder forms the intention (either at the time of taking possession or subsequently) to deprive the owner of them. Nor is it conversion when the finder takes reasonable

---

[61] Ante, p. 381 et seq.

[62] [1950] N.Z.L.R. 878, at 905, 914.

[63] *Morris* v. *C. W. Martin & Sons Ltd.* [1966] 1 Q.B. 716, at 731-732, 738; *Gilchrist Watt & Sanderson Pty. Ltd.* v. *York Products Pty. Ltd.* [1970] 3 All E.R. 825, at 830-831. Cf. Paton, p. 118; *Newman* v. *Bourne & Hollingsworth Ltd.* (1915) 31 T.L.R. 209; *Thompson* v. *Nixon* [1966] 1 Q.B. 103; [1965] C.L.J. 173; Stoljar, (1955) 7 *Res Judicatae* 160, at 169.

[64] As with a sub-bailment: Salmond, *Torts*, (15th ed.), p. 149.

[65] *Newman* v. *Bourne & Hollingsworth Ltd.* (1915) 31 T.L.R. 209, semble. Cf. *Helson* v. *McKenzies (Cuba St.) Ltd.* [1950] N.Z.L.R. 878, at 916. There seems to be no specific ruling on the finder's burden of proof, but it follows logically from the equation between findings and other bailments in *Morris* v. *C. W. Martin & Sons Ltd.* and *Gilchrist Watt & Sanderson Pty. Ltd.* v. *York Products Pty. Ltd.* ante, n. 63.

[66] *Newman* v. *Bourne & Hollingsworth*, ante.

[67] *Isaack* v. *Clark* (1615) 2 Bulst. 306, at 312; 80 E.R. 1143, at 1148.

[68] *Helson* v. *McKenzies (Cuba St.) Ltd.* [1950] N.Z.L.R. 878, where, however, the plaintiff's damages were reduced on the grounds of her own contributory negligence; sed quaere. See p. 135, ante. Cf. *Morris* v. *Third Avenue R.R. Co.* (1862) 1 Daly 202 (N.Y.), where a negligent misdelivery was required to ground liability.

[69] *Morris* v. *C. W. Martin & Sons Ltd.* [1966] 1 Q.B. 716. See further the comments on *depositum*, p. 306 et seq., ante.

steps for the preservation of the goods,[70] even though these steps, without negligence on his part, result in their loss to the owner. According to Coke[71] the prudent finder will endeavour to find the true owner and deliver the goods to him. This advice is given on the strength of Coke's conclusion that a misdelivery sounds in conversion: in fact, there seems to be no compelling obligation on the finder to do anything towards returning the goods to their owner,[72] other than to abstain from a dishonest concealment of his find and to keep them available for the owner to retrieve them. On the other hand, the fewer steps the finder takes toward the honest objective of returning the goods, the easier it will be to infer that he has converted them, particularly where the owner is known to him or could have been discovered by reasonable means. A court may also be alive to the fact that a secretive finder could be more likely to bring about the permanent loss of the goods to their owner than no finder at all. Clearly, the safest course is to advertise the find or to hand the goods to the police.[73]

The finder is entitled to refuse to deliver the goods to a claimant until the latter has established his right to them or reasonable enquiries have been made.[74] In so delaying, the finder therefore commits neither detinue nor conversion. Nor is it conversion to lose the goods, even through carelessness, although in such an event the finder will probably be in breach of his duty as a constructive bailee.[75] But conversion is committed whenever the finder uses the goods for his own benefit, or hires them to a third party, or intercepts and consumes the profits of them, or seriously mishandles them in any other manner that the owner cannot be taken to have impliedly authorised.[76] Even the abandonment of the goods, or the act of turning them out on the street, may amount to a conversion, at least where they are permanently lost as a result.[77] On the other hand, an exceptional act of destruction (such as the humane killing of a dog seriously injured by the roadside) may be justifiable on the grounds of an agency of necessity between the parties.[78]

Treasure Trove: Certain categories of goods belong, irrespective of the circumstances in which they are found, to the Crown. These goods are characterised as treasure trove. Three main conditions must be satisfied before they can be classified in this way:

1. The goods must be of gold or silver.
2. Their ownership must be unknown.

---

[70] *Hollins* v. *Fowler* (1875) L.R. 7 H.L. 757, at 766 per Blackburn J.
[71] *Isaack* v. *Clark* (1615) 2 Bulst. 306, at 312; 80 E.R. 1143, at 1148.
[72] Cf. Wyatt Paine, pp. 28-29.
[73] Or. in W. Australia, to utilise ss. 20-21 of the *Disposal of Uncollected Goods Act* 1970; ante, p. 407. Failure to take the goods to the police may be a criminal offence: see, for instance, *Police Offences Act* 1936 (Tas.), s. 43(1).
[74] *Isaak* v. *Clark*, ante.
[75] Cf. *Vandrink & Archer's* case (1590) 1 Leon 221; 74 E.R. 203.
[76] *Isaack* v. *Clark*, ante.
[77] See *Ryan* v. *Chown* (1910) 160 Mich. 204; 125 N.W. 46 (finder of turkeys later released them on the highway: *held*, guilty of conversion); cf. *Wilson* v. *McLaughlin* (1871) 107 Mass. 587 (servant found horse straying on highway and put it in his master's field; two days later the master found out and ordered him to turn it loose; the servant obeyed and the horse was lost: *held*, the servant was not liable as a bailee).
[78] *Palmer* v. *Stear* (1963) 113 L.Jo. 420.

3. They must have been hidden in the ground or in a building with the intention of subsequently being recovered, rather than having merely been lost.[79]

Although the identification of goods as treasure trove clearly obliterates all questions of title between finders and occupiers or employers, it is material to note that in many cases it will be advantageous to the finder for them to be identified in this way. The goods will then be valued by the British Museum and the finder will generally be rewarded by means of an ex gratia payment equivalent to their full market value.[80] There seems to be no reported instance in which an employer of the finder, or an occupier, has been held entitled to recover such a reward from the finder on the grounds of unjust enrichment; in many cases, such restitution would seem desirable, for as Blakeley points out,[81] the practice has recently grown up among certain people of searching, with metal detectors and similar devices, for treasure trove on land which does not belong to them.[82]

The present law of treasure trove is rife with anomalies. The limitation to gold and silver articles means that a leaden pot in which silver coins are found would be allocated according to the ordinary rules of finding, while the coins themselves would go to the Crown;[83] the distinction between abandoned goods and those which the owner intended to retrieve means that many antiquities (e.g. the Sutton Hoo treasure) are beyond the reach of the Crown altogether, except insofar as it may bid for them in competition with outsiders.[84] The case is strong for a national antiquities law which protects all archaeological finds irrespective of their constituency or of the circumstances in which they are lost.[85]

IV. THE DUTIES OF THE OWNER

The owner of lost goods is under no obligation to search for them or to collect them from the finder. If, however, he knows that they have been taken into custody and are awaiting his retrieval, the longer he waits the more likely a court is to conclude that the finder has become an involuntary bailee.[86]

---

[79] Report of the Committee on Death Certification and Coroners Cmnd. 4810, (1971), para. 13.22: a more elaborate definition, and one which seems universally accepted by the courts, is given by Chitty, Prerogatives of the Crown (1802), p. 152.

[80] Cmnd. 4810, para. 13.23; but cf. Godfrey Blakeley who, in a valuable article in the Daily Telegraph Magazine, 21 September, 1973, p. 9, contends that the rewards given by the Treasury "are much lower than the price the objects would fetch on the international fine art market."

[81] Op. cit., p. 13 (quoting from an interview with Charles Sparrow Q.C.).

[82] There seems no reason why the occupier or employer should not recover damages on the strength of his possessory interest merely because the goods belong to the Crown.

[83] Blakeley, ibid.

[84] In fact, in the Sutton Hoo case the landowner, Mrs. Pretty, donated the hoard to the nation.

[85] In Cmnd. 4810, para. 13.26-13.27 it is advocated that the coroner retain his present functions in this field until such a law is forthcoming. The coroner provides a useful first tribunal not only for deciding whether goods are treasure trove but also (if they are found not to be treasure trove) for declaring the party entitled to possession.

[86] Ante, p. 393. The owner may also be held to have abandoned the goods.

Although there seems to be no decision in point, a loser can presumably be made liable for negligence if the goods are likely to cause damage or injury and in fact have this effect. The foregoing observation may apply not only when the goods are in their lost state but when a finder picks them up and takes them home. Danger, be it to chattels or to the person, invites rescue,[87] and if it is reasonably foreseeable that a finder will take the goods into his custody and suffer loss as a result, the loser who has negligently created this situation should be answerable for the ensuing damage.[88] Possibly other actions, e.g. nuisance, will lie against the loser in appropriate cases.

The more difficult and common problem is whether the loser is under any duty to compensate the finder for his trouble and expense in taking the goods into custody and preserving them until the owner returns. American decisions on this point are prolific and generous. Finders have been allowed to recover not only their reasonable expenses in rescuing and preserving the chattel[89] but even on occasions storage fees[90] or compensation for time and trouble.[91] It is unlikely that a Commonwealth court would adopt so munificent a view. Certainly, the finder has no lien[92] for there is no general right of salvage at Common Law.[93] There are, admittedly, two decisions which might be construed as supporting the finder's entitlement to his expenses, but neither of them is conclusive. In one of them,[94] the bailment was involuntary; and there is a clear difference between a person who has no choice in the possession of goods and a finder who assumes it entirely of his own volition. In the other case, Eyre C.J. was prepared to treat the defendant as a finder and remarked that the law "would go as far as it could go" in recompensing him for the performance of a good and meritorious office.[95] The learned annotator to the report remarks that such expenses would probably be recoverable, if at all, on an assumpsit for work and labour; but he then goes on to observe that a mere voluntary courtesy will not support an action of this kind.[96] In view of the fairly exacting scale of conditions which must now be fulfilled to support an implied assumpsit[97] it seems improbable that the finder will

[87] *Wagner* v. *International R.R.* (1921) 232 N.Y. 176 (Cardozo J.).

[88] *Haynes* v. *Harwood* [1935] 1 K.B. 146: *Hyett* v. *G.W. Ry. Co.* [1948] 1 K.B. 345; *Baker* v. *T. E. Hopkins & Son* [1959] 1 W.L.R. 966; 3 All E.R. 225; *Horsley* v. *MacLaren* (1970) 11 D.L.R. (3d) 277; but cf. *Cutler* v. *United Dairies Ltd.* [1933] 2 K.B. 297.

[89] *Linscomb* v. *Goodyear Tire & Rubber Co.* (1952) 199 F. 431, at 438; *Meekins* v. *Simpson* 96 S.E. 894.

[90] *Auto Insurance Co. of Hartford, Conn.* v. *Kirby* (1932) 144 So. 123.

[91] *Reeder* v. *Anderson* 4 Dana. 193.

[92] *Binstead* v. *Buck* (1776) 2 Wm. Bl. 1117; 96 E.R. 660; *Nicholson* v. *Chapman* (1793) 2 H. Bl. 254; 126 E.R. 536; *Sorrell* v. *Paget* [1950] 1. K.B. 252; *R.* v. *Howson* (1966) 55 D.L.R. (2d) 582, at 593-594; and see *Castellain* v. *Thompson* (1862) 13 C.B. (N.S.) 105; *Wood* v. *Pierson* 1 Or. 686; 62 Am D. 299.

[93] Vaines, *Personal Property* (5th ed.), p. 140; Goff and Jones, *Law of Restitution*. p. 238.

[94] *R.* v. *Howson* (1966) 55 D.L.R. (2d) 582, at 593-594.

[95] *Nicholson* v. *Chapman* (1793) 2 H.Bl. 254; 126 E.R. 536 (where timber broke loose from a dock, floated downstream, was washed up on, and obstructed, a tow path within the manor of Wimbledon, and was removed by the defendant, on the instructions of the bailiff of the manor, to a place of safety).

[96] Ibid., citing *Lampleigh* v. *Braithwaite* (1615) Hob. 105; 80 E.R. 255.

[97] *In re Casey's Patents, Stewart* v. *Casey* [1892] 1 Ch. 115; *Casey* v. *Commissioner of Inland Revenue* [1959] N.Z.L.R. 1052.

have an action on this or any other ground; the influential decision in
Falcke v. *Scottish Imperial Insurance Co.*[98] embodies the characteristic
aversion of the Common Law to volunteers who seek to embroil the
beneficiaries of their exertions in liabilities to which they have given no
prior consent. In many respects this is an acceptable policy, for the finder
is under no compulsion to act as he does. On the other hand, there are
cases involving other unrequested services which allow recovery for benefits
conferred in circumstances of necessity[99] and there are obvious advantages
in ensuring that people who would otherwise act from altruistic motives
should not be deterred, by the thought of expense, from doing so. The
test proposed by Goff and Jones would seem to strike a proper balance
between the required immunity of the owner and the demands of justice
towards the finder:

> . . . the intervener . . . should . . . be entitled to reimbursement
> of his reasonable expenditure, provided that he acted in good faith
> and in the interests of the owner of the property, *and* his inter-
> vention was necessary to preserve the property, *and* he did not
> intend his services to be gratuitous.[1]

This formulation would effectively exclude most finders, including those
whose motives in taking possession were, though not dishonest, essentially
selfish. It would be undesirable if a person who kept the property for a
long period and had every intention of doing so indefinitely were able to
turn round to the owner, upon his retrieving it, and submit a large claim
for storage or other expenses.

Reward: If a reward has been offered for the return of lost goods, and
the finder returns them on the faith of that reward, he has a contractual
right of recovery.[2] However, it would appear that even in these circumstances the finder has no lien.

V. OTHER UNREQUESTED KEEPERS

There remains, as we have seen,[3] a motley collection of circumstances in
which one person may come into possession of another's goods without
the consent of the owner and without qualifying as a finder. Sometimes
he may do so honestly, as where he genuinely believes that the goods are
his own, or where he takes possession in the interests of the owner; on other
occasions, the dispossession will be dishonest, as where the goods are
obtained by theft or by deception. Leaving aside the involuntary bailee, it
is clear that the unrequested keeper resembles the bailee by consent in at
least three respects. First, he obtains possession of the goods and can

---

[98] (1886) 34 Ch. D. 234.
[99] *Re Rhodes* (1890) 44 Ch. D. 94 (supply of goods to a lunatic); *Matheson* v. *Smiley*
[1932] 2 D.L.R. 781; *Greenspan* v. *Slate* (1953) 97 Atl. (2d) 390 (medical aid in
an emergency); *Schneider* v. *Eisovitch* [1960] 2 K.B. 430 (visit by relations of
seriously injured person).
[1] *Law of Restitution,* p. 240.
[2] *R.* v. *Clarke* (1927) 40 C.L.R. 227; *Williams* v. *Carwardine* (1833) 4 B. & Ad.
621; *Gibbons* v. *Proctor* (1891) 64 L.T. 594 (as explained in Treitel, *Law of
Contract*) (4th ed.), p. 27); *Fitch* v. *Snedaker* (1868) 38 N.Y. 248; cf. *Neville* v.
Kelly (1862) 12 C.B.N.S. 740.
[3] *Ante,* p. 27.

exercise the possessory remedies against anyone who violates that possession, unless of course the defendant is the owner or enjoys a better right to possess.[4] Secondly, if he bails the goods to a third party, the bailee is obliged to comply with the terms of the bailment and cannot evade this duty by pleading jus tertii.[5] Thirdly, the unrequested keeper should owe towards the goods the responsibilities of a bailee and should be bound to show that any damage or destruction occurred through no failure on his part to exercise the appropriate degree of care.[6] In most cases this duty will be irrelevant because the unrequested keeper will have committed conversion by taking the goods out of the possession of the owner. Whether a constructive bailment created in these circumstances should qualify as gratuitous, or as one for reward, should depend upon the facts of the case, and particularly upon the intentions with which the bailee assumed possession.[7]

---

[4] *Jeffries* v. *G.W. Ry. Co.* (1856) 25 L.J. Q.B. 107; *Daniel* v. *Rogers* [1918] 2 K.B. 228, at 234; *Frances & Taylor, Ltd.* v. *Commercial Bank of Australia Ltd.* [1932] N.Z.L.R. 1028; *Bird* v. *Ford Frances* [1949] 2 D.L.R. 791; *Richard* v. *Nowlan* (1959) 19 D.L.R. (2d) 229 (Bridges J.A. dissenting); Pollock & Wright, at 92-93, 187; Goodeve, *Personal Property* (9th ed.), p. 41; cf. *Buckley* v. *Gross* (1863) 3 B. & S. 566; 122 E.R. 213, which is inconclusive on this point, and *Byrne* v. *Hoare* [1965] Qd. R. 135, where Hart J. (dissenting) held that the plaintiff's possession was unlawful because it was obtained through trespass, but did not appear to doubt that a direct incursion upon that "bare naked possession" would have been actionable.

[5] *Biddle* v. *Bond* (1865) 6 B. & S. 225; 122 E.R. 1179; *Chapman* v. *Robinson and Ferguson* (1969) 71 W.W.R. 515, at 522.

[6] *McCowen* v. *McCulloch* [1926] 1 D.L.R. 312; *Canadian Imperial Bank of Commerce* v. *Doucette* (1968) 70 D.L.R. (2d) 657; *Chesworth* v. *Farrar* [1967] 1 Q.B. 407; cf. *Mazullah Khan* v. *McNamara* (1911) 13 W.A.L.R. 151; *Palmisano* v. *Downey* (1970) 233 So. (2d) 697; *Aetna Casualty Co.* v. *Chisman and Hollandsworth* (1974) 528 P. (2d) 1317.

[7] Ante, p. 283 et seq.

CHAPTER 23

INNKEEPERS*

The liability of the innkeeper for loss of his guests' property does not depend upon bailment.[1] Both at Common Law and under statute,[2] he is strictly liable for the theft or disappearance of goods[3] irrespective of whether the guest has delivered them into his possession. Many innkeepers do, in fact, become bailees by special arrangement with their guests[4] and in most jurisdictions a delivery into the innkeeper's custody will deprive him of his statutory limitation of liability;[5] but the creation of a bailment of the guest's property is by no means the invariable consequence (or a necessary pre-requisite) of the relationship of guest and host.[6]

I. LIABILITY UNDER THE HOTEL PROPRIETORS ACT 1956[7]

Section 1(1) of the Act[8] provides that a hotel within the meaning of the Act shall be deemed to be an inn; that no other establishment shall be deemed to fall within the meaning of inn; and that the duties, liabilities and rights, which prior to the commencement of the Act attached to an innkeeper as such, shall now (subject to the provisions of the Act) attach only to the proprietor of a hotel as subsequently defined. "Hotel" is defined as follows:

> . . . an establishment held out by the proprietor as offering food, drink and, if so required, sleeping accommodation, without special contract, to any traveller presenting himself who appears able and willing to pay a reasonable sum for the services and facilities provided and who is in a fit state to be received.[9]

---

*Attention is drawn to the Paris Convention on the liability of hotel-keepers for the property of guests. U.K. ratification to this Convention was deposited on 12 July 1963, and the Convention entered into force 15 February 1967. See Cmnd. 3205.

[1] *Robbins & Co.* v. *Gray* [1895] 2 Q.B. 501, at 503-504 per Lord Esher M.R.; Paton, *Bailment in the Common Law*, p. 199; Vaines, *Personal Property* (5th ed.), p. 130.

[2] England: *Hotel Proprietors Act* 1956. For Australian statutes see p. 902 et seq., post.

[3] And, in most cases, for damage to goods: see post.

[4] One example is *Phipps* v. *New Claridge Hotel Ltd.* (1905) 22 T.L.R. 49; ante, p. 296; and see *Daniel* v. *Hotel Pacific Pty. Ltd.* [1953] V.L.R. 447; post, p. 884

[5] Post, p. 893 et seq.

[6] For one interesting modern implication of this, see *Kott and Kott* v. *Gordon Hotels Ltd.* [1968] 2 Lloyd's Rep. 228; post, p. 894.

[7] This is the contemporary English statute. Australian legislation will be discussed later in the present chapter: post, p. 902 et seq.

[8] Implementing, in general, the recommendations of the Second Report of the Law Reform Committee: (1954) Cmnd. 9161.

[9] Section 1(3).

This definition substantially embodies the Common Law, and it is within the Common Law decisions that concrete examples of the meaning of an inn or hotel are to be found. In *Thompson* v. *Lacy*[10] three varying definitions were offered by members of the court:

> . . . a house, where [the owner] furnishes beds and provisions to persons in certain stations of life, who may think fit to apply for them . . . he does not absolutely engage to receive every person who comes to his house, but only such as are capable of paying a compensation suitable to the accommodation provided.[11]
> . . . a house where the traveller is furnished with everything which he has occasion for whilst upon his way.[12]
> . . . a house, the owner of which holds out that he will receive all travellers and sojourners who are willing to pay a price adequate to the sort of accommodation provided, and who come in a situation in which they are fit to be received.[13]

Despite the individual variations and differences of emphasis between these statements, the cardinal elements clearly emerge as a willingness to receive all reasonable candidates for accommodation and the provision of such accommodation itself. In accordance with these requirements, it has been held that the following are inns at Common Law: the Ritz Hotel;[14] a temperance hotel[15] or "coffee palace";[16] a motel[17] and, in America, a sleeping-car express.[18] The presence of stables or (presumably) garaging facilities is not essential,[19] nor is the provision of spirituous liquors,[20] although the innkeeper must be prepared to offer his guests lodging, and not merely refreshment, if required.[21] The lack of a sign will not prevent an establishment from qualifying as an inn[22] and the name upon the sign is not conclusive evidence of its status.[23] Ale-houses

---

[10] (1820) 3 B. & Ald. 283; 106 E.R. 667; see the remarks in Beven, *Negligence* (2nd ed.), p. 1026.

[11] Ibid., at 285; 667, per Abbott C.J.

[12] Ibid., at 286; 668, per Bayley J.

[13] Ibid., at 287; 668, per Best J.; adopted by Kennedy J. in *Orchard & Co.* v. *Bush* [1898] 2 Q.B. 284.

[14] *Marsh* v. *Police Commissioner* [1945] K.B. 43; and the Dorchester: *Gates* v. *Dorchester Hotel* [1953] C.L.Y. 1789.

[15] *Cunningham* v. *Philp* (1896) 12 T.L.R. 352.

[16] *Miller* v. *Federal Coffee Palace* (1889) 15 V.L.R. 30; *Knox* v. *Victoria Coffee Palace Co.* (1895) 1 A.L.R. (C.N.) 33; but cf. *Doe d. Pitt* v. *Laming* (1814) 4 Camp. 73, at 77.

[17] *Turner* v. *Queensland Motels Pty. Ltd.* [1968] Qld. R. 189; *Theeman* v. *Forte Properties Pty. Ltd.* [1973] 1 N.S.W.L.R. 418; cf. *King* v. *Barclay's Motel* (1960) 24 D.L.R. (2d) 418.

[18] *Pullman Palace Car Co.* v. *Lowe* (1889) 28 Neb. 239; but the decision has not passed uncriticised. See Paton, op. cit., pp. 198-199 and cf. *Goldstein* v. *Pullman Co.* (1917) 220 N.Y. 549; 116 N.E. 376; *Sneddon* v. *Payne* (1921) 114 Misc. 587; 187 N.Y. Supp. 185; *Van Dike* v. *Pullman Co.* (1932) 145 Misc. 452; 260 N.Y. Supp. 292; (1932-1933) 7 *St. John's Law Review* 334.

[19] *Thompson* v. *Lacy* (1820) 3 B. & Ald. 283, at 286-287 106 E.R. 667, at 668.

[20] *Miller* v. *Federal Coffee Palace* (1889) 15 V.L.R. 30. Quaere whether the provision of food was essential at Common Law: *Nelson* v. *Johnson* (1908) 116 N.W. 828 suggests not, but *R.* v. *Zinburg* [1953] O.W.N. 601 holds to the contrary. The statutory definition now requires that food be available: see ante.

[21] *Thompson* v. *Lacy* ante. But this does not mean, at Common Law, that the relationship of innkeeper and guest will be prevented from arising because the latter does not sleep at the inn: see post.

[22] *Parker* v. *Flint* (1699) 12 Mod. 254, at 255.

[23] See *Thompson* v. *Lacy*.

and coffee-houses are not inns,[24] and a bar within an hotel may fail to
be part of that hotel if it is physically distinct and has a separate
entrance.[25]

In *Lamond* v. *Richard*,[26] Lord Esher M.R. suggested that large London
hotels, presumably exercising a strict power of discrimination over
potential guests, may not show that willingness to receive all comers that
is correlative to the concept of an inn; but this observation seems unlikely in the context of the modern chain hotel, and Lord Esher conceded that the issue was, in any event, one of fact. Conversely, there
seems no reason why institutions like the Y.M.C.A. or even, perhaps, the
Salvation Army might not be classified as hoteliers within the meaning of
the Act. But the lodging-house keeper (or the person who takes in paying
guests) will not be an innkeeper because such arrangements depend
upon special contract and are not open to the public indiscriminately.[27]
The decisions in question generally turn upon the status of the lodger
as a guest rather than that of the host as an innkeeper. Clearly, one
may be an innkeeper and yet have visitors who are lodgers rather than
guests, towards whom the traditionally strict insurer's liability will not
be owed. Not everyone who visits an inn will be a guest within the
meaning of the Act.

A. The meaning of guest

The Hotel Proprietors Act requires that, in order for the innkeeper's
strict liability to be imposed, the loss or damage to the goods must have
occurred:

> . . . during the period commencing with the midnight immediately
> preceding, and ending with the midnight immediately following, a
> period for which the traveller was a guest at the hotel and entitled
> to use the accommodation so engaged.[28]

This section operates upon the assumption that only guests sleeping
at the hotel will be entitled to rely upon the hotelier's strict liability.
This assumption is articulated by s. 2(1), which explicitly provides that
a guest, in order to enforce the liability imposed by the Act, must be a
traveller; that is, a person for whom, at the time of the loss or damage,
sleeping accommodation has been engaged. These provisions accordingly
render redundant a number of pre-1956 cases which had held that, at
Common Law, a person could qualify as a traveller although he was
not staying at the inn.[29]

---

[24] *Thompson* v. *Lacy; Q.R.S. Canadian Corporation Ltd.* v. *Coleman* [1931] 1
D.L.R. 277; [1931] 3 D.L.R. 577.
[25] *R* v. *Rymer* (1877) 2 Q.B.D. 136; see also *Sealey* v. *Tandy* [1902] 1 K.B. 296, at
299-300; *Strauss* v. *County Hotel Co.* (1883) 53 L.J.Q.B. 25; *Q.R.S. Canadian
Corporation Ltd.* v. *Coleman* ante; *Williams* v. *Linnitt* [1951] 1 K.B. 565, at 577;
cf. *Carey* v. *Deveaux* (1920) 53 D.L.R. 267; *King* v. *Barclay* (1961) 24 D.L.R.
(2d) 418.
[26] [1897] 1 Q.B. 541, at 545.
[27] *Houlder* v. *Soulby* (1860) 8 C.B.N.S. 254; *Railway Assessment Authority* v.
G.W. Rail Co. [1948] A.C. 234, 248; and see post.
[28] *Hotel Proprietors Act* 1956, s. 2(1)(b).
[29] *Bennett* v. *Mellor* (1793) 5 Term. Rep. 273 (visitor to inn for refreshment on
market-day); *Orchard* v. *Bush & Co.* [1898] 2 Q.B. 284; *Aria* v. *Bridge House
Hotel* (1927) 137 L.T. 299 (travellers stopping for meal at hotel); *Williams* v.

The law has traditionally drawn a distinction between a traveller and a lodger. A lodger is someone who lodges at the establishment not as an ordinary wayfarer, willing within reason to engage such accommodation as is offered and entitled to insist upon it within the limits of the innkeepers facilities, but in reliance upon a special contract with the proprietor and one which is generally contemplated to last for a considerable time: ". . . lodgers cannot come by authority of law upon their journey without a previous contract, and the (proprietor) may refuse any of them, if he pleases."[30] The question is one of fact, and is more instructive to look at individual cases than at extracted generalisations. In many instances, of course, the difference between a lodging-house and an inn will be self-evident, particularly from such criteria as the degree of discrimination shown in accepting visitors and the length of accommodation which visitors are permitted, or expected, to engage.[31] Much may also depend upon the capacity and occupation of the proprietor: the householder who takes in occasional guests as a side-line, or the seasonal seaside landlady,[32] can therefore in many cases be readily identified as beyond the Common Law notion of an innkeeper.

In *Alldis* v. *Huxley*[33] a horse-trainer engaged accommodation from the defendant hotelier for himself and his stable boys, at a lump sum per week. This arrangement was made two days before the arrival of the trainer and his lads to take up residence, and the trainer paid three months' charges in advance. The court held that this was a contract for the lodging of men and horses and did not give rise to the relationship of innkeeper and guest. Accordingly, the hotelier had no lien.[34] It was not denied that such a relationship might arise between an innkeeper and a weekly boarder, but in the present case the contract was of a very special nature and such a relationship could not be sustained.

Sometimes the words spoken at the time of contracting may provide an indicator to the nature of the parties' relationship. Thus, in *Hanson* v. *Barwise*,[35] where the defendant said to the female plaintiff: "I would

Linnitt [1951] 1 K.B. 565 (farmer living about a mile from inn calling for a drink on his way home); *Cryan* v. *Hotel Rembrandt* (1925) 41 T.L.R. 287 (guest of person staying at hotel); *Webster* v. *Opitz* [1917] V.L.R. 107, at 109-110; *Ex parte Coulson; re Jones* (1947) 48 S.R. (N.S.W.) 178, at 184-185. See also *O'Dea* v. *O'Hara* (1895) *South Australian Advertiser*, 17 May; *Tinsley* v. *Dudley* [1951] 2 K.B. 18; *Murphy* v. *Innes* (1877) 11 S.A.L.R. 56; cf. *Wright* v. *Anderton* [1909] 1 K.B. 209, at 213. Note, however, that the Common Law cases may still be relevant under individual State laws in Australia.

30 *Parkhurst* v. *Foster* (1700) 1 Ld. Raym. 479; 91 E.R. 1219. See also *Thompson* v. *Lacy* ante, per Best J.: "a lodging-house keeper makes a contract with every man that comes, whereas an innkeeper is bound, without making any special contract, to provide lodging and entertainment for all at a reasonable price." The guest-lodger distinction is an old one. One of the earliest decisions adverting to it was *Warbrook* v. *Griffin* (1609) 2 Br. & G. 254; see also *Gulielm's Case* (1625) Lat. 88.
31 But cf. n. (44) post.
32 Cf. *Daniel* v. *Hotel Pacific Pty. Ltd.* [1953] V.L.R. 447; post, p. 884.
33 (1891) 12 L.R. (N.S.W.) 158; see also *Hayes* v. *Story* (1853), 10 April, cited in the instant case but apparently unreported.
34 Post, p. 897.
35 [1930] St. R. Qld. 285; 24 Q.J.P.R. 91; see also *Caldecutt* v. *Piesse* (1932) 49 T.L.R. 26.

like you and your husband to come and board with me" and the plaintiffs
in consequence stayed on the defendant's premises from June till November,[36] it was held that they were not travellers but boarders and the
defendant accordingly had no lien upon their property. But of course,
words like "boarder" and "guest" are often used interchangeably and
the designation accorded to the visitor by the proprietor is of little value
where (unlike in *Hanson* v. *Barwise*) the general circumstances are
inconsistent with the terminology employed.

A similar case was *Ford* v. *Seligman*,[37] where the appellant booked in
at the respondent's hotel and obtained a reduction in the weekly rate on
the ground that he would be there "for quite some time". The appellant
did in fact stay for about five months but a few weeks after his arrival
goods were stolen from his room. Payment had been made by the week
and he seems to have used the hotel only for sleeping. It was held that he
was a mere lodger and the respondent was not (in the absence of
negligence) liable for his loss.[38]

At one time, it seems to have been thought that the making of a prior
contract for accommodation (as opposed to the creation of the contract
upon the traveller's arrival) was a strong factor against inferring an
innkeeper-guest relationship, at least in these cases where the prior
booking was for a finite term and where the visitor would not (in the
absence of cancellations) have otherwise been accommodated by the
proprietor. This was, to some extent, the view of the majority in the
Victorian Full Supreme Court in *Daniel* v. *Hotel Pacific Pty. Ltd.*,[39] a
case involving thirteen plaintiffs, all of whom had made prior arrangement with the defendant hotelier to stay at his hotel for fixed periods
over the Christmas season. While they were staying there, announcements
were made over the hotel's loudspeaker system advising guests to
deposit valuables with the management. This the plaintiffs did, and their
property was deposited in the safe in the hotel office. Thieves broke in
and removed the safe and the plaintiff's goods were never recovered. It
was held that the defendant was not liable as an innkeeper for their loss.
Herring C.J. appeared to rely upon the fact that accommodation was
charged at a weekly rate and could not be obtained other than by prior
arrangement.[40] Lowe J. conceded that it was impossible to answer the
case satisfactorily upon the question whether the plaintiffs were "travellers", for that requirement had itself, in his view, been reduced to

---

[36] The price of accommodation was computed by the week and the first payment
was made a month after moving in, at which time the charges were first
arranged. The defendant was a licensed victualler.
[37] [1953] 1 D.L.R. 796 (Ontario C.A.).
[38] Cf. *O'Neill* v. *Esquire Hotels Ltd.* (1973) 30 D.L.R. (3d) 589, at 595-596, where
the fact that the defendants normally let apartments only for periods of three
months or more was a factor in the court's holding that they were not under
an insurer's liability towards a guest who had booked a room for a month. It
may also be predicated upon this decision that the granting of special, independent
facilities to the visitor (e.g. by allowing him to cook in his own room) may be
influential in identifying him as a mere lodger.
[39] [1953] V.L.R. 447: noted, 17 M.L.R. 272; 28 A.L.J. 27; 48 Q.J.P. 31. Cf. *Ex
parte Coulson; re Jones* (1947) 48 S.R. (N.S.W.) 178, at 184.
[40] Ibid., at 453.

vestigial proportions as a result of the decision in *Williams* v. *Linnitt*.[41] But while the mere fact that accommodation had been reserved, or that the reservation was for a definite period, would not necessarily, of itself, rebut the prima facie assumption that one who is received into an inn is received as a guest, the present case contained additional circumstances justifying the conclusion that the parties had impliedly relieved the innkeeper of his obligations as an insurer:

> I am influenced in coming to that conclusion by the facts that, so far as the evidence disclosed, no one adverted to the special position of the innkeeper in relation to a guest, that it was common knowledge that Lorne was a seaside resort with many boarding-houses and several licensed hotels, that there was evidence of a definite opening of booking by the defendant of accommodation for the Christmas and New Year season, that this last fact was known to the plaintiffs and that they booked accommodation accordingly, that there was evidence that no one who had not booked could get accommodation for that period, unless in the unforeseen contingency of a cancellation of a prior booking, that the form of booking was notoriously usual for booking at a boarding-house, and that there was no evidence of what took place at the defendant's hotel on the arrival of any of the plaintiff's and their entry into the premises. It is the combination of these circumstances and not merely the fact that the plaintiffs had booked for a definite period which leads me to my conclusion of fact. I do not say, and I should hesitate long before saying, that an arrangement to stay for a short but definite period in itself prevents the person so arranging being received as a guest. As a guest the plaintiff could not have insisted on staying for any particular time, and it is clear that he wanted to stay for two weeks. What he did was precisely what he would have done if he were booking accommodation at a boarding-house. If he were faced with the position that, as a guest, the length of his stay would be precarious, while, as a lodger he might stay for two weeks, I think that he would surely have made the latter choice. I think I can and should infer that he claimed to enter the defendant's hotel as a lodger and was received as such.[42]

In addition, the court held that the defendant had not been negligent in his method of safekeeping the valuables and was not, therefore, in breach of his obligations as a bailee.

Scholl J., while concurring upon the bailment point, held that the plaintiffs were not lodgers but guests. He pointed out[43] that the mere length of a visitor's stay is not a conclusive guide since there have been decisions in which the visitor has been held to be a traveller or guest although he stayed for several months.[44] Nor is the existence of an antecedent contract conclusive, for there are several cases which accord the status of guest to one whose accommodation was arranged by letter or by a

---

[41] [1951] 1 K.B. 565.
[42] [1953] V.L.R. 447, at 455-456. The relevant periods of sojourn in the present case ranged from nine to twenty-one days.
[43] Ibid., at 462.
[44] *Thompson* v. *Lacy* ante (eighty-three nights); *Allen* v. *Smith* (1862) 12 C.B.N.S. 638 (seven months); *Robbins & Co.* v. *Gray* [1895] 2 Q.B. 501 and *Chesham Automotive Supply Co. Ltd.* v. *Beresford Hotel (Birchington) Ltd.* (1913) 29 T.L.R. 584 (four months in each case).

friend,[45] and any other conclusion would be both anachronistic and contrary to common sense.[46] Nor is such status to be lost merely on the strength of a weekly or monthly rather than a daily tariff or by a booking for a finite time.[47] The question in the present case was whether a conflation of these factors was sufficient to displace the conventional innkeeper-guest relationship. In the learned judge's view, it was not. The relevant test was:

> . . . whether there has been initially or subsequently: i.e., before, on or at some time after the visitor's reception, and either expressly or by implication, an arrangement (a) which contemplates or involves an intended "permanence" of stay, i.e. a stay for a long time, whether defined or left indefinite as to duration . . . especially (b) if accompanied by the absence of any other permanent home, as in the case of the country bankers, school teachers and solicitors to whom Lowe J. has referred, or (c) which in some other way makes the visitor a member of the innkeeper's household in a character differing from that of an ordinary hotel guest: e.g. a relative who goes to stay temporarily or indefinitely, and pays board, but is for the time being a member of the innkeeper's family circle.[48]

The approach adopted by Scholl J. seems to have been preferred by the Queensland Full Supreme Court in *Turner* v. *Queensland Motels Pty. Ltd.*[49] where Hart J. re-emphasised the anachronism of holding that a prior arrangement should negative the creation of a relationship of innkeeper and guest, and where it was held that such a relationship did exist between the defendant motel proprietor and the plaintiffs who had been booked in for an indefinite period of four days or possibly longer by a business acquaintance some six or seven weeks before their arrival. Hart J. defined the special contract necessary to cast the visitor in the role of lodger as one which, at the very least, involves his reception upon terms other than those on which the owner of the inn holds out that he will receive all travellers who are willing to pay a reasonable price and are fit to be received.[50]

Of course, a person who originally comes to an inn as a traveller or guest may lose that status and become a mere lodger during the course of his sojourn.[51] Moreover, certain categories of person seem to be

---

[45] *Constantine* v. *Imperial Hotels Ltd.* [1944] K.B. 693; 60 T.L.R. 510; 172 L.T. 128; *R.* v. *Higgins* [1948] 1 K.B. 165, at 171.

[46] [1953] V.L.R. 447, at 463: "Take the case . . . of a Judge on circuit, for whom it is the practice to reserve hotel accommodation in advance. He usually stays at least one night, and sometimes much longer. He, too, in my opinion is a traveller and a guest. Then there is the case of the lawyer, the doctor, the man of commerce, or the man in public life, who intends attending a convention or conference in another city. In his case it is usually essential to book hotel accommodation in advance and for a stated minimum time. In my opinion, he is nevertheless a transient, a traveller and a guest, according both to current social ideas and customs and to the ordinary use of language."

[47] *Chesham Automobile Supply Ltd.* v. *Beresford Hotel (Birchington) Ltd.* ante; cf. *R.* v. *Hinton, ex parte M'Manus* (1884) 6 A.L.T. 12; *Fisher* v. *Bonneville Hotel Co.* (1920) 12 Am. L.R. Ann. 255; *Pinkerton* v. *Woodward* (1867) 33 Cal. 557; 91 Am. Dec. 657.

[48] [1953] V.L.R. 447, at 467.

[49] [1968] Qd. R. 189.

[50] Ibid., at 200.

[51] An example is *Lamond* v. *Richard* [1897] 1 Q.B. 541.

excluded almost as a matter of law from the definition of a guest. These were listed by Herring C.J. in *Daniel* v. *Hotel Pacific Pty. Ltd.*[52] as including inhabitants of the house, private guests of the innkeeper or his family, servants of the innkeeper and persons who visit the inn for purposes unconnected with its facilities as such, such as an electrician who comes to repair the wiring. But in all cases the identification is a question of fact.[53]

There are two main, antithetical reasons for distinguishing between lodgers and guests. The person who acts as host to a mere lodger is not, in the absence of special agreement, entitled to a lien on the lodger's goods, nor does he owe them an insurer's liability. In certain cases,[54] lodging-house keepers have been held liable for the loss of visitors' goods, but only on the basis of negligence.

B. Commencement of relationship

The time-points laid down in s. 2(1)(b) of the *Hotel Proprietors Act*[55] have rendered redundant a number of authorities which dealt with the question whether the innkeeper's liability had begun, or ceased to operate at the material time.[56] However, it has been suggested[57] that these authorities may still be relevant in helping to establish whether the innkeeper has become a bailee. Moreover, there are a number of Australian jurisdictions which do not have this clarifying period and in which the commencement or cessation of liability is still a question of fact.[58]

C. The scope of liability

Formerly, it was thought that the innkeeper's liability extended only to loss of the traveller's goods and not to mere damage unless caused by the negligence of the innkeeper.[59] This rule was endorsed by Swift and MacNaghten JJ. in *Winkworth* v. *Raven*.[60] In this case, the plaintiff's car had become damaged through the freezing of the radiator while parked in the garage at the defendant's inn. The garage was an abnormally cold

---

[52] [1953] V.L.R. 447, at 451, relying in part upon *Orchard & Co.* v. *Bush* [1898] 2 Q.B. 284, at 289 per Kennedy J.

[53] *Turner* v. *Queensland Motels Pty. Ltd.* [1968] Qd. R. 189, at 192 per Mack C.J.

[54] Post, p. 909 et seq.

[55] Ante, p. 882.

[56] *Drope* v. *Thaire* (1626) Benl. 173; *York* v. *Grindstone* (1703) 1 Salk. 388; *Allen* v. *Smith* (1863) 12 C.B.N.S. 638; *Day* v. *Bather* (1863) 2 H. & C. 14; *Strauss* v. *County Hotel Co.* (1883) 12 Q.B.D. 27; *Medawar* v. *Grand Hotel Co.* [1891] 2 Q.B. 11; *Wright* v. *Anderton* [1909] 1 K.B. 209; *Portman* v. *Griffin* (1913) 29 T.L.R. 225; *Grant* v. *Cardiff Hotels Co. Ltd.* (1921) 37 T.L.R. 775; and see ante, n. 29.

[57] Vaines, *Personal Property* (5th ed.), p. 132.

[58] Post, p. 903 et seq.

[59] *Dawson* v. *Chamney* (1843) 5 Q.B.D. 164; 114 E.R. 1210; but note that the decision is ambivalent and can be taken to suggest that the innkeeper's liability in all events is dependent upon his failure discharge the prima facie presumption of negligence. It was disapproved in *Morgan* v. *Ravey* (1861) 6 H. & N. 277; 158 E.R. 109, where Pollock C.B. suggested that it might be explained by reference to the lack of evidence showing show the chattel received its injury: a suggestion repudiated by the learned annotator of 158 E.R. 109, at 114. *Morgan* v. *Ravey* reaffirmed the strict liability of the innkeeper and appeared to extend that liability to damage or injury as well as loss.

[60] [1931] 1 K.B. 652; see also Cmnd. 9161 (1954).

one and had only three walls, the fourth side being exposed to the elements; a fact which was clearly known to the plaintiff. The court held that the defendant was not a bailee and was not, as an innkeeper, liable for the damage to the goods of his guest without negligence on his part. Such negligence had not been established in the present case because the garage was reasonably fit for its use under ordinary weather conditions and the plaintiff was aware of its defects in cold weather.[61] If anything, the negligence was the plaintiff's in not draining the radiator himself.[62]

The decision seems equitable on its facts, but it may be that it should be confined to situations in which the injury is due to the passive condition of the innkeeper's premises and that condition is both generally adequate for the purposes expected of it and clearly known to the traveller. MacNaghten J. suggested[63] that the plaintiff may well have had a legitimate complaint if the defendants' caretaker had contributed to the damage by interfering with the car. It is possible that as a general rule of the Common Law the innkeeper should be liable for damage as well as loss, at least in these cases where the injury is caused (or apparently caused) by positive conduct or by phenomena unknown to the traveller.

The latter proposition is, however, confuted by the decision of Finnemore J. in *Williams* v. *Owen*,[64] where the defendant innkeeper was held not liable for the destruction of the plaintiff's car by fire, arising through an unexplained cause in a garage adjoining the inn. Finnemore J. held that the innkeeper's liability did not extend to damage to the chattels of guests, and that even if it had originally so extended, it was mitigated in the case of fire by the *Fires Prevention (Metropolis) Act* 1774, which made him liable only for negligence. A different approach was adopted in the Queensland case of *Kellett* v. *Cowan*,[65] where liability was imposed under the Act upon an innkeeper for a fire caused without negligence on his part in the course of fumigating the hotel, which fire destroyed the plaintiff's goods. The court held that the defendant should be liable unless he could prove that the fire was the result of vis major, but the decision is weakened on this point by later interpretations of the Act which allow the defendant to escape if he can prove that he was not negligent.[66] The Queensland court does not appear to have specifically considered the innkeeper's liability as an insurer, or to have examined whether this liability had been attenuated by the Act.

Against these cases stands the decision of Heydon D.C.J. in *Nott* v. *Maclurcan*,[67] holding innkeepers liable even for accidental fires which damage property belonging to their guests and stating that the *Prevention of Fires (Metropolis) Act* 1774 does not extend to innkeepers: "That

---

[61] Cf. *Brabant & Co.* v. *King* [1895] A.C. 632, which held that such knowledge on the part of a bailor does not excuse the bailee for reward; ante, p. 460.
[62] [1931] 1 K.B. 652, at 662 per Swift J.
[63] Ibid., at 664.
[64] [1956] 1 All E.R. 104 (Exeter Assizes); see also *Seccombe* v. *Clarke Baker* (1953) 103 Law Jo. 624 (Mayor's Court); *Douglas Iron Works* v. *Owen* [1951] Ir. R. 93; 102 L.J. 284; *Bradley* v. *Stewart* [1954] C.L.Y. 1630 (N.I. Cty. Ct.).
[65] [1906-1907] Qd. St. R. 116.
[66] E.g. *Williams* v. *Owen* ante, at 107.
[67] (1902) 20 W.N. (N.S.W.) 135 (see also *Loyer* v. *Plante* [1960] Que. Q.B. 443; *Seigman* v. *Choquette* [1960] Que. Q.B. 335).

Act . . . was only intended to alter the Common Law in respect of the public generally and does not apply to the liability of innkeepers in respect of the goods of their guests."[68] The relationship estops the innkeeper from pleading or proving due care.

There is a clear conflict between this decision and *Williams* v. *Owen*[69] and it may be that, even in Australia, the latter decision would carry the greater weight. Finnemore J.'s conclusion seems to have been based principally upon a provision in s. 86 of the 1774 Act, stating that there shall be no liability for an accidental fire "any law, usage or custom to the contrary notwithstanding." In the learned judge's view, the innkeeper's strict liability was plainly a custom of the realm, albeit one embodied in the rules of the Common Law. It seems likely that this reasoning will prevail and that in the case of damage or even destruction by fire, the innkeeper will not be liable without fault on his part.[70]

So far as concerns other causes of damage, it seems that the decision in *Winkworth* v. *Raven*,[71] as upheld in *Williams* v. *Owen*,[72] again limits the innkeeper's liability to cases in which he is at fault. But *Winkworth* v. *Raven* is based upon extremely weak authority[73] and *Williams* v. *Owen* can be limited to the special case of fire. To the contrary stands *Nott* v. *Maclurcan*[74] and some dicta of the South Australian Supreme Court in *O'Dea* v. *O'Hara*.[75] Since *Winkworth* v. *Raven* was a case in which the traveller had full knowledge of the relevant risk, it is submitted that that decision should not be construed as relieving the innkeeper from liability for damage in cases where such knowledge was lacking.

In England, the question is now academic because of the wording of the statute. Section 2(1) of the *Hotel Proprietors Act* states that the proprietor of an hotel, as an innkeeper, is an insurer against the loss of or damage to the goods and chattels of his guest, unless he can prove that the loss arose from some default or negligence on the part of the guest, or his servant or agent.

D. Negligence of the guest

The latter exception has not proved easy to establish. "Negligence" in this context means no more than the guest's own carelessness:[76] that is, a failure to exercise the ordinary care a prudent man could reasonably have been expected to exercise in the circumstances.[77] The courts seem

---

[68] Ibid., at 136. Cf. Paton, op. cit., pp. 200-201.
[69] [1956] 1 All E.R. 104.
[70] Similarly, in relation to his duty as an occupier. He may be subject to strict liability under the rule in *Rylands* v. *Fletcher* (1865) 3 H. & C. 774; (1866) L.R. 1 Ex. 265; (1868) L.R. 3 H.L. 330, but the application of the rule in such cases will be rare because an ordinary household fire is not a non-natural user (*Sochaki* v. *Sas* [1941] 1 All E.R. 344) and because of the need for an escape (*Read* v. *Lyons & Co. Ltd.* [1947] A.C. 156).
[71] [1931] 1 K.B. 652.
[72] [1956] 1 All E.R. 104.
[73] *Dawson* v. *Chamney* (1843) 4 Q.B.D. 164; 114 E.R. 1210.
[74] (1903) 20 W.N. (N.S.W.) 135.
[75] (1895) *South Australian Advertiser*, 17 May.
[76] *Shacklock* v. *Ethorpe Ltd.* [1939] 3 All E.R. 372, at 374 per Lord MacMillan. The defence is a venerable one: see *Burgess* v. *Clements* (1815) 4 M. & S. 306; 105 E.R. 848.
[77] *Shacklock* v. *Ethorpe Ltd.* ante; *Cashill* v. *Wright* (1856) 6 E. & B. 391; *Levy* v. *Curran* (1909) 9 S.R. (N.S.W.) 725; 26 W.N. 157.

to have been willing to regard minor acts of carelessness on the part of the guest as less important, in a causal sense, than the inadequacy of the innkeeper's own facilities.[78] Thus, in *Brewster* v. *Drennan*[79] the innkeeper was held liable when a guest, having asked him about the absence of a lock on the door of her room and having been told that nobody would steal anything, left her fur cape hanging behind the bedroom door, whence it was stolen. Guests have also been acquitted of negligence for such conduct as leaving a valuable ring in a latched but unlocked suitcase in the bedroom, and locking the door of the room but disregarding a notice that valuables should be deposited with the management;[80] leaving jewels in a locked container under the luggage-stand in the bedroom and failing to lock the bedroom door;[81] or failing to put a vehicle in the hotel garage when staying overnight.[82]

Conduct which has been held to amount to negligence on the guest's part includes leaving open a balcony-window and leaving the door of the room unlocked, having previously displayed in a public room a bag containing money;[83] ostentatiously rolling up banknotes and allowing people to see them being put away in a badly secured box;[84] and leaving the key in the outside lock of a room in which jewellery is deposited.[85] The question is clearly one of fact and general conclusions cannot be predicated from individual cases: "What would be prudent in a small hotel, in a small town, might be the extreme of imprudence at a large hotel in a city like Bristol . . ."[86]

There is no authority upon the question whether the guest's negligence is now a ground for apportionment of damages under the *Law Reform*

[78] Cf. *Levy* v. *Curran* ante: the want of care must have "conduced to or brought about" the loss. The burden of proving both this and the want of care itself rests upon the innkeeper: *Medawar* v. *Grand Hotel Co.* [1891] 2 Q.B. 11; *Gee, Walker & Slater Ltd.* v. *Friary Hotel (Derby) Ltd.* (1949) 66 T.L.R. 59.

[79] [1945] 2 All E.R. 705.

[80] *Carpenter* v. *Haymarket Hotel Ltd.* [1931] 1 K.B. 364. Cf. *Jones* v. *Jackson* (1873) 29 L.T. 399, where the failure to take advantage of a notice, hung in the bedroom, declaring that "the proprietor will be happy to take charge of any valuables" was held to relieve the innkeeper. In *Marchioness of Huntley* v. *Bedford Hotel Co.* (1891) 7 T.L.R. 641, however, it was held that plaintiff (who had failed to comply with such a notice) was not negligent and that the notice itself was not evidence of a special contract between the parties, although it was read by the plaintiff. Cf. *Sanders* v. *Spencer* (1567) 3 Dyer 266b.

[81] *Shacklock* v. *Ethorpe Ltd.* [1939] 3 All E.R. 372; see also *Mitchell* v. *Woods* (1867) 16 L.T. 676 and *Filipowski* v. *Merryweather* (1860) 2 F. & F. 285; 175 E.R. 1063 where it was held that the mere failure to lock the door in which the guest is sleeping does not amount to negligence; likewise, *Laing* v. *Allied Innkeepers Ltd.* (1970) 8 D.L.R. (3d) 708. Cf. *Carey* v. *Long's Hotel Co.* (1891) 7 T.L.R. 213.

[82] *Gee, Walker & Slater Ltd.* v. *Friary Hotel (Derby) Ltd.* (1949) 66 T.L.R. 59; cf. *Douglas Iron Works* v. *Owen* [1951] Ir. R. 93 (failure to lock vehicle prevented plaintiff from recovering).

[83] *Oppenheim* v. *White Lion Hotel Co.* (1871) 6 L.R.C.P. 515; followed in *Semeloff* v. *Carlson* (1900) 18 N.Z.L.R. 757, but cf. *Laing* v. *Allied Innkeepers Ltd.* (1970) 8 D.L.R. (3d) 708.

[84] *Armistead* v. *Wilde* (1851) 17 O.B. 265; cf. *Portman* v. *Griffin* (1913) 29 T.L.R. 225.

[85] *Herbert* v. *Markwell* (1881) 45 L.T. 649. See also *Turner* v. *Queensland Motels Pty. Ltd.* [1968] Qd. R. 189, at 201, where Hart J. was prepared to hold that the leaving of a sum of £268 in a motel bedroom was negligent, but was precluded from doing so by the finding of trial judge.

[86] *Oppenheim* v. *White Lion Hotel Co.* ante per Montague Smith J.

(Contributory Negligence) Act 1945. Lord Macmillan has said that to describe this defence as one of contributory negligence is technically inaccurate,[87] but this designation has been applied in several cases[88] and in *Turner* v. *Queensland Motels Pty. Ltd.*[89] Hart J. seems to have been content to leave the question open. Undoubtedly, the field seems an ideal one for the operation of a rule of apportionment[90] and there is, of course, no difficulty about the defence having been a total one before the passing of the 1945 Act.[91] But the definition of "fault" in s. 4 of that Act would appear to exclude the strict liability of an innkeeper from the ambit of its operation: ". . . fault means negligence, breach of statutory duty or other act or omission which gives rise to a liability in tort or would, apart from this Act, give rise to the defence of contributory negligence."

It is difficult to see what act or omission on the part of the innkeeper gives rise to his traditional liability, and accordingly it appears that the principle of apportionment would, in cases of innkeepers' liability, be excluded.[92]

E. Retention by guest

The Common Law recognised a further defence to the innkeeper, viz., that the guest kept the goods in his exclusive possession. This does not mean, of course, that the innkeeper is liable only where exclusive possession of the chattel has been entrusted to him. Whereas the defence would almost certainly succeed if a guest's wallet were stolen from him by a pick-pocket in the hotel lounge, it was held to fail in *Carpenter* v. *Haymarket Hotel Ltd.*,[93] where the guest had left her property in a locked room during her absence from the hotel. In *Farnworth* v. *Packwood*[94] the innkeeper was exonerated where the guest was a commercial traveller who hired a room for the exclusive purpose of displaying his wares; but in *Richmond* v. *Smith*[95] it was held that a mere expression of choice by the traveller as to where his goods shall be placed did not (in the absence of any objection by the innkeeper) give the traveller exclusive possession. The question is one of fact[96] and in difficult cases, such as the leaving of a coat upon a rack in the restaurant[97] or of a watch upon

---

[87] *Shacklock* v. *Ethorpe Ltd.* [1939] 3 All E.R. 372, at 374: the reason being that the guest is in breach of no duty to the innkeeper.
[88] E.g. *Herbert* v. *Markwell* (1881) 45 L.T. 649; *Medawar* v. *Grand Hotel Co.* [1891] 2 Q.B. 11; *Carey* v. *Long's Hotel Co.* (1891) 7 T.L.R. 213; *Portman* v. *Griffin* (1913) 29 T.L.R. 225.
[89] [1968] Qd. R. 189, at 201.
[90] Contrast *Herbert* v. *Markwell* ante and *Petrovitch* v. *Callingham's Ltd.* [1969] 2 Lloyd's Rep. 386.
[91] Cf. *Wilton* v. *Commonwealth Trading Bank* [1973] 2 N.S.W.L.R. 664.
[92] There is, however, no reason why it should not operate where the statutory limitation is forfeited by the act or default of the innkeeper: post, p. 893.
[93] [1931] 1 K.B. 364.
[94] (1816) 1 Stark 249.
[95] (1828) 8 B. & C. 9.
[96] *Burgess* v. *Clements* (1815) 4 M. & S. 306.
[97] Cf. Vaines, op. cit., p. 13; *Orchard* v. *Bush & Co.* [1898] 2 Q.B. 284; *Ultzen* v. *Nichols* [1894] 1 Q.B. 92; ante, p. 205.

a ledge in the washroom,[98] it seems likely that the courts will lean against the hotelier.[99]

F. "Infra hospitium"

In order for the innkeeper's strict liability to operate, the goods must be infra hospitium: within the bounds of his house. This requirement has given rise to some of the most difficult decisions in this area,[1] but its importance is now greatly reduced in England as the result of s. 2(1) of the *Hotel Proprietors' Act*. This subsection excludes the innkeepers' liability as an insurer in relation to "any vehicle or any property left therein, or any horse or other live animal or its harness or other equipment."

Nevertheless, the Common Law rule may still require to be invoked when goods are kept within the building itself but in a place in which it was obviously not intended that they should be kept:[2] for instance, a coat left on the balcony of a room or a camera left hanging from an outside door-handle. But it is difficult to envisage applications of this rule which do not simultaneously point to an act of negligence by the guest.

G. Other defences

The only remaining defences open to the innkeeper against the total, strict liability imposed by the Common Law are Act of God and act of the Queen's enemies.[3] There does not seem to be any modern decision in which these defences have been successfully invoked.

Subject, therefore, to the foregoing defences, and to any statutory limitation of liability,[4] the innkeeper is an insurer of the property of guests brought to the inn. Moreover, it seems that action can be brought not only by the guest but by the true owner of the goods who bailed them to the guest.[5] The innkeeper's liability is independent of contract and incapable of classification as a tort.[6] Its Draconian effect has not passed uncriticised in recent decisions. In *Turner* v. *Queensland Motels*

---

[98] Cf. *Grant* v. *Cardiff Hotels Co. Ltd.* (1921) 37 T.L.R. 775.

[99] As where goods are stolen from the guest's room while he is asleep: e.g. *Laing* v. *Allied Innkeepers Ltd.* (1970) 8 D.L.R. (3d) 708.

[1] Both *Williams* v. *Linnitt* [1951] 1 K.B. 318 and *Watson* v. *People's Refreshment House Association* [1952] 1 K.B. 318 contain a useful review of the authorities; see also Paton, op. cit., pp. 208-209; *Aria Bridge House Hotel* (1927) 137 L.T. 299; *Gee, Walker & Slater Ltd.* v. *Friary Hotel (Derby) Ltd.* (1949) 66 T.L.R. 59; *Davies* v. *Clarke* [1953] C.L.Y. 1790; *Gresham* v. *Lyon* [1954] 2 All E.R. 786; *O'Dea* v. *O'Hara* (1895) *South Australian Advertiser*, 17 May; *Park* v. *Berkery* (1930) 25 Tas. L.R. 67; *George* v. *Williams* (1956) 5 D.L.R. (2d) 21 ante, p. 000); Murray (1956) 34 *Can. Bar Rev.* 1203; cf. *Adams (Durham)* v. *Trust Houses Ltd.* [1960] 1 Lloyd's Rep. 380.

[2] Cf. *Sanders* v. *Spencer* (1567) 3 Dyer 266b; *Williams* v. *Linnitt* [1951] 1 K.B. 318; *Gresham* v. *Lyon* [1954] 1 W.L.R. 1100 (luggage left in car in car park not infra hospitium).

[3] *Morgan* v. *Ravey* (1861) 6 H. & N. 265, at 277 (Pollock C.B.); *Butler & Co.* v. *Quilter* (1900) 17 T.L.R. 159; *Daniel* v. *Hotel Pacific Pty. Ltd.* [1953] V.L.R. 447, at 458 per Scholl J.

[4] Post, p. 893.

[5] E.g. *Gee, Walker & Slater Ltd.* v. *Friary Hotel (Derby) Ltd.* (1949) 66 T.L.R. 59.

[6] *Robbins & Co.* v. *Gray* [1895] 2 Q.B. 501, at 503-504; cf. *Carriss* v. *Buxton* (1958) 13 D.L.R. (3d) 689.

Pty. Ltd.[7] Hart J. castigated the anachronism of a principle that owed its origins to the immemorial liaison (if not equation) between inn-keepers and robbers: "The very idea of the appellant in this case being in league with ruffians or pilferers or highwaymen is ridiculous . . . if I did not think this judgment was not strictly required by precedent, I would not give it."[8]

It must, in conclusion, be reiterated that even in those cases in which the innkeeper's strict liability does not apply, he may be held liable for breach of his duty as an occupier or because he has become a bailee. In the latter event, it seems beyond question that he will be a bailee for reward.[9]

H. Limitation of liability

Under the *Hotel Proprietors Act*, the innkeeper may limit his liability by notice, but only if he does so in the manner prescribed by the Act. Any other method is ineffective, and it has been stated that the innkeeper (unlike the common carrier) has no power to contract out of liability at Common Law.[10] Section 2(3) provides that where a hotel proprietor is liable, as an innkeeper, to make good the loss of or damage to property brought to his hotel, his liability to any one guest shall not exceed £50 in respect of any one article, or £100 in the aggregate, provided he has properly exhibited the prescribed notice to that effect. In three specified events, however, the proprietor will remain strictly liable in full to his guests, despite the foregoing limitation. These events are:

(a) the theft, loss or damage of the property through the default, neglect or wilful act of the proprietor or his servant; or

(b) the depositing of the property by or on behalf of the guest expressly for safe custody with the proprietor or some servant of his who is authorised, or appears to be authorised, for the purpose: in this event, the proprietor or his servant is entitled to require that the goods be placed in a container fastened or sealed by the depositor; or

(c) a refusal by the proprietor or his servant to receive the property for deposit, or the inability of the guest or some other guest acting on his behalf, through the default of the proprietor or his servant, to offer and deliver the goods for deposit; such offer must in both cases be made at a time after the guest has arrived at the hotel.

The first two exceptions have given rise to some interesting case-law. In *Olley* v. *Marlborough Court Ltd.*[11] the first exception was held to

---

[7] [1968] Qd. R. 189.
[8] Ibid., at 198, 210. The criticism was especially acute in this case because the appellants, not being licensed victuallers, were not entitled to limit their liability under Queensland law; see post, p. 908.
[9] *Daniel* v. *Hotel Pacific Pty. Ltd.* (ante), at 457-458 per Scholl J.; cf. Lowe J. at 456, who preferred to leave the question undecided, and see Chapter 8, ante; *Mitchell* v. *Coffee* (1880) 5 O.A.R. 525.
[10] *Williams* v. *Linnitt* [1951] 1 K.B. 318; cf. *Williams* v. *Owen* [1956] 1 All E.R. 104, at 108, where Finnemore J. declined to commit himself but agreed that probably exclusion was not possible; and *Winkworth* v. *Raven* [1931] 1 K.B. 652. There is at least one old case, *Brand* v. *Glasse* (1584) Moore (K.B.) 158, which indicates to the contrary, but as Stirling (1931) 4 A.L.J. 319, at 320-321 points out, this is difficult to reconcile with *Harland's Case* (1641) Clay. 97. See further *Sanders* v. *Spencer* (1567) 3 Dyer 266b.
[11] [1949] 1 K.B. 532.

apply because the defendant's negligence had resulted in the theft of a key from their reception desk, thereby enabling the thief to enter the plaintiff's room.[12] In *Bonham-Carter* v. *Hyde Park Hotel Ltd.*[13] a similar finding was made, and the innkeeper forfeited the protection of the Act, because the only locking device attached to the plaintiff's door was an ineffective turnbuckle which was easily forced by a thief.

In *Belleville* v. *Palatine Hotel and Buildings Co. Ltd.*,[14] on the other hand, it was held not to be negligent on the part of an innkeeper to fail to suspect that a person arriving with an apparently empty suitcase might be a hotel-thief; even where the warping of the jamb on the plaintiff's door facilitated the thief's entry into a room for which he had no key.[15] Asquith J.'s dictum in the latter case, that the word "wilful" in the *Innkeeper's Liability Act* 1863, qualifies only the word "act" and not the words "default or neglect" is clearly irrelevant to the position under English Law in the light of the revised wording of s. 2(3)(a) of the 1956 Act.

In *Kott and Kott* v. *Gordon Hotels Ltd.*[16] valuables were stolen from the plaintiff's room by the defendants' floor-waiter, a convicted thief. Counsel for the defendants sought to argue that s. 2(3)(a) should be limited in its operation to those cases in which the servant was one to whom a duty of care over the goods had been delegated, and for whom the innkeeper would accordingly have been liable at Common Law under the decision in *Morris* v. *C. W. Martin & Sons Ltd.*[17] It followed, in his contention, that where the servant had not been entrusted with the goods but had merely been afforded an opportunity of stealing them by virtue of his employment, no liability should ensue.[18] But this argument, which was foreign to the innkeeper's traditionally strict liability, was rejected by the court.

In *Whitehouse* v. *Pickett*[19] a traveller was held to be precluded from relying upon a former equivalent of s. 2(3)(b)[20] when he handed a bag containing jewellery worth £1800 to the "boots" of the hotel upon arrival, without offering any description of its contents. The bag was placed in an alcove in a room used as a bar, in accordance with a practice which had been followed with the same traveller over the past eighteen years. The statute was held to demand, not merely that the guest himself should intend to deliver up the goods, but that this intention should "be brought to the mind of the bailee or his agent in some

---

[12] The foregoing conclusion was reached on the assumption that the establishment was an inn. See further, *Cryan* v. *Hotel Rembrandt Ltd.* (1925) 133 L.T. 395.
[13] (1948) 64 T.L.R. 177.
[14] (1944) 171 L.T. 363; see also *Squire* v. *Wheeler* (1867) 16 L.T. 93; *Behrens* v. *The Grenville Hotel (Bude) Ltd.* (1925) 69 Sol. Jo. 346.
[15] The burden of proving neglect or default on the part of the hotelier or his servants for the purposes of s. 2(3)(a) rests upon the guest: *Medawar* v. *Grand Hotel Co.* [1891] 2 Q.B. 11; *Hawkins* v. *Dominion Breweries Ltd.* [1948] N.Z.L.R. 15.
[16] [1968] 2 Lloyd's Rep. 228.
[17] [1966] 1 Q.B. 716; ante, p. 480.
[18] For the immunity of the employer in these circumstances at Common Law, see *De Parrell* v. *Walker* (1932) 49 T.L.R. 37; *Leesh River Tea Co. Ltd.* v. *British Indian Steam Navigation Co. Ltd.* [1967] 2 Q.B. 250.
[19] [1908] A.C. 357 (H.L.).
[20] *Innkeepers Liability Act* 1863, s. 1(2).

reasonable and intelligible manner, so that he may, if so minded, insist on the precautions specified in the Act."[21] This decision may be contrasted with that of the Court of Appeal in *Moss* v. *Russell*,[22] where, in very similar circumstances, the innkeeper was permitted to rely upon the statutory limitation of liability because the "boots" was clearly not a person who had authority to receive the goods for safe custody within the meaning of the 1863 Act.[23] It may be questioned whether the same result would be reached today. Ostensibly, it may be thought that any servant of the hotel who willingly accepts the goods for deposit has authority (or at least apparent authority) to do so. Even in cases of bailment the courts have been liberal in allowing the bailor to claim that delivery to a servant constitutes delivery to his employer as a bailee,[24] and it is evident in other respects that the innkeeper's liability under an express deposit is not necessarily dependent upon his becoming a bailee.

Certainly, it is not an essential pre-requisite of s. 2(3)(b) that the guest should notify the innkeeper of the value of the goods, even when that value far exceeds what would normally or reasonably be expected. In *Theeman* v. *Forte Properties Pty. Ltd.*[25] the plaintiff (who had visited the defendants' motel on several previous occasions) asked the defendant's receptionist to put her jewellery in the motel safe. The receptionist agreed and a bag containing the jewellery was handed over, without any disclosure that the jewellery was worth c.$21,000. It was stolen from the safe and the defendants (having, apparently, displayed the statutory notice)[26] claimed that their liability was limited to $100. They argued that the exception relating to express deposit[27] should not apply because the value of the goods was vastly in excess of their normal experience and because the non-disclosure prevented them from regulating the extent of their care over the goods in relation to their liability; this being the purpose of the statutory exception, according to Lord James in *Whitehouse* v. *R. & W. Pickett*.[28] The argument succeeded before McClemens J. but was rejected by the New South Wales Court of Appeal. Hope J.A. pointed out[29] that Lord James had merely required that the innkeeper should possess *or at any rate have the opportunity of possessing* knowledge of the nature and value of the goods deposited. Provided,

---

21 [1908] A.C. 357, at 361 per Lord James of Hereford. The principal case was largely anticipated by the decision of the Irish Queen's Bench Division in *O'Connor* v. *Grand International Hotel Co. Ltd.* [1898] 2 Ir. R. 92.

22 (1884) 1 T.L.R. 13. Cf. *Carey* v. *Deveaux* (1920) 53 D.L.R. 267.

23 See p. 241 et seq., ante.

24 The court went on to hold that the servant had not been negligent in his treatment of the parcel. See also *O'Connor's* case (ante), where the same conclusion was reached. The latter decision also recognises that the right to recover even the limited sum may be forfeited by the guest's contributory negligence (while acknowledging that mere failure to disclose value is not itself evidence of such default). It seems, since the innkeeper's default is clearly a factor in destroying this limitation, that the apportionment principle laid down in the *Law Reform (Contributory Negligence) Act* 1945, should apply: cf. p. 890, ante.

25 [1973] 1 N.S.W.L.R. 418.

26 Ibid., at 423.

27 *Innkeepers Liability Act* s. 7(3)(a); the equivalent to s. 2(3)(b) of the English (1956) Act (ante).

28 [1908] A.C. 357, at 361.

29 [1973] 1 N.S.W.L.R. 418, at 426.

therefore, that the innkeeper knew the goods were being expressly committed to his care and safekeeping, the statute would in most cases be satisfied, because he could then take advantage of the custody thus awarded to verify the value of the goods. Reliance was placed upon the judgment of Gibson J. in *O'Connor* v. *Grand International Hotel Co. Ltd.*[30] who had observed:

> No doubt the plaintiff, in making a deposit, was not bound to disclose the contents or to fix a value. If it had been a deposit under the Act it would have lain on the custodian to ascertain the value, and take proper care accordingly.

Since in the present case the plaintiff had, by asking the defendants to put the jewellery in the safe, clearly indicated to them that she was entrusting them with its custody, the requirement of express deposit was held to have been fulfilled and the non-disclosure of the value was held irrelevant. Hope J.A. did concede, however, that in special cases the failure to make such a disclosure might have evidential value in entitling the court to negate the occurrence of an express deposit; for example:

> If a bag of jewellery is handed by a guest to the manager of a hotel and nothing is said as to what is to be done with it, it may be that a statement as to its value will, in the circumstances, be sufficient to entitle a jury to find that there was a deposit expressly for safe custody.[31]

The requirements relating to notice, for the purpose of claiming the limitation allowed by the Act, are rigorous. The notice must be in the form set out in the Schedule to the Act[32] and a copy thereof, printed in plain type, must have been conspicuously displayed in a place where it could be conveniently read by the guest at or near the reception office or desk or, where there is no reception office or desk, at or near the main entrance to the hotel. Such display must take place at the time when the property in question was brought to the hotel.[33] In *Spice* v. *Bacon*[34] the omission of the word "act" from the phrase "wilful act, neglect or default" in the 1863 Act was held to deprive the innkeeper of the protection of the statute because there was nothing to show from the notice that Common Law liability for wilful acts causing loss by the innkeeper or his servant remained in force under the Act.[35] There have been a number of cases in which the defence of statutory limitation has

---

[30] [1898] 2 I.R. 92, at 100; see also Madden J. at 102, and *Behrens* v. *Grenville Hotel (Bude) Ltd.* (1925) 69 Sol. Jo. 346.
[31] [1973] 1 N.S.W.L.R. 418, at 428. Cf. the American case of *Millhiser* v. *Beau Site Co.* (1929) 251 N.Y. 290; 167 N.E. 447, where recovery was allowed in full for jewellery worth $300,000 deposited, without notification of value, with the defendant innkeepers; and *Hagerstrom* v. *Brainard Hotel Corporation* (1930) 45 F. (2d) 130.
[32] Set out in Vaines, op. cit., p. 133n.
[33] Section 2(3)(a).
[34] (1877) 2 Ex. D. 463.
[35] Cf. *Laing* v. *Allied Innkeepers Ltd.* (1970) 8 D.L.R. (3d) 708, where the omissions merely took the form of definite or indefinite articles. It was held that they did not detract in any way from the quality of the notice as a statement of all of the rights and liabilities of the parties as required under the relevant statute, and that the innkeeper's limitation was not forfeited on this ground.

failed because the requisite notices were not sufficiently prominent or proximate to the reception area to satisfy the demands of the Act.[36] In general, it seems that these demands are more stringent than those which would govern the ordinary incorporation of contractual terms at Common Law.[37]

II. The Innkeeper's Lien

The innkeeper occupies a rather singular position, in that he enjoys a lien over the goods of his guest without any specific agreement and without having expended any labour upon them or increased their value. Further, the *Innkeeper's Act* 1878, confers upon him the right to sell the property to which the lien attaches.[38]

A. The extent of the lien

The innkeeper's lien is a general one and extends to all goods which are received as part of the guest's luggage. However, in keeping with the cessation of his strict liability for such items as vehicles and their contents,[39] the proprietor of an hotel shall not *as an innkeeper*[40] have any lien or any vehicle or any property left therein, or on any horse or other live animal or its harness or other equipment. To some extent this provision, like others within the 1956 Act, has rendered some of the older authorities less relevant today; but even within the aforementioned categories of chattel, there are decisions of general application. One such case was *Mulliner* v. *Florence*[41] where it was held that the lien over horses brought by a guest to the inn was not limited to the cost of boarding the horses themselves but extended to sums which were owing for the accommodation enjoyed by the guest. The lien is general in character and therefore encompasses all chattels which have in fact been received as part of the luggage of the guest.

It is now abundantly clear, despite early suggestions to the contrary[42] that the innkeeper's lien can extend to property belonging to third parties and brought to the inn by the guest.[43] The reasons for this are probably

---

[36] *Carey* v. *Long's Hotel Co. Ltd.* (1891) 7 T.L.R. 213 (notice on first floor); *Shacklock* v. *Ethorpe* [1939] 3 All E.R. 372 (six feet above floor in corridor, over glass exhibition case); *Brewster* v. *Drennan* [1945] 2 All E.R. 705; *Olley* v. *Marlborough Court Ltd.* [1949] 1 K.B. 532; *Laing* v. *Allied Innkeepers Ltd.* (1970) 8 D.L.R. (3d) 708.

[37] Cf. *Olley* v. *Marlborough Court Ltd.* (ante), where one notice was held inadequate on both counts; *Knox* v. *Victoria Coffee Palace Co.* (1895) 1 A.L.R. (C.N.) 33; *Caldecutt* v. *Piesse* (1932) 49 T.L.R. 26.

[38] There is no right of sale at Common Law (*Mulliner* v. *Florence* (1878) 3 Q.B.D. 484) except perhaps by custom in the City of London and Exeter: *Robinson* v. *Walter* (1616) 3 Buls. 269; *Moss* v. *Townsend* (1612) 1 Buls. 207; *Warbrooke* v. *Griffin* (1609) 2 Brownl. & Golds 254; *Jones* v. *Pearle* (1736) 1 Stra. 557; Paton, op. cit., p. 218.

[39] Ante, p. 892.

[40] This is without prejudice to any other right: *Hotel Proprietors Act* 1956, s. 2(2).

[41] (1878) 3 Q.B.D. 484.

[42] E.g., *Skipwith* v. *J.S.* (1611) 1 Buls. 170; 3 Buls. 271; *Robinson* v. *Walter* (1616) 3 Buls. 269.

[43] *Yorke* v. *Greenaugh* (1703) 2 Ld. Raym. 866; *Sneed* v. *Watkins* (1856) 1 C.B.N.S. 267; *Turrill* v. *Crawley* (1849) 13 Q.B. 197; *Goodyear* v. *Klemm*

two fold. The innkeeper is obliged to accept the guest and his accompanying luggage and becomes an insurer of the latter in any event; and it would be unreasonable to expect him to conduct examinations into title.[44] But it seems that the lien attaches irrespective of whether the innkeeper knows that the goods belong to a third party,[45] and can extend to property which the innkeeper is not obliged to accept, if it is in fact accepted.[46]

The goods must, in any event, have been accepted by the innkeeper as part of the luggage of the guest and have come into his possession as the direct result of that relationship.[47] Thus, whereas the lien has been held to apply to race-horses[48] and "a piano, a sewing-machine, or other goods of a weighty or unusual character, which the innkeeper would not have been bound to receive"[49] it would not extend, for instance, to a chattel lodged with him by the police pending the discovery of its owner.[50] It has further been held the innkeeper's lien does not extend to money lent to or spent on behalf of, the guest.[51] It is confined to the

---

(1874) 5 A.J.R. 136; *Gordon* v. *Silber* (1890) 25 Q.B.D. 491; *O'Connor* v. *Grand International Hotel Co.* [1898] 2 Ir. Rep. 92; *Mercer* v. *Lowery* (1916) 181 S.W. 1050; *Park* v. *Berkery* (1930) 25 Tas. L.R. 66; *R.R. Cunningham Enterprises Ltd.* v. *Vollmers* (1973) 35 D.L.R. (3d) 761. In *Marsh* v. *Commissioner of Police* [1944] 2 All E.R. 392 and *Yorke* v. *Greenaugh* (supra) this rule was held to apply even to goods stolen by the guest; cf. *M. & M. Hotel Co.* v. *Nichols* (1935) 32 N.E. (2d) 463 (noted (1936) 10 *University of Cincinnati Law Review* 495) where the court declined to award the appellant hoteliers a lien over a stolen adding machine because "no case is found wherein the lien . . . has been sustained over inanimate property which was stolen from the owner who lost possession without any act of his, whether induced by fraud or not."

44 *Gordon* v. *Silber* (ante); property belonging to wife of guest.
45 *Robins & Co.* v. *Gray* [1895] 2 Q.B. 501; *Snead* v. *Watkins* ante; cf. *Johnson* v. *Hill* (1822) 3 Stark. 173, which had laid down the contrary rule.
46 *Park* v. *Berkery* (1930) 25 Tas. L.R. 67; see post, n. 49.
47 *Smith* v. *Dearlove* (1848) 6 C.B. 132, at 135 per Wilde C.J. No lien attaches, otherwise than by express agreement, to the goods of a mere lodger: *Alldiss* v. *Huxley* (1891) 12 L.R. (N.S.W.) 158; 8 W.N. 23; *Hanson* v. *Barwise* [1930] Q.S.R. 285; 24 Q.J.P.R. 91; *McInerny* v. *O'Neill* (1862) 1 Q.S.C.R. 84; *R.* v. *Hinton, ex parte M'Manus* (1884) 6 A.L.T. 12.
48 *Binns* v. *Pigot* (1840) 9 Car. & P. 208; but see now *Hotel Proprietors Act* 1956 s. 2(2) and cf. *Alldiss* v. *Huxley* ante.
49 *Threlfall* v *Borwick* (1875) L.R. 10 Q.B. 210. In this decision, Lord Coleridge C.J. rejected the statement by Parke B. in *Broadwood* v. *Granara* (1854) 10 Ex. 417 that the lien encompassed only those goods which the innkeeper was bound to receive. The chattel in question in the latter case was a grand piano lent to the guest by a third party and Paton, op. cit., p. 221 suggests that the case may be better explained on the ground that the innkeeper did not accept the piano as part of the goods of the guest. On the other hand, in *Threlfall* v. *Barwick* (ante) it was held that whether or not the innkeeper was bound to accept the goods (also, in this case, a piano) the lien attaches once they are in fact accepted. In *Robins* v. *Gray* [1895] 2 Q.B. 501, where the innkeeper was held to possess a lien over some sewing machines sent to the inn for a guest who was a commercial traveller, *Broadwood* v. *Granara* was distinguished on the above ground; but Kay L.J. appeared to prefer the argument of Parke B. that the innkeeper was not bound to accept the goods. However, in *Park* v. *Berkery* (1930) 25 Tas. L.R. 67, Clark J. clearly recognised that the innkeeper's lien is independent of any duty to receive the goods over which that lien extends. See further, *L.E. Lines Music Co.* v. *Holt* (1933) 60 S.W. (2d) 32; 61 S.W. (2d) 326.
50 *Binns* v. *Pigot* (1840) 9 C. & P. 208.
51 *Chesham Automobile Supply Ltd.* v. *Beresford Hotel (Birchington) Ltd.* (1913) 29 T.L.R. 584.

remuneration owed to him qua innkeeper and does not encompass moneys due on any other account.[52]

The innkeeper may include, within the debt secured by the lien, the reasonable cost of repairing a vehicle preparatory to its sale by auction[53] but not his expenses in keeping the chattel after the commencement of the lien.[54]

B. The exercise of the lien

In *R.* v. *Hough*,[55] the New South Wales Full Supreme Court held that it was unnecessary for the innkeeper to perform any positive act in order to assert his lien, because the right of lien attaches when the goods are deposited at the inn and the debt incurred.

During the currency of the lien, the innkeeper's duty towards the goods is that of reasonable care, as in the case of an ordinary bailee for reward.[56] This view is consistent with principle and seems to be supported by the unreported case of *Queen Anne's Mansions and Hotel Co.* v. *Butler*.[57] The amount of care exacted from the innkeeper may, however, decrease with the passage of time or with the deterioration of the goods.[58] Certainly he is not liable for natural deterioration or depreciation during the period of the lien, if he has exercised proper care and skill.[59]

The innkeeper is not entitled to detain the guest in person, nor to forcibly divest him of clothing or other articles of decoration.[60]

C. Loss of lien

Certain circumstances cause the innkeeper to lose an established lien over the property of a guest, while other circumstances prevent such a lien from arising in the first place. The innkeeper is not deemed to have waived his right to a lien merely because he adopts the added precaution of exacting a security from the guest; for the lien to be lost, there must be some element in the taking of the security, or in the security itself, which is inconsistent with the initial creation of a lien or with its continued existence.[61] The innkeeper's lien may even, therefore, extend over stolen

[52] *Park* v. *Berkery* (1930) 25 Tas. L.R. 67; and see *Matsuda* v. *Waldorf Hotel Co. Ltd.* (1910) 27 T.L.R. 153 (no lien over goods pledged with innkeeper); *Ferguson* v. *Peterkin* 1953 S.L.T. 91 (no lien for damage by guests to wardrobe).
[53] *Chesham Automobile Supply Ltd.* v. *Beresford Hotel (Birchington) Ltd.* (1913) 29 T.L.R. 584, at 586.
[54] *Park* v. *Berkery* (ante); *Somes* v. *British Empire Shipping Co.* (1860) 8 H.L.C. 338; *Re Rauf* (1975) 49 D.L.R. (3d) 345.
[55] (1894) 15 L.R. (N.S.W.) 204; 10 W.N. 205.
[56] *Angus* v. *McLachlan* (1883) 23 Ch.D. 330, which requires the landlord to be no more careful of the goods than he would towards his own goods of a similar description must be regarded as out-dated on this point; cf. *Canadian Imperial Bank of Commerce* v. *Doucette* (1968) 70 D.L.R. (2d) 657 (bank seizing goods by way of security owes duty of reasonable care); *Giblyn* v. *Hanf* (1911) 126 N.Y. Supp. 581, cited by Paton, op. cit., p. 222; *Re Rauf* (1974) 40 D.L.R. (3d) 362, at 365; reversed on different grounds (1975) 49 D.L.R. (3d) 345; *Frank* v. *Berryman* (1894) 3 B.C.R. 506.
[57] Cited by Wyatt Paine, *Bailment* (1901), at 211-212.
[58] Cf. p. 393 et seq., ante (involuntary bailments).
[59] *Angus* v. *McLachlan* (1883) 23 Ch.D. 330, at 333 per Kay J.
[60] *Sunbolf* v. *Alford* (1838) 3 M. & W. 248; *Grinnell* v. *Cook* (1842) 3 Hill 485; 38 Am. Dec. 663 (N. Yk. Supreme Court); contra, *Newton* v. *Trigg* (1691) 1 Shower 268. Cf. *R.* v. *Stewart* (1895) 59 J.P. 650; *R.* v. *Burton* (1886) 54 L.T. 765.
[61] *Angus* v. *McLachlan* (1883) 23 Ch.D. 330; *Park* v. *Berkery* (1930) 25 Tas. L.R. 67 (post, p. 901).

property which is expressly proffered to the innkeeper, and accepted by him, as security for the guest's bill.[62]

In *Goodyear* v. *Klemm*[63] a solicitor, Martin, left behind at the defendant's inn a portmanteau which contained inter alia a deed belonging to the plantiff. The plaintiff attorney asked the innkeeper to surrender up the deed and was told that he would do so if the attorney obtained authority from Martin. The plaintiff's attorney returned with Martin's authority and two promissory notes, which the innkeeper had given Martin in order to allow him to sue upon them. The innkeeper then refused to deliver the deed unless these promissory notes were returned to him, and was told that these could not be yielded up unless the portmanteau and its entire contents were handed over. No agreement was reached, and the plaintiff sued for detinue and conversion. Her claim failed, the Supreme Court of Victoria holding that these negotiations did not amount to a waiver of the lien.

The mere demand, by an innkeeper who has exercised his lien, of sums in excess of the amount owing to him in his capacity as innkeeper does not destroy the lien insofar as it extends to expenditure incurred by the guest under the innkeeper-guest relationship.[64] However, if the guest is mentally incapable or is an infant, no lien will probably arise,[65] unless presumably the accommodation could be classed in the latter case as necessaries.

Generally, an innkeeper who surrenders possession of goods that are the subject-matter of his lien loses therewith that lien. Certainly, this result follows if he allows the guest to depart with the goods, even though the guest returns later with the same goods:[66] once the chain of continuous possession is broken, it permanently obliterates the right to claim a lien in respect of the debt for which that possession was originally assumed. On the other hand, the mere fact that the guest is permitted to depart with certain of his goods does not preclude the innkeeper from asserting a lien in respect of those that are left behind;[67] occasional or casual absences with the chattel in question on the part of the guest may be disregarded if he departs intending to return;[68] and the bailment of the chattel to a repairer or auctioneer in preparation for the exercise of his statutory power of sale does not disable the innkeeper from exercising that power, despite the requirement in s. 1 of the *Innkeepers Act* 1878 that "no such sale shall be made until after the said goods . . . shall have been for the space of six weeks in such charge or custody or in or upon such premises without such debt having been paid or satisfied."[69]

The innkeeper's lien is also lost if the guest tenders the amount due

[62] *Marsh* v. *Commissioner of Police* [1944] 2 All E.R. 392; but cf. *Theft Act* 1968, s. 28 and Paton, op. cit., p. 223.

[63] (1874) 5 A.J.R. 136.

[64] *Park* v. *Berkery* (1930) 25 Tas. L.R. 67; *Chesham Automobile Supply Ltd.* v. *Beresford Hotel (Birchington) Ltd.* (1913) 29 T.L.R. 584.

[65] *Proctor* v. *Nicholson* (1835) 7 C. & P. 67, at 69.

[66] *Jones* v. *Pearle* (1736) 1 Stra. 557.

[67] *Snead* v. *Watkins* (1856) 1 C.B. (N.S.) 267.

[68] *Allen* v. *Smith* (1862) 12 C.B. (N.S.) 638.

[69] *Chesham Automobile Supply Ltd.* v. *Beresford Hotel (Birchington) Ltd.* ante; see post, p. 902.

under his bill and this is unreasonably refused. In *Park* v. *Berkery*[70] the defendant innkeeper claimed a lien over a motor-car which the guest had brought to the hotel. This vehicle did not belong to the guest but to an insurance company which had leased it on hire-purchase to H. H, in breach of this hire-purchase agreement, had leased it to the plaintiff, who in turn had lent it to the guest, a commission agent who worked for him but was not his servant and therefore held the car under a bailment at will.

The sums in respect of which the innkeeper claimed a lien were 13 guineas for accommodation;[71] four pounds advanced to the guest to defray his current expenses; a further three pounds allegedly advanced after the innkeeper first informed the guest that he was exercising the lien; and some £3 extra for storing the vehicle during the period of lien. The guest signed a document acknowledging his indebtedness in respect of the first two sums and stating that he was leaving the car as security for that debt. During the course of several interviews, the plaintiff and the defendant negotiated for the release of the car and the plaintiff made various offers of settlement, culminating in a promise to pay £10 down and £10 at a future date. The defendant expressed himself willing to accept these terms but demanded a full indemnity in the event of any action against him by the true owner of the car. This was refused, and the plaintiff sued in detinue for the car, contending that since he had made a tender of the full amount the innkeeper was entitled to claim under his lien, that lien was now discharged.

Clark J. agreed that the only sum which could properly be included in the lien was the charge of thirteen guineas for accommodation, but he held that the plaintiff never actually tendered this sum to the defendant. The innkeeper's lien was not destroyed merely because he claimed an amount larger than could be legitimately be included within that lien, nor because he had extracted the acknowledgment of security from the guest; for the latter would obliterate the lien only if inconsistent or repugnant thereto. Further, the lien was not abandoned or waived by the innkeeper during his conversations with the plaintiff. His demand for an indemnity was entirely reasonable in the circumstances since to have delivered the vehicle in contravention of the rights of the owner would have constituted conversion. The mere taking of such a precaution, and discussing of proposals for discharging the lien, could hardly be construed as a waiver of that lien itself. Finally, there was no tender by the plaintiff of the cost of accommodation, nor any dispensation of the need for a tender, because the plaintiff had at no time shown himself ready and willing to pay the sum there and then. Accordingly, the lien survived and the writ for detinue failed:

> When it is said that a person, having a lien on goods for the payment of a sum of money, has dispensed a person claiming the goods from making a tender of the amount secured by the lien, it is assumed

---

[70] (1930) 25 Tas. L.R. 67.

[71] The claim varied during the course of negotiations and at one point was stated to be for £15. The components of the claim also oscillated, but the total remained at c£23.

that the person claiming the goods was ready and willing to pay the amount owing. What is dispensed with, is an actual tender, not the readiness and willingness to pay the sum in respect of which the lien exists. A dispensation of readiness and willingness to pay the amount secured by the lien only occurs where the lien itself is abandoned or waived.

Paton cites a number of older decisions which suggest that the lien is forfeited if the innkeeper misuses the goods, for instance, by pledging or selling them.[72] Although the status of these authorities cannot be regarded as certain, there is much to be said for the view that a radical or fundamental misuse of the property both terminates the lien and revives the innkeeper's liability as an insurer. However, these decisions must be read subject to the statutory right of sale now conferred upon innkeepers in England and Australia.

D. Power of sale

The Innkeepers Act 1878 confers upon the innkeeper the right to sell by public auction the property to which the lien attaches, so as to recover the price for accommodating the guest or the keep of any animal left at livery in his stables or fields. It is assumed[73] that the latter power still applies although the lien itself no longer extends to animals. The innkeeper may include reasonable costs of advertisement and repair[74] in the amount he is entitled to deduct before paying the surplus to the guest on demand. However, the power of sale may not be exercised until six weeks after the debt became outstanding and the sale itself must be advertised, at least one month before it takes place, in one London and one country newspaper.[75] The six-week moratorium does not prohibit the innkeeper from making arrangements for sale while it is still subsisting, nor from putting the vehicle in the hands of repairers or auctioneers for that purpose. In neither case, unless there are special circumstances to the contrary,[76] will such arrangements offend the requirement of s. 1 that the goods shall be, during that period, in the charge or custody of the innkeeper or in upon his premises.[77]

III. The Liability of the Innkeeper under Australian Law[78]

The Australian Common Law relating to innkeepers is virtually indistinguishable from that applied by the English courts. There is, however, some significant divergence among the various State enactments, and a brief summary of the relevant legislation is provided in the following pages.

---

[72] Op. cit., p. 224, citing *Scott* v. *Newington* (1833) 1 M. & Rob. 252; *Jones* v. *Thurloe* (1723) 8 Mod. 172.

[73] *Vaines*, op. cit., p. 136.

[74] *Chesham Automobile Supply Ltd.* v. *Beresford Hotel (Birchington) Ltd.* ante; cf. *Munro* v. *Willmott* [1949] 1 K.B. 295.

[75] *Innkeepers Act* 1878, s. 1.

[76] E.g. where the bailee does not hold as agent for the innkeeper.

[77] *Chesham Automobile Supply Co. Ltd.* v. *Beresford Hotel (Birchington) Ltd.* ante. Lush J. at 584, held also that the words "in such charge or custody" in the proviso to s. 1 of the 1878 Act apply to things left upon the innkeeper's premises as well as to things deposited with him.

[78] Badger, *The Licensing Law of Australia;* Redshaw, *Liquor Law in New South Wales.*

A. New South Wales

The Innkeepers Act 1968 (repealing the *Innkeepers Liability Act* 1902) is almost identical to its English counterpart. Thus, the innkeeper's liability is expressed to cover damage as well as loss of property[79] but does not extend to vehicles and their contents or to live animals and their harness or other equipment[80] over which, correspondingly, the innkeeper has no lien.[81] Again, the traditional liability is owed only to travellers who have engaged sleeping accommodation at the inn, and subsists during times broadly equivalent to these laid down in the English statute.[82] Liability may be limited to a flat rate of one hundred dollars per guest by a notice which conforms with s. 7(2) of the Act: again, the requirements for limitation of liability follow closely upon the English model, except that the notice prescribed in the Schedule to the Act must additionally be exhibited (at a place in which it can conveniently be read) in the guest's room.[83] The ordinary limitation may also be lost (as in England) by express deposit,[84] inability of the guest to make such deposit, or "default, neglect or wilful act" of the innkeeper or his servant.[85]

It will be noted that the New South Wales Act speaks not in terms of hotel proprietors but in terms of "the keeper of an inn". The effect, however, is the same as in England, which is to preserve the relevance of the Common Law authority as to what is an inn.[86] S. 3(1) provides that, for the purposes of the Act, "inn" means a common inn and "innkeeper" means the keeper of an inn.[87]

Section 3(2) of the Act provides that nothing in the Act shall be construed as affecting:

(a) any right, liability or legal proceeding saved by the Interpretation Act of 1897, as subsequently amended;
(b) any lien that took effect before the commencement of this Act; or
(c) the liability of any person for loss of, or damage to, property caused before or after the commencement of this Act by his default, neglect or wilful act, or that of his servant.

---

[79] *Innkeepers Act* 1968, s. 5.
[80] Ibid., s. 6(a).
[81] Section 8.
[82] See ss. 6(b) and 4 of the N.S.W. Act, the latter of which (apart from transitional provisions catering for accommodation engaged before the coming into force of the Act) provides that the traveller shall be deemed to be a guest during the period commencing with the day on which he is entitled to use the sleeping accommodation and ending on the expiration of the day upon which he ceases to be so entitled.
[83] Section 7(2)(b).
[84] See *Theeman* v. *Forte Properties Pty. Ltd.* [1973] 1 N.S.W.L.R. 418; ante, p. 000.
[85] Section 7(3).
[86] Ante, p. 880 et seq.
[87] Note, however, that under s. 72 of the *Liquor Act* 1912, the innkeeper's liability is expressed to apply to every holder of a publican's licence. This extension is preserved and updated by s. 10(a) of the 1968 Act, but is clearly of decreasing importance in view of the rule that, to qualify as a guest, a person must now have engaged sleeping accommodation. It could mean, however, that a licensed publican who does not offer accommodation to all the sundry but who does so on a particular occasion, would come within the strict liability imposed by the 1968 Act.

Section 3(2)(c), which would of course cover the situation where the innkeeper becomes a bailee, is complemented by the proviso to s. 6, which renders the innkeeper liable even where the traveller has not engaged sleeping accommodation or where the chattel lost or injured is within the category excluded from the ambit of his strict liability by s. 6(a), if the loss or damage complained of is due to some default, neglect or wilful act of the innkeeper or his servant.[88]

The innkeeper's right to sell property belonging to his guests is laid down in s. 73 of the *Liquor Act* 1912. His lien is regulated primarily by the rules of the Common Law[89] but is extended by the statute to the property of lodgers:[90]

> If any guest or lodger leaves any licensed premises without first paying a reasonable sum for his accommodation, the licensee of such licensed premises may, with the consent of a licensing magistrate, and upon such magistrate being satisfied by affidavit or statutory declaration of the amount of debt, after the expiration of three months from the date of such guest or lodger absconding (having first given fourteen days' notice by an advertisement in some newspaper circulating in the police district within which such licensed premises are situated), proceed to sell by public auction all goods, chattels, and effects which have been left in the custody of such licensee by such guest or lodger; and any excess that is realised over and above the amount of such indebtedness and expenses shall be paid over to the Consolidated Revenue Fund in trust for such person or persons as may thereafter be proved to the satisfaction of the Colonial Treasurer to be entitled thereto.

B. Victoria

Formerly, the Victorian legislation attempted to deal with innkeeper's liability on the same basis as that relating to common carriers. The equation was not particularly felicitous[91] and the two forms of liability are now dealt with separately, albeit within the perimeter of a single statute. The contemporary law is to be found in ss. 26-31 of the *Carriers and Innkeepers Act* 1958, a revised body of rules inserted by s. 2 of the *Carriers and Innkeepers (Amendment) Act* 1970. Again, these rules correspond broadly with the *English Hotel Proprietors Act* 1956 and with the New South Wales Act of 1968, but a number of independent differences should be noted:

(a) There is a more detailed definition of "inn", which endeavours (to some extent) to codify and to update the Common Law.[92] Establishments

---

[88] Including, presumably, a servant for whom he would not be "vicariously" liable: cf. *Kott and Kott* v. *Gordon Hotels Ltd.* ante, p. 894). In this respect, the innkeeper's liability would still seem to be in excess of the ordinary liability of comparable tradesmen (e.g. restaurant-keepers) at common law.

[89] Ante, p. 897 et seq.

[90] *Alldiss* v. *Huxley* ante; and see ante, p. 883.

[91] E.g., *Miller* v. *Federal Coffee Palace Co.* (1889) 15 V.L.R. 30; and see Stirling (1931) 4 A.L.J. 319.

[92] By s. 26(1), "Inn" means "any hotel or motel and includes any establishment held out by the proprietor as offering food, drink and, if so required, sleeping accommodation, without special contract, to any traveller presenting himself who appears able and willing to pay a reasonable sum for the services and facilities provided and who is in a fit state to be received."

within this definition are the only establishments to whose proprietors shall attach the duties, liabilities and rights which immediately before the commencement of the Act attached by law to an innkeeper as such.[93]

(b) Instead of prescribing specific time-points for the commencement and cessation of the innkeeper's liability, s. 27(2) provides simply that for the purposes of the Act a traveller shall be deemed to be a guest "only on days during which he is entitled to use a room at the inn that has been engaged by or for him for sleeping." The effect of this section does not seem to be different, however, from that of the more elaborate section in the New South Wales Act.[94]

(c) The requirements as to notice claiming statutory limitation of liability[95] are the same as those contained in s. 7(2) of the New South Wales Act, but the consequence of an express deposit (or the inability of the guest to make such deposit) is not to make the innkeeper fully liable for ensuing loss or damage[96] to the goods but merely to limit his liability to the higher level of $2000 per guest.[97] However, no limitation applies when the cause of loss or damage was some default, neglect or wilful act of the innkeeper or his servant.

(d) The statutory limitation notice[98] does not (as in the case of the English and New South Wales statutes) contain a coda advising that the notice does not constitute an admission either that the Act applies to the premises in question or that liability thereunder attaches in any particular case. In all other respects, the Victorian legislation seems to be congruent to that of New South Wales, excepting only insofar as the latter statute also covers licensed publicans and makes some specific provision for the sale of guests' property, which the Victorian Act does not.

C. Western Australia

The position under Western Australia law is radically different from the rule of the Common Law. Section 173(1) of the *Liquor Act* 1970, provides:

> Without affecting the application of any other rule of law, a rule of law that imposes a duty or liability upon a person, by reason only of his being an innkeeper, no longer supplies in the State.

Accordingly, the innkeeper's strict liability is abolished and his liability would appear to depend solely upon his duties (if any) as a bailee, as a licensor of space upon which guests' belongings are placed,[99] as an occupier and under general principles of the law of contract and tort respectively.[1]

---

[93] Section 27(1).
[94] Section 4, *Innkeepers Act* 1968; ante, p. 903.
[95] Section 30(4). The limitation is to $100 per guest, unless the goods were expressly deposited or a guest was unable to make such deposit.
[96] Sections 28, 30(3).
[97] Section 30(1)(a).
[98] Schedule 4 to the (1958) Act.
[99] Chapter 5, ante.
[1] Section 173(2) preserves any duty or liability imposed upon an innkeeper by this or any other Act, but the remaining provisions of the Act do not touch upon his liability for loss of, or damage to, the property of his guests.

However, there seems no reason why he should not be additionally subject to a general duty of care on the same basis as the boarding-house keeper. This liability is discussed in the ensuing chapter. The foregoing provision also presumably deprives the Western Australian innkeeper of his right to an innkeepers' lien.

D. Tasmania

The Tasmanian legislation is contained in ss. 122-128 of the *Licensing Act* 1932. Section 122(1) enacts that every hotel and every public-house shall be deemed to be a common inn, and the licensee thereof to be an innkeeper;[2] the expressions "hotel" and "public-house" being defined to mean any house in respect of which a hotel or public-house licence has been issued under the Act.[3] An overall limitation of liability is afforded by s. 123: if any person lodging in any licensed premises shall lose any goods or chattels the licensee shall not be held responsible to a greater extent than £20[4] unless they have been lodged with him and a receipt obtained. Below this amount, the licensee's liability is presumably as an insurer. But although s. 123 applies to lodgers and weekly boarders as well as to more transient guests[5] it remains exceptionally generous to the hotel or public-house licensee. There are no requirements as to notice, the relevant limitation is anachronistically low and the circumstances in which this can be displaced are narrower than in other jurisdictions. It is possible to argue that, by referring only to persons "lodging" at the premises, s. 123 does not apply to persons who are not lodgers at Common Law but merely travellers or guests, in respect of whom the strict liability of the innkeeper would presumably be preserved in full. However, the definition of "lodger" would seem to encompass even the transient guest.

By referring only the *loss* of goods and chattels, s. 123 appears to assume that the innkeeper is not strictly liable for damage to guests' property at Common Law.[6] There is no exclusion of liability for animals or vehicles and the old decisions as to whether goods are infra hospitium are therefore still relevant in Tasmania.[7]

A wide power of sale is conferred by s. 124. The sale must be by public auction and can be exercised only for debts incurred in respect of board or lodging or the keep or care of animals. The debt must have remained unpaid, and the goods in the licensee's custody or possession for six weeks before sale.[8] Further, the licensee must make a statutory

---

[2] Cf. *Williams* v. *Linnitt* [1951] 1 K.B. 565.
[3] *Licensing Act* 1932, s. 3(1).
[4] Converted by s. 5(1) of the *Decimal Currency Act* 1965 (Tas.) to $40.
[5] Lodger is defined by s. 3(1) as "a person actually and in good faith lodging in the licensed premises in relation to which the term is used whether as a customer or as a servant of the licensee or as a member of his household; and includes a weekly boarder who habitually from day to day takes his meals in the licensed premises so long only, between the hours specified in any permit under s. 64(a) that is in force for the time being in relation to the premises, as he is on such premises in good faith for the purpose of obtaining such meals."
[6] See ante, p. 887.
[7] Ante, p. 892; and see s. 124 (power to sell, inter alia, animals left on "precincts").
[8] Cf. p. 902, ante.

declaration of the indebtedness and must give notice in a newspaper of the impending sale. Astonishingly, the power of sale does not apply to goods belonging to a ratepayer resident in Tasmania. Further subsections define the procedure to be followed prior to, or after, sale. Section 128 forbids the seizing of a lodger's goods by way of distress for rent.

E. South Australia

The position in South Australia is remarkably straightforward. Sections 120 (2) and (3) of the *Licensing Act* 1967, provide as follows:

120(2) No licensee[9] shall be liable to make good to any guest of such licensee any loss of or injury to goods or property brought on the licensed premises to any greater amount than the sum of sixty dollars, except in the following cases:

(a) Where the goods or property has been stolen, lost, or injured through the wilful act, default, or neglect of the licensee or any servant in his employ;

(b) Where the goods or property has been deposited with or entrusted to the licensee expressly for safe custody: Provided that in such case the licensee may, if he thinks fit, require as a condition of his liability that the goods or property shall be deposited or placed in a box, room, outhouse, or other receptacle or place fastened and sealed or locked by the person depositing the same.

(3) Every licensee shall cause at least one copy of the second subsection of this section printed in plain type to be exhibited in a conspicuous part of the hall or entrance to his licensed premises, and he shall be entitled to the benefit of this section in respect of such goods or property only as are brought to his licensed premises while the copy is so exhibited.

The licensee's power of sale is contained in s. 121, which contains similar safeguards and procedures to those laid down in the Tasmanian Act, except that a copy of the statutory newspaper notice must go to the owner of the goods;[10] the relevant waiting period is two months;[11] and no immunity is granted to South Australian ratepayers. Section 119 exempts travellers' goods from distress for rent.

F. Queensland

Under s. 92 of the *Liquor Act* 1912,[12] no licensed victualler shall be liable to make good to any guest or lodger[13] any loss of or injury to goods or property brought to his licensed premises, unless *either* the goods have been stolen, lost or injured through the wilful act,[14] default or neglect of such licensed victualler or any servant or person in his employ; *or* the goods have been deposited with him expressly for safe custody. In the latter event, the licensee may refuse to accept the goods unless they are sealed or fastened in a box or other receptacle. To produce this

---

[9] Defined by s. 120(1) as the holder of a full publican's or limited publican's licence.

[10] Section 121(2)(c).

[11] Section 121(2)(a).

[12] As amended by *Liquor Acts Amendment Act* 1965, s. 39.

[13] As defined by s. 4; see *Liquor Acts Amendment Act* 1965, s. 3.

[14] Ante, p. 893.

total exemption, a copy of s. 92 must be exhibited conspicuously near the principal entrance to the premises. The limitation is not available to innkeepers who are not licensed victuallers.[15]

A power of sale over lodgers' property is conferred by s. 93;[16] the waiting period is three months and the sale must be by public auction. The power no longer extends to horses and carriages and the licensee can no longer reimburse himself from the proceeds of sale for the maintenance of horses. Section 94 enacts that every house in respect of which a licensed victuallers' licence has been granted shall be held in law to be a common inn[17] and that no property belonging to a stranger shall be seized by way of distress for rent.

---

[15] *Turner* v. *Queensland Motels Pty. Ltd.* [1968] Qd. R. 191.
[16] As amended by *Liquor Act Amendment Act* 1973, s. 53.
[17] This does not, of course, prevent other houses from being designated inns.

CHAPTER 24

BOARDING-HOUSE KEEPERS

I. THE DUTY OF CARE

The boarding-house proprietor's responsibility for the safety of his guests' belongings rests approximately midway between the strict liability of the innkeeper and the almost vestigial duties owed by a mere licensor of space.[1] Whereas other occupiers who allow their premises to be used for occupation and for the incidental storing of goods have been held to owe no general duty to safeguard such goods from theft,[2] boarding-house proprietors have been held liable for the loss by theft of boarders' property when occasioned by a failure to take reasonable care,[3] irrespective of whether they are bailees.[4] However, whereas a bailor need not prove negligence but need only prove the loss and require the bailee to refute it, the boarder clearly carries the burden of proving that the loss of his goods was the result of the proprietor's neglect.

A number of decisions illustrate the duty of care in action. In *Dansey* v. *Richardson*[5] the main question was whether the proprietor should be liable for an act of negligence by her servant, and upon this issue the court was evenly divided. It was, however, acknowledged that the conduct complained of in this case, viz., leaving the front door of the house ajar while on an errand, could constitute a breach of the proprietor's duty (undertaken "by implication of law") to take proper care of baggage belonging to the guest.[6] Nowadays, the proprietor would undoubtedly be vicariously liable for any such act of negligence, provided it were committed in the course of that servant's employment or in discharge of a duty delegated to him.[7]

---

[1] Ante, Chapter 5.

[2] E.g. *Deyong* v. *Shenburn* [1946] K.B. 227 (actor's dressing-room at theatre): *Edwards* v. *West Herts. Group Hospital Management Committee* [1957] 1 All E.R. 541 (resident house physician's room in management committee's hostel); ante, p. 223 et seq.

[3] In *Edwards* v. *West Herts. etc. Committee* (ante) it was acknowledged that the boarding-house keeper owes a duty of care to all his guests, but held that in the present case the relationship was not one of boarding-house keeper and guest.

[4] Generally, in the absence of delivery of the goods for safekeeping, they will not be: *Dansey* v. *Richardson* (1854) 3 E. & B. 144, at 155 per Wightman J.; cf. Coleridge J. at 158-159.

[5] Ante.

[6] Cf. Lord Campbell C.J., at 170: "gross negligence"; Erle C.J. at 150: "such care of the house and things in it as a prudent owner would take"; Wightman J. at 155: such care "as a prudent owner would take with respect to his own"; Coleridge J. at 160: "ordinary care".

[7] Cf. *Morris* v. *C. W. Martin & Sons Ltd.* [1966] 1 Q.B. 716; and see n. 10, post.

The general duty was reaffirmed by the Court of Appeal in *Scarborough* v. *Cosgrove*.[8] The boarders in this case were appealing against a direction of Darling J. that boarding-house keepers were under no duty to take care of their boarders' goods unless handed to them for safe custody and were therefore liable only for misfeasance.[9] The Court of Appeal repudiated this ruling and granted the application for a new trial, holding that there was sufficient evidence to go to the jury as to whether the duty of care had been broken.[10] The alleged negligence in this case consisted in the failure or the management to supply keys to rooms or to cupboards within rooms, their refusal to allow boarders to take the keys that were already in the apartment doors and their admission of the thief as an inmate of the boarding-house without any reference or introduction, when they had told the plaintiff that all their boarders were known and could be trusted.

The alleged acts of negligence in *Paterson* v. *Norris*[11] were similar to those in *Dansey* v. *Richardson* except that the failure to close the front door was alleged to be a continuing one which persisted despite warnings from the defendant's guests, and to be a personal rather than a vicarious failure. Because of this, a thief was apparently able to enter the plaintiff's room (for which no key was supplied) and steal some jewellery locked in the **dressing-table drawer.** Coleridge J., while affirming the general duty of care, held that the plaintiff had failed to discharge the burden of proving a breach of that duty. He further held that the guest had retained the goods in her own custody[12] and hinted that she herself may have been less careful than was necessary in the circumstances. The decision seems a harsh one which may, however, be justified on the grounds that the failure to keep the front door shut could have been the fault of another guest,[13] or that the defendant was not shown to have knowledge of the jewellery.[14]

Certainly, the failure to provide an efficient lock to the boarder's room may constitute negligence, as is shown by the decision in *Caldecutt*

---

8 [1905] 2 K.B. 805. See the discussion of this case in *Tinsley* v. *Dudley* [1951] 1 K.B. 18, at 23.
9 This seems to be the modern rule as regards the ordinary licensor, at least so far as concerns loss by theft: see p. 195 et seq., ante.
10 In so deciding, the Court preferred *Dansey* v. *Richardson* to the later decision in *Holder* v. *Soulby* (1860) 8 C.B.N.S. 254, holding further that the boarding or lodging house proprietor was liable for the negligence of his servants and not merely for direct or personal negligence: see especially Collins M.R. [1905] 2 K.B., at 809-813. Romer L.J. acknowledged (at 814) that there may be cases in which the arrangement between the parties is to the effect that the boarder takes upon himself the sole custody of his property; in all other cases the proprietor owes a duty of reasonable care.
11 (1914) 30 T.L.R. 393.
12 Sed quaere: cf. *Carpenter* v. *Haymarket Hotel Ltd.* [1931] 1 K.B. 364; ante, p. 891.
13 "The defendant was bound to take reasonable care that the door should be kept shut but she did not guarantee that it should be": (1914) 30 T.L.R. 393, at 394; cf. *Appah* v. *Parncliffe Investments Ltd.* [1964] 1 All E.R. 838; post, p. 911.
14 Value £55. If the goods stolen are beyond the boarding-house keeper's reasonable contemplation, the lack of specific knowledge of them would in many cases negate a duty of care. Of course, the class of clientele and the status of the boarding-house may be relevant to the proprietor's duty of care: thus, in *Caldecutt* v. *Piesse* (post, n. 28), the plaintiff was allowed to recover for the loss of a diamond ring worth £50; see further, p. 499 ante.

v. *Piesse*.[15] In this case, the plaintiff had repeatedly asked for the lock on her door to be repaired and had been assured that the repair would be made. The plaintiff's ring, which she had left in a box on the dressing table while dining downstairs, was stolen by a fellow-guest and the defendants were held liable for her loss:

> The defendant was not fulfilling her duty if she provided a room for a guest who came with the expressed intention of making her residence there and in which she would probably keep such valuables as she had got if that room could not be locked from the outside by the guest.[16]

Equally, a boarding-house keeper may be negligent if he or his servant leaves the key in the outside lock of the guest's room;[17] or allows it to be left on a keyboard in the foyer of the building without providing anyone to scrutinise incoming persons;[18] or wrongfully allows another person to use the boarder's room during his absence.[19]

II. LANDLORDS AND LICENSORS DISTINGUISHED

Occasionally, the true analysis of the parties' relationship may be that of landlord and tenant rather than that of licensor and licensee. In this event, the landlord's duty is reduced and in general circumstances he owes no duty to protect his tenants' property from theft. Although boarding-house keepers are not normally bailees, they do retain some measure of control over the premises occupied by their boarders[20] and, through this, over their belongings. This control, which justifies in part the imposition of their duty of reasonable care,[21] is lacking from the landlord-tenant relationship where the tenant gets exclusive possession of the land subject to the lease.

This distinction, which raises questions more directly germane to the law of real property than to the present work, fell to be considered in *Appah* v. *Parncliffe Investments Ltd.*[22] Here, the plaintiff was considered to be a licensee for reward, and not a tenant, for the following reasons: the daily rate of payment for her room, the reservation of a right of entry by the proprietor, the cleaning and servicing of individual rooms by the defendants, the requirement that all visitors leave by 10.30 p.m. and the fact that instructions to quit could be given without notice. The defendants admitted that if their relationship were found to be one of licensor and licensee they would be under a duty of reasonable care. The Court of Appeal accepted this and held them liable for the theft of the

---

[15] (1932) 49 T.L.R. 26.
[16] Ibid., at 28 per Swift J.
[17] *Cole* v. *Lejeune* [1951] 2 T.L.R. 308, at 312.
[18] *Olley* v. *Marlborough Court Ltd.* [1949] 1 K.B. 532.
[19] Cf. *Warner* v. *Cameron* (1911) 19 W.L.R. 461.
[20] E.g. by a right of entry for cleaning purposes etc.
[21] *Cole* v. *Lejeune* ante, at 310 per Evershed M.R.
[22] [1964] 1 All E.R. 838. See also *O'Neill* v. *Esquire Hotels Ltd.* (1973) 30 D.L.R. (3d) 589; *Luganda* v. *Service Hotels Ltd.* [1969] 2 Ch. 209; *Marchant* v. *Charters* [1977] 1 W.L.R. 1181; *R.* v. *South Middlesex Rent Tribunal, ex parte Beswick* (1976) *The Times* March 26th; *Mayflower Cambridge Ltd.* v. *Secretary of State for the Environment* (1975) 30 P. & C.R. 28.

plaintiff's belongings from her room, the theft being facilitated by a defective lock on the door of her room.[23] Although none of the decisions concerning the liability of boarding-house keepers for theft was cited by the court, it seems clear that the defendants' establishment was capable of being characterised as a boarding-house. The decision is therefore of considerable importance, since hybrid establishments of the kind involved in *Appah* v. *Parncliffe Investments Ltd.* have proliferated greatly in London and other cities during the last ten or fifteen years, particularly, perhaps, for the accommodation of overseas visitors and students. On a different level, there seems no reason why an old people's home should not also be classed as a boarding-house for the purpose of imposing upon the proprietor a duty of reasonable care.[24]

III. DAMAGE TO GOODS

North observes[25] that there is no apparent authority on the boarding-house keeper's liability for damage to goods. It may be ventured that his Common Law duty of care would extend to destruction or damage and that he would be liable qua boarding-house keeper for a lack of reasonable care. However, this question is less important than the question of loss by theft, partly because the proprietor's liability as an occupier could cover many if not all cases of damage resulting from a failure to take reasonable care, and partly because he might be held liable on ordinary principles of negligence.[26]

IV. DEFENCES

The boarding-house keeper will be relieved from liability if the boarder kept the goods within his own exclusive custody,[27] or contributed to their loss, damage or destruction through his own neglect.[28] The latter question

---

[23] Other grounds of negligence were the failure to keep the front door closed during both day and night (cf. ante): the failure to provide an efficient porter or receptionist or to take other steps to prevent the entry of unauthorised persons; the failure to provide keys for cupboards or drawers in rooms; and the failure to provide the plaintiff with a key to the mortice lock on her door.

[24] In *Abbeyfield (Harpenden) Society Ltd.* v. *Woods* [1968] 1 W.L.R. 374 an elderly person living in an unfurnished bed-sitting room at an Abbeyfield Home was held not to be a tenant, but a mere licensee, for the purposes of the *Rent Restrictions Act*. It seems unlikely that a hospital would be held to be a boarding-house keeper for the purpose of liability for patients' belongings (cf. *Martin* v. *L.C.C.* [1947] K.B. 628; *Edwards* v. *West Herts. Group Hospital Management Committee* [1957] 1 All E.R. 541) but such liability may well attach to a school boarding-house (cf. *Poulton* v. *Notre Dame College* (1976) 60 D.L.R. (3d) 501) and *possibly* to a students' hall of residence: cf. *Edwards'* Case (ante) and see the *Mayflower Cambridge* and *Beswick* cases, ante. Quaere as to aeroplanes, army barracks, ocean-going liners and prisons. See generally Chapter 5 ante and, as to the distinction between licences and tenancies, Megarry & Wade, *Law of Real Property* (4th ed.), pp. 618-620.

[25] *Occupiers' Liability*, p. 109n.

[26] See further, p. 214 et seq., ante.

[27] *Scarborough* v. *Cosgrove* [1905] 2 K.B. 805, at 814 per Romer L.J.; *Paterson* v. *Norris* (1914) 30 T.L.R. 393; *Cole* v. *Lejeune* [1951] 2 T.L.R. 308, at 310.

[28] Cf. *Paterson* v. *Norris* (ante) with *Caldecutt* v. *Piesse* (1932) 49 T.L.R. 26, where Swift J. held that the plaintiff had not been contributorily negligent in

is one of fact to be decided by reference to such factors as the value of the property, the nature of the boarding-house and its clientele, and the alternative methods for safe-keeping made available by the proprietor of the establishment.[29] It would seem incontrovertible that the *Law Reform (Contributory Negligence) Act* 1945 applies in this context and that the boarder's negligence is no longer a total defence.[30] The proprietor may, under the ordinary rules of Common Law, limit or exclude his liability by notice.[31]

V. THE NATURE OF THE DUTY

Assuming that the boarding-house keeper's liability is not founded on bailment, there remains the further question of deciding whether it arises ex contractu, or is merely one dimension of the tort of negligence, or like the innkeeper's liability comprises an independent cause of action. This question could become important for several reasons, not least because it may affect the rights of someone whose board and lodging are paid for by a third person. It would be undesirable if privity of contract were necessary in order to establish the innkeeper's duty to take care. Although the courts could apply this requirement leniently, by discovering an implied or collateral contract with the non-paying boarder[32] or by allowing the party who pays for the lodging to recover the boarder's losses in a personal action for breach of contract,[33] the necessity to prove a contractual relation could well prove undesirably restrictive. It is not yet settled whether contributory negligence is a defence to an action for breach of contract[34] and yet such negligence clearly relieved the boarding-house proprietor before 1945 and would undoubtedly constitute a ground for apportionment after that date. For these and other reasons, it is suggested that the duty in question should not be regarded as exclusively contractual.

befriending the fellow guest who subsequently stole her ring. In *Olley* v. *Marlborough Court Ltd.* [1949] 1 K.B. 532, at 548 the female plaintiff was held not to have been negligent in leaving her key upon an unattended key-board in the reception office.

[29] A failure to disclose the value of goods may (if it is exceptional) be evidence of contributory negligence: *Paterson* v. *Norris* ante.

[30] But cf. post.

[31] Subject to the rules set out in Ch. 25 post. Cf. *Caldecutt* v. *Piesse,* where the notice could not apply because it was exhibited in an obscure position. Of course, there is no statutory requirement as to the position and content of the notice but often a notice which fails to satisfy the *Hotel Proprietors Act* will also be invalid at Common Law: cf. *Olley* v. *Marlborough Court Ltd.* ante, and p. 896 ante.

[32] *Olley* v. *Marlborough Court Ltd.* ante, at 547 per Singleton L.J. Cf. *Lockett* v. *A. & M. Charles Ltd.* [1938] 4 All E.R. 170 (presumption that where two people enter a restaurant and order a meal a contract is made between the restauranteur and each of them individually: this presumption not rebutted in the instant case although the husband paid for both meals); *Regensteiner* v. *Canuto's Restaurant Ltd.* (1938) *The Times* 6 May; *Forster* v. *Taylor* (1811) 3 Camp. 49; *Smith and Wife* v. *Inns of Court Hotel* (1900) *The Times,* 15 June; *Andrews* v. *Home Flats* [1945] 2 All E.R. 698.

[33] *Jackson* v. *Horizon Hotels Ltd.* [1975] 3 All E.R. 92.

[34] Ante, p. 55.

Nevertheless, this is the interpretation favoured by most of the authorities,[35] and in *Morris* v. *C. W. Martin & Sons Ltd.*[36] Lord Denning M.R. cited the case of the boarding-house keeper as an example of a contractual duty to protect goods from theft or depredation: "He is under an implied contract to take reasonable care for the safety of property brought into the house by a guest."

If such a term can be so readily implied into contracts for board and lodging it seems strange that the courts have refused to imply it into other contracts which involve the incidental provision of similar facilities and under which it is evident that the person receiving the use of such facilities must (to comply with the contract) leave his property unattended.[37] Possibly the duty of care arises only when the provision of facilities is a substantial part of the consideration; but although the principle can be extended too far, it seems illogical to discriminate against one type of contracting party who has an interest in the use of his accommodation and not against another. Despite the occasional references to "special contract" in the cases dealing with boarding-houses, the courts do not seem to have delved very deeply into the terms of individual contracts to ascertain whether the duty has, on the particular facts, been undertaken. Instead, they seem to have taken the duty for granted. It may be preferable to regard the boarding-house proprietor's liability as sui generis and founded, like that of the innkeeper, upon the custom of the realm.

VI. Liens

In the absence of special agreement, the boarding-house keeper enjoys at Common Law no lien over his boarders' goods.[38]

VII. Bailment of Room-key

It has already been stated that the boarder carries the onus of proving that his loss results from a want of reasonable care.[39] One interesting method of reversing this burden in certain circumstances is suggested by the judgment of Denning L.J. in *Olley* v. *Marlborough Court Ltd.*[40] In that case the boarder, on departing from the boarding house, placed her key on an unattended key-board in the foyer of the hotel. The lack

---

[35] Both *Dansey* v. *Richardson* (1854) 3 E. & B. 144 and *Scarborough* v. *Cosgrove* [1905] 2 K.B. 805 refer to the duty as one undertaken "by implication of law". North, op. cit., p. 109, suggests that this points to a contractual basis of liability and this explanation of *Scarborough* v. *Cosgrove*, as a decision in which the duty to guard against theft was created by implied or special contract, was accepted in *Tinsley* v. *Dudley* [1951] 2 K.B. 18, at 23 per Evershed M.R. See also *Olley* v. *Marlborough Court Ltd.* at 547.

[36] [1966] 1 Q.B. 716, at 727.

[37] *Deyong* v. *Shenburn* [1946] K.B. 227; *Edwards* v. *West Herts. etc. Committee* [1957] 1 All E.R. 541. And see further *Lee Cooper & Co. Ltd.* v. *C. H. Jeakins Ltd.* [1976] 2 Lloyd's Rep. 215.

[38] *& Sons Ltd.* [1967] 2 Q.B. 1; *Johnson Matthey Ltd.* v. *Constantine Terminals* Ante, p. 883.

[39] Ante, p. 909. Almost every decision in this area expresses the rule.

[40] [1949] 1 K.B. 532, at 548-549.

of supervision over the taking of keys enabled a thief to enter the boarder's room and steal a quantity of personal belongings. Denning L.J. held that by putting the key in the charge of the defendants the plaintiff placed upon them the onus of proving that they took reasonable care of the key; if they could not prove this, they were liable for those consequences "which might reasonably have been foreseen".

Although Denning L.J. did not expressly say so, it seems that this statement proceeds on the assumption that the boarding-house proprietors were bailees of the key under a bailment at will from their own bailee, the plaintiff. In these circumstances the plaintiff would be perfectly justified in requiring them to prove reasonable care[41] and in holding them responsible for the consequences of a failure to do so. The implications of this theory could be of significance not only in the immediate context of boarding-house proprietors but in all cases of licensor-licensee relationships where the licensor does not become a bailee of the principal chattel stolen but merely of its key or other means of access; especially since Lord Denning has subsequently stated that the bailee's measure of damages comprises all loss flowing directly from the failure to take reasonable care.[42] Had this argument been applied in *B.G. Transport Service Ltd.* v. *Marston Motor Co. Ltd.*[43] that case may well have been differently decided.

---

[41] They would, of course, be bailees for reward: see generally, Chapter 8 ante.
[42] *Building and Civil Engineering Holidays Scheme Management Ltd.* v. *Post Office* [1966] 1 Q.B. 247, at 261.
[43] [1970] 1 Lloyd's Rep. 371; ante, p. 201. Cf. *In re United Service Co., Johnstone's Claim* (1870) 6 Ch. App. 212 at 218.

CHAPTER 25

EXCLUSION CLAUSES [1]

For centuries, bailees have sought to guard against liability for loss or damage to goods by means of protective or exclusory clauses introduced into the contract of bailment. An early illustration is to be found in the report to *Southcot* v. *Bennet* in 1601,[2] where Coke's note to the proceedings warns that a depositary of goods should "take them in a special manner, Scil to keep them as he keeps his own goods . . . for . . . otherwise he may be charged by his general acceptance". Although a century later we find Powell J. somewhat peevishly observing that "half mankind" never heard of this distinction,[3] we may safely assume that professional bailees were increasingly aware of the possibilities of contracting out of liability imposed by contract or at common law. Nor, of course, is the practice confined to bailees. At a later stage, exclusion clauses were regularly utilised by lessors of chattels and other bailors to protect themselves against the consequences of defective or dangerous goods.

Nowadays, the breadth and particularity of standard-form conditions represent a recurrent social problem, in response to which the courts have devised a varied and occasionally counter-productive armoury.[4] Statute has also intervened in many areas, either by outlawing such clauses entirely or by defining strictly the species of liability which they can exclude.[5] This chapter will concern itself mainly with the requirements that are necessary to uphold exclusion clauses at Common Law.

Exclusion clauses are normally easy to identify, although they operate under a variety of pseudonyms: exemption, exception or exculpatory clauses are the most popular variations. Loosely, they are devices whereby one party to a contract or other relationship giving rise to duties and

---

[1] Coote, *Exception Clauses;* Yates, *Exclusion Clauses in Contracts* (1978); Laskin, "Limitation and Exclusion of Liability in Bailment" [1956] *University of Toronto Law Journal,* p. 202; Treitel, *Law of Contract* (4th ed.), Chapter 7; Law Commission No. 69 and Scottish Law Commission No. 39, *Exemption Clauses, Second Report* (1975).

[2] (1601) Cro. Eliz. 815; 4 Co. Rep. 83b; Co. Lit. 89. The initial stimulus seems to have been the stricter liability placed upon bailees prior to *Coggs* v. *Bernard* (1703) 2 Ld. Raym. 909; 92 E.R. 107. See further (1473) Y.B. 9 Ed. IV 40, pl. 22; Holmes, *The Common Law,* p. 178 *et seq.*

[3] *Coggs* v. *Bernard,* ante, at 912, 109.

[4] Other institutions have occasionally taken an adverse view of exclusion clauses. Winthrop's *Journal "History of New England", 1630-1649* (1908, ed. J. K. Hosmer), vol. i, pp. 315-318, cites the example of a sermon directed partly against provisions designed to exclude liability for loss from perils of the sea.

[5] Special rules affecting individual types of bailment are discussed in the appropriate chapters: see, for instance, Chapters 15-18, ante and *Unfair Contract Terms Act* 1977, post.

obligations attempts to immunise himself against liability for their breach, by means of terms inserted into the relationship and secured by the other party's assent. As such, they must be distinguished from certain other terms or variations, to which they bear a greater or lesser degree of resemblance.

I. Limitation Clauses

Under a limitation clause, the protected party seeks not to evade liability altogether for a breach of duty but merely to limit that liability to a specific or determinable amount.[6] Generally, the courts will approach a limitation clause in the same manner as they approach a clause which excludes liability in toto. However, the operation of the conventional rules may vary when the clause is of a purely limiting character, for reasons which will presently appear. In addition, what appears to be a limitation clause will sometimes represent an attempt by the parties to pre-estimate the damages resulting from a breach. In this event, the clause will normally escape the stricter rules that apply to clauses of limitation.[7]

II. Indemnity Clauses

Occasionally, one party to a contract will insert provisions which entitle him to recover any losses or liability suffered while carrying out the contract. Such clauses are a common method of insulating sub-bailees against the permanent loss of moneys paid to a consignor or other owner of the goods, with whom they have no contractual relationship, for loss or damage suffered during storage or in transit.[8] But the effectiveness of the indemnity clause is not confined to tripartite situations. It may also exist in a purely two-party situation, as where the parties to a contract of hire seek to apportion in advance the cost of returning the machine or of retrieving it from the scene of a disaster.[9] Insofar as indemnity clauses represent no more than the converse aspect of the ordinary exclusion clause, there is authority for the view that they will be treated by the courts in substantially the same way as exclusion clauses and will need to fulfil broadly the same conditions before they can be upheld.[10]

---

[6] For example, under a laundering contract, twenty times the cost of laundering: *Alderslade* v. *Hendon Laundry Ltd.* [1945] K.B. 189.

[7] *Suisse Atlantique Société D'Armement Maritime S.A.* v. *N.V. Rotterdamsche Kolen Centrale* [1967] 1 A.C. 361. Cf. Coote, op. cit., pp. 153-154.

[8] *Gillespie Bros. Ltd.* v. *Roy Bowles Transport Ltd.* [1973] Q.B. 400 (indemnity between forwarding-agents and carriers).

[9] *British Crane Hire Corporation Ltd.* v. *Ipswich Plant Hire Ltd.* [1975] 1 Q.B. 303.

[10] *Gillespie Bros. Ltd.* v. *Roy Bowles Transport Ltd.* ante; *British Crane Hire Corporation* v. *Ipswich Plant Hire Ltd.* ante; *Clark* v. *Sir William Arrol & Co. Ltd.* 1974 S.L.T. 90; *Blake* v. *Richards & Wallington Industries Ltd.* (1974) 16 K.I.R. 151; *Smith* v. *South Wales Switchgear* [1978] 1 All E.R. 18. See further *Unfair Contract Terms Act 1977*, s. 4.

III. TIME CLAUSES

Provisions which impose an individual limitation-period, and require the victim of a breach to take action within a certain time, have been regarded as exclusion clauses in at least four recent decisions.[11]

IV. CLAUSES WHICH DEFINE THE PARTIES' OBLIGATIONS

As Coote remarks,[12] the courts have assumed that an exclusion clause "provides merely a shield to a claim for damages and . . . does not in itself affect the obligations undertaken by the promisor". It should follow that any term which seeks merely to delineate the extent of one party's obligation, rather than to mitigate or qualify the effects of its breach, is not to be treated as an exclusion clause. However this differentiation is often difficult to make, and in two recent decisions little importance seems to have been attached to the distinction. In *Thomas National Transport (Melbourne) Pty. Ltd.* v. *May & Baker (Australia) Ltd.*[13] Windeyer J. (dissenting) acknowledged that the clause in question did not operate to qualify the effect of a breach of obligation but to determine the total content of that obligation. He nevertheless referred to the clause as an exemption clause and appeared to concede that a "radical breach" would have rendered it ineffective. Likewise, in *Anglo-Continental Holidays Ltd.* v. *Typaldos Lines (London) Ltd.*[14] both Lord Denning M.R. and Davies L.J. seem to have regarded a clause stating that "Steamers, Sailing Dates, Rates and Itineraries are subject to change without prior notice" as an exclusion clause, while Russell L.J., denying this conclusion, still held that the propounder "cannot be enabled thereby to alter the substance of the arrangement".[15]

In borderline cases such as these, there are powerful reasons for renouncing a strictly literal translation of the expression "exclusion clause" and for looking more generally to what the other contracting party could reasonably have expected to have been promised. Conversely, there are difficulties in subjecting a contract to some repugnant and ineradicable minimum content, when the term in question has clearly adopted a prophylactic attitude by stating that this content shall not obtain. The Law Commission and the Scottish Law Commission have recommended that legislative action should be taken with regard to certain types of delineating clause, but suggest that such action may need to be different in approach from that adopted towards the orthodox exclusion clause.

[11] *Smeaton Hanscomb & Co. Ltd.* v. *Sassoon I. Setty & Co. Ltd.* [1953] 1 W.L.R. 1468; *New Zealand Shipping Co. Ltd.* v. *A. N. Satterthwaite & Co. Ltd.* [1975] A.C. 154; (majority judgment); *H. & E. Van der Sterren* v. *Cibernetics (Holdings) Pty. Ltd.* (1970) 44 A.L.J.R. 157; *The New York Star* [1977] 1 Lloyd's Rep. 445; see further Coote, op. cit., pp. 154-155.
[12] Op. cit., p. 1.
[13] (1966) 115 C.L.R. 353, at 385-387; cf. *Council of the City of Sydney* v. *West* (1965) 114 C.L.R. 481, at 495-496 per Kitto J.
[14] [1967] 2 Lloyd's Rep. 61; discussed in the Law Commission's *Second Report*, at 55-56.
[15] [1967] 2 Lloyd's Rep. 61, at 67.

We have felt impelled to consider the possibility of controlling the exclusion or restriction not merely of obligations that have been undertaken but also of obligations which the promisee might honestly believe to have been undertaken, but we do not think we can go beyond provisions which in some way deprive persons against whom they are invoked of contractual rights which those persons reasonably expected to enjoy . . . We propose that a term should be subject to control if it has the effect of enabling the promisor to offer in purported fulfilment of the contract a performance which is substantially different from that which the promisee reasonably expected when he entered into the contract, or if it has the effect of enabling the promisor to refuse to render any performance.[16]

At Common Law, it seems that most of the problems arising from permissive or delineating clauses can be answered by means of construction, so that the clause will be read (so far as is consonant with its language) as leaving unaffected the central obligations of the contract.[17] Whether such a reconciliation or subordination can be imposed regardless of the wording of the clause is more doubtful and may depend, in some degree, upon the technically irrelevant question of whether a substantive doctrine of fundamental breach survives in English or Australian law. Although it seems that any kind of anti-commitment clause will be construed against the proferens, there are strong reasons for allowing such clauses to take effect whenever their meaning and importance have been made sufficiently plain, at least in cases where the event against which exoneration is sought is one which does not occur through the default of the defending party.[18]

V. Elements of Validity

The following requirements must be satisfied before an exclusion, indemnity or limitation clause can take effect. For the sake of clarity, the party relying on the clause will be described as the defendant and the party against whom it is invoked as the plaintiff.

A. Incorporation[19]

No exclusion clause can take effect unless the plaintiff has expressly or impliedly consented to its imposition. The defendant must show that the plaintiff enjoyed actual or imputable knowledge of its terms and that such knowledge was received before the bailment was created.[20] If these requirements are satisfied and the plaintiff has rendered no objection, the bailment will be subject to the clause. A formal or particular acceptance will not, in most cases, be required.

The imputation of knowledge and consent is readily made when the plaintiff has perused and acknowledged the terms of the exemption. If he

---

[16] *Second Report,* Exemption Clauses (1975), at 56-57. See now *Unfair Contract Terms Act* 1977, s. 3(2).
[17] See *Naviera de Canarias S.A.* v. *Nacional Hispanica Asegourada S.A.* (1976) *The Times,* 15 April; reversed [1977] 1 All E.R. 625 (H.L.); p. 940 post.
[18] *The Angelia* [1973] 1 W.L.R. 210, at 227-232.
[19] Clarke, *Notice of Contractual Terms* [1976] C.L.J. 51.
[20] Subject to a possible exception discussed at p. 923, post.

signs the document in which the clauses are contained without reading them, his signature will count as an acceptance[21] unless, perhaps, he had no reason to suppose that the document was of an exclusory nature[22] or the defendant has varied or misrepresented its effect.[23] Greater difficulties arise when the plaintiff has given no specific indication of his awareness or acceptance of the terms. An obvious example is the issue of a ticket to a passenger by public transport, or to the user of a car-park, or to a visitor to a dance-hall, who may put the ticket in his pocket without pausing to consult its contents. In this event, the benefiting party will be protected provided three preliminary requirements are fulfilled. First, he must have taken reasonable steps to draw the relevant clauses to the other party's attention; without this he is not entitled to conclude that they have been accepted. Adequate notice has been found when the surface of a ticket issued for transportation or storage refers the customer to legible conditions printed on the obverse[24] or within the company's excursion bills and timetables;[25] where prominent sign-boards at the entrances to land indicate the occupier's refusal to be liable for injury or damage to property;[26] where a document containing gratuitous advice is prefaced

---

[21] *L'Estrange* v. *F. Graucob Ltd.* [1934] 2 K.B. 394, discussed by Spencer [1973] C.L.J. 104; *Fong Gaep* v. *Reynolds* (1863) 2 W. & W. (L) 80 (where a signature by a Chinaman who could speak, but could not read, English, was held binding); *Jones* v. *Aircrafts Pty. Ltd.* [1949] St. R. Qd. 196; *Levison* v. *Patent Steam Carpet Cleaning Co. Ltd.* [1977] 3 W.L.R. 90.

[22] For instance, where a competitor in a motor race signs what he believes to be an attendance register without realising that exclusion clauses are attached: cf. *White* v. *Blackmore* [1972] 3 All E.R. 158, where there was no clear evidence that the clauses were ever attached, and see *D. J. Hill & Co. Pty. Ltd.* v. *Walter H. Wright Pty. Ltd.* [1971] V.R. 749. As to the defence of non est factum, which requires the signatory to prove (a) that there was a radical difference between what he thought he was signing and what he actually signed, and (b) that he was not careless in signing, see *Saunders* v. *Anglia Building Society Ltd.* [1971] A.C. 1004; *Petelin* v. *Cullen* (1975) 6 A.L.R. 129; *United Dominions Trust Ltd.* v. *Western* [1975] 3 All E.R. 1017.

[23] *Curtis* v. *Chemical Cleaning and Dyeing Co. Ltd.* [1951] 1 K.B. 805; *Mendelssohn* v. *Normand Ltd.* [1970] 1 Q.B. 177; see further: p. 000, post.

[24] *Parker* v. *S.E. Ry. Co.* (1877) 2 C.P.D. 416; see also *Herrick* v. *Leonard & Dingley Ltd.* [1975] 2 N.Z.L.R. 566; *MacRobertson Miller* v. *Commissioner of State Taxation* (1975) 8 A.L.R. 131; *Watkins* v. *Rymill* (1883) 10 Q.B.D. 178; *Ashby* v. *Tolhurst* [1937] 2 K.B. 242; *Heffron* v. *Imperial Parking Canada Ltd.* (1974) 46 D.L.R. (3d) 642; *Birmingham* v. *White* [1943] Q.W.N. 26; 37 Q.J.P.R. 75; *Davis* v. *Pearce Parking Stations Pty. Ltd.* (1954) 91 C.L.R. 642.

[25] *Smith* v. *South Wales Switchgear Ltd.* [1978] 1 All E.R. 18 *Thompson* v. *L.M. & S. Ry. Co.* [1930] 1 K.B. 41 (where the plaintiff was illiterate and her ticket was obtained by her niece). See also *Gray* v. *L.N.E. Ry. Co.* 1930 S.C. 989; *Fong Gaep* v. *Reynolds* (1863) 2. W. & W. (L) 80; *Geier* v. *Kiyawa* [1970] 1 Lloyd's Rep. 364; *Firchuk* v. *Waterfront Cartage* [1969] 2 Lloyd's Rep. 533; and cf. *Richardson, Spence & Co. Ltd.* v. *Rowntree* [1894] A.C. 217 (no incorporation where conditions printed on ticket issued to steerage passenger, of a class known to be illiterate: a decision of diminishing importance). Lord Denning M.R. has gone so far as to assert that an indication to the reverse side of the ticket is always necessary when the clauses do not appear on its surface: *White* v. *Blackmore* [1972] 3 All E.R. 158, at 165; sed quaere. It seems preferable to regard adequate notice as in every instance a question of fact rather than of law: *Burke* v. *S.E. Ry. Co.* (1879) 5 C.P.D. 1.

[26] *Ashdown* v. *Samuel Williams & Sons Ltd.* [1957] 1 Q.B. 409; *White* v. *Blackmore* [1972] 3 All E.R. 158; cf. ss. 2(1), 2(4)(a), *Occupier's Liability Act* 1957 (U.K.). And see *Balmain New Ferry Co. Ltd.* v. *Robertson* (1906) 4 C.L.R. 379; [1910] A.C. 295.

by a clear disclaimer;[27] where a course of dealing between the parties indicates a recurrent intention (or willingness) to contract on certain terms although there is no specific notification or acceptance on a particular occasion;[28] and where, even in the absence of a course of dealing or specific notification, the plaintiff can be taken to have contemplated that clauses equivalent to those in question would be imposed.[29] On the other hand, there has been held to be insufficient notice of incorporation where the plaintiff and his agent contracted several times previously with the defendant on different sets of conditions but with no specific knowledge and no attempt (other than an inadequate noticeboard) to apprise the plaintiff of the clauses on the relevant occasion;[30] where the clause is in a foreign language[31] or obscured by ink;[32] or where it is printed on the back of a holiday brochure.[33] In addition, Lord Denning has contended that no exclusion clause should operate unless it actually appears within the larger contract between the parties, rather than being imposed by some extraneous method[34] and Else-Mitchell J. has argued that the logic of the railway-ticket cases should be confined to contracts which are evidenced solely by the ticket or other written document, and should not (except, perhaps, in the face of very strong proof of assent) assist a party to an oral contract who seeks to superimpose integral terms by handing over a printed piece of paper.[35] To the general question, whether the defendant has done what would normally and reasonably suffice to bring the conditions to the notice of the plaintiff, the courts have added the important corollary that the degree of notice required may

---

[27] *Hedley Byrne & Co. Ltd.* v. *Heller & Partners Ltd.* [1964] A.C. 465. The same logic would probably operate to protect most contracting parties whose writing paper either contains conditions or refers the customer to some available source.

[28] *J. Spurling Ltd.* v. *Bradshaw* [1956] 1 W.L.R. 461, 467; *McCutcheon* v. *David MacBrayne Ltd.* [1964] 1 W.L.R. 125; *B.R.S. Ltd.* v. *Arthur V. Crutchley Ltd.* [1968] 1 All E.R. 811; *Hardwick Game Farm Ltd.* v. *S.A.P.P.A.* [1969] 2 A.C. 31; *Mendelssohn* v. *Normand Ltd.* [1970] 1 Q.B. 177; *Eastman Chemical International A.G.* v. *N.M.T. Trading Ltd.* [1972] 2 Lloyd's Rep. 25; *Levison* v. *Patent Steam Carpet Cleaning Co. Ltd.* ante; cf. *Hollier* v. *Rambler Motors (A.M.C.) Ltd.* [1972] 2 Q.B. 71 (three or four occasions over the past five years insufficient to amount to a cause of dealing); *British Crane Hire Corporation Ltd.* v. *Ipswich Plant Hire Ltd.* [1975] 1 Q.B. 303 (two occasions over previous sixteen months likewise insufficient). The statement of Lord Devlin (at 135) in *McCutcheon's* case that no implication can arise by course of dealing unless the plaintiff has *actual* knowledge of the terms imposed was repudiated by the House of Lords in *Hardwick's* case and by Salmon L.J. in *Hollier's* case (at 77-78); but cf. *D. J. Hill & Co. Pty. Ltd.* v. *Walter H. Wright Pty. Ltd.* [1971] V.R. 749, where it was approved.

[29] *British Crane Hire Corporation Ltd.* v. *Ipswich Plant Hire Ltd.* ante; *Smith* v. *South Wales Switchgear Ltd.* [1978] 1 All E.R. 18. Cf. *Trenoweth* v. *Cox* (1911) 13 W.A.L.R. 205; *D. J. Hill & Co. Pty. Ltd.* v. *Walter H. Wright Pty. Ltd.* [1971] VR 749; *Grayston Plant Hire Ltd.* v. *Plean Precast Ltd.* 1975 S.L.T. (O.H.). Notes 83.

[30] *McCutcheon* v. *David MacBrayne Ltd.* ante.

[31] *Parker* v. *S.E. Ry. Co.* (1877) 2 C.P.D. 416, at 423; *Thompson* v. *L.M. & S. Ry. Co.* [1930] 1 K.B. 41, at 56; cf. *Geier* v. *Kiyawa* [1970] 1 Lloyd's Rep. 364.

[32] *Sugar* v. *L.M. & S. Ry. Co.* [1941] 1 All E.R. 172.

[33] *Anglo-Continental Holidays Ltd.* v. *Typaldos Lines (London) Ltd.* [1967] 2 Lloyd's Rep. 61, per Lord Denning M.R.; see also *Walls* v. *Centaur Co. Ltd.* (1921) 126 L.T. 242; *Hollingworth* v. *Southern Ferries* [1977] 2 Lloyd's Rep. 70.

[34] *White* v. *Blackmore* [1972] 3 All E.R. 158, at 165-168: sed quaere.

[35] *Rozsasi* v. *Swinton Industries Pty. Ltd.* (1959) 59 S.R. (N.S.W.) 375 at 380-381; see also *Fosbroke-Hobbes* v. *Airwork Ltd.* [1937] 1 All E.R. 108.

vary in proportion to the breadth or savagery of the clause itself.[36] Clearly, the more ambitious or unreasonable the clause, the less likely the plaintiff may be (in the absence of direct knowledge) to assume that it has been incorporated. Trade experience and even equality of bargaining-power may be relevant to this inquiry.[37]

Secondly, the defendant must have done what is reasonable to indicate that the necessary clauses are conditions of exemption; it is not enough that the plaintiff merely knows of their existence, and has access to their contents, if he is given no reason to conclude that they are designed to confer an immunity.[38] In many cases, the nature of the document will militate against this necessary assumption. Thus, a receipt given to the hirer of a deck-chair in return for the hiring-fee,[39] a delivery-note presented for the plaintiff's signature after his goods have been transported,[40] a dry-cleaning docket,[41] a cheque book[42] and a programme given in part exchange for the admission-fee to an entertainment[43] have all been stated to lie beyond the class of document in which a plaintiff could reasonably expect to find exclusory conditions. Again, however, it is entirely a question of fact.[44]

Thirdly, the necessary notification must precede, or coincide with, the creation of the bailment. For this reason, the courts have struck down exemption clauses which were sought to be imposed upon the hirer of a deck-chair, who had already concluded a contract by taking a chair from the stack;[45] upon the charterer of a plane when the hiring contract had already been made and the plane was about to take off;[46] upon a visitor to a multi-storey carpark by means of a ticket issued from an automatic machine which referred the customer to conditions displayed within the

---

[36] *Parker* v. *S.E. Ry. Co.* (1877) 2 C.P.D. 416, at 428; *Thompson* v. *L.M. & S. Ry. Co.* [1930] 1 K.B. 41, at 53, 56; *J. Spurling Ltd.* v. *Bradshaw* [1956] 1 W.L.R. 461, at 466; *Thornton* v. *Shoe Lane Parking Ltd.* [1971] 2 Q.B. 163, at 170, 172-173, 174; *British Crane Hire Corporation Ltd.* v. *Ipswich Plant Hire Ltd.* ante; *Aluminium Industrie Vaassen B.V.* v. *Romalpa Aluminium Ltd.* [1976] 2 All E.R. 552, at p. 567. Cf. *Rozsasi* v. *Swinton Industries Pty. Ltd.* ante, at 381.

[37] *British Crane Hire Corporation Ltd.* v. *Ipswich Plant Hire Ltd.* ante.

[38] *Parker* v. *S.E. Ry. Co.* (1877) 2 C.P.D. 416; *Thornton* v. *Shoe Lane Parking Ltd.* ante.

[39] *Chapelton* v. *Barry U.D.C.* [1940] 1 K.B. 532.

[40] *D. J. Hill & Co. Pty. Ltd.* v. *Walter H. Wright Pty. Ltd.* [1971] V.R. 749.

[41] *Causer* v. *Browne* [1952] V.L.R. 1; *Rozsasi* v. *Swinton Industries Pty. Ltd.* ante; cf. *Birmingham* v. *White* [1943] Q.W.N. 26: 37 Q.J.P.R. 75.

[42] *Burnett* v. *Westminster Bank Ltd.* [1966] 1 Q.B. 742.

[43] *White* v. *Blackmore* [1972] 3 All E.R. 158, where the exclusion was in small type on page 2 of the programme and Lord Denning M.R. held it to be ineffective. The other members of the Court of Appeal did not decide the point. Cf. *Skrine* v. *Gould* (1912) 29 T.L.R. 19; *Taylor* v. *Glasgow Corporation* 1952 S.C. 440.

[44] Cf. *J. Spurling Ltd.* v. *Bradshaw* [1956] 1 W.L.R. 461 (landing account); *United Fresh Meat Co. Ltd.* v. *Charterhouse Cold Storage Ltd.* [1974] 2 Lloyd's Rep. 286 *Hollingworth* v. *Southern Ferries* ante.

[45] *Chapelton* v. *Barry U.D.C.* [1940] 1 K.B. 532; see also *McWhinnie* v. *United Steamship Co. of New Zealand* (1887) 9 L.R. (N.S.W.) 1; cf. *Pharmaceutical Society of Great Britain* v. *Boots Cash Chemists Ltd.* [1952] 2 Q.B. 795.

[46] *Fosbroke-Hobbes* v. *Airwork Ltd.* [1937] 1 All E.R. 108.

car-park itself;[47] and upon a hotel guest by means of a notice displayed in the bedroom.[48]

Most of the difficulties arising from the requirements of contemporaneity and communication are approached through the medium of offer and acceptance.[49] This analysis may prove helpful where one party seeks to substitute his conditions for the other's and neither party explicitly acknowledges assent.[50] In *B.R.S.* v. *Arthur V. Crutchley Ltd.*[51] the plaintiffs' driver arrived at the defendants' warehouse with a load of whiskey for warehousing. He gave their servant a receipt to sign, which incorporated the plaintiffs' standard trading conditions. The servant signed the receipt but added in writing that it was subject to the defendants' own conditions. It was held that this constituted a counter-offer which nullified the original "offer" and was accepted by the driver's subsequent unqualified delivery of the goods. It would be interesting to observe the application of this principle to consumer contracts. If consumer associations were to devise and disseminate their own standard trading conditions, and persuade their members to attach them to every contract presented for signature or perusal, it might be said that the tradesman who offered no objection would be bound by them in preference to his own.

When clear notification of the clause is given *after* the bailment has been created, and the plaintiff agrees to it or raises no objection, his liberty to disregard it is probably best explained on the grounds of absence of consideration.[52] It is no more open to a defendant to superimpose unilateral terms upon a concluded agreement than it is (for instance) to a buyer to sue upon a warranty given after the sale has taken place.[53] But it may be otherwise when there is a gratuitous licence which the licensor has the power to revoke or vary by notice at any time.[54] It is uncertain how far this power of variation should apply to gratuitous bailments. Probably it can be admitted, provided two conditions are fulfilled: (a) only the non-benefiting party should be able to impose the variation, and (b) the power must not be exercised if to do so is repugnant to any express (or possibly implied) promise to safeguard the goods without

---

[47] *Thornton* v. *Shoe Lane Parking Ltd.* ante; see also *Rozsasi* v. *Swinton Industries Pty. Ltd.* ante, at 380; cf. *Mendelssohn* v. *Normand Ltd.* [1970] 1 Q.B. 177; *Sydney City Council* v. *West* (1965) 114 C.L.R. 481, at 485-486, 491-493.

[48] *Olley* v. *Marlborough Court Hotel Ltd.* [1949] 1 K.B. 532. See further *Hollingworth* v. *Southern Ferries* ante.

[49] *Nunan* v. *Southern Ry. Co.* [1923] 2 K.B. 703, at 707; *Thompson* v. *L.M. & S. Ry. Co.* [1930] 1 K.B. 41, at 47; *Chapelton* v. *Barry U.D.C.* [1940] 1 K.B. 532; *Charles Davis (Metal Brokers) Ltd.* v. *Gilyott & Scott Ltd.* [1975] 2 Lloyd's Rep. 422, at 424-425; *Causer* v. *Browne* [1952] V.L.R. 1; *MacRobertson Miller* v. *Commissioner of State Taxation* (1975) 8A.L.R. 131.

[50] Although it may fall down on occasions: e.g. where two companies simultaneously send out printed conditions and each proceeds to trade on the assumption that its own conditions apply: see *Charles Davis (Metal Brokers) Ltd.* v. *Gilyott & Scott Ltd.* [1975] 2 Lloyd's Rep. 422, where this difficulty was obviated by construction.

[51] [1968] 1 All E.R. 811.

[52] Cf. *Burnett* v. *Westminster Bank Ltd.* [1966] 1 Q.B. 742; *Stilk* v. *Myrick* (1809) 2 Camp. 317; *Cook Islands Shipping Co. Ltd.* v. *Colson Builders Ltd.* [1975] 1 N.Z.L.R. 422.

[53] *Roscorla* v. *Thomas* (1842) 3 Q.B. 234.

[54] *White* v. *Blackmore* ante; cf. *Junner* v. *Farquhar* [1909] S.A.L.R. 116.

exclusion or to keep them for a finite time.[55] It would be undesirable if a depositary, having agreed to store goods for a month and knowing that they cannot readily be moved, should be entitled during that time to subtract by notice from the responsibility he has undertaken. At all events, the notice of variation must be clear and unequivocal and must allow the licensee or other beneficiary of the gratuitous service sufficient time to accommodate himself to the altered situation.

B. Adverse construction

It is an established rule that exclusion clauses are to be construed strictly contra proferentem.[56] Nominally this principle is confined to cases of ambiguity,[57] but the courts have shown a remarkable aptitude for discovering this phenomenon. Sometimes they conclude that a clause is meaningless and therefore void for uncertainty; sometimes, that it is capable of several different meanings, of which the narrowest and least favourable should apply. To a large extent, this practice is responsible for the complex and incomprehensible character of the modern exclusion clause, wherein the draftsman is seeking eternally to repair the loopholes made by the courts.[58]

The reports abound with illustrations of the contra proferentem principle. Five examples should suffice for present purposes.

(i) *Morris* v. *C. W. Martin & Sons Ltd.*:[59] A contract between the sub-bailee of a mink stole and an intermediate bailee purported to exonerate the sub-bailee for loss or damage to "goods belonging to customers". *Held* that even assuming the clause to be capable of applying in an action between the owner of the goods and the sub-bailee,[60] the defendant would not be protected because his only customer was the intermediate bailee.

(ii) *Charles Davis (Metal Brokers) Ltd.* v. *Gilyott & Scott Ltd.*:[61] A carrying company sent out notices stating: "All business is undertaken subject to the company's conditions of contract" (viz., the 1961 edition of the Conditions of Road Haulage Association Ltd.). Some time later they sent goods to be carried by a second company, who were one of the recipients of the earlier notice. *Held* in the resulting contract the 1961 Conditions could not apply because the first company were "giving" business and not "undertaking" it.

(iii) *Hollier* v. *Rambler Motors (A.M.C.) Ltd.*:[62] The defendants resisted an action for the destruction by fire of a customer's car while it was

---

[55] It is argued (ante) that such promises should be binding even in the absence of consideration.

[56] *Wilson* v. *Darling Island Stevedoring Co. Ltd.* (1956) 95 C.L.R. 43; *Mendelssohn* v. *Normand Ltd.* ante, n. 47; *Gillespie Bros. Ltd.* v. *Roy Bowles Transport Ltd.* [1973] Q.B. 400. Practically every decision on exclusion clauses adverts to this principle.

[57] Coote (1970) 28 C.L.J. 238 et seq.

[58] Contrast, for instance, *Andrews Bros. (Bournemouth) Ltd.* v. *Singer & Co. Ltd.* [1934] 1 K.B. 17 and *L'Estrange* v. *F. Graucob Ltd.* [1934] 2 K.B. 394; and see further *Hope* v. *R.C.A. Photophone of Australia Ltd.* (1937) 59 C.L.R. 348, at 363; see pp. 209-211 ante (licenses and bailments).

[59] [1966] 1 Q.B. 716, at 730, 731, 741.

[60] Post, p. 1000.

[61] [1975] 2 Lloyd's Rep. 422, at 424-425.

[62] [1972] 2 Q.B. 71, disapproving *Turner* v. *Civil Service Supply Association Ltd.* [1926] 1 K.B. 50; *Fagan* v. *Green & Edwards Ltd.* [1926] 1 K.B. 102. See also

bailed to them for repairs, on the strength of a clause which stated inter alia that "The company is not responsible for damage caused by fire to customers' cars on the premises". *Held* that even assuming the clause to have been incorporated (which it was not), it represented no more than a mere statement by way of warning to customers that if cars were destroyed by fire *without* negligence on the defendants' part, no liability would accrue.

(iv) *Mendelssohn* v. *Normand Ltd.*[63] The defendant car-park operators invoked the following conditions in defence to the plaintiff's action for valuables stolen from the back seat of a car during the currency of the bailment:

> (1) The garage proprietors will not accept responsibility for any loss or damage sustained by the vehicle its accessories or contents however caused . . . (6) No variation of these conditions will bind the garage proprietors unless made in writing signed by their duly authorised manager.

The Court of Appeal held that the effect of the clause had been modified by the attendant's promise to lock the car, and that any failure to observe this undertaking constituted a fundamental departure from the agreed method of performance, in which event none of the exclusion clauses could apply. Moreover, since clause 1 could be taken to mean that all losses (however caused) were protected *or* that the latter phrase applied only to damage sustained by the vehicle, its accessories or contents, the narrower meaning should prevail.

(v) *Thomas National Transport (Melbourne) Pty. Ltd.* v. *May & Baker (Australia) Pty. Ltd.*[64] The first defendants agreed to collect goods for the plaintiff and deliver them interstate. They delegated the collection process to the second defendant, who finished his rounds too late to take the goods to the first defendants' transit depot in Melbourne. Instead, he took them home and left them, still inside the truck, in his garage, where they were later destroyed by fire. The first defendants claimed that they were protected from liability by a clause authorising them to "carry all goods or to have them carried by any method" which they, in their absolute discretion, should deem fit, and by a further clause exonerating them and their agents from responsibility for loss, damage or misdelivery "in transit or in storage" for any reason whatsoever. *Held* (Windeyer J. dissenting) that the first defendants were under an implied obligation to store the goods in their depot after each collection round, and that the clauses must be read subject to this obligation. The first clause therefore applied only when the first defendants were carrying the goods or having them carried, and not when they were being stored at an unauthorised destination; the second clause was inapplicable insofar

---

Olley v. *Marlborough Court Hotel Ltd.* ante, at 550; *Paterson* v. *Miller* [1923] V.L.R. 36, at 47-49.

[63] [1970] 1 Q.B. 177. Cf. *Garnham, Harris & Elton Ltd.* v. *Afred J. Ellis Transport Ltd.* [1967] 1 W.L.R. 940: clause excluding liability for mis-delivery however arising does not extend to conversion by unauthorised and negligent selection of sub-bailee.

[64] (1966) 115 C.L.R. 353; see also *Akerib* v. *Booth* [1961] 1 W.L.R. 367; *Sydney City Council* v. *West* (1965) 114 C.L.R. 481.

as its application was repugnant to the *personal* duty of storage in their depot.

The contra proferentem rule has produced two important tributary doctrines. The first of these (which we will discuss later)[65] requires that no exclusion clause shall be construed so as to entitle the proferens to render a performance totally different from that for which he has contracted (or to render no performance at all) unless this result is clearly and unequivocally warranted by the terms of the contract. The second relates to the exclusion of liability for negligence. In *Rutter* v. *Palmer*[66] Scrutton L.J. propounded three guidelines for ascertaining whether a defendant has successfully excluded such liability. First, he must use clear and adequate words; second, his liability apart from the exclusion clause must be identified; and third, the effect of the clause must be considered: if the sole basis of liability on which the defendant might have been inculpated is liability in negligence, the clause will "more readily" operate to protect him.

Two things will be noted about these principles. The first is that they are peculiarly relevant to the position of the ordinary bailee, whose sole liability (in the absence of contractual modification) rests in detinue, conversion[67] and a breach of the duty of reasonable care. The second is that they are not dogmatically expressed. They do not mean that where the only potential liability against the defendant lies in negligence, the clause must *as a matter of law* be construed as excluding such liability;[68] nor do they mean that where negligence is merely one of a number of potential heads of liability, the clause must necessarily be construed as failing to exclude liability for negligence.[69] Rather, they are principles of interpretation, reflecting a judicial scepticism that any party who has shrunk from specifying negligence in his exclusion clauses should be taken as having excluded liability for it; a scepticism that may be relaxed when negligence represents the sole ground upon which his liability might have rested. In the final analysis, everything depends upon the

[65] Post, p. 930. Cf. s. 3, *Unfair Contract Terms Act* 1977.
[66] [1922] 2 K.B. 87, at 92; for a fuller list of relevant authorities see p. 248, n. 71, ante; Coote, op. cit., 30-31.
[67] Which is not dependant upon possession, ante, p. 127.
[68] As Lord Greene M.R. seems to have suggested in *Alderslade* v. *Hendon Laundry Ltd.* [1945] 1 K.B. 189, at 192; explained by Salmon L.J. in *Hollier* v. *Rambler Motors (A.M.C.) Ltd.* [1972] 2 Q.B. 71, at 80. It is submitted that the adherence to the substantive principle in *Thomas National Transport (Melbourne) Pty. Ltd.* v. *May & Baker (Australia) Pty. Ltd.* (1966) 115 C.L.R. 353, at 376-377 per Windeyer J. and *Sydney City Council* v. *West* (1965) 114 C.L.R. 481, at 493-494, 499-500 per Kitto and Menzies JJ. is misconceived: see *Moran* v. *Lipscombe* [1929] V.L.R. 10; *Oriental Bank Corporation* v. *The Queen* (1869) 8 S.C.R. (N.S.W.) 171; cf. *Crouch* v. *Jeeves* (1938) *Pty. Ltd.* (1946) 46 S.R. (N.S.W) 242; *Paterson* v. *Miller* [1923] V.L.R. 36; *Cheeke* v. *Commissioner of Railways* (1869) 8 S.C.R. (N.S.W.) 111; 9 S.C.R. (N.S.W.) 31.
[69] *Gillespie Bros. Ltd.* v. *Roy Bowles Transport Ltd.* [1973] Q.B. 400, at 414-415, 420-421, per Lord Denning M.R. and Buckley L.J. explaining *Canada Steamship Lines Ltd.* v. *R.* [1952] A.C. 192, at 208. See also *Levison* v. *Patent Steam Carpet Cleaning Co. Ltd.*, ante; *White* v. *John Warwick & Co. Ltd.* [1953] 1 W.L.R. 1285; *Western Australian Bank Ltd.* v. *Royal Insurance Co. Ltd.* (1908) 5 C.L.R. 533, at 574; *Commissioner for Railways (N.S.W.)* v. *Quinn* (1946) 72 C.L.R. 345, at 371-372; *Moran* v. *Lipscombe* [1929] V.L.R. 10; cf. *Webb* v. *Agricultural Society of New South Wales* (1893) 14 L.R. (N.S.W.) 333; *Brown* v. *National Bank of Australasia Ltd.* (1890) 16 V.L.R. 475.

wording of the clause.[70] Although liability for negligence may not be excluded in the absence of "very clear words",[71] a widely-drawn clause may produce this effect without referring to negligence specifically[72] and without necessitating any protracted inquiry into the other possible grounds upon which the bailee might be liable.[73] Thus, whereas the Court of Appeal have held that a clause in a contract of hire which purports to exclude the lessor's liability "for any personal injury" extends only to his contractual liability and not to his liability for negligence,[74] a later decision from the same Court makes it clear that a clause excluding liability "for all claims and demands whatsoever", or "arising from any cause whatsoever" or "for all losses or injuries howsoever caused" may produce a more total immunity.[75] Insofar as the existence of other heads of liability is relevant at all, it is to show that sufficient meaning or content can be given to an ambiguous clause without expanding it to cover liability for negligence.[76] In this event, the narrower (or more reasonable)[77] construction may be preferred. But when both intention and wording clearly point to the exclusion of liability for negligence, this unequivocal meaning must prevail.[78]

Onus of Proof: The authorities are unanimous that the party relying upon an exclusion clause must establish that it carries the construction for which he contends.

---

[70] *Hollier* v. *Rambler Motors (A.M.C.) Ltd.* [1972] 2 Q.B. 71, at 80; *Smith* v. *South Wales Switchgear Ltd.* [1978] 1 All E.R. 18.

[71] *British Crane Hire Corporation Ltd.* v. *Ipswich Plant Hire Ltd.* (ante), at 311 per Lord Denning M.R.; see also *Price & Co. Ltd.* v. *Union Lighterage Co. Ltd.* [1903] 1 K.B. 750 ("express, plain and unambiguous terms") cited with approval by the High Court in *Davis* v. *Pearce Parking Station Pty. Ltd.* (1954) 90 C.L.R. 642, at 649.

[72] For a case where this was done, see *Rosin & Turpentine Import Co. Ltd.* v. *Jacob & Sons Ltd.* (1901) 100 L.T. 266; 101 L.T. 56; 102 L.T. 81. Cf. the *Levison* case, ante.

[73] As occurred in the *Gillespie* case (ante), where five additional grounds were listed by counsel.

[74] *White* v. *John Warwick & Co. Ltd.* (ante, n. 69); see also *Imperial Furniture Pty. Ltd.* v. *Automatic Fire Sprinklers Pty. Ltd.* [1967] N.S.W.R. 29.

[75] *Gillespie Bros. Ltd.* v. *Roy Bowles Transport Ltd.* ante (where the clause was one of indemnity); see also *Ashby* v. *Tolhurst* [1937] 2 K.B. 242; *J. Archdale Ltd.* v. *Comservices Ltd.* [1954] 1 W.L.R. 459; *Travers & Sons Ltd.* v. *Cooper* [1915] 1 K.B. 73; *M.S. & L. Ry. Co.* v. *Brown* (1883) 8 App. Cas. 703; *Gibaud* v. *G.E. Ry. Co.* [1921] 2 K.B. 426. But cf. now the *South Wales Switchgear* case, ante.

[76] *Gillespie Bros. Ltd.* v. *Roy Bowles Transport Ltd.* (ante), at 415 per Lord Denning M.R. This may be particularly material in relation to common carriers.

[77] Ibid., at 421 per Buckley L.J. See also *New Zealand Shipping Co. Ltd.* v. *A. N. Satterthwaite & Co. Ltd.* [1974] 1 All E.R. 1015, at 1029 per Lord Simon of Glaisdale; *Hair & Skin Trading Co. Ltd.* v. *Norman Airfreight Carriers Ltd.* [1974] 1 Lloyd's Rep. 443, at 446 per Bean J.

[78] *Blake* v. *Richards & Wallington Industries Ltd.* (1974) 16 K.I.R. 151; *Davis* v. *Pearce Parking Station Pty. Ltd.* (1954) 91 C.L.R. 642; *Gallaher Ltd.* v. *B.R.S. Ltd.* [1974] 2 Lloyd's Rep. 440, at 447-449; *Hair & Skin Trading Co. Ltd.* v. *Norman Airfreight Carriers Ltd.* ante. But note that in the *South Wales Switchgear* case (ante) the House of Lords stressed the need for specific or synonymous reference to negligence.

C. Non-variation by conduct of defendant

A defendant may lose the protection of an exclusion clause if he or his servant misrepresents its effect[79] or otherwise leads the plaintiff to believe that the clause will not be relied upon in the particular circumstances of the loss. Sometimes this forfeiture may occur because the defendant has made a collateral contract which is not subject to the exclusion clauses contained in the principal transaction;[80] sometimes (which amounts to much the same thing) it may occur because the representation implies that the clauses are intended to operate only when the defendant is performing the contract in a particular way.[81] In *Mendelssohn* v. *Normand Ltd.*[82] the Court of Appeal went so far as to apply this principle against a clause which asserted that no variation by its servants should bind the defendant company. The Court did not advert to counsel's argument on this point and it may be questioned whether a clause which is in all other respects competent to protect the defendant can be neutralised by a patently unauthorised variation.[83]

D. Reasonableness

The question here is whether a properly incorporated exclusion clause, which clearly encompasses the particular loss suffered by the plaintiff, can be struck down solely upon the ground that it is unreasonable as between the parties. The idea is an attractive one, which has been adopted by the legislature on a number of occasions in particular areas.[84] Judicial authority is, however, slender and seems to rest almost entirely upon

---

[79] *Curtis* v. *Chemical Cleaning & Dyeing Co. Ltd.* [1951] 1 K.B. 805; *Jacques* v. *Lloyd D. George & Partners Ltd.* [1968] 2 All E.R. 187; cf. *Cheshire & Fifoot, Law of Contract* (8th ed.), p. 129; *Birch* v. *Thomas* [1972] 1 All E.R. 905; *Hall* v. *Queensland Truck Centre Pty. Ltd.* [1970] Qd. R. 231.

[80] *Gallaher Ltd.* v. *B.R.S. Ltd.* [1974] 2 Lloyd's Rep. 440 (carriers, who were employed regularly by the plaintiff manufacturers under standard conditions of carriage, agreed after negotiation to introduce special security precautions: *held*, this collateral promise was not governed by the standard conditions and the defendants were liable in full for losses resulting from their failure to implement the precautions). See also *Couchman* v. *Hill* [1947] K.B. 554; *Webster* v. *Higgin* [1948] 2 All E.R. 127; Anson, *Law of Contract*, (24th ed.), pp. 183-184.

[81] *Mendelssohn* v. *Normand Ltd.* [1970] 1 Q.B. 177 (promise to keep car locked meant that defendants could not escape liability for theft of contents resulting from their failure to do so); *J. Evans & Son (Portsmouth) Ltd.* v. *Andrea Merzario Ltd.* [1976] 2 All E.R. 930 (collateral promise by forwarding-agents that plaintiffs' goods would be carried below deck took precedence over printed conditions of carriage, which were accordingly displaced when the promise was broken and the goods were carried on deck. Lord Denning M.R. observed in this case that the traditional reluctance to imply collateral contracts may need to be relaxed now that the *Misrepresentation Act* 1967, s. 2 (U.K.) permits recovery of damages for innocent misrepresentation). See further, p. 932 et seq., post.

[82] [1970] 1 Q.B. 177.

[83] Cf. *Overbrooke Estates Ltd.* v. *Glencombe Properties Ltd.* [1974] 1 W.L.R. 1335; [1975] C.L.J. 17.

[84] *Misrepresentation Act* 1967, s. 3, criticised by Fairest [1967] C.L.J. 239, at 246-248, and by Atiyah and Treitel (1967) 30 M.L.R. 369, at 379-385; *Sale of Goods Act* 1893, ss. 55(4), 55(5), as amended by *Supply of Goods (Implied Terms) Act* 1973, s. 4; *Supply of Goods (Implied Terms) Act* 1973, ss. 12(3), 12(4) as amended by Schedule 4, para. 35, *Consumer Credit Act* 1974; *Unfair Contract Terms Act* 1977; see further *Commissioner for Railways (N.S.W.)* v. *Quinn* (1946) 72 C.L.R. 345.

certain statements of Lord Denning M.R. In *Gillespie Bros. Ltd.* v. *Roy Bowles Transport Ltd.*[85] he explained the requirement as follows:

> When a clause is reasonable, and is reasonably applied, it should be given effect according to its terms. I know that the judges hitherto have never confessed openly to the test of reasonableness. But it has been the driving force behind many of the decisions. And now it has the backing of the Law Commissions of England and Wales, and of Scotland.[86] I venture to suggest that the words of such a clause (be it an exemption clause, or a limitation clause, or an indemnity clause) should be construed in the same way as any other clause. It should be given its ordinary meaning, that is, the meaning which the parties understood by the Clause and must be presumed to have intended. The courts should give effect to the clause according to that meaning, provided always (and this is new) that it is reasonable between the parties and is applied reasonably in the circumstances of the particular case.[87]

It may, with respect, be questioned whether a proposed (or effectuated) reform by the legislature in analogous areas provide sufficient justification for the judicial adoption of the principles upon which that reform is based.[88] The weight of English[89] and Australian[90] authority is against Lord Denning's proposal and a number of earlier decisions which appear at first sight to pay regard to the reasonableness of an exclusion clause are properly explained as decisions in which the reasonableness of the clause went not to its substantive validity but to its incorporation.[91] Admittedly, the test is not without acknowledgment in Australian law, for in his dissenting judgment in *Thomas National Transport (Melbourne) Pty. Ltd.* v. *May & Baker (Australia) Pty. Ltd.*[92] Windeyer J. observed: "This was no hasty engagement, and there was no inequality between the parties to trouble a court as to the justice of enforcing the contract according to its terms". Again, however, it is possible to read this remark as relating to the question of incorporation. In the absence of any authoritative judicial pronouncement, it would seem unlikely that an exclusion clause can be struck down at common law on the ground that it is unreasonable alone.[93]

---

[85] [1973] Q.B. 400, at 416. This passage was cited with approval by Bean J. in *Hair & Skin Trading Co. Ltd.* v. *Norman Airfreight Carriers Ltd.*, ante.

[86] See Working Paper No. 39, paras. 57-65.

[87] See also *John Lee & Son (Grantham) Ltd.* v. *Railway Executive* [1949] 2 All E.R. 581, at 584; *Bonsor* v. *Musicians' Union* [1954] Ch. 479, at 485; cf. *Lee* v. *Showmen's Guild* [1952] 2 Q.B. 329.

[88] Lord Denning has subsequently reiterated the reasonableness principle in the *Levison* case, ante, at 95; applied in *Davidson* v. *Three Spruces Realty* [1977] 6 W.W.R. 460; and in *Photo Productions* v. *Securicor* (1978) *The Times* March 16.

[89] *Van Toll* v. *S.E. Ry. Co.* (1862) 12 C.B.N.S. 75, at 85; *Grand Truck Ry. of Canada* v. *Robinson* [1915] A.C. 740, at 747; *F. A. Tamplin S.C. Co. Ltd.* v. *Anglo-Mexican Petroleum Products Co. Ltd.* [1916] 2 A.C. 397, at 404; *Faramus* v. *Film Artistes' Association* [1963] 1 All E.R. 636, at 650-652; *Kenyon, Son & Craven Ltd.* v. *Baxter Hoare & Co. Ltd.* [1971] 2 All E.R. 708; *Blake* v. *Richards & Wallington Industries Ltd.* (1974) 16 K.I.R. 151, at 155; cf. *Gillespie Bros. Ltd.* v. *Roy Bowles Transport Ltd.* (ante), at 421 per Buckley L.J.

[90] *Hirsch* v. *Zinc Corporation Ltd.* (1917) 24 C.L.R. 34, at 52.

[91] These are set out ante, p. 922, n. 36.

[92] (1966) 115 C.L.R. 353, at 373.

[93] Cf. Coote (1975) 125 N.L.J. 752; Waddams (1976) 39 M.L.R. 369 at 378-380.

VI. Deviation and Fundamental Breach[94]

The most difficult question in the field of exclusion clauses concerns the extent to which reliance upon such a clause may be forfeited as a matter of law by the nature or consequences of the defendant's breach. In this regard, a number of concurrent but intersecting developments and ideas call for consideration.

A. Deviation

Originally, the doctrine of deviation arose in the context of carriage of goods by sea. A carrier who deviated without authority from the stipulated itinerary became an immediate insurer of the cargo and forfeited automatically the protection conferred upon him by exceptions in the bill of lading.[95] It seems that the original justification for the rule lay in the question of insurance, for a cargo-owner lost the protection of his policy once the vessel had departed from the agreed route.[96]

From these limited beginnings, the doctrine of deviation expanded to encompass carriers by land and, eventually, every category of bailee. Any radical departure from the terms of the bailment displaced the immunity conferred on the bailee and rendered him strictly liable for the ensuing loss. Negligence was irrelevant in this context. The only way in which the bailee could avert the legal consequences of his misconduct lay in proving that the loss must have occurred even if the deviation had not taken place,[97] or that it was the result of the owner's default.[98] Naturally, the circumstances in which this defence would be worth pleading were exceedingly rare.

Thus, it has been held that a bailee who wrongfully retains possession of goods after the term of the bailment has expired,[99] or who stores them in a different place from that agreed by the bailor,[1] or who carries them

---

[94] Yates op. cit. provides the best modern account.
[95] The authorities were discussed in depth in *Hain S.S. Co. Ltd.* v. *Tate & Lyle Ltd.* [1936] 2 All E.R. 597.
[96] Ibid., at 608; Legh-Jones and Pickering (1971) 87 L.Q.R. 515, at 525-528; *Thomas National Transport (Melbourne) Pty. Ltd.* v. *May & Baker (Australia) Pty. Ltd.* (1966) 115 C.L.R. 353, at 380 per Windeyer J.
[97] Jones, *Bailments* (1781), p. 70; *U.S. Shipping Board* v. *Bunge y Born* (1925) 31 Com. Cas. 118; *Morrison (James) & Co. Ltd.* v. *Shaw, Savill & Albion Co. Ltd.* [1916] 2 K.B. 783. The bailee would not be allowed to contend that the misfortune *might* have occurred irrespective of the deviation, for this would be to allow him to qualify his own wrong: *Davis* v. *Garret* (1830) 6 Bing. 716; 130 E.R. 1456; *Edwards* v. *Newland & Co. Ltd.* [1950] 1 All E.R. 1072, at 1081. A negligent deviation would suffice to bring the principle into play: *Hughes* v. *Rooke* [1954] St. R. Qd. 45, at 52-56. Cf. *Mitchell* v. *Ealing L.B.C.* (1978) *The Times*, Feb. 21st.
[98] Jones, loc. cit.
[99] *Shaw* v. *Symmons* [1917] 1 K.B. 799; *Crouch* v. *Jeeves* (1938) Pty. Ltd. (1946) 46 S.R. (N.S.W.) 242, at 245.
[1] *Lilley* v. *Doubleday* (1881) 7 Q.B.D. 510 (assumed to be a decision upon exclusion clauses by Scrutton L.J. in *Gibaud* v. *G.E. Ry. Co.* [1921] 2 K.B. 426, at 435 and by Viscount Dilhorne in *Suisse Atlantique* [1967] 1 A.C. 361, at 392; but cf. Coote, op. cit., p. 99); *Edwards* v. *Newland & Co. Ltd.* [1950] 1 All E.R. 1072; *Kenyon, Son & Craven Ltd.* v. *Baxter Hoare & Co. Ltd.* [1971] 2 All E.R. 708, at 720; *A/s Rendal* v. *Arcos Ltd.* (1937) 53 T.L.R. 953, at 958; *Thomas National Transport (Melbourne) Pty. Ltd.* v. *May & Baker (Australia) Pty. Ltd.* (1966) 115 C.L.R. 353.

by a different route or in a different conveyance[2] or wrongfully deputes
a third-party to discharge the task for which the goods were originally
entrusted to him,[3] is denied the protection of his contract. A similar
principle would seem to apply to hirers or borrowers who use the goods
for an unauthorised purpose, such as an unauthorised journey or an
unauthorised loan to a third-party.[4]

As a result of these cases, deviation came to signify any departure
from the limitations imposed upon the bailee's right to possession.[5] Once
the bailee transgressed the bounds of his authority, the ordinary principles of liability ceased to apply, because he had repudiated the very
terms upon which his status as bailee had been conferred.[6]

The logic of the deviation cases holds good today, but its operation
is subject to certain essential limitations. It applies only to bailees,[7]
and it can prove difficult to invoke when there has been a mere meta-
phorical deviation, i.e. something less than a physical or geographical
divergence from an agreed situs or itinerary or sequence of events. One
decision which seems to have applied the principle metaphorically was
Alexander v. *Railway Executive*,[8] where reliance upon a limitation clause
was forfeited because the defendant bailees had wrongfully allowed a
third party to have access to the goods, and had subsequently despatched
them to him without the owner's authority. Devlin J., relying in part upon
the deviation cases, characterised this misconduct as a fundamental
breach. Later judicial attempts to construct analogies or metaphors
around the doctrine of deviation are less felicitous, and have been responsible for much obscurity and confusion.[9]

---

[2] *Sleat* v. *Fagg* (1822) 5 B. & A. 242; 106 E.R. 1216; *Mallett* v. *G.E. Ry.* [1899]
1 Q.B. 309; *L.N.W. Ry. Co.* v. *Neilson* [1922] A.C. 263; *Gunyan* v. *S.E.C. Ry. Co.*
[1915] 2 K.B. 370; cf. *Gallaher Ltd.* v. *B.R.S. Ltd.* [1974] 2 Lloyd's Rep. 440;
Mayfair Photographic Co. Ltd. v. *Baxter Hoare & Co. Ltd.* [1972] 1 Lloyd's Rep.
410; *Gore* v. *Australasian Steam Navigation Co. Ltd.* (1873) 12 S.C.R. (N.S.W.)
14; *Cocking* v. *Hoffman* [1932] S.A.S.R. 108.

[3] *Edwards* v. *Newland & Co. Ltd.* ante (warehousing); *Davies* v. *Collins* [1945]
1 All E.R. 247; *Martin* v. *H. Negin Ltd.* (1945) 172 L.T. 275; *Causer* v. *Browne*
[1952] V.L.R. 1 (dry-cleaning); *Von Minden* v. *Pyke* (1865) 4 F. & F. 533 (agent
for sale); *Garnham, Harris & Elton Ltd.* v. *Alfred W. Ellis (Transport) Ltd.*
[1967] 1 W.L.R. 940 (carriage—the sub-contractors being negligently chosen in
any event).

[4] *Coggs* v. *Bernard* (1703) 2 Ld. Raym. 909, at 913; 92 E.R. 107, at 111; *Isaack*
v. *Clarke* (1615) 2 Bulst. 306, at 309; 80 E.R. 1143, at 1145; *Roberts* v.
MacDougall (1887) 3 T.L.R. 666; *Hughes* v. *Rooke* [1954] St. R. Qd. 45; *Chapman*
v. *Robinson and Ferguson* (1969) 71 W.W.R. 515 (none of them involving
exclusion clauses, but each acknowledging the resultant insurer's liability). See
further: *McKenna & Armistead Pty. Ltd.* v. *Excavations Pty. Ltd.* [1957] S.R.
(N.S.W.) 515; *Knight* v. *Wilson* 1949 S.L.T. 26. Cf. *Fawcett* v. *Smethurst* (1914)
112 L.T. 309.

[5] Coote, op. cit., p. 92. The limitation must be clear and unequivocal: cf. *Tobin*
v. *Murison* (1845) 5 Moore 110; *Gibaud* v. *S.E. Ry. Co.* [1921] 2 K.B. 426;
Mayfair Photographic case (ante), at 415.

[6] Coote [1970] C.L.J. 221, at 234.

[7] Coote, op. cit., pp. 83-84.

[8] [1951] 2 K.B. 882; see also *United Fresh Meat Co. Ltd.* v. *Charterhouse Cold
Storage Ltd.* [1974] 2 Lloyd's Rep. 286, at 291.

[9] Whether (as seems possible) the deviation cases were originally the product of a
substantive principle, or merely emanated from the necessary construction of the
contract, they were clearly assisted by the bailee's failure to specify the particular unauthorised act as within the realm of the exclusion. Devlin J.'s treatment of the subject in *Alexander* v. *Railway Executive* (ante) suggests a substantive

B. The "four corners" rule

Coalescent with the concept of deviation, and in many respects indissociable from it, there arose the somewhat wider assumption that no exclusion clause could apply unless the defendant was endeavouring to perform or carry out his contract at the time of the breach. Any substantial or radical departure from the agreed mode of performance took the defendant outside the four corners of his contract and precluded him from relying on its protection. The strongest statement of this principle was given by Scrutton J. in *Gibaud* v. *G.E. Ry. Co.*;[10] and despite the difficulties of distinguishing between conduct within, and conduct beyond, the agreed path of performance, the principle has been endorsed in many subsequent decisions.[11] Thus, it has been held that the protection of an exclusion clause may be lost when the bailee leaves the goods unattended for a substantial period[12] or misdelivers them to a third party[13] or fails to keep them upon his own premises,[14] but not when he merely leaves the vehicle in which they are contained unlocked[15] or commits some other momentary inadvertence.[16]

Although the rule is closely analogous to deviation, there is clear authority against confining its operation to bailees.[17] An example of its effect in a non-bailment situation might occur where a builder or agent sub-contracts work which he is under a duty to perform personally; in

principle, but it now seems that the decisions are to be explained as essays in construction: see *Suisse Atlantique* [1967] 1 A.C. 361, discussed at p. 934 et seq., post.

10 [1921] 2 K.B. 426, at 435: "The principle is well known, and perhaps *Lilley* v. *Doubleday* is the best illustration, that if you undertake to do a thing in a certain way, or to keep a thing in a certain place, with certain conditions protecting it, and have broken the contract by not doing the thing contracted for in the way contracted for, or not keeping the article in the place in which you have contracted to keep it, you cannot rely on the conditions which were only intended to protect you if you carried out the contract in the way which you had contracted to do it."

11 E.g. *Alderslade* v. *Hendon Laundry Ltd.* [1945] 1 K.B. 189, at 192; *Bontex Knitting Works Ltd.* v. *St. John's Garage* [1943] 2 All E.R. 690, at 695, aff'd (1944) 60 T.L.R. 253; *Tozer Kemsley & Millbourne (Australasia) Pty. Ltd.* v. *Collier's Interstate Transport Service Ltd.* (1956) 94 C.L.R. 384; *J. Spurling Ltd.* v. *Bradshaw* [1956] 1 W.L.R. 461, at 465; *Hunt & Winterbotham (West of England) Ltd.* v. *B.R.S. (Parcels) Ltd.* [1962] 1 Q.B. 617, at 626; *Sydney City Council* v. *West* (1965) 114 C.L.R. 481; *Thomas National Transport (Melbourne) Pty. Ltd.* v. *May & Baker (Australia) Pty. Ltd.* (ante) at 366, 377-378.

12 *Bontex Knitting Works Ltd.* v. *St. John's Garage Ltd.* (ante); cf. *Davis* v. *Pearce Parking Station Pty. Ltd.* (1954) 91 C.L.R. 642; *B.R.S. Ltd.* v. *Arthur V. Crutchley Ltd.* [1968] 1 All E.R. 811.

13 See the *Tozer Kemsley* and *Sydney City Council* cases ante; *Ashby* v. *Tolhurst* [1937] 2 K.B. 242 (not a case of bailment); cf. *Alexander* v. *Railway Executive* [1951] 2 K.B. 882; *Hollins* v. *J. Davey Ltd.* [1963] 1 Q.B. 844.

14 *Thomas National Transport (Melbourne) Pty. Ltd.* v. *May & Baker (Australia) Pty. Ltd.* ante. See also *Sze Hai Tong Bank Ltd.* v. *Rambler Cycle Co. Ltd.* [1959] A.C. 576.

15 *Colverd & Co. Ltd.* v. *Anglo Overseas Transport Co. Ltd.* [1961] 2 Lloyd's Rep. 352; cf. *L. R. Harris (Harella) Ltd.* v. *Continental Express Ltd.* [1961] 1 Lloyd's Rep. 251 and *Mendelssohn* v. *Normand Ltd.* [1970] 1 Q.B. 177, where there was an express promise that the vehicle would be locked and the failure to do so took the defendants beyond the terms of their exclusion.

16 *J. Spurling Ltd.* v. *Bradshaw* [1956] 1 W.L.R. 461, at 465; but cf. *Eastman Chemical International A.G.* v. *N.M.T. Trading Ltd.* [1972] 2 Lloyd's Rep. 25.

17 Coote, op. cit., p. 102.

such an event, the courts may be less ready to apply in his favour exclusion clauses which are clearly competent to protect him while undertaking the work in person.[18] Moreover, the principle is one of construction,[19] its basis being the presumption that no contracting party intends to grant an immunity which is to operate when the other party has deliberately disregarded the essential terms of the contract. Accordingly, it must give way in the face of clear words indicating a contrary effect. Both points were recognised by Windeyer J. in his dissenting judgment in *Thomas National Transport (Melbourne) Pty. Ltd.* v. *May & Baker (Australia) Pty. Ltd.*:[20]

> Thirdly, there is a rule or guide to construction which has in recent writings sometimes been treated as absorbed within the generalised modern term "fundamental breach", but which is itself far from new. It is that a condition absolving a party from liability, in particular exonerating a bailee from liability for the loss of goods in his care, is construed as referring only to a loss which occurs when the party is dealing with the goods in a way that can be regarded as in intended performance of his contractual obligation. He is not relieved of liability if, having obtained possession of the goods, he deals with them in a way that is quite alien to his contract.

C. A substantive doctrine of fundamental breach

A further principle, not confined to the responsibilities of bailees and operating independently of construction, was developed by certain English decisions during the post-war years. It was in these decisions, perhaps, that the formula "fundamental breach" first found extensive recognition and expression.[21] Dealing primarily with a series of actions which involved the leasing on hire-purchase of defective goods, the Court of Appeal held that any breach which went "to the root" of the contract, and rendered performance totally different from that contracted for, automatically invalidated an exemption clause, however widely drafted or construed.[22] This approach had the advantage of rendering construction otiose,[23] but it lacked authority[24] and created some important difficulties of its own. Not least of these was the task of identifying what

---

[18] Cf. *J. Evans & Son (Portsmouth) Ltd.* v. *Andrea Merzaria Ltd.* [1976] 2 All E.R. 930, (forwarding-agent).

[19] Coote, loc. cit.; *Suisse Atlantique* ante, at 434 per Lord Wilberforce.

[20] (1966) 115 C.L.R. 353, at 377.

[21] Although it was used in the context of deviation by Lord Wright in *Hain S.S. Co. Ltd.* v. *Tate & Lyle Ltd.* [1936] 2 All E.R. 597; and by Lord Esher M.R. in *Balian & Sons* v. *Joly, Victoria & Co. Ltd.* (1890) 6 T.L.R. 345.

[22] *Karsales (Harrow) Ltd.* v. *Wallis* [1956] 1 W.L.R. 936; *Yeoman Credit Ltd.* v. *Apps* [1962] 2 Q.B. 508; *Astley Industrial Trust Ltd.* v. *Grimley* [1963] 1 W.L.R. 584; *Charterhouse Credit Co. Ltd.* v. *Tolly* [1963] 2 Q.B. 683. *Smeaton Hanscomb & Co. Ltd.* v. *Sassoon I. Setty, Son & Co. Ltd.* (No. 1) [1953] 1 W.L.R. 1468, although appearing to be based upon construction, is probably best explained as the first manifestation of the substantive principle: see *Suisse Atlantique* (ante) at 400 per Lord Reid. Further possible authority for this principle is to be found in *Philip Boshali* v. *Allied Commercial Exporters Ltd.* (1961) Unrep. 14 November (P.C.); *Sze Hai Tong Bank Ltd.* v. *Rambler Cycle Co. Ltd.* [1959] A.C. 576, at 587 per Lord Denning (P.C.).

[23] Except insofar as the courts may have had to decide what, in fact, the defendant was promising; but in the cases under discussion, this question does not appear to have arisen.

[24] *Suisse Atlantique* (ante) at 401 per Lord Reid, 434 per Lord Wilberforce.

constituted a fundamental breach and how, if at all, this differed from the breach of a fundamental term.[25]

D. Construction as the universal rule

In 1965, the House of Lords sought to explain these cases on the basis of construction and to establish the rule that whether an exclusion clause applies to a particular breach is, in all cases, a question of construction to be answered by the terms of the contract, the language of the parties and the intentions that can be drawn from the transaction as a whole. In so doing, they denied the existence of a substantive doctrine of fundamental breach, and confirmed that the deviation cases were merely part of the general law of contract, rather than representing a special rule:[26]

> In my view, it is not right to say that the law prohibits and nullifies a clause exempting or limiting liability for a fundamental breach or breach of a fundamental term. Such a rule of law would involve a restriction on freedom of contract and in the older cases I can find no trace of it . . . In each case not only have the terms and scope of the exempting clause to be considered but also the contract as a whole.[27]
> It cannot be said as a matter of law that the resources of the English language are so limited that it is impossible to devise an exclusion clause which will apply to at least some cases of fundamental breach without being so widely drawn that it can be cut down on any ground by applying ordinary principles of construction . . . If this new rule of law is to be adopted, how far does it go? In its amplest form it would be that a party is not permitted to contract out of common law liability for a fundamental breach . . . In my view no such rule of law ought to be adopted.[28]
> The conception, therefore, of "fundamental breach" as one which, through ascertainment of the parties' contractual intention, falls outside an exceptions clause is well-recognised and comprehensible. Is

---

[25] See on this point *Hong Kong Fir Shipping Co. Ltd.* v. *Kawasaki Kisen Kaisha Ltd.* [1962] 2 Q.B. 26; *Direct Acceptance Finance Ltd.* v. *Cumberland Furnishing Pty. Ltd.* [1965] N.S.W.R. 1504; *Suisse Atlantique* at 392, 393 (Viscount Dilhorne), 397-398 (Lord Reid), 421-422 (Lord Upjohn), 431 (Lord Wilberforce); *Wathes (Western) Ltd.* v. *Austins (Menswear) Ltd.* [1976] 1 Lloyd's Rep. 14.

[26] *Suisse Atlantique* at 391 (Viscount Dilhorne), 399-400 (Lord Reid), 423-425 (Lord Upjohn), 434 (Lord Wilberforce). The statements are technically obiter as the demurrage clause in this case was characterised as an agreed damages clause and thus held not to fall within the definition of an exclusion or limitation clause. The substance of the appellants' complaint was that the respondents, who had chartered the appellants' ship for a period of two years' consecutive voyages from 31 December 1956, had failed to perform their contractual obligation of making the full total of voyages. A clause in the charterparty provided that, in the event of the respondents' exceeding the agreed periods of laytime, demurrage was to become payable at the rate of $1000 per day. The appellants claimed that the delays caused by the respondents constituted a fundamental breach of contract and entitled the appellants to recover damages over and above the quantum laid down by the demurrage clause. The House of Lords held that the appellants had no contractual right to any certain number of voyages and that the demurrage clause regulated entirely the respondents' liability for delay. Further, the appellants had not repudiated the contract and its original construction prevailed.

[27] At 392 per Viscount Dilhorne.

[28] At 399, 405 per Lord Reid.

there any need, or authority, in relation to exeptions clauses for extension of it beyond this? In my opinion there is not.[29]

The reception of Suisse Atlantique: two kinds of fundamental breach: At first sight, the dicta in *Suisse Atlantique* seemed to permit only one conclusion viz. that the substantive doctrine of fundamental breach had been permanently banished to the realms of nostalgia. Unfortunately, a number of elements detracted from the finality and clarity of this decision. First, both Lord Reid and Lord Wilberforce hinted that there may be breaches so fundamental, or so destructive of the main purpose of the transaction, that no exclusion clause could ever reach them without mutilating the agreement beyond recognition as a contract.[30] Secondly, the appellants in *Suisse Atlantique* had affirmed the contract after the relevant breach; this, coupled with certain statements that the acceptance of a fundamental breach immediately brings that contract to an end,[31] left room for the inference that if the victim of such a breach prefers to *terminate* the contract, a different rule from that of construction might become applicable, because the exclusion clauses will have disappeared along with the agreement in which they are contained.

It was this inference that subsequently enabled the Court of Appeal to hold that the construction analysis applies only when the plaintiff has affirmed the contract after, and with knowledge of, the fundamental breach.[32] Where, on the other hand, he elects to terminate the contract, or where (according to Lord Denning)[33] the results of the breach are so total that he is given no effective option either way, construction becomes irrelevant because the very contract upon which the clause relies for its subsistence has ceased to exist. This decision, in seeking to revive the substantive doctrine of fundamental breach, was at variance with both the philosophy and the express language of *Suisse Atlantique*. The statements of Lord Reid and Lord Upjohn upon which the Court of Appeal relied[34] were not intended to refer to the exclusion of liability already accruing before termination, but to the exclusion of liability accruing thereafter.[35]

---

[29] At 434 (Lord Wilberforce); see also at 409-410 (Lord Hodson) and 425 (Lord Upjohn). The construction analysis had previously been put by Pearson L.J. in *U.G.S. Finance Ltd.* v. *National Mortgage Bank of Greece and National Bank of Greece S.A.* [1964] 1 Lloyd's Rep. 446, at 453. The passage in question was cited with approval in most of the speeches in *Suisse Atlantique*.

[30] [1967] 1 A.C. 361, at 399 (see ante), 431-432.

[31] Ibid., at 398 (Lord Reid), 419, 425 (Lord Upjohn). The point was conceded by counsel: Coote [1970] C.L.J. 221, at 233.

[32] *Harbutt's "Plasticine" Ltd.* v. *Wayne Tank & Pump Co. Ltd.* [1970] 1 Q.B. 447; Legh-Jones and Pickering (1970) 86 L.Q.R. 513; Weir [1970] C.L.J. 189; Coote [1970] C.L.J. 221. The case did not involve bailment. It arose through the defendants' installation in the plaintiffs' factory of a defective feed-pipe, through the malfunctioning of which the factory was burned down.

[33] [1970] 1 Q.B. 447 at 465.

[34] Ante, n. 31.

[35] Legh-Jones and Pickering loc. cit., at 518; *Kenyon Son & Craven Ltd.* v. *Baxter Hoare & Co. Ltd.* [1971] 1 W.L.R. 519, at 530; *United Fresh Meat Co. Ltd.* v. *Charterhouse Cold Storage Ltd.* [1974] 2 Lloyd's Rep. 286, at 294-295; Handford (1975) 38 M.L.R. 577, at 578. Cf. Treitel, op. cit., p. 156, who suggests that a clause which restricts liability for damages may not, unless expressly worded, affect the victim's right to terminate. It is conceded, however, that a deprivation of this right should be possible in principle.

A similar approach was taken by Lord Denning M.R. in *Farnworth Finance Facilities Ltd.* v. *Attryde*.[36] Here the appellant finance company sought to avoid responsibility for a defective motor-cycle by relying on a clause which excluded all conditions and warranties, express and implied. Lord Denning found that they had broken a fundamental term by failing to supply a roadworthy machine and were accordingly prevented from relying upon the exclusion clause: the hirer could disregard it "at any rate if (he) had not affirmed the contract". Fenton Atkinson L.J. decided the question solely by reference to the terms of contract[37] and did not refer to *Harbutt's "Plasticine"*.[38] The existence of these two decisions created a clear anomaly, which provoked one commentator to remark that one no longer needed hard cases in order to make bad law.[39]

The task of reconciling them with *Suisse Atlantique* fell to Donaldson J. in *Kenyon, Son & Craven Ltd.* v. *Baxter Hoare & Co. Ltd.*[40] In this case, the plaintiffs had bailed nuts to the defendants for storage in their warehouse. The warehouse was defective and prone to rats, which consumed a large quantity of the nuts. The defendants were aware of the problem and had made some attempt to deal with it, but these efforts fell "far short of what the plaintiffs had a right to expect". The plaintiffs sued for the loss and were met by the defendants standard conditions, which exempted the bailees from liability unless due to their "wilful neglect or default" and limited their liability in any event to a specified sum. The plaintiffs in response pleaded fundamental breach.

The contention that the defendants' misconduct was so serious as to destroy reliance upon the clauses as a matter of law was dismissed by Donaldson J. In so deciding, he relied upon the speech of Lord Wilberforce in *Suisse Atlantique*,[41] where it was observed that a fundamental breach of contract may take one of two distinct forms: either "a performance totally different from that which the contract contemplates" or "a breach of contract more serious than one which would entitle the other party to damages and which (at least) would entitle him to refuse performance or further performance under the contract". In Donaldson J.'s view it was only in the former case that the construction of the clause was immaterial; and even here, the question might become relevant if the injured party had affirmed. Breaches of this kind were characterised as "non-contractual performance"; they were akin to deviation and represented the sole area in which no exclusion clause, however widely drafted, could protect the party in breach. *Harbutt's "Plasticine"* and *Farnworth Finance Facilities Ltd.* v. *Attryde* were explained as turning upon this category of fundamental breach.[42] Only

---

[36] [1970] 1 W.L.R. 1053, esp. at 1059.
[37] Ibid., at 1060. Megaw L.J. concurred with both judgments.
[38] [1970] 1 Q.B. 447.
[39] Weir [1970] C.L.J. 189.
[40] [1971] 1 W.L.R. 519; Legh-Jones and Pickering (1971) 87 L.Q.R. 515.
[41] [1967] 1 A.C. 361, at 431.
[42] Cf. (1971) 87 L.Q.R. 515, at 522-523, where it is conceded that the *Farnworth Finance* case will withstand such a construction but doubted whether the same is true of *Harbutt's "Plasticine"*. *Mendelssohn* v. *Normand Ltd.* [1970] 1 Q.B. 177 may also be regarded as falling within this category, since Lord Denning M.R. held that the failure to keep the car safe was "a totally different thing"

if the injured parties in those cases had affirmed the contract with knowledge of the breach would the true construction of the clause have become a relevant subject of inquiry.

In the present case, however, the defendants' breach did not amount to a deviation. It fell (if anywhere) within Lord Wilberforce's minor category of fundamental breach. In this area the question was purely one of construction; if, on a true analysis, the clause in question covered the breach, then the breach could not destroy reliance upon the exclusion.

The defendants had gone some way towards carrying out their obligations, had kept the goods in the agreed place and had expended some effort in counteracting the cause of the damage. Accordingly, they had committed neither a deviation nor a "wilful neglect or default" within the meaning of the clause and were entitled to the protection it purported to confer.

The decision is interesting because it seems to suggest that the legal consequences of deviation can operate in relationships other than that of bailor and bailee;[43] but its subsequent history, even in cases of bailment, has been unsatisfactory and inconsistent. In *Mayfair Photographic Co. Ltd.* v. *Baxter Hoare & Co. Ltd.*[44] a fundamental breach was alleged to have occurred when sub-contractors employed by the defendant forwarding agents failed to deliver the plaintiffs' goods in a vehicle set aside exclusively for that purpose, to fit their lorry with an immobiliser, to provide their driver with a mate and to ensure that the vehicle was attended at all times. MacKenna J. expressed grave doubts as to whether *Harbutt's "Plasticine" Ltd.* v. *Wayne Tank & Pump Co. Ltd.* could be reconciled with *Suisse Atlantique*, but held that the alleged breaches were not fundamental and that the relevant clauses exonerated the forwarding agents. Although he did not specifically refer to *Kenyon, Son & Craven Ltd.* v. *Baxter Hoare & Co. Ltd.* he remarked that the exclusions might have ceased to operate if their conduct had amounted to a deviation.[45] His decision is therefore consistent with the analysis propounded by Donaldson J. Insofar as the alleged breaches were capable of being fundamental, they clearly fell within Lord Wilberforce's second category.

In *Gallaher Ltd.* v. *B.R.S. Ltd.*[45a] Kerr J. specifically accepted the dichotomy laid down by Donaldson J. but held that on present facts there was no need to decide whether the failure to adopt certain agreed security arrangements constituted a greater or lesser form of fundamental breach. The security precautions were enshrined in a collateral

from what the defendants had undertaken. Alternatively, it could be regarded simply as a decision on construction, applying the four corners rule.

---

[43] See (1971) 87 L.Q.R. 515, at 524-526 for some of the difficulties presented by this approach; and cf. Coote [1970] C.L.J. 221, at 234 et seq. where it is argued that deviation and quasi-deviation are principles peculiar to bailment "in bringing about an automatic non-application of the exception clauses from the moment the deviation commences, without the need for an election to that effect by the injured party".
[44] [1972] 1 Lloyd's Rep. 410.
[45] At 416.
[45a] [1974] 2 Lloyd's Rep. 440.

agreement which was not subject to the first defendants' standard conditions of carriage in the first place.

Two further decisions of the English High Court provide a less harmonious impression. In the first of these,[45b] the Deputy Judge applied *Harbutt's "Plasticine"* to nullify exclusion clauses in a contract between the bailors of goods and a carrier who had legitimately sub-contracted the work to third parties. The latter negligently failed to provide a vehicle with adequate tyres and the judge held that the resultant destruction of the plaintiffs goods by fire brought their contract with the principal contractors to an end and precluded reliance upon the defendants' conditions of carriage. *Kenyon's* case was not cited and the two decisions are not easy to reconcile.

Equally unsatisfactory is the decision of Wien J. in *United Fresh Meat Co. Ltd.* v. *Charterhouse Cold Storage Ltd.*[46] In this case the court seems to have applied *Harbutt's "Plasticine"* while repudiating the very interpretation of *Suisse Atlantique* upon which that decision was based.[47] Although the *United Fresh Meat* case can be justified upon two alternative grounds advanced by the court, viz. that the clause did not on its true construction protect the defendants and that their failure to keep the plaintiff's meat at a proper temperature was in any event akin to deviation,[48] it does not lend clarity to the law of fundamental breach.[49]

[45b] *Eastman Chemical International A.G.* v. *N.M.T. Trading Ltd.* [1972] 2 Lloyd's Rep. 25.

[46] [1974] 2 Lloyd's Rep. 286.

[47] Handford (1975) 38 M.L.R. 577. The statement of Lord Reid in [1967] 1 A.C. 361, at 398 as to the effects of a fundamental breach upon the efficacy of exclusion clauses was recognised as applying only to losses occurring after repudiation: [1974] 2 Lloyd's Rep. 286, at 294-295. But it was upon a mis-construction of this passage that the Court of Appeal had reached its conclusion in *Harbutt's "Plasticine"* that a fundamental breach automatically brings the contract to an end and prevents reliance upon exclusion clauses in respect of past as well as future loss.

[48] [1974] 2 Lloyd's Rep. 286, at 291.

[49] The question of fundamental breach has been briefly considered in three further English decisions. In *The Angelia* [1973] 1 W.L.R. 210, at 234, Kerr J. contented himself with observing that the implications of *Harbutt's "Plasticine"* and *Farnworth Finance Facilities* v. *Attryde* "should be considered and the law rationalised at a higher level". In *Birch* v. *Thomas* [1972] 1 All E.R. 905, at 908 (a case involving a "passenger's risk" notice displayed on the dashboard of a car) Lord Denning M.R. held that the defendant's misconduct (careless overtaking) was not a fundamental breach and therefore fell within the protection of the clause. He continued: "In order to come within the doctrine of fundamental breach, the conduct would have to be something quite outside the contemplation of the parties, such as the instance I put in the course of the argument of a man who drove off the road across a field, or who drove up the wrong carriageway, and met with disaster. If a driver was guilty of that sort of conduct, he could not rely on the exemption clause." In *Levison* v. *Patent Steam Carpet Cleaning Co. Ltd.* [1977] 3 W.L.R. 90 Lord Denning M.R. again affirmed his support for a substantive doctrine of fundamental breach, at least in cases of standard-form contracts where there is a perceptible inequality of bargaining power between the parties. At p. 97, he observed: "If a party uses his superior power to impose an exception or limitation clause on the weaker party, he will not be allowed to rely on it if he has himself been guilty of a breach going to the root of the contract. In other cases, the court will, whenever it can, construe the contract so that an exemption or limitation clause only avails the party when he is carrying out the contract in substance: and not when he is breaking it in a manner which goes to the very root of the contract: see *United Fresh Meat Co. Ltd.* v. *Charterhouse Cold Storage Ltd.* [1974] 2 Lloyd's Rep. 286; and this is

More recently, the practice appears to have developed of reverting to construction in answer to a plea of fundamental breach, but of phrasing the relevant construction principles in especially imperative and ungenerous terms. *Wathes (Western) Ltd.* v. *Austins (Menswear) Ltd.*[50] seems to be such a case. This decision is significant because it holds that when the victim of a fundamental breach elects to affirm the contract, the affirmation does not destroy the character of the breach as fundamental for the purposes of ascertaining whether the exclusion clause does, in fact, apply to a fundamental breach.[51] In so doing, the Court of Appeal appear to have acknowledged that although an exclusion clause will be construed only in very exceptional circumstances as excusing liability for a fundamental breach,[52] whether it does operate to exclude such liability is ultimately a question of construction; and that this analysis holds good not only where the contract has been affirmed, but where the innocent party invokes the fundamental breach as a ground of rescission:

> It does not appear to me to have been suggested by their Lordships that *Charterhouse* v. *Tolly* was wrong in its decision that an exemption clause did not survive, or did not revive, where there was a fundamental breach, but no rescission, of the contract: at any rate if, as in the present case, it is accepted that the exemption clause would not have availed the party in breach of contract if the contract had been rescinded for fundamental breach . . . since cl. 14 would not as a matter of construction have availed the plaintiffs if the contract had been treated as rescinded for a fundamental breach, on Lord Reid's reasoning[53] it would not avail the plaintiffs when there is a fundamental breach, but no rescission.[54]
> What is the effect on a fundamental breach of the innocent party electing to affirm the contract? He does not waive the breach or his right to claim damages for it, but he waives his right to treat it as fundamental for the purpose of rescinding or discharging the whole contract and his right to claim rescission of it. On the authorities cited by my Lords, he apparently does not waive his right to treat it as fundamental for the purpose of defeating that part of the contract which excludes or limits the liability of the guilty party. A clause in the affirmed contract which does that does not cover fundamental breaches unless expressed to do so in the plainest terms and cannot be made to do so by extending its construction to cover a particular fundamental breach. This, which may look like a device to prevent a guilty

---

so, even though the injured party has not repudiated the contract for the breach, but has affirmed it afterwards: see *Wathes (Western) Ltd.* v. *Austins (Menswear) Ltd.* [1976] 1 Lloyd's Rep. 14." The remaining members of the Court of Appeal apparently preferred to treat the doctrine as one of pure construction (see infra). Cf. *Davidson* v. *Three Spruces Realty Ltd.* [1977] 6 W.W.R. 460.

---

[50] [1976] 1 Lloyd's Rep. 14 (C.A.); Reynolds, (1976) L.Q.R.; cf. *Guarantee Trust of Jersey Ltd.* v. *Gardner* (1973) 117 Sol. Jo. 564, which can arguably be put forward as evidence of this approach.

[51] Following *Charterhouse Credit Ltd.* v. *Tolly* [1963] 2 Q.B. 683; the Court of Appeal did not consider the decision to have been disapproved on this point in *Suisse Atlantique*.

[52] Cf. Lord Denning M.R. in *Harbutt's "Plasticine"* at 467, who sanctions this approach only in cases of affirmation.

[53] *Suisse Atlantique* at 399.

[54] [1976] 1 Lloyd's Rep. 14, at 22 per Megaw L.J.

party to a contract from escaping liability for a fundamental breach of it, is an illustration of the rule that the construction of a writing is not for the parties but for the Court. The innocent party cannot alter the meaning of a clause in a contract by affirming it: if the clause did not apply to what the guilty party has done and the damage which he has caused, it cannot be made to apply by the innocent party going on with the contract—or with another contract which appears to be regarded by the authorities as the same contract, though varied in a fundamental respect.[55]

I think it clear upon authority that apart from express words, such as are not to be found in this condition, an exemption clause is to be treated as inapplicable in respect of liability resulting from a fundamental breach notwithstanding that the injured party elects to affirm the contract . . . The current of authority has now set, as I read the cases, in favour of the view that where a contract is affirmed after fundamental breach an exemption clause is treated as inapplicable to liability resulting from that breach, not upon a substantive principle of law, but upon construction, the clause being construed, in the absence of some plain indication of a different intention, as by implication inapplicable to such liability. The distinction between the two grounds of inapplicability can, so far as I can see, make no difference to the result where there is no such indication of intention.[56]

Although the plaintiffs in *Wathes (Western) Ltd.* v. *Austins (Menswear) Ltd.* had specifically conceded that a rescission would have rendered the exclusion clause inapplicable, the decision does seem to cast doubts upon the rationale (if not the result) of Donaldson J.'s endeavours to segregate a variety of breach so fundamental as to be beyond the redemption of any clause as a matter of law.[57]

Further evidence that the attempted division of fundamental breach into "substantive" and "construable" breaches has fallen largely on unresponsive ground may be found in *Naviera de Canarias S.A.* v. *Nacional Hispanica Asegouradora S.A.*[58] In this case, which involved an exclusion clause in a marine insurance policy, Lord Denning M.R. refused to sanction an interpretation of the clause which would "defeat the very purpose of the contract."[59] In his view, the clause must be construed so as to render it consistent with the cardinal object and intent of the agreement. It is unclear whether this approach involves the use of interpretation to attain the same results as a substantive rule of law, or the use of a substantive rule of law to obtain the required interpretation. In either event, there are obvious perils in phrasing what purports to be a rule of construction in too mandatory or imperative a manner.

[55] Ibid., at 24, per Stephenson L.J.
[56] Ibid., at 25, per Sir John Pennycuick; and see further the *Levison* case, ante, at 98, 99, where Sir David Cairns and Orr L.J., while acknowledging the question to be one of construction, both stressed that great clarity and strength of language is required to exclude liability for fundamental breach.
[57] *Wathes'* case was not a case of bailment, but involved a contract for the installation of air-conditioning equipment. *Kenyon's* case was not cited in the judgments, except on one occasion and in a context different from that presently under discussion. Quaere whether the breach in *Wathes* would have fallen within Lord Wilberforce's first category of fundamental breach.
[58] (1976) *The Times*, 14 April (C.A.).
[59] Similar to *Anglo-Continental Holidays Ltd.* v. *Typaldos Lines Ltd.* [1967] 1 Lloyd's Rep. 61; as to which, see Treitel, op. cit.

It is significant that the remaining judges in *Naviera de Canarias* preferred to confine their solution to the ordinary and literal meaning of the clause. The "four corners" rule (or any other rule of construction) can hardly constitute an indomitable gloss upon every exclusion clause, irrespective of its wording and literal effect.[59a]

E. The Australian approach

Compared to recent developments in England, the Australian courts seem to have preserved an enviable integrity of approach. In the year preceding *Suisse Atlantique* the High Court anticipated the logic of that decision by affirming that an exclusion clause, once incorporated, should stand or fall upon its true construction.[60] The dispute in this case[61] concerned the loss of the plaintiff's car, which had been bailed to the defendant parking-lot operators and which they had subsequently permitted a third party to drive away. They claimed the relief of conditions printed on the parking ticket but the court, by a majority, denied them this protection. The reasons are clearly stated in the joint judgment of Barwick C.J. and Taylor J.[62] which explicitly subordinates the doctrines of quasi-deviation and performance within the contract to the express language of the contract itself:

> There is no doubt, of course, that in the case where a contract of bailment contains an exempting clause such as we have to consider the protection afforded by the clause will be lost if the goods the subject of the bailment are stored in a place or in a manner other than that authorized by the contract or if the bailee consumes or destroys them instead of storing them or if he sells them. But we would deny the application of such a clause in those circumstances simply upon the interpretation of the clause itself. Such a clause contemplates that loss or damage may occur by reason of negligence on the part of the warehouseman or his servants in carrying out the obligations created by the contract. But in our view it has no application to negligence in relation to acts done with respect to a bailor's goods which are neither authorized nor permitted by the contract . . . To our minds the clause clearly appears as one which contemplates that, in the performance of the Council's obligations under the contract of bailment, some loss or damage may be caused by reason of its servants' negligence but it does not contemplate or provide an excuse for negligence on the part of the Council's servants in doing something which it is neither authorised nor permitted to do by the terms of the contract.[63]

Both here and in the concurring judgment of Windeyer J. serious doubts are expressed as to the value or coherence of any substantive

---

[95a] The actual decision in the *Naviera de Canarias* case was reversed by the House of Lords: [1977] 1 All E.R. 625, relying on the plain and unambiguous wording of the clause.

[60] For earlier decisions to similar effect, see *Davis v. Pearce Parking Station Pty. Ltd.* (1954) 91 C.L.R. 642; *Tozer Kemsley & Millbourn (Australasia) Pty. Ltd. v. Collier's Interstate Transport Service Ltd.* (1956) 94 C.L.R. 384.

[61] *Sydney City Council v. West* (1965) 114 C.L.R. 481.

[62] Ibid., at 488-490. Kitto and Menzies JJ. dissented on the grounds that the conditions applied to the particular loss suffered.

[63] (1965) 114 C.L.R. 481, at 488-489.

doctrine of fundamental breach or breach of a fundamental term.[64] Clearly such concepts are otiose when the contract can be construed as protecting the defendant only when he acts within certain limits of behaviour, and when any breach of a fundamental character falls beyond that agreed realm of protection. This was the position in *Thomas National Transport (Melbourne) Pty. Ltd.* v. *May & Baker (Australia) Pty. Ltd.*,[65] where the High Court repeated its earlier technique. The majority held that the failure by the first defendants to warehouse the goods in their own building after collection involved a species of performance substantially different from that contemplated by the contract, and in respect of which the exclusion clauses were accordingly incapable of applying. Even in this, a pronounced case of deviation, the inquiry centred solely upon the linguistic ambit of the clauses and the obligations imposed by the contract as a whole.[66]

Likewise, in *H. & E. Van der Sterren* v. *Cibernetic (Holdings) Pty. Ltd.*,[67] where a warranty of quality was expressed to apply "provided that the company shall not be liable for any claim under this clause or in any other way whatsoever" if such claim were not made within fourteen days of delivery, the High Court held that the defendants were protected, even though the product was incapable of performing its function, because of defects which were not apparent at the time when it was delivered:

> The question is one of construction . . . The language is quite definite and clear . . . The terms of exception clauses must sometimes be read down if they cannot be applied literally without creating an absurdity or defeating the main object of the contract . . . But such a modification by implication of the language which the parties have used in an exception clause is not to be made unless it is necessary to give effect to what the parties must be understood to have intended.[68]

Consistently with this theory, a least one Australian court has shown itself prepared to extend the shelter of an exclusion clause to a defendant who is unable to provide evidence as to the cause of loss and therefore

---

[64] Ibid., at 488, 500-501. Such a doctrine had been invoked by the New South Wales Full Supreme Court; *West* v. *Sydney City Council* (1964) 82 W.N. (N.S.W.) Pt. 1 139.

[65] (1966) 115 C.L.R. 353. The facts are outlined ante, at p. 000.

[66] Note the somewhat different approach taken by Windeyer J. both here and in *West's* case. In *West*, he inferred from the use of the word "redelivered" on the ticket an undertaking by the defendants to redeliver the vehicle only to the person producing the ticket; breach of this obligation in the instant case meant that the defendants "did not do the thing it had contracted to do in the way in which it had contracted to do it" and accordingly, on the construction of the document, lost the protection of the clause: (1965) 114 C.L.R. 481, at 503. In *Thomas National Transport* Windeyer J. dissented because he could discern no obligation on the defendant's part to house the goods on their own premises in the first place. This analysis is interesting in that it moves towards a conception of exclusion clauses as substantive rather than procedural phenomena, which define the parties' obligations rather than mitigate the effect of their breach: see Coote, *Exception Clauses*, Chapter 1; [1970] C.L.J. 221, at 228 et seq. and cf. Kitto J. in *Sydney City Council* v. *West* (1965) 114 C.L.R. 481, at 495-496.

[67] (1970) 44 A.L.J.R. 157.

[68] Ibid., at 158 per Walsh J.

to deny that it resulted from a deliberate conversion by his servants.[69] The clause in question was widely framed to exclude responsibility "for any damage, including injury, delay, or loss of any nature . . . whether due or alleged to be due to misconduct or negligence on the part of the carrier or not and whether the cause of damage is known or unknown to the carrier". The defendants conceded that it should not apply to such extreme events as loss from criminal action to which they were a party, or wilful destruction; but the judgment of Winneke C.J. and Gowans J., while acknowledging the fairly imperative nature of the relevant rules of construction, attaches pre-eminent importance to the wording of the clause itself:

> It is now established doctrine that the language of such an exempting clause is to be construed strictly and its ambiguities resolved against the party seeking its protection. It is also to be read, *if its language so requires and its language so permits,* as subject to an implied limitation which would not allow that party to disregard performance of the main obligation of the contract . . . The proper approach . . . appears to be to endeavour to ascertain the intention of the parties by applying the language used as understood in its ordinary sense to the subject-matter and preferring a narrower operation to a wider operation where both are open . . .[70]

In the result, the defendants were relieved not only from the ordinary rules of bailees' liability but from the traditional operation of the bailees' burden of proof. *Metrotex* thus provides a vivid example of the willingness of Australian Courts to adopt a laissez-faire philosophy in the analysis of bailees' exclusions and to extend such exclusions where appropriate to quite severe or aggravated forms of breach. In such an environ-

---

[69] *Metrotex Pty. Ltd.* v. *Freight Investments Pty. Ltd.* [1969] V.R. 9 (Sup. Ct. F.C.); cf. *Hunt & Winterbotham (West of England) Ltd.* v. *B.R.S. (Parcels) Ltd.* [1962] 1 Q.B. 617; *Levison* v. *Patent Steam Carpet Cleaning Co. Ltd.* [1977] 3 W.L.R. 90.

[70] [1969] V.R. 9, at 12-13 (emphasis added). The later observations (at 15), concerning the different effects of a deviation or fundamental breach, must presumably be read subject to the construction of the clause itself which in this case would not have been wide enough to encompass such events. Lush J. (at 18) seems to have specifically adopted the rule that whether a fundamental breach vitiates an exclusion clause is exclusively a question of construction. A similar approach can be discerned in the dicta of the New South Wales Court of Appeal in *Salmond & Spraggon (Australia) Pty. Ltd.* v. *Joint Cargo Services Pty. Ltd., The New York Star* [1977] 1 Lloyd's Rep. 445. In this case the Court were prepared to exonerate the defendants for the loss of goods from their warehouse, had they been able to show that the clause in question actually extended to them under the bill of lading (See on this point, p. 993 post). The Court held that despite the fact that the loss had occurred through an unauthorised delivery without production of the necessary documents, the plaintiffs' allegation of fundamental breach would not have been fatal to any defence under the clause because the clause was capable on its proper construction of applying to a breach of this character. Citing the *Suisse Atlantique, May and Baker* and *Cibernetic* cases, Glass J. concluded (at 450-451): "There is therefore no rule of law which stipulates that a party in fundamental breach forfeits the protection of all exception clauses. The protection will only be lost if the fundamental breach is of such a character if the application to it of a given exception clause would defeat the whole purpose of the contract. I am not persuaded that the contractual substratum of the contract of sea carriage would be destroyed if liability for the wrongful delivery of goods to a person who had no documents were to become unenforceable after the lapse of 12 months." See also Hutley J. at 452-453 and the later decision of the H.C. in (1978) 18 A.L.R. 335.

ment, fundamental breach has little part to play as an effective rule of law.[71]

F. Summary

Two observations, at least, can be made with certainty. In most cases where there has been a fundamental breach, the defendant will be disentitled from relying upon an exclusion clause on principles of pure construction; and in many cases where such protection is available, it will be by virtue of a clause which effectively casts his undertaking in optional rather than compulsory terms and thus renders non-performance (or even perhaps grievous mis-performance) no breach at all. The latter phenomenon will be a rare and (to the proferens) a doubtfully advantageous event.

As regards construction, there is, as we have seen, a whole menagerie of rules heavily weighted against the proferens.[72] As Kitto J. has said,[73] ". . . an unexpressed qualification is not to be implied unless the implication is necessary in the sense that it introduces what is only 'so obvious that it goes without saying'."

The more serious the breach (or the term broken) the greater the degree of clarity and specificity that will be required to excuse it; indeed, it is suggested in *Wathes (Western) Ltd.* v. *Austins (Menswear) Ltd.*[74] that express words may be required to exclude liability for fundamental breach. Added to the rule that an exclusion clause must be construed,

---

[71] See also *Hall* v. *Queensland Truck Centre Pty. Ltd.* [1970] Qd. R. 231, at 235 where Hoare J. remarked that "The principle of fundamental breach . . . must now be regarded as substantially demolished." This was not a case of bailment but of the supply of goods totally different from the contract description. It was held, applying *Andrews Bros. (Bournemouth) Ltd.* v. *Singer & Co. Ltd.* [1934] 1 K.B. 17, that the defendants' clauses did not on their construction apply to such an event. Cf. *Direct Acceptance Finance Ltd.* v. *Cumberland Furnishing Pty. Ltd.* [1965] N.S.W.R. 1504, at 1510-1510, where Walsh J. was concerned only with the effect of a fundamental breach upon future obligations under a contract of indemnity or guarantee. He doubted whether such a breach had occurred and held that the defendants had failed in any event to terminate the contract. Canadian authority is not entirely consistent on this issue: see inter alia *B. G. Linton Construction Ltd.* v. *Canadian National Railway Co.* (1974) 49 D.L.R. (3d) 548, where the Canadian Supreme Court appeared by a majority to favour the construction approach (but cf. Laskin C.J.C., at 550); *Heffron* v. *Imperial Parking Co. Ltd.* (1974) 46 D.L.R. (3d) 642, where the survival of a substantive doctrine was left open by the Ontario Court of Appeal but Estey J.A. remarked (at 651) that the phenomenon of fundamental breach "is alive and prospering in the law of this Province"; *R. G. McLean Ltd.* v. *Canadian Vickers Ltd.* (1971) 15 D.L.R. (3d) 15 (Ont. C.A.); *Davidson* v. *North America Business Equipment Ltd.* (1975) 49 D.L.R. (3d) 533; *Burlington Leasing Ltd.* v. *de Moura* (1976) 60 D.L.R. (3d) 71; *Inelco Industries Ltd.* v. *Venture Well Services Ltd.* (1975) 59 D.L.R. (3d) 458; *Peters* v. *Parkway Mercury Sales Ltd.* (1975) 58 D.L.R. (3d) 128.

[72] These rules are summarised by Professor Coote [1970] C.L.J. 221, at 238-240.

[73] *Sydney City Council* v. *West* (1965) 114 C.L.R. 481, at 493; see also *H. & E. Van der Sterren Ltd.* v. *Cibernetics (Holdings) Pty. Ltd.* (1970) 44 A.L.J.R. 157, at 158 per Walsh J.

[74] [1976] 1 Lloyd's Rep. 14; see especially Sir John Pennycuick, at 25 and the *Levison* case (ante) at 98, 99. Cf. Treitel, op. cit., p. 156 (ante, p. 935) and *The Cap Palos* [1921] P. 458, at 471, 472 per Atkin L.J.: "I am far from saying that a contractor may not make a valid contract that he is not to be liable for any failure to perform his contract, including even wilful default; but he must use very clear words to express that purpose." Cf. now *Unfair Contract Terms Act* 1977, s. 3(2).

so far as is possible, with the main obligation of the contract,[75] these principles will continue to confront the perpetrator of a fundamental breach with a formidable task. For practical purposes, the impossibility of excluding such liability will depend upon the limits of language and the fact that the wider a clause becomes, the easier it may be to apply it solely to minor breaches falling short of non-contractual performance:

> Such a clause must, ex hypothesi, reflect the contemplation of the parties that a breach of contract, or what apart from the clause would be a breach of contract, may be committed, otherwise the clause would not be there: but the question remains open in any case whether there is a limit to the type of breach which they have in mind. One may safely say that the parties cannot, in a contract, have contemplated that the clause should have so wide an ambit as in effect to deprive one party's stipulations of all contractual force: to do so would be to reduce the contract to a mere declaration of intent. To this extent it may be correct to say that there is a rule of law against the application of an exceptions clause to a particular type of breach. But short of this it must be a question of contractual intention whether a particular breach is covered or not and the courts are entitled to insist, as they do, that the more radical the breach the clearer must the language be if it is to be covered.[76]

This dictum illustrates the second facet of the problem as well as the first. By phrasing his contract so as to exclude liability for fundamental breach, the proferens may find himself walking the tightrope between defining his apparent duties out of existence and rendering the contract void for uncertainty. The antithesis is epitomised by two statements of Lord Devlin:

> It is illusory to say, "we promise to do a thing but we are not liable if we do not do it".[77]
> If an anxious hostess is late in the preparation of a meal, she can perfectly well say: "send me peas or if you haven't got peas send beans; but for heaven's sake send something." That would be a contract for peas, beans or anything else ejusdem generis and is a perfectly sensible contract to make.[78]

If the purported contract becomes void for uncertainty, or is reduced to the mere status of a declaration of intent, neither party can sue upon it. Thus the proferens will be unable to sue for payment and the other party (unless he sues under a bailment) may be unable to recover for breach of the proferens' duty.[79] However, in many cases the putative exclusion will operate quite acceptably as a demarcation of the relevant duty; and although a clause of this kind will be treated as an exclusion clause for the purposes of strict construction, no question of forfeiture

---

[75] *Sze Hai Tong Bank Ltd.* v. *Rambler Cycle Co. Ltd.* [1959] A.C. 576; *Anglo-Continental Holidays Ltd.* v. *Typaldos Lines Ltd.* [1967] 2 Lloyd's Rep. 61; *Naviera de Canarias S.A.* v. *Nacional Hispanica Asegouradora S.A.* (1976) *The Times*, 14 April; reversed [1977] 1 All E.R. 625. See also the *Salmond & Spraggon* case, ante.

[76] *Suisse Atlantique* [1967] 1 A.C. 361, at 431-432 per Lord Wilberforce.

[77] *Firestone Tyre & Rubber Co. Ltd.* v. *Vokins & Co. Ltd.* [1951] 1 Lloyd's Rep. 32, at 39.

[78] [1966] C.L.J., at 212.

[79] Cf. Legh-Jones and Pickering (1971) 87 L.Q.R. 515, at 524-526.

through fundamental breach can arise when there is no obligation to be broken. This analysis may be particularly appropriate where the events against which protection is sought are events which occur without misbehaviour on the part of the excluding party.[80] In such a case, a denial of protection could operate to displace the doctrine of frustration:

> It is an impossible argument, and one which puts the cart before the horse, for the owners to say that the supply of a cargo is prima facie an absolute and fundamental obligation and that they can therefore get rid of clause 2 by treating the charterers' failure to supply a cargo as a repudiatory and fundamental breach, although clause 2 expressly provides that such failure shall be no breach at all if due to unavoidable hindrances. The correct analysis is that under this charterparty the charterers did not undertake an absolute obligation to supply a cargo, but merely the qualified obligation to do so unless prevented by any unavoidable hindrances within clause 2. . . . The conclusive answer to any allegation of fundamental breach is in my view that the relevant provision (whether it be properly described as an exception clause or as a qualification of the obligation) excuses nonperformance due to circumstances which are not the fault of the charterers. No case was cited on either side, nor have I been able to find one, in which it has ever been suggested that a party can commit a fundamental breach when the breach occurs due to circumstances beyond its control and the contract provides that non-performance due to such circumstances is to be excused. It seems to me that by its nature the doctrine cannot have any application in such a case. . . it was also rightly pointed out on behalf of the charterers that the owners' contention is in principle inconsistent with the doctrine of frustration and also with vast numbers of decided cases of settled authority. The essence of the doctrine of frustration is that a party will be excused from performance, even of absolute and fundamental obligations, if such performance has been rendered impossible by circumstances beyond its control. Since this is the position at common law without any exception clause, how can it be said that an express exception of unavoidable hindrances can be ousted by treating the non-performance as a fundamental breach? The owners answered this by saying that the exception would still operate if, but only if, the occurrence of the excepted causes would in any event have resulted in frustration. But in my view this is not a tenable proposition.[81]

It follows that, at its most extreme elevation, the problem of reconciling the doctrine of deviation with the constructional approach to exclusory clauses is an illusory one. It will be rare (if not impossible) for a contract to exclude liability for deviation without, in the same breath, creating a permission to deviate. Since deviation is thus qualified out of existence, there can be no forfeiture of the protection of the bailment by an "unauthorised" act. Of course, "liberty to deviate" clauses will be very strictly construed and a case of true deviation is distinguished by the resultant insurer's liability on the part of a bailee. This rule depends upon historical and practical considerations and should not affect the

---

[80] Treitel, *Law of Contract* (4th ed.), p. 159.
[81] *The Angelia* [1973] 1 W.L.R. 210, at 227-232 per Kerr J.

relief to which, on a true construction of the contract, the party allegedly in breach may be entitled.

G. The burden of proof

There remains one difficult question which has never been satis-factorily answered. It is whether a bailee, from whose premises goods are lost through some unidentified circumstance, must discharge the onus of proving that the loss occurred without a fundamental breach of contract on his part. This question is important for two reasons: first, because the survival of a substantive doctrine of fundamental breach would entail the automatic non-application of any exclusion clauses within the contract of bailment upon proof or inference of such breach; and secondly because, on modern rules of construction, it would be most unlikely that an exclusion clause would be construed as excluding liability for a funda-mental breach unless (if at all) the clause referred to this form of breach specifically.

Authority now strongly favours the view that if the plaintiff has specifically pleaded a fundamental breach the defendant will be answer-able unless he can disprove it. The decisions in point appear to regard this as a proper extension of the bailee's normal burden of proof (i.e. to show that any loss or damage to the goods did not occur through a breach of his duty of care), and as one which is peculiar to cases of bailment. Thus in *Woolmer* v. *Delmer Price Ltd.*[82] the defendant bailees (who had agreed to store the plaintiff's fur coat "at customer's risk") were held liable for its unexplained loss from their premises because they had failed to show that this did not result from a fundamental breach of the bailment on their part. Reaction to this decision was unenthusiastic[83] and until recently its authority could be regarded as open to doubt. It was, however, upheld and applied by the Court of Appeal in *Levison* v. *Patent Steam Carpet Cleaning Co. Ltd.*[84] In that case, a valuable Chinese carpet was lost by the defendant cleaners. The defendants relied upon their standard conditions but the Court held that these could apply only insofar as they were not displaced by a fundamental breach of the bailment. The defendants bore the burden of negativing such a breach because they, rather than the plaintiff, were the parties who knew or ought to have known what had happened to the carpet.[85] In thus appearing to extend the bailee's traditional burden of proof to include the rebuttal of a fundamental breach, the Court preferred a dictum of Denning L.J., in *J. Spurling Ltd.* v. *Bradshaw*[86] and the recent East African decision in

---

[82] [1955] Q.B. 291; see also *Vincent* v. *B.T.C.* (1957) 107 Law Jo. 202 (Southwark County Court).

[83] See *J. Spurling Ltd.* v. *Bradshaw* [1956] 1 W.L.R. 461 at 470, where Parker L.J. preferred to leave the question open; Treitel, op. cit., who observes that the decision is hard to reconcile with *Alderslade* v. *Hendon Laundry Ltd.* [1945] K.B. 189; and the later decision of the Court of Appeal in *Hunt & Winterbotham (West of England) Ltd.* v. *B.R.S. (Parcels) Ltd.* [1962] 1 Q.B. 617 (post, p. 948).

[84] [1977] 3 W.L.R. 90.

[85] Ibid., at 97, per Lord Denning M.R. This is markedly similar to the explanation for the bailee's standard burden of proving that he was not negligent: ante, p. 40.

[86] [1956] 1 W.L.R. 461 at 466, where Denning L.J. distinguished the *Alderslade* case (ante) on the ground that the Court did not specifically consider the question of burden of proof.

United Manufacturers Ltd. v. *WAFCO Ltd.*[87] to a series of shipping cases which had held that once a shipowner makes a prima facie case that loss to goods arose through one of his excepted perils the shipper then carries the burden of showing that the cause of loss was beyond the exceptions.[88] The decision in *Levison's* case has since been followed by the British Columbian Supreme Court in *Davidson* v. *Three Spruces Realty Ltd.*[89]

> . . . I am clearly of opinion that, in a contract of bailment, when a bailee seeks to escape liability on the ground that he was not negligent or that he was excused by an exception or limitation clause, then he must show what happened to the goods. If it appears that the goods were lost or damaged without any negligence on his part, then, of course, he is not liable. If it appears that they were lost or damaged by a slight breach—not going to the root of the contract—he may be protected by the exemption or limitation clause. But, if he leaves the cause of loss or damage undiscovered or unexplained—then I think he is liable: because it is then quite likely that the goods were stolen by one of his servants; or delivered by a servant to the wrong address; or damaged by reckless or wilful misconduct—all of which the offending servant will conceal and not make known to his employer. Such conduct would be a fundamental breach against which the exemption or limitation clause will not protect him.[89a]

Even if this principle be accepted as reliable, there remains the further question whether the burden of disproving fundamental breach should be imposed upon a bailee against whom such a breach has *not* been specifically pleaded. This question was answered in the negative by the Court of Appeal in *Hunt & Winterbotham (West of England) Ltd.* v. *B.R.S. (Parcels) Ltd.*,[90] a decision which casts some doubt upon the validity of *Levison* itself. Three parcels of woollen goods, part of a larger consignment carried by the defendant carriers, were lost in transit. The cause of the loss was never ascertained and, in defence to an action by the consignors, the carriers pleaded their written conditions of carriage. The consignors then contended that, in order to bring themselves within these conditions, the defendants were obliged to prove that they applied to the specific loss in question; since (as the law then stood) no exclusion clause could survive the occurrence of a fundamental breach, it followed that the defendants were likewise bound to refute the commission of such a breach on their part. They further contended that since they (the consignors) did not know the circumstances of the loss, they could not plead that a fundamental breach had been committed and it would have been unfair to have expected them to do so. The Court held against them on both points. They held that the relevant clauses could not, on a true construction, be regarded as importing a condition precedent that the defendants should (before being entitled to rely upon them) negative the

---

[87] [1974] E.A. 233.
[88] *The Glendarroch* [1894] P. 226; *Munro, Brice & Co.* v. *War Risks Association Ltd.* [1918] 2 K.B. 78; cf. *Joseph Constantine Steamship Line Ltd.* v. *Imperial Smelting Corporation Ltd.* [1942] A.C. 154.
[89] [1977] 6 W.W.R. 460.
[89a] [1977] 3 W.L.R. 90, at 98, per Lord Denning M.R.
[90] [1962] 1 Q.B. 617.

occurrence of a fundamental breach; and that the burden of proving such a breach should, in the present case, follow the general principles applicable to burden of proof.[91]

As to what would have been the position if such a breach had been specifically pleaded, no concluded opinion was expressed. Donovan L.J. did, however, observe that in *J. Spurling Ltd.* v. *Bradshaw*[92] Morris L.J. had remarked that in the present case there was "no material before us for finding that the claim results from some act of the plaintiffs outside what they contracted to do"; whereas if the burden of proof had been upon the bailees such positive material would have been unnecessary.[93] A similar observation was made more recently by Kerr J., in *Gallaher Ltd.* v. *B.R.S. Ltd.*[94] where, in an action against a carrier for the loss of goods by theft, it was held that an allegation of fundamental breach could not be sustained because the plaintiffs had adduced insufficient evidence to support it. But in *Hunt & Winterbotham* Donovan L.J. had further implied that a distinction may be permissible, for the purposes of the rule in *Woolmer* v. *Delmer, Price Ltd.*, between contracts for the hire of custody and contracts for the carriage of goods;[95] a distinction which, it is respectfully submitted, it would be difficult to justify. The learned Lord Justice continued:[96]

> The position might no doubt be different where a fundamental breach of the contract is specifically pleaded by the consignor as the cause of the loss, or where by his pleading the consignor in terms puts the carrier to proof of performance of the contract of carriage. In such a case the plea would be likely to be met by a demand for particulars to which in an appropriate case the answer might properly be that, in the nature of things, no such particulars could be given till after discovery, and that the paucity of the carrier's answers to inquiries made of him by the consignor fairly led to the inference that there might have been a deviation from, or a fundamental breach of, the contract of carriage by the carrier. What in such a case would be the result as to the onus of proof at any stage in the proceedings will have to be decided when such a case arises; but it would appear that, in such a case, the consignor would have clearly to claim, at least alternatively, damages for his loss otherwise than arising out of the contract of carriage.

There is, therefore, some prior appellate authority for the principle relied upon in *Levison* v. *Patent Steam Carpet Cleaning Co. Ltd.* But in *Levison* itself, the judgments of Lord Denning M.R. and Orr L.J. appear to go further and to imply that the relevant burden should apply whether or not a fundamental breach has been specifically pleaded.[97] Certainly

---

[91] Ibid., at 636-637. In *Metrotex Pty. Ltd.* v. *Freight Investments Pty. Ltd.* [1969] V.R. (ante, p. 943) the validity of this decision in Australia was explicitly left open by Winneke C.J. and Gowans J. It seems, however, that insofar as the rule is relevant to Australian law it should be adopted.
[92] [1956] 1 W.L.R. 461, at 469.
[93] [1962] 1 Q.B. 617, at 631-632.
[94] [1974] 2 Lloyd's Rep. 440. Cf. *Apang Ice Ltd.* v. *Paria Ship Suppliers Ltd.* (1972) 19 W.I.R. 337.
[95] [1962] 1 Q.B. 617, at 629, 631.
[96] Ibid., at 636-637.
[97] [1977] 3 W.L.R. 90, at 97-99.

no express qualification is entered for cases in which such a plea is absent and their Lordships' description of the circumstances in which the burden can arise are phrased in general terms. Unless the learned members of the Court of Appeal were adopting Donovan L.J.'s proposed differentiation between deposit and carriage, it is difficult to understand how they could consider themselves entitled to depart from the earlier Court of Appeal decision on this point in *Hunt & Winterbotham*.[98] In fact, the only member to advert specifically to this distinction was Sir David Cairns, who appears at one point to leave open the location of the burden of proof when fundamental breach is not specifically pleaded.[99] On the other hand, he cites with approval the dictum of Denning L.J. in *J. Spurling Ltd.* v. *Bradshaw*[1] which, like Lord Denning's later observations in *Levison,* was not confined to cases where fundamental breach is pleaded.

The difficulty is that in cases of this kind one is really dealing with at least three countervailing burdens. They are: the onus upon the party asserting a particular breach of contract to establish it; the onus upon a bailee to show that any loss or damage to goods in his possession was not caused by negligence on his part; and the onus upon any proferens to prove that, on a proper construction, his exclusion clauses apply to the particular loss sustained. At first sight it would appear that the *Levison* case is misconceived. It is not necessary, as Lord Denning suggests during the course of his judgment, for a bailee to establish the exact cause of loss or damage.[2] Traditionally, it has been held that when goods are lost from the possession of a bailee he need only prove that he took reasonable care to prevent such loss.[3] The burden of establishing this rests upon him, but his failure to discharge the burden raises against him an inference of negligence and no more. Such an inference is clearly irrelevant to his liability when (as in the *Levison* case itself) liability for negligence has already been adequately excluded. In such a case, the bailees separate responsibility to prove that his exclusion clauses apply to any other form of liability alleged against him should arise only when the liability against which protection is sought is affirmatively established by the bailor. In other words, the only material burden in cases of unexplained loss, where negligence is detonated as a source of liability by a clause excluding liability for negligence, is the burden upon a party asserting a particular form of breach to adduce positive evidence thereof. It is only when such a breach is established that any obligation arises upon the proferens to prove that his exemptions are competent to exonerate him from the resultant liability. If this were not the case, one would expect the bailee's burden to apply to minor as well as to fundamental breaches, and for it to be sufficient for a bailor, by making any assertion of a breach of contract, to cast the burden of disproving such breach upon the bailee. But such a rule would clearly be absurd.

---

[98] Cf. the extension upon the Court of Appeal's power to depart from earlier decisions proposed by Lord Denning M.R. and Sir George Baker, in *Davis* v. *Johnson* (1977) *The Times,* November 29th.

[99] [1977] 3 W.L.R. 90, at 100.

[1] [1956] 1 W.L.R. 461, at 466.

[2] [1977] 3 W.L.R. 90, at 98; cf. ante, p. 587.

[3] Or, that his negligence was unconnected with the loss: ante, p. 440.

Whereas, however, it is submitted that the general principle evolved from *Levison* is misconceived (and that this is so, whether fundamental breach is alleged in the pleadings or not), the decision itself can be justified on a separate ground. The bailee's liability for the theft of goods by his servants (which was one of the reasons suggested by the defendants for the loss of the Chinese carpet) has consistently been treated as a form of liability for failure to take reasonable care of the goods.[4] Whereas it qualifies as a form of liability in negligence for the purposes of the bailees burden of proof, however, it can equally qualify as a form of liability for fundamental breach for the purposes of any rule (substantive or constructional) which renders an exclusion clause inoperative upon proof of such breach. A conflation of these two principles would render the bailee liable, irrespective of a clause excluding liability for 'ordinary' or 'general' negligence, if he were unable to discharge the burden of proving (a) that the goods were not lost by the theft or complicity of his servants, or (b) that such theft or complicity is in any event within the contemplation of his exclusion clauses. The latter will, presumably, be fairly difficult to prove.[5]

There remains the problem of cases in which the bailee's conventional burden does not encompass an event which could be regarded as a fundamental breach. Suppose, for example, that the bailee has managed to show that no servant of his stole the goods, or misdelivered them negligently, but is unable to identify the precise cause of their loss, so that there remains a speculative margin of events in relation to which it can merely be surmised, without any evidence, that a fundamental breach has been committed.

Treitel has suggested that whereas it may be unfair to permit a plaintiff to cast the burden of proof upon the defendant merely by pleading fundamental breach, the burden might appropriately pass "if the plaintiff could support his allegation by *some* evidence that the defendant *might* have been guilty of a fundamental breach." The need for some initial evidence to justify such a finding becomes especially acute, perhaps, if the courts continue to accept the dual quality of fundamental breach propounded by Lord Wilberforce in *Suisse Atlantique* and amplified by Donaldson J. in *Kenyon, Son & Craven Ltd.* v. *Baxter Hoare & Co. Ltd.*[6] In such a context, it is essential to establish (and to have firm rules for establishing) not only whether a fundamental breach has occurred but whether it is of a kind that destroys reliance upon the relevant exclusion clauses outright, or falls within the principle of pure construction. Accordingly, it is submitted that the decision in *Levison* v. *Patent Steam Carpet Cleaning Co. Ltd.* should be confined to cases in which *either* the evidence *or* established authority permits a clear inference both that the loss may have occurred as the result of a fundamental breach by the defendant, and that such a breach would either fall outside the contemplation of the clause, or is of such a kind as to preclude reliance upon the clause in

[4] Ante, p. 471. Cf. *Port Swettenham* v. *Wu* (1978) *The Times,* June 22nd.
[5] Cf., however, the *Metrotex* decision, ante.
[6] [1971] 1 W.L.R. 519.

any event.[7] In some cases, the bailee may be able to demonstrate that his conditions are wide enough to cover even the commission of a fundamental breach, although it must be recalled that even on a purely constructional approach to exclusion clauses there will be a presumption against their applying to a breach of this character.[8] In any event, there should be at least some evidence to suggest that a debilitating breach has occurred before the relevant clauses are dismissed altogether and the bailee's ordinary burden of proof is extended to more radical breaches.[9]

VII. Need the Parties be in a Contractual Relation?

In *Adler* v. *Dickson*[10] both Morris and Denning L.JJ. said that a contract was essential to the derogation from the rights of one party that result from an exclusion clause. Lord Denning has since reiterated this statement[11] and has attempted to distinguish *Ashdown* v. *Samuel Williams & Sons Ltd.*,[12] which clearly favoured the contrary rule. In many cases, however, such clauses have been allowed to take effect in the absence of contract[13] and Lord Denning himself advocated such a result in his dissenting speech in *Scruttons Ltd.* v. *Midland Silicones Ltd.*[14] It therefore seems that no contract is necessary, provided the clause has been adequately brought to the other party's notice and is competent to cover the loss.[15]

VIII. The Unfair Contract Terms Act, 1977[16]

This Act, which came into force on February 1, 1978, represents the outcome of the Law Commission's advocacy of profound statutory reform in this area of the law. In the Second Report on Exemption Clauses compiled jointly by the Commission and its Scottish counterpart[17]

---

[7] See Vaines, *Personal Property* (5th ed.) pp. 101-102, where this approach is amplified.

[8] *Wathes (Western) Ltd.* v. *Austins (Menswear) Ltd.* [1976] 1 Lloyd's Rep. 14; *Levison* v. *Patent Steam Carpet Cleaning Co. Ltd.* [1977] 3 W.L.R. 90, at 98, 99.

[9] In theory, an exclusion clause could specifically provide for a reversal of whatever burden of proof rests on the bailee at Common Law; see the *Metrotex* case ante, but cf. now ss. 13, 25(3), *Unfair Contract Terms Act* 1977. Section 9 of the Act appears to have been intended to render questions of fundamental breach irrelevant under English Law, but it is doubtful whether it will necessarily have this effect: see infra.

[10] [1955] 1 Q.B. 158, at 184, 201.

[11] In *White* v. *Blackmore* [1972] 3 All E.R. 158, at 164-168.

[12] [1957] 1 Q.B. 409.

[13] Most notably in the field of gratuitous services; see *Hedley Byrne & Co. Ltd.* v. *Heller & Partners Ltd.* [1964] A.C. 465; *Birch* v. *Thomas* [1972] 1 All E.R. 905. For a decision in which the wife of the holder of a free pass on the railways was held bound by the terms of the pass although she had not seen it, see *McDonald* v. *Victorian Railways Commissioners* (1887) 13 V.L.R. 399; cf. on this point *Fosbroke-Hobbs* v. *Airwork Ltd.* [1937] 1 All E.R. 108.

[14] [1962] A.C. 446, at 481 et. seq.

[15] The question whether a sub-bailee can invoke clauses within the contract of sub-bailment against his principal bailor is discussed at p. 1000 et seq., post.

[16] See David Yates, *Exclusion Clauses in Contracts* (1978).

[17] Law Com. No. 69, Scot. Law Com. No. 39 (1975).

the function, object and effect of exclusion clauses in a wide range of service and supply industries had undergone close examination, and a variety of methods for bringing such clauses within reasonable bounds of control had been examined. The Commissions had annexed to their Report a draft Bill; though what has eventually been enacted differs in places from these suggestions, like them, it substantially affects the law of bailment in a number of important ways.

A. The test of "reasonableness" and the absolute ban

The Report had expressed support for a general criterion of "reasonableness" in the upholding or de-activating of exclusion clauses. The Commissions had denied that the resultant uncertainties would be any greater or more prejudicial to contracting parties than the other methods adopted by the courts in dealing with exclusion clauses (e.g. the doctrine of fundamental breach). Further, they had pointed out that a similar principle had long been in operation in other areas (e.g. restraint of trade, misrepresentation) without producing conspicuous uncertainty or injustice. It had, however, been felt that there should be a total ban on certain types of exclusion clauses.[18]

In general the Act implements these recommendations, thereby introducing a test of "reasonableness"; something which Lord Denning M.R. has often, though generally unsupported, stated to be part of the Common Law.[19]

1. *Clauses in contracts*: Section 3 provides that in contracts where one party is dealing on the other's written standard terms of business or where one party is dealing as consumer:[20]

As against that party, the other cannot by reference to any contract term:

(a) when himself in breach of contract, exclude or restrict any liability of his in respect of the breach; or

(b) claim to be entitled:

(i) to render a contractual performance substantially different from that which was reasonably expected of him, or

(ii) in respect of the whole or any part of his contractual obligation, to render no performance at all,

except in so far as (in any of the cases mentioned above in this subsection) the contract term satisfies the requirement of reasonableness.[21]

It is important to note that since s. 3 applies only between parties to a contract it would appear to be ineffective to protect a principal bailor against clauses contained in a sub-bailment even where, under the principle enunciated by Lord Denning M.R. in *Morris* v. *C. W. Martin and Sons Ltd.*,[22] he is held to be bound by such clauses. Although s. 3 clearly applies to a wide range of bailments, such as storage, work and labour,

---

[18] Ibid., at pp. 26-29.
[19] Most recently in *Levison* v. *Patent Steam Carpet Cleaning Co. Ltd.* [1977] 3 W.L.R. 90 at 94-5.
[20] Section 3(1).
[21] Section 3(2). Note the distinction between delineating and exclusory clauses, ante, p. 918.
[22] [1966] 1 Q.B. 716 at 729-730.

carriage and contracts of hire, the necessity for a contract would seem to exclude all gratuitous bailments as well as sub- and quasi- bailments. Again, not all contracts are within the prohibition. Where the contract is not one involving a consumer, it is necessary that the party against whom the clause is relied on is "dealing on the other's written standard terms of business";[23] a phenomenon which is nowhere defined in the Act. It may well be unclear whether a given contract is in standard form.[24] It also remains to be seen whether a court will be prepared to hold outside the ambit of s. 3 a cleverly constructed clause which, while achieving an end clearly outlawed by the spirit of the section, does so in a way not caught by the words of that section. Although s. 13[25] gives "exemption clause" an extended meaning, no amplification is provided as to the sort of term which will satisfy the description in s. 3(2)(b), and it is possible to envisage lengthy disputes as to whether the contractual performance which has been rendered differs substantially from the consumer's reasonable expectation.[26]

Section 7 governs cases where the possession or ownership of goods passes under or in pursuance of a contract (not being one of sale or hire-purchase).[27] It thus covers the following bailments: contracts of hire, contracts of exchange and contracts of work and labour—even, apparently, where the materials remain the property of the bailor throughout.

In favour of a person dealing as consumer under such a transaction, any term of the contract which purports to exclude or restrict liability for breach of obligation arising under the contract in respect of the goods' correspondence with their description or sample or their quality and fitness for any particular purpose is void.[28] In favour of anyone else such a term is ineffective except to the extent that the reasonableness principle is satisfied.[29] Likewise, those terms are ineffective which are intended to exclude or restrict liability in respect of:

(a) the right to transfer ownership of the goods or give possession; or
(b) the assurance of quiet possession to a person taking goods in pursuance of the contract,

and fail to satisfy the test of reasonableness.[30]

---

[23] Section 3(1).

[24] See, for example, the various sets of "standard form" conditions used from time to time by the defendants in *Smith* v. *South Wales Switchgear Ltd.* [1978] 1 All E.R. 18, and quaere whether the dealing in *British Crane Hire Corporation* v. *Ipswich Plant Hire* [1975] 1 Q.B. 303 was on "written" terms of business.

[25] Post p. 959.

[26] For an example of the sort of clause which would (presumably) fall victim to s. 3 (2), see *Anglo-Continental (Holidays) Ltd.* v. *Typaldos Lines (London) Ltd.* [1967] 2 Lloyd's Rep. 61. Presumably the presence of the clause will itself be one factor to be taken into account in deciding whether the consumer was entitled reasonably to expect a substantially different mode of performance. If, for instance, the clause has actually been drawn to the attention of the plaintiff who has realised its full implications it seems unlikely that the latter will be able to take advantage of this provision, for though the performance is not that which he sought, it is very probably not substantially different from the sort of performance to which he was alerted by the clause.

[27] Section 7(1).

[28] Section 7(2).

[29] Section 7(3).

[30] Section 7(4).

The provisions of s. 7 apply to those obligations which arise by implication or law from the nature of the contract.[31] The Act does not purport to alter the extent of this implication: indeed, s. 7(1) refers to the "effect (if any)" of such terms arising by implication, thereby suggesting that such terms may not exist in some contracts; given the absence of legislation corresponding to ss. 12 to 15 of the *Sale of Goods Act* 1893 governing contracts of sale, it is clearly for the courts to determine the nature of these implied terms.[32] In regard to contracts for work and materials the section was clearly intended to cover the strict liability for non-fitness of materials for their purpose but incidentally it seems also to cover the implied terms that the workmanship itself must be reasonably fit for its purpose and that the work must be performed with due care and skill. This means that, as against a consumer, these terms also cannot be excluded.

The notion of "dealing as a consumer", which is so important in both of these sections, is defined in s. 12(1):

> A party to a contract "deals as consumer" in relation to another party if:
> (a) he neither makes the contract in the course of a business nor holds himself out as doing so; and
> (b) the other party does make the contract in the course of a business; and
> (c) in the case of a contract governed by . . . s. 7 of this Act, the goods passing under or in pursuance of the contract are of a type ordinarily supplied for private use or consumption.

The burden of proof lies on the party claiming that a party does not deal as a consumer.[33] Auction sales and sales by competitive tender are not consumer transactions.[34]

2. *Liability for negligence*: Section 2(2) provides that a contract term or a notice (whether given to persons individually or generally) which purports to restrict or exclude liability for loss or damage to property caused by negligence shall be ineffective except in so far as it satisfies the reasonableness requirement. "Negligence" is, however, quite restrictively defined by the Act. It means the breach:

(a) of any obligation, arising from the express or implied terms of a contract, to take reasonable care or exercise reasonable skill in the performance of the contract;

(b) of any common law duty to take reasonable care or exercise reasonable skill (but not any stricter duty).

(c) of the common duty of care imposed by the *Occupiers' Liability Act* 1957 . . . .[35]

Section 2(2) thus applies to the basic custodial duty of reasonable care imposed on such bailees as warehousemen, dry-cleaners, removal men and private carriers generally, whether they hold as against the

---

[31] Section 7(1).
[32] The Law Commission has begun to review (in W.P. No. 71, 1977) the scope and purpose of such terms with a view to their being put on a statutory basis.
[33] Section 12(3).
[34] Section 12(2).
[35] Section 1(1).

owner by direct or sub-bailment.[36] It may also apply to gratuitous or unrewarded bailees, as well as between borrowers and lenders, if the law now imposes on such parties a duty of reasonable care.[37] It may further apply to operators of car parks even where they are not bailees but mere licensees, in so far as they now appear to owe a duty of reasonable care in respect of damage to (if not theft of) vehicles left on their premises.[38]

Section 2(1) places an absolute ban on contract terms or notices excluding or restricting liability for death or personal injury resulting from negligence. This is of only remote relevance to bailors and bailees as such.[39]

Section 2(3) states that in the case of clauses of either kind the fact that a person has agreed to, or is aware of, it is not, of itself, sufficient to indicate voluntary acceptance of any risk. This endorses the Law Commission's refusal to assimilate a deprivation of rights by notice within the tortious defence of volente non fit injuria.

It is important, at this point, to notice the restrictive effect of s. 1(3). This states that all the provisions so far considered apply only to "business liability" which is defined as "liability for breach of obligations or duties arising:

(a) from things done or to be done by a person in the course of business (whether his own business or another's); or

(b) from the occupation of premises used for business purposes of the occupier."

'Business' is, however, quite widely defined to include—

a profession and the activities of any government department or local or public authority.[40]

Moreover, the Act covers both inadvertent and intentional breaches and liability arising vicariously as well as directly.[41]

3. *The reasonableness 'guidelines'*: The concept of "reasonableness" used in the Act is "explained" in s. 11. The requirement is said to mean that:

> the term shall have been a fair one to be included having regard to the circumstances which were, or ought reasonably to have been, known to or in the contemplation of the parties when the contract was made.[42]

The onus of proof lies on the party asserting that the term is reasonable.[43] That what is important is what was reasonable at the time of contracting and not what is reasonable given all the circumstances at the time of trial is clear. Section 11(3) makes the relevant time for non-contractual notices the time at which liability arose or (but for the

---

[36] Under *Morris* v. *C.W. Martin and Sons Ltd.* [1966] 1 Q.B. 716.
[37] See Chapters 9-11 ante.
[38] Ante p. 214.
[39] It may, however, become relevant as against a lessor of goods if the lessor's duty to supply a reasonably fit chattel is held to be discharged at Common Law by the exercise of reasonable care: ante p. 724.
[40] Section 14.
[41] Section 1(4).
[42] Section 11(1).
[43] Section 11(5).

notice) would have arisen. Two situations are given more detailed consideration. Where the clause seeks to restrict liability to a specified sum particular regard is to be had to:

(a) the resources which he [*the person seeking to restrict liability*] could expect to be available to him for the purpose of meeting the liability should it arise; and

(b) how far it was open to him to cover himself by insurance.[44]

The other special provisions cover clauses caught by s. 7[45] (and also by s. 6[46]). Section 11(2) provides that particular regard should here be paid to the matters specified in Schedule 2. These are such of the following as appear to be relevant:

(a) the strength of the bargaining positions of the parties relative to each other, taking into account (among other things) alternative means by which the customers' requirements could have been met;

(b) whether the customer received an inducement to agree to the term or in accepting it had an opportunity of entering into a similar contract with other persons but without having to accept a similar term;

(c) whether the customer knew or ought reasonably to have known of the existence and extent of the term (having regard, among other things, to any custom of the trade and any previous course of dealing between the parties);

(d) where the term excludes or restricts any relevant liability if some condition is not complied with, whether it was reasonable at the time of the contract to expect that compliance with that condition would be practicable;

(e) whether the goods were manufactured, processed or adapted by the special order of the customer.

B. Fundamental breach

The Report had conceded that there was no ground for interference with the rule that liability for a fundamental breach will be excluded by an exclusion clause if, on its proper and strict construction, the clause is competent to cover the breach; and it had endorsed the principle that such questions are to be decided upon grounds of construction alone. Its concern had been with what has been called the substantive doctrine of fundamental breach, and, in particular, with the rule that, where a contract comes to an end as a result of a breach, exclusion clauses, like other terms, cease to operate.[47]

---

[44] Section 11(4).
[45] Ante p. 955.
[64] Post p. 960.
[47] Ibid., p. 77. It may be noted, in passing, that, by citing as authority for this proposition the statements of Lords Reid and Upjohn in *Suisse Atlantique* at p. 398 and 425 and the decision of the Court of Appeal in *Harbutt's "Plasticine"*, the authors of the Report seem to draw no distinction between the extinction of exclusion clauses in relation to loss suffered after the fundamental breach and consequent termination and their retrospective extinction so as to render them incapable of applying to prior losses, suffered while the contract was still on foot. It has been suggested earlier (p. 938) that it was the failure to draw such a distinction which produced the unsatisfactory decision in *United Fresh Meat Ltd.* v. *Charterhouse Cold Storage Co. Ltd.* [1974] 2 Lloyd's Rep. 286.

The authors of the Report had considered that the continued existence of a substantive doctrine of fundamental breach could run counter to, and impair the operation of, a statutory "reasonableness" principle upon exclusion clauses.

> The object of a reasonableness test is to do justice to both parties and its virtue is its flexibility. If the doctrine of fundamental breach were still to be applied as a rule of law where the contract comes to an end, a party might find that an exemption clause was ineffective even though he could show that the clause was reasonable. This would be a most unreasonable result.[48]

Section 9 is the section intended to cater for the problem posed by such a substantive doctrine of fundamental breach. Section 9(1) states:

> Where for reliance upon it a contract term has to satisfy the requirement of reasonableness, it may be found to do so and be given effect accordingly notwithstanding that the contract has been terminated either by breach or by a party electing to treat it as repudiated.

Clearly, the court's first task remains that of construing the clause. If, on construction, the court finds that the clause does not cover the breach that is the end of the matter. If it does cover the breach, then, given that it is a clause to which the Act applies the test of reasonableness, that test is applied. If it is reasonable it stands, and s. 9(1) is meant to ensure that it stands even in the face of arguments that it cannot be relied on because there has been a fundamental breach which has negated the contract (and, with it, its exception clauses) so that no reliance on any clause in it is possible. It might be thought that, in seeking to do this, s. 9(1) is superfluous. It has been argued above[49] that there is no substantive doctrine of fundamental breach. But basing their views on dicta in *Harbutt's "Plasticine"*,[50] judges have held that there are breaches capable of preventing reliance on exclusion clauses as a defence to past breaches (as opposed to just preventing reliance on them for any future breach after the fundamental one). For instance, in *Eastman Chemical International A.G. v. N.M.T. Trading Ltd. and Eagle Transport Ltd.*,[51] Deputy Judge Tudor Evans Q.C. managed to hold this to be the law[52] by relying on a dictum of Cross L.J. in *Harbutt's "Plasticine"*[53] even though he had clearly been talking about future breaches.[54] In so far as these cases are considered wrongly decided s. 9(1) is ineffective: the provision was clearly inserted lest they represent the law. If this is, indeed, the law, a clause which has been required to be found to be reasonable, and which has been so found, will not be ruled out on this ground. There would seem, however, to be some room for the continued existence of the substantive doctrine of fundamental breach since clauses not required to be reasonable by the Act are not covered by s. 9(1). If these decisions

---

[48] Ibid., p. 77.
[49] Ante p. 934.
[50] *Harbutt's "Plasticine" Ltd.* v. *Wayne Tank and Pump Co. Ltd.* [1970] 1 Q.B. 447.
[51] [1972] 2 Lloyd's Rep. 410.
[52] Ibid., p. 416.
[53] [1970] 1 Q.B. 447 at p. 475.
[54] A similar conclusion was reached after consideration of dicta of Lord Denning M.R. in the same case by Wien J. in *United Fresh Meat Co. Ltd.* v. *Charterhouse Cold Storage Ltd.* [1974] 2 Lloyd's Rep. 286.

do represent the law, there seems to be scope for this part of the common law to apply, though given the rigours of the construction process plus the quite wide range of the Act, it seems to be a very limited scope indeed.

Section 9(2) provides that where there has been affirmation of a contract after a breach, this will not mean that the reasonableness test is not to be applied. In *Wathes (Western) Ltd.* v. *Austin's (Menswear) Ltd.*[55] the Court of Appeal held that the presence of affirmation does not change the character of a breach; the question of construction is just the same as it would have been had there been no affirmation. Now there can be no argument that the reasonableness test does not fail to be considered because affirmation has somehow caused the breach to lose its "fundamental" character.

C. Other provisions

The most important for present purposes of the remaining sections are those which provide against evasion of the new statutory rules.

The term "exemption clause" is defined widely by s. 13 to include clauses:

(a) making the liability or its enforcement subject to restrictive or onerous conditions;

(b) excluding or restricting any right or remedy in respect of the liability, or subjecting a person to any prejudice in consequence of his pursuing any right or remedy;

(c) excluding or restricting rules of evidence or procedure and (to that extent) ss. 2 and 5 to 7 also prevent excluding or restricting liability by reference to terms and notices which exclude or restrict the relevant obligation or duty.[56]

Though this wide definition then covers the case where a party is required to give an indemnity in consequence of his pursuing any right or remedy, sometimes a party may be required to give an indemnity which is not so limited (e.g. where he is required to indemnify against losses which might ensue to a third party from the negligent handling of his property).

Section 4 subjects indemnity clauses to the test of reasonableness. It does not matter whether the person to be indemnified is a party to the contract.[57] The section applies whether the liability:

(a) is directly that of the person to be indemnified or is incurred by him vicariously;

(b) is to the person dealing as consumer or to someone else.[58]

Section 10, which appeared during the passage through Parliament of the Bill, provides against evasion of the statutory provisions by means of a secondary contract.

> A person is not bound by any contract term prejudicing or taking away rights of his which arise under, or in connection with, the performance of, another contract, so far as those rights extend to the

55 [1976] 1 Lloyd's Rep. 14.
56 Section 13(1).
57 Section 4(1).
58 Section 4(2).

enforcement of another's liability which . . . this Act prevents that other from excluding or restricting.[59]

Other sections, albeit sections of importance, are of less immediate interest in a consideration of the law of bailment. Section 5 is concerned with guarantees of consumer goods, setting out to remove the possibility of seemingly providing perfect goods and reducing obligations in respect of them by a subsequent contract of guarantee or a notice of guarantee. Section 6 re-enacts the requirements that ss. 13, 14 and 15 of the 1893 Act and ss. 9, 10 and 11 of the *Supply of Goods (Implied Terms) Act* cannot be excluded as against consumers. Otherwise they can now be excluded only in so far as the new test of reasonableness is satisfied. Section 8 of the Act also has the aim of bringing an already existing reasonableness test under the Act so that the same test applies: this time it is s. 3 of the *Misrepresentation Act* 1967 which sets a reasonableness requirement for clauses purporting to exclude liability for misrepresentation.[59a]

Schedule 2 excludes certain contracts from the Act's provisions and international supply contracts[60] and contracts in which the objective proper law is other than the law of England and Wales[61] are also excluded. Section 28 makes temporary provision for the carriage by sea of passengers.

As well as ss. 15-25 which amend the Scottish law similarly, there are sections dealing with definitions,[62] commencement,[63] citation and extent[64] saving for other legislation,[65] and consequent amendments[66] and repeals.[67]

---

[59] If a bailor is suing a sub-bailee under the rule in *Morris* v. *C.W. Martin & Sons Ltd.* (or under the wider statement of the rule made by Donaldson J. in *Johnson Matthey & Co. Ltd.* v. *Constantine Terminals Ltd. and International Express Co. Ltd.* [1976] 2 Lloyd's Rep. 215) any exclusion clause upon which the sub-bailee might rely is not subjected to the reasonableness test by s. 3, which section covers only clauses excluding or restricting contractual liability. It seems also that s. 10 would be inapplicable: it too covers only exclusion clauses limiting or excluding a contractual liability. Thus, if the bailor were to sue on a proto- or quasi-contractual term in the bailment (for which concept see ante p. 821) an excluding term on which the sub-bailee relied would not be covered by any section in the Act. It is, of course, true that in many cases the action might be one in negligence; in which case s. 2 would operate to impose the reasonableness test on any exception clause relied on in defence.

[59a] See *Howard Marine & Dredging Co. Ltd.* v. *A. Ogden & Sons (Excavations) Ltd.* [1978] 2 W.L.R. 515.

[60] Section 26.

[61] Section 27.

[62] Section 14.

[63] Section 31.

[64] Section 32.

[65] Section 29.

[66] Sections 30 and 31; Schedule 3.

[67] Section 31; Schedule 4.

CHAPTER 26

BAILMENTS AND THIRD PARTIES

In this chapter, we discuss a series of miscellaneous questions which have in common the single denominator that they involve the extent to which the existence of a bailment can affect the rights and obligations of third parties.

I. LIABILITY OF BAILOR TO THIRD PARTIES

When a chattel is bailed and, through misuse or imperfection, causes injury or damage to a party other than the bailee, the bailor's liability to the victim rests solely in negligence. This is so whether the injured party is a servant of the bailee or a mere independent bystander; for if there be neither contract nor bailment between the parties there can be no warranty of safety and no stricter remedy than that conferred by the ordinary law of tort.[1] The third party must therefore prove that the injury in question was foreseeable to the bailor and occurred because of his failure to take reasonable precautions to avert it.

The action will not generally succeed where the alleged act of negligence consists in the misuse of the chattel by the bailee or his servants. The bailor has no effective control over the manner in which his bailee, with an independent possession, employs the chattel and is not vicariously answerable for the bailee's misdeeds because the latter is not generally identifiable as his servant or agent.[2] Thus, to take an obvious example drawn from an American case, a publisher who bails a book-rack to a retailer is not liable if the negligent positioning of the rack in the retailer's shop causes injury to a customer.[3] But to this general rule there

---

[1] Occasionally it may be possible to discern a collateral contract between the bailor and the third party, but this will be unusual, at least when the third party is not simultaneously a bailee. Of course, we do not discount the possibility that the third party may be a non-contractual bailee and as such entitled to the benefit of strict warranties of safety and fitness under the terms of the extended or subsidiary bailment; see *Lovely* v. *Burroughs Corporation* (1974) 527 P. (2d) 557; ante, p. 48; post.

[2] *Smith* v. *Bailey* [1891] 2 Q.B. 403; *Gibson* v. *O'Keeney* [1928] N.I.66; *Wainio* v. *Beaudreault* [1927] 4 D.L.R. 1131; and see further, pp. 109, 235 ante. It follows that in an action by the bailor against a negligent third party for damage to the bailor's immediate or reversionary interest the bailee's contributory negligence is not effective in reducing the bailor's damages, even when bailor and bailee are husband and wife: *Wellwood* v. *King* [1921] 2 I.R. 274: *Berrill* v. *Road Haulage Executive* [1952] 2 Lloyd's Rep. 490; *France* v. *Parkinson* [1954] 1 W.L.R. 581; *Drive-Yourself Lessey's Pty. Ltd.* v. *Burnside* (1959) 59 S.R. (N.S.W.) 391, at 413; *Pierard* v. *Wright* [1933] N.Z.L.R. s. 120; *Krahn* v. *Bell* [1930] 4 D.L.R. 480; *Fletcher* v *Thomas* [1931] 3 D.L.R. 142. American authority, after early flirtations with the opposite view, now seems to accept this principle; see *York* v. *Day's Inc.* (1959) 140 A. (2d) 730.

[3] *Oklahoma Publishing Co.* v. *Autry* (1969) 463 P. (2d) 334.

are exceptions, and it seems that the owner of the chattel will be liable for its negligent operation in at least three cases: when the bailee is acting simultaneously as the bailor's agent, as where he agrees to drive the bailor's lorry from one place to another in return for free transportation for himself and his goods;[4] when the bailor is guilty of personal negligence, such as by bailing a powerful car to a drunken or inexperienced driver or by giving directions for the use of the chattel which are incompatible with the bailee's exercise of reasonable care; and when, despite the description of the contract as one of hire, possession of the chattel and the employment of its operator remain with the owner and do not pass to the hirer. Generally the loan or charter of a complicated machine with a qualified operator will not bring about a change in the operator's service from contractor to customer, and the bailor remains responsible for his negligence.[5]

The third party is more likely to succeed when his injury results from a defect in the chattel itself. As Denning L.J. once observed,[6] this is a straightforward application of the decision in *Donoghue* v. *Stevenson*;[7] and authorities in point can be found which date from the time before that case was decided.[8] Establishing liability is simple enough if it can be shown that the defect was in existence when the chattel was bailed and that the bailor either knew or ought to have known of it. Thus in *White* v. *Steadman*[9] the supplier of a horse, carriage and driver was held liable for injuries caused to the charterer and his wife by the shying of the animal at a traction-engine. Lush J. held that the owner ought to have known of its nervous disposition and that this imputed knowledge cast a duty upon him to warn the plaintiff's wife of the possible danger; a duty which arose independently of contract and could therefore be enforced by her although she was not a party to the original hiring. She was a person contemplated as likely to be in the vicinity of the horse during the period of hire and a responsibility accordingly arose to protect her from foreseeable dangers.

It will be noticed that in *White* v. *Steadman* the owner had retained control of the horse and carriage through his servant, so that the hirer was not technically a bailee. This meant that Lush J. could impose upon the owner a duty to provide a *direct* warning to the non-contracting passenger as to the unsafe character of the animal; and it further enabled him to find for the female plaintiff on the alternative ground that, having accepted her as a passenger in his carriage, the owner was under a duty to take reasonable care to carry her safely. A duty of the latter kind would, of course, make the owner responsible for a defect which developed after the contract was entered into, provided that it was one of which he knew or ought to have known. But when the chattel passes entirely out of the owner's control and possession as well as use is given

---

[4] Cf. *Roufos* v. *Brewster and Brewster* [1971] 2 S.A.S.R. 218; ante, p. 243.
[5] Ante, p. 246 et seq.
[6] *White* v. *John Warwick & Co. Ltd.* [1953] 2 All E.R. 1021, at 1025-1026 (obiter).
[7] [1932] A.C. 562 (H.L.) Cf. *Hill* v. *J. Crowe Ltd.* [1978] 1 All E.R. 812.
[8] E.g. *Hawkins* v. *Smith* (1896) 12 T.L.R. 532; *Oliver (or Chapman)* v. *Sadler & Co.* [1929] A.C. 584 (ante, p. 354).
[9] [1913] 3 K.B. 340.

to a bailee, the causal link between the defect and the bailor's alleged default becomes substantially harder to establish. In this event, a number of elements in the bailor-bailee transaction may reduce the causal impetus of the bailor's default and thus diminish the third-party's prospects of a successful action against him. The bailor may have warned the bailee of the defect and have relied quite reasonably upon him to transmit this warning to a subsequent user; he may reasonably have contemplated that the bailee would conduct an intermediate test or inspection which would bring the defect to light and enable him to take steps for the protection of third parties; he may have specifically declined responsibility for its upkeep and safety during the period of the bailment; or he may have forbidden its use by anyone other than the bailee. Any one of these factors may exonerate the bailor, provided that their presence establishes his exercise of reasonable care. But it is not enough for him to rely upon the circumspection of others in detecting or rectifying defects of which he was negligently ignorant or which he negligently failed to communicate to the bailee, unless it was foreseeably likely that such a precaution would actually be employed. Nor will the concurrent negligence of the bailee, in misusing the chattel or in failing to inspect or maintain it, necessarily absolve the bailor if the injury results from a defect existent at the time when possession was transferred and still operative at the time of the misadventure.

This is made clear from the decision of Chapman J. in *Griffiths* v. *Arch Engineering Ltd.*[10] The defendants were a firm of sub-contractors, engaged by the plaintiff's employer. They hired a grinding machine from the third-party owners for use in performance of their sub-contract. The speed at which the machine was governed was too great for the size of the wheel and when the plaintiff borrowed the machine to smooth a piece of metal the wheel shattered and injured his hand.[11] Chapman J. held that the liability of the owners of the machine depended upon three preliminary questions: was there a reasonably foreseeable risk that the machine would be used by the plaintiff; if so, was there a reasonably foreseeable risk that he would sustain injury as a result; and were the owners within the category of persons who were under a duty to take reasonable precautions against that risk? The first question could be answered in the negative if the use of the machine by third-parties had been strictly forbidden, or if the machine were of so specialised and technical a nature that the lessor could not reasonably anticipate that it would be used by anyone other than the immediate hirer or his suitably qualified servant. But a simple grinding machine did not fall within this category, and the owners must be taken to have known that other people might use it. Such use was foreseeably likely to cause injury to the user because the machine was governed incorrectly and any reasonably competent engineer would have been alert to the possibility of injury when the machine was brought into contact with an unsecured metal object.

---

[10] [1968] 3 All E.R. 218, at 221-222.
[11] He was not a gratuitous bailee and therefore the old decisions imposing a lower duty on the lender did not apply, even assuming that they were still reliable; ante, p. 356.

It was no defence to show that the officer of the lessor's company who delivered the machine to the hirers was by profession an accountant and did not have sufficient technical knowledge to appreciate the risks involved; the duty on him was that of a competent engineer, and in the absence of his acting in accordance with that standard, or of any reasonable expectation on his part that the hirer would make a sufficiently searching inspection of the chattel to safeguard any subsequent users, the lessors were liable for the injury. The mere existence of an *opportunity* for intermediate inspection by the hirer was not enough, because in this case the machine was wanted for immediate use and both parties to the bailment assumed that it was fit for such use. The result was that they owed a duty to protect the plaintiff from the consequences of the defect and, through failing to do so, were liable in part for his injuries.[12]

In this case, as in *White* v. *Steadman,* the defect was present at the time when the chattel was delivered to the bailee. If the defect does not develop until after the bailment was created, and the bailor has made it clear that he is not to be responsible for the continued safety of the chattel during the bailment, he will normally be exonerated;[13] at least in all but those exceptional cases where he knows he cannot rely upon the bailee to undertake the necessary maintenance in person. Even if the chattel is subject to a material imperfection at the time of delivery, the bailor may be entitled to an apportionment of damages between himself and the bailee if it can be shown that this defect was exacerbated by the bailee's own failure to observe an obligation to maintain the chattel;[14] or, if he warned the bailee about its present imperfections and reasonably expected that his warning would be passed on to a later user.

Occasionally, the injury to the third-party may be caused, not by the condition of the chattel itself or by the manner in which it is used, but by some other event, such as misleading packaging. In *Smith* v. *Southwark Offset Ltd.*[15] the sender of goods by Post Office bulk delivery service despatched them in bags of a greater weight than the Post Office recommended in its circular. A postal worker, assuming that the package was lighter than it was, injured himself while loading it and sued the sender for negligence. It was held that a duty of care not to send bags in excess of the recommended weight would arise only if the Post Office had made it clear to the sender that their statement as to weight was mandatory rather than advisory, and that it was made for the protection of their employees. As neither of these requirements was satisfied in the present case, the plaintiff's action failed.

---

12 Liability was eventually apportioned at 40 per cent against the owners, 40 per cent against the hirers and 20 per cent against the plaintiff himself.

13 *Hopkins* v. *G.E. Ry. Co.* (1895) 12 T.L.R. 25 (C.A.); not strictly a case of bailment but one of landlord and tenant or licensor and licensee.

14 *Hadley* v. *Droitwich Construction Co. Ltd.* [1968] 1 W.L.R. 37 (where liability was apportioned at 50 per cent each between lessor and hirer: post, p. 966). It seems that as a general rule the lessor of a chattel does not undertake its continued maintenance during the lease: post, p. 732, *Hopkins* v. *G.E. Ry. Co.* at 806, where the bailor specifically covenanted to be responsible for repairs and was held liable for the ensuing injury to the hirer's workman; similarly, *Scott* v. *Foley Aikman & Co.* (1899) 5 Comm. Cas. 53; and see *Dube* v. *Algoma Steel Corporation* (1916) 31 D.L.R. 178.

15 (1975) 119 Sol. Jo. 258.

In exceptional cases, the victim may find it possible to exact a stricter duty from the bailor than that of reasonable care. One method, which we have already mentioned, proceeds by use of the collateral contract. If, for instance, the guest of a diner in a restaurant can be said to enjoy a collateral contract with the restaurateur whereunder he is strictly liable for defects in the quality of his food,[16] it may be argued that a similar relationship might be discovered between (for example) the lessor of a vehicle and the hirer's wife, at least if she is present when the vehicle is selected, intends to derive as much benefit from it as her husband, and is a material influence upon his decision to hire it. There is an American case in which the guest passengers of a bailee to whom a car was loaned by a garage while his own car was being repaired were held entitled to enforce a strict warranty of safety and fitness against the garage proprietor;[17] but American refinements to the doctrine of privity are greatly advanced upon those in England or Australia and it is doubtful whether anything so ambitious would be attempted by a Commonwealth Court.

The second possibility involves the use of the bailee's own contractual right of action to recover damages on behalf of all those persons for whose benefit the contract of bailment was made. The prospect of his doing so is supported by a recent decision of the Court of Appeal in a non-bailment case[18] which would, if applied to the context of commercial bailments for the use and enjoyment of chattels, entitle the hirer to recover for such heads of damage as loss of enjoyment and the cost of hiring a replacement chattel, not only on his own behalf but on behalf of his family or of anyone else for whose benefit the contract was made. Indeed, the application of the principle to cases of this kind was expressly contemplated by Lord Denning M.R.[19] It remains to be seen whether this doctrine could be further extended into the field of non-contractual bailments.

It should be noted, in conclusion, that a third-party's action against the bailor of a motor vehicle may be further assisted by the implementation of certain special rules relating to agency and insurance. Thus, irrespective of their common law relationship, the registered proprietor of a licensed hackney carriage is statutorily deemed to be the master of

---

[16] *Lockett* v. *A. & M. Charles Ltd.* [1938] 4 All E.R. 170; *Conklin* v. *Hotel Waldorf* (1957) 161 N.Y.S. (2d) 205. Cf. *Smith* v. *Rae* (1919) 51 D.L.R. 323 (wife unable to proceed in contract against physician engaged by her husband for her benefit; if there had been an act of misfeasance, she could proceed in tort); and see further, Chapter 24; (1977) *The Times* Oct. 8th, 14th.

[17] *Whitfield* v. *Cooper* (1972) 298 A (2d) 50. Cf. *Miller* v. *Hand Ford Sales Inc.* (1959) 340 P. (2d) 181 (Oregon Supreme Court) where on similar facts it was held that the bailment was merely gratuitous and not for the mutual benefit of the parties; that the bailor was under a duy merely to disclose those defects in the car of which he knew; and that no warranty could therefore be implied in favour of the bailee's wife.

[18] *Jackson* v. *Horizon Holidays Ltd.* [1975] 3 All E.R. 92; Yates (1976) 39 M.L.R. 202. Cf. *The Albazero* [1976] 3 All E.R. 129 (ante, p. 187).

[19] [1975] 3 All E.R. 92, at 95, where one of the examples given of its use was the case of the vicar who hires a coach for the church outing. If the bus breaks down and the party are stranded the vicar may, in appropriate cases, be able to recover damages for loss of enjoyment and taxi-fares home on behalf of the entire party.

the driver for purposes of vicarious liability;[20] the driver of a car is presumed to be the servant or agent of the owner until proof of facts to the contrary;[21] and if the owner of a car lends it to another in circumstances where he is not insured in respect of third party risks, the owner is guilty of a breach of statutory duty and can be sued by the victim.[22]

The bailor's rights of recovery against third-party tortfeasors are discussed in Chapter 3.

II. LIABILITY OF BAILEE TO THIRD PARTIES

The bailee's responsibility for injury or loss inflicted upon a stranger to the bailment by the chattel is a simple facet of the ordinary law of negligence or trespass and does not necessitate exhaustive discussion. He will be liable if, through the negligent misuse of the chattel by himself or his servants acting in the course of their employment, a third party is foreseeably injured or property is foreseeably damaged.[23] Often, the bailee's negligence will operate concurrently with that of the bailor and liability will be apportioned to the extent of their respective default; thus, in *Griffiths* v. *Arch Engineering Ltd.*[24] the hirers of the grinding machine were held liable for forty per cent of the plaintiff's total damage because they failed adequately to enquire whether he had sufficient experience before allowing him to use the machine, failed to supervise his use of it, and failed to provide a sufficiently explicit explanation of the evident dangers involved in its employment. A similar apportionment was made in *Hadley* v. *Droitwich Construction Co. Ltd.* where a crane collapsed because of excessive clearance between the hook rollers and the steering wheel. This defect was already in evidence when the crane was delivered to the hirers, at which time the clearance stood at about one eighth of an inch;[25] but through the hirers' breach of their obligation to maintain the crane regularly and to put a competent man in charge of it, the excessive clearance was increased threefold by the time of the accident. The Court of Appeal upheld the County Court judge's apportionment of damages at fifty per cent each, but disagreed with his decision that the hirers could recover the extent of their damages by way of indemnity from the owner. The decision invoked in favour of this indemnity was that

---

[20] *London Hackney Carriages Act* 1843 and *Town Police Clauses Act* 1839; Vaines, *Personal Property* (5th ed.), p. 117. The rule has not been adopted in Australia: see ante, p. 111.

[21] *Barnard* v. *Sully* (1931) 47 T.L.R. 557; and see *Laycock* v. *Grayson* (1939) 55 T.L.R. 698.

[22] *Road Traffic Act* 1972 (U.K.) s. 143: *Monk* v. *Warbey* [1935] 1 K.B. 75; *Martin* v. *Dean* [1971] 2 Q.B. 208; and see *Wagner* v. *Lambert* (1976) 67 D.L.R. (3d) 264. When the driver is driving with the owner's permission and the owner *is* covered by third-party insurance, the bailee generally has the protection of the policy when sued by a third party.

[23] For an early example, see *Wheatley* v. *Patrick* (1837) 2 M. & W. 650, which involved the negligent management of a horse and chaise by the borrower and his passenger; cf. *Dever* v. *South Bay Boom Co.* (1872) 14 N.B.R. 109, where a bailee of timber was held not liable for damage caused by its drifting downstream on to adjoining lands.

[24] [1968] 3 All E.R. 218; ante, p. 936.

[25] The accepted maximum being one-sixteenth.

of the Court of Appeal in *Mowbray* v. *Merryweather*[26] where, as in the present case, the owner had been in breach of his Common Law duty to the hirer to provide a chattel that was reasonably safe and fit for use. But the two decisions were distinguishable because the present facts disclosed an obligation on the hirers' part to service and maintain the machine; and as Winn L.J. observed:[27]

> . . . in a case where A has been held liable to X, a stranger, for negligent failure to take a certain precaution, he may recover over from someone with whom he has a contract only if by that contract the other contracting party has warranted that he *need not*—there is no necessity—take the very precaution for the failure to take which he has been held liable in law to the plaintiff.

Occasionally the question as to third-party liability will depend upon whether the bailment has been effectively terminated and whether the bailor or the bailee was in possession at the material time. This problem arose in a New Zealand case,[28] in which both facts and judgments were finely balanced between two opposing conclusions. The defendants' mare was sent to one Maxted to be covered and was killed without negligence on his part when, after the service had been completed and the mare was being led by Maxted's groom along a road, it suffered a collision with a motorcycle. The wife of one of the defendants heard of the accident and arrangements were made to pull the mare to the roadside; but the creature was left exposed to view and while the same defendant was on his way to remove it the following morning (the accident having occurred at night) the mare was seen by the horses pulling the plaintiffs' chaise. The horses bolted, the chaise was damaged and the plaintiffs sued the defendants for their loss. At first instance, Chapman J. held that by informing the defendants of the accident and by showing that he regarded it as their responsibility to shift the mare, Maxted had effectively renounced possession of the creature before the accident occurred; moreover, there was apparently nothing wrongful in this renunciation because the accident was one for which he was not answerable to them[29] and which terminated the bailment between them. By taking steps to effect such removal and by treating it as their responsibility to do so, the defendants simultaneously resumed possession; and since the mare was therefore in their possession before the mishap occurred, they were under a duty to take reasonable precautions to ensure that it was not a hazard to people using the road. They were in breach of this duty because they knew that the plaintiffs' chaise passed along the road at the material time and because they knew that live horses invariably panic upon sighting dead ones. Even if they could not have removed the horse in time, they could at least have warned the plaintiffs that it was there. On appeal, the Court was evenly divided and the decision of Chapman J. was (on broadly similar grounds) affirmed. The case is a strange one and similar facts are unlikely to recur; but it seems not unreasonable that if the

---

[26] [1895] 2 Q.B. 640; cf. *Southland Harbour Board* v. *Vella* [1974] 1 N.Z.L.R. 526.
[27] [1968] 1 W.L.R. 37, at 43.
[28] *Fly & Young* v. *Percy Bros.* [1916] N.Z.L.R. 837; affirmed sub nom. *Percy Bros.* v. *Fly & Young* [1917] N.Z.L.R. 451
[29] Cf. ante, p. 756.

bailee is under no duty to salvage the chattel (which will by no means always be the case)[30] he is not the party who should be generally answerable if, in its unsalvaged state, it causes mischief to third parties.[31]

If the chattel which is the subject-matter of the bailment belongs to someone other than the bailor, and the bailee refuses to return it to the true owner or acts inconsistently with that owner's title, he may be liable to the owner in detinue or conversion, for a bailee has no better title than his bailor. In cases where an adverse claim is made upon the goods, the bailee should endeavour to interplead.[32]

The bailee's rights of action against third parties are discussed in Chapter 4.

III. BAILMENTS AT THE INSTRUCTION OF INSURANCE COMPANIES

Nowadays it is common for bailments by way of repair to assume a tripartite character[33] and to arise upon the following sequence of events:

A's car, which is insured with the B Insurance Company, is damaged in an accident. At the instruction of B, A obtains estimates for repair and one of these, submitted by C Garage, is accepted by B. Accordingly, A leaves his car with C and instructs them to proceed with the repairs. He knows from previous experience that once the repairs are completed and he has signed the garage's satisfaction note, B will compensate C for the repairs, minus perhaps the amount of any excess liability, for which A will be liable in person.

The first point to note is that A has bailed his car to the garage and that they, as bailees from him, owe him a duty of reasonable care. Even where the full cost of the repairs is to be borne by the insurance company, and nothing is to be paid by the owner of the car in person, the garage should still be regarded as bailees for reward. As we have seen,[34] a person may owe the duties of a bailee for reward to another notwithstanding that his reward emanates from a third party.[35] Acknowledgement that this is an accurate definition of the relationship between an owner and a repairer when the repairer's reward emanates from the owner's insurance company is apparently afforded by a Canadian

---

[30] Cf. *British Crane Hire Corporation Ltd.* v. *Ipswich Plant Hire Ltd.* [1975] 1 Q.B. 303; (ante, p. 756).

[31] For an interesting extension of this point, see *Mills* v. *Continental Parking Co.* (1970) 475 P. (2d) 673, which strongly suggests that the bailee is not his bailor's keeper. An action was brought by the heirs of a deceased pedestrian against the operator of a parking lot for allowing an obviously inebriated driver to recover and drive away in his car; in the course of the journey, the driver killed the pedestrian. It was held that the bailment ended when the car-owner reclaimed possession of the car and paid for the parking services, at which point the operator lost the right to control the car. The action accordingly failed.

[32] See generally, p. 786 et seq., ante.

[33] The word is employed thus by Sachs L.J. in *Brown & Davis Ltd.* v. *Galbraith* [1972] 1 W.L.R. 997, at 1007.

[34] See Chapter 8.

[35] *Morris* v. *C. W. Martin & Sons Ltd.* [1966] 1 Q.B. 716; *Phillip Morris (Australia) Pty. Ltd.* v. *The Transport Commission* [1975] Tas. S.R. 128.

decision[36] and may suggest a method of identifying the obligations of the parties without resort to the notion of a collateral contract. A bailment of this kind is a consensual relationship into which it should be possible to imply terms which are necessary to its commercial efficacy and which are comparable, if not synonymous, with the terms implied in contract. Thus, it may be an implied term of the bailment that the repairer should perform the work with reasonable care and skill and that any materials used in its performance should be of good quality and reasonably fit for their purpose.[37] It would not seem essential to the implication of such terms that there be a contract between the parties.

In fact, it is upon a contractual analysis that the courts have quantified the duties of the owner and the repairer under a tripartite arrangement of this kind. Hitherto, two questions have confronted them: can the car-owner be made to pay the repairer in full if the insurance company becomes insolvent before it has reimbursed the repairer, and can the owner sue the repairer for failing to repair the car competently and within a reasonable time? Not surprisingly, both questions have been answered in favour of the owner. But it has been constantly stressed that each case depends upon its own facts and upon the agreement (if any) that can be inferred from them.

The owner's liability for the full cost of repair was considered and rejected in two cases which arose on the collapse of the Brandaris Insurance Company. In the first of these cases,[38] the car was delivered to the repairers by its owners and correspondence was not entered into between the repairers and the owners' insurance company until almost a month later; but this correspondence invited the repairers to send the residual account, after deduction of the owners' excess contribution under the policy, to the insurers for payment by them, and in an earlier letter to the owners the repairers had shown their willingness to enter into a contract with either them or their insurer by inviting the owners to arrange for instructions to be sent by themselves or by their insurance company. Coupled with the repairers' method of invoicing, which billed the owners only for their excess contribution and a trifling amount relating to the repair of a tyre and invoiced the insurance company for the residual cost, these facts pointed clearly to an exclusive liability on the part of the insurance company for the substantial cost of repair. The Court accordingly refused to hold that the contract was made by the insurance company as agents for the owners (although it conceded that this may occasionally be possible) *or* that there was a contract of indemnity or guarantee between the owners and the repairers, whereunder the owners agreed to step in and discharge the insurance company's liability if it failed to do so in person. The result was that, as between two innocent parties, the loss should lie where it fell.

---

[36] *Saskatchewan Government Insurance Office* v. *Mid-West Motors Ltd.* (1961) 36 W.W.R. 254, at 256-258 (Saskatchewan District Court) citing *Andrews* v. *Home Flats Ltd.* [1945] 2 All E.R. 698 (ante, p. 276).

[37] See p. 821 et seq., and p. 000 ante.

[38] *Godfrey Davis Ltd.* v. *Culling & Hecht* [1962] 2 Lloyd's Rep. 349; both were decisions of the Court of Appeal.

A similar conclusion was reached in the second case,[39] where again there was some delay in corresponding with the insurers and repairs to the car had already been commenced. Both Ormerod and Pearson L.JJ. pointed out that it was clearly in the interests of the insurance company to contract as principals with the repairers because this gave them a greater control over the work that was done.[40] Pearson L.J. further pointed out that such an arrangement carries advantages for the repairer insofar as an insurance company will normally be a more affluent debtor than a private citizen;[41] and for the owner, who need not sign the repairer's satisfaction note (upon which the insurance company's liability is contingent) unless the repairs have been properly completed.

Neither of these decisions decided anything beyond the owner's contractual liability for the full cost of repair;[42] and in *Charnock* v. *Liverpool Corporation*[43] the Court of Appeal held that they were not authority against allowing the owner to recover in contract from the repairer for his failure to perform the work with reasonable skill and despatch. The plaintiff in this case was a union official whose car was damaged in collision with a Corporation bus. He took it to the defendants, of whom he was a regular customer and upon whose reputation he relied. The following morning he met his insurance company's assessor at the garage and an agreement was reached with the repairers as to the work to be done and the price to be paid. There was little doubt that the cost was to be borne (subject to any excess) by the insurance company and not by the plaintiff himself. However, this did not inhibit the implication of a secondary contract between the plaintiff and the repairers whereunder, in consideration for the plaintiff's leaving the car at the garage for repair, the repairers undertook to repair it with reasonable skill and expedition. The plaintiff could accordingly recover damages for their delay in completing the work.

> The practice has grown up that the insurance company shall agree the sum for which it will stand surety and a contract is very often made by the repairer with the insurance company. Let it be so in this case. That does not, in my view, at all rule out the existence of a contract between the person who owns the car and the repairer. The owner takes the car into the repairers and he asks them to repair it, at whatever cost the insurance company will be willing to go to, and everybody knows that the insurance company will within that limit pay. Whether there is any obligation on the owner himself to pay if the insurance company does not is another matter, but I cannot see why there is as regards the owner not a contract on which the repairer is liable, first, if he does not do the work with reasonable skill and, secondly, if he does not do it within a reasonable time.[44]

---

[39] *Cooter & Green Ltd.* v. *Tyrrell* [1962] 2 Lloyd's Rep. 377.
[40] Ibid., at 383, 386.
[41] Ibid., at 386. See also *Brown & Davis Ltd.* v. *Galbraith* [1972] 1 W.L.R. 997, at 1008 per Sachs L.J.
[42] See especially the *Godfrey Davis* case [1962] 2 Lloyd's Rep., at 354 per Upjohn L.J., who pointed out that there was, at least, a contract between owners and repairers for the amount of the excess; cf. Ormerod L.J. at 352-353.
[43] [1968] 1 W.L.R. 1498.
[44] Ibid., at 1502-1503 per Harman L.J.

Charnock's case was approved by the Court of Appeal in *Brown & Davis Ltd.* v. *Galbraith*,[45] a case which again involved the owner's liability to reimburse the repairer for the full cost of repairs. In the present instance, the owner had put in a counterclaim alleging delay and defective workmanship; and it was, perhaps, the convergence of these two claims in one situation that led the judge at first instance to assume that the contracts upon which each was allegedly based must stand or fall together. In the event he awarded the repairers £402 on the claim and the owner £51 on the counterclaim; the owner appealed as to the claim alone, and his appeal was allowed. The Court held that there was nothing inconsistent in allowing an owner to recover contractually from the repairer for inferior workmanship, while simultaneously denying that he was liable in full for the cost of the repairs. So far as concerned the latter question, the insurance company had been involved from a fairly early stage and their correspondence with the repairers showed clearly that, apart from the owner's excess of £25 and a further small towing charge, they were contracting as principals rather than as agents for the owner. The fact that the repairers wrote to the owner after he had taken the car without signing their satisfaction note, stating that unless he returned the note and paid the excess amount they would take action for the entire cost of repairs, did not affect the question. Far more important were the facts that the repairers knew the owner had comprehensive insurance cover and that in their written description of the work and its cost (described as an estimate) they had asked the insurance company to obtain the insured's confirmation (inter alia) of his liability for the excess amount.[46] Moreover, in cross-examination the repairers had stated that they were dealing with the insurance assessor. "The insurance company were going to meet the claim and the owner to meet the excess and the balance of towing".[47] These facts clearly militated against the liability for which the repairers contended, and it was evident that business efficacy demanded no other conclusion:

> In order to imply a promise by the owner to pay for these repairs, it is necessary to say not merely that it would be a businesslike arrangement to make but that any other arrangement would be so unbusinesslike that sensible people could not be supposed to have entered into it. It appears to me that it is very doubtful whether it could be said that it would be a businesslike arrangement to make, and I certainly am not prepared to say that it was so obvious a term that it ought to be implied in order to give business efficacy to the transaction.[48]

> . . . the inference of such an implied contract can, in my judgment, only be drawn if it is a matter of necessary inference, that is to say, if it is an inference which the business realities of the situation really make necessary to make sense of the dealings between the parties so that they can be implemented in a sensible manner. In my judgment,

---

45 [1972] 1 W.L.R. 997. This case arose from the collapse of the Vehicle and General Insurance Company.

46 Ibid., at 1005 per Cairns L.J.

47 Ibid. Cf. Sachs L.J. at 1008, who stressed that one material criterion lies in identifying the party to whom credit was given.

48 [1972] 1 W.L.R. at 1005 per Cairns L.J.

there is not sufficient material to be found either in the documentation in this case or in the oral evidence of the witnesses to support such an inference.[49]

It was left to Sachs L.J. to observe[50] that there was nothing in *Charnock v. Liverpool Corporation*[51] which could be regarded as controverting the decisions in *Godfrey Davis Ltd.* v. *Culling & Hecht*[52] and *Cooter and Green Ltd.* v. *Tyrrell*.[53] It would therefore seem that repairers should take pains to create a distinct and explicit contract with the owner of the vehicle if they wish to enjoy the kind of supplementary indemnity that was rejected in these decisions; and that they should attempt, so far as possible, to minimise their own obligations thereunder. But both the *Trade Practices Act* 1974 in Australia and the *Unfair Contract Terms Act* 1977 in England, impose substantial restrictions upon their power to do so in the field of consumer dealings.[54]

IV. THE TRANSMISSION OF COVENANTS WITH CHATTELS[55]

There is considerable advantage in a rule which enables covenants to run with chattels, and considerable commercial pressure in its favour.[56] The law of real property has long permitted the burden of a restrictive covenant, for example, to be enforced against subsequent alienees of the burdened land;[57] a rule which seems to have been originated as an early form of environmental protection.[58] It would be difficult to advance a similar reason in favour of extending this doctrine to chattels, but other equally compelling reasons of policy can be urged in support of the analogy. Unfortunately, few factors have been more influential in inhibiting the evolution of a doctrine that allows covenants to run with chattels than the supposed parallel with land; for land law has not stood still since the transmission of covenants was first permitted, and its progress has taken it into areas, or required it to assume shapes, which by their very nature are beyond the reach of the law of personal property.

Of course, not every situation in which a covenant is alleged to run with a chattel will involve, either originally or eventually, a bailment. One of the commonest manifestations of the problem occurs in the case of price-fixing agreements, whereunder A will sell a chattel to B on condition that B resell it only above a certain price and extract a covenant from the subsequent purchaser that he will do the same. The Courts have

---

[49] Ibid., at 1006 per Buckley L.J.
[50] Ibid., at 1009.
[51] Ante, n. 43.
[52] [1962] 2 Lloyd's Rep. 349. (ante, p. 969).
[53] [1962] 2 Lloyd's Rep. 377. (ante, p. 970).
[54] Post, pp. 527, 537, 952.
[55] Vaines, *Personal Property* (5th ed.), Chapter 8.
[56] Treitel (1958) 21 M.L.R. 433, at 435, citing Chafee (1929) 41 *Harvard Law Review* 945.
[57] *Tulk* v. *Moxhay* (1848) 2 Ph. 774.
[58] Ibid.; the case was decided at a time of intensive metropolitan development, and it was clearly thought that to enlarge the range of parties against whom, for example, a covenant against building could be enforced, would lead to greater protection of urban amenities.

steadfastly refused to hold the sub-purchaser liable for breach of such covenants at the suit of the original covenantee.[59] The reason for such refusal is, of course, the absence of contractual privity between the parties; but with cases of bailment, it may be that privity of bailment is enough. Although at first sight there seems to be little reason for distinguishing between conveyances of the whole interest in a chattel and conveyances of that limited interest that constitutes a bailee, sufficient justification may be found in the ability of bailment to exist without contract and to arise, for instance, between an owner and a sub-bailee. Between the seller and the sub-purchaser there exists no legal relationship at all.[60] Between the owner and a sub-bailee a certain relationship does exist, and upon this relationship it may be possible to construct certain obligations which transcend the restraints of privity of contract.

A. The priority of the purchaser over an earlier bailee for hire

So far as decided cases are concerned, it is not upon sub-bailments that the notion of transmissible covenants has had the greatest influence, but upon cases in which the ownership of a chattel changes during the subsistence of a contract of hire. The question thus arises: will the purchaser of a chattel, who knows that the chattel is subject to an existing contract of hire made by the former owner, be bound to honour that contract of hire upon acquisition of his ownership? The arguments against permitting him to disregard the prior contract are, of course, considerable; the purchaser may well have acquired the chattel at a lower price in consideration of there being a "sitting tenant"; he may have promised the seller that he will honour the hirer's interest; and it would be inequitable to allow him to evict the hirer if he knew all along that he was there. But generally the question has been rephrased as whether a person (the purchaser) who is not a party to a contract (the contract of hire) can be bound by its terms; and generally, of course, the answer has been "no". Unfortunately, even on this level the answer has not been as consistent or unambiguous as may have been expected.

If a parallel is to be found in the law of land, it might have been thought that this should be drawn from the cases which deal with a tenant's rights against his landlord's assignee. In fact, it is the law relating to outright dispositions between vendor and purchaser that seems to have supplied the greater inspiration. The generally accepted starting-point is a dictum of Knight Bruce L.J. in *De Mattos* v. *Gibson.*[61] In this case a ship was chartered to the plaintiff and subsequently mortgaged to the defendant. The plaintiff alleged that the mortgagee was threatening to sell the ship in violation of his charter-party, and applied for an interlocutory injunction to restrain him from doing so. In allowing the injunction, the learned Lord Justice observed:

[59] *Taddy* v. *Sterious* [1904] 1 Ch. 354; *McGruther* v. *Pitcher* [1904] 2 Ch. 306; *Dunlop* v. *Selfridge* [1915] A.C. 487; *National Phonograph Co. of Australia* v. *Menck* [1911] A.C. 336. The question is now covered by statute: see *Resale Prices Act* 1964, as amended by *Restrictive Trade Practices Act* 1968, s. 9, and *Fair Trading Act* 1973 (England); *Trade Practices Act* 1974, s. 48 (Australia).
[60] Except, perhaps, a duty of care in tort on the part of the seller.
[61] (1858) 4 De G. & J. 276, at 282.

Reason and justice seem to prescribe that, at least as a general rule, where a man, by gift or purchase, acquires property from another, with knowledge of a previous contract, lawfully and for valuable consideration made by him with a third person, to use and employ the property for a particular purpose in a specified manner, the acquirer shall not, to the material damage of the third person, in opposition to the contract and inconsistently with it, use and employ the property in a manner not allowable to the giver or seller.

He went on to remark that this principle should apply alike to moveable and immoveable property; at least, in the former case, when the subject-matter was something valuable such as a trading ship or any other costly machine.[62]

Now this was far from conclusive authority, for a variety of reasons,[63] but it seems to have been endorsed by the Lord Chancellor in a later appeal which went against the charterer on the ground that the mortgagee was guilty of no effective interference[64] and was accepted on several later occasions before the fallacy of equating land and chattels in this context was exposed.[65] The fallacy lay in assuming that in either case the transmission of a covenant depended upon mere notice; for although this was at first the only qualification envisaged in cases of land,[66] later decisions made it plain that something extra must be proved. One requirement was that the covenant must be negative or prohibitive in character;[67] another, far more important to the supposed analogy with chattels, was that the original covenantee must retain adjacent land that was capable of benefiting from the covenant.[68] It was at this point that the law of real property began to leave the law of personal property behind.

That this divergence had occurred, and that covenants could in no circumstances run with chattels without privity of contract, was emphatically endorsed by Scrutton L.J. in *Barker* v. *Stickney*.[69] He cited the example of the price-maintenance cases[70] to show that the application of the rules of real property to chattels was misconceived and "quite impracticable", and he held it to be settled that "the purchaser of a

---

[62] Ibid., at 283.

[63] The other member of the Court refused to commit himself upon the principle outlined by Knight Bruce L.J., and observed that it would require careful consideration; see Turner L.J. at 284. Moreover, the question was raised early in proceedings for an interlocutory injunction, and Wood V.C. (from whom the present appeal was made) was evidently not convinced that such a principle existed. For a lucid account of the course of proceedings in this case, see Cheshire & Fifoot, *Law of Contract* (3rd Australian ed.), p. 537.

[64] (1858) 4 De G. & J. 276, at 295-297, and see the *Swiss Bank* case, ante.

[65] See *The Messageries Imperiales Co.* v. *Baines* (1863) 7 L.T. 763; *Sevin* v. *Deslandes* (1861) 30 L.J. Ch. 457; *The Celtic King* [1894] P. 175; and the authorities cited by counsel in *Lord Strathcona S.S. Co. Ltd.* v. *Dominion Coal Co. Ltd.* [1926] A.C. 108, at 110-111.

[66] *Tulk* v. *Moxhay* (1848) 2 Ph. 774; a case, incidentally which was cited neither to nor by Knight Bruce L.J. in *De Mattos* v. *Gibson* ante.

[67] *Hayward* v. *Brunswick Permanent Benefit Building Society* (1881) 8 Q.B.D. 403.

[68] *L.C.C.* v. *Allen* [1914] 3 K.B. 642; and see *Werderman* v. *Société Générale d' Electricité* (1881) 19 Ch. D. 246. The same rule obtains in Australia: Sackville & Neave, *Property Law* (2nd ed.), passim.

[69] [1919] 1 K.B. 121, at 131-132. The principle propounded by Knight Bruce L.J. was also criticised as too wide by the Court of Appeal in *L.C.C.* v. *Allen* (ante), at 658.

[70] Ante, n. 59.

chattel is not bound by mere notice of stipulations made by his vendor unless he was himself a party to the contract in which the stipulations were made". This rule applied not only to tangible property but to mere choses in action.

In view of this authoritative condemnation, it was somewhat surprising to find the Privy Council applying Knight Bruce L.J.'s dictum a mere seven years after *Barker* v. *Stickney*. The resultant decision, *Lord Strathcona S.S. Co. Ltd.* v. *Dominion Coal Co. Ltd.*[71] became one of the most intensely criticised in the law of contract and has been variously condemned as incoherent and wrong. In this it resembled the House of Lords decision, of similar vintage, in *Elder, Dempster & Co. Ltd.* v. *Paterson, Zochonis & Co. Ltd.*[72]

The facts of the *Lord Strathcona* case were similar to those in *De Mattos* v. *Gibson*,[73] except that the ship in question was mortgaged several times before it was mortgaged in favour of the appellants. Each succeeding mortgagee had actual notice of the respondents' charter-party[74] and in the case of the final mortgage at least there was a specific provision in the bill of sale whereunder the appellants agreed to honour the respondents' interest. The charter-party was a seasonal one, intended to last from 1915 to 1924; the mortgage in favour of the appellants was executed in 1920. By this time the ship had been requisitioned for some three years by the British Government, and although the ship was released from requisitioning in July 1919 the appellants claimed that this had frustrated the charter-party. Alternatively, they argued that they were not bound by its terms because they were not a party to it. The Supreme Court of Nova Scotia dismissed both contentions, and their decision was upheld on appeal.

Lord Shaw, having rejected the plea of frustration, pointed out that since the appellants had not acquired the ship as a free ship it would be unfair to allow them to treat it as if it were.[75] Its acquisition had been sub conditione[76] and the matter could be answered on an analogy with the equivalent rule in cases of land. This equation had been acknowledged in *De Mattos* v. *Gibson* and, despite criticism, that decision was still good law. The principle it created, and the principle laid down by *Tulk* v. *Moxhay*[77] for cases of land, were consonant with justice and did no more than embody a rule of universal fairness and commonsense:

> In the opinion of the Board these views, much expressive of the justice and good faith of the situation, are still part of English equity jurisprudence and an injunction can still be granted thereunder to compel, as in a court of conscience, one who obtains a conveyance or

[71] [1926] A.C. 108.
[72] [1924] A.C. 522.
[73] (1858) 4 De G. & J. 276.
[74] Cf. *Tulk* v. *Moxhay* (1848) 2 Ph. 774, where an intermediate alienee of the land did not have notice of the covenant but the defendant did. It seems that this would be sufficient in a case concerning chattels, provided the rule were otherwise capable of applying, in order to affix the covenant upon an ultimate purchaser.
[75] [1926] A.C. 108, at 117, 120.
[76] Ibid., at 116.
[77] (1848) 2 Ph. 774.

grant *sub conditione* from violating the condition of his purchase to the prejudice of the original contractor. Honesty forbids this; and a court of equity will grant an injunction against it.[78]

It was, however, recognised that over and above the requirement of notice, relief against the purchaser was subject to three main limitations: the remedy sought must be an injunction,[79] the covenant enforced must be negative or restrictive upon use,[80] and the plaintiff must retain an interest in the chattel.[81] All three limitations were translated from the law of real property, and in the case of the third the translation was notably infelicitous. Lord Shaw appears to have thought that a mere interest in the use of the ship[82]—i.e. some commercial stake in its continued availability—would suffice to sustain the analogy with such cases as *L.C.C.* v. *Allen.* Clearly it was impossible to apply the adjacency test necessitated by that decision, and Lord Shaw did not attempt to do so. His equation was based more upon commercial expectation than upon proprietary propinquity. But it must be conceded that the respondents' "interest" in the ship was more extensive than is generally enjoyed by the temporary user of a chattel: the charter-party was a ten-year one and the ship had originally been built to the charterers' own specifications. Nor can it be disputed that the decision itself, and the principle contained therein, were equitable:

> If a man acquires from another rights in a ship which is already under charter, with notice of rights which required the ship to be used for a particular purpose and not inconsistently with it, then he appears to be plainly in the position of a constructive trustee with obligations which a Court of Equity will not permit him to violate. It does not matter that this Court cannot enforce specific performance. It can proceed if there is expressed or clearly implied a negative stipulation.[83]

Nevertheless, the decision left many questions unanswered and many conflicts of authority unresolved. Was the rule confined to cases involving ships? The foregoing statement suggests that it was, but the noun might be employed in a purely illustrative sense, and in *De Mattos* v. *Gibson*[84] Knight Bruce L.J. was clearly not prepared to draw the scope of the principle so narrowly. Was the rule confined to restrictions upon use? It may be that some other restriction might be enforceable without transforming the covenant from negative to positive. And what was meant by the use of the expression "constructive" trustee? At first sight, this suggests that Lord Shaw was deciding the case as a simple exception to the doctrine of privity of contract, via the notion that the ultimate bill of sale created a trust of the appellants' promise not to violate the charter-party, upon which trust the respondents, as beneficiaries, could sue. But if this were so (and on the facts the notion is not an unappealing

[78] [1926] A.C. 120; applied in the *Swiss Bank* case, ante, n. 62.
[79] Ibid., at 119.
[80] Ibid., at 119, 121, 125.
[81] Ibid., at 121-123.
[82] Ibid., at 123.
[83] [1926] A.C., at 125.
[84] (1858) 4 De G. & J. 276, at 283.

one) there would have been no reason to impose the additional demand that the promise should be a restrictive one and that the beneficiary should proceed solely by way of injunction. When Lord Shaw discussed the notion of a trust earlier in his judgment, he seemed to do so principally in the context of an assignment by the charterer;[85] in this event he evidently thought that the charterer could become a trustee of the assignee's rights and that the assignee could therefore sue the ship-owner to enforce them. Elsewhere, Lord Shaw referred to the need to keep separate the various equitable doctrines that might impinge upon a single case.[86] It seems that it was the equitable rule in *De Mattos* v. *Gibson*, and not the distinct concept of the trust, that provided the foundation for the Privy Council's opinion.[87]

This foundation was not strong, and over the next four decades *Strathcona* enjoyed a generally unenthusiastic reception.[88] Even in Canada, where the decision originated and where its reception has perhaps been more favourable than elsewhere, at least one court has refused to extend its principle.[89] But the strongest attack upon its validity came in an

---

[85] [1926] A.C., at 124-125.

[86] Ibid., at 123. Cf. *Binions* v. *Evans* [1972] Ch. 359.

[87] *Port Line Ltd.* v. *Ben Line Steamers Ltd.* [1958] 2 Q.B. 146, at 166 per Diplock J.

[88] *Greenhalgh* v. *Mallard* [1943] 2 All E.R. 234, at 239, per Lord Greene (who thought that the validity of the *Strathcona* and *De Mattos* decisions may need to be reconsidered at an authoritative level); *County Laboratories Ltd.* v. *J. Mindel Ltd.* [1957] Ch. 295, at 297 per Harman J. (who thought that the doctrine in *Tulk* v. *Moxhay* (1848) 2 Ph. 774 could not apply to the sale of chattels); *Clore* v. *Theatrical Properties Ltd.* [1936] 3 All E.R. 483, at 490-491 per Lord Wright (who thought that the rule would be confined to the very special case of a ship under charter-party); *Shell Oil of Australia Ltd.* v. *McIlwraith McEacharn Ltd.* (1944) 45 S.R. N.S.W.) 144, at 150 per Jordan C.J. (who thought that since a contract of hire conferred no proprietary interest upon the hirer, the *Strathcona* decision could be justified only on the grounds that a ship and the right to its use were a peculiarly valuable species of personal property which would accordingly be protected against anyone who took with notice of that right, insofar as was possible by means of an injunction); *Howie* v. *New South Wales Lawn Tennis Ground Ltd.* (1956) 95 C.L.R. 132, at 156 per Dixon C.J. and McTiernan and Fullagar JJ. (who considered that the requirement of adjoining land would alone have been fatal to the charterer's claim in the *Strathcona* case to be entitled to require the mortgagee, on an analogy with the real property decisions, to observe the charterparty, and who expressed no final opinion upon the capacity of covenants to run with chattels); and see further *Toohey* v. *Gunther* (1928) 41 C.L.R. 181, at 208 per Higgins J.; *Tooth & Co. Ltd.* v. *Barker* [1960] N.S.W.R. 51, at 64 per McLelland J.

[89] *Meeker Cedar Products Ltd.* v. *Edge* (1967) 61 D.L.R. (2d) 388, at 395-396 (B.C. Supreme Court) where Seton J. did, however, acknowledge that the *Strathcona* decision was binding him and did not appear to doubt that it was correct. Cf. *Canadian Brotherhood of Railway Transport and General Workers* v. *B.C. Airlines Ltd.* [1971] 1 W.W.R. 39 (B.C. Supreme Court) where *Strathcona* was applied so as to bind the acquirers of a commercial enterprise to agreements made by the previous management with the plaintiff union. Dohm J. remarked (at 44) that Canadian courts "will not apply rigid common-law doctrines in the field of labour relations, in the face of what is plainly equitable, reasonable and necessary". He cited the leading United States authority of *John Wiley & Sons Inc.* v. *Livingston* (1964) 376 U.S. 543, where the Supreme Court had held that "the disappearance by merger of a corporate employer which has entered into a collective bargaining agreement with a union does not automatically terminate all rights of the employees covered by the agreement, and that, in appropriate circumstances, present here, the successor employer may be required to arbitrate with the union under the agreement". At first sight, the decision of the British Columbia Court of Appeal in *Marquest Industries Ltd.* v. *Willows Poultry*

English decision at first instance. *Port Line Ltd.* v. *Ben Line Steamers Ltd.*[90] again involved the sale and subsequent requisition of a ship under charter. The contract was for a period of thirty months and took the form of a gross time charter between the plaintiff charterers and Silver Line, the current owners of the ship. Later the ship was sold to the defendants and chartered back to Silver Line for the residue of the plaintiffs' charter-party; a course of events of which the plaintiffs were informed, and to which they raised no objection. Later still the ship was requisitioned by the Ministry of Transport and the defendants, as owners, were paid compensation. The plaintiffs then claimed to be entitled to share in this compensation, on the ground that the defendants were bound to honour the original charterparty and were therefore liable for its breach. The defendants countered by alleging that the charterparty was frustrated and that since they were, in any event, strangers to it they could not be bound by its terms. Diplock J. held against them on the first argument[91] but found for them on the second. He advanced a series of reasons for holding that the decision in the *Lord Strathcona* case should not be followed; chief among them were the unsound doctrinal basis of the decision and the extreme difficulty of extracting a coherent ratio from it. But in addition to holding that the decision was wrong, Diplock J. discovered no fewer than four reasons for refusing to apply it on the facts before him. These were as follows:—

(i) In *Strathcona*, the defendants had full actual knowledge of the existence and terms of the plaintiffs' charterparty; in the present case the defendants merely knew of its existence and were not fully aware of its terms. More especially, the present defendants were unaware that the charterparty did not contain a clause (as did their own with Silver Line)

Farms Ltd. (1969) 1 D.L.R. (3d) 513, reversing (1967) 63 D.L.R. (2d) 753, appears to sanction the enforceability of a covenant to pay a certain sum upon termination of an agreement against the successors in title to the original covenantor. In fact, the covenant was a highly beneficial one to the successors because it enabled them to terminate the agreement upon payment of compensation for the installation of certain machinery by the covenantee on the premises, and the profits they could make elsewhere far exceeded the cost of such compensation. At first instance Ruttan J. held that the new owners were strangers to the agreement and could not cancel thereunder; on appeal, this point was held to be immaterial because it was the company itself that was being sued. The case was accordingly approached as one which illustrated that parties to a contract may provide that it shall be terminated upon the occurrence of any event, including the decision of someone who is not a party to that contract: see especially (1969) 1 D.L.R. (3d) 513, at 518 per Bull J.A., and cf. Robertson J.A. dissenting, at 527-528, 532. Finally, in *General Securities Ltd.* v. *Brett's (Lillooet) Ltd.* (1956) 5 D.L.R. (2d) 46, a principle akin to that in *Strathcona* was held to protect the holder of a lien from an action by the true owner of the chattel, even though the lien-holder had apparently known that the original bailee who left the chattel with him for repair was forbidden to create a lien. Manson J. suggested that to subject the defendant to the inter-mediate bailee's limitation of authority would amount to binding him by a contract to which he was not a party. Quaere, however, whether this can be reconciled with the requirement that the lien-holder's original possession must be lawful; post, p. 1009.

---

[90] [1958] 2 Q.B. 146; (1958) 74 L.Q.R. 338; Treitel (1958) 21 M.L.R. 433; MacCormack (1959) 3 *Sydney Law Review* 395.
[91] The requisitioning lasted for only three months at a time when there were ten left to run.

whereunder the agreement was to be automatically frustrated upon requisition of the vessel; and they did not (as in the *Strathcona case*) take the vessel from Silver Line on the express condition that the plaintiffs' rights were to be honoured.[92]

(ii) The *Strathcona* case, if it possesses any validity at all, merely confers upon the aggrieved contracting party the right to sue for an injunction against interference with his rights. In the present case, the remedy sought was not an injunction but monetary compensation.[93]

(iii) Likewise, *Strathcona* is confined to cases in which the defendant third-party has broken the relevant agreement; the present defendants had not broken the charterparty and were accordingly beyond the putative ambit of the rule.[94]

(iv) The present case involved a gross time charter, and not a charter by demise. It therefore gave the plaintiffs no right in the vessel, and no right to its possession. Without such a proprietary or possessory interest, they were reduced to asserting against the defendants a mere contractual right, enshrined in an agreement to which the defendants were not parties. Such a demand contravened the doctrine of privity and must inevitably fail.[95]

Diplock J. examined in some depth the endeavours of the Privy Council to identify the plaintiffs' interest in the vessel, for without an interest of some kind there could be no application by analogy of the decisions which enabled restrictive covenants to run with land. He concluded, reluctantly, that the interest perceived by the Privy Council was little more than a commercial expectation or advantage; and that the word seemed to have been used more colloquially than legally throughout Lord Shaw's opinion. According to Diplock J. the projection of a pre-existing contractual relationship upon a subsequent purchaser of the subject-matter of that contract could not be achieved merely by showing that the plaintiff had a contractual right that the chattel shall be employed in a particular way, and that he stood to lose financially if performance of the contract were rendered impossible by the refusal of a non-party to be governed by its terms.

> If . . . the ship is the "subject-matter" of the covenant of which the violation by another is to be restrained, it is difficult to see in what sense a charterer under a gross time charter has an interest in that subject-matter except in the broad sense that it is to his commercial advantage that his convenantor should continue to use the ship to perform the services which he has convenanted to perform. But the time charter is a contract for services. The time charterer has no proprietary or possessory rights in the ship, and if the covenantee's commercial advantage in the observance of the covenant is sufficient to constitute an interest in the chattel to which the covenant relates, it is difficult to see why the principle does not apply to price-fixing cases . . . The Board explain cases like *Dunlop's* case . . . as cases where the plaintiff had no interest in the subject-matter of the con-

---

[92] [1958] 2 Q B. 146, at 167-168, 172.
[93] Ibid., at 168, 172-173.
[94] Ibid., at 172.
[95] Ibid., at 163-164, 166-167.

tract. They say that the charterer has and will have during the maintenance of the charterparty "a plain interest" (in the ship) "so long
as she is fit to go to sea".[96] Plain though it be, if the expression
"interest" is used colloquially, the Board nowhere explain what the
legal nature of that interest is.[97]

Diplock J. clearly thought that the *Lord Strathcona* case was an
aberration; an exercise in doctrinal necromancy which should, like the
doctrine it purported to exhume, be decently interred.[98] Two factors
militate against this conclusion and suggest that the *Lord Strathcona* case
may still survive in some vestigial form. The first is the authority of the
decision itself, as an opinion of the Privy Council. The second is the
elaborate set of distinctions which Diplock J. drew between the generalisations upon which the case was decided and the limits of its own facts.
Support for some form of protection against the incursions of third-party
purchasers upon established contractual rights is afforded by a number
of writers[99] and is undoubtedly desirable. The problem lies in squaring
this protection with the conceptual integrity of privity of contract. With
the proliferation in recent years of methods for circumnavigating that
doctrine, it may be that the necessary reconciliation can finally be
achieved.[1]

Certainly the hirer of a chattel is in a more favourable position than
the time-charterer. Although he acquires no proprietary interest,[2] he will
generally enjoy possession or at least the immediate right to possess.
Either of these may qualify as the "possessory interest" envisaged by
Diplock J. as sufficient to safeguard the contracting party against the
incursions of a subsequent alienee.[3] Admittedly, no concluded opinion
was expressed upon the adequacy of such an interest, but it has been
argued that its protection would accord with the doctrine nemo dat quod
non habet. Thus, it is said that the lessor who has already conferred
possession or an immediate right of possession upon a hirer cannot subsequently confer a superior right of possession upon a third-party; for
in so doing he purports to alienate an interest he no longer has.[4]

If this is true, there would indeed be a distinction between possessory
rights and other purely contractual rights which have as their subject-
matter the use or deployment of a chattel. Possessory rights would attach
to the chattel itself and could not generally be pre-empted or usurped
by any subsequent disponee. Whether they could be lost upon alienation
at all would presumably depend upon whether they are legal or equitable
in character; a prior legal estate prevails against the world whereas a prior
equitable estate prevails only against all except a bona fide purchaser

[96] [1926] A.C., at 121, 123.
[97] [1958] 2 Q.B. 146, at 166-167.
[98] Ibid., at 165. But it was revived in the *Swiss Bank* case, ante, n. 62.
[99] See Treitel, op. cit. and the *Swiss Bank* case, ante.
[1] E.g. *Jackson* v. *Horizon Holidays Ltd.* [1975] 3 All E.R. 92; *The Eurymedon*
[1975] A.C. 154; *Beswick* v. *Beswick* [1968] A.C. 58.
[2] *Australian Provincial Assurance Co. Ltd.* v. *Coroneo* (1938) 38 S.R. (N.S.W.) 700;
Shell Oil Co. of Australia Ltd. v. *McIlwraith McEacharn Ltd.* (1944) 45 S.R.
(N.S.W.) 144, at 150.
[3] Ante, p. 979.
[4] Thorneley (1974) 13 J.S.P.T.L. 150, at 151.

for value of the legal estate without notice. If the sole method of protecting the hirer's interest were the equitable doctrine laid down in *Strathcona* it may seem logical to identify his interest as an equitable one; certainly in *Port Line* Diplock J. did not expressly contemplate that even a possessory right should survive against a purchaser without actual notice. But if the right of possession is classified as a legal interest, notice would seem inessential. The difficulty is that possessory rights straddle the boundary between property and contract and are not fully comparable, for instance, with the right in rem which arises by operation of law in the case of a workman's lien.[5] There can be little doubt that if the owner of a chattel subject to such a lien sells it to a third party, the third party takes subject to the lien whether he is aware of it or not. The trend of decisions suggests that in the case of a simple contract of hire it would be necessary to prove notice on the part of the purchaser in order to protect the hirer, even when he is in possession at the material time.[6] However, it may well be preferable to allow the hirer to assert his rights against the purchaser irrespective of notice, whenever the contract of hire has conferred upon him possession of the chattel or the immediate right to possess. Such an approach would apparently accord with the exercise of the hirer's remedies in tort against the third-party usurper. If the hirer has possession, the purchaser who retakes the goods in violation of the lease will be liable in trespass or conversion regardless of whether he is aware of the interest he is usurping. If the hirer has merely an immediate right to possess, it seems that the purchaser may still be liable in conversion,[7] because no later transaction between lessor and purchaser can deprive the lessee of what he has already been given. It might, therefore, be anomalous if notice of the potential hirer's right to possess were unnecessary to render the purchaser liable in damages for conversion and yet essential to the purchaser's duty to honour the contract of hire; for liability in conversion may itself depend upon the prevailing validity of the hirer's right to possess against an equivalent right purportedly transferred from the lessor to the purchaser. If the innocent purchaser does not acquire such a right merely by lack of notice that it has already been distributed elsewhere, the right that *has* been previously distributed would appear to prevail against him for all purposes and not merely for the purposes of the law of tort. This view accords, perhaps, with our earlier suggestion that an immediate right to possess should entitle the person upon whom that right is conferred to sue for wrongs committed upon the chattel, to the extent of his limited interest.[8] It does not create a right in rem in the full sense, but it does recognise both possession and the immediate right to possess as interests whose protection goes

---

[5] *Tappenden* v. *Artus* [1964] 2 Q.B. 185, at 194-195 per Diplock L.J. See also *General Securities Ltd.* v. *Brett's (Lillooet) Ltd.* (1956) 5 D.L.R. (2d) 46, at 53 and, in relation to pawns, ante, p. 65.

[6] Thus in *Shell Oil Co. of Australia Ltd.* v. *McIlwraith McEacharn Ltd.* (1944) 45 S.R. (N.S.W.) 144, at 150, Jordan C.J. said that the hirer's interest was purely contractual, and regarded maritime vessels as a special exception to the ordinary contractual principle that a person who is not a party to a contract cannot be bound by its terms.

[7] Thorneley, loc. cit.

[8] See Chapter 4.

beyond the ordinary rules of contract and the ordinary remedies in tort. Thus a bailment, whether consummated or unconsummated by the delivery of possession, may be said to produce an attenuated species of property.

Even if the hirer cannot be said to enjoy a legal interest capable of transmission against third parties without notice, it seems clear from *Port Line* and *Strathcona* that his interest may prevail in cases where the subsequent purchaser has actual notice of its terms. Beyond this point, however, it is difficult to elicit any concrete rules. It may be that the purchaser must have specifically promised, in the conveyance of the chattel, that he would honour the hirer's interest; and that without possession or the immediate right to possess the plaintiff has no projectable interest in the chattel. The answer depends to a large degree upon whether the factual limitations placed upon the *Strathcona* case of Diplock J. are alternative or cumulative; but the emphatic reassertion of the need for some extra-contractual interest suggests that nothing short of a possessory right will suffice. Thus, if a society agrees to charter a particular bus and driver for its annual outing, and the bus is sold to a third party on the morning the trip is due to begin, mere notice of the pre-existing contract would not bind the purchaser to an observance of its terms. Such a conclusion could at least be expected to follow in England; in Australia, the protection of the charterer may be rendered additionally difficult by judicial opinion that the plaintiff must enjoy a *proprietary* interest[9] and that the *Strathcona* principle should in any event be confined to cases involving ships.[10]

Of course, the hirer may pursue other remedies to safeguard his interest. If, in the contract of sale, the purchaser has covenanted not to interfere with the contract of hire, the seller himself may be persuaded to bring an action for breach of this covenant and may be entitled to recover, as under a contract made partially for the hirer's benefit, damages for injury to the hirer's interest.[11] Alternatively, he may be entitled to specific performance.[12]

The hirer may also have an action in tort; for trespass or conversion if the purchaser violates a possessory right over the chattel, or for unlawfully procuring a breach of the lease if the purchaser has induced the lessor to sell in knowing contravention of the contract.[13] A further remedy may lie against the lessor for breach of the implied covenant of quiet enjoyment;[14] the prospects of success are more favourable in modern jurisdictions which restrict the lessor's right to exclude liability for

---

[9] *Tooth & Co. Ltd.* v. *Barker* [1960] N.S.W.R. 51, at 64; cf. *Toohey* v. *Gunther* (1928) 41 C.L.R. 181.

[10] *Shell Oil Co. of Australia Ltd.* v. *McIlwraith McEacharn Ltd.* (ante), at 150. Cf. Cheshire & Fifoot, *Law of Contract* (3rd Australian ed.), p. 541, where it is suggested that the principle may also apply in the analogous case of aircraft; and see ante, n. 88.

[11] Cf. *Jackson* v. *Horizon Holidays Ltd.* ante.

[12] Which according to *Swiss Bank* (ante) creates an equitable interest.

[13] For discussions of the use of the remedy in this context (which will not be examined in detail) see Treitel, op. cit.; Vaines, op. cit., pp. 146, 156.

[14] Ante, p. 721 et seq.

breach of the covenant[15] and recognise, apparently, the cause of the disturbance need not be existent at the time of the original contract in order for the hirer to sue.[16] But of course the lessor may have disappeared, or he may have persuaded the hirer to accept only such limited rights of possession as he was personally entitled to confer.

In exceptional cases it may also be possible to persuade the court that a substitutional relationship of bailor and bailee has arisen between the original lessee and the subsequent purchaser. Thus, if the purchaser agrees initially to accept the hirer as a bailee with a safeguarded interest, there may be said to arise some obligation, or reverse attornment, whereunder the "bailor" is prohibited from subsequently denying the bailee's title. Certainly it would be unfair if the bailee were liable at the suit of the purchaser for such wrongs as negligent damage to the chattel, while enjoying no reciprocal advantage from the relationship which gave rise to the duty. It may be argued that the relationship of bailor and bailee would itself depend upon the hirer's having attorned to the purchaser; but the bailee's duty of care would seem to be unaffected by this requirement, for the alternative view would necessitate any action for injury to the chattel to be brought by the original lessor. Provided the hirer voluntarily continues in possession of a chattel which he knows to belong to the third party, and provided the third party takes the chattel with a similar initial acquiescence in the hirer's interest, it should be permissible to argue the existence between these parties of an implied bailment upon terms: the relevant term in the bailee's favour being the security of his tenure. A similar phenomenon may be observed in cases where goods in the possession of a warehouseman are sold to a third party; once the warehouseman has attorned, the third party is bound by the exclusory conditions in the original contract of bailment.[17] Admittedly, these cases are contractual in character and do depend upon an act of attornment; but even if the latter preliminary is imposed upon the hirer (who is in a very different commercial position from the professional warehouseman of goods) the existence of a contract between him and the purchaser would not seem essential to the transmission of restrictive duties against the purchaser himself. A bailment may exist without a contract, and a non-contractual bailment may yet contain enforceable promissory terms. Sometimes, as in the case of a sub-bailment, these terms may arise from a promise which the succeeding bailee has given to an intermediary;[18] a similar enlargement of duty should therefore be capable of applying as against a substitutional or succeeding bailor. The purchaser who undertakes (at least, with the consent of the bailee) to honour the terms of an existing bailment should accordingly be bound by those terms; they are among the conditions upon which he has defined and assumed his status as bailor, and he should not be entitled to enjoy the beneficial aspects of that status without submitting to its burdens.

[15] *Trade Practices Act* 1974, ss. 68, 69(1)(b) (Australia); *Unfair Contract Terms Act* 1977, s. 7(4) (England).
[16] *Microbeads A.C.* v. *Vinhurst Road Markings Ltd.* [1975] 1 All E.R. 529 (a case of sale).
[17] Ante, p. 851; and see Weir (1977) 36 C.L.J. 24, at 27.
[18] Ante, p. 821 et seq.

This subjection is not an extension of the decision in *Halsall* v. *Brizell*[19] into the realm of personal property, nor is it dependent upon a contract between the parties; rather, it depends upon the existence (in implied or constructive form) of a bailment, a concept which provides an essential connecting relationship, within which necessary terms can be constructed or implied. On this approach, there may be no reason to limit the hirer to the enforcement of restrictive covenants; and, as we hope to have shown, there should be grounds for enforcing positive promissory obligations upon the bailee.

B. The alienation of the bailor's interest under contracts of hire-purchase

It has long been acknowledged that a contract of hire-purchase entails more than the simple lease of a chattel coupled with a separate option to purchase. Although this analysis has not infrequently been made to answer particular legal problems, the predominant conception of hire-purchase is not so much as a specialised form of bailment as a delayed contract of sale.[20] One manifestation of this lies in the judicial treatment of third-parties who intervene and discharge the outstanding debt owed by the hirer; usually because the hirer has become unable to discharge the debt in person. At first sight, this would seem to constitute a purchase of the chattel by the third party and therefore to raise problems of the kind discussed in the preceding subsection. But if the contract of hire-purchase is still, despite the hirer's default, subsisting at the time of payment, it is clear that the option to purchase belongs exclusively to him. Accordingly, it has been held that any such payment is deemed to be made on behalf of the hirer and operates to vest the full title to the chattel in him.[21] The party discharging the debt has therefore no right to possess the chattel and must rely upon a personal enforcement of the debt assigned to him by the original bailor. In one unreported case, the Court of Appeal went so far as to hold that this conclusion should apply although the hirer had wrongfully disposed of the chattel prior to the discharge of his debt.[22] It is difficult to understand why the hirer's option to purchase was not forfeited and why full ownership had not re-vested in the owners to be disposed of as they desired.[23]

C. Other cases

Elsewhere, we have discussed at length the use of the relationship between an owner and a sub- or quasi-bailee to create terms, or covenants, which may be enforceable without resort to the contractual relationships enjoyed by each of them with the intervening party.[24] Thus, instead of a chain of indemnity covenants, a restriction on use may be made directly actionable as between the parties at each extremity of an extended relationship, if such a restriction forms an essential part of the considera-

[19] [1957] Ch. 169.
[20] Vaines, op. cit., p. 374 et. seq.
[21] *Bennett* v. *Griffin Finance Ltd.* [1967] 2 Q.B. 46; *Snook* v. *London & West Riding Investments Ltd.* [1967] 2 Q.B. 796, at 797.
[22] *Hodge Industrial Securities Ltd.* v. *Hynes* (1971), 7th October; Vaines, op. cit., p. 410.
[23] See *Bennett* v. *Griffin Finance Ltd.* [1967] 2 Q.B. 46, at 50 per Winn L.J.
[24] Ante, p. 821 et seq.

tion for the sub-bailment or a condition upon which the sub-bailee's possession was assumed. On this analysis, which admittedly has not been advanced before a court in England or Australia to date, the bailor would be entitled not merely to obtain an injunction against misuse of the chattel but to gain damages for breach of the covenant. A right of this kind would, of course, be particularly necessary in cases of short-term sub-lease or sub-borrowing, where the damage is done before the owner knows that it is even threatened. But the principle may be extended to include positive as well as negative obligations: thus in a bailment by way of sub-lease, a covenant of reasonable fitness may run with the chattel and be enforceable against the owner by both the original and the subsidiary lessee,[25] while under a sub-bailment for work and labour covenants of reasonable skill and reasonable fitness of materials may likewise apply as between the owner and the ultimate bailee.

The operation of exclusion clauses within a relationship of sub-bailment may similarly be seen as an example of the transmission of covenants with chattels. Thus, it is said that if the owner of goods bails them on certain terms to a principal bailee, and authorises the principal bailee to sub-bail the goods on equivalent terms, the owner will be bound by those terms as against the sub-bailee although there is no contractual relationship between them.[26]

While some authorities have seen this as an operation of the doctrine volenti non fit injuria, it is clear that the two principles are distinguishable; indeed, successive Law Commission Working papers have regarded the non-contractual consent to exclusions of liability and the consent to the risk of an event against which exclusion may be sought as subjects to be given independent treatment.[27] An alternative rationalisation may be found in the notion of a transmissible immunity; the owner covenants not to exact full liability from any person who lawfully and upon the conditions specified in the covenant comes into possession of the chattel, and possession of the chattel in these circumstances serves to transmit the benefit of the covenant. Admittedly, the analogy is not a perfect one because the sub-bailee's immunity may not depend upon total identity of covenant between the owner and the principal bailee on the one hand, and the owner and himself on the other; moreover, a recent decision suggests that the sub-bailee may protect himself by a central definition of his responsibilities in the contract with the intermediary, regardless of whether the owner has given his consent to that definition or not.[28] But this is a separate doctrine; and there is much to be said for the view that an immunity against suit may be attached to the chattel by the owner and invoked by anyone who later obtains the required possessory qualification.

[25] Cf. *Lovely* v. *Burroughs Corporation* (1974) 527 P. (2d) 557 with *Southland Harbour Board* v. *Vella* [1974] 1 N.Z.L.R. 526; and see the discussion of *Penfolds Wines Pty. Ltd.* v. *Elliott* (1946) 74 C.L.R. 204 ante, p. 147.
[26] Post, p. 1000 et seq.
[27] E.g. Law Commission No. 79 (Exemption Clauses) (1975); Working Paper on Liability to Trespassers (1971); cf. Furmston (1960) 23 M.L.R. 373, at 386 et seq.; Coote (1977) 36 C.L.J. 18-20.
[28] *Johnson, Matthey & Co. Ltd.* v. *Constantine Terminals Ltd.* [1976] 2 Lloyd's Rep. 215; ante, p. 819; post, p. 1004.

A further potential example may be drawn from the realm of liens. A lien may be created by a bailee with authority to do so.[29] There is no resulting contract between the lien-holder and the owner but the authority granted to the intermediate bailee operates to support the lien-holder's proprietary right to the chattel, and again resembles the passing of the benefit of a promise by the owner, attached to a particular chattel. Of course, liens are not fundamentally consensual animals but arise by operation of law; moreover, a total absence of actual authority on the part of the bailee may not prove fatal to the lien, if he enjoyed an ostensible authority to create it. But no lien can arise without a lawful possession and no party can assert a lien if he knew at the time when possession was transferred to him that the owner had forbade its creation. Thus, even in its most non-consensual phases, the third-party lien does bear some resemblance to a beneficial right which originates in an implied or constructive covenant by the owner and can move, along with the chattel to which it is allied, in favour of a subsequent, lawful possessor.

To some extent, the preceding illustrations are oddities of the law. Some of them may fit into several legal categories; others may fit into none. But it may be that a denominator can be found in their recognition, however qualified, of a doctrine that covenants may occasionally run with chattels. Such a doctrine seems especially apt amidst the possessory interests and the consensual, albeit non-contractual, relationship that can exist between the parties to a bailment.

V. EXCLUSION CLAUSES AND THIRD PARTIES[30]

Contracts are not always performed exclusively by the contracting parties. In commercial life, it is clearly essential that a large organisation should be entitled to delegate performance of its contractual duties to servants, agents or even independent contractors. As strangers to the original contract, such employees will encounter difficulty in claiming the protection of any exclusion clauses contained therein. In this section we discuss some of the methods by which such protection may be achieved.

Of course, this problem is not peculiar to the law of bailment. It may arise in cases of passenger carriage, or in cases where neither the original contractor nor his deputy acquires possession of the goods that are the subject-matter of the contract. But many of the authorities do involve the vicarious performance of a contract of bailment by a servant or agent of the bailee, and others raise questions as to the existence of special principles which may protect the sub-bailee other than by contract in an action brought by the owner.

The general rule is straightforward. No person who is a stranger to a contract can take advantage of its terms, whether it is expressed to be for his benefit or not; he cannot sue upon them and he cannot invoke

---

[29] Post, p. 1008, et seq.
[30] Battersby [1975] *University of Toronto Law Journal* 371; Rose (1975) 4 *Anglo-American Law Review* 7; Reynolds (1972) 88 L.Q.R. 179, and 464; (1974) 90 L.Q.R. 301; Coote (1974) 37 M.L.R. 453; Palmer [1974] J.B.L. 101, and 220.

them in his defence.[31] Thus if a servant or agent, while assisting in the performance of a contract between his master and the plaintiff, negligently injures the plaintiff or damages his goods, he will be directly liable at the suit of the plaintiff and cannot shelter behind the protective provisions contained in his employer's contract. The same conclusion applies a fortiori when the defendant is not assisting in the performance of the contract but is merely performing some independent act, unconnected with any duty arising thereunder.

The general principle has been applied so as to enable the plaintiff to recover in full from a negligent employee in a wide variety of cases. They include an action for negligence against the master and boatswain of a ship, by a passenger whose sole contract was with the shipping company who employed them;[32] an action for negligence against the driver of a bus, by a passenger in another bus who was employed by the same company and was travelling on a free pass at the time of the collision;[33] and numerous actions against stevedores[34] or sub-contracting carriers,[35] who negligently lose or damage goods belonging to a consigner or consignee with whom they enjoy no direct contractual relation.

The commercial inconvenience of this rule has provoked academic and judicial criticism and has given rise to a varied sequence of attempts to circumvent it. Some of these are more reliable than others, and one at least is mentioned solely in order to warn that it is now defunct. The vital element in all but one of them is the construction and drafting of the original contract between the plaintiff and the defendant's employer. By framing this contract in a particular way, it is possible to extend its protection to persons who were not present when it was concluded and who had no contract or communication with the plaintiffs throughout.

A. Vicarious immunity

In *Mersey Shipping and Transport Co. Ltd.* v. *Rea*,[36] Scrutton L.J. laid down the following principle:

> Where there is a contract which contains an exemption clause, the

---

[31] The argument that privity of contract prohibited only the positive enforcement of contractual terms by a stranger to the contract, and did not prohibit the use of such terms as a shield or a defence, was firmly rejected by Lord Reid in *Scruttons Ltd.* v. *Midland Silicones Ltd.* [1962] A.C. 445, at 473.

[32] *Adler* v. *Dickson* [1955] 1 Q.B. 158.

[34] The following are the most important recent authorities: *Scruttons Ltd.* v. *Midland Silicones Ltd.* [1962] A.C. 445 (H.L.): *Wilson* v. *Darling Island Stevedoring and Lighterage Co. Ltd.* (1956) 95 C.L.R. 43 (High Court of Australia): *Gilchrist, Watt & Sanderson Pty. Ltd.* v. *York Products Pty. Ltd.* [1970] 3 All E.R. 825 (P.C.); [1970] 2 Lloyd's Rep. 3 (Supreme Court of N.S.W.); *Canadian General Electric Co. Ltd.* v. *The Lake Bosomtwe and Pickford & Black Ltd.* [1970] 2 Lloyd's Rep. 81 (Supreme Court of Canada); *Moyer Stainless & Alloy Co. Ltd.* v. *Canadian Overseas Shipping Ltd.* [1973] 2 Lloyd's Rep. 420 (Quebec District Ct.); *The Suleyman Stalskiy* [1976] 2 Lloyd's Rep. 609 (British Columbia Supreme Court); *The New York Star* [1977] 1 Lloyd's Rep. 445 (C.A. of N.S.W.); (1978) 18 A.L.R. 335 (H.C. of A.) for American authorities, see [1974] J.B.L. 101, at 104.

[35] E.g. *Lee Cooper & Co. Ltd.* v. *C. H. Jeakins Ltd.* [1967] 2 Q.B. 1; *Philip Morris (Australia) Pty. Ltd.* v. *Transport Commission* [1975] Tas. S.R. 128.

[33] *Cosgrove* v. *Horsfall* (1945) 62 T.L.R. 140; and see *Gore* v. *Van Der Lann*

[36] (1925) 21 Ll.L.R. 375, at 378.

[1967] 2 Q.B. 31.

servants or agents who act under that contract have the benefit of the exemption clause.[37]

This principle was both a paraphrase and an extension of what Scrutton L.J. had said in his earlier dissenting judgment in the Court of Appeal in *Elder, Dempster and Co. Ltd.* v. *Paterson Zochonis and Co. Ltd.*[38] When that case came before the House of Lords the Court of Appeal's decision was reversed and the view of Scrutton L.J. was (by Lords Cave and Finlay at least) preferred.[39] But the interpretation he propounded (which was rejected by Bankes L.J. in the *Mersey Shipping* case) has now been firmly discredited. It was disapproved, inter alia, by Diplock J. at first instance in *Midland Silicones Ltd.* v. *Scruttons Ltd.*;[40] by the House of Lords in the same case;[41] by Jenkins and Morris L.JJ. in *Adler* v. *Dickson*;[42] by Fullager and Kitto JJ. in *Wilson* v. *Darling Island Stevedoring and Lighterage Co. Ltd*;[43] and by the Supreme Court of the United States in *Krawill Machinery Corporation* v. *Robert C. Herd and Co. Inc.*[44] Vicarious immunity is therefore a defunct doctrine, and one which can no longer be invoked under modern law.

Much of the difficulty in expunging it from the Common Law arose from the intensely obscure quality of the decision in *Elder, Dempster* itself. In that case shipowners were held not answerable for defective stowage of the plaintiff's goods. The plaintiffs had contracted for carriage of the goods with the charterers of the defendants ship and enjoyed no apparent contractual relationship with the defendants themselves. The defendants were nevertheless held entitled to the protection contained in the bill of lading between the owners and the charterers. In so holding, the House of Lords were no doubt influenced by the fact that the master of the ship had signed the bill of lading: but the opaque character of the speeches may be inferred from the fact that in *Scruttons Ltd.* v. *Midland Silicones Ltd.* the *Elder, Dempster* case was put forward as supporting at least three independent notions. These were: (a) the doctrine of vicarious immunity; (b) the principle of an implied contract, which was said to arise whenever an employee of the original contracting party performs his employer's contract, and was said to transfer by implication all the protection of that original contract into the secondary contract between plaintiff and tortfeasor; and (c) the doctrine of a bailment upon terms. Only the last of these rationalisations was left standing after *Midland Silicones*; the first was condemned as doctrinally unsound and the second was dismissed as factually impossible. As Viscount Simonds trenchantly observed, it is one thing to imply a term into an established contract in order to give that contract business efficacy, but it is a very different matter to infer a contractual relation between parties who have

---

[37] "Servants or agents" must be taken here to encompass independent contractors.
[38] [1923] 1 K.B. 420, at 441-442.
[39] [1924] A.C. 522, at 533-534, 547-548.
[40] [1959] 2 Q.B. 171, at 187.
[41] *Scruttons Ltd.* v. *Midland Silicones Ltd.* [1962] A.C. 445.
[42] [1955] 1 Q.B. 158.
[43] (1956) 95 C.L.R. 43, at 69-70, 74-75, 80-81; cf. Williams J. at 57-61.
[44] [1959] 1 Lloyd's Rep. 305; cf. *Carle & Montanari Inc.* v. *American Export Isbrandtsen Lines Inc. and McGrath* [1968] 1 Lloyd's Rep. 260.

never entered into a contract at all.[45] The result in *Midland Silicones* itself was that the defendant stevedores, who had negligently damaged a drum of chemicals during the course of unloading, were held unable to invoke, as their defence to an action by the owner, the terms of the bill of lading between the consignors and the carriers.[46] The relevant terms had referred only to the protection of the "carrier" and there was nothing in them to show that they were intended to apply to the stevedores. Of course, it was by no means conceded that such intention alone would have been enough.

B. The unilateral contract

The third party tortfeasor may be able to persuade the court that the terms of the original contract represent a simultaneous offer to him (and to anyone else who properly comes forward to perform the contract) that he will be granted the immunity from action specified in the contract from the moment he embarks upon performance. Thus, it has been held that where a bill of lading contains a clause in "Himalaya" form,[47] a stevedore who unloads goods which have been shipped subject to the bill of lading will be entitled to claim the protection of its terms in the event of any negligent loss or damage.[48] This approach has a number of limitations and disadvantages. It would mean that there was no contract, and therefore no immunity, until the stevedores began the task of loading. Thus, the owners of the goods might be able to withdraw their standing offer of immunity before that time, and if the stevedores injured the goods before beginning to unload, such as by carelessly colliding with them or by dropping other goods on top of them, their protection would not yet have crystallised and they could be made liable in full for the damage.[49]

More importantly, the original contract must make it plain that it represents an offer of immunity; it must clearly extend to the particular defendants; and it must, apparently, comply with the five conditions laid down by Lord Reid in *Scruttons Ltd.* v. *Midland Silicones Ltd.*[50] These conditions were phrased in response to an argument by counsel for the stevedores that the carriers had acted as their agents in creating a subsidiary contract of immunity between themselves (the stevedores) and the owners of the goods. Lord Reid, after observing that there was no evidence of such an arrangement in the present case, continued:

> I can see a possibility of success of the agency argument if (first) the bill of lading makes it clear that the stevedore is intended to be protected by the provisions in it which limited liability, (secondly) the bill of lading makes it clear that the carrier, in addition to con-

45 [1962] A.C. 446, at 466-467.
46 The same conclusion was reached, on very similar facts, by the High Court of Australia in *Wilson* v. *Darling Island Stevedoring & Lighterage Co. Ltd.* (1956) 95 C.L.R. 43.
47 The name is borrowed from the name of the ship in *Adler* v. *Dickson* [1955] 1 Q.B. 158.
48 *New Zealand Shipping Co. Ltd.* v. *A. M. Satterthwaite & Co. Ltd.* [1975] A.C. 154 (P.C.); reversing the decision of the New Zealand C.A. in [1973] 1 N.Z.L.R. 174 and restoring that of Beattie J. in [1972] N.Z.L.R. 385.
49 Reynolds (1974) 90 L.Q.R. 301, at 303.
50 [1962] A.C. 446, at 474.

tracting for these provisions on his own behalf, is also contracting
as agent for the stevedore that these provisions should apply to the
stevedore, (thirdly) the carrier has authority from the stevedore
to do that, or perhaps later ratification by the stevedore would suffice,
and (fourthly) that any difficulties about consideration moving from
the stevedore were overcome. And then to affect the consignee it
would be necessary to show that the provisions of the *Bills of Lading
Act* 1855, apply.[51]

There is some doubt as to whether Lord Reid was actually contem-
plating a post-active or "unilateral" contract between the owner and the
stevedore when he formulated these proposals. It seems likely that the
contract he had in mind, like the contract which the stevedores had alleged
to exist, took the form of an immediate "bilateral" one, arising as soon
as the bill of lading was signed and uniting the consignor and the stevedores through the agency of the shipowners. The invocation of Lord
Reid's requirements by the Privy Council in *Satterthwaite's* case[52] clearly
suggests that in their view these requirements apply equally to the unilateral as to the bilateral contract theory; thus, Lord Wilberforce remarked: "The question in this appeal is whether the contract satisfies
these propositions".[53] But this is little more than a description of how
the case was argued and is not authority for holding that, if counsel for
the stevedores had argued against them, Lord Reid's conditions must
necessarily have been held to apply. Moreover, it is by no means certain
that the Privy Council in *Satterthwaite's* case based their decision exclusively upon the theory of a unilateral contract. Undoubtedly this is the
rationalisation which emerges most strongly from the majority opinion. It
is supported by the citation of *Carlill v. Carbolic Smoke Ball Co. Ltd.*[54]
and *G.N. Ry. Co. v. Witham*,[55] and is lucidly enshrined in the following
principle:

> . . . the bill of lading brought into existence a bargain initially uni-
> lateral but capable of becoming mutual, between the shipper and the
> appellant, made through the carrier as agent. This became a full con-
> tract when the appellant performed services by discharging the goods.[56]

But four factors, at least, suggest that the unilateral contract theory is
not a sound exclusive foundation for the Privy Council's opinion. First,
the majority seem to commit themselves to an ambiguous identification
of the stevedores' necessary consideration under the unilateral contract,
by remarking at one point that an agreement to do an act which one is
already obligated to a third party to perform may, and this case does,
amount to valid consideration,[57] whereas if it were *performance* of the
obligated act that constituted the necessary consideration, such a pro-

---

[51] This point, which will not be separately considered, was answered in the
stevedores' favour by the majority of the Privy Council in the *Satterthwaite*
case [1975] A.C. 154 and, apparently, by the N.S.W.C.A. in *The New York
Star* [1977] 1 Lloyd's Rep. 445; infra. See now (1978) 18 A.L.R. 337.
[52] [1975] A.C. 154.
[53] Ibid., at 166.
[54] [1892] 2 Q.B. 484; [1893] 1 Q.B. 256.
[55] (1873) L.R. 9 C.P. 16.
[56] [1975] A.C. 154, at 167-168.
[57] Ibid., at 168.

mise would have been irrelevant. Secondly, the final analysis distilled by Lord Wilberforce is equally consistent with either theory;[58] thirdly, Lord Wilberforce conceded that there might be more than one way of analysing the transaction;[59] and fourthly the construction of the Himalaya clause as a unilateral offer to be accepted by performance of an act is difficult to reconcile with the language of the clause itself.[60] All in all, it is by no means certain as to what the *Satterthwaite* case decided; but the majority were clear that, insofar as was necessary, all five of Lord Reid's qualificatory conditions had been fulfilled.[61]

A similar failure to differentiate between the competing varieties of contracts occurs in the decision of McMullin J. in *Herrick v. Leonard and Dingley Ltd.*[62] In this case, where the plaintiff's Jaguar had been negligently damaged by the defendant stevedore, the learned judge applied each of Lord Reid's four main requirements seriatim (the fifth being irrelevant[63]) and held that only the fourth requirement, that of consideration, was satisfied. The first failed because the bill of lading, by referring only to the charterer, the carrier, and their servants or agents, did not make it clear that the defendants (who were independent contractors) were to be included within the covenanted orbit of protection.[64] The second failed because there was nothing in the contract of carriage to indicate that the carrier was acting as agent for the stevedore; the third, because the stevedores had supplied neither authority nor ratification for the entry into a contract by the carriers on their behalf. But McMullin J. thought that the requirement of consideration might be fulfilled because:

> ... the contract whereby the stevedore was engaged by the charterer was plainly a commercial contract from which it might be assumed that consideration moved both ways—from the stevedore to the charterer in unloading the ship at its request and from the charterer to the stevedore in paying for that work to be done.[65]

It is interesting that McMullin J. considered the requirements of consideration to be fulfilled by the exchange of benefits or obligations between the stevedores and the party who engaged them. How this might afford consideration under the consignor-stevedore contract, and the very character of that contract itself, are unfortunately left unexplained. Of course it could be vitally important for the stevedore to know. He will want to know when his contract has begun to operate and what sort of consideration he must provide. No certain guidance can be drawn on this point from either of the foregoing decisions.

---

[58] Ibid., at 167.
[59] Ibid., at 167-168.
[60] See especially on this point Lord Simon of Glaisdale at 175, 180, citing with approval the New Zealand C.A. at [1973] 1 N.Z.L.R. 174, at 185. It is submitted, with respect, that Lord Simon's other objections to the majority conclusion are less well-founded: [1975] A.C. 154, at 179-180, 181; [1974] J.B.L. 101, at 111-114.
[61] [1975] A.C. 154, at 166-167, 168.
[62] [1975] 2 N.Z.L.R. 566; (1976) 39 M.L.R. 466.
[63] Because there was no change in ownership of the damaged goods after the bill of lading was signed.
[64] Cf. on this point *Mason Bros. v. A.G.F. Transport* [1969] N.Z.L.R. 1.
[65] [1975] 2 N.Z.L.R. 566, at 575.

Herrick's case does, however, confirm that the Privy Council did not abolish the need for Lord Reid's principal requirements to be fulfilled; a confirmation which is echoed in a more recent decision from the Supreme Court of British Columbia.[66] Counsel for the defendants in *Herrick* had argued that the majority of the Privy Council laid down a rule which circumvented these decisions, or rendered them redundant; and that the majority opinion comprised an unqualified acceptance of Lord Denning's dissenting speech in *Scrutton's Ltd.* v. *Midland Silicones Ltd.*[67] Lord Denning had urged upon the House a much wider route to protection, based upon the owner's consent to the making of a subsidiary contract which relieved the third-party from liability for negligence. In fact, an approach not dissimilar to this was advanced by counsel in *Satterthwaite*; but the majority declined to comment upon it[68] and it is impossible to collect from their opinion any compelling endorsement of so wide a rule.[69]

The fact remains that one is left with no conclusive guidance upon three important points: (a) whether *Satterthwaite* represents an application of the bilateral theory, the unilateral theory, or a compound of the two; (b) whether Lord Reid's four conditions apply to both kinds of contract; (c) what precise consideration the stevedore or other third party can be said to supply under either. The second area of doubt may perhaps account for the decision of the Tasmanian Supreme Court in *Philip Morris (Australia) Pty. Ltd.* v. *The Transport Commission*,[70] a decision which is remarkable chiefly for its failure to consider *Satterthwaite* a mere eighteen months after it was decided. This case involved a sub-bailment by a principal carrier to a sub-contractor, and could best have been decided upon special principles which apply between owner and sub-bailee. The principal contract made it clear that the sub-contractors were to be protected from suit in the event of loss or damage, but Nettlefold J. held that since they were not parties to this contract they could not claim its protection. In so holding, he recited two earlier decisions of high authority, neither of them involving a contract which expressly mentioned, or purported to confer protection upon, a nominated or identifiable third party.[71] He did not consider the application of Lord Reid's four conditions, and the only passage which can be taken to suggest that he regarded *Satterthwaite* as distinguishable is one in which he remarks that there was nothing in the principal contract of carriage to show that the principal carriers were active, or were authorised *by the consignors* to act, as agents for the sub-contractors.[72] This objection has some force when applied to the bilateral theory but less when applied to the unilateral theory. When a "unilateral offer" is conveyed from A to C by the intermediary B, B is not necessarily acting as an agent in the strict sense because his duties are as a transmitter rather than

---

[66] *The Suleyman Stalskiy* [1976] 2 Lloyd's Rep. 609; and see *The New York Star* [1977] 1 Lloyd's Rep. 445; (1978) 18 A.L.R. 337.
[67] [1962] A.C. 446, at 491.
[68] [1975] A.C. 154, at 168; cf. Lord Simon of Glaisdale at 182.
[69] See further, p. 995 et seq., post.
[70] [1975] Tas. S.R. 128.
[71] *Scruttons Ltd.* v. *Midland Silicones Ltd.* ante; *Wilson* v. *Darling Island Stevedoring & Lighterage Co. Ltd.* (1956) 95 C.L.R. 43.
[72] [1975] Tas. S.R. 128, at 131-132.

as a negotiator or as a participant in the conclusion of the resultant contract. Thus, in *Carlill's* case there was no suggestion that the company in whose newspaper the advertisement first appeared was an agent of the defendant, nor that in order to take advantage of the offer the plaintiff must have authorised or ratified them to act as they did in transmitting the offer to her. Provided that the offeror knew that the offer was to be transmitted or raised no objection to its occurrence, and provided that the offer itself is construable as a promise which becomes binding upon performance of an act, it would seem unnecessary that the intermediate party should have described himself as an agent or that the third-party should have authorised him so to act. Thus it may be that Lord Reid's second and third conditions apply only to those cases in which an immediate bilateral contract is alleged between the plaintiff and the third party.

Leaving these problems aside, it is evident that the third party may enjoy an independent, contractual immunity if he can clearly demonstrate that the original contract was additionally framed as an offer of immunity,[73] that it was addressed or intended to be communicated to him, and that he had both accepted it and supplied the necessary consideration by commencing to perform the tasks undertaken by his immediate employer, and delegated by his immediate employer to him.[74] The only remaining difficulty concerns the ordinary contractual requirement that the offeree should perform the relevant act of acceptance with knowledge of the offer, and intending to accept it. It may be hazarded that the courts would be fairly willing in cases of this kind to infer the necessary knowledge on the part of the stevedore;[74a] if not, the constitution of the carrier as his agent may assume importance as a means of establishing such knowledge vicariously.[74b]

[73] The problem of detecting two separate and differently-synchronised agreements within the perimeter of what appeared to be a single contract was one of the strongest grounds for the minority opinion in *Satterthwaite*: [1975] A.C. 154, at 170, 172, 175, 180. The stevedores attempted to surmount it by alleging an immediate but non-binding agreement, or nudum pactum, within the bill of lading, which later became binding upon commencement of the unloading. The majority (at 168) found this formulation unnecessary; the minority, unacceptable.

[74] The decision in *Satterthwaite*, confirming *Scotson* v. *Pegg* (1861) 6 H. & N. 295; *Chichester* v. *Cobb* (1866) 14 L.T. 433; and *Shadwell* v. *Shadwell* (1860) 9 C.B. (N. S.) 159, is authority for the view that performance of an existing contractual obligation towards a third party may constitute adequate consideration as against the immediate promisee. It has been suggested in [1974] J.B.L. 101, at 115, that the necessary consideration could be reinforced if it were stated in the bill of lading that the consignor's offer shall be accepted as soon as the stevedore *contracts* with the carriers to unload. This may also solve the problem of damage inflicted prior to commencement of the work.

[74a] Or to distil a contract although there is no formal offer or acceptance: cf. *The Satanita* [1895] P. 248 and *Satterthwaite* ante.

[74b] It was upon this ground that the New South Wales Court of Appeal, adopting the opinion of the Privy Council in *Satterthwaite* and apparently considering that Lord Reid's five conditions in *Midland Silicones* applied equally to the unilateral contract argument, held against the stevedores in *Salmond & Spraggon (Australia) Pty. Ltd.* v. *Joint Cargo Services Pty. Ltd., The New York Star*, [1977] 1 Lloyd's Rep. 445. The facts of this case (which was reported after the present chapter was written) were broadly similar to those in the *Satterthwaite* and *Midland Silicones* decisions, except that the stevedores may have gained possession of the goods. The Court held that Lord Reid's fourth condition (that of consideration) was unfulfilled in the present case because the stevedores had failed to prove that their unloading of the goods (and thus their alleged accep-

C. The immediate bilateral contract

If the contract between an owner of goods and a person who is obliged to perform work upon them contains a specific clause under which the owner promises not to sue any servant, agent or independent contractor engaged by the contractor for the purpose of performing that contract, it may be possible to discern a secondary contract of immunity between the owner and any third party by whom the work may be performed. Such a contract would, in theory, come into existence simultaneously with the principal agreement, and would have the advantage of protecting the third-party during the period prior to his commencement of the work.

It seems clear that this was the type of arrangement Lord Reid had in mind when he propounded his five conditions in *Scruttons Ltd.* v. *Midland Silicones Ltd.*[75] and that, in order for a bilateral contract to arise, the stevedores must satisfy all of those conditions. In *Satterthwaite*[76] the minority members of the Privy Council foresaw insuperable objections to the application of these conditions on the facts before them. Chief among these objections was the problem of consideration, for at the time the original contract is made the stevedores will have promised the consignors nothing and may not even have known that they would be helping to perform it. While it cannot be unreservedly accepted that such consideration must, ex necessitate, take the form of a promise by the stevedores to the owners to perform the very act as against the mis-performance of which exemption is now claimed,[77] it must be conceded that the requirement raises considerable problems. Possibly it will be solved by relying on the commercial nature of the overall transaction and upon modern judicial attitudes that men in the market do not make promises without both a palpable prospect of benefit from them and a reasonably firm intention to keep them.[78] Other objections to the bilateral theory in the context of a consignee-stevedore action seem, with respect, less well-founded.[79] But the acknowledged difficulty of invoking this method of protection may well mean that it is surpassed by other and more simple

tance of the unilateral offer of immunity) was actually motivated or influenced by the offer itself: *The Crown* v. *Clarke* (1927) 40 C.L.R. 227 applied. At [1977] 1 Lloyd's Rep. 449, Glass J. observed: "I find that the stevedore knew of the shipper's offer to exempt. But it was bound to carry out stevedoring operations under its contract (*with the carrier*). For all that appears there may have been no relationship whatever between the conduct of the stevedore and its knowledge of the offer: *Australian Woollen Mills Pty. Ltd.* v. *The Commonwealth* (1953-1954) 92 C.L.R. 424 at 457. It is quite consistent with the facts proved that the stevedore acted as it did solely because of the contract it had made with the carrier. For these reasons I conclude that there is a fatal gap in the stevedores' proofs of the fourth condition on which *The Eurymedon* doctrine depends. Having shown no consideration for it, the defendant is unable to claim against the plaintiff the protection of the exemption clauses contained in the bill of lading." See further Hutley J. at 452 and now (1978) 18 A.L.R. 337.

75 [1962] A.C. 446, at 474; ante, p. 989.
76 [1975] A.C. 154, at 171, 179-180; and see [1973] 1 N.Z.L.R. 174, at 178; [1972] N.Z.L.R. 385, at 397.
77 As proposed by Lord Simon of Glaisdale [1975] A.C. 154, at 179; cf. [1974] J.B.L. 101, at 113-114.
78 E.g. *Woodhouse A.C. Israel Cocoa Ltd. S.A.* v. *Nigerian Produce Marketing Co. Ltd.* [1972] 2 All E.R. 271, at 282 per Lord Hailsham L.C.
79 See [1975] A.C. 154, at 178-179, discussed in [1974] J.B.L. 101, at 111-113.

methods. Certainly the *Satterthwaite* decision seems not so much to inflict a radical inroad upon accepted legal doctrine, as to indicate a fairly narrow path along which the confines of privity of contract may be evaded by virtue of careful drafting. Some quantification of its impact upon the general question of third-party protection may perhaps be made from the fact that in the five Commonwealth cases in which the question has subsequently arisen, three courts have distinguished *Satterthwaite*,[80] one has circumvented it[81] and one has disregarded it completely.[82]

D. Volenti non fit injuria, authorised sub-contracts of exclusion and the non-contractual disclaimer of rights

In *Wilson* v. *Darling Island Stevedoring & Lighterage Co. Ltd.*[83] Kitto J. advanced the view that a person who has voluntarily and unequivocally consented to the risk of negligence on the part of another person should be debarred from subsequently recovering against him in tort, notwithstanding that the relevant consent was expressed in a transaction to which the potential defendant was not a party. On this principle, it would not be necessary to show that the defendant was privy to an exclusion or limitation clause, provided the clause was made for his benefit or protection and clearly expressed the consent of the plaintiff to undergo without redress an act of negligence on his part. Indeed, the same defence could apply although the critical consent was not expressed contractually at all:

> Hence, if A in his contract with B agrees expressly or impliedly that C need take no care to avoid injuring A in carrying out particular work which (as he knows) involves danger to A and that B may so inform C, and B does so inform C who then proceeds with the work and in the course of it injures A, the defence of *volenti* is as clearly made out as it would have been if A had himself told C that he accepted, in exoneration of C, the whole risk of injury from C's activities. The absence of privity of contract between A and C would be irrelevant. It is all a question of consent or no consent.[84]

This view was taken up and elucidated by Professor Furmston four years later.[85] It coincided to some extent with certain dicta of Lord Denning in the decade prior to *Scruttons Ltd.* v. *Midland Silicones Ltd.* Thus, in *White* v. *John Warwick & Co. Ltd.*[86] he had remarked:

> When a party to a contract has deliberately in plain words agreed to exempt a third party from negligence, intending that the third party

[80] *Herrick* v. *Leonard & Dingley Ltd.* [1975] 2 N.Z.L.R. 566; *The Suleyman Stalskiy* [1976] 2 Lloyd's Rep. 609 (where the stevedores' claim to immunity failed on the ground that the carriers were not their agents); *The New York Star* [1977] 1 Lloyd's 445; (1978) 18 A.L.R. 335; and see Waddams (1977) 55 *Can. Bar Rev.* 327; *Eisen und Metall* v. *Ceres Stevedoring* [1977] 1 Lloyd's Rep. 665.
[81] *Johnson, Matthey & Co. Ltd.* v. *Constantine Terminals Ltd.* [1976] 2 Lloyd's. Rep. 215.
[82] *Philip Morris (Australia) Pty. Ltd.* v. *The Transport Commission* [1975] Tas. S.R. 128.
[83] (1956) 95 C.L.R. 43, at 81-83, 85.
[84] Ibid., at 82.
[85] (1960) 23 M.L.R. 373, at 392 et. seq.
[86] [1953] 1 W.L.R. 1285, at 1294.

should have the benefit of the exemption, he cannot go back on his plighted word and disregard the exemption.[87]

The pronouncements of Lord Denning suffered from a number of unfortunate associations which (perhaps unjustly) tended to detract from their weight. Among these were: their affinity with the *Elder, Dempster* case;[88] his Lordship's own endorsement of the doctrine of vicarious immunity;[89] the contemporary view that an exclusion clause could not take effect unless contained in a contract between the plaintiff and the proferens;[90] and Lord Denning's contemporaneous assaults upon the wider validity of the doctrine of privity of contract.[91] It was not, therefore, surprising that in *Midland Silicones Ltd.* v. *Scruttons Ltd.*[92] Diplock J. unequivocally condemned the approach advocated by Lord Denning throughout the previous decade. But no such condemnation was applied to the observations of Kitto J. which were based more squarely upon the doctrine of volenti non fit injuria than upon the notion of allowing a stranger to a contract to directly enforce its terms. If, in fact, Lord Denning's own expressions of principle are regarded as directing attention to whether a plaintiff has consented to run the risk of damage, rather than as perpetrating some more ambitious erosion of the doctrine of privity of contract, it is by no means clear that they are as unacceptable as Diplock J. believed.[93] Certainly not every judge before whom this question has arisen has been prepared to say that the construction of the clause is wholly irrelevant because the defendant is not a party to it.[94] Its relevance may lie in establishing a consent which has nothing to do with the law of contract at all.

When *Midland Silicones* came before the House of Lords, Lord Denning delivered a dissenting judgment in which he expressly advocated the application of the volenti doctrine to situations of this character, but conceded that on the present facts the defence could not apply. The reason for this was not privity of contract but the wording of the clause itself:

---

[87] See also *Adler* v. *Dickson* [1955] 1 Q.B. 158, at 181-184, where similar observations were expressly disclaimed by his fellow members of the Court of Appeal. Morris and Jenkins LJJ., at 186 et. seq., and 198. Note, however, that insofar as the latter members were applying to the validity of any exclusion clause the necessity that it should be contained in a contract, their opinions would now seem to be misconceived: ante, p. 952. Some oblique support for the view expressed in the text may be drawn from a dictum of Goddard J. in *Fosbroke-Hobbes* v. *Airwork Ltd.* [1931] 1 All E.R. 108, at 112. See also *Alsey Steam Fishing Co. Ltd.* v. *Hillman* [1957] P. 51, at 64-67; *Hollingworth* v. *Southern Ferries* [1977] 2 Lloyd's Rep. 70.

[88] [1924] A.C. 522; ante, p. 988.

[89] Not shared by Kitto J.: see (1956) 95 C.L.R. 43, at 80-81. Lord Denning re-affirmed his support for this doctrine in his dissenting speech in *Scruttons Ltd.* v. *Midland Silicones Ltd.* (ante), at 486-487.

[90] See ante, n. 87; disapproved by Kitto J. in the *Darling Island* case (1956) 95 C.L.R. 43, at 82.

[91] E.g. *Smith & Snipes Hall Farm Ltd.* v. *River Douglas Catchment Board* [1949] 2 K.B. 500, at 514.

[92] [1959] 2 Q.B. 171, at 189-193 (first instance).

[93] (1960) 23 M.L.R. 373, at 392-398.

[94] See for instance, the *Darling Island* case (1956) 95 C.L.R. at 60, 81-83, 85 (Williams and Kitto JJ.); cf. Fullager J. at 79.

Even though negligence is an independent tort, nevertheless it is an accepted principle of the law of tort that no man can complain of an injury if he has voluntarily consented to take the risk of it on himself. This consent need not be embodied in a contract.[95] Nor does it need consideration to support it. Suffice it that he consented to take the risk of injury on himself. So in the case of through transit, when the shipper of goods consigns them "at owner's risk" for the whole journey, his consent to take the risk avails the second carrier as well as the first, even though there is no contract between the goods owner and the second carrier. Likewise in the *Elder, Dempster* case the shipper, by exempting the charterers from bad stowage, may be taken to have consented to exempt the shipowners also. But I am afraid that this reasoning would not avail the stevedores in the present case: for the simple reason that the bill of lading is not expressed so as to protect the stevedores but only the "carrier". The shipper has therefore not consented to take on himself the risk of the negligence of the stevedores and is not to be defeated on that ground.[96]

Having dismissed this defence, however, Lord Denning went on to hold that a quite separate principle could be invoked in the defendants' favour. This principle, which he drew from the law relating to bailment[97] but applied to the handling of goods by a non-bailee,[98] was not directed to ascertaining whether the *original* contract had conferred a specific protection upon the third-party tortfeasor, but inquired instead whether any protection conferred by the *secondary* contract between the third-party and the intermediary was authorised by the plaintiff. If so, the defendant should be protected, just as he would be protected if he were a lien-holder whose lien had been conferred by a bailee with authority to do so:

> . . . when the owner of goods allows the person in possession of them to make a contract in regard to them, then he cannot go back on the terms of the contract, if they are such as he expressly or impliedly authorised, that is to say, consented to be made, even though he was no party to the contract and could not sue or be sued on it. It is just the same as if he stood by and watched it being made. And his successor in title is in no better position.[99]

It seems, with respect to Lord Denning, that the latter principle may be confined to cases in which the tortfeasor himself has become a bailee, and may represent one peculiarity of that branch of the law which is not evident in comparable areas. Unfortunately, the validity of Lord Denning's theory in a non-bailment action has never been satisfactorily tested, for in *New Zealand Shipping Co. Ltd.* v. *A. M. Satterthwaite & Co. Ltd.* the stevedores preferred to invoke a third, independent principle which paid no regard to the carrier-stevedore contract and which they were at pains to distinguish from the doctrine of volenti non fit injuria: a doctrine upon

[95] Cf. ante, p. 952.
[96] [1962] A.C. 446, at 488-489. The reasoning and conclusion enjoy a marked correspondence with that of Kitto J. in the *Darling Island* case (ante), at 80 et seq.
[97] Post, p. 1000 et seq.
[98] Relying on *The Kite* [1933] P. 154.
[99] [1962] A.C. 446, at 491.

which they expressly declined to rely.[1] This defence (the fourth contention) drew its inspiration from a series of cases in which the plaintiff had been held, without entering into any contract with the defendant, to have consented to forgo any remedy in tort by acquiescing in a notice or disclaimer to that effect, published by the party from whom a duty would otherwise have been extracted. Examples are the posting of a noticeboard on land, warning that no liability would be accepted for injury to licensees;[2] the placing of a sign on a car dashboard which likewise renounces any responsibility for injury to passengers;[3] and the publication of a clear disclaimer for the accuracy of certain gratuitous advice at the head of a letter in which that advice was given.[4] This notion is, as we have previously remarked,[5] distinct from volenti non fit injuria: the victim consents not to the risk of negligence but to the absence of redress. But Lord Simon of Glaisdale, the only member of the Privy Council to consider the contention at length, held that the distinction was immaterial.[6] He refused to entertain any defence based upon the respondents' non-contractual consent to the limitations contained in the bill of lading, on the ground that such an approach would render Lord Reid's four principal conditions in *Midland Silicones*[7] entirely redundant. He further remarked that the same approach was inconsistent with the reasoning and conclusion in *Cosgrove* v. *Horsfall*[8] and would, if valid, have produced a different result in *Midland Silicones* itself. In his view, the decisions which support the doctrine of a non-contractual disclaimer could be distinguished on the ground that they involved promises, licenses or services that were essentially gratuitous: and "any person making a gift can delimit its extent". If this were so, one might have expected the principle to apply in cases like *Genys* v. *Matthews*,[9] and one would be surprised to find it applying in a case like *White* v. *Blackmore*. In fact, it would not seem essential that the service from which the alleged tort arises should be gratuitous; and it is clear from Lord Simon's own reasoning in *Satterthwaite* that the stevedores were there performing, vis-à-vis the consignees, a gratuitous act. This follows from his observations that no consideration passed between the parties and that the stevedores had not entered into any binding contract with the consignees to unload.[10] Nor can *Midland Silicones* and *Cosgrove* v. *Horsfall* be regarded as conclusive

[1] [1975] A.C. at 158.
[2] E.g. *Ashdown* v. *Samuel Williams Ltd.* [1957] 1 Q.B. 409: cf. *White* v. *Blackmore* [1972] 3 All E.R. 158.
[3] E.g. *Bennett* v. *Tugwell* [1971] 2 W.L.R. 847; *Birch* v. *Thomas* [1972] 1 All E.R. 905.
[4] *Hedley Byrne & Co. Ltd.* v. *Heller & Partners Ltd.* [1964] A.C. 465.
[5] Ante, p. 44.
[6] [1975] A.C. 154, at 182. At 173 Viscount Dichorne expressed his concurrence in these observations. At 168 the majority refused to commit themselves upon the fourth contention, observing that it required "elaborate discussion".
[7] [1962] A.C. 446, at 474; ante, p. 989.
[8] (1945) 175 L.T. 334. Cf. Lord Denning in *Midland Silicones* [1962] A.C. 446, at 489, who, while conceding that *Cosgrove's* case "appears to suggest the contrary", sought to distinguish it on the ground that it is harder to infer consent to the risk of injury in the case of carriage of passengers than in the case of carriage of goods.
[9] [1965] 3 All E.R. 24.
[10] [1975] A.C. 154, at 179-180.

authority against the principles in question. In the first case, volenti at least does not seem to have been pleaded;[11] in the second, the issue was touched upon only indirectly in the course of a discussion as to whether the plaintiff, having rejected the conditions of his free bus pass, should be regarded as a trespasser ab initio and therefore unable to recover.[12] It is submitted that there is still no authoritative foundation for the rejection of either the volenti doctrine or the theory of the non-contractual disclaimer in cases of this character. The inapplicability of volenti non fit injuria was baldly assumed by Beattie J. at first instance in the *Satterthwaite* case, but no reasons were given for this assumption.[13] The existence of any alternative non-contractual doctrine was discountenanced entirely by Nettlefold J. in *Philip Morris (Australia) Ltd.* v. *The Transport Commission*.[14]

The latter decision does, however, contain one interesting reflection upon the likely success of a defence of volenti based exclusively upon the terms of a written document. Having found as a fact that the necessary consent could not be inferred from the documentary facts before him (a somewhat harsh conclusion in view of the explicit manner in which the principal contract of carriage sought to protect the defendants) and having questioned whether the statements of Kitto J. in the *Darling Island*[15] case were not inconsistent with the *ratio* in *Midland Silicones* (where even Lord Denning held that the defence was unavailable) he cited a proposition of Turner J. in a New Zealand case[16] to support his conclusion that volenti was inapplicable:[17]

> That in an action alleging negligence to which the defence volenti non fit injuria is raised the defence cannot succeed in the absence of express agreement, or at least of some transaction or intercourse between the parties which may be short of contract but from which the plaintiff's assent may be freely inferred, that the plaintiff will freely and voluntarily accept the risk of negligent acts on the part of the defendant which are still in the future when the plaintiff is said to have shown himself to be volens.

Certainly it would appear that for a defence of volenti to arise it may be necessary to show that the plaintiff consented to the actual risk of damage and therefore that he had some knowledge of the circumstances creating that risk. But no such qualification seems to arise in the alternative defence of a non-contractual disclaimer, although the relevant notice will, no doubt, be strictly construed against the defendant. Again, there may be difficulties in applying the volenti doctrine to a mere time-clause or a mere limitation of damages;[18] but the alternative theory presents no

---

[11] Cf. [1962] A.C. 446, at 458-459.

[12] As counsel for the stevedores pointed out in *Midland Silicones, Elder, Dempster* was not cited in *Cosgrove* v. *Horsfall*: counsel contended that the latter decision should accordingly be overruled.

[13] [1972] N.Z.L.R. 385, at 395: the issue was not mentioned in the New Zealand Court of Appeal.

[14] [1975] Tas. S.R. 128, at 139.

[15] (1956) 95 C.L.R. 43, at 81-83.

[16] *Morrison* v. *U.S.S. Co. Ltd.* [1964] N.Z.L.R. 468.

[17] At 138.

[18] Cf. Rose (1975) 4 *Anglo-American Law Review* 7, pp. 28-32.

such difficulty and it may be questioned whether volenti itself necessarily demands some "transaction" between the parties. Both methods of protection are somewhat neglected in recent pronouncements and it would be unsafe to dismiss them out of hand.

E. The bailment on terms

Whatever the uncertainty surrounding the third-party performance of contracts in general, bailments would appear to generate a special rule. There is considerable judicial support for the view that a bailor of goods is bound by the terms of any subsidiary bailment which he has authorised his bailee to enter into and cannot, irrespective of the lack of any contractual relation, disregard those terms in his action against the sub-bailee.

The principal advocate of this view has been Lord Denning. In his dissenting speech in *Midland Silicones*,[19] and later in the Court of Appeal in *Morris* v. *C. W. Martin & Sons Ltd.*,[20] he stressed the independent legal character of the bailment relation and pointed out that to enable the non-contractual bailee to set up this defence was consistent with the principles which enable the creation of a third party lien. Just as the repairer in possession of a chattel may enjoy a lien although the chattel was delivered to him by an intermediate bailee with authority to do so from the actual owner,[21] so a sub-bailee may rely upon an immunity contained in his contract of sub-bailment if the owner of the goods had authorised the intermediate bailee to contract on those terms. This conclusion is not dependent upon the existence of a contract between the owner and the sub-bailee, nor is it synonymous with the defence of volenti non fit injuria.[22] It is one of the aspects of bailment that are independent from the rules of contract or tort.[23]

There has been very little direct disapproval of this principle and a considerable degree of oblique support. In *Morris* v. *C. W. Martin & Sons Ltd.*[24] Salmon L.J. professed himself strongly attracted by it, but declined to offer any decided conclusion because, as Lord Denning himself observed, the relevant clause could not in any event encompass the loss.[25] Diplock L.J. was more non-committal and refrained from expressing any opinion, however tentative;[26] he agreed that the clause relied upon could not extend to the particular wrongdoing even if it were binding on the plaintiff. At first sight it might appear surprising that Diplock L.J. was not more enthusiastic about the notion of a non-contractual immunity, since it was his own judgment in *Tappenden* v. *Artus* that had authoritatively endorsed an analogous principle in the

---

[19] [1962] A.C. 446 at 489-491.
[20] [1966] 1 Q.B. 716, at 729-730.
[21] *Tappenden* v. *Artus* [1964] 2 Q.B. 185: p. 1009, post.
[22] Cf. Reynolds (1972) 88 L.Q.R. 179, at 183.
[23] In *Midland Silicones* Lord Denning appears to ascribe the principle to the identification of bailment with the law of property. He reiterated the bailee's power of protection more recently in *Gillespie Bros. Ltd.* v. *Roy Bowles Transport Ltd.* [1973] Q.B. 400, at 412. The doctrine is supported by a number of academic writers: see, for instance, Weir (1977) 36 C.L.J. 24, at 27: Coote (1977) 36 C.L.J. 18, at 19-20; Reynolds, loc. cit.
[24] [1966] 1 Q.B. 716, at 741.
[25] See, on this point, p. 924 ante.
[26] At 731.

case of the third-party lien.[27] In *Tappenden* v. *Artus*[28] he made it plain
that the lien is not the product of an implied contract between the parties
but a right arising by operation of law. But this characterisation extends
only so far as enabling the lien to arise when the intermediate party had
no more than ostensible authority to create it; if the person asserting
the lien knows of the lack of authority (at least, at the time when the
chattel was initially delivered) no lien can arise because his possession
must be lawful. Thus there is a close resemblance between the third-
party lien and the sub-bailment subject to exclusions of liability, because
both produce possessory rights or defences which are independent of
contract and are based upon the semblance of consent. Moreover, it
seems probable that if an intermediate bailee has *ostensible* authority to
create a sub-bailment upon terms which exonerate the sub-bailee, the sub-
bailee may rely upon those terms regardless of the owner's absence of
actual consent.

Possibly the strongest endorsement of this principle appears in the
speeches of the House of Lords in *Scruttons Ltd.* v. *Midland Silicones
Ltd.* Quite apart from the opinion of Lord Denning (who was prepared to
extend the defence to a wrongdoer who was not a bailee) at least two
of the four majority members of the House were prepared to distinguish
the *Elder, Dempster* case[29] on the ground that it involved a bailment
upon terms:

> It may be difficult to discover any common ratio decidendi in the
> speeches of their Lordships who decided the *Elder, Dempster* case
> . . . But I take the preferred view of Lord Sumner, which had the
> support of Lord Dunedin and Lord Carson, as meaning that in the
> circumstances of that case, including the fact that the bills of lading
> were signed by the master of the ship, the cargo was received by the
> ship and the owners, with the assent of the shippers, on the same
> conditions as regards immunity in respect of stowage as had been
> obtained by the charterers under their contract of carriage.[30]

Clearly this principle could not apply in *Midland Silicones* itself
because the stevedores had never obtained possession of the goods and
therefore, as Diplock J. had remarked at first instance, were not bailees
"sub, bald or simple".[31]

---

[27] Diplock L.J. did in fact cite *Tappenden* v. *Artus* in *Morris* v. *C. W. Martin &
Sons Ltd.* (at 732), but only, apparently, as authority for the proposition that a
person may owe the duties of a bailee without any contractual relationship with
the person entitled to enforce those duties.

[28] At 195.

[29] [1924] A.C. 522.

[30] [1962] A.C. 446, at 481 per Lord Keith of Avonholm; see also at 470, per
Viscount Simonds; cf. at 494 per Lord Morris of Borth-y-Gest and at 479 per
Lord Reid, neither of whom was conclusively opposed to the principle but
both of whom experienced some difficulty in extracting it (or any other ratio) from
the decision in *Elder, Dempster*.

[31] [1959] 2 Q.B. 171, at 189, 301; cited with approval by Viscount Simonds at [1962]
A.C. 470. In fact, it is by no means clear that Diplock J. himself accepted the
existence of a special principle for non-contractual bailees. He seems to have
regarded the existence of a bailment as relevant only in establishing whether the
plaintiff had genuinely consented to the risk of damage or the absence of
redress. Cf. further *Gilchrist Watt & Sanderson Pty. Ltd.* v. *York Products
Pty. Ltd.* [1970] 3 All E.R. 825 (P.C.) where the stevedores became bailees by

In so restricting the *Elder, Dempster* case, Lord Keith and Viscount Simonds expressed a clear preference for the principle enounced by Lord Sumner over the wider basis of vicarious immunity supported by Viscount Cave.[32] It is difficult to extract any clear majority within the decision itself for either view, since Lord Dunedin agreed with Lord Sumner, Lord Finlay agreed with Viscount Cave, and Lord Carson apparently agreed with them all.[33] Other interpretations of *Elder, Dempster*, while almost unanimously disapproving the doctrine of vicarious immunity,[34] seem generally to endorse the view of Lord Sumner; although it must be conceded that the width of that endorsement varies from judgment to judgment. Thus, in *Wilson* v. *Darling Island Stevedoring and Lighterage Co. Ltd.*[35] Fullager J. arrived at an explanation of *Elder, Dempster* which was almost identical to that of Lord Keith in *Midland Silicones* and was itself cited, with full approval, by Viscount Simonds in the same case; but Fullager J. laid emphasis upon the fact that the master in *Elder, Dempster* actually signed the bill of lading and, while declining to state that this fact was necessarily decisive, elsewhere refused to accept *Elder, Dempster* as authority for "a general rule of the law of bailment".[36] In the same case Kitto J.[37] accepted as authoritative the speech of Lord Sumner in *Elder, Dempster*, but seemed to regard the transfer of possession as merely an important factor in establishing whether the plaintiff had manifested sufficient consent to sustain a defence of volenti non fit injuria. Taylor J. (dissenting) declined to discover a special principle for bailments because he considered it illogical to distinguish between defendants who were and those who were not in possession of the goods, and because he supported the doctrine of vicarious immunity which would of course encompass either eventuality;[38] while Williams J. (also dissenting) implied that the principle was peculiar to bailment only insofar as the party engaging the defendant must be a bailee.[39] In effect, Williams J. also approved the doctrine of vicarious immunity, while confining it to the third-party performance of contracts of bailment.

---

warehousing the stolen property, but the defence does not seem to have been pursued; *The New York Star* [1977] 1 Lloyd's Rep. 454; (1978) 18 A.L.R. 335.

[32] [1924] A.C. 522, at 534, 564.

[33] In *Midland Silicones* Lord Denning (at 487) took this to mean that both rationes were valid.

[34] The principal exceptions are Lord Denning in *Midland Silicones* and Taylor J. in the *Darling Island* case (1956) 95 C.L.R. 43, at 91-93; see also Williams J. ibid., at 60-61, 62.

[35] At 68-69, 78, Dixon C.J. concurring.

[36] (1956) 95 C.L.R. 43, at 74; in the next sentence, however, he questions whether the principle, if sound, should be confined to bailments by way of carriage; doubting on this point a statement by Owen J. in *Gilbert Stokes & Kerr Pty. Ltd.* v. *Dalgety & Co. Ltd.* (1948) 48 S.R. (N.S.W.) 435, at 443. Fullagar J. seems in fact merely to have been saying that an exemption could not be claimed by anyone who performed work delegated to him by a bailee unless he, in turn, possessed the goods under a bailment. Cf. the views of Williams J. post. There would have been no point in the stevedores raising any other argument because they themselves were never bailees.

[37] (1956) 95 C.L.R. 43, at 85

[38] Ibid., at 92-93. Taylor J. saw no difference between the views of Lord Sumner and Lord Finlay in *Elder, Dempster*.

[39] At 60-61.

Nothing decisive can therefore be collected from the *Darling Island* case, and it cannot be seen as an authoritative denial of the principle more recently propounded by Lord Denning.[40] Indeed, it may be observed that an earlier decision of the New South Wales Supreme Court,[41] which seemed to provide clear support for the special exemption of a subsidiary bailee, was expressly disapproved by only two members of the High Court[42] in the *Darling Island* case and not, as the headnote suggests, by a majority. These two members were in fact those whose judgments provide the most persuasive support for the separate identity of the principle in question.[43]

There are a number of first instance decisions prior to *Morris* v. *C. W. Martin & Sons Ltd.*[44] in which a sub-carrier was held unable to rely upon the terms of the relevant contract of carriage, but these do not seem to have been decided with reference to the principles of bailment, and were argued solely (if at all) on the question of privity of contract.[45] Immediately after *Morris's* case, first instance judges seem to have been conspicuously neutral in their attitude to this question: thus in *Mayfair Photographic Supplies (London) Ltd.* v. *Baxter Hoare and Co. Ltd.*[46] and *Moukataff* v. *B.O.A.C.*[47] both MacKenna and Browne JJ. refused to commit themselves as to whether the bailee could rely upon the terms of a contract to which either he or the owner of the goods was not a party. But in the first case, MacKenna J. was referring only to the possibility of the defendant's reliance upon the terms of the principal contract of carriage and not to the alternative prospect of a defence based upon the plaintiff's consent to the terms of exclusion within the subsidiary contract; and he had already held that the terms of the latter contract were of relevance in establishing whether the defendants had broken any duty towards the plaintiffs.[48] In *Moukataff's* case Browne J. saw as one of the difficulties of applying Lord Denning's principle to the facts before him the fact that there was no contract (exclusory or otherwise) between the original bailor and the intermediate bailee.[49] But, with respect, this element would not appear to be essential: the central factor in Lord Denning's test is the original bailor's consent to the making of the exclusory contract between the intermediate and the subsidiary bailee. The principal contract may provide evidence of the intermediate bailee's

[40] See p. 1000, ante.

[41] *Gilbert Stokes & Kerr Pty. Ltd.* v. *Dalgety & Co. Ltd* (ante), at 437; see also *Waters Trading Co. Ltd.* v. *Dalgety & Co. Ltd.* (1951) 52 S.R. (N.S.W.) 4.

[42] Dixon C.J. and Fullagar J. See especially the comments of Fullagar J. (in (1956) 95 C.L.R. 43, at 73), who very reasonably observes that it was unlikely that the stevedores in the *Gilbert Stokes* case were actually bailees of the goods.

[43] See ante, p. 1002, n. 36.

[44] [1966] 1 Q.B. 716.

[45] E.g. *L. Harris (Harella) Ltd.* v. *Continental Express Ltd.* [1961] 1 Lloyd's Rep. 251; *Lee Cooper & Co. Ltd.* v. *C. H. Jeakins & Sons Ltd.* [1964] 1 Lloyd's Rep. 300; [1967] 2 Q.B. 1; cf. *W.L.R. Traders Ltd.* v. *B. & N. Shipping Agency Ltd.* [1955] 1 Lloyd's Rep. 554.

[46] [1972] 1 Lloyd's Rep. 410, at 417.

[47] [1967] 1 Lloyd's Rep. 396, at 418. Cf. *James Buchanan & Co. Ltd.* v. *Hay's Transport Services Ltd.* [1972] 2 Lloyd's Rep. 535, where the point was not argued.

[48] [1972] 1 Lloyd's Rep. 410, at 416; ante, p. 817.

[49] The Post Office: see *Triefus & Co. Ltd.* v. *The Post Office* [1957] 2 Q.B. 352.

permission to sub-contract upon similar terms, and it may be difficult to infer such authority unless there is substantial correspondence between the terms contained in the principal contract and those contained in the secondary contract; but in theory the rule should be capable of being satisfied by any evidence which shows that the ultimate transaction was one into which the intermediary was authorised to enter.

In 1976, however, Donaldson J. advocated a new approach which had as its foundation the origins of the duty which the non-contractual bailee was alleged to have broken. In *Johnson, Matthey and Co. Ltd.* v. *Constantine Terminals Ltd.*[50] he approved Fullager J's explanation of the *Elder, Dempster* case and endorsed the statements of Lord Denning M.R. in *Morris* v. *C. W. Martin & Sons Ltd.* This alone would have been sufficient to dispose of the case before him, because the ultimate bailees' conditions were not materially different from those imposed upon the owner by the original bailee, and it was therefore legitimate to infer that the goods had been sub-bailed on terms which operated to exonerate the sub-bailee.[51] But impressed by certain differences between the present facts and those in *Elder, Dempster,*[52] Donaldson J. went further and propounded a separate principle under which the original bailor's consent was immaterial to the protection of the ultimate bailee. According to this principle, the non-contractual bailee who is sued for breach of any duty which would not have arisen but for the bailment under which he is sued may rely upon the essential terms upon which he assumed posses- sion, even though these are contained in a contract to which the plaintiff is not a party, as a defence to the action.[53] In so holding, Donaldson J. disapproved the decision of Marshall J. in *Lee Cooper and Co. Ltd.* v. *C. H. Jeakins and Sons Ltd.*[54] and left open the question whether the same rule could apply where the act complained of was of a kind (such as negligently-inflicted damage) in relation to which the existence of a bailment was not a pre-requisite to liability. Elsewhere, we submit that the rule may apply to such a case.[55]

Johnson, Matthey is the first English decision to afford direct con- sideration of the special problems of the non-contractual bailee's immunity, and it is submitted that it should be accepted as authority for two distinct principles: first, that a principal bailor is bound by the terms upon which he has authorised an intermediate party to contract with the secondary bailee, and secondly that the principal bailor is bound (at least in any action which arises out of the extended bailment) by any terms which represent the consideration upon which the secondary bailee accepted the goods, irrespective of whether the intermediate party was authorised to enter into a transaction on those terms. Both principles are consistent with the hybrid and independent character of the non-con-

---

[50] [1976] 2 Lloyd's Rep. 215; ante, p. 819 et seq.; Coote (1977) 36 C.L.J. 18; cf. *Charles Davis (Metal Brokers) Ltd.* v. *Gilyott & Scott Ltd.* [1975] 2 Lloyd's Rep. 422.
[51] At 221.
[52] Set out in [1976] 2 Lloyd's Rep. 215, at 220.
[53] Ibid., at 222; set out more fully ante, p. 820.
[54] [1964] Lloyd's Rep. 300; [1967] 2 Q.B. 1.
[55] Ante, p. 821.

tractual bailment and with the capacity of that relationship to engender duties and defences that are not assignable to the ordinary forms of action in contract or in tort.

The remaining Commonwealth authority is less ambitious and less consistent. The more orthodox of these two principles, i.e. that sanctioned by Lord Denning M.R. in *Morris* v. *C. W. Martin & Sons Ltd.*,[56] was approved obiter by the Guyanan Court of Appeal in *B.W.I.A.* v. *Bart*[57] but firmly disapproved by Nettlefold J. in the Tasmanian case of *Philip Morris (Australia) Pty. Ltd.* v. *The Transport Commission.*[58] The latter is in fact the only decision in which the dicta of Lord Denning M.R. have been directly repudiated. In reaching his conclusion that the sub-bailees were not entitled to shelter behind their own contract of carriage with the main bailee in resisting the consignor's action for the loss of a quantity of cigarettes by theft, the learned judge preferred to rely upon the earlier first instance decisions in *Lee Cooper & Co. Ltd.* v. *C. H. Jeakins and Sons Ltd.* and *L. Harris (Harella) Ltd.* v. *Continental Express Ltd.*[59] and the "basic approach" of Fullager J. in *Wilson* v. *Darling Island Stevedoring & Lighterage Co. Ltd.*, remarking that the latter judge and Lord Denning M.R. were, on this point, "very much in conflict". The conflict is difficult to identify when it is recalled that it was Fullager J's own rationalisation of the *Elder, Dempster* case that came closest to the recognition of a special principle for those defendants who have come into possession of the relevant goods. This rationalisation was, as we have seen, approved by Viscount Simonds in the House of Lords in *Midland Silicones* and bears a marked resemblance to Lord Denning's own alternative explanation of *Elder, Dempster.*[60] It was his own interpretation of *Elder, Dempster*, and the special conclusions he drew therefrom as applying to cases of bailment, that Lord Denning reiterated in *Morris* v. *C. W. Martin & Sons Ltd.* These conclusions seem perfectly consistent with the approach of Fullager J. and Dixon C.J. in the *Darling Islands* case. In cases where the defendant is a bailee, there is no conflict at all.

The decision of Nettlefold J. is open to question on a number of different levels. The learned judge pays no regard to the problems of finding a vestigial ratio for the *Elder, Dempster* case and apparently overlooks the fact that the principle for which the defendant sub-bailees contended has been endorsed by at least three members of the House of Lords.[61] The notion that bailment may be an independent concept and may give rise to special liabilities or defences was peremptorily dismissed with a statement that the defendants could not succeed unless they could raise a defence which arose from the law of contract or of tort. But the idea that bailment is sui generis was acknowledged in at least two of the decisions upon which the learned judge relied[62] and the

---

[56] At 729-730.
[57] (1966) 11 W.I.R. 378, at 399, 412.
[58] [1975] Tas. S.R. 128.
[59] [1961] 1 Lloyd's Rep. 251.
[60] I.e. an interpretation not based on the doctrine of vicarious immunity: see [1962] A.C. 446, at 487.
[61] Ante, p. 1001.
[62] *Scruttons Ltd.* v. *Midland Silicones Ltd.* ante; *Hobbs* v. *Petersham Transport Co. Pty. Ltd.* (1971) 45 A.L.J.R. 356, at 364 per Windeyer J.

alternative view fails to explain the obvious analogy of the third-party lien; a phenomenon which, like the sub-bailee's defence, is independent of contractual or tortious remedies and is centred upon an authorised possession. This phenomenon was recognised obiter by the Full Supreme Court of Victoria a mere eleven months before the *Philip Morris* case was decided.[63]

On the facts of the case before Nettlefold J. there would seem to have been cogent reasons for exempting the defendants. The principal contract of carriage conferred specific immunity upon "the carrier" and stipulated that this expression should include the immediate carrier's servants, agents and independent contractors. This immunity specifically included liability for negligence, which was the ground of the plaintiffs' action against the sub-bailee. The exemptions in the principal contract corresponded substantially with those contained in the secondary contract of carriage between the original carriers and the defendant sub-contractors. Admittedly, negligence was not specifically mentioned in the latter contract, but the relevant clause relieved the defendants "from all liability for loss, injury, damage, non-delivery, mis-delivery, delay or detention except on proof that the same arose from the wilful misconduct of the (defendants') servants". There was therefore clear evidence that the plaintiffs had consented to a sub-bailment upon terms which exonerated the sub-bailees from the liability in question. There was certainly no evidence that any form of sub-contracting was forbidden, and the only form that was logical in the circumstances was one which corresponded substantially with the principal transaction.

The secondary bailee's immunity should not depend upon the intermediate party's own possession: he may be a forwarding agent and the same rule would apply. But it no longer seems sufficient that the intermediary alone should be a bailee:[64] the defendant's immunity does depend upon possession and until possession is transferred his role is that of an ordinary tortfeasor, subject of course to the prospect of his raising a defence of volenti non fit injuria against the plaintiff.

The principles we have expounded in this section are supported to a certain degree by authority which entitles the warehouseman of goods to rely upon exclusion clauses in the original contract of bailment as against any subsequent purchaser of the goods to whom he has attorned.[65] In theory, there is no reason why this principle should be limited to bailments which are contractual in character.

F. The trust device

The trust device is a long established method of evading the doctrine of privity, but its value in the context of our present discussion seems negligible. The bill of lading in *New Zealand Shipping Co. Ltd.* v. *A. M. Satterthwaite & Co. Ltd.* attempted to utilise the concept of the trust by

---

[63] *Protean Enterprises (Newmarket) Pty. Ltd.* v. *Randall* [1975] V.R. 327, at 334-336. Nettlefold J's assertion (at [1975] Tas. S.R. 128, at 137) that Lord Denning's dicta are consistent with *Cosgrove* v. *Horsfall* (1945) 62 T.L.R. 140 seems likewise to discount that fact that *Cosgrove's* case was not a case of bailment.

[64] Ante, p. 1002.

[65] Ante, p. 851.

providing that the ship-owners should be trustees of the promise not to exact full liability from their own servants, agents and independent contractors. If this contention were sustained, it would presumably enable such employees to invoke the promise directly in their own defence, as beneficiaries of the trust. But this conclusion alone serves to show the artificiality of alleging a trust in such circumstances: for as Beattie J. pointed out at first instance[66] a trust of this kind provides the beneficiary with nothing to enforce. Moreover, it would seem anomalous, if not impossible, for a person who is on the one hand the beneficiary of a trust to be at the same time "a principal contractor in respect of the same subject-matter".[67] These objections, coupled with the increasing reluctance of the Courts to imply trusts in a purely commercial context, would seem fatal to a defence based upon this ground.

G. Stay of action

In most cases where the original contract seeks to confer its protection upon a third party, the plaintiff will by proceeding against him be in breach of a promise to the other contracting party. In such a case, it appears that the plaintiff may be restrained from acting in violation of his contract, at least where his action will cause loss to the other contracting party because of an indemnity clause between the latter and the defendant. This possibility was acknowledged by Harman and Willmer JJ. in *Gore* v. *Van der Lann*,[68] where they remarked:

> Since it has not been shown that there was any contract between the corporation and the conductor making the corporation liable in law to indemnify the conductor, there is no ground upon which the corporation could be held to have an interest entitling them to relief under s. 41 of the *Judicature Act* 1925.[69]

In fact, it is by no means clear that the restraint of the plaintiff's action should be contingent upon some potential loss to the other contracting party in the event of the action's proving successful. Further discussion of this question is, however, beyond the realm and confines of the present work.[70]

H. Indemnity clauses[71]

This device proceeds more upon cure than upon prevention. Its circuitous nature was recognised by Lord Reid in *Midland Silicones Ltd.* v. *Scruttons Ltd:*[72]

> It may be that in a roundabout way the stranger could be protected. If A, wishing to protect X, gives to X an enforceable indemnity, and contracts with B that B will not sue X, informing B of the in-

---

[66] [1971] 2 Lloyd's Rep. 399, at 408.
[67] [1975] A.C. 154, at 182 per Lord Simon of Glaisdale.
[68] [1967] 2 Q.B. 31; see also *Cosgrove* v. *Horsfall* (1945) 175 L.T. 334.
[69] Such an indemnity was apparently present in *Philip Morris (Australia) Pty. Ltd.* v. *The Transport Commission* (ante, p. 1005) and it is surprising that the defendants did not appear to request the intermediate parties (Ansett) from moving to stay the action. Cf. *The Elbe Maru* [1978] 1 Lloyd's Rep. 206.
[70] See further, *Snelling* v. *John G. Snelling Ltd.* [1972] 1 All E.R. 79.
[71] See generally, p. 917 ante.
[72] [1962] A.C. 446, at 473.

demnity, and then B does sue X in breach of his contract with A, it may be that A can recover from B as damages the sum which he has to pay X under the indemnity, X having had to pay it to B.

In some respects this resembles the chain of indemnity covenants which may be inserted into dispositions of land to overcome the rule that the burden of a positive covenant is not transmissible upon subsequent alienees. The difficulty from the third party's point of view is that the indemnity clause will be treated in the same manner as an exclusion clause and therefore construed strictly *contra proferentem*.[73] Moreover, Lord Denning M.R. has recently stated that such clauses must be reasonable as between the parties,[74] in a passage which was cited with approval by Bean J. in a subsequent decision.[75] The question of reasonableness is perhaps unlikely to cause undue difficulty where both parties to the indemnity are commercial enterprises, or where at least the potential indemnified falls within the description.[76]

VI. THIRD-PARTY LIENS[77]

In most cases in which an artificer acquires a lien over goods bailed to him for improvement or repair, the delivery will have been made by the owner of the goods in person and the lien will exist alongside some direct contract between the owner and the repairer. The artificer may, however, acquire a valid lien although neither the contract of labour nor the bailment of the goods was made by the owner personally. Such a lien may arise when someone to whom the owner has bailed the goods (for example, a hirer or a principal repairer) is given actual or ostensible authority to confer possession of the chattel on a third person for a purpose which the law acknowledges as giving rise to a lien. In such a case, it may be immaterial that the owner is a stranger to the contract for work and labour or that the owner has, without the repairer's knowledge, specifically prohibited the creation of a lien. A lien is not a right that necessarily arises by virtue of an implied contract, but one which arises (upon the occurrence of specified events) by operation of law.[78]

Actual authority: No difficulty arises when the bailee is expressly empowered to create a lien; but it is clear that such explicit authority is not essential.[79] The problem lies in identifying those circumstances in which the necessary authority will be implied. The implication has been made in

---

[73] See pp. 917, 924 ante; *Gillespie Bros. Ltd.* v. *Roy Bowles Transport Ltd.* [1973] Q.B. 400.
Levison v. *Patent Steam Carpet Cleaning Co. Ltd.* [1977] 3 W.L.R. 90 and *Unfair Contract Terms Act* 1977.
[74] *Gillespie Bros. Ltd.* v. *Roy Bowles Transport Ltd.* [1973] Q.B. 400.
[75] *Hair & Skin Trading Co. Ltd.* v. *Norman Airfreight Carriers Ltd.* [1974] 1 Lloyd's Rep. 443, at 446.
[76] E.g. where it is a large commercial employer entering into such contracts with its employees. As to the implication of a right to indemnity, see *Herrick* v. *Leonard & Dingley Ltd.* [1975] 2 N.Z.L.R. 566.
[77] As to liens generally, see p. 543 et seq., ante.
[78] *Tappenden* v. *Artus* [1964] 2 Q.B. 185, at 194-195 per Diplock L.J.; and see *General Securities Ltd.* v. *Brett's (Lillooet) Ltd.* (1956) 5 D.L.R. (2d) 46, at 53.
[79] *Tappenden* v. *Artus* ante, at 197 per Diplock L.J., disapproving the statement by McCardie J. in *Pennington* v. *Reliance Motor Works Ltd.* [1923] 1 K.B. 127, at 129; *Fisher* v. *Automobile Finance Co. of Australia Ltd.* (1928) 41 C.L.R. 167.

a number of cases in which the bailee was the hirer of goods under a hire-purchase agreement which expressly imposed upon him the duty of keeping the goods (at his own expense) in good condition and repair.[80] In *Green* v. *All Motors Ltd.*[81] Swinfen Eady L.J. stressed that an obligation of this kind could not be discharged unless the bailee vacated possession of the chattel in favour of a competent repairer; the repairer could hardly be expected to perform the work otherwise than upon his own premises and in the abesnce of the hirer. This necessity produced an implied authority in the hirer to perform the acts which gave rise to a lien, and entitled the repairer to assert such a lien against the owner. Presumably, the duty to repair prevailed over the other duty imposed on the hirer under the agreement, to keep the chattel at all times in his possession.[82]

Even when there is no express obligation to repair, the implied authority to create a lien may be discovered by looking to the purpose for which the chattel was bailed and to the conduct which is necessarily incidental to the fulfilment of that purpose. The most notable application of this approach is to be found in the decision of the Court of Appeal in *Tappenden* v. *Artus*. Under an informal contract of bailment, designed to accommodate the bailee until he could raise a sufficient deposit to acquire the vehicle on hire-purchase, the plaintiffs allowed the prospective hirer to use a certain motor-van on condition that he licensed and insured it. The bailment was one for the mutual benefit of the parties and not a gratuitous bailment in the nature of a loan.[83] The van broke down and the bailee ordered the defendants to tow it away and effect the necessary repairs. The defendants never saw him in possession of the vehicle but assumed that he was the owner. After the repairs were completed, the bailor located the van and demanded its return. The defendants refused to surrender it until they were paid and, in reply to the bailor's action for detinue, counterclaimed for a declaration that they were entitled to a repairer's lien. The Court of Appeal, upholding the counterclaim, dismissed an argument that the lien should be treated as equivalent to an implied contractual term and thus regarded as capable of arising only when its existence was essential to the efficacy of the contract of repair.[84] They further rejected the argument that an authority to create a lien should be displaced when the bailor himself is in the business of carrying out repairs. As Diplock L.J. observed, there could be many cases in which the parties would not reasonably contemplate that repairs would be carried out by the bailor alone: for example, when the vehicle breaks down a long way from the bailor's premises.[85]

The court conceded that the lien can be exercised by an artificer only if his possession of the chattel is lawful at the time when the lien was alleged to have arisen. To demonstrate this it was necessary to show

---

[80] E.g. *Keene* v. *Thomas* [1905] 1 K.B. 136; *Green* v. *All Motors Ltd.* [1917] 1 K.B. 625.
[81] [1917] 1 K.B. 625, at 630-631.
[82] Ibid., at 625 (statement of facts).
[83] At 201; see generally, Chapter 8.
[84] At 195.
[85] At 202.

that the original delivery was lawful, and the criterion to be applied in this context is whether "the owner authorised (or is estopped as against the artificer from denying that he authorised) the bailee to give possession of the goods to the artificer".[86]

Such authority, while not arising automatically from the existence of a bailment,[87] could be discovered in the present case because it was inherent in the purpose of the bailment and in the terms of the agreement under which the chattel was bailed.[88] When the object of a bailment is to enable the bailee to use the goods, the bailee is entitled to enjoy all reasonable aspects of their use; and if it is reasonably incidental to such use for him to confer possession of the goods upon a third party in circumstances which may result in the creation of a lien, the bailee may be deemed to enjoy authority to create the lien itself. This was clearly the situation in the present case, where the full use and enjoyment of the vehicle impliedly included a power to bail it for repairs. Diplock L.J. observed that an express prohibition would have been necessary in order to remove this authority:

> The grant of authority to use goods is itself to be construed as authority to do in relation to the goods all things that are reasonably incidental to their reasonable use. If the bailor desires to exclude the right of the bailee to do in relation to the goods some particular thing which is reasonably incidental to their reasonable use, he can, of course, do so, but he must do so expressly.
> In the case of a bailment for use, therefore, where there is no express prohibition upon his parting with possession of the goods (and no question of ostensible authority arises), the relevant inquiry is whether the giving of actual possession of the goods by the bailee to the person asserting the common law lien was an act which was reasonably incidental to the bailee's reasonable use of the goods.[89]

An implied authority of this kind is not necessarily restricted to subbailments by way of repair but may extend to storage,[90] to carriage,[90a] or to any other purpose reasonably incidental to the use of the chattel. It is, however, unlikely that such authority would be implied into a gratuitous bailment by way of loan;[91] and it may be harder to establish in the case of an original bailee who is entrusted with the task of improvement or repair. The bailee for work and labour generally undertakes a personal service and is not entitled to sub-contract the work;[92] thus sub-contractors to

---

[86] At 196.
[87] *Buxton* v. *Baughan* (1834) 6 C. & P. 674; *Associated Securities Ltd.* v. *Cocks* (1975) *Australian Current Law* D.T. 181 (N.S.W. Sup. Ct., Begg J.).
[88] [1964] 2 Q.B. 185, at 197 citing Collins J. in *Singer Manufacturing Co.* v. *L. & S.W. Ry. Co.* [1894] 1 Q.B. 833, at 837.
[89] [1964] 2 Q.B., at 198. Diplock L.J. went on to stress (at 202) that it was a statutory offence to drive an unroadworthy vehicle; and he pointed out that different considerations might apply when the relevant repairs were not necessary to put the vehicle in a roadworthy condition.
[90] *Singer Manufacturing Co. Ltd.* v. *L. & S.W. Ry. Co.* [1894] 1 Q.B. 833: but note that generally the mere custodian has no lien (ante, p. 493).
[90a] *K. Chellaram & Sons (London) Ltd.* v. *Butlers Warehousing & Distribution Ltd.* [1977] 2 Lloyd's Rep. 192.
[91] *Tappenden* v. *Artus* [1964] 2 Q.B. 185, at 201.
[92] Ante, p. 514 et seq.

whom goods have been bailed for such purposes as bleaching,[93] or the fitting of a new body to a motor chassis,[94] have been denied a lien against the owner.[95] But whereas the implied authority to create a lien cannot be taken to be *necessarily* incidental to an original bailment by way of work and labour (and thus need not in ordinary circumstances be expressly excluded) it seems that, if an authority can be implied to sub-contract the work itself, this should carry the further authority to create a lien.

Ostensible authority: Although counsel in *Tappenden* v. *Artus* expressly declined to rely upon the existence of a separate, ostensible authority, the Court of Appeal acknowledged in passing that such authority might itself be sufficient to sustain the lien. It would therefore follow that a lien may arise between a sub-bailee of goods and their owner, even when there is an express prohibition upon its creation within the primary contract of bailment, provided the bailor's conduct has induced the artificer to believe that his bailee had actual authority to perform the acts which caused the lien to attach. An ostensible authority is a matter of estoppel and must be expressly pleaded.[96]

In accepting the validity of an estoppel in this context, the Court of Appeal upheld statements in two earlier English cases which involved vehicles bailed under contracts of hire-purchase. The first was *Albermarle Supply Co. Ltd.* v. *Hind & Co. Ltd.*,[97] where the bailor who had expressly prohibited the creation of a lien was held estopped from denying its validity after a lengthy period of acquiescence in the bailee's practice of stabling the relevant vehicles with an artificer. This case was accepted without question in New Zealand as importing a separate doctrine of ostensible authority into the realm of tripartite liens.[98] The second authority was a dictum by Goddard C.J. in *Bowmaker Ltd.* v. *Wycombe Motors Ltd*:[99]

> . . . an arrangement between the owner and the hirer that the hirer shall not be entilted to create a lien does not affect the repairer. A repairer has a lien although the owner has purported to limit the hirer's authority to create a lien in that way. That seems to me to depend upon this: Once an artificer exercises his art upon a chattel, the law gives the artificer a lien upon that chattel, which he can exercise against the owner of the chattel if the owner of the chattel is the person who has placed the goods with him or has authorised another person to place the goods with him.

Australian authority was, until recently, less favourably inclined to the creation of a lien by estoppel. Thus in *Fisher* v. *Automobile Finance*

---

93 *Cassils & Co.* v. *Holden Wood Bleaching Co. Ltd.* (1914) 84 L.J.K.B. 834; cf. the *Chellaram* case, ante.

94 *Pennington* v. *Reliance Motor Works Ltd.* [1923] 1 K.B. 127.

95 See also *Protean Enterprises (Newmarket) Pty. Ltd.* v. *Randall* [1975] V.R. 327.

96 [1964] 2 Q.B., at 200.

97 [1928] 1 K.B. 307.

98 *Moyes* v. *Magnus Motors Ltd.* [1927] N.Z.L.R. 905; cf. *Lamonby* v. *Foulds Ltd.* 1928 S.C. 89.

99 [1946] 2 All E.R. 113, at 115; see also *General Securities Ltd.* v. *Brett's (Lillooet) Ltd.* (1956) 5 D.L.R. (2d) 46, at 53.

Co. of Australia Ltd.[1] the majority of the High Court relied upon early
English case-law for their pronouncement that the artificer's lien can
arise only when "the work in respect of which the charges arose was
done by the order or at the request of the owner or some person
authorised by him"; and a similar rule was more recently articulated by
the Victorian Full Supreme Court in *Protean Enterprises (Newmarket)
Pty. Ltd.* v. *Randall.*[2] In *Lombard Australia Ltd.* v. *Wells Park Motors
Pty. Ltd.*[3] Herring C.J. disapproved the dictum of Goddard C.J. in
Bowmaker Ltd. v. *Wycombe Motors Ltd.* and endorsed an earlier observation by Isaacs J.[4] that the right to create a lien could not be spelt out
from the mere fact that the hirer of a chattel had been entrusted with its
full and unrestricted use. But even within these authorities there is clear
recognition that an estoppel or ostensible authority may operate to
confer a lien upon the artificer, notwithstanding an express prohibition to
that effect within the original contract of bailment. Such recognition is
given by both Isaacs and Higgins JJ. in *Fisher* v. *Automobile Finance Co.
of Australia Ltd.;*[5] by Herring C.J. in *Lombard Australia Ltd.* v. *Wells
Park Motors Pty. Ltd.;*[6] and by Begg J. in the recent unreported case of
Associated Securities Ltd. v. *Cocks,*[7] where the principle was directly
applied and the lien was actually upheld. In *Cocks'* case the plaintiffs
leased a Lamborghini car under a three-year agreement. The lessee took
it to the defendants for repairs on about twenty-two occasions during a
period of eighteen months. The defendants, who were the sole distributors of Lamborghini cars in New South Wales, knew of the leasing agreement but were apparently unaware of an express provision in the agreement which forbade the creation of a lien. Begg J. held that they were
entitled to a lien for the cost of their unpaid repairs because the lessee
had given ostensible authority to have the car repaired by them and,
as an incident of such authority, to allow the assertion of their lien.
In so holding, the learned judge distinguished *Fisher* v. *Automobile
Finance Co. of Australia Ltd.* and seems to have preferred the wider
formulations of the appropriate authority given by Isaacs and Higgens JJ.
to that of the majority of the High Court. He conceded that an ostensible authority could not be inferred from the mere placing of a chattel
in the hands of a bailee over an extensive period of time, but held that
facts additional to this, even though they did not add substantially to the
facts in *Fisher's* case, might justify the inference of such authority. On
the present facts, particularly insofar as it was reasonable for the
repairer to suppose that the lessor would wish the car to be maintained
by the principal distributor, Begg J. felt able to conclude that a lien
had arisen.

---

[1] (1928) 41 C.L.R. 167, at 174; see generally the discussion in Elliott, *The Artificer's Lien*, p. 29 et. seq.
[2] [1975] V.R. 327, at 335.
[3] [1960] V.R. 693, at 700.
[4] In *Fisher* v. *Automobile Finance Co. of Australia Ltd.* (1928) 41 C.L.R. 167,
at 176.
[5] (1928) 41 C.L.R. 167, at 175, 176-177, 179-180.
[6] [1960] V.R. at 695, 698, 699.
[7] [1975] *Australian Current Law* D.T. 181 (N.S.W. Sup. Ct.).

This decision would appear to bring Australian law into line with that in England and New Zealand; and there seems no reason why an ostensible authority to create a lien should not be inferred within the limits outlined by Goddard C.J. in *Bowmaker Ltd.* v. *Wycombe Motors Ltd.* There is a wide difference between the mere entrustment of a chattel to a bailee and the granting to him of an authority to confer possession upon a third party in pursuance of a contract of repair. The latter requirement (whether the authority is actual or ostensible) is necessary because the artificer's own possession must be lawful; a rule which debars the creation of the lien when the artificer has knowledge of the limitation on the bailee's authority[8] or when the original bailment has already been terminated by the bailor by the time the artificer takes delivery.[9] But if these conditions are present, there should be no further obligation to prove that the bailee was actually authorised to perform the acts which give rise to the lien, or that the owner actually requested the performance of the work. Nor should it be essential (as was actually the position in *Bowmaker*) that the bailment should specifically impose upon the bailee the duty of effecting repairs; it should be sufficient that he had the right to do so.

Finally, it should be noted that under the uniform Australian hire-purchase legislation, a lien is granted to any workman who performs work upon goods that are the subject-matter of a hire-purchase agreement, unless he has notice, prior to the commencement of the labour, of any provision within the hire-purchase agreement prohibiting the creation of such a lien by the hirer.[10]

VII. BAILMENTS AND TITLE

Under certain conditions, a seller or buyer in possession of goods may transmit a valid title in those goods to a third party by way of exemption to the general principle nemo dat quod non habet. A similar exception may result in the extinction of a bailor's title through the operation of an estoppel as to the authority of his bailee. The reader is referred to more specialised works for discussion of these issues.[11]

---

[8] *Tappenden* v. *Artus* [1964] 2 Q.B. 185, at 201.
[9] *Bowmaker Ltd.* v. *Wycombe Motors Ltd.* ante; *Green* v. *All Motors Ltd.* [1917] 1 K.B. 625 (obiter, per all three members of the C.A.); *Tappenden* v. *Artus* ante, at 201.
[10] *Hire-Purchase Act* 1960-1970, s. 34 (N.S.W.); *H.P. Act* 1959-1971, s. 26 (Vic.); *H.P. Agreements Act* 1960-1971, s. 26, and *Consumer Transactions Act* 1972-1973, s. 37 (S.A.); *H.P. Act* 1959-1974, s. 26 (W.A.); *H.P. Act* 1959, s. 31 (Qld.); *H.P. Act* 1959-1971, s. 35 (Tas.); *H.P. Ordinance* 1961-1969, s. 31 (A.C.T.) *H.P. Ordinance* 1961-1974, s. 38 (N.T.).
[11] E.g. Atiyah, *The Sale of Goods* (5th ed.), Chapter 19.

APPENDIX I

THE TORTS (INTERFERENCE WITH GOODS) ACT, 1977

This enactment received the Royal Assent on 22nd July, 1977.[1] It follows
in part from the Report of the Law Reform Committee on Conversion
and Detinue, published in 1971.[2] There is, however, some divergence
between the recommendations of the Committee and the provisions of
the Act. Indeed, certain areas of proposed reform (such as the rights
of finders[3]) have not been affected at all.

The Act makes relatively few substantive changes to the Common
Law rights and duties of bailees. An exception is the disposal of uncollected goods, where the Act repeals the former legislation[4] and replaces it
with provisions of greater adaptability and scope.[5] These provisions are
discussed later in the present account.

The main purpose of the Act is to eradicate certain specific anomalies
which had infiltrated the traditional torts to chattels. To alleviate these
anomalies, the draftsman has found it necessary to regroup existing
remedies (such as trespass, negligence and conversion) within a larger
collective concept and to extend the reforms of the Act to all members
of that concept. The draftsman has not, however, attempted a comprehensive redefinition of the traditional remedies and in the case of certain
minor reforms the Act continues to refer to individual torts.[6]

I. The Concept of Wrongful Interference with Goods

The Act employs the novel and composite notion of "wrongful interference with goods". In so doing it does not create any new substantive
tort, nor does it generally seek to extinguish the conventional torts or
merge them within a single, comprehensive remedy.[7] It merely creates
a common denominator for the purpose of certain generalised reforms,
much in the same way as the *Consumer Credit Act* 1974, utilises the
concept of the regulated agreement. Within that overall concept, most of
the traditional torts (and the traditional demarcations between them)
are preserved.

[1] It did not come into force immediately but upon such days as the Lord Chancellor
should appoint: s. 17(2). See *Torts (Interference with Goods) Act* 1977 (Commencement No. 3) Order (No. 1910 (C. 64)), which brings ss. 12 to 16 and
s. 17(1) and (2) and Schedule 1 into force from 1st January, 1978.
[2] Cmnd. 4774. The main recommendations are set out in Chapter 3.
[3] Discussed in Cmnd. 4774 Appendix I.
[4] *Disposal of Uncollected Goods Act* 1952. The criticisms of the Law Reform
Committee against this Act are set out ante, pp. 399-400.
[5] Sections 12 and 13 and Schedule 1 to the Act.
[6] See s. 11; infra.
[7] The one exception is the tort of detinue, which is abolished and merged with
conversion: see ss. 2(1) and 2(2), discussed infra.

The expression "wrongful interference" or "wrongful interference with goods" is therefore defined to include:[8]

    (a) conversion of goods (also called trover),

    (b) trespass to goods,

    (c) negligence so far as it results in damage to goods or to an interest in goods,

    (d) subject to section 2,[9] any other tort so far as it results in damage to goods or to an interest in goods.

One immediate question is whether this definition includes the action by a bailor against his bailee for breach of his Common Law duty of care. At first sight such an action is a simple illustration of the tort of negligence, but to classify it exclusively as an action in negligence for the purposes of the Act is to invite the following problems:

(i) Even when the bailee's responsibility is founded upon the ordinary duty of care, there may be substantial differences (both conceptual and practical) between an action for breach of this duty and a typical action in negligence.[10] If bailment gives rise to independent obligations and to independent remedies to enforce those obligations, it might be argued that the bailee's liability is characteristically different from negligence or from 'any other tort' and therefore outside the categories of wrong set out in section 1[10a].

(ii) Does the word 'negligence' in s. 1(c) include the gross and slight degrees of neglect for which the unrewarded bailee and the borrower are traditionally held to be liable?

(iii) Does the word 'negligence' similarly encompass a bailee whose ordinary Common Law liability would be less onerous than a liability for failure to take reasonable care, but who has consensually enlarged that liability so as to impose upon himself a greater duty of care, commensurate with that which is reasonable?

(iv) Likewise, does it include an action against a bailee who has consensually *reduced* his liability to a liability for failing to exercise reasonable care?

(v) Does the same word cover an action *in contract* against a contractual bailee for reward for breach of the duty of reasonable care?

(vi) Does the same word include an action against the bailee for failure to safeguard the goods against theft, this being a duty which is normally

---

[8] Sections 1(a), (b), (c) and (d).

[9] Which abolishes detinue.

[10] See generally Chapter 1.

[10a] A similar argument, applied to s. 29(1) of the *Post Office Act* 1969, found some favour in the Court of Appeal in *Harold Stephen & Co. Ltd.* v. *Post Office* [1977] 1 W.L.R. 1172. The appellants had sought to argue that s. 29(1), which provides that ". . . no proceedings in tort shall lie against the Post Office in respect of any loss or damage suffered by any person . . .", could be circumvented by bringing an action in bailment. Lord Denning M.R., at pp. 1177-1178, declined to pronounce upon the matter finally but remarked "I would like to think that that may be so." Browne L.J., at p. 1179, expressed neutrality on the point, while Geoffrey Lane L.J. contented himself with observing, at pp. 1179-1180, "that liability in bailment, if it were to exist, would see to render largely meaningless section 29 of the Act of 1969." The question did not fall for final decision because the Court decided that the remedy sought (a mandatory injunction) could not, in the circumstances, be granted. See further Palmer (1978) 41 M.L.R.

imposed only by contract or by bailment and is not a general facet of the law of negligence itself?

The existence of these questions suggests that there are a number of ways in which bailors could frame actions so as to avoid the provisions of the Act. This is particularly likely when the bailment is contractual, for recent authority confirms that when there is a contract creating a duty of reasonable care the victim of a breach of that duty may elect to proceed either in contract or in tort.[11] Moreover, the courts should be reluctant to construe the Act as imposing an imperative classification of actions according to their substance (as in the case of the *Limitation Acts*) rather than according to their form. Even if this approach were taken, the substance of such an action may well be said to lie not in negligence but in bailment; and it would be as great an oversimplification to classify an action for breach of bailment as arising out of "any other tort" within the meaning of s. 1(d) as it would be to classify an action for breach of contract in the same way. In many cases the action against a bailee cannot be characterised as tortious at all. It is sui generis; sometimes promissory, sometimes consensual or proto-contractual, but fundamentally arising from the bailee's voluntary acceptance of the possession of goods. In other cases an action in tort (usually for negligence) is merely one of the methods by which the bailor can enforce the bailee's responsibility for the goods. An obvious alternative is an action for breach of the bailee's promise to redeliver them in the condition in which they were bailed; and in those cases (at least) in which the bailment is contractual the bailee appears entitled to choose between three distinct remedies: in tort, in contract and in bailment.

The concept of interference is an active one and conveys impressions of some positive misconduct. Most forms of negligence involve such misconduct (for example, driving a hired car faster than its capacity allows) but many actions against bailees are based upon mere omission: the failure to lock doors, or to employ proper watchmen to safeguard the goods, are common examples. In terms of common speech, it seems fanciful to say that a warehouseman who loses goods by theft because he did not install a burglar-alarm is guilty of interfering with those goods. It may be, however, that the word interference is construed to include loss by passive neglect.

We have earlier mentioned another problem which arises from the loss of goods by theft. Such loss would normally be evidence of negligence provided there were a pre-existing duty of care. Does the breach of that duty, however, and the consequent loss of the goods amount to "negligence . . . (which) . . . results in damage to goods or to an interest in goods"?[12] The latter phrase is ambiguous but seems capable of including that form of economic loss that results from the theft of goods owned by the plaintiff. It is unfortunate, however, that no explanation is offered as to the *sort* of interest that s. 1(c) refers to; and it is an open question whether a purely contractual interest (such

[11] Ante, p. 53.
[12] Section 1(c).

as the passing of risk unaccompanied by the passing of property[13]) would suffice to bring the section into play. Presumably the answer would depend upon whether the violation of such an interest could give rise to an action for negligence at Common Law; and whereas direct authority suggests otherwise,[14] more recent decisions suggest a softening in the former limits to liability for economic loss.[15]

II. THE ABOLITION OF DETINUE AND THE EXPANSION OF CONVERSION

At first sight, it would appear that the circumvention suggested in the preceding section would not be possible in every case because of s. 2 of the Act. Under s. 2(1), "Detinue is abolished". Section 2(2) attempts, in the face of the resulting vacuum, to make alternative provision for the situation where a bailee has wrongfully lost or brought about the destruction of his bailor's goods. It provides that an action for loss or destruction of goods "which a bailee has allowed to happen in breach of his duty to his bailor" now lies in conversion. This statutory re-characterisation therefore brings such actions within the larger concept of wrongful interference as defined by s. 1. However, there seems no reason why the bailor could not frame his action so as to avoid the appearance of what would formerly have been an action in detinue and therefore to avoid inclusion within s. 1(a). The most obvious method, again, would be by suing in contract, or in bailment. Such a device should also enable him to circumvent the confusing explanatory parenthesis to s. 2(2). This parenthesis explains that, synonymously with the foregoing provision, an action for conversion lies "in a case which is not otherwise conversion but would have been detinue before detinue was abolished". If "would have been detinue" means "must necessarily and could only have been brought in detinue" then clearly s. 2(2) fails to subsume all actions against bailees who have allowed loss or destruction to happen in breach of their duty to their bailors within the extended tort of conversion; in many cases the action could just as safely have been brought for breach of the bailee's promise to redeliver. If, on the other hand, these words mean merely "could, as one alternative, have been brought or characterised as an action in detinue" then the assimilation is more complete. It is submitted that the former construction is emphatically to be preferred. Even on the latter, the artificial characterisation of such actions as actions for conversion does not extend to cases involving the mere negligent *damage* of goods.

It is, perhaps, significant that the draftsman of s. 2(2) chose to group such actions within a tort to which they do not bear any affinity at Common Law. The fact that he did so suggests that he did not regard them as capable of constituting actions in negligence within s. 1(c). If this assumption holds good, it would seem to follow that an action based upon negligent damage which the bailee has allowed to happen in

---

[13] Cf. *Margarine Union G.m.b.H.* v. *S.S. Cambay Prince* [1969] 1 Q.B. 219.
[14] Ibid.
[15] *Caltex Oil (Aust.) Pty. Ltd.* v. *The Tug "Willemstad"* (1977) 11 A.L.R. 227; (1977) 93 L.Q.R. 333.

breach of his duty to the bailor cannot amount to an action for wrongful interference at all.

Three further problems are raised by the interaction of ss. 2(1) and 2(2). First, what wrongs are contemplated by the requirement that the occasion of damage or destruction be one "which a bailee has *allowed* to happen in breach of his duty to his bailor"? The primary target of s. 2(2) is the bailee who, through failure to exercise reasonable care in safeguarding the goods, enables them to be stolen or destroyed. It would seem unnecessary for s. 2(2) to apply to bailees who, by malicious or positive misconduct, bring about the loss or destruction of the goods. Such conduct would, in all but exceptional cases, fall within the traditional frontiers of trespass or conversion,[16] and the ensuing loss can hardly be described as something which the bailee has "allowed" to happen. Between these extremes there lies the intermediate situation of a bailee whose initial deviation has led, without negligence on his part, to the loss or destruction of his bailor's goods. The bailee is strictly liable for such loss or destruction and this liability would seem to follow both when goods are merely damaged and when they are lost or destroyed. Does the act of deviation, when it leads to loss or destruction, fall within s. 2(2)? It may be doubted whether the element of passivity inherent in the expression "has allowed to happen" can encompass an initially positive act of deviation; and conversely whether the bailee "allows to happen" a degree of subsequent loss or destruction which no amount of reasonable care on his part could have prevented. It seems to have been accepted that a deviation does not automatically render the bailee liable *in conversion* for the loss of the goods,[17] but it is probable that he could be sued for detinue. It is unfortunate that the inclusion or exclusion of this form of liability was not more explicitly stated. If the words "breach of his duty" in s. 2(2) included breach of any *contractual* duty the expansion of the tort of conversion would appear at first sight to be remarkable. But not every breach of contract by a bailee "would have been detinue" as apparently required by the parenthesis to s. 2(2), and if an action in bailment or in contract is brought the bailor may thereby avoid characterisation of his remedy as one for wrongful interference altogether.

Secondly, there is the question whether ss. 2(1) and 2(2) abolish that form of the action for detinue which is based upon a simple demand and refusal, unaccompanied by loss or destruction of the goods.[18] Evidently a refusal of this kind will no longer, per se, constitute a tort, and the question will be whether the refusal to return the goods amounts

---

[16] A possible exception is the situation where a bailee deliberately does something (for instance, leaves the door of his warehouse open) which he knows will enable someone else to steal the bailor's goods. Such conduct may well give rise to an action in detinue; but it really amounts to a breach of his duty of care and, while not constituting trespass or conversion, would certainly render him liable for negligence. Cf. the other cases of deviation, discussed infra, which are unaccompanied by a lack of reasonable care on the part of the bailee.

[17] Cf. *Lilley* v. *Doubleday* (1881) 7 Q.B.D. at 511, 512.

[18] Except insofar as the bailee's refusal to return them necessarily predicates at least their temporary loss to the bailor. Even here there is the problem whether the bailee has merely "allowed" such loss to happen. It would be anomalous if a bailee who merely failed to return the goods were guilty of conversion within s. 2(2) whereas a bailee who overtly refused to do so were not.

to a conversion. It can hardly be argued that the parenthesis to s. 2(2) expands the action for conversion to all cases of what would, prior to the Act, have been detinue. Rather, the parenthesis must be taken to be qualified by the specific situation described earlier in s. 2(2), and thus confined to cases where the bailee has allowed the loss or destruction to occur in breach of his duty to the bailor. Of course, most cases involving a wrongful refusal to redeliver goods to one's bailor will involve commission of the tort of conversion. This is not, however, a necessary equation, and it may be questioned whether the abolition of this aspect of detinue is a desirable consequence of s. 2(1).

Thirdly, it seems unclear whether that form of liability for detinue which is substantially preserved by s. 2(2) continues to require that the bailor should have demanded the return of the goods. By recharacterising the action as one for conversion, the draftsman seems to have intended that this prefatory requirement should no longer be imposed. However, the parenthesis to s. 2(2) continues to require that the action be one which (apart from the Act) "would have been detinue"; and the general rule is that no action lies in detinue unless the plaintiff can establish both demand and refusal. Thus it may be that in order to bring an action against a negligent bailee within s. 2(2), and consequently within s. 2(1), the bailor must still prove that the bailee failed to comply with a reasonable demand for the return of the goods. If the bailor would be at liberty to enforce the obligation in some other way (e.g. by suing in contract or by bringing a separate action on the bailment) the action will apparently escape being classified as an action for wrongful interference within the meaning of s. 2(1).[19]

III. Forms of Judgment for Detention of Goods

In this and in the ensuing paragraphs we shall assume that the foregoing questions have been resolved and the relevant action is unequivocally characterised as an action for wrongful interference with the terms of s. 1. Section 3 sets out the forms of relief which may be given (so far as is appropriate) in proceedings for wrongful interference against a person who is "in possession or in control of the goods". This expression was evidently intended to include a bailee in possession; but it might also include a possessor whose possession is not founded upon bailment, a servant, and a bailee who has sub-bailed the goods to a third party, provided in the last case that he remains in control of the goods. The relief that may be given is:

(a) an order for delivery of the goods, and for payment of any consequential damages, or

(b) an order for delivery of the goods, but giving the defendant the alternative of paying damages by reference to the value of the goods,

[19] Presumably those actions in detinue which do *not* escape such characterisation will now carry the measure of damages appropriate to conversion; alternatively, it may well be argued that the action is assimilated to that of conversion only for the purposes of the Act itself.

together in either alternative with payment of any consequential damages, or

(c) damages.[20]

Subject to the rules of the court relief can only be given in an action for wrongful interference in any particular instance under one of the preceding paragraphs.[21] Paragraph (a) differs from paras. (b) and (c) in that relief given under it is at the discretion of the court, whereas a successful claimant is given the power to elect between the other two forms of relief contained in paras. (b) and (c): again, however, this principle is subject to rules of the court.[22]

If it is shown to the satisfaction of the court that an order for delivery under para. (a) has not been complied with, the court is given further powers under ss. 3(4)(a) and 3(4)(b) of the Act to revoke the order (or the relevant part thereof) and to make instead an order for the payment of damages by reference to the value of the goods.

When an order has been made under para. (b),[23] the defendant may satisfy that order by returning the goods at any time before execution of judgment. However, this is without prejudice to any liability on his part for the payment of consequential damages.[24]

An order for the delivery of goods, whether made under paras. (a) or (b), may be made subject to such conditions as the court determines. One particular instance of the possible imposition of conditions upon an order for delivery occurs when damages awarded by reference to the value of the goods would not amount to the whole of the value of the goods.[25] In such an event the court may require that the difference be reflected in an allowance made by the claimant to the defendant.[26] A specific example is given in s. 3(6):

> For example, a bailor's action against the bailee may be one in which the measure of damages is not the full value of the goods, and then the court may order delivery of the goods, but require the bailor to pay the bailee a sum reflecting the difference.

The measure of a bailor's damage may fail to equate with the full value of the goods for two principal reasons. First, the bailor may not be the owner; and since s. 8(1) of the Act apparently seeks to abolish the former principle that a bailee is estopped from disputing his bailor's title, it would seem to follow that in a bailor-bailee suit the bailee who commits a tort against the goods is no longer liable to the bailor as if the latter were the owner. This may of course affect the level of damages he would otherwise be compelled to pay, and the statutory disparity brings in s. 3(6). Thus, for example, where a sub-hirer wrongfully detains goods in contravention of the principal hirer's title, an order requiring delivery of the goods by the sub-hirer to the principal hirer may be accompanied by a condition that the principal hirer make some adjustive

---

[20] Sections 3(2)(a), (b) and (c).
[21] Section 3(3)(a).
[22] Section 3(3)(b).
[23] Ante.
[24] Section 3(5).
[25] Section 3(6).
[26] Ibid.

allowance representing the difference between the value of the goods thus delivered and his own lesser interest therein. Otherwise, of course, the intermediate party (the bailor-bailee) might be unjustly enriched; although it should be noticed that even at Common Law he would be required to account to his own bailor for any profit resulting from the action.

Secondly, a bailee who has committed an act of wrongful interference may nevertheless retain some outstanding interest in the goods; and in such an event it could again be contended (in the words of s. 3(6)) that the damages capable of being awarded to the bailor, against him, would not amount to the whole value of the goods. Thus where a bailee has leased for a term and has subsequently interfered with the goods without forfeiting the remainder of his term (e.g. by an act of negligent damage which permanently injures the bailor's reversion) the court may, in ordering delivery to the bailor, require the bailor to make allowance for the bailee's outstanding interest; for the measure of the bailor's damages is the value of his reversionary interest alone. Of course, it may be otherwise when the misconduct in question has caused the forfeiture of the bailee's immediate right of possession, and thus the loss of any interest in the goods such as to create a margin between the value of the lessor's own interest and the value of the goods themselves.

In certain cases, the defendant to an action for wrongful interference may be entitled to an allowance for any improvement he has made to the goods.[27] If this is so, the court may (in making an order under ss. 3(2)(a) or (b) of the Act) assess the allowance which is to be made and by the order required, as a condition for delivery of the goods, that that allowance be made by the claimant.[28]

Nothing in s. 3 derogates from the remedies afforded by s. 133 of the *Consumer Credit Act* 1974; from the remedies afforded by ss. 35, 42 and 44 of the *Hire Purchase Act* 1965 (so long as those sections remain in force): or from any jurisdiction of the courts to afford ancillary or incidental relief.[29]

Section 4, which will not be discussed in detail, deals with the power to grant interlocutory relief in cases where goods are wrongfully detained.

IV. DAMAGES

A judgment in conversion has been described as effecting a compulsory sale of the converted chattel to the defendant.[30] Section 5(1) of the *Torts (Interference with Goods) Act* seeks to clarify the proprietary consequences of a satisfied action for wrongful interference with goods. Broadly, it enacts the rule that satisfaction of such a claim extinguishes the claimant's title to his interest in the goods. However, a general limitation is placed upon this principle, confining it to cases in which the claimant's damages are assessed, or would fall to be assessed, on the

[27] Sections 6(1) and (2) of the Act; infra.
[28] Section 3(7).
[29] Section 3(8).
[30] Ante, p. 127.

footing that he is being compensated for the whole of his interest in the goods. The section reads as follows:

5.-(1) Where damages for wrongful interference are, or would fall to be, assessed on the footing that the claimant is being compensated—

(a) for the whole of his interest in the goods, or

(b) for the whole of his interest in the goods subject to a reduction for contributory negligence,

payment of the assessed damages (under all heads), or as the case may be settlement of a claim for damages for the wrong (under all heads), extinguishes the claimant's title to that interest.

Clearly, not every action for wrongful interference involves a claim for damages that would fall to be assessed upon the total value of the plaintiff's interest in the goods. For example, the goods may merely be damaged, in which event the claimant must obviously be entitled to retain his title to them in addition to receiving damages for the partial impairment of his interest. Nor, it seems, is the operation of s. 5(1) solely dependent upon a mathematical parity between the damages recoverable by the claimant and the value of his interest in the chattel. An owner (for instance) may recover damages for consequential loss, resulting from a partial impairment of his interest, which far exceed the value of that interest itself. Nevertheless, if his claim is not one for compensation for the whole of his interest, he retains his title thereto upon recovery of such damages, even though the latter far exceed the value of the former. The test is one of identity or synonymity rather than of mere equivalence.

Conversely, the following are illustrations of claims which (when satisfied) may fall within the operation of s. 5(1): the action on the case by a reversionary owner out of possession for destruction or total deprivation of his reversionary interest; the action by an outright owner of goods for their conversion upon sale to, and receipt by, an innocent purchaser; and the action by a bailee for deprivation, during the whole remainder of the bailment, of his limited interest, by the bailor or by a third party. In practice, of course, s. 5(1) will be important only in the context of those wrongs to chattels (such as conversion) which do not result in the total destruction thereof; for in cases of destruction it is generally immaterial to consider questions of the extinction or relocation of title at all.

The meaning of a settlement of a claim within s. 5(1) is amplified by s. 5(2):

(2) In subsection (1) the reference to the settlement of the claim includes—

(a) where the claim is made in court proceedings, and the defendant has paid a sum into court to meet the whole claim, the taking of that sum by the claimant, and

(b) where the claim is made in court proceedings, and the proceedings are settled or compromised, the payment of what is due in accordance with the settlement or compromise, and

(c) where the claim is made out of court and is settled or compromised, the payment of what is due in accordance with the settlement or compromise.

Section 5(1) (which may be varied by agreement inter partes and is subject to any order of the court)[31] does not apply to cases where, although damages are assessed on the footing that the claimant is being compensated for the whole of his interest in the goods, the damages paid are limited to some lesser amount by virtue of any enactment or rule of law;[32] aliter, it seems, when they are limited to some agreement between the parties.

Special provision is made by s. 5(4) to cater for cases in which the claimant accounts over to a third party; this will be discussed in due course.

V. Improvements to Goods

The restitutionary rights of a person who expends money or labour in the improvement of another's chattel are uncertain at Common Law. A recent New Zealand case underlines this confusion by referring to at last three separate tests for the determination of disputes in cases where one person has added his own goods to those of another and the composite or overall product is indivisible.[33] The 1977 Act does not affect questions of title, but it does provide for an allowance to be made when someone with an established interest in goods recovers them (or damages for wrongful interference with them) from an innocent improver. The drafting of these provisions is designed to exclude those improvers who are aware that they have no title to the goods, so that the defendant in a case like *Munro* v. *Willmott*[34] would not be entitled to claim their protection. Such a case would continue to be governed by the principles of Common Law.

> 6—(1) If in proceedings for wrongful interference against a person (the "improver") who has improved the goods, it is shown that the improver acted in the mistaken but honest belief that he had a good title to them, an allowance shall be made for the extent to which, at the time as at which the goods fall to be valued in assessing damages, the value of the goods is attributable to the improvement.
> (2) If, in proceedings for wrongful interference against a person ("the purchaser") who has purported to purchase the goods—
> (a) from the improver, or
> (b) where after such a purported sale the goods passed by a further purported sale on one or more occasions, on any such occasion,
> it is shown that the purchaser acted in good faith, an allowance shall be made on the principle set out in subsection (1).
> For example, where a person in good faith buys a stolen car from the improver and is sued in conversion by the true owner the damages may be reduced to reflect the improvement but if the person who bought the stolen car from the improver sues the improver for failure of consideration, and the improver acted in

---

[31] Section 5(5).
[32] Section 5(3).
[33] *Thomas* v. *Robinson* [1977] 1 N.Z.L.R. 385.
[34] [1949] 1 K.B. 295.

good faith, subsection (3) below will ordinarily make a comparable reduction in the damages he recovers from the improver.

(3) If in a case within subsection (2) the person purporting to sell the goods acted in good faith, then in proceedings by the purchaser for recovery of the purchase price because of failure of consideration, or in any other proceedings founded on that failure of consideration, an allowance shall, where appropriate, be made on the principle set out in subsection (1).

(4) This section applies, with the necessary modifications, to a purported bailment or other disposition of goods as it applies to a purported sale of goods.

Section 6 is confined to instances of improvement, so that the mere maintenance of a chattel would not activate the section. Difficult questions could arise from the need to determine whether a certain course of conduct has produced an improvement to the goods.

VI. DOUBLE LIABILITY

The Law Reform Committee devoted considerable attention to the problems of potential double liability under the existing Common Law remedies for the vindication of interests in chattels, and gave several examples of situations in which such liability could arise.[35] Section 7 of the 1977 Act seeks to cure these defects. It defines 'double liability' for the purposes of the section as the double liability of the wrongdoer which can arise:

(a) where one of two or more rights of action for wrongful interference is founded on a possessory title, or

(b) where the measure of damages in an action for wrongful interference founded on a proprietory title is or includes the entire value of the goods, although the interest is one of two or more interests in the goods.[36]

and states the governing principle that in proceedings for wrongful interference to which any two or more claimants are parties, the relief shall be such as to avoid double liability of the wrongdoer as between those claimants.[37] The attainment of this objective is set out in ss. 7(3) and 7(4). Under the former, it is provided that whenever any claim is satisfied (in whole or in part) for an amount which exceeds the amount which would be recoverable if the principle against double liability were implemented, the claimant is liable to account over, to the other person having a right to claim, to such extent as will avoid double liability. Thus if a finder of goods, relying upon his possessory title, recovers damages from a converter, the finder shall be bound to pay any amount by which these damages exceed the value of his own interest in the goods (which will normally be nil) to the true owner. Under s. 7(4), any claimant who is unjustly enriched to any extent as the result of enforcement of a double liability is liable to reimburse the

[35] Cmnd. 4774, paras. 51 et seq.
[36] Section 7(1).
[37] Section 7(2).

wrongdoer to the extent of that unjust enrichment. A specific example is given by the draftsman, again involving a finder:

> For example, if a converter of goods pays damages first to a finder of the goods and then to the true owner, the finder is unjustly enriched unless he accounts over to the owner under subsection (3); and then the true owner is unjustly enriched and becomes liable to reimburse the converter of the goods.

VII. Pleading Jus Tertii

There were two principal situations in which the Common Law forbade a defendant in an action for wrongful interference to chattels to plead jus tertii, and in so doing allowed the plaintiff to recover more than his actual loss. The first arose when a subsisting possession, residing in someone other than the general owner, was violated by the wrongful act of an outsider. An example is the conversion of found goods by someone other than the finder or owner. The possessor could recover at Common Law for the full value of the chattel (or the full cost of its depreciation) irrespective of whether he was a conventional bailee, a finder, or a thief; and irrespective of whether the impairment of which he complained was one for which he was answerable to the owner.[38] The second situation arose when goods were damaged, converted or detained by the default of a bailee. The bailee was deemed to have promised, as part of his consideration for being given possession, that he would not question his bailor's title. This implied undertaking could be displaced by a clear agreement to the contrary; but in the absence of such agreement the inability to plead jus tertii took effect as an implied term in every bailment.[39] It was one of the reasons for the importance of discovering the exact identity of the bailor, and indirectly, perhaps, for the development of the doctrine of attornment discussed in Chapter 21.

In both of the foregoing situations the defendant's incapacity to plead jus tertii could be justified on grounds of policy. It allowed a possessor to bring a single consolidated action for the loss of a large number of chattels of individually trivial value, and it led to security in the relations between bailors and bailees; a warehouseman, for example, could not avoid liability for negligence merely by proving that since the person who had delivered goods to him was no longer their owner he had suffered no personal loss. Indeed, it seems to have been thought that the transaction of commercial bailments would be unworkable on any other basis.[40]

Conversely, the foregoing rules could prove disadvantageous. If, as seems correct, the recovery of full damages by a possessor from an outside interferer, or by a bailor from his bailee, relieved the defendant from all further liability in respect of his wrongdoing, there was a clear disadvantage to the general owner. Although the successful plaintiff was under a fiduciary obligation to account to the owner for the proceeds of

[38] Chapter 4, ante.
[39] Ante, p. 163 et seq.
[40] Ante, p. 164.

litigation above and beyond his personal interest, the plaintiff may well have disappeared or have become insolvent before doing so, and his possession of the monetary equivalent of the goods could give him an unfair disadvantage in any later dispute with the owner or with any other person who had a superior right to the goods. Moreover, even in those cases where a full recovery by the non-owner did not discharge the defendant from liability to the owner himself, there was a corresponding disadvantage to the defendant, who might become subject to a double liability and therefore obliged to pay for the same goods twice. This problem may have arisen in the case of a sub-bailee, who apparently owes at Common Law the duties of a bailee (including the obligation not to impugn his bailor's title) both to the original and to the immediate, or intermediate, bailor.[41]

Despite the Law Reform Committee's recommendation that the bailee's estoppel should be preserved[42] (as it is in the case of landlord and tenant) both of the foregoing principles have apparently been changed by the 1977 Act. By s. 8(1), the defendant in an action for wrongful interference shall be entitled to show in accordance with rules of court that a third party has a better right than the plaintiff as respects all or any part of the interest claimed by the plaintiff or in right of which he sues. The section concludes flatly: "and any rule of law (sometimes called jus tertii) to the contrary is abolished."

It may be that it would have been better to have retained the bailee's estoppel, while abolishing merely the principle that (as against third-parties) possession counts as title. The removal of the estoppel could give rise to inconvenience in cases of commercial bailment where the bailor has ceased to own the goods and the bailee has not yet attorned to any subsequent owner. At Common Law the bailee's responsibilities qua bailee are solely to the original bailor until the latter's displacement and substitution upon an attornment. Now there may be a danger that bailees, sued upon the original bailment, will be able to engage in delaying tactics by adducing evidence of a series of later changes of ownership and by requiring later owners to be made parties to the proceedings; whereas if such owners may be unknown to the bailee the value of s. 8(1) may, even in terms of its own apparent objectives, be reduced. In view of s. 7 a bailee has little to fear from double liability, even if the wrong he has committed is one for which he could be sued by a later purchaser to whom he has not attorned. Indeed such later purchasers could well be said, until attornment occurs, to have conferred impliedly upon the seller-bailor a power to recover full damages on their behalf. It could be argued that since s. 8(1) abolishes *"any rule of law"* creating an incapacity to plead jus tertii it does not apply to the relationship of bailor and bailee because the bailee's estoppel is the product of an implied agreement inter partes. However, such agreement does not encompass the ulterior owner of the goods for whose protection s. 8 is obviously intended; since he is a stranger to any such consensual estoppel, such estoppel could well be said to operate upon him as a rule

---

[41] Ante, p. 175.
[42] Cmnd. 4774, paras. 62 et seq.

of law and accordingly to fall within the prohibition proclaimed by
s. 8(1). Perhaps it is for this reason that s. 8 is not (like some other
sections in the 1977 Act) made subject to any contrary agreement.

Section 8(2) provides for the making of the relevant rules of court;
this is to be without prejudice to any other power of making such rules
(s. 8(3)):

> 8(2)—Rules of court relating to proceedings for wrongful inter-
> ference may—
> (a) require the plaintiff to give particulars of his title
> (b) require the plaintiff to identify any person, who, to his know-
> ledge, has or claims any interest in the goods,
> (c) authorise the defendant to apply for directions as to whether
> any person should be joined with a view to establishing
> whether he has a better right than the plaintiff, or has a claim
> as a result of which the defendant might be doubly liable,
> (d) where a party fails to appear on an application within para-
> graph (c), or to comply with any direction given by the court
> on such an application, authorise the court to deprive him of
> any right of action against the defendant for the wrong either
> unconditionally, or subject to such terms or conditions as may
> be specified.

Section 8 applies only to actions for wrongful interference and not,
for example, to actions for breach of contract. This suggests at least two
types of situation in which a defendant may still be answerable in extra-
compensatory damages. The first arises where a defendant causes loss
or impairment to goods without committing an independent tort, for
example, a bailee may be guilty of negligent delay in the delivery of
goods, thereby causing a fall in their market value;[43] or a third party
may, through breach of his contract with the bailee, become responsible
for the deterioration of goods in the bailee's possession, as where he
fails to build a road allowing them to be moved.[44] In such cases s. 8(1)
would seem wholly inapplicable. A more difficult question arises when
the defendant's wrongdoing simultaneously constitutes both a "wrongful
interference" within s. 1 and a breach of contract or of bailment. It is
submitted[45] that the plaintiff can elect to sue in contract or in bailment
and avoid any imperative classification of the action as one for wrongful
interference. In permitting him to do so, the courts would therefore
apparently hold that he takes himself beyond the scope of s. 8.

For similar reasons, s. 8 does not affect the bailee's right to recover
the full value of the goods under an appropriately worded contract of
insurance. Such a right sounds solely in contract and does not proceed
from any wrongful interference by the defendant insurer. Of course the
bailee remains liable to account to his bailor for the residual value of
the latter's interest in the goods.[46]

[43] B.W.I.A. Ltd. v. Bart (1966) 11 W.I.R. 378.
[44] Tanentaum v. W. J. Bell Paper Co. Ltd. (1956) 4 D.L.R. (2d) 177; ante, p. 181.
[45] Ante, p. 1015.
[46] See generally ante, p. 193 et seq.

VIII. Concurrent Actions

Procedural provisions designed to deal with concurrent actions are set out in s. 9 of the Act. This section may be passed over briefly. It provides as follows:

> 9—(1) This section applies where goods are the subject of two or more claims for wrongful interference (whether or not the claims are founded on the same wrongful act, and whether or not any of the claims relates also to other goods).
>
> (2) Where goods are the subject of two or more claims under section 6 this section shall apply as if any claim under section 6(3) were a claim for wrongful interference.
>
> (3) If proceedings have been brought in a county court on one of those claims, county court rules may waive, or allow a court to waive, any limit (financial or territorial) on the jurisdiction of county courts in the County Courts Act 1959 or the County Courts Act (Northern Ireland) 1959 so as to allow another of those claims to be brought in the same county court.
>
> (4) If proceedings are brought on one of the claims in the High Court, and proceedings on any other are brought in a county court, whether prior to the High Court proceedings or not, the High Court may, on the application of the defendant, after notice has been given to the claimant in the county court proceedings—
>
> (a) order that the county court proceedings be transferred to the High Court, and
>
> (b) order security for costs or impose such other terms as the court thinks fit.

IX. Conversion, Trespass and Problems of Co-ownership

Actions between co-owners are dealt with by s. 10, which has already been set out in Chapter 3.[47]

X. Minor Amendments

Section 11 seeks to resolve three specific areas of uncertainty within the law of trespass and conversion. Two of the solutions are straightforward and do not call for comment. Section 11(2) declares that the receipt of goods by way of pledge now amounts to conversion if the delivery of those goods itself constitutes conversion.[48] Under s. 11(3) a mere denial of title is no longer deemed, of itself, to be conversion.[49]

At first sight, s. 11(1) appears equally straightforward. It states that contributory negligence is no defence in proceedings founded in conversion, or on intentional trespass to goods. This provision follows the recommendation of the Law Reform Committee[50] and shows a legislative

---

[47] Ante, p. 162.
[48] Cf. ante, p. 128 (Chapter 3).
[49] The position at Common Law is discussed ante, pp. 129-130.
[50] Cmnd. 4774, paras. 48, 81; ante, p. 137.

preference for the position taken by Samuels J. in the *Wilton* case,[51] to that previously adopted by Donaldson J.[52] and by the New Zealand Court of Appeal.[53] It is uncertain, however, whether the prohibition applies to an action against an involuntary bailee for misdelivery of goods. The 'bailee' in such a case appears to be liable only if he mis-delivers the goods without exercising reasonable care.[54] Whether such liability sounds in conversion (thereby attracting s. 11(1)) or in negligence (allowing contributory negligence still to be pleaded) is an open question. It is submitted that the courts are entitled to apply the defence in such a case and should do so. Admittedly, s. 11(1) refers to proceedings founded on conversion and not merely to proceedings *in* conversion; but negligence remains as essential an ingredient of liability as the act of mis-delivery itself, and it will be observed (in a somewhat parallel vein) that only *intentional* trespasses, and not those which are negligently committed, are likewise brought within the section. It is unfortunate that this question was not more clearly answered by the Act.

XI. THE DISPOSAL OF UNCOLLECTED GOODS

The *Disposal of Uncollected Goods Act* 1952[55] was an unsatisfactory statute. The procedures it laid down were unnecessarily complicated and the types of bailment to which it applied were strictly limited. The 1977 Act affords a broader and more imaginative solution. Its defects are those of complexity and uncertainty rather than of narrowness. Every variety of bailment seems to be included but nowhere is the concept of bailment defined. It is therefore unclear whether cases of involuntary bailment, sub-bailment and bailment without the consent of the owner qualify as bailments for the purposes of the Act. The draftsman would have been well advised to study the Western Australian legislation, which applies to every case in which one person is in lawful possession of goods which belong to another.[56]

The Act allows for two types of disposal: sale without authority of the court and sale with such authority. No provision is made for any other form of disposal, such as by gift or by destruction. In view of the problems of perishable or malodorous goods the latter omission is to be regretted.

A. Non-Judicial sale

Section 12(3) of the Act confers a general power of sale upon bailees when certain conditions are fulfilled. This power applies only to goods bailed after the commencement of the Act.[57] The bailee must show that the following requirements are satisfied:

[51] *Wilton* v. *Commonwealth Bank of Australasia Ltd.* [1973] 2 N.S.W.R.
[52] *Lumsden* v. *London Trustee Savings Bank Ltd.* [1971] 1 Lloyd's Rep. 114.
[53] *Helson* v. *McKenzies (Cuba St.) Ltd.* [1950] N.Z.L.R. 878.
[54] Ante, p. 387.
[55] Ante, p. 396.
[56] Ante, p. 407.
[57] Section 12(9).

(i) The terms of the bailment do not provide to the contrary.[58]

(ii) The goods must be in the possession or under the control of the bailee.[59] Thus a bailee who no longer possesses the goods but has sub-bailed them to a third-party on terms that he may call for their redelivery at will is apparently entitled to the protection of the Act.

(iii) Some actual or constructive date for redelivery to the bailor must have passed. The bailee may satisfy this in one of several ways:

(a) By showing that the bailor is actually in breach of an obligation to take delivery of the goods, or, if the terms of the bailment so provide, to give directions for their redelivery;[60]

(b) By showing that the bailee would be able to impose such an obligation by giving notice to the bailor but that the bailee is in fact unable to trace or communicate with them;[61]

(c) By showing that the bailee could reasonably expect to be relieved of any duty to safeguard the goods by giving notice to the bailor but is unable to trace or communicate with him.[62]

Few bailments impose a positive obligation upon the bailor to collect the goods at any particular time. A projection of the period of custody beyond that originally contemplated will sometimes serve to reduce the bailee's own level of responsibility for the goods but will rarely place the bailor in breach of contract.[63] Accordingly, s. 12(2) and Schedule 1 Part 1 of the Act enable the bailee under certain types of bailment to impose such an obligation by notice to the bailor. Such notice may alternatively impose an obligation upon the bailor to give directions for redelivery of the goods.

The notice must be in writing and may be given either by delivering it to the bailor, or by leaving it at his proper address (as defined in Schedule 2 Part II para. 8), or by post.[64] The requirement that it should be 'given' and not merely sent suggests that the notice must be actually received by the bailor and that mere proof of posting would be insufficient. To comply with Schedule 1 the notice must:

(a) specify the name of the bailee, and give sufficient particulars of the goods and the address or place where they are held;

(b) state that the goods are ready for redelivery to the bailor, or, where combined with a notice terminating the contract of bailment, state that they will be ready for redelivery when the contract is terminated; and

(c) specify the amount, if any, which is payable by the bailor to the bailee in respect of the goods and which became due before the giving of the notice.[65]

The times at which such notice may be given vary according to the purpose of the bailment. They are also, by virtue of para. 6 of Schedule 1, Part 1, to the Act, subject to the terms of the bailment.

---

58 Section 12(8); and see Schedule 1, Part 1 para. 6.
59 Section 12(1).
60 Section 12(1)(a).
61 Section 12(1)(b).
62 Section 12(1)(c).
63 See generally ante, p. 437.
64 Schedule 1, Part 1, para. 1(2).
65 Schedule 1, Part 1, para. 1(3); see also para. 1(4).

Purpose of bailment	Exact description of bailment	Time for notice.
I Goods accepted for repair or other treatment.	"If a bailee has accepted goods for repair or other treatment on the terms (expressed or implied) that they will be redelivered to the bailor when the repair or other treatment has been carried out . . ."	". . . at any time after the repair or other treatment has been carried out."[66]
II Goods accepted for valuation or appraisal.	"If the bailee has accepted goods in order to value or appraise them . . ."	". . . at any time after the bailee has carried out the valuation or appraisal."[67]
III Storage, warehousing etc.	"If a bailee is in possession of goods which he has held as custodian, and his obligation as custodian has come to an end . . ."	". . . at any time after the ending of the obligation or may be combined with any notice terminating his obligation as custodian."[68]

BUT: "This paragraph III shall not apply to goods held by a person as mercantile agent, that is to say by a person having in the customary course of his business as a mercantile agent authority either to sell goods or to consign goods for the purpose of sale, or to any goods, or to raise money on the security of goods."

Under para. 5 of Schedule 1 to the Act, it is provided that the fore-going provisions (paras. 2, 3 and 4) "apply whether or not the bailor has paid any amount due to the bailee in respect of the goods, and whether or not the bailment is for reward, or in the course of business or gratuitous."

Thus the power to impose an obligation upon the bailor to take delivery of the goods is not limited to commercial bailments. It could apply, for example, to the man who takes charge of his neighbour's budgerigar while the neighbour is on holiday only to find, upon the neighbour's return, that he is reluctant to reclaim it. It is interesting that para. 5 extends these provisions to bailments that are purely gratui-tous, thereby providing at least some tacit legislative assumption that promissory obligations are enforceable upon gratuitous bailments. Else-where, it is to be noticed that the statute refers, notwithstanding this extension, to the *contract* of bailment.[69]

(iv) The bailee must next give notice to the bailor of his intention to sell the goods, or must have failed to trace or communicate with the bailor with a view to giving him such notice, after having taken reason-able steps for that purpose.[70] If these conditions are fulfilled *and* the bailee is reasonably satisfied that the bailor owns the goods,[71] he then becomes entitled to sell them. The notice of intention to sell must, however, specify the following information:[72]

[66] Ibid., para. 2.
[67] Ibid., para. 3.
[68] Ibid., para. 4.
[69] Ibid., para. 1(3); supra.
[70] Section 12(3).
[71] Ibid.
[72] Schedule 1, Part II, para. 6(1).

(a) the name and address of the bailee; and it must give sufficient particulars of the goods and the address or place where they are held;

(b) the date on or after which the bailee proposes to sell the goods;

(c) the amount, if any, which is payable by the bailor to the bailee in respect of the goods, and which became due before the giving of the notice.

Moreover, the period specified in this notice as that after which the bailee proposes to sell the goods must be "such as will afford the bailor a reasonable opportunity of taking delivery of the goods;"[73] and if any amount is payable in respect of the goods by the bailor to the bailee, and became due before the notice of intention to sell was given, the period allowed shall not be less than three months.[74]

The notice must be in writing and must be sent by post in a registered letter, or by recorded delivery.[75]

(v) The final obstacle to be surmounted by the bailee arises from Schedule 1, Part II, para. 7. According to this:

7—(1) The bailee shall not give notice under Section 12(3), of exercise his right to sell the goods pursuant to such a notice, at a time when he has notice that, because of a dispute concerning the goods, the bailor is questioning or refusing to pay all or any part of what the bailee claims to be due to him in respect of the goods.

(2) This paragraph shall be left out of account in determining under section 13(1) whether a bailee of goods is entitled to sell the goods under section 12, or would be so entitled if he had given any notice required in accordance with this Schedule.

(vi) When the bailee has exercised his authority to sell under s. 12(3), he must account to the bailor for the proceeds of the sale, after first deducting the expenses thereof.[76] The account shall be taken on the footing that the bailee should have adopted the best method of sale reasonably available in the circumstances.[77] When this occurs, the bailee may also deduct any sum which is payable by the bailor to the bailee in respect of the goods and which "accrued due" before the bailee gave notice of his intention to sell.[78]

A sale, properly effected under s. 12, gives the purchaser of the goods a good title *as against the bailor* alone.[79] If the bailor did not own the goods, no good title is conferred by sale under the Act either against the true owner or against anyone claiming under him.[80]

By s. 12(7)(a), the words "bailor" and "bailee" as used in ss. 12 and 13 and in Schedule 1 include their respective successors in title.[81]

---

[73] Ibid., para. 6(2).
[74] Ibid., para. 6(3).
[75] Ibid., para. 6(4).
[76] Section 12(5).
[77] Section 12(5)(a).
[78] Section 12(5)(b).
[79] Section 12(6).
[80] Section 12(4).
[81] See also, as to the definition of charges payable in respect of the goods, s. 12 (7)(b).

B. Judicial Sale

The procedures for a sale authorised by the Court are set out in s. 13:

13—(1) If a bailee of the goods to which section 12 applies satisfies the court that he is entitled to sell the goods under section 12, or that he would be so entitled if he had given any notice required in accordance with Schedule 1 to this Act, the court—

(a) may authorise the sale of the goods subject to such terms and conditions, if any, as may be specified in the order, and

(b) may authorise the bailee to deduct from the proceeds of sale any costs of sale and any amount due from the bailor to the bailee in respect of the goods, and

(c) may direct the payment into court of the net proceeds of sale, less any amount deducted under paragraph (b), to be held to the credit of the bailor.

(2) A decision of the court authorising a sale under this section shall, subject to any right of appeal, be conclusive, as against the bailor, of the bailee's entitlement to sell the goods, and gives a good title to the purchaser as against the bailor.

(3) In this section "the court" means the High Court or a county court, and a county court shall have jurisdiction in the proceedings if the value of the goods does not exceed the county court limit.

XII. Supplemental and Transitional Provisions

The remainder of the *Torts (Interference with Goods) Act* 1977, provides as follows:

14—(1) In this Act, unless the context otherwise requires—
"county court limit" means the current limit on jurisdiction in s. 39 of the County Courts Act 1959, or in Northern Ireland the current amount mentioned in section 10(1) of the County Courts Act (Northern Ireland) 1959.

"enactment" includes an enactment contained in an Act of the Parliament of Northern Ireland or an Order in Council made under the Northern Ireland (Temporary Provisions) Act 1972, or in a Measure of the Northern Ireland Assembly,

"goods" includes all chattels personal other than things in action and money,

"High Court" includes the High Court of Justice in Northern Ireland.

(2) References in this Act to any enactment include references to that enactment as amended, extended or applied by or under that or any other enactment.

15—(1) The Disposal of Uncollected Goods Act 1952 is hereby repealed.

(2) In England and Wales that repeal shall not affect goods bailed before the commencement of this Act.

(3) In Scotland that repeal shall not affect the rights of the person with whom the goods are deposited where the notice of intention to sell the goods under s. 1(3)(c) of the said Act of 1952 was delivered before the commencement of this Act.

16—(1) Section 15 shall extend to Scotland, but otherwise the Act shall not extend to Scotland.

(2) This Act, except s. 15, extends to Northern Ireland.

(3) This Act shall bind the Crown, but as regards the Crown liability in tort shall not bind the Crown further than the Crown is made liable in tort by the *Crown Proceedings Act* 1947.

17—(1) This Act may be cited as the *Torts (Interference with Goods) Act* 1977.

(2) This Act shall come into force on such day as the Lord Chancellor may by order contained in a statutory instrument appoint, and such an order may appoint different dates for different provisions or for different purposes.

(3) Schedule 2 to this Act contains transitional provisions.

SCHEDULE 2.

Transitional

1. This Act shall not affect any action or arbitration brought before the commencement of this Act or any proceedings brought to enforce a decision in the action or arbitration.

2. Subject to paragraph 1, this Act applies to acts or omissions before it comes into force as well as to later ones, and for the purposes of the *Limitation Act* 1939, the *Statute of Limitations (Northern Ireland)* 1958, or any other limitation enactment, the cause of action shall be treated as having accrued at the time of the act or omission even if proceedings could not have been brought before the commencement of this Act.

3. For the purposes of this Schedule, any claim by way of set-off or counterclaim shall be deemed to be a separate action, and to have been brought on the same date as the action in which the set-off or counterclaim is pleaded.

THE TRADE PRACTICES AMENDMENT ACT 1977 (AUSTRALIA)

This statute makes substantial amendments to the *Trade Practices Act* 1974. Most of the amendments are beyond the scope of this book. This is because we have been required to pay regard only to those portions of the 1974 Act which provide for the implication and non-exclusion of undertakings as to quality, fitness, title etc. under contracts for the supply of goods or services.[1] The largest single amendment of relevance occurs in relation to the statutory definition of 'dealing as a consumer'. This was originally contained in ss. 4(3) and 4(4) of the 1974 Act. That part of s. 4 is now repealed and a new section is added—s. 4B—which greatly expands the statutory notion of the consumer. It provides as follows:

4B (1) For the purposes of this Act, unless the contrary intention appears—
(a) a person shall be taken to have acquired particular goods as a consumer if, and only if—
    (i) the price paid or payable by the person for the goods did not exceed the prescribed amount; or
    (ii) where that price exceeded the prescribed amount—the goods were of a kind ordinarily acquired for personal, domestic or household use or consumption,
and the person did not acquire the goods, or hold himself out as acquiring the goods, for the purpose of re-supply or for the purpose of using them up or transforming them, in trade or commerce, in the course of a process of production or manufacture or of repairing or treating other goods or fixtures on land; and
(b) a person shall be taken to have acquired particular services as a consumer if, and only if—
    (i) the price paid or payable by the person for the services did not exceed the prescribed amount; or
    (ii) where that price exceeded the prescribed amount—the services were of a kind ordinarily acquired for personal, domestic or household use or consumption.
(2) For the purposes of sub-section (1)—
(a) the prescribed amount is $15,000 or, if a greater amount is prescribed for the purposes of this paragraph, that greater amount;
(b) if a person acquired goods together with other property or with services, or with both other property and services, and a specified price was not allocated to the goods in the contract under which they were acquired, the price paid or payable by the person for the goods shall be taken to have been the amount that was the market value of the goods at the time when that contract was entered into; and

---

[1] Ante, pp. 527, 531, 603 et seq.

(c) if a person acquired services together with property or with other services, or with both property and other services, and a specified price was not allocated to the first-mentioned services in the contract under which they were acquired, the price paid or payable by the person for the first-mentioned services shall be taken to have been the amount that was the market value of those services at the time when that contract was entered into.

(3) Where it is alleged in any proceeding under this Act or in any other proceeding in respect of a matter arising under this Act that a person was a consumer in relation to particular goods or services, it shall be presumed, unless the contrary is established, that the person was a consumer in relation to those goods or services.

The concepts of acquisition, supply and re-supply are amplified by a further new section—s. 4c—added to the 1974 statute by the amending Act of 1977.[2]

4c. In this Act, unless the contrary intention appears—
(a) a reference to the acquisition of goods includes a reference to the acquisition of property in, or rights in relation to, goods in pursuance of a supply of the goods;
(b) a reference to the supply or acquisition of goods or services includes a reference to agreeing to supply or acquire goods or services;
(c) a reference to the supply or acquisition of goods includes a reference to the supply or acquisition of goods together with other property or services, or both;
(d) a reference to the supply or acquisition of services includes a reference to the supply or acquisition of services together with property or other services, or both; and
(e) a reference to the re-supply of goods acquired from a person includes a reference to—
(i) a supply of the goods to another person in an altered form or condition; and
(ii) a supply to another person of goods in which the first-mentioned goods have been incorporated.

The important remaining provisions of the 1977 Act are those which modify (albeit only slightly) the statutory terms as to title, fitness, quality etc. originally implied by ss. 69 to 72 and 74 of the 1974 Act. These sections (and the relevant implied terms) remain, but are varied in the following manner:

(i) There is no longer the exemption for sales by competitive tender from the operation of the statutory terms as to correspondence with description,[3] fitness for purpose and merchantable quality[4] and correspondence with sample.[5] Such sales appear to have become a regular feature of the used-car market in the three years after the passing of the parent statute. However, this removal of protection for sales by tender occurs only in relation to contracts made after the commencement

---

[2] Section 6.
[3] Section 70 of the 1974 Act; exemption removed by s. 40(1) of the 1977 Act.
[4] Section 71 of the 1974 Act; exemption removed by s. 41(1) of the 1977 Act.
[5] Section 72 of the 1974 Act; exemption removed by s. 42(1) of the 1977 Act.

of the Act[6] and still applies, of course, only in contracts between a corporation and one who deals as a consumer.

(ii) The supply of services by way of competitive tender is likewise now included within the operation of the terms implied by s. 74[7] in relation to contracts made after July 1st 1977.[8]

(iii) Section 74(3), which defines the types of services that are made subject to the terms implied by ss. 74(1) and (2), is revised and re-enacted as follows:

(3) In this section, "services" means services by way of—
(a) the construction, maintenance, repair, treatment, processing, cleaning or alteration of goods or of fixtures on land;
(b) the alteration of the physical state of land; or
(c) the transportation of goods otherwise than for the purposes of a business, trade, profession or occupation "carried" on or engaged in by the person for whom the goods are transported.[9]

(iv) Special rules for the rescission of contracts for breach of a condition implied by ss. 69 to 72 and 74 of the 1974 Act are enacted by a new section (s. 75A) added by s. 44 of the 1977 Act. This new section provides that:

44. After section 75 of the Principal Act the following section is inserted in Part V:—

75A. (1) Where—
(a) a corporation supplies goods to a consumer in the course of a business; and
(b) there is a breach of a condition that is, by virtue of a provision of Division 2, implied in the contract for the supply of the goods,
the consumer is, subject to this section, entitled to rescind the contract by—
(c) causing to be served on the corporation a notice in writing signed by him giving particulars of the breach; or
(d) causing the goods to be returned to the corporation and giving to the corporation, either orally or in writing, particulars of the breach.

(2) Where a consumer purports to rescind under this section a contract for the supply of goods by a corporation, the purported rescission does not have any effect if—
(a) the notice is not served or the goods are not returned within a reasonable time after the consumer has had a reasonable opportunity of inspecting the goods;
(b) in the case of a recission effected by service of a notice, after the delivery of the goods to the consumer but before the notice is served—
   (i) the goods were disposed of by the consumer, were lost, or were destroyed otherwise than by reason of a defect in the goods;

---

[6] Sections 40(2), 41(2) and 42(2) of the 1977 Act. The Act itself came into force on July 1st, 1977; see s. 3, ibid.
[7] Section 43(1)(a) of the 1977 Act.
[8] Section 43(2) ibid.
[9] Sections 43(1)(b) and (c) ibid.

        (ii) the consumer caused the goods to become unmerchant-
            able or failed to take reasonable steps to prevent the
            goods from becoming unmerchantable; or
       (iii) **the goods were damaged by abnormal use; or**
  (c) in the case of a rescission effected by return of the goods,
      while the goods were in the possession of the consumer—
         (i) the consumer caused the goods to become unmerchant-
            able or failed to take reasonable steps to prevent the
            goods from becoming unmerchantable; or
        (ii) the goods were damaged by abnormal use.

(3) Where a contract for the supply of goods by a corporation to
a consumer has been rescinded in accordance with this section—
  (a) if the property in the goods had passed to the consumer before
      the notice of rescission was served on, or the goods were
      returned to, the corporation—the property in the goods re-
      vests in the corporation upon the service of the notice or the
      return of the goods; and
  (b) the consumer may recover from the corporation, as a debt, the
      amount or value of any consideration paid or provided by
      him for the goods.

(4) The right of rescission conferred by this section is in addition
to, and not in derogation of, any other right or remedy under this
Act or any other Act, any State Act, any law of a Territory or
any rule of law.".

The foregoing are the principal amendments likely to affect transactions of bailment. The Australian reader is, however, advised to consult the amending Act for a fuller account of its provisions.

INDEX